Lecture Notes in Computer Science 2885

Edited by G. Goos, J. Hartmanis, and J. van Leeuwen

T0205308

Springer
Berlin
Heidelberg
New York
Hong Kong
London
Milan
Paris
Tokyo

Jin Song Dong Jim Woodcock (Eds.)

Formal Methods and Software Engineering

5th International Conference
on Formal Engineering Methods, ICFEM 2003
Singapore, November 5-7, 2003
Proceedings

Springer

Series Editors

Gerhard Goos, Karlsruhe University, Germany
Juris Hartmanis, Cornell University, NY, USA
Jan van Leeuwen, Utrecht University, The Netherlands

Volume Editors

Jin Song Dong
National University of Singapore, Computer Science Department
3 Science Drive 2, Singapore 117543
E-mail: dongjs@comp.nus.edu.sg

Jim Woodcock
University of Kent, Computing Laboratory
Canterbury, Kent, CT2 7NF, UK
E-mail: J.C.P.Woodcock@kent.ac.uk

Cataloging-in-Publication Data applied for

A catalog record for this book is available from the Library of Congress.

Bibliographic information published by Die Deutsche Bibliothek
Die Deutsche Bibliothek lists this publication in the Deutsche Nationalbibliografie;
detailed bibliographic data is available in the Internet at <http://dnb.ddb.de>.

CR Subject Classification (1998): D.2.4, D.2, F.3, D.3, F.4

ISSN 0302-9743
ISBN 3-540-20461-X Springer-Verlag Berlin Heidelberg New York

Springer-Verlag is a part of Springer Science+Business Media

springeronline.com

© Springer-Verlag Berlin Heidelberg 2003
Printed in Germany

Typesetting: Camera-ready by author, data conversion by Olgun Computergrafik
Printed on acid-free paper   SPIN: 10967843   06/3142   5 4 3 2 1 0

Preface

This volume contains the proceedings of the 2003 International Conference on Formal Engineering Methods (ICFEM 2003). The conference was the fifth in a series that began in 1997. ICFEM 2003 was held in Singapore during 5–7 November 2003.

ICFEM 2003 aimed to bring together researchers and practitioners from industry, academia, and government to advance the state of the art in formal engineering methods and to encourage a wider uptake of formal methods in industry.

The Program Committee received 91 submissions from more than 20 countries in various regions. After each paper was reviewed by at least three referees in each relevant field, 34 high-quality papers were accepted based on originality, technical content, presentation and relevance to formal methods and software engineering. We wish to sincerely thank all authors who submitted their work for consideration. We would also like to thank the Program Committee members and other reviewers for their great efforts in the reviewing and selecting process.

We are indebted to the three keynote speakers, Prof. Ian Hayes of the University of Queensland, Prof. Mathai Joseph of the Tata Research, Development and Design Centre, and Dr. Colin O'Halloran of QinetiQ, for accepting our invitation to address the conference.

ICFEM 2003 was well organized. It could not have been successful without the hard work and efforts of our organization, program and steering committee members. We would particularly like to thank Jifeng He and P.S. Thiagarajan for overseeing general issues of the conference, Martin Henz for handling local organization, Hugh Anderson and Aminah Ayu for handling registrations, Hai Wang for maintaining the conference Website, Shengchao Qin and Zongyan Qiu for taking care of publicity, and Yuanfang Li for his excellent assistance in preparing the proceedings with Jun Sun and in setting up and maintaining the Web review system CyberChair (developed by R. van de Stadt). Finally, our thanks to Springer-Verlag for their help with the publication.

ICFEM 2003 was sponsored and organized by the Computer Science Department, National University of Singapore. More information on this conference can be found at: http://nt-appn.comp.nus.edu.sg/fm/icfem2003/

November 2003   Jin Song Dong and Jim Woodcock

Organization

Conference Committee

Conference Co-chairs:	Jifeng He (IIST, United Nations U.)
	P.S. Thiagarajan (National U. of Singapore)
Program Co-chairs:	Jin Song Dong (National U. of Singapore)
	Jim Woodcock (U. of Kent)
Publicity Co-chairs:	Shengchao Qin (National U. of Singapore)
	Zongyan Qiu (Peking University)
Local Organization Chair:	Martin Henz (National U. of Singapore)
Registration:	Hugh Anderson (National U. of Singapore)
Webmasters:	Yuanfang Li (National U. of Singapore)
	Wang Hai (National U. of Singapore)
Proceedings Assistant Editor:	Yuanfang Li (National U. of Singapore)

Program Committee

Vasu Alagar	Kyo Chul Kang	Thomas Santen
Richard Banach	Kung-Kiu Lau	Klaus-Dieter Schewe
Jonathan Bowen	Shaoying Liu	Wolfram Schulte
Manfred Broy	Zhiming Liu	Graeme Smith
Michael Butler	Huimin Lin	Paul Swatman
Ana Cavalcanti	Peter Lindsay	Kenji Taguchi
Dan Craigen	Brendan Mahony	Sofiène Tahar
Jim Davies	Huaikou Miao	T.H. Tse
Jin Song Dong	Jeff Offutt	Farn Wang
Kai Engelhardt	Richard Paige	Yi Wang
John Fitzgerald	Abhik Roychoudhury	Jim Woodcock
Marc Frappier	Motoshi Saeki	Hongjun Zheng
Andy Galloway	Augusto Sampaio	Hong Zhu

Referees

Parosh Abdulla	Alessandra Cavarra	Danielle Fowler
Otmane Ait-Mohamed	Sungdeok Cha	Benoit Fraikin
Behzad Akbarpour	Haiming Chen	Frédéric Gervais
Juan Carlos Augusto	Yifeng Chen	Andy Gravell
Ho-Jung Bang	Hung Dang Van	Jim Grundy
Luis. S. Barbosa	Neville Dean	Stefan Gruner
Phil Brooke	Roger Duke	Ali Habibi
Zining Cao	Colin Fidge	Ping Hao

John Harrison
Sven Hartmann
Ian Hayes
Steffen Helke
David Hemer
Shui-Ming Ho
Xiaoning Huang
Ralf Huuck
Cornelia Inggs
Czeslaw Jeske
Jan Jürjens
Florian Kammüller
Siau-Cheng Khoo
Moonjoo Kim
Soon-Kyeong Kim
Tai-Hyo Kim
Markus Kirchberg
Leonid Kof
Ming Siem Kong
Maciej Koutny
Kevin Lano
Mohamed Layouni
Reinhold Letz
Martin Leucker
Yuan Fang Li

Hui Liang
Sebastian Link
Jim McCarthy
Alistair McEwan
Sun Meng
Yassine Mokhtari
Alexandre Mota
Tohru Naoi
Muan Yong Ng
Naoya Nitta
Olga Ormandjieva
N. Paramesh
Joey Paquet
Anup Patnaik
Hong Peng
Kasi Periyasamy
Paul Pettersson
Mike Poppleton
Stephane Lo Presti
Shengchao Qin
S. Ramesh
Ken Robinson
Jan Romberg
Dirk Seifert
Adnan Sherif

Harold Simmons
Carlo Simon
Jing Sun
Jun Sun
Pasha Shabalin
Linda Yue Tang
P.S. Thiagarajan
Alexei Tretiakov
Mark Utting
Frank D. Valencia
Sergiy Vilkomir
Hai Wang
Yan Wang
Guido Wimmel
Kirsten Winter
Satoshi Yamane
Roland Yap Hock Chuan
Hirokazu Yatsu
Hongnian Yu
Ling Yuan
Patryk Zadarnowski
Wenhui Zhang
Mao Zheng

Steering Committee

Chair:	Jifeng He (IIST, United Nations U.)
Members:	Keijiro Araki (Kyushu U.)
	Jin Song Dong (National U. of Singapore)
	Chris George (IIST, United Nations U.)
	Mike Hinchey (NASA)
	Shaoying Liu (Hosei U.)
	John McDermid (U. of York)
	Carroll Morgan (U. of NSW)
	Tetsuo Tamai (U. of Tokyo)
	Jim Woodcock (U. of Kent)

Table of Contents

Petri Nets

Timed Automata

System Modeling and Checking

Semantics and Synthesis

Author Index

Programs as Paths:
An Approach to Timing Constraint Analysis

Ian J. Hayes

School of Information Technology and Electrical Engineering,
The University of Queensland, Brisbane, 4072, Australia
ianh@itee.uq.edu.au

Abstract. A program can be decomposed into a set of possible execution paths. These can be described in terms of primitives such as assignments, assumptions and coercions, and composition operators such as sequential composition and nondeterministic choice as well as finitely or infinitely iterated sequential composition. Some of these paths cannot possibly be followed (they are dead or infeasible), and they may or may not terminate.

Decomposing programs into paths provides a foundation for analyzing properties of programs. Our motivation is timing constraint analysis of real-time programs, but the same techniques can be applied in other areas such as program testing. In general the set of execution paths for a program is infinite. For timing analysis we would like to decompose a program into a finite set of subpaths that covers all possible execution paths, in the sense that we only have to analyze the subpaths in order to determine suitable timing constraints that cover all execution paths.

1 Introduction

The semantics of a program is usually given in terms of an input-output relation [14, 15] or in terms of weakest preconditions [6]. These semantics are well suited to reasoning about the correctness of a program with respect to its specification, but for analyzing properties of programs, such as their timing behaviour, it is more appropriate to decompose a program into its possible execution paths. The motivation for our work comes from timing constraint analysis of machine-independent real-time programs in order to determine execution-time constraints on paths through the program that guarantee that all deadlines within the program will be met [8, 17]. The "path" view of a program is also well suited to analyzing the worst-case execution time of programs [4], as well as program testing [3] and static analysis of programs [9].

The primitives we use to define paths come from the refinement calculus [1, 18]. The primitives are assignments, coercions and assumptions and these primitives are combined using sequential composition and nondeterministic choice, as well as finitely or infinitely iterated sequential composition. For example, in refinement calculus circles it is well known that an "if" command,

if b **then** s **else** t **fi**,

can be decomposed into more primitive constructs using binary nondeterministic choice ($\sqcap$), binary sequential composition (;), and coercions of the form $[b]$, where b is a boolean expression.

J.S. Dong and J. Woodcock (Eds.): ICFEM 2003, LNCS 2885, pp. 1–15, 2003.

$$([b] \,;\, s) \sqcap ([\neg b] \,;\, t) \tag{1}$$

Nondeterministic choice demonically chooses between its two alternatives [6]. A coercion $[b]$ acts like **skip** (the no-operation statement) if b is true but is equivalent to **magic** if b is false. To simplify the presentation here we assume all expressions are well defined. The command **skip** is the identity of sequential composition:

$$\textbf{skip}; \, s = s = s; \, \textbf{skip} \tag{2}$$

The command **magic** is miraculous in that it implements any specification whatsoever. It cannot be implemented, and hence (unless b is the predicate *true*) a coercion $[b]$ cannot be implemented in isolation. The command **magic** is the identity of nondeterministic choice:

$$\textbf{magic} \sqcap s = s = s \sqcap \textbf{magic} \tag{3}$$

and a left zero of sequential composition:

$$\textbf{magic}; \, s = \textbf{magic} \tag{4}$$

as well as a right zero provided s terminates:

$$s; \, \textbf{magic} = \textbf{magic} \tag{5}$$

For example, an "if" command with a constant guard of *true* can be decomposed as follows.

> **if** *true* **then** s **else** t **fi**
> $=$ by (1)
> $\quad ([\textit{true}] \,;\, s) \sqcap ([\textit{false}] \,;\, t)$
> $=$ as $[\textit{true}] = \textbf{skip}$ and $[\textit{false}] = \textbf{magic}$
> $\quad (\textbf{skip}; \, s) \sqcap (\textbf{magic}; \, t)$
> $=$ by (2) and (4)
> $\quad s \sqcap \textbf{magic}$
> $=$ by (3)
> $\quad s$

Note how the "else" branch is eliminated because the false coercion is equivalent to **magic** and **magic** is the identity of nondeterministic choice. Of course the elimination only works for constant guards and is not applicable to guards that are dependent on the program state.

The above decomposition (1) of an "if" command splits the "if" command into its two possible execution paths. This "path" view can be exploited for analyzing, for example, timing constraints on paths through a program.

In Section 2 we introduce of our path primitives and composition operators, and define a simple programming language in terms of these. Section 3 defines the path view of a repetition. Section 4 considers dead path and Section 5 extends to approach to real-time programs.

2 Path Primitives and Composition Operators

Given a predicate p, a vector of variables $\vec{x}$, and a vector of expressions $\vec{e}$, that is assignment compatible with $\vec{x}$, the following are path primitives.

$$\{p\} \text{ — Assumption} \tag{6}$$

$$[p] \text{ — Coercion} \tag{7}$$

$$\vec{x} \leftarrow \vec{e} \text{ — Multiple assignment} \tag{8}$$

The assumption command either acts like **skip** if p is true, or aborts if p is false. The coercion command either acts like **skip** if p is true, or like **magic** if p is false. The following can be defined in terms of the primitives.

$$\mathbf{abort} \mathrel{\hat{=}} \{false\} \tag{9}$$

$$\mathbf{skip} \mathrel{\hat{=}} \{true\} \tag{10}$$

$$= [true] \tag{11}$$

$$\mathbf{magic} \mathrel{\hat{=}} [false] \tag{12}$$

In terms of the refinement lattice **abort** is the bottom program (i.e., it is refined (implemented) by all other programs) and **magic** is the top program (i.e., it refines all other programs). Because the coercion $[p]$ guarantees to establish p, p may be assumed to hold immediately after the coercion, that is,

$$[p] = [p] ; \{p\} \tag{13}$$

The composition operators are given in Figure 1. We have already seen the binary versions of nondeterministic choice and sequential composition. These can be generalised. The general nondeterministic choice

$$\bigsqcap i : T \bullet s_i \tag{14}$$

is a choice over all the commands s_i for i ranging over all the values of type T. If T is empty then the general choice is equivalent to **magic** (the identity of nondeterministic choice).

Given commands s and t the following composition operators can be defined.

$$s \sqcap t \text{ — Binary demonic nondeterministic choice} \tag{15}$$

$$\bigsqcap i : T \bullet s_i \text{ — General demonic nondeterministic choice} \tag{16}$$

$$s; \ t \text{ — Sequential composition} \tag{17}$$

$$s^i \text{ — Finite iteration of } s, i \text{ times} \tag{18}$$

$$s^\infty \text{ — Infinite iteration of } s \tag{19}$$

Fig. 1. Path composition operators.

Sequential composition can be generalised to any finite number of iterations or even an infinite number of iterations. Finite iteration, s^i, satisfies the following properties

$$s^0 \mathrel{\widehat{=}} \mathbf{skip} \tag{20}$$
$$s^{i+1} \mathrel{\widehat{=}} s;\ s^i \tag{21}$$

where i is a natural number. Iteration satisfies the following properties.

$$s^1 = s \tag{22}$$
$$s^{i+j} = s^i;\ s^j \tag{23}$$

Infinite iteration, s^∞, is the least-refined command that satisfies

$$s^\infty = s;\ s^\infty \tag{24}$$

Unfolding using (24) i times gives

$$s^\infty = s^i;\ s^\infty \tag{25}$$

Any nonterminating command followed by another command is equivalent to the non-terminating command and hence

$$s^\infty;\ t = s^\infty \tag{26}$$

Infinite iteration also satisfies the following property.

$$(s;\ t)^\infty = s;\ (t;\ s)^\infty \tag{27}$$

Table 1. Comparison with regular expressions.

Construct	Regular expression	Program
Alternation	$e \mid f$	$s \sqcap t$
Sequence	$e\,f$	$s;\ t$
Kleene star	e^*	s^*
Identity of alternation	$\varnothing$	**magic**
Identity of sequence	ϵ	**skip**

In order to define programming language repetitions we introduce the Kleene star iterator, s^*, to stand for the nondeterministic choice between any finite number (zero or more) of iterations of s. It can be defined in terms of finite iteration and general nondeterministic choice.

$$s^* \mathrel{\widehat{=}} (\textstyle\bigcap i : \mathbb{N} \bullet s^i) \tag{28}$$

Kleene star has the usual properties that we associate with it from regular expressions. Table 1 compares regular expressions (for matching strings) with the operators on programs: sequential composition of commands corresponds to concatenation of regular expressions, nondeterministic choice corresponds to a choice between alternative regular expressions, **magic** corresponds to the empty language, and **skip** corresponds to the empty string. One can split out the empty case of a Kleene star:

$$\begin{aligned}
s^* &= s^0 \sqcap \left(\bigsqcap i : \mathbb{N} \bullet s^{i+1}\right) \\
&= \mathbf{skip} \sqcap \left(\bigsqcap i : \mathbb{N} \bullet s;\ s^i\right) \\
&= \mathbf{skip} \sqcap \left(s;\ \left(\bigsqcap i : \mathbb{N} \bullet s^i\right)\right) \\
&= \mathbf{skip} \sqcap \left(s;\ s^*\right)
\end{aligned} \tag{29}$$

and the following *sliding* law holds (the step in the middle can be proved by induction).

$$\begin{aligned}
t;\ (s;\ t)^* &= t;\ \left(\bigsqcap i : \mathbb{N} \bullet (s;\ t)^i\right) \\
&= t;\ \left(\mathbf{skip} \sqcap \left(\bigsqcap i : \mathbb{N} \bullet s;\ t;\ (s;\ t)^i\right)\right) \\
&= t \sqcap \left(\bigsqcap i : \mathbb{N} \bullet t;\ s;\ t;\ (s;\ t)^i\right) \\
&= t \sqcap \left(\bigsqcap i : \mathbb{N} \bullet t;\ s;\ (t;\ s)^i;\ t\right) \\
&= \left(\mathbf{skip} \sqcap \left(\bigsqcap i : \mathbb{N} \bullet t;\ s;\ (t;\ s)^i\right)\right);\ t \\
&= \left(\bigsqcap i : \mathbb{N} \bullet (t;\ s)^i\right);\ t \\
&= (t;\ s)^*;\ t
\end{aligned} \tag{30}$$

We assume the Kleene star operator has the highest precedence followed by sequential composition and then nondeterministic choice.

3   Defining a Repetition Command

A repetition with guard b and body s,

    do $b \to s$ **od**

can now be defined as the choice between any finite number of iterations (including zero) of the guarded command, and an infinite iteration of it. If the guard is initially false the body of the repetition is never executed and repetition is equivalent to the path containing just the coercion $[\neg b]$. If the repetition executes exactly one iteration before terminating it is equivalent to the path

$$[b] ;\ s;\ [\neg b]$$

If the repetition executes exactly two iterations before terminating it is equivalent to the path

$$[b] ;\ s;\ [b] ;\ s;\ [\neg b] = ([b] ;\ s)^2;\ [\neg b]$$

More generally if it executes exactly i iterations before terminating it is equivalent to the path

$$([b] ;\ s)^i;\ [\neg b]$$

To allow for any finite number of iterations we take the nondeterministic choice over all possible number of iterations (including zero).

$$\left(\bigsqcap i : \mathbb{N} \bullet ([b] ;\ s)^i\right);\ [\neg b] \tag{31}$$

The nondeterministic choice in the above chooses from alternatives corresponding to zero or more iterations of the guarded body. This has exactly the properties of the Kleene star operator introduced earlier. Hence (31) can be rewritten as

$$([b] ; s)^*; \; [\neg b]$$

Assuming the command s terminates, this defines all the finite execution paths of the repetition. If the number of iterations taken by a repetition before terminating is deterministic and, say, j then b will be true on the first j iterations and false on the next. Hence

$$([b] ; s)^j; \; [\neg b] = ([true] ; s)^j; \; [\neg false] = (\textbf{skip}; s)^j; \; \textbf{skip} = s^j$$

and for i less than j

$$
\begin{aligned}
&([b] ; s)^i; \; [\neg b] \\
&= ([true] ; s)^i; \; [\neg true] \\
&= (\textbf{skip}; s)^i; \; \textbf{magic} \\
&= s^i; \; \textbf{magic} \\
&= \textbf{magic}
\end{aligned}
$$

The last step relies on the property that **magic** is a right zero of sequential composition provided s^i terminates (5), and s^i terminates because s terminates. For i greater than j

$$
\begin{aligned}
&([b] ; s)^i; \; [\neg b] \\
&= ([true] ; s)^j; \; [false] ; s; \; ([b] ; s)^{i-(j+1)}; \; [\neg b] \\
&= s^j; \; \textbf{magic}; \; s; \; ([b] ; s)^{i-(j+1)}; \; [\neg b] \\
&= \textbf{magic}
\end{aligned}
$$

Again the last step requires that s terminates and uses property (5). If the number of iterations, j, executed by the repetition is deterministic and finite, all other the alternative numbers of iterations within the nondeterministic choice are equivalent to **magic**. Because **magic** is the identity of nondeterministic choice, the choice over all i reduces to just the single path

$$([b] ; s)^j; \; [\neg b]$$

If the number of iterations is finite but nondeterministic then, rather than ending up with a single path, we end up with a nondeterministic choice over all possible number of iterations of the repetition for which it may terminate.

If the repetition never terminates (still assuming s terminates) then for all i

$$([b] ; s)^i; \; [\neg b] = ([true] ; s)^i; \; [\neg true] = s^i; \; \textbf{magic} = \textbf{magic}$$

To allow for a nonterminating repetition we use an infinite iteration of the guarded body:

$$([b] ; s)^\infty$$

This represents the infinite path that repeatedly evaluates the coercion (to true) and executes s, forever. If b ever becomes false, say after j iterations, then this is equivalent to **magic** because using (25)

$$
\begin{aligned}
& ([b] \,;\, s)^\infty \\
= & ([true] \,;\, s)^j; \, [false] \,;\, s; \, ([b] \,;\, s)^\infty \\
= & (\textbf{skip};\, s)^j; \, \textbf{magic};\, s; \, ([b] \,;\, s)^\infty \\
= & \,\textbf{magic}
\end{aligned}
$$

For the last step we are still assuming that s always terminates and using property (5).

The whole iteration can be defined via the following.

$$
\textbf{do } b \rightarrow s \textbf{ od} \;\widehat{=}\; (([b] \,;\, s)^*;\, [\neg b]) \sqcap ([b] \,;\, s)^\infty \tag{32}
$$

Above we assumed that the body of the repetition, s, always terminates, but if s terminated on the first j iterations and did not terminate on iteration $j + 1$, then paths with less than $j + 1$ iterations are equivalent to **magic** (as before), but paths with i iterations, where i is at least $j + 1$, satisfy the following (because if t does not terminate t; $u = t$ for any u).

$$
\begin{aligned}
& ([b] \,;\, s)^j; \, [b] \,;\, s; \, ([b] \,;\, s)^{i-(j+1)}; \, [\neg b] \\
= &\ \text{as } s \text{ does not terminate on iteration number } j + 1 \\
& ([b] \,;\, s)^j; \, [b] \,;\, s
\end{aligned}
$$

Hence the definition above also covers the case in which the body of the repetition fails to terminate on some iteration.

The definition of a repetition using an approach similar to the above was used by Back and von Wright [2] and in the real-time context in [11]. Earlier work on using Kleene algebra with tests has been done by Kozen [16] and Cohen [5].

4   Dead Paths

Identifying *dead* paths in a program is useful in contexts such as devising test cases and timing constraint analysis (see Section 6). Dead paths are paths that cannot possibly be followed (they are infeasible) or paths that do not terminate. In the testing context one would like to avoid trying to devise test cases for paths that cannot possibly be followed, or for paths that do not terminate. For timing analysis, including paths that cannot possibly be followed leads to more pessimistic timing estimates, and there is no point analyzing the time taken by a path that does not terminate.

As an example with dead paths, consider the following program.

if b **then** s **else** t **fi**; u; **if** b **then** v **else** w **fi**

The path view of this program can be calculated as follows.

$$
\begin{aligned}
& ([b] \,;\, s \sqcap [\neg b] \,;\, t); \, u; \, ([b] \,;\, v \sqcap [\neg b] \,;\, w) \\
= & [b] \,;\, s; \, u; \, [b] \,;\, v \,\sqcap \\
& [b] \,;\, s; \, u; \, [\neg b] \,;\, w \,\sqcap \\
& [\neg b] \,;\, t; \, u; \, [b] \,;\, v \,\sqcap \\
& [\neg b] \,;\, t; \, u; \, [\neg b] \,;\, w
\end{aligned}
$$

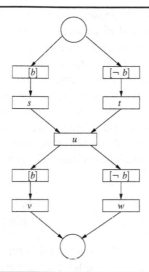

Fig. 2. Control-flow graph for the example.

This decomposes the program into its four possible execution paths. Paths that cannot possibly be followed are equivalent to **magic** and can be eliminated from the nondeterministic choice. If we assume that none of the commands s, t, and u modify variables used in b, then the second path is dead because if b is true at the start of the path then $\neg b$ will be false (and hence $[\neg b]$ will be equivalent to **magic**) later in the path. The third path is also dead for similar reasons.

The same four paths would be extracted with a conventional control-flow analysis of the control-flow graph of the program. Here the extraction is done using algebraic properties of programs and the resulting paths are valid constructs in the primitives of the language. Fig. 2 gives an control-flow graph of the example. When drawing control-flow graphs we draw the conditions differently to the most common form (a diamond with edges labeled *true* and *false* emanating from it). Instead we represent the true and false forms of the condition by separate boxes labeled with the condition that must hold to follow the path. This form of graph is more general because it is able to represent "case"-like commands with no additional primitives.

A dead path is either equivalent to **magic** or nonterminating (including aborting). In earlier work [12] we characterised dead paths using Dijkstra's weakest liberal preconditions. A path s is dead if and only if

$$wlp.s.false \equiv true \qquad (33)$$

Alternatively $wlp.s.false$ characterises those initial states from which the path s is dead.

5   Extending to Real-Time

To extend to path view to real-time programs we introduce a special real-valued variable, τ, to stand for the current time. In order to remain the identity of sequential composition, the command **skip** must take no time to execute, i.e., it does not change τ.

In the real-time language we distinguish between local (state) variables, including auxiliary variables (see below), and external inputs and outputs, in that the latter are represented by a timed trace, a function from time to their value at that time, whereas the former are just represented by their current value. For a real-time program we are not just interested in the final value of an external variable but the relationship between the traces of inputs and outputs over the execution time of the program.

We introduce a new command, **idle**, that may take some finite time to execute, but changes no variables or program outputs. Using **idle** as well as our existing constructs we can define a real-time version of the "if" command, in which the times taken to evaluate the guard and exit the branches of the "if" command are represented by **idle** commands.

$$\textbf{if } b \textbf{ then } s \textbf{ else } t \textbf{ fi} \mathrel{\widehat{=}} \left([b \mathbin{@} \tau] \; ; \; \textbf{idle}; \; s; \; \textbf{idle} \right) \sqcap \qquad (34)$$
$$\left([\neg\, b \mathbin{@} \tau] \; ; \; \textbf{idle}; \; t; \; \textbf{idle} \right)$$

The evaluation of the guard of the "if" command is represented by "$[b \mathbin{@} \tau]$; **idle**" for the "then" branch and "$[\neg\, b \mathbin{@} \tau]$; **idle**" for the "else" branch. In this paper the coercion primitives are defined to take no time to execute; this differs from earlier work [13] but makes algebraic reasoning easier. Here additional **idle** commands are used to represent the passage of time. The guard b is evaluated at the current time τ. Hence we use the expression $b \mathbin{@} \tau$ in the definition; this stands for the expression b with every occurrence of an external input or output, v, replaced by its value at time τ, i.e., $v(\tau)$. In order to ensure that the evaluation of the guard is independent of the time taken to evaluate the guard, we require that the guard expression is *idle-stable*, that is, its value does not change with the passage of time, assuming that the program's state variables and outputs do not change. An expression b is idle-stable provided

$$[b] \; ; \; \textbf{idle} = \textbf{idle}; \; [b] \qquad (35)$$

In practice this means the guard b must be independent of the current time variable, τ, and of external inputs.

For an implementation on a particular target machine the guard evaluation will take a particular (range of) time to execute. Because we are working with a machine-independent language, we allow any finite execution time to allow for any conceivable target machine. In order to guarantee that the program performs in a timely manner we make use of a deadline command [7] of the form **deadline** d. In our context a deadline command can be represented by a coercion of the form $[\tau \leq d]$, where τ represents the current time. Like other coercions, a deadline command cannot be implemented in isolation because it always guarantees to meet its deadline, even if executed at a time later than its deadline.

We introduce a real-time specification command,

$$\vec{x}, \vec{o} \colon [Q] \,,$$

with a frame consisting of the vector of state variables $\vec{x}$ and the vector of outputs $\vec{o}$, and postcondition Q. The predicate Q is a *relation*, in the sense that it may refer to both the initial value of a state variable v via v and its final value via v'. The specification command guarantees to establish Q and only change the variables in the frame and the current time variable τ. Furthermore it guarantees that time does not go backward ($\tau \leq \tau'$) and that it terminates ($\tau' < \infty$). Because outputs are traces over time, in order to ensure that the value of an output, y, that is not in the frame does not change during the execution of the command we introduce the predicate $stable(y, S)$ to state that the value of y is the same for all times in the set S,

$$stable(y, S) \cong S \neq \varnothing \Rightarrow (\exists z \bullet y(\!| S |\!) = \{z\}) \tag{36}$$

where $y(\!| S |\!)$ is the image of the set S through the function y. We allow $stable$ to be applied to a set of variables, in which case every variable in the vector is stable over S.

The specification command can be defined in terms of our existing constructs. We assume that ρ is the environment consisting of all the variables in scope and that $\rho.out$ consists of all the outputs in scope and hence $\rho.out \setminus \vec{o}$ is the set of output variables that are not in the frame.

$$\vec{x}, \vec{o}: [Q] \cong \left(\prod \tau', \vec{x}' \bullet \begin{bmatrix} Q \wedge \tau \leq \tau' < \infty \wedge \\ stable(\rho.out \setminus \vec{o}, [\tau \ldots \tau']) \end{bmatrix} ; \ \tau, \vec{x} \leftarrow \tau', \vec{x}' \right) \tag{37}$$

The specification nondeterministically chooses the final time, τ', and the final values of the state variables in the frame, $\vec{x}'$, so that $Q \wedge \tau \leq \tau' < \infty$ is satisfied. Q may also refer to inputs and outputs, and hence the values of τ' and $\vec{x}'$ may be constrained by this. Q may constrain the traces of outputs (usually over the execution time of the command). See [13, 19] for more details. Those outputs that are not in the frame are stable for the duration of the command.

Given a vector of state variables, $\vec{x}$; a vector of idle-stable expressions $\vec{e}$ that are assignment compatible with $\vec{x}$; an idle-stable, time-valued expression d that does not refer to τ; a time-valued variable t; a state variable v; an input i that is assignment compatible with v; an output o; and an idle-stable expression f that is assignment compatible with o, then

$$\mathbf{idle} \cong \varnothing: [true] \tag{38}$$

$$\vec{x} := \vec{e} \cong \mathbf{idle}; \ \vec{x} \leftarrow \vec{e} \tag{39}$$

$$\mathbf{delay\ until}(d) \cong \mathbf{idle}; \ [d @ \tau \leq \tau] \tag{40}$$

$$t : \mathbf{gettime} \cong t: [\tau \leq t \leq \tau'] \tag{41}$$

$$v : \mathbf{read}(i) \cong v: [v' \in i(\!| [\tau \ldots \tau'] |\!)] \tag{42}$$

$$o : \mathbf{write}(f) \cong o: [o(\tau') = f @ \tau] \tag{43}$$

Fig. 3. Real-time commands.

Other real-time commands can be defined using the constructs we have introduced already (see Figure 3). The specification command $\varnothing: [true]$, where $\varnothing$ indicates an empty frame, differs from the coercion $[true]$ in that τ is implicitly in the frame of the former and hence **idle** allows time to pass. The primitive assignment $\vec{x} \leftarrow \vec{e}$ takes no time; hence an **idle** command is needed in the definition of the real-time assignment to allow for the passage of time. In the real-time language the primitive assignment is only used for auxiliary variables (see below).

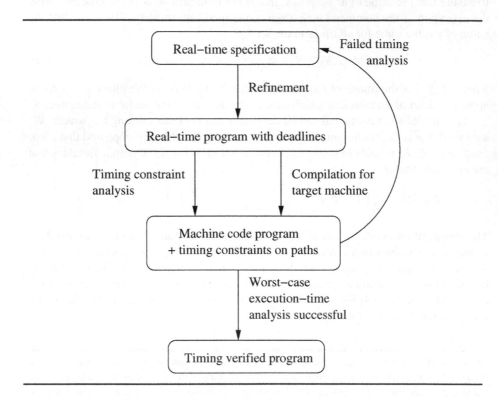

Fig. 4. Development process for real-time programs.

6   Timing Constraint Analysis

Deadline commands provide a mechanism for specifying timing constraints in a machine-independent manner. Fig. 4 gives an overview of the program development approach. A real-time specification is refined to a machine-independent real-time program, which includes deadline commands to guarantee the timely operation of the program. In order to show that a program compiled for a particular target machine implements the machine-independent program, one must show that all deadlines in the program are reached before their specified deadline. Showing that all deadlines are met can be split into two phases:

timing constraint analysis a machine-independent phase that partitions the program into a set of subpaths ending in deadlines, along with an execution-time constraint on each path, and

execution-time analysis a machine-dependent phase that checks whether or not the compiled code corresponding to each path meets its execution-time constraint.

Here we concentrate on the first machine-independent phase and show how representing programs as paths can facilitate the timing constraint analysis. We use an example of a repetition containing a deadline.

$$\textbf{do } b \rightarrow s_1;\ [\tau \leq d]\ ;\ s_2 \textbf{ od}$$

Before manipulating this we note that, using (13), the predicate in the coercion can be assumed after the coercion, and hence the above is equivalent to the following.

$$\textbf{do } b \rightarrow s_1;\ [\tau \leq d]\ ;\ \{\tau \leq d\};\ s_2 \textbf{ od} \tag{44}$$

In the real-time refinement calculus a repetition is defined in a manner similar to (32), except that additional **idle** commands are included to allow for the time taken to evaluate the guard of the repetition and for the branch back to the start of the repetition.

$$\textbf{do } b \rightarrow s \textbf{ od} \mathrel{\widehat{=}} ([b]\ ;\ \textbf{idle};\ s;\ \textbf{idle})^*;\ [\neg b]\ ;\ \textbf{idle} \sqcap ([b]\ ;\ \textbf{idle};\ s;\ \textbf{idle})^\infty \tag{45}$$

Applying (45), our example (44) is equivalent to the following.

$$([b]\ ;\ \textbf{idle};\ s_1;\ [\tau \leq d]\ ;\ \{\tau \leq d\};\ s_2;\ \textbf{idle})^*;\ [\neg b]\ ;\ \textbf{idle}$$
$$\sqcap\ ([b]\ ;\ \textbf{idle};\ s_1;\ [\tau \leq d]\ ;\ \{\tau \leq d\};\ s_2;\ \textbf{idle})^\infty$$

If we introduce the following abbreviations

$$t \mathrel{\widehat{=}} [b]\ ;\ \textbf{idle};\ s_1$$
$$u \mathrel{\widehat{=}} [\tau \leq d]$$
$$v \mathrel{\widehat{=}} \{\tau \leq d\};\ s_2;\ \textbf{idle}$$

then the above can be rewritten as

$$(t;\ u;\ v)^*;\ [\neg b]\ ;\ \textbf{idle} \sqcap (t;\ u;\ v)^\infty$$
$$= \text{unfolding the Kleene star (29) and using (27)}$$
$$(\textbf{skip} \sqcap t;\ u;\ v;\ (t;\ u;\ v)^*);\ [\neg b]\ ;\ \textbf{idle} \sqcap t;\ u;\ (v;\ t;\ u)^\infty$$
$$= \text{using the sliding law (30)}$$
$$(\textbf{skip} \sqcap t;\ u;\ (v;\ t;\ u)^*;\ v);\ [\neg b]\ ;\ \textbf{idle} \sqcap t;\ u;\ (v;\ t;\ u)^\infty \tag{46}$$

Recalling that u stands for the deadline command, we have rewritten the program so that the subpaths appearing in the program end with the deadline (u). We introduce a new construct, $s\langle x \rangle$, into the real-time language that allows one to specify an execution-time limit, x, on a command s so that $s\langle x \rangle$ is the same as s except that it guarantees to execute in at most x time units. If one can show that there exist upper time limits x and y such that

$$t;\ u \sqsubseteq t\langle x \rangle \tag{47}$$
$$v;\ t;\ u \sqsubseteq (v;\ t)\langle y \rangle \tag{48}$$

then (46) can be refined to

$$(\textbf{skip} \sqcap t\langle x \rangle;\ ((v;\ t)\langle y \rangle))^*;\ v);\ [\neg b]\ ;\ \textbf{idle} \sqcap t\langle x \rangle;\ ((v;\ t)\langle y \rangle)^\infty$$

Expanding our abbreviations for t, u, and v, (47) and (48) become

$$[b] \; ; \; \mathbf{idle}; \; s_1; \; [\tau \le d] \sqsubseteq ([b] \; ; \; \mathbf{idle}; \; s_1) \langle x \rangle$$

$$\{\tau \le d\}; \; s_2; \; \mathbf{idle}; \; [b] \; ; \; \mathbf{idle}; \; s_1; \; [\tau \le d] \sqsubseteq (\{\tau \le d\}; \; s_2; \; \mathbf{idle}; \; [b] \; ; \; \mathbf{idle}; \; s_1) \langle y \rangle$$

What we have done is to replace the deadline commands by time limits on subpaths in such a way the the result is a refinement of the original repetition. When the program is compiled, the code corresponding to each time-limited subpath needs to be analyzed to show that its worst-case execution time meets its time limit.

To make our example more concrete, consider the following simple program which repeatedly reads a value from an input i and writes some function of the input to the output o. Each cycle is limited to a time of D milliseconds. The variable T is an auxiliary variable; no code needs to be generated for the commands involving auxiliary variables; they are used only to express timing constraints [10].

$$
\begin{aligned}
& T \leftarrow \tau; \\
& \mathbf{do} \; true \; \rightarrow \\
& \qquad x : \mathbf{read}(i); \\
& \qquad o : \mathbf{write}(f(x)); \\
& \qquad [\tau \le T + D] \; ; \\
& \qquad T \leftarrow \tau \\
& \mathbf{od}
\end{aligned}
\tag{49}
$$

It is of a structure similar to (44). Using a decomposition similar to (46), the interesting paths are

$$T \leftarrow \tau; \; [true]; \; \mathbf{idle}; \; x : \mathbf{read}(i); \; o : \mathbf{write}(f(x)); \; [\tau \le T + D]$$

and

$$T \leftarrow \tau; \; \mathbf{idle}; \; [true]; \; \mathbf{idle}; \; x : \mathbf{read}(i); \; o : \mathbf{write}(f(x)); \; [\tau \le T + D]$$

For this simple example both paths can be refined by removing the deadlines and adding an execution-time limit of D milliseconds. For example, the first path becomes:

$$(T \leftarrow \tau; \; [true]; \; \mathbf{idle}; \; x : \mathbf{read}(i); \; o : \mathbf{write}(f(x))) \langle D \rangle$$

The auxiliary variable T could also be eliminated at this stage because it no longer serves a useful purpose. Note that it is not possible to introduce the execution-time limit into the original program (49) expressed using a repetition. This is because the paths do not correspond directly to subcomponents visible in the original program. The first path starts before the repetition and finishes at the deadline in its body, and the second path starts at the auxiliary assignment at the end of the repetition continues back to the start of the repetition and finishes at the deadline. Only using the path-oriented view of the program can we introduce the appropriate time limits that guarantee that the deadlines will always be met.

7 Conclusion

In the program analysis world, analyzing programs in terms of their control-flow graph, including paths through the control-flow graph, is common place [9]. The approach taken in this paper has been to decompose programs into their constituent paths that are defined in terms of primitives derived from the refinement calculus, in particular, nondeterministic choice, coercions and iteration.

Our use of a path-oriented view of programs is motivated by the need to consider timing constraints on subpaths of a program that guarantee that all deadlines in the program will be met. The path-oriented view allows us to manipulate the program into a form suitable for imposing timing constraints. The manipulation makes use of the algebraic properties of the primitives. For repetitions we make use of the Kleene star operator which allows a simple definition of a repetition with nice algebraic properties for manipulation of programs written in this form, e.g., the use of the sliding law.

Acknowledgments

This research was supported by Australian Research Council (ARC) Discovery Grant DP0209722, *Derivation and timing analysis of concurrent real-time software*. I would like to thank Kirsten Winter for feedback on earlier drafts of this paper, and Colin Fidge, Karl Lermer and Joachim von Wright for fruitful discussions on the topic of this paper. I would also like to thank the members of IFIP Working Group 2.3 on Programming Methodology, especially Ernie Cohen, for introducing me to Kleene algebra for programs.

References

1. R.-J. Back and J. von Wright. *Refinement Calculus: A Systematic Introduction*. Springer, 1998.
2. R.J.R. Back and J. von Wright. Reasoning algebraically about loops. *Acta Informatica*, 36:295–334, 1999.
3. B. Beizer. *Software Testing Techniques*. Thomson Computer Press, second edition, 1990.
4. R. Chapman, A. Burns, and A. J. Wellings. Integrated program proof and worst-case timing analysis of SPARK Ada. In *ACM Workshop on language, compiler and tool support for real-time systems*. ACM Press, 1994.
5. E. Cohen. Hypotheses in Kleene algebra. Technical report TM-ARH-023814, Bellcore, 1994.
6. E. W. Dijkstra. *A Discipline of Programming*. Prentice-Hall, 1976.
7. C. J. Fidge, I. J. Hayes, and G. Watson. The deadline command. *IEE Proceedings—Software*, 146(2):104–111, April 1999.
8. S. Grundon, I. J. Hayes, and C. J. Fidge. Timing constraint analysis. In C. McDonald, editor, *Computer Science '98: Proc. 21st Australasian Computer Sci. Conf. (ACSC'98)*, Perth, 4–6 Feb., pages 575–586. Springer, 1998.
9. E.L. Gunter and D. Peled. Path exploration tool. In W.R. Cleaveland, editor, *Tools and Algorithms for the Construction and Analysis of Systems (TACAS/ETAPS'99)*, volume 1579 of *Lecture Notes in Computer Science*, pages 405–419. Springer, 1999.

10. I. J. Hayes. Real-time program refinement using auxiliary variables. In M. Joseph, editor, *Proc. Formal Techniques in Real-Time and Fault-Tolerant Systems*, volume 1926 of *Lecture Notes in Comp. Sci.*, pages 170–184. Springer, 2000.

11. I. J. Hayes. Reasoning about real-time repetitions: Terminating and nonterminating. *Science of Computer Programming*, 43(2–3):161–192, May–June 2002.

12. I. J. Hayes, C. J. Fidge, and K. Lermer. Semantic characterisation of dead control-flow paths. *IEE Proceedings—Software*, 148(6):175–186, December 2001.

13. I. J. Hayes and M. Utting. A sequential real-time refinement calculus. *Acta Informatica*, 37(6):385–448, 2001.

14. E. C. R. Hehner. *A Practical Theory of Programming*. Springer, 1993.

15. C. A. R. Hoare and He Jifeng. *Unifying Theories of Programming*. Prentice Hall, 1998.

16. Dexter Kozen. Kleene algebra with tests. *ACM Transactions on Programming Languages and Systems*, 19(3):427–443, May 1997.

17. K. Lermer, C. J. Fidge, and I. J. Hayes. Linear approximation of execution time constraints. Technical Report 02-31, Software Verification Reseach Centre, The University of Queensland, Oct 2002.

18. C. C. Morgan. *Programming from Specifications*. Prentice Hall, second edition, 1994.

19. M. Utting and C. J. Fidge. A real-time refinement calculus that changes only time. In He Jifeng, editor, *Proc. 7th BCS/FACS Refinement Workshop*, Electronic Workshops in Computing. Springer, July 1996.

Model Based Code Verification

Colin O'Halloran

QinetiQ, Trusted Information Management, Systems Assurance Group,
Malvern Technology Park, UK
cmohalloran@qinetiq.com

Abstract. Model based development languages, such as Simulink and UML, are increasing in popularity. Simulink is a de-facto standard in control systems engineering and UML is the subject of a significant standardisation effort. These "standardised" model based languages have commercial tool support, which primarily address the customer's immediate demands. In this paper I shall discuss the trends that are leading to an opportunity for formal methods to deliver significant benefits to industrial software development. Insights are drawn from an industrial application of formal methods and an experiment that compares a formal and a conventional development.

1 Introduction

In this paper I shall refer to model-based design to mean a design environment that lets engineers use a single model of their entire system to work through data analysis, model visualization, testing and validation, and ultimately production deployment.

1.1 The Potential of Model-Based Design

Increasing processing power and memory at reduced costs have led to powerful design tools for software and system engineering. For example Simulink from The MathWorks allows the block diagram idiom that control law engineers have used on paper to be simulated and to facilitate computational analysis techniques. Several industries, especially the aerospace and automotive sectors, were early adopters of simulation technologies.

Previously control law engineers would have written a Fortran or C program to simulate a specification. Software engineering issues of, for example, efficiency of execution would then become entangled with control engineering issues. The simulation program would become the specification and much of the initial development work would be hard to maintain because it had been done in Fortran, Ada, or C. The design of algorithmic languages makes them good for developing efficient simulations, but they are not ideal for a specification hence the rapid rise in popularity of a language like Simulink. UML is an analogous approach to Simulink for Software Engineering to separate the "what is required" from the "how to achieve the requirements".

Developing algorithms and software manually can be a time-consuming and error-prone process. Processes based on paper specifications can lead to misinterpretation, slow communication between groups, and difficulty in responding to changes in design and requirements. Model-based design addresses these issues, with executable specifications transferred in the form of, for example, Simulink and Stateflow models. By reducing errors from design ambiguities, running real-time simulations for rapid prototyping, hardware-in-the-loop testing, and generating production code from models, development time and costs can potentially be dramatically reduced.

1.2 The Commercial Pressure for Model Based Code Generation

Increasing processing power and memory has also led to an increase in the size and complexity of software applications. These software applications are growing in their pervasiveness leading to a greater dependence by society. This has also led to an increase in the criticality of software. For example automotive control systems for power management, traction control and engine control. In this case the criticality does not usually lie in safety, since they can be designed to be fail safe, but in the monetary issue of the manufacturers' warranty.

Due to the explosion in the pervasiveness of software there will be a shortage in skilled software engineers, this was experienced recently during the ".com" boom. At the same time the issues such as warranty have led to more rigorous and labour intensive software development processes. As a consequence the costs and timescales for development of software intensive projects have increased significantly, or have failed to deliver.

Automatic code generation from modeling languages such as Simulink is attractive if the code generation process can be trusted. However, because of commercial pressures, the modelling languages and their support tools are constantly being upgraded requiring the constant evolution or complete re-work of the associated automatic code generators. The issue of trust in the validity of the models and in particular the fidelity of the code generated from the models is the subject of this paper. In the next section I shall discuss the general issues of trust in automatic code generation. In section 3 I will give a brief overview of an experiment in formally verifying automatically generated code and give preliminary results, the experiment and its final results will be the subject of a full paper in the future. Finally I will discuss the implications of the results of the experiment and how formal methods might be able to build on the approach taken to establishing the validity of models.

2 Code Generation from Models

In this section three broad approaches for establishing trust in automatic code generation are discussed and compared.

2.1 Verified Automatic Code Generators

There does not appear to be any reference in the literature to work on verification of conventional automatic code generators, except for compilers. The most significant work in the area of compiler verification is reported in the book by Susan Stepney [1]. The origins of this work go back to a study commissioned by QinetiQ (previously

DERA) Malvern into how to develop a trusted compiler for high integrity applications.

In that study, the source language was SPARK [2], a subset of Ada designed for safety critical applications, and the target was Viper [3,4], a high integrity processor. Logica developed a mathematical technique for specifying a compiler and proving it correct, and developed a small proof of concept prototype [5].

This work was subsequently extended for another simple high integrity processor for a subset of Pascal [6]. A high integrity compiler was produced and is being incrementally extended to enlarge the subset of Pascal, to include for example separate compilation (without any sharing).

It is important to appreciate the scope of the work that was required, in order to assess verifying an automatic code generator. The development of a high integrity code generator, following the same approach, would involve the following steps: mathematically specifying the generator; implementing this specification; providing a mathematical semantics for the input and target language; proof that the generator's semantics are meaning preserving.

The compiler specification consisted of an operational semantics of the source language in the form of a set of target language templates described in the formal language Z [7]. This is a rigorous version of the way many automatic code generators currently operate. The compiler was implemented by translating the Z description into Prolog that was then executed. Executing the semantics essentially provided a trusted compilation.

The source and target languages were specified by providing a denotational semantics for both the source and target language, again expressed in Z. The proof in Z consisted of demonstrating that the compiler's operational semantics were equivalent to the source language's denotational semantics. That is, the denotational meaning of a transformed source program, using templates, in the target language is equivalent to the denotational meaning of the source program. The compiler was shown to be meaning preserving and hence correct.

For the particular project this high integrity compiler work has been a success and proved to be cost effective [6]. However the proofs, although undoubtedly useful, were carried out by hand. Furthermore no optimizations were performed on the generated target code.

More recently there has been promising work being undertaken by the VERIFIX project [8]. The aim of the VERIFIX project is the construction of mathematically correct compilers, which includes both the development of formal methods for specification and implementation of a compiler, and also the implementation of concrete compilers and development tools. However it is unclear at this time whether they will be able to achieve their aims. The main problem is the rapid obsolescence of target processors.

2.2 Correct by Construction

The correct by construction approach works by transforming the description in the input language into the target. It is most associated with proof where proving a specification also constructs a program that is guaranteed to implement that specification.

A related approach is taken by techniques such as the B method [9]. A high level specification is refined towards a low-level design from which code is generated. The key point here is that the refinement is supported by proof and bridges the large gap between the high level specification and the low-level design. The automatic code generation introduces only a small gap with less risk of introducing errors.

These approaches to code generation do not fit into the usual paradigm of automatic code generation. However when high assurance is required, these approaches have the advantage that the verification effort also produces the required code. This is equivalent to the "automatically generate and verify" approach.

The process can even be automated in some cases. For example using the proof-planning paradigm recursive functional programs can be automatically generated [10]. Automated code generation becomes equivalent to automatic theorem proving. However the implementation languages tend to be constraint or functional programming languages.

2.3   Verifying the Generated Code

The third approach to provide the necessary assurance for automatically generated safety critical code is to take the generated code and construct a proof of correctness. This involves constructing a proof that the observed behaviour of the code is a subset of the observed behaviour of the design. Like the other two approaches it requires a mathematical meaning for the input design and target language.

Assessing the generated code for correctness is a reverse engineering exercise, as opposed to the top down synthesis approach. However a refinement approach, as practiced in the B method or refinement calculi [10,11], can also be used to underpin the reverse engineering approach. This particular approach, called "conjecture and verify", fell out of favour but is suited for verifying automatically generated code.

2.4   Comparing the Approaches

The three broad approaches outlined in sections 2.1 to 2.3 cover how assurance for automated code generation might be achieved, but which one is the best? Of course there is no absolute "best approach", it depends upon the timescale constraints and project circumstances. For example the high integrity compiler work of Stepney has proven to be the best approach for the particular project it was developed for. This is because the application is so critical it was worth the investment just for that particular project. Further the microprocessor design and fabrication, the software development process and the compiler were all under the control of the same people.

For the compiler work the specification of the compiler templates were approximately 100 pages of Z, with a further 20 pages to specify linking for separate compilation. The Z specification of the Pascal subset was 150 pages, the specification of the target language was 50 pages. In comparison the static semantics for SPARK, that could be a target language, is 300 pages of Z and the dynamic semantics is 500 pages of Z. This indicates that verifying an automated code generator is at least at the edge of commercial viability.

The correct by construction approach suffers from the problem that it is still largely manual and requires a particular development process to be adopted by industry. In the longer-term automatic code synthesis (i.e. code generation based upon constructing the code via a proof) promises much and has proven useful for control systems [12]. There is a lack of support for current mainstream languages, like C and Ada, however in the longer term this could become irrelevant.

Automatic code synthesis based on automatic proof suffers from the problems of automated theorem proving. In general it is difficult to guarantee that a proof and hence code will be generated. However by constraining the problem space, which would happen quite naturally for domains such as control laws, automatic synthesis could be very effective [13]. By the same token automatic verification strategies, for code that has been generated by another tool, should be possible in such constrained domains.

The soundness of the theorem prover is an issue because it is directly responsible for the generation of the code. The veracity of the proof for a verified automated code generator is also a problem. This moves the assurance problem elsewhere, but it might well be more appropriate to address it in the domain of theorem proving tools.

Verification of the code that has been automatically generated is less of a problem. A view, which has been taken in UK safety clearance, is that it would be incredible if a flaw in post verification tool exactly masked a flaw in the software that was being assessed. Of course errors will be present, but they will either prevent verification or be so gross that they will reveal themselves. This is an appeal to software diversity between, for example, system control software and verification software. Although only limited quantitative evidence can be demonstrated there are very strong qualitative arguments that can be made for independence of truly diverse software.

If automated code generation of safety critical software is to become more widespread then they will have to be commercial tools. The possible legal liabilities mean that claims made about the tool (that it is verified or is guaranteed to generate correct code) carry significant commercial risk. This makes the first two approaches to automatic code generation, verification of the generator and "correctness by construction", commercially unattractive.

Verifying the code independently from the automated code generator moves the risk elsewhere. With this approach the code generator adds no assurance and is just a tool to reduce costs, of both development **and verification**. Where does the risk go? It goes to either the developer of the safety critical system, such as an aircraft manufacturer, or to the customer, such as the UK MOD, or is shared between both.

In the next section I shall present some evidence in favour of independently verifying the automatic code generator.

3   Verification of Automatically Generated Code

The Systems Assurance Group at Malvern has applied verification techniques and tools to two previous versions of a control system. The specification of the control system is estimated to be of the order of 800 pages of A4 Simulink diagrams. It is hierarchical and was transcribed from another representation. The transcription process included a significant validation effort that takes advantage of Simulink's simulation capabilities. The specification in Simulink is suitable for review by independent control engineers, which the previous representation was not, although it could be executed. The implementation of the control system consisted of approximately 18,000 lines of non-blank, non-comment code. The verification was conducted on an implementation of the control system that had already been subjected to a mature software verification and validation process. Further details of the results of the verification exercise can be found in [14].

Although the formal post-development verification was successful in providing extra evidence of the correctness of the implementation (as well as identifying a handful of minor issues and one major one) there was little justification for using the approach to replace parts of a development process. The techniques and tools did not have a stable baseline and time measurements for the various activities were not taken. As a result, it was not easy to assess the potential impact on any other project. For this reason an experiment was proposed and funded by the UK MOD's Corporate Research Programme to provide evidence for deciding whether to use the QinetiQ tool set in development with respect to potential benefits, risks and costs.

3.1 Aims of the Experiment

The principal aims for the experiment were:

1. Could automatic code generation be integrated with the existing verification tools to give a software development process that would pass the existing functional unit tests?
2. Would the code be of sufficient quality to be flown, i.e. was it certifiable?
3. What were the cost implications of adopting the process as part of a development lifecycle?

In September 2002, QinetiQ agreed to run the experiment to replace a third of the functional modules of the latest verified version of the control system with auto-generated, machine assisted formally proven SPARK Ada code. The experiment was conducted in conjunction with the company that had developed the original software. The selected modules represented various types of code including complexity, runtime (both long and short), size and the applicability to a proprietary PowerPC benchmark. These modules represented approximately 8,500 lines of code of a total of approximately 18,000 lines of code (roughly 47% of the manually developed code and all non-blank and non-comment). Throughout the Malvern work, time measurements were taken for each part of the process and compared to industry norms and the equivalent from the original work undertaken by the company.

3.2 Results of the Experiment

The functional unit testing revealed changes in the structure of the code and minor problems with instrumenting the code for testing with the legacy code. The most significant issue that functional unit testing showed was a small deviation from the numerical accuracy required. Floating point numbers are represented within the QinetiQ verification approach as mathematical real numbers; hence numerical accuracy is not in the scope of our verification. This is no different from the use of, for example, the SPARK examiner and its associated verification tools. This means that the conventional testing for numerical accuracy is still required. However the use of retrenchment refinement techniques offers the promise of addressing this formally in the future [15].

Of the autocoded functional modules analysed, when compared with the original hand code, 15 showed an improved Worst Case Run Time (WCRT), 12 had identical WCRT and 53 had greater WCRT. Overall approximately 28% more run-time was consumed by the autocode and approximately 30% more storage was required.

The true WCRT figures are likely to be somewhat higher than those calculated, as the automatically generated code does not contain a specific optimisation for the target processor. Running the code without the optimisation typically causes instruction times to double. The optimisation is not required for the PowerPC microprocessor.

The Worst Case Run Time analysis indicated that overall the one third of the functional modules would not fit into the very stringent real time performance requirements. This is because of the severe limitations of the processor being used with respect to the demands of the control system. For this reason 18 functional modules were selected as a sample to be compiled and executed on the Power PC (the MPC 565 microprocessor) using the Green Hills compiler.

Of the 18 functional modules that were timed: 9 had longer run-times to the original hand code; 7 had shorter run-times; and 2 were identical. Of the 9 procedures that had longer run-times, 4 of these took roughly an additional 50% of the (manually developed code) execution time to execute, with one taking slightly more than double the time of the manually developed code. The remaining 5 procedures were on average around 11% slower. Those procedures that had shorter run-times were on average about 4% faster. The procedures that took 50% or longer than the manually developed code would bear further investigation into how the automatic code generator could produce more efficient code.

In summary the results of the experiment demonstrated that the first two aims of the experiment were essentially positively satisfied, however more work needs to be done. In answer to the third question the broad comparison is that in terms of person hours the QinetiQ process is between 2 ½ and 4 ½ times faster in that part of the software development that includes Design, Implementation and Unit Tests. This is a significant impact on overall costs of a development, which can easily form over 50% of software project cost. No credit has been taken for further reductions of costs in the Design or Rig Tests.

4 Conclusions

There has always been tension between modelling and developer led processes. Typically modelling and development are separate processes carried out by different individuals. The modeller produces specifications, but the developer treats them as broad guidelines rather than precise specifications, or misinterprets them. Platform considerations often force developers to compromise good partitioning of functionality to achieve acceptable performance and integrity. Perfectly reasonable changes made to the implementation are not reflected back into the design or specification, rendering these not merely out of date, but dangerously inconsistent.

Model-based design is vulnerable to these problems. For example in the preparation for the experiment it was necessary to significantly re-structure the Simulink specification for integration with the legacy software and architecture. This implementation oriented Simulink was then used to generate the software, however the original validated Simulink was still used as the specification. The formal verification not only detected errors in the automatic code generation process, but also errors in the Simulink re-structuring process. This means that the potential for divergence between modelling and development, that is not special to model-based design, can be managed and consistency enforced.

The experiment has shown that the "conjecture and verify" approach is a means of reducing development and warranty costs within the model-based design paradigm. Although QinetiQ's experience has been with Simulink there is no reason why it should not be possible to reap benefits from other model based languages. Indeed the Systems Assurance Group at QinetiQ Malvern is working on extending the approach to The MathWorks' Stateflow language and aspects of the UML. Further the formal basis for code verification also provides a platform for applying formal techniques to validate a specification in a model-based language.

To this end QinetiQ has sponsored research into symbolically reasoning about control laws in Simulink [16]. We are also working with our colleagues at QinetiQ Bedford in joining our verification technology with their technology for assessing global stability properties of control laws using bifurcation analysis. There is related work on employing formal methods at SRI and York University for Simulink and Stateflow [17]. The UML is another candidate for reasoning about specifications for the purpose of validation [18].

I believe that we have an opportunity to inject formal methods into mainstream software engineering via the model-based development paradigm. Rather than continuing to be regarded as "gold plating" technology affordable only within security or safety critical niches, we should aim to reduce the "cost" of applying formal methods and increase its ubiquity. The objective should be to be cheaper and more effective than conventional testing and to be more flexible and re-usable for requirements changes.

Model-based design provides an opportunity because much of the formality can be made invisible and it has the potential for widespread acceptance by industry. Current acceptance practices do not have to be replaced suddenly, testing can still be used for acceptance. The costs can still be largely neutral over the lifecycle even with current testing, because of reduced iteration of testing and correction cycles as well as re-use of verification evidence due to changes in requirements. Significant cost reductions can then accrue from replacing conventional verification and validation leading to reduced manual effort, time and warranty issues. The experiment in verifying automatically generated code indicates that this is plausible. There are still significant commercial challenges and prejudices to be addressed, but the technical and economic climate is such that the long promised impact of formal methods could occur in the next five years.

Acknowledgements

This paper is due to the work funded by the UK MOD's CRP CISP domain. I would also like to acknowledge the work and support of a number of people who have been involved in this work. I am immensely grateful to both Mark Adams and Phil Clayton who have taken my original ideas and considerably extended them, much of the success I have reported here are due to them. My colleague Alf Smith has been a bedrock of technical support for the work reported here. Liz Whiting has also contributed much through the application of static analysis for run-time errors and Jaspal Sagoo made my ideas on distributed scheduling verification into an industrial process. Howard Manning lifted the burden of project managing the tasks and members of the Systems Assurance Group have all contributed over the past three years to developing this verification technology. John Burnell at QinetiQ Bedford has also been invaluable with his Simulink expertise. Paul Caseley was one of the first to recognise the potential for this work and originally had the thankless task of project managing the work. Finally my thanks goes to Squadron Leader Nick Tudor for believing in this work and championing a vision of model-based development within the UK MOD.

References

1. Stepney S.: High Integrity Compilation
2. Barnes J.: High integrity Ada, The SPARK approach, Addison-Wesley, 1997.
3. Pygott C.: Formal Specification of the VIPER microprocessor in HOL, RSRE report 90009.
4. Cohn A.: The notion of proof in hardware verification. Journal of automated reasoning 5, 127-139.
5. Stepney S., Whitley D., Cooper D, and Grant C.: A demonstrably correct compiler. BCS Formal Aspects of Computing, 3:58-101, 1991.
6. Stepney S. Incremental development of a high integrity compiler: experience from an industrial development. Third IEEE High-Assurance Systems Engineering Symposium (HASE'98), Washington DC 1998.
7. Davies J., Woodcock J.: Using Z. Prentice Hall International series in computer science, 1996.
8. http://www.info.uni-karlsruhe.de/~verifix/index.html
9. Storey A. C. and Haughton H. P.: A strategy for the production of verifiable code using the B method, Springer-Verlag, FME94.
10. Armando A., Smaill A., and Green I.: Automatic Synthesis of Recursive Programs: The Proof-Planning Paradigm, 12th IEEE ASE, 1997. IEEE Computer Society Press.
11. Morgan C.: Programming from specifications. Prentice-Hall International series in computer science, 1990.

12. Tronci E.: Automatic synthesis of control software for an industrial automation control system. 14th IEEE ASE, 1999. IEEE Computer Society Press.
13. Garbett P., Parkes J., Shackleton M., and Anderson S.: Secure synthesis of code: a process improvement experiment. FM99, LNCS 1709, Springer. 1999.
14. O'Halloran C.: Acceptance Based Assurance. Proceedings of the IEEE conference on Automated Software Engineering 2001.
15. Poppleton M., Banach R.: Retrenchment: Extending the Reach of Refinement. Proceedings of IEEE conference on Automated Software Engineering 1999: 158-165.
16. Boulton Richard J., Hardy R., Martin U.: A Hoare Logic for Single-Input Single-Output Continuous-Time Control Systems. HSCC 2003: 113-125
17. Blow J., Galloway A.: Generalised Substitution Language and Differentials. ZB 2002: 396-415.
18. Davies J., Crichton C.: Concurrency and refinement in the UML. ENTCS 70(3): (2002)

Adding Formalism to Methods
or
Where and When Will Industry Use Formal Reasoning?

Mathai Joseph

Tata Research Development and Design Centre,
54B Hadapsar Industrial Estate, Pune 411 013, India
`mathai@pune.tcs.co.in`

1 Introduction

Twenty years and more after the term 'formal methods' was introduced, their use in industrial software engineering is still so limited that it raises the question: is there indeed a 'method' to the use of formal theories in solving practical problems? In comparison, the practice of large-scale software development abounds in methods, some requiring no more than the systematic use of paperwork, some based on graphical notations with annotations and some tightly wired into project management tools. None of these is a 'formal' method; equally, no application of formal reasoning into the development process resembles a 'method' as known in software engineering.

Large-scale software development is being undertaken successfully today with the use of semi-formal methods and tools. Likewise, formal modeling has been used very effectively for critical and complex applications to identify and solve problems that would otherwise have remained undiscovered. The difficulty is that though the barriers to extending these successes towards each other have moved slightly in the last few years, they now seem to have reached limits. The kinds of applications where formal reasoning is used remain quite distinct. For example, it would need the triumph of unbounded optimism over good sense to propose to use formal specification for the software for a complete stock-exchange trading system. (It would be no less unwise to propose the use of just 'traditional' software development methods for guaranteeing the correctness of a safety-critical system.)

Critics of the use of formal reasoning cite the prevalence of too many different complex notations without ways to link them to engineering practice, the lack of automated tools and uncertainties about scalability as reasons for not using formal methods in practical projects. There is very little inclination from practical software engineers towards changing that situation. The design notation in most widespread use today, UML, does not have a well-defined semantics, and plans for the radically enhanced UML 2.0 show that even that will have very little by way of a formal semantic model.

J.S. Dong and J. Woodcock (Eds.): ICFEM 2003, LNCS 2885, pp. 26–33, 2003.

In this talk, I argue that there is a great deal more that formal reasoning can do for software development. There are many problems in large-scale software development where the existing methods are quite inadequate and any contribution from formal reasoning would result in great improvement. Some of these methods will benefit from the systematic use of lightweight formalisms, others from the insights that can come from the kind of analysis that formal reasoning makes possible (e.g. discovering 'missing scenarios'). There may be no obvious method to the use of formal reasoning itself in these cases, i.e. no 'formal method', but instead there can be the addition of formal analysis to some existing method.

I will first describe two systems built in the last few years. *System One* is a cross-border trading system of considerable size and complexity which was built using modern software development techniques and tools. *System Two* is a safety critical system built for a highly automated freight railway network using formal specification and an automated tool to develop the final software system. I will then describe where formal reasoning could have played a role in the development of the first system and how 'standard' software development methods were used along with formal reasoning in the second.

2   *System One*

International trading in securities is still largely manual and lacks agreed standards. In practice, a number of system-level problems are caused by the use of different protocols and incompatible platforms and these lead to various integration problems. Any system that will solve these problems must reduce the end-to-end completion time for trades and do this in a framework in which there are many different service providers, practices and standards.

System One is an example of such a trading system and it is probably among the most complex systems built in recent times. Two major areas of work stand out and were undoubtedly the most important.

a   Requirements analysis: It took a team of 20-30 experienced people about eight months to define the requirements and build the analysis models in UML. This was a period when extensive discussions were needed before commonly agreed requirements were defined in full detail.

b   Software development: After the requirements analysis was completed, the time left for the software development was another six months. The team had 60 people with a range of abilities, from a few experts to people with no previous experience of such work. As often happens, there were many changes in this team of 60 during the six months.

Broadly, therefore, 40% of the effort on this project went into defining the requirements and 60% into building and testing the software system. This distribution of effort deserves to be examined more closely. How complex was the requirement and how large was the final software system? The following table gives a summary of some of the details.

Summary Details of *System One*

- 180K lines of operation specification
- 1200 classes
- 5M lines of C++ Code (for IBM S/390, using CICS and DB2) generated
- 1.5M lines of C++ code (for SUN Solaris/Windows NT and DB2) generated
- Average of 250 lines of C++ produced and tested per person per day

A period of three more months was spent for system and performance testing and for final acceptance by the user.

It will be obvious that this level of programmer productivity was not achieved using manual coding. A highly automated software development environment was used to generate code from UML models. Unit-testing templates were also generated automatically, so much of what usually takes manual effort and time was reduced substantially.

3   *System Two*

In small railway networks, it is possible to use a high level of automation and remote control of trains to achieve high throughput. There are several examples of such networks in urban transport. *System Two* was developed for a small freight railway transporting ore from the mine-head for loading into large freight wagons for long-distance transport.

In a network of 8.5 miles of track, there were 9 driver-less trains to be controlled, each with up to 20 wagons. Inputs from about 100 track sensors and 36 power sensors were used to control 24 switches. The system had to tolerate failures of some sensors. In a tight 1-second cycle, control commands had to be sent to all locomotives and inputs from all sensors read in order to prepare the commands for the next cycle. One safety condition was that any locomotive that failed to receive its regular 1-second cycle command would be stopped automatically. The task was to specify, design and develop a safety-critical checker function that would ensure, with a specified level of confidence, that if the system were initially in a safe state, the issuance and execution of the next set of commands would leave the system in a safe state.

This is a system where formal techniques were used at several places in the software development process.

a Requirements analysis: Roughly 6 person months were spend on analyzing the requirements and building the prototypes. Specifications were written in the Z notation and consisted of around 50 schema (or roughly 1000 lines of Z).

b Prototyping: The Z specifications were validated by transcribing them into a logic programming notation and executing them in this form. Prototyping enabled the construction of possible operational scenarios and these were used to develop the user's acceptance test cases.

c Review and analysis: There was an independent review by a consultant. Fault-tree analysis was used to check for specific cases. This resulted in some amendments to the specifications. An important part of the analysis phase was to standardize the form of the Z schema structure, decide on naming conventions, and plan the conversion of the specifications to design specifications. This required further rework of the specifications and the addition of design and implementation details. This phase took 4 person months.

d Software construction: By the time the software construction began, there were 70 schema (or about 2000 lines of Z). In addition, around 7000 lines of C code were hand-written for various software and hardware interfaces. This phase took 16 person months.

e Testing: The system was tested using standard unit-test, module-test and system- test steps, finally using the test scenarios developed during the prototyping phase. This required 4 person months.

Roughly 33% of the effort was spent on analyzing the requirements, prototyping and reviewing the specifications, with the remaining 66% spent on software construction and testing.

There was a high degree of traceability between specifications and code. For example, there was one C function for every 'operation' schema. Further, the predefined schema structure allowed code to be hand written in a straightforward way: preconditions and postconditions were converted into tests and quantifier expressions into loops.

4   Comparison

System One is typical of many large commercial systems. These systems are complex, have many internal and external interfaces and must be developed and delivered following tight schedules. The 'standard' steps of software development must be followed, if only to permit close and effective project management (alignment to ISO 9000 and CMM Level-5 standards requires all of these and a great deal more of detailed information). Given the high productivity that can be achieved using a modern, automated software development environment, it is clear that there is little that formalisms could have done to improve productivity. To take just one example, attempts to formally specify and verify the complete program would be wasted here. By comparison, the relative time and effort (40%) spent on requirements analysis do suggest that this is an area where even a modest improvement could make a major contribution[1].

[1] Note that the software construction cycle was greatly accelerated in this case. Using 'industry-standard' norms, the development of software of this size would normally require an effort that is an order of magnitude greater; the relative cost of the requirements analysis would then reduce to less than 5%. This would not alter the improvement that use of formalisms can make as errors are harder to detect and correct in a manually built system.

This is not an isolated example. Industry-wide experience shows that errors in requirements analysis are widespread and the cause of a large proportion of the 'bugs' reported in the field. Automating requirements 'capture' using an easily understood notation, and followed by analysis, would have quickly provided the users with reports that otherwise took months and many meetings to generate. It could also have led to the generation of some acceptance tests that would have provided precise definitions of what the system had to achieve.

System Two is fairly typical of a different class of problem, and one that seems to almost demand the use of formal methods. In this particular case, the user had pre-ordained some choices, such as the use of Z for specification and C for the program, so the formal approach had to be built using these choices. This meant that automated proof assistance was hard to obtain, as indeed was automated help for refinement of specifications into code. There were some experimental tools available to do one or the other of these steps but none that had been tried in an industrial-scale software development process (and given the risks, this was not a project in which to attempt such use for the first time). Other requirements were for full traceability between specifications and code, and for the C program was to be documented and independently maintainable. Thus any automated refinement method that may be demonstrably correct but which produced code using intricate patterns could not be used[2]. The user was willing to ensure that changes made in the code were always accompanied by corresponding changes in the specification, and vice-versa.

Program Size

The generated program for *System One* had a code size of around twice that of high quality hand code. This is less alarming than it sounds. Experience shows that most programs of similar size have enormously varying internal quality; while some parts may be said to be well written, there are invariably other parts that are not and added to this, notably for legacy systems, is the dead code that no longer serves any function. Moreover, *System One* did meet very demanding performance requirements, so the code size did not affect the execution speed in any substantial way The program for *System Two* was refined manually from the specifications. The final code size (not counting the interface code) was around 10,000 lines of C, or an average of around five lines of code per line of specification. It is hard to see how this size could be reduced, given the need to preserve traceability and simplicity of maintenance.

Bugs and Errors

Some of the complexity of *System Two* came from need to distribute the application over two different platforms: OS/390 and Solaris. The early versions of the program ran into difficulties with the way the interface was modeled, and

---

[2] This requirement is fairly universal and is one that is not easy to meet with any automated refinement method.

tracking and correcting such errors was difficult. Once the interface had been correctly modeled, no further errors were observed during testing or subsequently. The rest of the generated code was remarkably free of bugs and the testing time was spent in systematically executing testing procedures, rather than in correcting bugs.

In *System Two*, the use of formalisms to enhance the software development method was very effective. The software system was tested under a simulator using tests defined during the prototyping phase. Four errors only were discovered, and these were easily corrected. Once again, the testing time was spent in gaining assurance about the program and not in fixing problems.

Formalism and Method

There are some well-accepted steps in the development of a software system:

a Requirements analysis;
b Functional definition of software system (sometimes called 'software specification');
c System design (high level and low level);
d Coding and review; and
e Testing (unit, module and system).

There are different methods for supporting each of these steps, either individually or as part of a development process. Replacing any of these steps by a formal 'method' will require demonstration of a capability that is beyond formal techniques today. On the other hand, complementing a step with formal analysis to improve the way it is performed, or the quality of what is achieved, is a contribution that will have widespread acceptance.

There are few documented cases of complete programs that have been developed from mathematical specifications; most of these are small in size and for safety-critical systems, where the increased costs for software development are justified by the criticality of the application. Model checking has been used to verify critical parts of programs, e.g. to detect the possibility of deadlock, and there are compilers, e.g. from specifications to automata that allow other properties to be checked. Once again, with few exceptions, these are usually for small but undoubtedly complex applications.

It is now important to move formal techniques from the world of small programs into the far more encompassing world of large programs. There are some good examples of where there can be a substantial payoff in using lightweight formal techniques.

(i) Program review: While the use of automated code generation is increasing, most programs today are still hand written and therefore subject to a wide variety of clerical and coding errors. Programming standards have been developed (e.g. especially for Java and C) to reduce the possibility of many such errors. However, checking compliance against standards is usually done after program development is over, and for programs of any size is limited to manual inspection.

Static analysis of programs can be automated, thus checking rigorously against programming standards and greatly reducing the amount of testing that needs to be performed. Such analysis leads to detection of common errors (ranging from the use of un-initialized variables to poor program structure) and can be used very effectively during development, and not in a 'final checkout' step.

Evidence collected from the static analysis of programs that did not pass through automated checking is testimony to the value of such a step. In one case, subsequent automated analysis of an operational program identified errors that were classified as 39% fatal errors, 49% weaknesses in program structure and 12% other errors, all of which could have been detected before the release of the program.

(ii) Use of assertions: There is increasing awareness of the value of using assertions to specify expected program properties, e.g. in terms of pre- and post-conditions to function or procedure calls. Automated validation of assertions, at compile-time where possible and otherwise at run-time can add greatly to the programmer's understanding of actual program behaviour and of course to the assurance about the quality of a program. Few compilers will actually check assertions, either at compile-time or by generating the appropriate code for a run-time check. However, it is possible to augment the compilation process by using an analysis tool in a preceding pass to interpret assertions and generate code where necessary.

(iii) Modelling requirements: One of the greatest contributions of formal techniques would be in the area of requirements analysis, since errors in requirement specification are among the most common and most difficult errors to remove. At the requirements level, some problems may be stated in a reasonably abstract form and be of a size that is amenable to formal analysis. For example, in a transaction processing system, from an analysis of the requirements, some critical global properties were specified as invariants. Each process step was specified separately as a pre- and post-condition pair. These pre- and post-condition pairs must be shown to be consistent with the global invariants and this was checked for using model checking. The results helped to uncover several gaps in the requirements.

The challenge for formal methods today is to influence the way that mainstream software engineering is done. There are a variety of techniques that can be applied there leading to obvious and measurable improvements in software quality and reliability.

5   Conclusions

Many of the barriers to extending the use of formalisms in software development are attributed to limitations of capability (inability to scale-up, or to handle the size of the state-space). This has led to the use of formal techniques in smaller applications where the additional cost is justified because of the criticality of the application. There are many other areas where formal techniques can enrich software development methods and these have often been ignored. The emphasis on program specification, refinement and verification has meant that other forms of specification have received less attention.

It is critical to move formal techniques out of the limited sphere in which they have been confined and into the wider context of general software development. This will require the application of formal techniques into non-formal methods. In this talk, I have discussed a few areas where formal techniques can be used to good effect in developing large programs and where they can make a qualitative difference to the software development process.

Acknowledgments

I would like to thank Purandar Bhaduri, Vinay Kulkarni, and R. Venkatesh for their help and their comments.

References

1. G. Palshikar, Safety checking in an automatic train operation system, *Inf. & Softw. Tech.*, 43, pp.325-338, 2001.
2. G. Palshikar, Applying formal specifications to real-world software development, *IEEE Software*, pp.89-97, November/December 2001.
3. A. Sreenivas, R. Venkatesh and M. Joseph, Meta-modeling for formal software development, *Proc. CATS 2001*, Gold Coast, Australia, pp.1-11, 2001.

Using Formal Methods
to Serialize Synchronization Events

Jessica Chen

School of Computer Science, University of Windsor
Windsor, Ont. Canada N9B 3P4
xjchen@cs.uwindsor.ca

Abstract. One of the difficulties in testing concurrent systems comes from the fact that executions with internal nondeterministic choices make the testing procedure non-repeatable. A natural solution is to artificially enforce and direct the execution to take the desired path so that a test can be *reproduced*. With a reproducible testing technique, we use a set of test scenarios which consist of pairs of test cases and path constraints, the latter expressing the ordering among certain interesting events during the execution. We consider the automated generation of significant sets of path constraints with a given test case, and we are interested in those sets of path constraints that reflect the possible serializations upon synchronization events during the executions of different processes in the program. Here we present our study on exploring *formal engineering methods* to generate path constraints when the synchronization events are governed by monitors.

Keywords: Reproducible Testing, Nondeterminism, Formal Engineering Method, Labelled Transition Systems.

1 Motivation

Concurrent systems have imposed a lot of new challenges on software testing. In particular, due to the nondeterminism appeared in concurrent systems, the behavior of the program is no more predictable even with the same input: with given input, the system may still have many different paths depending on the factors such as the different speeds of the process[1], the interactions among different processes. As a consequence, testing turns out to be non-repeatable: If we observed a certain erroneous phenomenon during a testing procedure, we may not be able to see it again or check whether it is corrected during the regression testing. A natural way to tackle this problem is to artificially enforce some of the internal nondeterministic choices so as to *direct* the program executions with each given input [1,2,5,6,7,14,18,17]. Then we are able to *reproduce* the same observations. Of course, we can realize such a control via debugging techniques, but

---

[1] We use the term *process* in a general sense that subsumes *thread* in multithreaded programs.

J.S. Dong and J. Woodcock (Eds.): ICFEM 2003, LNCS 2885, pp. 34–47, 2003.

that normally requires manual control of the executions. Another possible approach is via specification-based testing techniques that consider the automated control over the orders of some predefined points of the internal execution of each process. This is often called *reproducible testing*.

Obviously, for reproducible testing, we assume that we are given in a test scenario, not only a test case but also a *path constraint*. The test case, as usual, describes the external input and the expected observations. For simplicity, we do not consider distributed applications now, so the test case to a program is just a sequence of input and output. The additional path constraint describes some further control information on the execution paths according to the given test case. Such path constraint can be expressed as a partial or total order among some internal events such as certain statements in the program, and actually we can *predefine* in general, the events we are interested in controlling their time of occurrences. Apparently, the path constraints are often designed to denote the typical or representative scenarios in which possible errors or bugs may reside, and the internal events that we are interested in here are the synchronization events [6], such as to access a shared object, or to coordinate with another process. Our interest is based on the observation that different outputs with same inputs are very often concurrency-related: they are typically caused by the different orders of accesses to the shared objects by various processes, or by the coordination among processes. As the input sequence may be used to feed multiple processes, the timing of the input may effect the ordering of the synchronization events. Thus, we will consider path constraints of both synchronization events and input events.

As we discussed previously [5], given a test scenario, we can force the Program Under Test (PUT) to take an execution path that satisfies both the given input and the given path constraint. This can be achieved by introducing some control mechanism into the system during the execution: the execution of the PUT is augmented by additional communications between the control mechanism and all the processes in the PUT. Such additional communications happen at the control points which are, in our setting, *right before* and *right after* the synchronization events, *right before* and *right after* input events.

In the present work, we consider the automated generation of significant sets of path constraints with a given test case when the synchronization events are governed by monitors. Each path constraint is a sequence of synchronization events and input events. These events *correspond* to the control points in the PUT and their ordering can be controlled by the test control mechanism. The generation of these path constraints is accomplished by exploring *formal engineering methods* to systematically and automatically generate control models that contain paths of all possible serializations of the executions with respect to the synchronization events and input events. We consider the PUTs of static set of processes and we assume that the design abstract of the program is given in terms of process terms [15]. We define structural operational semantics on the processes in terms of labelled transition systems. The control model is obtained from the above-derived labelled transition system constructed according to the

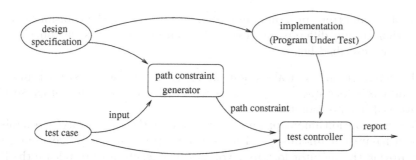

Fig. 1. Reproducible testing architecture.

given test case, by removing irrelevant events according to trace equivalence [10], leaving only those labels of the synchronization events and input events. A path constraint then corresponds to a sequence of labels along a path in the control model, and we can adopt various existing coverage criteria to generate significant sets of path constraints from it.

The structure of this paper is as follows. We first give a brief overview of the architecture of the reproducible testing and our existing test control mechanism. Then we introduce the operational semantics for the construction of the labelled transition systems. This is followed by the discussion on how to obtain the control model and to generate significant sets of path constraints. Finally we conclude the present work and compare it with other related ones.

2   Test Architecture

Our reproducible testing architecture is illustrated in Figure 1. We assume that a design specification is given that describes the abstract behavior of the application in terms of process algebras [3,9,15]. The PUT is actually the implementation of this design specification. It is executed under the control of the test controller to check for its correctness with respect to a given test scenario. A test scenario consists of test case, i.e. a sequence of inputs and expected outputs, and a path constraint for this test case, which is, in current setting, a sequence of synchronization events and input events. The former comes from the test user, while the latter comes from the path constraint generator, which generates the path constraints from the design specification and the given test case. The test controller directs the execution according to the input part of the test case and the path constraint, and compares the actual outputs with the expected ones from the test case.

As we mentioned in the Introduction, during the execution of the PUT, there will be communications between the PUT and the test controller at the control points, and this enables the controller to realize the *desired* execution path. We explain below how the control points for synchronization events are determined.

There are typically two kinds of concurrency control in existing programming practice: one is to guarantee the mutual exclusion of the executions of a critical section of a concurrent program, and another is to realize the coordination and cooperation among different processes. A monitor provides such functionality generally as described below:

- The access to the critical sections is protected by the locks. Each monitor maintains a lock queue of processes who wish to access the critical section governed by this monitor.
- The coordination among processes is realized by the wait/notify[2] mechanism. Each monitor maintains a waiting queue of processes. A process currently occupying the monitor lock may voluntarily execute *wait* to release the lock and put itself into the waiting queue of this monitor. When a process *notifies* a monitor, and the waiting queue of the monitor is nonempty, the first process in the queue is removed and re-enabled for execution. The awakened process will compete in the usual manner with any other processes that might be actively competing for the lock on this monitor. When a process *notifies* a monitor whose waiting queue is empty, the notification signal is simply discarded. There exists in some existing programming languages the execution of *notifyAll* that wakes up all instead of one of the waiting processes. We do not consider this case here. If necessary, it can be analogous accommodated into our discussion straightforwardly. As each monitor maintains a separate waiting queue of processes, it can be used to realize the coordination and cooperation among different groups of processes.

Consequently, our test controller can suspend the program execution at the points (i) before and after a process obtains a monitor lock; (ii) before and after a process executes *wait*; (iii) before and after a process executes *notify*; (iv) before and after an external input to the program. Correspondingly, a path constraint shows the desired ordering among four kinds of events: to obtain a monitor lock, to execute *wait*, to execute *notify*, and to get an input from outside.

For details on how the test controller work, see [5]. In this paper, we explain how the path constraint generator is built. As we mentioned in the Introduction, the path constraints are generated from control models derived from the labelled transition systems. In the next section, we define operational semantics which can be used to construct the labelled transition systems from the given design specification in terms of process terms [15]. In doing so, it is essential that a path constraint is composed of the abovementioned four kinds of events that correspond to the control points that existing test control tool can handle. This is achieved by ignoring other irrelevant labels in the control model as denoted by invisible action τ. We discuss this point in Section 4.

3 Operational Semantics

We define the operational semantics of the abstract behavior of the PUT in terms of labelled transition systems. Basically, a labelled transition system is a quadruple *(State,Label,$\rightarrow$,s_0)* where

---

[2] With different names in various concurrent programming languages.

- *State* is the set of possible states of the program computation;
- *Label* is a set of labels showing the information about the state changes;
- $\rightarrow\ \subseteq State \times Label \times State$ is a transition relation that describes the system evolution. $(s, l, s') \in \rightarrow$ (also written as $s \xrightarrow{l} s'$) expresses that the system may evolve from state s to state s' with the information of the state change described in l.
- $s_0 \in State$ is the initial state.

A state contains all the information we are interested in for the computation. Note, however, that such information will not be used in the path constraint: all information we eventually need should be put into the labels. In our setting, a state configuration is composed of the following elements:

- *A sequence of input data derived from the given test case.* As we mentioned, the formal design abstract we derive is in regard of *given input*. With different program input, we will obtain different control models. Thus, the program input is an essential element in generating the abstract model. The input can be easily derived from the given test case by ignoring the expected output. In case the program is multi-tasked or multi-threaded, this sequence of input data will be used to feed a *set* of processes.
- *A set of states of shared variables.* The processes share a set of variables. Each variable state consists of a variable name and its corresponding value.
- *A set of states of monitor locks and a set of states of monitor queues.* A state of a monitor lock expresses the current status of the lock of the monitor. A state of a monitor queue expresses the current queue of processes waiting on this monitor to be notified.
- *A set of processes.* A process consists of a process identifier and a process term. We use $pid : p$ to denote a process with identifier pid and process term p. A process identifier is an integer that uniquely identifies the process in the program. We need this information because the generated model should contain the process identifier on the labels. A process term expresses the state of the behavior of a sequential process, and the state of the behavior of the entire system is expressed via a set of processes. The structure of process terms will be explained in more details below.

Assume that we are given a set V of variables, $MID \subset N$ as a set of monitor identifiers, and $PID \subset N$ as a set of process identifiers. Let $x \in V$, $m, m_1, m_2 \in MID, pid \in PID$. A *process term p in the design specification* can be constructed by the following BNF:

$$p = stop \mid s; p$$
$$s = x := e \mid if\ c\ then\ q_1\ else\ q_2 \mid while\ c\ do\ q \mid input(x) \mid lock(m, q)$$
$$\mid wait(m_1, m_2) \mid notify(m)$$
$$q = s \mid s; q$$

where s is a statement[3], q, q_1, q_2 are intermediate sequences of statements, e is an arithmetic expression over V and c is a boolean expression over V.

- $input(x)$ means to get the next input into variable x.
- $lock(m,q)$ means to execute segment q using monitor m to realize the mutual exclusion of the execution.
- $wait(m_1, m_2)$ means to give up the current lock on m_1 and wait on the waiting queue of monitor m_2.
- $notify(m)$ means to notify the first process on the waiting queue of monitor m.

Apart from the above statements, we also need to introduce some additional internal statements for our computation:

- $lock\_restart(m)$: to regain the lock on monitor m after being notified.
- $lock\_end(m)$: to end a critical section governed by monitor m.
- $waiting(m)$: to stay on waiting queue of monitor m.

These internal statements are essential to our computation to simulate the behavior of the system with respect to the monitors. In the following, a *process term* is constructed on statements including these additional ones.

Our primary goal in constructing the control model is to generate path constraints as sequences of its labels. Consequently, the set of labels in the labelled transition systems contains and only contains the synchronization events and input events that we need to control. Precisely, the labels we consider can be described as:

$$A = \{(pid, lock, m), (pid, wait, m), (pid, notify, m), (pid, input)$$

$$\mid pid \in PID, m \in MID\} \cup \{\tau\}$$

This set of labels corresponds to the set of events we mentioned in the previous section, with one additional label τ which is used as an internal action for the computation [15]. The use of τ facilitates the construction of the control model and we will explain in the next section how it is eventually removed from the model.

Let us use I to denote the set of input values as well as the set of variable values. I^* thus represents the set of sequences of inputs. $E \subseteq V \to I$ represents the mapping from variables to their values. $L \subseteq MID \to \{true, false\}$ represents the set of locking status of the monitors. $Q \subseteq MID \to PID^*$ represents the mapping from the monitors to sequences of processes (waiting on the monitors). Let P be the set of process terms over MID and V. $PR \subseteq 2^{PID \times P}$ represents the set of the status of the processes. Then the labelled transition system is a quadruple $\langle S, A, \to, s_0 \rangle$, where

---

[3] Note that although we call them statements, the process terms built on top of them represent design abstracts rather than program code.

- $S \subseteq I^* \times E \times L \times Q \times PR$
- $s_0 \in S$ is the initial state
- $A \subseteq (PID \times \{lock, wait, notify\} \times MID) \cup (PID \times \{input\})$

The transition relation $\_ \longrightarrow \_$ is defined as the least relation satisfying the following twelve *structural rules*. For clarity, we split these rules into four groups. All the structural rules have schema:

$$\frac{\text{ANTECEDENT}}{\text{CONSEQUENT}}$$

which is interpreted logically as: $\forall$(ANTECEDENT $\longrightarrow$ CONSEQUENT), where $\forall(\ldots)$ stands for the universal closure of all free variables occurring in $(\ldots)$. Observe that, typically, ANTECEDENT and CONSEQUENT share free variables. When ANTECEDENT is missing, they are interpreted as *true*.

We adopt the interleaving semantics. This is based on two facts: (i) it is simple; (ii) the test control tool can only realize the *sequential control*: it cannot enforce two events to occur simultaneously. Thus, the following structural rules enjoy a common feature: the system moves from one state to another according to the move of one of the processes, while the others remain unchanged. The only exception is R_{11} and we will explain it later.

The evolution caused by the execution of an assignment, a choice statement, or a while-loop statement of one of the processes is described in the first group of structural rules (Figure 2). We use $pid_1 : p_1 \parallel \ldots \parallel pid_n : p_n$ for $\{pid_1 : p_1, \ldots, pid_n : p_n\}$. $P \parallel pid : a; p$ (where a is an assignment, a choice statement, or a while-loop statement) denotes a set of processes consisting of process term $a; p$ with process identifier pid and some other processes expressed in P. x, c and e are as defined above. p, p_1, p_2 and p_3 are process terms. pid is a process identifier. We use $Eval(E, e)$ and $Eval(E, c)$ to denote the evaluation of e and c in E respectively. $E[x/v]$ denotes the status E of the variables with the value of x replaced by v. All the moves caused by these structural rules are invisible, as labelled by τ, because they do not contribute to the path constraints.

The evolution of the system states caused by the input action is reflected in Rule R_6 (Figure 3): The first input data in I is read into variable x in E. We use *first(I)* to denote the first input data in I and *rest(I)* the input status obtained from I by removing the first one.

Rules R_7, R_8 and R_9 (Figure 4) simulates the execution of a process with mutual exclusion. R_7 is to start a critical section guarded by monitor m. This move is possible only if m has not yet been locked by others ($Eval(L, m) = false$). We use $Eval(L, m)$ to denote the lock value of m in L, and $L[m/v]$ to denote the status L with the value of m replaced by v. Here process pid needs to execute a critical section p_1 followed by p_2. Note that we have inserted an additional statement *lock_end(m)* right after the execution of p_1. This is necessary because we need to know for our computation *when* the lock is released. The system move according to *lock_end(m)* is given in Rule R_9. Here, since the *lock_end(m)* is used only for the computation and we do not need such

Rule R_1 (Assignment)

$$\frac{(x, f) \in E}{\langle I, E, L, Q, P \parallel pid : (x := e); p \rangle \overset{\tau}{\longrightarrow} \langle I, E[x/Eval(E, e)], L, Q, P \parallel pid : p \rangle}$$

Rule R_2 (Deterministic Choice - Condition True)

$$\frac{Eval(E, c) = true}{\langle I, E, L, Q, P \parallel pid : (if\ c\ then\ p_1\ else\ p_2); p_3 \rangle \overset{\tau}{\longrightarrow} \langle I, E, L, Q, P \parallel pid : p_1; p_3 \rangle}$$

Rule R_3 (Deterministic Choice - Condition False)

$$\frac{Eval(E, c) = false}{\langle I, E, L, Q, P \parallel pid : (if\ c\ then\ p_1\ else\ p_2); p_3 \rangle \overset{\tau}{\longrightarrow} \langle I, E, L, Q, P \parallel pid : p_2; p_3 \rangle}$$

Rule R_4 (Loop - Continue)

$$\frac{Eval(E, c) = true}{\langle I, E, L, Q, P \parallel pid : (while\ c\ do\ p_1); p_2 \rangle \overset{\tau}{\longrightarrow} \langle I, E, L, Q, P \parallel pid : p_1; (while\ c\ do\ p_1); p_2 \rangle}$$

Rule R_5 (Loop - End)

$$\frac{Eval(E, c) = false}{\langle I, E, L, Q, P \parallel pid : (while\ c\ do\ p_1); p_2 \rangle \overset{\tau}{\longrightarrow} \langle I, E, L, Q, P \parallel pid : p_2 \rangle}$$

Fig. 2. Structural Rules: choice and loop.

Rule R_6 (Receive Input)

$$\frac{I \neq \emptyset}{\langle I, E, L, Q, P \parallel pid : input(x); p \rangle \xrightarrow{(pid, input)} \langle rest(I), E[x/first(I)], L, Q, P \parallel pid : p \rangle}$$

Fig. 3. Structural Rules: input.

information in the path constraint, the transition is labelled as τ. Rule R_8 is for the regain of the monitor after being notified, and we will explain it later. Again, the transition is labelled as τ because we do not need any information in path constraints regarding this move.

Figure 5 shows the evolution of the system caused by the coordination among processes via the use of set Q of waiting queues. We use (i) *enqueue(Q,m,pid)*

Rule R_7 (Lock Begin)

$$Eval(L, m) = false$$

$$\langle I, E, L, Q, P \parallel pid : lock(m, p_1); p_2 \rangle \xrightarrow{(pid, lock, m)}$$
$$\langle I, E, L[m/true], Q, P \parallel pid : p_1; lock\_end(m); p_2 \rangle$$

Rule R_8 (Lock Restart)

$$Eval(L, m) = false$$

$$\langle I, E, L, Q, P \parallel pid : lock\_restart(m); p \rangle \xrightarrow{\tau} \langle I, E, L[m/true], Q, P \parallel pid : p \rangle$$

Rule R_9 (Lock End)

$$Eval(L, m) = true$$

$$\langle I, E, L, Q, P \parallel pid : lock\_end(m); p \rangle \xrightarrow{\tau}$$
$$\langle I, E, L[m/false], Q, P \parallel pid : p \rangle$$

Fig. 4. Structural Rules: mutual exclusion.

Rule R_{10} (Wait)

$$\langle I, E, L, Q, P \parallel pid : wait(m_1, m_2); p \rangle \xrightarrow{(pid, wait, m_2)}$$
$$\langle I, E, L[m_1/false], enqueue(Q, m_2, pid), P \parallel pid : p' \rangle$$
$$\text{where } p' = waiting(m_2); lock\_restart(m_1); p$$

Rule R_{11} (Notify with Nonempty Queue)

$$first(Q, m) = pid_2$$

$$\langle I, E, L, Q, P \parallel pid_1 : notify(m); p_1 \parallel pid_2 : waiting(m); p_2 \rangle \xrightarrow{(pid, notify, m)}$$
$$\langle I, E, L, dequeue(Q, m), P \parallel pid_1 : p_1 \parallel pid_2 : p_2 \rangle$$

Rule R_{12} (Notify with Empty Queue)

$$first(Q, m) = null$$

$$\langle I, E, L, Q, P \parallel pid : notify(m); p \rangle \xrightarrow{(pid, notify, m)} \langle I, E, L, Q, P \parallel pid : p \rangle$$

Fig. 5. Structural Rules: coordination.

to denote the set of waiting queues derived from Q by adding pid into the queue of m; (ii) $dequeue(Q,m)$ to denote the set of waiting queues derived from Q by removing the first element from the queue of m; (iii) $first(Q,m)$ to denote the first process on the waiting queue of m in Q. In R_{10}, process pid releases its lock on m_1 and puts itself into the waiting queue of m_2. The next state of process pid in the process term is changed into $waiting(m_2)$. This is to be executed together with another process who can perform $notify(m_2)$, as expressed in Rules R_{11} and R_{12}.

R_{11} expresses the rule to allow the system to evolve when one of the processes pid_1 performs notification to the waiting queue of monitor m and the later is nonempty. In R_{11}, if a process pid_1 is capable of moving to its next state by notifying the first process pid_2 on the waiting queue of m, and process pid_2 is capable of performing a $waiting$ statement, then the system can move into a state where both processes pid_1 and pid_2 make a move to their next states, and pid_2 is removed from the waiting queue of m. This is the typical *hand-shaking* mechanism where the system's move comes from the movement of *two* synchronizing processes. Note that the $waiting(m)$ statement is artificially inserted: it does not belong to the four kinds of events and we do not need to control it. From the test user's viewpoint, the system's move is only made from the move of the notifying process. Thus, this hand-shaking mechanism is consistent with the test control mechanism in the sense that there are no two events in the label to be controlled to happen at the same time.

R_{12} shows the rule analogous to R_{11} when the waiting queue to be notified is empty, as denoted by $first(Q,m) = null$. The system can make a move to the next one corresponding to the move of the notifying process without making any effect to the global state.

Note that in R_{10}, we have inserted a statement $lock\_restart(m_1)$ after the $waiting(m_2)$ statement. This is for the waiting process to regain the lock on m_1, as expressed in R_8.

Given an initial state, the above structural rules allow us to associate to it a labelled transition system whose states are those reachable from the initial state, via the transitions inferred by using these rules.

4 Test Case Generation

A labelled transition system may have infinite number of states or infinite number of transitions. Here we only consider finite-state labelled transition systems. As the set of labels is finite, the finite-state model can also contain only finite number of transitions.

The control of the test is over the serializations of the executions of different processes based on the afore-mentioned four kinds of events. As we can see, apart from these events, the labels also contain τ in the constructed model. Thus, the derived labelled transition system needs to be further simplified by reducing the τ-transitions. There are several equivalence notions in the literature, for example, bisimilation [15], trace equivalence [10], testing equivalence [16]. Since the test control tool can recognize neither the program state, nor the set of possible next actions (i.e. statements), our simplification is based on *trace equivalence*. That is, whenever we have $s_1 \xrightarrow{\tau} s_2$ ($s_1 \neq s_2$) we can remove this transition and merge s_1 and s_2 into one state. In addition, τ-loop transitions, i.e. $s \xrightarrow{\tau} s$, can be removed. We call the simplified labelled transition system the control model.

Now with the control model, we can generate various sets of possible paths according to different criteria similar as those we have in the general test case generation techniques according to given control flow diagrams. For example, we can use *state coverage criterion* or *edge coverage criterion* to guarantee that in the set of generated paths, each state or each transition is visited at least once. There are two major differences between our control models and the control flow diagrams:

- In the control flow diagrams, the choices (different edges going out from the same state) is deterministic, in the sense that they correspond to the *if-then-else* statement or *case* statement, and the choice depends on the external input. In our setting, since the input to the program is given, there is no state with deterministic choice. Instead, two different transitions from the same state represent the internal nondeterministic choice of the execution of the program.
- The control flow diagrams can be cyclic and the number of times a test case passes a loop may depend on the input. In our setting, since the input is given, the circles in the transition systems are due solely to the *infinite* loops in the program.

These two major points however, make no difference in terms of adopting the similar criteria for generating test cases or path constraints.

5   Related Work

Monitoring or controlling nondeterministic behavior of a system during software testing has been studied extensively recently [1,2,5,6,7,8,11,12,13,14,18,17]. Many researchers have realized that for testing concurrent systems, we need to consider both test data and the sequence of statements [1,2,5,6,7,8,14,18,17]. In particular, we should consider sequences of statements related to the concurrency control [1,2,5,6,7,14] and statements of remote method invocations [5,8,18,17]. Our present work also followed such lines and considered sequences of statements with respect to concurrency control. There are mainly two issues here: one is to generate the test scenarios, and the other is to realize the desired executions. The focus of the present work is the former.

In the work of [7], it has been proposed a specification-base methodology for testing concurrent programs. With this methodology, people use a set of *sequencing constraints* to specify the restrictions on the allowed sequences on synchronization events. Given a set of sequencing constraints in terms of CSPE (Constraints on Succeeding and Preceding Events), it is discussed [12] how to generate a set of test sequences so that each sequencing constraint is covered at least once. This coverage criterion is based on the fact that a CSPE constraint expresses a temporal property and it is hard to browse the space of the test sequences to find out all possible serializations of the synchronization events that satisfy the given set of constraints. In our work, no such restrictions on the allowed test sequences are assumed. The path constraints are derived directly from the given design abstract from which we generate a labelled transition system that contains all possible serializations of the synchronization events.

In [18,17], the authors have discussed the generation of the alternations of remote method invocations in the execution of a PUT. However, different serializations of executions based on *synchronization events* are not considered there, and the work does not involve the study of formal engineering method.

Developing formal engineering method and integrate it into reproducible testing is the most prominent feature in our work. Another example of embedding formal methods into reproducible testing can be found in [8] where we have developed a formal method in order to obtain *deadlock-free test model* for middleware-based PUT.

Labelled transition systems are well defined models for concurrent systems. Adopting labelled transition systems to conduct testing has been extensively studied in the past decade. For example, a test derivation algorithm is given [19] for conformance testing on labelled transition systems. For an annotated bibliography, see [4]. Along this line of research, the labelled transition systems are used to describe the allowed behavior of the system with possible inputs and outputs. Correspondingly, the labels are assumed to be divided into input and output ones. As the focus is on input and output, a classical complete testing assumption is often used: after a sufficient number of executions of the same test, all the paths according to this test in the implementation will be taken. With reproducible testing, we gain control over the internal choice instead of using the complete testing assumption. In our work, labelled transition system is used to express the allowed behavior of *given input*, and rather than generating test cases, we have discussed the generation of different ways of controlling the internal choices.

6   Conclusion and Final Remarks

For reproducible testing, the generation of test scenarios means to generate not only test cases but also path constraints. Our initial idea is to follow the principle of divide-and-conquer and to consider test case generation and path constraint generation *separately*. Based on this, we have focused here on the automated generation of path constraints when a test case is given. The starting point is that the significant sets of path constraints with respect to each given test case can be fully determined if the design specification is available that describes the abstract behavior of the system. Most importantly, the present work shows a possible way to explore formal engineering method for test scenario generation in software reproducible testing.

The process language we used to describe the abstract behavior of the system is very primitive: It only allows us to define the behavior of a static set of processes. It is possible to extend this language to allow for dynamic process creation, by modifying correspondingly the structural rules. However, since the path constraint generation is based on test criteria defined on a finite model, the generated labelled transition systems have to be finite.

The implementation of the path constraint generator is in progress and it will be integrated into the toolset of our automated environment for reproducible testing. A further extension of the present work is to consider generation of the path constraints when the test control is not only over the synchronization events but also over remote method invocation events in distributed applications.

Acknowledgements

The author would like to thank the anonymous reviewers for helpful comments on the preliminary version of this paper submitted to ICFEM 2003. This work is supported by the Natural Sciences and Engineering Research Council of Canada under grant number RGPIN 209774.

References

1. P. Bates. Debugging heterogeneous distributed systems using event-based models of behavior. *ACM Transactions on Computer Systems*, 13(1):1–31, Feb. 1995.
2. A. Bechini and K. Tai. Design of a toolset for dynamic analysis of concurrent Java programs. In *Proc. of the 6th International Workshop on Program Comprehension*, Ischia, Italy, June 1998.
3. J. Bergstra and J. Klop. Process algebra for synchronous communication. *Information and Control*, 60:109–137, 1984.
4. E. Brinksma and J. Tretmans. Testing transition systems: An annotated bibliography. In *Lecture Notes in Computer Science Vol. 1067*, pages 187–195. Springer-Verlag, 2001.
5. X. Cai and J. Chen. Control of nondeterminism in testing distributed multi-threaded programs. In *Proc. of the First Asia-Pacific Conference on Quality Software (APAQS 2000)*, pages 29–38. IEEE Computer Society Press, 2000.
6. R. Carver and K. Tai. Replay and testing for concurrent programs. *IEEE Software*, pages 66–74, Mar. 1991.
7. R. Carver and K. Tai. Use of sequencing constraints for specification-based testing of concurrent programs. *IEEE Transactions on Software Engineering*, 24(6):471–490, June 1998.
8. J. Chen. On using static analysis in distributed system testing. In *Proc. of the 2nd International Workshop on Engineering Distributed Objects (EDO 2000). Lecture Notes in Computer Science Vol. 1999*, pages 145–162. Springer-Verlag, 2000.
9. C. A. R. Hoare. *Communicating Sequential Processes*. Prentice Hall Int., London, 1985.
10. C. Hoare. A calculus of total correctness for communicating processes. *Science of Computer Programming*, 1:49–72, 1981.

11. E. Itoh, Z. Furukawa, and K. Ushijima. A prototype of a concurrent behavior monitoring tool for testing concurrent programs. In *Proc. of Asia-Pacific Software Engineering Conference (APSEC'96)*, pages 345–354, 1996.
12. B. Karacali and K. Tai. Automated test sequence generation using sequencing constraints for concurrent programs. In *Proc. of the International Symposium on Software Engineering for Parallel and Distributed Systems*, pages 97–106. IEEE Computer Society Press, 1999.
13. S. Kenkatesan and B. Dathan. Testing and debugging distributed programs using global predicates. *IEEE Transactions on Software Engineering*, 21(2):163–177, Feb. 1995.
14. T. Leblanc and J. Mellor-Crummey. Debugging parallel programs with instant replay. *IEEE Transactions on Computers*, 36(4):471–482, Apr. 1987.
15. R. Milner. *Communication and Concurrency*. Prentice Hall, London, 1989.
16. R. Nicola and M. Hennessy. Testing equivalences for processes. *Theoretical Computer Science*, 34:83–133, 1984.
17. H. Sohn, D. Kung, P. Hsia, Y. Toyoshima, and C. Chen. Reproducible testing for distributed programs. In *Proc. of the 4th International Conference on Telecommunication Systems, Modeling and Analysis*, pages 172–179, Nashiville, Tennessee, Mar. 1996.
18. H. Sohn, D. Kung, and P. Hsia. State-based reproducible testing for CORBA applications. In *Proc. of IEEE Internaltional Symposium on Software Engineering for Parallel and Distributed Systems (PDSE'99)*, pages 24–35, LA, USA, May 1999.
19. J. Tretmans. Testing transition systems: A formal approach. In *Proc. of the 10th International Conference on Concurrency Theory. Lecture Notes in Computer Science Vol. 1664*, pages 46–65. Springer-Verlag, 1999.

An AMBA-ARM7 Formal Verification Platform

Kong Woei Susanto[1] and Tom Melham[2]

[1] Department of Computing Science, University of Glasgow
Glasgow, G12 8QQ, UK
`susanto@dcs.gla.ac.uk`
[2] Computing Laboratory , Oxford University
Oxford, OX1 3QD, UK
`Tom.Melham@comlab.ox.ac.uk`

Abstract. The pressure to create a working System on Chip design as early as possible leads designers to consider using a platform based design method. In this approach, designing an application is a matter of selecting from a set of standard components with compatible specifications. Subsequently, a formal verification platform can be constructed. The formal verification platform provides an environment to analysed the combined properties of the design. In this paper, we present a methodology to do formal System on Chip analysis by developing generic formal components that can be integrated in a formal verification platform. First, we develop reusable formal properties of standard components. Second, we define a generic formal platform in which components of System on Chip design can be integrated. The platform contains basic components such as a standard bus protocol and a processor. Third, we combine the properties of standard components and obtain a set of refined properties of the system. We use these properties to develop the required specifications of the remaining components.

1 Introduction

The effort to implement a single chip system from scratch is enormous and only a few companies have the needed competency in all design areas. In most cases, designers will have to use *Intellectual Property* (IP) blocks or *Virtual Components* (VCs). IP blocks are predefined, large grained logic blocks, (such as processors, memories, and peripherals) whose function has been precisely specified. They can be developed in–house or originate from external vendors. When IP blocks become widely available, the design focus will shift to reuse. Chip design is becoming much more a matter of design composition than of design creation.

These compositional or reuse based design methodologies will be the issue addressed by *System on Chip* (SoC) designers. A standard platform and application specific architectural context will play a major role in achieving a plug and play environment using reusable components. Such an *integration environment* will typically be a design platform for a specific application domain. The IP blocks will be the standard building blocks that can be easily integrated within the application domain [6,16].

J.S. Dong and J. Woodcock (Eds.): ICFEM 2003, LNCS 2885, pp. 48–67, 2003.
© Springer-Verlag Berlin Heidelberg 2003

The verification of SoC design is arguably the biggest challenge for designers. Complexity has made design validation the bottleneck in the completion of a design project. A new design and validation methodology is needed to address this problem [4]. This must be capable of reducing the amount of analysis and debugging that takes place in the early development stages. The new validation methodology should emphasise reusing existing validation code. This reduces the time needed in recreating the validation code. The use of an abstract representation of IP models could help to speed up the validation process.

The limits of traditional validation methods have prompted the industrial community to consider formal verification methodologies for verifying hardware system specifications and models [19]. The inclusion of formal verification will remove uncertainty, increasing confidence in the design, and reduce verification time. Advances in design and validation methodologies for system level verification will make changes to the current formal verification approach necessary.

In this paper, we present one methodology to do formal SoC verification. The core of this methodology is in the development of reusable formal properties or proofs that can be used in the development of an SoC design. The properties contain the operational conditions for the system and specify its input/output relations. These properties are used as the behavioural representations of the components. We use these properties to define the requirements for each components used in the design of an application. The methodology is based on the combination of semiformal [1] and hybrid systems [5]. Tool support for the methodology is constructed from a selection of formal tools.

The contents of the paper are as follows: In Section 2 we briefly describe the integration platform approach for system on chip technology. In Section 3 we explain our idea of a verification platform, followed by a brief description of the formal tools environment. The AMBA and ARM platform is described in Section 4. In Section 5, we describe the specification development for an Ethernet Switch system built on this platform. A summary and discussion of future work is presented in Section 6.

2   Typical SoC Architecture

Cadence, Synopsys, and Mentor Graphics, three major providers of Electronics Design Automation (EDA) tools, have proposed similar systems that support or are based on the integration platform concept. A typical integration platform [21] is presented in Figure 1. A simple general-purpose processor core is the basic component. The platform is customisable with a collection of IP blocks which can be either user-defined logic blocks or third party IP blocks. All the IP blocks communicate through busses that also communicate with the processor.

Within this environment, two kinds of busses are introduced: the processor local bus (PLB) and the on-chip peripheral bus (OPB). There will be only one PLB but there may be more than one OPB. The OPB is connected to the PLB through a module interface called the OPB bridge. The PLB arbiter controls

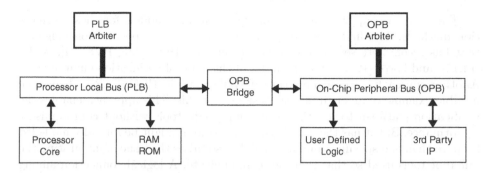

Fig. 1. A Typical Integration Platform.

the PLB communications among the processor, memory and OPB bridge. The OPB arbiter controls the OPB communications among the IP blocks.

Typically, an integration platform will come as a platform for a specific application domain. The platform will consists of components such as a target hardware and software architecture, a portfolio of VCs, and a design validation methodology. Its IP blocks are standard building blocks that can be easily integrated together into a system in the platform.

The design validation methodology determines the kinds of test-benches required for system level verification. These test-benches must be started early in the design process to avoid the possibility having a working chip but a failed system. The methodology determines which verification tools (event-driven simulation, cycle-based simulation, emulation) can be used. This information is very useful as each selected tool may have specific coding style requirements. Finally, the methodology defines a way to validate the system with an application running on it.

3   A Verification Platform Approach to SoC

In parallel with the system integration platform described above, we suggest that a *formal verification platform* is constructed. A formal verification platform is a standardised platform where a verification engineer can easily integrate various formal models in a single environment and perform formal validation of the system [26]. In this, each of the building blocks is represented as a formal specification model. There is a model for the processor core, for the bus and its protocol, and for all IP blocks available. Then the different models are integrated as a single system description in the verification platform.

Similar to validation, which commonly uses simulation, the formal verification platform may apply a variety of verification techniques. For example, a processor core formal model can be verified by symbolic simulation or by formal proof [10]. A bus protocol formal model is normally verified using a property checker [23]. The verification platform needs to accommodate all these various verification techniques.

There are two approaches to defining the formal models for these verification methods. The first is to define them all in a single specification language that has a complete set of verification techniques. HOL [8,9], PVS [24], ACL2 [14,15], and Forte [12] are the examples of this kind of verification environment. Another approach is to use a mixture of available tools, PROSPER [7] being one notable example of an environment designed for this. This approach enables the verification platform to use the most appropriate tools without compromising performance. But it has the drawback that a system might be formally modelled in more than one specification language. It also raises the issue of integrating the different tools used so that they can communicate. A logical connection among the tools is required in which the formal models can be integrated as a single system, using a kind of glue logic to connect them.

Our work uses the second approach, a mixed tools environment. We construct *a verification environment* which has the capabilities of various formal verification technologies, such as a theorem prover, a symbolic simulator, and a model checker. The verification environment combines the HOL98 theorem prover, the ACL2 theorem prover and the SMV model checker [17]. HOL98 is the centre of the tools environment. ACL2 and SMV are connected to HOL98 through a layer of interfaces. Through these interfaces, users can send commands from HOL98 to instruct ACL2 and SMV to perform formal proof. HOL98 also accepts proved theorems and properties from ACL2 and SMV as theorems in its own logic. Detailed descriptions of the system are given in the reminder of this section.

3.1 Theorem Prover

The theorem prover is the central tool to perform an integrated system level verification. Its command language is treated as the implementation language for interfacing various formal tools in the platform. It also provides the environment for orchestrating the proofs.

The theorem prover includes an integration interface that provides the communication protocol for the verification tools. It consists of several parts: a datatype for all logical and control data transferred between tools, a datatype for the results of remote calls and support for installing and calling procedures, and a low-level communication manager.

The verification environment uses HOL98, a modern descendent of HOL, as the theorem prover component. HOL98 is a higher order logic theorem prover. Its logic is built on the predicate calculus of ML style typed system. Higher order logic is used as the glue logic to connect and integrate formal components. HOL's command language, ML, allows a developer to have a full programming language available in which to develop custom verification procedures. The tools integration interface library in HOL is provided by PROSPER.

3.2 Symbolic Simulator

The common design practice of validation by simulation has encouraged us to choose the ACL2 theorem prover as a component for the verification environment. ACL2 offers the capability of simulating test vectors and performing symbolic simulation. An interface (ACL2PII [25]) for PROSPER has been developed to allow results from ACL2 to be interpreted in HOL. ACL2PII is a dynamic link for translating theorems between two *live sessions* of HOL and ACL2, with communications going in both directions. The interface also allows a user to run ACL2 from within HOL.

The ACL2 and HOL theorem provers use different languages and different logics. ACL2 uses untyped s-expressions [27] to represent first order logics, whereas the HOL system uses typed terms for higher order logic. The interface implements a scheme for translating ACL2 s-expressions into HOL terms. A set of basic translation has been implemented so that the appropriate s-expressions can be automatically translated into booleans, natural numbers, integers, simple arithmetic expressions, characters, strings, lists and tuples. The interface also provides an environment to extend and add new translation clauses for new ACL2 theories.

Logically, ACL2 is being used as an *axiom–server* for facts about constants that are uninterpreted in HOL but have definitions in ACL2. The consistency of the axioms are assured by proofs being conducted in ACL2. This way of connecting ACL2 and HOL is pragmatic, but sound for the purposes of our application. The automatic transformation reduces the possibility of inconsistency when importing definitions and theorems from ACL2 into HOL.

3.3   Model Checker

The HOL98 distribution includes an early version of McMillan's SMV symbolic model checker as part of the temporal logic library. The model checker is embedded in HOL as one of the decision procedures for HOL's tactic language. Using this library, temporal properties specified in LTL notations can be validated in two ways, either by proving the properties using HOL tactics or by using the external model checker. When the model checker is used and the formula can be verified then the result from the model checker is represented as a HOL theorem using HOL's oracle mechanism. If the model checker reports an error, then a counterexample is provided. A detailed description of the embedding of LTL in HOL is presented in [22]

We replace the SMV model checker with the latest version from Cadence. This re–implementation of SMV uses LTL instead of CTL. Although for backward compatibility it supports CTL, the developers suggest to use LTL to achieve maximum performance. We extended the temporal library so that it is possible to use the Cadence SMV model checker with LTL notations. We embed a subset of SMVL in HOL using the deep embedding technique. In a deep embedding, the semantics of the language is constructed and an interpretation of the language is provided. This makes the system more modular. Previously, when we used model checker we had to specify formal models and properties which are to be verified in HOL. Now, we can define and verify the SMV model on its own and then automatically import the proved properties as HOL theorems.

4 Case Study: AMBA Bus Protocol and ARM7 Processor Based Verification Platform

We use RAPIER to describe our experience in the development of a reusable SoC verification platform. RAPIER is an integration platform architecture developed by the Institute for System Level Integration (ISLI) in Scotland [20]. It is based on the ARM *Advanced Microcontroller Bus Architecture* (AMBA) [3]. The platform contains an *Advanced High–Performance Bus* (AHB) and an *Advanced Peripheral Bus* (APB), an external memory controller, two timers, a UART, an Interrupt Controller, a System Controller, a system watchdog, a general purpose I/O block, five AHB masters, four AHB slaves, and four APB slaves. The AHB bus is the processor local bus (PLB) and the APB is the on–chip peripheral bus (APB). The architectural block diagram of the RAPIER platform is shown in Fig. 2.

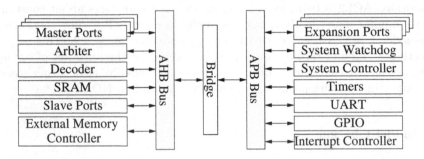

Fig. 2. Block diagram of RAPIER Platform.

4.1 AMBA Bus Protocol

AMBA is an on–chip bus specification that defines interconnection, communication, and management of functional blocks for SoC design. It is a technology independent specification. This ensures that the modules are reusable across diverse IC processes and technologies. It encourages standardise modular system design using a common bus protocol. This enhances the reuse design methodology for the modules.

Typically, AMBA based SoC design contains a high performance bus system such as the AHB. The bus is capable of handling high–bandwidth communication with the external memory interface, processor, on–chip memory, *Direct Memory Access* (DMA) module, and a bridge to the lower speed bus APB, where most peripherals in the system are located. An SoC system can have one or more masters. A typical system contains at least one processor. A DMA controller or a *Digital Signal Processor* (DSP) are also standard bus master devices. The external memory interfaces, on–chip memory, and APB bridge are typical AHB slaves. Most of the peripherals can be part of the system as AHB slaves, but more likely they are part of the AMBA APB.

4.2   The Protocol

In this case study, we partition the RAPIER platform and use only the AHB module. RAPIER's AHB contains an arbiter with five master ports and one slave port. We develop reusable properties for this module. The properties give the operational conditions for the system and the input/output behavioural relations.

The AMBA AHB process starts when a master asserts a bus request signal (req_m_i) to AHB arbiter. Then the AHB arbiter performs the arbitration process to determine which master is granted ($grant\_m_i$) the access to the bus. The granted master starts the data transfer process by sending control signals and an address. Control signals provide information about the transfer. One of these control signals is the type of transfer (HTRANS). There are four types of transfer: IDLE (mst_i_idle), BUSY (mst_i_busy), NONSEQ (mst_i_nonseq), and SEQ (mst_i_seq). In an IDLE transfer, the active master does not perform any data transfer. BUSY transfer is similar to IDLE, but it also indicates that the active master is inserting an IDLE cycle in the middle of a BURST operation. NONSEQ and SEQ signals indicate the control signal and address relation between current transfer and the previous one.

When the active master has started the transfer, the selected slave will respond with information on the transfer using HREADY and HRESP signals. Whenever slaves need to assert one or more wait states, the HREADY (slv_ready) signal is set to LOW. The HRESP signal is used to determine the status of transfer. There are four possible HRESP responses: OKAY (slv_ok), ERROR (slv_error), RETRY (slv_retry), and SPLIT (slv_split). The OKAY response indicates the slave's transfer is progressing without any problem. The ERROR response indicates that an error has occurred during the transfer. The RETRY response indicates that the transfer is not finished yet and the bus master has to retry the transfer until it is completed. The SPLIT response indicates that the transfer is not completed successfully; the bus master must retry the transfer when it is next granted access to the bus. In a SPLIT condition, the slave takes the responsibility to initiate a request to access the bus when the transfer can be completed.

The arbiter manages the arbitration processes. It monitors requests to access the bus from masters and to complete the split transfer from slaves. Then it decides which master has the highest priority to be granted the access. The arbiter is also responsible for ensuring that at any time there is only one master is granted access to the bus.

SMV is used to verify the implementation of AHB bus protocol. SMV uses the SMV Language (SMVL) and Verilog as its modelling languages. When the source is in Verilog, it needs to be translated into SMVL before it is model checked. The translation from Verilog to SMVL is done by using the translation tool *vl2smv*. The tool comes as part of the Cadence SMV distribution.

RAPIER AHB is implemented in Verilog. We needed to slightly modify the code to satisfy our system level verification methodology, which considers all components are black box components. The black box approach does not allow the use of any internal nodes or signals. One approach to overcoming this requirement is by bringing all internal nodes needed in the verification to the output interfaces. We also need to do abstractions to the data–bus and address–bus of the bus protocol to eliminate one source of explosion in BDD sizes during formal verification. The n-bit bus is replaced with a special scalar–set datatype called num [11].

4.3   ARM7 Processor

ARM7 is a 32–bit microprocessor from Advanced RISC Machines (ARM) [2]. It is based on the Reduced Instruction Set Computer (RISC) architecture. The processor features a three–stages pipeline architecture. Typically, in one cycle one instruction is being executed while the next one is being decoded, and the one after that is being fetched.

In our platform the formal model of the ARM7 processor is specified in LISP, the programming language of ACL2. Implementing the processor in LISP enables the model to be used in classical simulation test by executing the functional model with input test vectors. In the ACL2 environment, the LISP model is used as a formal model which enables user to perform symbolic simulation.

ARM7 is modelled as a finite state machine at the Micro–Architectural (MA) level. The model is a clock–cycle accurate model of the pipeline machine implementation. Every internal state transition corresponds to a hardware clock cycle. The MA is modelled using a state function, which is a mapping of *(f: inputs → state → state)* [18]. The *inputs* argument are the input interfaces of the processor. The *state* defines the internal state of the processor at a given time. It contains a list of all state–holding components of the processor, such as the registers, and flags. Our processor model does not feature Thumb and co–processor instructions.

The bus protocol and the processor are the core components of the verification platform. The platform is used in the development of an application, the Ethernet Switch. The system uses only two master modules.

5   Formal Properties

In this section, we explain the development of a verification platform for the system just described. The platform is based on specifications for the AMBA AHB bus protocol and the ARM7 processor. We then use these to develop platform specifications for two AHB masters. We require that the resulting system should have certain liveness properties.

The development stages are as follows: first, we establish generic properties of the platform which are based only on RAPIER's AMBA protocol properties. Second, we develop properties of the processor. Third, we integrate the bus arbiter and the processor by combining their properties. The result of this combination is used to define specifications for the remaining components. In effect, these specifications are the test–benches to define components' compatibilities with the system.

5.1   AMBA AHB Properties

Our verification platform is built around the AMBA bus protocol. In this first stage mentioned above, we define the environmental constraints for the protocol. These constraints provide operational conditions whereby the expected behaviours of the protocol are reached or proven correct. Conditions are proved using the SMV model checker; then they are imported into HOL98 as theorems (axioms).

All verification has been performed using a Linux machine with an Intel Xeon 2.4GHz processor with 3G RAM. The time used to import theorems from SMV into HOL is negligible compared to the time used to model check. Model checking of Theorems 1, 2, and 3 took approximately 25 seconds, 25 seconds, and 59 minutes of CPU time respectively.

From the documentation [13], we learn that the request from all masters connected to the AMBA AHB can be activated or de–activated by setting the clock blocking signals ($clocken\_m_i$). When a master is de–activated, the clock signal is blocked for that master. Consequently, its requests to access the bus will be ignored and no grant signal can be assigned to it. To achieve maximum coverage of all masters' activities, all masters need to be activated. This is done by setting off the blocking control for the input clock of each module ($clocken\_m_i$) with a HIGH signal.

One way to assure behavioural consistency of the system is by applying an initialisation sequence. This is achieved by triggering the reset signal. The environmental constraint express this by saying that the reset signal is active for at least one cycle and no reset is applied afterwards. We only analyse the behaviour of the model after the system is reset and all masters are active. This constraint is defined in *Assumption 1*.

Assumption 1.

$$Reset \land XG \neg Reset \land G(\bigwedge_{1 \leq i \leq 5} clocken\_m_i)$$

In SMV, *Assumption 1* is declared as a fairness condition for the system. The SMV code for this fairness condition is *SMV_Assumption1*. The fairness properties are enforced by assuming them to be true, using the SMV *assume* construct.

```
SMV_Assumption1:
    assert (Reset & XG ~Reset & G(clocken_m₁ &
        clocken_m₂ & clocken_m₃ & clocken_m₄));
    assume SMV_Assumption1;
```

The AHB arbiter receives requests from up to five AHB masters. It then uses a fixed priority rule to determine which master should be granted bus ownership. Master m_5 is assigned the highest priority and master m_0 the lowest priority. If no master is requesting the bus, then unless m_1 is in the split mode [3], bus ownership is granted to m_1. If default master (m_1) is in split mode, the bus is granted to dummy master (m_0). The AHB arbiter has the responsibility to ensure that at any time only one master is being granted bus ownership. The arbiter also guarantees that at any time there is one master which is granted the bus. This is shown in *SMV_Theorem1*. The mutual exclusion properties are described in *SMV_Theorem2*.

SMV_Theorem1:
    assert G(grant_m$_0$ | grant_m$_1$ | grant_m$_2$ |
            grant_m$_3$ | grant_m$_4$ | grant_m$_5$);
using SMV_Assumption1 prove SMV_Theorem1;

SMV_Theorem2:
    assert G($\sim$(grant_m$_0$ & grant_m$_1$) &
            $\sim$(grant_m$_0$ & grant_m$_2$) &
            . . .
            $\sim$(grant_m$_4$ & grant_m$_5$));
using SMV_Assumption1 prove SMV_Theorem2;

SMV_Theorem1 and *SMV_Theorem2* are proved using the fairness condition *SMV_Assumption1*. We instruct SMV to use the constraints by a **using** *assumptions* **prove** *theorems* statement.

The interface between SMV and HOL enables users to automatically import properties proved in SMV into HOL. The interface analyses the SMV code to find relevant information about the properties being verified. It also gathers which components or modules and assumptions are used in the verification. The modules and assumptions become the antecedents and the properties being proved as the conclusions of implications in HOL. For example, SMV_Theorem1 is imported into the HOL environment by using the command *get_smv_theorem*. The HOL theorem is:

HOL_Theorem1:
(AHB $\wedge$ Reset $\wedge$ XG $\neg$Reset $\wedge$
 G(clocken_m$_1$ $\wedge$ clocken_m$_2$ $\wedge$ clocken_m$_3$ $\wedge$ clocken_m$_4$))
$\rightarrow$
(G(grant_m$_0$ $\vee$ grant_m$_1$ $\vee$ grant_m$_2$ $\vee$
   grant_m$_3$ $\vee$ grant_m$_4$ $\vee$ grant_m$_5$) $\wedge$
 G($\neg$(grant_m$_0$ $\wedge$ grant_m$_1$)$\wedge$
   $\neg$(grant_m$_0$ $\wedge$ grant_m$_2$)$\wedge$
   . . .
   $\neg$(grant_m$_4$ $\wedge$ grant_m$_5$))

Another style of *HOL_Theorem1* is presented in *Theorem 1*. The theorem says that when AHB is initialised with conditions described in *Assumption 1*, there will be exactly one master being granted bus ownership.

Theorem 1.
$$(\textbf{AHB} \wedge Assumption(1)) \rightarrow (G(\bigvee_{0 \leq i,j \leq 5} grant\_m_i) \wedge$$
$$G(\bigwedge_{0 \leq i,j \leq 5, i \neq j} \neg(grant\_m_i \wedge grant\_m_j)))$$

For the reminder of Section 5.1, we use the notations employed in *Assumption 1* to describe the SMV fairness constraints and *Theorem 1* to describe SMV theorems when they are imported into HOL.

After defining the initialisation process, we need to learn about the specific behaviour of the system. The resources we have for this are the documentation and the circuit itself. In most cases, however, the existing documentation is not detailed enough to provide the specific information needed. Furthermore, the system may come as a black box system where minimum information of the circuitry are available. One approach that can be taken is by performing experimental verifications using the documented specifications as the guidelines. In our case, we use SMV to learn about our AHB system. When incorrect constraints are used in the verification, SMV generates a counter example. We use the documentation and feedback from SMV to determine the operational conditions of the system that can lead to the expected behaviours.

One of master's behaviours is that it can request the arbiter to perform a burst process or a lock process. When the arbiter allows the master to perform those processes, the arbiter state machine goes into either burst mode or lock mode state. In these states, the system goes into an internal loop and continues to grant the bus to the active master until the process is finished. The only exception is when the arbiter goes into a lock–split state, which forces the arbitration to grant the bus to the dummy master until the split process is completed. Lock–split state is a condition when the arbiter is serving active master lock request, slave responds with a split signal. The arbiter starts a new arbitration when the process in burst mode or lock mode is completed.

At this stage, we need to find the general conditions that ensure that all process modes can be completed. When a master is granted the bus, the completion of the process depends on the response from the slave. The slave informs the arbiter and the master that the data is ready by emitting a *slv_ready* signal. We assume slaves have the fairness property of eventually responding to any request. At the same time, the master must be able to acknowledge the slave response. This requires a condition where if master m_i is granted the bus then eventually the active master is not in a busy mode and slave issues a ready signal. This fairness constraint is described in *Assumption 2*.

Assumption 2.

$$GF\ slv\_ready \wedge G(\bigwedge_{1 \leq i,j \leq 5} grant\_m_i \rightarrow XF(\neg mst_i\_busy \wedge slv\_ready))$$

The transition of the arbiter's state machine into lock mode can be observed from the response on grant and lock signals of each masters. When an active master is sending a lock signal, then the arbiter will go to lock mode. We define this condition as $(\bigvee_{1 \leq i \leq 5} (grant\_m_i \wedge lock\_m_i))$ and abbreviate it as the *lock_req* signal. When *lock_req* goes HIGH then the arbiter will be in the lock mode. Whenever the system enters a lock mode, there is a possibility that the system is trapped and has reached a deadlock condition. We prevent this condition by stating that every master which asserts a lock signal will eventually de–assert it.

There is also a possibility that the lock mode operation goes into an alternating sequence in which the master sends the lock/unlock signal and the slave sends the split/retry-ok/error signal. For examples, everytime active master de–

assert lock signal, slave responds with split/retry signal. This condition forces arbiter to go back into lock or lock–split mode state. If this condition always occurs, the system will be trapped in the lock mode. We choose to allow this condition to happen and examine the possible sequences needed to break this loop–trap. The requirement to exit from the loop–trap is described in *Assumption 3*.

Assumption 3.

G *(lock_req $\rightarrow$ F $\neg$lock_req) $\wedge$*
GF *(lock_mode $\rightarrow$ ($\neg$grant_m$_0$ $\wedge$ slv_ok/slv_error $\wedge$ $\neg$lock_req $\wedge$*
X(slv_ready $\wedge$ slv_ok/slv_error $\wedge$ $\neg$lock_req)))

The description of the above assumption is as follows: first, when the active master asserts a lock signal, it will eventually de–assert it. Second, lock mode will always be terminated after two cycles. In the first of these cycles, it is required that the bus is not granted to m_0. In the second cycle, the slave module has to acknowledge that it is ready to complete the transfer. In both cycles, the master has to be able to retract the lock signal (unlock), and the slave must not issue a split or retry response.

A new arbitration is achieved when the system is in burst mode or able to exit from the lock–trap while in lock mode. This condition is indicated by *new_cycle* signal. When HIGH output on this signal indicates that the arbiter is performing a new arbiration process. The exit requirements are defined in *Assumption 1,2,* and *3*. Assuming the exit requirements are fair, we prove that the arbiter will always eventually perform a new arbitration. The theorem is described below:

Theorem 2.

*(**AHB** $\wedge$ Assumption(1,2,3)) $\rightarrow$ GF new_cycle*

There is a possibility that a granted master is forced by a slave into split mode. When this condition occurs, the arbiter memorises which master has been split using the *split_m$_i$* signal. In this case, arbiter will ignore all incoming requests from master m$_i$ until it receives *un–split* signal from the slave. The *un–split* signal indicates that the data for the master is ready for transfer. To avoid the scenario that a master remains in split mode indefinitely, we define a new fairness condition described in *Assumption 4*.

Assumption 4.

$G \bigwedge\limits_{1 \leq i \leq 5}$ *(split_m$_i$ $\rightarrow$ F un–split_m$_i$)*

Every clock cycle, the arbiter evaluates the latest input signals and decides what action it will take. When a request send by a master module is not granted, the module needs to keep requesting. This is because the arbiter does not memorise any incoming signals. If the master retracts its request signal, the arbiter will assume the corresponding master has cancelled its request.

The arbiter uses a fixed priority scheme to decide which master is granted access to the bus. The fixed priority scheme will always prevent any lower priority master being granted bus ownership. We need to create a situation where the possibility of granting control to this master exists. A request from m_i can only be granted whenever no higher priority master is sending a request signal or when the higher priority master is in split mode. The request constraints are described in *Assumption 5*.

Assumption 5.

$$G \bigwedge_{1 \leq i \leq 5} ((req\_m_i \wedge X \neg grant\_m_i) \rightarrow X \ req\_m_i) \wedge$$

$$G \bigwedge_{1 \leq i \leq 4} (req\_m_i \rightarrow F (\bigwedge_{i < j \leq 5} (\neg req\_m_j \vee split\_m_j) \wedge X \ new\_cycle))$$

After we successfully create the general scenario for a new arbitration, we can use it to obtain the requirements for the arbiter to grant every incoming master request. The additional rules are described in Assumption 4 and 5. The general request-grant theorem is described in *Theorem 3*. The theorem says that every master request will eventually be granted, provided all requirements defined in *Assumption 1* through *Assumption 5* are satisfied:

Theorem 3.

$$(\mathbf{AHB} \wedge Assumption(1,2,3,4,5)) \rightarrow G (\bigwedge_{1 \leq i,j \leq 5} req\_m_i \rightarrow F \ grant\_m_i)$$

Theorem 3 defines only the liveness condition of every master's request. In order to guarantee liveness of the system, all constraints must be satisfied. This means that all masters have to operate fairly so that every master has the chance to access the bus. In Section 5.3, we describe how we refine *Theorem 3* to construct an application specific verification platform.

5.2   ARM7 Properties

ARM7 processor is the second core component of the verification platform. In AMBA AHB, processor is defined as the default master and connected to the ports of m_1. The processor is modelled in ACL2 using functional modelling style. In this style, the output signals of a component are given as a function of the input signals.

ARM7execute is a single–step execution function for the ARM7 processor. The function takes five arguments. The first is the input signal for reset. The second is the signal from the arbiter to grant the access to the bus. The third argument is the interrupt input signal. The fourth is the data–in from the AHB bus. The last argument is the internal state function of the processor. Evaluating *ARM7execute* will compute the updated initial internal state and return this updated state.

Similar to the bus protocol, we also need to obtain properties of the processor. They are obtained by proving facts using the ACL2 theorem prover. In this paper, we describe three features of the processor that have been verified.

All analysis was performed under the condition that no reset is applied to the processor. The processor's properties are as follows:

- A *busy* signal is emitted only when the processor is executing co–processor instructions. Since our processor model does not implement co–processor instructions, it will never send a *busy* signal.

  $\neg reset \rightarrow (\neg\ Pbusy\ (ARM7execute\ 0\ grant\ interrupts\ data\ Pstate))$

- The processor will continue its evaluation only when it recieves a grant signal. If it does not, then it goes to an idle state and maintains its internal state. This means that the processor holds its request signal whenever it is not granted.

  $(\neg reset \wedge \neg grant) \rightarrow (ARM7execute\ 0\ 0\ interrupts\ data\ Pstate) = Pstate.$

- The ARM7 processor is capable of performing a lock sequence. We prove that after at most three execution cycles, the processor will release the bus.

  $(P1 = (ARM7execute\ reset0\ grant0\ interrupts0\ data0\ P0) \wedge$
  $P2 = (ARM7execute\ reset1\ grant1\ interrupts1\ data1\ P1) \wedge$
  $P3 = (ARM7execute\ reset2\ grant2\ interrupts2\ data2\ P2)) \rightarrow$
  $((\neg reset0 \wedge grant0) \rightarrow$
  $(\neg Plock(P1) \vee ((\neg reset1 \wedge grant1) \rightarrow$
  $(\neg Plock(P2) \vee ((\neg reset2 \wedge grant2) \rightarrow \neg Plock(P3))))))$

In our methodology, all components are combined and integrated in HOL. They are specified as relational models in higher order logic by defining predicates that state which combinations of values can appear on their external ports. When a component is defined as a functional model, as is the case with our ACL2 model of ARM7, it needs to be transformed into a relational one. A wrapper is created to bridge the functional model and the relational model.

The ACL2 processor function *ARM7execute* is transformed in HOL into the relational model called *ARM7*. The relational model of the processor is defined as follows:

$$ARM7 \overset{def}{=} (Pst_0 = P_0) \wedge$$
$$(Pst_{(t+1)} = ARM7execute\ reset\ grant\ interrupts\ data\ Pst_t)$$

Pst is a function from time to the processor's state. The index subscript to Pst indicates the relative time at which the state occurs. Pst_0 is the state of the processor at time 0 and P_0 is the initial state of the processor. As discussed above, ACL2 theorems for the processor are automatically imported into HOL as trusted axioms. A small amount of very simple theorem proving is needed to simplify the HOL properties obtained from ACL2 theorems. The final HOL theorem is as follows:

Theorem 4.

$(\mathbf{ARM7} \wedge (\mathrm{G} \ \neg\mathrm{reset})) \rightarrow$
$((G \ (\neg mst_1\_busy) \ \wedge$
$\quad G \ (\neg grant\_m_1 \rightarrow (Pst_{(t+1)} = Pst_t)) \ \wedge$
$\quad G \ (grant\_m_{1(t)} \rightarrow (\neg Plock(Pst_{(t+1)}) \vee (grant\_m_{1(t+1)} \rightarrow$
$\quad\quad (\neg Plock(Pst_{(t+2)}) \vee (grant\_m_{1(t+2)} \rightarrow \neg Plock(Pst_{(t+3)}))))))))$

5.3 Application Specific Platform

RAPIER is an environment used in teaching at the ISLI. One application case study was to build an Ethernet Switch using the platform. The Ethernet Switch system uses two AHB masters: the ARM7 processor and a memory controller. In this platform, all slaves are required to give an immediate response for any master's request. The slaves are not allowed to respond with a split or retry signal. Our goal is to find the specifications or requirements for the memory controller and the slaves so that all desired properties are satisfied.

Interconnection of the components in the verification platform is a straight-forward step. The formal models are connected and integrated with logical conjunction in higher order logic. The integration of the AHB bus protocol and the ARM7 processor are just defined as ($\mathbf{AHB} \wedge \mathbf{ARM7}$).

We set our goal to have a system which has liveness properties. In this condition, all requests are always granted. *Theorem 3* shows the general rules or constraints for granting master's requests. We use these constraints to define the specifications of a system which has the desired liveness properties.

The Ethernet Switch system uses only two masters. The other masters are left inactive. This fact is the new constraint for the AHB bus. We use this constraint to refine existing AHB properties. The refinement is performed either using the model checker (SMV) or the theorem prover (HOL). In either case, we use existing properties and simplify the constraints of the AHB bus protocol. We do not need to re–model check the bus protocol from scratch for the system with two masters. We choose to import all proofs about AHB into HOL where we perform system level integration and verification.

The non–existence of m_3 to m_5 means that there is no request from any of these modules. One of the implications of this is that no grant signals are ever sent for these masters. The slave requirement of not allowing *split* or *retry* means a slave can only respond with *ok* or *error*. Because a slave is never emitting a *split* signal, no split condition will ever occur. In SMV we prove the system has these properties. The properties are used as the refinement constraints to simplify the generic properties of AMBA AHB. These constraints are defined as follows:

$$\bigwedge_{3 \leq i \leq 5} (G\neg req\_m_i \rightarrow G\neg grant\_m_i) \ \wedge$$

$$(G \ slv\_split/slv\_retry) \rightarrow G(\bigwedge_{1 \leq i \leq 5} \neg split\_m_i \wedge \neg grant\_m_0 \wedge slv\_ok/slv\_error)$$

The constraints eliminate the need for *Assumption 4*. They also simplify *Assumption 1,3,5* with *Assumption 6,7,8* respectively. The new assumptions eliminate all properties related to m_0, m_3, m_4, m_5, and slave *split/retry* response.

The clock enable signals in Assumption 1 are only needed when they are used. If there is no master connected to the corresponding port, the condition of these signals can be ignored or turned off. The new assumption is shown below:

Assumption 6.

$Reset \land XG \neg Reset \land G(\bigwedge_{1 \leq i \leq 2} clocken\_m_i)$

The restriction on slave modules not allowing them to send split or retry signals reduces *Assumption 3* dramatically. It eliminates the need to include a dummy master module. Furthermore, the exit constraints when the arbiter is in lock mode depend only on the slave's ready signal and master's lock request signal. The reduced fairness constraints are as follows:

Assumption 7.
$G\ (lock\_req \rightarrow F \neg lock\_req) \land$
$GF\ (lock\_mode \rightarrow (\neg lock\_req \land X(slv\_ready \land \neg lock\_req)))$

The properties of *Assumption 5* are reduced to m_1 and m_2. In the specialized platform, the system's liveness constraints only depend on the fairness condition of m_2 not infinitely requesting the bus. Because m_1 is the default master, when m_2 does not request the bus, arbiter will always grant the bus to the default master. The simplified assumption is described in *Assumption 8*.

Assumption 8.

$G \bigwedge_{1 \leq i \leq 2} ((req\_m_i \land X \neg grant\_m_i) \rightarrow X\ req\_m_i) \land$
$G\ (req\_m_1 \rightarrow F(\neg req\_m_2 \land X\ new\_cycle))$

The behaviour of the ARM7 processor is given by *Theorem 4*. One of the properties is that the processor never sends a *busy* signal. This fact eliminates the dependency of *Assumption 2* on the processor's behaviour. The new constraints are given in *Assumption 9*.

Assumption 9.
$GF\ slv\_ready \land G(grant\_m_2 \rightarrow XF(\neg mst_2\_busy \land slv\_ready))$

When the processor is in a wait state, it maintains all of its properties. This means when the processor sends a request signal and the arbiter tells the processor to wait, the processor will keep sending the request signal. This property refines *Assumption 8* into *Assumption 10*.

Assumption 10.
$G\ ((req\_m_2 \land X \neg grant\_m_2) \rightarrow X\ req\_m_2) \land$
$G\ (req\_m_1 \rightarrow F(\neg req\_m_2 \land X\ new\_cycle))$

Theorem 4 also shows that when the processor is locking the bus, it will eventually unlock it in at most three execution cycles. The arbiter also guarantees that in lock mode the active master always keeps the bus. These conditions refine *Assumption 7* to *Assumption 11*.

Assumption 11.

$G((grant\_m_2 \wedge lock\_m_2) \rightarrow F(grant\_m_2 \wedge \neg lock\_m_2)) \wedge$
$GF \ (lock\_mode \rightarrow (\neg lock\_req \wedge X(slv\_ready \wedge \neg lock\_req)))$

Finally, the Ethernet Switch platform is defined in *Theorem 5*. It says the platform has two masters. It is constructed from the AHB bus protocol and the ARM7 processor. When the system is initialised with the sequence described in *Assumption 6* and the constraints described in *Assumption 9,10,11* are satisfied, the system will always provide fair services for its two masters. Light weight theorem proving is needed to prove *Theorem 5*.

Theorem 5.

(AHB $\wedge$ ARM7 $\wedge$ Assumption(6,9,10,11)) $\rightarrow$
$G \ (req\_m_1 \rightarrow F \ grant\_m_1 \wedge req\_m_2 \rightarrow F \ grant\_m_2)$

Based on *Theorem 5*, we can analyse the requirements and define the specifications for each module. The second master (memory controller) has to satisfy the following specifications:

- The module has to be capable in maintaining its request signal until it is granted.
- The module has to be able to accept a response from a slave by not always engaging in a busy mode.
- If the module is capable asserting a lock signal, it has to be able to de-assert it until a new arbitration cycle is reached.
- In order to let a lower priority master access the bus, the module should not infinitely request the bus. One way to achieve this is by introducing one additional rule: every completed request sequence must be followed by a sequence of idle states. In this way, the system can guarantee that all requests can be served.

The slaves in this platform have to satisfy specifications as follows:

- By definition, all slaves are not allowed to send a retry or split signal.
- They have to be able to respond to all requests.
- To prevent any erratic behaviours of the slave, we define one additional rule which controls the behaviour of the slave: when all input are stable, the output of the slaves will eventually become stable. This means that when a slave is ready to respond to a master's request, afterwards the slave's output remains stable as long as the input does not change.

In this methodology, we obtain specialised specifications for both master and slave modules. This specifications feature tighter requirements in comparison to the standard ones. The specifications are geared to satisfy the application specific requirements. Designing the modules under these specifications guarantee the system to fulfil the application's specific requirements.

6   Conclusions and Future Work

We have presented a tool architecture and methodology to perform formal verification for system on chip designs. The verification environment combines various formal tools which enable verification engineers to perform symbolic simulation, model checking, and theorem proving. The mechanism for sharing information reduces the possibility of errors being made during the translation of theorems from one formal tool to the other. It also allows each component to be modelled in the most suitable formalism.

The methodology is based on the development of a generic formal verification platform in which applications can be developed. The generic platform behaviours are described as a set of formal properties. The generality of the properties make them reusable in the development of platform specific applications. The properties can be used to develop the specifications of the components of the platform. They can also be used to analyse the behaviour of the platform with a set of components.

We have developed a standard integration platform containing the AMBA–AHB bus protocol and a ARM7 processor. We described the development of reusable formal properties for this platform. The properties define the generic behaviour of the system. We used this platform to build an application. By evaluating the platform's properties with the application requirements, we obtain the specification for the remaining components.

Our future research will build a more comprehensive verification platform on top of our proof environment. The platform will be based on the full specification of the AMBA bus protocol and the ARM7 processor. We are aiming for a 'plug and play' verification environment, involving a collection of reusable proofs. The verification platform will enable the possibility to be used as a workbench to develop detailed specifications.

Acknowledgements

The authors thank the Institute for System Level Integration for providing the RAPIER platform for this work, the Veriscope research group for the use of their machine, Michael Dales for helpful comments on a draft of this paper, and the reviewers for their feedback.

This work has been supported in part by SHEFC RDG grant 85, *Design Cluster for System Level Integration*, and the ESPRIT PROSPER project LTR 26241.

References

1. Mark D. Aagaard, Robert B. Jones, and Carl-John H. Seger. Combining Theorem Proving and Trajectory Evaluation in an Industrial Environment, in *the 35th Design Automation Conference*, San Francisco, California, June 1998, pp. 538–541.
2. ARM, ARM-7 Datasheet, DDI 0020C, December 1994.

3. ARM, AMBA specification ver 2.0, IHI-0011A, May 1999.
4. Mark Birnbaum and Howard Sachs, How VSIA Answers the SOC Dilemma, *IEEE Computer* magazine, June 1999, pp. 42–50.
5. A.J. Camilleri, A Hybrid Approach to Verifying Liveness in a Symmetric Multi-Processor, Eds Elsa L. Gunter and Amy Felty in *Theorem Proving in Higher Order Logic*, Murray Hill, New Jersey, August 1997, Springer-Verlag LNCS 1275, pp. 49–67.
6. Henry Chang, Larry Cooke, Merrill Hunt, Grant Martin, Andrew McNelly, and Lee Todd. *Surviving the SOC Revolution. A Guide to Platform-Based Design*, Kluwer, 1999.
7. Louise A. Dennis, Graham Collins, Michael Norrish, Richard Boulton, Konrad Slind, Graham Robinson, Mike Gordon, and Tom Melham. The PROSPER Toolkit, Eds S. Graf and M. Schwartzbach in *Tools and Algorithms for the Construction and Analysis of Systems: 6th International Conference, TACAS 2000*, Berlin, March/April 2000, Springer-Verlag LNCS 1785, pp. 78–92.
8. M.J.C. Gordon and T.F.Melham, editors. *Introduction to HOL: A theorem proving environment for higher order logic*, Cambridge University Press, 1993.
9. *The HOL System Description, HOL98 Taupo-6*, University of Cambridge, February 2000.
10. W.A. Hunt. *FM8501: A Verified Microprocessor*, 1994, Springer-Verlag LNCS 795.
11. C.N.Ip and D.L.Dill. Better Verification Through Symmetry, Eds D. Agnew, L. Claesen, and R. Compasano, *Computer Hardware Description Languages and their Applications*, Elsevier Science Publishers B.V., Amsterdam, Netherland, pp. 87–100.
12. R.B. Jones, J.W. O'Leary, C.-J.H. Seger, M.D. Aagaard, and T.F. Melham. Practical Formal Verification in Microprocessor Design, *IEEE Design & Test of Computers* magazine, July/August 2001, pp. 16–25.
13. Mark Litterick, ARM Integration Platform Power Management, The Institute of System Level Integration, Scotland, November 2001.
14. Matt Kaufmann, Panagiotis Manolios, and J Strother Moore. *Computer-Aided Reasoning, An Approach*, Kluwer, 2000.
15. Matt Kaufmann, Panagiotis Manolios, and J Strother Moore. *Computer-Aided Reasoning, ACL2 Case Studies*, Kluwer, 2000.
16. Michael Keating and Pierre Bricaud, *Reuse Methodology Manual For System−On−a−Chip Designs*, Kluwer Academic Publisher, Norwell Massachussetts, 1999.
17. Kenneth L. McMillan, *Symbolic Model Checking*, Kluwer Academic Publisher, Norwell Massachussetts, 1993.
18. J Strother Moore, Symbolic Simulation: An ACL2 Approach. Eds Ganesh Gopalakrishnan and Phillip Windley in *Formal Methods in Computer-Aided Design*, PaloAlto, California, November 1998, Springer–Verlag LNCS 1522, pp.334–350.
19. Carl Pixley, Formal Verification of Commercial Integrated Circuits, *IEEE Design & Test of Computers* magazine, July/August 2001, pp.4–5.
20. RAPIER, The Institute of System Level Integration, Scotland, 2001.
21. Ann Marie Rincon, Cory Cherichetti, James A. Monzel, David R. Stauffer, and Michael T. Trick. Core Design and System-on-a-Chip Integration, *IEEE Design & Test of Computers* magazine, October–December 1997, pp. 26–35.
22. K. Schneider. Yet another look at LTL model checking. Eds Laurence Pierre, and Thomas Kropf, in IFIP WG10.5 Advanced Research Working Conference on *Correct Hardware Design and verification Methods*, Bad Herrenalb, Germany, September 1999, Springer–Verlag LNCS 1703, pp.321–325.

23. Kanna Shimizu, David L. Dill, and Ching-Tsun Chou. A Specification Methodology by a Collection of Compact Properties as Applied to the Intel Itanium Processor Bus Protocol. Eds Tiziana Margaria, and Tom Melham, In *Correct Hardware Design and verification Methods*, September 1999, Springer–Verlag LNCS 2144, pp.340–354.
24. Madayam Srivas, Harald Rueβ, and David Cyrluk. Hardware Verification using PVS in *Formal Hardware Verification Methods and Systems in Comparison*, edited by Thomas Kropf , July 1997, Springer Verlag LNCS 1287, pp: 156–205.
25. Mark Staples, *Linking ACL2 and Hol*, Computer Laboratory, University of Cambridge, Technical Report No. 476, November 1999.
26. Kong Woei Susanto, An integrated Formal Approach for System on Chip, In *IP based Design*, Grenoble, France, October 2002, pp: 119–123.
27. Patrick Henry Winston and Berthold Klaus Paul Horn, *LISP*, Addison–Wesley Pub.Co., 1989.

Formalization, Testing and Execution of a Use Case Diagram⋆

Wuwei Shen[1] and Shaoying Liu[2]

[1] Department of Computer Science, Western Michigan University, USA
wwshen@cs.wmich.edu
[2] Department of Computer Science, Hosei University, Tokyo, Japan
sliu@k.hosei.ac.jp

Abstract. Errors in a requirements model have prolonged detrimental effects on reliability, cost, and safety of a software system. It is very costly to fix these errors in later phases of software development if they cannot be corrected during requirements analysis and design. A use case diagram, as a requirements model, plays an important role in giving requirements for a software system. It provides a communication tool between software requirements developers and prospective users to understand what requirements of a software system are. However most descriptions of a use case diagram are written in some informal language, leading to possible misunderstanding between developers and users. In this paper, we propose a new rigorous review technique which can be applied to software requirements models. Using this new technique before a software system is fully designed will help us find some potential errors in a requirements model, resulting in reduced time, labor and expenditure in software development.

1 Introduction

The Unified Modeling Language (UML) [12] has been proposed as a modeling language which can be applied in software development from software requirements and specification to software code generation through model design under the same framework. UML has become a standard modeling language in software development. As the first step in software development, the quality of requirements analysis is of great importance to the later phases of software development. High quality of a requirements model can most likely reduce many potential errors occurred in later phases of software development.

According to recent error investigation in software development, researchers have found that more errors are introduced during requirements analysis and design than any other phase in software development. Furthermore, requirements errors have prolonged effects on reliability, cost, and safety of a software system [14,13]. Requirements errors are more costly to fix during later phases of software development than during the requirements analysis and design phase [2].

⋆ This work is supported by the Ministry of Education, Culture, Sports, Science, and Technology of Japan under Grant-in-Aid for Scientific Research on Priority Areas (No. 15017280).

J.S. Dong and J. Woodcock (Eds.): ICFEM 2003, LNCS 2885, pp. 68–85, 2003.

Central to software requirements analysis and design is a use case diagram. A use case diagram has been proposed in UML as a notation to describe a software system's requirements and behavior. It has been served as a communication tool between software developers and users. After talking with potential users of a software system, software requirements developers should transform what users expect in a software system into a requirements model given by use case diagrams, representing what the system is expected to do from a perspective of software developers.

Use case diagrams play an important role during software development. On the one hand, software users can understand whether the software system satisfies their need at the very beginning in software development when they see use case diagrams. Their complaints about a system can be directly reported to requirements developers and some necessary changes can be made in the requirements model accordingly. Use case diagrams make it possible for users to evaluate the system behavior before code is written. On the other hand, use case diagrams can be used as blueprints during the whole software development. Besides requirements developers, other software developers such as model designers and testers can further design and test the software system based on these use case diagrams.

Most requirements models given by a use case diagram consist of two parts. One is a diagram part and the other is a textual description. The diagram part gives the relationship among use cases and actors. The textual description part informally presents the description for each use case. Most descriptions are written in informal language such as English. Although UML accepts any level of formality for use cases, we think a high level of formality for use cases can reduce many confusion and misunderstanding between software developers and users. The reduction of confusion and misunderstanding can be very helpful in improving software quality.

Formalizing a requirements model has aroused some attention in software research community [2,7,15,1,17]. Although most research works are based on some UML diagrams except for use case diagrams, we find there are a few research works about use case diagrams. Operation schemas [16] have been proposed to formalize use cases based on the fact that use cases provide the informal description of interactions between a system and its actors, whereas operation schemas precisely describe a particular system action which executes atomically. Since operation schemas are more precise and formal than natural language, they offer some rigorous basis which makes some reasoning possible. We also provided a new formal language (High-level Constraint Langauge) [18] which can be used to give the pre- and post- condition for a use case. We want to use some formal language to describe some requirements model and ultimately to reduce some confusion and ambiguity in software requirements description.

In spite of non-ambiguity in formal languages, many software practitioners complain about the impracticality of many formal languages when the formal verification has been applied in some industry applications. Due to this reason we are looking for some new method, called "rigorous reviews". Instead of some convincing formal proofs, required by most formal methods, to ensure some correctness, rigorous reviews employ some sound and practical review technique to ensure the correctness. Thus rigorous reviews can be done either by means of systematic checking of specification manually or by execution of specification with some tool support. Practitioners can easily learn these techniques without some special training. Especially in this paper we propose a new rigorous reviews technique which can be achieved by means of manual checking and some software tool together, and so practitioners can observe the result directly.

Among the rigorous reviews techniques, testing and execution are the most powerful methods because the behavior of a system can be tested and observed. Execution is a powerful and direct mechanism to observe a system. When practitioners execute a system and find some results which are not what they expect in the system, it usually means that there are some errors in the system.

However one of the sapient differences between a requirements model and an execution model is a requirements model presents what a system should do, while an execution model presents how a system can do. Because of this difference, it is almost impossible to execute a requirements model during software requirements analysis and design; therefore some requirements errors are really hard to detect when they are first introduced, and they usually cannot be found until the software system is tested. Even worse, some of them may not be found after the software system is delivered.

Unfortunately we find there is almost no research work about really using some rigorous reviews techniques to find some requirements errors during requirements analysis and design based on use case diagrams. After observing the lasting impact of requirements errors on software development, we proposed a new language (High-level Constraint Language) (HCL) [18] to which a requirements model given by use case diagrams can be mapped. In that paper, we used the "execution", the most obvious rigorous reviews technique, to check whether or not a high-level model based on a use case diagram satisfies users' requirements. However, the execution techniques cannot be used to check all high-level models because some specifications are not executable.

Fortunately testing, especially specification testing as a rigorous review technique, can be used to attack the weakness of the execution approach. By specification testing, we mean presentation of inputs and outputs to a specification, and evaluation to obtain a result—usually a truth value, as described in detail in the second author's previous publication [9]. As the post-condition of an operation usually describes the relation between its inputs and outputs, an evaluation of the post-condition needs both input and output values. This is slightly different from program testing in the sense that program testing needs to run the program with test cases only for input variables, while testing specifications (especially for those written in terms of pre and post-conditions) require test cases for both input and output variables, and there is no need to run any program but just to evaluate the related predicate expressions (e.g., pre and post-conditions). When testing an operation, it is necessary to treat the state variables before and after the operation, for example, $\overleftarrow{x}$ and x in VDM [6]; x and x' in Z [3], and $\tilde{x}$ and

x in SOFL [10,8], as inputs and outputs of the operation, respectively. This will allow the evaluation of the post-condition of the operation and an examination of whether the change of the state made by this operation is satisfactory in its consistency.

The remainder of this paper is organized as follows. Section 2 gives the rigorous reviews techniques used in this paper. In section 3 we first introduce a use case diagram and then a vending machine example is used to show the application of our rigorous reviews techniques. Section 4 draws some conclusions and suggests future work.

2   Rigorous Reviews Overview

After a requirements model is given by a use case diagram together with HCL specification for each use case, we can use specification testing and execution to find whether any errors exist in the requirements model. Specification testing is used first to check whether there are some inconsistencies in a requirements model. If no inconsistencies are found, then requirements model developers can move to the second stage, i.e. execution of the requirements model.

Although a requirements model can pass specification testing, it cannot guarantee that the model totally satisfies users' needs. One example is that one of the plausible requirements in a vending machine example is the change returned to a customer plus the price of a product the customer would like to buy times the number of the product the customer buys should be equal to the amount of money he pays to the machine. But according to this requirement, the machine can always return all the coins the customer pays to the machine as change when the product is still available. But this solution cannot be acceptable and the specification testing may not find any error in this requirement. Thus, users of the vending machine may not find the problem until they run the prototyping system. Therefore only when users run a prototyping system do they find some more subtle errors in a requirements model.

Therefore the rigorous reviews technique consists of two parts: test a requirements model and execute a requirements model. Fig. 1 gives a use case diagram to show what our technique can do. From this diagram, we can know that software developers are an actor who can get a result from use case *Test a Req. Model* and *Execute a Req. Model.*, while software users are another actor who can observe the system behavior by use case *Execute a Req. Model.* Based on the results, software developers can redesign a requirements model if necessary.

Fig. 2 is a state chart diagram which shows a software development process to which our rigorous reviews can be applied. After designing a use case diagram and giving a pre- and post- condition, software developers can use the specification testing and execution proposed in this paper to find errors in a requirements model. If an error is found, software developers can return to the first state, redesigning the requirements model. If no error is found and the requirements model is executable, then the developers can execute the model to find more potential errors. If no error is found and the model is non-executable, then

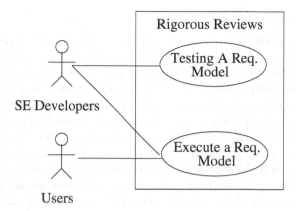

Fig. 1. A use case diagram representing the rigorous reviews presented in this paper.

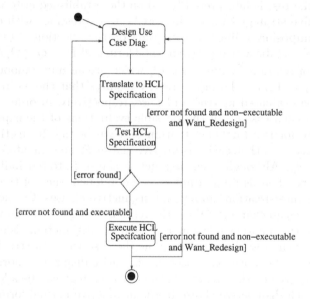

Fig. 2. A state chart diagram showing how our rigorous reviews can be applied to software requirements developement.

the developers can have two choices. One is they can further refine the model to make the new model executable. In this case the developers return to the first state. The second choice is that the developers can leave the requirements analysis and design phase and go to the next phase to further develop the model. Since software development process is iterative, the process shown in Fig. 2 can always be repeated when a requirements model is designed.

2.1 Requirements Model Testing

The specific approach to testing a requirements specification (representing a model of the system) consists of two steps. The first step is to derive the properties from the specification as targets for testing. For example, the properties may include the satisfiability of operations, consistency between invariants and operations, and the consistency between different operations when they are integrated. The second step is to test the properties for their consistency. Similar to conventional program testing [19], testing a target property also takes three steps: (1) generate test cases; (2) evaluate the property with the test cases; and (3) analyze the test results to determine whether faults are detected. For the testing of internal consistency of the target properties, test cases are mainly generated based on the structure of the specification. This is similar to *structural testing* for programs where test cases are generated by examining the program structure. In this method, there is no need to provide expected test results, because the nature of the test is interpreted based on the established criteria.

There are five strategies for testing predicate expressions with different objectives, each imposing a different constraint on the selection of test cases. Let $P \equiv P_1 \vee P_2 \vee \cdots \vee P_n$ be a disjunctive normal form and $P_i \equiv Q_i^1 \wedge Q_i^2 \wedge \cdots \wedge Q_i^m$ be a conjunction of relational expressions Q_i^j which are atomic components, where $i = 1...n$ and $j = 1...m$. The first strategy requires that the entire disjunctive normal form be evaluated as true and false, respectively, in order to allow the examination of each case of all the possible evaluations of the expression. The second strategy focuses further attention on each of the disjunctive clause of the form and requires that each disjunctive clause P_i be evaluated as true and false, respectively. Although each disjunctive clause is tested individually using this strategy, there is no guarantee of the independency of the testing due to the possible inter-relation among the disjunctive clauses. Consider the form $x \leq 20 \vee x > 10$ as an example. When the relation $x \leq 20$ evaluates with the test case $x = 15$ as true, another relation $x > 10$ in the disjunction also evaluates as true. Therefore, this test does not examine the case when the truth evaluation of $x \leq 20$ leads to the truth evaluation of the entire disjunctive normal form individually. To overcome this weakness, the third strategy can be adopted, which requires that each disjunctive clause in the disjunctive normal form evaluate as true while all the other clauses evaluate as false. The fourth and fifth strategies give guidelines for the generating of test cases to examine the effectiveness of each atomic expression in each conjunction of the disjunctive normal form, with a little difference in emphasizing the independency of testing each atomic expression.

2.2 Requirements Model Execution and Its Implementation

The next step following the specification testing is to execute the model. Even though not all requirements models can be executable due to high-level specification, the execution of an executable model is important in find errors in a requirements model. We will discuss the executable part in the following. After passing the testing, we will execute the model, trying to find some subtle errors undetected during the specification testing. For those executable part of requirements model, All HCL specifications used to give a requirements model are mapped into AsmL specifications.

AsmL [11] is a formal language based on the theory of Abstract State Machines [5], which was first presented by Dr. Yuri Gurevich more than ten years ago. An ASM is a state machine which computes a set of updates of the machine's variables by firing all possible updates based on the current state. The computation of a set of updates occurs at the same time and the result of computation leads to a new state to be generated. AsmL itself is an executable language and the control flow in AsmL includes many structures such as parallel, sequence, loop, choice and exception. Due to the executability in AsmL, we use AsmL as our target language to execute a use case diagram.

The translation from HCL into ASML consists of two steps. First, each use specification is translated into a method in AsmL. The method body is implemented based on the pre- and post- condition given by HCL. Each pre-condition is translated into a **require** structure in AsmL, which means that the pre-condition should be satisfied before the method is executed. All the definitions given in the description parts in a requirements model are mapped into declarations in AsmL specifications.

Second, the order of execution of use cases is implied by the inputs and outputs given in a requirements model. Every input which is given in a pre-condition and has no relation to other outputs for the rest of use cases is treated as an input in a requirements model. A use case with a model input variable should first be executed. Similarly, any output variable which occurs in a post-condition of a use case but does not appear in any other use case's pre-conditions is regarded as a requirements model output. A use case with a model output should be last executed. The other input and output variables are called internal inputs and outputs respectively. A use case, say A, whose output variable is an input of another use case B, then the use case A should be executed before the use case B. Based on the above strategies, we translate a requirements model into an AsmL specification and then execute the specification.

3   Use Case Diagrams and a Vending Machine Example

A requirements model as the first model designed by requirements developers during software development is usually represented by a use case diagram. A use case diagram usually consists of set of use cases, actors and their relationships. An actor is an external user or another system who can initiate a business represented by a use case diagram. A use case represents a sequence of actions which can be performed due to some events triggered by an actor. A use case in a use case diagram only describes one aspect of a software system without presuming any specific design or implementation. A use case only describes what it can do instead of how to do.

There are three relationships which can be defined in a use case diagram, "extend", "include" and "generalization". These relationships try to direct software developers towards a more object-oriented view of the world so as to avoid some duplicate work. But a use case diagram itself does not provide how a requirements model should be structured. Therefore, the description for each use case has become very important in a requirements model. Here we use pre- and post- condition to represent the behavior of each use case. How to use give a pre- and post- condition based on HCL can be found in [18].

In the following we use a vending machine example [4] to illustrate how to give a requirements model by our rigorous reviews. A vending machine consists of a money box, a change box, a keypad and a container containing all products to be sold. The vending machine sells sodas, chips and sandwiches whose prices are 60 cents, 50 cents and 100 cents respectively in its container. The keypad provides a mapping between a number and a product. We assume that 0 represents sodas, 1 represents chips and 2 represents sandwiches. We assume that the maximum amounts of the money for the change box, which is used to return change to a customer, and money box, which is used to keep a customer pay, are both 1000 cents. Every purchase only returns one product to a customer.

3.1 A High-Level Model

In the highest level we abstract the problem as follows: a customer can buy a product from the vending machine if (s)he provides a number, which represents the amount of money (coins) to be inserted, and the product code. Then the vending machine can sell the product and return change to the customer if exists. Therefore, the model involves only one actor, i.e. *customer*, and one use case, i.e. *Buy_product*. So the highest use case diagram for the vending machine is shown in Fig. 3, where the stick figure represents the actor who can interact with the system and the oval, named *Buy_product*, represents the use case and provides a service to the actor.

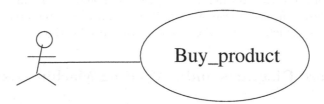

Fig. 3. The highest level model for the vending machine.

In order to give a complete requirements model, we need to give a pre- and post- condition for each use case in the diagram. Before giving these conditions, we need to find out the requirements of the use case *Buy_product*. After a customer inserts an amount of money and provides a product code, then the vending machine can sell the product and return an integer which represents the amount of change returned to the customer if exists. So the pre- and post- condition for the above use case can be given by the HCL specification in Fig. 4.

---

usecase VendingMachine1 (in money, product,
*   out num_product, changes)*
pre: money in Integer, product in Indices(code)
*   where money > 0*
post: (num_product in RAN, changes in[0..1000]) |
*   num_product * price(product) + changes = money*
description:
*   PRODUCT = {soda, chip, sandiwich}*
*   RAN = [0..1]*
*   code: Integer → PRODUCT = {0→ soad,*
*   1 → chip, 2 → sandwich}*
*   price: PRODUCT → Integer = { soda → 60,*
*   chip → 50, sandwich → 100}*

Fig. 4. The highest requirements model for the vending machine.

The main requirement for this highest level model is that the price of the product a customer buys plus the change if returned should be equal to the amount of money (s)he pays to the vending machine. The other requirement includes the number which represents an amount of money a customer provides should be positive and the product code should be valid. Therefore the *precondition* for the use case *VendingMachine1* requires that the amount of money a customer pays be a positive integer and the product (s)he chooses be a valid product stored in the vending machine. The valid products stored in the vending machine are defined by the set *PRODUCT* which is defined in the *description* part. To ensure that a code input by a customer is valid, we use a built-in function *Indices(code)* which represents the domain for the function *code*.

The post-condition for the use case *VendingMachine1* gives a relation among the amount of money a customer pays, the price of the product (s)he chooses and the change returned to a customer if exists. This is usually what a user of the vending machine expects.

The pre-condition and post-condition of a use case concentrate on some constraints on variables. In order to make the requirements model complete, we use the *description* part to give all the necessary information missed in the precondition and post-condition. Thus, we include the definitions for *PRODUCT*, *RAN*, *code* and *price* in the *description* part.

Before we execute the requirements model, we can use specification testing technique to find some inconsistency in the conditions of a use case. According to the criteria mentioned in the previous section, we can automatically generate some test data to check whether there is some inconsistency in the specification for each use case. Table 1 gives a test generated by trying to use the second strategy (i.e., evaluate each disjunctive clause as true and false, respectively) from Fig. 4. The symbol **nil** in tables denotes *undefined*.

Table 1. A test for VendingMachine1.

money	product	num_product	changes	pre	post	pre => post
20	2	1	20	true	nil	nil
60	0	0	60	true	nil	nil
100	2	1	0	true	nil	nil
50	1	1	0	true	nil	nil

usecase VendingMachine2 (in money, product,
                    out num_product, changes)
pre: money in Integer, product in Indices(code)
        where money > 0
post: (num_product in RAN, changes in [0..1000]) |
            num_product * price(code(product)) + changes = money
description:
        PRODUCT = {soda, chip, sandiwich}
        RAN = [0, 1]
        code: Integer → PRODUCT = {0→ soad,
        1 → chip, 2 → sandwich}
        price: PRODUCT → Integer = { soda → 60,
        chip → 50, sandwich → 100}

Fig. 5. The revised highest requirements model for the vending machine.

Because of the "strange" results when the pre-condition evaluates as true, the post-condition is unable to evaluate as a truth value, we have quickly realized that there must be something wrong in the post-condition. In fact, by this test we have found a type-mismatching fault in the post-condition. In the pre-condition, the variable *product* is defined as an index (natural number or zero) in the set *indices(code)* (the domain of the function *code* {0, 1, 2}), but in the post-condition the function *price*, whose domain is $PRODUCT = \{soda,$ *chip, sandwich*} and range is the set of integers {60, 50, 100}, is applied to the variable *product* whose value cannot be a member of the type *PRODUCT*.

3.2   A Revised Model

Based on the error we have found, we correct this mistake by replacing the original function application *price(product)* with the new function application *price(code(product))* and redefine the use case *VendingMachine1* shown in Fig. 5.

To ensure that the modified specification does not introduce new errors and no other kinds of inconsistency problems remain in it, we generate another test given in Table 2 for the modified specification *VendingMachine2*.

In this test the similar phenomena to the test given in table 1 appears again: for the last three test cases in table 2 while the pre-condition evaluates as true the post-condition becomes undefined. After analyzing the reason, we have found

Table 2. A test for VendingMachine2.

money	product	num_product	changes	pre	post	pre => post
20	2	0	20	true	true	true
30	1	1	0	true	false	false
60	0	1	0	true	true	true
50	1	1	0	true	true	true
0	0	0	0	false	true	true
200	2	1	100	true	true	true
1100	1	1	1050	true	**nil**	**nil**
1200	2	1	1100	true	**nil**	**nil**
1300	0	1	1240	true	**nil**	**nil**

that the problem is caused by neglecting that the amount of 1000 cents is the maximum capacity for the money box. This problem can be resolved by imposing the further restriction on the range of input variable *money* as *money > 0 and money <= 1000* in the pre-condition. Thus, the use case *VendingMachine2* can be modified into the following specification:

> *usecase VendingMachine3 (in money, product,*
> *out num_product, changes)*
> *pre: money in Integer, product in Indices(code)*
> *where money > 0 and money <= 1000*
> *...   /*the same as that of VendingMachine2 */*

A consistent specification for a use case does not necessarily mean that the specification really satisfies the requirements given by a user. Some design errors in a requirements model cannot be found until users see the execution. Therefore, after checking that a specification for a use case does not include inconsistency, we can execute the specification by translating it into Asml specification. By running the AsmL specification, a user of the system can interact with the prototype system immediately, shown in Fig. 6. The system returns a solution set after execution. Let us assume that a user chooses 0 ("soda") and pays 76 cents. For this given input, there are two solutions which can be observed by this customer. One is to return 76 cents to this customer and the other is return one "soda" and 16 cents as a change to the customer. Obviously, the first solution is not really what a user expects from the vending machine system.

3.3   A Further Revised Model

When we return to the HCL requirements model, we find that there exists a problem in the post-condition. The post-condition actually accepts one solution which is that the change to be returned to a customer is equal to the money the customer pays and no product the customer chooses is sold. In any case, this solution should not be accepted. Therefore we should modify the post-condition

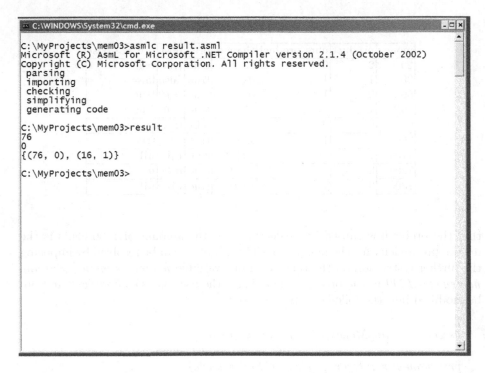

Fig. 6. The result of running the first level model.

for the use case *VendingMachine3* and the complete specification is shown in Fig. 7.

In the revised HCL requirements model shown in Fig. 7, we include an `exists` condition in the `if` statement in the post-condition part. The revised post-condition says that if there exists a solution which can return a product to a customer then the vending machine should perform this purchase instead of returning all the money to the customer; otherwise the vending machine should return all the money to the customer.

Before we execute the revised model, we need to check whether there is any inconsistency in our specification. Again this specification can be tested based on the same approach to testing use case *VendingMachine2*. Since giving the specific test data does not add any value in helping explain the principle of our rigorous reviews technique, the test data for testing use case *VendingMachine4* in Fig. 7 are omitted. After the specification testing, we can execute the revised HCL requirements model and find the solution is what a user of the vending machine expects.

3.4   A Refined Model

After giving the highest model for the vending machine example, we can further develop it by refining the diagram shown in Fig. 3. The refined model is presented

usecase VendingMachine4(in money, product,
                              out num_product, changes)
    pre: money in Integer, product in Indices(code)
        where money > 0 and money <= 1000
    post: (num_product in [0..1], changes in[0..1000]) |
        if (exists (num in [0..1], ret in [0..1000]) | num > 0
            and num *price(code(product)) + ret = money) then
            num_product > 0 and num_product * price(code(product))
                + changes = money
        else
            num_product = 0 and changes = money
    description:
        PRODUCT = {soda, chip, sandiwich}
        code: Integer → PRODUCT = {0→ soad,
            1 → chip, 2 → sandwich}
        price: PRODUCT → Integer = { soda → 60,
        chip → 50, sandwich → 100}

Fig. 7. The revised HCL requirements model for the Vending Machine.

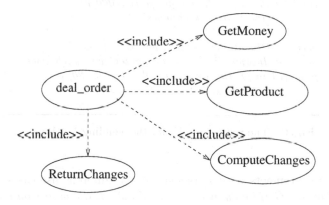

Fig. 8. The refined model for the Vending Machine.

by a use case diagram shown in Fig. 8. In the refined model, we concentrate on how the model can support the input and output closer to the real vending machine. Usually a customer first provides the code for a product, and then inserts some coins into the machine. The machine figures out and then returns the change to the customer if any according to the money the customer pays and the price of the product.

According to UML, an include relationship between use cases means that the base use case explicitly incorporates the behavior of another use case at a location specified in the base. The included use case never stands alone, but is only instantiated as part of some larger base that includes it. Thus we distribute the responsibility of the use case *deal_order* to its four including use cases. There-

usecase GetMoney(in n1, n2, n3, out total)
pre: n1 in Integer, n2 in Integer, n3 in Integer where
        n1 > 0 and n2 > 0 and n3 > 0
post: (total in [0..1000]) |
        *total = n1 * 5 + n2 * 10 + n3 * 25*

usecase GetProduct(in choice, out product_price)
pre: choice in Indices(code)
post: (product_price in [0..100]) |
        product_price = price(code(choice))
description:
        code: Integer → PRODUCT = {0→ soad,
            1 → chip, 2 → sandwich}
        price: PRODUCT → Integer =
            {soda→60, chip→50, sandwich→100}

usecase ComputeChanges(in total, price, out changes)
pre: total in Integer, price in Integer where
        total = GetMoney::total and
        price = GetProduct::product_price
post: (num in [0..1], changes in [1..1000]) |
        total = price + changes)

usecase ReturnChanges(in c, out o1, o2, o3)
pre: c in Integer where c = ComputeChanges::changes
post: (o1 in [0..10], o2 in [0..20], o3 in [0..30] |
        *o1 * 5 + o2 * 10 + o3 * 25 = c)*

Fig. 9. The refined model for the Vending Machine.

fore the new requirements model consists of five different use cases, which are use case *deal_order*, *GetMoney*, use case *GetProduct*, use case *ComputeChanges* and use case *ReturnChanges*; the latter four use cases are included in the use case *deal_order*. The HCL specification for each included use case in the refined requirements model is shown in Fig. 9.

The input, *i.e. money*, to the highest level model has been replaced by a set of numbers, representing a set of numbers of each denomination a customer pays. We assume that the machine can only accept 5-cent coins, 10-cent coins and 25-cent coins. The input parameter n1, n2 and n3 represent the number of 5-cent coins, 10-cent coins and 25-cent coins paid by a customer respectively. These numbers have become inputs to the use case *GetMoney* as well as our incremental model. We deliberately miss the restriction for use case *GetMoney* on the number of coins whose total amount should not exceed 1000 cents. The use case *GetProduct* whose input is a product choice is used to output the price for the product which a customer chooses. Similarly the output *changes* to the highest level model has been replaced by a set of integers, representing a number

Table 3. A test for GetMoney.

n1	n2	n3	total	pre	post	pre => post
5	10	15	450	true	true	true
10	100	5	1175	true	**nil**	**nil**
100	200	30	999	true	false	false
150	20	10	1200	true	nil	nil

Table 4. A test for GetProduct.

choice	product_price	pre	post	pre => post
0	60	true	true	true
1	50	true	true	true
2	100	true	true	true

of each denomination (5-cent coins, 10-cent coins and 25-cent coins) returned to the customer. This set of integers has become outputs in the use case *Compute Changes*. Also we should follow the restriction on the maximum amount (1000 cents) of money returned to a customer. Here we assume the maximum capacities for 5-cent coins, 10-cent coins and 25-cent coins in the change box are 10, 20 and 30.

The use case *Compute Changes* is the main part in the vending machine. It accepts the amount of money paid by a customer, which is returned by the use case *GetProduct*. The constraint $total = GetMoney::total$ in the pre-condition of the use case *Compute Changes* asserts that *total* should be from the output *total* in the use case *GetProduct* and so should $p = GetProduct::product\_price$. This gives a potential order to execute the use cases when we want to execute a requirements model. According to these inputs, the use case *Compute Changes* can have the post-condition shown in Fig. 9 to achieve the main requirements for the vending machine.

The use case *Return Changes* computes the number of each denomination which should be returned to a customer as change if exists. The pre-condition shows that the input c comes from the use case *ComputerChanges*. Based on the conditions for each use case, we can use specification testing to check whether any inconsistency exists in these use cases.

Based on the conditions for each use case, we can use specification testing to check whether any inconsistency exists in these use cases. Two tests for the use cases *GetMoney* and *GetProduct* are given in Table 3 and 4, respectively, and tests for another two use cases *Compute Changes* and *Return Changes* are omitted for brevity.

3.5   A Final Model

Since the post-condition evaluates as either nil or false while the pre-condition evaluates as true for three test cases in which the value of the variable *total* is beyond 1000, the test shows the possibility of involving an error in the post-condition. After a careful analysis, we have realized that the specification is

---

usecase GetMoney(in n1, n2, n3, out total)
pre: n1 in Integer, n2 in Integer, n3 in Integer where
    $n1 > 0$ and $n2 > 0$ and $n3 > 0$ and $n1 * 5 + n2 * 10 + n3 * 25 \leq 1000$
post: (total in [0..1000]) |
    $total = n1 * 5 + n2 * 10 + n3 * 25$

Fig. 10. The revised HCL specification for use case GetMoney.

---

usecase ReturnChange2(in c, out n1, n2, n3)
pre: c in Integer where c = ComputeChanges::changes
post: (n1 in [0..10], n2 in [0..20], n3 in [0..30]) | $n1 * 5 +$
    $n2 * 10 + n3 * 25 = c$ and
    forall o1 in [0..10] holds
    forall o2 in [0..20] holds
    forall o3 in [0..30] holds
    $o1*5+o2*10+o3*25= c$ implies
    $n1+n2+n3 <= o1+o2+o3)$

Fig. 11. The revised version for use case *ReturnChanges*.

not satisfiable because of the missing requirements for the maximum amount of money which the machine can accepts. To make this specification satisfiable, we add a further constraint on the pre-condition to ensure that no value of the variable *total* can exceed 1000 according to the formula computing *total* in the post-condition. The modified precondition of use case *GetMoney* is shown in Fig. 10.

As far as the test in Table 4 is concerned, since the post-condition evaluates as true while the pre-condition evaluates as true for all the test cases, there is no indication of potential faults in the specification. After testing, we can further execute the model. For brevity, we skip the execution result, and actually this is a valid model.

The requirements model can be further refined. For brevity, we only refine the use case *ReturnChanges*. In this case we consider more requirements in the new refined model while not changing the inputs and outputs for the use case *ReturnChanges*. In the refined use case, the refined requirement is to return the fewest number of denominations to the customer; and therefore we rewrite the post-condition to satisfy the fewest numbers of denominations returned to a customer without changing any input and output in the previous use case. Fig. 11 gives the revised version for the use case *ReturnChanges*. After giving this model, both developers and users can run the HCL specification and check the solution set, which is omitted for brevity.

4   Conclusion

After observing the impact requirements errors on software development, we propose a rigorous reviews technique, based on specification testing and execution, attempting to find errors in a requirements model during the early phase of software development. Based on our previous work about formalization of a use case diagram, we present in this paper that a requirements model given by a use case diagram together with a pre- and post- condition for each use case can be first tested, trying to find whether there exists any kind of errors such as inconsistency in a requirements model. In order to implement specification testing, we proposed several strategies for these pre- and post- conditions for use cases.

Furthermore, if the pre- and post- condition in a use case diagram are executable, then the requirements model can be executed and some undesirable effects can be directly observed. We also outline the execution model based Abstract State Machine Language. Due to the executability of a requirements model, some necessary changes can be made accordingly. A vending machine example has been illustrated to show how the rigorous reviews technique works.

Our rigorous review technique proposed in this paper can also be applied to the later phases of software development, such as a software model design. A design model given by a class diagram which includes a pre- and post- condition for each method defined in classes can also be tested. If the conditions are executable, then the design model can be executed as well. On the other hand we will look for some software development process to which our rigorous review technique can be applied. Especially we will investigate some possibility to apply this technique to some use case driven software development processes.

Furthermore, we will work on a tool based on the rigorous reviews technique, which will be very crucial to software practitioners. Also, more examples, especially some industrial applications, will be studied to make our technique more practical in software development in the near future.

Acknowledgement

The first would like to appreciate Professor James Huggins and Kevin Compton who read the draft of the paper and provided some valuable comments. Also, the first author would like to express his gratitude to Ronald Miller and Bert Greve who helped to improve the English text of this paper.

References

1. Aynur Abdurazik and Jeff Offutt. Using UML collaboration diagrams for static checking and test generation. In Andy Evans, Stuart Kent, and Bran Selic, editors, *UML 2000 - The Unified Modeling Language. Advancing the Standard. Third International Conference, York, UK, October 2000, Proceedings*, volume 1939, pages 383–395. Springer, 2000.
2. R. Bourdeau and B. Cheng. A formal semantics for object model diagrams. In *IEEE Transactions on Software Engineering*, volume 21 of *No. 10*, pages 799–821, October 1995.
3. Antoni Diller. *Z: An Introduction to Formal Methods*. John Wiley & Sons, 1994.

4. Microsoft FSE Group. Vending machine case study. Technical report, Microsoft FSE Group, June, 2002.
5. Yuri Gurevich. Evolving algebras 1993: Lipari guide. In E. Börger, editor, *Specification and Validation Methods*, pages 9–36. Oxford University Press, 1995.
6. Cliff B. Jones. *Systematic Software Development Using VDM*. Prentice-Hall International(UK) Ltd., 1990.
7. Lionel C. Briand and Yvan Labiche. A uml-based approach to system testing. In *Software and System Modeling*, volume 1 of *1*, pages 10–42. Springer, 2002.
8. Shaoying Liu. Developing Quality Software Systems Using the SOFL Formal Engineering Method. In *Proceedings of 4th International Conference on Formal Engineering Methods (ICFEM2002), LNCS 2495*, pages 3–19, Shanghai, China, October 21-25 2002. Springer-Verlag.
9. Shaoying Liu. Verifying Consistency and Validity of Formal Specifications by Testing. In Jeannette M. Wing, Jim Woodcock, and Jim Davies, editors, *Proceedings of World Congress on Formal Methods in the Development of Computing Systems*, Lecture Notes in Computer Science, pages 896–914, Toulouse, France, September 1999. Springer-Verlag.
10. Shaoying Liu, A. Jeff Offutt, Chris Ho-Stuart, Yong Sun, and Mitsuru Ohba. SOFL: A Formal Engineering Methodology for Industrial Applications. *IEEE Transactions on Software Engineering*, 24(1):337–344, January 1998. Special Issue on Formal Methods.
11. Microsoft FSE Group. Introducing AsmL: A Tutorial for the Abstract State Machine Language. Technical report, Microsoft FSE Group, Dec, 2001.
12. OMG. Unified Modeling Language Specification, version 1.3. June 1999.
13. R. R. Lutz. Analyzing software requirements errors in safety-critical embedded systems. In *SIGSOFT '93 Symposium on the Foundation of Software Engineering*, 1993.
14. R. R. Lutz. Targeting safety-related errors during software requirements analysis. In *SIGSOFT '93 Symposium on the Foundation of Software Engineering*, 1993.
15. Mark Richters and Martin Gogolla. Validating UML models and OCL constraints. In *UML 2000 - The Unified Modeling Language. Advancing the Standard. Third International Conference, York, UK, October 2000*, volume 1939 of *LNCS*, pages 265–277. Springer, 2000.
16. S. Sendall, A. Strohmeier. From Use Cases to System Operation Specification. In *UML 2000 - The Unified Modeling Language. Advancing the Standard. Third International Conference, York, UK, October 2000*, volume 1939 of *LNCS*, pages 1–15. Springer, 2000.
17. Wuwei Shen, Kevin Compton, and James Huggins. A Toolset for Supporting UML Static and Dynamic Model Checking. In *Proceedings of the 26th Annual International Computer Software and Applications Conference*, pages 147–152. IEEE Computer Society, Aug 26-29, 2002, Oxford, England.
18. Wuwei Shen, Kevin Compton, and James Huggins. Execution of a requirement model in software development. March, 2003.
19. Lee J. White. *Software Testing and Verification*, volume 26. Academic Press, ADVANCES IN COMPUTERS, 1987.

Service-Based Systems Engineering: Consistent Combination of Services

Bernhard Schätz[1] and Christian Salzmann[2]

[1] Fakultät für Informatik, TU München, 80290 München, Germany
schaetz@in.tum.de
[2] BMW Car IT GmbH, Petuelring 116, 80809 München, Germany
christian.salzmann@bmw-carit.de

Abstract. Using service-based system descriptions simplifies the specification of complex reactive systems as found in the domain of web-services as well as embedded systems. To support a service-based development process applicable in safety-critical areas, a precise understanding of the notions *service, component* and *interface* is introduced as well as methodical steps like composition, and consistency and completeness validation. The applicability of our definitions is demonstrated in the context of tool-supported feature interaction detection.

Keywords: Service, component, specification, behavior, partiality, consistency, completeness, implementation, interaction, formalization, application, tool-support, model checking.

1 Introduction

Using *services* as basic concept eases the specification of reactive systems with a high degree of interaction with its environment as found, e.g., in the telecommunication or web services domain. This approach allows breaking up complex system functionality into smaller functional modules. This modularity supports a more manageable and comprehensible description of the functionality. This shift from a structural architecture (using *components* as the main building blocks) to a behavioral architecture (using *services* instead) is, e.g., applied in the domain of web services. There, systems do not consist of a fixed set of components, but are dynamically composed from services. However, using a service-based engineering process is not only useful in the field of dynamic networks, but also in domains with static structure supplying complex interacting functionalities. In the automotive domain, e.g., a large number of functionalities like ABS (anti-lock braking system) and ABC (active body control) are combined, interacting with each other and resulting in a complex overall behavior requiring a high level of safety. Here, too, services can help to structure the behavior of the complete system and make those interactions more explicit, thus leading to improved safety.

To enable a service-based engineering process, however, in both domains a precise definition of the notion of a service as well as the corresponding methodical steps (checking their compatibility, combining services into components) is required. In

J.S. Dong and J. Woodcock (Eds.): ICFEM 2003, LNCS 2885, pp. 86–104, 2003.
© Springer-Verlag Berlin Heidelberg 2003

Section 3 we will give such a definition, based on the preliminaries introduced in Section 2. Targeting service-based software engineering in general, we furthermore show the relationship between services and components in Section 4 including the implementation of a service (network) by a component (network). Since safety-related issues play an important role in embedded systems, in Section 5 we define methodical properties like completeness and consistency of services; issues more specific to dynamic networks (e.g., dynamic allocation of services) are not discussed here. For the practicability of the introduced concepts it is important to evaluate their applicability in a in a tool supported service-based development process. Therefore, in each section we apply the introduced definitions by translating them into a form suitable for a model checker for the relational μ calculus.

The basic techniques introduced are not specific to the semantic model used here but can be easily transferred to others like I/O-Automata [LT89] or TLA [Lam93] as well as other tools like bounded model checking or CLP based approaches. The contribution of the formalization therefore rather lies in the transfer of the formal techniques than in the introduction of new formal concepts. Basic principles behind this formal model have been applied in a service-engineering environment [Sal02] and in a model-checking approach to detect feature interaction [Sch02].

2 Preliminaries

To relate our definition of service to other forms, we will first look at some definitions found in other work, identifying the essential difference between services and components and the advantages of a service-based approach. Furthermore, we give a short introduction in the semantic model that is used to give a precise definition of the notions of service and component.

2.1 Services vs. Components and Interfaces

There are several different definitions of what a service is; generally more pragmatically described than precisely defined. The web service definition language (WSDL) defines a service "*as collections of network endpoints, or ports*" [CCM+], basically corresponding to a typed interface or signature description. In the Open Systems Interconnection-Reference Model (OSI-RM) a service is defined as, "*a capability of a given layer, and the layers below it, that (a) is provided to the entities of the next higher layer and (b) for a given layer, is provided at the interface between the given layer and the next higher layer*". A very general definition is "*A service is an abstract protocol*" [BL01].

While these definitions are quite diverse, all of the above-cited definitions have in common that they focus on *interfaces* and *interactions* but exclude *structure*. Therefore, focusing on interface behavior instead of system structure is the fundamental difference between a component-based and a service-based development process. Components and services own *interfaces* in form of signatures defining the types of messages that flow via these interfaces (e.g., interfaces in Java or the interface of a hardware interfaces). *Components* are defined as reusable units of behavior and structure [BS01,Müh96]. Structure is defined by assigning subcomponents including their behavior to a component. To reuse a component, it is structurally composed with other components, restricted only by structural compatibility conditions and supporting only a restricted form of behavioral combination (through communication). In contrast, a *service* represents a more abstract behavioral specification, its behavior depending on other services in the form of *needed services*. For reuse, services require a much stronger (behavioral) compatibility; however they also support a stronger form of (behavioral) combination.

In a nutshell, a service is a clipping of the behavior of a component that is under-specified concerning internal structure and – making assumptions about the environment – supports the definition of partial behavior. However, there is also a strong relation between services and components: both an abstract component as well as an abstract service can be realized by a network of communication components or services, resp. And – most importantly - a *service* (or network of services) *can be implemented by a component* (or network of components) making it an offered service of the component.

2.2 Semantic Model: FOCUS

In the following we use the model of stream-processing functions to introduce our definitions. However, the definitions are not specific to this model but directly carry over to other formalisms focusing on system interaction and supporting message-asynchronous communication, concurrent input as well as output actions, and time-ordered interactions[1]. Thus, TLA [Lam93] or Reactive Modules [AH99] are suitable models as well. Furthermore, when applying the concepts, we do not operate on the mathematical model itself. We rather use more structured and intuitive description techniques like state-transition or sequence diagrams as shown in Figure 2. Besides a more structured description, these techniques support reuse of modularized behavior, e.g., by encapsulating services in partial state-transition descriptions [HS99].

Here, we use an adapted version of the general model introduced in [BS01]. Basically, the mathematical model of a component (or service) consists of its externally observable behavior, i.e. the messages received from the environment or sent to it. Messages are sent and received via channels. We use a timed model, splitting the observable behavior into time slots; during each time slot, an arbitrary (but finite) number of messages can be received or sent via each channel. The behavior of a component or service can then be described by channel histories, assigning a sequence of messages to each channel and time slot. In the following, we introduce stream relations to model those forms of behaviors.

For a given set of messages M, the set M^* defines the set of *finite sequences* of messages including the empty sequence consisting of no messages. To model complete interactions of exchanged messages, we use the set of *infinite streams* of finite sequences, with notation M^ω. Those infinite streams of finite sequences can be identified with functions from the natural numbers Nat to finite sequences M^*, i.e. $M^\omega \equiv Nat \to M^*$. Thus, for a time slot $t \in Nat$, s_t describes the finite message sequence assigned to time slot t of a stream $s \in M^\omega$.

---

[1] See [KS03] for classification of models of reactive systems.

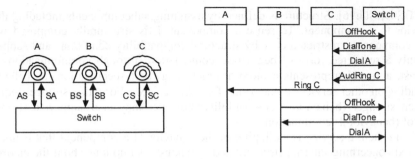

Fig. 1. Example of the POTS Interface and Description of an Observation

To combine observation with channels, we introduce the notion of a channel history. Given a set C of channel identifiers, a channel history is a mapping from those identifiers to message streams M^{ω}. The set of all *channel histories* for a given set of channel identifiers is described by $\vec{C}$, i.e., $\vec{C} \equiv C \to M^{\omega}$. Furthermore, we define the restriction $h \uparrow C'$ of a channel history h to subset $C' \subseteq C$ by standard function restriction. Restriction corresponds to the hiding of channels. Finally, using channel histories, we define the behavior of a component or service with a given interface by a relation of channel histories.

For sets of input and output channels I, O, a *stream relation s* over these input and output channels is defined as a (partial) function $s : \vec{I} \to \wp(\vec{O})$ [2]. For a stream relation over I, O, we define its *restriction* $s \uparrow (I', O')$ to (I', O') with $I' \subseteq I, O' \subseteq O$ by

$$s \uparrow (I', O') = \{(i \uparrow \vec{I'}, o \uparrow \vec{O'}) \mid (i, o) \in s\}$$

using restriction of channel histories.

Note that – since we focus on the introduction of a service notion - in this short introduction we did not impose additional requirements to be fulfilled by a stream function or relation to be realizable or implementable, e.g. a weak causality constraint or a strong realizabilty constraint as defined in [BS01]. In the following, we use the notation $\vec{I} \mapsto \wp(\vec{O})$ for total stream functions respecting those additional properties. Note that the properties defined in [BS01] are union stable, i.e. for functions $s_1, s_2 : \vec{I} \mapsto \wp(\vec{O})$, also $s_1 \cup s_2 \in \vec{I} \mapsto \wp(\vec{O})$. Therefore, for a partial function $s : \vec{I} \to \wp(\vec{O})$ we can define $\hat{s} \equiv \bigcup_{c \in \vec{I} \mapsto \wp(\vec{O}) \land c \subseteq s} c$ as the most general causality respecting function implementing s.

2.3 Application: Telecommunication Services

Throughout the following sections, we illustrate our approach by applying it to the analysis of feature interaction, using automatic analysis by the symbolic model checker tool μcke [Bie97]. We illustrate our approach using an example from the telecom domain, because telecom services are more familiar to most readers than,

---

[2] Instead of relational notation, we will use functional notation for this set-valued function for ease of reading.

e.g., automotive services; nevertheless they have a similar level of interactions between services, and require a similar safety level concerning completeness and consistency of services without introducing additional aspects like hard real-time bounds. To simplify matters, we will use a more basic formal model as introduced in Section 2.2 allowing only one (or no) message to be transported via a channel in a single time slot.

The left side of Figure 2 shows the Chisel representation of a part of the basic telephone service. Telecordia/BellCor introduced Chisel as a graphical notation to describe telecom features ([AG+98]). Informally, each diagram, as described in [GB+99], represents a behavior of the system as a decision tree, describing a possible course of actions. In following we show some tool-support for service-based specifications using Chisel diagrams. Note that this approach is not Chisel specific. It carries over to other notations describing a course of actions like, e.g., (high level) sequence diagrams or even state-based description of services.

To describe a system with services enhancing the plain ordinary telephone system (POTS), a collection of Chisel diagrams is used. Each diagram describes an additional service by extending the original POTS diagram to describe features like Terminating Call Screening (TCSC) or Call Forward on Busy Line (CFBL):

- Terminating Call Screening (TCSC): A subscribing user can prohibit calls from other users adding their terminals to a Screen List. Calls from screened terminals are not announced at the callee; the caller is informed by a corresponding message.
- Call Forwarding on Busy Line (CFBL): A subscribing user can redirect calls to a third party if a call occurs while his terminal is busy.

However, in general those services are not independent of each other. Thus, when combined to form a complete system description, they influence each other, resulting in feature interaction. In the worst case, the combined services may be incompatible, resulting in an inconsistent specification.

3 Service Formalization

In this section we present a formalization of the notions of service and component, based on the introduced FOCUS model. Furthermore, we apply these notions to the POTS example using relational μ calculus.

3.1 Interfaces, Behaviors, Components, and Services

An *interface* of a system or a service consists of the access points (channels) that are used by the system or service to communicate with its environment. Those access points are directed (i.e., either *input* or *output* channels) and typed (i.e. have an associated type describing what messages can be sent/received at this channel).

Definition (Interface). An interface (I,O) consists of two disjoint sets of channels I, O that represents the directed input and output channels of the interface. Each channel $(c,M_c) \in I \cup O$ consists of a channel identifier c as well as a set $M_c \subseteq M$ of messages that can flow via the channel.

For reasons of simplicity, in the following we assume an interface has disjoint sets of input and output channel identifiers. Considering the example of the POTS system depicted in the left half of Figure 1, the interface of the switch component contains a input channel with identifier *AS* and carrying the set of messages {*OffHook, Dial A X, OnHook*} to component A as well as an output channel with identifier SA carrying messages {*DialTone, LineBusyTone, Ring X, ...*} from component A. To describe this interface information, the FOCUS CASE tool prototype AutoFOCUS [HSE97] uses a similar notation (including typing of channels) as shown in the left half of Figure 1. To assign behavior to interfaces, we introduce the notion of a channel history, basically corresponding to a complete observation of messages exchanged over a channel.

Definition (Channel History, Execution, Behavior). Given a set of channel identifiers as well as for each identifier c its type M_c, a channel history is a (total) mapping from each identifier c to a message stream M_c^∞. The set of all *channel histories* for a given set C of channels is described by $\vec{C}$. A *(system) execution* $e \in \overrightarrow{(I \cup O)}$ for a given interface (I, O) consists of a channel history for each channel identifier of the interface. A (system) behavior for a given interface (I, O) is a set of executions $B \subseteq \overrightarrow{(I \cup O)}$.

Since a behavior can also be interpreted as relation (or a set-valued function) between input and output channel histories, we will use the notation $B : \vec{I} \to \wp(\vec{O})$ in the following. Based on the definition of a behavior, we introduce the notion of a *system/component* as well as a *service*. Since – as shown in Section 3.2 – a system can be broken up into components, we use the terms 'system' and 'component' synonymously.

Of course, there are different forms of description of behavior. The right side of Figure 2 shows a (incomplete) state-transition-based description of a behavior using a similar notation as in AutoFOCUS [HSE97]. Using a state-based description including control state and data variables, e.g., the transition between the *OffHook* and the *Ring* state describes a step where

- in the previous state the data variable *BusyB* has the value false,
- on the input channel *AS* the signal *DialB* is received,
- on the output channel *SA* the signal *AudibleRingB* and the output channel *SB* the signal *RingA* is sent, and
- in the following state the data variable *BusyB* is set to true.

To generate a behavior from such a state-transition-based description, sequences of such steps forming channel and variable assignments are constructed.

A component communicates with its environment via its interface. A component has a *completely specified behavior*: for each behavior of the environment (presenting a history of input messages on the input channels of the component) its reaction (in terms of histories of messages of the output channels) is defined. More formally, this is defined as input completeness or totality, in the following definition.

Definition (Component). A *component* $c = ((I, O)_c, B_c)$ is defined by its interface $(I, O)_c$ as well as its behavior $B_c : \vec{I} \to \wp(\vec{O})$. The behavior is input complete, i.e. for each input $i \in \vec{I}$ there exists (at least) one corresponding output $o \in \vec{O}$: $\forall i \in \vec{I}. \exists o \in \vec{O}. o \in B_c(i)$

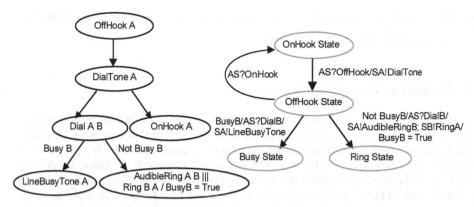

Fig. 2. A Chisel Diagram and its State/Transition Representation

Since the empty output set corresponds to undefined output behavior, input complete-ness corresponds to the *totality* of the behavior function. Note that we do not require a component to be deterministic (i.e. $\forall i \in \vec{I}. \exists o \in \vec{O}. o = B_c(i)$). While this is a reason-able requirement for a component to be implemented, on a more abstract level, non-determinism can be helpful when specifying a component.

In contrast to a component, a service behavior needs not be totally defined. For a partial specification, it is possible to have a behavior of the environment where no behavior of the component is defined by the specification. From a formal point of view, we have two different possibilities to deal with those 'undefined spots' when constructing a behavior from such a partial specification:

- **"Underspecification = Non-determinism"**: Using this approach, each reaction is considered legal for the 'undefined spots' since the specification does not restrict the behavior. As a result, the behavior of the component cannot be distinguished from completely non-deterministic behavior in these spots.
- **"Underspecification = Partiality"**: Here, we explicitly state that no behavior has been defined. As a result, for these inputs from the environment, the empty set of outputs is assigned when constructing a behavior.

Consequently, in the context of services we choose the second interpretation of under-specification and obtain the following definition of a service:

Definition (Service). A *service* $s = ((I,O)_s, B_s)$ is defined by its interface $(I,O)_s$ as well as its behavior $B_s : \vec{I} \rightarrow \wp(\vec{O})$.

A service describes *partial interaction behavior*. By allowing arbitrary behavior (i.e. partiality), we can use services to describe only a partial behavior offered by a com-ponent. This means there are *some inputs* of a service where the specification of the service does *not make any assertion* how the service behaves. According to these definitions a component is also a service, but not the other way round.

Definition (Subinterface, Subinterface Behavior). A (service) interface (I_{s_1}, O_{s_1}) is said *to be a subinterface of* an interface (I_{s_2}, O_{s_2}) if $I_{s_1} \subseteq I_{s_2} \wedge O_{s_1} \subseteq O_{s_2}$, i.e. if the subinterface is a subset (of the channels) of the interface. The behavior

$B_{S_1} : \vec{I}_{S_1} \to \wp(\vec{O}_{S_1})$ is the corresponding subinterface behavior of the service behavior $B_{S_2} : \vec{I}_{S_2} \to \wp(\vec{O}_{S_2})$ with $B_{S_1} = B_{S_2} \uparrow (I_{S_1}, O_{S_1})$.

3.2 Application: Formalizing Services

The first step of the tool support – besides the modeling of the interfaces and behaviors - consists in supplying a translation of a service description into the μ calculus. Additional information (system interface description, used variables) is needed for a translation as described in [HSE97]. The μ calculus-translator of AutoFocus/Quest [BL+00] can be used to translate the automaton representation of diagrams described by AutoFocus STDs to its μ calculus form. The μ calculus form of the state description is generated from SSD descriptions used by AutoFocus to describe the interface and the data state of a system or component. To formalize a service behavior in a state-based fashion as mentioned in Section 3.1, we use a relation typed according to the interface of the service. In case of the basic telephone service POTS for caller A and callee B, the interface is

$$(\{(AS, In), (BS, In)\}, \{(SA, Out), (SB, Out)\})$$

i.e., input channels with identifiers AS, BS of type In and output channels with identifiers SA, SB of type Out.

Besides the channels, the state of the service is needed as additional argument of the relation. In case of the basic telephone service POTS (for callee B) the type of the control state is $S = \{OnHook\ State, OffHook\ State, Busy, Ring, ...\}$ and a data state consists of the Boolean variable BusyB. Thus this transition relation describing the behavior of the system for one time slot is typed

$$R_{POTS_{(A,B)}} \subseteq S \times B \times In^{\perp} \times In^{\perp} \times Out^{\perp} \times Out^{\perp} \times B \times S$$

with B denoting Boolean values, In the input, and Out the output channel type[3]. In this simplified example we restrict sending and receiving to at most one message per time slot. Therefore, instead of In^* (or Out^*) we only use $In^{\perp}$ (or $Out^{\perp}$) to describe the message sent/received during a transition[4]. Furthermore, since this feature considers two parties (initiating/called party), two input and two output lines are needed.

To specify the behavior of a service, we use a notation described in [HSE97], as shown in the right half of Figure 2. To go from *OffHookState* to *Ring* - when A is calling B with B being not busy – we obtain a transition with precondition (*Not BusyB*), input pattern (*AS?Dial B*; *Dial B* received on channel *AS*), output pattern (*SA!AudibleRing B;SB!Ring A*; *AudibleRing B* sent on channel *SA* while *Ring B* sent on channel SB), and postcondition (*BusyB* = *True*). While a diagram represents only one call, a system characterized by diagrams accepts an arbitrary sequence of such calls. Thus, the final states of the automaton are identified with initial states, allowing

---

[3] Note that in the example all input channels carry the same messages as the output channels.

[4] The notation $In^{\perp}$ is used to describe one-element messages as well as the empty message $\perp$, i.e. $In^{\perp} = In \cup \{\perp\}$.

a repetition of a service during system execution. Figure 2 shows an example of such a feedback loop triggered by the *OnHook* signal.

A transition is formalized as the conjunction of pre- and postcondition as well as the channel predicates. Channel predicates are simply the equality between the channel variable and the value assigned to or read form the channel as described by the channel patterns. Thus, for the transition described above with a formal parameter list of

$$State\ C; BusyB\ B; AS\ I; BS\ I; SA\ O; SB\ O; BusyB'\ B; State'\ C$$

we obtain the formalization

$$State = OffHook \land \neg BusyB \land AS = Dial\ B\ \land$$
$$SA = AudibleRing\ B \land\ SB = Ring\ A \land BusyB' = True \land State' = Busy$$

with *State* and *State'* denoting the control state as well as *BusyB* and *BusyB'* the data state before and after the transition. The transition relation is constructed via the disjunction of the formalization of each transition. In a state-based description, additionally, the initial state of the transition relation has to be described:

$$Init_{POTS_{(A,B)}}(State, BusyB) \equiv (State = OnHook \land BusyB = False)$$

The behavior of a service describes as transition relation is constructed in the usual manner by generating an infinite sequence of transition steps and abstracting from the control and data space. Since in this section we only consider channels transporting at most a single value per time slot, channels and state variables can be treated alike. Thus the associated behavior of a the transition relation can be formalized as

$$B_{POTS_{(A,B)}}(\{AS, BS\}, \{SA, SB\}) \equiv \exists State, BusyB.\ Init_{POTS_{(A,B)}}(State_0, BusyB_0) \land$$

$$\forall t.\ R_{POTS_{(A,B)}}(State_t, BusyB_t, AS_t, BS_t, SA_t, SB_t, BState_{t+1}, BusyB_{t+1})$$

4 Combination and Implementation

In the previous section we discussed the differences between services and components. For a service-based engineering process, however, we must relate services to components. Intuitively, a component providing a service reacts as the service on the channels and inputs taken into account by the service. Having introduced the basic notions of service and component, the following questions arise:

- How are components (or services) combined to build composed components (or services)?
- How are services implemented by components?

4.1 Combining Networks

For reasons of simplicity, in the following, we only define binary composition and combination of components or services, resp., which – of course – can be simply generalized to finite sets. *Composition* of components corresponds to combining components by connecting their common channels; Figure 1 shows such a networks consisting of three receivers and a switch including their linking channels.

Definition (Composition). For components c_1, c_2 with interfaces (I_1, O_1) and (I_2, O_2), resp., we define the *composition* $c_1 \otimes c_2$ to be the stream relation with interface $(I, O) = (I_1 \cup I_2 \setminus (O_1 \cup O_2), O_1 \cup O_2)$ and behavior

$$B_{c_1 \otimes c_2} \equiv \bigcup \{ B \in \vec{I} \mapsto \wp(\vec{O}) \mid B \uparrow (I_1, O_1) \subseteq B_{c_1} \land B \uparrow (I_2, O_2) \subseteq B_{c_2} \}$$

given the syntactic compatibility $O_1 \cap O_2 = \emptyset$.

Note that the syntactic compatibility condition $O_1 \cap O_2 = \emptyset$ ensures that the combination of two components again is a component (i.e., a total function). For services, we can also define an analogue notion of a *combination*.

Definition (Combination). For services s_1, s_2 with interfaces (I_1, O_1) and (I_2, O_2), resp., we define the *combination* $s_1 \oplus s_2$ to be the stream relation with interface $(I, O) = (I_1 \cup I_2 \setminus (O_1 \cup O_2), O_1 \cup O_2)$ and service behavior

$$B_{s_1 \oplus s_2} \equiv \bigcup \{ B \in \vec{I} \rightarrow \wp(\vec{O}) \mid B \uparrow (I_1, O_1) \subseteq B_{s_1} \land B \uparrow (I_2, O_2) \subseteq B_{s_2} \}.$$

Note that the composition of components is a special case of the combination of services by restricting it to components (complete services) with disjoint output channels. Furthermore note that besides combining them in a network-like fashion, services using the same output channels can also be combined. This form of combination is needed if services with a common subinterface are to be implemented by a single component. Table 1 shows a combination of eight services to be implemented by the switch component of Figure 1; here, e.g., the POTS service for subscriber B (with originator B and further party C) and for subscriber C (with originator C and further party B) both have AS and BS as input channels and SA and SB as output channels.

Combination is 'strict' in the sense that partial behavior of one service can 'knock out' defined behavior of the other service. This is reasonable from a methodical point of view, since we cannot rely on the undefined behavior.

4.2 Implementing Behavior

To implement an abstract component by a more concrete one, we use the notion of behavioral refinement. Basically, behavioral refinement is used to remove nondeterminism from a component specification:

Definition (Behavioral Refinement). Given two components c_1, c_2 with the same interface, the behavior of c_1 is said to *refine* the behavior of c_2, written as $B_{c_1} \leq B_{c_2}$ if c_1 is more deterministic than c_2. More formally, we require:

$$B_{c_1}, B_{c_2} : \vec{I} \mapsto \wp(\vec{O})$$

$$B_{c_1} \leq B_{c_2} \quad \equiv \quad \forall i \in \vec{I}, o \in \vec{O}. \; o \in B_{c_1}(i) \Rightarrow o \in B_{c_2}(i)$$

Analogously, c_1 is said to refine c_2 if the behavior of the former is a refinement of the latter.

The refinement relation orders components according to their degree of non-determinism, with the top element being the completely nondeterministic component. Note that behavioral refinement requires respecting the limitations of a component like input closure or the causality restrictions.

To relate components and services, we use the notion of implementation. Intuitively, this corresponds to behavioral refinement extended to services and requiring 'improved input behavior':

Definition (Implementation). Given two services s_1, s_2 with the same interface, the behavior of s_1 is said to *implement* the behavior of s_2, written as $B_{s_1} \prec B_{s_2}$ if s_1 is more deterministic and less partial than s_2. More formally, we require:

$$B_{s_1}, B_{s_2} : \vec{I} \to \wp(\vec{O})$$

$$B_{s_1} \prec B_{s_2} \equiv B_{s_1} \le B_{s_2} \wedge dom(B_{s_2}) \subseteq dom(B_{s_1})$$

where

$$dom(B_S) \equiv \{ i \mid \exists o \in \vec{O}. o \in B_S(i) \}$$

Analogously, s_1 is said to implement s_2 if the behavior of the former is an implementation of the latter.

Note that the implementation relation between components corresponds to a refinement relation between them. For a more general version of the notion of implementation we can make use of the notion of subinterfaces. A service with interface (I_{s_1}, O_{s_1}) and corresponding behavior $B_{s_1} : \vec{I}_{s_1} \to \wp(\vec{O}_{s_1})$ *implements* a service with subinterface (I_{s_2}, O_{s_2}) and behavior $B_{s_2} : \vec{I}_{s_2} \to \wp(\vec{O}_{s_2})$ if $B_{s_1} \prec_{(I_{s_1}, O_{s_1})} B_{s_2}$ with

$$B_{s_1} \prec_{(I_{s_1}, O_{s_1})} B_{s_2} \equiv B_{s_1} \le (B_{s_2} \uparrow (\vec{I}_{s_1}, \vec{O}_{s_1})) \wedge dom(B_{s_2} \uparrow (\vec{I}_{s_1}, \vec{O}_{s_1})) \subseteq dom(B_{s_1})$$

Based on this notion of implementation we can define what it means for a component to offer or to require a service.

Definition (Provided Service, Required Service). A service s_1 (or component) is said to *provide a service* s_2 if s_2 is implemented by s_1. A service s_1 (or component) is said to *require a service* s_2 if the complementary service $\overline{s_2}$ is implemented by s_1. A complementary service $\overline{s}$ of a service $s = ((I_s, O_s), B_s)$ is defined by $\overline{s} = ((O_s, I_s), B_{\overline{s}})$ and the behavior $B_{\overline{s}} : \vec{O}_s \to \wp(\vec{I}_s)$ defined by

$$\forall i \in \vec{I}_s, o \in \vec{O}_s. i \in B_{\overline{s}}(o) \Longleftrightarrow o \in B_s(i)$$

If a component c provides and requires a set of services $s_i...s_j$, we demand that these services fulfill additional compatibility constraints. The simplest form of compatibility is called *interface compatibility*, defined by

$$\forall m, n \in \{i, ..., j\}. m \ne n \Rightarrow (I_m \cap I_n = \varnothing \wedge O_m \cap O_n = \varnothing)$$

This means that the input channels of the services as well as the output channels are pairwise disjoint. Further forms of compatibility are discussed in the following section. Note that formally there is no difference whether a service is provided by an

Table 1. Service Instantiations for the TCSC/CFBL Interaction

Subscriber	Service	Instance: Originator, further parties	Parameters
A	TCSC	B, A	Screen List = {B}
A	TCSC	C, A	Screen List = {B}
A	CFBL	B, A, C	Forward = C
A	CFBL	C, A, C	Forward = C
B	POTS	A, B	-
B	POTS	C, B	-
C	POTS	A, C,	-
C	POTS	B, C	-

atomic component or by a network of components, since the latter can be substituted by the combined component as defined in Section 4.1.

4.3 Application: Combining Components and Services

As described in Subsection 4.1, from the formal point of view it makes no difference whether we construct a network of components, combine services to create a more complex service, or construct a network of (needed and provided) services. Basically, components and service are combined alike by (interface-adjusted) conjunction of their behaviors. Since in this example services (or rather service schemes) are described using parameters like caller, callee, or screen list, these must be instantiated prior to combination. To build a configuration of services, as shown in Table 1, service instances are combined.

As in the case of a single service, we define the specification of the combined services by a transition relation for the complete system. Thus, the type of this relation is defined by the product of

- all variables used by services for each instance (e.g., *BusyA*, *BusyB* and *BusyC* for the terminals A,B, and C), representing the system state prior to the transition
- all input channel variables as defined by the system interface
- all output channel variables as defined by the system interface
- all variables used by services for each instance representing the state after the transition

In a state-based approach, service are defined using input and output channels, and additionally using control and date states. While components can only be combined using communication and thus cannot share their local state space, service support a more general form of combination. Therefore, we additionally allow sharing the state space between services[5]. Thus, finally, the combination of service instances is simply formed by conjunction of the service transition relation instantiated with the necessary parameters (Screen List, e.g.) and applied to the corresponding elements of the system state and adjusted according to their interfaces. On the automaton level this is equivalent to constructing the product automaton.

---

[5] Note that in this example all service instances make only use of non-overlapping parts of the state space.

5 Methodical Issues

From a methodical point of view, the following questions remain when building a component specification from a collection of service specifications:

- Which services are (reasonably) combinable?
- What makes a service a component?

In this section we investigate how the explicit representation of the domain of a service helps in combining services and constructing complete component behavior. We introduce the notion of *consistency* of a collection of services (basically stating that a collection can be implemented by a component) as well as the notion of *completeness* of a service (stating that each action of the environment is accounted for by an reaction of the service). Since completeness and consistency are essential prerequisites for the robustness and reliability of safety-critical systems, the validation of these properties is a decisive aspect of a service-based development process.

5.1 Completeness

Informally, a service is said to be complete, if its behavior is already detailed enough to define a component (ignoring some causality aspects).

Definition (Completeness). A *service* $s = ((I,O)_S, B_S)$ with interface $(I,O)_S$ as well as behavior $B_S : \vec{I} \to \wp(\vec{O})$ is called *complete*, if $dom(B_S) \equiv \vec{I}$.

To form a component specification out of a (combined) service description, the service description must be extended from a partial to a total specification. From a methodical point of view, different forms of canonical completions $\hat{s}$ are possible for a service s. Three prominent examples are:

- *Chaotic completion*: If the service exhibits some undefined behavior at some time point, in the completion any behavior is possible afterwards.
- *Operational completion*: If the service exhibits some undefined behavior at some time point, in the completion the empty output is produced at that time point.
- *Error completion*: If the service exhibits some undefined behavior at some time point, it will produce an error message.

Chaotic completion is associated with a loose interpretation of a specification. Basically, we use a kind of Assumption-Commitment scheme to construct components from services by chaotic completion (c.f. [SDW93]). The domain part of a service forms the assumption; the service specification forms the commitment part. However, since for a given service behavior $B_S : \vec{I} \to \wp(\vec{O})$, the total function defined by

$$B_{S_{chaos}}(i) \equiv \begin{cases} B_S(i) \Leftarrow i \in dom(s) \\ \vec{O} \Leftarrow i \notin dom(s) \end{cases}$$

generally is not a causality-respecting function, a component for this service is defined by the behavior $\hat{B}_{S_{chaos}}$ as defined in Section 2.2.

Operational completion is associated with an operational interpretation; it is, e.g., used in [HS01]. As mentioned in the following subsection, completions can be schematically constructed in the μ calculus.

5.2 Application: Detecting Incompleteness

According to our definition of service, the formalization of a service makes explicit the part where no behavior is defined by the description of the service. This explicit representation of the domain of a service (or a combination of services) can be exploited when checking for completeness. When translating the definition of completeness to our μ calculus based description of a service as shown in the previous subsection, a service is incomplete if it has a non-input closed relation. Checking for input-enabledness requires the calculation of all reachable states of the transition. A service is not input enabled if either its initial states relation is unsatisfiable or its transition relation is not input-enabled. Using the above formalization, in the first case we have

$$\forall s, v.\neg Init(s,v)$$

stating that there is no defined initial (control or data) state, thus leading to the completely undefined behavior. In the second case, we have to check whether there is a reachable state that does not define an output or a successor (control or data) state for a given input. With the set of reachable states used to mark those trace positions identified by s, incompleteness of a transition relation in terms of the μ calculus for transition relation R is

$$\exists s, v.Reach(s,v) \wedge \exists i_1,\ldots i_m.\forall o_1,\ldots o_n, v', t.$$

$$\neg R(s,v,i_1,\ldots,i_m,o_1,\ldots,o_n,v',t)$$

where $Reach$ denotes the set of reachable states defined by

$$\mu Reach(s) \equiv Init(s) \vee \exists i_1,\ldots i_m, o_1,\ldots o_n, t.\ Reach(t) \wedge R(t,i_1,\ldots i_m,o_1,\ldots o_n,s)$$

with μ denoting the least fixed point used as interpretation of this recursive definition and $Init$ the set of initial states.

Note that this definition does not exclude nondeterministic behavior if the nondeterministic behavior is explicitly stated by the service specification. In early phases nondeterminism is often introduced into service specifications by abstracting from internal aspects of a system: an ATM may seemingly nondeterministically provide a customer with cash if abstracting from the current balance of the account. Therefore, from a methodical point of view it is necessary to support both nondeterminism and underspecification but to distinguish between them.

When applying the approach to the example of the POTS, the model checker can detect several incompletenesses. E.g., in the specification is not defined which reaction of the system should occur if the callee picks up the phone in the same instance the caller dials his number.

As mention in Section 5.1, an incomplete service specification can be transformed into a (complete) system behavior by adding a behavior for each possible input sequence to the set of executions of the service. This canonical transformation can also be carried out on the level of the transition relation: simply adding a transition with arbitrary output and successor state for each undefined input to the transition relation leads to a highly nondeterministic relation. To support a more operational interpretation for partial behavior, as, e.g., used in [HS01], undefined output is substituted by *nil* modeling that no signal is send; undefined successor control or data states are defined to remain unchanged. Again, such a canonical transformation can be easily defined on the level of the transition relation.

5.3 Consistency

An important issue when dealing with the combination of services is the problem of service interaction. While each service exposes the intended behavior if used separately, when combined unforeseen interaction patterns may show up.

The combination of services is linked to the concept of compatibility of services: A compatible collection of services can be combined without exhibiting unwanted behavior. Therefore, a notion of compatibility of services is needed to combine services to form a component. In formal approaches dealing with the combination of features or services (e.g., [KB00] or [Sch02]), compatibility of services is defined in terms of consistency of the (specifications of) services. As usual, services are considered to be consistent if the specifications are not contradicting.

Definition (Consistency). Two services s_1, s_2 with interfaces $(I_1, O_1), (I_2, O_2)$ and

$$dom(B_{s_1}) \subseteq dom((B_{s_1} \oplus B_{s_1}) \uparrow (I_{s_1}, O_{s_1})) \wedge dom(B_{s_2}) \subseteq dom((B_{s_1} \oplus B_{s_1}) \uparrow (I_{s_2}, O_{s_2}))$$

are called *consistent*.

From a methodical point of view, consistency of services can be interpreted by the fact that the combined service is not more restricted than each of the services. The immediate methodical consequence is, that the combination of consistent services is an implementation of each service:

$$s_1, s_2 \; consistent \Rightarrow ((s_1 \oplus s_2) \uparrow (I_1, O_1) \prec s_1 \wedge (s_1 \oplus s_2) \uparrow (I_2, O_2) \prec s_2)$$

In the development process this corresponds to the fact that a consistent service can safely be added to a system without leading to unexpected results.

Consistency of services describes the most general intuitive form of compatibility, however rather sophisticated notion to be checked. For practical use, simpler forms of compatibility (ensuring consistency) are useful, e.g.:

- *Syntactic consistency*: This form required the disjointness to the output channels of services. For services s_1, s_2, their output interface has to be disjoint, i.e. $O_{s_1} \cap O_{s_2} = \varnothing$. While this form is very restricted, it has the advantage that compatibility is guaranteed by a design rule that can be check syntactically.
- *Pointwise consistency*: If service behavior is described in a state-based fashion, consistency of services boils down to consistency of their transition relations. Section 5.4 treats this form of consistency in more detail.

Note that there is a simple relation between consistency of services and the completeness of the combination of their chaos-completions:

$$s_1, s_2 \; consistent \Longleftrightarrow s_{1Chaos} \oplus s_{2Chaos} \; complete$$

This due to the fact that (completely) chaotic behavior is a 'neutral element' when combining services.

5.4 Application: Detecting Inconsistency

As introduced in Subsection 5.3, we define a service interaction problem to occur if the behavior defined by the combined services is inconsistent. Therefore, a service configuration is considered to expose a service interaction if the service instances are contradictory for at least one behavior of the environment. Therefore we have to check whether there exists an input channel history that has no behavior assigned by the combined services but has a behavior assigned by the services in isolation.

Instead of checking this property directly, we check for the completeness of the chaotic completion of the services of the configuration, as noted in Subsection 5.2. Thus, services exhibit an interaction problem if their chaotic completions have a non-input closed relation. In the relational μ calculus, chaotic completion CR of a transition relation R can simply be constructed by

$$CR(s,v,i_1,\ldots,i_m,o_1,\ldots,o_n,w,t) \equiv$$

$$R(s,v,i_1,\ldots,i_m,o_1,\ldots,o_n,w,t) \vee \forall o_1',\ldots o_n',w',t'. \neg R(s,v,i_1,\ldots,i_m,o_1',\ldots o_n',w',t')$$

Using suitable blocking (starting with the input variables) and interleaving when ordering the argument variables, the corresponding OBDD representation of the chaotic completion is of the same complexity.

If services are described using shared variables, a possible source of interaction is the assignment of values to variables. If two services assign different values to a shared variable, there is no interpretation for this assignment. Similar observations hold for communication actions, modeled by values assigned to channels. Note that feature interaction may as well occur combining two instantiations of the same feature (in case of the POTS specification, e.g., the service behaves differently if the initiator is being called prior to service start) as with the combination of two different features like call forwarding and call blocking.

Since this example uses simple signals the system has a finite state space accessible to symbolic verification. Using a schematically generated variable order, OBDDs representing the transition relations can be kept sufficiently small to allow the generation of the set of reachable states. The check for an interaction problem is carried out using the relational μ calculus symbolic model checker μcke ([Bie97]). Here, all reachable states of the system transition starting from the initial state are checked for input actions missing an appropriate transition. Again, the μ calculus term can be generated schematically from interface and data space of the system. If such a missing transition is found, the counterexample component of μcke is used to generate execution traces leading to system states with conflicting feature requirements including the input actions that have no defined output actions.

Combining TCSC and CFBL as described by Table we obtain a simple four-step execution trace leading to a feature interaction problem: If user A subscribes to both CFBL with Forward C and TCSC with a Screen List containing B, what happens if B calls A while A is busy? Should B be forwarded resulting in a ring tone played to B or screened resulting in a screening message played to B?

μcke generates a counterexample given by assignments for the variables and channels of the system for each execution step starting from the initial state of the system and ending with the input action generating the conflict. However, μcke generates a μ calculus tableau representation. For a transparent use of this formalization, a different representation of the counterexample is needed, for example, in an MSC-like form. Figure 1 shows such a visualization of the counterexample for the TCSC/CFBL conflict.

6 Conclusion

In this article we introduced a formal definition of the notion *service* and related it to formal model of interacting components. Essential aspects of our service notion are its partiality and its separation between functionality and structure. The introduction of different notions of compositionality and combination lays a first foundation for a methodical service-based development process. To support practical application, the formal model is used transparently to the engineer: for the specification of a service (or component) intuitive description techniques like state transition diagrams or sequence diagrams are used; for suitable systems, mechanized techniques like model checking are used to ensure consistency; finally, generic completion techniques are applied to transform the partial behavior of a service into a complete component behavior.

6.1 Service-Based Development Process

Besides defining services, their combination, and their implementation by a component network, the main advantage of the formalization of services is that it enables the support of services as a specification technique in a development process. In the following we give a brief sketch out how a possible process could be structured and what advantages services would bring to the systematic development of software systems.

Services allow modelling of the functionalities of the system without tailoring the structure of the system at the beginning of the development process. They can be extracted from very abstract specifications of the system functionality, for example UML use cases, which do not narrow the later structure of the system either.

After modelling the service functionality – using Sequence Diagrams or a state-based description - the different services can be deployed to component networks by composing services into a component type. During this step, structural attributes are added to the system specification. Since a service specification can be realized by many component networks, different architectures are possible.

As shown in the previous sections, certain aspects of such a deployment step (like checking from completeness or consistency) can be automated. Here, the precise notion of services and components and their composition helps to avoid problems like unwanted service interaction as described above.

A service based development process makes use of the separation of functionality and structural architecture of a system using the following steps:

1. Specification of use cases (i.e. UML)
2. Encapsulation of services out of the use cases
3. Modeling of the service architecture of the system (without defining a technical structure)
4. Deployment of the services on a given set of components
5. Choice of realization and alternatives.

Note that until step four the system is specified without fixing its structure. The result of the deployment is a *set* of various possible realizations that offer the same functionality but differ in the structure (e.g. which component provides which service). So structural issues can be delayed to latter steps in the development process that gives the development more flexibility and better applicability.

6.2 Related Work

As mentioned in Section 1, a precise as well as abstract definition of service has not been widely addressed so far; most work in this area is focused on implementational issues. However, several aspects of services and their methodical treatment have been addressed in other approaches.

The description of partial behavior is, e.g., addressed in the context of description techniques like Message Sequence Charts (MSC) [Krü00]. Here, however, rather the interpretation of sequence diagrams is discussed; the issue of combining partial descriptions of a system is not in the main focus.

As mentioned above, the combination of partial descriptions to form a complete specification is closely related to the problem of feature interaction. Since this problem has been studied carefully in the context of telecommunication, especially the issue of consistent specifications has been addressed there ([KB+98], [CM00]). However, besides being more complex, those approaches generally add implementation details or other restrictions. Furthermore, the issue of the incompleteness of combined service descriptions is treated here, which is generally not considered in the other approaches.

6.3 Outlook

Services allow modeling of the functionalities of the system without tailoring the structure of the system at the beginning of the development process. They can be extracted from very abstract specifications of the system functionality, for example UML use cases combined with sequence diagrams, which do not narrow the later structure of the system either. After modeling the service functionality the different services can be deployed to component networks by composing services into a component type, adding structural information to the system specification. Furthermore, services allow to structure complex functionalities of a system to modularize its specification. Using consistent composition, services can be used to support reuse on a behavioral rather than an architectural level, enabling a shift from component-based to service-based development. Validation of completeness and consistency makes this approach suitable even for safety-critical systems.

However, several issues – specific to a service-based development process in certain application domains – were not addressed here, e.g.:

- Dynamic networks: How is the dynamic change concerning an interface of a component as well as the services implemented by a component described in the semantic model? While [GS96] gives a general outline, more conceptual support is needed for an application of the approach in this domain.
- Service properties: How are aspects concerning Quality of Service (e.g., response times, loss of signals) incorporated in the semantic model? While the basic model is capable of expressing such aspects like time constraints, special analysis techniques for these properties like [KS01] can be supplied to reduce the complexity of the analysis.

For other domains focusing on the issues of modular description of behavior and the related aspects of completeness and consistency (e.g., in the automotive domain), the results here supply a suitable basis for a methodical development process. Current research is directed on integrating this approach in a support tool for the development of embedded automotive software.

References

[AG+98] Aho, A. Gallagher, N. Griffeth, N. Schell, C. Swayne D. *SCF3/Sculptor with Chisel.* In: Kimbler, K. et al. (eds.) Proc. 5th Feature Interactions in Telecommunications and Software Systems. IOS Press, 1998.

[AH99]   Alur, R. Henzinger, T. *Reactive Modules*. In: Formal Methods in Systems Design. 1(15). Kluwer Academic Publishers, 1999.

[Bie97]   Biere, A. Effiziente *Modellprüfung des μ-Kalküls mit binären Entscheidungsdiagrammen*. Ph.D. Thesis. Universität Karlsruhe, 1997.

[BL01]   Berners-Lee, T. *Are we done yet?*. http://www.w3.org/2001/Talks/0501-tbl/

[BS01]   Broy, M. Stoelen, K. *Specification and Development of Interactive Systems*. Springer, 2001.

[CCM+]   E. Christensen, F. Curbera, G. Meredith, S. Weerawarana: *Web Services Description Language (WSDL) 1.1*, W3C Note http://www.w3.org/TR/wsdl

[CM00]   Calder, M. et Magill, E. (eds.) Proc. 6ᵗʰ Feature Interactions in Telecommunications and Software Systems. IOS Press, 2000.

[GB+99]   Griffeth, N. et al. Feature Interaction Detection Contest. Instructions. http://www-db.research.bell-labs.com/user/nancyg/instructions.ps, 1999.

[GS96]   Grosu, R. Stoelen, K. *Specification of Dynamic Networks*. In: Proceedings of the 8th Nordic Workshop on Programming Theory, Oslo, Norway. University of Oslo, 1996.

[HS99]   Huber, F. Schätz, B. *Integrating Formal Description Techniques*. In: FM'99 -- Formal Methods, Volume II. Wing, J. et al. (eds.). Springer, 1999.

[HSE97]   Huber, F. Schätz, B. Einert, G. *Consistent Graphical Specification of Distributed Systems*. In: Fitzgerald, J. et al. (eds.) Proceedings of FME'97. LNCS Vol. 1313. Springer, 1997.

[JZ00]   Jackson, M. Zave, P. *New Feature Interactions in Mobile and Multimedia Telecommunication Services*. In: Calder, M. et al. (eds.) Proc. 6ᵗʰ Feature Interactions in Telecommunications and Software Systems. IOS Press, 2000.

[KB00]   Koshumi, A. Bevelo, R.J. *A Detection Method Developed after A Thorough Study of the Contest Held in 1998*. In: Calder, M. et al. (eds.) Proc. 6ᵗʰ Feature Interactions in Telecommunications and Software Systems. IOS Press, 2000.

[KB98]   Kimbler, K. et Bouma, L. (eds.) Proc. 5th Feature Interactions in Telecommunications and Software Systems. IOS Press, 1998.

[Krü00]   Krüger, I. *Distributed System Design with Message Sequence Charts*, Dissertation, Technische Universität München, 2000.

[KS01]   Logothetis, G. Schneider, K. *Symbolic Model-Checking of Real-Time Systems*. In: Eighth International Symposium on Temporal Representation and Reasoning (TIME'01). IEEE Computer Society, 2001.

[KS03]   Kof, L. Schätz, B. *Dimensions of Design: Combining Aspects of Reactive Systems*. In: Perspectives Of System Informatics (5ᵗʰ Andrei Ershov International Conference). LNCS Springer, 2003.

[Lam93]   Lamport, L. *Specification and Verification of Concurrent Programs*. In: de Bakker, J.W. et al. (eds.). A Decade of Concurrency. LNCS Vol. 803. Springer, 1993.

[LT89]   Lynch, N. Tuttle, M. *An Introdcution to Input/Output Automata*. CWI Quaterly 3(2). 1989.

[Müh96]   Mühlhäuser, M. (Ed.): *Special Issues in Object- Oriented Programming* – Proceedings of WCOP 96, dpunkt Verlag, Heidelberg, Gemany, 1997

[Oas02]   OASIS Web Page http://www.oasis-open.org/committees/wscm

[Sal02]   Christian Salzmann *Modellbasierter Entwurf spontaner Komponentensysteme*. PhD Thesis Technische Universität München 2002.

[Sch02]   Schätz, B. *Towards Service-Based Systems Engineering: Formalizing and mu-Checking Service Specifications*. Tech. Report TUMI-0602, TU München, 2002

[SDW93]   Stoelen, K. Dederichs, F. Weber, R. *Assumption/Commitment Rules for Networks of Asynchronously Communicating Agents*. Technical Report TUM-I9303, TU München, 1993.

Using State Diagrams
to Describe Concurrent Behaviour

Jim Davies and Charles Crichton

Oxford University Computing Laboratory
Wolfson Building Parks Road, Oxford, OX1 3QD, UK
{jdavies,crc}@comlab.ox.ac.uk

Abstract. The state diagram notation, a derivative of Harel's State-Charts, is an important component of the Unified Modeling Language (UML). It is the primary means of describing object behaviour: by associating a state diagram with a particular class, a designer may specify how objects of that class should perform sequences of actions in response to incoming events.

This paper explains that, under the default interpretation, state diagrams are adequate only for designs in which: each object may admit at most one thread of execution; different threads of execution could never interfere; and it is impossible for an object to invoke an operation upon itself. The paper argues that these limitations are unsatisfactory.

An alternative interpretation is then presented, in which separate diagrams are used to describe the object state and the transient, operation state. The resulting separation of concerns – between control flow and state abstraction – produces a simpler, more scalable approach to specification, and one that is adequate for the precise description of concurrent behaviour.

1   Introduction

The Unified Modeling Language (UML) is a *de facto* standard for object modelling. It includes several different notations for the description of behaviour, and one of these – the language of *state diagrams* – can be used to completely characterise the behaviour of objects of a particular class. However, if the state diagram language is used and interpreted in the obvious fashion, the resulting models may not be adequate for the description of concurrent behaviour.

There are two potential sources of inadequacy. The first concerns the possibility of intra-object concurrency – the concurrent execution of multiple operations upon a single object. A single state diagram cannot properly describe this phenomenon. The second is a matter of complexity: even where operations are executed in sequence, an attempt to incorporate their effects within a single state diagram may result in a description that is difficult to complete.

In this paper, we show how the state diagram notation can be used to produce adequate models: by associating collections of diagrams with each class; one diagram for the chosen state abstraction; and one diagram for each of the

J.S. Dong and J. Woodcock (Eds.): ICFEM 2003, LNCS 2885, pp. 105–124, 2003.
© Springer-Verlag Berlin Heidelberg 2003

compound operations. We explain how the resulting descriptions may be given a formal semantics – using the language of Communicating Sequential Processes (CSP) – and analysed using the refinement-checking tool Failures–Divergences Refinement (FDR).

The paper begins with an explanation of why it is important that an object modelling language should allow for a precise description of the effects of intra-object concurrency. This is followed by a review of the state diagram notation, and an informal explanation of its semantics. In Section 4, we show how the notation can be used to produce adequate descriptions of intra-object concurrency; in Section 5, we show how these descriptions can be given a formal, process semantics, and analysed using a notion of process refinement.

2   Intra-object Concurrency

Object-oriented designs are naturally concurrent: unless thread or control classes are explicitly included, the assumption is that any combination of operations might execute together. In the class diagram notation of UML, operations have a *concurrency* attribute; an operation may be described as

- *sequential*: concurrent calls on the same object are forbidden;
- *guarded*: concurrent calls are permitted, but each execution will be blocked until the previous call has completed;
- *concurrent*: concurrent execution is permitted, and the corresponding sequences of transitions and actions may be arbitrarily interleaved.

That is, the concurrency attribute makes explicit the possibility of concurrent execution of multiple operations upon a single object.

It is tempting to exclude this possibility, and insist instead that all operations are labelled *sequential* – the specification says nothing about the effect of concurrent calls – or *guarded* – the specification says that calls will be sequentialised. Either way, we can then ignore the problems of concurrent access to the state of an object. However, there are two reasons why this course of action, although appealing, is not appropriate:

1. most object-oriented designs, realised as object-oriented programs, would not conform to this ideal;
2. the effect of calling an operation on the current object – a common practice – needs to be considered as a special case.

The first results either from a compromise in design, or from the (sensible) use of abstraction; the second is fundamental to object-oriented modelling.

2.1   Design and Abstraction

Intra-object concurrency can always be avoided by a wider distribution of the state information. However, this increases the complexity of the design: in terms of the number of classes; in terms of the actions required to access or update the information. In many cases, intra-object concurrency appears – to the designer, or programmer – a reasonable compromise, and it seems unreasonable for our modelling tools to refuse to address the consequences.

More importantly, the emerging Model-Driven Architecture (MDA) [5] approach to software development involves the definition or generation of a hierarchy of models of the same system, at different levels of abstraction. It is likely that a component described as a single class at one level will be realised as a collection of classes at another: to be effective, the MDA approach requires a language that supports intra-object concurrency.

Similarly, in the commonly-advocated practice of *refactoring* – restructuring a design without introducing any new behaviour on the conceptual level [12] – two operations that are members of the same class will often be distributed into two separate classes: to afford a proper comparison between behaviours, the language must admit the possibility of these operations being executed concurrently – in both designs.

2.2   Calling the Current Object

It is common for the execution of an operation to require one or more calls upon the current object: these may involve subsidiary functions, alternative versions of the operation expecting different argument vectors, or even a recursive invocation of the operation itself. At the implementation level, this does not require intra-object concurrency: the current operation is suspended until the called operation completes. At the modelling level, however, we might hope that the suspension mechanism has been abstracted away.

If our modelling notation is unable to describe the effects of intra-object concurrency, then it will be unable also to describe the effect of calling an operation on the current object, unless this is made a special case. The 'special case' approach is particularly undesirable, as the target of an operation call, an object reference, may be updated during the lifetime of an object.

2.3   Effects and Precision

It is important to note that we are concerned here with the description of *effects*. A model written in UML may indicate that intra-object concurrency is possible, by setting the concurrency attribute to **concurrent** for one or more of the operations of a class. Furthermore, each operation may be completely specified in terms of a sequence of actions: in a target programming language, or in a more abstract notation.

However, the UML modelling language also includes *dynamic* modelling notations, and with good reason. To communicate and analyse the essential properties of a design, we would wish to describe the intended effects of operations executing together. The state diagram notation allows us to do this in terms of an abstraction of the state space; executing operations may produce events that trigger transitions from one abstract state to another.

It is important also to note that we are concerned with *precise* descriptions: sufficient to support automated analysis of behavioural properties. At present, most applications of UML are imprecise, or even unfaithful: diagrams may include features or annotations that, if taken literally, would contradict the design intention. The resulting models serve a valuable purpose in raising issues, explaining architectures, and communicating intentions.

However, where diagrams are intended as precise, faithful representations of behaviour, we may apply model-checking and theorem-proving tools to establish properties, or check the consistency, of object models; the benefits of formal engineering techniques are then accessible within the context of the Unified Modeling Language.

3   State Diagrams

A state diagram describes a pattern of behaviour in terms of transitions within and between abstract states. Each transition may be labelled with a trigger event, a guard, and a sequence of actions: each of these components is optional. There are several different kinds of trigger event, but the most important are: signal events, representing abstract communication between objects; and call events, representing (the beginning of) operation execution.

In either case, if an event occurs, and there is a suitably-labelled transition starting from the current state, then the guard on that transition is evaluated. Should the guard prove to be true, based on the values of the object attributes, and any attributes associated with the event itself, then the sequence of actions will be performed. Should the guard prove to be false, then the event will be discarded, and the object will remain in the current (source) state.

Some of the transitions in a diagram may have no trigger events: these are called *completion* transitions. An enabled completion transition – one whose guard is true – will be fired as soon as the sequence of actions leading to its source state is complete. If a state has more than one completion transition leading from it, then the resulting behaviour may be nondeterministic.

A key feature of the state diagram language, inherited from Harel's STATE-CHARTS notation [8], is the *run-to-completion property*: following the occurrence of an event, no further events will be accepted until every action triggered by that event, including those associated with any subsequently-enabled completion transitions, has been performed.

3.1   Factorisation Mechanisms

The information contained within a state diagram may be factorised using a variety of mechanisms: entry and exit actions, deferred event queues, composite and history states. For example, if all the transitions leading from a particular state begin with the same action, we may make this action an *exit* action for the state, rather than prepending it to the action sequence of each transition.

One of these mechanisms deserves particular attention. A 'concurrent composite state' is a state divided into a number of regions by a broken line – see

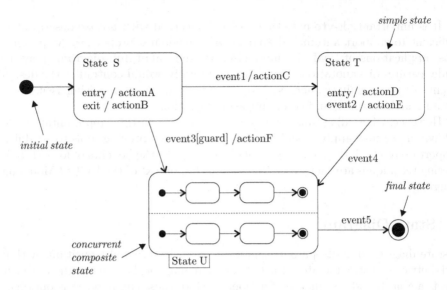

Fig. 1. State diagram notation.

State U in Figure 1. When an object enters a concurrent composite state, more than one transition may be triggered, and the resulting sequences of actions may be arbitrarily interleaved.

A deferred event is held in a local queue – one that cannot be accessed outside the current region of the state diagram – and will occur immediately after the next transition. Each region has its own queue for deferred events, and this queue is checked, and filtered, at each transition.

Figure 5 illustrates some of the features of the state diagram notation. In this example, if an object is in *State S* when *event3* occurs, and *guard* is true, then the sequence of actions *actionB ; action F* will be performed, and the object will enter *State U*: a composite state, describing a pattern of behaviour that may be interrupted at any point by an occurrence of *event5*.

The use of entry and exit actions is convenient and helpful; use of the other mechanisms, however, can easily result in diagrams whose semantics may be quite different from that intended by the author, or those understood by the readers. For this reason, we will focus our attention upon the core features of the language: simple states and labelled transitions.

3.2   Actions and Events

A *call* action represents the invocation of an operation. This invocation may be synchronous or asynchronous. In the first case, the action will not complete until the operation has finished executing: there is an implicit return mechanism. In the second, the action completes immediately; there is no return. The call action $t.op(args)$ produces a corresponding call event $op(args)$, for operation op with arguments $args$, at the target object t.

A *send* action represents the sending of a UML signal. This is a more abstract means of communication, used to indicate that the behaviour of one part of a system can affect another. The send action *send t.sig(args)* produces a corresponding send event *sig(args)* at the target object *t*.

The events associated with objects of a particular class are introduced in the class diagram for the model: the third component of a class box declares the operations, and thus the call events, that objects of that class may process; the fourth, optional compartment lists the set of signals that objects of that class should be capable of receiving.

The transport mechanism that connects the performance of an action to the reception of the corresponding event is left unspecified in UML: it is a *semantic variation point*. However, the description of the run-to-completion property makes it clear that received events can be stored for *processing* when the current action sequence has been completed.

Other forms of action, whose effects are local to the current object, may be described in a particular *action language*, chosen to suit the application domain. In this paper, we will assume that the action language includes a notion of assignment, and we will write $a := E$ to indicate that the value of expression E is assigned to the attribute a.

3.3   Concurrency

The run-to-completion property states that the state machine described by a state diagram must complete all of the actions associated with one event before it can process another. This means that a single state diagram cannot be used to describe the effects of concurrent execution: each call event will be held until the actions triggered by the previous call are complete.

Similarly, a single state diagram cannot be used to describe the effects of self-invocation of an synchronous operation. A synchronous call action cannot complete until the call event has been processed by the target, but – if the target is the current object – then that call event cannot be processed until the call action has been completed; the stated semantics suggests a deadly embrace.

Even if the operation is asynchronous, a single state diagram would provide an unsatisfactory description of the effects: the actions resulting from the call can begin only after the current sequence of actions has been completed, when we might expect to find that this sequence could be interleaved with the actions resulting from the call.

The concurrent composite state mechanism cannot be used to solve this problem, as – with the current semantics – the corresponding state machine cannot process another event until activity in every concurrent region has ceased. An alternative semantics, in which the run-to-completion property were relaxed, would allow a fixed degree of intra-object concurrency. In the following section, we present a more general solution.

4   Operation Diagrams

An adequate description of the effects of concurrent execution can be obtained if we describe the behaviour of objects of a particular class using a collection of state diagrams. One of these diagrams, the *object state diagram*, will be used to describe the chosen abstraction of the state space. The others, *operation state diagrams*, will be used to describe the effects of operations.

This affords a clear separation of concerns: the object state diagram presents only the state abstraction; the operation state diagrams explain the possible flows of execution. Accordingly, the transitions in the object diagram will be labelled only with send (or signal) events. Indeed, call events will appear only as labels for the corresponding operation diagrams.

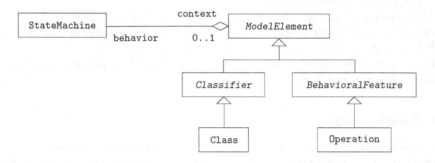

Fig. 2. Metamodel components.

The operation diagrams will have neither call nor send events: every transition will be a (possibly-guarded) completion transition. The same information could be conveyed by an activity diagram, or even inferred from a sequence diagram; the advantage of using state diagrams is that we have no need to introduce a second, graphical notation.

Call and send actions can appear in either kind of diagram, as can other kinds of action, such as assignment. The arguments supplied to these actions, and any guards that appear, can refer to any of the object attributes, as well as to the actual parameters of any call and send events processed within the current diagram.

This approach to the description of behaviour is permitted by the UML metamodel [7]. The relevant part of the metamodel is shown in Figure 2: a state machine has an optional *context*, a model element. The following constraint, included with the metamodel, insists that if this context is not null, then the model element must be either a classifier or a behavioural feature:

```
self.context.notEmpty implies
  (self.context.oclIsKindOf(BehavioralFeature) or
    self.context.oclIsKindOf(Classifier))
```

In this paper, we restrict our attention to classifiers that are instances of `Class`, and behavioural features that represent `Operations`, but the same approach could be adopted if the classifier were an actor or a use case, and if the behavioural feature were a (more concrete) method.

4.1 A Simple Example

As a simple example, consider how we might describe the behaviour of objects of the class `Counter`, shown in the class diagram of Figure 3. Objects of this class have two integer-valued attributes, `a1` and `a2`, and three operations, `m1()`, `m2(b:int)`, and `getTotal()`.

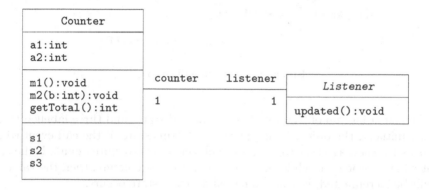

Fig. 3. A class diagram.

A `Counter` object can be in one of two abstract states: `count`, in which case the value of `a1` is non-zero, and may be repeatedly incremented; and `hold`, in which case the value of `a1` is unimportant, and `a2` is used to hold the running total (of increments). Transitions between these two states may be triggered by signals `s1`, `s2`, and `s3`.

The effect of `m1()` is to increment the value of `a1`; if this is the first time that `m1()` has been executed since the last 'successful' execution of `m2(b:int)`, then the value of `a1` is set to zero before the increment takes place. It is this issue, whether the last execution of `m2` was 'successful' or not, that is reflected in our abstraction of the state space.

The effect of `m2(b:int)` depends upon the result of comparing the value of parameter `b` with the current value of `a1`. If `a1` is greater than `b`, then the value of `a2` is increased by that of `a1`, and a listening object is informed that an update has taken place; if not, then the operation simply terminates.

The third operation, `getTotal()`, can be used by a listening object to obtain the current value of `a2`. Unlike the other two operations, this operation has a return value.

4.2   Using a Single State Diagram

If the `concurrency` attribute of each operation is set to *sequential* or *guarded*, and we can be sure that an object of class `Counter` will never call an operation upon itself, then we may obtain an adequate description of object behaviour using a single state diagram.

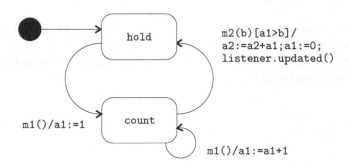

Fig. 4. A single state diagram.

The state diagram of Figure 4 has two named states and three labelled transitions. Initially, the object is in state `hold`. In this state, if the call event `m1()` is processed, then `a1` is set to `1`, and the object moves to state `count`. If the call event `m1()` is processed while the object is in the state `count`, then the value of `a1` will be incremented, but no change of abstract state occurs.

In state diagrams, as in STATECHARTS, if an event is processed in a state where there is no matching transition, then that event is simply discarded. Accordingly, if the call event `m2(b)` is processed when the abstract state of the object is `hold`, no actions will be performed.

If `m2(b)` is processed in `count`, and `a1` is greater than `b`, then a new total is established in `a2`, the listener is informed, and the object returns to state `hold`. If, however, the value of `a1` is less than or equal to `b`, then no actions are performed, and the object remains in state `count`.

For simplicity, we have omitted two self-transitions: the call event `getTotal()` may be processed in either state, resulting in a single *return* action with the value of `a2` as an argument. As no change of state is involved, these transitions could be declared as *internal*, and included within the two named state boxes.

4.3   A Combination of Diagrams

The state diagram of Figure 4 cannot be used to describe the effect of concurrent execution. The sequence of actions corresponding to a call event must be completed before the next call event can be processed. To consider the effects of concurrent execution of operations upon this object, we must describe each operation as a separate diagram.

These operation state diagrams may use signals s1, s2, and s3 to capture the relationship between operation execution and the chosen state abstraction. The assignment actions, and the call action listener.updated(), may be included either in the operation diagrams, or in object state diagram.

Figure 5 shows an object state diagram for the Counter class, in which a transition from hold to count is triggered by s1, and a transition from count to hold is triggered by s2. These transitions have corresponding actions, assignments to the object attributes. In addition, when the object is in state count, an occurrence of the event s3 will increment the value of a1.

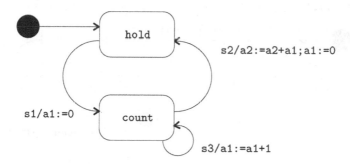

Fig. 5. An object state diagram.

Figure 6 presents a matching collection of operation state diagrams. The first of these describes the effects of an execution of operation m1(). The object state is updated in a way that corresponds to signal s1, and then in a way that corresponds to signal s3. In each case, the target of the send action is self, indicating the current object.

The second diagram explains the execution of operation m2(b:int). The value of parameter b is compared with the current value of attribute a1 – each of these state diagrams may refer to the values of attributes within the current object. If a1 is greater than b, signal s2 is sent, and a call action listener.updated() is performed to inform the listener of the expected change in the value of a2. Otherwise, the execution terminates immediately.

The informal interpretation of state diagrams [7] is given in terms of state machines: each diagram corresponds to sequential machine that accepts events and performs actions. To address the issues of intra-object concurrency, it is necessary to extend this interpretation: an *operation* state diagram corresponds to a state machine *factory*; each invocation of the operation may be given its own state machine. This interpretation is formalised in Section 5.

The third diagram explains the execution of getTotal(); this operation does nothing except return the current value of a2. Such a simple operation could reasonably be regarded as atomic: we could have decided instead to include the call event getTotal() in the object state diagram, and dispense with the state diagram for the operation.

m1():void

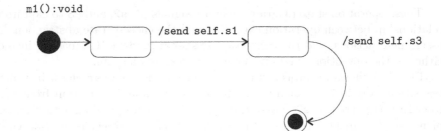

m2(b:int):void

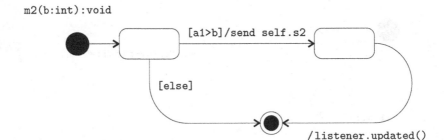

getTotal():int

Fig. 6. Operation state diagrams.

An analysis of this description reveals a behaviour that is not possible for the single state diagram of Figure 4: in terms of actions and events,

```
< m1(), send self.s1, s1, a1:=0, send self.s3, s3, a1:=1,
  m1(), send self.s1,
    m2(0), send self.s2, s2, a2:=a2+a1; listener.updated(),
      s1, send self.s3, s3 >
```

Here, the second execution of m1() is interleaved with an execution of m2(0). The expected second increment of a1 never occurs; the final value of a2, accessible through the getTotal() operation, is not 2, but 1.

If our intention was that any call of getTotal() immediately following a call of m2(0) should return the total number of (m1()) increments performed thus far, then this behaviour is unsatisfactory. It becomes clear that executions of m1() and m2 should be mutually exclusive.

The single state diagram of Figure 5 would not admit such an analysis; it cannot describe the effects of executing m1 and m2 concurrently. A model using a single state diagram is adequate only for an analysis of sequential or guarded operations.

4.4   A Complete Separation

In Figures 5 and 6, actions were distributed between the state and operation diagrams, and the relationship between the values of the object attributes and the abstract state was made explicit. If we wish to focus instead upon the abstract representation – the partitioning into `count` and `hold` – then the object state diagram of Figure 7 may be more convenient.

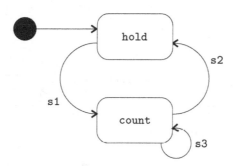

Fig. 7. Object state diagram without assignments.

Here, the transitions are labelled only with trigger events; the actions have been included instead in the operation state diagrams of Figure 8. In this version of the model, the diagram for operation `m1()` makes a reference to the abstract state: the actions of sending `s1`, and setting `a1` to zero, should be performed only if the object is in a state corresponding to `hold`.

The send actions of Figure 6 have been composed with the assignments that followed the corresponding send events in Figure 5. The resulting operation state diagrams explain the effects of operation calls upon attribute values; the object state diagram explains the effect of operation calls upon the abstract representation of the state.

The reader might be wondering whether or not these two descriptions admit the same range of behaviours. A careful analysis confirms the suspicion that, indeed, they do not: for example, the behaviour

```
< m1(), send self.s1(),
    m1(), send self.s1(), s1, s1,
      s1:=0, send self.s3(), a1:=a1+1,
        s1:=0, send self.s3(), a1:=a1+1 >
```

is admitted by the behavioural description of Figures 7 and 8, but not by that of Figures 5 and 6. When the second `m1()` call event occurs, the object state is still `[hold]`: the `s1` signal from the first `m1()` call has yet to be processed. As a result, the second call proceeds to set `a1` to zero, and does so *after* the first call has performed the increment.

That is, when the assignment actions are placed on the operation state diagrams, it is possible for two complete executions of `m1()` to leave the object in

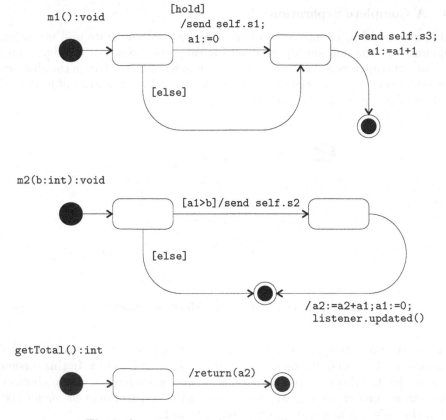

Fig. 8. Operation state diagrams with assignments.

a state in which attribute a1 has the value 1. When the assignment actions are placed on the object state diagram, two complete executions of m1() will always result in a state in which a1 has the value 2, assuming that operation m2 is not executing at the same time.

By placing the assignment actions within the object state diagram, we impose a degree of atomicity upon access to the shared state. For example, in the diagram of Figure 5, nothing can happen between the processing of signal s1 and the assignment a1:=0; more importantly, in this case, no other event will be accepted until the object is in state Count.

By placing all assignments with the operation state diagrams, we obtain a model that admits the maximum degree of concurrency: a model that will reveal every potential disadvantage of allowing more than one operation to execute concurrently. In deciding where to place assignment actions, we can express different assumptions about access to the shared, attribute state.

5 Process Semantics

The example of the previous section, however artificial and simplistic it might seem, should be enough to convince the reader that the effects of concurrent execution upon shared state can be unpredictable. For this reason, we might – as suggested in Section 2 – feel tempted to forbid it, and insist that every operation is either *sequential* or *guarded*.

However, as Section 2 goes on to explain, this form of concurrent execution is an essential ingredient of the Model-Driven Architecture approach to software development, in which a single abstract class might later be replaced by a collection of smaller, more concrete classes. It is also essential to the theory of refactoring, and to a homogeneous treatment of self-invocation.

It is important, therefore, that our ability to describe concurrent execution is properly complemented by an ability to analyse the consequences. Manual analysis is costly and error-prone; if we wish to conduct comprehensive analyses in an industrial context, we require highly-automated tool support. In this section, we explain how such support might be obtained using machine-readable CSP [11] and the refinement-checking tool FDR [6].

5.1 The Language of CSP

In the language of CSP, processes are defined in terms of the occurrence and availability of abstract events: atomic, synchronous, communications. In the machine-readable dialect, CSP events are introduced as elements of *channels*: for example, the declaration

```
channel c : A . B
```

introduces a set of events, each of the form c.a.b, where a is drawn from the set A and b is drawn from the set B. We may use the expression {| c |} to refer to all of the events whose names start with the prefix c.

The process a -> P is ready to perform the event a; if this event is performed, the future behaviour of this process is described by term P. The binary operator [] represents an external choice of processes, and can be used to describe a menu of possible interactions.

The input choice c?x -> P(x) represents an external choice in which every alternative begins with an event from the channel set {| c |}. The corresponding output c!v -> P is no choice at all: any variables appearing in the value expression v must already have been declared.

Processes may be composed using a binary parallel operator, which specifies the set of events to be shared between its two arguments: the set of events that can occur only if performed simultaneously by both processes. The expression P[|A|]Q denotes the parallel combination of two processes, P and Q, sharing every event in the set A. If A is empty, we may write P|||Q instead.

The hiding operator is used to conceal sets of events: P \ A is a process that behaves exactly as P, except that events from the set A are no longer visible, and do not require the cooperation of other processes. The `let...within...` construct allows for the scoping of process names; definitions made between `let` and `within` apply only for the term immediately following `within`.

5.2   Actions and Events

Each action or event in UML can be modelled as a separate abstract event in CSP. As we wish to analyse the behaviour of concurrent operations over a shared state, we must also introduce CSP events to represent the points at which these operations read the values of shared attributes.

Each call action, call event, send action, or send event will be represented as a CSP event of the form `type_source_target_member.arguments`, where `type` is one of `callAction`, `callEvent`, `sendAction`, and `sendEvent`, `source` and `target` are object references, `member` is the name of the operation or signal, and `arguments` represents the values passed.

Assignment actions are represented by CSP events of the form `set_a`, where `a` is the name of the attribute concerned. The implicit action of reading the current value of the same attribute is represented a CSP event of the form `get_a`. In our example, the process semantics involves the following channels.

The use of a separate channel for each UML action or event facilitates subsequent analysis – the number of CSP events shared by each process is kept to a minimum. Other measures adopted include the replacement of the infinite type `int` with a finite set, and the imposition of bounds upon the number of simultaneous executions of each operation. In our example, `Integer = {0..maxint}` and `maxint = 4`.

These other measures produce processes that are finite approximations to the actual semantics, and additional reasoning may be required before the results of analysis can be translated into properties of the original, object model. To make this clear, an `Error` state is introduced, to indicate that the scope of the current, finite approximation has been exceeded.

CSP events are used also to represent signal communication within an object. In our example, we will use this representation to illustrate another means of facilitating automated analysis: the abstraction of UML action–event pairs into a single, synchronous CSP events: `s1`, `s2`, and `s3`. The resulting semantics is adequate only for the analysis of models in which the occurrence of an action or event between the sending of an internal signal and its subsequent processing is either impossible, or immaterial.

5.3   Processes

We use a simple memory process, shown in Figure 9, to represent the attribute state of an object: the last value received on a `set` channel will be available on `get`. In our example, the integer attributes have been initialised to zero.

The process semantics of our first model, the one whose behaviour is defined by the single state diagram of Figure 4, is given in Figure 10. The correspondence

```
Attributes =
  let
    Attribute_a1 =
      let Store(value) =
            get_a1!value -> Store(value)
            []
            set_a1?new -> Store(new)
      within Store(0)
    Attribute_a2 =
      let Store(value) =
            get_a2!value -> Store(value)
            []
            set_a2?new -> Store(new)
      within Store(0)
  within
    Attribute_a1
    |||
    Attribute_a2
```

Fig. 9. A memory process.

between this process and the state diagram is quite clear: the state names have become the names of separate equations in the definition of ObjectState.

Each call event is followed by a sequence of other events; all of these must be completed before the process returns to either the Hold or Count states – only then can another call event be processed. If the process is in state Hold, and the call event for m2 is performed, then the resulting sequence is empty: the process returns immediately to Hold: this reflects the semantics of state diagrams; if there is no suitable transition, events are simply discarded.

The process semantics of our second model, that of Figures 5 and 6, is given in Figure 11. Again, the object state diagram corresponds to a process with two defining equations, Hold and Count. This time, however there are no action or signal events within the process definition; these appear instead within the processes describing the operations.

Each operation process begins with a call event, and terminates successfully as soon as its work is done. (Successful termination is denoted by the special process SKIP; the future behaviour is then determined by whatever follows the next semicolon). An idealised process semantics would employ an infinite interleaving of these processes: for example,

$$||| \, i : 0 \, .. \, \infty \bullet Operation\_m1$$

However, such a process cannot be written in machine-readable CSP, and would be poorly received by a model-checking tool.

```
CounterObject_sequential =
  let
    ObjectState =
      let Hold = callEvent_listener_counter_m1 -> set_a1!1 -> Count
                 []
                 callEvent_listener_counter_m2?b -> Hold
                 []
                 callEvent_listener_counter_getTotal ->
                   get_a2?a2 ->
                     returnAction_counter_listener_getTotal!a2 -> Hold

          Count = callEvent_listener_counter_m1 ->
                    get_a1?a1 -> (if a1+1 > maxint then Error
                                   else set_a1!a1+1 -> Count)
                  []
                  callEvent_listener_counter_m2?b ->
                    get_a1?a1 ->
                      if (a1 > b) then
                        get_a2?a2 ->
                          ( if (a1+a2 > maxint) then Error
                            else set_a2!(a1+a2) -> set_a1!0 ->
                                     callAction_counter_listener_updated ->
                                     Hold )
                      else
                        Count
                  []
                  callEvent_listener_counter_getTotal ->
                    get_a2?a2 ->
                      returnAction_counter_listener_getTotal!a2 -> Count
      within Hold
  within
    (ObjectState [| {| set_a1, set_a2, get_a1, get_a2 |} |] Attributes)
      \ {| set_a1, set_a2, get_a1, get_a2 |}
```

Fig. 10. Sequential counter process.

Instead, we must place a finite bound upon the number of simultaneous executions. For example, we might define

```
Operations =
  let
    Operations_m1 = Operation_m1 ; Operations_m1
    ...
  within
    Operations_m1 ||| Operations_m2 ||| Operations_getTotal
```

to produce a semantics in which no more than one copy of each operation may be executing at any one time.

```
CounterObject_concurrent =
  let
    ObjectState =
      let Hold = s1 -> set_a1!0 -> Count
                 []
                 s2 -> Hold
                 []
                 s3 -> Hold
                 []
                 stable -> Hold

          Count = s1 -> Count
                  []
                  s2 -> get_a1?a1 -> get_a2?a2 ->
                      if (a1+a2 > maxint) then Error
                      else set_a2!(a1+a2) -> set_a1!0 -> Hold
                  []
                  s3 -> get_a1?a1 -> if a1+1 > maxint then Error
                                     else set_a1!a1+1 -> Count
                  []
                  stable -> Count
      within Hold

    Operation_m1 =
      callEvent_listener_counter_m1 -> s1 -> s3 -> SKIP

    Operation_m2 =
      callEvent_listener_counter_m2?b -> get_a1?a1 ->
                    if (a1 > b) then
                        s2 -> callAction_counter_listener_updated -> SKIP
                    else SKIP

    Operation_getTotal =
      callEvent_listener_counter_getTotal -> get_a2?a2 ->
        returnAction_counter_listener_getTotal!a2 -> SKIP

    Operations =
      ( Operation_m1 [] Operation_m2 [] Operation_getTotal )
        ; stable -> Operations

  within
    ( ( ( ObjectState [| {| s1, s2, s3, stable |} |] Operations ) \
          {| s1, s2, s3, stable |} )
      [| {| set_a1, set_a2, get_a1, get_a2 |} |] Attributes )
    \ {| set_a1, set_a2, get_a1, get_a2 |}
```

Fig. 11. Concurrent counter process.

The definition of `Operations` used in Figure 11 is quite restrictive. Operations may be called in any order, but each operation must terminate before the next can begin execution. Moreover, all internal activity within the current object must have ceased: a condition that is represented here by the availability of the CSP event `stable`: observe that this event is blocked by the `ObjectState` process during transitions; it is available only in states `Hold` and `Count`.

The point of this restriction is quite simple: if we compare the two processes using failures–divergences refinement, the FDR tool confirms that they are equivalent: that is,

```
CounterObject_sequential [FD= CounterObject_concurrent
CounterObject_concurrent [FD= CounterObject_sequential
```

By choosing a suitable definition for the `Operations` process, we may explore the consequences of different levels of concurrent execution, and identify any assumptions that may need to be made about the order in which the different operations will be called.

6 Discussion

We have presented, in some detail, a novel approach to the specification of object behaviour in UML. We have been able to develop and refine the observations made in an earlier paper [1], clarifying the roles and composition of each kind of diagram, introducing a suitable characterisation of attribute state, and presenting a more convincing, more representative example.

We have also been able to identify and explain the need for the approach, and locate it within the UML metamodel. We have explored the consequences of placing assignment actions in the object state diagram, and shown how the abstract state representation of that diagram may be linked to the execution patterns of the operations.

Finally, we have used the worked example to show how a precise UML model, described as a combination of class and state diagrams, may be translated into the process language of CSP. A tool has been written to automate this translation, taking UML models in XMI format to machine-readable CSP: however, more sophisticated mechanisms are required – in particular, for namespaces and dynamic binding – before this tool can be applied to models any more complex than the example presented here.

As far as we are aware, no other author has proposed or investigated the use of operation state diagrams. Most of the work on behavioural semantics of UML models is inspired by that of Harel and Gery, in their paper *Executable Object Modeling with Statecharts* [8]. As a result, none of the semantics offers an adequate treatment of concurrent execution of more than one operation upon the same object.

The issue of concurrent execution in UML is discussed by Ober and Stan [10], who consider the notion of *active* and *passive* objects, and conclude that the semantics suggested by the UML documentation [7] is inadequate with regard to concurrency. They recommend that that passive objects should not be associated with state machines, and that an explicit treatment of threading should be included in the model; this is necessarily more concrete, and more restrictive, than the approach adopted here

[2], [3], and [9] show how machine-readable CSP may be used to check consistency in UML–RT [4]: although they consider neither operation invocation nor concurrent execution, the approach taken – mapping UML models (or fragments) into CSP, and then applying failures–divergences refinement – is the same as the one employed here; again, a tool has been written to automate the translation from UML to CSP.

Acknowledgements

The authors would like to acknowledge the contribution made by our colleagues in the AGEDIS project (EU IST 1999–20218). They are grateful also to QinetiQ and to IBM (Faculty Partnership Program) for their support.

References

1. J. Davies and C. Crichton. Refinement and concurrency in UML. In *Proceedings of REFINE'02*. Springer, 2002.
2. G. Engels, J. M. Küster, and L. Groenewegen. Consistent interaction of software components. In *Integrated Design and Process technology*. Society for Design and Process Science, June 2002.
3. G. Engels, J. M. Küster, R. Heckel, and L. Groenewegen. A methodology for specifying and analyzing consistency of object-oriented behavioral models. In *8th European Software Engineering Conference, and ACM SIGSOFT Symposium on the Foundations of Software Engineering*, 2001.
4. C. Fischer, E.-R. Olderog, and H. Wehrheim. A CSP view on UML-RT structure diagrams. In H. Hussmann, editor, *Fundamental Approaches to Software Engineering, 4th International Conference, FASE 2001*, volume 2029 of *LNCS*, pages 91–108. Springer, 2001.
5. D. Frankel. *Model Driven Architecture: Applying MDA to Enterprise Computing*. Wiley, 2003.
6. FSEL – Formal Systems (Europe) Ltd. The FDR2 refinement checker. http://www.fsel.com.
7. Object Management Group. UML 2.0 Superstructure Draft Adopted Specification. http://www.omg.org/cgi-bin/doc?ptc/2003-07-06, 2003.
8. D. Harel and E. Gery. Executable object modeling with Statecharts. *IEEE Computer*, 30(7):31–42, 1997.
9. J. M. Küster and J. Stehr. Towards explicit behavioral consistency concepts in the uml. In *Proceedings of SCESM 2003 workshop*. IEEE, 2003.
10. I. Ober and I. Stan. On the concurrent object model of UML. In *Proceedings of EuroPar99*, volume 1685 of *LNCS*. Springer, 1999.
11. A. W. Roscoe. *Theory and Practice of Concurrency*. Prentice Hall, 1997.
12. G. Sunyé, D. Pollet, Y. Le Traon, and J.-M. Jézéquel. Refactoring UML models. In M. Gogolla and C. Kobryn, editors, *UML 2001: Modeling Languages, Concepts, and Tools*, volume 2185 of *LNCS*, pages 134–148. Springer, 2001.

The Equivalence of Statecharts*

Quan Long[1], Zongyan Qiu[1], and Shengchao Qin[2]

[1] LMAM, Department of Informatics
School of Mathematical Sciences
Peking University, Beijing, China 100871
lq@is.pku.edu.cn,zyqiu@pku.edu.cn
[2] Singapore-MIT Alliance
National University of Singapore
qinsc@comp.nus.edu.sg

Abstract. This paper proposes a compositional operational semantics for a nontrivial subset of Statecharts and defines an equivalence relation between Statecharts using bisimulation on configurations. An input/response trace model is also investigated at the level of observable behaviour.

1 Introduction

Statecharts is a visual synchronous specification language introduced by David Harel originally in the early 1980s [4], which is an extension of the finite state machine by hierarchy, concurrency and broadcasting communication. Quoting the words of D.Harel [4],

> **Statecharts = state diagram + depth +**
> **orthogonality + broadcast communication**

Statecharts was invented originally for the development of the avionics system for an Israeli aircraft, and has seen widespread use since then (e.g. [11]). It is desirable to be a tool for specifying real-time, reactive and embedded systems. Some development environments, such as STATEMATE [4,5], are developed to support the specification of applications with Statecharts. The formalism acts now also as one of the major components of UML [2].

Statecharts can be thought as an enrichment of finite-state transition systems. Here the states can have hierarchical structures and may consist of several sub-states, in fact, sub-Statecharts. These sub-Statecharts can themselves have embedded sub-Statecharts too. Statecharts may be composed sequentially or in parallel to form *Or-Statecharts* or *And-Statecharts* respectively.

The execution of Statecharts is defined by the active states and transitions. In a Statechart, there are usually several simultaneously active states (sub-Statecharts) at a time instant, they communicate with each other via broadcasting events in a global environment. The transitions defined determine the

---

* Supported by National Natural Science Foundation of China (No. 60173003)

J.S. Dong and J. Woodcock (Eds.): ICFEM 2003, LNCS 2885, pp. 125–143, 2003.

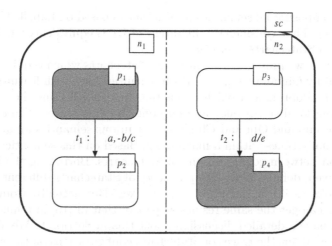

Fig. 1. A simple Statechart.

transference of active states. Each of the transitions is labeled by a pair of sets of events, where the first set of events is called the *trigger* of the transition which may include both positive and negative events, and the second is referred to as the *action* which can in turn act as triggers to fire other transitions. A transition connects a pair of states, with the first one as its source state and the second one as its target. Intuitively, if the source state of a transition is active, and all positive events from its trigger are present while all negative ones are absent, the transition is enabled and may be performed. When a transition is performed, the events in its action will be generated, and the target state of the transition becomes active afterward.

Fig. 1 shows a simple Statechart. It consists of only one *And-Statechart* named sc. The Statechart sc is composed of two parallel sub-Statecharts named n_1 and n_2. Both n_1 and n_2 are *Or-Statecharts*. Or-Statechart n_1 is refined to basic Statecharts p_1 and p_2, which are connected by transition t_1 with trigger $\{a, -b\}$ (Here we use $-b$ to indicate that event b is absent.) and action c. The figure shows that, in the current situation, the active state of n_1 is p_1. When event a occurs but b does not, t_1 can be performed, thus the event c is generated as the action of t_1, and the active state will be transferred to p_2. On the other side, Or-Statechart n_2 is composed of two basic Statecharts p_3 and p_4, which are connected by transition t_2. The active state of n_2 is p_4.

In literatures, there exist a number of different semantics for variants of Statecharts. M. von der Beeck discussed about twenty variants of Statecharts in [1], each of these variants can be regarded as a subset of the originally proposed language. The version discussed in [5] for STATEMATE has a powerful semantics. But the semantics defined in that paper is neither formal, nor compositional. The work presented in [12] gives a compositional semantics of Statecharts, whereas their version does not contain data states. In [16], M.Schettini, A.Peron and S.Tini had a discussion about the equivalence of Statecharts. They presented a compositional semantics of Statecharts based on Labelled Transition Systems(LTSs). They considered a hierarchy of LTSs equivalences and gave the congruences to Statecharts operators.

In this paper, we present a semantics for Statecharts which is quite similar to that proposed by Qin and Chin [15]. Both semantics have such features as being compositional, adopting an asynchronous time model, reflecting the causality of events, obeying local consistency and covering the data states. The only difference between ours and Qin and Chin's is that in our semantics an active event can be used many times within a macro-step. Based on this semantics, we build a bisimulation between configurations of Statecharts. Borrowing the idea of [9] and [7], we give a definition of the equivalence of Statecharts different from that in [16]. It looks as if our definition were weaker. But actually, from this new definition, we can get the same results as part of that in [16] in a much simpler way. We will have a detailed discussion about this in Section 6. We also have a brief discussion about the traces of Statecharts configurations on the macro-step level.

The next section gives a brief description of term-based syntax of Statecharts. In Section 3, we present our new semantics by a set of operational transition rules. In Section 4, we define the equivalence of Statecharts and prove that the definition is appropriate for getting the needed properties of equivalence. Discussed in Section 5 are the definition and properties of traces of Statecharts configurations. The related works are discussed in Section 6. Finally, Section 7 contains our conclusions and directions for future research.

2   Term-Based Syntax of Statecharts

To facilitate our discussion, we use the textual representation for Statecharts that was also given in Qin and Chin [15]. The formal term-based syntax definition for Statecharts is depicted in what follows.

Suppose we have the following sets:

- N: The set of names used to denote Statecharts. We assume that the set is large enough for all the Statecharts.
- Π_e: The set of all positive events.
- $\Pi_{\bar{e}}$: The set of all negative events, that is, $\Pi_{\bar{e}} =_{def} \{\bar{e}|e \in \Pi_e\}$. We assume that $\bar{\bar{e}} = e$.
- Π_a: The set of all assignment actions. These actions have the form $\nu = exp$.
- $\mathcal{T}$: The set of all possible transitions, $\mathcal{T} \subseteq N \times 2^{\Pi_e \cup \Pi_{\bar{e}}} \times 2^{\Pi_e \cup \Pi_a} \times N$, where the first N denotes the source sub-state, the last N is the target sub-state, $2^{\Pi_e \cup \Pi_{\bar{e}}}$ the trigger and $2^{\Pi_e \cup \Pi_a}$ the new events and assignments which were generated and performed by the transition of $\mathcal{T}$.

Definition 2.1. The set SC of Statecharts is defined inductively as follows:

1. Basic: $N \rightarrow SC$:

$$Basic(n) =_{def} [n]$$

2. Or: $N \times \langle SC \rangle \times SC \times 2^{T} \to SC$:

$$Or(n, \langle P_1, \cdots, P_l, \cdots, P_m \rangle, P_l, T) =_{def} [n, (P_1, \cdots, P_m), P_l, T]$$

3. And: $N \times 2^{SC} \to SC$:

$$And(n, \{P_1, \cdots, P_m\}) =_{def} [n, (P_1, \cdots, P_m)]$$

Note that we use square brackets to enclose a Statechart, use $\langle SC \rangle$ to denote all sequences of Statecharts of SC. Following are some explanations of the constructions of Statecharts.

- $Basic(n)$ denotes a basic Statechart named n.
- $Or(n, \langle P_1, \cdots, P_l, \cdots, P_m \rangle, P_l, T)$ denotes an Or-Statechart named n with a sequence of sub-states $\langle P_1, \cdots, P_m \rangle$, where P_1 is the default sub-state and P_l is the active sub-state currently. Notice that the sub-states are defined as a sequence rather than a set, to indicate that P_1 is the default sub-state. The order of other sub-states is arbitrary. T is the set composed of all possible transitions among the sub-states of n.
- $And(n, \{P_1, \cdots, P_m\})$ denotes the And-Statechart named n, which contains a number of parallel sub-states $P_1, \cdots, P_m$, where $P_1, \cdots, P_m$ are basic Statecharts or Or-Statecharts (but not And-Statecharts).

Example 2.1. The term-based syntax for the Statechart shown in Fig. 1 is given below:

1. $N = And(sc, \{n_1, n_2\}) = [sc, (n_1, n_2)]$;
2. $n_1 = Or(n_1, \langle p_1, p_2 \rangle, p_1, \{t_1\}) = [n_1, (p_1, p_2), p_1, \{\langle p_1, \{a, \bar{b}\}, \{c\}, p_2 \rangle\}]$;
3. $n_2 = [n_2, (p_3, p_4), p_4, \{\langle p_3, \{d\}, \{e\}, p_4 \rangle\}]$;
4. Definition of p_1, p_2, p_3, p_4, etc.

Note that we use $\langle p_i, E, A, p_j \rangle$ to represent a transition from state p_i to p_j with trigger set E and action set A. □

It should be noticed that our version is a subset of Harel's original definition. We do not include timeout events, inter-level transitions and some other minor features.

3   Operational Transition Rules

Before presenting the semantics for Statecharts, we define configurations of Statecharts first. A configuration of Statecharts is defined as a triple $\langle P, \nu, E \rangle$, where

- P is the syntax of the Statechart of interest.
- ν is a snapshot of data items (data state).
- $E \subseteq \Pi_e$ is a set of active events.

The behavior of a Statechart is composed of a sequence of macro-steps, each of which comprises a sequence of micro-steps which are triggered by the external or internal events. A Statechart reacts to any stimulus from the environment at the beginning of each macro-step by performing a sequence of transitions and generating some internal events (by the actions of the transitions it performs), which can in turn fire other state transitions and lead to a chain of micro-steps without advancing time. During this chain of micro-steps, the Statechart does not respond to any (potentially) further external stimulus. In case that no more transitions, except for the clock tick, are enabled, the macro-step comes to the end. The clock tick transition then occurs, which empties the set of currently active events and advances time by one unit. Then, the Statechart is ready again to accept another external stimuli and start off the next macro-step. The relationship of macro-step and micro-step was discussed in details by G. Lüttgen, M. von der Beeck and R. Cleaveland [12].

We explore the following transition rules, consisting of state transitions rules and time advance transitions rules.

The first transition rule initiates a macro-step for a Statechart. It is the first micro-step of a macro-step. It performs only when a set of events E arrives (due to the environment) and the Statechart is ready to accept them.

Rule 3.1 (*Initiate*). $\langle P, \nu, \phi \rangle \xrightarrow{E} \langle P, \nu, E \rangle$ □

In an Or-Statechart, if a transition between two immediate connected substates is enabled, the transition can be performed.

Rule 3.2 (*Or*). Suppose P is an Or-Statechart and $P = [n, (P_1, \cdots, P_m), P_l, T]$, $\tau \in En(P, E)$. Then we can have

$$\langle P, \nu, E \rangle \xrightarrow{\tau} \langle [n, (P_1, \cdots, P_m), a2d(tgt(\tau)), T], \nu', E \cup act^e(\tau) \rangle$$

where

- $En(P, E) =_{def} \{\tau \in T | sre(\tau) = P_l \wedge trig^+(\tau) \subseteq E \wedge trig^-(\tau) \cap E = \phi\}$ is the set of transitions enabled in current configuration on the "highest level".
- $sre(\tau)$ and $tgt(\tau)$ are the source and target states of transition τ, respectively.
- $act^e(\tau)$ denotes the set of events generated by transition τ.
- $trig^+(\tau)$ and $trig^-(\tau)$ are respectively the set of positive events and the set of negative ones that form the trigger of the transition τ.
- The function $a2d(P)$ maps the sub-state p of P to its default sub-state (recursively). Its definition is:

  $a2d([n]) =_{def} [n]$
  $a2d([n, (P_1, \cdots, P_m), P_l, T]) =_{def} [n, (P_1, \cdots, P_m), a2d(P_1), T]$
  $a2d([n, (P_1, \cdots, P_m)]) =_{def} [n, (a2d(P_1), \cdots, a2d(P_m))]$

- ν' denotes the new data states which might be updated by actions of τ. □

If no transition among immediate sub-states of an Or-Statechart is enabled, then the transitions in its active sub-state can be performed.

Rule 3.3 (*Or-Substate*). Suppose $P = [n, (P_1, \cdots, P_m), P_l, T]$ is an Or-State-chart, $En(P, E) = \phi$, and $\langle P_l, \nu, E \rangle \xrightarrow{\tau} \langle P_l', \nu', E' \rangle$, then

$$\langle P, \nu, E \rangle \xrightarrow{\tau} \langle [n, (P_1, \cdots, P_m), P_l', T], \nu', E' \rangle$$

□

From **Rule 3.3** we know that, the enabled transitions of the higher level Stat-echart will have the relative higher priority of being chosen, while simultaneously enabled transitions of the embedded Statecharts will be discarded.

Notice that the transition τ in above rule may be the conjunction of a set of transitions, because P_l can be an And-Statechart (See **Rule 3.4** below). We use also symbol τ to denote that case for convenience and shall follow this convention when needed. On the other hand, the fired transition(s) τ is (are) definitely on the highest possible level in P_l due to **Rule 3.2** and **Rule 3.3**.

If each variable can be modified by only one transition of an And-Statechart, then all enabled transitions of those sub-states can perform together. We use $WV(\tau_i)$ to denotes the variables that can be modified by τ_i. Here we avoid the racing conflicts only for simpleness. Adding it will not bring essential changes to the main parts of this paper.

Rule 3.4 (*And*). Suppose P is an And-Statechart, $P = [n, (P_1, \cdots, P_m)]$. For $i = 1, 2, \cdots, m$, P_i is a Basic Statechart or Or-Statechart,

$$\langle P_i, \nu, E \rangle \xrightarrow{\tau_i} \langle P_i', \nu_i', E \cup act^e(\tau_i) \rangle$$

If $En^*(P_i, E) = \phi$ for some i, then the sub-configuration is considered as staying the same. That is

$$\langle P_i, \nu, E \rangle \rightarrow \langle P_i, \nu, E \rangle$$

where En^* is defined as follows

$$En^*([n], E) =_{def} \phi$$
$$En^*(P = [n, (P_1, \cdots, P_m), P_l, T], E) =_{def} En(P, E) \cup En^*(P_l, E)$$
$$En^*(P = [n, (P_1, \cdots, P_m)], E) =_{def} \bigcup_{i=1}^{m} En^*(P_i, E)$$

We have further condition that for all $i \neq j$, $WV(\tau_i) \cap WV(\tau_j) = \phi$, we denote $\nu' = \bigoplus_{i=1}^{m} \nu_i'$ the direct sum of all ν_i', then we have

$$\langle P, \nu, E \rangle \xrightarrow{\wedge_{i=1}^{m} \tau_i} \langle [P, (P_1', \cdots, P_m')], \nu', E \cup \bigcup_{i=1}^{m} act^e(\tau_i) \rangle$$

□

If no transition is enabled in a Statechart and all of its embedded sub-states, the current macro-step comes to the end. The Statechart will clear the set of events and advance the time (Here σ is used to denote the clock tick transition), and is ready to perform **Rule 3.1** to start another macro-step.

Rule 3.5 (*Empty and Time Advance*). If $En^*(P, E) = \phi$, then we have

$$\langle P, \nu, E \rangle \xrightarrow{\sigma} \langle P, \nu, \phi \rangle$$

□

Here is a simple example of how these operational rules work.

Example 3.1. In the Statechart of Fig. 1, the default configuration is

$$\langle [sc, ([n_1, (p_1, p_2), p_1, t_1], [n_2, (p_3, p_4), p_3, t_2])], \nu, \phi \rangle$$

When the external events set $\{a, d\}$ appears. **Rule 3.1** works.

$$\langle [sc, ([n_1, (p_1, p_2), p_1, t_1], [n_2, (p_3, p_4), p_3, t_2])], \nu, \phi \rangle$$
$$\xrightarrow{\{a,d\}} \langle [sc, ([n_1, (p_1, p_2), p_1, t_1], [n_2, (p_3, p_4), p_3, t_2])], \nu, \{a, d\} \rangle$$

This is an And-Statechart. Following the **Rule 3.4**, we need to consider its sub-Statecharts. According to **Rule 3.2**, the following two potential transitions are ready to be fired:

$$\langle [n_1, (p_1, p_2), p_1, t_1], \nu_1, \{a, d\} \rangle \xrightarrow{t_1} \langle [n_1, (p_1, p_2), p_2, t_1], \nu_1', \{a, d, c\} \rangle$$
$$\langle [n_2, (p_3, p_4), p_3, t_2], \nu_2, \{a, d\} \rangle \xrightarrow{t_2} \langle [n_2, (p_3, p_4), p_4, t_2], \nu_2', \{a, d, e\} \rangle$$

The conditions of **Rule 3.4** hold. Therefore,

$$\langle [sc, ([n_1, (p_1, p_2), p_1, t_1], [n_2, (p_3, p_4), p_3, t_2])], \nu, \{a, d\} \rangle$$
$$\xrightarrow{t_1 \wedge t_2} \langle [sc, ([n_1, (p_1, p_2), p_2, t_1], [n_2, (p_3, p_4), p_4, t_2])], \nu', \{a, d, c, e\} \rangle$$

where $\nu' = \nu_1' \oplus \nu_2'$.

Now the set $En^*(sc, \{a, c, d, e\})$ is empty, hence the **Rule 3.5**, that is,

$$\langle [sc, ([n_1, (p_1, p_2), p_2, t_1], [n_2, (p_3, p_4), p_4, t_2])], \nu', \{a, d, c, e\} \rangle$$
$$\xrightarrow{\sigma} \langle [sc, ([n_1, (p_1, p_2), p_2, t_1], [n_2, (p_3, p_4), p_4, t_2])], \nu', \phi \rangle$$

A macro-step comes to the end.   □

4   Equivalence

For the sake of convenience, we will use the capital letter C (or C_i) to denote the configuration $\langle P, \nu, E \rangle$ and let $\mathbb{C}$ be the space of all possible configurations of a set of Statecharts.

For the description of the set of events used in one micro-step to trigger the transition, we give the following definition.

Definition 4.1. We use $C \xrightarrow{E} C'$ to denote that, the configuration C evolves to C' in one **micro-step** by some fired transitions (There might be more than one fired transitions because of **Rule 3.4**), and E is the set of all the positive events of the triggers of all the transitions performed in this micro-step.

The following definition describes the configurations which will execute micro-steps infinitely and, therefore, makes the Statecharts no chance to participate further stimuli from the environment.

Definition 4.2 (*Divergent*). A configuration C is divergent if there is an infinite sequence of configurations $\{C_n\}_{n=1}^{\infty}$ such that $C = C_1$ and $C_n \xrightarrow{E_n} C_{n+1}$, where E_n is the corresponding set of events. That is, there is an infinite sequence of micro-steps started from C.

In what follows we depict the relationship of two configurations to express their equivalent property.

Definition 4.3 (*Bisimulation*). A binary relation $\mathcal{S}$ over a configuration space $\mathbb{C}$ is a bisimulation iff it satisfies the following conditions:

1. $\mathcal{S}$ is an equivalence relation.
2. Given $C_i = \langle P_i, \nu_i, E_i \rangle, i = 1, 2$. If $C_1 \mathcal{S} C_2$ then
   (a) $var(P_1) = var(P_2)$, where $var()$ denotes the variable set
   (b) $\nu_1 = \nu_2$
   (c) $E_1 = E_2$
   (d) if C_1 is not divergent, For any set of events E, whenever there exists a C_1' such that $C_1 \xrightarrow{E} C_1'$, then there exists C_2', such that
   $$(C_2 \xrightarrow{E} C_2') \wedge (C_1' \mathcal{S} C_2')$$
   (e) If $C_1 \xrightarrow{\sigma} C_1'$ (**Rule 3.5**), then there exists C_2', such that
   $$(C_2 \xrightarrow{\sigma} C_2') \wedge (C_1' \mathcal{S} C_2')$$
   □

In this definition, we do not mention the actions of the performed transitions. However, from 2 (b), (c) and (d) we know that, the data states and sets of active events of C_1' and C_2', i.e. ν_1' and ν_2', E_1' and E_2' (which reflect the effects of the actions of the micro-step), are the same.

The following lemma shows our definition of bisimulation preserves normal operations.

Lemma 4.4. If $\{\mathcal{S}_i\}$ are bisimulations, then the following relations are also bisimulations.

1. $\bigcup_i \mathcal{S}_i$
2. $\mathcal{S}_i \circ \mathcal{S}_j$

Proof. The proof of 1 and 2 are similar. We prove 2 as an example.

What needs to be checked are the two conditions of **Definition 4.3** in turn. The condition 1 and (a), (b) and (c) of condition 2 are trivial, let's see the condition 2 (d).

If $C_1(\mathcal{S}_i \circ \mathcal{S}_j)C_3$, then there exists a configuration C_2 such that

$$(C_1 \mathcal{S}_i C_2) \wedge (C_2 \mathcal{S}_j C_3)$$

So if there exists a configuration C_1' such that $C_1 \xrightarrow{E} C_1'$, then

$$\exists C_2' \cdot (C_2 \xrightarrow{E} C_2') \wedge (C_1' \mathcal{S}_i C_2')$$

For $C_2 \mathcal{S}_j C_3$ and $C_2 \xrightarrow{E} C_2'$, we have

$$\exists C_3' \cdot (C_3 \xrightarrow{E} C_3') \wedge (C_2' \mathcal{S}_j C_3')$$

So we have $C_1'(\mathcal{S}_i \circ \mathcal{S}_j)C_3'$. Now we have proved that $C_1 \xrightarrow{E} C_1'$ implies

$$\exists C_3' \cdot (C_3 \xrightarrow{E} C_3') \wedge (C_1'(\mathcal{S}_i \circ \mathcal{S}_j)C_3')$$

In case of condition (e), it is similar to condition (d).   □

Using **Definition 4.3**, we give the definition of the equivalence of two configurations as follows.

Definition 4.5 (*Configuration Equivalence*). Two configurations C_1 and C_2 are equivalent, denoted by $C_1 \sim C_2$, iff there exists a bisimulation $\mathcal{S}$ such that $C_1 \mathcal{S} C_2$.

Furthermore, we give the definition for the equivalence of two Statecharts as follows. It seems that this definition is a little weak. In fact, this definition is sufficient. The validity of this statement will be embodied by later theorems and corollaries.

Definition 4.6 (*Statechart Equivalence*). Two Statecharts P and Q are equivalent, denoted by $P \sim Q$, iff $D(P) \sim D(Q)$, where $D(P)$ denotes the default configuration of P. That is, the configuration where the set of active states is exactly the set of default states of P.

Example 4.1. $[sc_1, ([n_{11}, (p_1, p_2), p_1, t], [n_{12}, (p_3, p_4), p_3, t])]$ and $[sc_2, ([n_{21}, (p_1, p_3)], [n_{22}, (p_2, p_4)]), n_{21}, t]$ are two Statecharts, where p_1, p_2, p_3, p_4 are their embedded Statecharts. Assuming $var(sc_1) = var(sc_2)$, $\nu(D(sc_1)) = \nu(D(sc_2))$ and $E(D(sc_1)) = E(D(sc_2))$, these two Statecharts are equivalent.

Fig. 2 and Fig.3 shows these two Statecharts. The only micro-step can be fired of sc_1 is to transfer p_1, p_3 to p_2, p_4 parallelly by **Rule 3.4** and the only micro-step can be fired of sc_2 is to transfer n_{21} to n_{22} by **Rule 3.2**. It is easy to check that their default configurations can bisimulate each other.   □

Lemma 4.7. $\sim$ on the Statechart space is an equivalence relation.
The proof of this lemma is trivial.   □

To illustrate the validity of our definition of the equivalence, we shall show the result that for every possible configuration of a Statechart P, we can find a configuration from a Statechart Q which is equivalent to P, these configurations bisimulate each other. We give the following definition first.

Definition 4.8. Suppose $tr = \langle E_1, E_2, \cdots \rangle$, where $E_i \subseteq \Pi_e$ (Recall that Π_e is the set of all possible events) or $E_i = \{\sigma\}$ is a sequence of sets of events. We use $C_1 \xrightarrow{tr} C_2$ to denote the fact that the configuration C_1 evolves into C_2 by performing micro-steps $\langle step_1, step_2, \cdots \rangle$ in turn and the set of positive events out of triggers of the transitions fired in $step_i$ is E_i.

Given two equivalent statecharts P and Q ($P \sim Q$), the following theorem states that, for any reachable configuration in a run of P (or Q respectively), there exists a bisimular configuration in a run of Q (or P respectively).

Theorem 4.9. Suppose $P \sim Q$. Let tr be any finite length sequence of sets of events. If there exists a configuration C_p such that $D(P) \xrightarrow{tr} C_p$, then there exists a configuration C_q such that $D(Q) \xrightarrow{tr} C_q$ and $C_p \sim C_q$.

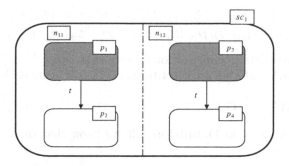

Fig. 2. Statechart sc_1.

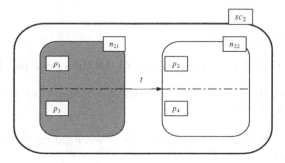

Fig. 3. Statechart sc_2.

That is, we have the following commuting diagram:

$$\begin{array}{ccc} D(P) & \xrightarrow{\;tr\;} & C_p \\ \sim \downarrow & & \downarrow \sim \\ D(Q) & \xrightarrow[\;tr\;]{} & C_q \end{array}$$

Proof. By induction on n, the length of tr.

(1) $n = 1$. By **Definition 4.5** and **Definition 4.6**, there exists a bisimulation S such that

$$D(P)\,S\,D(Q),$$

and we have

$$D(P) \xrightarrow{E_1} C_p$$

From 2.(d) and 2.(e) in **Definition 4.3**, we get that there exists C_q such that

$$(D(Q) \xrightarrow{E_1} C_q) \wedge (C_p S C_q)$$

(2) Assume the result holds for $n = k$. We prove that it also holds for the case of $n = k + 1$.

Suppose $tr = \{E_1, E_2, \cdots, E_{k+1}\}$. We denote $tr' = \{E_1, E_2, \cdots, E_k\}$. Then there exists C'_p such that $D(P) \xrightarrow{tr'} C'_p$ and $C'_p \xrightarrow{E_{k+1}} C_p$. Using the inductive assumption, there exists a configuration C'_q such that $D(Q) \xrightarrow{tr'} C'_q$ and $C'_p \sim C'_q$. By **Definition 4.5** and **Definition 4.6**, there exists a bisimulation $\mathcal{S}$ such that

$$(C'_p \mathcal{S} C'_q) \wedge (C'_p \xrightarrow{E_{k+1}} C_p)$$

From 2.(d) and 2.(e) in **Definition 4.3**, we know that there exists C_q such that

$$(C'_q \xrightarrow{E_{k+1}} C_q) \wedge (C_p \mathcal{S} C_q)$$

That is

$$(D(Q) \xrightarrow{tr} C_q) \wedge (C_p \mathcal{S} C_q)$$

Now with (1) and (2) done, we have come to the end of our proof. $\square$

From the above theorem we can prove the following property which expresses the above mentioned idea easily.

Corollary 4.10. Suppose $P \sim Q$. Then for each legal configuration C_p of P, there exists a configuration C_q of Q such that $C_p \sim C_q$.

Proof. Consider the micro-step sequence $\langle step_1, \cdots, step_k \rangle$ which leads $D(P)$ to C_p and the corresponding sequence of sets of events $\langle E_1, \cdots, E_k \rangle$. $\square$

The following theorem shows that the equivalence relation is preserved by the constructors of Statecharts.

Theorem 4.11 (*Congruence*). $P_i \sim Q_i$ $(i = 1, \cdots, m)$ implies

1. $And(N_p, \{P_1, \cdots, P_m\}) \sim And(N_q, \{Q_1, \cdots, Q_m\})$;
2. $Or(N_p, \langle P_1, \cdots, P_m \rangle, P_l, T) \sim Or(N_q, \langle Q_1, \cdots, Q_m \rangle, Q_l, T')$. where there exist a bijection f between T and T', such that for any $\tau \in T$
   (a) $act^e(\tau) = act^e(f(\tau))$
   (b) $trig^+(\tau) = trig^+(f(\tau)) \wedge trig^-(\tau) = trig^-(f(\tau))$
   (c) $P_i \xrightarrow{\tau} P_j \Longleftrightarrow Q_i \xrightarrow{f(\tau)} Q_j$

That is, we have following commuting diagram in which the symbol op denotes the Statechart construction operators *And* or *Or*:

$$
\begin{array}{ccc}
\{P_1, \cdots, P_m\} & \xrightarrow{\ op\ } & N_p \\
\sim\downarrow & & \downarrow\sim \\
\{Q_1, \cdots, Q_m\} & \xrightarrow[\ op\ ]{} & N_q
\end{array}
$$

Proof. 1. For $P_i \sim Q_i$, we have $D(P_i) \sim D(Q_i)$, then $\exists S_i \cdot D(P_i)S_iD(Q_i)$, where S_i is a bisimulation. So we have:
For any set of events E, whenever there exists a configuration $(D(P_i))'$ such that

$$D(P_i) \xrightarrow{E} (D(P_i))',$$

there exists $(D(Q_i))'$, such that

$$(D(Q_i) \xrightarrow{E} (D(Q_i))') \wedge ((D(P_i))'S_i(D(Q_i))')$$

Now we define the relationship

$$S = \{\langle D(And(N_p, \{P_1, \cdots, P_m\})), D(And(N_q, \{Q_1, \cdots, Q_m\}))\rangle \\ \text{where } D(P_i)S_iD(Q_i)\} \ \cup Id$$

We prove that S is a bisimulation as follows.
It is trivial that S is an equivalence relation.   (†)
Now we check the conditions 2(a) – 2(e) in **Definition 4.3**. 2(a), 2(b) and 2(c) are trivial. Since 2(e) is similar to 2(d), we check condition 2(d) in details here.
Since our discussion is at the micro-step level, the actions of transitions in $D(P_i)$ do not have effect on $D(P_j)$. Thus we have the following fact.

For any set of events E, whenever $D(N_p) \xrightarrow{E} (D(N_p))'$,

there exists $(D(N_q))'$, such that

$$(D(N_q) \xrightarrow{E} (D(N_q))') \wedge ((D(N_p))'S(D(N_q))') \tag{‡}$$

We then have $N_p \sim N_q$ from (†) and (‡).

2. Similar to 1, we have $\exists S_i \cdot D(P_i)S_iD(Q_i)$, where S_i is a bisimulation, and the following result:
For any set of events E, whenever there exists a configuration $(D(P_i))'$ such that

$$D(P_i) \xrightarrow{E} (D(P_i))',$$

there exists a $(D(Q_i))'$, such that

$$(D(Q_i) \xrightarrow{E} (D(Q_i))') \wedge ((D(P_i))'S_i(D(Q_i))')$$

Now we define the relationship

$$S = \{\langle D(Or(N_p, \langle P_1, \cdots, P_m\rangle, P_l, T)), \\ D(Or(N_q, \langle Q_1, \cdots, Q_m\rangle, Q_l, T'))\rangle, \text{ where } D(P_i)S_iD(Q_i)\} \\ \cup \ Id$$

It is trivial that S is an equivalence relation.   (∗)

Analogically, to check condition 2 in **Definition 4.3**, we need a formula similar to (‡). It can be divided into two cases:
(a) If the micro-step triggered by E is between the immediate sub-state P_l and P_k, i.e.

$$D(N_p) \xrightarrow{E} (D(N_p))' = D(Or(N_p', \langle P_1, \cdots, P_m \rangle, P_k, T))$$

Because of there is a bijection f between the transitions sets of N_p and N_q which satisfies the three conditions, we have

$$D(N_q) \xrightarrow{E} (D(N_q))' = D(Or(N_q', \langle Q_1, \cdots, Q_m \rangle, Q_k, T'))$$

(b) If the micro-step triggered by E is in the active sub-state P_l, i.e.

$$P_l \xrightarrow{E} P_l'$$

For $P_l \mathcal{S}_l Q_l$, we have there exits Q_l', such that

$$(Q_l \xrightarrow{E} Q_l') \wedge (P_l' \mathcal{S}_l Q_l')$$

We take

$$(D(N_q))' = D(Or(N_q', \langle Q_1, \cdots, Q_m \rangle, Q_l', T'))$$

In both case (a) and case (b) it is trivial that

$$(D(N_q) \xrightarrow{E} (D(N_q))') \wedge ((D(N_p))' \mathcal{S} (D(N_q))') \qquad (**)$$

From $(*)$ and $(**)$, we obtain $N_p \sim N_q$. $\square$

5   Traces

As shown in the **Definition 4.8**, suppose $tr = \langle E_1, E_2, \cdots \rangle$ is a sequence of sets of events. We use $C_1 \xrightarrow{tr} C_2$ to denote the fact that the configuration C_1 evolves into C_2 by performing micro-steps $\langle step_1, step_2, \cdots \rangle$ in turn and the set of positive events from the triggers of the transitions fired in $step_i$ is E_i. In this section we investigate some properties on the level of **macro-step**.

Definition 5.1. We use Π_{ex} to denote all possible external events. Suppose $E \subseteq \Pi_{ex}$ and $C_i = \langle P_i, \nu_i, \phi \rangle$, $i = 1, 2$, we use $C_1 \xRightarrow{E} C_2$ to denote a macro-step from C_1 to C_2 with the set of initial external events E by a sequence of micro-steps, where only the last micro-step is the clock tick σ.

We use $(2^{\Pi_{ex}})^*$ to denote the set of all the possible finite-length sequences of sets of external events. Suppose $tr = \langle E_1, E_2, \cdots, E_m \rangle \in (2^{\Pi_{ex}})^*$. We use also $C_1 \xRightarrow{tr} C_2$ to denote the fact that the configuration C_1 can evolve into C_2 by performing a sequence of macro-steps $\langle Mstep_1, Mstep_2, \cdots, Mstep_m \rangle$ in turn and the set of events E_i is the set of initial events stimulating the $Mstep_i$.

When a finite sequence of sets of external events comes sequentially, a Statechart starts to respond the first set of events from its current configuration. As reactions to this finite sequence of stimuli, it may perform a sequence of transitions which are triggered by these stimuli directly or indirectly, go through a number of macro-steps and reach another configuration eventually, or it may fall into divergence in some macro-step on the way, and is not able to participate the next macro-step. We address these issues in this section.

We give two definitions to formalize the aforementioned ideas.

Definition 5.2 (*Trace*). A trace $tr \in (2^{\Pi_{ex}})^*$ is a finite sequence of external events in which a particular Statechart participates with its environment.

What follows is our definition of specific trace sets. We propose two type of sets with respect to configurations. For a configuration C_P, set $Div(C_P)$ includes all the traces that **may** lead the configuration C_P to divergence, while the another set is $Prg(C_P)$ which includes all traces which definitely lead configuration C_P to a steady configuration. We use Prg to hint that the configuration will progress normally while "consuming" a trace of $Prg(C_P)$ and will be ready to accept other external events.

Definition 5.3 (*Trace Sets*). Suppose P is a Statechart and C_P is one of its configurations with empty set of events, we define two sets of sequences of set of events as follows:

$$Div(C_P) =_{def} \{ tr \in (2^{\Pi_{ex}})^* |$$
$$\exists s, C' \cdot s \prec tr \wedge (C_P \xrightarrow{s} C') \wedge div(C', tr(\#s + 1))\}$$
$$Prg(C_P) =_{def} \{ tr \in (2^{\Pi_{ex}})^* | \exists C' \cdot (C_P \xrightarrow{tr} C'))\}$$

where $s \prec tr$ means s is a proper prefix of tr. We use $div(C', E)$ to represent that C' is divergent after receiving set of events E according to **Rule 3.1**. Note that $\#s$ is the length of s, while $tr(n)$ denotes the nth element of tr.

Form the definition we have the following property immediately.

Lemma 5.4. Suppose C_P is a configuration of a Statechart P with empty set of events, then

$$Prg(C_P) \cup Div(C_P) = (2^{\Pi_{ex}})^*$$

Proof. By **Definition 4.2**, we have the fact that if a trace tr is not in $Div(C_P)$, then there exists a steady configuration C as the end configuration after preforming all the macro-steps triggered by tr. From the transition **Rule 3.1** $\sim$ **3.5**, we can see that only the configuration with the form $\langle P, \nu, \phi \rangle$ can be the end configuration of a macro-step. Therefore tr lies in $Prg(C_P)$. So we have

$$Prg(C_P) \cup Div(C_P) = (2^{\Pi_{ex}})^*$$

$\square$

Two equivalent configurations of Statecharts should have the same trace sets Div and Prg as one may expect. The following theorem tells us the truth.

Theorem 5.5 (*Trace*). Suppose $P \sim Q$ and C_p is the configuration of P with empty set of events. If C_q is the configuration of Q which is equivalent to C_p. Then

$$Div(C_p) = Div(C_q) \quad \text{and} \quad Prg(C_p) = Prg(C_q)$$

Proof. If $tr \in Prg(C_p)$ is a trace, then there exists a configuration C'_p such that

$$C_p \stackrel{tr}{\Longrightarrow} C'_p$$

Because a macro-step can be considered as a sequence of micro-steps, by **Theorem 4.9**, we see that there exists a configuration C'_q, such that

$$C_q \stackrel{tr}{\Longrightarrow} C'_q$$

So $tr \in Prg(C_q)$, Then we have

$$Prg(C_p) \subseteq Prg(C_q)$$

For the same reason , we have

$$Prg(C_q) \subseteq Prg(C_p)$$

So we come to

$$Prg(C_p) = Prg(C_q)$$

From **Lemma 5.4**, we obtain $Div(C_p) = Div(C_q)$. $\qquad\qquad\square$

We considered above the *external traces* or *input traces*, which are provided by the environment. Now we take into account the responses of a statechart to these stimuli from the environment, and introduce the *response traces*.

According to our definition of transition rules, before a clock tick transition, all events generated by those transitions in one macro-step are accumulated in the set of active events. This reflects the reaction of the statechart to environmental stimuli arrived at the beginning of the macrostep. We use it to specify a statechart's response behaviour to the environment.

Definition 5.6 (*Response*). We use $C \stackrel{E/\hat{E}}{\Longrightarrow} C'$ to denote a macro-step from C to C' with the set of initial external events E by a sequence of micro-steps, where only the last micro-step is the clock tick σ, and the set of events in the configuration before the clock tick is $\hat{E}$. We call $\hat{E}$ the set of response events in this macro-step.

Definition 5.7 (*Response Trace*). Suppose P is a Statechart and C_p is one of its configuration with empty set of events. Suppose $tr = \langle E_1, E_2, \cdots, E_m \rangle \in (2^{\Pi_{ex}})^*$ and there is a configuration C' such that $C \stackrel{tr}{\Longrightarrow} C'$. We collect the sets of response events along the way, which form a sequence of sets of events $\hat{tr} = \langle \hat{E}_1, \hat{E}_2, \cdots, \hat{E}_m \rangle \in (2^{\Pi})^*$, and call the sequence a *response trace* of tr with respect to C and C', and denote the fact as $C \stackrel{tr/\hat{tr}}{\Longrightarrow} C'$.

Obviously, due to possible non-determinism, for a certain C and a fixed tr, there might be more than one pair of C' and $\hat{tr}$ such that $C \overset{tr/\hat{tr}}{\Longrightarrow} C'$.

In the remainder of this section, we shall prove that, if two configurations are equivalent, $C_1 \sim C_2$, or two Statecharts are equivalent, $P \sim Q$, then for an external event trace tr, they will generate the same set of response traces.

Lemma 5.8. Suppose $P \sim Q$, C_p is a configuration of P with empty set of events and C_q is a configuration of Q which is equivalent to C_p. Suppose $E \in 2^{\Pi_{ex}}$ and $\hat{E} \in 2^{\Pi}$. Then we have that, if there exists a configuration C'_p of P such that $C_p \overset{E/\hat{E}}{\Longrightarrow} C'_p$, then there exists a configuration C'_q of Q such that $C_q \overset{E/\hat{E}}{\Longrightarrow} C'_q$. That is we have the following commuting diagram:

$$
\begin{array}{ccc}
C_p & \overset{E/\hat{E}}{\Longrightarrow} & C'_p \\
{\scriptstyle\sim}\downarrow & & \downarrow{\scriptstyle\sim} \\
C_q & \overset{E/\hat{E}}{\Longrightarrow} & C'_q
\end{array}
$$

Proof. A macro-step can be considered as a sequence of micro-steps, so if we have $\exists C'_p \cdot C_p \overset{E/\hat{E}}{\Longrightarrow} C'_p$, then by **Theorem 4.9**, we see that

$$\exists C'_q \cdot C_q \overset{E}{\Longrightarrow} C'_q \qquad\qquad (*)$$

Suppose the macro-step from C_p to C'_p is $Mstep_p = \langle step_1, \cdots, step_{k-1}, step_k \rangle$, the macro-step from C_q to C'_q is $Mstep_q = \langle step'_1, \cdots, step'_{k-1}, step'_k \rangle$, and the configuration sequences with respect to these steps are $\langle C_{p,1}, \cdots, C_{p,k-1}, C'_p \rangle$ and $\langle C_{q,1}, \cdots, C_{q,k-1}, C'_q \rangle$ respectively, where $step_i$ and $step'_i$ $(i-1, \cdots, k)$ are all micro-steps. For $\hat{E}$ is the response set of $Mstep_p$, from **Definition 5.6**, we know that the set of events in $C_{p,k-1}$ is $\hat{E}$. For $C_{p,k-1} \sim C_{q,k-1}$, from **Definition 4.3,4.5** we get that the event set of $C_{q,k-1}$ is also $\hat{E}$. So we have $\hat{E}$ is the response set of $Mstep_q$. Then from $(*)$ we have come to

$$\exists C'_q \cdot C_q \overset{E/\hat{E}}{\Longrightarrow} C'_q$$

So there is

$$\exists C'_p \cdot C_p \overset{E/\hat{E}}{\Longrightarrow} C'_p \text{ implies } \exists C'_q \cdot C_q \overset{E/\hat{E}}{\Longrightarrow} C'_q$$

$\square$

Theorem 5.9 (*Response Trace*). Suppose $P \sim Q$, C_p is a configuration of P with empty set of events and C_q is a configuration of Q which is equivalent to C_p. Suppose $tr \in (2^{\Pi_{ex}})^*$ and $\hat{tr} \in (2^{\Pi})^*$ is a sequence with the same length of tr. Then we have that, if there exists a configuration C'_p of P such that $C_p \overset{tr/\hat{tr}}{\Longrightarrow} C'_p$, then there exists a configuration C'_q of Q such that $C_q \overset{tr/\hat{tr}}{\Longrightarrow} C'_q$.

Proof. Suppose $tr = \langle E_1, E_2, \cdots, E_m \rangle$ and $tr = \langle \hat{E}_1, \hat{E}_2, \cdots, \hat{E}_m \rangle$, By **Lemma 5.8** and the following commuting diagram,

$$
\begin{array}{ccccccccccc}
C_p & \xrightarrow{E_1/\hat{E}_1} & C_{p,1} & \xrightarrow{E_2/\hat{E}_2} & C_{p,2} & \xrightarrow{E_3/\hat{E}_3} & \cdots & \xrightarrow{E_{m-1}/\hat{E}_{m-1}} & C_{p,m-1} & \xrightarrow{E_m/\hat{E}_m} & C_p' \\
\sim\downarrow & & \sim\downarrow & & \sim\downarrow & & \sim\downarrow & & \sim\downarrow & & \sim\downarrow \\
C_q & \xrightarrow{E_1/\hat{E}_1} & C_{q,1} & \xrightarrow{E_2/\hat{E}_2} & C_{q,2} & \xrightarrow{E_3/\hat{E}_3} & \cdots & \xrightarrow{E_{m-1}/\hat{E}_{m-1}} & C_{q,m-1} & \xrightarrow{E_m/\hat{E}_m} & C_q'
\end{array}
$$

One can see the existence of C_q'.   □

Corollary 5.10. Given a pair of configurations C_p, C_q with empty sets of events, $C_p \sim C_q$, tr is a sequence of sets of external events. Then the sets of all possible response traces of C_p and C_q with respect to trace tr are the same.

Proof. Using the above theorem it is trivial.   □

Corollary 5.11. Given two Statecharts P and Q, $P \sim Q$, tr is a sequence of sets of external events. Then the sets of all possible response traces of $D(P)$ and $D(Q)$ with respect to trace tr are the same.

6   Related Work

The original Statecharts semantics is present by Harel et al. [6]. It obeys causality and synchrony, but not compositionality. The synchrony implies that the system is definitely faster than its environment, and can always finish computing its response before the next stimulus from the environment arrives. In 1991, A.Pnueli and M.Shalev [14] presented a way of defining the notion of step in the execution of Statecharts. This semantics maintains the synchrony hypothesis. They defined the function $En(\tau)$ and used it to describe the synchrony, causality and global consistency formally. They also gave a step-construction procedure to compute $En(\tau)$ for a Statechart with respect to a certain environment. In 1996, M. Schettini, A.Peron and S.Tini [16] gave a new definition which covered the definition in [14] and included a new restriction named compatibility, such that their step-construction procedure will not fail.

    With regard to a semantics for Statecharts, it is very important whether it is compositional or not. Because the compositionality ensures that the semantics for a Statechart can be defined in terms of its component-charts. This is important especially when only a few components of a large Statechart change, a waste of resources by re-compiling the large Statechart will not take place. Theoretical studies constructed by Huizing [10] showed that one cannot combine the features of causality, synchrony hypothesis and compositionality with a step semantics which labels transitions by sets of "input/output" events. G. Lüttgen, M. von der Beeck and R. Cleaveland [12] presented an approach to define Statecharts' semantics. Their semantics achieved compositionality on the explicit micro-step level and causality and synchrony on the implicit macro-step level. Our semantics is compositional. It adopts an asynchronous time model, in which a macro-step is defined as a sequence of micro-steps taking place instantaneously. To be more intuitive, our semantics obeys local consistency rather than global one. Furthermore, our semantics supports the data-states issues of Statecharts, i.e. the actions in a transition can contain assignments.

In [16], the equivalences of Statecharts are investigated. The authors associated a Labeled Transition System (LTS) with each Statechart term in a syntax directed way, and defined the semantics of Statecharts based on the LTS. They defined a causal order over events to express the causality. Using these notions, they defined four levels of equivalence of Statecharts and proved the properties of congruence respectively. The main difference between our work and what presented in [16] is as follows. The first definition of equivalence in [16] needs a bijection between all possible configurations of the two Statecharts whose equivalence is under consideration. It causes much troublesome in proving the property of congruence. Our concept of equivalence is similar to the second definition of equivalence of [16]. We only need the bisimulation of the default states of the Statecharts, which makes it much easier to prove the congruence property (**Theorem 4.11**). It seems that our definition is weaker in comparison to the first definition of equivalence in [16], but, in fact, it is not. As we have proved in **Theorem 4.9**, our concept has all the expected properties of equivalence stated in the first definition of equivalence in [16] and, at the same time, can get rid of the redundant statements in proving the properties of congruence for that level of equivalence, thus, getting the same results in a much simpler way.

C.A.R.Hoare [8] defined the trace notations of CSP. Many scholars defined the trace notations for other languages, for instance [9,3,13,7], to describe observable behaviours of systems. Borrowing the ideas from these work we define the trace notations for Statecharts as sequences of sets of external stimuli and sequences of responses of the Statechart to these stimuli. Some properties with respect to the trace model for Statecharts are also explored. We believe these definitions can be valuable in further investigation of Statecharts' properties at behavioural level of traces.

7   Conclusions and Future Work

In this paper we have explored a set of transition rules so as to describe the operational semantics of Statecharts. We introduced the bisimulation to illustrate the equivalence between Statecharts' configurations. Ulteriorly we defined the equivalence between Statecharts and studied congruence properties with respect to the construction operators of Statecharts (*And* and *Or* constructions). In the end we introduced the notions of traces of Statecharts. It is foreseeable that we can describe the equivalence of Statecharts at the level of observable traces. As part of future work, the trace model should be further refined to comprise more information on behaviours of Statecharts, like causal orders of events generated in one instant, instantaneous updates of data state. The simulation between Statecharts needs also to be investigated to describe the refinement of Statecharts.

Acknowledgement

We would like to thank anonymous referees for many helpful comments.

References

1. M. von der Beeck, A comparison of Statecharts variants, *Formal Tech. in Real-Time and Fault-Tolerant Systems*, LNCS 863, pp.128-148, Springer-Verlag, 1994.
2. G. Booch, J. Rumbaugh and I. Jacobson, *The Unified Modeling Language User Guide*, Addison-Wesley Longman, Reading, MA, USA, 1998.
3. J. Davies and S. Schneider. A brief history of Timed CSP. *Theoretical Computer Science*, 138:243–271, 1995.
4. D. Harel, Statecharts: a visual formalism for complex systems, *Science of Computer Programming*, 8(3), pp.231-274, 1987.
5. D. Harel and A. Naamad, The STATEMATE semantics of Statecharts, *ACM Trans. on Software Engineering and Methodology*, 5(4), pp.293-333, Oct. 1996.
6. D. Harel, A.Pnueli, J.Schmidt, and R.Sherman, On the formal semantics of Statecharts, *Symp. on Logis in Computer Science*, pp.56-64, IEEE CS Press, 1987.
7. J. He, An algebraic approach to the VERILOG programming, *Proc. of 10th Anniversary Colloquium of the United Nations University / International Institute for Software Technology*, Springer-Verlag, 2002.
8. C. A. R. Hoare, *Communicating Sequential Processes*, Prentice Hall, 1985.
9. C. A. R. Hoare and J. He, *Unifying Theory of Programming*, Prentice Hall, 1998.
10. C. Huizing, *Semantics of Reactive Systems: Comparison and Full Abstraction*, Ph.D. thesis, Eindhoven University of Technology, The Netherlands, 1991.
11. N. G. Leveson, M. Heimdahl, H. Hildreth, and J. Reese, Requirements specifications for process control systems, *IEEE Trans. on Software Engineering*, 20(9), pp.684-707, Sept. 1994.
12. G. Lüttgen, M. von der Beeck, and R. Cleaveland, A compositional approach to Statecharts semantics, NASA/ICASE Report No.2000-12, March 2000.
13. B. Mahony and J. S. Dong. Overview of the semantics of TCOZ. *IFM'99: Integrated Formal Methods*, pp. 66–85. Springer-Verlag, 1999.
14. A. Pnueli and M. Shalev, What is in a step: on the semantics of Statecharts, *Theo. Aspects of Computer Software*, LNCS 526, pp.244-264, Springer-Verlag, 1991.
15. S. Qin and W. N. Chin, Mapping Statecharts to VERILOG for hardware/software co-specification, *FM03: the 12th International FME Symposium (to appear)*, 2003.
16. M. Schettini, A. Peron, and S. Tini, Equivalences of Statecharts, *7th International Conference on Concurrency*, LNCS 1119, pp.687-702, Springer-Verlag, Aug. 1996.

Generic Interacting State Machines and Their Instantiation with Dynamic Features

David von Oheimb and Volkmar Lotz

Siemens AG, Corporate Technology, D-81730 Munich
{David.von.Oheimb,Volkmar.Lotz}@siemens.com

Abstract. Interacting State Machines (ISMs) are used to model reactive systems and to express and verify their properties. They can be seen both as automata exchanging messages simultaneously on multiple buffered ports and as communicating processes with explicit local state.

We introduce generic ISMs, extending the ISM formalism with global state. We give a typical instantiation, namely support for dynamically changing communication. Other instantiations, e.g. an implementation of boxed mobile ambients, can be used alternatively or in combination, which demonstrates the flexibility of the framework. As an application example we model a simple multi-threaded client/server system.

ISMs and all their derivations are formally defined within the theorem prover Isabelle/HOL. The development, textual documentation, and verification of their applications is supported by Isabelle as well, and graphical design and documentation is available via the CASE tool AutoFocus. The conventional state-based approach, its expressiveness and flexibility, and freely available multi-level tool support makes our framework well-suited for practical formal system analysis even in an industrial setting.

Keywords: modeling, verification, composition, semantics, dynamic communication, mobile ambients, Interacting State Machines, Isabelle/HOL, AutoFocus.

1 Introduction

State-based approaches, e.g. [LT89,HLN$^+$90,Spi92,HSSS96,Gur97,EHS97] have turned out to be an adequate means to model and analyze properties of interest in many of today's IT systems, including communication networks, database systems, and industrial control systems. In particular, the authors have introduced basic Interacting State Machines (ISMs) [OL02,Ohe02] and successfully applied them to security analysis, ranging from the specification and validation of security requirements with respect to very abstract system models to verification of low-level protocols. ISMs can intuitively be seen as a variant of I/O automata [LT89] offering high-level transitions allowing for simultaneous, buffered I/O on multiple ports. The resulting concepts have proved to be adequate for supplying formal security models for real-world smart card processor systems and healthcare applications. In particular, the recent version of the LKW security model

J.S. Dong and J. Woodcock (Eds.): ICFEM 2003, LNCS 2885, pp. 144–166, 2003.

for the Infineon SLE 66 smart card chip has been developed using ISMs and their Isabelle [Pau94] tool support, see [OL02] for details.

However, ISMs as introduced so far lack expressiveness wrt. system dynamics. These may occur in a variety of flavors, comprising varying communication interfaces, the activation and deactivation of processes, and changes to the visibility context or execution environment of a component. All of these aspects are of practical relevance, e.g. in a middle-ware system where objects get to know additional communication channels by requesting a directory object, a multi-threaded system where the system components, along with their ports, are created and terminated dynamically, or a mobile agent system where the current execution environment determines the communication abilities of a hosted agent.

Driven by the above motivation, we generalize ISMs, introducing global state and commands that generic ISMs can execute in order to change it. By instantiating generic ISMs in a suitable way, one can handle dynamic communication interfaces as well as dynamic component contexts. Such extensions may be hierarchical or orthogonal, or they may combine other extensions while interrelating features as appropriate. The global state may express e.g. port ownership and the activation status of ports and ISMs, with the commands allowing to change port ownership and to (de-)activate ISMs and ports. We thus arrive at dynamic ISMs (dISMs). Alternatively, we may borrow the concepts of boxed ambients [BCC01] to treat dynamic contexts. Doing so, the global state is given by an ambient structure whose nodes refer to those ISMs that share the same administrative domain and thus can interact with each other. Commands include introducing and deleting contexts and moving them around. The resulting automata are called Ambient ISMs (AmbISMs). By combining the two concepts in the appropriate way, we arrive at dynamic Ambient ISMs (dAmbISMs). Figure 1 shows how the just mentioned dynamic extensions relate. The advantage of this "construction kit" approach is flexibility: the user may select either one of the two styles of dynamics (if not both of them are required) or their combination.

Generic ISMs (and their descendants) are supported by the same tools as basic ISMs: in a typical application of our framework, the user first specifies a system graphically with the CASE tool AutoFocus [HSSS96], then translates the model to theories of the theorem prover Isabelle/HOL [Pau94] using a tool program [Nan02,ON02], and then uses the facilities of Isabelle for conducting proofs and for textual documentation.

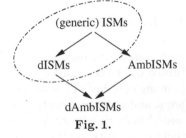

Fig. 1.

In this paper, we define generic and dynamic ISMs in detail and just introduce the concepts of ambient and dynamic ambient ISMs. The formal definition of the latter is subject of an accompanying paper [KO03]. The present paper is structured as follows. §2 formally defines generic ISMs and describes their representation with AutoFocus and Isabelle/HOL. In §3, we informally describe the different extensions and lay out the foundations of their semantics. A full definition of dynamic ISMs is given in §4. §5 contains a typical example of their use, namely a model of a multi-threaded client-server system where threads are activated dynamically on demand, and §6 comments on related and future work.

2   Generic Interacting State Machines (ISMs)

In §2.1 we introduce the notion of *generic ISMs*, which is a generalized (and partially simplified) version of the original ISM notion [Ohe02]. §2.2 gives the details of the semantics, which (as well as §4) may be safely skipped by readers solely interested in ISM application. Next, we describe how ISMs are represented as AutoFocus diagrams (in §2.3) and in Isabelle/HOL theories (in §2.4).

2.1   Concepts

An *Interacting State Machine (ISM)* is an automaton whose state transitions may involve multiple input and output simultaneously on any number of ports. As the name suggests, the key concepts of ISMs are states (and in particular the transitions between them) and interaction. By *interaction* we mean explicit buffered communication via named ports (which are also called connections), where on each *port*, (typically) one receiver listens to possibly many senders.

Any number of ISMs may be composed in parallel by interleaving their transitions and forming I/O connections among peer ISMs. The local state of the resulting ISM is essentially the Cartesian product of the local states of its components. The top-level composition is called an ISM *system*. It may hold additional *global state*, which may be affected by *commands* contained in the transitions of any (sub-)component.

A *configuration* of an ISM consists of its input buffer state and local state. The *local state* may have arbitrary structure but typically is the Cartesian product of a *control state* which is of finite type and a *data state* which is a record of named fields representing local variables. Each ISM has a single[1] local *initial state*.

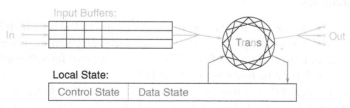

Fig. 2. ISM structure.

The input buffers of an ISM are a family of (unbounded) message FIFOs, indexed by port names. The buffers are not actually part of an ISM but exist

---

[1] If a non-singleton set of initial states is required, this may be simulated by nonde-terministic spontaneous transitions from a single dummy initial state.

merely as intermediate data structures within parallel composition during ISM runs. Input buffers can (but in most applications should not) be shared among ISMs, which leads to competition on the input without fairness constraints.

Message exchange is triggered by an output operation of any ISM within the system. Input from the environment may be modeled with suitable ISMs. Inputs cannot be blocked, i.e. they may occur at any time, appending the received value to the corresponding FIFO. Values stored in the input buffers related to an ISM are received and processed by the ISM when it is ready to do so.

The actions of ISMs are given as user-defined *transitions*, which may be nondeterministic and can be specified in any relational style. Thus for each transition the user has the choice to define it in an operational (i.e., executable) or axiomatic (i.e., property-oriented) fashion or a mixture of the two. Transition rules specify that – potentially under some precondition that typically includes matching of messages in the input buffers – the ISM consumes some input, makes a local state transition, issues a list of commands affecting the global state, and produces some output. The output is appended to the respective input buffers specified by port names. Direct or indirect feedback is possible. Multicast is not directly supported but may be explicitly modeled easily.

A *run* of an ISM system is any prefix of the sequence of configurations reachable from the initial configuration. The length of a run is not bounded but finite. Finiteness allows for a simple trace semantics, but on the other hand implies that we cannot handle liveness properties. Yet we do not feel this as a real restriction because most practically relevant properties are essentially safety properties: if at all they involve guarantees about the existence of future events, these typically involve timeouts.

Transitions of different ISMs that are composed in parallel cannot directly interfere with each other but are related only by the causality wrt. the messages interchanged, and by the effects of commands on the global state which may in effect block certain transitions. Execution gets stuck (i.e., deadlocks) when there is no component that can perform any step. As is typical for reactive systems, there is no built-in notion of final or accepting states.

2.2   Semantics

This subsection gives the logical meaning of (generic) ISMs, which is both an extension and a slight simplification of the definitions given in [Ohe02]. As the modifications pervade all parts of the ISM definitions, and for self-containedness, it appears mandatory to rephrase all of them.

First some general remarks on the presentation: all definitions and proofs have been developed as a hierarchy of Isabelle/HOL theories and machine-checked using this tool. One important effect of this approach is that many kinds of mistakes like type mismatches can be ruled out. Using the LATEX documentation feature of Isabelle would even preclude typographic slips in the presentation but on the other hand would introduce some technicalities many readers would not be familiar with. Therefore, we give the semantics in the traditional "mathematical" style in order to enhance readability. We sometimes make use of λ-abstraction borrowed from the λ-calculus, but write (multi-argument) function application in the conventional form, e.g. $f(a, b, c)$. Occasionally we make use of partial application (aka. *currying*), such that, in the example just given, $f(a, b)$ is an intermediate function value that requires a third parameter to be given before yielding the actual function result.

Message Families. Let $\mathcal{M}$ be the type of all messages potentially exchanged by ISMs and $\mathcal{P}$ the type of port names. Then the *message families*, which are used to denote both input[2] buffers and input/output patterns, have type $MSGs = \mathcal{P} \to \mathcal{M}^*$ where $\mathcal{M}^*$ is any finite sequence of elements of $\mathcal{M}$. We will make use of the following operations on message families:

- the term $\underline{\mathcal{U}}$ denotes the empty message family $\lambda p. \langle \rangle$ where $\langle \rangle$ denotes the empty sequence
- the term $mdom(m)$ abbreviates $\{p. \, m(p) \neq \langle \rangle\}$, i.e. the domain of m
- the infix operation $.@.$ concatenates two message families m and n pointwise: $(m \, .@. \, n)(p) = m(p) \, @ \, n(p)$

States and Transitions. Let $\mathcal{C}$ be the type of commands. Then the set of ISM transitions has type $TRANS(\mathcal{C}, \Sigma) = \wp((MSGs \times \Sigma) \times \mathcal{C} \times (MSGs \times \Sigma))$ where the parameter Σ stands for the type of the local state and the two occurrences of $MSGs$ stand for input and output patterns, respectively. Each element has the form $((i, \sigma), c, (o, \sigma'))$ and means that the ISM can (nondeterministically) perform a step from local state σ to σ', consuming input i, executing command c, and producing output o. Simultaneous input and/or output on multiple channels can be specified because both i and o each denote whole message families. In contrast to the original definition of ISMs [Ohe02], within a transition, input is described by patterns of messages consumed in the given step — not by a transition between the state of the input buffer before and after the transition. This simplifies the definition of single ISMs and shifts the concept of input buffering to the places where it is indispensable: at the definitions of parallel composition and automata runs.

Elementary ISMs. An ISM is given as a quadruple[3] $a = (In(a), Out(a), \sigma_0(a), Trans(a))$ of type $ISM(\mathcal{C}, \Sigma) = \wp(\mathcal{P}) \times \wp(\mathcal{P}) \times \Sigma \times TRANS(\mathcal{C}, \Sigma)$ where

- $In(a)$ is the set of input port names
- $Out(a)$ is the set of output port names
- $\sigma_0(a)$ is the initial local state
- $Trans(a)$ is the transition relation

---

[2] Recall that output buffers are not required.

[3] The definition pattern $x = (sel_1(x), sel_2(x), \ldots)$ should not be understood as a recursive definition of x but as a shorthand introducing a tuple with typical name x and with selectors (i.e., projection functions) sel_1, sel_2, ...

Such an ISM is *well-formed* iff all the port names actually used in the transitions for input or output respect the I/O interface of the ISM, i.e. $ipns(a) \subseteq In(a)$ and $opns(a) \subseteq Out(a)$ where

- $ipns(a) = \bigcup_{t \in Trans(a)} mdom((\lambda((i, \sigma), c, (o, \sigma')).\ i)(t))$
- $opns(a) = \bigcup_{t \in Trans(a)} mdom((\lambda((i, \sigma), c, (o, \sigma')).\ o)(t))$

Note that $In(a)$ and $Out(a)$ may overlap, which allows for direct feedback within parallel composition.

Runs. Below we will define composite ISM runs, i.e. the parallel composition and execution of a family of ISMs, directly in one step. Nevertheless, we first define the two notions of ISM runs and parallel composition independently. Defining parallel composition in isolation not only makes it easier to understand but also enables hierarchical analysis and design.

The *open runs* of an ISM a, denoted by $Runs(a) \in \wp(\Sigma^*)$, are finite sequences of states that are inductively defined as

$$\overline{\langle \sigma_0(a) \rangle \in Runs(a)}$$

$$\frac{\text{centering } ss ^\frown \sigma \in Runs(a)}{ss ^\frown \sigma ^\frown \sigma' \in Runs(a)}$$

The operator $^\frown$ appends elements to a sequence. Commands c are ignored here as we consider global state only for composite runs.

This form of runs is called *open* because in each step the environment provides arbitrary input to the ISM, and any output of the ISM is discarded. If feedback from output to input is desired, one can achieve this by applying the parallel composition operator to the singleton family of ISMs consisting just of a, described next.

Parallel Composition. Any number of ISMs can be combined in parallel to form a single composite ISM, which may be further combined with others, etc.

The *parallel composition* $\|_{i \in I} A_i$ of a family of ISMs $A = (A_i)_{i \in I}$ is an ISM of type $ISM(\mathcal{C}, CONF(\Pi_{i \in I} \Sigma_i))$ where for any X, the type of an ISM *configuration* $CONF(X)$ is defined as $MSGs \times X$. Here $MSGs$ stands for the type of input buffers. The composite ISM is defined as the quadruple $(AllIn(A) \backslash AllOut(A),$ $AllOut(A) \backslash AllIn(A),\ (\varnothing, S_0(A)),\ PTrans(A))$ where

- $AllIn(A) = \bigcup_{i \in I} In(A_i)$
- $AllOut(A) = \bigcup_{i \in I} Out(A_i)$
- $\varnothing$ denotes the initially empty input buffers, which are used to handle I/O among peers as well as direct feedback
- $S_0(A) = \Pi_{i \in I}(\sigma_0(A_i))$ is the Cartesian product of all initial local states
- $PTrans(A)$ of type $TRANS(\mathcal{C}, CONF(\Pi_{i \in I} \Sigma_i))$ is the parallel composition of their transition relations.

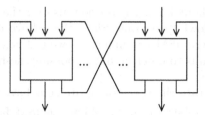

Fig. 3. General pattern of feedback within parallel composition.

The pre- and post-states in the composed transition relation refer not only to the Cartesian product of the local states involved but also to a message family b. As already mentioned above for the initial state, the role of b is to buffer internal I/O. Apart from this, the composed transition relation is defined simply as the interleaving of the transitions of the component ISMs:

$$\frac{j \in I \\ ((i, \sigma), c, (o, \sigma')) \in \mathit{Trans}(A_j)}{((i_{|\overline{\mathit{AllOut}(A)}}, (i_{|\mathit{AllOut}(A)} \cdot @. \, b, S[j := \sigma \,])), c, \\ (o_{|\overline{\mathit{AllIn}(A)}}, (b \cdot @. \, o_{|\mathit{AllIn}(A)}, \; S[j := \sigma'\,]))) \in \mathit{PTrans}(A)}$$

where

- $S[j := \sigma]$ denotes the replacement of the j-th component of the tuple S by σ
- $m_{|P}$ denotes the restriction $\lambda p.$ if $p \in P$ then $m(p)$ else $\langle\rangle$ of the message family m to the set of ports P
- $o_{|\overline{\mathit{AllIn}(A)}}$ denotes those parts of the output o provided to any outer ISM
- $o_{|\mathit{AllIn}(A)}$ denotes the internal output to peer ISMs or direct feedback, which is added to the current buffer contents b

Note that commands c are simply forwarded to the outer level of transitions.

A parallel composition is *well-formed* iff the inputs of the individual components do not overlap: $\forall i \, j. \, i \neq j \longrightarrow \mathit{In}(A_i) \cap \mathit{In}(A_j) = \emptyset$. On the other hand, outputs may overlap, which allows the outputs of different ISMs to interleave nondeterministically.

A family A of ISMs is called *closed* iff $\mathit{AllIn}(A) = \mathit{AllOut}(A)$, i.e. there is no interaction with any outside ISMs. If a system is modeled with a closed ISM family and input from the environment is important, this may be modeled with an ISM that belongs to the family and does nothing but generating all possible input patterns.

When composing ISMs, it is occasionally necessary to prevent name clashes or to hide connections, which can be achieved by suitable renaming of ports.

Composite Runs. We define ISM runs not only for single (possibly composite) ISMs but also directly for closed families of ISMs intended to run in parallel. The below definition is generic wrt. ISM commands and the global state Γ, such that it may be used without further extension also for the specialized styles of ISMs defined in the following sections. Since the above definition of parallel composition is generic wrt. ISM commands as well, it may be used in combination with composite runs to describe inner (possibly nested) levels of parallel composition.

For handling global state changes, composite runs have three parameters:

- a function $As(\gamma) = (As(\gamma)_i)_{i \in I(\gamma)}$ yielding an ISM family for any global state γ, which enables dynamic changes to the ISM system
- the initial global state γ_0
- a transition relation $gtrans(j)$ that takes as its parameter the index of the ISM whose transition is currently performed and yields a transition between the global pre-state γ, the command c, and the global post-state γ'

The set of all possible *composite runs* is denoted by $CRuns(As, \gamma_0, gtrans)$ and has type $\wp((CONF(\Gamma \times \Pi_{i \in I} \Sigma_i))^*)$ corresponding to the generic ISM type $ISM(\mathcal{C}, \Gamma \times \Pi_{i \in I} \Sigma_i)$. Its elements are finite sequences of configurations, inductively defined as

$$\overline{\langle (\varnothing, (\gamma_0, S_0(As(\gamma_0)))) \rangle \in CRuns(As, \gamma_0, gtrans)}$$

$$\frac{
\begin{array}{c}
j \in I(\gamma) \\
cs ^\frown (i\ .@.\ b, (\gamma, S[j := \sigma])) \in CRuns(As, \gamma_0, gtrans) \\
((i, \sigma), c, (o, \sigma')) \in Trans(As(\gamma)_j) \\
mdom(i) \subseteq In(As(\gamma)_j) \cap AllOut(As(\gamma)) \\
mdom(o) \subseteq Out(As(\gamma)_j) \cap AllIn(As(\gamma)) \\
(\gamma, c, \gamma') \in gtrans(j)
\end{array}
}{
cs ^\frown (i\ .@.\ b, (\gamma, S[j := \sigma])) ^\frown (b\ .@.\ o, (\gamma', S[j := \sigma'])) \in CRuns(As, \gamma_0, gtrans)
}$$

Note that the changes to the local state σ and the global state γ are independent of each other, except that the transition $Trans(As(\gamma)_j)$ may block $gtrans(j)$ and vice versa. The restrictions on the input and output domains are the dynamic counterparts for the static well-formedness of the family components and the closedness of the system. They ensure in particular that ISMs can use only ports they are allowed to according to their I/O interface which may depend on the current global state[4]. An ISM family function – together with the initial global state and the global transition associated with it – that fulfills the restrictions on the input and output domains already by its construction is called *dynamically closed*.

Traces of composite runs have the form $\langle (\varnothing, (\gamma_0, S_0(As(\gamma_0)))), (b_1, (\gamma_1, S_1)),$ $(b_2, (\gamma_2, S_2)), \dots \rangle$ where each element of the sequence is a nested tuple of the current input buffer contents, the current global state, and the Cartesian product of all the currently relevant local states.

---

[4] Note that this restriction is defined wrt. γ and not γ' for both input and output, which makes the definition technically slightly simpler. A viable alternative would be to use instead γ' for restricting the output, which would implement the idea that the effects of the command c are already visible to the output operations.

One can show that composite runs of any closed family $As(\gamma)$ of well-formed ISMs are equivalent to the runs of the parallel composition of the same family if the global transition relation is the identity and the global state is projected away from the traces:

$$wf\_isms(As(\gamma)) \wedge closed(As(\gamma)) \longrightarrow Runs(\|_{i \in I(\gamma)} As(\gamma)_i) =$$
$$\{map_{(\lambda(b,\gamma,\sigma).\ (b,\sigma))}(cs) \mid cs \in CRuns(As, \gamma, (\lambda i.\ \{(\gamma, c, \gamma')\mid \gamma = \gamma'\}))\}$$

2.3 Graphical Representation

When designing and presenting system models, a graphical representation is very helpful since it gives a good overview of the system structure and a quick intuition about its behavior. This is particularly important in an industrial setting: models are developed in collaboration with clients and documented for their further use, where strong familiarity with formal notations cannot be assumed.

Unfortunately, we do not have a graphical tool available that could cover the dynamic port connections and ambient structures described in the following sections. Nevertheless, we have designed the structure of generic ISMs in a way such that their basic features can be displayed using the CASE tool AutoFocus.

One may use AutoFocus as a graphical front-end to our Isabelle implementation of ISMs: the user first specifies ISMs using AutoFocus and translates them into suitable Isabelle theory files, described in §2.4 below, utilizing a tool program [Nan02,ON02]. ISM commands, which are not directly supported by AutoFocus automata, may be simulated by output to special channels.

AutoFocus [HSSS96] is a freely available prototype CASE tool for specification and simulation of distributed systems. Components and their behavior are specified by a combination of *System Structure Diagrams (SSDs)*, *State Transition Diagrams (STDs)* and auxiliary *Data Type Definitions (DTDs)*. Their execution is visualized using *Extended Event Traces (EETs)*.

As an illustrating example, take a multi-threaded client/server architecture: a server spawns a new working thread for each request received from a client. The system structure diagram in Figure 4 shows one client, the server, and two threads with their local variables and the named connections between them, all including type information. The meaning of the diagram, i.e. the mapping to the ISM semantics, should be obvious.

The state transition diagram in Figure 5 shows the three control states of a Thread ISM and the transitions between them, which have the general format precondition : inputs : outputs : assignments. Each input is given by a port name, the ? symbol, and a message pattern, while each output is given by a port name, the ! symbol, and a message value. The initial control state is marked with a black bullet. The output to the special port cmd represents dynamic ISM commands as described in §4. The example will be described in detail in §5.

The simulation, code generation and model checking capabilities of AutoFocus cannot be used for (our extended versions of) ISMs because its underlying semantics is clock-synchronous and does not deal with commands and global state. Anyway, if one is interested mainly in the graphical capabilities of AutoFocus, the AutoFocus syntax is general enough to cover most aspects of ISMs.

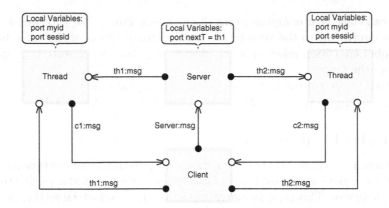

Fig. 4. Client/Server System Structure Diagram.

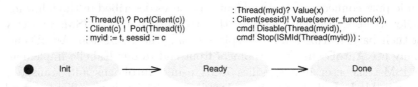

Fig. 5. Client/Server State Transition Diagram: **Thread**

2.4   Isabelle/HOL Representation

When aiming at rigorous formal modeling or even system verification, tools performing syntactic checks, type checks, and mechanized proofs are essential. We employ the theorem proving system Isabelle/HOL because of excellent experience with this tool.

Isabelle [Pau94] is a generic interactive theorem prover that has been instantiated to many logics, in particular the very practical *Higher-Order Logic (HOL)*. Despite of one nuisance[5], we consider Isabelle/HOL the most flexible and mature modeling and verification environment available. Using it, system properties can be expressed easily and adequately and can be verified using powerful proof methods. Furthermore, Isabelle offers good facilities for textual presentation and documentation.

ISMs can be defined in special sections of Isabelle theories. This abstract representation has essentially a one-to-one correspondence to the AutoFocus representation. The standard interpretation of these syntactical entities is the

---

[5] The only drawback of Isabelle/HOL for applications like ours is the lack of dependent types: for each system modeled there is a single type of message contents into which all message data has to be injected, and the same holds for the local ISM states. The alternative prover PVS supports dependent types, but on the other hand it is less flexible, in particular, user-defined theory sections are not possible.

meta theory described in §2.2. This theory is formalized as a hierarchy of Isabelle theories, to which also the tool program [Nan02] refers.

An ISM section is introduced by the keyword **ism** and has the following general structure[6]:

```
ism name =
  ports pn_type
    inputs    I_pns
    outputs   O_pns
  messages msg_type
  [commands cmd_type [default cmd_expr']]
    states    [state_type]
    [control cs_type [init cs_expr0]]
    [data     ds_type [init ds_expr0] [name ds_name]]
  [transitions
    (tr_name [attrs]: [cs_expr -> cs_expr']
    [pre   (bool_expr)+]
    [in    (I_pn I_msgs)+]
    [out   (O_pn O_msgs)+]
    [cmd   cmd_expr]
    [post  ((lvar_name := expr)+ | ds_expr')]
    )+
  ]
```

The meaning of the individual parts is as follows.

- The type expression *pn_type* gives the Isabelle/HOL type of the port names, while *I_pns* and *O_pns* denote the set of input and output port names, respectively. If ports can be changed dynamically, like with dynamic ISMs, the sets given here specify the initial or maximal interface.
- The type expression *msg_type* gives the type of the messages, which is typically an algebraic datatype with a constructor for each kind of message.
- The optional *cmd_type* specifies the type of ISM commands. It must be given if commands are used in the transitions. The optional default command *cmd_expr'*, which typically is the empty list of commands, can be used to shorten the specification of transitions that do not actually issue commands.
- The optional *state_type* should be given if the current ISM forms part of a parallel composition and the state types of the ISMs involved differ. In this case, *state_type* should be a free algebraic datatype with a constructor for each state type of the ISMs involved.
  The type expressions *cs_type* and *ds_type* give the types of the control and data state, respectively, while the optional terms *cs_expr0* and *ds_expr0* specify their initial values — if not given, they default to some arbitrary value. Either (i.e., not both) the control state or the data state may be absent.
  The optional logical variable name *ds_name*, which defaults to *s*, may be used to refer to the whole data state within transition rules.

---

[6] *[...]* marks optional parts, *(...)+* means one or more comma-delimited occurrences.

Transitions are given via named rules where *attrs* is an optional list of attributes, e.g. [**intro**]. The control states (if any) before and after the transition are specified by the expressions[7] *cs_expr* and *cs_expr'*.

Expressions within a rule may refer to the logical data state variable mentioned above. In particular, assuming that **s** is the name of the data state variable, then the value of any local variable **lvar** of the ISM may be referred to by **lvar s**. The scope of free variables appearing in a rule is the whole rule, i.e. free variables are implicitly universally quantified (immediately) outside each rule. All the following parts of a transition rule are optional:

- The **pre** part contains guard expressions *bool_expr*, i.e. preconditions constraining the enabledness of a transition.
- The **in** part gives input port names *I_pn*, each in conjunction with a list *I_msgs* of message patterns expected to be present in the corresponding input buffer. When an ISM executes a transition, any free variables in message patterns are bound to the actual values that have been input. Each port name should be used at most once within each **in** part. Any input port not explicitly mentioned is left untouched.
- The **out** part gives output port names *O_pns*, each in conjunction with an expression *O_msgs* denoting a list of values designated for output to the corresponding port. Each port name should be used at most once within each **out** part. Any output port not mentioned does not obtain new output.
- The **cmd** part gives the ISM command *cmd_expr* associated with the current transition. Such a command can be given in each transition if the **commands** subsection is present.
- The **post** part describes assignments of values *expr* to the local variables *lvar_name* of the data state. Variables not mentioned remain invariant. Alternatively, an expression *ds_expr'* may be given that represents the entire new data state after the transition. Assignments to the local variables suit an operational style, whereas an axiomatic style can be achieved using *ds_expr'* (in conjunction with suitable constraints in the preconditions).

An **ism** theory section is translated to Isabelle/HOL concepts in a straightforward way using an extension to Isabelle, as described in [Nan02]. In particular, each ISM section is translated to a record definition with the appropriate fields, the most complex one being the transition relation, which is defined via an inductive (but not actually recursive) definition.

The meta theory of ISMs that we have defined in Isabelle/HOL includes all concepts mentioned in §2.2, in particular well-formedness, renaming, parallel composition, runs, and composite runs. Further auxiliary concepts are introduced as well, in particular reachability and induction schemes related to ISM runs. The characteristic properties of these concepts, as required for system verification, are derived within Isabelle/HOL. All details of the meta theory may be found in [ON02]. Example **ism** sections will be given in §5.

---

[7] These need not be constant but may contain also variables, which is useful for modeling generic transitions. In this case, one such transition has to be represented by a set of transitions within AutoFocus.

3 Extensions

In this section we give a conceptual overview of the instantiations of generic ISMs available so far, namely by dynamic ports and running state of ISMs, by ambient structures, and the combination of these features.

3.1 Dynamic ISMs

Dynamic ISMs (dISMs) are an instantiation of generic ISMs offering dynamic creation, transfer, enabling and disabling of ports. They also offer activation and deactivation of dISMs. This may be used to emulate ISM creation and deletion, provided that all possible ISMs of the desired form are part of the system. Note that "genuine" creation and deletion would not only be beyond the limits of the underlying logic and its type system, but also less general: it would not give the possibility to "reawaken" ISMs. These dynamic features show the power of the generalization of ISMs. An application example that makes use of all these features is given in §5.

A system of dynamic ISMs uses the global state to keep track of the currently running dISMs, enabled ports, and port ownership. Changes to this state are made by members of the system issuing suitable commands: a dynamic ISM may request that a dISM not yet running is activated or a running dISM (including itself) is stopped. Moreover, a dynamic ISM may create a new port and become its initial owner. An owner of a port may receive input on the port, allow or forbid others to output to it, or convey it to any other dISM. The facility to enable or disable ports can be used to model e.g. flow control.

3.2 Ambient ISMs

An instantiation of generic ISMs quite different from dynamic ISMs are *Ambient ISMs (AmbISMs)* [KO03]. They give a novel form of operational semantics to the ambient calculus [CG98] where we extend the ability to communicate along the lines of boxed ambients [BCC01]. Most importantly, by combining ambient processes with ISMs, we introduce a concept of process state.

Ambients are nested administrative domains that contain *processes* which (in our case) are ISMs. As usual, the ambient structure determines the ability of the processes to communicate with each other. Ambients are *mobile* in the sense that an ISM may move the ambient it belongs to, together with all ISMs and sub-ambients contained in it, out of the parent ambient or into a sibling. Moreover, an ambient may be deleted ("opened") such that its contents are poured into the surrounding ambient, or a new ambient may be created as a child of the current one. Finally, (new) ISMs may be assigned to ambients.

All these operations are implemented by ISM commands manipulating a particular instantiation of the global state, which is given by a tree structure representing the ambient hierarchy.

In the ambient literature, ambient operations are called *capabilities* since their "possession" can be seen as a qualification to perform the respective action.

Semantically speaking, the qualification simply boils down to knowing the name of the ambient involved.

3.3   Dynamic Ambient ISMs

As the name suggests, *dynamic Ambient ISMs (dAmbISMs)* [KO03] combine dynamic ISMs and Ambient ISMs.

Dynamic Ambient ISMs inherit port handling and dAmbISM (de-)activation from dynamic ISMs and ambients from Ambient ISMs. The concepts are mostly orthogonal, except for one new feature: it is reasonable to offer the operations that affect other dAmbISMs j (by activating or deactivating them or conveying ports to them) only to dAmbISMs that are in the vicinity of j, by restricting the respective dISM commands. We call this *locality* of dAmbISM manipulation.

We have taken care in designing dynamic ISMs and Ambient ISMs such that their combination is painless both on implementation and application levels.

4   Semantics of Dynamic ISMs

In this section, we define the semantics of dynamic ISMs in detail and comment on some of their properties. In doing so, we build immediately on the definitions given in §2.2. Readers focusing on ISM application may just note the six dynamic ISM commands (with their obvious parameters) and skip the details.

Dynamic State and Commands. The global state of dynamic ISMs has the form $\delta = (running(\delta), enabled(\delta), owned(\delta))$, instantiating the generic global state Γ to $dSTATE = \wp(\Im) \times \wp(\mathcal{P}) \times (\Im \to \wp(\mathcal{P}))$ where $\Im$ is the type of dISM identifiers. $running(\delta)$ is the set of dISMs currently active, $enabled(\delta)$ the set of ports currently enabled, and $owned(\delta, i)$ the set of ports currently owned by the dISM i.

The ISM type parameter $\mathcal{C}$ gets instantiated to dynamic ISM commands $dCMD^*$ where $dCMD = \{Run(i)|i \in \Im\} \cup \{Stop(i)|i \in \Im\} \cup \{New(p)|p \in \mathcal{P}\} \cup \{Convey(p,i)|p \in \mathcal{P} \wedge i \in \Im\} \cup \{Enable(p)|p \in \mathcal{P}\} \cup \{Disable(p)|p \in \mathcal{P}\}$.

Dynamic Transitions. Let i be the current dISM and js be the set of dISMs that it is allowed to start or stop or convey ports to. The global transition relation $dTrans(js, i)$ is defined as $\{(\delta, dcmds, \delta') \mid i \in running(\delta) \wedge \delta \xrightarrow{i:js:dcmds} {}^* \delta'\}$ where the single-step command execution relation $\delta \xrightarrow{i:js:dcmd} \delta'$ means that the command $dcmd$ issued by i transfers the dynamic state δ to δ', as defined by the rules

$$\frac{j \notin running(\delta) \ \wedge \ j \in js}{\delta \xrightarrow{i:js:Run(j)} \delta(\!|running := running(\delta) \cup \{j\}|\!)}$$

$$\frac{j \in running(\delta) \ \wedge \ j \in js}{\delta \xrightarrow{i:js:Stop(j)} \delta(\!|running := running(\delta) \setminus \{j\}|\!)}$$

$$\frac{p \in owned(\delta, i) \ \wedge \ p \notin enabled(\delta)}{\delta \xrightarrow{i:js:Enable(p)} \delta (\!| enabled := enabled(\delta) \cup \{p\} |\!)}$$

$$\frac{p \in owned(\delta, i) \ \wedge \ p \in enabled(\delta)}{\delta \xrightarrow{i:js:Disable(p)} \delta (\!| enabled := enabled(\delta) \setminus \{p\} |\!)}$$

$$\frac{p \notin \bigcup i. \ owned(\delta, i)}{\delta \xrightarrow{i:js:New(p)} \delta (\!| owned := ((owned(\delta))[i := owned(\delta, i) \cup \{p\}] |\!)}$$

$$\frac{p \in owned(\delta, i) \ \wedge \ p \notin owned(\delta, j) \ \wedge \ j \in js}{\delta \xrightarrow{i:js:Convey(p,j)} \delta (\!| owned := ((owned(\delta))[j := owned(\delta, j) \cup \{p\},}$$
$$i := owned(\delta, i) \setminus \{p\}]) |\!)$$

where $\_(\!| \_ := \_ |\!)$ is the component update operator on tuples.

Marking non-existing dISMs as running is possible but harmless. A dISM j may be put into the running state only if it is not currently running and stopped only if it is currently running. Ports may be conveyed also to dISMs not currently running. Common to the $Run(j)$, $Stop(j)$, and $Convey(p, j)$ commands is that the range of ISMs j affected by them can be restricted by the set js. In the definition of $dCRuns$ below, js is instantiated to the universal set (implying no restrictions), but in the definition of dynamic Ambient ISMs [KO03], js is used to implement a locality constraint.

A port p may be enabled only if it is not currently enabled and disabled only if it is currently enabled. Only a current owner may receive from, enable, disable, and convey a port. Freshness of a new port is guaranteed by requiring that it is not currently owned by any dISM. The definition of set_In_Out below implies that input may be received also from ports not currently enabled, while output may be sent only to enabled ports owned by currently running dISMs. The initial input interface of an ISM determines its initial port ownership, whereas the initial output interface serves as an upper limit of the output interface throughout the life of the ISM.

Composite Runs. Finally, we instantiate the generic composite runs operator for ISMs according to the needs of dynamic ISMs: for any dISM family A and any set $r \subseteq I$ of ISM identifiers describing those dISMs that shall be running initially, $dCRuns(A, r)$ gives the (set of traces of) composite runs of dynamic ISMs. It has type $\wp((CONF(dSTATE \times \Pi_{i \in I} \Sigma_i))^*)$, corresponding to the dISM type $ISM(dCMD^*, dSTATE \times \Pi_{i \in I} \Sigma_i))$, and is defined as

$$dCRuns(A, r) \equiv CRuns((set\_In\_Out(A)), init\_dSTATE(A, r), (dTrans(\overline{\emptyset})))$$

where

- $\overline{\emptyset}$ is the complement of the empty set, i.e. the universal set.
- $init\_dSTATE(A, r) = (r, \overline{\emptyset}, (\lambda i. \ if \ i \in I \ then \ In(A_i) \ else \ \emptyset))$ yields the initial dynamic state where the set of running dISMs is r, all ports (even those not yet existing) are enabled, and port ownership is according to the input interfaces of the members of A.

– $set\_In\_Out(A, \delta) = (A_i(\![In := owned(\delta, i), Out := Out(A_i) \cap enabled(\delta) \cap \bigcup_{j \in running(\delta)} owned(\delta, j)]\!))_{i \in I}$ transforms the initial ISM family A according to the dynamic state δ by setting the input interface of each member i to the ports it currently owns and the output interface to the subset of the initial output ports that are currently enabled and owned by some running dISM j.

As a consequence of these definitions, and the generic definition of *CRuns*, a family A of dISMs runs as follows. Initially, a subset r of the members of A is active, all ports are enabled, and port ownership is determined by the corresponding input interfaces. According to this initial dynamic state δ_0 produced by *init_dSTATE*, a new dISM family A' is determined by *set_In_Out*. When a member of A' performs a transition, the dynamic commands contained in the transition transform the dynamic state to δ_1, from which the next dISM family A'' is determined and used for the next transition, and so on.

Basic Properties. Since port ownership is used to defined the input interface of the ISMs, the notion of well-formedness of parallel compositions introduced in §2.2 means in the context of dynamic ISMs that port ownership is unique. This nice property is preserved by the dynamic commands, as can be seen easily: in the case of port creation, only one dISM becomes the owner of the new port, and in the case of port transfer, port ownership is removed from the initial owner and given to a single new owner. All other commands do not affect port ownership.

According to the definition of *CRuns*, the ports that a dynamic ISM is allowed to use in its transitions are determined by the initial dynamic state of the transition at hand. This implies for example that ports newly created by (the commands part) of a transition can be communicated to peer dISMs immediately (i.e. in the same transition), but cannot immediately be used for sending or receiving messages on it. Yet this is not a restriction of expressiveness because the port will be available for I/O in any further transitions, and communicating via a newly created port usually makes sense only if the port has already become known to some peer ISM, which typically incurs some delay anyway.

5   Application Example

We present a typical application of dynamic ISMs for modeling dynamically communicating systems: the multi-threaded client/server architecture introduced in §2.3. It demonstrates dISM activation and deactivation, port creation, port transfer, and disabling of ports.

Our translation tool converts the AutoFocus diagrams to an Isabelle theory as outlined in §2.4. Typically, the user then edits that theory file in order to enhance the presentation and augments it with commenting texts and proofs. We reproduce here the complete textual documentation of the resulting Isabelle theory, as automatically produced by the LATEX documentation facility of Isabelle.

theory `ClientServer = ISM_package:`   — including dISM definitions

The example consists of a client that concurrently opens two sessions with a server. The sessions are identified by the reply ports provided by the client. The server spawns a working thread for each connection request received, creates a port for the thread, conveys the port to it, sends the client port to the new thread port, and awaits any new requests. Each thread receives its own port as well as the client port it is responsible for and sends the thread port to the respective client. The client receives the thread port and uses it to send the value it wants to be processed. The thread receives the value, computes the response value, sends it to the client, disables its port, and stops itself. Finally, the client collects the responses from the two server threads.

First we define the type of ports and dISM identifiers and a mapping between the two. There is one server with one port, several threads with one port each, and one client with several ports. The tags (i.e., datatype constructors used in the definitions of *port* and *id*) help us to statically map ports to dISM identifiers, which we do using the auxiliary function *ISMId*. Furthermore, we define a type abbreviation *cs_cmds* for the instance of dynamic ISM commands used here.

```
typedecl sid   — session identifier
typedecl tid   — thread identifier
datatype port = Server | Thread tid | Client sid
datatype id   = iServer | iThread tid | iClient
consts    ISMId :: "port ⇒ id"
primrec "ISMId Server    = iServer"
        "ISMId (Thread t) = iThread t"
        "ISMId (Client c) = iClient"
types cs_cmds = "(id, port) dcmd list"
```

The type of user data is called *val*. The server threads perform a function (taking values to values) called *server_function* which is not further specified. Messages sent within the system consist of either a port name or a value.

```
typedecl val   — value
consts server_function :: "val ⇒ val"
datatype msg = Port port | Value val
```

The server has a data state holding the identity of the next thread to be created. A thread may be in one of three control states and has two local variables in its data state: the thread identifier and the client session identifier indicating the session the thread is engaged in. Clients have a control state but no data state. For technical reasons, namely the lack of dependent types in Isabelle/HOL, we have to construct the union type *state* of all different local ISM states which will be used in each **ism** section and the definition of the overall *System* below.

```
types Server_data = tid
datatype Thread_control = Init | Ready | Done
record Thread_data =
  myid   :: "tid"
  sessid :: "sid"
```

```
datatype Client_control = Open | Send | Close | Halt
datatype state = SS Server_data
              | TS "Thread_control × Thread_data"
              | CS Client_control
```

The server dISM, as well as all other dISMs, declares the type *port* for its port interface, *msg* for the messages it sends and receives, and *cs_cmds* for the dISM commands it issues. It listens only to the port *Server* but potentially talks to all threads that may ever come into existence. The name of its data state is *nextT* identifying the next thread to be dispatched, with the initial value *th1*. We let the server pre-compute (and store for the next connection request) the identity of the next thread because this saves us from defining two transitions where in the first transition the server receives the client port, stores it and creates a new thread as well as a new port, and in the second transition the server sends the newly created port and the client port to the thread.

```
consts th1 :: tid
ism Server =
  ports port
    inputs   "{Server}"
    outputs  "{Thread c |c. True}"
  messages msg
  commands cs_cmds
  states state
    data Server_data init "th1" name "nextT"   — next thread to be created
  transitions
  dispatch:
    pre "tp = Thread nextT"   — just used as an abbreviation mechanism
    in   "Server"         "[Port cl]"
    out  "Thread nextT"  "[Port cl]"
    cmd  "[Convey tp (ISMId tp), Run (ISMId tp), New (Thread th')]"
    — the thread identifier th' is fresh by the semantics of New
    post "th'"   — the new value of nextT is th'
```

The initial input interface of a thread is empty because the server supplies a port to the thread dynamically. The output interface is the set of (potentially) all clients ports. The thread holds its two local variables (with arbitrary initial values) in the data state variable *s* and sets them according to the ports received in its first transition. The definition of this transition does not give a **cmd** subsection and thus makes implicit use of the default command, which is the empty list here.

```
ism Thread =
  ports port
    inputs   "{}"   — the thread port will be supplied by the Server
    outputs  "{Thread c |c. True}"
  messages msg
  commands cs_cmds default "[]"
```

```
states state
  control Thread_control init "Init"
  data     Thread_data
transitions
"init":
  Init → Ready
  in  "Thread t" "[Port (Client c)]"
  — the thread identifier t (and thus the thread port) is implicitly learned here
  — the input message pattern Port (Client c) guarantees to the thread that
     the port received actually is a client port (where c identifies the session)
  out "Client c" "[Port (Thread t)]"
  post myid := "t", sessid := "c"  work:
  Ready → Done
  in  "Thread (myid  s)" "[Value x]"   — s denotes the current data state
  out "Client (sessid s)" "[Value (server_function x)]"
  cmd "[Disable (Thread (myid s)), Stop (ISMId (Thread (myid s)))]"
```

We declare two session identifiers used as the input interface of the client. The client may output to the server and any threads. It sends the two connection requests immediately one after the other to the server port, waits until it has received the thread ports on its two ports, uses the two thread ports to concurrently send two (arbitrary) request values, and collects the two responses. Note the use of the control state to serialize the I/O operations. This example client synchronizes its two sessions. Of course, one could add further clients whose (single or multiple) sessions do not interfere at all with the other sessions.

```
consts c1 :: sid
consts c2 :: sid
ism Client =
  ports "port"
    inputs  "{Client c1, Client c2}"
    outputs "{Server} ∪ {Thread c |c. True}"
  messages msg
  commands cs_cmds default "[]"
  states state
    control Client_control init "Open"
  transitions
"open":
  Open → Send
  out Server "[Port (Client c1), Port (Client c2)]"
send:
  Send → Close
  in "Client c1" "[Port (Thread t1)]", "Client c2" "[Port (Thread t1)]"
  out "Thread t1" "[Value x1]       ", "Thread t2" "[Value x2]"
close:
  Close → Halt
  in "Client c1" "[Value y1]"        , "Client c2" "[Value y2]"
```

The overall system maps the dISM identifiers to the corresponding dISMs. Note that the parallel composition already includes all the threads that may become active at some time. When defining the composite runs of the system, we specify that initially the client and the server, but no thread, is running.

constdefs

```
System :: "(id, (cs_cmds, port, msg, state) ism) family"
"System ≡ (λi. case i of iServer     ⇒ Server.ism
                       | iThread tid ⇒ Thread.ism
                       | iClient     ⇒ Client.ism,
              {iServer, iClient} ∪ {iThread t |t. True})"
Runs :: "((port, msg, (id,port) dstate × (id ⇒ state)) conf list) set"
"Runs ≡ d_comp_runs System {iClient, iServer}"
```

The parallel composition of all dISMs in the system is (at least initially) well-formed, i.e. their inputs do not overlap:

theorem `wf_comp_System: "wf_comp System"`

The proof of this property is routine and essentially automatic.

The system components are (statically) well-formed if the input interfaces of the threads are not taken into account. The system is dynamically closed because the server augments the input interface of each thread with the `Convey` command *before* the thread is activated, the thread receives input only from the port conveyed to it, and all input and output operations of all system components have their counterparts within the system.

This ends our small application example. It should demonstrate that dynamic ISMs are adequate means to describe dynamically changing communication patterns and that the abstraction level of ISMs is high enough for focusing on the essential aspects of reactive systems and low enough for making the transition to the technical implementation straightforward.

6   Discussion

Since dynamic ISMs provide a stateful notion of both dynamic and reactive systems, it is interesting to compare them both with well-known notions of dynamic systems and with state automata used for modeling reactive systems.

The π-calculus [MPW92] and its descendants have a built-in notion of communication channels and handle dynamics by passing channel identifiers and instantiating channel variables. Restricting the calculus to a small number of basic concepts leads to a concise and very abstract formalism still bearing a rich metatheory. This makes the π-calculus particularly suited to study general concepts, but lacks feature for adequately specifying complex industrial-scale systems. In particular, state information is cumbersome to encode, as is local computation: even basic data types like numbers and the operations on them, which naturally occur *within* processes, have to be translated to auxiliary processes that need to interact via extra channels — an utterly inadequate representation that renders practical applications incomprehensible. Moreover, communication is synchronous via global channels without support for simultaneous multiple I/O and ownership restrictions like in dISMs. There is some basic tool support for verification but not for graphical design and documentation of complex specifications, as offered by AutoFocus. We conclude that the quite abstract π-calculus is well-suited for academic research, while the more operational-style dynamic ISM approach with its rather concrete structure tailored for stateful reactive systems makes practical system analysis easier to conduct and to understand.

In the area of state-based automata, there are approaches particularly addressing the complexity of industrial-scale systems like StateCharts, which are supported by the CASE tool StateMate [HLN+90]. Statecharts offer rich structuring notions like hierarchical states as well as a notion of time. On the other hand, the communication facilities offered by are rather basic: messaging is achieved via synchronous events that are distributed globally, i.e. in an undirected (and uncontrollable) way. Though the advanced concepts of Statecharts like hierarchical states could at least partially be encoded in the (dynamic) ISM setting, Statecharts seem to be more adequate in the area of modeling non-distributed systems. On the other hand, they do not offer asynchronous communication with controlled dynamics that is desirable to model systems like the one given in §5. Moreover, tool support for verification is very poor, which is partially due to the fact that the precise semantics of Statecharts (intentionally) had been left underspecified such that various interpretations exist.

Compared to dISMs, also most other state based automata approaches are more basic with respect to communication. Recall that the development of the ISM notion has been originally motivated by the need to extend I/O automata [LT89] with more advanced communication concepts.

There is other related work addressing the extension of state based approaches with particular aspects of dynamic behavior, e.g., [GR95,HS97,Zap02], however, we are not aware of any flexible approach, supported by CASE and verification tools, that can handle several kinds of dynamics in combination.

The ISM instantiations with dynamic features introduced in this paper are intended for modeling and analyzing security aspects of dynamic systems including multi-threaded and mobile agent systems. When modeling such systems, additional restrictions may apply with respect to the type of manipulation of the global state that a single ISM can perform, or with respect to the structure of the whole system, e.g., the existence of pre-defined components. Future work will include the provision of d(Amb)ISM frameworks for particular application scenarios and system paradigms, leaving the analyst only with the task of specifying those component ISMs that are specific for the application at hand.

As applications of generic ISMs evolve, new instantiations may turn out to be useful and may be implemented by ourselves and/or third parties.

We plan to extend the proof support offered by our Isabelle implementation of the ISM meta theory, as far as required by applications. Since our aim is to prove security, which typically is a collection of safety (but not liveness) properties, the most important next steps will be proof support for refinement and compositionality, i.e. proof decomposition wrt. parallel composition.

7   Conclusion

We have generalized Interacting State Machines, instantiated them with dynamic features, and demonstrated how to employ them for system modeling.

The extension is based on the introduction of global state for a system of ISMs. While generic ISMs do not further specify the structure of the global state and the type of the commands, different instantiations supporting different kinds of dynamics can be given. We have done so by defining dynamic ISMs allowing for mutable communication interfaces and a form of creation and deletion of components, as well as Ambient ISMs considering mutable contexts of components and components moving between contexts. The latter variant gives an operational semantics to the (boxed) ambient calculus. Furthermore, both variants can be combined to form dynamic Ambient ISMs, thus giving a very expressive and flexible approach to dynamic automata. We have defined generic and dynamic ISMs fully and formally, while the formalization and use of Ambient and dynamic Ambient ISMs is the subject of the companion paper [KO03].

By providing the concept of a global state appearing in different flavors, the ISM approach can be tailored to the analysis task at hand. Each of the extensions presented can be used on its own or be combined depending on the system that is to be analyzed. This is seen as an important practical advantage, since it does not leave users with the burden of additional structure if there is no need to, but on the other hand gives high expressive power where required.

Since we have fully formalized generic ISMs and their descendants in Isabelle/ HOL, we both inherit its advanced interactive and semi-automatic proof support features and achieve maximal reliability of the results. Experience already gained with real-world application examples, e.g. [OL02,OWL03] using basic ISMs, indicates that a high degree of proof automation can be achieved in this way, even though typical reactive systems have infinite state space and transitions heavily depend on message buffer contents and other (local and global) data.

Acknowledgments

Thomas Kuhn has provided invaluable input motivating the design of the ISM extensions. We thank him as well as some anonymous referees for their suggestions on early versions of this paper.

References

[BCC01]   Michele Bugliesi, Giuseppe Castagna, and Silvia Crafa. Boxed ambients. In *TACS 2001, 4th. International Symposium on Theoretical Aspects of Computer Science*, volume 2215 of *LNCS*, pages 38–63. Springer-Verlag, 2001.

[CG98]   Luca Cardelli and Andrew D. Gordon. Mobile ambients. In Maurice Nivat, editor, *Foundations of Software Science and Computational Structures: First International Conference, FOSSACS '98*, volume 1378 of *LNCS*, pages 140–155. Springer-Verlag, 1998.

[EHS97]   Jan Ellsberger, Dieter Hogrefe, and Amardeo Sarma. *SDL: Formal Object-Oriented Language for Communicating Systems*. Prentice Hall, 1997.

[GR95]   Radu Grosu and Bernhard Rumpe. Concurrent timed port automata. Technical Report TUM-I9533, Technische Univerität München, 1995.

[Gur97]   Y. Gurevich. Draft of the asm guide. Technical Report CSE-TR-336-97, EECS Dept., University of Michigan, 1997.

[HLN⁺90] David Harel, Hagi Lachover, Amnon Naamad, Amir Pnueli, Michal Politi, Rivi Sherman, Aharon Shtull-Trauring, and Mark B. Trakhtenbrot. STATE-MATE: A working environment for the development of complex reactive systems. *Software Engineering*, 16(4):403–414, 1990.

[HS97]   Ursula Hinkel and Katharina Spies. Spezifikationsmethodik für mobile, dynamische FOCUS-Netze. In A. Wolisz, I. Schieferdecker, and A. Rennoch, editors, *Formale Beschreibungstechniken für verteilte Systeme, GI/ITG-Fachgespräch 1997*, 1997.

[HSSS96] Franz Huber, Bernhard Schätz, Alexander Schmidt, and Katharina Spies. Autofocus - a tool for distributed systems specification. In *Proceedings FTRTFT'96 - Formal Techniques in Real-Time and Fault-Tolerant Systems*, volume 1135 of *LNCS*, pages 467–470. Springer-Verlag, 1996. See also http://autofocus.in.tum.de/index-e.html.

[KO03]   Thomas Kuhn and David von Oheimb. Interacting State Machines for mobility. In *Proc. of the 12ᵗʰ International FME Symposium (FM'03)*. Springer, September 2003. http://ddvo.net/papers/ISMfM.html, to appear.

[LT89]   Nancy Lynch and Mark Tuttle. An introduction to input/output automata. *CWI Quarterly*, 2(3):219–246, 1989. http://theory.lcs.mit.edu/tds/papers/Lynch/CWI89.html.

[MPW92] Robin Milner, Joachim Parrow, and David Walker. A calculus of mobile processes. *Information and Computation*, 100(1):1–77, September 1992.

[Nan02]   Sebastian Nanz. Integration of CASE tools and theorem provers: a framework for system modeling and verification with AutoFocus and Isabelle. Master's thesis, TU München, 2002. http://home.in.tum.de/nanz/csthesis/.

[Ohe02]   David von Oheimb. Interacting State Machines: *a stateful approach to proving security*. In Ali Abdallah, Peter Ryan, and Steve Schneider, editors, *Proceedings from the BCS-FACS International Conference on Formal Aspects of Security 2002*, volume 2629 of *LNCS*. Springer-Verlag, 2002. http://ddvo.net/papers/ISMs.html.

[OL02]   David von Oheimb and Volkmar Lotz. Formal Security Analysis with Interacting State Machines. In Dieter Gollmann, Günter Karjoth, and Michael Waidner, editors, *Proc. of the 7ᵗʰ European Symposium on Research in Computer Security (ESORICS)*, volume 2502, pages 212–228. Spinger, 2002. http://ddvo.net/papers/FSA_ISM.html. A more detailed journal version is submitted for publication.

[ON02]   David von Oheimb and Sebastian Nanz. *ISM Homepage: Documentation, sources and distribution*, 2002. http://ddvo.net/ISM/.

[OWL03] David von Oheimb, Georg Walter, and Volkmar Lotz. A formal security model of the infineon SLE 88 smart card memory management. In *Proc. of the 8ᵗʰ European Symposium on Research in Computer Security (ESORICS)*. Spinger, 2003. http://ddvo.net/papers/SLE88_MM.html, to appear.

[Pau94]   Lawrence C. Paulson. *Isabelle: A Generic Theorem Prover*, volume 828 of *LNCS*. Springer-Verlag, 1994. For an up-to-date documentation, see http://isabelle.in.tum.de/.

[Spi92]   J. Mike Spivey. *The Z Notation: A Reference Manual*. Prentice Hall International Series in Computer Science, 2nd edition, 1992.

[Zap02]   Júlia Zappe. Towards a mobile TLA. In *Proc. of the 7th ESSLLI Student Session, 14th European Summer School in Logic, Language and Information, Trento, Italy*, 2002.

Using PVS to Prove Properties of Systems Modelled in a Synchronous Dataflow Language*

Sanjai Rayadurgam, Anjali Joshi, and Mats P.E. Heimdahl

Department of Computer Science and Engineering
University of Minnesota, Minneapolis
{rsanjai,ajoshi,heimdahl}@cs.umn.edu

Abstract. We report on our experience with using the PVS theorem prover as a verification tool for analyzing systems modelled in $RSML^{-e}$ – a synchronous dataflow language. $RSML^{-e}$ is a formal specification language particularly well-suited for specifying requirements of reactive systems. We advocate a *specification-centered approach* to system development, in which various development activities like prototyping, analysis, verification, testing, and code-generation are based on a formal model of the system requirements. To support the analysis and verification activities, we developed a translator from $RSML^{-e}$ to PVS as part of our toolset. We used these tools to successfully verify properties of the mode logic of a flight-guidance system specified in $RSML^{-e}$ by our industrial partner, Rockwell Collins Inc. The results from this exercise are encouraging. This paper describes our approach to formalizing $RSML^{-e}$ in PVS and discusses briefly the strategies adopted in proving properties as well as some experiences.

1 Introduction

Software development for critical control systems, such as the software controlling aeronautics applications and medical devices, is a costly and time consuming process. Verification and validation of such systems must be an ongoing process throughout the development life-cycle. Currently, inspections and testing are the validation and verification methods used. We advocate that these methods be complemented with model checking and theorem proving. Also, other early life-cycle approaches like prototyping and specification simulation helps the analyst to evaluate and address poorly understood aspects of the system behavior. We advocate a specification-centered approach to development, in which a formal model of the system requirements is used to drive these life-cycle activities.

To realize a concrete instantiation of this approach, we have constructed a framework for developing tools to support specification-centered development using $RSML^{-e}$ as the requirements specification language. $RSML^{-e}$ [15] is a formal specification language particularly well-suited for specifying requirements of reactive systems. The NIMBUS toolset [14] provides the capability to execute

---

* This work has been partially supported by NASA contract NCC-01-001.

RSML^{-e} specifications. We have extended the analysis capabilities of the toolset by constructing translators to various verification tools such as NuSMV [12] and PVS [7]. Having the capacity to use different techniques like model-checking and theorem-proving to analyze the same RSML^{-e} model helps us leverage the unique advantages of each of these techniques. We have conducted case-studies using realistic industrial models to validate our approach.

In this report we present our formalization of RSML^{-e} in PVS. We have implemented a translator in the NIMBUS tool and used NIMBUS and PVS to verify various interesting properties of the mode logic of a realistic flight guidance system. Our motivation for the translation project and in general for using PVS as a verification tool was to help us prove classes of properties we could not prove using model-checking techniques. We also wanted to evaluate: (1) the feasibility of using a theorem prover as an *analysis back-end* to a specification tool, (2) the difficulty of constructing proofs, and (3) the scalability of the approach to industrial size systems.

In constructing translators to different verification tools our goals for the translation were driven by the specific capabilities of the tool and the expected user-interaction with the tools. Thus, when translating to the model-checker [5], we built in certain conservative abstractions that would make model-checking feasible by sacrificing some accuracy and expressiveness of the original RSML^{-e} specification. This was an acceptable trade-off since model-checking, when feasible, is completely automated and does not require any user interaction.

On the other hand, theorem-proving is essentially an interactive process. Thus, readability of the translated output and maintaining a close correspondence with the source specification were of importance. Further, there is no need to abstract away details in the source specification. Thus, the requirements for the translation were that it should fully capture the semantics of the source language in an elegant way producing readable PVS specifications.

Our formalization of RSML^{-e} in PVS is built around the concept of *objects as streams*, an idea similar to that of [2]. All entities in the specification – such as, variables, expressions and assignments – are viewed as state-indexed sequences of values. The specification, taken in totality, is considered as a set of constraints on the possible execution traces (*histories*) of the system. Verification, in this context, is checking whether the set of possible histories as constrained by the specification, satisfy a given predicate. Our formalization has the advantage of retaining both the structure and the semantics of the RSML^{-e} source specification in the translated PVS output. With some carefully chosen syntax, this makes the full power of the theorem prover available to the user at a level of representation that is in direct correspondence with the source specification. In our experience this has been of practical significance when constructing PVS proofs.

Our experience so far has been encouraging. Currently, the proof construction part is essentially a manual process. Even though the proofs are typically large, they are straightforward to construct. The complexity of the proofs does not seem to grow excessively with the increased complexity of the models. Where the model checking efforts increase exponentially, our experiences indicate that the effort involved in constructing PVS proofs will exhibit a more *linear growth pattern*. We are in the process of empirically testing our hypothesis about the scalability of PVS proofs.

The rest of the paper is organized as follows. The next section briefly discusses the related efforts in this area. Section 3 provides an overview of the formal specification language RSML^{-e} and the PVS theorem prover. Section 4 describes our translation scheme in detail. Section 5 discusses our approach to proving properties. We then conclude the paper with a brief discussion in Section 6.

2   Related Work

We briefly discuss some of the related works in the area of using theorem proving for verifying reactive systems.

Owre *et al.* [13] discuss a systematic way to represent state-machine specifications of reactive systems in PVS, such as specifications written in SCR [6]. Extending that approach to RSML^{-e}, however, made reasoning with large systems a bit cumbersome. This was primarily due to the difficulty in understanding the mechanically translated PVS output and relating it to the original RSML^{-e} specification, a task that was often required during proof construction.

Bensalem *et al.* [2] discuss a methodology for proving control systems specified in LUSTRE using PVS. Their approach involves representing LUSTRE objects as streams in PVS, similar to the one that we describe here. They present a method for constructing provably correct control programs using LUSTRE and PVS in combination. An advantage of this approach is that property specification is not different from the specification of the system requirements.

TAME [1] is an interface for verifying properties of automata like, I/O automata, Lynch-Vaandrager timed automata and SCR. It provides a set of templates for specifying these automata and also a set of specializing strategies for reasoning about these automata in PVS. An advantage of this approach is that users can construct proofs using template strategies which are more meaningful and intuitive in the context of automata verification, without having to understand the underlying PVS steps. In our work, we only have a few hand-crafted specialized strategies that are used in reasoning about RSML^{-e} specifications. But this has been adequate to construct proofs of non-trivial properties on fairly complex models. We are currently working on constructing specialized strategies and investigating auto-generation of model-specific strategies to speed-up the proof construction process.

3   Framework

Figure 1 shows an overview of our verification framework. The user builds a behavioral model of the system in the fully formal and executable specification language RSML^{-e}. The specification is then fed to the NIMBUS simulator which

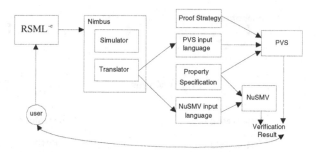

Fig. 1. Verification Framework.

checks that the specification is well formed and type correct. After the specification is checked, the user can translate the specification to the PVS or NuSMV input languages. The specification can then be analyzed for various properties using the theorem prover. The user can also input proof strategies to aid the proof process.

3.1   Flight Guidance System

A Flight Guidance System (FGS)[1] is a component of the overall Flight Control System (FCS). It compares the measured state of an aircraft (position, speed, and altitude) to the desired state and generates pitch and roll guidance commands to minimize the difference between the measured and desired state. The FGS can be broken down to mode logic, which determines which lateral and vertical modes of operation are active and armed at any given time, and the flight control laws that accept information about the aircraft's current and desired state and compute the pitch and roll guidance commands. We will be using a scaled down version of FGS as a running example in these discussions, but the equivalent properties to the examples in this paper have been proven on larger FGS models.

Figure 2 illustrates a graphical view of a FGS in the NIMBUS environment. The figure shows the hierarchical and parallel state machines representing the different modes in the FGS. The arrows represent the possible transitions between states. The primary modes of interest in the FGS are the horizontal and vertical modes. The horizontal modes control the behavior of the aircraft about the longitudinal, or roll, axis, while the vertical modes control the behavior of the aircraft about the vertical, or pitch, axis. In addition, there are a number of auxiliary modes, such as half-bank mode, that control other aspects of the aircraft's behavior.

---

[1] We thank Dr. Steve Miller and Dr. Alan Tribble of Rockwell Collins Inc. for the information on flight control systems and for letting us use the RSML^{-e} models they have developed during our collaboration.

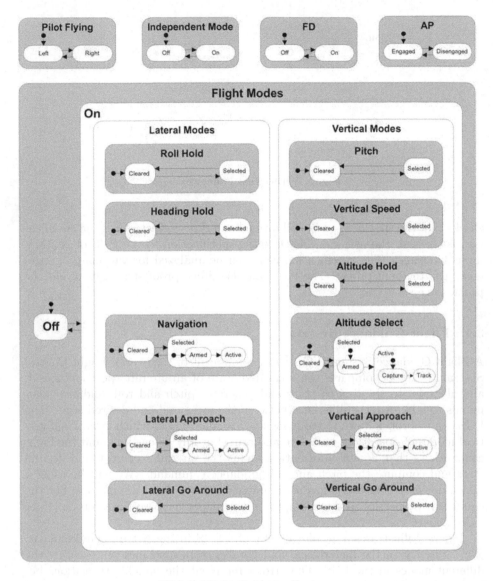

Fig. 2. Flight Guidance System.

3.2 Overview of RSML^{-e}

RSML^{-e} stands for Requirements State Machine Language without Events. It is based on the Statecharts [8] like language Requirements State Machine Language (RSML) [11]. It is fully formal and a synchronous data-flow language without any internal broadcast events, which have been found to be error-prone [10].

An RSML^{-e} specification consists of a collection of input variables, state variables, input/output interfaces, functions, macros, and constants; *input variables*

```
STATE_VARIABLE ROLL : Base_State
        PARENT           : Modes.On
        INITIAL_VALUE    : UNDEFINED
        CLASSIFICATION   : State
        TRANSITION UNDEFINED TO Cleared IF NOT Select_ROLL()
        TRANSITION UNDEFINED TO Selected IF Select_ROLL()
        TRANSITION Cleared TO Selected IF Select_ROLL()
        TRANSITION Selected TO Cleared IF Deselect_ROLL()
END STATE_VARIABLE

MACRO Select_ROLL() :
        TABLE
                Is_No_Nonbasic_Lateral_Mode_Active()    : T;
                Modes = On                              : T;
        END TABLE
END MACRO

MACRO Deselect_ROLL() :
        TABLE
                When_Nonbasic_Lateral_Mode_Activated()  : T *;
                When(Modes = Off)                       : * T;
        END TABLE
END MACRO
```

Fig. 3. A small portion of the FGS specification in RSML^{-e} .

are used to record the values observed in the environment, *state variables* are organized in a hierarchical fashion and are used to model various states of the control model, *interfaces* act as communication gateways to the external environment, and *functions and macros* encapsulate computations providing increased readability and ease of use.

Figure 3 shows a specification fragment of an RSML^{-e} specification of the Flight Guidance System[2]. The figure shows the definition of a state variable, ROLL. ROLL is the default lateral mode in the FGS mode logic. The state variable ROLL is declared as a child state of Modes and is active when the variable Modes has the value On – this notion of hierarchical variables provides the same abstractions and structuring mechanism as the AND and OR states in Statecharts , but the semantics is much simpler [15].

The conditions under which the state variable changes value are defined in the TRANSITION clauses in the definition. The condition tables are encoded in the macros, Select_ROLL and Deselect_ROLL. The use of macros not only improves the readability of the specifications but also helps localize errors and future changes. The conditions are represented in the AND-OR table format. The tables are adopted from the original RSML notation – each column of truth values represents a conjunction of the propositions in the leftmost column (a '*' represents a "don't care" condition). If a table contains several columns, we take the disjunction of the columns; thus, the table is a way of expressing conditions in a disjunctive normal form.

---

[2] We use here the ASCII version of RSML^{-e} since it is much more compact than the more readable typeset version.

Frequently we might need to refer to values of the variables at a certain point in the variable *history*. RSML^{-e} provides a construct for doing this, as shown in the following example.

```
MACRO Were_Modes_Off() :
        PREV_STEP(Modes) = Off
END MACRO
```

In the above example, `PREV_STEP(Modes)` refers to the previous value of the state variable `Modes`.

Data-Flow Semantics: RSML^{-e} transitions are purely condition-based and free of internal events – as soon as the guards in a variable definition can be evaluated, it will take on its new value. The variables are partially ordered based on the data dependency induced by the guard conditions – a similar semantics is adopted in the programming language LUSTRE [2]. Data-flow semantics removes complex issues caused by internal events, such as infinite triggering events or analysis of micro-steps [4], from the language.

Use of Undefined *Values:* Startup behavior and behavior in the face of sensor failures pose particular challenges when specifying control systems – under these circumstances we simply do not know what the state of the environment might be. RSML^{-e} supports modeling of this uncertainty by providing the concept of *Undefinedness*. One can explicitly specify the initial value of variables at startup to be *Undefined*, such as `ROLL=UNDEFINED` in Figure 3. Also, when a parent variable takes on a new value, each child variable of the parent value that was just changed are no longer relevant and must not be used – these child variables are *Undefined*. RSML^{-e} supports both explicit and implicit *Undefinedness*.

3.3   Properties of Interest for Theorem Proving

Most of the FGS properties could be expressed as state invariants for verification. State invariants are suitable for model checking and indeed around 290 FGS properties have been successfully model checked for the largest FGS model [5]. However, there were also some other types of interesting properties, like the FGS mode confusion properties [3], some of which cannot be model checked. As an example, consider the following property:

> Any two states that do not have the same modes, have different mode annunciations.

This property compares two arbitrary states, with no particular values specified for modes or mode annunciations, other than saying that the values are either same or different [9]. This property cannot be expressed in the temporal logics used by conventional model-checkers. Proving such mode confusion properties was a motivation for the current work in exploring the application of a theorem prover like PVS.

3.4   Overview of PVS

PVS [7] (Prototype Verification System) provides an environment for effective proof construction in addition to writing specifications. Its input language is based on simply-typed higher-order logic with function, record and product types and recursive type definitions. The language provides a powerful mechanism to specify and use sub-types. The powerful type system means that type-checking a PVS specification is in general an undecidable problem. Type-checking could require guidance to the theorem prover from the user in dismissing type correctness conditions. PVS specifications are organized into theories that can be parameterized. The primitive proof steps are composed of efficient decision procedures, rewriting rules and BDD based propositional simplifications.

4   Translating from RSML^{-e} to PVS

We considered two competing approaches for representing RSML^{-e} specifications in PVS.

The first approach is to view the *state-space as a cross product of the domains* of system variables. The specification is viewed as a collection of constraints determining the set of possible initial states and the set of possible transitions between states. Then, the transitive closure of the initial states under the transition relation constitutes the reachable state-space of the system. The system will satisfy a certain property of interest if it can be established that every reachable state satisfies this property. This view is usually adopted when one is verifying state-based specifications using model-checkers like SMV or the μ-calculus model-checker of PVS. Owre *et al.* [13] discuss such an approach to translate requirement specifications written in SCR to PVS.

The second approach is to consider *state as a point of observation of certain quantities of interest* in the system. The system variables represent quantities of interest, i.e., they are mappings from states (the observation points) to values of those quantities (at those observation points). When the system responds to changes in its environment, it moves to a new observation point, i.e., to a new state. So each state has an associated (finite) *history* of observations up to that point. In this view, the system specification is a set of constraints on the histories of observations at each state. If we think of constraints as Boolean valued quantities constructed using system variables, then the specification lists a set of such quantities that are given to be true in every state. Properties of interest that one wants to prove are also similar to constraints but one has to establish that these are true. Bensalem *et al.* [2] adopt such an approach for proving properties of control system specified in LUSTRE using PVS.

In an earlier version of our translation we adopted the former approach to translate RSML^{-e} specifications to PVS. However, we found that it was difficult to construct proof of properties in PVS for large systems using such an approach. Part of the difficulty arose from the fact that one had to carry around the complete state construct in proofs, even though, much of the reasoning and proof steps involved only a few variables at any given time. Also, the translated output was quite difficult to comprehend. The latter approach, which we adopted subsequently, overcomes these shortcomings.

In the current approach, objects defined in RSML^{-e} are treated as sequences of values over states in PVS, also called *streams*. Operations over values are uniformly lifted to operations over streams by applying the operation to values at each state. The resulting translation to PVS retains a close correspondence with the original RSML^{-e} specification making it easy to understand and follow. In the next two subsections we discuss the translation scheme in detail.

4.1   Translation Foundation

As the first step to translation, we defined a library *rsmlne.pvs* containing definitions for various constructs of the RSML^{-e} language in PVS. These RSML^{-e} constructs include the basic types, operations to lift RSML^{-e} objects to streams, RSML^{-e} specific operations, and so on. This PVS library will then be imported into every translated RSML^{-e} specification, so that the basic definitions can be reused across all specifications. Due to space constraints, we present only the most relevant aspects of the translation scheme here.

Undefined and Defined Values: In RSML^{-e} variables may be *undefined* in certain configurations (global states) of the system. To capture this notion, we uniformly lift all RSML^{-e} types to include a null element. Defined values are accessed using a C-like address/contents (&/*) syntax:

```
rType[T: TYPE]: DATATYPE
 BEGIN
  null    :  undef?
  &(*: T) :  def?
 END rType
```

A generic function `ext` extends operation on T-values to null-extended-T-values by applying the operation to the contents when the value is defined and otherwise returning null.

States and History States: As explained earlier, states are just points of observations of quantities of interest in the system. The only properties that we require of states are that: 1) There is some starting point for observations - initial state, and 2) There is a unique history for each state - previous state. In our theory, we define State as a natural number: the initial state being zero and n being the predecessor of n + 1, and zero being the predecessor of itself.

```
State: TYPE = nat
init: State = 0
```

RSML^{-e} specifications may use certain types of history operations on objects like variables and interfaces. These operations may access values of variables at certain points in their history (for example, when the value changed the second previous time). To uniformly translate such expressions, we define a single history operation on States called `last`. This is a higher order recursive function, which results in a state transformer, i.e., the result is a mapping from a state to a (previous) state. It returns the zth last state at which the take function was true.

```
prev(s: State): State = pred(s)
history?(s: State)(x: State):bool= x <= s
Filter: TYPE = [State -> bool]
last(take: Filter, z: posnat)(s:State): RECURSIVE (history?(s)) =
   IF s = init OR (z = 1 AND take(s)) THEN s
   ELSE last(take, IF take(s) THEN z - 1 ELSE z ENDIF) (prev(s))
   ENDIF
 MEASURE s
```

Objects as Streams: RSML^{-e} objects are implemented as streams that map State to (null-extended) values:

```
Object: TYPE = [State -> rType[T]]
```

In certain contexts, objects may have to be constrained to be defined (or undefined) at every state. The predicates defined? and undefined? are used for this purpose. The object UNDEFINED returns *null* at each state. The L operator lifts the RSML^{-e} constants to streams.

```
L(x: T): (constant?[T]) = LAMBDA s: &(x)
```

The RSML^{-e} entities, state variables and input variables and the return types of functions and macros, are simply objects of the appropriate type; constants are constant objects of their respective types; and, conditions (such as those guarding assignments to variables) are defined Boolean objects.

```
rSTVAR__:   TYPE = Object[T]
rINVAR__:   TYPE = Object[T]
rFUNCT__:   TYPE = Object[T]
rMACRO__:   TYPE = Object[bool]
rFIELD__:   TYPE = (defined?[T])
rCONST__:   TYPE = (constant?[T])
rCOND__ :   TYPE = (defined?[bool])
```

Messages in RSML^{-e} are data received and sent by the system at the interfaces and such data are always defined. We represent Messages from RSML^{-e} as records in PVS, with fields having rFIELD__[T] type for the appropriate type T.

RSML^{-e} Basic Types: The RSML^{-e} types, BOOLEAN, REAL, INTEGER have equivalent types in PVS. RSML^{-e} type TIME is simply of type nonnegative real in PVS. TIME is an intrinsic object in RSML^{-e} that is always defined and is monotonically increasing with respect to State.

RSML^{-e} Specific Operations: Here we define a few RSML^{-e} specific operations on objects. Equality comparison is a safe-operation even if one or both of its operands are Undefined. That is its result will always be defined. We use the symbolic operator == to distinguish it from the normal equality operator =.

```
==(obj1, obj2: Object[T]): (defined?[bool]) =
    LAMBDA (s: State): &(obj1(s) = obj2(s))
```

The unary operator PREV yields an object that gives the value of its operand in the previous state:

```
PREV(obj: Object[T]): Object[T] = LAMBDA (s: State): obj(prev(s))
```

We require a binary BECAME? operation on objects, with the intuitive meaning "did the first object's value change to that of the second object in this state?". Also required is a unary CHANGED? that simply checks if the object's value changed in this state.

```
BECAME?(obj1, obj2: Object[T]): (defined?[bool]) =
    LAMBDA s: &(obj1(s) /= PREV(obj1)(s) AND obj1(s) = obj2(s));

CHANGED?(obj: Object[T]): (defined?[bool]) =
    LAMBDA (s: State): &(obj(s) /= PREV(obj)(s));
```

With this formulation, one could express SCR style operators like @T(expr), @F(expr) and @C(expr) as BECAME?(expr, true), BECAME?(expr, false) and CHANGED?(expr) respectively. Also note that these could be used to determine history states in a general fashion, such as, the nth last time variable A changed. The function PREV_STATE takes an object representing a condition and the step count to compute the appropriate history state:

```
PREV_STATE(c: Object[bool], z: posnat):[s:State -> (history?(s))] =
    last(* o (c == L(TRUE)), z)
```

A LUSTRE style followed-by operator (->) is useful in expressing initial state values for RSML^{-e} entities. We overload the ANDTHEN infix operator in PVS for this purpose, which conveys the intuitive meaning of followed-by:

```
ANDTHEN(obj1, obj2: Object[T]): Object[T] =
    LAMBDA (s: State): IF s = init THEN obj1(s) ELSE obj2(s) ENDIF
```

Similarly, we also overload the WHEN infix operator in PVS to express parent state constraint. The expression (A WHEN B) will have the value of A when the condition B is true in a state and otherwise be undefined:

```
WHEN(obj: Object[T], p: (defined?[bool])): Object[T] =
    LAMBDA (s: State): IF *(p(s)) THEN obj(s) ELSE UNDEFINED(s) ENDIF
```

Guards and Guarded Expressions: Computation in RSML^{-e} specifications is expressed in terms of guarded assignments to variables. An assignment is triggered if its corresponding guard evaluates to true. Thus, for *consistency* (or to avoid non-determinism), the guards of different assignments of a variable must be disjoint at each state. Also, for *completeness*, the disjunction of the guards of all assignments of a variable must be a tautology. The construct, COND ... ENDCOND in PVS, is typically used to capture such guarded expressions. It is equivalent to a series of if-then-else expressions, except that it generates disjointedness and completeness constraints as type-correctness obligations to be proved by the user. One could lift this construct state-wise to streams (and thus to RSML^{-e} objects) by evaluating the guard and the expressions at each state. The RSML^{-e} library for PVS defines operators `[| |]`, `>>`, `/\` and `ELSE?`, such that,

```
[|   ... >> ... /\ ... /\ ELSE? >> ... |]
```

is equivalent to lifting,

```
COND ... -> ... ,  ... ,  ELSE  -> ... ENDCOND
```

to RSML^{-e} objects, state-wise. The translator can be set to generate default `ELSE?` cases that just stutter previous state values. This is useful when the specification is written assuming the implicit behavior of "no change in value when none of the guards are true".

4.2   RSML^{-e} to PVS Translation

On the basis of the translation foundation discussed above, we will now illustrate the actual translation of various RSML^{-e} constructs. The *rsmlne.pvs* library will be imported into the translated PVS specification. The basic construct in RSML^{-e} is the variable and the transition relation defined on the variable – the translation of these constructs is discussed in detail below.

Type Definitions: Basic RSML^{-e} types are defined in the *rsmlne.pvs* library. RSML^{-e} enumerated types are defined in a straightforward way in PVS.

```
TYPE_DEF Base_State   {Cleared, Selected}
```

translates to

```
Base_State: TYPE =   {Cleared, Selected}
```

Variable Declarations: Input variable declarations create equivalent PVS definitions for the type, if necessary. The expected_min and expected_max specifications, if they exist, are not declared, but just translated as constants wherever those are used. The unit and classification definitions are ignored since they are primarily present for documentation purposes.

```
IN_VARIABLE FD_Switch: Switch
            INITIAL_VALUE : UNDEFINED
            CLASSIFICATION: MONITORED
        END IN_VARIABLE
```

translates to

```
FD_Switch:  rINVAR__[Switch]
```

The state variable declarations are handled in a similar way as the input variables. The declaration for the state variable ROLL from figure 3 translates to

```
ROLL:  rSTVAR__[Base_State]
```

Functions and Macros: Functions and macros are both defined as functions, with macros being functions returning Boolean values. The macro Deselect_ROLL from figure 3 translates to

```
Deselect_ROLL: rFUNCT__[BOOLEAN] =
     When_Nonbasic_Lateral_Mode_Activated
     OR
     BECAME?((Modes == L(Off)), L(TRUE))
```

State Variable Assignments: The bulk of the computation in an RSML^{-e} specification is in the assignments and their guard conditions expressed as AND/OR tables. While there could be no cycles in the dependency among variable values at a given state in a correct RSML^{-e} specification, assignment expressions and guards may frequently refer to one or more history state values of any number of variables. Thus, variable histories are defined by a set of mutually recursive equations. This mutual recursion cannot be directly represented in PVS. This problem is also addressed in the [2] as the *feedback loop problem*. To handle the mutual recursion, we split the definitions for variables into three parts:

- Declaration of the variable
- Defining equation for the variable
- Assertion that the variable is equal to the value given by its defining equation.

The declarations of variables is explained earlier. For the rest of the definition: First the guard conditions are translated to individual condition objects. While this is not necessary, it makes the translator output readable and easy to follow. If the assignment is given as a transition from one state to another, it is internally rewritten to an assignment form where the guard includes the previous state as a constraint. As an example, the first guard condition for the ROLL state variable from figure 3,

```
TRANSITION UNDEFINED TO Cleared IF NOT Select_ROLL()
```

    translates to

```
ROLL__T1:   rCOND =
        (NOT Select_ROLL)
        AND
        (PREV(ROLL) == UNDEFINED)
```

The transition relation needs to consider the hierarchical relationship between variables. The transition relation for child variables needs to check if the parent variable has the right value. If the parent has the right value, the child variable is relevant and its transition relation is evaluated normally. If the parent variable has the wrong value, then the child will be *undefined*. This is captured using the WHEN operator.

The complete definition of the ROLL state variable is translated as,

```
ROLL__DEF: rFUNCT__[Base_State] =
   (UNDEFINED
    ANDTHEN ([|   ROLL__T1 >>  L(Cleared)
             /\  ROLL__T2 >>  L(Selected)
             /\  ROLL__T3 >>  L(Selected)
             /\  ROLL__T4 >>  L(Cleared)
             /\  ELSE?   >>  PREV(ROLL)
             |]
             WHEN  (Modes == L(On))))
```

```
ROLL__DECL: AXIOM ROLL = ROLL__DEF
```

Finally, an axiom is generated to assert that the variable is equivalent to the value given by its defining equation. However, this axiom could seldom be used as an auto-rewrite unconditionally, for this could easily cause rewrite loops. So, two additional conditional equations - one for the initial state and one for the non-initial states - are generated, which could be used as auto-rewrites in proof strategies:

```
s: VAR State
ROLL__INIT: AXIOM  (s = init)  IMPLIES  ROLL(s) = ROLL__DEF(s)
ROLL__NEXT: AXIOM  (s /= init) IMPLIES  ROLL(s) = ROLL__DEF(s)
```

While the indiscriminate use of axioms could lead to inconsistent specifications, the type-correctness of RSML^{-e} specifications is sufficient to guarantee that this is not the case with the translated PVS output. In particular, RSML^{-e} language disallows cyclic dependency among variables.

The input variable assignments are handled similar to the state variable assignments. Although input variables have a different syntax and their assignments appear under handlers for input interfaces, the PVS translation produced is similar to that of state variables. In other words, input variables are treated very much like top-level state variables in the PVS interpretation.

Messages, Interface Declarations and Handlers: The translator can be set to skip interfaces altogether when one is interested in reasoning about the specification independent of input and output. In that case the input variables are all left unconstrained so that they may assume any value at each step.

Messages are declared to be of a record type in PVS. The interfaces are declared to be constants of the type of the messages handled. The interface message separation times are translated to constant objects wherever they are used. The input interface handlers define the values of the input variables and thus provide the transition conditions for the input variable assignments.

One-Input Interface Assumption: In RSML^{-e} step computation is assumed to take place when and only when an input is received by one of the input receivers. Also, it is assumed that two input receivers do not receive messages from the environment at the same instant and that input values do not change before computation is completed. Thus, the trigger for computation of a step is receipt of a single message. It is implicitly assumed that there is a system clock interface, which periodically receives clock ticks, so that even if there are no other receivers, computation still proceeds. To capture the one-input assumption when there is more than one receiver, a system input variable INPUT? is declared, whose possible range of values are the different input receivers in the specification. Its value at each state is understood to be the receiver that triggered the step computation for that state.

5   Proving Properties

Currently, the proof construction is essentially a manual process. The most common properties we encountered during the verification of the flight-guidance mode logic were *state invariants* (p is true is always true) or *transition invariants* (if p is true in the current state, p will be true in the next state). While proofs for transition invariants begin with a CASE split for the *init* and *next* states, those for state invariants begin with instantiation of a simple induction schema over states. After the first steps, the proofs of the subgoals, follow a similar pattern in both types of proofs, the details of which follow. The subgoals that one has to address typically could involve the current (or previous) state either in the *init* or the *next* state configuration. Most proofs do not require reasoning beyond one previous state in the history. However, RSML^{-e} allows the use of state history of any bounded length, and, therefore, there could be specifications for which proofs may require reasoning beyond one history state. Below, we discuss briefly how to proceed with a proof after we have instantiated an induction schema, so that we have two subgoals to dismiss: one to show that the property holds in the initial state and one to show that is holds in the next state.

Example Proof: Our motivation for using the theorem proving approach were the *mode confusion* properties. Though they are really interesting properties, they have rather involved proofs. For the purpose of illustration, we will consider here a simple *state invariant* that we may wish to verify on a toy model of the Flight Guidance System. Though this property is clearly suited for model checking, we use it here as a simple example to explain the general proof process. The proofs for the mode confusion properties [9] follow a similar pattern.

```
At_Least_One_Lateral_Mode_Active : THEOREM
    verify(Mode_Annunciations_On IMPLIES
                (Is_ROLL_Selected OR Is_HDG_Selected))
```

Informally, the property states, as the name implies, that whenever modes are turned on, at least one lateral mode is active. In more realistic models, there would be several of those modes, some classified as lateral and some classified as vertical. The proof of this property for our much larger models, follows a similar sequence of steps.

Invocation of basic auto-rewrite strategies (described later) followed by simplification, reduces the goal to:

```
|-------
{1}   FORALL (s: State):
        IMPLIES(*(Modes(s)) = On,
                OR((ROLL(s) = &(Selected)),(HDG(s) = &(Selected)))))
```

Since this is a state invariant, we decide to induct on state s. This yields two
subgoals: 1) s is an *init state*, and 2) s is a *next state*. The *init* branch can be
dismissed trivially by invoking Modes_INIT which asserts that Modes = Off in
the init state. Since the left-hand-side of the implication is false, the subgoal will
be immediately dismissed.

The *next* state branch, after skolemization and simplification, becomes:

```
[-1]  IMPLIES(*(Modes(j!1)) = On,
              OR((ROLL(j!1) = &(Selected)),(HDG(j!1) = &(Selected)))))
{-2}  *(Modes(1 + j!1)) = On
  |-------
{1}   (ROLL(1 + j!1) = &(Selected))
{2}   (HDG(1 + j!1) = &(Selected))
```

Note that [−1] formula in the antecedent is the induction hypothesis. State
(j!1) is the previous state and (1 + j!1) is the current state[3] in the induction process. Proceeding with the proof, we may now instantiate the transition
relation for the ROLL (or, symmetrically, HDG) state variable assignments in the
current state and simplify to obtain:

```
{-1}  ROLL(1 + j!1) =
        IF *(ROLL__T1(1 + j!1))  THEN &(Cleared)
        ELSE IF *(ROLL__T2(1 + j!1))  THEN &(Selected)
            ELSE IF *(ROLL__T3(1 + j!1))  THEN &(Selected)
                ELSE IF *(ROLL__T4(1 + j!1))  THEN &(Cleared)
                    ELSE ROLL(j!1)
                    ENDIF
                ENDIF
            ENDIF
        ENDIF
[-2]  IMPLIES(*(Modes(j!1)) = On,
              OR((ROLL(j!1) = &(Selected)),(HDG(j!1) = &(Selected)))))
[-3]  *(Modes(1 + j!1)) = On
  |-------
[1]   (ROLL(1 + j!1) = &(Selected))
[2]   (HDG(1 + j!1) = &(Selected))
```

Now, the value of ROLL in the current state depends on the guard conditions
satisfied. Dismissing the conditions one by one, CASE splitting as required,
would result in a sub-goal like the following:

---

[3] For clarity of presentation we talk of previous/current states, instead of current/next
states to avoid confusing with init/next states.

```
[-1]   *(When_HDG_Switch_Pressed(1 + j!1))
{-2}   *(ROLL(1 + j!1)) = Cleared
[-3]   *(Modes(1 + j!1)) = On
  |-------
[1]    HDG(j!1) = &(Selected)
[2]    *(ROLL(j!1)) = Cleared
[3]    ROLL(j!1) = null
[4]    (ROLL(1 + j!1) = &(Selected))
[5]    (HDG(1 + j!1) = &(Selected))
```

Instantiation of the transition relation on ROLL led to the value of Cleared for the variable in the current state. At this point, it is clear that more information from the specification is necessary to proceed further with proof construction: we have not yet reasoned with the value of HDG variable in the current state. We, therefore, instantiate the transition relation for HDG in current state and introduce it into the sequent. Dismissing the various guard conditions for HDG_NEXT and further simplification of the consequent formulas, yields HDG = Selected for the current state, which is one of the consequents. This completes the outline of the proof of the invariant.

As mentioned earlier, the most common properties we encountered during the verification of the FGS were state and transition invariants. The proofs were fairly straightforward, though long. Most proofs followed a structure similar to the one explained above, where the analysis faces with two cases:

init State Invoke the *StateVar*_INIT condition to dismiss the proof branch. These sub-goals are trivial to dismiss.

next State Invoke the *StateVar*_NEXT transition condition on one of the State variables involved in the property. Since the transition condition is composed of *COND* statement, each branch, corresponding to each transition would have to be dismissed to obtain the value assigned for the state variable in the next state. If after simplification of the transition condition, the proof is not yet complete, we may have to deal with one of the following cases:

1. A subgoal is reached, whose consequent is provable but requires additional information to prove it. In this case, it may be necessary to invoke new initial/transition conditions on some other relevant state variables on which the value of the present state variable depends. We then repeat the above process.

2. A subgoal is reached, in which one of the newly introduced antecedents is false. This may again require introduction of more information into the proof branch through the initial/transition conditions to discharge the subgoal by contradiction.

3. A subgoal is reached, which is unprovable. This would typically point to a scenario in which the property being analyzed is false. The counter-example, could typically be easily gleaned from the formulas in the sequent. However, some familiarity with the system being verified may be necessary to determine that a sub-goal is unprovable.

The `At_Least_One_Lateral_Mode_Active` example proof described above is for a scaled down version of the FGS. This version of FGS is about 900 lines of PVS code, when translated from the RSML^{-e} specification. The complete proof is 93 proof steps and runs in approximately 6 seconds on a 1.5 GHz Linux workstation with 1.5 GB main memory. The largest FGS model that we have worked on is about 3900 lines of translated PVS code. In this version of FGS, there are five lateral modes instead of the two in our example property. The `At_Least_One_Lateral_Mode_Active` proof for this version of FGS is 380 proof steps and runs in approximately 40 seconds on the same machine. We also constructed around six elaborate proofs analyzing the mode logic of the FGS. One of those proofs, which is especially interesting, could not be verified using model checking techniques.

One of the authors was involved in constructing these proofs manually. The author had no prior experience in theorem proving before starting this exercise. An interesting observation from this exercise is that the effort involved in constructing these proofs, although large, increases roughly linearly with the size of the model. The experience so far has been very encouraging as we were successful in constructing non-trivial proofs of useful properties of a critical system model used in the avionics industry. We are cautiously optimistic that the theorem proving approach may well scale up to much larger systems than what we can handle using model-checking techniques.

6   Discussion

In our experience, the proofs we dealt with, have been typically *long, but straightforward to understand*. To make the translation specific details transparent to the user and increase readability of the sub-goals, we invoke the RSML^{-e} specific definitions from the library file as lazy, eager or macro auto-rewrites in PVS. Those are automatically brought in whenever the ASSERT primitive is used in the proof. To further reduce the tediousness of constructing proofs, we have attempted to construct certain non-trivial strategies that are specific to proofs of properties for RSML^{-e} models, as well as, generating model-specific strategies along with the translation. As a first step, we identified simple patterns of rule invocations and encoded these patterns as strategies. For example, a simple strategy EXPAND_SIMP is frequently used in these proofs. This strategy expands certain definitions and simplifies the result using a few other rewrite rules and lemmas. Simple strategies, such as this, have helped greatly in reducing the length of the proofs and remove the intermediate clutter while rendering the proof more readable. Since extensive automation is the goal of all our analysis work, the next step is to pursue construction of more powerful strategies that are both language and model specific. In the example proof discussed earlier, it is rather straightforward to determine that one has to introduce ROLL and HDG transition relations to complete the proof. But generating this automatically as a strategy from the specification is rather involved. It requires identifying patterns in the sub-goal and invoking the right set of rules and lemmas, while at the same time, providing a fine-grained control to the user in choosing the proof steps to apply. Experience from our preliminary work in this area seems to suggest that such automated strategy generation is difficult. Manual proof construction provides a certain level of flexibility that lets the user determine the level of detail to which the specification must be drilled down during proof construction on a per subgoal basis. This flexibility has been critical for keeping the proofs readable and manageable. Construction of more powerful strategies seem to trade-off some of this flexibility. Our current efforts are directed towards finding the right balance between the two for typical proofs for RSML^{-e} models.

In conclusion, in this paper we presented a method for formalizing a synchronous dataflow language in PVS, based on which a mechanical translator was implemented. A salient feature of the translation scheme is that it reflects the structure and the semantics of the source specification, which has been useful in proof construction. We have been successful in verifying non-trivial properties of the mode logic in a flight-guidance system. Some of these properties could not be model-checked. We also observed that the proof complexity did not grow exponentially with the size of the model.

References

1. Myla Archer, Constance Heitmeyer, and Steve Sims. TAME: A PVS interface to simplify proofs for automata models. In *User Interfaces for Theorem Provers*, 1998.
2. S. Bensalem, P. Caspi, C. Parent-Vigouroux, and C. Dumas. A methodology for proving control systems with Lustre and PVS. In *Proceedings of the Seventh Working Conference on Dependable Computing for Critical Applications (DCCA 7)*, 1999.
3. Ricky W. Butler, Steven P. Miller, James N. Potts, and Victor A. Carreno. A formal methods approach to the analysis of mode confusion. In *17 th AIAA/IEEE Digital Avionics Systems Conference*, October 1998.
4. W. Chan, R.J. Anderson, P. Beame, S. Burns, F. Modugno, D. Notkin, and J.D. Reese. Model checking large software specifications. *IEEE Transactions on Software Engineering*, 24(7):498–520, July 1998.
5. Yunja Choi and Mats Heimdahl. Model checking RSML^{-e} requirements. In *Proceedings of the 7th IEEE/IEICE International Symposium on High Assurance Systems Engineering*, October 2002.
6. P. Clements. *Software Cost Reduction through Disciplined Design*. 1984 Naval Research Laboratory Review, Washington D.C., 1985. Available as National Technical Information Service order number AD-A1590000, pp. 79-87, July 1985.
7. J. Crow, S. Owre, J. Rushby, et al. A tutorial introduction to PVS. In *WIFT 95: Workshop on Industrial-Strength Formal Specification Techniques*, 1995.
8. D. Harel. Statecharts: A visual formalism for complex systems. *Science of Computer Programming*, 8(3):231–274, June 1987.
9. Anjali Joshi, Steve P. Miller, and Mats P.E. Heimdahl. Mode confusion analysis of a flight guidance system using formal methods. In *To appear in Digital Avionics Systems Conference*, 2003.

10. Nancy G. Leveson, Mats P.E. Heimdahl, and Jon Damon Reese. Designing Specification Languages for Process Control Systems: Lessons Learned and Steps to the Future. In *Seventh ACM SIGSOFT Symposium on the Foundations on Software Engineering*, volume 1687 of *LNCS*, pages 127–145, September 1999.
11. N.G. Leveson, M.P.E. Heimdahl, H. Hildreth, and J.D. Reese. Requirements Specification for Process-Control Systems. *IEEE Transactions on Software Engineering*, 20(9):684–706, September 1994.
12. NuSMV: A New Symbolic Model Checking. Available at http://nusmv.irst.itc.it/.
13. S. Owre, J. Rushby, and N. Shankar. Analyzing tabular and state-transition requirements specifications in PVS. Technical Report SRI-CSL-95-12, SRI International, June 1995.
14. Jeffrey M. Thompson and Mats P.E. Heimdahl. An integrated development environment prototyping safety critical systems. In *Tenth IEEE International Workshop on Rapid System Prototyping (RSP) 99*, pages 172–177, June 1999.
15. Michael W. Whalen. A formal semantics for RSML^{-e}. Master's thesis, University of Minnesota, May 2000.

Formalising an Integrated Language in PVS

Gwen Salaün and Christian Attiogbé

IRIN, Université de Nantes
2 rue de la Houssinière, B.P. 92208
44322 Nantes Cedex 3, France
{salaun,attiogbe}@irin.univ-nantes.fr

Abstract. System verification is one of the main topics of interest in formal methods. In this paper, we especially focus on equivalence proofs between abstract specification and more concrete ones. We propose an encoding into PVS of an integrated specification language. This language integrates the CCS process algebra extended to manage algebraic terms written from datatype definitions. Such an integrated language is useful to specify large size systems and to cover the different involved aspects. This encoding makes it possible the use of PVS for verification of nontrivial systems.

Keywords: Formal Method Integration, Process Algebra, Algebraic Specifications, Embedding, PVS, Equivalence Proof.

1 Introduction

Complex systems are composed of several different aspects, mainly the data (or static) aspects and the behaviour (or dynamic) aspects. It is interesting to allow the developer to specify each aspect of the system with suitable formalisms. Algebraic specification languages and process algebras are respectively appropriate to specify the static and the dynamic aspects. The material of this paper is issued from a series of work concerning integration of formal specification techniques [32–34]. These works aim at integrating process algebras with algebraic specifications. Algebraic terms enhanced the process algebra through the value passing. The global semantics is given in an operational way. Alternative integration approaches exist, especially the one combining state oriented languages (mainly Z and B) with process algebra, see [16, 15, 25, 36, 38] for instance. Currently, we prefer an algebraic description of data since their translation to PVS, our target proof environment, is easier than for state oriented languages.

We focus on the behavioural semantics of such integrated languages, that means the axiomatisation which describes the bisimulation or observational equivalence of two processes. This is essential if we aim to achieve equivalence proofs between processes. That can be achieved using tools like PVS [12], HOL [19] or Isabelle [30]. We refer to higher order theorem provers because classical ones such as the Larch Prover [17] lack expressive input forms and automated proof capabilities. This automation, particularly developed in PVS, guided our choice of this tool. Similarly, the existing model-checkers are not sufficient as target tools. Indeed, most of them only take into account dynamic aspects, but not data ones (algebraic terms in our framework). Though it is not the case of the CADP toolbox [14], its limit is the state explosion problem.

J.S. Dong and J. Woodcock (Eds.): ICFEM 2003, LNCS 2885, pp. 187–205, 2003.

Our goal is to embed an integrated specification language into PVS so as to perform equivalence proofs. This kind of proof is necessary for different reasons such as minimizing systems or refining them. Refinement means two versions of a same specification, one abstract and one more concrete, are proved to be equivalent. For this study, we choose the axiomatisation for only one precise process algebra, CCS. However, our approach could be considered as guidelines for the translation in PVS of other integrated languages which have similar features (process algebra and abstract datatypes of which LOTOS [6, 22] is another example).

In previous works, only partial verification was performed on the independent parts of the specification. As far as the dynamic part is concerned, specifications obtained using our approach may be animated or verified using model-checking. They may be translated in specific tools – such as CWB-NC [11] – input languages abstracting away from the datatypes. As far as the static part is concerned, one may use theorem provers or toolboxes dedicated to the static languages that are being used within the integration (*e.g.* CATS[1] for CASL, Larch Prover for Larch). We also have developed a tool, ISA [2], dedicated to the animation of specifications combining CCS with abstract datatypes. In this paper, we show that equivalence proofs on the global specification could be performed in an homogeneous context such as the PVS one. The algebraic specification part will be expressed using the PVS abstract datatypes. About the dynamic part, we choose the CCS process algebra and we take as a starting point of our formalisation some existing works [3, 29].

The organization of this paper is as follows. Section 2 introduces the formal foundations underlying our proposal: the integrated specification technique, its behavioural semantics, the PVS theorem prover and the embedding techniques. Section 3 deals with the embedding of the language into PVS. Then, we show in Section 4 how abstract specifications could be written and proved to be equivalent to more concrete ones. Finally, Section 5 makes the assessment of our approach.

2   Formal Foundations Underlying Our Proposal

2.1   The Integrated Formal Specification Language

We present our formalism which combines CCS and algebraic specifications. More comprehensive presentations are reported in [32, 34].

Syntax. CCS is a process algebra introduced by Milner [27]. It permits to describe communicating systems called processes or agents. Each CCS process is defined by a behaviour made of actions composed using operators. CCS has operators for prefixing (.), nondeterministic choice (+), parallel composition (|), restriction to enforce synchronization (\) and *if* structure. Relabeling and extended sum are not taken into account in our proposal for sake of conciseness. CCS allows synchronous, binary and oriented communication. We emphasize that our approach is control driven and CCS is called the main formalism because it gives the behaviour of the full specification. Concerning algebraic specifications, different concrete language could be considered such as

---

[1] http://www.tzi.de/cofi/Tools/CATS.html

Larch [18] or CASL [1]. Interactions between algebraic terms and CCS agents are located at five levels: the parameterized agent declarations and calls, the input and output parameterized actions, and the condition of the *if* operator.

Let us now present an example of a CCS agent including algebraic data terms. It describes a process called $Agent_0$ parameterized by a natural number. If the number is greater or equal to 5, the process outputs it (an overlined action indicates an output, otherwise it is an input) and recursively behaves as itself with a decreasing of the x value.

$$Agent_0(x : Nat) \stackrel{def}{=} \text{if } x \geq 5 \text{ then } \overline{send}(x).Agent_0(x - 1)$$

Semantics. The global operational semantics of our formalism is defined following an approach similar to Galloway's one for ZCCS [16]. The precise meaning of the different CCS constructions with algebraic value passing is given using inference rules. The environment E is a context storing various informations used to define the inference rules. E is a tuple composed of the rewrite rules R deduced from the axioms of the algebraic part and of a set of tuples $CCSE$ for CCS agents. This set is built from the full specification (*i.e.* both algebraic sorts and CCS agents).

$$\boxed{E \triangleq\ < R, CCSE >}$$

The semantics of the independent algebraic specifications is as described initially for each language (*e.g* see [18] for Larch). However, the meaning of algebraic terms appearing in the CCS agents is given by term rewriting. This choice is justified since it is suitable to an operational semantics. The rewriting is performed using a set R of rewrite rules deduced from the datatype definitions. As an example, rewriting of Larch terms can be achieved using the Larch Prover [17].

The set $CCSE$ contains informations recorded during the agent declaration. More precisely, for each agent declaration, we store in this set a tuple containing the agent name (or agent constant) AC, its whole behaviour H and the list of the agent parameters (identifiers) AP.

$$\boxed{CCSE \triangleq \{< AC_1, H_1, AP_1 >, \ldots, < AC_n, H_n, AP_n >\}}$$

These three values, associated with each agent, are useful in presence of agent call. In such a case, the agent constant is substituted by the behaviour corresponding to this call. Moreover, for a parameterized agent, the identifiers stored during the declaration are substituted in the whole behaviour by the terms used as parameter.

There are two groups of inference rules in our operational semantics. The first group corresponds to the construction of the E environment from the agent definitions and the algebraic specification part. The E environment, after being completely built, is never modified. The second group gives the meaning for each (possibly extended) CCS operator. For this second group, the global specification is seen as a Labelled Transition System (LTS) which evolves by the application of the inference rules. For instance, the next rules give the meaning of the parallel composition.

```
BEHAVIOUR ::= BEHAVIOUR|BEHAVIOUR
```

$$\frac{F \overset{\alpha}{\to} F'}{F|G \overset{\alpha}{\to} F'|G}$$

$$\frac{F \overset{a}{\to} F' \quad G \overset{\bar{a}}{\to} G'}{F|G \overset{\tau}{\to} F'|G'}$$

$$\frac{F \xrightarrow{a(x_1:S_1,\ldots,x_n:S_n)} F' \quad G \xrightarrow{\bar{a}(t_1,\ldots,t_n)} G'}{F|G \overset{\tau}{\to} F'[\overset{R}{\downarrow} t_1/x_1,\ldots,\overset{R}{\downarrow} t_n/x_n]|G'}$$

The reading of the last rule is: if a behaviour F evolves in F' after the firing of an input parameterized action, and if a behaviour G evolves in G' by an output parameterized action, then $F|G$ evolves in $F'|G'$ by τ. The input variables x_i are substituted in the behaviour F' by the terms t_i received during the synchronization. These terms are rewritten in their normal forms (when possible) thanks to the R rewrite rules.

2.2 Axiomatisation

We recall here the material we need to support rewriting of CCS processes. Equivalence relations were introduced by Milner [27] and Hennessy and Milner [23]. Equivalences are formalised using axiomatic rules. Equivalences between behaviours are proved through rewriting of behaviours with respect to equalities defining a precise equivalence relation. Observational semantics is given through equivalence relations. Examples of such a semantics are strong equivalence, observation equivalence / congruence, trace / testing equivalences and branching bisimulation.

Now, we give an axiomatisation describing an observational semantics for CCS. To prove the equivalence between two agents, we will apply the next laws following the principle of *substituting equals for equals*. This is only possible if the equivalence is a congruence [29] (relation preserved by all CCS operators). Laws for observation congruence (written = in the following) are shown below. These laws have been proved correct and complete [23,27]. We start with the basic laws for choice, tau (τ), parallel composition and restriction. As an illustration, the first four axioms below are defined for the nondeterministic choice and respectively mean the commutativity, the associativity and two reduction rules.

$$
\begin{aligned}
P + Q &= Q + P \\
P + (Q + R) &= (P + Q) + R \\
P + P &= P \\
P + 0 &= P \\
\alpha.\tau.P &= \alpha.P \\
P + \tau.P &= \tau.P \\
\alpha.(P + \tau.Q) + \alpha.Q &= \alpha.(P + \tau.Q)
\end{aligned}
$$

$$
\begin{aligned}
P|Q &= Q|P \\
P|(Q|R) &= (P|Q)|R \\
P|0 &= P
\end{aligned}
$$

$$
\begin{aligned}
0\backslash L &= 0 \\
(X+Y)\backslash L &= X\backslash L + Y\backslash L \\
(\alpha.X)\backslash L &= \alpha.(X\backslash L) \text{ if } \alpha \notin L \\
(\alpha.X)\backslash L &= 0 \text{ if } \alpha \in L
\end{aligned}
$$

The expansion law was initially introduced by Milner [27]. This law formalises the possible evolutions of processes combined with the parallel composition and the restriction operators. One evolution step is either an independent evolution of one behaviour or a binary synchronization of two behaviours. Other formulations of the expansion law exist [29, 21]. The difference in formulation is worthy of interest because Milner considers parallel composition and restriction in the same rule (that seems rather convenient for communication in CCS) whereas the others deal with them separately.

$$
\text{if } P \equiv (u_1.P_1|...|u_n.P_n)\backslash L \text{ then}
$$
$$
P = \sum \{u_i.(u_1.P_1|...|P_i|...|u_n.P_n)\backslash L : u_i, \overline{u_i} \notin L\} +
$$
$$
\sum \{\tau.(u_1.P_1|...|P_i'|...|P_j'|...|u_n.P_n)\backslash L : u_i = \overline{u_j}\}
$$

Note that these axioms allow only equational reasoning on simple CCS agents. In the current work, CCS is extended with data expressions. Nevertheless, that is the same equivalence relation which is enhanced with an equality relation on terms similar to the common equalities of the algebraic specifications rewriting.

2.3   The PVS Theorem Prover

PVS[2] is a verification system that is an interactive environment for writing formal specifications and checking formal proofs. PVS provides an expressive specification language that enhances classical higher order logic with a sophisticated type system containing predicate subtypes and dependent types. It also proposes parameterized theories and a mechanism for defining and using abstract datatypes. The PVS typechecker is undecidable due to the combination of the previous features. It copes with this undecidability by generating proof obligations (TCC, Type-Correctness Conditions) for the PVS theorem prover (that are discharged automatically for most of them). PVS has a powerful interactive theorem prover / proof checker. User-defined proof strategies can be used to enhance the automation of the proof checker. Model-checking capabilities used for automatically verifying temporal properties of finite-state systems have recently been integrated in PVS. An input PVS specification is a collection of theories containing types, functions, lemma and theorems.

2.4   Embedding Techniques

An embedding [7] is an encoding or a translation of a specification language into another one, especially to reuse existing tools of the target language. Embeddings are

---

[2] http://pvs.csl.sri.com/

also useful to combine strengths of formal methods and verification systems. Two main kinds of embedding are distinguished. The *shallow embedding* is a syntactic translation of the formal specification in semantically equivalent objects in the language of the verification system. The *deep embedding* encapsulates the language and its semantics as an object in the logic of the target system. The latter approach is rather dedicated to prove meta-theoretical properties (that are proofs on the encoded language) of the embedded method whereas the shallow approach favours the reasoning on particular applications. Other kinds of embeddings exist such as the *structural embedding* [28] which mixes both previous approaches. Our proposal aims to encode the integrated specification language following the shallow embedding approach which must be augmented with the axiomatisation encoding.

3 Embedding of One Integrated Language into PVS

We focus in this section on the different steps of our embedding into the PVS logic. We remind that we chose a shallow embedding. This choice is justified because we focus on a mechanical support oriented towards verification of concrete applications. Nevertheless, proofs of meta-theoretical properties are possible too since we add the encoding of a behavioural axiomatisation formalising the meaning of the operators.

The main guidelines we perform to reach the encoding of the integrated specification language and proofs of concrete specifications are the following. First, actions, CCS operators and their axioms are expressed using the PVS logic. We start the embedding with a small set of operators (possibly without value passing) and then we enhance this initial set of constructions (addition of operators and corresponding axioms). Afterwards, we implement the extended CCS version, particularly the algebraic value passing and the substitution of variables by real terms in behaviours. A transverse work is the abstract datatype definitions in PVS and the term rewriting in this context.

3.1 Basic Actions

In a first step, we introduce the theory `BasicA` corresponding to the encoding of basic actions, *i.e.* actions without value passing. Two types are defined, `Name` and `Action`, representing the action name and the action in general (possibly with value passing in the sequel). At this level, a constant and two functions describe respectively the tau action, an input action and an output action. Three additional functions (`the_name`, `eq_action`, `eq_name`) are implemented to respectively recover the name of a global action, to test the equality of two actions and to test the equality of two action names. Some axioms formalise the meaning of these functions. In this work, we choose to specify functions using an axiomatic style and not a definitional one (which could be used too). In our opinion, axiomatic style is more suitable to perform behavioural rewriting. Indeed, rewriting could be handled step by step in a more manageable way.

```
BasicA: THEORY
  BEGIN
    Name: TYPE+
    Action: TYPE+
    tau: Action
    input: [ Name -> Action ]
    output: [ Name -> Action ]
    the_name: [ Action -> Name ]
    eq_action: [ Action, Action -> bool]
    eq_name: [Name, Name -> bool]
    m, m1, m2: VAR Name
    tn1: AXIOM the_name(input(m)) = m
    tn2: AXIOM the_name(output(m)) = m
    eq1: AXIOM eq_action(tau,tau) = true
    eq2: AXIOM eq_action(tau,input(m)) = false
    eq3: AXIOM eq_action(tau,output(m)) = false
    eq4: AXIOM eq_action(input(m),tau) = false
    eq5: AXIOM eq_action(input(m1),input(m2)) = eq_name(m1,m2)
    eq6: AXIOM eq_action(input(m1),output(m2)) = false
    ...
  END BasicA
```

3.2 Value Passing Actions

The VpA theory completes the previous one with value passing actions. This theory is parameterized by the type of the parameter bound to the action. This typing is required by the PVS typechecker. Consequently, actions (in a general sense) are labelled by the type of data that one action can send or receive. New functions for input and output are defined and overload the previous ones. Axioms for the the_name and eq_action functions are enhanced with respect to the new declarations.

```
VpA [T: TYPE]: THEORY
BEGIN
   IMPORTING BasicA
   input: [ Name, T -> Action ]
   output: [ Name, T -> Action ]
   n, n1, n2: VAR Name
   x, x1, x2: VAR T
   tn3: AXIOM the_name(input(n,x)) = n
   tn4: AXIOM the_name(output(n,x)) = n
   eq10: AXIOM eq_action(tau,input(n,x)) = false
   eq11: AXIOM eq_action(tau,output(n,x)) = false
   ...
END VpA
```

3.3 Basic Process Algebra

The BasicPA1 theory embeds the basic process algebra into the PVS logic. The value passing extension is dealt with in the next subsection. First of all, we note the use of a datatype describing generic sets (see [35] for its definition). This datatype is needed to describe the set of restricted actions. Generic sets also exist in the PVS prelude, but we prefer a datatype parameterized by an explicit equality function (and not just to use a syntactic one). A set is made of two constructors `empty` and `add`. A function `member` is defined to test the membership of an element in a set.

The type `Behaviour` is now defined. The `nil` behaviour is declared as well as the CCS operators: the nondeterministic choice +, the prefixing o, the parallel composition /, the `ifthen` structure and the restriction `res`. The `bhv` function makes implicitly the conversion of action in behaviour. Some variables have also to be declared for the forthcoming definition of axioms.

```
BasicPA1: THEORY
BEGIN
    IMPORTING BasicA
    IMPORTING Set_op[Name,eq_name]
    Behaviour: TYPE
    nil: Behaviour
    bhv: [ Action -> Behaviour ] CONVERSION bhv
    +, o, /: [ Behaviour, Behaviour -> Behaviour ]
    ifthen: [ bool, Behaviour -> Behaviour ]
    res: [ Behaviour, Set[Name,eq_name] -> Behaviour ]
    a, b: VAR Action
    F, G, H, I: VAR Behaviour
    b: VAR bool
    L: VAR Set[Name,eq_name]
    n1, n2: VAR Name
    ...
```

Afterwards, axioms defining the behavioural semantics are encoded into PVS. They correspond to the rules introduced in subsection 2.2 (axioms B1 to B15b). Some axioms are added to deal with the parenthesizing (not included here). Finally, the expansion law is encoded using different axioms to depict the possible cases (axioms BM16 to BM63). Below, the BM16 axiom denotes the synchronization between two agents on the same action name. The BM63 axiom is devoted to an interleaving case between two parallel output actions where just one is possible (the other pertaining to the restriction set). Agent call is not straightforwardly implemented in the theory but is expressed during the concrete agent writing (see Section 4). Furthermore, the embedding of a CCS notation into PVS could be simply generalized to any kind of process algebra following a similar approach.

```
B1: AXIOM F + G = G + F
B2: AXIOM F + (G + H) = (F + G) + H
B3: AXIOM F + F = F
B4: AXIOM F + nil = F
B5: AXIOM a o (tau o F) = a o F
B6: AXIOM F + tau o F = tau o F
B7: AXIOM a o (F + tau o G) + a o G = a o (F + tau o G)
B8: AXIOM F / G = G / F
B9: AXIOM F / (G / H) = (F / G) / H
```

```
B10:  AXIOM F / nil = F
B11:  AXIOM ifthen(b,G) = IF b THEN G ELSE nil ENDIF
B12:  AXIOM res(nil, L) = nil
B13:  AXIOM res(F + G, L) = res(F, L) + res(G, L)
B14:  AXIOM F = res(a o G, L) AND NOT eq_action(a,tau)
  AND not member(the_name(a), L) IMPLIES F = a o res(G, L)
B15:  AXIOM F = res(a o G, L) AND NOT eq_action(a,tau)
  AND member(the_name(a), L) IMPLIES F = nil
B15b: AXIOM F = res(tau o G, L) IMPLIES F = tau o res(G,L)
BM16: AXIOM eq_name(n1,n2) AND F = input(n1) o H
  AND G = output(n2) o I
    IMPLIES res(F / G, L) = tau o (H / I)
  ...
BM63: AXIOM F = output(n1) o H AND G = output(n2) o I
  AND not member(n1, L) AND member(n2, L)
    IMPLIES res(F / G, L) = output(n1) o res(H / G, L)
END BasicPA1
```

Let us show an example of a basic agent described in CCS and then encoded into PVS using our theory.

$$Agent_1 \stackrel{def}{=} n.(\overline{m}.0 + \overline{p}.Agent_1)$$

```
Agent1 = input(n) o (output(m) o nil + output(p) o Agent1)
```

3.4   Value Passing Process Algebra

We start with the description of a theory encoding the substitution of a variable by a term in a whole behaviour. As illustration, we show a piece of behaviour with value passing. In this example, we rewrite the behaviour using the Milner's expansion law. We stress that, after communication on the action name n, the variable x is substituted in the remaining of the behaviour ($x + 3 \rightsquigarrow 2 + 3$) and then rewritten as 5.

$$(n(x).(\overline{m}(x+3).0)/\overline{n}(2).0)\backslash\{n\} = \tau.(\overline{m}(5).0)\backslash\{n\}$$

Now, we describe the dynsubst function performing the substitution. This function substitutes a term by another with the same typing in a behaviour. It is defined inductively on the different operators of the embedded process algebra as written in the axioms identified by DSij in the PVS theories. We highlight that this function depends on another substitution function concerning the static part. Indeed, the statsubst function performs the substitution of a variable by a value in a term (for instance substituting x with 2 in $x + 3$). This function is needed because this kind of substitution is not achieved by the PVS equational reasoning capabilities.

The statsubst function is a tedious task to be faced during this embedding because this kind of function have to be defined by the user for each new datatype. Moreover, in our encoding we only take into account a simple static substitution case in which the substitution is achieved in an expression with the same type as the variable to be substituted, whereas in real cases it seems also natural to replace for instance a natural number in a boolean expression (*e.g.* $x + 3 < 5$). This disadvantage is discussed in more details in Section 5.

The axiom DS11 expresses that the substitution of x by the term t in the process τ. F is equal to the process F, in which the previous substitution has to be performed, prefixed by τ. The axioms DS12 and DS13 denote the absence of effective substitution for input and output actions without parameter. DS21 and DS22 depict the appropriate application of the statsubst function for parameterized actions, and so on.

```
DynSubst [T: TYPE, statsubst: [T, T, T-> T]]: THEORY
BEGIN
    IMPORTING BasicPA1
    IMPORTING VpA[T]
    dynsubst: [Behaviour, T, T -> Behaviour]
    n: VAR Name
    x, x1, x2, t: VAR T
    F, G, H, I: VAR Behaviour
    L: VAR Set[Name,eq_name]
    b: VAR bool
    DS11: AXIOM dynsubst(tau o F, x, t) =
      tau o dynsubst(F, x, t)
    DS12: AXIOM dynsubst(input(n) o F, x, t) =
      input(n) o dynsubst(F, x, t)
    DS13: AXIOM dynsubst(output(n) o F, x, t) =
      output(n) o dynsubst(F, x, t)
    DS21: AXIOM dynsubst(input[T](n, x1) o F, x2, t) =
      input[T](n, statsubst(x1, x2, t)) o dynsubst(F, x2, t)
    DS22: AXIOM dynsubst(output[T](n, x1) o F, x2, t) =
      output[T](n, statsubst(x1, x2, t)) o dynsubst(F, x2, t)
    DS31: AXIOM dynsubst(nil, x, t) = nil
    DS32: AXIOM dynsubst(F+G, x, t) =
      dynsubst(F, x, t) + dynsubst(G, x, t)
    ...
END DynSubst
```

The value passing process algebra theory mainly contains the supplementary axioms to cope with the expansion law in case of parameterized actions. Thus, we enumerate the possible cases of behaviours rewriting using the definition of subsection 2.2 extended with data management. In the expansion law, the parallel composition and restriction operators are considered at the same time. Therefore, synchronization and interleaving cases are not split in a different set of rules. That is illustrated below with the axioms for τ actions. As far as the communication is concerned, the dynsubst function is called so as to perform the substitution in the remainder of the behaviour. Parenthesizing rules are added too in order to simplify parenthesized behaviours. The VpPA1 theory is parameterized by two types and two possible static substitution functions. This double typing is needed to make it possible the interleaving of different type parameterized actions. We only permit single parameterized action in this work because it is sufficiently expressive. The multi-parameterized case could be expressed in the simpler one, so it is not fundamentally necessary.

The VPM1 and VPM2 axioms below denote the synchronization between two agents. The VMP3i axioms express the three possible interleaving cases depending on the pertaining (or not) of the action name to the restriction set. The VPM4i axioms are the same but considering the reverse sense between input and output.

```
VpPA1 [T, T1: TYPE, statsubst: [T, T, T -> T],
    statsubst1: [T1, T1, T1 -> T1]]: THEORY
BEGIN
    IMPORTING DynSubst[T,statsubst]
    IMPORTING DynSubst[T1,statsubst1]
    n, n1, n2: VAR Name
    x, y, t, r: VAR T
    x1, y1, t1, r1: VAR T1
    F, G, H, I: VAR Behaviour
    L: VAR Set[Name,eq_name]
VPM1: AXIOM eq_name(n1,n2) AND F = input[T](n1,x) o H
      AND G = output[T](n2,t) o I
    IMPLIES res(F / G, L) = tau o res(dynsubst(H,x,t) / I, L)
VPM2: AXIOM eq_name(n1,n2) AND F = output[T](n1,t) o H
      AND G = input[T](n2,x) o I
    IMPLIES res(F / G, L) = tau o res(H / dynsubst(I,x,t), L)
VPM31: AXIOM NOT eq_name(n1,n2) AND F = input[T](n1,x) o H
    AND G = output[T](n2,t) o I
      AND not member(n1, L) AND not member(n2, L) IMPLIES
    res(F / G, L) = input[T](n1,x) o res(H / G, L)
      + output[T](n2,t) o res(F / I, L)
VPM32: AXIOM NOT eq_name(n1,n2) AND F = input[T](n1,x) o H
    AND G = output[T](n2,t) o I
      AND member(n1, L) AND not member(n2, L) IMPLIES
    res(F / G, L) = output[T](n2,t) o res(F / I, L)
VPM33: AXIOM NOT eq_name(n1,n2) AND F = input[T](n1,x) o H
    AND G = output[T](n2,t) o I
      AND not member(n1, L) AND member(n2, L) IMPLIES
    res(F / G, L) = input[T](n1,x) o res(H / G, L)
VPM41: AXIOM NOT eq_name(n1,n2) AND F = output[T](n1,t) o H
    AND G = input[T](n2,x) o I
      AND not member(n1, L) AND not member(n2, L) IMPLIES
    res(F / G, L) = output[T](n1,t) o res(H / G, L)
      + input[T](n2,x) o res(F / I, L)
...
END VpPA1
```

Let us illustrate on an example of a value passing behaviour described in CCS and then encoded into PVS.

$$Agent_2 \stackrel{def}{=} n(x). \text{ if } x = 2 \text{ then } \overline{p}(x+1).Agent_2$$

```
Agent2 = input[Nat](n,x) o (ifthen(egal(x,succ(succ(zero))),
         output[Nat](p,plus(x,succ(zero))) o Agent2))
```

3.5   Datatype Definitions and Rewriting

The integrated specification language uses algebraic specifications for the modelling of static aspects. Our shallow embedding of data aspects is straightforward thanks to the datatype possibilities of the PVS input logic. As a well-known example, consider the Nat and Nat_op theories. The first one only contains the constructors zero and succ. The operations on natural numbers are the usual ones such as plus or minus. PVS also generates a theory from the Nat datatype containing several axioms and definitions. We stress that the definition of the natural number substitution (replacing one natural by another in a natural number expression) is defined inductively on the different operators of the datatype.

```
Nat_op: THEORY
BEGIN
   IMPORTING Nat
   plus: [Nat, Nat -> Nat]
   minus: [Nat, Nat -> Nat]
   ...
   natsubst: [Nat, Nat, Nat -> Nat]
   x, y, z, t, x1, x2: VAR Nat
   plus1: AXIOM plus(x,zero) = x;
   plus2: AXIOM plus(x,succ(y)) = succ(plus(x,y));
   ...
   SS1: AXIOM natsubst(zero,x,t) = zero
   SS2: AXIOM natsubst(succ(y),x,t) = succ(natsubst(y,x,t))
   SS3: AXIOM natsubst(plus(x1,x2),x,t) =
       plus(natsubst(x1,x,t),natsubst(x2,x,t))
   SS4: AXIOM natsubst(minus(x1,x2),x,t) =
       minus(natsubst(x1,x,t),natsubst(x2,x,t))
   SS5: AXIOM x1=x2 IMPLIES natsubst(x1,x2,t) = t
   ...
END Nat_op
```

Real-size examples have also been specified using the PVS datatypes, for example a stock of drink with its available quantity. Concerning the rewriting of algebraic terms, it could be performed either manually or automatically (using one of the auto-rewrite command) thanks to the rewrite capabilities of PVS. Theorems could be proved on this part using the PVS prover. The reader may refer to [35] for a comprehensive PVS specification of a vending machine and for examples of theorems on this data part.

4   Concrete Specification and Equivalence Proof

In this section, we illustrate how our embedded language may be used to specify and refine concrete systems. We focus on the specification of a small but realistic example: the coupling of an adder with a multiplier. This system is refined using the axiomatic definitions introduced in Section 3.

Specification. The current system is made of two communicating parts. Each involved process manages natural terms as value passing. We do not manage more complex

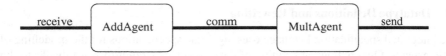

Fig. 1. Adder/Multiplier.

datatypes for sake of readability and comprehension of the system specification and proof steps. The first agent is an adder that receives a value (x) and adds to this value another one (u, parameter of the agent). The second part is a multiplier which receives a value (plus(x,u)) from the adder and multiplies this value by another one (v). Figure 1 schematizes the general idea of this simple system. The specification is then written in the source integrated specification language.

$$AddAgent(u : Nat) \stackrel{def}{=} receive(x : Nat).(\overline{comm}(x + u).AddAgent(u))$$
$$MultAgent(v : Nat) \stackrel{def}{=} comm(y).(\overline{send}(y * v).MultAgent(v))$$

We introduce now the PVS specification written using the theories presented previously. In the agent definitions, axiomatic specifications make it possible the agent call avoiding the use of recursive function and measure function to ensure termination. The Nat_op theory is imported in order to use its contents and especially the natsubst function. The VpPA1 theory is also imported with the parameters Nat and natsubst. The action names are defined as well as the variables used to write the agent behaviours. Afterwards, agents are declared. Inputs and outputs are explicitly typed using Nat.

```
EXAMPLE: THEORY
BEGIN
   IMPORTING Nat_op
   IMPORTING VpPA1[Nat,Nat,natsubst,natsubst]
   receive, send, comm: Name
   x, y: VAR Nat

   u: VAR Nat
   AddAgent: [Nat -> Behaviour]
   defAddAgent: AXIOM AddAgent(u) =
      input[Nat](receive,x) o
         (output[Nat](comm,plus(x,u)) o AddAgent(u))
   v: VAR Nat
   MultAgent: [Nat -> Behaviour]
   defMultAgent: AXIOM MultAgent(v) =
      input[Nat](comm,y) o
         (output[Nat](send,mult(y,v)) o MultAgent(v))
   ...
```

Equivalence Proof. We show how one equivalence between a behaviour and its refined form could be proved by rewriting one to the other. We write below the theorem ThM to be proved. An intermediate lemma is used. The goal is to prove the equivalence between an abstract specification (the AddAgent and MultAgent parallel composition communicating on the comm name) and a more concrete one where the communication is hidden and the parallel composition expanded. In the proof, we replace the agent

call by a termination behaviour to simplify the proof steps to a finite case. This issue is
discussed in Section 5.

```
LM: LEMMA
   AddAgent(u)  / MultAgent(v)  =
      input[Nat](receive,x) o
         (output[Nat](comm,plus(x,u)) o nil) /
      input[Nat](comm,y) o
         (output[Nat](send,mult(y,v)) o nil)
ThM: THEOREM
   res(input[Nat](receive,x) o
      (output[Nat](comm,plus(x,u)) o nil) /
   input[Nat](comm,y) o
      (output[Nat](send,mult(y,v)) o nil), add(comm, empty)) =
   input[Nat](receive,x) o
      (output[Nat](send,mult(plus(x,u),v)) o nil)
```

The above LM lemma is proved using the agent definitions and the grind strategy.
Then, the theorem ThM (and some alternative formulations) is proved as follows. After
running the skosimp command, we apply one rule of Milner's expansion law (VPM53)
and instantiate this rule with adequate concrete parameters. Rewritings on the member
function are performed to simplify the active antecedent and this formula is replaced in
the consequent. The VPM2 axiom expresses the synchronization between both agents.
Dynamic and static substitution rewritings are performed. Several simplifications of the
antecedent are done with the B5, B10, B14, B12 axioms on one hand and the eq_name,
the_name, eq_action and member axioms on the other hand. The detailed proof steps
are reported in [35].

Several variants of this theorem have been proved too. For instance, we work with
more concrete parameters of behaviours: AddAgent(succ(zero)) / MultAgent(su
cc(succ(zero))). In such a case, rewriting of terms may be done. That is made
using the axioms defining the datatype operations. Nevertheless, we cannot make proofs
with a generic action (input[T](...)). Indeed, the statsubst function needs to be
instantiated. Then, meta-theoretical proofs are possible but limited to the use of this
function. To end, we highlight that debugging steps are performed in the PVS context
and not in the specification input language. Accordingly, expertise of the specifier is
needed at this level.

5   Discussion

In this paper, we advocate an embedding of an integrated specification language (the
CCS process algebra and algebraic specifications) into PVS. The encoding follows a
shallow embedding accompanied with an encoding of the axiomatisation to be used
for equivalence proofs. That results in some PVS theories. Specifications can be written using the implemented theories. Equivalence proofs on these specifications can be
achieved thanks to behavioural rewriting. Besides, meta-theoretical proofs are possible
too but in a limited way due to the extension of the process algebra to manage data
terms (and especially due to the underlying static substitution). Our proposal can be
viewed as guidelines to embed other (extended or not) process algebra into PVS.

Concerning existing works related to mixed bisimulation (*i.e.* bisimulation involving a static and a dynamic part), Calder *et al.* [10, 9] propose a symbolic semantics and bisimulation for Full LOTOS. This work is strongly related to ours but we do not completely follow their formalisation (*e.g.* the management of free and bound variables). As [24], our work could be viewed as an instantiation of this theoretical proposal.

Nesi [29] proposes a formalisation of Milner's value passing calculus in the HOL proof assistant in order to describe and reason about communicating systems. The resulting formalisation supports both meta-theoretic reasoning and verification strategies for CCS specifications. Compared to our, her work only deals with simple data and the proof steps are more tedious than using PVS. These two works also share common issues such as the recursion encoding. A work similar to the Nesi's one is [26]. This paper proposes a mechanized formal theory of the π-calculus in higher order logic using the HOL theorem prover.

Another work, strongly related to ours, is the one of Basten and Hooman [3]. The idea is to apply equational reasoning to ACP-style processes. Two alternatives for the modelling of process algebra in PVS are investigated in this paper. First, mechanical support is proposed for the verification of concrete applications (verifying that an implementation satisfies a specification). Secondly, mechanical support is suggested for the proof of theoretical properties of a process algebra (meta-reasoning). Two different features of the PVS logic are used to reach both previous mechanizations: process terms as uninterpreted types or as abstract datatypes. In comparison, our input language is more expressive, but consequently makes more difficult the meta-theoretical properties.

Van de Pol *et al.* [37] propose a specification of requirements using invariants on state for data, temporal assertions for behaviours and a simple glue between views. The support of this approach is developed and implemented in PVS. We may also note the proposal of Dutertre and Schneider [13]. They provide an effective mechanical support to the modelling and analysis of authentication protocols using PVS. They develop a general proof strategy for verifying authentication properties. This approach is quite different because close to a precise application domain. Brooke's work [8] takes inspiration in the previous one, but deals with timed-CSP as input language.

Bodeveix *et al.* [5, 4] formalise an embedding of the B abstract machine notation into Coq and PVS. Rather than translating the notation in PVS (the prover considered for concrete experiment), they add the notation as a layer over the PVS language. This embedding has been fully implemented in a front-end tool called PBS. Another similar work is the one of Pratten [31]. Gravell and Pratten [20] automate the embedding of Z specifications into the PVS and HOL theorem provers using the JavaLIL tool.

Our contribution with reference to the previous ones is the expressiveness of the integrated language we embed into PVS. This expressiveness makes it possible the specification of the different aspects involved in complex systems. We also show that verification (especially equivalence proof here) of such systems is tractable.

The mechanical support presented in this paper enables us to point out some issues faced during the encoding into PVS. A first drawback is the static substitution. The specifier have to implement for each new datatype the corresponding variable substitution function (because this substitution is strongly linked to the datatype definition).

In fact, this encoding is rather restricting. As an example, if we consider a datatype `T` which is a set of tuple, each tuple containing three values of type `T_1`, `T_2`, `T_3`, then there exist several possible variable substitution functions:

1. `statsubst_1: T, T_1, T_1 -> T`
2. `statsubst_1: T, T_2, T_2 -> T`
3. `statsubst_1: T, T_3, T_3 -> T`

In the case of more complex datatype, the number of possible functions increases. There are also possible nested calls of other static substitution functions. Moreover, the definition of such a function is systematic but error-prone and becomes harder with the number of static operations. The substitution function is not yet satisfactory. It would be better to define a higher order substitution function which use both terms and types as parameters. That is also a bolt to achieve meta-theoretic proofs because they need implementations of this function to complete the proof.

Another issue met during proof steps is the redundant problem of variable equality. Indeed, the inequality between variables cannot be proved with the PVS prover. Thus, to finish one proof and avoids these blocking steps, axioms have to be added in the suitable theories (for example `eqn1` and `eqn2` in the `BasicA` theory). This kind of axioms is essential but error-prone if badly used (the `eqn2` axiom may also matched with equal values).

```
eqn1: AXIOM eq_name(m,m)  = true
eqn2: AXIOM eq_name(m1,m2) = false
```

Next, proving theorems involving recursive agents is limited. A solution could be the one of Dutertre and Schneider [13]. In the context of their mechanical support for CSP, they implement a (generic) least fixed point operator. This operator allows one to define recursive processes and need induction rules for reasoning about such processes.

Finally, we emphasize that proving nontrivial examples of equivalence theorems could be reached with limited efforts, but efforts for complex system equivalence proofs are really time-consuming. Indeed, automated rewritings are rather problematic in PVS because the prover regularly faces difficulties on nontrivial proofs to resolve substitutions.

Many directions are interesting for future work. A first perspective is the scalability, *i.e.* we wish to improve our proposal and to have at our disposal a complete framework making it possible specifications and equivalence proofs of real size systems. The different drawbacks discussed above have to be think about to enhance the expressiveness and ease of use of our mechanized support. Besides, an alternative idea may be to experiment a deep (or semantic) embedding of the objects to be reasoned about. Another direction for future work is the increasing of the proof automation. That would simplify the restricting steps of behavioural rewriting. The main idea is to develop tactics which could be systematically applied and therefore could enhance the automation.

Acknowledgments

The authors would like to thank Michel Allemand for his support on initial versions of this work, Bruno Dutertre, Christoph Berg and Karim Berkani for judicious comments on the substitution issue, Mamoun Filali for fruitful remarks on this work, Pascal

Poizat for the discussion we had on this approach, and the anonymous referees for their numerous advice which increased the comprehension and readability level of the paper.

References

1. E. Astesiano, M. Bidoit, H. Kirchner, B. Krieg-Brückner, P. D. Mosses, D. Sannella, and A. Tarlecki. CASL: The Common Algebraic Specification Language. *Theoretical Computer Science*, 286(2):153–196, 2002.
2. C. Attiogbé, A. Francheteau, J. Limousin, and G. Salaün. ISA, a Tool for Integrated Specifications Animation. Available at http://www.sciences.univ-nantes.fr/info/perso/permanents/salaun/ISA/isa.html.
3. T. Basten and J. Hooman. Process Algebra in PVS. In W. R. Cleaveland, editor, *Proc. of the International Conference on Tools and Algorithms for the Construction and Analysis of Systems (TACAS '99)*, volume 1579 of *Lecture Notes in Computer Science*, pages 270–284, The Netherlands, 1999. Springer-Verlag.
4. J.-P. Bodeveix and M. Filali. Type Synthesis in B and the Translation of B to PVS. In *Proc. of the 2nd International Z and B Conference (ZB'02)*, volume 2272 of *Lecture Notes in Computer Science*, pages 350–369, France, 2002. Springer-Verlag.
5. J.-P. Bodeveix, M. Filali, and C. Muñoz. A Formalization of the B Method in Coq and PVS. In *Proc. of the B Users Group Meeting – Applying B in an industrial context: Tools, Lessons and Techniques (FM'99)*, pages 32–48. Springer-Verlag, 1999.
6. T. Bolognesi and E. Brinksma. Introduction to the ISO Specification Language LOTOS. In P. H. J. van Eijk, C. A. Vissers, and M. Diaz, editors, *The Formal Description Technique LOTOS*, pages 23–73. Elsevier Science Publishers North-Holland, 1989.
7. R. Boulton, A. Gordon, M. J. C. Gordon, J. Herbert, and J. van Tassel. Experience with Embedding Hardware Description Languages in HOL. In *Proc. of the International Conference on Theorem Provers in Circuit Design: Theory, Practice and Experience*, pages 129–156, The Netherlands, 1992. IFIP TC10/WG 10.2, North-Holland.
8. P. Brooke. *A Timed Semantics for a Hierarchical Design Notation*. PhD Thesis, University of York, 1999.
9. M. Calder, S. Maharaj, and C. Shankland. A Modal Logic for Full LOTOS Based on Symbolic Transition Systems. *The Computer Journal*, 45(1):55–61, 2002.
10. M. Calder and C. Shankland. A Symbolic Semantics and Bisimulation for Full LOTOS. In M. Kim, B. Chin, S. Kang, and D. Lee, editors, *Proc. of the International Conference on Formal Description Techniques for Networked and Distributed Systems (FORTE'01)*, volume 197 of *IFIP Conference Proceedings*, pages 184–200, Korea, 2001. Kluwer Academic Publishers.
11. R. Cleaveland, T. Li, and S. Sims. *The Concurrency Workbench of the New Century (Version 1.2)*. Department of Computer Science, North Carolina State University, 2000.
12. J. Crow, S. Owre, J. Rushby, N. Shankar, and M. Srivas. A Tutorial Introduction to PVS. In *Proc. of the Workshop on Industrial-Strength Formal Specification Techniques (WIFT'95)*, USA, 1995. Computer Science Laboratory, SRI International.
13. B. Dutertre and S. Schneider. Using a PVS Embedding of CSP to Verify Authentication Protocols. In E. Gunter and A. Felty, editors, *Proc. of the 10th International Conference on Theorem Proving in Higher Order Logics (TPHOLs '97)*, volume 1275 of *Lecture Notes in Computer Science*, pages 121–136, USA, 1997. Springer-Verlag.
14. J.-C. Fernandez, H. Garavel, A. Kerbrat, L. Mounier, R. Mateescu, and M. Sighireanu. CADP: A Protocol Validation and Verification Toolbox. In R. Alur and T. A. Henzinger, editors, *Proc. of the Eighth International Conference on Computer Aided Verification (CAV'96)*, volume 1102 of *Lecture Notes in Computer Science*, pages 437–440, USA, 1996. Springer-Verlag.

15. C. Fischer. CSP-OZ: a Combination of Object-Z and CSP. In H. Bowman and J. Derrick, editors, *Proc. of the 2nd IFIP Workshop on Formal Methods for Open Object-Based Distributed Systems (FMOODS'97)*, pages 423–438, UK, 1997. Chapman and Hall, London.

16. A. J. Galloway and W. Stoddart. An Operational Semantics for ZCCS. In M. G. Hinchey and S. Liu, editors, *Proc. of the 1st International Conference onf Formal Engineering Methods (ICFEM'97)*, pages 272–282, Japan, 1997. IEEE Computer Society Press.

17. S. J. Garland and J. V. Guttag. A Guide to LP, the Larch Prover. Technical Report, Palo Alto, California, 1991.

18. S. J. Garland, J. V. Guttag, and J. J. Horning. *An Overview of Larch*, volume 693 of *Lecture Notes in Computer Science*, pages 329–348. Springer Verlag, 1993.

19. M. J. C. Gordon and T. F. Melham. *Introduction to HOL: A Theorem Proving Environment for Higher Order Logic*. Cambridge University Press, 1993.

20. A. M. Gravell and C. H. Pratten. Embedding a Formal Notation: Experiences of Automating the Embedding of Z in the Higher Order Logics of PVS and HOL. In J. Grundy and M. Newey, editors, *Proc. of the 11th International Conference on Theorem Proving in Higher Order Logics (TPHOLs '98)*, volume 1479 of *Lecture Notes in Computer Science*, pages 73–84, Australia, 1998. Springer-Verlag.

21. A. Ingólfsdóttir and H. Lin. A Symbolic Approach to Value-Passing Processes. In J. A. Bergstra, A. Ponse, and S. A. Smolka, editors, *Handbook of Process Algebra*, pages 427–478. Elsevier, 2001.

22. ISO. LOTOS: a Formal Description Technique based on the Temporal Ordering of Observational Behaviour. Technical Report 8807, International Standards Organisation, 1989.

23. M. Hennessy and R. Milner. Algebraic Laws for Non-Determinism and Concurrency. *Journal of the ACM*, 32:137–161, 1985.

24. S. Maharaj. A PVS Theory of Symbolic Transition Systems. In R. J. Boulton and P. B. Jackson, editors, *TPHOLs 2001: Supplemental Proceedings*, pages 255–266, UK, 2001.

25. B. Mahony and J. S. Dong. Blending Object-Z and Timed CSP: An Introduction to TCOZ. In *Proc. of the International Conference on Software Engineering (ICSE'98)*, pages 95–104, Japan, 1998. IEEE Computer Society Press / ACM Press.

26. T. F. Melham. A Mechanized Theory of the π-calculus in HOL. *Nordic Journal of Computing*, 1(1):50–76, 1995.

27. R. Milner. *Communication and Concurrency*. International Series in Computer Science. Prentice Hall, 1989.

28. C. Muñoz and J. Rushby. Structural Embeddings: Mechanization with Method. In J. Wing and J. Woodcock, editors, *Proc. of the The World Congress in Formal Methods (FM'99)*, volume 1708 of *Lecture Notes in Computer Science*, pages 452–471, France, 1999. Springer-Verlag.

29. M. Nesi. Formalising a Value-Passing Calculus in HOL. *Formal Aspects of Computing*, 11(2):160–199, 1999.

30. T. Nipkow and L. C. Paulson. Isabelle-91. In D. Kapur, editor, *Proc. of the 11th International Conference on Automated Deduction (CADE'92)*, volume 607 of *Lecture Notes in Computer Science*, pages 673–676, USA, 1992. Springer-Verlag.

31. C. H. Pratten. An Introduction to Proving AMN Specifications with PVS and the AMN-PROOF Tool. In H. Habrias, editor, *Proc. of Z Twenty Years on - What is its Future*, pages 149–165, France, 1995.

32. G. Salaün, M. Allemand, and C. Attiogbé. Formal Framework for a Generic Combination of a Process Algebra with an Algebraic Specification Language: an Overview. In *Proc. of the 8th Asia-Pacific Software Engineering Conference (APSEC'01)*, IEEE Computer Society Press, pages 299–302, Macau, 2001.

33. G. Salaün, M. Allemand, and C. Attiogbé. A Method to Combine any Process Algebra with an Algebraic Specification Language: the π-Calculus Example. In *Proc. of the 26th Annual International Computer Software and Applications Conference (COMPSAC'02)*, IEEE Computer Society Press, pages 385–390, England, 2002.

34. G. Salaün, M. Allemand, and C. Attiogbé. Specification of an Access Control System with a Formalism Combining CCS and CASL. In *Proc. of the 7th International Workshop on Formal Methods for Parallel Programming: Theory and Applications (FMPPTA'02)*, IEEE Computer Society Press, USA, 2002.

35. G. Salaün, C. Attiogbé, and M. Allemand. Verification of Integrated Specifications using PVS. Technical Report 03.02, University of Nantes, February 2003. Available at http://www.sciences.univ-nantes.fr/info/perso/permanents/sala un/papers/verif_ifm_with_pvs.ps.

36. H. Treharne and S. Schneider. Using a Process Algebra to Control B OPERATIONS. In K. Araki, A. Galloway, and K. Taguchi, editors, *Proc. of the 1st International Conference on Integrated Formal Methods (IFM'99)*, pages 437–457, UK, 1999. Springer-Verlag.

37. J. van de Pol, J. Hooman, and E. de Jong. Modular Formal Specification of Data and Behaviour. In K. Araki, A. Galloway, and K. Taguchi, editors, *Proc. of the 1st Conference on Integrated Formal Methods (IFM'99)*, pages 109–128, UK, 1999. Springer.

38. J. Woodcock and A. Cavalcanti. The Semantics of Circus. In D. Bert, J. P. Bowen, M. C. Henson, and K. Robinson, editors, *Proc. of the 2nd International Z and B Conference (ZB'02)*, volume 2272 of *Lecture Notes in Computer Science*, pages 184–203, France, 2002. Springer-Verlag.

Modeling SystemC Fixed-Point Arithmetic in HOL

Behzad Akbarpour and Sofiène Tahar

Dept. of Electrical & Computer Engineering, Concordia University
1455 de Maisonneuve W., Montreal, Quebec, H3H 1M8, Canada
{behzad,tahar}@ece.concordia.ca

Abstract. SystemC is a new C-based system level design language whose ultimate objective is to enable System-on-a-Chip (SoC) design and verification. Fixed-point design based on the SystemC data types is rapidly becoming the standard for optimizing DSP systems. In this paper, we propose to create a formalization of SystemC fixed-point arithmetic in the HOL theorem proving environment. The SystemC fixed-point number representation which contains a new generalized format and different rounding and overflow modes is described, and then it is formalized in higher-order logic. This formalization is then compared with the formalization of IEEE standard based floating-point arithmetic in HOL. A set of theorems are proved to bound the error in fixed-point rounding and to verify the fixed-point arithmetic operations against their abstract mathematical counterparts. Finally, we show by an example how this formalization can be used in verification of the translation from floating-point and fixed-point algorithmic, down to register transfer and netlist gate levels in the design flow of SoC systems.

1 Introduction

High complexity of modern digital signal processing systems versus increasing demand for a short time-to-market are current challenges of today's VLSI designers. With improvements in silicon technology and the increase in the number of logic gates that can be implemented on a single chip, various functionalities such as memories, logic gates, analogue blocks, CPU and digital signal processing (DSP) cores can be integrated into a single silicon chip. These functionalities are implemented by using System-on-a-Chip (SoC) [7] solutions that generally integrate diverse hardware and software. On the other hand, the use of inexpensive, high speed, and low power DSPs is on the rise. For DSP the problem is to decide whether a fixed-point or a floating-point math unit should be used [17]. Several factors should be taken into account in this regard. An important first step is to gain an understanding of how the hardware representations differ and how they affect precision and range. Also needed is a grasp of the types of applications to which particular chips are best suited and which hardware vendors provide these chips. Performance is also a driving factor behind the use of DSPs for which cost, speed, and power consumption are key ingredients.

J.S. Dong and J. Woodcock (Eds.): ICFEM 2003, LNCS 2885, pp. 206–225, 2003.
© Springer-Verlag Berlin Heidelberg 2003

The final consideration is the availability of development tools and the programming paradigms they support. Recently, significant effort has gone into building high level languages for both fixed- and floating-point DSPs. The most popular language has been C. Since C has a built-in type for floating-point, this is an attractive solution for those chips. The standard ANSI C language, however, does not support fixed-point data types, thus forcing programmers to write in assembly language and to deal with complicated and error-prone scaling issues. A significant breakthrough to allow a systematic approach for fixed-point design has been achieved by the Open SystemC Initiative. Fixed-point design based on the SystemC [31] data types is rapidly becoming the standard for optimizing DSP systems, and Electronic Design Automation (EDA) tools supporting this design flow are available today.

With ever increasing complexity of the design of digital systems the role of design verification has gained a lot of importance. Design errors can cause serious failures, resulting in the loss of time and money. It takes a very large amount of time and effort to correct the error, especially when the error is discovered late in the process. For these reasons, we need approaches that enable us to discover errors and validate designs as early as possible. Verification is defined as the validation of the circuit for its correctness. The verification of floating-point hardware has always been an important part of processor verification. The importance of arithmetic circuit verification was illustrated by the famous floating-point division bug in Intel's Pentium processor [18]. Floating-point algorithms are usually very complicated. They are composed of many modules where the smallest flaw in the design or the implementation can cause a very hard-to-discover bug, as occurred in Intel's case. Traditional approaches for verifying floating-point circuits are based on simulation. However, these approaches cannot exhaustively cover the input space of the circuits. Therefore, new methods are needed for the economical and reliable verification of digital systems. Formal verification [19] have recently paved a path, showing the utility of finding bugs early in the design cycle. Formal verification techniques are usually classified in two categories: interactive theorem proving and automatic decision diagram based model checking and equivalence checking. Theorem proving consists in expressing the specification and implementation in a formal logic. Their relationship, stated as equivalence or implication, is regarded as a theorem to be proven within the logic system, using axioms and inference rules. Powerful mathematical techniques such as induction and abstraction are strengths of theorem proving and make it a very flexible verification technique. In model checking, one checks if the design satisfies some properties (formal specification). With equivalence checking, we check if two designs exhibit the same behavior. The latter techniques have been successfully applied to real industrial designs. However, since most of the tools are based on Binary Decision Diagrams (BDDs), they require the design to be described at the Boolean level. In practice, they often fail to verify a large-scale design because of the so-called state space explosion.

There exist several related works in the open literature on the formalization and verification of floating-point arithmetic. For instance, Barett [3] specified parts of the IEEE-754 [15] standard in Z, and Miner [25] formalized the IEEE-854 [16] floating-point standard in PVS. Carreno [6] formalized the same IEEE-854 standard in HOL. Harrison [12] defined and formalized real numbers using HOL. He then developed a generic floating-point library [14] to define and verify the most fundamental terms and lemmas of the IEEE-754 standard. This former library was used by him to formalize and verify floating-point algorithms such as the square root and the exponential function [13] against their behavioral specification.

Moore et al. [26] have verified the AMD-K5 floating-point division algorithm using the ACL2 theorem prover. Also, Russinoff [28] has developed a library for ACL2 prover and applied it successfully to verify the K5 square root, and the Athlon multiplication, division, square root, and addition algorithms. Daumas et al. [10] have presented a generic library for reasoning about floating-point numbers within the Coq system. Berg et al. [4] have formally verified a theory of IEEE rounding presented in [27] using the theorem prover PVS, and then used the theory to prove the correctness of a fully IEEE compliant floating-point unit used in the VAMP processor.

Aagaard and Seger [1] combined BDD based methods and theorem proving techniques to verify a floating-point multiplier. Chen and Bryant [9] used word-level SMV to verify a floating-point adder. Miner and Leathrum [24] verified a general class of subtractive division algorithms with respect to the IEEE-754 standard in PVS. Leeser et al. [20] verified a radix-2 square root algorithm and its hardware implementation using theorem proving methods. Cornea-Hasegan [8] used iterative approaches and mathematical proofs to verify the correctness of the IEEE floating-point square root, division and remainder algorithms. O'Leary et al. [21] reported on the verification of the Intel's floating-point unit at the gate level using a combination of model-checking and theorem proving.

While the above works are concerned with floating-point representation and arithmetic, in [2] we proposed the first machine-checked formal development on properties of fixed-point arithmetic according to Cadence SPW (Signal Processing WorkSystem) tool. Unlike floating-point arithmetic which is standardized in IEEE-754 [15] and IEEE-854 [16], current fixed-point arithmetic does not follow any particular standard and depends on the tool and the language used to design the DSP chip. Based on higher-order logic, we proposed to encode a fixed-point number by a pair composed of a boolean word, and a triple indicating the word length, the length of the integer portion and the sign format. Then, we formalized the concepts of valuation and rounding as functions that convert respectively a fixed-point number to a real number and vice versa, taking into account different rounding and overflow modes. Fixed-point arithmetic operations are formalized as functions performing operations on the real numbers corresponding to the fixed-point operands and then applying the rounding on the real number result. We supported three kinds of exceptions, two overflow modes and five rounding modes as described in SPW documentation. Finally, we proved different lemmas regarding the error analysis of the fixed-point quantization and correctness of the basic operations like addition, multiplication, and division. The formalization of the fixed-point arithmetic has been inspired mostly by the work done by Harrison [13]. Indeed we followed similar steps as in formalization of floating-point arithmetic for modeling fixed-point arithmetic, and used an analogous set of lemmas to his work to check the validity of operation results and to carry out the error analysis of the fixed-point rounding.

In this paper, we significantly extend this work to the SystemC fixed point description. In comparison to SPW, SystemC represents the numbers in a different more comprehensive format. SystemC also covers a more complete set of overflow, rounding, and exception handling parameters. SystemC supports seven rounding modes, of which four correspond exactly to the rounding modes of SPW. The other three modes are specific to SystemC and are not supported by the other tools. SystemC supports five overflow modes covering those of SPW. These features motivated EDA companies, including Cadence, to adapt SystemC for fixed-point design and verification[1]. In the new fixed-point theory, we have included the parameters representing the overflow, rounding mode, and the number of saturation bits which have been introduced in SPW theory in the definition of arithmetic operations, directly in the format to make a generalized SystemC fixed-point attributes. Also new enumerated data types are defined to cover the SystemC rounding and overflow modes. Specific functions are then defined to handle the overflow in SystemC wrap around modes. Finally new theorems are proved to bound the error in SystemC special rounding modes. The modularity of SPW theory has facilitated the extension process. This is of great importance since the design of modular and reusable theories remains a big challenge in the theorem proving era.

The organization of this paper is as follows: Section 2 describes the SystemC fixed-point arithmetic including the format of the fixed-point numbers, and overflow and quantization modes. Section 3 describes in detail their formalization in HOL in parallel with the formalization of IEEE-754 based floating-point arithmetic in HOL. In Section 4, we discuss the rounding error analysis and the verification of the SystemC fixed-point arithmetic operations. Section 5 presents an illustrative example on how this formalization can be used through the modeling and verification of a Notch filter algorithm. Finally, Section 6 concludes the paper.

2   Fixed-Point Types in SystemC

In this section we describe SystemC based fixed-point arithmetic. SystemC is a C++ based modeling platform supporting design abstractions at the register-transfer, behavioral, and system levels. Consisting of a class library and a simulation kernel, the language is an attempt at standardization of a C/C++ design methodology, and is supported by the Open SystemC Initiative (OSCI), a consortium of a wide range of system houses, semiconductor companies, intellectual property (IP) providers, embedded software developers, and design automation

---

[1] In fact the latest release of the Cadence SPW tool supports both the old SPW fixed-point arithmetic as well as the SystemC one.

tool vendors. The advantages of SystemC include the establishment of a common design environment consisting of C++ libraries, models and tools, thereby setting up a foundation for hardware-software co-design; the ability to exchange IP easily and efficiently; and the ability to reuse test benches across different levels of modeling abstraction. An important element of SystemC is the support for fixed-point data-types, which is essential for the refinement of complex algorithms to a hardware or software implementation.

The SystemC fixed-point library contains basic types for both unconstrained, constrained, signed and unsigned fixed-point data types [30]. Constrained data types use static arguments to specify the functionality of the type while unconstrained data types can use argument types that are nonstatic. Static arguments must be known at compile time, while nonstatic arguments can be variables. In addition to the standard fixed-point types which use arbitrary precision in calculations, SystemC also provides limited precision fixed-point types to speed simulation when limited precision is all that is required. With standard fixed-point types the mantissa can be virtually any size. With limited precision fixed-point types the mantissa is limited to 53 bits. Limited precision fixed-point types are implemented with double precision floating-point values. The fixed-point format used by the fixed-point data types consists of the following parameters:

- *wl:* Total word length, used for fixed-point representation. Equivalent to the total number of bits used in the type. Word length must be greater than 0.
- *iwl:* Integer word length, specifies the number of bits that are to the left of the binary point (.) in a fixed-point number. Integer word length can be positive or negative, and larger than the word length. If this number is negative, repeated leading sign bits or zeros are added to the object. If this number is greater than the total number of bits, trailing zeros are added to generate the equivalent binary value.
- *q_mode:* Quantization mode, determines the behavior of the fixed point type when the result of an operation generates more precision in the least significant bits (LSB) than is available as specified by the word length and integer word length parameters.
- *o_mode:* Overflow mode, determines what happens when the result of an operation generates more bits on the most significant bits (MSB) side than are available for representation.
- *n_bits:* Number of saturated bits, only used for overflow mode and specifies how many bits will be saturated if a saturation behavior is specified and an overflow occurs.

In comparison with the fixed-point format defined in SPW [29], the parameters *wl* and *iw* in SystemC correspond to parameters *#bits* and *#integer_bits* in SPW fixed-point attributes. The parameters *q_mode* and *o_mode* which have been used in SPW during the definition of arithmetic operations, are inserted directly in the format to make a generalized fixed-point attributes for SystemC. Also the argument *n_bits* is not used by SPW and is specific to SystemC. In SPW the type of the fixed-point numbers as *signed* or *unsigned* are defined by the parameter *sign_format* in the attributes; however, in SystemC there is not such a parameter in the format and separate types are defined for signed and unsigned fixed-point numbers.

Operations performed on fixed-point data types are done using arbitrary and full precision. After the operation is complete, the resulting operand is cast to fit the fixed-point data type object. The casting operation applies the quantization behavior of the target object to the new value and assigns the new value to the target object. Then, the appropriate overflow behavior is applied to the result of the process which gives the final value.

Quantization effects are used to determine what happens to the LSBs (Least Significant Bits) of a fixed-point type when more bits of precision are required than are available. The quantization modes available in SystemC are shown in Table 1:

Table 1. SystemC Quantization Modes

Quantization Mode	Name
Rounding to plus infinity	SC_RND
Rounding to zero	SC_RND_ZERO
Rounding to minus infinity	SC_RND_MIN_INF
Rounding to infinity	SC_RND_INF
Convergent Rounding	SC_RND_CONV
Truncation	SC_TRN
Truncation to zero	SC_TRN_ZERO

Figure 1 shows the behavior of each quantization mode. The diagonal line represents the ideal number representation given infinite bits. The small horizontal lines show the effect of the rounding. Any value of the X axis within the range of the line will be converted to the value of the Y axis. The symbol q in the figure refers to the quantization step, that is, the resolution of the data type. As shown in this figure modes *SC_RND*, *SC_RND_ZERO*, *SC_RND_MIN_INF*, *SC_RND_INF*, and *SC_RND_CONV* will round the value to the closest representable number if the two nearest representable numbers are not an equal distance apart. Otherwise, rounding towards plus infinity, to zero, towards minus infinity, towards plus infinity if positive or minus infinity if negative, and towards nearest even will be performed respectively (Figure 1 (a-e)). *SC_TRN* mode is the default for fixed-point types and will be used if no other value is specified. The result is always rounded towards minus infinity (Figure 1 (f)). In other words, the result value is the first representable number lower than the original value. Finally, for *SC_TRN_ZERO* the result is the nearest representable value towards zero (Figure 1 (g)). Rounding modes *SC_RND*, *SC_RND_CONV*, *SC_TRN*, and *SC_TRN_ZERO* in SystemC correspond exactly to *Round*, *Convergent_Round*, *Truncate*, and *Round_To_Zero* loss of precision modes in SPW, respectively. The other three rounding modes are specific to SystemC and are not supported by SPW.

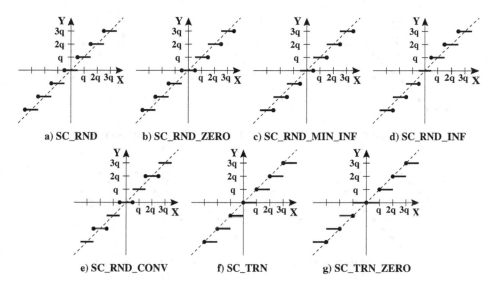

Fig. 1. The Behavior of SystemC Quantization Modes

In addition to quantization modes, we can use overflow modes to approximate a higher range for fixed-point operations. Usually, overflow occurs when the result of an operation is too large or too small for the available bit range. Specific overflow modes can then be implemented to reduce the loss of data. Overflow modes are specified by the o_mode and n_bits parameters to a fixed point type. The supported overflow modes are listed in the Table 2.

Table 2. SystemC Overflow Modes

Overflow Mode	Name
Saturation	SC_SAT
Saturation to zero	SC_SAT_ZERO
Symmetrical Saturation	SC_SAT_SYM
Wrap-around	SC_WRAP
Sign magnitude wrap-around	SC_WRAP_SM

Figure 2 shows the behavior of each overflow mode for a 3 bit type. The diagonal line represents the ideal value if infinite bits are available for representation. The dots represent the values of the result. The X axis is the original value and the Y axis is the result. From this figure it can be seen that $MAX = 3$ and $MIN = -4$ for a 3 bit type. SC_SAT mode will convert the specified value to MAX for an overflow or MIN for an underflow condition (Figure 2 (a)). SC_SAT_ZERO mode will set the result to 0 for any input value that is outside the representable range of the fixed point type. If the result value is greater than MAX or smaller than MIN the result will be 0 (Figure 2 (b)). In SC_SAT_SYM

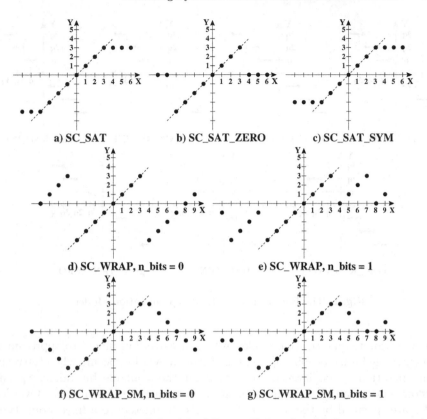

Fig. 2. The Behavior of SystemC Overflow Modes

mode, positive overflow will generate MAX and negative overflow will generate $-MAX$ for signed numbers or MIN for unsigned numbers (Figure 2 (c)). With SC_WRAP mode the value of an arithmetic operand will wrap around from MAX to MIN as MAX is reached. There are two different cases within this mode. The first is with the n_bits parameter set to 0 or having a default value of 0. All bits except for the deleted bits are copied to the result number (Figure 2 (d)). The second is when the n_bits parameter is a nonzero value. In this case the specified number of most significant bits of the result number are saturated with preservation of the original sign, the other bits are simply copied. Positive numbers remain positive and negative numbers remain negative. A graph showing this behavior with $n\_bits = 1$ is shown in Figure 2 (e). Notice that positive numbers wrap around to 0 while negative values wrap around to -1. The SC_WRAP_SM overflow mode uses sign magnitude wrapping. This overflow mode behaves in two different styles depending on the value of parameter n_bits. When n_bits is 0 no bits are saturated. This mode will first delete any MSB bits that are outside the result word length. The sign bit of the result is set to the value of the least significant deleted bit. If the most significant remaining bit is different from the original MSB then all the remaining bits are inverted. If MSBs are the same, the other bits are copied from the original value to the result value. A graph showing the result of this overflow mode is shown in Figure 2 (f). As the value of X increases, the value of Y increases to MAX and then slowly starts to decrease until MIN is reached. The result is a sawtooth like waveform. With n_bits greater than 0, n_bits MSB bits are saturated to 1. A graph showing this behavior with $n\_bits = 1$ is shown in Figure 2 (g). Notice that while the graph looks somewhat like a sawtooth waveform, positive numbers do not dip below 0 and negative numbers do not cross -1. Overflow modes SC_SAT and SC_Wrap in SystemC cover the two overflow modes *Clip* and *Wrap* in SPW. The other three overflow modes are not supported by SPW and are specific to SystemC.

3   Modeling SystemC Fixed-Point Arithmetic in HOL

In this section, we present the formalization of SystemC based fixed-point arithmetic in higher-order logic, based on the general purpose HOL theorem prover [11]. HOL's basic types include the natural numbers and booleans. It also includes other specific extensions like John Harrison's reals library [12] which proved to be essential for our fixed-point arithmetic formalization.

Fixed point numbers are modeled in HOL as a pair of elements composed of a bit string (*string*) and a set of attributes (*attrib*). The bit string is represented by a boolean word and the set of attributes is itself a combination of six elements representing the word length (*wordlength*), integer word length (*integerwordlength*), sign type (*signtype*), rounding mode (*roundmode*), overflow mode (*overflowmode*), and the number of saturation bits (*satbits*), respectively. In comparison to the SPW formalization we have included three extra parameters to define a generalized fixed-point format. The fixed-point numbers are then partitioned using special predicates into signed (*is_signed*) and un-signed (*is_unsigned*) numbers. The validity of a fixed-point number (*is_valid*) and a set of attributes (*validAttr*) is defined using special predicates. In a valid set of attributes the word length is in the range of 1 and 53 corresponding to fast fixed-point data types, in comparison to 256 in SPW. Also, the sign type in a valid set of attributes is either 0 or 1, and the number of saturation bits is less than the word length. The fixed-point data types are defined in bijection with the appropriate subset of $boolword \times \mathbb{N}^3 \times roundingmode \times overflowmode \times \mathbb{N}$ using functions *Fxp* and *deFxp*. Then, we defined the valuation function (*value*) to specify a real value to fixed-point numbers using separate formulas for signed and unsigned numbers. The constants for the smallest (*bottomfxp*) and largest (*topfxp*) fixed-point numbers for a given format together with their corresponding real values (*MIN,MAX*) are also defined using specific functions. Then, we defined enumerated data types for seven rounding modes and five overflow modes in SystemC fixed-point arithmetic. The rounding function (*fxp_round*) is then defined case by case on the rounding modes and special functions are defined to handle the overflow in Wrap-around (*WRAP*) and Sign magnitude wrap-around (*WRAP_SM*) modes. Then, we defined the operations on fixed-point numbers (*fxpAdd,fxpSub,fxpMul,fxpDiv*) which performed using the arbitrary precision in real domain and then the result is casted to the output format.

Our effort in formalization of fixed-point arithmetic can be compared to the formalization of IEEE standard based floating-point arithmetic in HOL [13] which is performed as in the following steps:

- **Floating Point Numbers:** A floating-point number is modeled as a triple of natural numbers interpreted as a sign, an exponent, and a fraction. The exponent is usually added to a constant (bias) to make the biased exponent's range nonnegative. The floating-point numbers are partitioned into not a numbers (NaN), infinities, normalized numbers, denormalized but nonzero numbers, and zeros as specified in IEEE-754 standard. Predicates for testing the validity and finiteness of a triple for a given format are defined. Also extractors for the three fields of a floating-point number together with constants for convenient values such as largest representable positive number and the most negative number in a format are defined.
- **Format Parameters:** The floating-point format for single, double precision, and extended numbers is defined as a pair of two natural numbers representing the width in bits of the exponent field, and the width in bits of the significand field. From these parameters three other characteristic numbers are defined for the total word length, the maximum exponent value, and the bias in the exponent.
- **Representation and Valuation:** The next step in formalization of floating-point numbers is the definition of the concrete representation of the numbers as the fields are laid out with the sign as the most significant bit, the exponent in the middle and the fraction in the bottom. Then, a real value is specified to non exceptional numbers. The valuation is meaningless when applied to infinities and NaNs. The denormalized numbers and normalized numbers are treated separately. Then, a few significant real values such as the real value of the largest representable number, the overflow threshold, and the notion of the unit in the last place for a given floating-point number are defined.
- **Rounding:** The definition of the valuation function is fundamental of the definition of the inverse operation of rounding which coerces a real number into a given floating-point format. The rounding is controlled by a rounding mode, specifying whether a real number is to be mapped to the nearest floating-point number (using round to even to choose a unique number if necessary), towards zero, or towards positive or negative infinity. The modes are represented in HOL via an enumerated type definition.
- **Arithmetic Operations:** Then, the arithmetic operations are defined where they first deal with the exceptional cases, either where the arguments involve a NaN or infinity, or are invalid for other reasons (e.g. $\infty - \infty$) and generate a NaN. Apart from that, they basically just take the values of the arguments, perform the mathematical operations and then round the result according to the desired rounding mode.
- **Float and Double Types:** Finally, the above considerations are specified to actual HOL type of single precision and double precision numbers called *float* and *double*. These types are defined to be in bijection with the

appropriate subset of $\mathbb{N}^3$, with the bijections written in HOL as *float* and *defloat*. The operations are defined by mapping out of the type, performing the operations, and mapping back.

4   Verification of SystemC Arithmetic Operations

The correctness of fixed-point operations can be specified by comparing the operation's output with the true mathematical result. Since the operations are defined as if they first performed using infinite precision and then the result is rounded to fit in the destination format, the verification of operations is closely related to bounding the error in rounding function. On the other hand, the analysis of error in fixed-point rounding is very similar to the error analysis in floating-point rounding. In the following discussion, we first explain the details of floating-point rounding error analysis and then describe how similar steps are followed and analogous theorems are proved to bound the error in fixed-point rounding and to verify the fixed-point arithmetic operations.

4.1   Floating-Point Verification

The steps in analysis of floating-point rounding error in HOL [13] are as follows[2]:

- **Lemmas for Analyzing the Rounding Operation:** In the first step, prove some lemmas about the properties of the approximating a real number with a floating-point number. First, prove a theorem that ensures the existence of the best approximation to a given real number in a finite non empty set of floating-point numbers. Then, prove that the chosen best approximation to a real number satisfying a property p from a finite and non empty set of floating-point numbers is unique and is itself a member of the set and is itself the best approximation of the real number. Then, prove that the set of all valid and finite floating-point numbers are finite and non empty. Then, prove that the chosen best approximation to a real number satisfying a property p from the set of all finite floating-point numbers is a finite and valid floating-point number. Finally, prove that the result of rounding a real number to a floating-point number is valid.
- **Preliminary Theorems about Rounding Error:** In the second step, define the error as the difference between a real number and the value of its rounding result for rounding to nearest even. Then, prove that if the absolute value of a real number is less than the threshold value of a given floating-point format, then the rounding result is the nearest value to the real number and the corresponding error is minimum comparing to the other floating-point numbers. Also, if for a given real number we can find a floating-point number with equal value then the rounding-error is zero.
- **General Error Bound Theorems:** Next, prove two main theorems quantifying the error. In the first theorem, prove that if the absolute value of a real

---

[2] This analysis is performed using the HOL Light theorem prover which is an older version of the tool. The code is recently ported by the first author from HOL Light to HOL4 which is the latest version of HOL tool.

number is in the representable range of normalized floating-point numbers and located in the j'th binade, i.e. its absolute value is less than $2^{j+1}/2^{126}$ and greater than or equal to $2^j/2^{126}$, then the absolute value of error is less than or equal to $2^j/2^{150}$. In the second theorem, prove that if the real number is in the denormal range, i.e. its absolute value is less than 2^{-126}, then the error is less than or equal to 2^{-150}. To prove these main theorems, a set of eight lemmas and four theorems about general rounding error are established.

The error bounding theorems can be explained as follows. The single precision format in IEEE standard for binary floating-point numbers is 32 bits wide and has an 8 bit exponent field with the exponent bias of 127 and has a 23 bit significand considering the hidden bit which is always 1. The single precision floating-point numbers are distributed on the real axis as shown in Figure 3. Figure 3(a) shows the number distribution pattern and the various subranges in this format. Figure 3(b) illustrates the relative magnitudes of normalized and denormalized numbers. In the context of numbers of a specific precision, it is useful to speak of rounding in terms of units in the last place (ulp). A ulp is naturally understood as the magnitude of the least significant digit, or in the other words, the distance between the floating point number a and the next floating point number of greater magnitude. For example, one ulp of the denormalized region in the single precision format of IEEE standard is 2^{-149}, and one ulp for the j'th binade in the normalized region is equal to $2^{j+1}/2^{150}$ as shown in Figure 3(b). The rounding error can be easily bounded in term of ulps. For rounding to nearest the absolute value of error is less than or equal to half a ulp. This means that the absolute value of error is less than or equal to 2^{-150} for denormalized region, and less than or equal to $2^j/2^{150}$ for the j'th binade in the normalizerd region as stated in the last two main theorems mentioned before.

– **Rounding Error in Arithmetic Operations:** At the end, prove theorems that relate the arithmetic operations such as addition, subtraction, multiplication, division, reminder, square root, negation and absolute value to their abstract mathematical counterparts according to the corresponding errors. The theorems are composed of two parts. In the first part which is about the finiteness of the floating-point operation output prove that for each pair of finite floating-point numbers, if the real result is less than the overflow threshold value then the output result is also finite. In the second part of the theorems, prove that the value of the floating-point result is equal to the value of the real result plus an error which is already quantified using the previous error bound theorems.

4.2   Fixed-Point Verification

Similar steps are followed for the error analysis of fixed-point rounding:

– **Lemmas for Analyzing the Fixed-Point Rounding Operation:** We first proved lemmas concerning with the approximation of a real number

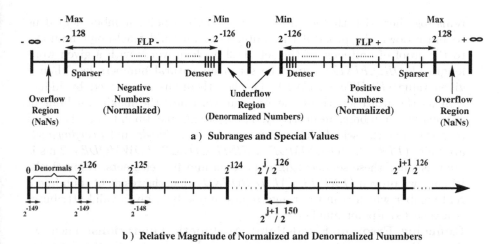

Fig. 3. Single Precision Floating-Point Numbers on the Real Number Line

with a fixed-point number. We proved ($FXP\_IS\_CLOSEST\_EXISTS$) that in a finite nonempty set of fixed-point numbers we can find the best approximation to a real number based on a given valuation function. Then, we proved that the chosen best approximation to a real number satisfying a property p from a finite and non empty set of fixed-point numbers is unique ($FXP\_CLOSEST\_IS\_EVERYTHING$) and is itself a member of the set ($FXP\_CLOSEST\_IN\_SET$) and is itself the best approximation of the real number ($FXP\_CLOSEST\_IS\_CLOSEST$). Finally, we proved ($FXP\_IS\_VAL ID\_CLOSEST$) that the chosen best approximation to a real number satisfying a property p from the set of all valid fixed-point numbers with a given attributes is itself a valid fixed-point number. Since in the definition of fixed-point rounding we have used the same approximating functions ($is\_closest$, $closest$) as in floating-point case, the proof of these theorems are very close to their corresponding floating-point lemmas. Then, we proved that the set of all valid fixed-point numbers with a given attributes is finite ($FI-NITE\_VALID\_ATTRIB$). We also proved ($FXP\_IS\_VALID\_NONEMPTY$) that the set of all valid fixed-point numbers is nonempty. The proof of the first lemma is a bit complicated. For this purpose we made use of some built-in theorems about the finite sets in HOL *pred_sets* library [22]. Among these are the two fundamental theorems $FINITE\_EMPTY$ and $FI-NITE\_INSERT$, which state that the empty set is indeed finite and the insertion of an element to a finite set constructs a finite set. Other theorems state that the union of two finite sets ($FINITE\_UNION$), the image of a function on a finite set ($IMAGE\_FINITE$), a singleton set[3] ($FINITE\_SING$), the cross combination of two finite sets ($FINITE\_CROSS$), and any subset of a finite set ($SUBSET\_FINITE$) is itself a finite set. Using these theo-

---

[3] a set that contains precisely one element

rems together with the definition of a valid fixed-point number helped us to break down the proof of the finiteness of all valid fixed-point numbers to the proof of finiteness of the set of all boolean words with a given word length (*WORD_FINITE*) and the set of all natural numbers less than a given value (*FINITE_COUNT*). The last theorems are proved by induction on the word length of the boolean word and the maximum limit of the natural numbers, respectively. For SystemC fixed-point, we also need to prove that the set of all elements of type *roundmode* and *overflowmode* are finite (*FINITE_ROUNDMODE, FINITE_OVERFLOWMODE*). This is obvious since these sets contain only seven and five elements, respectively. Finally, we proved (*FXP_IS_VALID_ROUND*) that the result of rounding a real number which is in the range representable by a given valid attributes is a valid fixed-point number.

- **Rounding Error in Fixed-Point Arithmetic Operations:** Then, we defined the error resulting from rounding a real number to a fixed-point value (*fxperror*). Then, we established the first main theorems (*FXP_ADD_THM, FXP_SUB_THM, FXP_MUL_THM, FXP_DIV_THM*) on the correctness of fixed-point arithmetic operations. According to these theorems, if the input fixed-point operands and the output attributes are valid then the result of fixed-point operations is valid. Also the result of the operations is related to the real result considering the error.

- **General Fixed-Point Error Bound Theorem:** In the next step, we established the second main theorem on fixed-point rounding error analysis which concerns bounding the error. The error is absolutely quantified as in the theorem *FXP_ERROR_BOUND_THM*. According to this theorem, the error in rounding a real number which is in the range representable by a given set of attributes X is less than the quantity $1/2^{fracbits(X)}$. To explain the theorem, we consider the following fact which relates the definition of the fixed-point numbers to the rationals. An N-bit binary word, when interpreted as an unsigned fixed-point number, can take on values from a subset P of rationals of the form $p/2^b$ in which p is an integer in the range $0 \le p \le 2^N - 1$ for unsigned, and $-2^{N-1} \le p \le 2^{N-1} - 1$ for signed numbers, respectively. Note that P contains 2^N elements and b represents the fractional bits in each case. Based on this fact, we can depict the range of values covered by each case as shown by Figure 4. Thereafter, the representable range of fixed-point numbers is divided into 2^N equispaced quantization steps with the distance between two successive steps equal to $1/2^b$. Suppose that $x \in \mathbb{R}$ is approximated by a fixed-point number a. The position of these values are labeled in the figure. The error $| x - a |$ is hence less than the length of one interval, or $1/2^b$, as mentioned in the second theorem. In comparison to floating-point case, the fixed-point representation leads to equal spacing in the set of representable numbers. Thus the maximum absolute error is the same throughout (*ulp* with truncation and *ulp*/2 with rounding).

- **Lemmas about General Fixed-Point Rounding Error:** To prove the general fixed-point error bound theorem, a set of five lemmas is established. We first proved that the rounding result is the nearest value to a real number

(*FXP_BOUND_AT_WORST_LEMMA*) and the corresponding error is minimum (*FXP_ERROR_AT_WORST_LEMMA*) comparing to the other fixed-point numbers. Then, we proved (*FXP_ERROR_BOUND_LEMMA1*) that each representable real value x can be surrounded by two successive rational numbers. Also we proved (*FXP_ERROR_BOUND_LEMMA2*) that the difference between the real number and the surrounding rationals is less than $1/2^{fracbits(X)}$. Finally, we proved (*FXP_ERROR_BOUND_LEMMA3*) that for each real value we can find a fixed-point number with the required error characteristics. Since the rounding produces the minimum error as stated in *FXP_ERROR_AT_WORST_LEMMA*, the proof of the second main theorem (*FXP_ERROR_BOUND_THM*) is a direct consequence of *FXP_ERROR_BOUND_LEMMA3*. In these proofs, we have treated the case of signed and unsigned numbers separately since they have different definitions for *MAX*, *MIN*, and *value* functions. For signed numbers special attention needs also to be paid to dealing with the negative numbers.

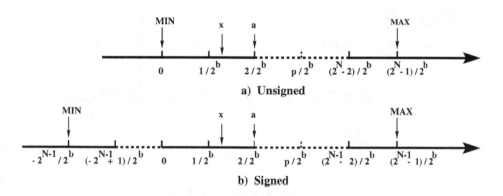

Fig. 4. Fixed-Point Values on the Real Axis

– **SystemC Fixed-Point Error Bound Theorem:** The theorem *FXP_ERR OR_BOUND_THM* is a general theorem for bounding the error in fixed-point rounding which is valid for all rounding modes. This theorem can then be extended to prove new theorems for different rounding modes in SystemC fixed-point arithmetic. For instance, for *SC_TRN, SC_RND_ZERO, SC_RND_MIN_INF,SC_RND_INF* and *SC_RND_CONV* modes which round to nearest representable values, the error is less than *ulp/2*. For these modes the error is bounded to $1/2^{fracbits(X)+1}$. This fact is proved as in theorem *SYSTEMC_FXP_ERROR_BOUND_THM*.

5   The Notch Filter Example

In this section we demonstrate how to apply the formalization of SystemC fixed-point arithmetic presented in the previous sections for the verification of DSP systems. We have chosen CoCentric Fixed-Point Designer [33] as the application tool and the case of a second order 60 Hz *Notch Filter* as an example circuit (Figure 5). The filter is first designed and simulated using floating-point operations and parameters (Figure 5(a)). The design is composed of *Add* (adder), *Gain* (multiply by a constant), and *Delay* blocks together with signal source and sink elements. The design is then converted to a fixed-point design (Figure 5(b)) in which each block is replaced with the corresponding fixed-point block. Fixed-point blocks are shown by double circles and squares to distinguish from floating-point blocks. The attributes of all fixed-point block outputs are set to $< 64, 31, t >$ to ensure that overflows and quantization do not affect the system operation. This means that we have used sixty four bits to represent the signal values, the numbers are in two's complement format in which the most significant bit is the sign bit, and the binary point is fixed at the thirty first position following the sign bit.

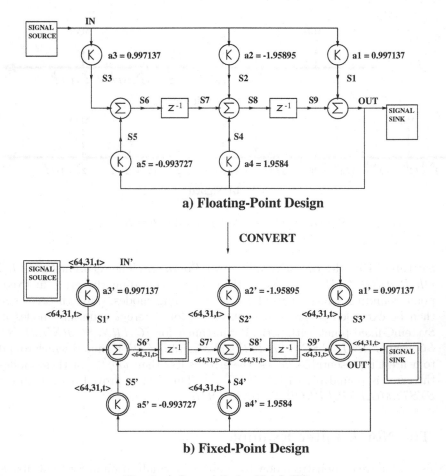

a) Floating-Point Design

CONVERT

b) Fixed-Point Design

Fig. 5. A Second Order Notch Filter

Figure 6 shows the proposed verification methodology. Based on this method-ology, we first modeled the design in different abstraction levels such as floating-point and fixed-point levels as predicates in higher order logic (*NOTCH_FILTER_FLOAT_IMP,NOTCH_FILTER_FXP_IMP*). The process of specifying a hardware description language in higher-order logic is commonly known as semantic embedding. There are two main approaches [5]: deep embedding and shallow embedding. In deep embedding, the abstract syntax of a design descrip-tion is represented by terms, which are then interpreted by semantic functions defined in the logic that assign meaning to the design. With this method, it is possible to reason about classes of designs, since one can quantify over the syntactic structures. However, setting up HOL types of abstract syntax and se-mantic functions can be very tedious. In a shallow embedding on the other hand, the design is modeled directly by a formal specification of its functional behavior. This eliminates the effort of defining abstract syntax and semantic functions, but it also limits the proofs to functional properties. In this example, since our main concern is to check the correctness of the design based on its functionality, we propose shallow embedding: translate the intended meaning of the design blocks into HOL and then complete the formal proof in HOL theorem prover. Primitive blocks are defined using the corresponding functions in floating-point and fixed-point theories in HOL. The whole filter is then implemented as a conjunction of these blocks.

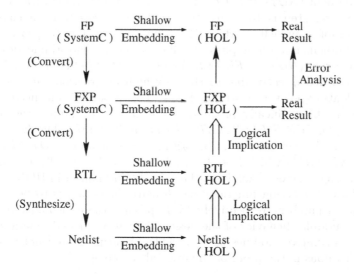

Fig. 6. Verification Methodology

In the next step, separately and independently from the actual implementa-tions, we described the designs as a difference equation relating the input and output samples (*NOTCH_FILTER_FLOAT_SPEC,NOTCH_FILTER_FXP_SPEC*). Then, we established lemmas that ensure the implementation at each level satisfies the corresponding specification (*NOTCH_FILTER_FLOAT_IMP_SPEC,*

NOTCH_FILTER_FXP_IMP_SPEC). For the error analysis of transition from floating-point to fixed-point levels, and based on the theorems *FXP_ADD_THM*, *FXP_MUL_THM*, and the corresponding ones in floating-point theory, we proved a theorem (*NOTCH_FILTER_FXP_TO_FLOAT_THM*) that states the error between the real values of the floating and fixed-point precision output samples. According to this theorem, for a valid and finite set of input and output sequences at times n - 1 and n - 2, we will have finite and valid outputs at time n. Also, the difference between the output real values at each sample time can be expressed as the difference in input and output values at previous sample times multiplied by the corresponding coefficients, taking into account the effects of finite precision in coefficients and arithmetic operations. Proper assumptions are set for both floating-point and fixed-point designs to guarantee the validity of output samples. Based on this theorem, three sources of error can be distinguished: errors due to the quantization of input samples, errors due to the rounding in arithmetic operations, and errors due to quantization of coefficients. The errors are already quantified using the theorem *SYSTEMC_FXP_ERROR_BOUND_THM* and the corresponding theorems for error analysis in floating-point case.

Next, we generated with CoCentric System Studio [32] the VHDL code corresponding to the Filter design, and used Synopsys to synthesize the code to reach to the logic gate level netlist. At this point, we used the well known formal techniques to model the design in each of these levels in higher-order logic within the HOL environment (*NOTCH_FILTER_RTL_IMP*, *NOTCH_FILTER_NETLIST_IMP*). The next step is to verify these different levels using a classical hierarchical proof approach in HOL [23]. Our final goal is to prove that the gate level implementation implies the floating-point algorithmic design considering the errors (*NOTCH_FILTER_NETLIST_TO_FLOAT_THM*). This goal cannot be reached directly, due to the very high abstraction gap between the gate and floating-point algorithmic levels. The proof scheme need hence to be changed to hierarchically prove that the gate level implies the more abstract RTL (*NOTCH_FILTER_NETLIST_TO_RTL_THM*). The latter is used to imply the high level fixed-point algorithmic specification (*NOTCH_FILTER_RTL_TO_FXP_THM*) which has already been related to the floating-point description through the error analysis. This can be formalized in HOL using *float* and *Fxp* data abstraction functions which map binary words to floating-point and fixed-point numbers, respectively. In the proof of these theorems we used the regular and modular behavior of the design, so that we proved separate lemmas for different primitive modules such as adder, multiplier, and delay and then used these lemmas in the proof of the original theorems.

6   Conclusions

As system-on-a-chip (SoC) designs become a driving force in electronics systems, current verification techniques are falling behind at an increasing rate. Verification of today's SoCs occurs at low levels of abstraction, typically RTL. As the complexity of SoCs grows, it is important to move the verification to higher levels of abstraction. In this paper, we proposed the formalization of SystemC based fixed-point arithmetic in the HOL theorem prover as a basis for modeling and verification of SoC designs at floating-point and fixed-point algorithmic levels against the implementations in RTL and netlist gate levels. The formalization presented in this paper is an extension to the previous work on formalization of IEEE standard based floating-point arithmetic and Cadence SPW based fixed-point arithmetic. We modeled the generalized SystemC fixed-point data types and extended the verification to cover the different rounding and overflow modes in SystemC fixed-point arithmetic. Finally, we used our formalization for modeling and verification of a second order Notch filter system.

References

1. M. D. Aagaard, and C.-J. H. Seger, "The Formal Verification of a Pipelined Double-Precision IEEE Floating-Point Multiplier," In International Conference on Computer Aided Design, San Francisco, CA, USA, pp. 7-10, Nov. 1995.
2. B. Akbarpour, S. Tahar, and A. Dekdouk, "Formalization of Cadence SPW Fixed-Point Arithmetic in HOL," In Integrated Formal Methods, Lecture Notes in Computer Science, Vol. 2335, Springer-Verlag, pp. 185-204, 2002.
3. G. Barrett, "Formal Methods Applied to a Floating Point Number System," IEEE Transactions on Software Engineering, SE-15(5): 611-621, May 1989.
4. C. Berg and C. Jacobi, "Formal Verification of the VAMP Floating Point Unit," In Correct Hardware Design and Verification Methods, Lecture Notes in Computer Science, Vol. 2144, Springer-Verlag, pp. 325-339, 2001.
5. R. Boulton, A. Gordon, M. Gordon, J. Harrison, J. Herbert, and J. Van-Tassel, "Experience with Embedding Hardware Description Languages in HOL," In Theorem Provers in Circuit Design, pages 129-156. North-Holland, 1992.
6. V. A. Carreno, "Interpretation of IEEE-854 Floating-Point Standard and Definition in the HOL System," NASA Technical Memorandum 110189, September 1995.
7. H. Chang et al., Surviving the SoC Revolution, A Guide to Platform-Based Design, Kluwer Academic Publishers, Boston, 1999.
8. M. Cornea-Hasegan, "Proving the IEEE Correctness of Iterative Floating-Point Square Root, Divide, and Remainder Algorithms," Intel Technology Journal, Q2, 1998, pp. 1-11.
9. Y.-A. Chen and R. E. Bryant, "Verification of Floating Point Adders," In Computer Aided Verification, Lecture Notes in Computer Science, Vol. 1427, Springer-Verlag, pp. 488-499, 1998.
10. M. Daumas, L. Rideau, L. Thry, "A Generic Library for Floating-Point Numbers and its Application to Exact Computing," In Theorem Proving in Higher Order Logics, Lecture Notes in Computer Science, Vol. 2152, Springer-Verlag, pp. 169-184, 2001.
11. M. J. C. Gordon and T. F. Melham, Introduction to HOL: A Theorem Proving Environment for Higher-Order Logic, Cambridge University Press, 1993.
12. J. R. Harrison, "Theorem Proving with the Real Numbers," Technical Report 408, University of Cambridge Computer Laboratory, New Museums Site, Pembroke Street, Cambridge, CB2 3QG, UK, December 1996.
13. J. R. Harrison, "Floating-Point Verification in HOL Light: The Exponential Function," Formal Methods in System Design 16(3): 271-305 (2000).

14. J. R. Harrison, "A Machine-Checked Theory of Floating-Point Arithmetic," In Theorem Proving in Higher Order Logics, Lecture Notes in Computer Science, Vol. 1690, Springer-Verlag, pp. 113-130, 1999.
15. IEEE, Standard for Binary Floating-Point Arithmetic, ANSI/IEEE Standard 754-1985, The Institute of Electrical and Electronic Engineers, Inc., 345 East 47th Street, New York, NY 10017, USA, 1985.
16. IEEE, Standard for Radix-Independent Floating-Point Arithmetic, ANSI/IEEE Std 854-1987, The Institute of Electrical and Electronic Engineers, Inc., 345 East 47th Street, New York, NY 10017, USA, 1987.
17. C. Inacio, D. Ombres, "The DSP Decision: Fixed Point or Floating?," IEEE Spectrum, 0018-9234, September 1996.
18. Intel Inc., "Pentium Processors, Statistical Analysis of Floating-Point Flaw," Intel White Paper, Sec. 3, November 1994.
19. C. Kern and M. Greenstreet, "Formal Verification in Hardware Design: A Survey," ACM Transactions on Design Automation of Electronic Systems, Vol. 4, pp. 123-193, April 1999.
20. M. Leeser, and J. O'Leary, "Verification of a Subtractive Radix-2 Square Root Algorithm and Implementation," In International Conference on Computer Design, Cambridge, MA, USA, pp. 526-531, October 1995.
21. J. O Leary, X. Zhao, R. Gerth, and C.-J.H. Seger, "Formally Verifying IEEE Compliance of Floating-Point Hardware," Intel Technology Journal, Vol. 1999-Q1, pp. 1-14.
22. T. F. Melham, "The HOL pred_sets Library," University of Cambridge, Computer Laboratory, February 1992.
23. T. Melham, Higher Order Logic and Hardware Verification, Cambridge Tracts in Theoretical Computer Science 31 (Cambridge University Press, 1993).
24. P. S. Miner, and J. F. Leathrum, "Verification of IEEE Compliant Subtractive Division Algorithms," In International Conference on Formal Methods in Computer-Aided Design, Lecture Notes in Computer Science, Vol. 1166, Springer-Verlag, pp. 64-78, 1996.
25. P.S. Miner, "Defining the IEEE-854 Floating-Point Standard in PVS," Technical Memorandum 110167, NASA, Langley Research Center, Hampton, VA 236810001, USA, June 1995.
26. J.S. Moore, T. Lynch, and M. Kaufmann, "A Mechanically Checked Proof of the Correctness of the Kernel of the AMD5K86 Floating-Point Division Algorithm," IEEE Transactions on Computers, Vol. 47, pp. 913-926, 1998.
27. S. M. Mueller and W. J. Paul, Computer Architecture. Complexity and Correctness, Springer-Verlag, 2000.
28. D. M. Russinoff, "A Case Study in Formal Verification of Register-Transfer Logic with ACL2: The Floating-Point Adder of the AMD Athlon Processor," In Formal Methods in Computer-Aided Design, Lecture Notes in Computer Science, Vol. 1954, Springer-Verlag, pp. 3-36, 2000.
29. Signal Processing WorkSystem (SPW) User's Guide, Cadence Design Systems, Inc., July 1999.
30. S. Swan, An Introduction to System Level Modeling in SystemC 2.0, Cadence Design Systems, Inc., May 2001.
31. http://www.systemc.org/.
32. CoCentric^{TM} System Studio User's Guide, Synopsys, Inc., USA, August 2001.
33. CoCentric Fixed-Point Designer User's Guide, Synopsys, Inc., USA, August 2002.

Adding Action Refinement
to Stochastic True Concurrency Models

Mila Majster-Cederbaum[1] and Jinzhao Wu[1,2]

[1] Fakultät für Mathematik und Informatik
Universität Mannheim, D7, 27, 68131 Mannheim, Germany
{mcb,wu}@pi2.informatik.uni-mannheim.de
[2] Chengdu Institute of Computer Applications
Chinese Academy of Sciences, Chengdu 610041, China

Abstract. Action refinement is an essential operation in the hierarchical design of concurrent systems, stochastic or not. In this paper we develop techniques of action refinement in a stochastic true concurrency causality based setting, stochastic bundle event structures. A stochastic LOTOS-like process algebra is used as the specification language, where the corresponding syntactic operation of action refinement is carried out. We show that the behaviour of the refined system can be inferred compositionally from the behaviour of the original system and from the behaviour of the systems substituted for actions with explicitly represented start points, that the stochastic versions of pomset trace equivalence and history preserving bisimulation equivalence are both congruences under the refinement, and that the semantic and syntactic action refinements coincide under these equivalence relations with respect to a cpo-based denotational semantics. Therefore, our refinement operations behave well. They meet the commonly expected properties.

1 Introduction

We consider the design of concurrent systems in the framework of approaches where the basic building blocks are actions. By an action we understand here any activity which is considered as a conceptual entity on a chosen level of abstraction.

Concentrating on functional issues of systems, traditional concurrency models have no performance information associated. To control the complexity of system specification, a well-founded theory of composition and a well-founded theory of hierarchy for traditional concurrent systems have both been significantly established. The former is usually realized by means of modular techniques, which are indeed the main features of process algebras [29], while the latter by *action refinement* [10], which allows the representation of systems in a hierarchical way, changing the level of abstraction by interpreting actions on a higher level by more complicated processes on a lower level until the implementation level is reached.

Traditional concurrency models lack the capability of performance evaluation that describes, analyses and optimises dynamic behaviour of the systems [12,3].

J.S. Dong and J. Woodcock (Eds.): ICFEM 2003, LNCS 2885, pp. 226–245, 2003.
© Springer-Verlag Berlin Heidelberg 2003

A lot of effort has been put into the stochastic extensions of formal methods to solve this problem. Prominent examples are various stochastic process calculi in which time and probability are integrated by considering delays of a continuous probabilistic nature [11,16,18,2,19].

A theory of composition has been successfully established for stochastic concurrent systems [4,16,18,14,13]. But how can a theory of hierarchy be achieved for such systems? Until so far we are unaware of any work in this regard. We believe that introducing action refinement is again a right way to reach a solution. This paper focuses on this topic. The main practical benefit from our work is that action refinement approach for stochastic concurrent systems is developed such that hierarchical specification of such systems is now possible.

The models of concurrency can be distinguished in two groups: interleaving models, in which the independent execution of two processes is modelled by specifying the possible interleaving of their actions, and true concurrency models, in which the causal relations between actions are represented explicitly.

Without further restrictions, even for traditional concurrency models most of the commonly used equivalence relations are not preserved under action refinement in the interleaving approach. These equivalence relations, however, are often used to establish the correctness of the implementation with respect to the system specification. In particular, stochastic interleaving models have to be restricted to the use of exponential distributions [3]. The interleaving of causally independent actions complicates the use of more general distributions considerably. But exponential distributions are not realistic for modelling many phenomena in an adequate way. These problems can be circumvented by moving to true concurrency models [11,18,9,19]. Moreover, in the system design phase the local causal dependencies between actions are important. Interleaving with actions of other parts of the system burdens the design. True concurrency models are considered to be much more appropriate here. In addition, a true concurrency setting does not suffer from the state explosion problem.

We study action refinement for stochastic true concurrent systems, where action occurrences are subject to a delay that is governed by a random variable. Our aim is to achieve system correctness with respect not only to functional aspects but also to performance issues.

A well accepted true concurrency model is event structures. We use stochastic bundle event structures [20,21,18] as the system model. Bundle event structures have been shown to adequately deal with e.g. parallel composition, and the method to equip performance information allows for more general distributions. A stochastic version of a LOTOS-like process algebra proposed in [4,18,5] is used as the specification language, which is a synthesis of CCS [25] and CSP [17].

There are essentially two interpretations of action refinement. One is called syntactic and the other semantic. Syntactic action refinement, where actions in a process are replaced by more complicated processes, yields a more detailed process description [1,10]. Due to its definitional clarity, syntactic action refinement can be easily used without too much insight on the semantics. Semantic action refinement is carried out in the semantic domain. It may avoid a confusion of the abstraction levels, which is possible in syntactic refinement and may result in undesirable situations [9,10].

We define both syntactic and semantic action refinements, and discuss three common issues of interest: *safety, congruence* and *coincidence* problems.

A refinement operation should be safe, that is, the behaviour of the refined system is the refinement of the behaviour of the original system, and the refinement of the behaviour of the original system is the behaviour of the refined system. Here, please do not confuse the safety notion with the usual one e.g. things like deadlock-freeness. Since equivalence relations are often used to capture when two systems are considered to exhibit the same behaviour, we have to try to find such equivalences which are congruences under the refinement. The result that syntactic and semantic refinements coincide gives a clear understanding of the concept of action refinement, and has important applications in system verifications [22]: the refined syntactic specification can be modelled by semantic refinement, and the refined semantic model can be specified by syntactic refinement.

We adopt the methodology to model action refinement as an operator. Our work is a further development of the work of [9,23,24]. In [9] action refinement approaches for traditional event structures were proposed, whereas in [23,24] action refinement for concurrent systems with deterministic real-time was studied. The main contributions of this paper are:

- the action refinement techniques in stochastic event structures and a stochastic process algebra;
- the verification of safety of refinement;
- the congruence result about pomset trace and history preserving bisimulation equivalences; and
- the coincidence result of semantic refinement with syntactic refinement.

The paper is structured as follows: We present some necessary notions and results in stochastic processes in Section 2. In Section 3, we extend stochastic event structures with action durations, and define on such a model some useful compositional operators and equivalences. An action refinement technique for stochastic event structures is developed in Section 4, where the refinement safety and the congruence result about pomset trace equivalence are also declared and given. In Section 5, we describe a stochastic LOTOS-like process algebra and define a cpo-based denotational semantics on which our coincidence result is based. An action refinement approach in the stochastic process algebra is proposed in Section 6, where we also demonstrate the coincidence result under pomset trace equivalence. Proofs of results are given in Section 7. Section 8 contains a brief discussion on synchronization as well as the congruence and coincidence results when history preserving bisimulation equivalence is taken.

2   Notations

We assume the reader to be familiar with the notions of *random variables* and their *(probability) distribution functions* [28]. In the following, we always use F_U to denote the distribution function of a random variable U.

If U and V are random variables, then so are $max(U, V)$ and $pU \pm qV$. Here, $p, q \in \mathbb{R}^+$ and $\mathbb{R}^+$ denotes the set of non-negative reals.

Let RV_0 be a set of independent random variables whose values are in $\mathbb{R}^+$ and characterized by their distribution functions, and RV be a set of random variables containing RV_0 and satisfying the conditions that if $U, V \in RV$ then

(1) $pU \in RV$ for $p \in \mathbb{R}^+$,
(2) $max(U, V) \in RV$.

Conditions (1) and (2) indicate that RV is closed under the number-multiple and maximum operation on random variables. Note that the distribution function of a random variable in RV can be obtained from the distribution functions of the random variables in RV_0, and 0 is in RV. Since $max(U, 0) = U$ holds for any $U \in RV$, 0 is the identity element of RV for the maximum operation.

Examples of such a set of random variables are the case where RV_0 consists of independent random variables of phase-type distributions [26,15] and the case where RV_0 consists of independent random variables of exponential polynomial form distributions [30]. In the first case, all the random variables in RV are phase-type distributed. In the second case, all the random variables in RV are of exponential polynomial form distributions.

3   System Model: Stochastic Event Structures

Assume a given set Θ of observable actions and an invisible internal silent action τ ($\tau \notin \Theta$). Action $\sqrt{}$ ($\sqrt{} \notin \Theta \cup \{\tau\}$) indicates the successful termination of a process. Let $Act = \Theta \cup \{\tau, \sqrt{}\}$. Unlike e.g. [4,18,5], actions are no longer instantaneous, they are viewed as compound happenings having durations, and the duration of an action is determined by a random variable. Let the *duration function* $k : \Theta \to RV$ assign random variables to observable actions. Moreover, we suppose $k(\tau) = 0$ and $k(\sqrt{}) = 0$, namely the durations of actions τ and $\sqrt{}$ are assumed to be zero. This assumption is reasonable: Action $\sqrt{}$ is used only to indicate the successful termination of a process, it is instantaneous and costs no time. A time interval in which the system is silent can be modelled by a run where one τ-action is put at the start and one at the end point of the interval, and the run executes τ-actions inside this interval.

3.1   What Are Stochastic Event Structures

We employ bundle event structures [20,21] with stochastic information associated as the system model. Bundle event structures consist of events labelled with actions, together with relations of causality and conflict between events. Symmetric conflict is a binary relation, denoted $\sharp$, between events, and the intended meaning of $e \sharp e'$ is that e and e' cannot both occur in a single system run. Causality is represented by a binary relation, the bundle relation denoted $\mapsto$. For an event e and a set X of events that are pairwise in conflict, $X \mapsto e$ means that if e happens in a system run, then exactly one event in X has happened before and caused e. X is called a *bundle-set*. Note that X can be empty.

Event and bundle delay functions Ed and Bd are assumed to associate random variables to events and bundles, respectively [4,18,5]. The intuitive interpretation of an event e equipped with a random variable $Ed(e) = U$ is that U may determine the minimal time at which e is enabled, i.e. the probability that this minimal time is within time t is $F_U(t)$. For a bundle $X \mapsto e$ equipped with a random variable $Bd(X, e) = V$, V may determine the minimal time elapse between the enabling of e and the end of its causal predecessor in X, that is, the probability that this minimal time elapse is within time t is $F_V(t)$. Here, "may determine" means "determines in case e is enabled".

Let EVENT be a universe of events, such that $* \notin EVENT$ and $(e, *), (*, e), (e, e') \in$ EVENT for $e, e' \in$ EVENT. The introduction of pair events is for conveniently defining refinement and other compositional operators on stochastic event structures. Formally, a *stochastic event structure* (abbr. *ses*) $\mathcal{E}$ is a tuple $(E, \sharp, \mapsto, l, Ed, Bd)$ with

> $E \subseteq$ EVENT, a set of *events*,
> $\sharp \subseteq E \times E$, the irreflexive and symmetric *conflict relation*,
> $\mapsto \subseteq 2^E \times E$, the *bundle relation*,
> $l : E \to Act$, the *action labelling function*,
> $Ed : E \to RV$, the *event delay function*, and
> $Bd : \mapsto \to RV$, the *bundle delay function*,
> such that for any bundle-set $X \subseteq E$, $(X \times X) \setminus Id_E \subseteq \sharp$.

Here 2^E denotes the power-set of E, $Id_E = \{(e, e) \mid e \in E\}$, and RV the set of random variables defined in Section 2. The constraint in the definition requires all events in a bundle-set to be mutually in conflict. This enables us to uniquely define a causal ordering between the events in a system run. Action durations are not made part of the tuple, this is because actions exist independently of any individual ses's. However, system runs of a ses rely heavily upon action durations. Also, the event delay function is not redundant with respect to the bundle delay function and action duration function. See the following description of system runs.

A ses is depicted as follows: Events are denoted by nodes. The action label is given inside or near the node. $e \sharp e'$ is indicated by a dotted line between events e and e'. A bundle $X \mapsto e$ is indicated by an arrow to e and to this arrow each event in X is connected via a line. Random variables belonging to events and bundles are depicted near the events and bundles, respectively. Delays 0 are usually omitted, and we identify events with their action labels if no confusion arises.

Example 3.1.1 $\mathcal{E}$ in Figure 1 is a ses. It models a message sender, where actions a, b and c can be understood as sending the message, returning the message and informing the user, respectively. The τ-events indicate the system becomes silent

after executing the action of sending or returning the message and then informs
the user. The random variables $U_1, U_2, V_1, V_2, V_3 \in RV$ have the following meaning that e.g. the event labelled with action a (send the message) is equipped
with random variable U_1: the minimal time when the sending begins to happen
is determined by U_1, namely the probability that this minimal time is within t
is $F_{U_1}(t)$. The bundle equipped with e.g. random variable V_1 has the meaning
that the minimal transition delay between the end of sending and the enabling of
the silent action is determined by V_1, namely the probability that this minimal
delay is not more than t is $F_{V_1}(t)$. It is assumed that the duration of sending the
message is W, i.e. $k(a) = W$, where $W \in RV$.

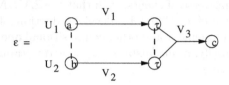

Fig. 1. An example ses

By SES we denote the set of all ses's. Elements of SES are denoted by $\mathcal{E}, \mathcal{E}_i$,
where $\mathcal{E} = (E, \sharp, \mapsto, l, Ed, Bd)$, $\mathcal{E}_i = (E_i, \sharp_i, \mapsto_i, l_i, Ed_i, Bd_i)$. When necessary, we
also use $E_\mathcal{E}$, $\sharp_\mathcal{E}$, $\mapsto_\mathcal{E}$, $l_\mathcal{E}$, $Ed_\mathcal{E}$ and $Bd_\mathcal{E}$ to represent the components of $\mathcal{E}$. $init(\mathcal{E})$
denotes the set of initial events of $\mathcal{E}$, and $exit(\mathcal{E})$ its set of successful termination
events, i.e.

$$init(\mathcal{E}) = \{e \in E \mid \neg(\exists X \subseteq E : X \mapsto e)\}, \text{ and } exit(\mathcal{E}) = \{e \in E \mid l(e) = \sqrt{}\}.$$

The positive events of $\mathcal{E}$ are those events that are annotated with non-zero
random variables, namely $pos(\mathcal{E}) = \{e \in E \mid Ed(e) \neq 0\}$. Let $pin(\mathcal{E}) = pos(\mathcal{E}) \cup init(\mathcal{E})$.

A system run of a ses is modelled by a sequence of random events, where each
event e_i is associated with a random variable U_i that uniquely determines the
minimal enabling time of this event. A *random event (of $\mathcal{E}$)* is formally defined
as a pair (e, U), where $e \in E$ and U is a random variable.

Let γ be a finite sequence $(e_1, U_1), \cdots, (e_n, U_n)$ of random events, where e_i
and e_j are distinct whenever $i \neq j$. We denote by $E(\gamma)$ the set of all events
appearing in γ, and $RV(\gamma, e_i)$ the random variable associated with event e_i.
That is, $E(\gamma) = \{e_1, \cdots, e_n\}$ and $RV(\gamma, e_i) = U_i$. Note that $E(\gamma)$ and $RV(\gamma, e_i)$
can be similarly defined when γ is a set of random events. Suppose $\gamma_{i-1} = (e_1, U_1), \cdots, (e_{i-1}, U_{i-1})$ is the $(i-1)$-th prefix of γ $(i = 1, \cdots, n)$.

In a system run, (i) any two events that occur should not be in conflict,
and (ii) predecessors should be closed with respect to the causality on events.
To meet these two requirements, we first figure out the events enabled after a
sub-sequence of random events. We say that an event is enabled after γ_{i-1} if
it is not disabled by one of the events in γ_{i-1} and some event in an arbitrary
bundle-set pointing to it occurs in γ_{i-1}. Let

$$en(\gamma_{i-1}) = \{e \in E \setminus E(\gamma_{i-1}) \mid (\forall e_j \in E(\gamma_{i-1}) : e \not\Vdash e_j) \wedge$$
$$(\forall X \mapsto e : X \cap E(\gamma_{i-1}) \neq \emptyset)\}.$$

$en(\gamma_{i-1})$ is then the set of *events enabled after* γ_{i-1}.

The random variable U_i is determined by the random variable in $\mathcal{E}$ annotated to e_i, the duration of the action labelled to e_i, the random variables linked to all bundles pointing to e_i and the random variables U_j associated with the causal predecessors of e_i in the system run. We use the following simple ses, say $\mathcal{E}$, as an example to illustrate our basic philosophy about the requirements on the random variable annotations in system runs, where a and b are the actions labelled to events, and U, V and W random variables from RV:

$$U \; a\circ \xrightarrow{\;V\;} \circ b \; W$$

Assume the sequence $(a, U_1), (b, U_2)$ is a system run of $\mathcal{E}$. Then U_1 and U_2 are explained as the random variables that determine the minimal time instants at which a and b begin to happen in this run, respectively. Since U determines, as aforementioned, the minimal time at which a is enabled, we require $U_1 = U$. Also, because the minimal time at which a starts to happen is determined by U and the execution period of a is determined by the random variable $k(a)$, the time at which a finishes should not be less than $U + k(a)$. However, since V determines the minimal transition delay from the end of a to the start of b, b should start to happen at time not less than $U + k(a) + V$. On the other hand, b has to start to happen at time not less than W. It is thus required that the minimal time at which b starts to happen is determined by $max(W, U + k(a) + V)$, namely we require that (iii) $U_2 = max(W, U + k(a) + V)$.

Bearing this in mind, one can easily understand the definition of configurations below, which are actually the underlying random event sets of system runs. Remark that the causality relations in the runs will be reflected in the notion of isomorphic configurations for convenience.

Let the sequence γ of random events satisfy the conditions that for $1 \leq i \leq n$,

(1) $e_i \in en(\gamma_{i-1})$, and (2) $U_i = max(\{Ed(e_i)\} \cup B_i)$ where $B_i = \{Ed(e_j) + k(l(e_j)) + Bd(X, e_i) \mid \exists X \subseteq E : X \mapsto e_i \wedge X \cap E(\gamma_{i-1}) = \{e_j\}\}$.

Then the set of random events occurring in γ is called a *(random) configuration* of $\mathcal{E}$.

The first condition takes care of the requirements (i) and (ii), and the second takes care of (iii). Note that the random variable U_i may not be in RV. It is a composition of the random variables in RV by the addition and maximum operations. By $C(\mathcal{E})$ we denote the set of all the configurations of $\mathcal{E}$.

A configuration σ of $\mathcal{E}$ *successfully terminates* if there exists $e \in E(\sigma)$ such that e is labelled with the successful termination action $\sqrt{}$. $\mathcal{E}$ is called *well-labelled* if $E(\sigma) \cap exit(\mathcal{E})$ is empty or a singleton for each configuration σ of it. Let $T(\mathcal{E}) = \{U \mid \exists \sigma \in C(\mathcal{E}) : \exists (e, U) \in \sigma : l(e) = \sqrt{}\}$. $T(\mathcal{E})$ consists of all the random variables determining the minimal time instants at which the system runs successfully terminate.

3.2   Compositional Operators on SES's

Here we only describe *action prefix* "a_U.", *parallel composition* "$\|_A$" and *abstraction* "$\backslash A$" in detail. For other operators such as *sequential composition* ";", *choice* "+" as well as *relabelling* "$[\lambda]$", we refer the reader to [4,18,5]. Notice also that in the definition of action prefix, we suppose event e is uniquely determined [31] to guarantee that it is really a function from SES to SES.

Action prefix: $a_U.\mathcal{E}_1 = (E_1 \cup \{e\}, \sharp_1, \mapsto, l_1 \cup \{(e,a)\}, Ed, Bd)$ for $a \in \Theta \cup \{\tau\}$ and $U \in RV$, where $e \in \text{EVENT} \setminus E_1$ and

$$\mapsto = \mapsto_1 \cup(\{\{e\}\} \times pin(\mathcal{E}_1)),$$
$$Ed = \{(e,U)\} \cup (E_1 \times \{0\}),$$
$$Bd = Bd_1 \cup \{((\{e\}, e_1), Ed_1(e_1)) \mid e_1 \in pin(\mathcal{E}_1)\}.$$

Parallel composition: For $A \subseteq \Theta$, $\mathcal{E}_1 \|_A \mathcal{E}_2 = (E, \sharp, \mapsto, l, Ed, Bd)$, where

$$E = (E_1^f \times \{*\}) \cup (\{*\} \times E_2^f) \cup \{(e_1, e_2) \in E_1^s \times E_2^s \mid l_1(e_1) = l_2(e_2)\} \text{ where}$$
$\quad E_i^s = \{e \in E_i \mid l_i(e) \in A \cup \{\sqrt{}\}\}$ and $E_i^f = E_i \setminus E_i^s$ $(i = 1, 2)$,
$(e_1, e_2)\sharp(e_1', e_2')$ iff $(e_1 \sharp_1 e_1') \vee (e_2 \sharp_2 e_2')\vee$
$\quad (e_1 = e_1' \neq * \wedge e_2 \neq e_2') \vee (e_2 = e_2' \neq * \wedge e_1 \neq e_1')$,
$X \mapsto (e_1, e_2)$ iff $(\exists X_1 : X_1 \mapsto_1 e_1 \wedge X = \{(e, e') \in E \mid e \in X_1\}) \vee$
$\quad (\exists X_2 : X_2 \mapsto_2 e_2 \wedge X = \{(e, e') \in E \mid e' \in X_2\})$,
$l((e_1, e_2)) = $ if $e_1 = *$ then $l_2(e_2)$ else $l_1(e_1)$,
$Ed((e_1, e_2)) = max(Ed_1(e_1), Ed_2(e_2))$ with $Ed_1(*) = Ed_2(*) = 0$,
$Bd((X, (e_1, e_2))) = max(Bd_1((pr_1(X), e_1)), Bd_2((pr_2(X), e_2)))$
with $Bd_1((\emptyset, e_1)) = Bd_2((\emptyset, e_2)) = 0$ where
$\quad pr_1(X) = \{X_1 \subseteq E_1 \mid X_1 \mapsto_1 e_1 \wedge X = \{(e, e') \in E \mid e \in X_1\}\}$,
$\quad pr_2(X) = \{X_2 \subseteq E_2 \mid X_2 \mapsto_2 e_2 \wedge X = \{(e, e') \in E \mid e' \in X_2\}\}$.

For more explanations of these operators, we refer the reader to [18]. Also, we can see from these two definitions why RV is required to be closed under the maximum operation and to contain the identity element 0 for this operation.

Since actions are no longer instantaneous, the abstraction operator proposed in [4,18,5] has to be modified. In fact, both relabelling and abstraction can be viewed as certain action refinements for the system. Our idea to abstract an observable action a is that we insert two τ-events, one at the time when a starts and the other at the time when a finishes. We suggest to the reader to come back to the following definition after reading the next section.

Abstraction: $\mathcal{E}_1 \backslash A = f(\mathcal{E}_1)$, the refinement of $\mathcal{E}_1$, where $Act_0 = Act \setminus A$, and for $a \in A$, $f(a) = (\{e_\sqrt{}\}, \emptyset, \emptyset, \{(e_\sqrt{}, \sqrt{})\}, \{(e_\sqrt{}, k(a))\}, \emptyset)$, namely the ses $\circ\sqrt{}\{k(a)\}$.

By our Theorem 4.1.1 in the next section, $\mathcal{E}_1 \backslash A$ is a ses. The definition of ses's is independent of the assumption that actions have durations. As has been proved in [18], all the other operators mentioned are also well defined, i.e. $\circ\mathcal{E}_1(\circ \in \{a_T., [\lambda]\})$ and $\mathcal{E}_1 \circ \mathcal{E}_2(\circ \in \{;, +, \|_A\})$ are all ses's.

3.3 Equivalences

The behaviour of a system may be described by equivalence classes of partially ordered multisets of actions (pomsets). We define in this section a linear-time equivalence, termed pomset trace equivalence, on ses's. A branching-time equivalence, termed history preserving bisimulation equivalence, can be similarly defined to further record where choices are made [9]. Here we only describe the former in detail. The latter is briefly discussed in the discussion part. For linear-time and branching-time equivalences the reader is referred to [8].

Assume that σ is a configuration of $\mathcal{E}$ and $e_i, e_j \in E(\sigma)$. By $e_j \mapsto e_i$ we mean that there exists a bundle-set X such that $e_j \in X$ and $X \mapsto e_i$. We use $\to |_\sigma$ to represent the reflexive and transitive closure of this relation, which is in fact the causality relation in σ. We also use $l|_\sigma$ as the restriction of l on $E(\sigma)$, i.e. $l|_\sigma(e) = l(e)$ for $e \in E(\sigma)$. In addition, $e_j \in E(\sigma)$ is said to be *maximal* in σ, if there does not exist $e_i \in E(\sigma)$ such that $e_j \mapsto e_i$.

A configuration σ_1 of $\mathcal{E}_1$ and a configuration σ_2 of $\mathcal{E}_2$ are said to be *isomorphic*, denoted $\sigma_1 \approx \sigma_2$, if there exists a bijection $h : E(\sigma_1) \to E(\sigma_2)$, such that for arbitrary $e, e' \in E(\sigma_1)$,

(1) $RV(\sigma_1, e) = RV(\sigma_2, h(e))$,
(2) $l_1|_{\sigma_1}(e) = l_2|_{\sigma_2}(h(e))$, and
(3) $e \to_1 |_{\sigma_1} e'$ iff $h(e) \to_2 |_{\sigma_2} h(e')$.

The bijection h is called an *isomorphism* between σ_1 and σ_2. Constraint (1) requires the minimal time instants at which the two corresponding events in isomorphic configurations start to happen to be determined by the same random variable. Therefore the probabilities that the minimal time instants are within a given time are the same. Constraints (2) and (3) require the action labels of the corresponding events and the causality relations of the events in isomorphic configurations to be the same.

By $C(\mathcal{E}_1) \approx C(\mathcal{E}_2)$ we denote that any configuration of $\mathcal{E}_1$ has an isomorphic correspondence in $\mathcal{E}_2$, and vice versa. $\mathcal{E}_1$ and $\mathcal{E}_2$ are said to be *pomset trace equivalent*, denoted $\mathcal{E}_1 \cong_p \mathcal{E}_2$, if $C(\mathcal{E}_1) \approx C(\mathcal{E}_2)$.

4 Semantic Action Refinement for SES's

For our purpose, we have first to re-arrange the ses's used to substitute actions. Given a random variable $U \in RV$, we call $\tau_U.\mathcal{E}$, denoted $r(\mathcal{E}, U)$, the *rooted ses* of $\mathcal{E}$ with start random variable U. In $r(\mathcal{E}, U)$, the new event corresponding to the prefix τ is called the *start event* of $\mathcal{E}$ (or $r(\mathcal{E}, U)$) and denoted by $o_{r(\mathcal{E},U)}$. This new event resembles the specially introduced events utilized in [23,7,24], and can be viewed as the start point of system. It executes the internal silent action and the earliest time to be triggered is determined by U.

Example 4.1 Let $\mathcal{E}_a$ be the ses given in the left hand of Figure 2, where action a' can be understood as sending the message by channel 1, and action a'' sending the message by channel 2. $r(\mathcal{E}_a, U)$ is the ses depicted in the right hand of Figure 2. We suppose $k(a') = \frac{1}{5}W$ and $k(a'') = \frac{3}{10}W$.

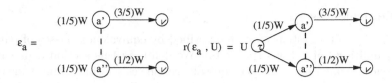

Fig. 2. A ses and its rooted ses with start random variable U

4.1   Refining a SES

A refinement of an observable action a, say $\mathcal{E}_a$, should be a ses. Since action $\sqrt{}$ only represents the successful termination of a process, a system run should contain at most one $\sqrt{}$-event. So we require $\mathcal{E}_a$ to be well-labelled. Our requirement on the random variable annotations is that the "duration" of a successful termination system run of $\mathcal{E}_a$ is the duration of action a. We thus require the minimal termination time points of the successful termination runs of $\mathcal{E}_a$ to be determined by the random variable $k(a)$.

Let Act_0 be a subset of Act, representing the set of actions that need not or cannot be refined, and $\{\tau, \sqrt{}\} \subseteq Act_0$. A function $f : Act \setminus Act_0 \to SES$ is called a *refinement function* if for any action $a \in Act \setminus Act_0$, the following conditions hold:

$$\text{(1) } f(a) \text{ is well-labelled,}$$
$$\text{(2) } T(f(a)) = \{k(a)\}.$$

We call $f(a)$ the *refinement of action* a (with respect to f). Note that the properties of RV described in its definition ensure the existence of refinement of an action. Additionally, in practice it is reasonable to require that $f(a)$ is finite. If so and if the relations between the random variables annotated to events and bundles in $f(a)$ and the duration $k(a)$ of action a are clear, Constraints (1) and (2) can be checked and easily enforced.

Let f be a refinement function. Our basic idea to use f to refine a ses $\mathcal{E}$ is, if event e is annotated with random variable U and labelled with action a in $\mathcal{E}$ then e is "replaced" by the rooted ses of $f(a)$ with start random variable U. For simplicity we use $rfl(e)$ or $rf(a)$ in the following to abbreviate the rooted ses of $f(a)$ with an already fixed start random variable. Without loss of generality we suppose that $E \cap E_{rf(a)} = \emptyset$ for any $a \in Act \setminus Act_0$.

Definition 4.1.1 (*Refinement of a ses*) The refinement of ses $\mathcal{E}$ is defined as $f(\mathcal{E}) = (E_f, \sharp_f, \mapsto_f, l_f, Ed_f, Bd_f)$, where

- $E_f = \{(e, e') \mid (e \in E) \wedge (l(e) \notin Act_0) \wedge (e' \in E_{rfl(e)})\} \cup \{(e, e) \mid (e \in E) \wedge (l(e) \in Act_0)\}$;

- for any $(e_1, e_2), (e_1', e_2') \in E_f$, $(e_1, e_2) \sharp_f (e_1', e_2')$ iff
  if $(e_1 = e_1')$ then $(e_2 \sharp_{rfl(e_1)} e_2') \vee (e_2, e_2' \in exit(rfl(e_1)) \wedge e_2 \neq e_2')$,
  if $(e_1 \neq e_1')$ then

if $(e_2 = e_1) \wedge (e'_2 = e'_1)$ then $(e_1 \sharp e'_1)$,

if $(e_2 \neq e_1) \wedge (e'_2 = e'_1)$ then $(e_1 \sharp e'_1) \wedge (e_2 \in \{o_{rfl(e_1)}\} \cup exit(rfl(e_1)))$,

if $(e_2 = e_1) \wedge (e'_2 \neq e'_1)$ then $(e_1 \sharp e'_1) \wedge (e'_2 \in \{o_{rfl(e'_1)}\} \cup exit(rfl(e'_1)))$,

if $(e_2 \neq e_1) \wedge (e'_2 \neq e'_1)$ then $(e_1 \sharp e'_1) \wedge (e_2 \in \{o_{rfl(e_1)}\} \cup exit(rfl(e_1))) \wedge$
$(e'_2 \in \{o_{rfl(e'_1)}\} \cup exit(rfl(e'_1)))$;

- for any $X \subseteq E_f$ and $(e_1, e_2) \in E_f$, $X \mapsto_f (e_1, e_2)$ iff
  if $(e_2 \neq e_1) \wedge (e_2 \in E_{rfl(e_1)} \setminus \{o_{rfl(e_1)}\})$ then
  $(\pi_1(X) = \{e_1\}) \wedge (\pi_2(X) \mapsto_{rfl(e_1)} e_2)$,
  if $((e_2 \neq e_1) \wedge (e_2 = o_{rfl(e_1)})) \vee (e_2 = e_1)$ then $(\pi_1(X) \mapsto e_1) \wedge$
  $(\pi_2(X) = \cup_{e \in \pi_1(X), l(e) \notin Act_0} exit(rfl(e)) \cup (\cup_{e \in \pi_1(X), l(e) \in Act_0} \{e\}))$;

- for any $(e_1, e_2) \in E_f$, if $(e_2 \neq e_1)$ then
  if $(e_2 \notin exit(rfl(e_1)))$ then $(l_f((e_1, e_2)) = l_{rfl(e_1)}(e_2))$,
  if $(e_2 \in exit(rfl(e_1)))$ then $(l_f((e_1, e_2)) = \tau)$,
  if $(e_2 = e_1)$ then $(l_f((e_1, e_2)) = l(e_1))$;

- for any $(e_1, e_2) \in E_f$, if $(e_2 = e_1)$ then $Ed_f((e_1, e_2)) = Ed(e_1)$,
  if $(e_2 \neq e_1)$ then
      if $(e_2 = o_{rfl(e_1)})$ then $Ed_f((e_1, e_2)) = Ed(e_1)$,
      if $(e_2 \neq o_{rfl(e_1)})$ then $Ed_f((e_1, e_2)) = 0$;

- for any $X \subseteq E_f$ and $(e_1, e_2) \in E_f$, if $(X \mapsto_f (e_1, e_2))$ then
  if $(e_2 \neq e_1) \wedge (e_2 \in E_{rfl(e_1)} \setminus \{o_{rfl(e_1)}\}) \wedge (\pi_1(X) = \{e_1\})$ then
  $Bd_f(X, (e_1, e_2)) = Bd_{rfl(e_1)}(\pi_2(X), e_2)$,
  if $(e_2 \neq e_1) \wedge (e_2 = o_{rfl(e_1)})$ then $Bd_f(X, (e_1, e_2)) = Bd(\pi_1(X), e_1)$,
  if $(e_2 = e_1)$ then $Bd_f(X, (e_1, e_2)) = Bd(\pi_1(X), e_1)$.

Here $\pi_1(X) = \{e \mid (e, e') \in X\}$ and $\pi_2(X) = \{e' \mid (e, e') \in X\}$.

Figure 3 demonstrates intuitively how $f(\mathcal{E})$ is obtained. In the original ses, a, b and c are "replaced" by $rf(a)$, $rf(b)$ and $rf(c)$ respectively. The event set of the refined ses consists of all the events of $rf(a)$, $rf(b)$ and $rf(c)$. In the original ses, a and b are in conflict with each other, therefore in the refined ses a dotted line, namely a conflict relation, is introduced between the start-events of $rf(a)$ and $rf(b)$. In the original ses, a and b form a bundle-set pointing to c, thus in the refined ses all the successful termination events of $rf(a)$ and $rf(b)$, i.e. $exit(rf(a)) \cup exit(rf(b))$, form a bundle-set pointing to the start-event of $rf(c)$. For this all the events in this bundle-set are relabelled with action τ and dotted lines, i.e. conflict relations, are introduced pairwise between them. In order to guarantee that events in a bundle-set have to be pairwise in conflict for the case when for example action a is not allowed to be refined, dotted lines, namely conflict relations, between the events of $exit(rf(a))$ [$exit(rf(b))$] and the start-event of $rf(b)$ [resp. $rf(a)$] are introduced. Except that the successful termination events of $rf(a), rf(b)$ and $rf(c)$ are relabelled with τ-actions, the other events in the refined ses are labelled with the same actions as they are in $rf(a), rf(b)$ and $rf(c)$. In the original ses, since random variable U_3 may determine the minimal time at which c starts to happen, the start event of $rf(c)$ is annotated with U_3 in the refined ses. In the original ses, random variable V determines the minimal delay from the end of a or b to the start of c. Therefore in the refined ses V is annotated to the bundle from the end events of $rf(a)$ and $rf(b)$ pointing to the start event of $rf(c)$. The random variables annotated to the start events of $rf(a)$ and $rf(b)$ can be explained analogously.

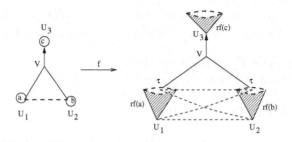

Fig. 3. Illustration of the refinement of a ses

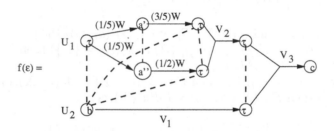

Fig. 4. The refined ses

Theorem 4.1.1 Suppose that $\mathcal{E} \in SES$, and f is a refinement function. Then $f(\mathcal{E}) \in SES$.

Example 4.1.1 Assume $Act_0 = Act \setminus \{a\}$, and $\mathcal{E}$ the ses of Example 3.1.1 (Figure 1). The ses $\mathcal{E}_a$ defined in Example 4.1 (Figure 2) satisfies the two conditions in the definition of $f(a)$. Let $f(a) = \mathcal{E}_a$. That means sending the message is required to be decomposed into the left-hand system of Figure 2 so that the sending can be done by channel 1 or channel 2 satisfying the performance information associated. The refinement $f(\mathcal{E})$ of $\mathcal{E}$ is then the ses depicted in Figure 4.

4.2 Safety and Congruence Result

Let σ be a configuration of $\mathcal{E}$, $e \in E(\sigma)$ with $l(e) \notin Act_0$, and σ_e a configuration of $rfl(e)$. We further assume that $rfl(e)$ satisfies the condition that σ_e successfully terminates if event e is not maximal in σ. Let

$$\sigma_f = \{((e, e_j), U_j) \mid e \in E(\sigma) \text{ and } \text{ if } l(e) \in Act_0 \text{ then } e_j = e, U_j = RV(\sigma, e)$$
$$\text{otherwise } e_j \in E(\sigma_e), U_j = RV(\sigma, e) + RV(\sigma_e, e_j) - RV(\sigma_e, o_{rfl(e)})\}.$$

We call σ_f a *refinement of configuration* σ. It is derived by replacing each random event (e, U) with $l(e) \notin Act_0$ in configuration σ by a configuration σ_e of $rfl(e)$, where the accompanying random variables of events are adjusted according to the random variable U associated to event e.

Theorem 4.2.1 (*Safety*) Suppose that f is a refinement function, and $\mathcal{E} \in SES$. Then $C(f(\mathcal{E})) = \{\sigma_f \mid \sigma_f \text{ is a refinement of } \sigma \in C(\mathcal{E})\}$.

Remark that all the constraints in the definition of refinement functions are needed for the correctness of this theorem.

It is natural to use the rooted ses $rfl(e)$ rather than $f(l(e))$ to substitute action $l(e)$ in $\mathcal{E}$. The start event introduced is the recognizer of the start of system. If necessary, it can be neglected by considering the observable behaviour of the system, i.e. abstracting the system away from the internal τ-events.

Also, it is straightforward to see that the causality relations in each σ_e are respected in the corresponding refinement of σ. The causality relations in σ are respected as well in the meaning that if e causes e' in σ then the successful termination event of σ_e causes the start event of $\sigma_{e'}$.

The behaviour of the refined ses can thus be inferred compositionally from the behaviour of the original ses and from the behaviour of those substituted for actions. Our refinement is safe when defining safety in this sense.

Theorem 4.2.2 (*Congruence result*) Suppose that $\mathcal{E}_1$, $\mathcal{E}_2$ are two ses's such that $\mathcal{E}_1 \cong_p \mathcal{E}_2$, and f_1, f_2: $Act \setminus Act_0 \to SES$ are two refinement functions such that $f_1(a) \cong_p f_2(a)$ for any $a \in Act \setminus Act_0$. Then $f_1(\mathcal{E}_1) \cong_p f_2(\mathcal{E}_2)$.

This theorem indicates that pomset trace equivalence is a congruence under the refinement. Our concept of action refinement is thus well-defined with respect to this equivalence relation.

5   A Stochastic Process Algebra

Let $a \in \Theta \cup \{\tau\}$, $A \subseteq \Theta$, and $\lambda: \Theta \to \Theta$ a relabelling function. $dom(\lambda) = \{a \in \Theta \mid \lambda(a) \neq a\}$ represents the set of actions really relabelled by λ. We further assume that an action a can only be relabelled by an action with the same duration, i.e., $k(\lambda(a)) = k(a)$. Let $x \in Var$, where Var is a set of process variables, and $U \in RV$.

5.1   Syntax

We use the stochastic version of a LOTOS-like process calculus. The set of *(random) expressions* is generated by the following grammar:

$$P ::= 0 \mid 1_U \mid a_U.P \mid P; P \mid P + P \mid P \parallel_A P \mid P \backslash A \mid P[\lambda] \mid x \mid \mu x.P$$

The operators have the following intuitive meaning: 0 denotes inaction. 1_U represents the process that terminates successfully, and its minimal termination time is determined by U, i.e. the probability that this minimal termination time is no more than t is $F_U(t)$. In the stochastic process algebra defined in [4,18,5], the successful termination processes are always equipped with random variable 0. Now we need to label them with arbitrary random variables from RV, since actions are no longer instantaneous, and the minimal time at which an action may be enabled has thus to be specified.

$a_U.P$ denotes the prefix of action a before P where the minimal time when a starts to happen is determined by U, i.e. the probability that this minimal time is no more than t is $F_U(t)$. $P[\lambda]$ denotes the relabelling of P according to λ. $P \backslash A$ behaves as P, except that the actions in A are abstracted to be τ-actions.

$P_1; P_2$ denotes the sequential composition of P_1 and P_2, where the control is passed to P_2 by the successful termination of P_1. $P_1 + P_2$ indicates the choice between the behaviours described by P_1 and P_2. $P_1 \parallel_A P_2$ denotes the parallel composition of P_1 and P_2, where P_1 and P_2 must perform any actions in $A \cup \{\sqrt{}\}$ simultaneously, while the other actions are executed independently from each other.

Recursive behaviour is described by $\mu x.P$. It can be understood through $x := P$, where $x \in Var$ may occur in the body P.

By SPA we denote the set of all the expressions of our language, and $A_P \subseteq \Theta$ the set of all observable actions occurring in an expression P. The random variable attachments of actions, if they are 0, are omitted in an expression.

Example 5.1.1 The following P and P_a are expressions:
$$P = (a_{U_1}.1_{V_1} + b_{U_2}.1_{V_2}); (c_{V_3}.0) ,$$
$$P_a = a'_{\frac{1}{5}W}.1_{\frac{3}{5}W} + a''_{\frac{4}{5}W}.1_{\frac{1}{2}W} .$$
We will see later that P and P_a specify the ses of Figures 1 and the left-hand ses of Figure 2, respectively.

5.2   Denotational Semantics

An expression is said to be *closed*, if any process variable x that occurs has to be in the scope of a μx-operator. Let s be the cpo-based denotational semantics defined in [6], which is an improvement of [18,5]. Basically, the semantic model of a closed expression is a ses, which is derived as follows:

$$s(0) = (\emptyset, \emptyset, \emptyset, \emptyset, \emptyset, \emptyset);$$
$$s(1_U) = (\{e_{\sqrt{}}\}, \emptyset, \emptyset, \{(e_{\sqrt{}}, \sqrt{})\}, \{(e_{\sqrt{}}, U)\}, \emptyset);$$
$$s(\circ P) = \circ s(P) \text{ for } \circ \in \{a_U., \backslash A, [\lambda]\};$$
$$s(P_1 \circ P_2) = s(P_1) \circ s(P_2) \text{ for } \circ \in \{;, +, \parallel_A\}; \text{ and}$$

the semantic model of recursion is defined as the least upper bound of a set of ses's with a complete partial order (cpo):

$$s(\mu x.P) = (\cup_i E_i, \cup_i \sharp_i, \mapsto, \cup_i l_i, \cup_i Ed_i, Bd), \text{ where}$$

$\bot = (\emptyset, \emptyset, \emptyset, \emptyset, \emptyset, \emptyset), v_P(v_P^{i-1}(\bot)) = v_P^i(\bot) = (E_i, \natural_i, \mapsto_i, l_i, Ed_i, Bd_i),$
$\mapsto = \{(\cup_i X_i, e) \mid \forall i : (e \in E_i \Rightarrow X_i \mapsto_i e) \wedge (X_{i+1} \cap E_i = X_i)\},$
$Bd = \{((\cup_i X_i, e), U_i) \mid \forall i : (e \in E_i \Rightarrow Bd_i(X_i, e) = U_i) \wedge (X_{i+1} \cap E_i = X_i)\},$
and v_P is defined as the function that substitutes a ses for each occurrence of x in P, interpreting all operators in P as operators on ses's.

Remark that $s(1_U)$ is a modification of $s(1)$ defined in [18,5]. In the sequel, when the context depends upon $s(P)$ we always suppose that expression P is closed.

Example 5.2.1 Let $\mathcal{E}$ and $\mathcal{E}_a$ be the ses's given in Example 3.1.1 (Figure 1) and Example 4.1 (Figure 2, left-hand), and P and P_a be the expressions given in Example 5.1.1. Then $s(P) = \mathcal{E}$, and $s(P_a) = \mathcal{E}_a$.

6   Syntactic Action Refinement in Stochastic Processes

In this section, we define the syntactic refinement of a closed expression $P \in SPA$. For this we have to sort out some actions occurring in P that may not be refined. For a given expression P, $Sort(P)$ is defined as the smallest set of actions containing A $[A, dom(\lambda)]$ if the abstraction operator "$\backslash A$" [resp. parallel composition "$\|_A$", relabelling "$[\lambda]$"] occurs in P. All actions in $Sort(P)$ are not allowed to be refined, since otherwise it may lead to a confusion of the communication levels like in the traditional case [10]. Remark that the restriction on synchronization actions in the parallel composition can actually be relaxed. Some details about this is given in the discussion part. Here we exclude such actions for clarity.

6.1   Refining an Expression

Let $Act_0 \subseteq Act$, representing the set of actions that need not or cannot be refined such that $Sort(P) \cup \{\tau, \surd\} \subseteq Act_0$, and let $g : Act \setminus Act_0 \to SPA$ be a function. For convenience, we also use $A_{g(a)}$ to denote the action singleton $\{a\}$ when $a \in \Theta \cap Act_0$. It is defined as follows that g is a *refinement function for expression P*:

   g is a refinement function for 0, 1 and x;
   g is a refinement function for $a_U.P_1$ iff g is a refinement function for P_1;
   g is a refinement function for $P_1 \circ P_2$ iff g is a refinement function for P_1 and P_2, where $\circ \in \{; , +\}$;
   g is a refinement function for $P_1 \|_A P_2$ iff g is a refinement function for P_1 and P_2, and for any $a \in Act \setminus Act_0$, $A_{g(a)} \cap Sort(P) = \emptyset$;
   g is a refinement function for $\circ P_1$ iff g is a refinement function for P_1, and for any $a \in Act \setminus Act_0$, $A_{g(a)} \cap Sort(P) = \emptyset$, where $\circ \in \{\backslash A, [\lambda]\}$;
   g is a refinement function for $\mu x.P_1$ iff g is a refinement function for P_1.

We forbid the actions in $Sort(P)$ to occur in $g(a)$. Usually, like in the traditional case such constraints cannot be avoided for refinement on syntactic level. Otherwise a confusion of the communication levels may happen [10].

Hereafter, let g be a refinement function for expression P. We proceed to consider how g can be applied to P to obtain the refinement of P. Our basic idea is that the refinement of $a_U.P_1$, where $a \notin Act_0$, is defined as the sequential composition of $\tau_U.g(a)$ and the refinement of P_1.

Similarly, the prefix τ can be viewed as the start point of the process. Since the random variable U determines the minimal time when action a starts to happen in $a_U.P_1$, the minimal time at which the start point begins to happen in the refined expression should be determined by U.

Definition 6.1.1 (*Refinement of expression P*) The refinement $g(P)$ of expression P is defined as follows:

$$g(0) = 0; g(1_U) = 1_U; g(x) = x;$$

$$g(a_U.P_1) = \begin{cases} a_U.g(P_1) & \text{if } a \in Act_0; \\ (\tau_U.g(a)); g(P_1) & \text{otherwise}; \end{cases}$$

$$g(\circ P_1) = \circ g(P_1), \text{ where } \circ \in \{\backslash A, [\lambda]\};$$
$$g(P_1 \circ P_2) = g(P_1) \circ g(P_2), \text{ where } \circ \in \{;, +, \|_A\};$$
$$g(\mu x.P_1) = \mu x.g(P_1).$$

Theorem 6.1.1 Suppose that $P \in SPA$, and g is a refinement function for P. Then $g(P) \in SPA$.

Example 6.1.1 Assume $Act \setminus Act_0 = \{a\}$, and P and P_a are the expressions given in Example 5.1.1. Let $g(a) = P_a$. Then
$$g(P) = (\tau_{U_1}.(a'_{\frac{1}{5}W}.1_{\frac{3}{5}W} + a''_{\frac{4}{5}W}.1_{\frac{1}{2}W}); 1_{V_1} + b_{U_2}.1_{V_2}); (c_{V_3}.0) .$$

The refinement $g(P)$ is obviously closed if P is closed. In addition, our refinement operation is simultaneous, not step-wise.

6.2   Coincidence Result

Assume $g : Act \setminus Act_0 \to SPA$ is a syntactic refinement function for a given expression P as defined in Section 6.1 such that $g(a)$ is closed. We associate with g a semantic refinement function $f : a \mapsto s(g(a))$ $(a \in Act \setminus Act_0)$ as defined in Section 4.1. Notice that $s(g(a))$ is naturally well-labelled. Moreover, a syntactic characterization of $s(g(a))$ with property $T(s(g(a))) = \{k(a)\}$ is possible if $s(g(a))$ satisfies the similar finite variability property [27].

Theorem 6.2.1 (*Coincidence result*) Suppose that $P \in SPA$, $g : Act \setminus Act_0 \to SPA$ is a refinement function for P, and $f : Act \setminus Act_0 \to SES, f(a) = s(g(a))$ for $a \in Act \setminus Act_0$ is a refinement function. Then $f(s(P)) \cong_p s(g(P))$.

This theorem demonstrates that with respect to the cpo-based denotational semantics our syntactic and semantic refinement operations coincide up to pomset trace equivalence. Due to this result, under pomset trace equivalence and under the cpo-based denotational semantics we do not need to distinguish f

from g. Note that P should be closed and the constraint that actions in $Sort(P)$ are not allowed to be refined and to occur in the refinement of some actions is necessary for this theorem to hold.

Example 6.2.1 The semantic model $s(g(P))$ of $g(P)$, where $g(P)$ is the refinement of expression P described in Example 6.1.1, is pomset trace equivalent to the ses $f(\mathcal{E})$, the refinement of ses $\mathcal{E}$ given in Example 4.1.1 (Figure 4). Note that $\mathcal{E} = s(P)$ and $\mathcal{E}_a = s(P_a)$ as shown in Example 5.2.1.

7 Proofs

We sketch proofs of the theorems presented in the previous sections. Theorems 4.1.1 and 6.1.1 follow directly from the definitions of ses's, expressions and the corresponding refinement operations. We hereby focus on the remaining results.

Lemma 7.1 Suppose $\mathcal{E}_1 \cong_p \mathcal{E}_2$, $\mathcal{E}_3 \cong_p \mathcal{E}_4$. Then
$$\circ\mathcal{E}_1 \cong_p \circ\mathcal{E}_2 \ (\circ \in \{a_U., \backslash A, [\lambda]\}),$$
$$\mathcal{E}_1 \circ \mathcal{E}_3 \cong_p \mathcal{E}_2 \circ \mathcal{E}_4 \ (\circ \in \{;, +, \|_A\}).$$

Lemma 7.1 indicates that pomset trace equivalence is a congruence under the standard compositional operators on ses's.

Lemma 7.2 below shows that the rooted ses of a well-labelled ses remains well-labelled, the "duration" of this rooted ses remains invariant, and the rooted ses's of two pomset trace equivalent ses's with the same start random variables remain pomset trace equivalent.

Lemma 7.2 (1) $\mathcal{E}$ is well-labelled iff $r(\mathcal{E}, U)$ is well-labelled;
(2) $\{U + V \mid V \in T(\mathcal{E})\} = T(r(\mathcal{E}, U))$;
(3) If $\mathcal{E}_1 \cong_p \mathcal{E}_2$ then $r(\mathcal{E}_1, U) \cong_p r(\mathcal{E}_2, U)$.

Now suppose that σ_f is a configuration of $f(\mathcal{E})$. Let

$$\pi_1(\sigma_f) = \{(e, W) \mid \text{ there exists } (e, e_j) \in E(\sigma_f) \text{ and if } l(e) \notin Act_0$$
$$\text{then } W = RV(\sigma_f, (e, o_{rfl(e)})) \text{ otherwise } W = RV(\sigma_f, (e, e))\}.$$

For $e \in E(\pi_1(\sigma_f))$ with $l(e) \notin Act_0$, let

$$\pi_2(\sigma_f, e) = \{(e_j, W_j) \mid (e, e_j) \in E(\sigma_f) \text{ and }$$
$$W_j = RV(\sigma_f, (e, e_j)) - RV(\sigma_f, (e, o_{rfl(e)}) + U\}.$$

Here $rfl(e)$ stands for $r(f(l(e)), U)$. $\pi_1(\sigma_f)$ is actually the projection of σ_f on $\mathcal{E}$, and $\pi_2(\sigma_f, e)$ the projection of σ_f on $rfl(e)$, where the random variables attached to events are adjusted according to the random variable attached to the start-event of each $f(l(e))$ in σ_f.

From Lemma 7.2, we have the following

Lemma 7.3 (1) $\pi_1(\sigma_f)$ is a configuration of $\mathcal{E}$; (2) $\pi_2(\sigma_f, e)$ is a configuration of $rfl(e)$, and it successfully terminates if e is not maximal in $E(\pi_1(\sigma_f))$.

Lemma 7.4 $C(f(a_U.s(P_1))) = C(a_U.f(s(P_1)))$, if $a \in Act_0$;
$\qquad\qquad C(f(a_U.s(P_1))) = C((\tau_U.f(a)); f(s(P_1)))$, if $a \notin Act_0$;
$\qquad\qquad C(f(\circ s(P_1))) = C(\circ f(s(P_1))), \circ \in \{\backslash A, [\lambda]\}$;
$\qquad\qquad C(f(s(P_1) \circ s(P_2))) = C(f(s(P_1)) \circ f(s(P_1))), \circ \in \{;, +, \|_A\}$.

Lemma 7.4 follows from Lemma 7.3 and the constraint that the actions involved with the abstraction, relabelling and the parallel composition operators are not allowed to be refined and to occur in the refinement of actions.

In Lemma 7.4, if the ses appearing in the left-hand side of an equality is denoted by $\mathcal{E}_f$ and the ses in the corresponding right-hand side by $\mathcal{E}_g$, then for any configuration σ of $\mathcal{E}_f$, $\to_f |_\sigma = \to_g |_\sigma$ and $l_f|_\sigma = l_g|_\sigma$. Thus, trivially $C(\mathcal{E}_f) \approx C(\mathcal{E}_g)$ and so $\mathcal{E}_f \cong_p \mathcal{E}_g$.

Theorem 4.2.1 follows from Lemma 7.2(1)(2) and Lemma 7.3. Theorem 4.2.2 follows from Lemma 7.2(3), Lemma 7.3 and Theorem 4.2.1. Theorem 6.2.1 follows from Lemmas 7.1 and 7.4, where the result for recursion follows from the fact that $f(v_P^i(\bot)) \cong_p v_{f(P)}^i(\bot)$ for $i \geq 0$. This fact can be proved by means of the results for the other operators.

8 Discussions

In this paper, we introduced the notions of action refinement on stochastic event structures and a stochastic LOTOS-like process algebra. We have demonstrated that the refinement is safe, and so far pomset trace equivalence is a congruence under the refinement. We have also shown that the syntactic refinement and the semantic refinement coincide up to pomset trace equivalence with respect to a cpo-based denotational semantics.

8.1 Synchronization

In general Theorem 6.2.1 no longer holds if synchronization actions are allowed to be refined. The main reason is that it is impossible to require the newly introduced τ-events to be executed simultaneously. This problem can be solved by abstracting the system from the internal τ-events:

• Omitting the random τ-events that occur, we define as usual the concepts of observational configurations and observational pomset trace equivalence;

• The ses used to refine an observable action is required to be observable too. That is, any an observational configuration of it that terminates successfully contains at least an event labelled with an observable action;

• In the definition of g being a refinement function for expression $P_1 \|_A P_2$, we further require that $A_{g(a_1)} \cap A_{g(a_2)} = \emptyset$ for any two distinct $a_1 \in A$ and $a_2 \in \Theta$. Without this constraint, a confusion of communication levels may occur. Finally, we define $g(P_1 \|_A P_2) = g(P_1) \|_{g(A)} g(P_2)$, where $g(A) = \cup_{a \in A} A_{g(a)}$.

Under these conditions, Theorem 6.2.1 holds again for observational pomset trace equivalence.

8.2 History Preserving Bisimulation Equivalence

For an action a, a random variable U and two configuration σ and σ' of $\mathcal{E}$ such that $\sigma \subseteq \sigma'$, we say $\sigma \xrightarrow{a,U} \sigma'$ if $\sigma' \backslash \sigma = \{(e, U)\}$ with $l(e) = a$. As usual, a relation

$H \subseteq C(\mathcal{E}_1) \times C(\mathcal{E}_2) \times 2^{(E_1 \times E_2)}$ is called a *history preserving bisimulation* between $\mathcal{E}_1$ and $\mathcal{E}_2$, if $(\emptyset, \emptyset, \emptyset) \in H$ and when $(\sigma_1, \sigma_2, h) \in H$ then

(1) h is an isomorphism between $E(\sigma_1)$ and $E(\sigma_2)$,

(2) $\sigma_1 \xrightarrow{a,U}_1 \sigma_1' \Rightarrow \exists \sigma_2', h' : \sigma_2 \xrightarrow{a,U}_2 \sigma_2', (\sigma_1', \sigma_2', h') \in H$ and $h'|_{\sigma_1} = h$,

(3) $\sigma_2 \xrightarrow{a,U}_2 \sigma_2' \Rightarrow \exists \sigma_1', h' : \sigma_1 \xrightarrow{a,U}_1 \sigma_1', (\sigma_1', \sigma_2', h') \in H$ and $h'|_{\sigma_1} = h$.

Here $h'|_{\sigma_1}$ denotes the restriction of h' on $E(\sigma_1)$.

$\mathcal{E}_1$ and $\mathcal{E}_2$ are said to be *history preserving bisimulation equivalent*, denoted $\mathcal{E}_1 \cong_b \mathcal{E}_2$, if there is a history preserving bisimulation between $\mathcal{E}_1$ and $\mathcal{E}_2$.

Theorem 4.2.2 holds for history preserving bisimulation equivalence. Theorem 6.2.1 holds under history preserving bisimulation equivalence when no synchronization on observable actions occurs. Proofs are analogous and omitted.

References

1. L. Aceto. *Action Refinement in Process Algebra.* Cambridge Univ. Press, 1992.
2. M. Bernardo, R. Gorrieri. A Tutorial on EMPA: A Theory of Concurrent Processes with Nondeterminism, Priorities, Probabilities and Time. *Th. Comp. Sci.*, 202: 1 – 54, 1998.
3. E. Brinksma, H. Hermanns, and J-P. Katoen. *Lectures on Formal Methods and Performance Analysis.* Lecture Notes in Computer Science 2090, Springer, 2001.
4. E. Brinksma, J-P. Katoen, R. Langerak, and D. Latella. A Stochastic Causality-Based Process Algebra. *The Computer Journal*, 38(7): 552 – 565, 1995.
5. E. Brinksma, J-P. Katoen, R. Langerak, and D. Latella. Partial-Order Models for Quantitative Extensions of LOTOS. *Computer Networks & ISDN Systems*, 30(9/10): 925 – 950, 1998.
6. H. Fecher, M. Majster-Cederbaum, and J. Wu. Bundle Event Structures: A Revised Cpo Approach. *Information Processing Letters*, 83: 7 – 12, 2002.
7. H. Fecher, M. Majster-Cederbaum, and J. Wu. Action Refinement for Probabilistic Processes with True Concurrency Models. *PAPM-Promiv'02*, Lecture Notes in Computer Science, 2399: 77 – 94, 2002.
8. R. van Glabbeek. The Linear Time - Branching Time Spectrum. *Lecture Notes in Computer Science*, 458: 278 – 297, 1990.
9. R. van Glabbeek, U. Goltz. Refinement of Actions and Equivalence Notions for Concurrent Systems. *Acta Informatica*, 37: 229 – 327, 2001.
10. R. Gorrieri, A. Rensink. Action Refinement. *Handbook of Process Algebra*, Elsevier Science, 1047 – 1147, 2001.
11. N. Götz, U. Herzog, and M. Rettelbach. Multiprocessor and Distributed System Design: The Integration of Functional Specification and Performance Analysis Using Stochastic Process Algebra. *Lecture Notes in Computer Science*, 729: 121 – 146, 1993.
12. C. Harvey. Performance Engineering as an Integral Part of System Design. *Br. Telecom Technol. J.*, 4(3): 142 – 147, 1986.
13. B. Henrik. *Compositional Solution of Stochastic Process Algebra Models.* PhD Thesis, RWTH Aachen, 2002.
14. H. Hermanns. *Interactive Markov Chains.* PhD Thesis, Universität Erlangen-Nürnberg, 1998.

15. H. Hermanns, J-P. Katoen. Automated Compositional Markov Chain Generation for a Plain-Old Telephone System. *Science of Computer Programming*, 36: 97 – 127, 2000.
16. J. Hillston. *A Compositional Approach to Performance Modelling*. Cambridge University Press, 1996.
17. C. A. R. Hoare. *Communicating Sequential Processes*. Prentice-Hall, 1985.
18. J-P. Katoen. *Quantitative and Qualitative Extensions of Event Structures*. PhD Thesis, University of Twente, 1996.
19. J-P. Katoen, P. R. D'Argenio. General Distribution in Process Algebra. In E. Brinksma et al [3], 375 – 429.
20. R. Langerak. *Transformations and Semantics for LOTOS*. PhD Thesis, University of Twente, 1992.
21. R. Langerak. Bundle Event Structures: A Non-Interleaving Semantics for LOTOS. *Formal Description Techniques* (eds. M. Diaz and R. Groz), Elsevier Science Publishers, 331 – 346, 1993.
22. M. Majster-Cederbaum, F. Salger. Correctness by Construction: Towards Verification in Hierarchical System Development. *Lecture Notes in Computer Science*, 1885: 163 – 180, 2000.
23. M. Majster-Cederbaum, J. Wu. Action Refinement for True Concurrent Real Time. *Proc. ICECCS 2001*. IEEE Computer Society Press, 58 – 68, 2001.
24. M. Majster-Cederbaum, J. Wu. Towards Action Refinement for True Concurrent Real-Time. *Acta Informatica*, 39: to appear, 2003.
25. R. Milner. *Communication and Concurrency*. Prentice-Hall, 1989.
26. M. F. Neuts. *Matrix-Geometric Solutions in Stochastic Models - An Algorithmic Approach*. The Johns Hopkins University Press, 1981.
27. X. Nicollin, J. Sifakis. An Overview and Synthesis on Timed Process Algebra. In: *Real-Time: Theory in Practice*, Lecture Notes in Computer Science, 660: 526 – 548, 1992.
28. A. Papoulis. *Probability, Random Variables, and Stochastic Processes*. McGraw-Hill, 1991.
29. A. W. Roscoe. *The Theory and Practice of Concurrency*. Prentice Hall, 1998.
30. R. A. Sahner, K. S. Trividi. Performance and Reliability Analysis Using Direct Acyclic Graphs. *IEEE Tran. on Softw. Eng.*, 13(10): 1105 – 1114, 1987.
31. G. Winskel. An Introduction to Event Structures. *Lecture Notes in Computer Science*, 354: 364 - 397, 1989.

Incremental Derivation of Abstraction Relations for Data Refinement

Neil J. Robinson

Systems and Software Engineering Research Group
School of Information Technology and Electrical Engineering
The University of Queensland, Australia
njr@itee.uq.edu.au

Abstract. Data refinements are refinement steps in which a program's local data structures are changed. Data refinement proof obligations require the software designer to find an abstraction relation that relates the states of the original and new program. In this paper we describe an algorithm that helps a designer find an abstraction relation for a proposed refinement. Given sufficient time and space, the algorithm can find a minimal abstraction relation, and thus show that the refinement holds. As it executes, the algorithm displays mappings that cannot be in any abstraction relation. When the algorithm is not given sufficient resources to terminate, these mappings can help the designer find a suitable abstraction relation. The same algorithm can be used to test an abstraction relation supplied by the designer.

1 Introduction

Refinement is the process of deriving verifiably-correct software from its specification. Data refinement is concerned with refinement steps in which the program's local data structures are changed. Data refinement steps can be complex and difficult to prove correct. It is possible within a data refinement step to totally change the structure of the program, providing it is not possible to detect a change in the program's external behaviour.

Typically, in a data refinement, the designer may wish to replace an abstract data type, e.g., a set, with a more concrete one, e.g., an array. In some cases, given an abstraction relation that expresses the desired relationship between the two data types, the designer can *calculate* the least refined system from the abstract system and the abstraction relation [9].

In most cases however, the designer proposes a concrete system, expecting it to be a refinement of the abstract system. In order to prove this, the designer then needs to find a suitable abstraction relation — one that is sufficient to discharge the proof obligations. It is this case that we address in this paper.

The proof obligations for data refinement are in the form

$$\exists R \bullet p$$

where R is an abstraction relation between states of the concrete system and states of the abstract system and p is the particular obligation to be proven.

J.S. Dong and J. Woodcock (Eds.): ICFEM 2003, LNCS 2885, pp. 246–265, 2003.
© Springer-Verlag Berlin Heidelberg 2003

Usually, every reachable concrete state must be in the domain of the abstraction relation — that is, R must be total.

It is often very hard to find a suitable abstraction relation. In previous work [10,12], we showed published examples where abstraction relations were incorrect. Other authors, e.g., Butler [6], have also recognised this problem, and have proposed approaches to save time when looking for abstraction relations.

In a previous paper [11], we described an algorithm for finding the *weakest abstraction relation* for a proposed refinement. That algorithm worked at the semantic level, and required the construction of the complete transition relations for the abstract and concrete systems before it could be applied. In this paper we describe an algorithm that can find *minimal* abstraction relations. This algorithm works directly on the syntactic specifications, and is incremental in the sense that it builds the transition relations as it executes, and can produce useful intermediate output. Whilst time and space limitations may prevent the algorithm from finding an abstraction relation, the intermediate output from the algorithm can nevertheless help the designer find a suitable abstraction relation. In such cases, we anticipate the algorithm being useful as an aid to proving refinements with a theorem prover.

The same algorithm can also be used to test a supplied abstraction relation. If it is not a suitable abstraction relation, then the algorithm can find incorrect mappings in the relation. If the supplied relation is too weak, the algorithm can still use it to help find a minimal abstraction relation. An intelligent choice of a candidate abstraction relation can significantly cut down the search space. In this way a designer can use their insight into the refinement to improve the performance of the algorithm.

Our aim in this paper is to present the concept of how to derive abstraction relations. We use the action system formalism [2], since this is a comprehensive approach which deals with most of the issues that arise in data refinement within other formalisms.

2   Comparison with Previous Work

Butler [6] considers the problem of iteratively deriving and checking abstraction relations for data refinement. He observes that, typically, an abstraction relation is "invented", and then, using that relation, the proof obligations are checked. Often, the abstraction relation is found to be too weak, and so needs to be strengthened. Butler's work is aimed at reducing the "tedium" of rechecking all the proof obligations in this scenario. He shows that, in some cases, it is only necessary for the designer to recheck a subset of the proof obligations when the abstraction relation has been strengthened. This is different to our aims in this paper, although Butler's method would certainly complement our approach. We are more concerned with helping the designer "invent" the abstraction relation.

Doche and Gravell [7] consider the same problem that we address. Their work is based on the Csp2B approach, in which the CSP and B formalisms are used together in order to model both concurrency and state-changing operations. The CSP part of the specification deals with the ordering and synchronisation of events, and the B part deals with the specification of operations. Their method supports the conversion of the CSP part into B, and they use the B toolkit to discharge the data refinement proof obligations. They show how the refinement of the CSP part of the specification can also be model checked using the FDR tool. FDR constructs Labelled Transition Systems, which they can then use to automatically derive an abstraction relation for the CSP part of the specification. The derived relation is in the form of a set of mappings between individual states of the two specifications, i.e., it is not in predicate form. The method requires the designer to manually provide the abstraction relation for the B part of the specification. Together, the two parts of the abstraction relation are used to discharge the data refinement proof obligations in the B toolkit. Parts of the proof are discharged automatically, but parts must be carried out by hand. Doche and Gravell's results are clearly limited in that they only deal with the CSP part of the specification. Basically this covers the "guard enabledness" parts of the data refinement proof obligations that we use in this paper. Our aim is to derive the whole abstraction relation.

Bensalem et al. describe an approach designed to make model checking feasible for infinite state systems [5]. Given a concrete system and an abstraction function, they show how to compute an abstract system such that the concrete system simulates the abstract system. This is the same as Back and von Wright's concept of *decoding* [4]. Bensalem et al.'s work is relevant because it makes use of an elimination method based on simulation, which is similar in concept to the algorithm we define in this paper. Their method begins by defining the abstract system as the universal relation (one which relates every abstract state to every abstract state). Transitions are then deleted from the abstract system so as to preserve the simulation relation between the abstract and concrete systems. The method presented by Bensalem et al. is set in a different context to our work — it uses Hoare triples and a simple form of functional data refinement. However the main difference from our work is that their aim is to find an abstract system given a concrete system and an abstraction function, whereas our aim is to find an abstraction relation given an abstract system and a concrete system.

3   Background

3.1   Action Systems

Action systems [2] use Guarded Command Language notation to define an interleaving, state-machine simulation of concurrent behaviours. Each action appears as a (multiple) assignment protected by a Boolean guard. An outermost **do...od** loop nondeterministically selects actions with true guards until none remain.

An action system is defined by its *local*, or *internal* variables, the initial values of its local variables, its *global*, or *externally visible* variables, and its *actions*, where each action

$$A_i \stackrel{def}{=} gA_i \to sA_i$$

consists of a *guard* gA_i and a *statement* sA_i [1].

A simple action system, *Salvador's Bakery*, is shown in Figure 1. This models a bakery in which customers do not queue. The observable part of the state is the global variable *out* representing the set of customers outside the bakery. The internal part of the state consists of the local variables sb_in, representing the customers waiting inside the bakery and sb_th representing customers who are saying thank you. The local variables are declared within the **var** construct and the global variables are listed at the end of the **do..od** loop. The initial value of the local variables are defined by the **init** construct. There are four actions in the example, labelled SB_1 to SB_4, separated by the $\square$ symbol which represents nondeterministic choice. Action SB_1 models a customer entering the bakery, moving from outside the shop to inside. We use a multiple nondeterministic assignment in the form $x_1, x_2 := y_1, y_2 \bullet p$, where y_1 and y_2 are expressions, and p is a predicate that must hold for the assignments to succeed. Action SB_2 models a customer being served and saying thank you. Action SB_3 models a customer being served and leaving the shop without saying thank you, and thus moving from inside the shop to outside. Finally, action SB_4 models the customer who has said thank you leaving the bakery, and thus moving from inside the shop to outside.

$$
\begin{aligned}
&\textbf{var } sb\_in, sb\_th : \mathbb{P}\ Cust \\
&\textbf{init } sb\_in = \{\} \wedge sb\_th = \{\} \\
&\textbf{do} \\
&(\square \qquad out \neq \{\} \to sb\_in, out := sb\_in \cup \{c\}, out \setminus \{c\} \bullet c \in out \quad)\ [SB_1] \\
&(\square\ sb\_in \neq \{\} \wedge \\
&\qquad sb\_th = \{\} \to sb\_in, sb\_th := sb\_in \setminus \{c\}, \{c\} \bullet c \in sb\_in \qquad)\ [SB_2] \\
&(\square\ sb\_in \neq \{\} \wedge \\
&\qquad sb\_th = \{\} \to sb\_in, out := sb\_in \setminus \{c\}, out \cup \{c\} \bullet c \in sb\_in\ )\ [SB_3] \\
&(\square \qquad sb\_th \neq \{\} \to sb\_th, out := \{\}, out \cup sb\_th \qquad\qquad\qquad)\ [SB_4] \\
&\textbf{od} : out : \mathbb{P}\ Cust
\end{aligned}
$$

Fig. 1. Salvador's Bakery action system specification *SB*.

We model action systems using a relational model, based on Back and von Wright's semantics [2], but with a simplified treatment of stuttering actions. *Stuttering actions* are those which are guaranteed not to change the observable part of the state, for example action SB_2 in Salvador's Bakery. *Change actions* are those which *may* change the observable part of the state, for example action SB_3 in Salvador's Bakery.

An action system $\mathcal{A}$ is modelled by a sextuple

$$(S, T, initial, terminating, aborting, infstutter)$$

where:

- S is a set of states. Each state in S consists of a pair (a, b) in which the first element a represents the internal state, and the second element b represents the observable (or global) state.

- T is the transition (or *next-state*) relation over S, derived from the system's actions. Each transition in T represents a change of state of the action system of the form $(a, b) \mapsto (a', b')$. When constructing a transition relation from a syntactic action system, actions are chosen demonically. So if one of the enabled actions aborts, then the whole action system aborts, and there is no next state in the transition relation. *Reachable* states are those states which can be reached by starting from an initial state and then applying the transition relation zero or more times.

- *initial*, *terminating*, and *aborting* are subsets of S representing the initial, terminating and aborting states of the action system. These can be obtained from a syntactic action system as follows:
  - The *initial* states are all the states reachable by performing the **init** statement.
  - The *terminating* states are the states in which all of the guards of the action system are *false*.
  - The *aborting* states are the states (a, b) in which one of the guards is *true* but there is no next state (a', b') (as defined by T).

- *infstutter* is a subset of S, representing the states from which there may be infinite stuttering. It contains the states from which it is possible to take stuttering transitions of T, i.e., transitions of the form $(a, b) \mapsto (a', b)$, an infinite number of times.

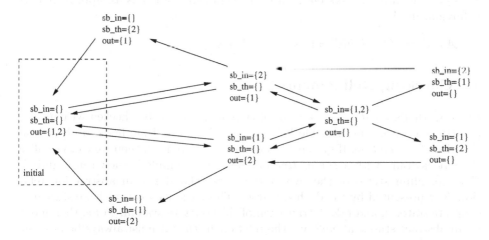

Fig. 2. Salvador's Bakery digraph, with initial value of observable variable $out = \{1, 2\}$.

We use digraphs to pictorially represent such systems, e.g., Figure 2 represents Salvador's Bakery action system in the case in which the initial value of the observable variable *out* is $\{1, 2\}$. The states are represented by vertices of the graph within which the values of the each of the state variables are shown. Possible transitions between states are shown by the edges of the graph.

Following Back and von Wright [2], the *behaviours*, $beh(T)$ of an action system, are all the possible sequences of system states, as defined by the initial states and the transition relation T. All behaviours begin in an *initial* state. Subsequent states in a behaviour are obtained by performing iterations of the loop. A behaviour can be:

- *terminating*, when its last element is a *terminating* state,
- *aborting*, when its last element is an *aborting* state, or
- *infinite*, when it has no last element.

A *trace*, $tr(s)$ of a behaviour s is obtained by removing the internal states and removing finite repetitions of observable states. The traces of a system represent all its possible observable behaviours.

3.2   Action System Refinement

Following Back and von Wright [2], we define refinement as follows:
Let '$\preceq$' be an approximation relation on behaviours. Behaviour s approximates t, denoted $s \preceq t$ if and only if:

- either s is aborting and $tr(s)$ is a prefix of $tr(t)$, or
- neither s nor t is aborting, and $tr(s) = tr(t)$.

Let '$\sqsubseteq$' be the refinement relation for action systems. Action system $\mathcal{C}$ is a refinement of action system $\mathcal{A}$ if every behaviour of $\mathcal{C}$ has an approximating behaviour in $\mathcal{A}$:

$$\mathcal{A} \sqsubseteq \mathcal{C} \stackrel{def}{=} \forall t \in beh(\mathcal{C}) \bullet (\exists s \in beh(\mathcal{A}) \bullet s \preceq t)$$

4   Checking Refinements

Proof methods for *data refinement* allow refinements to be checked without explicitly considering all possible behaviours. These proof methods are based on the idea of *simulation*. If system A is refined by system C, then we can visualise their behaviours with a *commuting diagram*. An example is shown in Figure 3. Corresponding states of the two systems are related via an abstraction relation R, represented by the dashed arrows. The basic idea is that if we start in a concrete state, c, and take a transition of the concrete system, to nc, then move to an abstract state, say $na2$, via the relation R, then it must always be possible to reach the same abstract state $na2$ by starting in the same concrete state c, moving to an abstract state via R, and taking a transition of the abstract system. This form of simulation is called a *forward simulation*. In certain situations, for example when non-determinism in the abstract specification is postponed in the concrete specification, *backward simulation* is required to prove the refinement. We do not consider backward simulation in this paper.

Note that refinement steps usually involve a reduction in nondeterminism. Simulation based proof obligations reflect this, and only require a single matching

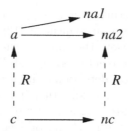

Fig. 3. Commuting diagram.

abstract transition for each concrete transition. Hence the abstract transition from state a to state $na1$ in Figure 3, is not necessary for the simulation to succeed.

4.1   Simulation Conditions for Action Systems

For action systems, Back and von Wright give a general definition of simulation using abstraction statements (predicate transformers), rather than abstraction relations. They then develop this into two more practical sets of proof obligations, using abstraction relations, for forward simulation and backward simulation. Their definitions make use of the explicit separation of an action system into stuttering and change actions, and can deal with changes in the amount of stuttering between the two action systems [2].

We do not follow Back and von Wright's approach to dealing with stuttering actions. This is because our algorithm relies on there being a continuous forward simulation from initial states onwards, whereas their approach allows for breaks in the forward simulation within sequences of stuttering concrete actions. For further details and an example see our previous paper [11].

We also limit our work to refinements in which there is the same or more stuttering in the concrete system as in the abstract system. This is not too severe a limitation, since in most cases we expect refinements to increase the number of stuttering steps, for example through decomposition of actions.

The approach we take is to transform the abstract action system so that, in the context of a simulation, it allows for additional stuttering in the concrete system. The abstract action system is thus transformed to make its transition relation reflexive, as follows:

$$(S, T, initial, terminating, aborting, infstutter)^{\triangle} \stackrel{def}{=}$$
$$(S, (T \cup \mathrm{id}(\mathrm{dom}\ T \cup \mathrm{ran}\ T \cup initial)),$$
$$initial, terminating, aborting, infstutter)$$

In terms of a syntactic action system, this is the same as adding a '$true \rightarrow SKIP$' action to the action system, where $SKIP$ is a transition of the action system in which the state does not change. When performing a simulation, these additional transitions allow the abstract system to stay in the same state while the concrete system performs stuttering actions. Von Wright uses a similar idea in an earlier paper on action system refinement [13]. As stated there, the traces of action system $\mathcal{A}^{\triangle}$ are precisely the same as the traces obtained by adding arbitrary amounts of stuttering to action system $\mathcal{A}$. He notes that a problem with this approach is that it prevents detection of infinite stuttering in the concrete system. In our transformation, we ensure that it is still possible to identify the states from which there is infinite stuttering, by using the previously defined set *infstutter*, thus distinguishing the newly-introduced stuttering transitions from those that already existed.

Thus, to check a refinement between action systems $\mathcal{A}$ and $\mathcal{C}$, we check forward simulation between $\mathcal{A}^{\triangle}$ and $\mathcal{C}$.

Concrete action system $\mathcal{C}$ is a refinement of abstract action system $\mathcal{A}$ if there exists an abstraction relation R from the concrete states $\mathcal{C}.S$ to the abstract states $\mathcal{A}.S$, such that the following conditions are satisfied:

$$(c, u) \in \mathcal{C}.initial \Rightarrow$$
$$(\exists a \bullet (a, u) \in \mathcal{A}^{\triangle}.initial \wedge (c, u) \mapsto (a, u) \in R) \ [F1]$$
$$(c, u) \mapsto (a, u) \in R \wedge (c, u) \mapsto (c', u') \in \mathcal{C}.T \Rightarrow$$
$$(a, u) \in \mathcal{A}^{\triangle}.aborting \vee$$
$$(\exists a' \bullet (a, u) \mapsto (a', u') \in \mathcal{A}^{\triangle}.T \wedge$$
$$(c', u') \mapsto (a', u') \in R) \qquad\qquad [F2]$$
$$(c, u) \mapsto (a, u) \in R \wedge (c, u) \in \mathcal{C}.aborting \Rightarrow$$
$$(a, u) \in \mathcal{A}^{\triangle}.aborting \qquad\qquad [F3]$$
$$(c, u) \mapsto (a, u) \in R \wedge (c, u) \in \mathcal{C}.terminating \Rightarrow$$
$$(a, u) \in \mathcal{A}^{\triangle}.aborting \vee (a, u) \in \mathcal{A}^{\triangle}.terminating \ [F4]$$
$$(c, u) \mapsto (a, u) \in R \wedge (c, u) \in \mathcal{C}.infstutter \Rightarrow$$
$$(a, u) \in \mathcal{A}^{\triangle}.aborting \vee (a, u) \in \mathcal{A}^{\triangle}.infstutter \quad [F5]$$

As a consequence of proof obligations $F1$ and $F2$, except when there are aborting states in the abstract system, abstraction relations for forward simulation need to be total.

Proof obligation $F1$ deals with initialisation. It requires that every concrete initial state is mapped, via the abstraction relation R, to at least one abstract initial state.

Proof obligation $F2$ is the main forward simulation condition. It requires that if a concrete state (c, u) is mapped to an abstract state (a, u) via the abstraction relation R, then either the abstract state it is mapped to via R is aborting, or every concrete state (c', u') reachable from (c, u) must be reachable from (a, u) via an abstract transition and a mapping in the abstraction relation.

Proof obligation $F3$ requires that every concrete aborting state is only mapped to abstract aborting states. Proof obligation $F4$ requires that concrete terminating states must only be mapped to abstract terminating states, or to abstract aborting states. Finally, proof obligation $F5$ requires that any concrete state from which there is infinite stuttering is only mapped to either abstract aborting states or abstract states from which there is infinite stuttering.

In practice, for ease of use with syntactic action systems, action system proof obligations are rewritten in a form that allows the designer to perform proofs by matching up single actions of the concrete system with single, or small groups of actions of the abstract system [2].

Forward simulation is not complete. Thus, even if there is no abstraction relation for which these proof obligations hold, there may still be a refinement by backward simulation [2].

4.2   Sets of Abstraction Relations

Assume concrete action system $\mathcal{C}$ is a refinement of abstract action system $\mathcal{A}$.

Definition 1. *The* **set of abstraction relations** $\overrightarrow{\Re}$ **for forward simulation** *contains only the relations, from $\mathcal{C}.S$ to $\mathcal{A}.S$, mapping observably identical states, for which conditions $F1$ to $F5$ are true.*

By definition, if the refinement is a forward simulation then $\overrightarrow{\Re}$ will be non-empty.

The structure $(\overrightarrow{\Re}, \subseteq)$ is a *poset*. In the following sections, when we refer to minimal, maximal, least and greatest elements of $\overrightarrow{\Re}$, it is with reference to this poset. Also when we refer to abstraction relations in the following sections, we are referring to members of $\overrightarrow{\Re}$, i.e., abstraction relations for forward simulation only.

Since $(\overrightarrow{\Re}, \subseteq)$ is a poset, it has at least one maximal element and at least one minimal element. In previous work [11] we showed that there is only one maximal element, i.e., there is a greatest element of the poset. However there may be many minimal elements. For example, if an abstract system has two possible behaviours, both of which produce the same trace, then this can be refined to a concrete system which has one possible behaviour which produces this trace. In such a case, there would be a choice of two minimal abstraction relations. This means that the existence of a least (or strongest) abstraction relation is not guaranteed.

5   A Monolithic Algorithm
for Finding Abstraction Relations

When performing data refinement proofs for forward simulations, it is necessary to find an abstraction relation for which the above conditions hold.

In earlier work [11], we presented a *monolithic algorithm* for finding abstraction relations. This algorithm works by examining the *complete* descriptions of the abstract and concrete action systems, including their transition relations. It populates a candidate abstraction relation that, if any abstraction relation exists, is guaranteed to contain all possible abstraction relations. The algorithm then deletes mappings from the candidate abstraction relation until either no further deletions can be made, in which case the resulting relation is the *weakest abstraction relation*, or a deletion is made which makes the proof obligations false, in which case there is no abstraction relation. We showed that the algorithm is sound and complete, and by construction, showed that, if an abstraction relation exists, then there is always a weakest abstraction relation. For convenience, we repeat the relevant propositions and definitions below. The proofs are provided in our earlier paper [11].

Proposition 1 *The set of relations $\overrightarrow{\Re}$ has a unique greatest element.*

Definition 2. *The* **weakest abstraction relation for forward simulation**, $\overrightarrow{\mathcal{R}}$, *is the greatest element in* $\overrightarrow{\Re}$.

Proposition 2 *The weakest abstraction relation for forward simulation $\overrightarrow{\mathcal{R}}$ exists if and only if C is a refinement of A by forward simulation.*

6 Incrementally Finding Abstraction Relations

In this section we define an *incremental* algorithm for finding an abstraction relation, given an abstract and a concrete syntactic action system. First we define the steps of the algorithm, and provide an explanation of its operation. We show a simple example application of the algorithm to illustrate its action when it is possible to run it to completion. We then explain how the algorithm relates to the monolithic algorithm we presented in our previous paper [11].

The algorithm tries to find a forward simulation between the two systems. As the simulation proceeds, the algorithm visits pairs of concrete and abstract states. For convenience, we refer to these pairs of states as *positions*.

6.1 Inputs to the Algorithm and Interpretation of Its Outputs

The algorithm uses the following inputs:

- The abstract syntactic action system $\mathcal{A}$
- The concrete syntactic action system $\mathcal{C}$
- A candidate abstraction relation R. This can be thought of as containing *matching* positions.

On termination, it supplies an answer "Yes" or "No". If the answer is "Yes" then this means there is a forward simulation, and in this case the algorithm also produces a minimal abstraction relation MR. As the algorithm executes it can delete pairs of states from R. These pairs are also printed as intermediate output.

If no candidate relation is supplied, the algorithm is called with a relation R that contains all the mappings from concrete to abstract states in which the global variables are identical, i.e., $R = \{(c, g) \mapsto (a, g)\}$, where values for c are drawn from possible values of the local part of a concrete state, a from the local part of an abstract state and g from the global part of the states. This relation is guaranteed to contain all other abstraction relations [11] (if there are any).

Cases in which a candidate abstraction relation is supplied are discussed in Section 7.

6.2   Steps of the Algorithm

The algorithm is defined in three parts. The first part defines the initialisation of
the algorithm. The second part of the algorithm generates all the concrete initial
states and initiates a search on each of them. The third part of the algorithm is
the definition of the subroutine *VISIT*, which performs a depth-first search on
a position.

  The steps of the algorithm are as follows:

Setting up

1. Transform the abstract specification, as described in Section 4.1.
2. Initialise relation MR to empty.

Checking Initial States

3. Generate the concrete initial states $C.initial$
4. If $C.initial$ is empty then this is a special case of a forward simulation. Exit
   with answer "Yes".
5. For each concrete initial state c_i in $C.initial$
   (a) if there is an abstract initial state a_i such that (c_i, a_i) is in both R
       and MR then go to next concrete state at step 5.
   (b) Find an abstract initial state a_i such that (c_i, a_i) is in R
   (c) If there is such a state then
         i. if $VISIT(c_i, a_i) = explored$, then go to next concrete state at step 5.
        ii. Otherwise, go back to step 5b
   (d) Otherwise, there is a concrete initial state with no matching abstract
       initial state. Exit with answer "No".
6. All the initial concrete states have been explored, so there is a forward simulation. Exit with answer "Yes", and print relation MR.

Subroutine $VISIT(c, a)$: *Explored | failed*.

7. Update relation $MR := MR \cup \{c \mapsto a\}$
8. Find the concrete and abstract actions enabled from the current state,
   $C\_enabled$ and $A\_enabled$
9. If one of the actions in $A\_enabled$ aborts (i.e., has no next state), then
   Return(explored).
10. If one of the actions in $C\_enabled$ aborts, then go to step 14.
11. If $C\_enabled$ is empty then
    (a) If $A\_enabled$ contains only *true* $\rightarrow$ *SKIP*, as added at step 1, then
        Return(explored).
    (b) Otherwise, the concrete system has terminated early, so go to step 14.
12. For each concrete state nc reachable from c via an action in $C\_enabled$
    (a) if there is an abstract state na reachable from a via an action in
        $A\_enabled$, such that (nc, na) is in both R and MR then go to next
        concrete state at step 12.

(b) Find an abstract state na reachable from a via an action in $A\_enabled$, such that (nc, na) is in R

(c) If there is such a state then

   i. If $VISIT(nc, na) = explored$ then go to next concrete state at step 12.

   ii. Otherwise, go back to step 12b

(d) Otherwise, go to step 14

13. All the next concrete states have been explored, so $Return(explored)$

14. Relation R is inconsistent with the current pair of states, so print mapping (c, a), remove it from R and MR, and $Return(failed)$.

6.3   Explanation of the Algorithm

The algorithm looks for a forward simulation between the two action systems, using the input relation R. The algorithm first generates the initial concrete states. It then tries to find a matching abstract initial state for each of them. For each potential match, the algorithm performs a depth-first search from that position using a call to subroutine $VISIT$. This subroutine is recursive and proceeds depth-first. The depth-first search can return either $explored$ meaning that the position was successfully explored, or $failed$ meaning that the relation R was inconsistent with the position. Failure can occur if either there is a concrete aborting state not matched by an abstract aborting state, or the concrete system terminates early, or if a reachable concrete state cannot be matched by a reachable abstract state. Note that to check termination of system $\mathcal{A}$, we check that the only enabled action in $A^\triangle$ is the $true \to SKIP$ action added during the transformation in step 1.

If the search is successful then the algorithm moves on to the next concrete initial state. If the search is unsuccessful, then this results in a reduction in potential choices of abstract state, through positions being deleted from relation R. The algorithm will then, using the updated relation R, try to find an alternative matching abstract initial state, and initiate a new search. If there is one concrete initial state without a match then this shows the input relation R cannot be an abstraction relation. If, however, a match can be found for every concrete initial state, then there is a forward simulation. The searches will have resulted in relation MR being populated with all those states visited by the search but not deleted from relation R. This forms a minimal abstraction relation. Note that, since the algorithm only looks for one successful match for each concrete state, it is nondeterministic in its operation.

We anticipate the algorithm being used to check refinements, and to assist designers who are trying to prove data refinement steps. When the algorithm terminates with a "Yes", this confirms that the refinement holds, and the minimal abstraction relation produced gives the designer insight into how the refinement works. Model checkers do not provide such insight. A common complaint with model checking is that, when a check succeeds, it does not give any assurance that the check performed was correct [8]. With our algorithm, the designer can examine the minimal abstraction relation to confirm that the check was as intended.

When the algorithm terminates with a "No", with the default relation R, as defined in Section 6.1, then this confirms that there is no forward simulation. The intermediate mappings printed by the algorithm show which states caused the simulation to fail, and thus provide justification of the failure to the designer.

If the algorithm does not terminate, and the supplied relation R was the default, then the intermediate mappings printed by the algorithm cannot be in any abstraction relation. These can be used to test any proposed abstraction relation, i.e., if any of those mappings are in the relation, then the relation is wrong.

6.4   An Example Application of the Algorithm

We illustrate the operation of the algorithm on a simple case, where the algorithm can terminate successfully. Figure 4 shows *Elena's Bakery* action system, which is intended to be a refinement of Salvador's Bakery. This models a bakery in which the customers queue in an orderly fashion, and always say thank you before leaving the shop. The local variable sb_in from Salvador's Bakery has been replaced by a queue eb_in, and there is no equivalent to action SB_3. Action EB_1 models a customer entering the bakery and joining the end of the queue. Stuttering action EB_2 models a customer being served and saying thank you. Finally action EB_3 models the customer that said thank you leaving the shop.

$$
\begin{aligned}
&\textbf{var } eb\_in : \text{seq } Cust;\ eb\_th : \mathbb{P}\ Cust \\
&\textbf{init } eb\_in = \langle\rangle \wedge eb\_th = \{\} \\
&\textbf{do} \\
&(\Box \qquad out \neq \{\} \rightarrow eb\_in, out := eb\_in \mathbin{+\!\!+} \langle c\rangle, out \setminus \{c\} \bullet c \in out\ )\ [EB_1] \\
&(\Box\ eb\_in \neq \langle\rangle \wedge \\
&\qquad eb\_th = \{\} \rightarrow eb\_in, eb\_th := tail(eb\_in), \{head(eb\_in)\} \qquad)\ [EB_2] \\
&(\Box \qquad eb\_th \neq \{\} \rightarrow eb\_th, out := \{\}, out \cup eb\_th \qquad\qquad)\ [EB_3] \\
&\textbf{od} : out : \mathbb{P}\ Cust
\end{aligned}
$$

Fig. 4. Elena's Bakery action system specification *EB*.

We now illustrate the operation of the algorithm by finding an abstraction relation that connects the states of Elena's Bakery action system with the states of Salvador's Bakery. For brevity, we restrict the type *Cust* to $\{1,2\}$, and we only show the search for the concrete initial state in which *out* is $\{1,2\}$.

We call the algorithm with the default value of the candidate abstraction relation R, as defined in Section 6.1. This contains all the mappings between the concrete and abstract states in which the value of the observable variable *out* is the same.

Figure 5 shows the first steps in the application of the algorithm to Salvador's and Elena's bakery example. Each step is labelled in bold, with the first number providing the order of the steps, and the subsequent number in brackets referring to a particular labelled step of the algorithm, as shown in Section 6.2.

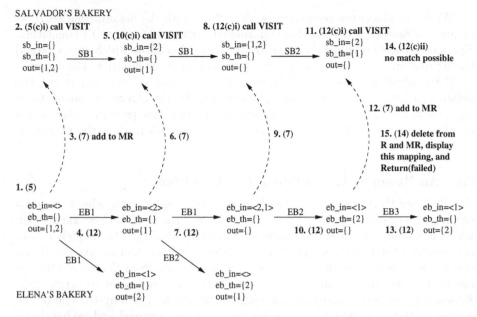

Fig. 5. First steps of the algorithm for Salvador's and Elena's bakeries.

The first step selects a concrete initial state. Step 2 selects a matching abstract initial state and initiates a search on the new position by calling subroutine *VISIT*. In step 3, a pair of initial states is added to the relation *MR*. Step 4 generates the next concrete states. The diagram shows the selection of one of these states. In step 5, the abstract system matches the concrete state and initiates another search on the new position. This causes the current pair of states to be added to relation *MR* in step 6. This pattern continues in a similar fashion until step 14, in which it is not possible for the abstract system to match the current concrete state. This is because, although in step 10 customer 2 was served in Elena's Bakery, in step 11 customer 1 was served in Salvador's Bakery. This results in customer 2 leaving Elena's Bakery in step 13, an action which cannot be matched by Salvador's Bakery. So, in step 15, the current pair of states

$$EB.state = ((eb\_in = \langle 1 \rangle, eb\_th = \{2\}), out = \{\})$$
$$SB.state = ((sb\_in = \{2\}, sb\_th = \{1\}), out = \{\})$$

is deleted from the relations R and MR, and printed. The algorithm then backtracks to try an alternative to step 11.

Figure 6 shows the continued application of the algorithm after the failure. In step 16, the algorithm has to match concrete state $eb\_in = \langle 1 \rangle$, $eb\_th = \{2\}$, $out = \{\}$ with a Salvador's Bakery action from abstract state $sb\_in = \{1,2\}$, $sb\_th = \{\}$, $out = \{\}$. From here the algorithm can either choose action SB_2, but this time serving customer 2, instead of 1, or it can choose to use the additional action $true \rightarrow SKIP$. For this example, we choose the *SKIP* action. Salvador's

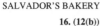

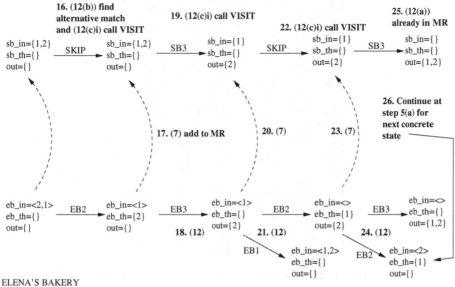

Fig. 6. Continued steps of the algorithm for Salvador's and Elena's bakeries.

Bakery can then match Elena's Bakery's next action with SB_3, in which the customer leaves the shop without saying thank you. The algorithm continues the exploration until, in step 25, it finds a position which is already in relation MR (in fact it is the initial position). This means there is no need to explore further in that direction. The algorithm now continues to explore the remaining concrete states.

In the remaining steps of the search on the selected concrete initial state, the algorithm consistently matches action EB_2 with a $SKIP$ in Salvador's Bakery. This generates three more mappings in relation MR, and no further failures. It is then necessary to search on the other concrete initial states. These steps generate seven further mappings in relation MR. The algorithm exits with "Yes", and the minimal abstraction relation shown in Figure 7. The relation is shown as a table of mappings between concrete and abstract states. The first part of the table shows the mappings that were generated when exploring the concrete initial state in which $out = \{1, 2\}$. Subsequent parts of the table, separated by horizontal lines, show the mappings generated from exploring the other concrete initial states, in which out is $\{1\}$, $\{2\}$ and $\{\}$ respectively.

As stated earlier, the operation of the algorithm is nondeterministic. The application of the algorithm to this particular problem can produce many different minimal abstraction relations. In Elena's Bakery, customers always say thank you, via action EB_2. Salvador's Bakery can simulate action EB_2 either by performing action SB_2, in which a customer says thank you, or by doing nothing (using the $true \rightarrow SKIP$ action). In our example above, the algorithm

Concrete (EB) state			Abstract (SB) state		
eb_in	eb_th	out	sb_in	sb_th	out
$\langle\rangle$	{}	{1,2}	{}	{}	{1,2}
$\langle 2 \rangle$	{}	{1}	{2}	{}	{1}
$\langle 2,1 \rangle$	{}	{}	{1,2}	{}	{}
$\langle 1 \rangle$	{2}	{}	{1,2}	{}	{}
$\langle 1 \rangle$	{}	{2}	{1}	{}	{2}
$\langle\rangle$	{1}	{2}	{1}	{}	{2}
$\langle 2 \rangle$	{1}	{}	{1,2}	{}	{}
$\langle 1,2 \rangle$	{}	{}	{1,2}	{}	{}
$\langle\rangle$	{2}	{1}	{2}	{}	{1}
$\langle\rangle$	{}	{1}	{}	{}	{1}
$\langle 1 \rangle$	{}	{}	{1}	{}	{}
$\langle\rangle$	{1}	{}	{1}	{}	{}
$\langle\rangle$	{}	{2}	{}	{}	{2}
$\langle 2 \rangle$	{}	{}	{2}	{}	{}
$\langle\rangle$	{2}	{}	{2}	{}	{}
$\langle\rangle$	{}	{}	{}	{}	{}

Fig. 7. The resulting minimal abstraction relation.

consistently chose the *SKIP* action (except in step 11 in Figure 5 which led to a failure in the search, and the subsequent deletion of the resulting mapping).

In practice, when performing data refinement proofs, designers make decisions in their choice of abstraction relation, based on how they wish to split up the proof of the main simulation proof obligation $F2$. For example, with our abstraction relation above, proof obligation $F2$ can be split into separate proofs that action EB_1 implements SB_1, action EB_2 implements $true \to SKIP$, and action EB_3 implements action SB_3.

There is clearly an alternative minimal abstraction relation in which action EB_2 is always simulated by action SB_2, i.e., each time a customer says thank you in Elena's Bakery, the same customer says thank you in Salvador's Bakery. There are also other alternative minimal abstraction relations in which inconsistent choices of Salvador's Bakery action are made during the simulation. Such relations would make it difficult for a designer to perform the data refinement proofs in the usual way.

6.5   Comparison with the Monolithic Algorithm

In this section we only consider the case in which the algorithm is called with the default relation R, as defined in Section 6.1.

The incremental algorithm described here is derived from the monolithic algorithm, which has been shown to be sound, and complete to the same extent Back and von Wright's proof obligations, except in the case of a reduction in stuttering in the concrete system [11]. However, the algorithm presented here is limited in that it does not deal with backward simulation and does not detect infinite stuttering — these are areas for future work.

A key difference in the operation of the algorithm in this paper is that it checks proof obligation $F3$ and $F4$ on the fly, as it incrementally explores the simulation. The monolithic algorithm checks these proof obligations before beginning to eliminate mappings from the relation R.

The monolithic algorithm is able to examine the *complete* transition relations and *all* mappings in the candidate abstraction relation. The incremental algorithm however can only check mappings in the candidate abstraction relation that are reachable through the simulation. Therefore it cannot generally reduce relation R to the weakest abstraction relation. Instead it uses the relation R to "steer" through the simulation. When it finds a failure, i.e., a case where a mapping in R causes the simulation to fail, it eliminates the inconsistent mapping from R, and thus closes off that path to the subsequent search. As the algorithm progresses, relation R gradually approaches $\overrightarrow{\mathcal{R}}$, but generally will not reach it.

If the incremental algorithm terminates with a "Yes", then the record of positions that have been successfully explored in relation MR forms a minimal abstraction relation, and is thus of interest to the designer. However the final value of R is of less interest — it is sufficient to steer a simulation, but when it is weaker than relation $\overrightarrow{\mathcal{R}}$ it will not be sufficient to make the forward simulation proof obligations true.

7   Starting with a Proposed Abstraction Relation

As stated earlier, the designer can supply a candidate abstraction relation, and use the algorithm to "test" it.

In such cases, when the algorithm terminates with a "No", this confirms that the supplied candidate abstraction relation is unsuitable. The intermediate mappings printed by the algorithm show which states in the input relation caused the simulation to fail, and so can provide the designer insight into why the supplied relation is incorrect.

If the algorithm does not terminate, and the designer supplied the candidate abstraction relation, then intermediate outputs are mappings that should not be in the supplied relation, so the designer can try to strengthen the relation to eliminate those mappings.

Considering the Bakery example, the designer could choose to call the algorithm with the relation R defined below.

$$R = \{((eb\_in, eb\_th), out) \mapsto ((sb\_in, sb\_th), out)) \mid sb\_th = \{\}\}$$

This would reduce the choices available to the algorithm whenever it tries to match the concrete action EB_2. It would not be able to use abstract action SB_2, since this causes customers in Salvador's Bakery to say thank you, and so makes variable sb_th non-empty. By supply this abstraction relation, the designer can make the algorithm avoid the potential failures in the simulation that can happen when the algorithm is called with the default value of R.

Alternatively, the designer could use the relation below.

$$R = \{(((eb\_in, eb\_th), out) \mapsto ((sb\_in, sb\_th), out)) \mid eb\_th = sb\_th\}$$

Again, this relation cuts down choices available to the algorithm. It prevents the algorithm matching concrete action *EB_2* with a *SKIP* in the abstract system, and it also prevents the potential failures in the simulation when the wrong customer is served in Salvador's Bakery. This choice of relation R will result in a different minimal abstraction relation to that shown in Figure 7.

Both the above suggestions help the operation of the algorithm in that they cut down choices. In general, an intelligent choice of supplied relation can improve the chances of the algorithm terminating. However, when the designer proposes an abstraction relation, a "Yes" answer does not mean that the proposed abstraction relation *is* an abstraction relation. As stated in Section 6.5, the proposed relation could contain mappings which are not reachable by simulation, but which could cause the proof obligations to fail. Such mappings are not tested by the algorithm.

When a designer proposes an abstraction relation that is wrong, a "No" answer only relates to the suitability of the proposed relation. For example, the designer could propose relation R_3 as follows.

$$R = \{((eb\_in, eb\_th), out) \mapsto ((sb\_in, sb\_th), out)) \mid eb\_th \neq sb\_th\}$$

This would cause the algorithm to exit with answer "No" (e.g., one of the concrete initial states cannot be matched), but we already know there is a forward simulation.

8 Discussion

We anticipate the intermediate mappings printed by the algorithm being useful to a designer, as explained in Section 6. However, we are also considering whether the record of actions used and states visited would be useful to the designer in cases when the algorithm does not terminate. This is the subject of ongoing work.

The abstraction relations that are usually used in data refinement proofs are expressed symbolically, i.e., as predicates. At present, our algorithm generates outputs expressed as mappings between individual states of the two systems. We have used a specification animation tool to prototype parts of the algorithm. This allows the candidate abstraction relation to be expressed as a predicate, but outputs from the algorithm are still in the form of mappings between individual states. Whilst it is possible, with tool support, to use such relations in proofs [7], it would be preferable if the outputs from the algorithm were expressed as predicates. Our next task is to investigate a symbolic approach to the same problem.

The algorithm presented in this paper does not detect infinite stuttering. It is clearly possible to extend the algorithm to detect infinite stuttering which results in a return to a previous state. However, we expect it will not be possible to detect infinite stuttering which results in an infinite series of different states. The algorithm also cannot check backward simulations. The monolithic algorithm we presented in our previous paper [11] provides a basis for dealing with these issues, and we intend to address them as part of our future work.

Lange and Stirling recently described an approach to model checking that makes use of game theory [8]. They describe how a game can be played by two players on the model and the properties to be checked. They show how a question about the properties being fulfilled is equivalent to finding a winning strategy for one of the players. Once such a strategy is found it can be used to enable an interactive play between a tool and the user [8]. Their work addresses some of the same issues as ours. For example, their approach can provide justification to the designer of a "Yes" answer from the model checker. Whereas our work is based on Back and von Wright's action system semantics [2], theirs is based on game theory and branching time logics. There may be parallels between the winning strategy their approach can identify in the case of a positive result from the model checker, and the minimal abstraction relation our algorithm can produce. It would be interesting to investigate such questions, and also to investigate whether we could make use of optimisations that they suggest. Work by Back and von Wright that examines the notion of games and their use in refinement theory [3] may also help with the interpretation of Lange and Stirling's results in our context.

9   Conclusion

We have presented an algorithm that can incrementally derive abstraction relations for data refinements. When time and space limitations prevent the algorithm from terminating, its intermediate output can nevertheless be useful to a designer when trying to prove the refinement step. The algorithm can also be used to test an abstraction relation supplied by the designer. An intelligent choice of this relation can cut down the search space for the algorithm, and thus improve the likelihood of it terminating. In future work we intend to investigate a symbolic version of the algorithm in which its outputs are expressed as a predicates, instead of sets of mappings between individual states of the two systems.

Acknowledgements

I would like to thank Colin Fidge and Graeme Smith for their advice and encouragement in preparing this paper.

References

1. R.-J. R. Back. Refinement of parallel and reactive programs. Technical Report Caltech-CS-TR-92-93, Computer Science Department, California Institute of Technology, 1992.
2. R.-J. R. Back and J. von Wright. Trace refinement of action systems. In B. Jonsson and J. Parrow, editors, *Proceedings of CONCUR '94: Concurrency Theory*, volume 836 of *Lecture Notes in Computer Science*, pages 367–384. Springer-Verlag, 1994.

3. R.-J. R. Back and J. von Wright. Contracts, games and refinement. *Information and Computation*, 156:25–45, 2000.
4. R.-J. R. Back and J. von Wright. Encoding, decoding and data refinement. *Formal Aspects of Computing*, 12:313–349, 2000.
5. S. Bensalem, Y. Lakhnech, and S. Owre. Computing abstractions of infinite state systems compositionally and automatically. In *Proceedings of the 10th International Conference on Computer Aided Verification, CAV98*, volume 1427 of *Lecture Notes in Computer Science*, pages 319–331. Springer, 1998.
6. M. Butler. On the use of data refinement in the development of secure communications systems. *Formal Aspects of Computing*, 14(1):2–34, 2002.
7. M. Doche and A. Gravell. Extraction of abstraction invariants for data refinement. In D. Bert, J. P. Bowen, M. C. Henson, and K. Robinson, editors, *ZB 2002: Formal Specification and Development in Z and B, Proceedings of the 2nd International Conference of B and Z Users*, volume 2272 of *Lecture Notes in Computer Science*, pages 120–139. Springer, 2002.
8. M. Lange and C. Stirling. Model checking games for branching time logics. *Journal of Logic and Computation*, 12:623–639, 2002.
9. C. Morgan and P. H. B. Gardiner. Data refinement by calculation. *Acta Informatica*, 27(6):481–503, 1989.
10. N. J. Robinson. Checking Z data refinements using an animation tool. In D. Bert, J. P. Bowen, M. C. Henson, and K. Robinson, editors, *ZB 2002: Formal Specification and Development in Z and B, Proceedings of the 2nd International Conference of B and Z Users*, volume 2272 of *Lecture Notes in Computer Science*, pages 62–81. Springer, 2002.
11. N. J. Robinson. Finding abstraction relations for data refinement. Technical Report TR03-03, Software Verification Research Centre, School of Information Technology and Electrical Engineering, The University of Queensland, Brisbane 4072, Australia, February 2003. http://www.itee.uq.edu.au/~njr/tr0303.pdf.
12. N. J. Robinson and C. Fidge. Animation of data refinements. In *Proceedings of the Asia-Pacific Software Engineering Conference, APSEC 2002, Gold Coast, Australia*, pages 137–146. IEEE Computer Society Press, December 2002.
13. J. von Wright. Data refinement and the simulation method. Technical Report Ser. A, No. 137, Abo Akademi, 1992.

Comparison of Data and Process Refinement

Steve Reeves and David Streader

Department of Computer Science, University of Waikato, Hamilton, New Zealand
{dstr,stever}@cs.waikato.ac.nz

Abstract. From what point of view is it reasonable, or possible, to refine a one place buffer into a two place buffer? In order to answer this
question we characterise refinement based on substitution in restricted
contexts. We see that data refinement (specifically in Z) and process refinement give differing answers to the original question, and we compare
the precise circumstances which give rise to this difference by translating
programs and processes into labelled transition systems, so providing a
common basis upon which to make the comparison. We also look at the
closely related area of sub-typing of objects. Along the way we see how
all these sorts of computational construct are related as far as refinement
is concerned, and discover and characterise some (as far as we can tell)
new sorts of refinement.

Keywords: data refinement, process refinement, labelled transition systems, Z, sub-typing.

1 Introduction

When considering just the process view, R. van Glabbeek [1] surveys 155 different testing semantics, each with an accompanying definition of refinement. One
reason for this interest is that by understanding how a process interacts with
its environment it is possible to select the corresponding testing semantics and
hence select a definition of refinement. With the advent of both the International
Standard on Open Distributed Processing [2] and aspect-oriented programming
[3], there has been increasing interest in using different formalisms to specify
different views or aspects of the same system. By considering more than one
view the selection of an appropriate refinement relation is made much harder.

One multi-view approach is to keep the different views/formalisms separate
in the development, *i.e.* refinement, of an abstract specification into a concrete
implementation and ensure the separate views are consistent [4]. Another approach is to use formalisms to define different components, with another to
"glue" the components together. A good first step, for either approach, is to
define a common semantics for the different views/formalisms.

Operational semantics, using labelled transition systems (LTSs), have been
defined for processes [5,6], abstract data types (ADTs) and objects [7,8,9]. Also,
we can use process operators defined directly on LTSs [5,10] to compose different
components regardless of the views/formalisms from which they originate.

J.S. Dong and J. Woodcock (Eds.): ICFEM 2003, LNCS 2885, pp. 266–285, 2003.

Unfortunately, state-based refinement and process-based refinement are defined in different styles and justifiably are not the same, hence the different answers to the question "is a two place buffer a refinement of a one place buffer?". The important point here is that the very meaning of a specification is given by (or is at least highly bound-up in) what it can be refined into. Consequently, the same LTS specification has different meanings depending upon the view (state/process) it originates from.

To develop the multi-view approach we clearly need a good understanding of the relationship between refinement as defined in different views and different styles.

The key observation of [8] is that different kinds of things can be placed in differing contexts. For example, in [8] ADTs can only be placed in contexts that are traces (*i.e.* sequences) of (calls to) operations, *i.e.* programs, whereas processes can be placed in contexts modelled by branching transition systems [11]. Using this observation we construct two general definitions of refinement of LTS that are parameterized on the contexts in which the LTS can be placed. One definition is in the style of process refinement. The other refinement is more in a state-based style. We then show when the two general definitions are equivalent.

The general definition of refinement can be applied to different kinds of things. That is to say, the general definition of refinement is made more concrete by fixing the contexts in which the things are to be placed. Doing this we find that our notion of refinement of processes, placed in **all** process contexts, is equivalent to failure refinement [11] and our notion of refinement of ADTs, placed in **all** ADT contexts, is equivalent to singleton failure refinement [8]. These are the results we would expect.

The actions of an ADT are passive and only occur when a program calls them. Consequently for ADT refinement, $A \sqsubseteq C$ (read "A is refined by C"), C is only placed in contexts "*where* A *is expected*". This is formalised by restricting the contexts in our general definition. This definition of refinement permits **feature addition** *i.e.* some traces of C are not traces of A, as in state-based refinement. In contrast the more restrictive, process view of refinement is the "reduction of non-determinism", feature addition being called *extension* [12], and both feature addition and reduction of non-determinism being called *conformance* [12]. So, here we use the word refinement in same way as the state-based approach does.

Although the process view is that refinement is the reduction of non- determinism this does not mean that all reduction of non-determinism is refinement. There are indeed well known definitions of process "refinement" such as testing refinement [13] and extension [14] which preserve the trace semantics.

We restrict contexts to "*where* A *is expected*" in the general setting and then, when we select a universe of contexts for ADTs and then again for processes, we have definitions of:

ADT refinement related to, but not equivalent to, LOTOS's *ext* [14],

process refinement equivalent to a definition of object-oriented *behavioural sub-typing* given in [15].

Although our approach is intentionally general (even abstract) we have been able to replace the questions: one - "what style do you want refinement to be specified in?" and two - "which of the very very many definitions of refinement do you wish to use?" by the less abstract question "how does this component interact with its context?".

We define the notation for labelled transition systems in Section 2 and review some definitions of refinement of processes from the literature in Section 2.1. We introduce our items of interest in Section 3 and then we define two formalisations, both parameterized by sets of contexts, of what we mean in general by refinement in Section 4.

In Section 5 we use Z to define data types and subsequently define the operational semantics for them based on the *guarded* interpretation (which models most closely what is usual in processes, as opposed to the more usual Z interpretation of chaos outside of preconditions).

In Section 6 we define the contexts in which we can place ADTs and use this and the definition of Section 4 to define ADT refinement. Similarly in Section 7 we define the contexts in which we can place processes and use this and the definition of Section 4 to define process refinement. In Section 8 we give pointers to prior work and in our conclusions in Section 9 we summarise our categorisation and our discoveries.

2   Labelled Transition Systems

In this section we define the notation we will use. It is a combination of notation from ACP [5] and Z [16]. We assume a universe of observable action names Act, from which we build $\overline{Act} \stackrel{\text{def}}{=} \{\overline{a} \mid a \in Act\}$, and then $Act^\tau \stackrel{\text{def}}{=} Act \cup \{\tau\}$. We are interested in finite but cyclic labelled transition systems.

Definition 1 *Labelled transition systems (LTS)*
$A \stackrel{\text{def}}{=} (Nodes_A, Tran_A, s_A)$ *where* $s_A \in Nodes_A$ *and* $Tran_A \subseteq \{(n, a, m) \mid n, m \in Nodes_A \wedge a \in Act^\tau\}$ *and both* $Nodes_A$ *and* $Tran_A$ *are finite.*

We write *lts* for the set of labelled transition systems. We lift "−" to sets of transitions, to $A \in lts$ and *lts* in the obvious way. Any single labelled transition system will either have transitions labelled from $Act \cup \{\tau\}$ or transitions labelled from $\overline{Act} \cup \{\tau\}$ (which are used as contexts).

Let $a \in Act$ and $\rho \in Act^*$. We write $\rho \mid_n$ for the nth element of ρ and $\rho \lceil_n$ for the first n elements of ρ. We write $\rho \lceil X$ for the sequence ρ with all elements not in set X removed, so $prefix(\rho) \stackrel{\text{def}}{=} \{\rho \lceil_n \mid n <\mid \rho \mid\}$.

Where A is obvious from context, we write: $n \stackrel{a}{\longrightarrow} m$ for $(n, a, m) \in Tran_A$, $n \stackrel{a}{\longrightarrow}$ for $\exists_m . (n, a, m) \in Tran_A$, $m_1 \stackrel{\rho}{\longrightarrow}$ for $\exists_{m_1 \ldots} . (m_1, \rho \mid_1, m_2), \ldots \in Tran_A$ and $m_1 \stackrel{\rho}{\longrightarrow} m_{i+1}$ for $\exists_{m_1 \ldots m_i} . (m_1, \rho \mid_1, m_2), \ldots (m_i, \rho \mid_i, m_{i+1}) \in Tran_A \wedge \mid \rho \mid = i$.

$\alpha(A) \stackrel{\text{def}}{=} \{a \mid n \stackrel{a}{\longrightarrow} m \in Tran_A\}$, $\pi(s) \stackrel{\text{def}}{=} \{a \mid s \stackrel{a}{\longrightarrow}\}$

The traces of A are $Tr(A) \stackrel{\text{def}}{=} \{\rho \mid s_A \stackrel{\rho}{\longrightarrow}\}$ and the complete traces of A are $Tr^c(A) \stackrel{\text{def}}{=} \{\rho \mid (s_A \stackrel{\rho}{\longrightarrow} n \wedge \pi(n) = \varnothing) \vee (s_A \stackrel{\rho}{\longrightarrow} \wedge \mid \rho \mid = \infty)\}$.

$(A)\delta_X \overset{\text{def}}{=} (Nodes_A, Tran_{(A)\delta_X}, s_A)$ where $Tran_{(A)\delta_X} \overset{\text{def}}{=} \{n \xrightarrow{a} m \mid n \xrightarrow{a} m \in Tran_A \wedge a \notin X\}$.

$(A)\tau_X \overset{\text{def}}{=} (Nodes_A, Tran_{(A)\tau_X}, s_A)$ where $Tran_{(A)\tau_X} \overset{\text{def}}{=} Tran_{(A)\delta_X} \cup \{n \xrightarrow{\tau} m \mid n \xrightarrow{a} m \in Tran_A \wedge a \in X\}$.

We treat the synchronisation of x and x̄ as giving the observable x̄. In order to do this, and allow the deletion of unsynchronised x̄ actions, we first (see Figure 1) map them to x̄^{o} (so γ_S contains $(x, \overline{x}) \mapsto \overline{x}^o$ for $x \in S$) then delete $\overline{x}$ via $\delta_{\overline{S}}$ and then rename x̄^{o} to x̄ via Ren_S. All this is brought together in the following definition (which we say more about in Section 3):

$$ \_ \|_S \_ \overset{\text{def}}{=} ((\_ \|_{\gamma_S} \_)\delta_{\overline{S}})Ren_S $$

$P = \overline{a}!1\overline{b}?x\overline{c}!2 \|_{\gamma_{\{\overline{a},\overline{c}\}}} a?yc?x \qquad Q = (P)\delta_{\{\overline{a},\overline{c}\}} \qquad R = (Q)Ren_{\{a,c\}}\delta_{Act}$

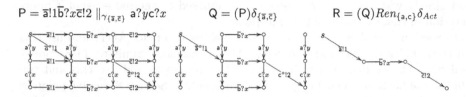

Fig. 1. $\overline{a}!1\overline{b}?x\overline{c}!2 \|_{\{a,c\}} a?yc?x$.

Finally we have refusal sets: $Ref(\rho, C) \overset{\text{def}}{=} \{X \mid s_C \xrightarrow{\rho} s \wedge X \subseteq Act - \pi(s)\}$ and singleton refusal sets: $Ref_s(\rho, C) \overset{\text{def}}{=} \{\{a\} \mid s_C \xrightarrow{\rho} s \wedge a \in Act - \pi(s)\}$.

2.1 Some Known Refinement Relations for Process-Based Systems

Hennessy's "may and must" testing refinement [13] $\sqsubseteq_{test}$ is the most constrained form of refinement we consider. A relaxation is LOTOS's extensional refinement $\sqsubseteq_{ext}$ [14] which allows feature addition in the form of both alphabet extension α^+ and the addition of new traces Tr^+ over the original alphabet. We define $\sqsubseteq_{pro}$, that only introduces alphabet extension α^+, from which we have $\sqsubseteq_{test} \Rightarrow \sqsubseteq_{pro} \Rightarrow \sqsubseteq_{ext}$.

Each of these can be relaxed by adding the ability to prune non-deterministic traces (note $A \sqsubseteq B$ in Figure 2). Adding this ability to $\sqsubseteq_{test}$ forms $\sqsubseteq_{Ftest}$ (failure refinement [11], which is known to be equivalent to must testing refinement [13]) and $\sqsubseteq_{Fpro}$, which is shown (Lemma 1) to be equivalent to "weak sub-typing" [15] and $\sqsubseteq_{Fext}$, which is *conf* [12].

Definition 2 *Process refinements. Let* $New = (\alpha(C) - \alpha(A))$:

$(A \sqsubseteq_{test} C) \Leftrightarrow Tr(A) = Tr(C) \wedge \forall \rho.Ref(\rho, C) \subseteq Ref(\rho, A)$.

$(A \sqsubseteq_{pro} C) \Leftrightarrow Tr(A) = Tr(C\delta_{New}) \wedge \forall \rho \in Tr(A).Ref(\rho, C) \subseteq Ref(\rho, A)$.

$(A \sqsubseteq_{ext} C) \Leftrightarrow Tr(A) \subseteq Tr(C) \wedge \forall \rho \in Tr(A).Ref(\rho, C) \subseteq Ref(\rho, A)$.

$(A \sqsubseteq_{Ftest} C) \Leftrightarrow \forall \rho.Ref(\rho, C) \subseteq Ref(\rho, A)$.

$(A \sqsubseteq_{Fpro} C) \Leftrightarrow Tr(A) \supseteq Tr(C\delta_{New}) \wedge \forall \rho \in Tr(A).Ref(\rho, C) \subseteq Ref(\rho, A)$

$(A \sqsubseteq_{Fext} C) \Leftrightarrow \forall \rho \in Tr(A).Ref(\rho, C) \subseteq Ref(\rho, A)$.

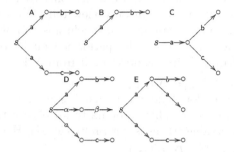

		Prune	α^+	**Tr**$^+$
[13]	test	×	×	×
	pro	×	√	×
[14]	ext	×	√	√
[11]	Ftest	√	×	×
[15]	Fpro	√	√	×
[12]	Fext	√	√	√
	A ⊑	B	D	E

Fig. 2. A $\sqsubseteq_{F....}$ B   A $\sqsubseteq_{test}$ C   A $\sqsubseteq_{pro}$ C, D   A $\sqsubseteq_{ext}$ C, D, E.

All the above are based on refusals $Ref(\rho, X)$. From [8,17] we see that ADTs are more appropriately based on singleton refusals $Ref_s(\rho, X)$. Consequently by replacing $Ref(\rho, X)$ with $Ref_s(\rho, X)$ in the above we have a whole new set of refinement relations $\sqsubseteq^s_X$ tailored for ADTs.

We find (as we shall see) that our definition of ADT refinement corresponds to a singleton version of $\sqsubseteq_{Fext}$ *i.e.* $\sqsubseteq^s_{Fext}$.

A $\sqsubseteq_{Ftest}$ Cδ_{New} has been used in *weak sub-typing* in [15] where they take as a requirement of behavioural sub-typing that if $New = \varnothing$ then refinement should be failure refinement. A consequence of this decision, as we shall see, is that a one place buffer cannot be refined into a two place buffer.

Lemma 1 A $\sqsubseteq_{Fpro}$ C $\Leftrightarrow$ A $\sqsubseteq_{Ftest}$ Cδ_{New}

3   Things and Contexts of Interest

Our 'things' could be abstract data types, processes or even objects, all of which we introduce and consider later. Both things and the contexts in which we place them are given a labelled transition system semantics. Different kinds of things can be placed in different contexts. The use of different contexts for different kinds of thing can be seen in [8,15].

Placing 'thing' T in a context built from thing X is written $[T]_X$ and must model the synchronisation between actions of things such as method m and actions of contexts such as calling method m, *i.e.* $\overline{m}$.

The resulting synchronised actions may be private, *i.e.* τ actions. Any action of the context that is not private is observable by an "independent observer". A consequence of this is that although communication between thing and context may be unobserved (τ) it is easy to amend any context by adding actions that make observable any of the unobservable synchronisations. Consequently, we will treat the synchronisation of x and $\overline{x}$ as giving the observable $\overline{x}$. In order to allow the deletion of unsynchronised $\overline{x}$ actions we use $\_ \parallel_S \_ \overset{\text{def}}{=} (\_ \parallel_{\gamma_S} \_)\delta_{\overline{S}})Ren_S$ (see Section 2 above).

We assume that all observable actions of T require synchronisation with some other thing in order to be performed. We can only view our things via their synchronisation with the context and we can view all synchronisation with the context. Hence, no observable action of T can be performed on its own (formalised by $(\_)\delta_{Act}$). So, placing 'thing' T in a context built from X is:

$$[\mathsf{T}]_X \;\overset{\text{def}}{=}\; (\mathsf{T} \|_{\alpha(\mathsf{T})} X)\delta_{Act}$$

Further, we assume that we can wait long enough so that if something observable will eventually happen we do see it. This amounts to an observation being a *complete trace* (the set of observable traces is not prefix closed). Hence:

$$Obs([\mathsf{T}]_X) \;\overset{\text{def}}{=}\; Tr^c([\mathsf{T}]_X).$$

Assumption 1 (*a*) *Things and their contexts can be given a LTS semantics.* (*b*) *The kind of a thing can be characterised by the set of contexts it can be placed in.* (*c*) *A thing's actions can only be executed in synchronisation with actions from the context.* (*d*) *All synchronisations of a thing with actions from the context are observed.* (*e*)*All that we can observe are the complete traces of context.*

4   Refinement, Observation and Contexts

Refinement is a step in the construction of an implementation from a specification. The refinement of A (something abstract) into C (something more concrete) will be written A $\sqsubseteq$ C. We allow the C to have new operations not found in A, $New \overset{\text{def}}{=} \alpha(\mathsf{C}) - \alpha(\mathsf{A})$. We will formalise refinement in two related styles:

Process-based style where the observation of an execution of $[\mathsf{A}]_X$ is interpreted as success or failure and refinement is based on a pre-order representing improvement.

State-based style refinement based on "substitutability", C being a refinement of A when the substitution of A, in a context *where* A *was expected*, by C, cannot be observed.

The first style is a small modification of Hennessy's [13], and when applied to processes it gives the same refinements as Hennessy's. This style generates different refinements depending on the pre-order used.

The second style appears [18,19,9,20,15] as behavioural sub-typing and hence could be thought of as object refinement. The *"not being able to tell"* will be formalised as subset of observations. In the case when the contexts are programs this becomes equivalent to the definition of data refinement as subset of the relational semantics of programs as found in [21,22,23]. For data refinement where operations are undefined (and so can have any behaviour, sometimes referred to as chaos) outside pre-conditions the restriction of programs to those *where* A *was expected* is redundant, but for data refinement where operations are guarded it is this restriction that permits feature addition.

Because of the links between the two styles of definitions we will apply the notion of *"where* A *was expected"* to the first style, thereby introducing the feature addition permitted by the second style. When applied to ADTs this will result in a refinement weaker than LOTOS's *ext* refinement.

4.1   Process-Based Refinement

A single observation of $[T]_X$ is a complete trace of T in context X and will be interpreted as $\top$ (success) if and only if it is also a complete trace of the context X. What can be observed of $[T]_X$ is the set of single observations $Tr^c([T]_X)$. Such observations are given one of the following three interpretations: $\{\top\}$—always succeed; $\{\top, \bot\}$—may succeed or may fail; and $\{\bot\}$—always fail.

There are three powerdomains on the two point lattice $\top > \bot$ (see Figure 3). We are only interested in two of them: we will ignore the *Hoare* powerdomain[1] and use the other two powerdomains to impose a pre-order on the observations.

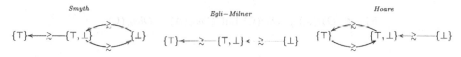

Fig. 3. Powerdomains.

Definition 3 $Obs([A]_X) \overset{\text{def}}{=} Tr^c([A]_X)$

$\top \in I([A]_X) \Leftrightarrow \exists_{\rho \in Obs([A]_X)} \cdot \rho \in Tr^c(X)$

$\bot \in I([A]_X) \Leftrightarrow \exists_{\rho \in Obs([A]_X)} \cdot \rho \in prefix(Tr^c(X))$ *and nothing else is in* $I([A]_X)$.

$Obs([C]_X) \gtrsim Obs([A]_X) \overset{\text{def}}{=} I([C]_X x) > I([A]_X) \vee (I([A]_X) = I([C]_X) \wedge Obs([A]_X) \supseteq Obs([C]_X))$

$A \sqsubseteq C \overset{\text{def}}{=} \forall_{[\_]X \in [\_]} \cdot Obs([C]_X) \gtrsim Obs([A]_X).$ •

This definition of refinement depends on :

1. the set of contexts used $[\_]$
2. and what pre-order $>$ we apply to our interpretations $I([\_]_X)$

Hennessy [13] uses a "*success state*" approach in which tests formalise the notion of observation. A special action ω is introduced and used to decorate the success states $\{s \overset{\omega}{\longrightarrow} \mid s \in Succ\}$. Then a test (an execution of a process in a context) is interpreted as being a success when it reaches a success state (when ω is observed).

Here end states ($\pi(n) = \varnothing$) can be viewed as our success states, but whereas Hennessy allows only ω to be visible, we allow the observation of the whole trace of executed actions. These two treatments can be shown (see Lemma 6 later) to result in the same refinement relation when applied to processes. But, as we now demonstrate, the two treatments define *different* refinements when applied to ADTs.

Applying the "*success state*" approach to ADTs (where contexts are traces) we interpret a test as being a success if the context reaches a success state.

---

[1] The *Hoare* powerdomain has been used [13] to define 'may' testing, which is equivalent to trace refinement. Here we can achieve the same results by restricting the LTS used to represent both things and contexts.

Clearly this is equivalent to restricting contexts to $\rho\omega$ and treating only ω as visible, $Obs_H(\_) \stackrel{\text{def}}{=} Obs(\_)\tau_{(Act-\{\omega\})}$. Using this definition of observation we can see that A and C in Figure 4 are observationally equivalent. But they are not observationally equivalent using our definition of observation as completed traces.

$$\begin{aligned}
Obs([A]_{abc\omega}) &= \{a, ab, abc\omega\} \\
Obs([C]_{abc\omega}) &= \{a, abc\omega\} \\
\hline
Obs_H([A]_{a\omega}) &= \{\omega\} = Obs_H([C]_{a\omega}) \\
Obs_H([A]_{ab\omega}) &= \{\omega, \langle\rangle\} = Obs_H([C]_{ab\omega}) \\
Obs_H([A]_{abc\omega}) &= \{\omega, \langle\rangle\} = Obs_H([C]_{abc\omega})
\end{aligned}$$

Fig. 4. $Obs(A) \neq Obs(C)$ but $Obs_H(A) = Obs_H(C)$.

Although the "success state" approach seems a perfectly reasonable way to define refinement we do not pursue this here.

4.2   Contexts Where A Is Expected

Our state-based notion of refinement is going to be based upon "substituting" A with C in contexts *where* A *was expected*. Here we will formalise this idea and apply it to our action-based definition of refinement.

Definition 4 A ⊑ C *iff* C *may be used in any context where* A *was expected, without the client being able to tell.*

Our contexts for things T are $[T]_X \stackrel{\text{def}}{=} (T \parallel_{\alpha(T)} X)\delta_{Act}$. Note the context synchronises on actions of T and then all unsynchronised actions get deleted (δ_{Act}).

Assumption 2 *Contexts where* A *is expected can only synchronise with (call) actions of* A

Consequently: $[\_]^A \subseteq \{(\_ \parallel_{\alpha(A)} X)\delta_{Act} \mid X \in \overline{lts}\}$.

Assumption 3 *"contexts where* A *is expected" are not contexts where* A *must fail.*

Definition 5 *"contexts where* A *is expected"*
$$[\_]^A \stackrel{\text{def}}{=} \{(\_ \parallel_{\alpha(A)} X)\delta_{Act} \mid X \in \overline{lts} \wedge I((\_ \parallel_{\alpha(A)} X)\delta_{Act}) \neq \{\bot\}\} .$$

Definition 6 A ⊑^{A} C $\stackrel{\text{def}}{=} \forall_{[\_]_a \in [\_]^A} . Obs([C]_a) \gtrsim Obs([A]_a)$.

Prior to restricting the contexts, our two definitions of refinement, applied to processes, will be the same as two of Hennessy's testing refinements. When we apply this definition, with restricted contexts, to ADTs and processes we will find that our definitions of refinement are very similar to that of LOTOS's *ext* refinement.

4.3 State-Based Refinement

Early work [21] defines refinement as subset on the relational semantics and quantifies over all contexts (programs). This can be rephrased as: for all inputs (contexts), we must have a subset of outputs (what can be observed). In a similar fashion we define refinement by explicitly defining contexts $[\_]^A$ or $[\_]$ and use subsets of observations.

Definition 7 $A \sqsubseteq_{State} C \stackrel{\text{def}}{=} \forall_{[\_]_a \in [\_]} . Obs([C]_a) \subseteq Obs([A]_a).$

$\quad A \sqsubseteq_{State}^A C \stackrel{\text{def}}{=} \forall_{[\_]_a \in [\_]^A} . Obs([C]_a) \subseteq Obs([A]_a).$

$[\![P]\!]_R \stackrel{\text{def}}{=} \{\langle [\_]_x, o \rangle \mid o \in Obs([P]_x), [\_]_x \in [\_]\} \quad A \sqsubseteq_R C \stackrel{\text{def}}{=} [\![C]\!]_R \subseteq [\![A]\!]_R$

$[\![P]\!]_R^A \stackrel{\text{def}}{=} \{\langle [\_]_x, o \rangle \mid o \in Obs([P]_x), [\_]_x \in [\_]^A\} \quad A \sqsubseteq_R^A C \stackrel{\text{def}}{=} [\![C]\!]_R^A \subseteq [\![A]\!]_R^A \qquad \circ$

Clearly $A \sqsubseteq_{State} C \Leftrightarrow A \sqsubseteq_R C$ and $A \sqsubseteq_{State}^A C \Leftrightarrow A \sqsubseteq_R^A C$. Definition 7 is, by design, closely related to Z data refinement [8].

It is easy to see that if we assume the Smyth powerdomain and use the previously computed contexts then the above definitions are a characterisation of our previously defined process-based refinements.

Once we have restricted the contexts to *contexts where* A *is expected*, as in Definition 6, then $\stackrel{\gtrsim}{\leftarrow}\{\perp\}$ is redundant. Consequently using the restricted relations in Figure 5 will have the same effect as using the powerdomains.

Fig. 5. Restrictions of powerdomains.

Lemma 2 *Assume the Smyth powerdomain*
$$A \sqsubseteq^A C \Leftrightarrow A \sqsubseteq_{State}^A C \Leftrightarrow A \sqsubseteq_R^A C.$$
$$A \sqsubseteq C \Leftrightarrow A \sqsubseteq_{State} \Leftrightarrow A \sqsubseteq_R C.$$

Thus refinements based on both the Smyth powerdomain and the Egli-Milner powerdomain reduce non-determinism, but refinements based on the Egli-Milner powerdomain (which will be a restriction of refinements based on the Smyth powerdomain) will also increase the likelihood of success.

An advantage of Definition 7 is that it is based on subsets of observations and not a more abstract interpretation of the observations and an $(\gtrsim)$ improve relation. On the other hand, starting from a definition of $\gtrsim$ we find that: 1— $[\_]^A$ the set contexts where A is expected can, based on stated assumptions, be computed; and 2—we have not excluded the Egli-Milner powerdomain. Hence we have not excluded testing refinement $\sqsubseteq_{test}$ [13] nor have we excluded LOTOS's extensional refinement $\sqsubseteq_{ext}$ [14].

Summary. Our process-based definition of refinement $\sqsubseteq$ depends upon:

1. what set of contexts [_] we use
2. what powerdomain we use—Smyth or Egli-Milner

The set of contexts [_] we use defines what kind of thing we model *e.g.* ADTs, processes *etc.* If we use the Smyth powerdomain then we can characterise refinement as a subset of observations. Based on the stated assumptions we can compute the contexts "where A is expected" ($[\_]^A$). If we restrict ourselves to these contexts we have refinement $\sqsubseteq^A$ which permits "feature addition".

Our relational or state-based refinement $\sqsubseteq_{State}$ starts with a definition of the contexts "where A is expected" ($[\_]^A$). If we choose the same set as those computed in the process-based style then, by Lemma 2, our state-based refinement has been proven to be the same as the process-based refinement with the Smyth powerdomain.

5   Using Z to Define Data Types

We might refer to a *one place buffer* as a data type, whether the buffer was empty or not. As an alternative we will follow the convention from the world of processes and regard a data type to define both its operational behaviour and an initial state. Thus, for us, strictly speaking, an *empty one place buffer* is a different data type from a *full one place buffer*.

5.1   Z Abstract Data Types

The state-and-operations style of Z specification can be *interpreted* as an ADT-specification style, but Z offers no structuring mechanisms to formalise this. Consequently we informally use the notation of [23] to group schemas.

Data types consist of a single state schema, an initialising operation schema and a set of operation schemas $A \stackrel{\text{def}}{=} (State_A, init_A, Op_A)$.

5.2   Z-ADT Relational Semantics

The normal interpretation of Z operation schemas is that they are *undefined* (*i.e.* specify arbitrary behaviour) outside their preconditions [22]. We use another interpretation (variously called *behavioural, abortive* or *guarded*) which is given a relational semantics $[\![\_]\!]_R$ in [8]. A detailed comparison of refinement of both interpretations of Z operations can be found in [24].

As is well known, each operation schema a can be given a partial relation $[\![a]\!]_R \subseteq (State \times input) \times (State \times output)$. From this we define:

$$[\![A]\!]_R \stackrel{\text{def}}{=} \langle State_A, init_A, \{\langle a, [\![a]\!]_R \rangle \mid a \in name_A\}\rangle$$

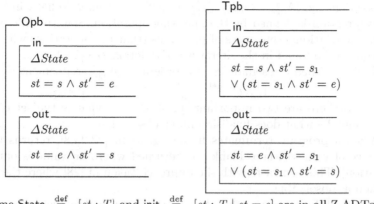

We assume State $\overset{\text{def}}{=}$ $[st : T]$ and init $\overset{\text{def}}{=}$ $[st : T \mid st = s]$ are in all Z ADTs.

Fig. 6. Z ADT Opb and Tpb.

5.3   Z-ADT Operational Semantics

We can assume the guarded semantics for a Z ADT A giving the LTS $[\![A]\!]_g$, the semantics from [25,26,27] simplified by not having value passing.

$$[\![A]\!]_g \overset{\text{def}}{=} \langle State_A, init_A, \{x \overset{n}{\longrightarrow} y \mid (n \in Op_A) \wedge x \in State_A \wedge n \wedge y \in State'_A\}\rangle$$

Note in above schema n is used, as with Z, to represent its predicate.

The relation between $[\![A]\!]_R$ and $[\![A]\!]_g$ is straightforward. The nodes of $[\![A]\!]_g$ and the states of $[\![A]\!]_R$ are Z bindings. The meaning of an operation a is a relation $[\![a]\!]_R$ between evaluations, labelled with a, which hence defines a set of a transitions of $[\![A]\!]_g$. The initialisation schema is restricted to a unique evaluation/node.

$$_g[\![[\![A]\!]_g]\!]_R \overset{\text{def}}{=} \langle State_A, init_{A,g} [\![Op_A]\!]_g]\!]_R\rangle$$
$$_g[\![[\![Op_A]\!]_g]\!]_R \overset{\text{def}}{=} \{\langle a, \langle\langle x, \_\rangle, \langle y, \_\rangle\rangle\rangle \mid x \overset{a}{\rightarrow} y\}$$
$$_R[\![\_]\!]_g \overset{\text{def}}{=} (_g[\![\_]\!]_R)^{-1}$$

Lemma 3 $_R[\![[\![A]\!]_R]\!]_g = [\![A]\!]_g$ and $_g[\![[\![A]\!]_g]\!]_R = [\![A]\!]_R$

5.4   Z Relational Semantics and Data Refinement

Data refinement, forward simulation and backward simulation are defined in [21]. Later on, *Z data refinement* [16] is defined and in [22] shown to be equivalent to forward simulation of [21]. We use data refinement as defined in [21,22,23] and think of forward and backward simulation to be techniques to compute refinement.

Data refinement of A is defined on *programs*, *i.e.* sequences ρ of 'calls' of operations. Each operation a is given a relational semantics $[\![a]\!]_R$ and the semantics of the programs $\rho \overset{\text{def}}{=} \overline{a1}\,\overline{a2}\dots$ on a data type is constructed from the relational semantics plus an initialisation and finalisation relation. Where operations cannot perform input and output the construction is simply relational composition, *i.e.* $[\![A_\rho]\!]_Z = init \circ [\![\mathsf{a1}]\!]_R \circ [\![\mathsf{a2}]\!]_R \ldots \circ final$. What can be observed of any program is defined by the finalising operation. Slightly different ways to define the relational semantics of programs (that use operations with input and output) can be found in the literature. For details see [22,23,8].

Having defined the semantics of a program, $[\![A_\rho]\!]_Z$, refinement is defined:

$$A \sqsubseteq_Z C \stackrel{\text{def}}{=} \forall_{\rho \in Prog} . [\![C]_\rho]\!]_Z \subseteq [\![A]_\rho]\!]_Z.$$

For us there are two important questions: 1—what is the set of programs *Prog*?; and 2—what does finalising make observable?

When a program terminates finalising, as in [22,23,8], returns the output sequence of values (where blank _ is returned where no value is output by an operation). This contrasts with the approach taken in [28] where the refusal set is taken as observable.

But in [8], for programs that do not terminate *final* returns a sequence of the same length as the sequence of operations that did terminate. We write $[\![A]_\rho]\!]_{Zg}$ for the relational semantics, defined in [8], of program ρ using data type A.

6   Sequential Data Types

An informal and common argument exists that a two place buffer Tpb is a refinement of a one place buffer Opb because "replacing a one place buffer with a two place buffer cannot be noticed". Similarly Opbdel Figure 7 can be seen as Opb with a delete feature added and hence we would like Opbdel to be a refinement of Opb. We consider these arguments further below.

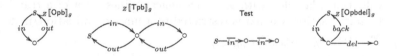

Fig. 7. Opb $\sqsubseteq_{Fext}^s$ Tpb Opb $\sqsubseteq_{Fext}^s$ Opbdel.

ADT Refinement. In order to apply our approach from Section 4 we need to define the contexts in which ADTs can be placed.

$$[\_] \stackrel{\text{def}}{=} \{(\_ \|_{\alpha(\_)} \rho))\delta_{Act} \mid \rho \in \overline{Act}^*\}.$$

We use these contexts throughout (see Section 6) and apply Definition 5 to compute "contexts where A is expected" to be:

$$[\_]^A = \{(\_ \|_{\alpha(A)} \rho))\delta_{Act} \mid \overline{\rho} \upharpoonright \alpha(A) \in Tr(A)\}$$

Now we can define ADT refinement as:

$$A \sqsubseteq_{DT} C \stackrel{\text{def}}{=} A \sqsubseteq C \text{ and } A \sqsubseteq_{DT^A} C \stackrel{\text{def}}{=} A \sqsubseteq^A C$$

Assuming the Smyth powerdomain then from Lemma 2 we have:

$$A \sqsubseteq_{DT} C \Leftrightarrow \forall_{[\_]_a \in [\_]} . Obs([C]_a) \subseteq Obs([A]_a).$$
$$A \sqsubseteq_{DT^A} C \Leftrightarrow \forall_{[\_]_a \in [\_]^A} . Obs([C]_a) \subseteq Obs([A]_a).$$

Data Refinements on Z. The semantic mapping $[\![\_]\!]_g$ defines the operational semantics of a Z ADT on which we can apply our definitions of refinement. By restricting the programs under consideration we have a definition of refinement that permits feature addition.

$$A \sqsubseteq_{Z^A} C \stackrel{def}{=} \forall_{\rho \in \{\rho \mid (\_ \|_{\alpha(A)} \rho)) \delta_{Act} \in [\_]_A\}} \cdot [\![C]\!]_\rho z \subseteq [\![A]\!]_\rho z.$$

Lemma 4 $A \sqsubseteq_Z C = [\![A]\!]_g \sqsubseteq_{DT} [\![C]\!]_g$ *and* $A \sqsubseteq_{Z^A} C = [\![A]\!]_g \sqsubseteq_{DT^A} [\![C]\!]_g$

Although Opb $\not\sqsubseteq_{DT}$ Tpb and Opb $\not\sqsubseteq_{DT}$ Opbdel, the restriction on contexts with $\sqsubseteq_{DT^A}$ prevents $z[\![Opb]\!]_g$ being placed in contexts (programs) such as $\overline{in};\overline{in}$ and $\overline{in};\overline{del}$. So, we have our desired results: Opb $\sqsubseteq_{DT^A}$ Tpb and Opb $\sqsubseteq_{DT^A}$ Opbdel.

Lemma 5 $A \sqsubseteq_{DT} C \Leftrightarrow A \sqsubseteq^s_F C$ $A \sqsubseteq_{DT^A} C \Leftrightarrow A \sqsubseteq^s_{Fext} C$

Z Refinement. In [8] they establish $A \sqsubseteq_Z C \Leftrightarrow A \sqsubseteq^s_F C$.

7 Processes in Sequential Branching Contexts

Processes in general can be placed in either branching or concurrent contexts. We are going to consider only sequential branching contexts.

A process can prevent a context from starting to execute an operation (action), whereas ADTs cannot prevent a context (program) from calling an operation, but it may be that the called operation will not terminate.

Because processes can be placed in more contexts than ADTs, we should expect process refinement to be different from ADT refinement (Test in Figure 8 is not an ADT context).

Consequently, from the process view, we find a two place buffer **not** to be a refinement of a one place buffer.

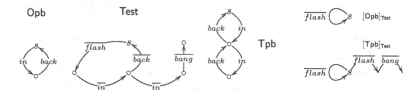

Fig. 8. Opb $\sqsubseteq_{ext}$ Tpb but $Obs([Tpb]_{Test}) \not\subseteq Obs([Opb]_{Test})$.

Refinement of Process in Sequential Contexts on LTS. In order to apply our approach from Section 4 we need to define the contexts in which processes can be placed.

$$[\_] \stackrel{def}{=} \{(\_ \|_{\alpha(\_)} p)\delta_{Act} \mid p \in \overline{lts}\}$$

We use these contexts throughout Section 7 and apply Definition 5 to compute "contexts where A is expected" to be:

$$[\_]^A = \{(\_ \|_{\alpha(A)} p)\delta_{Act} \mid \overline{Tr^c(p)} \cap Tr(A) \neq \varnothing\}$$

It can easily be seen (see Lemma 17) that we could have used $\{(\_ \|_{\alpha(A)} p)\delta_{Act} \mid true\}$ without affecting the refinement relation. This means that for processes, *i.e.* branching contexts, Assumption 3 has no effect on the definition of refinement. This is not very surprising as Assumption 3 originated from the state-based intuition of refinement and its relevance to process refinement is tenuous.

$$A \sqsubseteq_P C \stackrel{\text{def}}{=} A \sqsubseteq C \text{ and } A \sqsubseteq_{PA} C \stackrel{\text{def}}{=} A \sqsubseteq^A C$$

Assuming the Smyth powerdomain then from Lemma 2 we have:

$$A \sqsubseteq_P C \Leftrightarrow \forall_{[\_]_a \in [\_]} . Obs([C]_a) \subseteq Obs([A]_a).$$
$$A \sqsubseteq_{PA} C \Leftrightarrow \forall_{[\_]_a \in [\_]_A} . Obs([C]_a) \subseteq Obs([A]_a).$$

Lemma 6 $A \sqsubseteq_P C \Leftrightarrow A \sqsubseteq_{Ftest} C$ *and* $A \sqsubseteq_{PA} C \Leftrightarrow A \sqsubseteq_{Fpro} C$

8   Refinement in the Literature

The weakest precondition refinement can be formulated to coincide with failure divergence refinement [29,30] and provides a semantics for Circus [31]. In this paper it is Z's single predicate semantics and process refinement on an operational, not denotational, semantics that are compared. For a survey on the unification of Z with process algebras see [32].

Initially it was thought that Z data refinement and failure refinement were the same [33]. Then this was shown not be the case, *i.e.* that $\sqsubseteq_Z \neq \sqsubseteq_{Ftest}$, and singleton failures refinement $\sqsubseteq_{Ftest}^s$ was defined ([8]) and shown equivalent to $\sqsubseteq_Z$.

Data refinement, described in [22, page 241], uses the restricted contexts "every program of $P(A)$". Because the semantics mean an operation is undefined outside of its precondition, this restriction is redundant. Data refinement, described in [23], uses all contexts (programs). As their semantics says an operation is not undefined outside of its precondition the restriction of the contexts would not be redundant. Of the two definitions only refinement of [22] permits feature addition.

Using the data refinement of [23] a two place buffer is not a refinement of a one place buffer. This corresponds to the usual process notion of refinement. But for data types, where actions (methods) can only be executed when a program calls them, this is unnecessarily restrictive. As any program that works successfully with a one place buffer will work with the one place buffer replaced by a two place buffer.

For us the important insight of [8] was that data types could only be placed in sequential contexts. Here we have extended their work by permitting "feature addition" as is usual in the state-based approach.

When we are considering the refinement not of individual operations but of the whole ADT/process then non-determinism may still be unwanted, *i.e.* we may wish it to be designed away, yet the pruning of traces may not be desirable. Definitions of refinement that reflect this are testing refinement [13] and LOTOS's extension refinement [14]. These forms of refinement reduce non-determinism and the set of contexts in which the process will not terminate.

The definition of refinement found in [9] does not restrict the "contexts where A is expected" to $\alpha(A)$, consequently a feature (action) addition like $a + b \not\sqsubseteq a + b + c$ is not a refinement, whereas in ours and the definition in [19] it is.

In [9] they say "we'd like the two place buffer to be a subtype of a one place buffer" and they place their buffers in branching contexts. Like them we find this problematic. The solution suggested in [9] is that actions that are "not offered" are given an undefined semantics not a guarded semantics. Here we define data types that cannot be placed in branching contexts and for which a two place buffer is a refinement of a one place buffer. We give a separate definition of processes that can be placed in branching contexts and for which a two place buffer is **not** a refinement of a one place buffer.

Nierstasz [19] defines sub-typing in an equivalent way to extension refinement and obtains the result: Sequential clients (contexts), satisfied by an abstract object, will be satisfied by a subtype (refinement) of it. For concurrent (branching) contexts this result does not follow, whereas we restrict the contexts in which our processes can be placed.

In [15] several refinement definitions are given on the denotational semantics. **Weak** sub-typing, for not-shared objects, is equivalent to our $\sqsubseteq_{PA}$. But if we assume that not-shared objects can only be placed in sequential contexts then we would choose $\sqsubseteq_{DT^A} = \sqsubseteq^s_{Fext}$ as our definition of behavioural sub-typing. Their other definitions **safe**, **optimal** and **optimistic** sub-typing are for shared objects and extend **weak** sub-typing by treating actions, of the sharing object, as (τ) internal actions (other versions can be found in [23,18]).

9   Conclusion

We have provided a common framework in which to compare some of the many definitions of refinement/sub-typing. Using this we have shown that the state-based definition of data refinement more closely relates to process *conformance* than process refinement.

Data refinement defined on Z [22], where actions are undefined outside of preconditions, permit *feature addition*, whereas data refinement defined where actions are guarded outside of precondition [8] do not. From our general framework it is easy to see that the reason for the lack of feature addition is not the fact that actions are guarded but the fact that the contexts are not restricted to "*where* A *is expected*". Hence it is easy to see that a small amendment to the definition of Z refinement in [8] suffices for this state-based version of refinement to correspond to $\sqsubseteq^s_{Fext}$ (*singleton conformance*) and to consequently permit feature addition similarly to the original Z data refinement of [22].

Acknowledgments

Thanks to Greg Reeve, Moshe Deutsch, Mark Utting and Doug Goldson for many helpful discussions. Thanks to new Zealand Government's Foundation for Research, Science and Technology for funding to make this research possible.

References

1. van Glabbeek, R.J.: The Linear Time - Branching Time Spectrum II. In: International Conference on Concurrency Theory. (1993) 66–81
2. Standard, I.: Open Distributed Processing - Reference Model. Technical Report ISO/IEC 10746-1(E), International Electrotechnical Commission (1998)
3. Kiczales, G., Lamping, J., Menhdhekar, A., Maeda, C., Lopes, C., Loingtier, J.M., Irwin, J.: Aspect-oriented programming. In Akşit, M., Matsuoka, S., eds.: Proceedings European Conference on Object-Oriented Programming. Volume 1241. Springer-Verlag, Berlin, Heidelberg, and New York (1997) 220–242
4. Steen, M., Derrick, J., Boiten, E., Bowman, H.: Consistency of partial process specifications. Lecture Notes in Computer Science **1548** (1999) 248–262
5. Baeten, J.C.M., Weijland, W.P.: Process Algebra. Cambridge Tracts in Theoretical Computer Science 18 (1990)
6. Roscoe, A.: The Theory and Practice of Concurrency. Prentice Hall International Series in Computer Science (1997)
7. Derrick, J., Bowman, H., Boiten, E., Steen, M.: Comparing LOTOS and Z refinement relations. In: FORTE/PSTV'96, Kaiserslautern, Germany, Chapman & Hall (1996) 501–516
8. Bolton, C., Davies, J.: A singleton failures semantics for Communicating Sequential Processes. Research Report PRG-RR-01-11, Oxford University Computing Laboratory (2001)
9. Bowman, H., Briscoe-Smith, C., Derrick, J., Strulo, B.: On behavioural subtyping in LOTOS (1997)
10. Winskel, G., Nielsen, M.: Models for concurrency. Technical Report DAIMI PB 429, Computer Science Dept. Aarhus Universty (1992)
11. Hoare, C.: Communicating Sequential Processes. Prentice Hall International Series in Computer Science (1985)
12. Brinksma, E., Scollo, G., Steenbergen, C.: LOTOS specifications, their implementation and their tests. In Sarikaya, B., Bochmann, G.V., eds.: Protocol Specification, Testing and Verification. Volume VI., North-Holland (1986) 349–360
13. Hennessy, M.: Algebraic Theory of Processes. The MIT Press (1988)
14. Brinksma, E., Scollo, G.: Formal notions of implementation and conformance in LOTOS. Technical Report INF-86-13, Twente University of Technology, Department of Informatics, Enschede, The Netherlands (1986)
15. Fischer, C., Wehrheim, H.: Behavioural subtyping relations for object-oriented formalisms. Lecture Notes in Computer Science **1816** (2000) 469–483
16. Spivey, J.M.: The Z notation: A reference manual. Prentice Hall (1989)
17. Bolton, C., Davies, J.: A comparison of refinement orderings and their associated simulation rules. In Derrick, J., Boiten, E., Woodcock, J., von Wright, J., eds.: Electronic Notes in Theoretical Computer Science. Volume 70., Elsevier (2002)
18. Basten, T., van der Aalst, W.M.P.: Inheritance of behavior. JLAP **47** (2001) 47–145
19. Nierstrasz, O.: Regular types for active objects. In Nierstrasz, O., Tsichritzis, D., eds.: Object-Oriented Software Composition. Prentice-Hall (1995) 99–121
20. Liskov, B., Wing, J.: Family values: a behavioral notion of subtyping. Technical Report MIT/LCS/TR-562b, Massachusetts Institute of Technology (1993)
21. He, J., Hoare, C., Sanders, J.: Data refinement refined. ESOP 86 Lecture Notes in Computer Science **213** (1986) 187–196

22. Woodcock, J., Davies, J.: Using Z: Specification, Refinement and Proof. Prentice Hall (1996)
23. Derrick, J., Boiten, E.: Refinement in Z and Object-Z: Foundations and Advanced Applications. Formal Approaches to Computing and Information Technology. Springer (2001)
24. Deutsch, M., Henson, M., Reeves, S.: Results on Formal Stepwise Design in Z. In: Proceedings of APSEC2002, IEEE Computer Society (2002)
25. Smith, G.: A Semantic Integration of Object-Z and CSP for the Specification of Concurrent Systems. In Fitzgerald, J., Jones, C.B., Lucas, P., eds.: FME'97: Industrial Applications and Strengthened Foundations of Formal Methods (Proc. 4th Intl. Symposium of Formal Methods Europe, Graz, Austria, September 1997). Volume 1313., Springer-Verlag (1997) 62–81
26. Smith, G.: A Fully Abstract Semantics of Classes for Object-Z. Formal Aspects of Computing **7** (1995) 289–313
27. Derrick, J., Boiten, E., Bowman, H., Steen, M.: Specifying and Refining Internal Operations in Z. Formal Aspects of Computing **10** (1998) 125–159
28. Boiten, E., Derrick, J.: Unifying concurrent and relational refinement. In Derrick, J., Boiten, E., Woodcock, J., von Wright, J., eds.: REFINE 02: The BCS FACS Refinement Workshop. Volume 70(3) of Electronic Notes in Theoretical Computer Science., Elsevier Science Publishers (2002)
29. Woodcock, J., Morgan, C.: Refinement of state-based concurrent systems. LNCS 428 (1990) 340–351 Springer-Verlag.
30. Hoare, C., Jifeng, H.: Unifying Theories of Programming. Prentice Hall International Series in Computer Science (1998)
31. Woodcock, J.C.P., Cavalcanti, A.L.C.: The Semantics of Circus. In Didier Ber, Jonathan P. Bowen, M.C.H., Robinson, K., eds.: ZB 2002 Formal Specification and Development in Z and B LNCS 2272. Springer-Verlag (2002) 184–203
32. Fischer, C.: How to combine Z with a process algebra. In Bowen, J.P., Fett, A., Hinchey, M.G., eds.: 11th Int. Conf. ZUM'98: the Z Formal Specification Notation. LNCS 1492, Springer-Verlag (1998) 5–23
33. Bolton, C., Davies, J., Woodcock, J.: On the refinement and simulation of data types and processes. In Arak, K., Galloway, A., Taguchi, K., eds.: Proceedings of IFM '99. (1999) 273–292

A   Proofs

Lemma 7 $\mathsf{A} \sqsubseteq_{Fpro} \mathsf{C} \Leftrightarrow \mathsf{A} \sqsubseteq_{Ftest} \mathsf{C}\delta_{New}$

Proof   Step 1. $\mathsf{A} \sqsubseteq_{Fpro} \mathsf{C} \Rightarrow \mathsf{A} \sqsubseteq_{Ftest} \mathsf{C}\delta_{New}$. Assume $\mathsf{A} \sqsubseteq_{Fpro} \mathsf{C}$.

$\mathsf{A} \sqsubseteq_{Fpro} \mathsf{C} \stackrel{\text{def}}{=} Tr(\mathsf{A}) \supseteq Tr(\mathsf{C}\delta_{New}) \land \forall \rho \in Tr(\mathsf{A}).Ref(\rho, \mathsf{C}) \subseteq Ref(\rho, \mathsf{A})$.

1. $\forall \rho \in Tr(\mathsf{A}).Ref(\rho, \mathsf{C}) \subseteq Ref(\rho, \mathsf{A}) \Rightarrow \forall \rho \in Tr(\mathsf{A}).Ref(\rho, \mathsf{C}\delta_{New}) \subseteq Ref(\rho, \mathsf{A})$.

As $Tr(\mathsf{A}) \supseteq Tr(\mathsf{C}\delta_{New})$ if $\rho \notin Tr(\mathsf{A})$ then $\rho \notin Tr(\mathsf{C}\delta_{New})$. Hence 2. if $\rho \notin Tr(\mathsf{A})$ then $Ref(\rho, \mathsf{C}\delta_{New}) \subseteq Ref(\rho, \mathsf{A})$.

From 1 and 2. $\forall \rho.Ref(\rho, \mathsf{C}\delta_{New}) \subseteq Ref(\rho, \mathsf{A}) \stackrel{\text{def}}{=} (\mathsf{A} \sqsubseteq_{Ftest} \mathsf{C}\delta_{New})$.

Step 2. $\mathsf{A} \sqsubseteq_{Ftest} \mathsf{C} \Rightarrow \delta_{New}\mathsf{A} \sqsubseteq_{Fpro} \mathsf{C}$. Assume $\mathsf{A} \sqsubseteq_{Ftest} \mathsf{C}$.

$(\mathsf{A} \sqsubseteq_{Ftest} \mathsf{C}\delta_{New}) \stackrel{\text{def}}{=} \forall \rho.Ref(\rho, \mathsf{C}\delta_{New}) \subseteq Ref(\rho, \mathsf{A})$.

1. $\forall \rho.Ref(\rho, C\delta_{New}) \subseteq Ref(\rho, A) \Rightarrow Tr(A) \supseteq Tr(C\delta_{New})$.

2. $\forall \rho.Ref(\rho, C\delta_{New}) \subseteq Ref(\rho, A) \Rightarrow \forall \rho \in Tr(A).Ref(\rho, C\delta_{New}) \subseteq Ref(\rho, A)$.

As $New = (\alpha(C) - \alpha(A))$ then $Ref(\rho, C\delta_{New}) \subseteq Ref(\rho, A) \Rightarrow Ref(\rho, C) \subseteq Ref(\rho, A)$. Hence $\forall \rho \in Tr(A).Ref(\rho, C) \subseteq Ref(\rho, A)$. Hence from 1. and 2.

$$Tr(A) \supseteq Tr(C\delta_{New}) \wedge \forall \rho \in Tr(A).Ref(\rho, C) \subseteq Ref(\rho, A) \stackrel{\text{def}}{=} A \sqsubseteq_{Fpro} C.$$

•

Lemma 8 *Assume the Smyth powerdomain*
$$A \sqsubseteq^A C \Leftrightarrow A \sqsubseteq^A_{State} C \Leftrightarrow A \sqsubseteq^A_R C.$$

Proof   Second equivalence is obvious. For first equivalence:

1. By definition if $Obs([C]_a) \gtrsim Obs([A]_a)$ then $I([C]_a) > I([A]_a) \vee (I([A]_a) = I([C]_a) \wedge Obs([A]_a) \supseteq Obs([C]_a))$. As if $I([C]_a) > I([A]_a)$ then from Figure 5 $Obs([C]_a) \subseteq Obs([A]_a)$. Consequently if $Obs([C]_a) \gtrsim Obs([A]_a)$ then $Obs([C]_a) \subseteq Obs([A]_a)$.

$\forall_{[\_]_a \in [\_]^A} . Obs([C]_a) \gtrsim Obs([A]_a) \Rightarrow Obs([C]_a) \subseteq Obs([A]_a)$

2. Similarly $\forall_{[\_]_a \in [\_]^A} . Obs([C]_a) \subseteq Obs([A]_a) \Rightarrow Obs([C]_a) \gtrsim Obs([A]_a)$

From 1. and 2.

$\forall_{[\_]_a \in [\_]^A} . Obs([C]_a) \gtrsim Obs([A]_a) \Leftrightarrow Obs([C]_a) \subseteq Obs([A]_a)$

$A \sqsubseteq^A C \Leftrightarrow \forall_{[\_]_a \in [\_]^A} . Obs([C]_a) \subseteq Obs([A]_a)$ •

Because what can be observed in one context may restrict what can be observed in other "similar" contexts, and because refinement quantifies over a universe of contexts, we can show that, even without restricting the contexts, some of the powerdomain is redundant.

Lemma 9 *If* $I(A]_\rho) = \{\perp\} \wedge I([C]_\rho) \neq \{\perp\}$ $I([C]_\rho) \xrightarrow{\gtrsim} I([A]_\rho)$ *then* $Obs([A]_{\rho a}) \not\gtrsim Obs([C]_{\rho a})$

Proof

As $I([A]_\rho) = \{\perp\}$ then $\rho \notin Obs([A]_\rho)$ and as $I([C]_\rho) \neq \{\perp\}$ then $\rho \in Obs([C]_\rho)$. Hence $Obs([C]_\rho) \not\subseteq Obs([A]_\rho)$ i.e. $Tr^c([C]_\rho) \not\subseteq Tr^c([A]_\rho)$. Select an a such that $\rho a \notin Tr^c([C]_{\rho a})$ hence $Tr^c([C]_{\rho a}) = Tr^c([C]_\rho)$. As $I([A]_{\rho a}) = \{\perp\} = I([C]_{\rho a})$ and $Obs([A]_{\rho a}) \not\supseteq Obs([C]_{\rho a})$ we have $Obs([A]_{\rho a}) \not\gtrsim Obs([C]_{\rho a})$.

•

Lemma 10 *Assume the Smyth powerdomain*
$$A \sqsubseteq C \Leftrightarrow A \sqsubseteq_{State} \Leftrightarrow A \sqsubseteq_R C.$$

Proof   From Lemma 8 and Lemma 9   •

Lemma 11 $A \sqsubseteq_Z C = [A]_g \sqsubseteq_{DT} [C]_g$ *and* $A \sqsubseteq_{Z^A} C = [A]_g \sqsubseteq_{DT^A} [C]_g$

Proof   It is clear to see that knowing the program (trace) ρ and how many actions terminated is to know exactly the complete trace of an ADT run with context program ρ.   •

Lemma 12 $A \sqsubseteq_{DT} C \Leftrightarrow A \sqsubseteq^s_F C$

Proof $A \sqsubseteq_{DT} C \stackrel{\text{def}}{=} \forall_{[\_]_a \in [\_]} . Obs([C]_a) \subseteq Obs([A]_a)$

1. $\forall_{[\_]_a \in [\_]} . Obs([C]_a) \subseteq Obs([A]_a) \Leftarrow A \sqsubseteq_F^s C$:

Let $[\_]_a \stackrel{\text{def}}{=} (\_ \parallel_{\alpha(C)} \rho)\delta_{Act}$ and $\hat{\rho} \stackrel{\text{def}}{=} \overline{\rho} \upharpoonright \alpha(C)$ and $o \in Obs([C]_a)$.

If $\hat{\rho} = o$ then $o \in Tr(C)$ and from $A \sqsubseteq_F^s C$ we have $o \in Tr(C) \Rightarrow o \in Tr(A)$. hence we know that $o \in Obs([A]_a)$

else if $\hat{\rho} \upharpoonright_n = o$ then $\langle \hat{\rho} \upharpoonright_n, \{\hat{\rho} \upharpoonright_{n+1}\} \rangle \in Ref_s(C)$.

hence $\langle \rho \upharpoonright_n, \{\hat{\rho} \upharpoonright_{n+1}\} \rangle \in Ref_s(A)$ and $o \in Obs([A]_a)$.

2. $A \sqsubseteq_{DT} C \Rightarrow A \sqsubseteq_F^s C$: If $\langle \rho, \{a\} \rangle \in Ref_s(C)$ then $\rho \in Obs([C]_{\rho a})$ and $\rho \in Obs([A]_{\rho a})$ so $\langle \rho, \{a\} \rangle \in Ref_s(A)$ •

Lemma 13 $A \sqsubseteq_{DT^A} C \Leftrightarrow A \sqsubseteq_{F_{ext}}^s C$

Proof   The difference between this and Lemma 12 is that both sides of the equivalence are restricted to traces of A. Hence if $\rho \in Tr(A)$ the above proof holds and if $\rho \notin Tr(A)$ there is nothing to show.   •

Lemma 14 $A \sqsubseteq_{Zg} C \Leftrightarrow A \sqsubseteq_F^s C$

Proof   [8]   •

Lemma 15 $\forall_\rho . [\![C]\!]_\rho Zg \subseteq [\![A]\!]_\rho Zg \Leftrightarrow Obs([C]_a) \subseteq Obs([A]_a)$

Proof   In context ρ, *final* from [8] returns n blanks when n operations have terminated. Clearly this is true if and only if $\rho \upharpoonright_n$ will have been observed in our formalisation.   •

Because of the very close relation between $\sqsubseteq_{DTg}$ and $\sqsubseteq_{Zg}$ (see Lemma 15) we know how to amend the definition of $\sqsubseteq_{Zg}$ so as to permit feature addition with the guarded semantics.

$$A \sqsubseteq_{Zg}^A C \stackrel{\text{def}}{=} \forall_{[\_]_\rho \in [\_]_A} . [\![C]\!]_\rho Z \subseteq [\![A]\!]_\rho Z$$

From Lemma 15 and definitions we can conclude $A \sqsubseteq_{Zg}^A C \Leftrightarrow A \sqsubseteq_{DTg^A} C$.

Lemma 16 $A \sqsubseteq_{Zg} C \Leftrightarrow A \sqsubseteq_{DTg} C$.

Proof   From Lemma 12 and Lemma 14 or Lemma 15 and definitions.   •

Lemma 17 $[\_]^A = \{(\_ \parallel_{\alpha(A)} p)\delta_{Act} \mid \overline{Tr^c(p)} \cap Tr(A) \neq \varnothing\}$ *is a core set of contexts for* $[\_]^{A^+} = \{(\_ \parallel_{\alpha(A)} p)\delta_{Act} \mid true\}$

Proof   We need to show that if $[\_]_x \in [\_]^{A^+} - [\_]^A$ then we can infer what $Obs([\_]_x)$ would be from the observations of $[\_]^A$. To do this we build a context $x + a$ where "+" is choice[2]. $s_{x+a} \stackrel{\text{def}}{=} s_x$ and $Tran_{x+a} \stackrel{\text{def}}{=} Tran_x \cup \{(s_x, a, x) \mid \{(s_a, a, x)\} = Tran_a\}$.

Let $a \in \pi(A)$ then $a \notin Obs([A]_x)$, $Obs([A]_a) \stackrel{\text{def}}{=} \{a\}$ and $[A]_a \in [A]^A \wedge [A]_{x+a} \in [A]^A$. As $Obs([A]_{x+a}) = Obs([A]_x) \cup Obs([A]_a)$ and $Obs([A]_x) \cap Obs([A]_a) = \varnothing$ we know $Obs([A]_x) = Obs([A]_{x+a}) - Obs([A]_a)$.   •

---

[2] Although we could have used choice from ACP we, for brevity of definition, use that from [10].

Lemma 18 $A \sqsubseteq_P C \Leftrightarrow A \sqsubseteq_{Ftest} C$

Proof $A \sqsubseteq_P C \Rightarrow A \sqsubseteq_{Ftest} C$ follows from the observation that Hennessy's "essential tests" [13] are all contained in our process contexts [_].

$A \sqsubseteq_P C \Leftarrow A \sqsubseteq_{Ftest} C$ follows directly from folklore monotonicity of failure refinement with respect to the basic process operators ([6,13]).

$\bullet$

Lemma 19 $A \sqsubseteq_{P^A} C \Leftrightarrow A \sqsubseteq_{Fpro} C$

Proof   Part 1. $A \sqsubseteq_{P^A} C \Rightarrow A \sqsubseteq_{Fpro} C$ Let $\overline{\rho; (\Sigma X)}$ be the smallest context such that $s \xrightarrow{\overline{\rho}} s1 \wedge \forall_{x \in X} .s1 \xrightarrow{\overline{x}}$ (or use ACP's sequential composition ";" and choice "+").

We need to prove 1. $A \sqsubseteq C \Rightarrow \forall \sigma \in Tr(A).Ref(C, \sigma) \subseteq Ref(A, \sigma)$

Using contexts $\overline{\rho; (\Sigma X)}$ where $\rho \in Tr(C\delta_{New}) \wedge X \subseteq \alpha(C\delta_{New})$ we can see that $\rho \in Obs(C) \Rightarrow \rho \in Obs(A)$ hence $\forall \sigma \in Tr(C\delta_{New}).Ref(C\delta_{New}, \sigma) \subseteq Ref(A, \sigma)$.

and 2. $A \sqsubseteq C \Rightarrow Tr(A) = Tr(C\delta_{New})$

As failure refinement implies trace refinement ([13,11]) from Lemma 18 above we have: $A \sqsubseteq C \Rightarrow Tr(A) \subseteq Tr(C\delta_{New})$

Finally we prove: $A \sqsubseteq C \Rightarrow Tr(A) \supseteq Tr(C\delta_{New})$

Use contexts ρ where $\rho \in Tr(C\delta_{New})$ $\rho \in Obs([C]_\rho)$ and by assumption $\rho \in Obs([A]_\rho)$ hence $\rho \in Tr(A)$

Part 2. $A \sqsubseteq_{Fpro} C \Rightarrow A \sqsubseteq_{Pa} C$

From Lemma 7 $A \sqsubseteq_{Fpro} C \Leftrightarrow A \sqsubseteq_{Ftest} C\delta_{New}$.

From Lemma 18 $A \sqsubseteq_{Ftest} C\delta_{New} \Leftrightarrow A \sqsubseteq_P C\delta_{New}$.

From Lemma 17 the only difference between the contexts used in the definition of $\sqsubseteq_P$ and those in the definition of $\sqsubseteq_{Pa}$ is that one can synchronise with actions that do not appear in either A or $C\delta_{New}$. Consequently $A \sqsubseteq_P C\delta_{New} \Leftrightarrow A \sqsubseteq_{Pa} C\delta_{New}$

As $Obs([C\delta_{New}]_\rho^A) \overset{\text{def}}{=} Obs((C\delta_{New} \parallel_{\alpha(A)} p)\delta_{Act})$ and because $New \cap \alpha(A) = \varnothing$ we know: $Obs((C\delta_{New} \parallel_{\alpha(A)} p)\delta_{Act}) = Obs((C \parallel_{\alpha(A)} p)\delta_{Act})$

Hence from definition $A \sqsubseteq_{Pa} C\delta_{New} \Leftrightarrow A \sqsubseteq_{Pa} C$

From Part 1 and 2 we have the result.

$\bullet$

Compilation by Refinement
for a Practical Assembly Language

Geoffrey Watson[*]

School of Information Technology and Electrical Engineering,
The University of Queensland

Abstract. In this paper we extend the conventional framework of program refinement down to the assembler level. We describe an extension to the Refinement Calculus that supports the refinement of programs in the Guarded Command Language to programs in .NET assembler. This is illustrated by a small example.

1 Introduction

Program compilation is among the oldest and most well-explored aspects of computing technology. Nevertheless, modern optimising compilers are large and complex, and bugs are still found in well-used compilers. Consequently, programmers of mission and safety-critical systems are significantly distracted by concerns about compiler correctness. For instance, certification authorities for safety-critical systems require that program compilers are verified or, at least, rigorously validated [1]. Verifying the correctness of an industrial-size compiler has long been recognised as impractical with current proof technology [2, p. 146].

In this paper we approach this problem from the viewpoint of program refinement [3, 4]. A characteristic of the refinement approach is that it is done within a 'wide-spectrum' framework, using a single language that can express both specifications and programming constructs. In our case the language includes both high-level and assembler-level languages. Rather than develop a verified stand-alone compiler, the code generation phase is encoded in the repertoire of refinement laws that generate the assembler code. These laws are all verified in the semantic framework of the refinement theory. Just as the language is 'wide-spectrum' so is the refinement framework, and it supports the formal refinement of a program from its specification right down to executable code.

This concept is not new [5–7]. However, earlier work tended to focus on the principles of the approach and to use a highly simplified assembler. Here we seek to place earlier work [6, 8] in a more practical setting by targeting a realistic assembler language. We address such 'practical' compilation issues as:

- using runtime data structures rather than a flat address space,
- handling multiple variants of the basic instructions, and
- managing different addressing modes.

---

[*] This research has been funded by Australian Research Council Large Grant A00104650, *Verified Compilation Strategies for Critical Computer Programs*.

This is one step towards the goal of using this framework with a real assembler language. In this paper we target a limited subset of Microsoft's *Common Interface Language* (CIL [9]), which is part of the .NET framework [10, 11]. We propose a set of data structures that support a workable system of data refinement between the high-level language and assembler-level CIL constructs.

The paper takes the form of an example, which illustrates the approach that we are taking, followed by an assessment of the results. Section 2 discusses related work. Section 3 describes the refinement language used, and Section 4 describes its semantics in terms of the runtime data structures. Section 5 describes the compilation by refinement strategy and Section 6 gives an example of the proof of one of the refinement laws. Finally, the worked example is given in Section 7 and an assessment of the method and conclusions in Section 8.

2   Related Work

There is a large literature on the principles of the verification and certification of compilers [12, 5, 13–16]. Applications of these methods to larger-scale practical systems include the ESPRIT ProCoS project [17, 18] and work on the formal verification of Java Virtual Machine bytecode verifier [19, 20].

This paper focuses on using refinement as a compilation model, and continues earlier work by Sampaio [5] and Fidge and Lermer [6, 8] by applying the framework developed by the latter to a concrete example. Although our approach was motivated from the refinement framework, in practice it adopts the same philosophy as that of Müller-Olm [7] and the ProCoS project, in that it uses a layered approach to the semantic issues of compilation. However, whereas that work focused on verifying the compiler itself, the work presented here regards compilation as a phase in the total refinement process (from specification to machine code).

3   The Language

3.1   Specifications and the High-Level Language

The process of compilation by refinement is an incremental one — an initial specification is first refined to an implementable program in a high-level language, and this is then refined to an assembler program. This is all done in this a single 'wide-spectrum' language. We use the specification statement [4] to initially specify programs at an abstract level. The specification $\vec{w} : [A, B]$ achieves a state satisfying predicate B starting from a state that satisfies predicate A while changing only variables that appear in the list $\vec{w}$ (the frame).

Since our target is assembler code the high-level language is just an intermediate stage between the specification and the code. We can therefore use an idealised high-level language, introducing only the features necessary to support the refinement process. We use a version of Dijkstra's Guarded Command Language (GCL) [21] for this purpose. This language is simple, well known and expressive. Programs in this language can readily be rewritten in traditional block-structured programming languages.

Skip	**skip**
Sequential composition	$C_1; C_2$
Multiple assignment	$X_1, X_2 \cdots := E_1, E_2 \ldots$
Invariant	$\|[\ \mathbf{inv}\ I\ \bullet\ C\ ]\|$
Iteration	$\mathbf{do}\ \ G_1 \to C_1$
	$\vdots$
	$[]\quad G_m \to C_m$
	od
Alternation	$\mathbf{if}\ \ G_1 \to C_1$
	$\vdots$
	$[]\quad G_n \to C_n$
	fi
Constant declaration	$\|[\ \mathbf{con}\ c \colon T\ \bullet\ C\ ]\|$
Variable declaration	$\|[\ \mathbf{var}\ v \colon T\ \bullet\ C\ ]\|$
Procedure declaration	$\|[\ \mathbf{proc}\ P\,(X) = C_1\ \bullet\ C_2\ ]\|$
Procedure call	$\mathbf{call}\ P\,(X)$
Assertion	$\{P\}$
Coercion	$[P]$

Fig. 1. The High-Level Language.

The full set of constructs in our high-level language is shown in Figure 1. We include some non-implementable constructs which are used both to annotate refinements and to model assembler instructions (Section 4.2). An assertion $\{P\}$ records that the predicate P is true at that point in the program (if it is false the program aborts), while the coercion $[P]$ makes the predicate P true at that point in the program. In general the coercion $[P]$ may achieve P miraculously, but coercions are used in our modelling framework in such a way that this never occurs. The local invariant construct **inv** defines an predicate that is expected to be invariant throughout its block [22]. The remaining constructs are all familiar executable ones [21, 4].

3.2   Assembler Language

The assembler used was chosen on the basis of a number of criteria. Since we were addressing 'practical' issues it should be a subset of a real assembler language, and its formalisation be based on the published definition of that language. For this pilot study the language should be quite small, sufficient to support a basic imperative language such as GCL. We also decided that it should be stack-based, since a register-machine semantics had been used in earlier work [7, 23], and issues such as register allocation were not directly relevant to our main purpose.

The assembler language that we chose is based on a fragment of the CIL language from the .NET framework. This is defined as part of the Microsoft submission [9] to the 'Common Language Infrastructure' (ECMA TC39/TG3)[24] and provides us with an up-to-date stack-based assembler-like notation and a well-defined, and machine-independent, set of assembler-level data structures. The subset used included only basic instructions, such as loads, stores, tests and branches. CIL has the additional advantage that verification of its typing system has been considered elsewhere by Gordon and Syme [25].

A full, but informal, description of the CIL language can be found in the ECMA standard [9]. A typical instruction definition is the following (adapted from [9, Part III,2.38]).

> **ldarg** *num* - load argument onto the stack.
> **Description:**
> The **ldarg** *num* instruction pushes the incoming argument numbered *num* onto the evaluation stack. The **ldarg** instruction can be used to load a value type or a primitive value onto the stack by copying it from an incoming argument. The type of the value is the same as the type of the argument, as specified by the current method's signature.
> **Stack Transition:** $\ldots \mapsto \ldots$, value

The **ldarg** instruction, and the others in the subset of CIL instructions used, are included in our wide-spectrum language. Their semantics is described below in Section 4.3.

By compiling to CIL we are not compiling down to a machine-code level, since a CIL assembler language program undergoes two further stages before it is executed. Obviously programs produced in his way cannot be considered as 'fully verified', since if they were run they would depend on a unverified interpreter. However we are using CIL simply as a convenient vehicle for exploring the fundamental compilation-by-refinement framework in a more realistic setting. Our focus is on the method not the resultant code (and in a wider context our focus is on high-level compilation strategies, which can be studied satisfactorily in the framework presented here).

4   Semantics

In the refinement calculus, specifications and commands are given a semantics in terms of *predicate transformers* [4, Chap. 21]. To give a semantics to the assembler instructions we adopt the strategy, described by Lermer and Fidge [8], of interpreting these instructions in terms of high-level commands acting on runtime data structures. This enables the language to be extended to include assembler instructions without changing the underlying semantics.

4.1 The CIL Runtime Data Structures

In previous work Lermer and Fidge [8] targeted an idealised register machine, but in this paper we use the stack-based language CIL which has a different set of runtime data structures, namely an instruction pointer, an evaluation stack, a local-variable array and a parameter array. There is also a heap, but this is not required for the particular example.

Modelling these machine-level data structures involves addressing the representation of variable values in memory. There are many approaches to modelling memory [5, 26, 16, 27, 28]. One approach is to model it as an unstructured collection of *words* [28]. However, in .NET memory slots are allocated per variable, with a size that depends on the type. Slots are addressed on this basis, and individual words cannot be addressed directly. We therefore model the stack and arrays as sequences of polymorphic values, whose representation in terms of word-size is hidden.

In this paper we shall model the items on the stack as elements of the set *Values*. For simplicity we restrict types to just those used in the example of Section 7, so we define *Values* by:

$$Values = int32 \cup \mathbf{seq}\ int32 \cup Addr$$

(Where $int32$ is the type of CIL's 32-bit integers.) That is, it includes the integers ($int32$), arrays of integers ($\mathbf{seq}\ int32$) and the address type ($Addr$) (to handle reference parameters). The high-level language variables are modelled as functions of type: $identifier \nrightarrow Values\backslash Addr$, i.e., from identifiers to actual values, but not addresses. For example the variable X will be the tuple (X, v) where v is the value of X.

Our model of the CIL runtime data structures has four components.

1. An instruction pointer IP, which ranges over the instruction addresses. We model these by symbolic labels (See Section 5.2).
2. A local evaluation stack S, which we model by the partial function type $\mathbb{N}_1 \nrightarrow Values$ from positive numbers to values. S has an associated stack pointer SP which ranges over the natural numbers. On entry to a subroutine the stack is initialised to be empty $- SP = 0$.
3. A local-variable array L, which is of type $identifier \nrightarrow Values$.
4. A parameter array P of type $identifier \nrightarrow Values$. Indirectly addressed parameters are supported, since elements of P may be of type $Addr$. In this case we define the functions
   - val of type $Addr \nrightarrow Values\backslash Addr$ which retrieves the value of an indirectly addressed item, and which may only be evaluated on the right-hand side of an assignment.
   - loc of type $Addr \nrightarrow (identifier \nrightarrow Values\backslash Addr)$ which retrieves the identity of an indirectly addressed item, and which may only be evaluated on the left-hand side of an assignment. We have that $loc(P[\widehat{x}]) = x$, if $Ind(\widehat{P[\widehat{x}]}, \_)$, i.e. if $P[\widehat{x}]$ contains an address.

Note that we index the L and P arrays associatively, using the *name* of the high-level language variable as the index. We use the notation $\widehat{x}$ to denote the name of the high-level variable x. For example, high-level local variable i corresponds to assembler array element $L[\widehat{i}]$ of the array L.

4.2 Control Flow at the Assembler Level

In an assembler program there is no facility for large-scale control structuring. Instead control flow is determined by the behaviour of the runtime instruction pointer. As commands are executed this pointer moves sequentially through the program store, except when re-directed to a specific address by a jump or branch instruction. To handle this we introduce an explicit control emulation mechanism encoded in GCL, modelling the instruction pointer by IP [13, 29, 5, 8]. Specifically, the operation of the flow of control is emulated by embedding labelled commands in a **do** loop, the most general form of which is:

$$\textbf{do } IP \in L_1 \to C_1; [IP \in L'_1]$$
$$[\!]\ \ IP \in L_2 \to C_2; [IP \in L'_2]$$
$$\vdots$$
$$\textbf{od}$$

Here IP is the instruction pointer, L is a set of labels, and C is either a high-level command or an assembler instruction. Sequencing is controlled by the coercions which follow each command, which constrain the label values that IP may take after completion of the command. The rules for generating the labels ensure that any actual iteration of this loop is deterministic.

In this paper, for compactness of presentation, we make use of the notation:

$$l_1, \ldots, l_n : C|_x^{y_1, \ldots, y_k}$$

as a shorthand for:

$$IP \in \{l_1, \ldots, l_n\} \to C; [IP \in \{x, y_1, \ldots, y_k\}]$$

where x is the label of the next sequential instruction in the program store (if this is one of the possible values for IP after C is executed) and $y_1, \ldots, y_k$ are any other possible values for IP. A vertically-displayed list of such labelled statements is interpreted as residing in the context of an outer **do** loop as shown above.

We label *all* assembler instructions, and in the model there is no distinction between proceeding to an implicit 'next' instruction and an explicit jump or branch to a label elsewhere in the program. Both are handled by the loop mechanism. However the sequencing of instructions is explicit in the refinement laws which generate the assembler code, and it is convenient to retain the identity of the next sequential instruction, as in the notation used here, rather than lose it.

The following code fragment illustrates this notation.

$$a : X := E|_b$$
$$b : \textbf{brfalse } X|_c^p$$
$$c : \textbf{jmp } |^q$$

The first instruction, labelled a, will always be followed by the next, labelled b. The third instruction is an unconditional jump to a label q elsewhere in the program, while the middle instruction may direct execution to either the next instruction c or to the label p.

4.3 Instruction Semantics

Assembler instructions are modelled in GCL within a **do** loop of labelled instructions, as described in Section 4.2, and with CIL runtime data structures declared, as described in Section 4.1. For example, the **ldarg** instruction, whose informal definition was given in Section 3.2, is modelled by the following multiple assignment.

$$p : \textbf{ldarg } X|_{Nxt} \overset{def}{\underset{net}{=}} p : S, SP, IP{:=}(S \oplus (SP + 1 \mapsto P[X])), SP + 1, Nxt$$
$$\text{provided that } Par(X)$$

This definition formalises the description of **ldarg** given in Section 3.2. It increments the stack pointer SP, and assigns the value of the parameter X to the new slot, by extending the stack S. IP is set to the label Nxt of the next instruction. The proviso ensures that it is applied in the correct context — that is, when X is a subroutine parameter.

Note that we use the function override notation $\oplus$ [30] in assignments to array elements. Thus, rather than $A[i] := E$, we write $A := A \oplus (i \mapsto E)$. This makes the calculation of substitutions applied to array assignments more transparent.

All assembler instructions are modelled in this way. A jump instruction such as 'br' is simply modelled by an assignment of a label to IP. Ultimately the correctness of the compiler depends on the correctness of this formalisation, however, in the absence of a full formal definition of CIL, this can only be checked informally.

5 Compilation by Refinement

Refinement of a high-level program to assembler code is performed by the application of refinement laws which refine high-level statements to sequences of assembler instructions. Coping with a practical assembler language like CIL introduces the need for a large collection of refinement laws.

5.1 Refinement Laws

The refinement laws are parameterised by the variables and expressions that occur in the abstract syntax of the high-level commands. (Appendix A lists the laws used in this paper.) The generation of the assembler code for a program requires a recursive application of the laws to the components of compound commands and expressions. To incrementally compile expressions we use 'intermediate-level' instructions **Eval** and **Op** in the definitions of the laws that refer to expressions

[6]. For example, Law L.2 in Appendix A. These must be further refined to executable assembler instructions by the application of other laws. The semantics of **Eval** (X) is just X, since X is a high-level variable.

An important feature of the assembler is the handling of variables. At the high level a variable is simply referred to by name, but at the assembler level such references are implemented by explicit loads and stores, and the instructions for these have many variants. Instructions differ depending on whether the variable is a local variable or parameter, and whether it is addressed directly or indirectly. For example, **ldarg** loads a parameter value, but **ldloc** must be used for a local variable. In addition CIL store instructions, and some loads, must specify, by a suffix, the type of the variable being stored. In the current paper we are only considering variables of type $int32$, so only the suffix **.i4** is used.

This situation has the potential to lead to an explosion in the number of refinement laws if, for each high-level language statement, there is a separate law for every possible sequence of assembler language instructions that it may compile to. We solve this by using the **Load** and **Store** intermediate language instructions to factor out the handling of variable characteristics into a separate 'layer' of laws. The semantics of the intermediate instruction **Store** X is just $X, SP := S[SP], SP - 1$ and of **Load** X is $S, SP := S \oplus (SP + 1 \mapsto X), SP + 1$.

The situation whereby a single high-level command, such as an assignment, may be compiled by a number of variants of assembler code depending on the circumstances requires that many refinement laws are conditional. In such cases, each individual law handles one situation and in combination they cover all possibilities. An example is the two **Store** laws mentioned above, where L.12 handles the case where the variable is local, and L.13 the case where it is a directly addressed parameter (indirect addressing requires a different assembler 'template' and is handled differently — see Laws L.2 and L.3).

A refinement step is performed in a context which includes the current invariant. This contains type information and an indication of how each variable is stored at the assembler level. For clarity we use the following boolean-valued functions, which summarise the different possibilities for variables.

- $Par(x)$ is true if x is a parameter $(x = P[\widehat{x}])$.
- $Loc(x)$ is true if x is local $(x = L[\widehat{x}])$.
- $Ind(x, t)$ is true if x is addressed indirectly and is of type t. That is, if $x = val(P[\widehat{x}])$ and $val(P[\widehat{x}]) : t$ (and by implication, $P[\widehat{x}] : Addr$).
- $Ref(\widehat{x}, array)$ is true if x is a reference to an array.

Conditions on rules are not limited to those listed above. For instance Law L.11 includes the condition $I \in 0 \ldots size(A) - 1$, which ensures that the array element used is within bounds. The conditions could also be extended to include checks such as for integer overflow (for example, by a special conditional form of Law L.16 for arithmetic operators).

The set of refinement laws that we use for compilation is such that at most one law is applicable in any particular context. The compilation of a high-level program by the application of a set of code-generation refinement laws with this characteristic is an algorithmic process that can be done automatically.

5.2 Labelling

In the refinement by compilation formalism *all* instructions are labelled, and *all* sequencing of instructions is managed by labelling (via setting *IP* and the operation of the outer **do** loop). This differs from traditional assembler practice, where sequential control is implicit in the ordering of instructions, and labels are only used as the targets of jumps. Our mechanism is more akin to using code locations at the machine-code level, but code locations can only be determined after all the instructions have been generated.

Our symbolic labels are derived from a set (*lab*) of sequences on a base set. Set *lab* is constructed so that it has both a complete ordering of its elements and a hierarchical structure which allows the insertion of fresh labels. A formal description of this structure, and of the insertion construction, is given elsewhere [8]. There, labels are sequences of integers, written in the form: $n_1.n_2. \ldots$, e.g., 2.1.12.19. However we base our label sequences on the set $a \ldots z$, which restricts the number of sequences available, but is sufficient for the small example in Section 7. This also allows the label sequences to be represented by concatenation without ambiguity, e.g., *acd* rather than *a.c.d*. So our labels are just alphabetic strings.

The labelling mechanism allows us to either generate a set of children for a given label, e.g., you can add *acea*, *aceb*, etc. after *ace*, or, given a sequence of labels, you can add a sibling, e.g., given *aba*, *abb*, *abc* you can add *abd*. In refinements and the refinement laws this labelling system is presented using the following notational conventions:

- The variable $p*$ has, as its value, the first child of label p at the next level down in the hierarchy.
- The variable p' has as value the successor of label p at the same level in the hierarchy.

The mechanism that generates labels must ensure that labels are unique throughout the refinement. Labels are generated by the refinement laws, and it can be shown that the protocol used in these laws satisfies this requirement.

Technically, each labelling introduces a new local block with the fresh labels as local constants. However, such blocks can always be moved outwards to the maximum scope of the refinement, which will then introduce *all* the labels used in the emulation. For clarity we omit this level of detail in our presentation.

5.3 Justification of the Refinement Laws

Stepwise refinement is a process that guarantees that the resultant program (in this case the assembler code) is a valid refinement of the original specification, provided the refinement laws are sound and applied correctly. To justify our compilation strategy we must therefore justify the refinement laws that we use.

Overall the compilation of a GCL program is an application of data refinement. The process is initialised by the introduction of the runtime data structures described in Section 4 (including the **do**-loop which emulates control flow). The high-level program constructs are then refined in this context to sequences of assembler instructions using the laws listed in Appendix A. Thus the compilation refinement laws are only used in this context, and the justification of these laws assumes it.

We may divide the refinement laws into two groups. The first group of laws are those that set up and manipulate the basic compilation machinery. These laws are independent of the CIL-specific runtime data structures. Examples are the law to initially introduce the new data structures (which we do not show explicitly in this paper), and Law L.0 which labels a sequence of high-level commands. Similarly laws that just manipulate control flow, such as those which convert high-level iterations and alternations to assembler level instruction templates, refer only to branch instructions, which, although part of CIL, manipulate only IP. Examples are Laws L.4, L.5 and L.6. Such laws may be proven by exploiting the characteristics of the outer **do** loop which handles the instruction pointer. Proofs of these laws can be found in earlier work [8]. These proofs use techniques based on Back's method of refining action systems [31].

The second group of laws are those that refer to the details of the CIL runtime environment, and give effect to the data refinement from high-level variables to the CIL data structures. The left-hand side of such laws will normally be a high-level assignment statement. This aspect of compilation is not discussed by Fidge and Lermer [6], but Sampaio [5] handles it comprehensively, although in a different manner than is done here.

We justify such laws by showing that the high-level language statement has the same effect on high-level variables as the compiled assembler has on the corresponding low-level ones. The laws assume the emulation context and the mapping of high-level to low-level variables implied by the conditions on the law, for example, $x = P[\widehat{x}] \wedge i = L[\widehat{i}]$ if x and i are a parameter and a local variable respectively. The definitions of the assembler instructions in terms of high-level multiple assignments, described in Section 4.3, enable assembler instructions on the right-hand sides of laws to be eliminated in favour of multiple assignments involving the runtime data structures. Proving such a refinement is then an exercise in conventional data refinement, and can be done for the data manipulation laws in Appendix A. An example is given in Section 6.

6 An Example of the Justification of a Refinement Law

6.1 Proof Strategy

In this section we sketch the proof of Law L.3.

As was described in Section 5.3, for data manipulation commands (which do not involve branching), it is convenient to simplify sequences of stack manipulations before applying data refinement. This allows some of the complexity to be removed in a simpler semantic framework, with the more complex data refinement being applied only to the simplified form.

This type of refinement law often has the form:

$$p \ldots q : C|_x \underset{net}{\sqsubseteq} p \ldots q, r_1 : \ Y_1\ |_{r_2} \qquad (A)$$
$$r_2 \qquad : \ Y_2\ |_{r_3}$$
$$\vdots$$
$$r_k \qquad : \ Y_k\ |_x$$

where C is a high-level command and Y an assembler instruction.

We simplify the right-hand side of this law in a number of stages. First, the list of assembler instructions is converted to a single compound statement using Law C2 of [8]. This states that a sequence of assembler instructions with no branching is equivalent to a sequential composition. That is, where the Y_i are simple commands, and the q_i are fresh labels, we have the equivalence:

$$p \ : \ Y_1|_{q_2} \equiv p : \ Y_1; Y_2; \ldots; Y_k|_x$$
$$q_2 : \ Y_2|_{q_3}$$
$$\vdots$$
$$q_k : \ Y_k|_x$$

Applying this law gives a single compound statement, which is a sequential composition of the assembler instructions, rather than an iteration over a set of guarded commands implicitly sequenced by the value of the program counter.

The second step in the simplification is to replace all the assembler instructions by their definitions as assignments referring to the runtime data structures. The third step is to simplify this sequential composition of assignments, by combining them into a single multiple assignment.

All three of these operations are equivalences. So, if $p \ldots r : Z|_x$ is the result of applying them to Law A above, then a proof of:

$$p \ldots q : C|_x \underset{net}{\sqsubseteq} p \ldots r : Z|_x$$

is also a proof of the original Law A. This still leaves a data refinement from the abstract data of the high-level level to the concrete data of the runtime structures, but this is simpler than proving the original refinement law, since it only involves a single multiple assignment.

6.2   An Example of Simplification

As an illustration we show the simplification of the refinement law for $X := E$, where X is addressed indirectly via a parameter to the subroutine. This is law L.3 in Appendix A, namely:

$$p \ldots q : \ X := E|_x \underset{net}{\sqsubseteq} p \ldots q* : \textbf{ldarg } \hat{X}|_{q*\prime}$$
$$q*\prime \qquad : \textbf{Eval } E|_{q*\prime\prime}$$
$$q*\prime\prime \qquad : \textbf{stind.i4 } |_x$$
$$\text{provided } Par(\hat{X}) \wedge Ind(\hat{X}, int32)$$

Here the surrounding **do** loop, and the introduction of the label constants, is implicit.

Since this law does not contain any jumps or other changes of the flow of control, we apply the process described above. We first convert the right-hand side to the equivalent sequential composition:

$$p \ldots q* : \mathbf{ldarg}\ \widehat{X}|_{q*'} ; \mathbf{Eval}\ E|_{q*''} ; \mathbf{stind.i4}\ |_x$$
$$\text{provided } Par(\widehat{X}) \wedge Ind(\widehat{X}, int32)$$

The next step is to substitute the definitions of the assembler instructions. To do this we need translations for all the assembler instructions that appear in the law. The interpretation for **ldarg** was given above. The translation for **Eval** is:

$$\mathbf{Eval}\ E|_{Nxt} \quad \overset{def}{\underset{net}{=}} \quad S, SP, IP := S \oplus (SP + 1 \mapsto E), SP + 1, Nxt$$

and for **stind.i4** is:

$$\mathbf{stind.i4}\ |_{Nxt} \quad \overset{def}{\underset{net}{=}} \quad loc(S[SP-1]), SP, IP := S[SP], SP - 2, Nxt$$

Applying these definitions gives the right-hand side of the law in the following form.

$$p \ldots q* : S, SP, IP := S \oplus (SP + 1 \mapsto P[\widehat{X}]), SP + 1, q*' ;$$
$$S, SP, IP := S \oplus (SP + 1 \mapsto E), SP + 1, q*'' ;$$
$$loc(S[SP-1]), SP, IP := S[SP], SP - 2, x$$

This is subject to the provisos, $Par(\widehat{X})$ and $Ind(\widehat{X}, int32)$.

Two sequential assignments can be combined by applying the substitution implied by the first to the second. (We use the notation $T_{[A \backslash B]}$ to denote the term obtained from T by substituting the expression B for the variable A.) So we combine the first two assignments, and eliminate ineffective substitutions, to give:

$$p \ldots q* : S, SP, IP :=$$
$$(S \oplus (SP + 1 \mapsto E))_{[S, SP \backslash S \oplus (SP+1 \mapsto P[\widehat{X}]), SP+1]}, SP_{[SP \backslash SP+1]} + 1, q*'' ;$$
$$loc(S[SP-1]), SP, IP := S[SP], SP - 2, x$$

Combining the result with the third assignment gives:

$$p \ldots q* : loc((S[SP-1])_{[S, SP \backslash S \oplus (SP+1 \mapsto P[\widehat{X}]) \oplus (SP+2 \mapsto E), SP+2]}), SP, IP :=$$
$$(S[SP])_{[S, SP \backslash S \oplus (SP+1 \mapsto P[\widehat{X}]) \oplus (SP+2 \mapsto E), SP+2]}, SP - 2_{[SP \backslash SP+2]}, x$$

Applying the substitutions, and simplifying, gives:

$$p \ldots q* : loc(P[\widehat{X}]), SP, IP := E, SP, x$$

We can omit the assignment of SP to SP since this does nothing. (That the value of the stack pointer SP is unchanged by the sequence of assembler instructions is a check on the validity of the refinement, since the stack is not visible at the high level. Note, however, that the stack contents have been modified by the sequence of operations, and so it retains a partial history of the low-level operations.) Expressing the result using the '|' notation for the next address gives Law L.3 in the following form.

$$p \ldots q : \ X := E|_x \sqsubseteq_{\text{net}} p \ldots q * \ : \ loc(P[\widehat{X}]) := E|_x$$

Under the assumptions $Par(\widehat{X})$ and $Ind(\widehat{X}, int32)$ and in the context of the runtime data structures, we can apply the identity $loc(P[\widehat{X}]) = X$ to the left-hand side of the assignment on the right-hand side of the refinement, and in this simplified form the rule can readily be seen to be correct. Other refinement laws in Appendix A which do not alter the flow-of-control, can be handled in a similar way.

7   A Compilation Example

In this section we demonstrate the compilation technique which we have described. The example is necessarily small, and uses a handful of CIL instructions only. All the variables used are signed 32-bit integers, which are are represented in CIL by the type $int32$, and which are handled by instructions of type **i4**.

The example program finds the largest value in the first n elements of an array m of positive integers. It can be specified by the specification statement:

$$r : [true, (n \leq size(m) \wedge r = max\{m(j)|0 \leq j < n\}) \vee (n > size(m) \wedge r = -1)]$$

This specifies a final value for r that is is either the maximum value in the array m, or the value -1 if n exceeds the size of the array (which is zero-based — the .NET default). The frame only shows the variables that may be altered by the program, namely r. We assume that this specification is within a context that defines r, n and m with types integer, natural number and sequence of natural numbers, respectively.

We assume that this original specification has been refined, using conventional refinement techniques [4], to a call to the GCL procedure $MaxN$ shown in Figure 2, and we will use the method of compilation by refinement to compile the body of $MaxN$. For simplicity we consider compilation of the subroutine $MaxN$ in isolation. We assume the existence of the appropriate runtime data structures (which will have been introduced by the calling sequence). The initialisation also introduces the coupling invariant between the GCL and assembler level parameters to $MaxN$, which is expressed by the following symbol table-like invariant.

$$|[\ \mathbf{inv} \quad m = P[\widehat{m}] \wedge P[\widehat{m}] : \mathbf{seq} \ int32 \wedge$$
$$n = P[\widehat{n}] \wedge P[\widehat{n}] : int32 \wedge$$
$$r = val(P[\widehat{r}]) \wedge P[\widehat{r}] : Addr \wedge$$
$$val(P[\widehat{r}]) : int32 \ \bullet \ldots$$
$$]|$$

This invariant implies the following condition, used to select the applicable refinement laws.

$$
\begin{array}{l}
|[\mathbf{proc}\ MaxN\ (\ \mathbf{value}\ m : \mathbf{seq}\ \mathbb{N}_1,\\
\qquad\qquad\qquad \mathbf{value}\ n : \mathbb{N}_1,\\
\qquad\qquad\qquad \mathbf{result}\ r : \mathbb{Z}\ )=\\
\quad |[\mathbf{var}\ i : \mathbb{N}\ \bullet\\
\qquad i := 0;\\
\qquad r := 0;\\
\qquad \mathbf{if}\ n > size(m) \rightarrow r := -1\\
\qquad [\!]\ n \le size(m) \rightarrow\\
\qquad\qquad\qquad \mathbf{do}\ i < n \rightarrow\\
\qquad\qquad\qquad\qquad \mathbf{if}\ m[i] > r \rightarrow r := m[i]\\
\qquad\qquad\qquad\qquad [\!]\ m[i] \le r \rightarrow \mathbf{skip}\\
\qquad\qquad\qquad\qquad \mathbf{fi}\ ;\\
\qquad\qquad\qquad\qquad i := i + 1\\
\qquad\qquad\qquad \mathbf{od}\\
\qquad \mathbf{fi}\\
\quad]|\ \bullet \ldots\\
]|
\end{array}
$$

Fig. 2. The subroutine $MaxN$.

$$Par(\widehat{m}) \wedge Ref(\widehat{m}, array) \wedge Par(\widehat{n}) \wedge Par(\widehat{r}) \wedge Ind(\widehat{r}, int32)$$

We confine our discussion to the compilation of the body of $MaxN$, so the example starts with the subprogram body initialised to:

$$
\begin{array}{l}
IP = a;\\
\mathbf{do}\\
\quad a: Body|_z\\
\quad z: \mathbf{ret}\\
\mathbf{od}
\end{array}
$$

Here $Body$ is the body of the procedure $MaxN$ in Figure 2, and a and z are fresh labels. Label a marks the body of the subroutine, while z is the 'exit' label for the subroutine. In the full compilation system, this structure will be generated by the compilation of $MaxN$'s declarative block.

In the rest of this section we outline the process of transforming the body of $MaxN$ from high-level language to assembler, using the repertoire of transformation rules given in Appendix A.

The first step is the introduction of the local variable in $Body$. This is done by law L.1 (Appendix A) which generates a **.locals .NET** directive, and adds the local variables to the invariant. (We adopt the convention of annotating the refinement step with the law(s) used above the refinement symbol $\sqsubseteq$.)

$$a: |[\mathbf{var}\ i : \mathbb{N}\ \bullet Cmds]|\ |_z\ \overset{\text{L.1}}{\underset{\text{net}}{\sqsubseteq}}\ \#\ .\mathbf{locals}\ \mathbf{init}\ (\mathbf{int32}\ i)$$
$$a: |[\mathbf{inv}\ \ i = L[\widehat{i}] \wedge L[\widehat{i}] : int32\ \bullet Cmds|_z]|$$

Compiler directives, which do not correspond to executable commands, are represented by comments (indicated by '# ...') in the compiled program. The statement $Cmds$ is a sequential composition, so before we can proceed to refine its components, we must convert it to a list of labelled statements using law L.0 [6, Law 3][1].

$$a:(\; i := 0; \qquad\qquad \overset{\text{L.0}}{\underset{\text{net}}{\sqsubseteq}} \; a: \qquad i := 0|_{ab}$$
$$\quad\; r := 0; \qquad\qquad\qquad ab: \qquad r := 0|_{ac}$$
$$\quad\; \textbf{if} \; \ldots \qquad\qquad\qquad ac: \qquad \textbf{if} \; \ldots$$
$$\quad\; \textbf{fi} \;)|_z \qquad\qquad\qquad\qquad\quad \textbf{fi} \; |_z$$

Note that the sequential processing of the three commands, which was initially defined by the sequential composition operator, is now controlled by the **do** loop of the emulator. Law L.0 labels the first component with the original label, and generates fresh labels, which are children of the original label, for the other components. The other laws handle labels in a similar fashion.

We now proceed to refine each of the three sequential commands in turn. Variable i is a local variable with a direct address. It is initialised using law L.2.

$$a: i := 0|_{ab} \overset{\text{L.2}}{\underset{\text{net}}{\sqsubseteq}} a: \quad \textbf{Eval} \; 0|_{aab}$$
$$aab: \textbf{Store} \; i|_{ab}$$

To evaluate an integer constant we use law L.15.

$$a: \textbf{Eval} \;\; 0|_{aab} \overset{\text{L.15}}{\underset{\text{net}}{\sqsubseteq}} a: \textbf{Load} \;\; 0|_{aab}$$

and since $0 \subset int32$ we can apply law L.7:

$$a: \textbf{Load} \;\; 0|_{aab} \overset{\text{L.7}}{\underset{\text{net}}{\sqsubseteq}} a: \textbf{ldc.i4} \; 0|_{aab}$$

this compiles the **Eval** to code. The next instruction is a **Store** (labelled aab). There are two refinement laws in Appendix A that compile the **Store** instructions — laws L.12 and L.13. These are conditional, and the appropriate law is determined by checking which is applicable in the current situation. Since $Loc(\widehat{i})$ is true, law L.12 is applicable (and since $Par(\widehat{i})$ is false, law L.13 is not), so we use law L.12.

$$aab: \textbf{Store} \; i|_{ab} \overset{\text{L.12}}{\underset{\text{net}}{\sqsubseteq}} aab: \textbf{stloc} \; \widehat{i} \; |_{ab}$$

This completes the initialisation $i := 0$. Applying a similar procedure for the initialisation $r := 0$, gives the assembler code for the initial part of $MaxN$ as:

$$
\begin{array}{ll}
\# & \textbf{.locals} \;\; \textbf{init} \; (\; \textbf{int32} \; \widehat{i} \;) \\
a: & \textbf{ldc.i4} \; 0 \; |_{aab} \\
aab: & \textbf{stloc} \; \widehat{i} \; |_{ab} \\
ab: & \textbf{ldarg} \; \widehat{r} \; |_{abb} \\
abb: & \textbf{ldc.i4} \; 0 \; |_{abc} \\
abc: & \textbf{stind.i4} \; |_{ac}
\end{array}
$$

---

[1] We simplify the labelling by only showing the first label in a list. The omitted labels only contribute to label housekeeping, and are never the targets of jumps.

		.locals init (int32 i)		
a :	ldc.i4 0		$acebaaac$:	ldelem.i4
aab :	stloc i		$acebaab$:	ldarg r
ab :	ldarg r		$acebaabb$:	ldind.i4
abb :	ldc.i4 0		$acebaac$:	cgt
abc :	stind.i4		$acebab$:	brfalse $acebb$
ac :	ldarg n		$acebac$:	ldarg r
$acab$:	ldarg m		$acebacb$:	ldarg m
$acabb$:	ldlen		$acebacbb$:	ldloc i
$acabc$:	conv.i4		$acebacbc$:	ldelem.i4
$acac$:	cgt		$acebacc$:	stind.i4
acb :	brfalse ace		$acebb$:	ldloc i
acc :	ldarg r		$acebbb$:	ldc.i4 1
$accb$:	ldc.i4 -1		$acebbc$:	add
$accc$:	stind.i4		$acebbd$:	stloc i
acd :	br z		$acec$:	ldloc i
ace :	br $acec$		$acecb$:	ldarg n
$aceb$:	ldarg m		$acecc$:	clt
$acebaaab$:	ldloc i		$aced$:	brtrue $aceb$

Fig. 3. Final Assembler Code.

The main part of $MaxN$ is an iteration embedded in an alternation. We refine the latter using law L.6:

$$ac\colon \textbf{if} \quad \ldots \overset{\text{L.6}}{\underset{\text{net}}{\sqsubseteq}} \quad ac\colon \textbf{Eval} \quad n > size(m)|_{acb}$$
$$[\!] \neg \ldots \qquad acb\colon \textbf{brfalse} \ ace|_{acc}^{ace}$$
$$\textbf{fi} \ |_z \qquad acc\colon r := -1|_{acd}$$
$$acd\colon \textbf{br} \ z|^z$$
$$ace\colon \textbf{do} \ \ldots \textbf{od} \ |_z$$

The test is compiled using law L.16.

$$ac\colon \textbf{Eval} \ n > size(m)|_{acb} \overset{\text{L.16}}{\underset{\text{net}}{\sqsubseteq}} ac\colon \quad \textbf{Eval} \ n|_{acab}$$
$$acab\colon \textbf{Eval} \ size(m)|_{acac}$$
$$acac\colon \textbf{Op} \ > |_{acb}$$

The rest of the code can be handled in a similar fashion to give a final assembler program, which is shown in Figure 3. The generated assembler code is valid input to Microsoft's *ilasm* assembler program, which generates an executable file. The executable was successfully tested using a test harness written in the $C^\sharp$ language [32].

8 Conclusions

In this paper we have demonstrated how an assembler-level program can be derived from a high-level program using the mechanism of program refinement. We have indicated how the refinement laws used can be justified using a modelling of the assembler instructions into GCL. Unlike previous work, we have placed our model in the context of a 'practical' assembler-level language — a very restricted subset of .NET's CIL. To achieve this we were forced to extend the existing compilation-as-refinement frameworks with: intermediate instructions and conditional laws, to allow the large number of refinement steps to be managed effectively; and context invariants, to maintain essential scoping and typing information normally stored in the compiler's symbol table.

Traditionally program refinement starts from a specification and generates high-level code. Supplementing this with the compilation mechanism described here gives a methodology for the complete formal derivation of executable assembler code from a specification. The work to date shows that this is an achievable goal, but much is left to be done. In particular using a 'real world' assembler has greatly expanded the number of instructions and consequently in the number of laws that must be formulated and proven. The frameworks previously used in the literature are not ideal for this work.

Here we have only presented a very simple example, for instance we have limited data types to just the integers. The handling of more complex types raises a number of issues. Obviously it increases the number of laws, which will be conditional on the types of their operands. Also, where there is no longer a direct mapping of high-level data items to assembler-level ones, the simple scheme for the justification of data manipulation rules, described in Section 6, must be extended by a non-trivial data refinement step after the simplification has been carried out.

Even within the confines of the integers, we have presented a simplified picture. For instance, CIL has 'short' forms of some instructions for use when referring to small integers, but here we have always compiled to the general form. However, the identification of such instances is more efficiently left to post-compilation optimisation rather than extending the rule-set with special cases. Also we have only alluded to the issue of integer overflow, indicating how this might be done in Section 5.1. (Checking for *stack* overflow is another issue. Although it would be simple to ensure that, whenever the stack pointer is incremented there was a condition stating that the result must be in range, checking that this was satisfied would not be generally possible at compile-time.)

Existing approaches to compilation-by-refinement, including that presented here, have some drawbacks. One is the necessity to label every single instruction (see Figure 3!). Another is the difficulty of reasoning about the assembler code. Using the **do** loop emulation means that, although an assembler program might be compiled from a structured high-level program, all the structure has been hidden, and must be reconstructed if required. Even the normal instruction sequencing of an assembler program is hidden in the same way (although it is easier to retrieve this). This causes complications, for example, when constructing arguments to justify optimising transformations.

Finally the application of this type of detailed refinement requires tool support. Work has been done to adapt an existing tool to handle the compilation framework described here [33].

References

1. Ould, M. A. (1990) Software development under Def Stan 00-55: A guide. *Information and Software Technology*, **32**, 170–175.
2. Bowen, J. (ed.) (1994) *Towards Verified Systems*, vol. 2 of *Real-Time Safety Critical Systems*. Elsevier.
3. Back, R.-J. and von Wright, J. (1998) *Refinement Calculus: A Systematic Introduction*. Springer-Verlag.
4. Morgan, C. (1994) *Programming from Specifications*. Prentice-Hall, second edn.
5. Sampaio, A. (1997) *An Algebraic Approach to Compiler Design*, vol. 4 of *AMAST Series in Computing*. World Scientific.
6. Fidge, C. J. (1997) Modelling program compilation in the refinement calculus. Duke, D. J. and Evans, A. S. (eds.), *2nd BCS-FACS Northern Formal Methods Workshop*, Electronic Workshops in Computing, Springer-Verlag, http://www.bcs.org/ewic/.
7. Müller-Olm, M. (1997) *Modular Compiler Verification: A Refinement-Algebraic Approach Advocating Stepwise Abstraction*, vol. 1283 of *Lecture Notes in Computer Science (LNCS)*. Springer-Verlag.
8. Lermer, K. and Fidge, C. J. (1997) Compilation as refinement. Groves, L. and Reeves, S. (eds.), *Formal Methods Pacific '97*, pp. 142–164, Springer.
9. ECMA standardization - original submission. Web: http://msdn.microsoft.com/net/ecma/OctoberSubmission.asp, accessed 1 Nov. 2002.
10. Lam, H. and Thai, T. (2001) *.NET Framework Essentials*. O'Reilly & Associates.
11. Platt, D. S. (2001) *Introducing Microsoft .NET*. Microsoft Press.
12. Jones, C. B. (1989) *Systematic Software Development Using VDM*. Prentice-Hall International Series in Computer Science, Prentice-Hall International, second edn.
13. Hoare, C. A. R. (1990) Refinement algebra proves correctness of compiling specifications. Morgan, C. and Woodcock, J. (eds.), *3rd Refinement Workshop*, pp. 33–48, Springer-Verlag.
14. Hoare, C. A. R. and He Jifeng (1990) Refinement algebra proves correctness of a compiler. *Lecture Notes of International Summer School at Marktoberdorf*, Springer-Verlag.
15. Börger, E. and Durdanović, I. (1996) Correctness of compiling Occam to transputer code. *The Computer Journal*, **39**, 52–92.
16. Fränzle, M. and Müller-Olm, M. (1994) Towards provably correct code generation for a hard real-time programming language. Fritzson, P. (ed.), *Compiler Construction*, vol. 786 of *Lecture Notes in Computer Science*, pp. 294–308, Springer-Verlag.
17. Olderog, E.-R. (1993) ProCoS tutorial: Specifications to programs. *Formal Methods Europe'93 Tutorial Material*, Odense, Denmark, Apr., pp. 422–436.
18. He Jifeng (1995) *Provably Correct Systems: Modelling of Communication Languages and Design of Optimized Compilers*. McGraw-Hill.
19. Coglio, A., Goldberg, A., and Qian, Z. (1998) Towards a provably-correct implementation of the JVM bytecode verifier. *Proc. OOPSLA'98 Workshop on Formal Underpinnings of Java*, Oct.
20. Klein, G. and Nipkow, T. (2001) Verified lightweight bytecode verification. *Concurrency and Computation : Practice and Experience*, **13**, 1133–1151.
21. Dijkstra, E. W. (1976) *A Discipline of Programming*. Prentice-Hall.
22. Morgan, C. and Vickers, T. (1990) Types and invariants in the refinement calculus. *Science of Computer Programming*, **14**, 281–304.

23. Lermer, K. and Fidge, C. J. (2002) A formal model of real-time program compilation. *Theoretical Computer Science*, **282**, 151–190.
24. TC39 - programming and scripting languages.
    Web: http://www.ecma.ch/ecma1/memento/TC39-G3.htm, acc. 1 Nov. 2002.
25. Gordon, A. D. and Syme, D. (2000) Typing a multi-language intermediate code. Tech. Rep. MSR-TR-2000-106, MicroSoft Corporation.
26. Stepney, S. (1993) *High Integrity Compilation: A Case Study*. Prentice-Hall.
27. Morrisett, G., Crary, K., Walker, D., and Glew, N. (2002) Stack-based typed assembly language. *Journal of Functional Programming*.
28. Börger, E. and Schulte, W. (1998) Defining the Java virtual machine as platform for provably correct Java compilation. *23rd Int Symp on Math Found of Comp Sci*, vol. 1450 of *lncs*.
29. Mannasse, M. S. and Nelson, G. (1984) Correct comilation of control structures. Tech. rep., AT&T Bell Laboratories.
30. Spivey, J. M. (1992) *The Z Notation: A Reference Manual*. Prentice Hall International Series in Computer Science, 2nd edn.
31. Back, R.-J. R. (1992) Refinement of parallel and reactive programs. Tech. Rep. Caltech-CS-TR-92-23, California Institute of Technology.
32. Microsoft Corporation (2001) *Microsoft ♯ Language Specifications*. Microsoft Press.
33. Wildman, L. (2002) A formal basis for a program compilation proof tool. Eriksson, L.-H. and Lindsay, P. (eds.), *FME 2002*, vol. 2391 of *Lecture Notes in Computer Science*, pp. 491–510.

A   GCL to CIL Refinement Rules

These are the compilation laws used to compile the example in Section 7. Here X is a high-level variable (with name $\widehat{X}$), N is an integer constant, A is an array, E is an expression, B is a boolean-valued expression, I is an array-index-valued expression, O is a binary operator and C is a command, and p and q are labels.

L.0 $p \ldots q : C_1; C_2|_x \sqsubseteq_{net} p \ldots q* : \; C_1|_{q*'}$
$$q*' : \qquad C_2|_x$$

L.1 $p \ldots q : |[\mathbf{var}\; X_1, \cdots : \mathbb{Z} \bullet C]| \,|_x \sqsubseteq_{net} \#$ .locals init (int32 $\widehat{X_1}, \ldots$
$$p \ldots q \;: |[\;\; \mathbf{inv}\; X_1 = L[\widehat{X_1}] \wedge \ldots \; \bullet$$
$$C|_x]|$$

L.2 $p \ldots q : X := E|_x \sqsubseteq_{net} p \ldots q* : \; \mathbf{Eval}\; E|_{q*'} \; prov.\; \neg Ind(\widehat{X}, \_)$
$$q*' : \qquad \mathbf{Store}\; X|_x$$

L.3 $p \ldots q : X := E|_x \sqsubseteq_{net} p \ldots q* : \; \mathbf{ldarg}\; \widehat{X}|_{q*'} \; prov.\; Par(\widehat{X}) \wedge$
$$q*' : \qquad \mathbf{Eval}\; E|_{q*''} \qquad Ind(\widehat{X}, int32)$$
$$q*'' : \qquad \mathbf{stind.i4}\; |_x$$

L.4 $p \ldots q : \mathbf{do}\; B \rightarrow C\; \mathbf{od}\; |_x \sqsubseteq_{net} p \ldots q : \; \mathbf{br}\; q*''\,|^{q*''}$
$$q*' : \qquad C|_{q*''}$$
$$q*'' : \qquad \mathbf{Eval}\; B|_{q*'''}$$
$$q*''' : \qquad \mathbf{brtrue}\; q*'\,|^{q*'}_x$$

L.5 $p \ldots q :$ **if** $B \to C$ **fi** $|_x \sqsubseteq_{net} p \ldots q* :$ **Eval** $B|_{q*'}$

$\qquad\qquad\qquad\qquad\qquad q*' : \qquad$ **brfalse** $x|_{q*''}^{x}$

$\qquad\qquad\qquad\qquad\qquad q*'' : \qquad C|_x$

L.6 $p \ldots q :$ **if** $B \to C_1 \sqsubseteq_{net} p \ldots q* :$ **Eval** $B|_{q*'}$

$\qquad\qquad \llbracket \neg B \to C_2 \qquad q*' : \qquad$ **brfalse** $q*'''' \, |_{q*''}^{q*''''}$

$\qquad\qquad$ **fi** $|_x \qquad\qquad\; q*'' : \qquad C_1|_{q*'''}$

$\qquad\qquad\qquad\qquad\qquad\; q*''' : \qquad$ **br** $x|^x$

$\qquad\qquad\qquad\qquad\qquad\; q*'''' : \qquad C_2|_x$

L.7 $p \ldots q :$ **Load** $N|_x \sqsubseteq_{net} p \ldots q :$ **ldc.i4** $N|_x$ *prov.* $N \in int32$

L.8 $p \ldots q :$ **Load** $X|_x \sqsubseteq_{net} p \ldots q :$ **ldloc** $\widehat{X}|_x$ *prov.* $Loc(\widehat{X})$

L.9 $p \ldots q :$ **Load** $X|_x \sqsubseteq_{net} p \ldots q :$ **ldarg** $\widehat{X}|_x$ *prov.* $Par(\widehat{X}) \wedge \neg Ind(\widehat{X}, \_)$

L.10 $p \ldots q :$ **Load** $X|_x \sqsubseteq_{net} p \ldots q :$ **ldarg** $\widehat{X}|_{q*}$ *prov.* $Par(\widehat{X}) \wedge$

$\qquad\qquad\qquad\qquad\qquad q* : \qquad$ **ldind.i4** $|_x \qquad\qquad Ind(\widehat{X}, int32)$

L.11 $p \ldots q :$ **Load** $A[I]|_x \sqsubseteq_{net} p \ldots q* :$ **Load** $A|_{q*'}$ *prov.* $Ref(\widehat{A}, array) \wedge$

$\qquad\qquad\qquad\qquad\qquad q*' : \qquad$ **Eval** $I|_{q*''} \qquad\quad I \in 0 \ldots size(A) - 1$

$\qquad\qquad\qquad\qquad\qquad q*'' : \qquad$ **ldelem.i4** $|_x$

L.12 $p \ldots q :$ **Store** $X|_x \sqsubseteq_{net} p \ldots q :$ **stloc** $\widehat{X}|_x$ *prov.* $Loc(\widehat{X})$

L.13 $p \ldots q :$ **Store** $X|_x \sqsubseteq_{net} p \ldots q :$ **starg** $\widehat{X}|_x$ *prov.* $Par(\widehat{X}) \wedge \neg Ind(\widehat{X}, \_)$

L.14 $p \ldots q :$ **Eval** $X|_x \sqsubseteq_{net} p \ldots q :$ **Load** $X|_x$ *prov.* $Par(\widehat{X}) \vee$

$\qquad\qquad\qquad\qquad\qquad\qquad\qquad\qquad\qquad\qquad Loc(\widehat{X}) \vee Ref(\widehat{X}, array)$

L.15 $p \ldots q :$ **Eval** $N|_x \sqsubseteq_{net} p \ldots q :$ **Load** $N|_x$ *prov.* $N \in int32$

L.16 $p \ldots q :$ **Eval** $E_1 \; O \; E_2|_x \sqsubseteq_{net} p \ldots q* :$ **Eval** $E_1|_{q*'}$

$\qquad\qquad\qquad\qquad\qquad q*' : \qquad$ **Eval** $E_2|_{q*''}$

$\qquad\qquad\qquad\qquad\qquad q*'' : \qquad$ **Op** $O|_x$

L.17 $p \ldots q :$ **Op** $>|_x \sqsubseteq_{net} p \ldots q :$ **cgt** $|_x$

L.18 $p \ldots q :$ **Op** $<|_x \sqsubseteq_{net} p \ldots q :$ **clt** $|_x$

L.19 $p \ldots q :$ **Op** $+|_x \sqsubseteq_{net} p \ldots q :$ **add** $|_x$

L.20 $p \ldots q :$ **Eval** $size(A)|_x \sqsubseteq_{net} p \ldots q* :$ **Load** $A|_{q*'}$ *prov.* $Ref(\widehat{A}, array)$

$\qquad\qquad\qquad\qquad\qquad q*' : \qquad$ **ldlen** $|_{q*''}$

$\qquad\qquad\qquad\qquad\qquad q*'' : \qquad$ **conv.i4** $|_x$

Java Card Code Generation from B Specifications

Bruno Tatibouët[1], Antoine Requet[2],
Jean-Christophe Voisinet[1], and Ahmed Hammad[1]

[1] Laboratoire d'Informatique de l'université de Franche-Comté
16, route de Gray 25030 Besançon cedex
{tatibouet,hammad,voisinet}@lifc.univ-fcomte.fr
[2] Gemplus Research Laboratory
La Vigie, Avenue du Jujubier - ZI Athelia IV
13705 La Ciotat CEDEX
antoine.requet@gemplus.com

Abstract. The French BOM[1] (B with Optimised Memory) project has analysed issues related to code generation from B specifications. This analysis was built upon the shortcoming of the existing translators, and led to proposals to generate optimised code suitable for embedding in highly memory-constrained devices, such as smart cards. Two code translators have been developed: one targetting C, suitable for system or virtual machine development; the second targetting object oriented languages. This second translator enables the writing of Java Card[2] applications. This paper presents results of the BOM project related to the Open-Source Java/Java Card translator.

1   Introduction

As smart cards are usually used to provide security to information systems, their security requirements are very strong. With the advent of the new open cards such as Java Card [8][13], which allow downloading new applications to the card during its life cycle, the complexity of the security mechanisms has greatly increased. This motivated the use of formal modelling, in order to prove the correctness of those mechanisms as well as to provide correct implementations of those mechanisms. However, as applications are developed and those cards become increasingly used, it also becomes necessary to be able to formally ensure the correctness of the applications executed on those platforms. Such an assurance would even be required in the case of an applet certification at a high level.

The B method has already been used to specify and implement some smart card operating system components. Although the code generated by the current version (3.6) of *Atelier B*[3] is not suitable for embedding, using a dedicated

---

[1] http://lifc.univ-fcomte.fr/~tatibouet/WEBBOM.

[2] Java and Java Card are trademarks of SUN Microsystems, Inc.

[3] http://www.clearsy.com.

J.S. Dong and J. Woodcock (Eds.): ICFEM 2003, LNCS 2885, pp. 306–318, 2003.

converter already allowed embedding B code for parts of the virtual machine [2]. Therefore, as it has shown its usefulness for verifying the underlying platform, the B method could allow formal development of smart card applications. The platform targeted for those applications is Java Card.

However, Java Card virtual machines remain platforms with stringent constraints, due to the limited memory size and computing power of smart card (The chips used are usually 16-bit chips, and smart card memory rarely exceeds 64 kilobytes of ROM, 64 kilobytes of EEPROM, and 4 kilobytes of RAM), but also to the subset of the Java language supported. Thus, a converter meant to produce Java code embeddable in a smart card from B specifications would require both performing optimisations on the class produced and taking into account the Java subset supported by Java Card.

This paper presents a work aiming to provide such an optimising code translator, by converting B specifications to Java code. This work is a part of the BOM project whose objectives are to:

- Improve the B0 implementation language (similar to classical languages).
- Develop a reliable and memory-optimising code translator from B0 to C and Java
- Provide an Open Source code translator
- Validate the correctness of the designed optimisations (with a view to certifying the translator).
- Apply the B method on the Java Card architecture

Whereas the BOM project aims to develop both a C converter suitable for low-level development using B [6], and a Java converter for application development, this paper focuses to the Java translator. After a short presentation of the B development process, we present the general conversion scheme from B to Java. Then, a sample example is introduced, the translation in Java code is presented and the generation of a Java Card applet is discussed.

2   The B Development Process

The B method is a model oriented formal method based on first order logic, set theory and generalised guarded substitutions. It is fully described in [1] and introduced in [3][12][7]. This method encompasses the whole development process, from the specification down to the implementation (Figure 1). The B-method is supported by industrial tools such as *Atelier B* of *ClearSy*.

An important point with the B method is that every design step can and should be proved. Each specification has an associated set of proof obligations that correspond to the proofs that must be completed in order to ensure the consistency of the specification. The primary component of the B method is the abstract machine. A B specification consists of one or more abstract machines. An abstract machine encapsulates data, properties and operations that manipulate those data. In that way, abstract machines are a concept similar to modules, packages or classes.

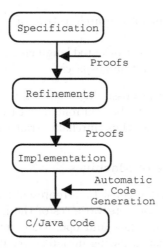

Fig. 1. B method process.

An abstract machine is gradually turned into an implementation using the refinement mechanism. Refinements allow transforming an abstract machine into a less abstract one, by adding implementation details to the specification. Informally, refining an abstract machine consists in replacing the machine by another machine that has the same interface and that preserves the meaning of the abstraction.

An implementation corresponds to the last refinement of an abstract machine, and can be used to generate executable code. It has to be expressed in a subset of the B language called B0. The B0 language matches a subset of imperative languages such as C or Pascal. Contrary to abstract machines, implementations have to be deterministic, parallel substitutions must have been replaced by sequencing, and all the variables must be concrete ones and have an implementable type.

Finally, an important point with the B method is that it clearly distinguishes the part of the specification that are needed for the implementation from the parts only used for specification purpose. This makes it well suited for realistic code generation [4].

3   Conversion Scheme

3.1   Followed Strategy

In the approach that we follow, we aim at a strategy in which:

- The translation of a machine by a class allows the generation of a comprehensible and reusable source code by the designer/developer.
- Low-level optimisations (replacement of the literal constants by the values,..) are left to the compiler of the target language.

- Optimisations dependent on the architecture of the B project are handled by the translator.
- The mechanisms of the object-oriented language are used to provide support for creation of instances and namespaces.

The reasonable use of the possibilities offered by the object-oriented languages makes it possible not to be confronted with constraints justifying the implementation of complex and thus unreliable translators.

3.2   Conversion Scheme of Machines

A natural scheme of conversion consists in representing each B implementation by a class. In this case, the concrete variables of the B machines are translated into instance variables of the class and operations into methods. The default constructor (or the mechanism allowing initialization at the moment of instantiation) allows to translate the *INITIALISATION* clause. This translation scheme has the advantage of proposing a simple management of machine instances, the complexity of this management being delegated to the object oriented language.

Conversion towards an object oriented language can benefit from a conversion scheme dedicated to machines which are not instantiated multiple times. In the case of machines that are instanciated only once in a project, the overhead associated to using instance variables and methods can be suppressed by using class variables and methods. In that case, the default constructor cannot be used for translating the *INITIALISATION* clause anymore. For Java, the static initialisation could be used for this purpose, but as this is unsuported by Java Card, a special class method is used instead. This class method will be called by the implementation which imports this machine.

3.3   Proposal for a Translation in Java

The Representation of a B Project. With each B implementation a class will be associated. As previously seen, if there is only one instance of the machine within the project, this class will only contain class method and variables. In order not to have to manage the access modifiers (public, private, protected, package) for methods and class variables, a package being used as namespace will be defined and each generated class belonging to the B project will be defined in this package. The access rights to the translated entities will be set to *package*.

B Machines and Java Translation Schemes. The use of another machine is done by *IMPORTS* clause. In a general way, the *IMPORTS* clause allows creating new instances of the imported machines. The concept of instance in B is similar to that of the object-oriented languages. A machine instance has data and operations which are defined in this machine and its refinements.

The characteristics of B are as follows:

- It is possible in B not to give a name to an instance, if there is only one instance of this type. For example, if an implementation *M1* instantiates once and only once the machine *M2*, and if the machine *M2* has an operation *f*, then the use in the M1 implementation of *f* is not ambiguous.
- It is necessary in B to give a name to the instances if there is in addition to one. Indeed if *M1* instantiates twice the machine *M2*, the use of *f* is ambiguous: what is the corresponding instance of *M2* ? The solution is to name the instances, for example *i1* and *i2*, and to prefix the call of the function by the name of the calling instance such as for example: *i1.f*.

Thus the general outline is to associate each B instance with an instance of a Java class. However, with the aim of optimization, a B machine which would not be instantiated more than once will be represented by a class and class variables. To carry out this optimization, information concerning the number of instances will have to be determined by the translator.

Two problems arise:

- The imported machine is named but there is only one instance: in the generation of code, this name disappears to leave only the name of the corresponding Java class.
- The machine is imported several times but one of the instances is not named: in the code generation, it will be necessary to choose a name for this machine. The selected name will reveal the name of the class and the fact that it is about an anonymous instance: *anonymous<NameOfClass>*.

Each Java class will include a function *INITIALIZATION*. This function will be preceded by the *static* modifier in the case of a class which will never be instantiated. This function will allow:

- the creation of machine instances in Java via the operator *new*: this operator calls the class constructor which calls the function *INITIALIZATION* of the instance,
- the initialization of variables (class or instance).

4   An Electronic Wallet Example

4.1   Presentation

This section illustrates the previously described translation schema by a simple applet corresponding to an electronic wallet. After a brief description of its functionalities, we present the associated B machines, as well as the corresponding generated code.

4.2   The Electronic Wallet

The wallet example is a Java applet corresponding to a simple electronic wallet application. This wallet stores electronic money by maintaining the current amount it contains, and supports the following three operations:

- credit, allowing adding electronic money to the wallet,
- debit, allowing to remove money from the wallet, and
- check balance, allowing to read the current balance of the wallet.

Those operations allow the user to add money to the wallet (credit), make purchase or withdrawals (debit), and inquire about the current available balance. The wallet has predefined limits on the maximum amount that it can contain, as well as on its maximum transaction amount.

4.3   The Associated B Machines

The B project is divided in two abstract machines and their implementations. One machine corresponds to the electronic wallet itself, and the second one to a sample user of the wallet. Figure 2 presents the BWallet abstract machine and his implementation. As the implementation of the BWallet is very close to the abstract machine, only the value of the constants is shown. Figure 3 presents the implementation of the UsingBWallet machine.

4.4   Corresponding Java Translation

The Java code translation (Figure 4) generates as many classes as B implementations. Those classes are defined in a dedicated package: *wallet* corresponding to the B project. A Java implementation of the BT_IO basic machine for input/output is automatically added to the project. As there is only one instance of the electronic wallet in the B specification, the optimisation allowing translating the variables and operations to static variables and methods is used: the electronic wallet is represented by a class with only static fields and methods.

5   Java Card Code Generation

5.1   Presentation

This section discusses the specificities of the Java Card code generation. It first describes the main differences between Java and Java Card. A possible Java Card implementation of the previous Wallet example is then presented.

5.2   Specificities of the Java Card Platform

As Java Cards are highly constrained devices, the Java Card standard [8] defines a simplified version of Java, more suitable for smart cards. This simplified version corresponds to a subset of Java that keeps the main object-oriented features of Java, but still introduces noticeable limitations impacting the design of a code converter. Among those differences, we can list the following ones:

- No dynamic class loading: all the classes used by an application must already be loaded in the card when the application is loaded.

```
MACHINE
  BWallet
CONSTANTS
  MAX_BALANCE, MAX_TRANSACTION_AMOUNT, DEFAULT_BALANCE
PROPERTIES
  MAX_BALANCE : NAT & MAX_BALANCE < 50000 &
  MAX_TRANSACTION_AMOUNT : NAT & DEFAULT_BALANCE : NAT &
  DEFAULT_BALANCE <= MAX_BALANCE
CONCRETE_VARIABLES
  balance
INVARIANT
  balance : 0..MAX_BALANCE
INITIALISATION
  balance := DEFAULT_BALANCE
OPERATIONS
  ...
  credit (creditAmount) =
    PRE
      creditAmount : NAT & (creditAmount >= 0 ) &
      (creditAmount <= MAX_TRANSACTION_AMOUNT) &
      ((balance + creditAmount) <= MAX_BALANCE)
    THEN
      balance := balance + creditAmount
    END
END

IMPLEMENTATION
  BWallet_imp
  ...
  VALUES
    MAX_BALANCE = 10000 ;
    MAX_TRANSACTION_AMOUNT = 100 ;
    DEFAULT_BALANCE = 0
  ...
END
```

Fig. 2. B specification for the wallet example.

- Static initialisation is only supported for constant values. So, it cannot be used to translate the B initialisation clause
- No garbage collection: the memory used by objects dynamically allocated cannot be reclaimed. Thus, allocating new objects should not be performed lightly. Especially, such allocations should not be introduced by the converter for temporary objects.
- The primitive types allowed are *byte* (8 bits), *short* (16 bits) and *boolean*. The *int* type is optional.
- Multidimensional arrays are not supported: only arrays of dimension 1 can be created.

```
IMPLEMENTATION
  UsingBWallet_imp
REFINES
  UsingBWallet
IMPORTS
  BWallet, BT_IO
OPERATIONS
  main =
    VAR balanceAmount, creditAmount, balanceFuture IN
      balanceAmount <-- getBalance ;
      INT_WRITE (balanceAmount) ;
      creditAmount := 100 ;
      balanceFuture := balanceAmount + creditAmount ;
      IF (creditAmount >= 0) & (creditAmount <= MAX_TRANSACTION_AMOUNT) &
         (balanceFuture <= MAX_BALANCE)
      THEN
        credit (creditAmount)
      END ;
        balanceAmount <-- getBalance ;
        INT_WRITE (balanceAmount)
      END
END
```

Fig. 3. B specification for the sample user of the wallet.

- Multithreading is not supported.
- The security policy is incorporated in the virtual machine.
- Java Card applets use a dedicated framework: a class must inherit from the Applet class and implement the install method (called when the applet is installed in a smart card), as well as the process method (called for processing commands). A transaction mechanism is provided, as well as an object sharing mechanism between applets.

Although Java Cards can appear as quite limited platforms, it must be kept in mind that Java Card is a fast evolving standard, and that those restrictions are usually reduced as technology increases and new specifications are developed.

5.3   The Java Card Wallet Application

This example is inspired from the classical wallet applet [13]. We can see in Figure 5 that the *Wallet* class inherits from the *Applet* class. After the applet is installed the applet can be selected and handle commands using the process method. This method receives data packets (APDU) sent by the terminal. Those APDU are then decoded before handling the real command. Part of the class containing the *credit* operation is provided on Figure 5.

```
/**** class BWallet.java * generated on 20 fvr. 2003 19:06:28 ****/
package wallet;
class BWallet {
  static final int MAX_BALANCE = 10000;
  static final int MAX_TRANSACTION_AMOUNT = 100;
  static final int DEFAULT_BALANCE = 0;
  static int balance;
  static void INITIALISATION() {
    balance = 0;
  }
  public static void  setBalance (int balanceInit) {
    balance = balanceInit;
  }
  public static void  debit (int debitAmount) {
    balance = balance - debitAmount;
  }
  public static void  credit (int creditAmount) {
    balance = balance + creditAmount;
  }
  public static int getBalance () {
    int amount = 0;
    amount = balance;
    return amount;
  }
}
/*** class UsingBWallet.java * generated on 20 fvr. 2003 19:06:28 ****/
package wallet;
class UsingBWallet {
  static void INITIALISATION() {
    BWallet.INITIALISATION();
    BT_IO.INITIALISATION();
  }
  public static void main (String Args[]) {
    INITIALISATION();
    int  balanceAmount;
    int  creditAmount;
    int  balanceFuture;
    balanceAmount = BWallet.getBalance();
    BT_IO.writeInteger(balanceAmount);
    creditAmount = 100;
    balanceFuture = balanceAmount + creditAmount;
    if (creditAmount >= 0
        && creditAmount <= BWallet.MAX_TRANSACTION_AMOUNT
        && balanceFuture <= BWallet.MAX_BALANCE) {
      BWallet.credit(creditAmount);
    }
    balanceAmount = BWallet.getBalance();
    BT_IO.writeInteger(balanceAmount);
  }
}
```

Fig. 4. Java code generated for the Wallet example.

```
package wallet ;
import javacard.framework.* ;
public class Wallet extends Applet {
  ...
  final static byte WALLET = 0xAA;
  // codes of INS byte in the command APDU header
  final static byte GET = 0x01;
  final static byte CREDIT = 0x02;
  final static byte DEBIT = 0x03;
  final static short MAX_BALANCE = 10000 ;
  final static short MAX_TRANSACTION_AMOUNT = 100;
  private short balance;
  public Wallet() { balance = 0; register(); }
  public static void install( APDU apdu ) { new Wallet(); }
  public void process( APDU apdu ) {
    byte[] buffer = apdu.getBuffer();
    if ( buffer[ISO.OFFSET_CLA] != WALLET )
      ISOException.throwIt(ISO.SW_CLA_NOT_SUPPORTED);
    switch (buffer[ ISO.OFFSET_INS]) {
      case GET    : getBalance(buffer)  ; break ;
      case CREDIT : credit(buffer); break ;
      case DEBIT  : debit(buffer) ; break ;
      default: ISOException.throwIt(ISO.SW_INS_NOT_SUPPORTED);
    }
  }
  void credit(Byte[] buffer) {
    byte byteRead = (byte) apdu.setIncomingAndReceive();
    if (byteRead != 1)  ISOException. throwIt( ISO.SW_WRONG_LENGTH);
    short creditAmount = (buffer[ISO.OFFSET_CDATA]<< 8)
                          | buffer[ISO.OFFSET_CDATA+1] ;
    // process data
    if ((creditAmount > MAX_TRANSACTION_AMOUNT)||(creditAmount < 0 ))
      ISOException.throwIt (INVALID_TRANSACTION_AMOUNT);
    // check the new balance
    if ((balance - creditAmount) < MAX_BALANCE)
      ISOException.throwIt(EXCEED_MAXIMUM_BALANCE);
    balance = balance - creditAmount;
  }
}
```

Fig. 5. The Java Card electronic wallet.

5.4   B and the Previous Example

Through the previous example, we can easily see that fully specifying those
applications with B would be a very complex task: the applet handles the low-
level protocol with the terminal as well as the application logic. Moreover, a large
amount of code is tied to the current technology, and so can evolve rapidly. This

is why we suggest that a B development of this application should be written using two separate classes:

- A first class defining the application logic: *BWallet*. This class should be specified and proved with B, and its code should be automatically generated using the converter.
- A second class handling the communication: *Wallet*. This class would handle the communication protocol with the terminal and is tied to the current Java Card technology. This class could be written manually and call the B generated code. In that case, it would however be necessary to check that the preconditions of the B operations are met when they are called.

This corresponds to the case where the B project is not self contained, but is used like a library. So, the code generator cannot determine whether a particular machine will be instantiated once or multiple times. This implies that the user has to manually decide which kind of conversion should be used by the converter. The default behaviour is to generate Java code allowing multiple instances of machines, corresponding to a safe, but potentially less efficient choice. The Java implementation of the Wallet class is given Figure 6.

```
package wallet ;
import javacard.framework.* ;
public class Wallet extends Applet {
  ...

  BWallet bw ;
  public Wallet() { bw = new BWallet() ; register(); }
  public static void install( APDU apdu ) { new Wallet(); }
  public void process( APDU apdu ) {
  ...
  }
  void credit(Byte[] buffer) {
  ...
    bw.credit(creditAmount) ;
  }
}
```

Fig. 6. Java implementation of the Wallet class.

6   Conclusions and Future Prospects

This work is a part of the BOM Project. The BOM Project is a precompetitive project over two years which finished in March, 2003. Many documents describing the reflexions, the approaches chosen, the processes of translation are available from the BOM site pages.

In this work we studied and developed an optimized code generator to translate B proved formal specifications into Java/Java Card language. The main part of the Java/Java Card code generator development is ended at the moment. It is publicly available since January 2003. It is based on the *jBTools*[4] [9][11] which is a B platform under the GPL license developed at the *Laboratoire d'Informatique de Franche-Comté (LIFC)*.

The main characteristics of the translation chain are as follows:

- It is currently based on the syntax of B and B0 supported by *Atelier B*.
- It supports the multi-instances of a B machines and is able to optimize the code if there is only one instance.
- It rather allows the passage of the arrays in parameter of the functions by reference than by copy under certain constraints. The validity proof of this possibility is detailed in [5].
- It allows to choose the type of basic integer for the target platform (short on the Java Card platform). This possibility should be used with precaution because the proof with a tool as *Atelier B* is done for integers on 32 bits.

The first results seem promising and we shall continue to improve the translator by using it on two more complex case studies in order to definitively validate the selected approach. We hope that this work will make it possible to formally develop safe and reliable applications for smart cards.

References

1. J.R. Abrial - The B Book: Assigning Programs to Meanings - Cambridge University Press, 1996 - ISBN 0521-496195.
2. L. Casset, L. Burdy, A. Requet - Formal Development of an Embedded Verifier for Java Card Byte Code - DSN 2002, International Conference on Dependable Systems & Networks, p. 51-56, Washington, D.C., USA, June 2002.
3. K. Lano - The B Language and Method: A Guide to Practical Formal Development - Springer-Verlag - 1996 - ISBN 3-540-19977-2.
4. K. Lano - Formal Object-Oriented Development - Springer-Verlag - 1995 - ISBN 3-540-19978-0.
5. M.-L. Potet - Etude du passage de paramètres dans la méthode B - Optimisation Mémoire - Technical report of BOM Project - URL: http://lifc.univ-fcomte.fr/~tatibouet/WEBBOM, 2001.
6. A. Requet, G. Bossu - Embedding Formally Proved Code in a Smart Card: Converting B to C - 3rd International Conference on Formal Engineering Methods (ICFEM'2000), p. 15-24, York, England.
7. S. Schneider - The B-Method an Introduction - Palgrave - 2001 - ISBN 0-333-79284-X.
8. Sun Microsystems - Java Card™ 2.2 Specification and Development Kit - URL: http://java.sun.com/products/javacard/
9. B. Tatibouet, J.C. Voisinet - jBTools and B2UML: a platform and a tool to provide a UML Class Diagram since a B specification - ICSSEA'2001, 14th International Conference on Software and Systems Engineering and Their Applications, Vol 2, Formal Methods Session, France, Paris (4-6 december 2001).

---

[4] http://lifc.univ-fcomte.fr/ ~tatibouet/JBTOOLS.

10. B. Tatibouet, J.C. Voisinet - Génération de code à partir du langage formel B vers des langages à objets: Etude de la Génération de code Java/Java Card - Technical report of BOM Project - URL: http://lifc.univ-fcomte.fr/~tatibouet/WEBBOM, 2002.
11. J.C. Voisinet, B. Tatibouet, A. Hammad - jBTools: An experimental platform for the formal B method - Principles and Practice of Programming in Java (PPPJ'02), p. 137-140, Trinity College, Dublin, Ireland, June 13-14 2002.
12. J.B. Wordsworth - Software Engineering with B - Addison-Wesley - ISBN 0-201-40356-0.
13. Zhiqun Chen - Java Card Technology for Smart Cards: Architecture and Programmer's Guide - Addison-Wesley - 2000 - ISBN 0-201-70329-7.

Efficient Path Finding with the Sweep-Line Method Using External Storage

Lars Michael Kristensen* and Thomas Mailund

Department of Computer Science, University of Aarhus
IT-parken, Aabogade 34, DK-8200 Aarhus N, Denmark
{lmkristensen,mailund}@daimi.au.dk

Abstract. The sweep-line method deletes states on-the-fly during state space exploration to reduce peak memory usage. This deletion of states prohibits the immediate generation of, e.g., an error-trace when the violation of a safety property is detected. We address this problem by combining the sweep-line method with storing a spanning tree of the explored state space in external storage on a magnetic disk. We show how this allows us to easily obtain paths in the state space, such as error-traces. A key property of the proposed technique is that it avoids searching in external storage during the state space exploration and gives the same reduction in peak memory usage as the stand-alone sweep-line method. We evaluate the proposed technique on a number of example systems, and compare its performance to a related technique. These practical experiments demonstrate how the suggested technique complements existing techniques based on using external storage.

1   Introduction

State space methods [6, 17] are based on calculating all reachable states and state changes of a finite-state system and representing these as a directed graph. One advantage of state space methods is that they allow most of the underlying mathematics to be encapsulated and hidden inside supporting computer tools. This makes state space methods highly automatic and easy to use. A second advantage of state space methods is that they can provide the analyst with constructive debugging information when an error in the system is detected. Debugging information can often be provided as an *error-trace*, which is a path in the state space leading from the initial state to a state violating a desired safety property. Recently, state space methods and path finding for timed automata [2] have been used for the synthesis of schedules in real-time control systems [3,10]. Generation of error-traces and synthesis of schedules can both be formulated as the problem of finding a path from the initial state leading to a state satisfying a certain state predicate. Supporting such *path finding* is hence an important requirement to state space methods.

The main disadvantage of state space methods is the inherent state explosion problem [39] which, for certain systems, implies that one rapidly runs out of

---

* Supported by the Danish Natural Science Research Council.

J.S. Dong and J. Woodcock (Eds.): ICFEM 2003, LNCS 2885, pp. 319–337, 2003.
© Springer-Verlag Berlin Heidelberg 2003

memory, thereby prohibiting state space analysis. A multitude of state space reduction methods have been developed to alleviate this problem (see [39] for a survey). Of particular relevance in the context of this paper are methods such as the *state space caching method* [20,13,15,23], the *pseudo-root* technique [29], *hash compaction* [41,32,34], and *bit-state hashing* [16,18]. These methods delete state information on-the-fly during state space exploration and support path finding by relying on a depth-first exploration of the state space. In depth-first exploration, a path from the initial state to a state currently being examined is always available on the depth-first stack. Other methods of relevance are methods exploiting external storage [35,33] such as magnetic disks for storage of the state space. With these methods, states are written to disk during state space exploration to free up main memory. The key problem with using disk storage is that searching for states on disk is time expensive. Hence, the number of searches for states stored on disk must be reduced to make the use of external storage applicable in practice.

The sweep-line method [5,25,26] is aimed at the verification of safety properties. It belongs to the family of state space methods which deletes information about states during state space exploration. It uses the notion of *progress measures* as a heuristic to delete states. The original sweep-line method was developed in [5] and later generalised in [25] to deal with reactive systems. The sweep-line method guarantees full coverage of the state space, but may explore states several times. The sweep-line method has been applied in practice on some example systems in [5,25,26], and on the WAP Transaction Protocol in [14]. The case studies have demonstrated that the sweep-line method provides a good trade-off between space reduction and time usage. It was shown in [26] how progress measures can be derived fully automatically for systems modelled in a compositional framework.

A main problem with the sweep-line method not addressed in any of the papers [5,25,26] is path finding. The sweep-line method inherently relies on exploration of the states according to the progress measure. Together with the deletion of states, this has the effect that when a path to a state currently being examined is desired, states on a path leading to this state cannot be assumed to be in memory. This prohibits the immediate generation of a path.

The first contribution of this paper is a technique which uses external storage on a disk to support path finding with the sweep-line method. The idea is to write a spanning tree for the explored states on disk during sweep-line state space exploration. The proposed technique avoids *any* searches for states in external storage during the state space exploration, and gives the same reduction in peak memory usage as the stand-alone sweep-line method. Subsequent path finding can be conducted by making a seek in the external storage for each state on the path. The second contribution is experiments with an implementation of the path finding technique comparing it to a related disk-based technique [35]. These experiments demonstrate that the overhead incurred by additionally writing states to disk is insignificant, and that the path finding technique complements existing techniques.

This paper is organised as follows. Section 2 introduces the notation for labelled transition systems and gives the necessary background on the sweep-line method. Section 3 introduces the path finding technique and presents the associated algorithms. The correctness of the algorithms is established in Sect. 4. Section 5 presents some variants of the path finding technique. In Sect. 6 we report on some experimental results obtained with an implementation of the algorithms. Finally, in Sect. 7 we draw the conclusions and give a further discussion of related work. The reader is assumed to be familiar with the basic ideas of state space methods.

2   The Sweep-Line Method

To make our presentation independent of any concrete modelling language, we formulate our results in the context of (finite) labelled transition systems.

Definition 1 (Labelled Transition System). *A labelled transition system (LTS) is a tuple $\mathcal{L} = (S, \Sigma, \Delta, \iota)$, where S is a finite set of states, Σ is a finite set of transition labels, $\Delta \subseteq S \times \Sigma \times S$ is the transition relation, and $\iota \in S$ is the initial state.* □

We will use the notation $s \xrightarrow{a} s'$ to mean $(s, a, s') \in \Delta$ and when not concerned with the label, we will write $s \to s'$ for $\exists a \in \Sigma : s \xrightarrow{a} s'$. We will also write $s_1 \xrightarrow{a_1} s_2 \xrightarrow{a_2} s_3 \ldots s_{n-1} \xrightarrow{a_{n-1}} s_n$ for $s_1 \xrightarrow{a_1} s_2 \wedge s_2 \xrightarrow{a_2} s_3 \wedge \cdots \wedge s_{n-1} \xrightarrow{a_{n-1}} s_n$ and use $\to^*$ for the transitive and reflexive closure of Δ, i.e., $s \to^* s'$ if there exists a sequence $s_1 \to s_2 \to s_3 \cdots \to s_n$ with $s = s_1$ and $s' = s_n$. In particular $s \to^* s$ for all $s \in S$. We say that s' is *reachable* from s if and only if $s \to^* s'$, and we let reach(s) denote the set of states reachable from s, i.e., reach(s) = $\{ s' \in S \mid s \to^* s' \}$.

In the following we are concerned with exploring the *state space* of a labelled transition system, by which we mean the set of states, reach(ι), reachable from the initial state. We will call this set the set of *reachable states*.

The sweep-line method reduces peak memory usage by deleting states when these are guaranteed not to be reached again during the exploration [5], or when they are unlikely to be reached again [25]. The sweep-line method is based on the notion of *progress measures*. A progress measure provides an ordering of the states of the transition system and can be seen as an approximation of the reachability relation. The reader is referred to [26] for a description of how to compute a progress measure in a compositional framework prior to state space exploration. Other sources of progress measures are sequence numbers and retransmission counters in communication protocols, control flow in processes, and time in certain formalisms with time [21].

Definition 2 (Progress Measure [25]). *A progress measure on an LTS $\mathcal{L} = (S, \Sigma, \Delta, \iota)$ is a tuple $\mathcal{P} = (O, \sqsubseteq, \psi)$ such that $(O, \sqsubseteq)$ is a total order and $\psi : S \to O$ is a progress mapping from states into a set of progress values O. A monotonic progress measure is a progress measure satisfying: $\forall s, s' \in$ reach(ι) : $s \to^* s' \Rightarrow \psi(s) \sqsubseteq \psi(s')$.* □

A monotonic progress measure provides a conservative estimate of reachability relation $\to^*$ in that if $\psi(s) \sqsubseteq \psi(s')$ for $s, s' \in S$, then it is impossible to reach s from s'. Conventional state space exploration keeps the set of explored states in memory to recognise already visited states. For a system with a monotonic progress measure it is safe to delete states from memory with a progress measure strictly smaller than the minimal progress value among the set of unprocessed states. Deleting such states is the basic idea of the sweep-line method. When the progress measure is not monotonic (which can be detected on-the-fly during state space exploration) the method still deletes states with a progress value smaller than the minimal progress among the unprocessed states. However, when a *regress edge* (s, a, s') violating monotonicity is encountered, i.e., $\psi(s) \sqsupseteq \psi(s')$, the state s' is marked as *persistent* preventing it from being deleted again.

The sweep-line method is illustrated in Fig. 1 (based on [25]) which shows three snapshots from a state space exploration. To simplify the figures we have omitted labels on the edges. The states are ordered left to right according to their progress value. In Fig. 1 (a) we have explored the states ι and s_1. Both of these states have been deleted from memory again since they have a progress measure which is smaller than the current minimal progress value among the unprocessed states s_2, s_3, and s_4. The conceptual sweep-line (the vertical dashed line) is immediately to the left of the unprocessed states.

The sweep-line method explores states in a least-progress-first order. Hence, either s_2 or s_3 will be selected for processing next. When both have been explored, the sweep-line moves to the right, s_2 and s_3 are deleted from memory, and the situation shown in Fig. 1 (b) is obtained. The states s_5, s_6, and s_4 will now be explored and eventually the situation depicted in Fig. 1 (c) is obtained. Now s_8 will be explored, and the unexplored state s_9 and the deleted state s_6 are discovered as successor states of s_8. The edges $s_8 \to s_6$ and $s_8 \to s_9$ are both *regress-edges* and the states s_6 and s_9 are marked as *persistent*. This ensures that they will not be deleted in subsequent sweeps. States s_6 and s_9 are also set aside as *roots* for the next sweep. When the current sweep terminates (which

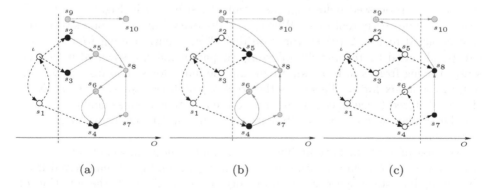

(a)   (b)   (c)

Fig. 1. Snapshots of sweep-line state space exploration.

will happen when s_8 has been explored), the algorithm initiates a new sweep using s_6 and s_9 as starting points (roots). When the regress-edge $s_8 \rightarrow s_6$ is rediscovered in this sweep, s_6 will not have been deleted since it was marked as persistent in the previous sweep. Similarly for the regress-edge from s_8 to s_9. Multiple sweeps are needed, since we cannot distinguish a regress-edge leading to a previously explored state (e.g., s_6) from a regress-edge leading to a state not explored in a previous sweep (e.g., s_9). For further details on the sweep-line method see [5, 25].

3   Path Finding with the Sweep-Line Method

It follows from Fig. 1 that path finding with the sweep-line method is problematic because of the least-progress-first exploration, and the way states are deleted. Suppose that we are interested in finding a path from the initial state to each of the terminal states of the system (i.e., states without outgoing arcs). When the terminal state s_{10} of Fig. 1 is discovered in the beginning of the second sweep, only the persistent states s_6 and s_9 will be stored in memory.

The basic idea in our path finding technique is to write a directed tree to a file on disk during state space exploration. This tree is rooted in the initial state ι. An edge from s to s' in the tree is represented by associating an index (file position) with s' which points to the index (file position) where the *parent* (predecessor) s is stored. Figure 2 illustrates how the tree is stored in a file. Figures 2 (a–c) correspond to the snapshots shown in Figs. 1 (a–c). Figure 2 (d) depicts the situation when s_{10} is discovered at the end of the second sweep. The parent index of a state is drawn as an arc. In the figures we have only indicated the storage of states. In the algorithm to be presented next, both labels and states will be written to disk.

In Fig. 2 (a) (corresponding to Fig. 1 (a)), states ι, and $s_1, \ldots, s_4$ have been written to disk. States s_2 and s_3 have a parent index pointing to the location of state ι. This corresponds to (ι, s_2) and (ι, s_3) being edges in the tree. Similarly, s_4 has a parent index pointing to s_1 which in turn has a parent index pointing to ι. If s_2 is processed before s_3, we obtain the situation in Fig. 2 (b). In this case s_2 will be the parent of s_5. When s_{10} is discovered in the second sweep, the tree depicted in Fig. 2 (d) is stored on disk. Now a path leading from ι to s_{10} can be obtained by recursively following the parent index associated with each state starting from s_{10}. From s_{10} we obtain the index for s_9 and from s_9 we can obtain the index for s_8. This gives the (reverse) path $(s_{10}, s_9, s_8, s_5, s_2, \iota)$. Note that s_6 is stored twice since it is discovered the first time from s_4, and once again (in the second sweep) from s_8 after it has been deleted, but before it is made persistent.

We now present the path finding algorithm introduced informally above. The state space exploration algorithm is shown in Fig. 3, and has been derived from the sweep-line state space exploration algorithm in [25] with the addition of writing a tree to external storage during state space exploration, and terminating the state space exploration when a state is encountered satisfying a given predicate ϕ on states. We assume a linear external storage (e.g., a file) in which data written is appended to the end.

The algorithm operates on four sets: N is the set of states (nodes) currently stored in memory, R is the set of nodes to be used as roots for the next sweep, P is the set of persistent states, and U is the set of unprocessed states, i.e., states for which successor states have not yet been calculated. The algorithm starts by writing the initial state ι to external storage using the procedure WRITE (line 5). The WRITE procedure takes the label and state provided as second and third argument, and write them to external storage together with the parent index provided as first argument. The WRITE procedure returns the index in external storage at which the state, label, and parent index were written. The initial state is (by convention) written at index 0 with parent index 0, and a no label (indicated by $\perp \notin \Sigma$).

The algorithm then performs a number of sweeps (procedure SWEEP in lines 12–44), newly discovered states are written to external storage (line 26) with the appropriate parent index. In each sweep regress-edges are identified (line 30), and the destination states of regress-edges are marked as persistent and are used as root states (lines 31–32) in the next sweep. Once a node has been marked as persistent, it is not deleted in line 41. If a state s' is found satisfying the state predicate ϕ, the index where s' is stored in external storage is returned. In lines 6,

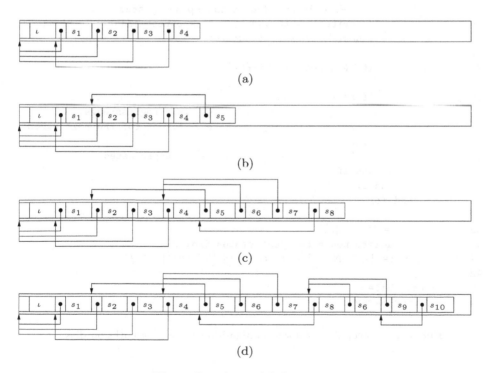

(a)

(b)

(c)

(d)

Fig. 2. Snapshots of disk storage.

```
1      R := {ι}    // the initial state is root in first sweep
2      N := {ι}    // create a node for the initial state
3      P := ∅      // initially there are no persistent states
4
5      index(ι) := WRITE(0,⊥,ι) // write ι to disk with index 0
6      if φ(ι) return index(ι)
7
8      while R ≠ ∅ do
9         SWEEP(R, N, P)
10     end while
11
12     where proc SWEEP(R, N, P) is
13        U := R // mark all root states for this sweep unprocessed.
14        R := ∅
15        while U ≠ ∅
16           // select s minimal wrt. ψ and ⊑ in U
17           select s ∈ U such that ∀ s' ∈ U : ψ(s) ⊑ ψ(s')
18
19           // explore successors of s
20           forall (a, s') such that s ─ᵃ→ s'
21              if s' ∉ N
22                 N := N ∪ {s'}
23
24                 // s ─ᵃ→ s' is an edge in the spanning tree
25                 // write s' with index of s as parent index
26                 index(s') := WRITE(index(s),a,s')
27
28                 if φ(s') return index(s')
29
30                 if ψ(s) ⊐ ψ(s')
31                    P := P ∪{s'}    // s ─ᵃ→ s' is a regress-edge
32                    R := R ∪{s'}    // make s' a root for the next sweep.
33                 else
34                    U := U ∪{s'}    // mark s' as unprocessed
35                 end if
36              end if
37           end for
38
39           U := U − {s}
40           // delete non-persistent states from N
41           N := {s ∈ N |∃ s' ∈ U : ψ(s') ⊑ ψ(s)} ∪ P
42
43        end while
44     end proc SWEEP
```

Fig. 3. The sweep-line exploration algorithm for storing paths on disk.

```
1    proc FINDPATH(i)
2
3    path : dynamic array of states
4    j := 0
5
6    do
7         (i, a, s) := READ(i) // read item stored at index i
8         path[j] := (a, s)
9         j := j + 1
10   until (a = ⊥)
11
12   return path
```

Fig. 4. Reading a path from external storage.

26, and 28 we use **index** to obtain the index in external storage at which the
state provided as argument is stored. Also, in lines 5 and 26 we record the index
at which a given state is stored.

From the above it follows that we only need to remember the index of states
currently stored in main memory. The index of a state s is therefore stored
together with the state itself, and deleted when the state is deleted in line 41.
This ensures that we only keep the index of states that are currently stored in
main memory.

If a state satisfying ϕ is found, the index returned by the algorithm can
then be used as argument to the procedure FINDPATH shown in Fig. 4. The
procedure FINDPATH uses the tree stored in external storage to obtain the path.
The procedure FINDPATH uses another procedure, READ, to fetch states from
external storage. Provided with an index in external storage, READ returns the
state s and label a stored at that index, and the parent index i associated with
the label and state. The procedure FINDPATH requires a seek in external storage
for each state on the path, but no searches.

4   Correctness of the Path Finding Technique

The algorithm in Fig. 3 differs from the sweep-line state space exploration algorithm in [25] only in the use of WRITE for storing the labels, states, and
parent index in external storage. The theorem from [25] concerning coverage
and termination of the sweep-line method therefore remains valid.

Theorem 1 ([25]). *The sweep-line algorithm in Fig. 3 terminates after having
explored at most* $(|D| + 1) \cdot |\mathsf{reach}(\iota)|$ *states, where D denotes the destinations of
regress-edges:* $D = \{ s' \in \mathsf{reach}(\iota) \mid s \to s' \land \psi(s') \sqsubset \psi(s) \}$. *Upon termination
all states reachable from ι have been explored at least once.*   □

In addition, we prove the following theorem regarding paths stored in external
storage and extracted by the algorithm in Fig. 4. The theorem states that the

path obtained for given state is finite and leads to the initial state, i.e., the reverse path is a path in the state space leading from the initial state to the given state.

Theorem 2. *Let (a, s) be the label and state in external storage at index i. The sequence (a_j, s_j) of states s_j and labels a_j obtained by following the stored indices backwards is finite. Furthermore, let $s_0, a_0, s_1, a_1, \ldots a_{n-1}, s_n$ be the finite sequence, with $s = s_0$ and $a = a_0$, then: $s_n = \iota$ and $s_j \xrightarrow{a_{j-1}} s_{j-1} \in \Delta$ for $j = 1, \ldots, n$.* $\square$

Proof. The theorem follows from the following invariant, which holds at any time in procedure SWEEP:

> *For all $s \in U \cup R$, s is in external storage and s has the property stated by the theorem.*

The invariant clearly holds initially since $R = \{\iota\}$, $U = \emptyset$, and ι has been written to external storage, where the empty sequence from ι to ι demonstrating the required property. The invariant is also preserved by line 13–14 when updating R and U. When s' is added to R in line 32 or U in line 34 it has previously been written to external storage in line 26. When writing s' to external storage we store $(\text{index}(s), a, s')$ at $\text{index}(s')$. Since $s \in U$ we have by the invariant that following the indices backwards yields a sequence: $s = s_1, a = a_1, s_2, a_2, \ldots a_{n-1}, s_n = \iota$. Following the indices backwards from s' hence yields the sequence: $s' = s_0, a = a_0, s = s_1, a = a_1, s_2, a_2, \ldots a_{n-1}, s_n = \iota$. Since from line 20: $s \xrightarrow{a} s' \in \Delta$ we have $s_j \xrightarrow{a_{j-1}} s_{j-1} \in \Delta$ for $j = 1, \ldots, n$. The state s' therefore satisfies the property expressed by the invariant. $\square$

The fact that a path can be obtained to any reachable state follows from the observation that the sweep-line method according to Thm. 1 explores all states. Hence if there exists a reachable state satisfying the state predicate ϕ, such a state will be in U at some point.

An important measure of the quality of paths is length: for error-traces shorter paths are preferred since they make it easier to identity the source of the error. The sweep-line method explores states in a least progress-first order which is done to move the sweep-line as soon as possible, and hence promote deletion of states in line 41. Since least-progress-first traversal (in general) is different from breadth-first traversal, a shortest path leading to a state satisfying ϕ is not necessarily obtained. For monotone progress measures regress-edges exist and only a single sweep is conducted. In this case, we obtain a path to the state with minimal progress value that satisfies ϕ (if such a state exists). If the progress value of a state is related to the number of transitions required to reach the state (which intuitively and in practice is often the case), then we can expect to get reasonably short paths.

The sweep-line algorithm generally conducts multiple sweeps, and it terminates in the earliest sweep at which a state s is found satisfying ϕ. The number of sweeps conducted therefore equals the minimal number of regress-edges required to reach a state satisfying ϕ with the sweep-line algorithm. Moreover, the state obtained has a minimal progress value among the states explored in that sweep since states are processed in a least-progress first order. Let for a path σ, $RE(\sigma)$ denotes the number of regress edges on σ, then we have the following proposition regarding the quality of paths obtained with the sweep-line path finding technique.

Proposition 1. *Let* $\sigma_\phi = (\iota = s_0, a_0, s_1, a_1, \ldots, a_{n-1}, s_n)$ *denote the path leading to a state satisfying the state predicate* ϕ *obtained via the sweep-line algorithm in Fig. 3. Let* $\sigma'_\phi = (\iota = s'_0, a'_0, s'_1, a'_1, \ldots, a'_{n-1}, s'_n)$ *be any path in the state space leading from the initial state to a state satisfying the state predicate* ϕ. *Then:* $RE(\sigma_\phi) \leq RE(\sigma'_\phi)$ *and if* $RE(\sigma_\phi) = RE(\sigma'_\phi)$ *then* $\psi(s_n) \sqsubseteq \psi(s'_n)$. $\qquad\square$

5   Variants of Sweep-Line Path Finding

The algorithm in Fig. 3 stores both states and labels in external storage. It is, however, sufficient to store the states. The labels can be reconstructed afterwards by computing for each state, s_i, on the path $\iota = s_0, s_1, \ldots, s_n$, the set of enabled transitions and selecting a transition which leads to s_{i+1}. For modelling languages where transitions are deterministic, it suffices to store the labels in external storage. When a path $a_0, a_1, \ldots a_{n-1}$ leading to s is obtained, the intermediate states can be determined uniquely since transitions are deterministic, i.e., for a given intermediate state, s_i, the transition label, a_i, determines a unique successor state, s_{i+1}. Petri nets [31] is an example of a modelling language where transitions are deterministic. Transitions in process algebra [28] may become nondeterministic due to renaming or hiding.

Both of the above variants which either stores states or transitions reduce the amount of information written to external storage, and hence will both save space in external storage and also time during state space exploration.

The use of external storage to achieve memory savings was also considered in [35]. The approach in [35] is based on breadth-first exploration of the state space. To reduce the run-time overhead when searching in external storage, all states in a given breadth-first level are generated before the external storage is linearly searched to filter out previously visited states. The run-time overhead incurred by the sweep-line method due to multiple exploration of states could be reduced by using a variant of the technique suggested in [35]: whenever a sweep has been conducted, the external storage is linearly searched for the root states, i.e., states which were at the end of regress-edges. Root states which have been seen before can then be eliminated in line 13 of the algorithm in Fig. 3 from the set of states used as roots in the sweep. This search could be optimised by storing states in external storage according to their progress value. We compare our path finding technique and the disk-based state space exploration method of [35] on a number of example systems in the next section.

6   Experiments

In this section we apply the path finding technique to a number of example systems and compare the results obtained to those that can be obtained with the closely related disk-based technique described in [35]. The results were obtained using an implementation in the Design/CPN tool [1], a tool for constructing and analysing *Coloured Petri nets* (CPN) [21]. The prototype is implemented in the *Standard ML* (SML) programming language [36]. The user provides a progress measure to the tool by writing an SML function mapping a state into an integer. The ordering on progress values is the usual total ordering on integers. Predicates are provided as SML functions mapping states into boolean values. The experiments were conducted on a 1Ghz Pentium III Linux PC with 1Gb of memory. We have implemented the path finding technique such that only transition labels are written to external storage since the modelling language used for the example systems is Petri nets. The reduction in peak memory usage reported below for the sweep-line method is better than the corresponding results in [5,25,14]. The reason is that the implementation uses the approach described in [26] when deleting states from memory.

Database Replication Protocol. The first example we consider is a database replication protocol [21]. The protocol describes the communication between a set of database managers for maintaining consistent copies of a distributed database. When a database manager updates its local copy of the database it broadcasts an update request to all other database managers. The other database managers then perform the update on their local copies and then acknowledge that the update has been performed. The progress measure for the protocol is based on the control flow of the database managers and an ordering on the database managers. See [25] for details.

The performance results obtained for full state space exploration, sweep-line exploration, and the disk-based breadth-first exploration of [35] is given in Table 1. Experiments were conducted for different numbers of database managers, shown in the $|D|$ column. The two *Full* columns show the total number of reachable states and the time it took to generate the full state space. The time is shown in the form *h:mm:ss* or *mm:ss*, where h denotes hours, mm denotes minutes, and ss seconds. The *Sweep-Line Method* columns show the *Total* number of states explored by the sweep-line method, and the peak (Pk) number of states stored during the exploration. The *Basic* column gives the time used to explore the state space using the basic sweep-line method from [25], i.e., without writing to external storage. The *Path* column gives the time used to explore the state space when writing to external storage, i.e., using the algorithm in Fig. 3. The difference between the *Basic* column and the *Path* column is hence the overhead added by writing to external storage.

For the protocol, we are interested in finding a path to a state where all the other database managers have performed the update. The column L gives the length of the path leading to such a state as obtained by the sweep-line path finding technique. The *Breadth-first Disk* columns show the performance of the disk-based breadth-first exploration from [35]. The Pk column gives in this case the widest breadth-first level encountered during state space exploration. The *Time* column gives the time for corresponding state space exploration. The L column gives (for this method) the length of a shortest path leading to a

Table 1. Database Replication Protocol.

|D|	Full		Sweep-Line Method					Breadth-first Disk		
	States	Time	Total	Pk	Basic	Path	L	Pk	Time	L
7	5,105	0:00:03	10,209	251	0:00:06	0:00:07	14	987	00:07	14
8	17,498	0:00:15	34,995	738	0:00:27	0:00:34	16	3,144	00:31	16
9	59,051	0:01:01	118,101	2,197	0:01:57	0:02:28	18	9,963	02:07	18
10	196,832	0:04:34	393,663	6,572	0:08:27	0:10:16	20	31,390	08:41	20
11	649,541	1:32:55	1,299,081	19,695	0:37:01	0:41:17	22	98,483	36:08	22
12	—	-:-:-	4,251,531	59,062	2:22:31	2:47:58	24	—	-:-	—

state where all the other database managers have performed their update. The number of states explored by the disk-based breadth-first exploration is equal to the number of states in the full state space.

The sweep-line method explores twice as many states as the full state space exploration. This is due to the fact that after an update has been completed the system returns to its initial state. The initial state is thus a destination of a regress edge (and in fact the only destination of regress edges in this system). This results in two sweeps of the entire state space. Since the sweep-line method explores twice as many states as the full exploration it is not surprising that it takes about twice as long to complete the sweep-line method compared to full state space exploration. We notice, however, that very little additional overhead is added by the path finding technique. The time used by the path finding technique is similar to the time used by the disk-based breadth-first exploration. The sweep-line method however achieves much better reduction in terms of peak number of states stored, and it also gives paths of the same length as the disk-based breadth-first exploration. Because of memory constraints, we were not able to generate the full state space for 12 database managers. For the disk-based breadth-first exploration with 12 database managers, state space generation was terminated after 10 hours.

The case for 11 database managers demonstrates that the sweep-line method can be faster than standard state space exploration. The reason for this is that with the sweep-line method there are fewer states to compare with, when determining whether a newly generated state has been visited before. For configurations up to 11 database managers, the sweep-line path finding technique outperforms the disk-based breadth-first exploration since the exploration time is essentially the same for the two methods, but the sweep-line method has a smaller peak memory usage and still gives a shortest path to the desired state. Only the sweep-line method was able to provide a result in reasonable time for 12 database managers.

Stop and Wait Communication Protocol. The second example is a stop-and-wait communication protocol [24]. One variant of the protocol is parameterised with the number of packets to be sent and the sequence numbers associated with packets are unbounded. In this case, we can use the number of packets

Table 2. Stop and Wait Communication Protocol.

	Full		Sweep-Line Method					Breadth-first Disk		
P	States	Time	Total	Pk	Basic	Path	L	Pk	Time	L
200	54,066	02:06	54,066	287	02:19	02:38	4,384	87	0:32:50	1,398
400	108,266	04:12	108,266	287	04:39	05:18	8,784	87	2:04:44	2,798
800	216,666	08:44	216,666	287	09:14	10:37	17,584	87	8:07:38	5,598
1000	270,866	10:44	270,866	287	11:33	13:15	21,984	—	—:—:—	—
2000	541,866	22:06	541,866	287	23:02	27:04	43,984	—	—:—:—	—
3000	812,866	33:18	812,866	287	34:19	40:20	65,984	—	—:—:—	—
4000	—	—:—	1,083,866	287	45:52	54:08	87,984	—	—:—:—	—

successfully transmitted as a monotonic progress measure [5]. For this system, we have obtained a path leading to a state where all packets have been received.

The performance is shown in Table 2 for different number of packets P sent from the sender to the receiver. It is worth noticing that the peak memory usage for the sweep-line method does not increase for larger configurations. Hence, main memory is no longer the bottleneck. The time overhead when using the disk-based sweep-line method is similar to what we observed for the database replication protocol.

The disk-based breadth-first exploration from [35] gives a better reduction in peak number of states for this system. Its performance in terms of exploration time is however much worse than the sweep-line method. The disk-based breadth-first exploration for 1,000 packets was terminated after 10 hours. The excessive use of time by the disk-based breadth-first exploration for this example is caused by the time expensive search for states on disk. The sweep-line path finding technique avoids these expensive searches altogether and is hence able to produce paths for large configurations of this system.

Another variation of the stop-and-wait protocol abstracts away from the actual packets to be sent and already transmitted, and uses a wrapping sequence number on packets. In this system we can use the sequence number as a non-monotonic progress measure. This system is parameterised with the bound on sequence numbers. The performance for this system is shown in Table 3 for the different values of the maximum sequence number S. As for the database replication protocol, the regress edges lead to re-processing roughly twice as many states when using the sweep-line method with the inevitable additional time overhead. The sweep-line method however performs much better in terms of exploration time than the disk-based breadth-first exploration because it avoid any searches for states on disk. For this system, we have obtained a path leading to a state where the sequence number wraps.

Wireless Transaction Protocol (WTP). This third example is taken from [14] where Coloured Petri Nets were used to model and verify the WTP [11]. WTP constitutes the transaction layer in the Wireless Application Protocol (WAP) architecture [12]. The progress measure used is based on the transaction control

Table 3. Stop and Wait Communication Protocol – with wrapping sequence numbers.

	Full		Sweep-Line Method					Breadth-first Disk		
S	States	Time	Total	Pk	Basic	Path	L	Pk	Time	L
200	54,201	02:26	108,202	335	04:32	05:20	3,184	87	0:29:59	1,393
300	81,301	03:36	162,402	335	06:47	08:00	4,784	87	1:06:14	2,093
400	108,401	04:59	216,602	335	09:05	10:45	6,384	87	1:56:42	2,793
500	135,501	06:12	270,802	335	11:25	13:26	7,984	87	3:02:47	3,493
800	216,801	10:04	433,402	335	18:10	21:26	12,784	—	–:–:–	—
1000	271,001	13:02	541,802	335	23:07	27:03	15,984	—	–:–:–	—
1500	406,501	18:31	812,802	335	34:22	40:32	23,984	—	–:–:–	—
2000	542,001	25:07	1,083,802	335	46:04	53:20	31,984	—	–:–:–	—

flow of the two protocol entities in WTP and the re-transmission counters used in the protocol. See [14] for details on the progress measure. The experimental results obtained for this system is given in Table 4. Configurations (Conf) are written in the form X-Y where X specifies the maximum value of the retransmission counters, and Y specifies whether *user acknowledgement* is on (T) or off (F). The WTP specification [11] suggests 4 as the maximum retransmission value for GSM networks and 8 as the maximum value for IP networks. For this system, we have obtained a path leading to a state where both protocol entities are in their terminating state. The sweep-line method performs slightly better in time than the disk-based breadth-first exploration. The breadth-first exploration, however, achieves slightly better memory reduction. The path obtained with the sweep-line method is only one longer than a shortest path.

This example shows that with sufficient memory, the full state space exploration can outperform both of the disk-based techniques. If sufficient memory is not available, the two disk-based are comparable in performance, with the sweep-line method performing slightly better in time and the breadth-first exploration performing slightly better in memory reduction.

7   Conclusions

We have presented a technique based on the use of external storage to support path finding with the sweep-line method. The missing support for path finding has until now been the main shortcoming of the sweep-line method. Our technique, due to the notion of progress, avoids costly search in external storage, but at the cost of possibly exploring the states several times. The practical experiments conducted have shown that writing the required path information to external storage adds a relatively small overhead of 10–20% in run-time. We have also shown a theoretical result quantifying the length of the paths obtained with the proposed technique.

We have compared the performance of the suggested technique with the performance of the closely related disk-based breadth-first exploration of [35].

Table 4. Wireless Transaction Protocol (WTP).

Conf	Full		Sweep-Line Method					Breadth-first Disk		
	States	Time	Total	Pk	Basic	Path	L	Pk	Time	L
1-T	1,838	0:00:04	1,838	677	0:00:04	0:00:05	6	570	0:00:06	5
2-T	10,333	0:00:36	10,333	2,780	0:00:50	0:00:54	6	2,679	0:01:04	5
3-T	30,978	0:02:31	30,978	7,052	0:03:53	0:03:52	6	6,668	0:04:41	5
4-T	65,873	0:06:17	65,873	12,417	0:09:14	0:09:59	6	11,882	0:11:58	5
5-T	113,343	0:11:32	113,343	18,660	0:17:15	0:19:04	6	17,283	0:22:21	5
6-T	172,657	0:18:07	172,657	26,068	0:27:42	0:31:06	6	22,697	0:35:54	5
7-T	243,765	0:27:03	243,765	34,742	0:40:25	0:44:10	6	28,111	0:52:44	5
8-T	326,667	0:36:35	326,667	44,690	0:55:37	1:00:05	6	33,525	1:12:38	5
1-F	4,232	0:00:15	4,232	1,658	0:00:19	0:00:20	6	1,324	0:00:23	5
2-F	24,905	0:02:51	24,905	7,195	0:04:40	0:04:37	6	6,713	0:05:27	5
3-F	74,017	0:11:41	74,017	17,111	0:18:55	0:20:24	6	16,633	0:23:43	5
4-F	154,231	0:28:59	154,231	29,157	0:46:41	0:51:25	6	28,813	0:57:11	5
5-F	262,442	0:54:32	262,442	42,964	1:26:54	1:35:11	6	41,390	1:45:24	5
6-F	397,583	1:25:58	397,583	59,323	2:19:11	2:30:10	6	53,990	2:49:45	5
7-F	559,604	2:07:58	559,604	78,404	3:22:57	3:39:49	6	66,590	4:06:18	5
8-F	748,505	2:52:29	748,505	100,215	4:39:02	5:01:38	6	79,190	5:37:42	5

These experiments have shown that the sweep-line method seems to have a better run-time profile than the method of [35], and in some cases gives better reduction results at the same time. The reason for this is that the sweep-line path finding technique avoids costly searches in external storage. The technique in [35] on the other hand obtains shortest paths whereas our technique obtain shortest paths subject to least-progress-first exploration. As our examples indicate, the least-progress-first exploration seems to give reasonably short paths in practice, and in some cases even a shortest path.

A general observation can be made about the relative performance of the sweep-line method and the disk-based breadth-first exploration of [35]. The disk-based breadth-first exploration performs well with respect to memory reduction when the breadth-first width of the state space is small. However, when the "width" of the state space is small, few states are generated at each breadth-first level. This is turn leads to many linear searches on disk, thereby making the run-time unacceptable. The sweep-line method seems to cope better with such narrow and long state spaces.

The run-time overhead for accessing disk was further reduced in [35] by using hash compaction. The use of hash compaction reduces run-time at the risk of not getting full coverage of the state space. The use of hash compaction however reduces the amount of information than must be written to disk, but the expensive linear searches still need to be conducted. An advantage of the sweep-line method is therefore that it guarantees full coverage of the state space. In conclusion, we have demonstrated that with path finding added the sweep-line method is a powerful alternative to other disk-based state space exploration methods such as [35].

The state space caching method [20,13,15] can also be used for path finding. Since state space caching is based on depth-first exploration, it has the advantage that a path from the initial state to the current state is always present on the depth-first search stack. The peak number of states with the state space caching method will be at least equal to the length of the shortest path leading to the state of interest. Our experiments with, e.g., the stop-and-wait protocol reported on in this paper show that the peak number of states stored with the sweep-line method can be far less than the length of a shortest path. This means that there will be systems, where the sweep-line path finding technique will outperform state space caching in terms of peak memory usage.

An interesting topic of future work is the combination of the sweep-line method with other state space reduction methods. State space reduction methods often exploit a certain characteristic of the system under consideration. Examples of this are the symmetry method [22,19,9,7] and partial order methods [30,37]. The symmetry method exploits that systems are often composed of components whose identities are interchangeable. Exploiting symmetry makes it possible to construct a condensed state space where each node represents an equivalence class of symmetric states, and each arc represents an equivalence class of symmetric actions. The condensed state space is typically orders of magnitude smaller than the ordinary full state space, and verification of properties can be done directly on the condensed state space, i.e., by considering only a representative from each equivalence class. Partial order methods are based on the observation that a key contributer to state explosion is the representation of all possible interleavings of independent actions. For verification of many properties it suffices to consider only some interleavings and hence it suffices to explore only a subset of the full state space.

It was shown in [38,8] how the symmetry method and partial order methods could be combined and that the state space reduction obtained when using the methods simultaneously was better than when either method was used in isolation. The reason for this is that symmetry (as exploited by the symmetry method) and independence between actions (as exploited by partial order methods) are orthogonal properties of the system. The progress exploited by the sweep-line method seems intuitively to be orthogonal to both symmetry and independence, making it attractive to pursue the combination of the sweep-line method and these other two reduction methods. It could also be considered to attempt to combine the sweep-line method with symbolic model checking techniques based on Binary Decision Diagram (BDDs) [27,4]. However, since there is no general correlation between the size of a set of states and the size of the BDD representing the set, it might be counter productive to combine BDDs with the sweep-line method.

Another topic of future work is to extend the properties of systems that can be verified with the sweep-line method. Currently, the sweep-line method can be used for the verification of safety properties. It would be of interest to investigate whether the sweep-line method could be used for, e.g., LTL and CTL model checking [6]. LTL model checking [40] is based on the detection of certain cycles in the state space. Hence, it should be possible to conduct LTL model checking for monotonic progress measures which have the property that all states on a given cycle will have the same progress value and hence be stored in memory simultaneously. It is currently an open question whether a variant of the generalised sweep-line method with non-monotonic progress measures can be developed to support full CTL and LTL model checking.

Acknowledgements

We would like to thank Stefan Sørensen for providing parts of the code for serialising states and events, and Jens Bæk Jørgensen, Guy Gallasch, and Jonathan Billington for providing comments on earlier versions of this paper.

References

1. Design/CPN. http://www.daimi.au.dk/designCPN.
2. R. Alur and D. Dill. A Theory of Timed Automata. *Theoretical Computer Science*, 126(2):183–235, 1994.
3. G. Behrmann, A. Fehnker, T. Hune, K. Larsen, P. Pettersson, and J. Romijn. Efficient Guiding Towards Cost-Optimaility in UPPAAL. In *Proc. of TACAS'01*, volume 2031 of *LNCS*, pages 174–188. Springer-Verlag, 2001.
4. R.E. Bryant. Graph Based Algorithms for Boolean Function Manipulation. *IEEE Transactions on Computers*, C-35(8):677–691, 1986.
5. S. Christensen, L.M. Kristensen, and T. Mailund. A Sweep-Line Method for State Space Exploration. In *Proceedings of TACAS'01*, volume 2031 of *LNCS*, pages 450–464. Springer-Verlag, 2001.
6. E. Clarke, O. Grumberg, and D. Peled. *Model Checking*. The MIT Press, 1999.
7. E.M. Clarke, T. Filkorn, and S. Jha. Exploiting Symmetries in Temporal Logic Model Checking. In *Proceedings of CAV'93*, LNCS, pages 450–462. Springer-Verlag, 1993.
8. E.A. Emerson, S. Jha, and D. Peled. Combining Partial Order and Symmetry Reduction. In E. Brinksma, editor, *Proceedings of TACAS'97*, volume 1217 of *Lecture Notes in Computer Science*, pages 35–49. Springer-Verlag, 1997.
9. E.A. Emerson and A.P. Sistla. Symmetry and Model Checking. *Formal Methods in System Design*, 9(1/2):105–131, 1996.
10. A. Fehnker. Scheduling a Steel Plant with Timed Automata. In *Proc. of RTCSA'99)*, pages 280–286. IEEE Computer Society, 1999.
11. WAP Forum. WAP Wireless Transaction Protocol Specification. June 2000 Conformance Release. Available via: http://www.wapforum.org/, 19 Feb. 2000.
12. WAP Forum. Wireless Application Protocol. Specifications available via: http://www.wapforum.org/.
13. P. Godefroid, G.J. Holzmann, and D. Pirottin. State-Space Caching Revisited. *Formal Methods in System Design*, 7(3):227–241, 1995.
14. S. Gordon, L.M. Kristensen, and J. Billington. Verification of a Revised WAP Wireless Transaction Protocol. In *Proc. of ICATPN'02*, volume 2360 of *LNCS*, pages 182–202. Springer-Verlag, 2002.
15. G.J. Holzmann. Tracing Protocols. *Bell System Technical Journal*, 64:2413–2434, 1985.

16. G.J. Holzmann. An Improved Protocol Reachability Analysis Technique. *Software, Practice and Experience*, 18(2):137–161, 1988.
17. G.J. Holzmann. *Design and Validation of Computer Protocols*. Prentice-Hall International Editions, 1991.
18. G.J. Holzmann. An Analysis of Bitstate Hashing. *Formal Methods in System Design*, 13:289–307, 1998.
19. C.N. Ip and D.L. Dill. Better Verification Through Symmetry. *Formal Methods in System Design*, 9(1/2):41–75, 1996.
20. C. Jard and T. Jeron. Bounded-memory Algorithms for Verification On-the-fly. In *Proc. of CAV'91*, volume 575 of *LNCS*, pages 192–202. Springer-Verlag, 1991.
21. K. Jensen. *Coloured Petri Nets - Basic Concepts, Analysis Methods and Practical Use. - Volume 1: Basic Concepts*. Springer-Verlag, 1992.
22. K. Jensen. Condensed State Spaces for Symmetrical Coloured Petri Nets. *Formal Methods in System Design*, 9(1/2):7–40, 1996.
23. S. Katz and H. Miller. Saving Space by Fully Exploiting Invisible Transitions. *Formal Methods in System Design*, 14:311–332, 1999.
24. L.M. Kristensen, S. Christensen, and K. Jensen. The Practitioner's Guide to Coloured Petri Nets. *International Journal on Software Tools for Technology Transfer*, 2(2):98–132, 1998.
25. L.M. Kristensen and T. Mailund. A Generalised Sweep-Line Method for Safety Properties. In *Proc. of FME'02*, volume 2391 of *LNCS*, pages 549–567. Springer-Verlag, 2002.
26. L.M. Kristensen and T. Mailund. A Compositional Sweep-Line State Space Exploration Method. In *Proc. of FORTE'02*, volume 2529 of *LNCS*, pages 327–343. Springer-Verlag, 2002.
27. K.L. McMillan. *Symbolic Model Checking*. Kluwer Academic Publishers, 1993.
28. R. Milner. *Communication and Concurrency*. Prentice-Hall International Series in Computer Science. Prentice-Hall, 1989.
29. A.N. Parashkevov and J. Yantchev. Space Efficient Reachability Analysis through use of Pseudo-root States. In *Proceedings of TACAS'97*, pages 50–64, 1997.
30. D. Peled. All from One, One for All: On Model Checking Using Representatives. In *Proceedings of CAV'93*, volume 697 of *LNCS*, pages 409–423. Springer-Verlag, 1993.
31. W. Reisig. *Petri Nets*, volume 4 of *EACTS Monographs on Theoretical Computer Science*. Springer-Verlag, 1985.
32. U. Stern and D.L. Dill. Improved Probabilistic Verification by Hash Compaction. In *Correct Hardware Design and Verification Methods*, volume 987 of *LNCS*, pages 206–224. Springer-Verlag, 1995.
33. U. Stern and D.L. Dill. A New Scheme for Memory-Efficient Probabilistic Verification. In *Proc. of Joint International Conference on Formal Description Techniques for Distributed Systems and Communication Protocols, and Protocol Specification, Testing, and Verification*, pages 333–348, 1996.
34. U. Stern and D.L. Dill. Combining State Space Caching and Hash Compaction. In *4. GI/ITG/GME Workshop zur Methoden des Entwurfs und der Verifikation Digitaler Systeme*, pages 81–90, Kreischa, 1996. Shaker Verlag, Aachen.
35. U. Stern and D.L. Dill. Using Magnetic Disk instead of Main Memory in the Murphi Verifier. In *Proc, of CAV'98*, volume 1427 of *LNCS*, pages 172–183. Springer-Verlag, 1998.
36. J.D. Ullman. *Elements of ML Programming*. Prentice-Hall, 1998.
37. A. Valmari. A Stubborn Attack on State Explosion. In *Proceedings of CAV'90*, volume 531 of *LNCS*, pages 156–165. Springer-Verlag, 1990.

38. A. Valmari. Stubborn Sets of Coloured Petri Nets. In G. Rozenberg, editor, *Proceedings of ICATPN'91*, pages 102–121, 1991.
39. A. Valmari. The State Explosion Problem. In *Lectures on Petri Nets I: Basic Models*, volume 1491 of *LNCS*, pages 429–528. Springer-Verlag, 1998.
40. M. Vardi and P. Wolper. An Automata-Theoretic Approach to Automatic Program Verification. In *In Proc. of IEEE Symposium on Logic in Computer Science*, pages 322–331, 1986.
41. P. Wolper and D. Leroy. Reliable Hashing without Collision Detection. In *Proceddings of CAV'93*, volume 697 of *LNCS*, pages 59–70. Springer-Verlag, 1993.

Formal Development
of a Distributed Logging Mechanism
Supporting Disconnected Updates

Yuechen Qian

Philips Research Laboratories, The Netherlands
and Eindhoven Embedded Systems Institute, The Netherlands
y.qian@tue.nl

Abstract. In mobile computing environments, logging systems are often used to record updates during device disconnection and logs are used in data synchronization on reconnection. Portable devices often have resource constraints and log truncation must be used to avoid log overflow. However, this method makes data synchronization vulnerable, due to information loss in truncating log files. Characteristic-entry logs record merely the most recent data access of each operation type per data item. They capture the minimum information needed to semantically resolve conflicting updates. They have been implemented in the MemorySafe system of Philips, a prototype distributed system supporting disconnected updates. In this paper, we present a formal model of characteristic-entry logs and investigate the relation between normal logs and characteristic-entry logs. We rigorously prove that characteristic-entry logs can be used in data synchronization, effectively in the same way as normal logs.

Keywords: Disconnected Updates, Consistency, Logs, Data Synchronization, Formal Methods, Z.

1 Introduction

As network technologies advance, it is becoming technically feasible to connect all consumer electronic devices to home networks and the Internet. Consequently, people will be able to access their data anytime and anywhere. This was an important requirement in the design of the MemorySafe system [1], a distributed data management system for future home environments. Portable devices and smart objects containing personal information, such as digital photos, can be used both at home and on the move [2]. In reality, however, devices will often be temporarily disconnected from the network, which is called *intermittent connectivity* [3] or *disconnected operation* [4]. This can be due to cost reasons, various technical limitations, administrative restrictions, human factors, or technical failures. The result is that data can be temporarily unavailable.

To overcome this unavailability, it is common practice to replicate data onto several reliable sites and/or onto the mobile devices that people carry. Data and their replicas can be updated independently when devices are disconnected. Such

J.S. Dong and J. Woodcock (Eds.): ICFEM 2003, LNCS 2885, pp. 338–358, 2003.

updates are called *disconnected updates*. Without precautions, data inconsistencies can occur. *Data synchronization* is the process of resolving inconsistencies of disconnected updates.

File synchronizers are user-level programs dealing with disconnected updates on hierarchical file systems. One example is the Unison File Synchronization [5]. In a formal model [6] of Unison, filenames are modelled as mappings between pathnames and contents. Predicate calculus is used to specify the behavior of Unison. Derived from this, filesystem algebra [7] provides options to combine several conflict-resolution policies into the specification of a file synchronizer.

Different from file synchronizers, distributed systems take advantage of access histories recorded in log files to resolve data inconsistencies. In this approach, the states of replicas are rolled back to a consistent state, the recorded disconnected updates are serialized, and the serialized updates are replayed in replicas. In the Coda system [8], resolution logs keep track of adding, removing, and updating activities on replicated directories. In the Ficus replicated file system [9,10], each file replica has its own version vector that records the history of updates to the file [11]. Conflicts are detected by comparing version vectors from two file replicas. In resolving inconsistencies of replicated data, both Coda and Ficus use semantic rules to resolve inconsistencies of replicated files. In database systems, system states can be rolled back and, then, uncommitted transactions recorded in logs are serialized and applied to all data copies [12]. The Bayou system [13] conducts application-specific conflict resolution.

When using logging mechanisms, log sizes are often determined by system administrators. Any realistic estimate of log size has to be derived from empirical data. With wrong estimations, logs may overflow due to frequent access during disconnection, which is especially the case for mobile devices with limited storage capacity. Truncating log files may cause information loss, making inconsistency resolution vulnerable. In the MemorySafe system [1], characteristic-entry logs [14] have been designed to address this problem. Such logs record merely the most recent data access of each operation type per data item.

So far log truncation and log-based data synchronization have been studied in empirical ways. Various log truncation methods are proposed and several semantic rules are applied in data synchronization, without rigorous definitions and proofs. In this paper, we present a formal model of characteristic-entry logs, formalize semantic rules, and present a correctness proof of using characteristic-entry logs in data synchronization. This formal model has played an essential role in conceiving the characteristic-entry log concept and in its implementation.

The rest of the paper is organized as follows. In Sect. 2, we give motivation of using characteristic-entry logs. In Sect. 3, we present an informal model of disconnected updates. In Sect. 4, we formalize both normal logs and characteristic-entry logs and present commutability between normal logs and characteristic-entry logs. The soundness of using characteristic-entry logs in data synchronization is presented in Sect. 5. Finally, we conclude this paper in Sect. 6.

2 Motivation

In most logging mechanisms, log length is restricted due to storage constraints. Sometimes it can also be the case that log length is purposely limited by system administrators. A log file grows linearly with the amount of data accesses performed. When the length of a log file reaches its limitation, any new data access will cause log overflow. This is especially the case for mobile computing devices with memory and storage constraints. To solve the problem of log overflow, system administrators, in practice, will be notified of such events and will take measures, such as manually compressing logs or deleting logs entries.

Alternatively, one solution is to discard new entries when log files reach their size limits. When using this approach, logs contain only the oldest accesses. Another solution to log overflow is to discard the oldest entries in logs when logs reach their limitation. In this approach, logs contain only the most recent accesses. In both cases, useful information can be lost when discarding log entries.

For example, suppose a storage device S and a data item x. S can be a personal digital assistant and x can be a file. The data item x can be added to S and, furthermore, can be accessed, modified, or deleted. We use A, W, R, and D for add, write, read, and delete accesses, respectively. Thus, $A(x)$ reads "add x to S". $W(x)1$ reads "write the value 1 to x" and the value is 1. $R(x)1$ reads "read the value of x and the value is 1". $D(x)$ reads "delete x from S". Let a log file l record all data accesses on the device S. For simplicity, timestamps are omitted in log entries. Assume that the length of l should never exceed 4, meaning that at most four accesses can be recorded. Suppose the following sequence of accesses will be consecutively performed on S, from left to right.

$$A(x), W(x)1, R(x)1, W(x)2, R(x)2, R(x)2, R(x)2, R(x)2.$$

Using the approach of discarding new entries in case of log overflow, the log l looks as follows, after the completion of the last access of the access sequence.

$$l = \langle A(x), W(x)1, R(x)1, W(x)2 \rangle.$$

This log does not show the last time x was read. Read accesses can be of relevance in synchronizing data copies. For instance, suppose that another copy of x was deleted from the device T, right after the $W(x)2$ access and before the first $R(x)2$ access on the device S. If the user expects that the most recent operation will be applied to all copies of x in synchronization, the deletion should be ignored. Because l does not reveal the four read accesses that occurred after the deletion, the deletion will be applied to S in this case, which introduces data loss. Therefore, a read access on a data item could not be replaced simply by the most recent write access on the same data item.

When using the method of discarding the oldest entries in case of log overflow, the log l looks as follows, after the completion of the access sequence.

$$l = \langle R(x)2, R(x)2, R(x)2, R(x)2 \rangle.$$

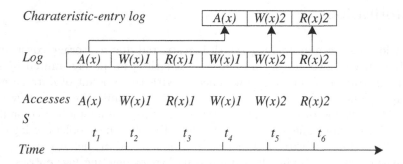

Fig. 1. Normal logs and characteristic-entry logs.

Obviously, this log does not tell when x was added and when x was modified. In both cases, the discarded log entries contain useful information that may be used in data synchronization.

Moreover, logs with length limits may contain only accesses of the most-frequently-visited data items while less-frequently-used data become "history-less". In other words, log spaces are not evenly distributed according to data items. Suppose that the following sequence of accesses will be applied on S. Again, assume the length limit of l is 4.

$$A(x), W(x)1, R(x)1, A(y), W(y)2, R(y)2, D(y).$$

Thus after the completion of the last access, the log l looks as follow, using the method of discarding the oldest entries in case of log overflow.

$$l = \langle A(y), W(y)2, R(y)2, D(y) \rangle.$$

In this case, l contains only access information of y. It has no information about x at all, which makes it difficult to synchronize x with its copies.

The above-mentioned examples make it clear that length limits of log files are of great importance in recording access information. Truncating logs may bring trouble in data synchronization. It is also shown that log spaces are not evenly distributed, which may introduce difficulties in data synchronization as well. Thus, in practice, length limits are often set as large as possible and are usually only constrained by storage capacities of devices. In mobile computing systems, however, this approach is not applicable, due to storage capacity limits of mobile hand-held devices. Setting realistic log limits is an empirical task. With wrong estimations, information loss in logs is inevitable.

Characteristic-entry logs record only the most recent add, read, write and delete accesses for each data item [14]. In this way, log length is not determined by the number of accesses any more, but by the number of data items and the number of access types. Therefore, log lengths become predicable and manageable. Moreover, log space is evenly distributed to all data items. Fig. 1 illustrates an example. In the figure, a sequence of accesses on the device S is shown horizontally, with a time line running from left to right. Each access is specified by its operation type and the value of the accessed data item. The normal log and the characteristic-entry logs of S are illustrated.

3   Disconnected Updates

A system supporting disconnected updates, called a DU system, consists of a collection of *data spaces*. Data spaces represent storage devices. For example, the DU system $\mathbf{S}_{DU}$ has three component data spaces.

$$\mathbf{S}_{DU} = \{S_1, S_2, S_3\}.$$

A data space contains a collection of *data items*. Each data item has a name part and a value part, called *key* and *value* respectively. A data item is uniquely identified by its key in a data space. Moreover, the key part of a data item is immutable while its value part can be modified. For example, the data space S_1 has three data items. x, y and z denote keys of data items. For simplicity, the values of data items are assumed to be natural numbers in this paper.

$$S_1 = \{(x, 1), (y, 2), (z, 3)\}.$$

Definition 1. *A DU system is a triple* ($\mathbf{S}$, $\mathbf{K}$, $\mathbf{V}$, *Store*). $\mathbf{S}$, $\mathbf{K}$ *and* $\mathbf{V}$ *are arbitrary sets. Store* : $\mathbf{S} \times \mathbf{K} \nrightarrow \mathbf{V}$ *is a partial function which describes where current values of data items are stored.*

In a DU system, *read, write, add, delete* are operations that can be performed on data spaces. All the four operations involve only one data space in the system and are assumed to be atomic.

Definition 2. *In a DU system, the following operations are allowed.*

- read, *read data from a data space.*
- write, *update the value of a data item in a data space.*
- add, *add a data item to a data space.*
- delete, *remove a data item from a data space.*

A data item can have copies in a DU system. Each copy is stored in one data space. A data item and its copies have a common key. A data item, or any of its copies, can be updated individually, as if its storing data space is disconnected from the other data spaces in the system.

Definition 3 (Disconnected update). *An operation is a disconnected update, if it changes the current value of a data item in a data space, independent of the other copies in other data spaces.*

Due to disconnected updates, a key may have different values in data spaces. For example, x has different values in S_1 and S_2.

$$S_1 = \{(x, 1), (y, 2), (z, 3)\}$$
$$S_2 = \{(x, 4), (y, 2)\}$$
$$S_3 = \{(x, 4), (u, 4), (v, 5)\}$$

Definition 4 (Data consistency). *Given a key x and two data spaces S_1 and S_2 of a DU system, x is* consistent *in S_1 and S_2, if x has the same value both in S_1 and in S_2 when both S_1 and S_2 have a data item with x as the key part.*

For example, x is not consistent in the data spaces S_1 and S_2, since it has different values in S_1 and S_2. z is considered to be consistent in S_1 and S_2, since z is not defined in S_2.

Definition 5 (System consistency). *A DU system is* consistent*, if given any key x and any two data spaces S_1 and S_2 of the DU system, x is consistent in S_1 and S_2.*

For example, the DU system $\mathbf{S}_{DU}$ is not consistent, due to the fact that x is not consistent in S_1 and S_2.

In order to resolve inconsistency, logs are introduced to record access histories of data spaces and a synchronization operation, *sync* (an abbreviation of "synchronize"), is introduced to bring the system into a consistent state.

Each data space of a DU system is associated with a log. A log is a sequence of log entries. A log entry contains information about the time, the operation, the accessed data item of an access. A log entry also keeps record of the values of the operated data item, before and after the access. For example, l is a log of a data space.

$$l = \langle A(x), W(x)1, R(x)1, A(y), W(y)2, D(x) \rangle.$$

We assume that system clocks of data spaces are synchronized. Thus timestamps in log entries are reliable.

Definition 6 (Synchronization). *Given any key x and any two data spaces S_1 and S_2 of a DU system, x will become consistent in S_1 and S_2 after performing the* sync *operation.*

For example, after performing the sync operation on the key x of the data space S_1 and S_2, x should have the same value in both S_1 and S_2. This is a rather loose specification of synchronization. What the eventual value should be and how the value is chosen are not specified at all. In data synchronization, semantic rules are often used. One semantic rule says that the value of x after the most recent update should be propagated to all copies of x, which is known as *no loss update semantics* in [9]. In this case, logs of S_1 and S_2 can be used to retrieve the most recent modification made on x. Later, the sync operation becomes an algorithmic specification to determine what operation should be applied to data spaces, based on the logs of the data spaces.

In models of distributed databases and file systems [15], there are logical data items and physical data items. Compared with those models, the concept of data items in the model of DU systems is close to that of physical data items in those models. The notion of logical data items is discarded for the following reasons. Firstly, the property of location-transparency is applicable in traditional distributed systems with reliable network connection, but not in living environments with dynamic network connection. Secondly, users conceptually associate data with locations (devices) and tend to have data copies stored in different locations (devices). Thus, data are also logically distributed. Thirdly, this treatment allows to focus on resolving inconsistencies of data copies, instead of on the mapping between logical data and physical data.

The objective of the next two sections is to prove that characteristic-entry logs can be used in data synchronization, effectively in the same way as normal logs. To achieve our goal, we firstly model normal logs and characteristic-entry logs. Then, we show that normal logs can be transformed to characteristic-entry ones. We formalize semantic rules that are used in data synchronization. Finally, we show that when applying the semantic rules on normal logs, the result is the same as the result obtained by applying the same rules on the transformed characteristic-entry logs of the normal logs. As usual in this kind of study, it is less the construction of the proofs as the choice of conjecture that is of interest.

4 Characteristic-Entry Logs

As mentioned in the previous section, each data space has a log that records performed data accesses. In this section, it is shown how characteristic-entry logs can be formally constructed. It is also shown that characteristic-entry logs can be generated from normal logs. Z-notation [16,17] is used in formalizing characteristic-entry logs.

4.1 Normal Logs

For the purpose of specification, two basic types are introduced. *KEY* denotes the set of keys of data items. *VAL* denotes the set of values of the keys.

$[KEY, VAL]$.

Additionally, *OP* defines a set of values that can be used for indicating operation types of log entries.

$OP ::= add \mid read \mid write \mid delete$.

add indicates an add operation. *read* indicates a read operation. *write* indicates a write operation. *delete* indicates a delete operation.

The type *TIME* is also introduced. The elements of *TIME* are used in logging the moments when accesses are performed. For simplicity, we assume the elements of *TIME* to be natural numbers, as in practical systems.

$TIME == \mathbb{N}$.

Logs consist of log entries. A log entry records information of an access. It contains the execution time, the performed operation, the key of the accessed data item, the value of the data item before the execution, and the value after the execution. Log entries can be formally defined as follows.

$$LogEntry == (((TIME \times OP) \times KEY) \times VAL) \times VAL.$$

Three projection functions, *time*, *op* and *key*, are defined for retrieving information from a log entry. Similar functions can be defined for retrieving pre- and post-value of a log entry.

$$time : LogEntry \rightarrow TIME$$
$$\forall e : LogEntry \bullet time(e) = first(first(first(first(e))))$$

$$op : LogEntry \rightarrow OP$$
$$\forall e : LogEntry \bullet op(e) = second(first(first(first(e))))$$

$$key : LogEntry \rightarrow KEY$$
$$\forall e : LogEntry \bullet key(e) = second(first(first(e)))$$

Logs can be modelled as sequences of log entries that are ordered by time[1].

$$Log == \{l : \text{seq } LogEntry \mid isOrdered(l)\}.$$

The predicate *isOrdered* checks whether the entries of a sequence of log entries are ordered by time[2].

$$isOrdered\_ : \mathbb{P}(\text{seq } LogEntry)$$
$$\lambda l : \text{seq } LogEntry \bullet isOrdered(l) \Leftrightarrow$$
$$\forall i,j : \text{dom } l \bullet i < j \Rightarrow time(l(i)) < time(l(j))$$

It requires that there may not be two entries in a log having the same timestamp. Recording an access is usually implemented by appending a log entry to the end of a log file. In practice, it is easy to guarantee that any two appending operations on the same log file are always sequentially executed.

One basic operation on a log is the *append* operation. When appending a entry to a log, it should be ensured that the timestamp of the log entry is larger than that of the last log entry of the log. In this way, the entries of the result log still preserve time order. To this end, the function *isAfterLast* is defined.

---

[1] One alternative model of a log would be a mapping (partial function), $l : TIME \nrightarrow (((OP \times KEY) \times VAL) \times VAL)$. In this way, the ordering could still be retrieved from the mapping. In our model, log entries can be ordered by their timestamps and they also preserve the time ordering in a log. The introduction of this redundancy is largely because this model is close to the data structure in implementation. Moreover, the most recent operation is often used in data synchronization, to be explained in Sect.5.2. In our model, this information can be easily retrieved from a log, since the last element of a log is the most recent access.

[2] The predicate is defined in terms of a set of objects that satisfy it. It is convenient to treat the name of the set as a unary operator. In this case, the definition includes an underscore to indicate the position of the argument.

$$isAfterLast\_ : \mathbb{P}(\text{seq } LogEntry \times TIME)$$

$$\lambda\, l : \text{seq } LogEntry;\ t : TIME \bullet isAfterLast(l, t) \Leftrightarrow$$
$$\text{if } l = \langle\rangle \text{ then } true \text{ else } time(last(l)) < t$$

The *append* function is defined as follows.

$$append : Log \times LogEntry \to \text{seq } LogEntry$$

$$append = \lambda\, l : Log;\ e : LogEntry \bullet$$
$$\text{if } isAfterLast(l, time(e)) \text{ then } l \frown \langle e \rangle \text{ else } l$$

Without difficulties, the following theorem can be proved. It says that the result of applying *append* on a log and a log entry is still a log.

Theorem 1. *Given any log, $l : Log$, and any log entry, $e : LogEntry$, $append(l, e)$ is still a log.*

4.2   Characteristic-Entry Logs

A characteristic-entry log records merely the last access of each operation type on a key. In other words, given a key and an operation type, there exists at most one log entry with the key and the operation type in a characteristic-entry log. This property is specified by the predicate *isCEL*.

$$isCEL\_ : \mathbb{P}(\text{seq } LogEntry)$$

$$\lambda\, l : \text{seq } LogEntry \bullet isCEL(l) \Leftrightarrow$$
$$\forall\, i, j : \text{dom } l \bullet (i \neq j \wedge key(l(i)) = key(l(j))) \Rightarrow op(l(i)) \neq op(l(j))$$

Thus, characteristic-entry logs can be formally specified as follows.

$$CELog == \{l : Log \mid isCEL(l)\}.$$

Note that this definition does not say that a recorded access is the last one of this sort. This "most recentness" property is ensured by the appending function of characteristic-entry logs.

Before appending a log entry to a characteristic-entry log, the log is checked whether it already contains an element, which has the same key and operation type as that of the log entry to be appended. If so, the element should be removed from the log. The *delete* function achieves this goal.

$$delete : CELog \times OP \times KEY \to \text{seq } LogEntry$$

$$delete = \lambda\, l : CELog;\ o : OP;\ k : KEY \bullet$$
$$\text{if } l = \langle\rangle \text{ then } \langle\rangle$$
$$\text{else if } op(last(l)) = o \wedge key(last(l)) = k \text{ then } front(l)$$
$$\text{else } delete(front(l), o, k) \frown \langle last(l) \rangle$$

Using *delete*, the function *concat* is defined for appending a log entry to a characteristic-entry log.

$$concat : CELog \times LogEntry \to \text{seq } LogEntry$$

$$concat = \lambda\, l : CELog;\ e : LogEntry \bullet$$
$$\quad \textbf{if } isAfterLast(l, time(e)) \textbf{ then } delete(l, op(e), key(e)) \frown \langle e \rangle \textbf{ else } l$$

For example, let l be the characteristic-entry log shown in Fig. 1, $l = \langle A(x), W(x)2, R(x)2 \rangle$. Suppose that we append a log entry e, where $op(e) = W$, $key(e) = x$, and $isAfterLast(l, time(e))$ hold. First, we apply the function $delete$. Then, we apply the function $concat$.

$$delete(l, op(e), key(e))$$
$$= delete(front(l), op(e), key(e)) \frown \langle last(l) \rangle$$
$$= delete(\langle A(x), W(x)2 \rangle, op(e), key(e)) \frown \langle R(x)2 \rangle$$
$$= front(\langle A(x), W(x)2 \rangle) \frown \langle R(x)2 \rangle$$
$$= \langle A(x), R(x)2 \rangle$$
$$concat(l, e)$$
$$= delete(l, op(e), key(e)) \frown \langle e \rangle$$
$$= \langle A(x), R(x)2 \rangle \frown \langle e \rangle$$
$$= \langle A(x), R(x)2, e \rangle$$

The function $delete$ has the non-creation, effectiveness, no-time-shift, and order-preservation properties.

Lemma 1 (Non-creation). *The result of the delete function contains no entries that were not present in the original log. Formally, given $l : CELog$, $k : KEY$ and $o : OP$, $\forall i : \text{dom } delete(l, o, k) \bullet \exists j : \text{dom } l \bullet delete(l, o, k)(i) = l(j)$.*

Lemma 2 (Effectiveness). *The result of the delete function contains no entries matching the specified operation and key[3]. Formally, given $l : CELog$, $k : KEY$ and $o : OP$, $\forall i : \text{dom } delete(l, o, k) \bullet op(delete(l, o, k)(i)) \neq o \lor key(delete(l, o, k)(i)) \neq k$.*

Lemma 3 (No-time-shift). *The result of the delete function does not violate the timing of the original log. Formally, given $l : CELog$, $k : KEY$, $o : OP$ and $t : Time$, $isAfterLast(l, t) \Rightarrow isAfterLast(delete(l, o, k), t)$.*

Lemma 4 (Order-preservation). *The result of the delete function preserves the order of the original log. Given $l : \text{seq } LogEntry$, $k : KEY$ and $o : OP$,*
$$l \in Log \Rightarrow delete(l, o, k) \in Log,$$
$$l \in CELog \Rightarrow delete(l, o, k) \in CELog.$$

These lemmas can be proved using structural induction on sequences of log entries. With help of these lemmas, the following theorem can be proven. It says that using $concat$ to concatenate a characteristic-entry log and a log entry, the result is still a characteristic-entry log.

---

[3] When applying $delete$ on a characteristic-entry log l, an operation o and a key k, the result sequence $delete(l, o, k)$ should have the following property, $\neg \exists i : \text{dom } delete(l, o, k) \bullet op(delete(l, o, k)(i)) = o \land key(delete(l, o, k)(i)) = k$. This property is equivalent to the formal definition of Effectiveness.

Theorem 2. *Given any characteristic-entry log, $l : CELog$, and any log entry, $e : LogEntry$, $concat(l, e)$ is still a characteristic-entry log.*

4.3 Converting Normal Logs to Characteristic-Entries Log

Characteristic-entry logs can be generated from normal logs. To do so, the *ce* function is defined.

$$ce : CELog \rightarrow \text{seq } LogEntry$$

$$ce = \lambda\, l : Log \bullet \text{if } l = \langle\rangle \text{ then } \langle\rangle \text{ else } concat(ce(front(l)), last(l))$$

Take the normal log in Fig. 1 as an example. Let $l = \langle A, W_1, R_1, W_1, W_2, R_2 \rangle$. In this example, we omit x in log entries and keep the values as subscripts, for simplicity. Thus A stands for $A(x)$, W_1 stands for $W(x)1$, and so on.

$$
\begin{aligned}
&ce(l) \\
={}& concat(ce(front(l)), last(l)) \\
={}& concat(ce(\langle A, W_1, R_1, W_1, W_2 \rangle), R_2) \\
={}& concat(concat(ce(\langle A, W_1, R_1, W_1 \rangle), W_2), R_2) \\
={}& concat(concat(concat(ce(\langle A, W_1, R_1 \rangle), W_1), W_2), R_2) \\
={}& concat(concat(concat(concat(ce(\langle A, W_1 \rangle), R_1), W_1), W_2), R_2) \\
={}& concat(concat(concat(concat(concat(ce(\langle A \rangle), W_1), R_1), W_1), W_2), R_2) \\
={}& concat(concat(concat(concat(concat(concat(ce(\langle\rangle), A), W_1), R_1), W_1), W_2), R_2) \\
={}& concat(concat(concat(concat(concat(concat(\langle\rangle, A), W_1), R_1), W_1), W_2), R_2) \\
={}& concat(concat(concat(concat(concat(\langle A\rangle, W_1), R_1), W_1), W_2), R_2) \\
={}& concat(concat(concat(concat(\langle A, W_1\rangle, R_1), W_1), W_2), R_2) \\
={}& concat(concat(concat(\langle A, W_1, R_1\rangle, W_1), W_2), R_2) \\
={}& concat(concat(\langle A, R_1, W_1\rangle, W_2), R_2) \\
={}& concat(\langle A, R_1, W_2\rangle, R_2) \\
={}& \langle A, W_2, R_2 \rangle
\end{aligned}
$$

Thus, applying *ce* on l has the result of $\langle A, W_2, R_2 \rangle$, that's $\langle A(x), W(x)2, \rangle$ $\langle R(x)2 \rangle$, which is exactly the characteristic-entry log of S in Fig. 1.

Formally, it can be proved that log sequences obtained by applying *ce* on characteristic-entry logs are still characteristic-entry logs. The proof format follows the one proposed by W.H.J. Feijen [18]. A justification is inserted between consecutive proof steps.

Theorem 3. *Given a log, $l : Log$, $ce(l)$ is a characteristic-entry log.*

Proof. The proof is done using structural induction[4] of l. **Base case** Trivial. **Inductive step** It should be proven that $ce(l \frown \langle e \rangle)$ is a characteristic-entry

---

[4] There are several versions of structural induction on sequences, as described in [19]. One version is that in order to show that some property $P(l)$ holds for all sequences $l : \text{seq } X$, it should be proven that (1) $P(\langle\rangle)$ holds. (2) If $P(l)$ holds for any sequence l, then so does $P(l \frown \langle x \rangle)$. Formally, $\forall x : X;\ l : \text{seq } X \bullet P(l) \Rightarrow P(l \frown \langle x \rangle)$. Because the *delete* function is recursively defined by checking the last element of a sequence, this version of structural induction on sequences is chosen to ease the proof.

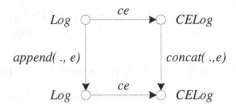

Fig. 2. The relations between logs and characteristic-entry logs.

log, on the assumption that $ce(l)$ is a characteristic entry log and that both l and $l \frown \langle e \rangle$ are logs.

$$ce(l \frown \langle e \rangle)$$
$$\equiv \{\text{Definition of } ce\}$$
$$concat(ce(front(l \frown \langle e \rangle)), last(l \frown \langle e \rangle))$$
$$\equiv \{\text{Definitions of } front \text{ and } ce\}$$
$$concat(ce(l), e)$$

Because of the induction hypothesis that $ce(l)$ is a characteristic entry log, $concat(ce(l), e)$ is a characteristic entry log according to Theorem 2. This establishes the inductive step. By structural induction, the theorem is proven. □

Similar to the *delete* function, the *ce* function has the property of non-creation as well. Moreover, the result log of the *ce* function and the original log end with the same log entry.

Lemma 5 (Non-creation). *The result of the ce function contains no entries that were not present in the original log. Formally, given $l : Log$,*
$\forall i : \operatorname{dom} ce(l) \bullet \exists j : \operatorname{dom} l \bullet ce(l)(i) = l(j)$.

Lemma 6 (Latest-equivalence). *Given any log, $l : Log$, and $t : Time$,*
$isAfterLast(l, t) = isAfterLast(ce(l), t)$.

It can be proven that the construction of a characteristic-entry log can be done on the fly and thus the long normal logs can be replaced by the compact characteristic-entry logs, as illustrated in Fig. 2.

Theorem 4 (Commutability). *Given any log, $l : Log$, and any log entry, $e : LogEntry$, $ce(append(l, e)) = concat(ce(l), e)$.*

Proof. Let LHS be $ce(append(l, e))$ and RHS be $concat(ce(l), e)$. The proof of the theorem is divided into three cases. **(1)** If $l = \langle \rangle$, trivial. **(2)** If $l \neq \langle \rangle$ and $isAfterLast(l, time(e)) = true$, $isAfterLast((ce(l), time(e))$ holds as well according to Lemma 6.

$$\text{LHS}$$
$$\equiv \{isAfterLast(l, time(e)) = true, \text{Definition of } append\}$$
$$ce(l \frown \langle e \rangle)$$
$$\equiv \{\text{Definition of } ce\}$$
$$concat(ce(l), e)$$
$$\equiv \text{RHS}$$

Therefore, it is proven that

$$isAfterLast(l, time(e)) = true \Rightarrow ce(append(l, e)) = concat(ce(l), e).$$

(3) If $l \neq \langle \rangle$ and $isAfterLast(l, time(e)) = false$, $isAfterLast((ce(l), time(e))$ does not hold either by Lemma 6.

$$\textit{LHS}$$
$$\equiv \{isAfterLast(l, time(e)) = false, \text{Definition of } append\}$$
$$ce(l)$$
$$\equiv \{isAfterLast(ce(l), time(e) = false), \text{Definition of } concat\}$$
$$\textit{RHS}$$

Thus, it is proven that

$$isAfterLast(l, time(e)) = false \Rightarrow ce(append(l, e)) = concat(ce(l), e)$$

In summary, the theorem holds for all l. $\qquad\qquad\qquad\qquad\qquad\qquad\qquad \square$

5   Data Synchronization Using Characteristic-Entry Logs

Disconnected updates may introduce inconsistencies to a DU system. In this section, it is rigorously proven that characteristic-entry log can be used in data synchronization in the same way as normal logs.

5.1   Semantic Rules

In data synchronization, basically, there are two ways of using logs.

- Serialization. In this approach, systems are rolled back to an initial consistent state. Then entries of logs of data spaces are serialized according to their timestamps. The serialized log entries are applied on all data spaces, after which the system state becomes consistent.
- Semantic synchronization. In this approach, semantic rules are defined to resolve inconsistencies, such as "propagating the latest update".

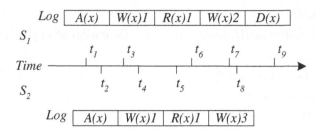

Fig. 3. Update loss when applying the up-to-date rule.

Serialization makes full use of information in logs. In this approach, however, rollback and applying serialized logs are expensive operations in terms of computing resources, especially to mobile devices. Semantic synchronization can incorporate user knowledge in data synchronization and provides flexibility of defining consistency. In this approach, however, only small portion of information stored in logs is used. There is much redundancy in logs. Characteristic-entry logs can be used in the same way as normal logs in semantic data synchronization while avoiding redundancy.

In semantic data synchronization, the up-to-date rule is often used for its simplicity, especially in file synchronization tools.

Definition 7 (Up-to-date). *When synchronizing a data item and its copies, the most recent operation will be propagated to all copies.*

Fig. 3 illustrates an example. The most recent operation on x at S_2 was $W(x)3$. After that, there was a $D(x)$ operation at S_1. According to the rule, the deletion is chosen for propagation. Thus x is deleted from both S_1 and S_2 after synchronization.

Using the up-to-date rule carelessly might result in unexpected data loss. Imagine the following scenario. A user modified a file at one computer. After that, he deleted a copy of the file at another computer, just in order to clean up local storage space. When synchronizing the two computers, the file is removed from both computers according to the up-to-date rule, since the deletion was performed most recently. This is not the user's initial intention. To avoid such data loss, Ficus introduced "no lost update" semantics [9].

Definition 8 (No-update-loss). *When synchronizing a data item and its copies, the most recent modification will be propagated to all copies.*

Take the example in Fig. 3. $W(x)3$ is chosen for propagation in synchronization, according to the no-update-loss rule. In this way, the latest modification made on S_2 become available on S_1, even though x was deleted already.

More subtle rules are used in semantic data synchronization, such as *weak-no-update-loss* and *read-delete-safety* in [14]. It can be rigorously proven that when applying the above-mentioned rules in semantic data synchronization, characteristic-entry logs can be used in the same way as normal logs. In the subsequent two sections, we use the up-to-date rule as an example to show how the soundness proof of using characteristic-entry logs is carried out. To do so, semantic rules need be to formalized.

5.2   Formalizing Semantic Rules

In DU systems, it is assumed that there is no dependency between data items. In such system, typically examples of data items are files. A file is usually accessed independent of the others. Moreover, in DU systems, there is no access dependency either. Data accesses are regarded as atomic and isolated events. These treatments make DU systems different from database systems, such as banking systems and flight reservation systems. In those systems, data-dependency and access-dependency exist widely.

By leaving those dependencies out of our model, we can obtain a better understanding of semantic rules. In future studies, we can extend our model to specify data dependency and access dependency. In this section, thus, we focus on a special type of logs, the logs whose entries are associated to the same key.

$$OneKeyLog == \{l : Log \mid onekey(l)\}$$

where

$$onekey\_ : \mathbb{P}(\text{seq } LogEntry)$$

$$\lambda\, l : \text{seq } LogEntry \bullet onekey(l) \Leftrightarrow \forall\, i, j : \text{dom } l \bullet key(l(i)) = key(l(j))$$

Semantic rules can be modelled as partial functions. The following abbreviation is introduced.

$$RULE == OneKeyLog \times OneKeyLog \nrightarrow \text{seq } LogEntry \times \text{seq } LogEntry$$

Such a function takes a pair of logs and computes what operations should be chosen for propagation. The results are captured in a pair of sequences of log entries, which should be applied to the data spaces that the logs are associated with, in a component-wise manner. Such a function is *totally defined* if it can be applied to any logs.

Moreover, a new data type OP_ϵ is introduced, which is an extension of the basic data type OP. OP_ϵ has an extra element ϵ, denoting an empty operation.

$$OP_\epsilon ::= OP \cup \{\epsilon\}$$

The function $last_\epsilon$ is also introduced, which returns the last operation of a sequence of log entries.

$$last_\epsilon : \text{seq } LogEntry \to OP_\epsilon$$

$$last_\epsilon = \lambda\, l : \text{seq } LogEntry \bullet \text{if } l = \langle\rangle \text{ then } \epsilon \text{ else } op(last(l))$$

When specifying a semantic rule, the operation of the most recent access is often needed. To obtain such information, using $op(last(l))$ would cause undefineness, where l is a sequence of log entries. This is because $last$ is a partial function on sequences in Z. The introduction of the empty operation ϵ and the $last_\epsilon$ function helps to simplify specifications, as illustrated below in the definition of the domain of $up_{\neg\epsilon}$.

When describing semantic rules, specification might become incomprehensible. Thus a compositional approach is devised. A semantic rule is decomposed into small pieces, which are modelled in terms of partial functions. A full specification of the given semantic rule can be built up by composing the partial functions. The composed function, a specification of the semantic rule, should be totally defined.

Using this compositional approach, the up-to-date rule can be specified by the following partial functions. $up_{\neg\epsilon}$ is a partial function, which takes pairs of non-ϵ logs as arguments. The domain of $up_{\neg\epsilon}$ is restricted by the function, dom. up_ϵ is a partial function, whose arguments involve at least one empty log.

$$
\begin{array}{|l}
\hline
up_{\neg\epsilon} : RULE \\
\hline
\text{dom } up_{\neg\epsilon} = \{(l_1, l_2) : OneKeyLog \times OneKeyLog \mid \neg endwithR(l_1, l_2) \wedge \\
\quad last_\epsilon(l_1) \neq \epsilon \wedge last_\epsilon(l_2) \neq \epsilon\} \\
up_{\neg\epsilon} = \lambda\, l_1, l_2 : OneKeyLog \bullet \\
\quad \textbf{if } time(last(l_1)) < time(last(l_2)) \textbf{ then } (\langle last(l_2)\rangle, \langle\rangle) \\
\quad \textbf{else if } time(last(l_2)) < time(last(l_1)) \textbf{ then } (\langle\rangle, \langle last(l_1)\rangle) \\
\quad\quad \textbf{else } (\langle\rangle, \langle\rangle)
\end{array}
$$

$$
\begin{array}{|l}
\hline
up_\epsilon : RULE \\
\hline
\text{dom } up_\epsilon = \{(l_1, l_2) : OneKeyLog \times OneKeyLog \mid \neg endwithR(l_1, l_2) \wedge \\
\quad (last_\epsilon(l_1) = \epsilon \vee last_\epsilon(l_2) = \epsilon)\} \\
up_\epsilon = \lambda\, l_1, l_2 : OneKeyLog \bullet \\
\quad \textbf{if } last_\epsilon(l_1) \neq \epsilon \textbf{ then } (\langle\rangle, \langle last(l_1)\rangle) \\
\quad \textbf{else if } last_\epsilon(l_2) \neq \epsilon \textbf{ then } (\langle last(l_2)\rangle, \langle\rangle) \\
\quad\quad \textbf{else } (\langle\rangle, \langle\rangle)
\end{array}
$$

In the definitions, the predicate $endwithR$ verifies whether either of given two logs ends with a read access.

$$
\begin{array}{|l}
\hline
endwithR\_ : \mathbb{P}(OneKeyLog \times OneKeyLog) \\
\hline
\lambda\, l_1, l_2 : OneKeyLog \bullet endwithR(l_1, l_2) \Leftrightarrow \\
\quad (last_\epsilon(l_1) = read \vee last_\epsilon(l_2) = read)
\end{array}
$$

In semantic data synchronization, read accesses are usually not taken into account, which is modelled by the up_r function. The up_r function takes two logs as arguments. If either of the logs ends with a read access, the access is ignored and the rest of the log is used in synchronization. Thus, the full specification of the up-to-date rule is the integration of up_ϵ, $up_{\neg\epsilon}$ and up_r [5].

$$up \stackrel{\wedge}{=} up_{\neg\epsilon} \oplus up_\epsilon \oplus up_r$$

where

$up_r : RULE$

dom $up_r = \{(l_1, l_2) : OneKeyLog \times OneKeyLog \mid endwithR(l_1, l_2)\}$
$up_r = \lambda\, l_1, l_2 : OneKeyLog \bullet$
    if $last_\epsilon(l_1) = read \wedge last_\epsilon(l_2) = read$ **then** $up(front(l_1), front(l_2))$
    else if $last_\epsilon(l_1) = read$ **then** $up(front(l_1), l_2)$
        else $up(l_1, front(l_2))$

To illustrate how to use up in data synchronization, we take the example in Fig. 3. Let l_1 and l_2 be the logs of the data spaces S_1 and S_2 in Fig. 3, respectively.

$$l_1 = \langle A(x)_1, W(x)1_1, R(x)1_1, W(x)2_1, D(x)_1 \rangle$$
$$l_2 = \langle A(x)_2, W(x)1_2, R(x)1_2, W(x)3_2 \rangle$$

Synchronization can be carried out by applying the function up to l_1 and l_2.

$$up(l_1, l_2)$$
$$= up_{\neg\epsilon}(l_1, l_2)$$
$$= (\langle\rangle, \langle last(l_1) \rangle)$$
$$= (\langle\rangle, \langle D(x)_1 \rangle)$$

Thus $D(x)$ should be applied to S_2 in synchronization.

To show that the function up can be used for synchronizing any two logs, it must be proven that given any two logs, $l_1, l_2 : OneKeyLog$, $up(l_1, l_2)$ is defined.

Theorem 5 (Totality). *up is a total function.*

Proof. It is sufficient to show that

    dom $up = OneKeyLog \times OneKeyLog$,

in order to prove that up is a total function.

    dom up
$=$ {Definition of $\oplus$. }
    dom $up_{\neg\epsilon} \cup$ dom $up_\epsilon \cup$ dom up_r
$=$ {Definitions of $up_{\neg\epsilon}$ and up_ϵ.}
    $\{(l_1, l_2) : OneKeyLog \times OneKeyLog \mid \neg endwithR(l_1, l_2) \wedge$

---

[5] The overriding operation is used here, instead of the union operation. The union operation can be used, only if two functions have disjoint domains. The disjointness of the domains of $up_{\neg\epsilon}$, up_ϵ, and up_r is proved in Theorem 6.

$$last_\epsilon(l_1) \neq \epsilon \wedge last_\epsilon(l_2) \neq \epsilon\} \cup$$
$$\{(l_1, l_2) : OneKeyLog \times OneKeyLog \mid \neg endwithR(l_1, l_2) \wedge$$
$$(last_\epsilon(l_1) = \epsilon \vee last_\epsilon(l_2) = \epsilon)\} \cup \operatorname{dom} up_r$$
$$= \{\text{Set theory. Predicate logic.}\}$$
$$\{(l_1, l_2) : OneKeyLog \times OneKeyLog \mid \neg endwithR(l_1, l_2)\} \cup \operatorname{dom} up_r$$
$$= \{\text{Definitions of } up_r.\}$$
$$\{(l_1, l_2) : OneKeyLog \times OneKeyLog \mid \neg endwithR(l_1, l_2)\} \cup$$
$$\{(l_1, l_2) : OneKeyLog \times OneKeyLog \mid endwithR(l_1, l_2)\}$$
$$= \{\text{Set theory. Predicate logic.}\}$$
$$\{(l_1, l_2) : OneKeyLog \times OneKeyLog \mid true\}$$
$$= OneKeyLog \times OneKeyLog \qquad \qquad \square$$

Moreover, our compositional approach of defining up makes sense only if the domains of its component functions disjoin from each other.

Theorem 6 (Disjointness). *The domains of $up_{\neg\epsilon}$, up_ϵ and up_r are disjoint.*

Proof. In order to prove the disjointness, it is sufficient to prove

$$\operatorname{dom} up_\epsilon \subseteq \operatorname{dom} up \setminus \operatorname{dom} up_r \qquad (1)$$
$$\operatorname{dom} up_{\neg\epsilon} \subseteq (\operatorname{dom} up \setminus \operatorname{dom} up_r) \setminus \operatorname{dom} up_\epsilon \qquad (2)$$

The proof of (1).

$$\operatorname{dom} up \setminus \operatorname{dom} up_r$$
$$= \{\text{Definition of } up \text{ and } up_r. \text{ Totality of } up. \text{ Definition of } \setminus.\}$$
$$\{(l_1, l_2) : OneKeyLog \times OneKeyLog \mid \neg endwithR(l_1, l_2)\}$$
$$\supseteq \{\text{Predicate logic.}\}$$
$$\{(l_1, l_2) : OneKeyLog \times OneKeyLog \mid \neg endwithR(l_1, l_2) \wedge$$
$$(last_\epsilon(l_1) = \epsilon \vee last_\epsilon(l_2) = \epsilon)\}$$
$$= \{\text{Definition of } up_\epsilon.\}$$
$$\operatorname{dom} up_\epsilon$$

The proof of (2).

$$(\operatorname{dom} up \setminus \operatorname{dom} up_r) \setminus \operatorname{dom} up_\epsilon$$
$$= \{\text{Definition of } up_\epsilon. \text{ Definition of } \setminus.\}$$
$$\{(l_1, l_2) : OneKeyLog \times OneKeyLog \mid \neg endwithR(l_1, l_2) \wedge$$
$$last_\epsilon(l_1) \neq \epsilon \wedge last_\epsilon(l_2) \neq \epsilon\}$$
$$= \{\text{Definition of } up_{\neg\epsilon}.\}$$
$$up_{\neg\epsilon} \qquad \qquad \square$$

5.3   Soundness of Using Characteristic-Entry Logs

When applying the formally specified up-to-date rule, characteristic-entry logs can be used in the same way as normal logs. To prove this, two lemmas are needed here.

Lemma 7. *Given any log, l : OneKeyLog, $last_\epsilon(l) = last_\epsilon(ce(l))$.*

Lemma 8. *Given any two logs, l_1, l_2 : OneKeyLog,*
$endwithR(l_1, l_2) = endwithR(ce(l_1), ce(l_2))$.

The soundness of using characteristic-entry logs for the up-to-date rule is proven in the following theorem.

Theorem 7 (Soundness). *Given any two logs, l_1, l_2 : OneKeyLog,*
$up(l_1, l_2) = up(ce(l_1), ce(l_2))$.

Proof. up is defined in a compositional way. Its domain consists of the domains of $up_{\neg\epsilon}$, up_ϵ and up_r, which are disjoint. Thus the proof of this theorem can be done case by case. **Case** $up_{\neg\epsilon}$. In this case, none of l_1 and l_2 is empty. According to Lemma 7 and Lemma 8, it can be easily verified that $(ce(l_1), ce(l_2)) \in$ dom $up_{\neg\epsilon}$. According to the definition of $up_{\neg\epsilon}$, the most recent one of $last(l_1)$ and $last(l_2)$ is chosen for propagation, which is the most recent one of $last(ce(l_1))$ and $last(ce(l_2))$. Thus $up_{\neg\epsilon}(l_1, l_2) = up_{\neg\epsilon}(ce(l_1), (l_2))$. **Case** up_ϵ. In a similar way, the case of up_ϵ can be proven. **Case** up_r. up_r filters out read accesses in logs and applies up to the rest of the log entries. When applying up to the rest of the log entries, $up_{\neg\epsilon}$ and up_ϵ are used. Due to the fact the cases of up_ϵ and $up_{\neg\epsilon}$ have been proven, it can be easily proven that $up_r(l_1, l_2) = up_r(ce(l_1), ce(l_2))$.   □

6   Conclusion

This work has been carried out in the Phenom project [2] of Philips Research Laboratories. One of Phenom's research topics is the design of a distributed data management system for future home environments. Our work is a direct contribution to producing a working research prototype. When the prototype is ready to be transferred to product divisions of Philips, either the author's code could become product code, or, at least, it will be used as a reference implementation. Moreover, the formal specification of data synchronization can be used in system testing and verification.

So far there have not been many applications of formal methods in studying disconnected updates. Semantic rules are expressed in an informal way and, thus, data synchronization is rather vulnerable. In our work, semantic rules are formally specified and synchronization is carried out in a rigorous way, which is helpful to researchers on data synchronization to improve their understanding on semantic rules and data synchronization.

In our project, we used Z-notation in formalization and proof. We extensively used axiomatic definitions of Z and purposely avoid using schemas and schema calculus, to make the specification and proof tasks easier. To manage the complexity of specifications and proofs, we used a compositional approach to define complex functions, namely using the built-in overriding operation of Z to compose partially defined functions. This practice turns out to be rather effective. Specifications of complex functions become comprehensible. Z-notation proves to be a powerful tool in modelling logs and semantic rules and in proving correctness of data synchronization. The mathematical machinery of Z is sufficient for our project. Our proofs are carried out as rigorously as possible. In the future, it would be nice to check them using theorem provers. This paper is an example of formal development work on a problem that is relevant in practice.

Acknowledgements

The author would like to thank L.M.G. Feijs, M. Bodlaender, E. van Loenen, and R. Udink for their comments on this paper.

References

1. Y. Qian, R. Udink, L.M.G. Feijs. A photo management system for future home environments. *Proc. of International ITEA Workshop on Virtual Home Environments*. Shaker Verlag, 2002, 93–101.
2. E. van Loenen, N. de Jong, E. Dijk, E. van den Hoven, Y. Qian, D. Teixeira: Phenom. In Aarts, E., Marzanon, S.(eds.): The New Everyday, Views on Ambient Intelligence. Koninklijke Philips Electronics N.V. 010 Publishers. (2003) 302–303.
3. E. Pitoura, B. Bhargava. Data Consistency in Intermittently Connected Distributed Systems, *Knowledge and Data Engineering*, 11(6), 1999, 896–915.
4. J.J. Kistler, M. Satyanarayanan. Disconnected Operation in the Coda File System, *Proc. 13th ACM Symp. on Operating Systems Principles*, 25(5), 1991, 213–225.
5. B.C. Pierce: Unison File Synchronizor.
   http://www.cis.upenn.edu/~bcpierce/unison/
6. S. Balasubramaniam, B.C. Pierce: What is a File Synchronizer? CSCI Technical Report #507. Indiana University (1998)
7. N. Ramsey, E. Csirmaz: An algebraic approach to file synchronization. Technical Report TR-05-01, Harvard University, Dept. of Computer Science, May 2001.
8. P. Kumar, M. Satyanarayanan. Log-Based Directory Resolution in the Coda File System, *Proc. 2nd International Conference on Parallel and Distributed Information Systems*, 1993, 202–213.
9. P. Reiher, J. Heidemann, D. Ratner, G. Skinner, G.J. Popek. Resolving File Conflicts in the Ficus File System, *Proc. USENIX Summer Conference*, 1994, 183–195.
10. G.R. Guy, J.S. Heidemann, W. Mak, T.W. Page, G.J. Popek, D. Rothmeier. Implementation of the Ficus Replicated File System, *Proc. USENIX Summer Conference*, CA, USA, June 1990, 63-71.
11. D.S. Parker, G.J. Popek, G. Rudisin, A. Stoughton, B. Walker, E. Walton, J. Chow, D. Edwards, S. Kieser, C. Kline. Detection of Mutual Inconsistency in Distributed Systems, *IEEE Trans. Software Engineering*, 9(3), 1983, 240–246.
12. S.B. Davidson, H. Garcia-Molina, D. Skeen. Consistency in Partitioned Networks, *ACM Computing Surveys*, 17(3), 1985, 341–370.

13. D.B. Terry, M.M. Theimer, K. Petersen, A.N. Demers, M.J. Spreitzer, C.H. Hauser. Managing Update Conflicts in Bayou, a Weakly Connected Replicated Storage System, *Proc. 15th Symp. on Operating Systems Principles*, 1995, 172–183.
14. Y. Qian, L.M.G Feijs, R. Udink. Characteristic-entry logs in the MemorySafe Information System. *Proc. 14th IASTED International Conference on Parallel and Distributed Computing and Systems*. ACTA Press. 2002, 185–190.
15. W. Cellary, E. Gelenbe, T. Morzy. Concurrency control in distributed database systems. North-Holland, 1988.
16. J.M. Spivey. The Z Notation: a reference manual: 2nd edition. Prentice Hall. 1992.
17. J. Woodcock, J. Davies. Using Z: Specification, Refinement, and Proof. Prentice Hall. 1996.
18. E.W. Dijkstra, C. Scholten. Predicate calculus and program semantics. Springer Verlag, 1990.
19. A. Diller. Z: An Introduction to Formal Methods. John Wiley & Sons. 1990.

Formal Proof of a Polychronous Protocol for Loosely Time-Triggered Architectures

Mickaël Kerbœuf[1], David Nowak[2], and Jean-Pierre Talpin[1]

[1] IRISA & INRIA Rennes
{kerboeuf,talpin}@irisa.fr
[2] LSV, CNRS & ENS Cachan
nowak@lsv.ens-cachan.fr

Abstract. The verification of safety-critical systems has become an area of increasing importance in computer science. The notion of reactive system has emerged to concentrate on problems related to the control of interaction and response-time in mission-critical systems. Synchronous languages have proved to be well-adapted to the verification of reactive systems. It is nonetheless commonly argued that real-life systems often do not satisfy the strong hypotheses assumed by the synchronous approach: they are not synchronous. Protocols have however been proposed (e.g. in [1]) to provide an abstract synchronous specification on top of real-time architectures (e.g. loosely time-triggered architectures or LTTA). This abstract model is designed so as to satisfy the synchronous hypotheses and meet the implementation architecture constraints. It makes it possible to design, specify and verify reactive systems in the context of the synchronous approach. In this aim, the present article formalizes the LTTA protocol in the theorem prover Coq and proves its correctness.

1   Introduction

The Synchronous Approach. The verification of safety-critical systems has become an area of increasing importance in computer science because of the constant progression of software developments in sensitive fields like medicine, communication, transportation and (nuclear) energy. The notion of reactive system has emerged to concentrate on problems related to the control of interaction and response-time in mission-critical systems. These strong requirements lead to the development of specific programming languages and related verification tools for reactive systems. The verification of a reactive system can be done by elaborating a discrete model of the system (i.e. as a finite-state machine) specified in a dedicated language (e.g. a synchronous programming language) and then by checking a property against the model (i.e. model checking). Model checking has been used at an industrial scale.

The Coq Proof-Assistant. When a property involves parameters or non-linear numerical terms, its verification by model checking is not straightforward and can sometimes be tedious. Another possibility to verify a reactive system is the

J.S. Dong and J. Woodcock (Eds.): ICFEM 2003, LNCS 2885, pp. 359–374, 2003.

use of a theorem prover such as Coq [9]. For instance, the semantics of the synchronous language Signal [8] has been formalized in Coq and the correctness of a steam-boiler implemented in Signal has been proved [6]. Coq [9] is a proof-assistant for higher-order logic. It allows the development of computer programs that are consistent with their formal specification. The logical language used in Coq is a variety of type theory, the *Calculus of Inductive Constructions* [10]. Due to the high expressive capability of this logic, proofs in Coq requires human-interaction to *direct* the strategy. The prover can nonetheless automate its most tedious and mechanical parts. Indeed, decisions procedures are implemented.

Synchronous languages (e.g. Esterel [3], Lustre [5], Signal [2]) have proved to be well adapted to the verification of reactive systems. Unfortunately, real systems often do not satisfy the strong hypotheses assumed by the synchronous approach: they are not synchronous.

Loosely Time-Triggered Architectures. A distributed real-time control system has a time-triggered nature just because the physical system for control is bound to physics. A loosely time-triggered architecture (LTTA) is one in which:

- Bus access is quasi-periodic and non-blocking
- Read and write operations are independent
- Values are sustained by the bus and periodically refreshed.

The clock rates at which data are, written to, updated by, read from the bus are not synchronous: a LTTA is a multi-clocked control system in which clocks are moreover bound to *physical* time and deviate one from each others. Here, the term *polychronous* refers to this multi-clocked feature. The LTTA has been extensively investigated in [4] and used in several major industries.

Logical Clocks on Top of LTTAs. That is why a protocol is proposed in [1] which provides an abstract level on top of an LTTA. This abstract level is such that the the synchronous hypotheses are satisfied. It is then possible to design, specify and verify reactive systems in the context of the synchronous approach.

Outline. In Section 2, we describe the protocol. Section 3 is devoted to previous work, especially partial proofs of the protocol by model checking. In Section 4, we explain our formalization in Coq, and we show in section 5 how this approach can be used as a generic formal framework to prove other implementations. Finally, we conclude in Section 6.

2   Description of the Protocol

The LTTA is composed of three devices, a *writer*, a *bus*, and a *reader*. Each device **d** is activated by its own, approximately periodic, clock (denoted by a function $t^{\mathbf{d}}$).

Writer. At the nth clock tick (time $t^{\mathbf{w}}(n)$), the *writer* generates the value $x^{\mathbf{w}}(n)$ and an alternating flag $b^{\mathbf{w}}(n)$ s.t.:

$$b^{\mathbf{w}}(n) = \begin{cases} \textit{false} & \text{if } n = 0 \\ \textit{not } b^{\mathbf{w}}(n-1) & \text{otherwise} \end{cases}$$

Both values are stored in its output buffer, denoted by $y^{\mathbf{w}}$. At any time t, the writer's output buffer $y^{\mathbf{w}}$ contains the last value that was written into it:

$$y^{\mathbf{w}}(t) = (x^{\mathbf{w}}(n), b^{\mathbf{w}}(n)), \text{ where } n = \sup\{n' \mid t^{\mathbf{w}}(n') < t\} \qquad (1)$$

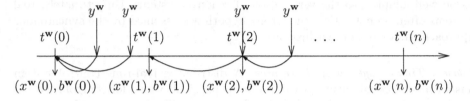

Bus. At $t^{\mathbf{b}}(n)$, the *bus* bus fetches $y^{\mathbf{w}}$ to store in the input buffer of the reader, denoted by $y^{\mathbf{b}}$. Thus, at any time t, the reader input buffer is defined by:

$$y^{\mathbf{b}}(t) = y^{\mathbf{w}}(t^{\mathbf{b}}(n)), \text{ where } n = \sup\{n' \mid t^{\mathbf{b}}(n') < t\} \qquad (2)$$

$$
\begin{array}{ccccc}
y^{\mathbf{b}} & y^{\mathbf{b}} & & y^{\mathbf{b}} & y^{\mathbf{b}} \\
t^{\mathbf{b}}(n) & t^{\mathbf{b}}(n+1) & t^{\mathbf{b}}(n+2) & & t^{\mathbf{b}}(p) \\
y^{\mathbf{w}}(t^{\mathbf{b}}(n)) & y^{\mathbf{w}}(t^{\mathbf{b}}(n+1)) & y^{\mathbf{w}}(t^{\mathbf{b}}(n+2)) & \cdots & y^{\mathbf{w}}(t^{\mathbf{b}}(p))
\end{array}
$$

Reader. At $t^{\mathbf{r}}(n)$, the *reader* loads the input buffer $y^{\mathbf{b}}$ into the variables $x(n)$ and $b(n)$:

$$y^{\mathbf{r}} = (x(n), b(n)) = y^{\mathbf{b}}(t^{\mathbf{r}}(n)) \qquad (3)$$

Then, in a similar manner as for an alternating bit protocol, the reader extracts $x(n)$ iff $b(n)$ has changed. This is by the sequence m of ticks where b changes:

$$m(0) = 0, \; m(n) = \inf\{k > m(n-1) \mid b(k) \neq b(k-1)\}$$
$$x^{\mathbf{r}}(k) = x(m(k)) \qquad (4)$$

$$
\begin{array}{cccc}
t^{\mathbf{r}}(n) & & t^{\mathbf{r}}(n+1) & \cdots & t^{\mathbf{r}}(p) \\
y^{\mathbf{r}}(n) = y^{\mathbf{b}}(t^{\mathbf{r}}(n)) & & y^{\mathbf{r}}(n+1) = y^{\mathbf{b}}(t^{\mathbf{r}}(n+1)) & & y^{\mathbf{r}}(p) = y^{\mathbf{b}}(t^{\mathbf{r}}(p))
\end{array}
$$

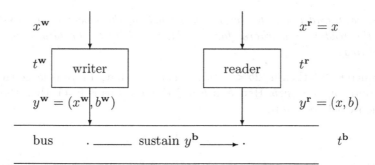

$x^{\mathbf{w}}$ $x^{\mathbf{r}} = x$

$t^{\mathbf{w}}$ writer   reader $t^{\mathbf{r}}$

$y^{\mathbf{w}} = (x^{\mathbf{w}}, b^{\mathbf{w}})$ $y^{\mathbf{r}} = (x, b)$

bus   . ——— sustain $y^{\mathbf{b}}$ ——→ . $t^{\mathbf{b}}$

Example. We illustrate the protocol by the following picture. Notice the role of the flag b: if the writer sends the same value along $x^{\mathbf{w}}$ twice, the boolean flag switch ensures that this value will be read twice on $x^{\mathbf{r}}$. On the opposite, if the value is sent once along $x^{\mathbf{w}}$ and read twice along $x^{\mathbf{r}}$, the boolean flag samples the excess of reading.

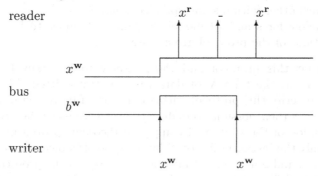

Flag switches are detected by the reader by a non predictable but bounded delay according to *physical* time: perfect physical synchrony is lost.

Correctness of the Protocol. We define here the expected behavior. In any execution of the protocol, the sequences $x^{\mathbf{w}}$ and $x^{\mathbf{r}}$ must coincide, i.e.,

$$\forall n \cdot x^{\mathbf{r}}(n) = x^{\mathbf{w}}(n) \tag{5}$$

In order to prove the correctness of the protocol, we need to prove that, under some hypotheses on the clocks, the property (5) is true.

3   Previous Work

In [1], the following theorem is proved by hand.

Theorem 1 (sampling theorem). *The LTTA protocol satisfies the property (5) if the following conditions hold:*

$$w \geq b \,, \text{ and } \left\lfloor \frac{w}{b} \right\rfloor \geq \frac{r}{b} \,, \tag{6}$$

where w, b and r are the respective periods of the clocks of the writer, the bus and the reader, and where, for $x \in \mathbb{R}$, $\lfloor x \rfloor$ denotes the largest integer less or equal to x.

Since $w \geq b$ then $w/2b < \lfloor w/b \rfloor$. Also note that, if w/b is large then $\lfloor w/b \rfloor \leq w/b$ and $\lfloor w/b \rfloor \sim w/b$. Hence, if $b \sim 0$ (i.e. the bus is fast), then the conditions of theorem 1 reduce to:

$$w \gg b \, , w > r.$$

In [1], it was shown using symbolic model-checking that a discrete SIGNAL model of the LTTA protocol (i.e. a finite-state approximation of the actual protocol) satisfied the desirable requirement of ensuring a coherent distribution of clocks. However, the assumptions ensuring correctness of the actual LTTA protocol are quantitative in nature (tolerance bounds for the relative periods, and time variations, of the different clocks). For the protocol to be correct, the clocks must be quasi-periodic (periods can vary within certain specified bounds), and must relate to each other within some specified bounds.

In order to allow for standard model checking techniques to be used, two kinds of abstractions of the protocol are necessary:

– It is clear that this protocol and the property to be verified are data-independent w.r.t. the type X of data which is transmitted. Therefore, it is sufficient to verify this protocol with a finite set of finite instantiations of the type X. It is then possible to deduce the correctness of the protocol for any instantiation of the type X, by applying theorems proved in [7]. However,in [1], only the instantiation of X by the type of booleans is considered. It is not proved and not evident that the correctness of the protocol for this instantiation is sufficient to prove the correctness of the protocol for any instantiation of X.

– Conditions (6) are abstraction by conditions on ordering between events. The first condition, $w \geq b$, is abstracted by the predicate:

$$w \geq b \leftrightarrow \text{never two } t^{\mathbf{w}} \text{ between two } t^{\mathbf{b}}. \tag{7}$$

The abstraction of the second condition, $\lfloor w/b \rfloor \geq r/b$ requires the following definition of the first instant (of the bus) $\tau^{\mathbf{b}}(n)$ where the bus can fetch the nth writing:

$$\tau^{\mathbf{b}}(n) \;=\; \min\{ \; t^{\mathbf{b}}(p) \mid t^{\mathbf{b}}(p) > t^{\mathbf{w}}(n) \; \}$$

The second condition is then restated as the requirement (8) that no two successive $\tau^{\mathbf{b}}$ can occur between two successive $t^{\mathbf{r}}$:

$$\left\lfloor \frac{w}{b} \right\rfloor \geq \frac{r}{b} \leftrightarrow \text{never two } \tau^{\mathbf{b}} \text{ between two successive } t^{\mathbf{r}}. \tag{8}$$

This verification has been done twice: with Lustre and its model checker Lesar; and with Signal and its model checker Sigali.

4   Abstraction and Formalization in Coq

We investigate the use of the theorem prover Coq as a general formal framework for any implementation of the protocol for LTTAs. In this section we describe our formalization in Coq. The translation of the specification is quite straightforward. We introduce some syntactical elements of Coq to illustrate this point.

4.1   Data, Time and Clocks

Data. The type of data is seen as an abstract data type $\mathcal{D}$ (`Data` in Coq). We do not need any relation or hypothesis on this type. It was not the case in the proof by model checking [1] where $\mathcal{D}$ was supposed to be the type of booleans.

```
Parameter Data : Set.
```

Physical Time. Physical time is also seen as an abstract data type i.e., a type $\mathcal{T}$ (`Time` in Coq), a binary predicate $\leq$ (`time_le` in Coq) and the assumption that $\leq$ is reflexive, transitive and total. We do *not* assume time is discrete. These are the only hypotheses on physical time we need for our proof.

$$\forall t \in \mathcal{T}, t \leq t$$
$$\forall t_1, t_2, t_3 \in \mathcal{T}, t_1 \leq t_2 \leq t_3 \;\Rightarrow\; t_1 \leq t_3$$
$$\forall t_1, t_2 \in \mathcal{T}, t_1 \leq t_2 \;\vee\; t_2 \leq t_1$$

In Coq, it is written

```
Variable Time : Type.
Variable time_le : Time->Time->Prop.
Hypothesis time_le_reflexive :
 (t:Time)(time_le t t).
Hypothesis time_le_transitive :
 (t1,t2,t3:Time)(time_le t1 t2)->(time_le t2 t3)->(time_le t1 t3).
Hypothesis time_le_total :
 (t1,t2:Time)(time_le t1 t2)(time_le t2 t1).
```

The keywords `Variable` and `Hypothesis` mean that it will be possible to instantiate those type (for example, by the type of reals available in Coq), relation and hypotheses in order to obtain specializations of the proved theorems. We will then be able to prove stronger theorems depending on particular instantiations.

Clocks. A clock c is modeled by two (possibly partial) functions. The first one, t_c (`time` in Coq), maps any natural number n in its domain to the instant $t \in \mathcal{T}$ when nth sampling tick occurs. The only assumption on this function is that it is strictly monotonic (`monotonicity` in Coq). The second function, l_c (`lTick` in Coq), maps any time $t \in \mathcal{T}$ to the number of the occurrence of the tick which immediately precedes the instant t. It is defined relationally by its characteristic property (`current_tick` in Coq):

$$\forall n \in \mathbb{N} \;\cdot\; \forall x \in \mathcal{T} \;\cdot\; t_c(n) < x \leq t_c(n+1) \;\Leftrightarrow\; n = l_c(x)$$

This function enables to access the value carried by the writer or by the bus at the *last tick* of its clock.

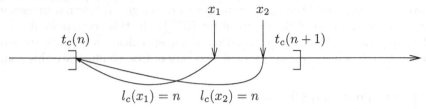

For instance, if t_c stands for t^b, then $l_c(x)$ (noted $l_b(x)$ in this case) correspond to $\sup\{n' \mid t^b(n') < x\}$. Thus, we have:

$$y^b(x) = y^w(t^b(n)), \text{ where } n = \sup\{n' \mid t^b(n') < x\}$$
$$= y^w(l_b(x))$$

A clock c is defined by the functions t_c and l_c. In Coq the type of clock is defined by a structure which embeds time (t_c), lTick (l_c) and two characteristic properties of t_c and l_c, namely `monotonicity` and `current_tick`.

```
Record Clock : Type := {
  time :> nat->Time;
  monotonicity : (n,n':nat)(lt n n')->(time_lt (time n) (time n'));
  lTick : Time->nat;
  current_tick :
   (n:nat; t:Time)
   (time_lt (time n) t)/\(time_le t (time (S n))) <-> n=(lTick t)
}.
```

The character ">" is used for the convenient mechanism of implicit coercion provided by Coq. Suppose that c is of type `Clock`. c is a record and not a function. Anyway we can apply it and Coq will instead apply the field `time` f the record c. It means we can simply write c n instead of `time` c n. It improves the readability.

Some useful results about monotonicity follow from the definition of clocks:

$$\forall c, \forall n, \forall n' \ (t_c(n) < t_c(n')) \Rightarrow (n < n')$$
$$\forall c, \forall n, \forall n' \ (n \leq n') \Rightarrow (t_c(n) \leq t_c(n'))$$

They are stated and proved in Coq:

```
Lemma monotonicity_inv :
  (c:Clock; n,n':nat)
  (time_lt (c n) (c n'))->(lt n n').
Lemma monotonicity_le :
  (c:Clock; n,n':nat)
  (le n n')->(time_le (c n) (c n')).
```

The following lemma is a fundamental property of l_c (lTick in Coq). It follows from its characteristic property. It guarantees that at any time t, $l_c(t)$ actually occurs after (or at the same time as) any tick n which itself occurs before t: $\forall c, \forall n, \forall t, \ (t_c(n) < t) \Rightarrow (t_c(n) \leq t_c(l_c(t)))$.

```
Lemma following_ticks :
  (c:Clock; n:nat;t:Time)
  (time_lt (c n) t) -> (time_le (c n) (c (1Tick c t))).
```

4.2   Writer, Bus and Reader

Following strictly definitions from [1], the three devices are formalized as follows:

```
Variable tw : Clock.
Variable xw : nat->Data.
Fixpoint  bw [n:nat] : bool :=
  Cases n of
    0 => false
  | (S p) => (negb (bw p))
  end.
Definition yw_x [t:Time] : Data := (xw (1Tick tw t)).
Definition yw_b [t:Time] : bool := (bw (1Tick tw t)).
```

We assume a clock `tw` for the writer and a sequence of values it writes `xw`. `bw` is the sequence of alternating booleans. It is used in order to implement the alternating bit protocol. `yw_x` (respectively, `yw_b`) maps a time $t \in \mathcal{T}$ to the last written value of `xw` (respectively, `bw`) at this time t.

We assume a clock `tb` for the bus. We define `yb_x` (respectively, `yb_b`) which maps a time $t \in \mathcal{T}$ to the last value (respectively, boolean) received by the bus at the time t.

```
Variable tb : Clock.
Definition yb_x [t:Time] : Data := (yw_x (tb (1Tick tb t))).
Definition yb_b [t:Time] : bool := (yw_b (tb (1Tick tb t))).
```

We assume a clock `tr` for the reader. We define `x` (respectively, `y`) to be the nth received value (respectively, boolean) by the reader.

```
Variable tr : Clock.
Definition x [n:nat] : Data := (yb_x (tr n)).
Definition b [n:nat] : bool := (yb_b (tr n)).
```

4.3   Abstraction

Two kinds of abstractions are needed for the automatic proofs of the protocol. The carried data are restricted to finitely enumerated types, and the quantitative assumptions (6) are abstracted into event ordering assumptions (7 and 8). In our approach, the first abstraction is avoided (thanks to the generic type $\mathcal{D}$), but we deliberately keep the second one. It appears to be more general than the initial statement. Indeed, whatever the respective quasi-periods of the writer, the bus and the reader (w, b and r) may be, it ensure all written values are actually fetched by the bus, and then read by the reader. Moreover, we aim at defining in Coq a kind of meta-model for data-flow encodings (like the Lustre and Signal ones proposed in [1]).

In order to be more general, and for more legibility, we did not introduce either the counter of bit alternations detected by the reader, nor the sequence x^r of validated values. Actually, b must be specified only for automatic proofs of the protocol. In this case, the written *values* and the read *values* are related, hence the necessity to implement a mechanism for values discrimination on the reader's side. Here, we aim at validating the protocol whatever the mechanism b for discrimination may be. In Coq, we can relate the *instants* when a value is written with the *instants* when a value is read. We suppose a part of the transmitted values enables the reader to sample correctly the received values. This is the case with b. Then, the correctness property (5) which handles *values* follows.

We define a function called *read_index* which maps to a given reading tick k the writing tick $read\_index(k)$ corresponding to the instant (on the writer's clock) when the writer emitted the value that can be read at the instant k (on the reader's clock). The following figure illustrates this function:

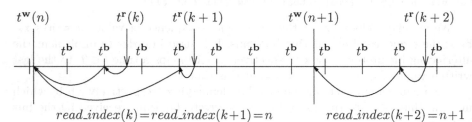

$$read\_index(k) = read\_index(k+1) = n \qquad read\_index(k+2) = n+1$$

This function is defined as follows:

$$read\_index \; : \; \left| \begin{array}{l} \mathbb{N} \to \mathbb{N} \\ k \mapsto l_{\mathbf{w}}(t^{\mathbf{b}}(l_{\mathbf{b}}(t^{\mathbf{r}}(k)))) \end{array} \right.$$

The moment of the kth reading tick is $t^{\mathbf{r}}(k)$. The last tick on the bus at this time $(l_{\mathbf{b}}(t^{\mathbf{r}}(k)))$ occurs at $t^{\mathbf{b}}(l_{\mathbf{b}}(t^{\mathbf{r}}(k)))$. The carried value at that time corresponds to the value sent by the writer at its previous tick: $l_{\mathbf{w}}(t^{\mathbf{b}}(l_{\mathbf{b}}(t^{\mathbf{r}}(k))))$. According to the protocol statement, we actually have the following relation:

$$\begin{aligned}
\forall k \in \mathbb{N}, \, (x(k), b(k)) \\
= y^{\mathbf{b}}(t^{\mathbf{r}}(k)) \\
= y^{\mathbf{w}}(t^{\mathbf{b}}(l_{\mathbf{b}}(t^{\mathbf{r}}(k)))) \\
= \left(\, x^{\mathbf{w}}(l_{\mathbf{w}}(t^{\mathbf{b}}(l_{\mathbf{b}}(t^{\mathbf{r}}(k))))) \, , \, b^{\mathbf{w}}(l_{\mathbf{w}}(t^{\mathbf{b}}(l_{\mathbf{b}}(t^{\mathbf{r}}(k))))) \, \right) \\
= (x^{\mathbf{w}}(read\_index(k)), b^{\mathbf{w}}(read\_index(k)))
\end{aligned}$$

Now, we focus on *read_index*, which relates the *instants* when a value is written with the *instants* when a value is read. To prove the correctness of the protocol, we only have to prove that *read_index* is increasing, and that it covers $\mathbb{N}$ (so that all written values are actually read):

$$\forall k_1, k_2 \in \mathbb{N}, \, k_1 < k_2 \Rightarrow read\_index(k_1) \leq read\_index(k_2)$$
$$\forall n \in \mathbb{N}, \, \exists k \in \mathbb{N} \text{ st. } n = read\_index(k)$$

Thus, all written values are actually read (and possibly more than once) in a correct order. Whatever the mechanism b for discrimination may be, it is possible to validate $x(0)$ and each $x(k+1)$ such that $b(k+1)$ and $b(k)$ are different.

$$\forall n \in \mathbb{N}, \; \exists k \in \mathbb{N}, \; \text{st. } x^{\mathbf{w}}(n) = x(k) \; \wedge \; b^{\mathbf{w}}(n) = b(k)$$

The property (5) follows when $\forall k \in \mathbb{N}$, $b^{\mathbf{w}}(k+1) \neq b^{\mathbf{w}}(k)$. It is actually the case with the alternating bit protocol.

4.4 Correctness of the Protocol

This result holds under the specific conditions (7) and (8). We state them in Coq with the unique following assumption:

$$\forall n \in \mathbb{N}, \; \exists k \in \mathbb{N}, \; \text{st. } \tau^{\mathbf{b}}(n) < t^{\mathbf{r}}(k) \leq \tau^{\mathbf{b}}(n+1)$$

It guarantees that all written values are actually fetched by the bus ($\tau^{\mathbf{b}}(n)$ always exists, and $\tau^{\mathbf{b}}(n+1) \neq \tau^{\mathbf{b}}(n)$ since there is at least one instant $t^{\mathbf{r}}(k)$ which occurs in between them), and all fetched values are actually read by the reader ($\tau^{\mathbf{b}}(n) < t^{\mathbf{r}}(k) \leq \tau^{\mathbf{b}}(n+1)$). This assumption is illustrated by the following picture:

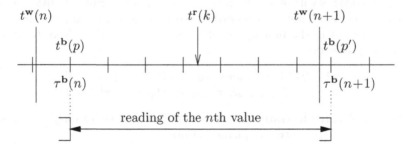

To state this condition, we formally define $\tau^{\mathbf{b}}$ as follows:

$$\forall n \in \mathbb{N}, \; \exists k \in \mathbb{N}, \; \text{st. } \begin{cases} \tau^{\mathbf{b}}(n) = t^{\mathbf{b}}(k) \\ \wedge \; t^{\mathbf{w}}(n) < t^{\mathbf{b}}(k) \\ \wedge \; \forall k' \in \mathbb{N}, \; k' < k \Rightarrow t^{\mathbf{b}}(k') \leq t^{\mathbf{w}}(n) \end{cases} \tag{9}$$

5   A Formal Framework for Any Implementation

Principles. The Coq encoding of the protocol for LTTAs we described in the previous section can be seen as a high level abstracted implementation. It is founded on the smallest set of physical requirements (e.g. time is an abstract domain which only comes with a reflexive, transitive and total relation) and logical requirements (e.g. no two successive writing ticks can occur without a bus tick in between them). Thus, any other implementation must provide at least these requirements. Its correctness then follows.

We can refine this approach by adding an intermediate level between Coq and the analyzed implementation. This interface details the expected form of the time domain (variable $\mathcal{T}$ in Coq) and its order (time_le in Coq), and the data domain (variable $\mathcal{D}$ in Coq). It must also make explicit the clocks, and the first instant $\tau^{\mathbf{b}}(n)$ where the bus can fetch the nth writing. Then the hypotheses concerning the time domain must be proved, and the assumptions concerning the correctness must be restated. To prove the correctness of any implementation built upon the model denoted by the intermediate level, we only have to prove its specification implies the assumptions of its interface.

Examples. Consider the manual proof of theorem 1 in [1]. It is built upon the explicit periods w, b and r (respectively of the writer, the bus and the reader) and the phases ψ and φ (respectively of the writer and the reader). The time domain (continuous) is denoted by $\mathbb{R}$. The logical statement of $\tau^{\mathbf{b}}$ (9) in Coq is implied by the functional statement $\tau^{\mathbf{b}}(n) = \lfloor (n + \psi)w \rfloor + 1$. In this approach, the correctness of the protocol comes from:

$$w \geq b \text{ , and } \left\lfloor \frac{w}{b} \right\rfloor \geq \frac{r}{b} \ \Rightarrow\ \forall n \in \mathbb{N}, \ \exists k \in \mathbb{N}, \ \text{st. } \tau^{\mathbf{b}}(n) < t^{\mathbf{r}}(k) \leq \tau^{\mathbf{b}}(n+1)$$

Now, in [1], another theorem is stated in order to take into account *approximately* periodic clocks. $t^{\mathbf{w}}$, $t^{\mathbf{b}}$ and $t^{\mathbf{r}}$ are restated including jitter terms $\delta^{\mathbf{w}}$ and $\delta^{\mathbf{r}}$ which denote the variations within a certain bound of w and b during execution. In this approach, the time domain and its order, the data domain and the clocks have the same nature as in the first approach without jitter. All we have to prove is the following property:

$$w(1 - 2\delta^{\mathbf{w}}) \geq 1 \text{ , and } \lfloor w(1 - 2\delta^{\mathbf{w}}) \rfloor \geq r(1 + 2\delta^{\mathbf{r}})$$
$$\Rightarrow \forall n \in \mathbb{N}, \ \exists k \in \mathbb{N}, \ \text{st. } \tau^{\mathbf{b}}(n) < t^{\mathbf{r}}(k) \leq \tau^{\mathbf{b}}(n+1)$$

The following picture illustrates the use of the Coq approach as a generic formal framework to prove these two implementations:

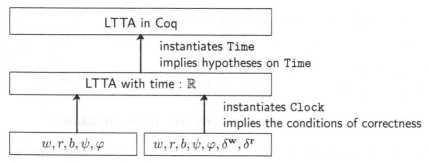

5.1   LTTA in Signal

We illustrate here the same principle for the Signal solution suggested in [1]. We first define the intermediate level of any synchronous data-flow approach. Then, we show how proving the Signal implementation matches these requirements.

To any device d of a LTTA is associated a clock which provides the sampling instants. It is possible to access a value at any time thanks to the function l_d associated to the device d which enables to access the value carried at the previous tick:

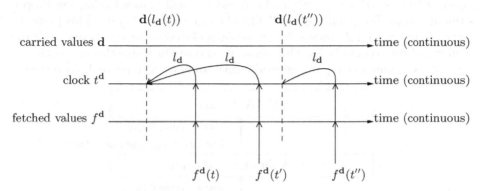

Data-Flow Synchronous Approaches. In these approaches, the time continuum is abstracted. Only the notions of precedence and simultaneity are relevant. It is therefore very simple to abstract the time domain using the sampling events. In synchronous data-flow approaches, the clock t^d only defines the ordered set of sampling instants, and the carried values d are represented by a *signal* synchronized with t^d. In order to make it possible to fetch the carried values *at any time*, we introduce a signal f^d whose clock[1] (noted $\hat{f}^d$) is completely free. For that purpose, we use the cell construct of Signal. It enables to memorize the last value carried by a given signal. f^d can be simply defined as follows:

$$f^d := (d \text{ cell } \hat{f}^d) \text{ when } \hat{f}^d$$

The following picture illustrates this abstraction:

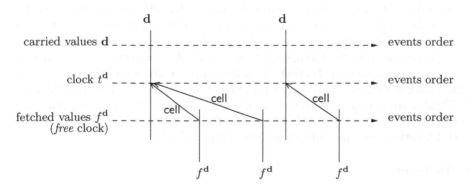

This abstraction can be encoded in Coq using the translation scheme detailed in [8].

---

[1] In a data-flow synchronous approach, by *clock* we mean the ordered set of instants where a signal is present.

LTTA in Signal. In the last step, we prove the specification suggested in [1] guarantees that no two successive writing ticks can occur without a bus tick in between them, and that no two successive τ^b can occur without a reading tick in between them. This implies the condition for correctness, i.e. $\forall n \in \mathbb{N}$, $\exists k \in \mathbb{N}$, st. $\tau^b(n) < t^r(k) \leq \tau^b(n+1)$. It can be easily proved using the Propositional Linear Temporal Logic (PLTL) also encoded in Coq [8]. This property comes from the shift_2 process. It introduces an interleaving constraint upon the reader and the writer clocks. The following picture illustrates this approach and underlines the use of Coq as a general formal framework to prove de correctness:

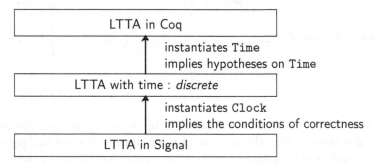

6   Conclusions and Future Work

We gave a formal proof of the correctness of a protocol for loosely time-triggered architectures using the Coq proof-assistant. Unlike [1], we did not have to restrict the model of the protocol to that of a finite-state system: we introduced a minimal set of assumptions about physical time. Since any other implementation of the LTTA protocol must at least guarantee these minimal requirements, our Coq model can be used as a generic formal proof framework. We illustrated this aspect by considering the Signal implementation of [1].

Directions of further studies comprise the specialization of our theorems by instantiating the abstract data type for time by the type for reals provided in Coq. Using the library of theorems and the decision procedures for reals, we could prove the numerical property from [1]. Another direction is to consider the verification of the synchronous data-flow implementation of the protocol. It could be done using the formalization of Signal in Coq and its library of theorem [8]. Finally, an attractive aspect of the use of Coq is the extraction of a reference implementation of the protocol. The only difficulty is that this protocol involves partial function that are difficult to deal with in Coq[2].

References

1. A. Benveniste, P. Caspi, P. L. Guernic, H. Marchand, J.-P. Talpin, and S. Tripakis. A protocol for loosely time-triggered architectures. In *Embedded Software Conference (EMSOFT'2002)*, volume 2491 of *Lecture Notes in Computer Science*, 2002.

---

[2] http://pauillac.inria.fr/pipermail/coq-club/2002/thread.html#569

2. A. Benveniste and P. Le Guernic. Synchronous Programming with Events and Relations: the SIGNAL Language and its Semantics. *Science of Computer Programming*, 16(2):103–149, 1991.

3. G. Berry and G. Gonthier. The ESTEREL Synchronous Programming Language: Design, Semantics, Implementation. *Science of Computer Programming*, 19:87–152, 1992.

4. P. Caspi, C. Mazuet, R. Salem, and D. Weber. Formal design of distributed control systems with lustre. In *Computer Safety, Reliability and Security, 18th International Conference, SAFECOMP'99, Toulouse, France, September, 1999, Proceedings*, volume 1698 of *Lecture Notes in Computer Science*, 1999.

5. N. Halbwachs, P. Caspi, P. Raymond, and D. Pilaud. The Synchronous Dataflow Programming Language LUSTRE. *Proc. of the IEEE*, 79(9):1305–1320, September 1991.

6. M. Kerbœuf, D. Nowak, and J.-P. Talpin. Specification and verification of a steam-boiler with Signal-Coq. In *Proceedings of the 13th International Conference on Theorem Proving in Higher Order Logics (TPHOLs 2000)*, volume 1869 of *Lecture Notes in Computer Science*, pages 356–371. Springer-Verlag, Aug. 2000.

7. R. Lazić and D. Nowak. A unifying approach to data-independence. In *Proceedings of the 11th International Conference on Concurrency Theory (CONCUR 2000)*, volume 1877 of *Lecture Notes in Computer Science*, pages 581–595. Springer-Verlag, Aug. 2000.

8. D. Nowak, J.-R. Beauvais, and J.-P. Talpin. Co-inductive axiomatization of a synchronous language. In *Proceedings of the 11th International Conference on Theorem Proving in Higher Order Logics (TPHOLs'98)*, volume 1479 of *Lecture Notes in Computer Science*, pages 387–399. Springer-Verlag, Sept. 1998.

9. The Coq development team. The Coq proof assistant reference manual : Version 7.3.1. Technical report, INRIA, 2002.

10. B. Werner. *Une Théorie des Constructions Inductives*. PhD thesis, Université Paris VII, 1994.

A   Model of the LTTA Protocol in SIGNAL

An Overview of SIGNAL. In SIGNAL, a process P consists of simultaneous equations over signals. A signal x describes a possibly infinite flow of discretely-timed values v. An equation $x = fy$ denotes a relation between a sequence of operands y and a sequence of results x by an operator f. Synchronous composition $P|Q$ consists of the simultaneous solution of the equations P and Q in time. SIGNAL requires three primitive operators: pre references the previous value of a signal in time (the equation $x = \text{pre}\, y$ or $x = y\$1\, \text{init}\, v$ initially defines x by v and then by the previous value of y in time), when samples a signal (the equation $x = y\, \text{when}\, z$ defines x by y when z is true) and default merges two signals (the equation $x = y\, \text{default}\, z$ defines x by y when y is present and by z otherwise).

$$P ::= x := fy \mid P|Q \mid P/x \qquad f \in F \supseteq \{\text{pre}\,v \mid v \in V\} \cup \{\text{when}, \text{default}, \ldots\}$$

As an example, we consider the definition of a counter: Count. It accepts an input event rst and delivers the integer output val. A local variable cnt, initialized to 0, stores the previous value of val (equation cnt := val\$1 init 0). When the event rst occurs, val is reset to 0 (i.e. 0 when rst). Otherwise, cnt is incremented (i.e. (cnt + 1)). The activity of Count is governed by the clock of its output val which differs from that of its input rst.

process Count = (? event rst ! integer val)	time	t_1	t_2	t_3	t_4	t_5	t_6	t_7	t_8	t_9	t_{10}	t_{11}	t_{12}
(| cnt := val\$1 init 0	rst		tt				tt					tt	tt
| val := (0 when rst) default (cnt + 1)	val	1	0	1	2	3	4	0	1	2	3	0	0
|) where integer cnt end;	cnt	0	1	0	1	2	3	4	0	1	2	3	0

SIGNAL Implementation of the LTTA. The methodology used in SIGNAL to implement the LTTA consists of the progressive and compositional refinement of the requirement expressed by theorem 1: $x^r(n) = x^w(n), \forall n \geq 0$ that preserves the property of flow equivalence: xr and xw hold the same successive values. This yields the process ltta.

process ltta = (? boolean xw; event cw, cb, cr ! boolean xr, i, zi)
   (\| (xb, bb, sbw) := bus (xw, writer(xw, cw), cb)
   \| (xr, br, sbb) := reader (xb, bb, cr)
   \| (i, zi) := prove (sbb, br, cr)
   \| objective (sbw, sbb, cb, cr)
   \|) where boolean bw, xb, bb, sbw, sbb, br;

The process ltta is decomposed into its three components reader, bus and writer connected by one-place buffers. The writer accepts an input x^w and defines the boolean flag b^w that will be carried along with it over the bus. The bus forward its inputs x^w and b^w to the reader as the result x^b and b^b of a one-place buffer. The reader loads its inputs x^b and b^b from the bus and samples x^r from x^b upon a switch of b^b. Each of the processes reader, bus and writer operate at independent (input) clocks c^w, c^b and c^r.

process writer = (? boolean xw; event cw ! boolean bw)
   (\| bw ^= xw ^= cw \| bw := not (bw\$1 init true) \|);
process bus = (? boolean xw, bw; event cb ! boolean xb, bb, sbw)
   (\| (xb, bb, sbw) := buffer (xw, bw, cb) \|);
process reader = (? boolean xb, bb; event cr ! boolean xr, br, sbb)
   (\| (yr, br, sbb) := buffer (xb, bb, cr) \| xr := yr when switch (br) \|)
   where boolean yr;
end;

The key switch process emits an output signal c iff two successive occurrences zb and b of the boolean flag differ (notice the importance of the initial condition: zb must be initialized to true).

process switch = (? boolean b ! event c)
   (\| zb := b\$1 init true \| c := (when b when not zb) default (when not b when zb) \|)
   where boolean zb;
end;

We now detail the definition of the desynchronizing one-place buffer which simulates asynchrony. The process buffer alternates between the receipt of an input (x, b) and the emission of an output (bx, bb). The alternate process makes these operations exclusive by using a boolean flip-flop signal b (notice, again, the importance of the initial condition: xb must be initialized to false for receive to precede send). The process current sustains its input signals (ux, ub) and allows to retrieve them at a given clock c.

```
process buffer = (? boolean x, b ; event c ! boolean bx, bb, sb)
  (| (sx, sb) := shift (x, b) | (bx, bb) := current (sx, sb, c) |)
  where boolean sx;
    process alternate = (? boolean x, sx ! )
      (| x ^= when b | sx ^= when not b | b := not (b$1 init false) |)
        where boolean b; end;
    process shift = (? boolean x, b ! boolean sx, sb)
      (| (sx, sb) := current (x, b, ^sb) | alternate (x, sx) |);
end;
process current = (? boolean wx, wb; event c ! boolean rx, rb)
  (| rx := (wx cell c init false) when c | rb := (wb cell c init true) when c |);
```

The process buffer introduces an unspecified delay (materialized by the input clock c), hence we can synchronize it with the output of the protocol xr without affecting the bus or the writer, and check whether they are equal.

A Z Based Approach to Verifying Security Protocols

Benjamin W. Long, Colin J. Fidge, and Antonio Cerone

School of Information Technology and Electrical Engineering
The University of Queensland, Brisbane, Australia
{benl,cjf,antonio}@itee.uq.edu.au

Abstract. Security protocols preserve essential properties, such as confidentiality and authentication, of electronically transmitted data. However, such properties cannot be directly expressed or verified in contemporary formal methods. Via a detailed example, we describe the phases needed to formalise and verify the correctness of a security protocol in the state-oriented Z formalism.

1   Introduction

Security protocols enable confidential and authenticated electronic transmission of sensitive data. Unfortunately, several such protocols thought to be secure have later been found susceptible to attacks [8], so formal proofs of their correctness are essential.

Security protocols are usually described informally using a 'standard notation' [7]. However, this notation provides no semantics or reasoning principles, and can be ambiguous when interpreted in isolation. In contrast, 'formal methods' allow for rigorous specification and verification of computer systems in order to verify system correctness. Therefore, several 'formal methods' have been promoted for verifying the correctness of security protocols [18]. However, non-functional security concepts such as 'confidentiality' and 'authentication' [23,15,21] have been found difficult to specify and analyse. Furthermore, formalising security protocols can seem quite intimidating to security practitioners with little or no formal methods experience.

In this paper we present an intuitive Z [25] based approach for formalising and verifying the correctness of the Needham-Schroeder Public Key Protocol [20], from its informal description, thus demonstrating the essential phases required to achieve such a proof.

2   Previous Work

Many formal methods have been proposed for the verification of security protocols [18,16]. This section provides an overview of the methods closely related to our research.

J.S. Dong and J. Woodcock (Eds.): ICFEM 2003, LNCS 2885, pp. 375–395, 2003.

Work already done in formal verification of security protocols is dominated by event-based methods, such as the spi calculus [1] and CSP [22], and logics [21,2,9], including specialised logics such as the BAN logic [5,26]. Other more popular methods include use of a new concept called *strand spaces* [27], and the purpose-built NRL Protocol Analyzer [17]. However, state-based methods such as B, Z, and VDM have seldom been used and we are interested in promoting the application of such methods since their rich data structures enable accurate modelling of message contents.

Previously, Kemmerer [13] used the Ina Jo formalism to analyse cryptographic protocols. The approach focussed on the assumptions and requirements pertaining to the operation of the cryptographic functions used for constructing cryptographic protocol messages.

Boyd [3] presented a formal design for describing secure communication architectures based on the concepts of 'confidentiality' and 'authentication' using Z. Here, the *communication channel* enabled the concept of message exchange between *users*. His approach was not for the purpose of any protocol in particular but a more general model that may be useful before particular protocols are considered.

Boyd and Kearney [4] explored protocol animation using Z for fair exchange protocols. For the purpose of modelling fair exchange protocols, each agent considers the other to be the intruder. Therefore, the possibility of an external attacker was ignored. Furthermore, the detailed structure of messages used in communication was not defined, thus making it difficult to model attacks made by clever manipulation of protocol messages.

Butler [6] used the B method to formally specify the Needham-Schroeder Protocol, incorporating event-based methodologies such as that of CSP into his model by defining possible event traces. Messages were modelled in some detail, however, an encrypted message was represented informally, merely by including the identity [6] of the agent to whom the key belonged as part of the message.

Inspired by this previous work, our goal is to show how the Z formalism can be used, without modification, to specify and verify security properties merely by careful design and application of appropriate data structures and operations.

3   The Needham-Schroeder Public Key Protocol

Needham and Schroeder [20] explain how public-key cryptography [11] can be used to distribute encryption keys to agents via a trusted third party. This protocol has become a classic example in the literature. Three of the seven steps from the protocol are concerned with authentication between two of the parties and are represented by the commonly used 'standard notation' [7] below.

1. $A \longrightarrow B : \{N_A, A\}_{K_B}$
2. $B \longrightarrow A : \{N_A, N_B\}_{K_A}$
3. $A \longrightarrow B : \{N_B\}_{K_B}$

Firstly, agent Antonio sends a message (step 1) to Ben consisting of a *nonce* N_A (a unique datum used for only one protocol run) [12] and his identity A

encrypted with the public key of the receiver (in this case Ben's public key K_B). This message indicates that someone claiming to be Antonio wishes to establish communication with Ben. At this point Ben does not know that Antonio actually created the message because an intruder could have forged it.

Ben replies by sending a message (step 2) consisting of the nonce received, and also a new nonce N_B generated by him, and encrypts both with the public key of the agent whose identity was part of the received message (in this case Antonio's public key K_A).

If the nonce that Antonio sent as part of the initial message in step 1 is in the message sent in step 2, Antonio knows that Ben received and decrypted the initial message because Ben is the only agent that can decrypt a message that has been encrypted with key K_B, and we assume that it is impossible for any other agent to forge the nonce N_A. (An agent's public key is known by everyone — messages encrypted with it can be decrypted only by the agent's secret private key [11].) However, Antonio can authenticate Ben as the creator of the message only if Antonio trusts that Ben will not reveal Antonio's nonce to any other agent. This requirement forms part of an invariant on the system that we will discuss in Section 7.

Antonio sends Ben's nonce back to him encrypted with Ben's public key (step 3). Ben then knows that Antonio received and decrypted the message sent in step 2. Again, Ben can authenticate the creator of the message only if he trusts that Antonio will not reveal Ben's nonce to any other agent. By receiving this message Ben can also assume that the initial message was from Antonio.

4 Formalising the Protocol

Based on the informal description above, we now illustrate the phases needed to accurately model this protocol in the Z notation [25], via its rich set of mathematical operators.

4.1 Define a Suitable Set of Data Types

The first phase in formalising the protocol is to define a suitable set of data structures that capture the types of data used in the standard notation description. We note that the left-hand side of the standard notation displays the agents whom the messages are being sent between, and the right-hand side displays the messages.

We define *AGENT* to be the set of all agents in the network, including Antonio (A), Ben (B), Colin (C) and a special symbol '$\perp$' to represent 'no agent'.

$AGENT ::= A \mid B \mid C \mid \perp$

The protocol messages are constructed from several data items. Therefore we assume the set of all such items as a given type.

[*ITEM*]

Given the set of all items, the set of all messages *MSG* is the set of all possible sequences of items.

MSG == seq *ITEM*

In the protocol, there are nonce, key, and address items. These can be encrypted individually, or in combination with one or more other items, producing a single encrypted item. To allow for these different types of data, we declare the following four subsets of *ITEM* as an 'axiomatic', global Z definition.

$$
\begin{array}{|l}
NON : \mathbb{P}\,ITEM \\
KEY : \mathbb{P}\,ITEM \\
ADR : \mathbb{P}\,ITEM \\
ENC : \mathbb{P}\,ITEM \\
\hline
\text{disjoint}\langle NON, KEY, ADR, ENC\rangle \\
NON \cup KEY \cup ADR \cup ENC = ITEM
\end{array}
$$

Z's 'disjoint' operator is used to ensure that the sets are pairwise disjoint, i.e., each element within a set is not an element of any other set. For completeness we also specify that each element in *ITEM* must be in one of the newly declared sets.

4.2 Define Supporting Functions

The second phase in formalising the protocol is to define operations on the components of messages. The method of encryption used in the protocol is public key encryption [11]. Therefore we introduce subsets of public and private keys from the set *KEY* of all keys.

$$
\begin{array}{|l}
PUB : \mathbb{P}\,KEY \\
PRV : \mathbb{P}\,KEY \\
pair : KEY \rightarrowtail\!\!\!\rightarrow KEY \\
\hline
disjoint\langle PUB, PRV\rangle \\
PUB \cup PRV = KEY \\
pair = pair^{\sim} \\
\forall\, k : KEY \bullet k \in PRV \Leftrightarrow pair(k) \in PUB
\end{array}
$$

The set *PUB* is the set of public keys, and *PRV* is the set of private keys. The first two predicates in the schema above state that the sets are pairwise disjoint and that every key may only be a public, or a private key. The total bijective function *pair* is introduced to define a one-to-one symmetric correspondence between keys. Symmetry is ensured by the predicate $pair = pair^{\sim}$ (that is, *pair* is identical to its inverse). Thus if the pair (k_1, k_2) exists in the *pair* function, then the pair (k_2, k_1) also exists in the *pair* function. The last predicate specifies that each private key corresponds to a public key and vice versa. Such a predicate, in combination with the symmetry of the *pair* function, ensures that each pair of keys in the *pair* function consists of one private key and one public key.

With these definitions, we now model important properties of the encrypt function *enc* and decrypt function *dec*. The encrypt function maps a key and a message to a unique encrypted item. The decrypt function maps a key k and a message m (that may contain encrypted items) to a message containing all items from m that are either non-encrypted or encrypted using a key other than k, plus items extracted from all encrypted items in m using k.

$$
\begin{array}{|l}
enc : (KEY \times MSG) \rightarrowtail ENC \\
dec : (KEY \times MSG) \rightarrowtail MSG \\
\hline
\forall k, \ell : KEY;\ m, m', m'' : MSG;\ s : ITEM \bullet \\
\quad dec(k, \langle\rangle) = \langle\rangle \wedge \hfill [1] \\
\quad ((m = \langle s \rangle \frown m' \wedge s \notin ENC) \Rightarrow \hfill [2] \\
\qquad dec(k, m) = \langle s \rangle \frown dec(k, m')) \wedge \\
\quad ((m = \langle s \rangle \frown m' \wedge s = enc(\ell, m'') \wedge \ell \neq pair(k)) \Rightarrow \hfill [3] \\
\qquad dec(k, m) = \langle s \rangle \frown dec(k, m')) \wedge \\
\quad (m = \langle enc(pair(k), m'') \rangle \frown m' \Rightarrow \hfill [4] \\
\qquad dec(k, m) = dec(k, m'') \frown dec(k, m'))
\end{array}
$$

The use of total injective functions ensure uniqueness and that all combinations of keys and messages have a mapping associated with them. Since the *enc* function maps an entire message (sequence of items) to a single encrypted item, arbitrary nesting of encrypted messages is allowed.

The predicates define the recursive nature of the decryption function. Given a message m and a key k, there are four possible cases depending on the structure of message m. Firstly, if the message is empty, then the result of the decryption is an empty message (conjunct 1). If the first item s in the given message is not an encrypted item (conjunct 2) or if the first item was encrypted using a key ℓ that does not correspond to the given key k (conjunct 3), then the item is unchanged and the result of the decryption is sequence $\langle s \rangle$ concatenated with the decryption of the remainder m' of the message. Lastly, if the first item of the given message is an encrypted item that was created using the key that corresponds (via function *pair*) to the given key (conjunct 4), then the result is the decryption of the secret message m'' from the encrypted item, concatenated with the decryption of the remainder of the message.

The use of the encrypt and decrypt functions together with the *pair* function allow:

- encryption using a public key $(pair(k) \in PUB)$ and decryption using the corresponding private key $(k \in PRV)$; and
- encryption using a private key $(pair(k) \in PRV)$ and decryption using the corresponding public key $(k \in PUB)$.

In the protocol, Antonio makes use of his address, Antonio and Ben make use of their nonces, and all three agents make use of their keys. For simplification, we can thus assume that each agent possesses one of each of these items. The declarations below include four total functions that map each agent[1] to a unique public key, private key, nonce and address. The predicate ensures that the pair of keys associated with each agent G are a matching pair in the *pair* function.

$$
\begin{array}{|l}
pub : AGENT \rightarrowtail KEY \\
prv : AGENT \rightarrowtail KEY \\
non : AGENT \rightarrowtail NON \\
adr : AGENT \rightarrowtail ADR \\
\hline
\forall\, G : AGENT \bullet pub(G) = pair(prv(G))
\end{array}
$$

4.3   Define the Global State

The third phase in formalising the protocol is to define its state space. The *InTransit* Z state schema below contains the content of the communications medium. It is often assumed in security analysis that protocol instances are independent, so modelling one instance is sufficient. Furthermore, we can also assume that one message only is in transit at a time for this protocol. The *to* and *from* variables represent whom the message is to and whom the message is from, respectively. (We use the 'no agent' value $\perp$ as the *to* address to indicate that no message is in transit.) These variables hold the agent identifiers corresponding to those on the left-hand side of the standard notation steps. The *msg* variable represents the content of the message, if any, corresponding to the message value in the standard notation steps.

$$
\begin{array}{|l}
\quad InTransit \\
\hline
to : AGENT \\
from : AGENT \\
msg : MSG \\
\end{array}
$$

To initialise the protocol, we merely need to state that no message is in transit, by setting the destination address to '$\perp$', in the following Z operation schema. An operation schema consists of a declaration part, above the line, and a predicate part, below. In this case the declaration part inherits the three global variable declarations from the *InTransit* state schema.

$$
\begin{array}{|l}
\quad Init \\
\hline
InTransit \\
\hline
to = \perp \\
\end{array}
$$

---

[1] To ensure that all predicates are well-defined, 'no agent' $\perp$ has dummy keys and a nonce, but these are never used.

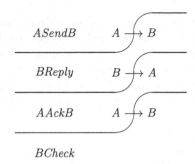

Fig. 1. Grouping of Needham-Schroeder protocol steps.

4.4 Specify the Agents' Operations

The fourth phase in formalising the protocol is to model its dynamic behaviour as a set of Z operations. A direct interpretation of the standard notation description above would urge us to model this protocol as three atomic operations corresponding to the three steps modelled by the standard notation: one for Antonio sending the first message to Ben, another for Ben's acknowledgement, and a final operation for Antonio's reply. However, we want to allow for the modelling of intrusions made whilst a message is in transit, and this particular partitioning would make it difficult to interpose an intrusion between a message's transmission and its subsequent receipt. Alternatively, the protocol could be broken into six operations — three sending operations and three receiving operations. However, assuming that an intruder cannot interfere with an agent's internal operations, we can more concisely model an agent's receipt and response to a message as part of a single 'atomic' operation [10,24]. Therefore we group the operations such that Ben receives and then sends his message within one operation, and also so that Antonio receives and acknowledges Ben's reply within one operation (see Fig. 1). Consequently, we can adequately model the whole protocol as four operations in Z: *ASendB*, *BReply*, *AAckB*, and *BCheck*.

Antonio Sends the First Message to Ben. We have defined the first operation specifically for Antonio sending the initial message to Ben. The message consists of Antonio's nonce $non(A)$ and his address $adr(A)$, and is encrypted using Ben's public key $pub(B)$ [2]. This operation is modelled in Z as follows:

$$
\begin{array}{l}
\underline{\;ASendB\;} \\
\Delta InTransit \\
\hline
to = \bot \wedge to' = B \wedge from' = A \\
msg' = \langle enc(pub(B), \langle non(A), adr(A) \rangle) \rangle
\end{array}
$$

---

[2] We assume that all public keys are known to all agents.

382 Benjamin W. Long, Colin J. Fidge, and Antonio Cerone

In the declaration part, Z's 'Δ' annotation is used to state that the variables in schema *InTransit* may change value by this operation. The undecorated (pre-state) variables specify the value of variables before the operation. The primed (post-state) variables specify the value of the variables after the operation. We want this operation to be applied only if there is no message in transit. This is checked by stating that the '*to*' address in the pre-state is no agent '$\perp$'. The post-state variables *to'* and *from'* are set to indicate that after the operation the message in transit is to Ben and from Antonio. The post-state value *msg'* of the message contains an encrypted item made from the appropriate structure of the message sent in step 1 of the protocol. The encrypted item is inside Z's sequence brackets '$\langle \cdots \rangle$' because a message always consists of a sequence of items, even though it contains only one item in this case. After this operation, Antonio is waiting for a reply message.

Ben Replies to the Message. The operation *BReply* is a generalised operation where Ben receives a message *msg* from an unknown agent X and replies to this agent. The reply message *msg'* contains the nonce N received and Ben's nonce. As the recipient of the message, Ben cannot control who it will come from, and thus accepts a message from any valid agent X. Similarly, Ben does not know the value of the incoming nonce and so uses an abitrary nonce N for this value.

$$
\begin{array}{|l}
\hline
\_BReply _____ \\
\Delta InTransit \\
\hline
to = B \wedge from' = B \\
(\exists\, X : AGENT;\ N : NON \bullet to' = X\ \wedge \\
\quad msg = \langle enc(pub(B), \langle N, adr(X) \rangle) \rangle\ \wedge \\
\quad msg' = \langle enc(pub(X), \langle N, non(B) \rangle) \rangle) \\
\hline
\end{array}
$$

The implicit precondition of the operation states that there is a message for Ben, the message is encrypted with Ben's public key (in other words Ben can decrypt it), and that the secret content of the message consists of a nonce N and an address $adr(X)$. Ben uses the arbitrary identity X as his way of identifying the unknown sender. Hence, the reply message, consisting of the nonce N and Ben's nonce $non(B)$, is encrypted using X's public key $pub(X)$.

Antonio Acknowledges the Message. In the next operation Antonio authenticates Ben's identity and sends the newly received nonce back to Ben in order to be authenticated by him.

$$
\begin{array}{|l}
\hline
\_AAckB _____ \\
\Delta InTransit \\
\hline
to = A \wedge to' = B \wedge from' = A \\
(\exists\, N : NON \bullet msg = \langle enc(pub(A), \langle non(A), N \rangle) \rangle\ \wedge \\
\quad msg' = \langle enc(pub(B), \langle N \rangle) \rangle) \\
\hline
\end{array}
$$

After sending the initial message, Antonio expects a message of a particular form from Ben. He knows that the message should contain the nonce that he sent in the initial message and another nonce N, which Antonio assumes to belong to Ben. This is checked as part of the implicit precondition. Antonio replies to this message by sending a reply back to Ben with the nonce assumed to be Ben's, N, and encrypts the message using Ben's public key, $pub(B)$. The fact that Antonio assumes that the nonce is from Ben is the weakness of this protocol and is demonstrated when the intruder's operations are introduced in Section 5.

Ben Checks the Message. Ben is now expecting a message of a particular form. Again this is implicitly checked as part of the required pre-state of the following operation which ensures that Ben's nonce is part of the incoming message, therefore allowing Ben to authenticate the identity of the agent he believes he is communicating with.

$$
\begin{array}{|l}
\hline
\;BCheck \\
\;\Delta In\,Transit \\
\hline
\;to = B \wedge to' = \bot \wedge msg = \langle enc(pub(B), \langle non(B) \rangle) \rangle \\
\hline
\end{array}
$$

Ben's receipt of the final message is modelled by setting the to variable in the post-state to 'no agent', allowing the protocol to start again.

5   An Attack on the Protocol

Lowe [14] identified an intrusion on this protocol whereby Antonio honestly communicates with Colin C (the intruder) not knowing that he has malicious intentions. Colin is able to masquerade as Antonio by sending modified messages to Ben.

1. $\quad A \longrightarrow C : \{N_A, A\}_{K_C}$
2. $\quad C_A \longrightarrow B : \{N_A, A\}_{K_B}$
3. $\quad B \longrightarrow C_A : \{N_A, N_B\}_{K_A}$
4. $\quad C \longrightarrow A : \{N_A, N_B\}_{K_A}$
5. $\quad A \longrightarrow C : \{N_B\}_{K_C}$
6. $\quad C_A \longrightarrow B : \{N_B\}_{K_B}$

When Ben receives the message from Colin in step 2, he believes that Antonio is initiating an instance of the protocol because Antonio's identity is in the message. He returns the message (step 3) to Antonio, following the protocol by encrypting the message with the key K_A of the agent whose identity was in the message. At this point Colin intercepts the message, but as he can't decrypt it, he merely forwards the message (step 4) to Antonio. Antonio believes that the nonce in the message belongs to Colin so he sends it back (step 5) to Colin for authentication. As Antonio sends Ben's nonce to Colin, Ben should not have

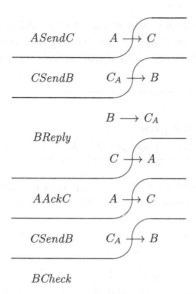

$$
\begin{array}{ll}
ASendC & A \dashrightarrow C \\[1.2em]
CSendB & C_A \dashrightarrow B \\[1.2em]
 & B \longrightarrow C_A \\
BReply \\
 & C \dashrightarrow A \\[1.2em]
AAckC & A \dashrightarrow C \\[1.2em]
CSendB & C_A \dashrightarrow B \\[1.2em]
BCheck
\end{array}
$$

Fig. 2. Grouping of protocol steps with the intrusion.

trusted Antonio. Now Colin can decrypt the message to gain access to Ben's nonce. Colin then sends Ben's nonce (step 6) to Ben to complete the protocol and to hide the intrusion.

6   Formalising the Attack

The fifth phase in analysing the protocol is to model the attacker's behaviour and any other operations required to enable the intruder's involvement in the protocol.

We explained above that Colin intercepts the message in step 3 but is unable to gain anything from it in its encrypted form. As he forwards the message without modification to Antonio in step 4, there is no change to the state. Therefore, we choose to ignore this operation in the sequence of protocol steps for the intrusion in our Z model. With this in mind we group the standard notation steps to create six Z operation schemas for modelling the intrusion as shown in Figure 2. Fortunately, we do not need to redefine Ben's operations as they are general enough for interaction with any agent.

The first operation needed to model the intrusion is *ASendC* which is similar to the *ASendB* operation, but where Antonio sends the initial message to Colin instead of Ben.

$$
\begin{array}{|l}
\hline
\_ASendC _____ \\
\Delta InTransit \\
\hline
to = \bot \wedge to' = C \wedge from' = A \\
msg' = \langle enc(pub(C), \langle non(A), adr(A) \rangle) \rangle \\
\hline
\end{array}
$$

The next operation is new and models Colin taking the message sent to him, encrypting it with Ben's public key, and sending it to Ben. This generic operation is used in both steps 2 and 6 when Colin sends a message M to Ben.

$$
\begin{array}{l}
\hline
\_CSendB_____ \\
\Delta InTransit \\
\hline
to = C \wedge to' = B \wedge from' = C \\
(\exists\, M : MSG \bullet msg = \langle enc(pub(C), M)\rangle \wedge msg' = \langle enc(pub(B), M)\rangle) \\
\hline
\end{array}
$$

Finally, we also need to define the operation $AAckC$, which is similar to $AAckB$ except that Antonio is interacting with Colin instead of Ben.

$$
\begin{array}{l}
\hline
\_AAckC_____ \\
\Delta InTransit \\
\hline
to = A \wedge to' = C \wedge from' = A \\
(\exists\, N : NON \bullet msg = \langle enc(pub(A), \langle non(A), N\rangle)\rangle \wedge \\
\quad msg' = \langle enc(pub(C), \langle N\rangle)\rangle) \\
\hline
\end{array}
$$

7 Verification of the Protocol

7.1 Specify Desired Property

The sixth phase in analysing the protocol is to specify properties that must be preserved for the protocol to operate securely. Previously, Butler [6] incorporated a variable containing nonces that are *critical* into his model. He specifies a property (invariant) stating that any critical nonces are to remain secret. With a run of the original flawed Needham-Schroeder Protocol in the presence of an intruder, this clause no longer holds, because at the end of the protocol, the protocol's critical nonce is no longer secret. Hence, the protocol is proven to be insecure.

We suggest that a simple property similar to Butler's should apply to nonces contained within a message to ensure confidentiality in authentication protocols. Each honest agent must be able to trust other honest agents to use nonces securely. Given this fact, our property is that each honest agent must not reveal a nonce to another agent unless it belongs to either the sender or the receiver. If it belongs to the sender then we may assume that the sender wants it to become a secret between the sender and the other agent, and if it belongs to the receiver, there is no harm in sending it to him. We restrict the invariant to honest agents only, because we know that an intruder can always choose to violate security properties, but we want to ensure that each honest agent always aims to maintain such a property. (An intruder should not be able to force an honest agent to violate security properties either.) The advantage of our invariant is that no extra variable containing critical nonces such as in Butler's model is required. For the Needham-Schroeder Protocol, it can be expressed by the following invariant.

$$
\begin{array}{|l|}
\hline
\textit{Inv} \\
\hline
\textit{InTransit} \\
\hline
(to \neq \perp \wedge \textit{from} \in \{A, B\}) \Rightarrow \\
\quad \{n : NON \mid n \textit{ in } dec(prv(to), msg)\} \subseteq \{non(\textit{from}), non(to)\} \\
\hline
\end{array}
$$

The invariant states that if there is a message in transit, which is sent from an honest agent (Antonio or Ben), and the recipient can decrypt it to reveal the secret content, then all 'decryptable' nonces in the message either belong to the sender or the recipient. Z's 'in' operator checks that the value on its left is in the sequence on its right [25].

7.2   Formal Proof

The seventh and final phase is to verify that the invariant is preserved by the protocol. This could be done by separately analysing each operation and proving that, in isolation, it preserves the invariant. However, this is an unnecessarily strong goal because it requires us to show that the operations preserve the invariant even from unreachable states. Instead, we show that the operations preserve the invariant when sequentially composed in their intended ordering, thus proving the weaker, but sufficient, goal that they preserve the invariant in their intended context.

   In the flawed version of the protocol described above, after the execution of $AAckC$, the invariant does not hold because there is a message from Antonio to Colin that is decrypted by Colin and contains Ben's nonce, which does not belong to either the sender or the receiver. To formally prove that the invariant does not hold at this point, we use Z's schema calculus [25]. We construct a schema from the composition of $ASendC$, $CSendB$, $BReply$, and $AAckC$, and prove that this sequence of operations contradicts the invariant.

   Given two schemas S and T, the composition '$S \,\raisebox{0.2ex}{$\scriptstyle\text{\tiny\raisebox{0.4ex}{$\cdot$}}_{\cdot}$}\, T$' of these schemas is the conjunction of the two where there exists an intermediate state which satisfies both the post-state of S and the pre-state of T [25]. This angelic form of composition provides a suitable basis for exploring the security implications of *potential* sequences of protocol steps. (We are not attempting to prove that the sequence of steps *can* be performed successfully, in which case a demonic composition operator would be needed.)

   After initialisation, only $ASendC$ is enabled because $to = \perp$. In fact, it is easy to check that only one operation is enabled at any stage of the protocol sequence in our model. As $CSendB$ is the enabled operation after $ASendC$ has been performed, we construct this particular sequence. Using the schema composition operator, the composition of schemas $ASendC$ and $CSendB$ is as follows.

$$
\begin{array}{l}
\_\_ASendC \,\S\, CSendB _____ \\
\Delta In\,Transit \\
\hline
to = \perp \land to' = B \land from' = C \\
(\exists\,In\,Transit'' \bullet to'' = C \land from'' = A \land \\
\quad msg'' = \langle enc(pub(C), \langle non(A), adr(A)\rangle)\rangle \land \\
\quad\quad (\exists\,M : MSG \bullet msg'' = \langle enc(pub(C), M)\rangle \land \\
\quad\quad\quad msg' = \langle enc(pub(B), M)\rangle)))
\end{array}
$$

To simplify this complicated schema, the nested quantifier can be removed by application of the one-point law [19] because we know that M must be $\langle non(A), A\rangle$.

$$
\begin{array}{l}
\_\_ASendC \,\S\, CSendB _____ \\
\Delta In\,Transit \\
\hline
to = \perp \land to' = B \land from' = C \\
msg' = \langle enc(pub(B), \langle non(A), adr(A)\rangle)\rangle \\
(\exists\,In\,Transit'' \bullet to'' = C \land from'' = A \land \\
\quad msg'' = \langle enc(pub(C), \langle non(A), adr(A)\rangle)\rangle)
\end{array}
$$

Now that none of the pre or post-state variables depend on the doubly primed variables, we can also remove these variables and the remaining quantifier.

$$
\begin{array}{l}
\_\_ASendC \,\S\, CSendB _____ \\
\Delta In\,Transit \\
\hline
to = \perp \land to' = B \land from' = C \\
msg' = \langle enc(pub(B), \langle non(A), adr(A)\rangle)\rangle
\end{array}
$$

Next we compose this schema with $BReply$.

$$
\begin{array}{l}
\_\_ASendC \,\S\, CSendB \,\S\, BReply _____ \\
\Delta In\,Transit \\
\hline
to = \perp \land from' = B \\
(\exists\,In\,Transit'' \bullet from'' = C \land to'' = B \land \\
\quad msg'' = \langle enc(pub(B), \langle non(A), adr(A)\rangle)\rangle \land \\
\quad\quad (\exists\,X : AGENT;\ N : NON \bullet to' = X \land \\
\quad\quad\quad msg'' = \langle enc(pub(B), \langle N, adr(X)\rangle)\rangle \land \\
\quad\quad\quad msg' = \langle enc(pub(X), \langle N, non(B)\rangle)\rangle)))
\end{array}
$$

By application of the one-point law we can simplify the schema because we know that agent X must be A, and nonce N must be $non(A)$.

$$\begin{array}{l} \underline{\quad ASendC \;_9^\circ\; CSendB \;_9^\circ\; BReply \quad\rule{5cm}{0.4pt}} \\ \Delta InTransit \\ \hline to = \bot \wedge to' = A \wedge from' = B \\ msg' = \langle enc(pub(A), \langle non(A), non(B)\rangle)\rangle \\ (\exists\, InTransit'' \bullet from'' = C \wedge to'' = B \wedge \\ \quad msg'' = \langle enc(pub(B), \langle non(A), adr(A)\rangle)\rangle) \end{array}$$

The remaining quantifier and doubly primed variables can be removed since the existence of such values is obvious.

$$\begin{array}{l} \underline{\quad ASendC \;_9^\circ\; CSendB \;_9^\circ\; BReply \quad\rule{5cm}{0.4pt}} \\ \Delta InTransit \\ \hline to = \bot \wedge to' = A \wedge from' = B \\ msg' = \langle enc(pub(A), \langle non(A), non(B)\rangle)\rangle \end{array}$$

Finally we compose this schema with $AAckC$.

$$\begin{array}{l} \underline{\quad ASendC \;_9^\circ\; CSendB \;_9^\circ\; BReply \;_9^\circ\; AAckC \quad\rule{4cm}{0.4pt}} \\ \Delta InTransit \\ \hline to = \bot \wedge to' = C \wedge from' = A \\ (\exists\, InTransit'' \bullet to'' = A \wedge from'' = B \wedge \\ \quad msg'' = \langle enc(pub(A), \langle non(A), non(B)\rangle)\rangle \wedge \\ \quad (\exists\, N : NON \bullet msg'' = \langle enc(pub(A), \langle non(A), N\rangle)\rangle \wedge \\ \quad msg' = \langle enc(pub(C), \langle N\rangle)\rangle)) \end{array}$$

Once again we can simplify the schema because we know that nonce N is $non(B)$.

$$\begin{array}{l} \underline{\quad ASendC \;_9^\circ\; CSendB \;_9^\circ\; BReply \;_9^\circ\; AAckC \quad\rule{4cm}{0.4pt}} \\ \Delta InTransit \\ \hline to = \bot \wedge to' = C \wedge from' = A \wedge msg' = \langle enc(pub(C), \langle non(B)\rangle)\rangle \end{array}$$

Using this schema, we will prove that this sequence of operations does not maintain the invariant. To do this we show that, assuming the invariant holds before the operations, the invariant does not hold afterwards. This is expressed by the following schema.

$$\begin{array}{l} \underline{\quad Inv \wedge ASendC \;_9^\circ\; CSendB \;_9^\circ\; BReply \;_9^\circ\; AAckC \Rightarrow \neg\, Inv' \quad\rule{3cm}{0.4pt}} \\ \Delta InTransit \\ \hline (((to \neq \bot \wedge from \in \{A, B\} \Rightarrow \\ \quad \{n : NON \mid n \text{ in } dec(prv(to), msg)\} \subseteq \{non(from), non(to)\}) \wedge \\ to = \bot \wedge to' = C \wedge from' = A \wedge msg' = \langle enc(pub(C), \langle non(B)\rangle)\rangle)) \\ \Rightarrow \\ \neg((to' \neq \bot \wedge from' \in \{A, B\}) \Rightarrow \\ \quad \{n : NON \mid n \text{ in } dec(prv(to'), msg')\} \subseteq \{non(from'), non(to')\}) \end{array}$$

We simplify this schema by eliminating the negation in the consequent of the schema.

$\_\_ Inv \wedge ASendC \, \mathring{,} \, CSendB \, \mathring{,} \, BReply \, \mathring{,} \, AAckC \Rightarrow \neg\, Inv' _____$
$\Delta\, In\, Transit$

$(((to \neq \perp \wedge from \in \{A, B\}) \Rightarrow$
$\qquad \{n : NON \mid n \,\text{in}\, dec(prv(to), msg)\} \subseteq \{non(from), non(to)\}) \wedge$
$to = \perp \wedge to' = C \wedge from' = A \wedge msg' = \langle enc(pub(C), \langle non(B)\rangle)\rangle))$
$\Rightarrow$
$((to' \neq \perp \wedge from' \in \{A, B\}) \wedge$
$\{n : NON \mid n \,\text{in}\, dec(prv(to'), msg')\} \not\subseteq \{non(from'), non(to')\})$

We distinguish two cases.

- If $to \neq \perp$, then the overall antecedent (the first three lines of the predicate above) is false and the whole schema is trivially true.
- If $to = \perp$, then the overall antecedent is simplified as follows:

$$to = \perp \wedge to' = C \wedge from' = A \wedge msg' = \langle enc(pub(C), non(B))\rangle \quad (1)$$

We distinguish two subcases.

- If predicate 1 is false, then the whole schema is trivially true.
- If predicate 1 is true, then both $to' \neq \perp$ and $from' \in \{A, B\}$ hold and the overall consequent (last two lines) can be simplified, in the context of predicate 1, as follows:

$$\{n : NON \mid n \,\text{in}\, dec(prv(to'), msg')\} \not\subseteq \{non(from'), non(to')\} \quad (2)$$

Since we have assumed that predicate 1 is true, we can evaluate predicate 2 by replacing $from'$ with A and to' with C and applying the decrypt function to the private key $prv(C)$ and the message in transit $msg' = \langle enc(pub(C), non(B))\rangle$.
Predicate 2 is then further simplified as follows:

$$\{non(B)\} \not\subseteq \{non(A), non(C)\} \quad (3)$$

Predicate 3 holds trivially and therefore the whole schema is true.

This completes the proof that the invariant is not maintained and the protocol is not secure. The proof relies on basic predicate logic only, and could be performed easily using a theorem prover.

8   The Fixed Needham-Schroeder Protocol

It is suggested by Lowe [14] that the protocol will operate securely if Ben's identity is included in the message he sends back to Antonio, i.e., if the message in Ben's reply is $\{N_A, N_B, B\}_{K_A}$. Then Antonio will be able to check the identity of the agent that created the message, which should be the agent with whom he is communicating. There can be no deception by an intruder modifying a message and claiming that it belongs to him. Furthermore, since the message is encrypted with Antonio's key, the intruder cannot insert his own address into the message.

To confirm this, we can repeat the phases above using the new version of the protocol, starting with the fourth phase. The operations that change to incorporate the new message structure are *BReply* and *AAckC*. Both play an important part in fixing the original protocol. The only difference in the new operation *BReply★* is that B adds his identity to msg' to conform to the new protocol.

BReply★
$\Delta InTransit$

$to = B \land from' = B$
$(\exists X : AGENT; \; N : NON \bullet to' = X \land$
$\quad msg = \langle enc(pub(B), \langle N, adr(X)\rangle)\rangle \land$
$\quad msg' = \langle enc(pub(X), \langle N, non(B), adr(B)\rangle)\rangle)$

Now that the responding agent's identity is part of the message, Antonio has the opportunity to check that this identity corresponds to the agent he is communicating with. So part of the pre-state for *AAckC★* is that Colin's identity is in the message.

AAckC★
$\Delta InTransit$

$to = A \land to' = C \land from' = A$
$(\exists N : NON \bullet msg = \langle enc(pub(A), \langle non(A), N, adr(C)\rangle)\rangle \land$
$\quad msg' = \langle enc(pub(C), \langle N\rangle)\rangle)$

Repeating the seventh phase in the analysis, we now show that each sequence of operations before *AAckC★* maintains the invariant and that the precondition of *AAckC★* is violated after *BReply★*, therefore indicating that *AAckC★* must not be performed. Firstly we show that *ASendC* maintains the invariant.

Inv $\land$ ASendC $\Rightarrow$ Inv'
$\Delta InTransit$

$(((to \neq \perp \land from \in \{A, B\}) \Rightarrow$
$\quad \{n : NON \mid n \text{ in } dec(prv(to), msg)\} \subseteq \{non(from), non(to)\}) \land$
$to = \perp \land to' = C \land from' = A \land$
$msg' = \langle enc(pub(C), \langle non(A), adr(A)\rangle)\rangle)$
$\Rightarrow$
$((to' \neq \perp \land from' \in \{A, B\}) \Rightarrow$
$\quad \{n : NON \mid n \text{ in } dec(prv(to'), msg')\} \subseteq \{non(from'), non(to')\})$

If $to \neq \bot$, then the overall antecedent is false and the whole schema is true. If $to = \bot$, the first conjunct is trivially true. The schema can be simplified by application of the one-point rule and the decrypt function.

$$
\begin{array}{|l}
\hline
\underline{\textit{Inv} \land \textit{ASendC} \Rightarrow \textit{Inv}'} \\
\Delta \textit{InTransit} \\
\hline
(to = \bot \land to' = C \land from' = A \land \\
\quad msg' = \langle enc(pub(C), \langle non(A), adr(A)\rangle)\rangle) \\
\Rightarrow \\
\{non(A)\} \subseteq \{non(A), non(C)\} \\
\hline
\end{array}
$$

As the consequent is true, the whole schema is trivially true thus confirming that the invariant is maintained. In other words, honest agent Antonio respects the invariant.

Using $\textit{ASendB} \, \mathbin{\raise.3ex\hbox{$_9$}} \, \textit{CSendB}$ calculated in Section 7, we prove that the sequence of these two operations maintains the invariant.

$$
\begin{array}{|l}
\hline
\underline{\textit{Inv} \land \textit{ASendC} \, \mathbin{\raise.3ex\hbox{$_9$}} \, \textit{CSendB} \Rightarrow \textit{Inv}'} \\
\Delta \textit{InTransit} \\
\hline
(((to \neq \bot \land from \in \{A, B\}) \Rightarrow \\
\quad \{n : NON \mid n \, \text{in} \, dec(prv(to), msg)\} \subseteq \{non(from), non(to)\}) \land \\
\quad to = \bot \land to' = B \land from' = C \land \\
\quad msg' = \langle enc(pub(B), \langle non(A), adr(A)\rangle)\rangle) \\
\Rightarrow \\
((to' \neq \bot \land from' \in \{A, B\}) \Rightarrow \\
\quad \{n : NON \mid n \, \text{in} \, dec(prv(to'), msg')\} \subseteq \{non(from'), non(to')\}) \\
\hline
\end{array}
$$

When the overall antecedent is false, the whole schema is trivially true. When the overall antecedent (the first four lines of the predicate above) is true, then $from' = C$, and therefore the antecedent of the implication in the overall consequent is false which makes the whole schema true. More simply, this just means that the invariant is satisfied because it places no constraint on the behaviour of dishonest agent Colin.

For the next test we firstly calculate $\textit{ASendC} \, \mathbin{\raise.3ex\hbox{$_9$}} \, \textit{CSendB} \, \mathbin{\raise.3ex\hbox{$_9$}} \, \textit{BReply}^\star$.

$$
\begin{array}{|l}
\hline
\underline{\textit{ASendC} \, \mathbin{\raise.3ex\hbox{$_9$}} \, \textit{CSendB} \, \mathbin{\raise.3ex\hbox{$_9$}} \, \textit{BReply}^\star} \\
\Delta \textit{InTransit} \\
\hline
to = \bot \land from' = B \\
(\exists \textit{InTransit}'' \bullet to'' = B \land from'' = C \land \\
\quad msg'' = \langle enc(pub(B), \langle non(A), adr(A)\rangle)\rangle \land \\
\quad (\exists X : AGENT; \ N : NON \bullet to' = X \land \\
\qquad msg'' = \langle enc(pub(B), \langle N, adr(X)\rangle)\rangle \land \\
\qquad msg' = \langle enc(pub(X), \langle N, non(B), adr(B)\rangle)\rangle))) \\
\hline
\end{array}
$$

Using the one-point rule we can simplify the schema because we know that X must be A and that N must be $non(A)$. Therefore, we can remove the remaining quantifier and doubly primed variables.

$$
\begin{array}{l}
\hline\ ASendC \mathbin{\raise1pt\hbox{$\scriptstyle\,_\circ^\circ\,$}} CSendB \mathbin{\raise1pt\hbox{$\scriptstyle\,_\circ^\circ\,$}} BReply^\star \underline{\hspace{6cm}} \\
\Delta In\,Transit \\
\hline
to = \bot \wedge to' = A \wedge from' = B \\
msg' = \langle enc(pub(A), \langle non(A), non(B), adr(B)\rangle)\rangle \\
\hline
\end{array}
$$

Using this schema we can prove that this sequence of operations also maintains the invariant.

$$
\begin{array}{l}
\hline\ Inv \wedge ASendC \mathbin{\raise1pt\hbox{$\scriptstyle\,_\circ^\circ\,$}} CSendB \mathbin{\raise1pt\hbox{$\scriptstyle\,_\circ^\circ\,$}} BReply^\star \Rightarrow Inv' \underline{\hspace{4cm}} \\
\Delta In\,Transit \\
\hline
((to \neq \bot \wedge from \in \{A, B\}) \Rightarrow \\
\quad \{n : NON \mid n\text{ in }dec(prv(to), msg)\} \subseteq \{non(from), non(to)\}) \wedge \\
to = \bot \wedge to' = A \wedge from' = B \wedge \\
msg' = \langle enc(pub(A), \langle non(A), non(B), adr(B)\rangle)\rangle) \\
\Rightarrow \\
((to' \neq \bot \wedge from' \in \{A, B\}) \Rightarrow \\
\quad \{n : NON \mid n\text{ in }dec(prv(to'), msg')\} \subseteq \{non(from'), non(to')\}) \\
\hline
\end{array}
$$

If $to \neq \bot$, then the overall antecedent is false and the whole schema is trivially true. Otherwise, if $to = \bot$, the first conjunct is trivially true and the remaining predicates can be simplified by application of the one-point rule and the decrypt function.

$$
\begin{array}{l}
\hline\ Inv \wedge ASendC \mathbin{\raise1pt\hbox{$\scriptstyle\,_\circ^\circ\,$}} CSendB \mathbin{\raise1pt\hbox{$\scriptstyle\,_\circ^\circ\,$}} BReply^\star \Rightarrow Inv' \underline{\hspace{4cm}} \\
\Delta In\,Transit \\
\hline
(to = \bot \wedge to' = A \wedge from' = B \wedge \\
msg' = \langle enc(pub(A), \langle non(A), non(B), adr(B)\rangle)\rangle) \\
\Rightarrow \\
\{non(A), non(B)\} \subseteq \{non(A), non(B)\} \\
\hline
\end{array}
$$

As the consequent is true, we know that the schema is true. This is expected because honest agent Ben obeys the invariant.

It is at this point that $AAckC$ was enabled in the flawed protocol. We now show that the precondition of the new operation $AAckC^\star$ is false at this point and hence not enabled. The precondition of an operation is calculated by assuming the existence of a final state in the operation [25].

$$
\boxed{\begin{array}{l}
\underline{\;\text{pre } AAckC^\star\;}\underline{} \\
InTransit \\
\hline
\exists\, InTransit' \bullet \\
\quad to = A \wedge to' = C \wedge from' = A \wedge \\
\quad (\exists\, N : NON \bullet msg = \langle enc(pub(A), \langle non(A), N, adr(C)\rangle)\rangle) \wedge \\
\qquad msg' = \langle enc(pub(C), \langle N\rangle)\rangle)
\end{array}}
$$

We know that such a post-state exists, so we can simplify the schema by removing the quantified post-state variables.

$$
\boxed{\begin{array}{l}
\underline{\;\text{pre } AAckC^\star\;}\underline{} \\
InTransit \\
\hline
to = A \wedge (\exists\, N : NON \bullet msg = \langle enc(pub(A), \langle non(A), N, adr(C)\rangle)\rangle)
\end{array}}
$$

To prove that the precondition of $AAckC^\star$ is not enabled, we prove that the sequence of operations leading up to $AAckC^\star$ in the fixed protocol imply the negation of the precondition of $AAckC^\star$. Z's 'pre' operator returns the implicit precondition of an operation schema by existentially quantifying the post-state variables.

$$
\boxed{\begin{array}{l}
\underline{\;ASendC \,\fatsemi\, CSendB \,\fatsemi\, BReply^\star \Rightarrow \neg(\text{pre } AAckC^\star)'\;}\underline{} \\
\Delta InTransit \\
\hline
(to = \bot \wedge to' = A \wedge from' = B \wedge \\
msg' = \langle enc(pub(A), \langle non(A), non(B), adr(B)\rangle)\rangle) \\
\Rightarrow \\
(to' \neq A \;\vee\; (\nexists N : NON \bullet msg' = \langle enc(pub(A), \langle non(A), N, adr(C)\rangle)\rangle))
\end{array}}
$$

If the antecedent is false, the whole schema is trivially true. If the antecedent is true, then there does not exist a message of the form specified in the consequent, which requires address C to be in the message, and hence the whole schema is true. Therefore, operation $AAckC^\star$ is not applicable at this point in the fixed protocol. Again, this formal proof matches our intuition. Operation $AAckC^\star$ expects Colin's address to be in the message but the sequence of operations leading up to this point put Ben's address in the message instead.

Note that if $AAckC^\star$ were performed, the invariant would be violated. We can therefore conclude that our invariant Inv is a desired property of the Needham-Schroeder Protocol, capable of formally distinguishing between successful and unsuccessful attacks.

9   Conclusion

Analysing security protocols is awkward because the security properties of interest are not directly expressible in typical formal methods. Although some researchers have attempted to remedy this by devising new, unfamiliar formalisms,

394   Benjamin W. Long, Colin J. Fidge, and Antonio Cerone

we instead prefer an approach which reuses widely-used methods. In this paper we demonstrated, via a worked example, that the Z notation is suitable, without change, for modelling and analysing a security protocol. This was done by systematically translating the protocol's informal 'standard notation' description into a Z model that accurately captured all essential features of the protocol. We then showed that Z's schema calculus provides a sound basis for formally reasoning about the protocol's correctness.

Acknowledgments

We wish to thank Luke Wildman for reviewing a draft of this paper and the anonymous reviewers for their helpful comments. This work was funded in part by Australian Research Council Discovery Grant DP0208046.

References

1. M. Abadi and A. D. Gordon. A calculus for cryptographic protocols: The spi calculus. In *Fourth ACM Conference on Computer and Communications Security*, pages 36–47. ACM Press, 1997.
2. G. Bella, F. Massacci, and L. C. Paulson. Verifying the SET registration protocols. *IEEE Journal On Selected Areas In Communications*, 21(5):77–87, January 2003.
3. C. Boyd. Security architectures using formal methods. *IEEE Journal On Selected Areas In Communications*, 11(5):694–701, June 1993.
4. C. Boyd and P. Kearney. Exploring fair exchange protocols using specification animation. In *Proceedings of the Information Security Workshop (ISW 2000)*, volume 1975 of *Lecture Notes in Computer Science*, pages 209–223. Springer-Verlag, 2000.
5. M. Burrows, M. Abadi, and R. Needham. A logic of authentication. Technical Report TR 39, Digital Equipment Corporation, February 1989.
6. M. Butler. On the use of data refinement in the development of secure communications systems. *Formal Aspects of Computing*, 14(1):2–34, 2002.
7. U. Carlsen. Generating formal cryptographic protocol specifications. In *Proceedings of the 1994 IEEE Computer Society Symposium on Research in Security and Privacy*, pages 137–146. IEEE Computer Society Press, 1994.
8. J. Clark and J. Jacob. A survey of authentication protocol literature: Version 1.0, 1997. http://www.cs.york.ac.uk/~jac/papers/drareviewps.ps. Accessed May 2003.
9. E. Cohen. Taps: A first-order verifier for cryptographic protocols. In *Proceedings of the 13th IEEE Computer Security Foundations Workshop (CSFW'00)*, pages 144–158. IEEE Computer Society Press, 2000.
10. G. Denker, J. K. Millen, A. Grau, and J. K. Filipe. Optimizing protocol rewrite rules of CIL specifications. In *Proceedings of 13th IEEE Computer Security Foundations Workshop (CSFW'00)*, pages 52–63. IEEE Computer Society Press, 2000.
11. W. Diffie and M. E. Hellman. Multiuser cryptographic techniques. In *Proceedings of AFIPS 1976 National Computer Conference*, pages 109–112, Montvale, New Jersey, 1976.
12. L. Gong. Variations on the themes of message freshness and replay — or the difficulty of devising formal methods to analyze cryptographic protocols. In *Proceedings of the Computer Security Foundations Workshop VI*, pages 131–136. IEEE Computer Society Press, 1993.

13. R. Kemmerer. Analyzing encryption protocols using formal verification techniques. *IEEE Journal On Selected Areas In Communications*, 7(4):448–457, May 1989.
14. G. Lowe. An attack on the Needham-Schroeder public-key authentication protocol. *Information Processing Letters*, 56(3):131–133, 1995.
15. G. Lowe. A hierarchy of authentication specifications. In *Proceedings of 10th IEEE Computer Security Foundations Workshop (CSFW'97)*, pages 31–43. IEEE Computer Society Press, 1997.
16. L. Ma and J. J. P. Tsai. *Formal Verification Techniques for Computer Communication Security Protocols*, volume 2. World Scientific Publishing Company, 2001. http://www.cs.uic.edu/~lma/abstract1.pdf. Accessed May 2003.
17. C. Meadows. The NRL protocol analyzer: An overview. *Journal of Logic Programming*, 26(2):113–131, February 1996.
18. C. A. Meadows. Formal verification of cryptographic protocols: A survey. In *Advances in Cryptology — ASIACRYPT '94*, volume 917 of *Lecture Notes in Computer Science*, pages 133–149. Springer-Verlag, 1995.
19. C. Morgan. *Programming from Specifications*. Prentice Hall International Series In Computer Science. Prentice Hall International, 1989.
20. R. Needham and M. Schroeder. Using encryption for authentication in large networks of computers. *Communications of the ACM*, 21(12):993–999, 1978.
21. L. C. Paulson. Proving properties of security protocols by induction. In *Proceedings of 10th IEEE Computer Security Foundations Workshop (CSFW'97)*, pages 70–83. IEEE Computer Society Press, 1997.
22. P. Ryan, S. Schneider, M. Goldsmith, G. Lowe, and B. Roscoe. *The Modelling and Analysis of Security Protocols: The CSP Approach*. Addison-Wesley, 2000.
23. S. Schneider. Security properties and CSP. In *Proceedings of the 1996 IEEE Computer Society Symposium on Research in Security and Privacy*. IEEE Computer Society Press, 1996.
24. V. Shmatikov and U. Stern. Efficient finite-state analysis for large security protocols. In *Proceedings of 11th IEEE Computer Security Foundations Workshop (CSFW'98)*, pages 106–115. IEEE Computer Society Press, 1998.
25. J. M. Spivey. *The Z Notation : A Reference Manual*. Prentice Hall International Series In Computer Science. Prentice Hall, London, 1992.
26. S. G. Stubblebine and R. N. Wright. An authentication logic with formal semantics supporting synchronization, revocation, and recency. *IEEE Transactions on Software Engineering*, 28(3):256–285, March 2002.
27. F. J. Thayer, J. C. Herzog, and J. D. Guttman. Strand spaces: Why is a security protocol correct? In *Proceedings of the 1998 IEEE Symposium on Security and Privacy*, pages 160–171. IEEE Computer Society Press, May 1998.

A Refinement Tool for Z

Angela Freitas[1], Carla Nascimento[1], and Ana Cavalcanti[2]

[1] Universidade Federal de Pernambuco/Centro de Informática
P.O. Box 7851, 50740-540 Recife PE, Brazil
{aff,cmpn}@cin.ufpe.br
[2] University of Kent/Computing Laboratory
Canterbury CT2 7NF, Kent, England
A.L.C.Cavalcanti@ukc.ac.uk

Abstract. Recently, a refinement calculus called ZRC has been proposed for Z; it follows the style and conventions of the Z notation and is completely formalised. As any other formal technique, however, it needs tool support to be of practical use. In this paper, we present such a tool, which we call ZRC-Refine. It is an interactive tool, whose design makes it distinctively user-friendly. We believe that ZRC-Refine is a significant encouragement to the extended application of ZRC and of Z itself.

Keywords: program development, calculation, ZRC.

1 Introduction

Since its original design, Z has significantly evolved; it is now a widely-accepted notation for specification and design [24, 29]. It has been applied in industry and an international standard is now available [1]. In spite of all this, Z does not include a well-defined formal technique for developing programs. This is in direct contrast to B [2], whose success owes much to the availability of commercial tools that cover the entire development life cycle.

Recently, a refinement calculus in the style of Morgan's work [21] has been proposed for Z. This calculus, which is called ZRC [11], builds up on existing work [19, 28, 29], but is distinctive in a few important points: it follows the styles and conventions of Z to avoid any notation translation, and is completely formalised. In [10], a weakest precondition semantics for Z is presented, which is calculated from its standard relational semantics. With basis on this semantics, the soundness of all refinement laws of ZRC have been proved. More than just a refinement calculus, ZRC is a theory of refinement for Z.

As with any other technique, however, a tool to support its application is essential for practical use. Many tools that support the application of a refinement calculus are available [16, 27, 23, 15]. As far as we know, none of them supports ZRC, or is in any way concerned with calculational refinement of Z specifications. Many are extensions of existing theorem provers [4, 30, 31, 6, 17, 5, 15].

In this paper, we present ZRC-Refine, an interactive user-friendly tool that supports the use of ZRC. Its design and implementation was motivated by the need to support teaching of ZRC. A major goal is to allow the development of

J.S. Dong and J. Woodcock (Eds.): ICFEM 2003, LNCS 2885, pp. 396–415, 2003.

programs in much the same way as it is done on paper. The ZRC-Refine design is based on another tool, Refine, which we have developed to support the application of Morgan's refinement calculus [12]. Refine has been used successfully in teaching for almost three years now.

ZRC-Refine is also useful as a development tool. We have used it in an industrial application, which we present here. Details of this work and of ZRC-Refine itself can be found in http://www.cin.ufpe.br/~aff/ZRC-Refine. We believe that ZRC-Refine is an incentive to the detailed application of ZRC and Z itself.

In an effort to conform to current trends, we have adopted the Z Standard syntax; we have also used Java as an implementation language. We hope to contribute to the CZT initiative: a project of the Z community to build a core for integration of Z tools and plug-in tools. ZRC-Refine is open-source and freely available. The design of ZRC-Refine encourages reusability and extendability. In fact, the implementation of ZRC-Refine has successfully reused the code of Refine; this is evidence of the good quality of the design of both tools.

In the next section we present ZRC. In Section 3, we present ZRC-Refine; we give an overview of its interface and the services it provides. Section 4 discusses one of our case studies: an Airbus cabin-illumination system [18]. Finally, in Section 5 we summarise related and future work.

2   ZRC

The Z Refinement Calculus (ZRC) is concerned with the derivation of code from a concrete Z specification, which is typically obtained by data refining an initial abstract specification. A development in ZRC considers each of the operations of the system independently; an implementation is developed for each of them.

The language of ZRC is called ZRC-L [11, 7]; it includes Z, the guarded command language [13], and extra constructs to handle procedures and recursion [8]. This is a uniform language of specification, design, and programming.

As with all refinement calculi, developments in ZRC are stepwise: typically, we gradually refine a schema that specifies an operation until we obtain an implementation. The target programming language is the idealised Dijkstra's language of guarded commands; translating the result programs to a real programming language syntax is a simple matter.

The specifications, the intermediary programs generated during stepwise refinement, which mix constructs of programming and specification, and the implementations are all written in ZRC-L. They are considered as programs and, in this more general sense, refinement is a relation between programs.

An important information in the refinement of an operation is its precondition. A specification using a Z schema includes this information, but it is not distinguished. ZRC-L includes specification statements $w : [pre, post]$. In such a construct, w, the frame, is a list of variables, and pre and $post$ are Z predicates: the precondition and the postcondition. Such an operation can change only the variables in w and, when executed in a state and with inputs that satisfy pre, terminates in a state and with outputs that satisfy $post$.

When refining an operation, the first step is to transform the schema into a ZRC-L construct more appropriate for refinement. In the simplest case, the target is a specification statement; in other situations, it is sequences, conditionals, or even procedures. ZRC includes laws to transform schema conjunctions and sequential compositions into sequences, and schema disjunctions into conditionals. We have also a law to structure the implementations of specifications defined using promotion in terms of procedures. In these cases, we take advantage of the structuring of the specification achieved with the schema calculus. These transformations are the object of a set of laws that we call conversion laws.

A program development is accomplished by the repeated application of refinement laws to an initial specification. Usually, the first step is the application of a conversion law, which is itself a refinement law. From then on, refinement laws similar to those of Morgan's calculus, but adapted to comply with the Z notation and style, are used. In Appendix A we present the ZRC refinement laws that we use throughout this paper. An extensive set can be found in [7].

3   ZRC-Refine

ZRC-Refine provides an interface composed by four windows; Figure 1 depicts this interface. The first window, named **Refinement**, shows the initial specification and all the steps carried out during the refinement process. In Figure 1, an operation specification has already been chosen for refinement.

The specifications are presented in the LaTeX markup that is part of the Z Standard. For example, in Figure 1 we have the following schema.

```
\begin{schema}{FindBirthday1}
\Xi BirthdayBook1 \\
name?: NAME \\
date!: DATE
\where
\exists i: 1 \upto hwm @ name? = names i \land date! = dates i
\end{schema}
```

This is LaTeX markup for the schema below.

$$
\begin{array}{l}
\hline
\_\,FindBirthday1\,\rule{4cm}{0.4pt} \\
\Xi\,BirthdayBook1 \\
name? : NAME \\
date! : DATE \\
\hline
\exists\,i : 1 \mathinner{\ldotp\ldotp} hwm \bullet name? = names\ i \wedge date! = dates\ i \\
\hline
\end{array}
$$

This is an operation of the concrete specification of the well-known birthday book presented in [24]. The use of the LaTeX markup is certainly not as satisfactory as the use of the usual graphical Z notation. Adding support for this notation, however, is a small matter, which we plan for the next version of ZRC-Refine.

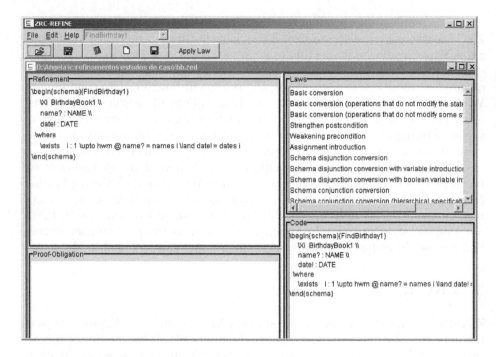

Fig. 1. ZRC-Refine interface

Our main concern, at this stage, is with the main design ideas of ZRC-Refine, which we discuss here. Many tool builders have chosen to delegate a graphical interface to later stages of development, and we adopt the same approach. As the case study presented in the next section show, ZRC-Refine is already usable as it is; while a graphical presentation of programs can certainly be of great benefit, its absence does not prevent us from considering even industrial application, and explore the several other facets of ZRC-Refine.

The second window in the interface of ZRC-Refine, **Laws**, contains a list of the laws of ZRC. The third, **Proofs**, shows the proof-obligations generated. And finally, the fourth window, **Code**, shows the resulting code of the refinement after each development step.

Our tool also has a main menu, through which the user can manage files that hold specifications and developments, and access the main services provided. The menu also offers a help to guide the users who are not familiar with the tool or ZRC itself; a documentation of the laws of ZRC is provided.

To start a development, a file that contains a Z specification should be loaded. The specification is checked for syntactic and typing errors, which, if found, are reported in a separate window. If the specification is correct, the schemas that specify operations and are, therefore, possible starting points for a refinement, are listed. These are the schemas whose signature includes only a dashed component for each undashed component there, and input and output variables, which are decorated with ? and !. For example, $FindBirthday1$ above specifies an operation, because its signature includes $names$, $dates$, and hwm, and $names'$, $dates'$, and hwm', which are included through $\Xi BirthdayBook1$, and $name?$ and $date!$. If $FindBirthday1$, had an extra undecorated component, it would not be listed.

With this filtering, we help the user to navigate through the specification, since all the operations that need to be refined are identified. Schemas used to specify states and types are left out. We do not rule out, however, auxiliary operation definitions that are used to define the main operations of the system. For example, in defining an operation Op in Z, it is usual to define the normal behaviour of the operation using a schema $OpNormal$, for instance, the error case using another schema $OpError$, and a third schema $Success$ that specifies a success message. The definition of Op itself is $(OpNormal \wedge Success) \vee OpError$, where the conjunction and the disjunction are schema calculus operators. In such a situation, ZRC-Refine identifies Op, $OpNormal$, $OpError$, and $Success$ as operations, even though the system operation is Op.

This is not a problem, since the user may choose to refine $OpNormal$, $Success$, and $OpError$ separately. It may be convenient to use conversion laws to refine Op to a conditional in which $OpNormal \wedge Success$ and $OpError$ appear as programs, and afterwards refine $OpNormal \wedge Success$ to the sequence $OpNormal; Success$, where the semi-colon is not the schema calculus operator, but the program operator of sequential composition. In summary, Op is refined to a conditional in which $OpNormal$, $Success$, and $OpError$ all apear as programs. At this stage, if they have already been refined to code, the development is concluded.

Alternatively, if the structure used in the specification is not convenient for the implementation, the user may decide to consider only Op itself for refinement. The fact that $OpNormal$, $Success$, and $OpError$ are listed does not imply that the user has to refine them.

After the operations are listed, the user can then choose one to be refined, which is shown in the **Refinement** window. To apply a law, we select a (part of a) program, and, in the **Law** window, the law we want to apply. Finally, we press the button APPLY. We cannot apply a law to an already refined program. If we choose a program to which a law has already been applied, the tool gives an error message when we press the button APPLY.

Some laws require parameters. For example, one of the simplest refinement laws is $assigI$ (assignment introduction), which we present in Figure 2. This law transforms a specification statement into a possibly multiple assignment. Its application requires two parameters: the list of variables to be assigned, and the corresponding list of assigning expression. When such a law is applied, ZRC-Refine opens a window where we must type the parameters.

ZRC-Refine checks parameters for syntactic and typing errors, and produces appropriate messages if necessary. Moreover, ZRC-Refine checks all implicit and explicit syntactic restrictions of a law before applying it. For example, $assigI$ can only be applied to specification statements whose frame includes the variables as parameters; these restrictions are implicit in the definition of the law. On the other hand, there is a number of explicit syntactic restrictions that are listed in

Law *assigI* Assignment introduction

　　$w, vl : [pre, post]$

$\sqsubseteq$ *assigI*

　　$vl := el$

provided $pre \Rightarrow post[el/vl'][\_/']$

Syntactic Restriction *vl* contains no duplicated variables; *vl* and *el* have the same length; *el* is well-scoped and well-typed; *el* has no free dashed variables; the corresponding variables of *vl* and expressions of *el* have the same type.

Fig. 2. Law assigI: assignment introduction

the definition of *assigI*; they guarantee that the assignment resulting from its application is well-formed and well-typed.

The provisos of the laws, if present, give rise to proof obligation when they are applied. These proof obligations are shown in the third window of the ZRC-Refine interface. Our tool does not provide assistance for theorem proving, but if an invalid proof obligation is generated, the user can undo the offending law application using the undo facility of ZRC-Refine. In the future, we plan to integrate ZRC-Refine with a theorem prover.

As the refinement progresses, the collected code is shown in the **Code** window. When the derivation ends up, this window contains the complete code that implements the original specification.

ZRC-Refine provides some facilities to help the user in the management of the refinement process. These include services as: possibility of undoing and redoing development steps; inclusion of comments associated the programs generated in the **Refinement** window; and printing and navigation facilities.

The possibility of undoing and redoing development steps is very useful. With this service, the user does not need to restart a development in the case of a wrong step. It is, of course, also possible to save the development at any stage, which is clearly useful in the refinement of large programs.

The refinement of programs is usually a long process, in which we manipulate large and, sometimes, complex formulas. It is fundamental to have explanations in parts of the refinement, to provide better understandability. ZRC-Refine offers the possibility to include comments associated to programs in the **Refinement** window. This can be done by clicking with the right button on the program. The tool opens a window where we include or edit comments. They are usually hidden; it is only when the user requests that the comments are shown.

ZRC-Refine allows the printing of the refinement steps, proof-obligation, comments, and collected code. The refinement steps are printed with the names of the applied laws. The lines are numbered, and each comment and proof obligation refers to the line of the program which generated it. It is also possible for the user to choose which parts (development, proofs or code) should be printed.

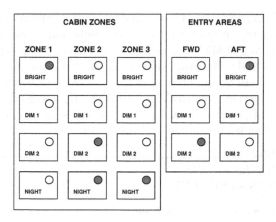

Fig. 3. Command Panel of the Illumination System

Another facility of ZRC-Refine is navigation between refinement and proof-obligations: by double-clicking in a proof-obligation in the **Proofs** window, the law application in the **Refinement** window that generated it is shown. This is very important when we have large developments, as that in the next section.

4   Case Study: Airbus Cabin-Illumination System

We describe how ZRC-Refine can be used in the refinement of an Airbus cabin-illumination system. Its specification, presented in [18], has been intentionally written at a concrete level, so that data refinement is not necessary. The Airbus cabin is divided into three zones and two entry areas. The illumination system provides separate control for each of these parts of the cabin. Figure 3, which has been extracted from [18], presents the panel used to command the system; a light indicator is associated with each of its buttons. The lights have three illumination levels; additionally, the cabin zones may have an extra set of special night lights.

The free types $ZONES$ and EA contain constants to identify the cabin zones ($z1$, $z2$, and $z3$) and the entry areas (fwd and aft). The set DIM_0 contains constants that represent the light indicators of a particular cabin zone or entry area ($dim1$, $dim2$, $bright$, off). They are elements of the free type DIM.

The BRIGHT, DIM1, and DIM2 buttons are used to switch on and off and to adjust the brightness of the lights in the cabin zones and entry areas. The function of the NIGHT buttons is determined by the global variable $CNLAUTO$. If the value of $CNLAUTO$ is $enabled$, then the night lights and their indicators in the command panel are automatically switched on (off) when the ordinary lights are switched off (on) and the NIGHT button is used only to switch off the night lights. If $CNLAUTO$ is equal to $disabled$, then the NIGHT buttons control the night lights. When a NIGHT button is pressed, the corresponding night light indicator is turned on, and the night light service is activated.

The schema *ZONEINDstate* below specifies part of the illumination system state. The component *zoneInd* represents the light indicators associated with the BRIGHT, DIM1, and DIM2 buttons that control cabin zone lights. For a zone z, *zoneInd* z is the light indicator that is on in that zone, or takes the value *off* when none of them is on. The component *nlInd* represents the night light indicators. It is a function from *ZONES* to *SWITCH*, a free type containing the constants *active* and *passive*; *nlInd* z is either *active* or *passive* depending on whether the NIGHT indicator of zone z is on or off.

_____ *ZONEINDstate* _____
$zoneInd : ZONES \rightarrow DIM_0$
$nlInd : ZONES \rightarrow SWITCH$
_____
$\forall z : ZONES \bullet nlInd\ z = active \Rightarrow$
$\quad (zoneInd\ z = off \lor CNLAUTO = disabled)$
_____

The invariant establishes that, in all zones, if the NIGHT indicator is on, then either the ordinary lights in the zone are off, or the night light autoservice is disabled: the NIGHT button has been pressed to pre-select the night light service.

The indicators of the entry areas are represented by the component *eaInd*.

_____ *EAINDstate* _____
$eaInd : EA \rightarrow DIM_0$
_____

The lights are identified by addresses in a bus: numbers in the interval from 1 to *maxad*. The addresses of the lights in each of the zones and entry areas are identified by tables: partial functions from $1 .. maxad$ to *ZONES* or *EA*.

| $CCAB : 1 .. maxad \nrightarrow ZONES;\ CEA : 1 .. maxad \nrightarrow EA$
| $CNL1 : 1 .. maxad \nrightarrow ZONES;\ CNL2 : 1 .. maxad \nrightarrow ZONES$
| _____
| $CNL1 \subseteq CCAB$
| dom $CCAB \cap$ (dom $CEA \cup$ dom $CNL2) = \varnothing$
| dom $CEA \cap$ dom $CNL2 = \varnothing$

The addresses in the table *CCAB* are those of the ordinary lights in the cabin zones; if the address a is in *CCAB*, it identifies a light in the zone *CCAB* a. Similarly, *CEA* contains the addresses of the lights in the entry areas. If the cabin zones have special night lights, then their addresses are recorded in *CNL2*. Otherwise, *CNL1* singles out ordinary lights used in the night light service.

The component *ill* represents the cabin zone, entry area, and night lights.

_____ *ILLstate* _____
$ill : 1 .. maxad \rightarrow DIM$
_____
$\forall a : 1 .. maxad \bullet ill\ a = onNl2 \Rightarrow a \notin$ (dom $CCAB \cup$ dom CEA)
_____

The constant *onNl2* represents the on state of a special night light. The invariant asserts that, for every a, if *ill* a is *onNl2*, then a is not an ordinary light.

The operation *EAop* controls the illumination of the entry areas; it is activated by pressing the DIM1, DIM2, or BRIGHT buttons. The input variables *ea?* and *dim?* determine the entry area and brightness level; DIM_1, is the subset of *DIM* containing *dim1*, *dim2*, and *bright*. The behaviour of *EAop* depends on the state of the light indicator associated with the button pressed. If it is on, the lights are at the brightness level chosen and are turned off, as is the light indicator. If it is off, then it is turned on and the lights are switched to the chosen brightness level. The effect on the light indicator is specified by *EAINDop*.

EAINDop

$\Delta EAINDstate$
$\Xi ZONEINDstate$
$ea? : EA;\ dim? : DIM_1$

$eaInd(ea?) = dim? \Rightarrow eaInd' = eaInd \oplus \{ea? \mapsto off\}$
$eaInd(ea?) \neq dim? \Rightarrow eaInd' = eaInd \oplus \{ea? \mapsto dim?\}$

EAILLopPassive defines the effect of *EAop* on *ill* if the light indicator is on.

EAILLopPassive

$\Delta ILLstate$
$EAINDstate$
$ea? : EA;\ dim? : DIM_1$

$eaInd(ea?) = dim? \wedge ill' = ill \oplus \{\ x : \mathrm{dom}(CEA \rhd \{ea?\}) \bullet x \mapsto off\ \}$

The effect of *EAop* on *ill* when the indicator is off is specified by *EAILLopActive*. If the cockpit door is open and the oil pressure is high, then there is an engine running, and the illumination of the *fwd* entry area cannot be changed arbitrarily to avoid blinding the cockpit personnel. The table *CEAD* establishes the maximum brightness to which the *fwd* entry areas lights can be switched.

$CEAD : 1 .. maxad \nrightarrow \{off, dim1, dim2\}$

$\mathrm{dom}\ CEAD \subseteq \mathrm{dom}(CEA \rhd \{fwd\})$

The state of the door (*open* or *closed*) and the oil pressure (*high* or *low*) are determined by the global variables *cockDoor* and *oilPres*, respectively.

EAILLopActive

$\Delta ILLstate$
$EAINDstate$
$ea? : EA;\ dim? : DIM_1$

$eaInd(ea?) \neq dim?$
$ill' = ill \oplus \mathbf{if}\ ea? = fwd \wedge cockDoor = open \wedge oilPres = high$
$\qquad \mathbf{then}\ \{\ x : \mathrm{dom}(CEA \rhd \{ea?\}) \bullet x \mapsto dim?\ \} \oplus$
$\qquad\qquad \{\ x : \mathrm{dom}\ CEAD \mid CEAD\ x <_{dim} dim? \bullet x \mapsto CEAD\ x\ \}$
$\qquad \mathbf{else}\ \{\ x : \mathrm{dom}(CEA \rhd \{ea?\}) \bullet x \mapsto dim?\ \}$

The operator $<_{dim}$ defines an order for the brightness levels.

Law bC Basic conversion (operations that do not modify some state components)

$$\langle \Delta S;\ \Xi T;\ di?;\ do! \mid p \rangle$$
$$\sqsubseteq bC$$

$$\alpha d_S, \alpha do! : \left[\left(\begin{array}{l} inv_S \\ inv_T \\ \exists\, d'_S;\ do! \bullet (inv'_S \wedge p)[\alpha d_T/\alpha d'_T] \end{array} \right),\ (inv'_S \wedge p)[\alpha d_T/\alpha d'_T] \right]$$

where $S \mathrel{\widehat{=}} \langle T;\ d_S \mid inv_S \rangle$ and $T \mathrel{\widehat{=}} \langle d_T \mid inv_T \rangle$

Fig. 4. Law bC: basic conversion

The definition of $EAop$ is as follows. Its precondition is true.

$$EAop \mathrel{\widehat{=}} EAINDop \wedge (EAILLopActive \vee EAILLopPassive)$$

In this example, the structure of the specification is not reflected in the intended implementation, which acts on the global system state: the conjunction of $ZONEINDstate$, $EAINDstate$, and $ILLstate$. For this reason, we start the refinement of $EAop$ with an application of the bC law presented in Figure 4, which can be used to derive a specification statement, taking advantage of the fact that it does not modify $zoneInd$.

The law bC applies to a schema $\langle \Delta S;\ \Xi T;\ di?;\ do! \mid p \rangle$, which specifies an operation. The state is S, which includes T. The operation modifies the state, but not the components of T. Therefore, the specification statement does not include them in its frame and does not enforce the maintenance of the state invariant of T. The predicate $\exists\, d'_S;\ do! \bullet (inv'_S \wedge p)[\alpha d_T/\alpha d'_T]$ is the precondition of $\langle \Delta S;\ \Xi T;\ di?;\ do! \mid p \rangle$.

The application of bC to $EAop$ yields the specification below.

$$
eaInd,\ ill : \left[\begin{array}{l} ZONEINDstate \wedge ILLstate, \\ \left(\begin{array}{l} ILLstate' \\ eaInd(ea?) = dim? \Rightarrow eaInd' = eaInd \oplus \{ea? \mapsto off\} \\ eaInd(ea?) \neq dim? \Rightarrow eaInd' = eaInd \oplus \{ea? \mapsto dim?\} \\ \left(\begin{array}{l} eaInd(ea?) = dim? \\ ill' = ill \oplus \{\, x : \operatorname{dom}(CEA \rhd \{ea?\}) \bullet x \mapsto off\,\} \end{array} \right) \vee \\ \left(\begin{array}{l} eaInd(ea?) \neq dim? \\ ill' = ill \oplus \mathbf{if}\ ea? = fwd \wedge cockDoor = open \wedge oilPres = high \\ \qquad\quad \mathbf{then}\ \{\, x : \operatorname{dom}(CEA \rhd \{ea?\}) \bullet x \mapsto dim?\,\} \oplus \\ \qquad\qquad\quad \{\, x : \operatorname{dom} CEAD \mid CEAD\ x <_{dim} dim? \bullet \\ \qquad\qquad\qquad\qquad\qquad\qquad\qquad x \mapsto CEAD\ x\,\} \\ \qquad\quad \mathbf{else}\ \{\, x : \operatorname{dom}(CEA \rhd \{ea?\}) \bullet x \mapsto dim?\,\} \end{array} \right) \end{array} \right) \end{array} \right]
$$

We implement this program with an alternation that distinguishes the cases $eaInd = dim?$ and $eaInd \neq dim?$. Before we introduce it, however, we use the law *prcI* (procedure introduction) to declare the procedure *updILL* presented below, which is used later on to update *ill*. The procedure block introduced by *prcI* has the specification statement above as its main program.

$$updILL \cong (\textbf{val } set : \mathbb{F}(1 \mathinner{..} maxad); \; dim : DIM \bullet$$
$$ill : [ill' = ill \oplus \{ \; a : set \bullet a \mapsto dim \; \}] \;)$$

The procedure *updILL* has two value parameters: *set* and *dim*. It updates *ill* by setting to *dim* the brightness level of the lights whose addresses are in *set*. The specification statement in the body of *updILL* can be implemented using an iteration. Its refinement is not difficult and, for conciseness, is omitted.

As far as we know, ZRC-Refine is one of the very few refinement tools to support the use of procedures. The tools reported in [25, 20] support the use of procedures in the context of a refinement calculus. They do not, however, support the calculational approach adopted in ZRC, in which parameters and procedures are introduced and treated independently.

Procedures are fundamental to the development of real systems, in which the control of the size of the code and of the refinement is essential. With a procedure construct, we can give a name to a specification, refine it, and introduce a call every time the specification is found in the main program. As well as adding structure to the code, we save refinement effort.

Procedures also allow us to preserve the structure of specifications that make use of the Z promotion technique. In this technique, we first define a local state with its corresponding operations. Afterwards, we define the global state of the system as a function from some index set to elements of the local state. The main advantage is the possibility of defining the operations of the global state in terms of, or rather, by promoting, the operations of the local state using the schema calculus. ZRC-Refine implements a conversion law that allows us to define procedures that correspond to the local state operations, and call such procedures to implement the global state operations.

To proceed, we apply *altI* (alternation introduction), and then *sP* (strengthen postcondition) and *wP* (weaken precondition) to simplify the specification statements in the branches of the alternation; we get the program below.

$\textbf{if } eaInd = dim? \rightarrow$

$$\begin{array}{l} eaInd, \\ ill \end{array} : \left[\left(\begin{array}{l} eaInd' = eaInd \oplus \{ea? \mapsto off\} \\ ill' = ill \oplus \{ \; x : \text{dom}(CEA \rhd \{ea?\}) \bullet x \mapsto off \; \} \end{array} \right) \right]$$

$[\!] \; eaInd \neq dim? \rightarrow$

$$\begin{array}{l} eaInd, \\ ill \end{array} : \left[\left(\begin{array}{l} eaInd' = eaInd \oplus \{ea? \mapsto dim?\} \\ ill' = ill \oplus \textbf{if } ea? = fwd \wedge cockDoor = open \wedge oilPres = high \\ \qquad \textbf{then } \{ \; x : \text{dom}(CEA \rhd \{ea?\}) \bullet x \mapsto dim? \; \} \oplus \\ \qquad \quad \{ \; x : \text{dom } CEAD \mid CEAD \; x <_{dim} dim? \bullet \\ \qquad \qquad \qquad \qquad \qquad \qquad x \mapsto CEAD \; x \; \} \\ \qquad \textbf{else } \{ \; x : \text{dom}(CEA \rhd \{ea?\}) \bullet x \mapsto dim? \; \} \end{array} \right) \right]$$

$\textbf{fi}$

We refine the second specification statement; the refinement of the first is similar.

Applying *fassigI* in order to introduce an assignment to *eaInd*, and *cfR* (contract frame) in order to simplify the remaining specification statement, we derive the following program.

$$
ill : \begin{bmatrix} ill' = ill \oplus \textbf{if } ea? = fwd \wedge cockDoor = open \wedge oilPres = high \\ \textbf{then } \{ \, x : \text{dom}(CEA \rhd \{ea?\}) \bullet x \mapsto dim? \, \} \oplus \\ \quad \{ \, x : \text{dom } CEAD \mid CEAD \; x <_{dim} dim? \bullet x \mapsto CEAD \; x \, \} \\ \textbf{else } \{ \, x : \text{dom}(CEA \rhd \{ea?\}) \bullet x \mapsto dim? \, \} \end{bmatrix} ;
$$
$$
eaInd := eaInd \oplus \{ea? \mapsto dim?\}
$$

The form of the postcondition of the above specification statement suggests the introduction of a conditional. With this purpose, we apply the law *altI* (alternation introduction) and, following the application of the laws *sP* (strengthen postcondition) and *wP* (weaken precondition) to the branches of the resulting alternation, we get to the program below.

$$
\textbf{if } ea? = fwd \wedge cockDoor = open \wedge oilPres = high \rightarrow
$$
$$
ill : \begin{bmatrix} ill' = ill \oplus \{ \, x : \text{dom}(CEA \rhd \{ea?\}) \bullet x \mapsto dim? \, \} \oplus \\ \quad \{ \, x : \text{dom } CEAD \mid CEAD \; x <_{dim} dim? \bullet x \mapsto CEAD \; x \, \} \end{bmatrix}
$$
$$
[] \; \neg \, (ea? = fwd \wedge cockDoor = open \wedge oilPres = high) \rightarrow
$$
$$
ill : [ill' = ill \oplus \{ \, x : \text{dom}(CEA \rhd \{ea?\}) \bullet x \mapsto dim? \, \}]
$$
$$
\textbf{fi}
$$

Using the laws *vS* (value specification) and *pcallI* (procedure call introduction), we can transform the second specification statement into a call to *updILL* with parameters dom($CEA \rhd \{ea?\}$) and *dim?*.

The application of the law *pcallI* requires that we collect the code refined until now, because this law is applied to a procedure block that includes a procedure declaration and the main program. We collect the code by clicking the right button of the mouse on the **Refinement** window and choosing the option Collect Code. This inserts in the window all the code refined so far, which can be a starting point of refinement. We select the procedure block and choose the law *pcallI*. ZRC-Refine searches for programs in the main program that match the body of the procedure, and replaces them with the procedure's name. The approach is based on the work in [8], where procedure bodies are parametrised commands in the style of Back [3].

As to the first specification statement above, since it does not switch lights to a common brightness level, we would rather implement it without using *updILL*. This development poses no difficulties and is not discussed here. The complete program is shown in Figure 5. This collected code is presented to the user by ZRC-Refine in the **Code** window.

When the Airbus is on the ground, the cabin illumination can be controlled from a MAIN button. Its indicator is represented by the state component

if $eaInd = dim? \rightarrow$

$\qquad updILL(\mathrm{dom}(CEA \rhd \{ea?\}), off)$; $eaInd := eaInd \oplus \{ea? \mapsto off\}$

$[\!]$ $eaInd \neq dim? \rightarrow$

$\qquad$ **if** $ea? = fwd \wedge cockDoor = open \wedge oilPres = high \rightarrow$

$\qquad\qquad |[$ **var** $i : 1 .. maxad + 1 \bullet$

$\qquad\qquad\qquad i := 1$;

$\qquad\qquad\qquad$ **do** $i \neq maxad + 1 \rightarrow$

$\qquad\qquad\qquad\qquad$ **if** $i \in \mathrm{dom}(CEA \rhd \{ea?\}) \rightarrow$

$\qquad\qquad\qquad\qquad\qquad$ **if** $i \in \mathrm{dom}\ CEAD \wedge CEAD\ i <_{dim} dim? \rightarrow$

$\qquad\qquad\qquad\qquad\qquad\qquad ill := ill \oplus \{i \mapsto CEAD\ i\}$

$\qquad\qquad\qquad\qquad\qquad [\!] \neg (i \in \mathrm{dom}\ CEAD \wedge CEAD\ i <_{dim}\ dim?) \rightarrow$

$\qquad\qquad\qquad\qquad\qquad\qquad ill := ill \oplus \{i \mapsto dim?\}$

$\qquad\qquad\qquad\qquad\qquad$ **fi**

$\qquad\qquad\qquad\qquad [\!]\ i \notin \mathrm{dom}(CEA \rhd \{ea?\}) \rightarrow$ **skip**

$\qquad\qquad\qquad\qquad$ **fi** ;

$\qquad\qquad\qquad\qquad i := i + 1$

$\qquad\qquad\qquad$ **od**

$\qquad\qquad]\!|$

$\qquad$ $[\!] \neg (ea? = fwd \wedge cockDoor = open \wedge oilPres = high) \rightarrow$

$\qquad\qquad updILL(\mathrm{dom}(CEA \rhd \{ea?\}), dim?)$

$\qquad$ **fi** ;

$\qquad$ $eaInd := eaInd \oplus \{ea? \mapsto dim?\}$

fi

Fig. 5. Collected code of $EAOp$

$mainInd$, which is introduced by the schema $MAININDstate$ that follows.

$MAININDstate$ _____

$ZONEINDstate$
$EAINDstate$
$mainInd : SWITCH$

$mainInd = passive \Leftrightarrow$
$\qquad \mathrm{ran}\ nlInd = \{passive\} \wedge \mathrm{ran}\ zoneInd = \{off\} \wedge \mathrm{ran}\ eaInd = \{off\}$

If $mainInd$ is equal to $passive$, the MAIN indicator is off and so are all other indicators.

The operation $MAINop$ is triggered by pressing the MAIN button. It has no effect if the Airbus is not on the ground. The global constant $LGEARst$ determines the current state of the landing gear: $downCompressed$, $downLocked$, or $upLocked$. The Airbus is in the air when the landing gear is either $downLocked$

or *upLocked*. This situation is characterised by the schema *MAINisBlocked*.

$$MAINisBlocked \mathrel{\widehat{=}} [\ LGEARst \in \{downLocked, upLocked\} \ ]$$

In this case, *MAINop* does not change the state: it behaves like *NOop* below.

$$NOop \mathrel{\widehat{=}} \Xi ZONEINDstate \wedge \Xi EAINDstate \wedge$$
$$\Xi MAININDstate \wedge \Xi ILLstate$$

If the Airbus is on the ground, the effect of *MAINop* depends on whether the MAIN indicator is on or off. If it is on, it is turned off, and so are all the other light indicators.

```
┌─ MAININDopPassive ─────────────────────────────
│ ΔMAININDstate
├────────────────────────────────────────────────
│ mainInd = active ∧ mainInd' = passive
└────────────────────────────────────────────────
```

The lights themselves are turned off as well. Also, if the MAIN indicator is turned off, then *MAINop* reinitialises the system. The MAIN indicator is turned on.

$$MAINILLopPassive \mathrel{\widehat{=}} [\ \Delta ILLstate \mid ill' = \{ \ a : 1 .. \ maxad \bullet a \mapsto \text{off} \ \} \ ]$$

$$MAININDINITop \mathrel{\widehat{=}} [\ MAININDstate' \mid mainInd' = active \ ]$$

The BRIGHT indicators are turned on and the NIGHT indicators are turned off. This is specified by the schemas *ZONEINDINITop* and *EAINDINITop*.

```
┌─ ZONEINDINITop ────────────────────────────────
│ ZONEINDstate'
├────────────────────────────────────────────────
│ zoneInd' = { z : ZONES • z ↦ bright }
│ nlInd' = { z : ZONES • z ↦ passive }
└────────────────────────────────────────────────
```

$$EAINDINITop \mathrel{\widehat{=}} [\ EAINDstate' \mid eaInd' = \{ \ z : EA \bullet z \mapsto bright \ \} \ ]$$

Finally, the ordinary lights are switched to bright and the special night lights, switched off.

```
┌─ ILLINITop ────────────────────────────────────
│ ILLstate'
├────────────────────────────────────────────────
│ { a : (dom CCAB ∪ dom CEA) • a ↦ bright } ∪
│ { a : dom CNL2 • a ↦ off } ⊆ ill'
└────────────────────────────────────────────────
```

The initialisation operation is defined as the conjunction of the last four schemas presented above.

$$INITop \mathrel{\widehat{=}} ZONEINDINITop \wedge EAINDINITop \wedge$$
$$MAININDINITop \wedge ILLINITop$$

410   Angela Freitas, Carla Nascimento, and Ana Cavalcanti

Law *sdisjC* Schema disjunction conversion

$Op_1 \vee Op_2$

$\sqsubseteq sdisjC$

if $pre_1 \rightarrow Op_1 \,[\!]\, pre_2 \rightarrow Op_2$ **fi**

where pre $Op_1 \equiv pre_1 \wedge inv \wedge t$; pre $Op_2 \equiv pre_2 \wedge inv \wedge t$; *inv* is the state invariant; and t is the restriction that is introduced by the declarations of the state components and input variables.

Syntactic Restriction Op_1 and Op_2 act over the same state and have the same input and output variables.

Fig. 6. Law *sdisjC*: schema disjunction conversion

This is used in the definition of the *MAINop* operation, which is specified by a disjunction, as shown below.

$MAINop \,\hat{=}\, (MAINisBlocked \wedge NOop) \vee$
$(\neg\, MAINisBlocked \wedge$
$(MAINILLopPassive \wedge MAININDopPassive \vee$
$[MAININDstate \mid mainInd = passive] \wedge INITop))$

The outer structure of the specification is carried out to the implementation. ZRC-Refine implements a conversion law *sdisjC* (schema disjunction conversion), which we present in Figure 6. It transforms a disjunction $Op1 \vee Op2$ into a conditional, in which, if the precondition of $Op1$ holds, then $Op1$ is executed, and if the precondition of $Op2$ holds, then $Op2$ is executed. If both preconditions hold, then $Op1$ and $Op2$ are nondeterministically chosen for execution.

For the application of *sdisjC*, it would not be necessary any parameters because the preconditions of the schemas can be calculated by ZRC-Refine. This, however, would generate long predicates, possibly involving existential quantifications. So, we take the preconditions as parameters. The requirement that the input predicates correspond to the preconditions of the operations is left as a proof obligation.

Applying *sdisjC* to *MAINop*, we can obtain the following conditional. The precondition of the first disjunct, $MAINisBlocked \wedge NOop$, can be expressed as $LGEARst = downLocked \vee LGEARst = upLocked$; the precondition of the second disjunct is $LGEARst = downCompressed$.

if $LGEARst = downLocked \vee LGEARst = upLocked \rightarrow$
        $MAINisBlocked \wedge NOop$

$[\!]$ $LGEARst = downCompressed \rightarrow$
        $\neg\, MAINisBlocked \wedge$
        $(MAINILLopPassive \wedge MAININDopPassive \vee$
        $[MAININDstate \mid mainInd = passive] \wedge INITop)$

fi

Law *seqcI* Sequential composition introduction

$w, x : [pre, post]$

$\sqsubseteq seqcI$

$w : [pre, mid[w'/w]\ ]\ ;\ w, x : [mid, post]$

Syntactic Restriction *mid* is well-scoped and well-typed; *mid* has no free dashed variables; and no free variable of *post* is in *w*.

Fig. 7. Law *seqcI*: sequential composition introduction

The development of the schemas in the branches of the conditional follows in much the same way as we have already illustrated, using the procedure *updILL*.

Our case studies give us confidence in the usability of our tool. The developments we tackled had been carried out by hand before. The use of ZRC-Refine revealed mistakes and points in which it would be beneficial to provide extra versions of the existing refinement laws. For example, one of the formulations of the law that introduces a sequential composition in ZRC is as presented in Figure 7. It does not deal with output variables explicitly; the requirement that the postcondition does not have free variables that are also in the frame makes it impossible to use this law if there is an output variable in the frame, which, typically, is also in the postcondition. A generalised version of this law is implemented in ZRC-Refine.

We also observed the need to provide support for transformations based on the schema calculus laws. In our developments, when a schema expression did not have the form required to apply a conversion law, we had to modify the specification to include an equivalent schema expression which was appropriate. For this reason, in the implementation of the laws, it was important to avoid unnecessary constraints in terms of the particular form of schema expressions. In most cases, however, simple properties of the schema calculus are useful to perform the necessary transformations.

5   Conclusions

We have presented ZRC-Refine, a tool to support a refinement calculus for Z in the style of Morgan; we have presented its main features and discussed an industrial case study. ZRC-Refine is still an academic exercise, but a very promising one, we believe.

ZRC-Refine is available in http://www.cin.ufpe.br/~aff/ZRC-Refine. It was developed using Java, and amounts to about 84000 lines of code, in 420 classes. In the site, we can also find UML documentation of the design, a tutorial, and example developments, including the complete refinement of the Airbus Cabin Illumination System presented here.

The design of ZRC-Refine is based on that of another tool that we developed to support Morgan's refinement calculus. The quality of the design has been confirmed by our ability to reuse code.

Several tools are reported in the literature. To the best of our knowledge, none of them is related to the development of programs from Z specifications, or to ZRC. Another distinguishing feature of ZRC-Refine is the treatment of procedures as illustrated in our case study. Due to the results presented in [9, 8], ZRC adopts Backs's approach to procedures [3], and includes some novel laws.

We drew many ideas from the design of the tools reported in [16, 27]. These are both interactive tools whose operation tries to mimic the way in which programs are developed on paper. The Proxac system is a transformation editor [23] driven by theory definitions; a refinement calculus tool was obtained with the definition of a theory based on the refinement calculus laws. The works described in [4, 30, 31, 6, 17, 5] are uses of a theorem prover, more specifically, HOL [14] and Ergo [26], to encode the refinement calculus theory. Except for the tool presented in [5], the interfaces provided are not adapted to the application of the refinement calculus supported. The B approach to refinement supported by its tools is based on verification rather than calculation: implementations are proposed and proof-obligations arise as a consequence.

We plan to further develop ZRC-Refine: inclusion of a graphical editor for Z and integration of a theorem prover are examples of tasks in our plans. We will also invest in extra facilities to support the management of the developments. We intend to include support for the definition and application of refinement tactics, in the style proposed in [22]. In that work, a refinement tactic language is presented; a tool that supports its use has already been integrated to Refine. Integrating this tool to ZRC-Refine as well is not a complex task.

A more substantial piece of future work is the addition of support for data refinement in Z, in the form of a proof-obligation calculator. Our plan is to produce a robust refinement calculator.

Acknowledgments

We would like to thank Ian Toyn for his Z grammar, and Fernanda Santos and André Barboza, for their participation in the implementation of the Z parser. Manuela Xavier has made herself constantly available to discuss the design of Refine. The work of Angela Freitas and Carla Nascimento is supported by CNPq. Ana Cavalcanti is also partly supported by CNPq, grants 520763/98-0 and 472204/2001-7.

References

1. ISO/IEC 13568:2002. Information technology—Z formal specification notation—syntax, type system and semantics. International Standard.
2. J-R. Abrial. *The B-Book: Assigning Progams to Meanings*. Cambridge University Press, 1996.

3. R. J. R. Back. Procedural Abstraction in the Refinement Calculus. Technical report, Department of Computer Science, Åbo, Finland, 1987. Ser. A No. 55.
4. R. J. R. Back and J. Wright. Refinement Concepts Formalised in Higher Order Logic. *Formal Aspects of Computing*, 2:247 – 274, 1990.
5. M. J. Butler, J. Grundy, T. Langbacka, R. Rukvenas, and J. Wright. The Refinement Calculator – Proof Support for Program Refinement. In *FMP'97 – Formal Methods Pacific*. Springer-Verlag, 1997.
6. D. Carrington, I. Hayes, R. Nickson, G. Watson, and J. Welsh. A program Refinement Tool. *Formal Aspects of Computing*, 10(2):97—124, 1998.
7. A. L. C. Cavalcanti. *A Refinement Calculus for Z*. PhD thesis, Oxford University Computing Laboratory, Oxford - UK, 1997. Technical Monograph TM-PRG-123, ISBN 00902928-97-X.
8. A. L. C. Cavalcanti, A. C. A. Sampaio, and J. C. P. Woodcock. Procedures and Recursion in the Refinement Calculus. *Journal of the Brazilian Computer Society*, 5(1):1 – 15, 1998.
9. A. L. C. Cavalcanti, A. C. A. Sampaio, and J. C. P. Woodcock. An Inconsistency in Procedures, Parameters, and Substitution the Refinement Calculus. *Science of Computer Programming*, 33(1):87 – 96, 1999.
10. A. L. C. Cavalcanti and J. C. P. Woodcock. A Weakest Precondition Semantics for Z. *The Computer Journal*, 41(1):1 – 15, 1998.
11. A. L. C. Cavalcanti and J. C. P. Woodcock. ZRC—A Refinement Calculus for Z. *Formal Aspects of Computing*, 10(3):267—289, 1999.
12. S. L. Coutinho, T. P. C. Reis, and A. L. C. Cavalcanti. Uma Ferramenta Educacional de Refinamentos. In *XIII Simpósio Brasileiro de Engenharia de Software*, pages 61 – 64, Florianópolis - SC, 1999. Sessão de Ferramentas.
13. E. W. Dijkstra. *A Discipline of Programming*. Prentice-Hall, 1976.
14. M. J. C. Gordon and T. F. Melham, editors. *Introduction to HOL: A Theorem Proving Environment for Higher Order Logic*. Cambridge University Press, 1993.
15. L. Groves. Adapting Formal Derivations. Technical Report CS-TR-95-9, Victoria University of Wellington, 1995.
16. L. Groves, R. Nickson, and M. Utting. A Tactic Driven Refinement Tool. In C. B. Jones, R. C. Shaw, and T. Denvir, editors, *5th Refinement Workshop*, Workshops in Computing, pages 272 – 297. Springer-Verlag, 1992.
17. J. Grundy. A Window Inference Tool for Refinement. In C. B. Jones, R. C. Shaw, and T. Denvir, editors, *5th Refinement Workshop*, Workshops in Computing, pages 230 – 254. Springer-Verlag, 1992.
18. U. Hamer and J. Peleska. Z Applied to the A330/340 CIDS Cabin Communication System. In M. G. Hinchey and J. P. Bowen, editors, *Applications of Formal Methods*, chapter 11, pages 253 – 284. Prentice-Hall, 1995.
19. S. King. Z and the Refinement Calculus. In D. Bjørner and C. A. R. Hoare, editors, *VDM'90 VDM and Z - Formal Methods in Software Development*, volume 428 of *Lecture Notes in Computer Science*, pages 164 – 188, Kiel - FRG, 1990. Springer-Verlag.
20. L. Laibinis. *Mechanised Formal Reasoning about Modular Programs*. PhD thesis, Turku Centre for Computer Science, 2000.
21. C. C. Morgan. *Programming from Specifications*. Prentice-Hall, 2nd edition, 1994.
22. M. Oliveira and A. L. C. Cavalcanti. Tactics of Refinement. In *14th Brazilian Symposium on Software Engineering*, pages 117 – 132, 2000.
23. J. L. A. Snepscheut. Mechanised Support for Stepwise Refinement. In J. Gutknecht, editor, *Programming Languages and System Architectures*, volume 782 of *Lecture Notes in Computer Science*, pages 35—48. Springer-Verlag, 1994.

24. J. M. Spivey. *The Z Notation: A Reference Manual.* 2nd. Prentice-Hall, 1992.
25. M. Staples. *A Mechanised Theory of Refinement.* PhD thesis, Cambridge University, 1999.
26. M. Utting. The ergo5 generic proof engine. Technical Report 97-44, Software Verification Research Centre, 1997.
27. T. Vickers. An Overview of a Refinement Editor. In *5th Australian Software Engineering Conference*, pages 39 – 44, Sidney - Australia, 1990.
28. J. C. P. Woodcock. Implementing Promoted Operations in Z. In C. B. Jones, R. C. Shaw, and T. Denvir, editors, *5th Refinement Workshop*, Workshops in Computing, London - UK, 1992. Prentice-Hall.
29. J. C. P. Woodcock and J. Davies. *Using Z—Specification, Refinement, and Proof.* Prentice-Hall, 1996.
30. J. Wright. Program Refinement by Theorem Prover. In D. Till, editor, *6th Refinement Workshop*, Workshops in Computing, pages 121 – 150, London - UK, 1994. Springer-Verlag.
31. J. Wright, J. Hekanaho, P. Luostarinen, and T. Langbacka. Mechanizing Some Advanced Refinement Concepts. *Formal Methods in System Design*, 3:49 – 81, 1993.

A   Laws

Law *altI* Alternation introduction

$$w : [pre, post]$$

$\sqsubseteq$ *altI*

if $[] \, i \bullet g_i \rightarrow w : [g_i \wedge pre, post]$ **fi**

provided $pre \Rightarrow (\bigvee i \bullet g_i)$

Syntactic Restriction Each g_i is a well-scoped predicate; no g_i has free dashed variables; $\{i \bullet g_i\}$ is non-empty.

Law *cfR* Contract frame

$$w, x : [pre, post]$$

$\sqsubseteq$ *cfR*

$$x : [pre, post[w/w']\,]$$

Syntactic Restriction The variables of w are not in x.

Law *fassigI* Following assignment introduction

$$w, vl : [pre, post]$$

$\sqsubseteq$ *fassigI*

$$w, vl : [pre, post[el[w', vl'/w, vl]/vl']\,] \; ; \; vl := el$$

Syntactic Restriction vl contains no duplicated variables; vl and el have the same length; el is well-scoped and well-typed; el has no free dashed variables; the corresponding variables of vl and expressions of el have the same type.

Law *pcallI* Call to a non-recursive procedure introduction

$\lVert \mathbf{proc}\ pn \mathrel{\widehat{=}} (fpd \bullet p_1) \bullet p_2[(fpd \bullet p_1)] \rVert$

$=$ *pcallI*

$\lVert \mathbf{proc}\ pn \mathrel{\widehat{=}} (fpd \bullet p_1) \bullet p_2[pn] \rVert$

Syntactic Restriction *pn* is not recursive.

Law *prcI* Procedure introduction

p_2

$=$ *prcI*

$\lVert \mathbf{proc}\ pn \mathrel{\widehat{=}} (fpd \bullet p_1) \bullet p_2 \rVert$

Syntactic Restriction *pn* is not free in p_2; $(fpd \bullet p_1)$ is well-scoped and well-typed.

Law *sP* Strengthen postcondition

$w : [pre, post]$

$\sqsubseteq$ *sP*

$w : [pre, npost]$

provided $pre \wedge npost \Rightarrow post$
Syntactic Restriction *npost* is well-scoped and well-typed.

Law *vS* Value specification

$w : [pre[el/vl], post[el, el'/vl, vl']\,]$

$=$ *vS*

$(\mathbf{val}\ dvl \bullet w : [pre, post])(el)$

where *dvl* declares the variables of *vl*.

Syntactic Restriction The variables of *vl* are not in *w* and are not dashed; the variables of *w* are not free in *el*; *el* has no free dashed variables.

Law *wP* Weaken precondition

$w : [pre, post]$

$\sqsubseteq$ *wP*

$w : [npre, post]$

provided $pre \Rightarrow npre$
Syntactic Restriction *npre* is well-scoped and well-typed.

The Common Semantic Constructs of XML Family

Hong Li Yang[1,2,*], Jun Gang Han[2], and Ke Gang Hao[1]

[1] Department of Computer Science
Northwest University, Xi'an China
yhl_ly@163.com
hkg@nwu.edu.cn
[2] Department of Computer Science
University of Xi'an Post & Telecomm. China
hjg@xiyou.edu.cn

Abstract. The most striking aspect of XML specifications released by
W3C is their mutual interdependence. At the time of this writing,
XSLT2.0, XPath2.0 and XQuery1.0 are all W3C working drafts. Standardizing each specification will be a major challenge. The formal semantics will be helpful to the standardization of languages. The key idea
of this paper is to model common semantic constructs of these languages
as Object-Z classes. The purpose is to reuse these semantic constructs to
specify the semantics of XML family languages and to understand the
common and difference between those languages.

1 Introduction

Extensible Markup Language(XML) [5] supports the standard formats for the
exchange of information among various applications on the Internet. As the importance of XML has increased, a series of lengthy specifications on various XML
languages appeared. The most striking aspect of XML specifications released
by World Wide Web Consortium (W3C)[1] is their mutual interdependence.
XSLT2.0[7], XPath2.0[2] and XQuery1.0[4] are all based on the type system of
XML Schema[14, 19, 3], and share same data model [15]. XSLT uses XPath expressions as a sublanguage, and XQuery is defined as a superset of XPath. The
numbers of dependencies between specifications have been expressed concern by
some members of XML-DEV [9]. At the time of this writing, XSLT2.0, XPath2.0
and XQuery1.0 are all W3C working draft. Standardizing each specification will
be a major challenge.

The development of formal semantics for these languages will bring any ambiguities about the language specifications to the fore so that they can be addressed
and resolved. There are some recent works in the research of the semantics of
XML related technologies. For instance, Wadler [21] presents a formal semantics of the patterns using traditional denotation semantics, Wadler [16] describes

---

* This paper was written during the first author's visit to the School of Computing of
National University of Singapore as part of the UNU/IIST Fellowship Programme.

J.S. Dong and J. Woodcock (Eds.): ICFEM 2003, LNCS 2885, pp. 416–431, 2003.

the formalization of XML Schema, and a formal semantics of the path expressions using judgments and inference rules are also defined in [20, 12]. We are interested in describing the mutual interdependence of XML family languages. In this paper, Object-Z [13, 17] is used as the meta language for presenting semantics. All common constructs of XML family languages, such as data types, data model and expressions, are specified as Object-Z classes. As example, we describes the dynamic semantics of partial XQuery by reusing these common semantic constructs. This object-oriented presentation of semantics will make sure all specifications fit together and make coherent sense. It not only leads to concise specification, but also to extensibility and reusability.

The remainder of this paper is organized as follows: Section 2 introduces XML family languages. Section 3 specifies the common semantic constructs of XML family languages. Section 4 presents the dynamic semantics of partial XQuery by reusing the common semantic constructs. Section 5 concludes the paper.

2   XML Family Languages Overview

XML is a simple, very flexible text format derived from SGML. Over the past few years, XML has rapidly gained popularity as a formatting language for exchanging information. XML family languages are a series of technologies proposed by W3C, which both develops and promotes standard technologies for the Web.

XML Schema is an XML based alternative to Document Type Definition (DTD). An XML schema defines the structure of elements and attributes that can appear in an XML document. It also defines data types for elements and attributes. XPath is a language for addressing parts of an XML document. XPath operates on the abstract, logical structure of an XML document. This logical structure is known as the Data Model, which is the data model of XSLT, XQuery, and any other specifications that reference it. The model treats XML documents as trees of nodes. Every value handled by the data model is a sequence of zero or more items. An item is either a node or a simple typed value, which is defined by the XML Schema data types. XPath uses path expressions to identify nodes in an XML document. XPath was designed to be used by XSLT, XQuery and other related XML languages.

XQuery is a query language that lets you retrieve data items from XML-formatted documents. XQuery1.0 is a superset of XPath2.0 in the sense that any valid XPath2.0 expression is also a valid XQuery1.0 expression and will return the same results. XQuery provides FLWR expressions for iterating over groups of nodes and for binding variables to intermediate results. XQuery uses element constructors to create elements that appear in the output or intermediate results of an expression.

XSLT is a language for transforming XML documents into other XML documents. The transformation is achieved by a set of template rules. A template rule associates a pattern, which matches nodes in the source document, with a content constructor, which can be evaluated to produce part of a result tree. A natural subset of XPath has been used in XSLT for matching (testing whether or not a node matches a pattern).

3   The Common Semantic Constructs

This section models the common semantic constructs of XML family languages. These constructs include the data types of XML Schema, the data model of XML document, and the expressions of XPath.

3.1   Data Types

XML Schema is a large and complex standard. In this section, we attempt to model only the most essential features. These include: atomic, list and union simple types; and derivation by restriction and by extension.

The class *Datatype* is modeled as a class union.

$$Datatype \ \widehat{=} \ atomicType \cup listType \cup unionType \cup derivedType$$

The atomic types are the nineteen primitive types of schema, such as xs:string and xs:integer, and the types derived from them.

$$atomicType \ ::=$$
$$String \mid QName \mid Bool \mid Int \mid Decimal \mid Float \mid Double \mid \cdots$$

The common attributes of all datatypes are modeled as class *baseType*, which contains attributes: type name, *name*, and set of values, *val*.

The type *Value* represents a set of values.

Value

```
┌─ baseType ────────────────────────────────────────
│ ┌──────────────────────────────────────────────
│ │ name : QName
│ │ val : ℙ Value
│ │
│ └──────────────────────────────────────────────
```

The class *unionType* is defined by inheriting class *baseType*. In addition, a set of members, *members*. The value space is the union of value spaces of their member data types. The class *listType* is defined by inheriting class *baseType*. In addition, a sequence of items, *items*. The value space of list type is composed of finite-length sequences of values from the value space of the item type.

```
┌─ unionType ──────────────────        ┌─ listType ────────────────────
│ ┌──────────────────────            │ ┌──────────────────────────
│ │ baseType                          │ │ baseType
│ └──────────────────────            │ └──────────────────────────
│ ┌──────────────────────            │ ┌──────────────────────────
│ │ members : ℙ Datatype              │ │ items : seq atomicType ∪ unionType
│ └──────────────────────            │ └──────────────────────────
│ │ val = ⋃{∀ m : Datatype ∣         │ │ val = ran items
│ │    m ∈ members • m.val}
```

$$val = \bigcup \{\forall\, m : Datatype \mid m \in members \bullet m.val\}$$

$$val = \operatorname{ran} items$$

A type derivation either restricts an atomic type, or restricts a named type to a given type, or extends a named type by a given type. The class *derivedType* is defined as class union.

$$derivedType \,\hat{=}\, res1\,Type \cup res2\,Type \cup extType$$

The definition of the class *res1Type* need define type *consFacets*, which is a set of constrains of data types, and function *satisfy*, which checks if a set of values satisfy a set of constrains.

$$consFacets == \{length, minLength, maxLength, pattern, enumeration,$$
$$whiteSpace, maxInclusive, maxExclusive, minExclusive,$$
$$minInclusive, totalDigits, fractionDigits\}$$

$$| \quad satisfy : \mathbb{P}\,Value \times \mathbb{P}\,consFacets \to \mathbb{B}$$

The class *res1Type* is defined by inheriting class *baseType*. In addition, it contains attributes: a type, *base*, and a set of consfacets, *cons*. The class *res2Type* is defined by inheriting class *baseType*. In addition, it contains attributes: a type, *base*, and a given type, *tp*.

res1Type	_res2Type_
baseType	*baseType*
base : *atomicType* *cons* : $\mathbb{P}$ *consFacets*	*base* : *Datatype* *tp* : *Datatype*
satisfy(*val*, *cons*) $\forall v : Value \bullet v \in val \Rightarrow v \in base.val$	*val* = *tp.val* $\forall v : Value \bullet v \in val \Rightarrow v \in base.val$

The class *extType* is defined by inheriting class *baseType*. In addition, it contains attributes: a type, *base*, and given type, *tp*.

The function *cat* is defined to concatenate two values.

$$| \quad cat : Value \times Value \to Value$$

extType
baseType
base : *Datatype*   *tp* : *Datatype*
$\forall v : Value \bullet v \in val \Rightarrow$ $\quad \exists v1, v2 : Value \bullet v1 \in base.val \wedge v2 \in tp.val \wedge v = cat(v1, v2)$

3.2 Data Model

This section presents the data model of an XML document. The data model is based on the XML Information Set [8], which specifies what information in the documents is accessible.

The basic data type is *Node*. Each node is one of seven kinds: document, element, attribute, text, comment, processing instruction, namespace. The node type is defined as Z free type definition.

$$nodeType ::= docType \mid elemType \mid attrType \\ \mid textType \mid commType \mid piType \mid nmType$$

The type *ID* is defined as a set of node identities.

ID

$$
\begin{array}{l}
\_\_Node_____ \\
\hline
type : nodeType \\
name : QName \\
value : String \\
parent : Node \\
children, attribute, namespace : \text{seq } Node \\
id : Node \rightarrow ID \\
\varDelta \\
doc : Node \\
descend, ancestor : \text{seq } Node \\
\end{array}
$$

A *Node* object contains a node type, *type*, a node name, *name*, a node value, *value*, a node parent, *parent*, a sequence of children nodes, *children*, a sequence of attribute nodes, *attribute*, a sequence of namespace nodes, *namespace*, a unique identity, *id*. In addition, the secondary attribute *doc* is a document node. *descend* is a sequence of descendant nodes. *ancestor* is a sequence of ancestor nodes.

3.3 Expressions

This section presents the dynamic semantics of XPath2.0 expressions. An expression is either a path expression, a sequence expression, an arithmetic expression, a comparison expression, a logic expression, a conditional expression or a quantified expression. The expression class *Exp* is defined as class union.

$$Exp \;\widehat{=}\; \\ pathExp \cup seqExp \cup arithExp \cup compExp \cup logicExp \cup condExp \cup quanExp$$

The value of an expression is always a sequence of items, which is either an atomic value or a node. There is no distinction between an item and a sequence of length one. The types *itemType* and *seqType* are defined as following:

$itemType ::= atomicType \mid Node$
$seqType == \text{seq } itemType$

The type of expressions are defined as scalar types $scalType$.

$scalType ::= itemType \mid seqType$

The set of scalar values is defined using the free-value construct.

$scalVal ::= atomicVal\langle\!\langle atomicType \rangle\!\rangle \mid nodeVal\langle\!\langle Node \rangle\!\rangle \mid seqVal\langle\!\langle seqType \rangle\!\rangle$

The function $type\_of$ returns the type of an expression value.

$$type\_of : scalVal \rightarrow scalType$$

$\forall\, a : atomicType;\ n : Node;\ s : seqType \bullet$
$type\_of(atomicVal(a)) = atomicType \wedge type\_of(nodeVal(n)) = Node \wedge$
$\qquad type\_of(seqVal(s)) = seqType$

The common properties of all expressions are specified as class $baseExp$. The context item $context$ is an object of class $Node$.

$baseExp$

$type : scalType$
Δ
$context : Node$
$val : scalVal$

$type\_of(val) = type$

$outVal$

$val! : scalVal$

$val! = val$

A path expression can be used to locate nodes within a XML document tree. The path expression class $pathExp$ requires the definition of the class $Step$, which represents step expressions.

Firstly, the type $Axis$ is defined as a free type definition

$Axis ::= child \mid desc \mid attr \mid self \mid desOrself \mid followSib \mid$
$\qquad follow \mid nmsp \mid parent \mid ance \mid preSib \mid preced \mid ancOrself$

The type $Test$ is defined as a free type definition

$Test ::= text \mid comm \mid pi \mid nd \mid qnm\langle\!\langle QName \rangle\!\rangle$

The type $Pred$ is simply defined as Exp type.

$Pred == Exp$

A step expression consists of an axis to express the relationship between the context node and the nodes to be selected, a node test, to actually specifies what is to be selected, and optionally, predicates, which filters the nodes selected by the node test. A step expression is defined as an object of class *Step*. A path expression contains a sequence of step expressions. It is defined as an object of class *pathExp*.

The function *evalStep* is defined to evaluate a step expression. Function *evalPath* is defined to evaluate a path expression.

$$evalStep : Node \times Axis \times Test \times Pred \rightarrow \text{seq } Node$$
$$evalPath : Node \times \text{seq } Step \rightarrow \text{seq } Node$$

```
┌─ Step ──────────────────            ┌─ pathExp ──────────────────
│ baseExp                             │ baseExp
│ ┌──────────────────────            │ ┌──────────────────────────
│ │ axis : Axis                      │ │ steps : seq Step
│ │ test : Test                      │ ├──────────────────────────
│ │ pred : Pred                      │ │ type = seq Node
│ ├──────────────────────            │ │ val = evalPath(context, steps)
│ │ type = seq Node                  │ └──────────────────────────
│ │ val = evalStep(context, axis, test, pred)
│ └──────────────────────
└──────────────────────────
```

A sequence expression is either a comma expression, a range expression or a combine expression. The class *seqExp* is defined as class union.

$$seqExp \mathrel{\widehat{=}} commaExp \cup rangeExp \cup combExp$$

The class *commaExp* contains a sequence of expressions *exps*. A comma expression object evaluates each of its operands and concatenates the resulting value into a single result sequence. The class *rangeExp* contains two integer operands *left* and *right*. The result sequence is constructed containing the two integers operands and every integer between the two operands. A combine expression is either an union expression, an intersect expression or an except expression. The class *combExp* contains two node sequences operands *left* and *right*, and a combine operator *op*, which is defined as Z free type definition.

$$combOp ::= union \mid intersect \mid except$$

The function *catExpVal* is specified to concatenate the value of sequence of expressions, to form a single sequence.

$$catExpVal : \text{seq } Exp \rightarrow \text{seq } atomicType \cup Node$$

```
┌─ commaExp ──────────────────
│ baseExp
│ ┌────────────────────────
│ │ exps : seq Exp
│ ├────────────────────────
│ │ type = seqType
│ │ val = catExpVal(exps)
│ └────────────────────────
```

```
┌─ rangeExp ──────────────────
│ baseExp
│ ┌────────────────────────
│ │ left : Exp
│ │ right : Exp
│ ├────────────────────────
│ │ type = seq Int
│ │ left.type = Int
│ │ right.type = Int
│ │ ∀ n ∈ ran val ⇒ n ∈ Int
│ │ ∧ n ≥ left.val ∧ n ≤ right.val
│ └────────────────────────
```

```
┌─ combExp ───────────────────
│ baseExp
│ ┌────────────────────────
│ │ left : Exp
│ │ op : combOp
│ │ right : Exp
│ ├────────────────────────
│ │ type = seq Node
│ │ left.type = seq Node
│ │ right.type = seq Node
│ │ op = union ⇒
│ │    val = left.val ⌢ right.val
│ │ op = intersect ⇒
│ │ ∀ n : Node • n ∈ ran val ⇒
│ │ n ∈ (ran left.val ∩ ran right.val)
│ │ op = except ⇒
│ │ ∀ n : Node • n ∈ ran val ⇒
│ │ n ∈ ran left.val ∧ n ∉ ran right.val
│ └────────────────────────
```

```
┌─ arithExp ──────────────────────────────────
│ baseExp
│ ┌────────────────────────────────────────
│ │ lf : Exp
│ │ op : arithOp
│ │ rg : Exp
│ ├────────────────────────────────────────
│ │ rg.type = lf.type
│ │ op = add ∧ lf.type = nmType ⇒ val = lf.val + rg.val ∧ type = lf.type
│ │ op = sub ∧ lf.type = nmType ⇒ val = lf.val − rg.val ∧ type = lf.type
│ │ op = mul ∧ lf.type = nmType ⇒ val = lf.val * rg.val ∧ type = lf.type
│ │ op = mod ∧ lf.type = nmType ⇒ val = lf.val mod rg.val ∧ type =
│ │                                                          lf.type
│ │ op = div ∧ lf.type = Int ⇒ val = lf.val div rg.val ∧ type = Decimal
│ │ op = div ∧ lf.type ∈ {Decimal, Float, Double} ⇒
│ │    val = lf.val div rg.val ∧ type = lf.type
│ └────────────────────────────────────────
```

XPath provides the usual arithmetic operators: $+, -, *,$ *div* and *mod*, which are defined on the values of numeric type *nmType*. An arithmetic expression is defined as an object of class *arithExp*, which contains two expressions operands *lf* and *rg*, and an arithmetic operator *op*, which is defined as type *arithOp*.

$$nmType ::= Int \mid Decimal \mid Float \mid Double$$
$$arithOp ::= add \mid sub \mid mul \mid mod \mid div$$

XPath provides four kinds of comparison expressions, called value comparisons, general comparisons, node comparisons and order comparisons. The result of a comparison expression is always true or false. The class *compExp* is defined as class union.

$$compExp \;\hat{=}\; valExp \cup genExp \cup nodeExp \cup orderExp$$

The common attributes of comparison expressions are defined as the class *baseCompExp*. Other class can be defined by inheriting this class.

```
┌─ baseCompExp ─────────────────────────────────────
│ baseExp
│ ┌──────────────────────────────────────────────
│ │ left : Exp
│ │ right : Exp
│ ├──────────────────────────────────────────────
│ │ left.type = right.type ∧ type = 𝔹
```

The value comparison operators type *valOp*, general comparison operators type *genOp*, node comparison operators type *nodeOp*, and order comparison operators type *orderOp* are defined as

$$
\begin{aligned}
valOp &::= eq \mid ne \mid lt \mid le \mid gt \mid ge \\
genOp &::= eq' \mid ne' \mid lt' \mid le' \mid gt' \mid ge' \\
nodeOp &::= is \mid isnot \\
orderOp &::= less \mid great
\end{aligned}
$$

The value comparison expression class *valExp* and node comparison expression class *nodeExp* are defined as

```
┌─ nodeExp ──────────────────           ┌─ valExp ────────────────────
│ baseCompExp                            │ baseCompExp
│ ┌─────────────────────────            │ ┌────────────────────────────
│ │ op : nodeOp                          │ │ op : valOp
│ ├─────────────────────────            │ ├────────────────────────────
│ │ left.type = Node                     │ │ left.type = itemType
│ │ op = is ⇒ val =                      │ │ op = eq ⇒ val =    (left.val = right.val)
│ │   (left.val.id = right.val.id)       │ │ op = ne ⇒ val =    (left.val ≠ right.val)
│ │ op = isnot ⇒ val =                   │ │ op = lt ⇒ val =    (left.val < right.val)
│ │   (left.val.id ≠ right.val.id)       │ │ op = le ⇒ val =    (left.val ≤ right.val)
│ │                                       │ │ op = gt ⇒ val =    (left.val > right.val)
│ │                                       │ │ op = ge ⇒ val =    (left.val ≥ right.val)
```

Each of the value comparison operators has a corresponding general comparison operator that is defined by adding existential semantics to the value comparison operator. The operands of a general comparison may be sequences of any length.

┌─ *genExp* ──
│ *baseCompExp*
│ ┌───
│ │ *op* : *genOp*
│ ├───
│ │ *left.type* = *seqType*
│ │ *op* = *eq'* ⇒ *val* = ($\exists\, x, y$: *itemType* •
│ │ $x \in$ ran *left.val* $\land$ $y \in$ ran *right.val* $\land$ *left.val* = *right.val*)
│ │ *op* = *ne'* ⇒ *val* = ($\exists\, x, y$: *itemType* •
│ │ $x \in$ ran *left.val* $\land$ $y \in$ ran *right.val* $\land$ *left.val* $\neq$ *right.val*)
│ │ *op* = *lt'* ⇒ *val* = ($\exists\, x, y$: *itemType* •
│ │ $x \in$ ran *left.val* $\land$ $y \in$ ran *right.val* $\land$ *left.val* $<$ *right.val*)
│ │ *op* = *le'* ⇒ *val* = ($\exists\, x, y$: *itemType* •
│ │ $x \in$ ran *left.val* $\land$ $y \in$ ran *right.val* $\land$ *left.val* $\leq$ *right.val*)
│ │ *op* = *gt'* ⇒ *val* = ($\exists\, x, y$: *itemType* •
│ │ $x \in$ ran *left.val* $\land$ $y \in$ ran *right.val* $\land$ *left.val* $>$ *right.val*)
│ │ *op* = *ge'* ⇒ *val* = ($\exists\, x, y$: *itemType* •
│ │ $x \in$ ran *left.val* $\land$ $y \in$ ran *right.val* $\land$ *left.val* $\geq$ *right.val*)
│ └───
└───

The order comparison expression uses operators '$\ll$' and '$\gg$' to compare the positions of two nodes. For instance, the '$\ll$' operator returns true if the first operand node is earlier than the second operand node in document order; otherwise, it returns false. The function *docOrder* defines the document order of a node in a document.

│ *docOrder* : *Node* → $\mathbb{Z}$

┌─ *orderExp* ──
│ *baseCompExp*
│ ┌───
│ │ *op* : *orderOp*
│ ├───
│ │ *left.type* = *Node*
│ │ *op* = *less* ⇒ *val* = *docOrder*(*left.val*) $<$ *docOrder*(*right.val*)
│ │ *op* = *great* ⇒ *val* = *docOrder*(*left.val*) $>$ *docOrder*(*right.val*)
│ └───
└───

A logical expression is either an and-expression or an or-expression. The logic operators are define as

│ *logicOp* ::= *and* | *or*

A logical expression is defined as an object of class *logicExp*.

┌─ logicExp ─────────────────────
│ baseExp
│ ┌────────────────────────────
│ │ left : Exp
│ │ op : logicOp
│ │ right : Exp
│ ├────────────────────────────
│ │ left.type = $\mathbb{B}$
│ │ right.type = $\mathbb{B} \wedge$ type = $\mathbb{B}$
│ │ op = and $\Rightarrow$
│ │   val = left.val $\wedge$ right.val
│ │ op = or $\Rightarrow$
│ │   val = left.val $\vee$ right.val
└─┴────────────────────────────

┌─ condExp ─────────────────────
│ baseExp
│ ┌────────────────────────────
│ │ test : Exp
│ │ then : Exp
│ │ else : Exp
│ ├────────────────────────────
│ │ test.type = $\mathbb{B}$
│ │ test.val $\Rightarrow$
│ │   type = then.type $\wedge$ val = then.val
│ │ $\neg$ test.val $\Rightarrow$
│ │   type = else.type $\wedge$ val = else.val
└─┴────────────────────────────

A conditional expression contains three sub-expressions: a test expression, a then-expression, an else-expression. It is defined as an object of class *condExp*.

Quantified expressions support existential and universal quantification. The quantified expression class *quanExp* requires the definition of variable reference class *VaRef*, which requires the definition of variable location class *VarLoc*.

┌─ VarLoc ─────────────────────
│ ┌────────────────────────────
│ │ type : scalType
│ │ cont : scalVal
│ ├────────────────────────────
│ │ type_of(cont) = type
│ └────────────────────────────
│ ┌─ INIT ─────────────────────
│ │ type = itemType $\Rightarrow$
│ │   cont = itemVal(NIL)
│ │ type = seqType $\Rightarrow$ cont = $\langle \ \rangle$
└─┴────────────────────────────

┌─ Assign ─────────────────────
│ $\Delta(cont)$
│ val? : scalVal
├──────────────────────────────
│ cont' = val?
└──────────────────────────────

Where *NIL* represents an initial item value.

┌─ VaRef ─────────────────────
│ baseExp
│ ┌────────────────────────────
│ │ nm : QName
│ │ vl : VarLoc
│ ├────────────────────────────
│ │ type = vl.type $\wedge$ val = vl.cont
│ └────────────────────────────
│ Assign $\widehat{=}$ vl.Assign
└──────────────────────────────

The quantified operators are defined as

quanOp ::= some | all

A quantified expression is modelled as an object of class $quanExp$, which contains an operator, op, a variable name, nm, an expression, ep, and a test expression, ts. In addition, a secondary attribute: a variable reference, ref.

$$
\begin{array}{l}
\underline{\_\,quanExp\,\underline{\hspace{8cm}}}\\
\quad baseExp\\
\quad \begin{array}{|l}
\hline
op : quanOp\\
nm : String\\
ep : Exp\\
ts : Exp\\
\Delta\\
ref : VaRef\\
\hline
type = \mathbb{B} \wedge ts.type = \mathbb{B} \wedge ep.type = seqType \wedge ref.nm = nm\\
op = all \Rightarrow val = \forall\, i : 1 \mathrel{..} \#ep.val \bullet ref.val = ep(i).val \wedge ts.val =\\
\hfill true\\
op = some \Rightarrow val = \exists\, i : 1 \mathrel{..} \#ep.val \bullet ref.val = ep(i).val \wedge ts.val =\\
\hfill true\\
\hline
\end{array}
\end{array}
$$

4   The Semantics of XQuery by Reusing

This section presents the dynamic semantics of partial XQuery by reusing the constructs in section 3. XQuery has several kinds of expressions. Except the expressions specified in section 3.3, there are FLWR expressions and constructors expressions. The expressions class $xqExp$ is defined as class union.

$$
xqExp \mathrel{\widehat{=}} xqpathExp \cup xqseqExp \cup xqarithExp \cup xqcompExp\cup\\
xqlogicExp \cup xqcondExp \cup xqquanExp \cup xqflwrExp \cup xqconsExp
$$

In XQuery, sequence expressions, arithmetic expressions, comparison expressions, logic expressions, conditional expressions and quantified expressions are all same with corresponding expressions in XPath.

$$
\begin{array}{l}
xqseqExp == seqExp\\
xqarithExp == arithExp\\
xqcompExp == compExp\\
xqlogicExp == logicExp\\
xqcondExp == condExp\\
xqquanExp == quanExp
\end{array}
$$

The path expressions in XQuery have little difference with ones in XPath. XQuery supports the following axes: $child$, $descendent$, $attribute$, $self$, $descendent\_or\_self$ and $parent$, the type $xqAxis$ is defined as

$$
xqAxis ::= child \mid desc \mid attr \mid self \mid desOrself \mid parent
$$

The XQuery step expressions class $xqStep$ is defined by replacing type $Axis$ with type $xqAxis$ in the class $Step$.

```
┌─ xqStep ─────────────────────────────────────────
│ Step[xqAxis/Axis]
└──────────────────────────────────────────────────
```

The XQuery path expressions class $xqpathExp$ is defined by replacing class $Step$ with class $xqStep$ in class $pathExp$.

```
┌─ xqpathExp ──────────────────────────────────────
│ pathExp[xqStep/Step]
└──────────────────────────────────────────────────
```

A $FLWR$ expression includes for, let, $where$ and $return$ clauses. The for and let clauses generate a sequence of variable references tuples. The $where$ clause serves to filter the tuples, retaining some tuples and discarding others. The $return$ clause constructs the result of the $FLWR$ expression.

A for clause may contain multiple variables, each with an associated expression. The for clause iterates each variable over the items that result from evaluating its expression. The class For contains a sequence of variable name nms, a sequence of expressions $exps$, and a secondary attribute $refs$, which is a sequence of variable references.

```
┌─ For ────────────────────────┐   ┌─ Let ────────────────────────┐
│ nms : seq String             │   │ nms : seq String             │
│ exps : seq Exp               │   │ exps : seq Exp               │
│ Δ                            │   │ Δ                            │
│ refs : seq VaRef             │   │ refs : seq VaRef             │
├──────────────────────────────┤   ├──────────────────────────────┤
│ #nms = #exps = #refs         │   │ #nms = #exps = #refs         │
│ ∀ i : 1 .. #nms •            │   │ ∀ i : 1 .. #nms •            │
│   refs(i).nm = nms(i) ∧      │   │   refs(i).nm = nms(i) ∧      │
│   refs(i).val ∈ ran exps(i).val │ │   refs(i).val = exps(i).val  │
└──────────────────────────────┘   └──────────────────────────────┘
```

A let clause may also contain one or more variables, each with an associated expression. Unlike a for clause, however, a let clause binds each variable to the result of its associated expression, without iteration.

The class $xqflwrExp$ need the defination of some auxiliary types and functions. The type $Binds$ defines a sequence of variable binding tuples.

$$Binds == \text{seq seq } VaRef$$

The function $binding$ is defined to construct a sequence of variable binding tuples.

$$binding : For \times Let \rightarrow Binds$$

The function *evalSingle* is defined to evaluate a FLWR expression which includes single variable binding tuple.

$$| \quad evalSingle : \text{seq } VaRef \times Exp \times Exp \to seq\,Val$$

The function *evalflwr* is defined to evaluate a FLWR expression.

$evalflwr : Binds \times Exp \times Exp \to seq\,Val$

$\forall\, b : Binds;\ wh : Exp;\ re : Exp;\ val : seq\,Val \bullet$
$\quad \#b = 1 \Rightarrow val = evalSingle(b(1), wh, re)$
$\quad \#b > 1 \Rightarrow val = evalSingle(b(1), wh, re) \frown evalFLWR(\text{tail } b, wh, re)$

The class *xqflwrExp* includes attributes: a *for* expression, a *let* expression, a *where* expression and a *return* expression. In addition, secondary attributes: a sequence of variable reference tuples *refs*, and *vscope*. The predicate *pred1* specifies that the whole access scope of a FLWR expression is the scope of variables in *for* and *let* clauses.

__*xqflwrExp*_____

baseExp

---
for : *For*
let : *Let*
wh : *Exp*
re : *Exp*
Δ
refs : *Binds*
vscope : *QName* $\rightarrowtail$ *VarLoc*

$type = seqType$
$val = evalflwr(binding(for, let), wh, re)$
$vscope = \{vr : \text{ran } for.refs \bullet vr.nm \mapsto vr.vl\} \cup$
$\quad \{vr : \text{ran } let.refs \bullet vr.nm \mapsto vr.vl\}$ $\qquad\qquad$ [pred1]

XQuery provides *constructors* that can create XML structures within a query. A special form of constructor called a computed constructor that can be used to create an element or attribute with a computed name.

The XQuery constructors class *xqConsExp* is defined as class union.

$$xqconsExp \mathrel{\widehat{=}} compElemCons \cup compAttrCons$$

A computed element constructor expression contains attributes: a name expression, *nm*, which is evaluated to produce the name of created element node; a content constructor expression, *cont*, which is evaluated to produce a sequence of children nodes of created element node.

A computed attribute constructor expression contains attributes: a name expression, *nm*, which is evaluated to produce the name of created attribute node; a content constructor expression, *cont*, which is evaluated to produce the value of created attribute node.

The function *create* is defined to create a new element node based on the given name and content. The function *catStr* is defined to concatenate a sequence of strings to form a single string.

$$create : QName \times \text{seq } Node \rightarrow Node$$
$$catStr : \text{seq } String \rightarrow String$$

┌─ *compElemCons* ─────────────────
│ *baseExp*
│ ├────────────────────────────
│ │ *nm* : *Exp*
│ │ *cont* : *Exp*
│ ├────────────────────────────
│ │ *type* = *Node*
│ │ *nm.type* = *QName*
│ │ *cont.type* = seq *Node*
│ │ *val.type* = *elemType*
│ │ *val* = *create*(*nm.val*, *cont.val*)
│ └────────────────────────────

┌─ *compAttrCons* ─────────────────
│ *baseExp*
│ ├────────────────────────────
│ │ *nm* : *Exp*
│ │ *cont* : *Exp*
│ ├────────────────────────────
│ │ *type* = *Node*
│ │ *nm.type* = *QName*
│ │ *cont.type* = seq *String*
│ │ *val.type* = *attrType*
│ │ *val.name* = *nm.val*
│ │ *val.value* = *catStr*(*cont.val*)
│ └────────────────────────────

5 Conclusion

In this paper, the common semantic constructs of XML family languages have been modeled as a semantic library based on object-oriented views of programming language semantics [10, 11]. The dynamic semantics of partial XQuery language has been specified by reusing this library. This highly structured approach will not only lead to an incremental and compact semantic models but also gain the extensibility and reusability.

One research direction will be to reuse this library to specify the semantics of all those XML related languages. For instance, Web Services Description Language(WSDL) [6] uses basic data type defined in [3] to define operations as typed message exchanges, so it is convenient to reuse the data type components in the semantic library to define the messages of this language.

One interesting aspect is that Object-Z itself has an XML environment [18] which supports automatic expansion of Object-Z inheritance and generation of UML diagrams. With this tool, the formal semantic model for XML family languages can be studied and understood more readily and visually.

Acknowledgements

This work is supported by the UNU/IIST fellowship programme.

References

1. see http://www.w3.org.
2. A. Berglund and S. Boag. *XML Path Language (XPath) 2.0*, 2002. http://www.w3.org/TR/xpath20/.
3. Paul V. Biron and A. Malhotra. *XML Schema Part 2: Datatypes*, 2001. http://www.w3.org/TR/2001/REC-xmlschema-2-20010502/.
4. S. Boag, D. Chamberlin, and M. Fernandez. *XQuery 1.0: An XML Query Language*, 15 November 2002. http://www.w3.org/TR/2002/WD-xquery-20021115/.
5. Tim Bray, Jean Paoli, and C. M. Sperberg-McQueen. *Extensible Markup Language (XML) 1.0 (Second Edition)*, 2000. http://www.w3.org/TR/REC-xml/.
6. R. Chinnici, M. Gudgin, J. J. Moreau, and S.Weerawarana. *Web Services Description Language (WSDL) Version 1.2*, 2002. http://www.w3.org/TR/2002/WD-wsdl12-20020709.
7. James Clark. *XSL Transformations (XSLT) Version 2.0*, 2002. http://www.w3.org/TR/xslt20/.
8. J. Cowan and R. Tobin. *XML Information Set*, 2001. http://www.w3.org/TR/xml-infoset/.
9. Leigh Dodds. *Time to Refactor XML?*, 2001. see http://www.xml.com/pub/a/2001/02/21/deviant.html.
10. J. S. Dong. *Formal Object Modelling Techniques and Denotational Semantics Studies*. PhD thesis, University of Queensland, 1995.
11. J. S. Dong, R. Duke, and G. Rose. An object-oriented approach to the semantics of programming languages. *Australian Computer Science Communications*, 16, 1994.
12. D. Draper, P. Fankhauser, and M. Fernández. *XQuery 1.0 and XPath 2.0 Formal Semantics*, 15 November 2002. http://www.w3.org/TR/2002/WD-query-semantics-20021115/.
13. R. Duke and G. Rose. *Formal Object Oriented Specification Using Object-Z*. Macmillan, 2000.
14. David C. Fallside. *XML Schema Part 0: Primer*, 2001. http://www.w3.org/TR/2001/REC-xmlschema-0-20010502/.
15. M. Fernández, A. Malhotra, and J. Marsh. *XQuery 1.0 and XPath 2.0 Data Model*, 15 November 2002. http://www.w3.org/TR/2002/WD-query-datamodel-20021115/.
16. J.Simeon and P. Wadler. The essence of xml. In *POPL'03, New Orleans, Louisiana, USA. ACM*, January 2003.
17. G. Smith. *The Object-Z Specification Language*. Kluwer Academic Publishers, 1999.
18. J. Sun, J. S. Dong, J. Liu, and H. Wang. Object-Z Web Environment and Projections to UML. In *WWW-10: 10th International World Wide Web Conference, refereed papers track*, pages 725–734. ACM Press, May 2001.
19. Henry S. Thompson, D. Beech, M. Maloney, and N. Mendelsohn. *XML Schema Part 1: Structures*, 2001. http://www.w3.org/TR/2001/REC-xmlschema-1-20010502/.
20. P. Wadler. *Two Semantics for XPath*, January 2000.
21. P. Wadler. *A formal semantics of patterns in XSLT, Markup Languages, MIT Press*, June 2001.

Controller Synthesis for Object Petri Nets

Berndt Farwer[1], Saraswati Kalvala[2], and Kundan Misra[2]

[1] Fachbereich Informatik
Universität Hamburg
D-22527, Hamburg, Germany
farwer@informatik.uni-hamburg.de
[2] Department of Computer Science
University of Warwick
Coventry, CV4 7AL, United Kingdom
{sk,kundan}@dcs.warwick.ac.uk

Abstract. A large class of real-world systems can be modelled as Petri nets, and complex systems are more conveniently modelled as object Petri nets. Ensuring that Petri net models avoid forbidden states has attracted much research effort. The work presented addresses the forbidden state problem for object Petri nets, through a method for controller synthesis. A simple illustrative example is given as well as an illustration in a flexible manufacturing system. The concept of place invariants plays an important role in Petri net theory. For the first time, place invariants are defined for object Petri nets.

1   Introduction

Petri nets [Pet66] are a type of discrete event system [HKG97] in which tokens represent objects moving through a net. A Petri net represents the dynamics of the system that it models. The most basic type of Petri net is the place/transition net ("**P/T net**") which has only black tokens. Coloured Petri nets ("**CPN**"s) are an extension of P/T nets in which values ("colours") are bound to tokens. Object Petri nets are a further extension in which nets can themselves be tokens of a net. An object Petri net is used to make a model of a complex system more understandable by breaking up the flat (P/T net or CPN) model and grouping components that belong together semantically. The result is a model comprising modules in the form of the token nets ("object nets"). These represent meaningful sub-parts of the system being modelled, while the overall system is represented by a higher level net called the system net. Conveniently, those modules are largely autonomous in their action and so each can be individually studied. Deeper nesting is appropriate when further modularization of object net modules delivers benefits in comprehensibility.

Petri nets are used to model real-world discrete event systems including telecommunications, manufacturing, business, biological, and chemical systems [LWC01,VG03,FMGV02,J03,Red94,Yam91]. Systems in these application domains are often forbidden from entering particular states. The problem of how

J.S. Dong and J. Woodcock (Eds.): ICFEM 2003, LNCS 2885, pp. 432–451, 2003.

to guarantee that constraints of a system are satisfied by a model is termed the *forbidden state problem*. The synthesis of supervisors or controllers for discrete event systems, and in particular for various classes of Petri nets, has been an active area of study. Only some of the work in this area will be mentioned, as space limits do not allow a comprehensive survey.

The work presented in this paper moves beyond CPNs to a richer Petri net formalism. In particular, the forbidden state problem is addressed for object Petri nets by introducing a method of controller synthesis for object Petri nets. The growing importance of object Petri nets motivates this research aim [LLKM95,Lak97,Val01,VG03,ADR01]. The benefits of object-based modelling have led to its central importance in modelling processes such as flexible manufacturing systems, though the complexity of Petri net analysis is not necessarily decreased by the object-based approach.

Ramadge and Wonham developed a theory [RW89] for modelling supervised discrete event systems and for synthesizing controllers for discrete event systems. Sreenivas [Sre97] showed how to use supervisory control to enforce liveness in discrete event systems that are modelled by Petri nets. Takai *et al* gave a necessary and sufficient condition for the existence of a unique maximally permissive feedback in Petri nets with external input places [TUK94]. Makungu *et al* developed a supervisory control theory and a method for supervisor synthesis for a class of CPNs [MBSD99].

Makungu *et al* also identified two main approaches to controller synthesis:

1. In the first, a discrete event system is described using a controlled Petri net [Kro97,IH88]. A controlled Petri net is an extension of a standard Petri net in which external control inputs can influence the enabling of transitions. Holloway and Krogh formulated the forbidden state problem for controlled Petri nets [HK91]. Boel *et al* addressed the forbidden state problem for a class of controlled Petri nets [BBNB95].
2. The second imposes control by synchronizing the main Petri net, also variously called the process Petri net and plant Petri net, with a controller which may be a P/T net.

The method of controller synthesis for Petri nets by Yamalidou *et al* [YMLA96] is essentially an example of the second approach identified by Makungu. The method of Yamalidou is based on place invariants and has the benefit that it is not limited to cyclic nets. In extending the approach of Yamalidou to object Petri nets, it will not be necessary to explicitly address the evolution of object nets *except* in the case of synchronization between an object net and the system net. At the same time, it certainly is critical to ensure that synchronization is accommodated. Given these factors, the authors favour the method of Yamalidou. Thus, the method will be extended below to address the forbidden state problem for object Petri nets.

In Section 2, object Petri nets are introduced, and the linear algebra-based calculus for P/T nets is extended to allow calculations on evolution of object Petri nets, as a foundation for the subsequent section. In particular, it will be shown how the new calculus accommodates the expression of synchronization.

In Section 3, the place invariant method for synthesizing controls for object Petri nets is explained. In Section 4, the method is illustrated using an example. Conclusions and and future research directions are given in Section 5.

2   Object Petri Nets

A variety of different high-level Petri nets are used for systems engineering (cf. [VG03]), all of which extend the basic formalism of place/transition nets or "P/T nets". Kis *et al*'s Chameleon nets [KNX97] and Valk's object systems [Val01] are two formalisms using the nets-within-nets paradigm of object Petri nets. A synchronization relation is commonly used in order to allow communication between objects (nets) at different levels of an object Petri net.

The definitions in Sections 2.1, 2.2 and 2.3 are from previous work [FM03, FM02], while novel concepts are presented and discussed in the sequel.

2.1   Basic Definitions

The definition of P/T nets is first recalled for reference.

Definition 1 (P/T net). *A P/T net is a tuple (P, T, F, W) with disjoint sets of places P and transitions T; the function $F \subseteq (P \times T) \cup (T \times P)$ defines the flow relation; and the function $W : (P \times T) \cup (T \times P) \to \mathbb{N}$ with $W(x, y) = 0$ if and only if $(x, y) \notin F$ defines the arc weights.*

A marked P/T net or P/T net system is a tuple (P, T, F, W, m_0) where (P, T, F, W) is a P/T net and $m_0 : P \to \mathbb{N}$ is the initial marking. The marking of place p is denoted $m(p)$.

Below, a subscript of 0 will be used to denote initial net markings. An arc with weight zero has the same practical effect as an arc that does not exist, and so these notions are regarded as equivalent. In the following, a P/T net is called an *ordinary Petri net* if $\forall (x, y) \in F.W(x, y) = 1$ is true for that P/T net.

Definition 2 (system net). *A system net is a tuple*

$$\mathrm{SN} = (\Sigma, P, T, F, C, V, E)$$

where the following hold:

(i)   *Σ is the set of types or colours with a subtype relation $\sqsubseteq$ that is reflexive and transitive.*

(ii)   *P is the set of* system net places *and T is the set of* system net transitions *such that $P \cap T = \emptyset$.*

(iii)   *$F \subseteq (P \times T) \cup (T \times P)$ is the* flow relation, *also called* the *set of arcs.*

(iv)   *$C : P \to \Sigma$ is a total function, called the* typing function *or* colouring function *of the system places.*

(v)   *V is the set of variable symbols and to every $v \in V$ there is associated a type $type(v) \in \Sigma$.*

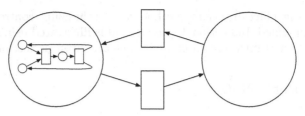

Fig. 1. An object Petri net with a system net and an object (token) net.

(vi) E : F → Multisets(V) is the arc labelling function.
(vii) The set of variables on the incoming arcs of transition t is denoted V_t and, for every variable v on an outgoing arc, $v \in V_t$ is true. of t. The set $V = \bigcup_{t \in T} V_t$ is the set of variables of SN.

In Definition 3 an object net is defined to be a P/T net. As with the system net from Definition 2 the marking is omitted and introduced in the respective net system. Object nets are also referred to as "token nets" since object nets are represented by tokens moving through a system net.

Definition 3 (object net or token net). *An object net $ON = (P, T, F, W)$ is a P/T net.*

Remark 1. It is assumed that different object nets have pairwise disjoint sets of places and transitions, and that the names of system net places and transitions are pairwise disjoint from the transitions and places of all object nets.

Informally, an object Petri net is a CPN with tokens which are P/T nets. The definitions given in this section are partly based on those of chameleon nets [KNX97] and object systems [Val98,Val01]. The following definition of an object Petri net refers to a synchronization relation, which is given in Definition 8. The other components of an object Petri net are a system net (Definition 2) and a set of object nets (Definition 3).

Definition 4 (object Petri net). *An object Petri net ("OPN") is a triple $OPN = (\text{SN}, \{ON_i\}_{i \in I}, \mathcal{S})$ where SN is a system net, for each $i \in I$ an indexing set ON_i is an object net, and $\mathcal{S}$ is a synchronization relation.*

An OPN is essentially a system net with an associated set of object net tokens and a synchronization relation between transitions of the system net and object nets. Throughout this paper, only two-level nesting of nets is allowed. Figure 1 portrays a simple example of an object Petri net.

Definition 5 (OPN marking). *A marking m of an OPN*

$$(\text{SN}, \{ON_i\}_{i \in I}, \mathcal{S})$$

is a function

$$\mathfrak{m} : P \to Multisets(\{(ON_i, m) \mid m : P_i \to \mathbb{N}\}_{i \in I}),$$

such that $\forall p \in P. \forall (x, m) \in \mathfrak{m}(p).type(x) \sqsubseteq C(p)$.

Recall that an object Petri net does not include reference to a marking. When an object Petri net marking is associated with an object Petri net, then something new is derived: an object Petri net *system*. The marking of place p in an object Petri net system is denoted $\mathfrak{m}(p)$.

2.2   Synchronization in Object Petri Nets

The synchronization relation from earlier work on object Petri nets was previously generalized [FM03] when *synchronization expressions* were introduced for each transition of the system net. This reflects the view that the system net may invoke a synchronization in several different ways. That is, the synchronization may require a finite set of object net transitions to occur simultaneously with its own firing. This more general approach to synchronization admits the standard *binary* synchronization as a special case.

Synchronization expressions from Definition 6 are used as a rule for synchronization of a transition t of a given net with other transitions of a (not necessarily distinct) net or nets. When reading Definition 6 the reader should be aware that:

(a) it assumes that the sets of transition labels for all nets in the object Petri net are pairwise disjoint, and

(b) it defines synchronization expressions in disjunctive normal form ("DNF").

These requirements are for convenience and are not onerous: (a) is a matter of relabelling and, for (b), it is clear that every formula containing only conjunctions and disjunctions can be transformed into DNF.

Definition 6 (synchronization expression). *Let $OS = (\text{SN}, \{ON_i\}_{i \in I}, \mathcal{S})$ be an object Petri net with system net $\text{SN} = (P, T, F)$ and object nets $ON_i = (P_i, T_i, F_i)$. Denote the set of object net transitions by $\hat{T} := \biguplus_{i \in I} T_i$ and define a context-free grammar $G = (V_N, V_T, R, D)$ where $V_N = \{A, C, D\}$, $V_T = \hat{T} \uplus \{(,), \wedge, \vee\}$, D is the initial symbol, and R comprises the following rules:*

$$D \to D \vee (C) \mid C$$
$$C \to C \wedge A \mid A$$
$$A \to u \ \text{for all } u \in \hat{T}.$$

The language generated by the grammar G is denoted $L(G)$. The synchronization expression of system net transition t is a pair (t, E_G) where $E_G \in L(G)$.

Definition 7 (synchronization evaluation). *The expression $E_G \in L(G)$ from Definition 6 is true if it is mapped to $\top$ under the evaluation function and is otherwise false. The evaluation function is given by:*

$$L(G) \to \mathbb{B}$$
$$u \mapsto \top \ \text{if and only if } u \text{ can fire in its net}[1]$$
$$E_{G1} \wedge E_{G2} \mapsto \top \ \text{if and only if } E_{G1} \text{ and } E_{G2} \text{ are simultaneously true}$$
$$E_{G1} \vee E_{G2} \mapsto \top \ \text{if and only if } E_{G1} \text{ or } E_{G2} \text{ (or both) are true.}$$

---

[1] For this definition the object net is viewed as an isolated ordinary net system.

The semantics of synchronization expressions is given by the synchronization evaluation function:

$$T \times L(G) \to \mathbb{B}$$

$(t, E_G) \mapsto \top$ *if and only if t is enabled in the system net[2] and E_G is true.*

A transition appearing in an interaction expression can fire if and only if the interaction expression evaluates to true. Only transitions of the system net or the object nets that do not appear in any synchronization expression of $\mathcal{S}$ may fire autonomously.

In Definition 6 the first component of a synchronization expression is a transition in T, i.e. from the system net. This portrays the view of the system net controlling the object Petri net and reflects locality conditions that should also be taken into account for the generalised case of multi-level object Petri nets. In restricting synchronizations to take place only between adjacent levels a locality condition is imposed. Object-object synchronization is prohibited in the present model. Object nets can synchronise among each other only indirectly by synchronizing with a net that takes the rôle of the system net.

If $u \in \hat{T}$ is not synchronised with a particular transition t, then this could be seen in the fact that u does not appear in the expression $E_G(t)$.

The following definition uses the notation of Definition 6.

Definition 8 (synchronization relation). *A **synchronization relation** for a system net with set of transitions T is given by:*

$$\{(t, E_G(t)) \mid t \in T \wedge E_G(t) \in L(G)\}.$$

To give an intuitive feel for synchronization expressions, if the synchronization expression for t were $(t, u_1 \wedge u_2)$ then both transitions u_1 and u_2 of the object net must simultaneously be able to fire in order that transition t of the system net be enabled. Thus enabled, transition t can fire, so changing the marking of the system net and the marking of the object net according to the firing of transitions u_1 and u_2 in the object net. If $(t, u_1 \vee u_2)$ were the element of the synchronization relation involving t, then it would be sufficient for either transition u_1 or u_2 of the object net to be enabled in order that transition t be enabled in the system net.

The simplest kind of synchronization is where t a system net transition is synchronised with u an object net transition, so that (t, u) is the synchronization expression. This is called *binary synchronization* and is sufficient for many purposes. The binary synchonization (t, u) is denoted in diagrams by labelling both t and u with a symbol $< n >$ for some n value. Where several such synchronizations are indicated, they are distinguished by different n values. This notation is used in Section 4.

---

[2] Enablement and transition firing in the system net is discussed below.

2.3   Transition Firing in Object Petri Nets

While synchronization is defined in terms of transition firing, enablement is a prerequisite to firing. Figure 2 illustrates how enablement of transitions varies under different synchronization relations.

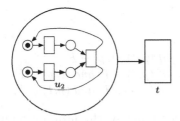

(a) t is enabled under both $(t, u_1 \vee u_2)$ and $(t, u_1 \wedge u_2)$.

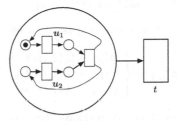

(b) t is enabled under $(t, u_1 \vee u_2)$ but not under $(t, u_1 \wedge u_2)$.

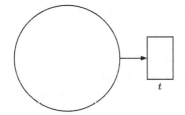

(c) t is not enabled under any synchronization relation.

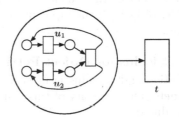

(d) t is enabled regardless of enablement of u_1 or u_2 when t does not appear in any synchronization pair (of the synchronization relation).

Fig. 2. Enablement of t varies with synchronization expression.

A variety of different firing rules have been discussed in earlier literature and the main differences are characterised by the proposed semantics of the respective approaches. Two main directions are noteworthy: reference semantics and value semantics (cf. [Far99], [Val99], [Val100]). The former views an object net as an integral item that cannot be locally modified without the knowledge of this being transferred to all referring instances. By contrast, the latter takes the viewpoint that local copies can act individually.

Having formally introduced synchronization, the OPN occurrence rule can now be given.

Definition 9 (OPN occurrence rule). *Consider* $(OPN, \mathfrak{m})$ *an OPNS with system net* SN $= (\Sigma, P, T, F, C, V, E)$. *Then transition* t *of the system net is enabled if and only if*

(i) E_G is true, where (t, E_G) is the synchronization expression of t from Definition 6, and

(ii) there exists a variable binding function

$$\beta_t : V_t \rightarrow \bigcup \Sigma \quad with \quad \forall x \in E(p,t).\beta_t(x) \in type(x)$$

such that image$(f) \subseteq \mathfrak{m}(p)$.

The successor marking is given by:

$$\mathfrak{m}'(p) = \begin{cases} \mathfrak{m}(p) - \beta_t(E(p,t)) + \beta_t(E(t,p)) & if\ (p,t), (t,p) \in F \\ \mathfrak{m}(p) - \beta_t(E(p,t)) & if\ (p,t) \in F\ and\ (t,p) \notin F \\ \mathfrak{m}(p) + \beta_t(E(t,p)) & if\ (t,p) \in F\ and\ (p,t) \notin F. \end{cases}$$

Object net transitions that are not subject to any synchronization requirements can occur autonomously according to the usual occurrence rule for P/T nets. Similarly, a system net transition t can occur autonomously if it is not subject to any synchronization requirement. An autonomous system net occurrence effectively moves the (unchanged) marked object nets bound to the respective variables of V_t from the input places to the output place of t according to β_t the binding.

2.4   Calculus for Object Petri Net Evolution

A notation and calculus is needed to describe and analyze evolution of object Petri nets. The necessity of this will become clear in Section 3 when the method is introduced.

Calculating the evolution of the system net is straightforward if the marking of any place of the system net is regarded as a multiset of object nets. However, it is necessary to ensure that whatever notation is used does not break down when applied to evolution of the object nets. The method that will be extended for synthesizing Petri net controllers relies on the transition matrix (also called the incidence matrix or change matrix). Thus, it would be convenient if there was an analogue of the P/T net transition matrix [Mur89] for object Petri nets.

The extended notation for object Petri nets is introduced using the example in Figure 1. System net places are ordered to allow a vectorial representation of any marking of the system net.

Definition 10. *A marked object net representation is a pair (ON, v) where ON is the name of the object net and v is the marking vector of the object net.*

Definition 11 (OPN marking vector). *The marking vector of an OPN is a column vector whose dimension equals the number of places in the system net of the OPN. Each entry of the vector is the multiset of marked object net representations corresponding to the marking of each place of the system net.*

The symbol $\mathfrak{m}$ which is used to denote OPN marking is also used to denote the OPN marking vector. When dealing with multisets of object nets, the multiset brackets are sometimes omitted for ease of reading.

The object Petri net in Figure 1 has marking $\begin{bmatrix} (ON, \begin{bmatrix} 0 \\ 0 \\ 0 \end{bmatrix}) \\ 0 \end{bmatrix}$. The transition

matrix of the object net is $\begin{bmatrix} -1 & -1 & 1 \\ 1 & 1 & -1 \end{bmatrix}$ while the transition matrix of the system

net is $\begin{bmatrix} -(ON, m^x) & (ON, m^x) \\ (ON, m^y) & -(ON, m^y) \end{bmatrix}$. The notation (ON, m^x) means that there
is a token in place x and in place x only of ON.

The only information that need be included about the marking of the object
net ON in the system net's transition matrix is that the marking is unchanged
when the transition of the system net fires. Of course, this would not necessarily
be the case if there was some synchronization between the system net transition
and an object net transition.

Now, suppose the object net in Figure 1 is marked, with a token in the two

leftmost places. Then the object Petri net has marking $\begin{bmatrix} (ON, \begin{bmatrix} 1 \\ 1 \\ 0 \end{bmatrix}) \\ 0 \end{bmatrix}$. The

only possible evolution of the object net can be calculated by:

$$\begin{bmatrix} (ON, \begin{bmatrix} 1 \\ 1 \\ 0 \end{bmatrix} + \begin{bmatrix} -1 & -1 & 1 \\ 1 & 1 & -1 \end{bmatrix}' \begin{bmatrix} 1 \\ 0 \end{bmatrix}) \\ 0 \end{bmatrix} = \begin{bmatrix} (ON, \begin{bmatrix} 0 \\ 0 \\ 1 \end{bmatrix}) \\ 0 \end{bmatrix}.$$

A prime denotes matrix transpose. For the matrix N the symbol N' denotes
the transpose of N. In this paper, the usual notation N^T for the transpose of N
might cause confusion with T the set of transitions.

The only possible evolution of the system net is calculated by:

$$\begin{bmatrix} (ON, \begin{bmatrix} 0 \\ 0 \\ 1 \end{bmatrix}) \\ 0 \end{bmatrix} + \begin{bmatrix} -(ON, m^x) & (ON, m^x) \\ (ON, m^y) & -(ON, m^y) \end{bmatrix}' \begin{bmatrix} 1 \\ 0 \end{bmatrix} = \begin{bmatrix} 0 \\ (ON, \begin{bmatrix} 0 \\ 0 \\ 1 \end{bmatrix}) \end{bmatrix}.$$

This calculus is nothing but a nesting, in the marking vector of the system
net, of the widely-used linear algebraic calculus for P/T net evolution [Mur89].
Thus, the method of Yamalidou et al can directly be applied to object nets since,
with two-level nesting, object nets are P/T nets.

It will be seen later that the above vector notation for object Petri nets is
convenient for calculations on object Petri net evolution. The above notation is
certainly adequate for calculations on system net evolution and this is what will
be required below.

3   Place Invariants and Feedback Control for OPNs

The method of controller synthesis using place invariants for object Petri nets will be described, borrowing heavily from Yamalidou *et al* though important differences will be clear when the extension is applied.

Definition 12. *The* token count vector *of an OPN is an integer vector with the same dimension as the marking vector of that OPN. Each entry is the size of the multiset in the corresponding entry of the marking vector of the OPN.*

If the marking vector of an OPN is $\mathfrak{m}$ then $\overline{\mathfrak{m}}$ denotes the token count vector of the same OPN.

Suppose a system must satisfy n_c constraints with jth constraint of the form:

$$k_{j_1}\overline{\mathfrak{m}}(p_{j_1}) + \cdots + k_{j_{n_j}}\overline{\mathfrak{m}}(p_{j_{n_j}}) \in M_j \tag{1}$$

where $k_j \in \mathbb{N}$ and $k_{j_i} \in \mathbb{N}$ for each $1 \le i \le n_j$, and $\overline{\mathfrak{m}}(p_{j_1})$, ..., $\overline{\mathfrak{m}}(p_{j_{n_j}})$ are the markings of the places $p_{j_1}, \ldots, p_{j_{n_j}}$ whose markings are to be constrained, and M_j is a set of multisets of marked object nets. This is the most basic kind of constraint and is the object Petri net analogue of the most basic form of constraint for P/T nets:

$$k_{j_1}m(p_{j_1}) + \cdots + k_{j_{n_j}}m(p_{j_{n_j}}) < k_j$$

where each k_{j_i} and $k_j \in \mathbb{N}$.

The n_c constraints in (1) can be combined into a single expression

$$L \cdot \overline{\mathfrak{m}}_p \in b \tag{2}$$

where L is a $n_c \times n$ matrix whose jth row comprises the coefficients of each place in the jth constraint and n is the number of places of the system net, and $\overline{\mathfrak{m}}_p = \begin{bmatrix} \overline{\mathfrak{m}}(p_1) \\ \vdots \\ \overline{\mathfrak{m}}(p_n) \end{bmatrix}$, and b is the vector $\begin{bmatrix} M_1 \\ \vdots \\ M_{n_c} \end{bmatrix}$. The symbol "$\in$" is used in the context of vectors as referring to inclusion in each corresponding row of the vector.

In $\overline{\mathfrak{m}}_p$ the subscript p refers to the original net or the "process" net, whereas the subscript c refers to the augmentation of the net or the "controller". This notation is borrowed from Yamalidou et al.

The constraints (2) can be expressed as an equality by introducing the vector for the marking of the n_c control places:

$$L \cdot \overline{\mathfrak{m}}_p + \overline{\mathfrak{m}}_c = b.$$

A place invariant is a set of places whose token count is constant, regardless of transition firing [Mur89] and are formally defined as follows.

Definition 13 (place invariant [YMLA96]). *A place invariant for a P/T net is an integer vector X which satisfies $X' \cdot \Delta = 0$ for Δ the transition matrix of the P/T net.*

Definition 14 (OPN place invariant). *A place invariant for an OPN is an OPN token count vector X which satisfies $X' \cdot \Delta = 0$ for Δ the transition matrix of the OPN.*

For such X as in Definition 14,

$$\mathfrak{m} \cdot X = \mathfrak{m}_0 \cdot X$$

for all reachable markings $\mathfrak{m}$ where $\mathfrak{m}_0$ is the initial marking of the net. referring to the marking of a single place p, whereas $\mathfrak{m}(A)$ is a column vector representing the marking of a set A of places of the system net.

The place invariant is to be the left-hand side of the constraint equations augmented to $X' = \begin{bmatrix} L\ I \end{bmatrix}$ where I is the identity matrix. The transition matrix of the net augmented with the control place is required. This is given by

$$\Delta = \begin{bmatrix} \Delta_p \\ \Delta_c \end{bmatrix}$$

where Δ_p is the transition matrix of the original net and Δ_c that of the augmentation to the net for the controller.

$$\text{Now } X' \cdot \Delta = 0, \tag{3}$$

$$\text{so } \begin{bmatrix} L\ I \end{bmatrix} \cdot \begin{bmatrix} \Delta_p \\ \Delta_c \end{bmatrix} = 0 \tag{4}$$

$$\text{or } L \cdot \Delta_p + \Delta_c = 0 \tag{5}$$

$$\text{or } \Delta_c = -L \cdot \Delta_p \tag{6}$$

Thus, the arcs connecting the control place to the existing transitions are specified. To find the initial marking of the control place c use:

$$L \cdot \mathfrak{m}_p + \mathfrak{m}_c = b$$

$$\text{which implies } \mathfrak{m}_0(p_c) = b - L \cdot \mathfrak{m}_{p_0}.$$

The initial marking then becomes $\mathfrak{m}_0 = \begin{bmatrix} \mathfrak{m}_{p_0} \\ \mathfrak{m}_0(p_c) \end{bmatrix}$.

The method just presented can be understood by considering the occurrence graph of the system. The forbidden states are isolated making it impossible for the system to enter those states. This is a result of additional restrictions being imposed on the firing of transitions which, in the original net, would allow the forbidden states to be entered. In the first example of Yamalidou *et al* the original net has the occurrence graph given in Figure 3. All states in the lower

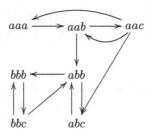

Fig. 3. Occurrence graph of original net in Yamalidou *et al.*

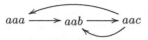

Fig. 4. Occurrence graph of controlled net in Yamalidou *et al.*

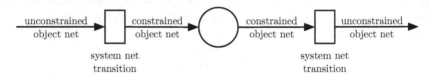

Fig. 5. Constraining object nets in some places of system net.

left square are forbidden, because the places b and c have more than one token between them. The occurrence graph of the controlled net is given in Figure 4 in which the forbidden states are no longer reachable.

If constraints are imposed on an individual object net using the methodology of Yamalidou *et al*, then the augmented object net is controlled wherever it may be in the system net. That is, there is no apparent practical method for ensuring that an object net is constrained when it is in one place while unconstrained when in another place, since to constrain an object net is to modify its structure.

An extended class of object Petri nets can be considered by slightly modifying the definition of object Petri nets. Marked object nets could be used as arc inscriptions so that transition firings *modify the constraints* to which an object net is subject depending on the place of the system net which the object net occupies. This is illustrated in Figure 5. The question of modifying properties of object nets brings into relief some benefits of linear logic Petri nets ("**LLPN**"s). An LLPN is obtained from an object Petri net by converting the object nets to linear logic formulae. Linear logic semantics can then be used to change the structure of object nets. Thus, intepreting an object Petri net as an LLPN, desirable properties can be forced onto the object Petri net. This line of research is currently being pursued [FM03].

Finally, if any object net were unbounded then, if a constraint such as that in expression (1) involves that unbounded object net, then the right-hand side M_j could be selected to be an infinite multiset. This would present difficulties

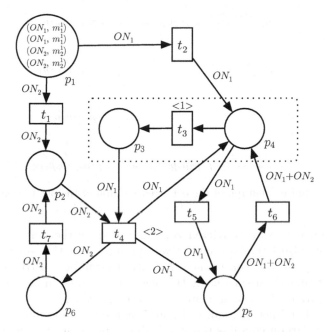

Fig. 6. System net with only one object net allowed in dotted region.

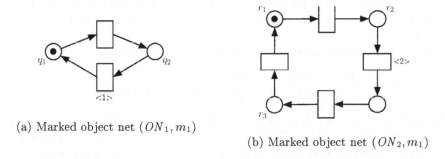

(a) Marked object net (ON_1, m_1)

(b) Marked object net (ON_2, m_1)

Fig. 7. Object net tokens of system net in Figure 6.

for computation of whether the constraint is satisfied. It would cause the control place to generally contain an infinite number of tokens, which does not lend itself to practical interpretation. In addition, there is no Petri net formalism allowing an infinite number of tokens to appear in a net. For these reasons, the treatment in this paper is restricted to bounded object nets.

4   Case Study: Feedback Controller Synthesis

A case study is presented using the object Petri net with system net in Figure 6 and object nets in Figure 7. This case study purports to model some characteristics of industrial processes, rather than to mimic an entire industrial process.

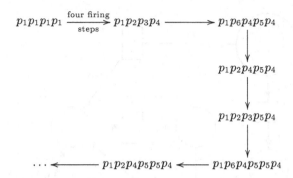

Fig. 8. Infinite subgraph of the occurrence graph of the net in Figure 6.

The system net has a restricted zone indicated by the dotted rectangle in Figure 6. The tokens that are collectively permitted in this zone—that is, in places p_3 and p_4—will be constrained. A controller will be constructed to ensure that the constraint is satisfied using the method presented in Section 3. Finally, the net in Figure 6 will be augmented with the controller.

The object Petri net in Figures 6 and 7 represents an infinite state system. The occurrence graph contains the graph shown in Figure 8 as a subgraph. In Figure 8 the object nets present in the places of the system net are not mentioned as these are evident by referring to Figure 6. The occurrence graph shows that the number of tokens will multiply without bound unless a controller is built for the net.

The tokens (i.e. marked object nets) that are available are:

$$(ON_1, m_1^1), (ON_1, m_1^2) \text{ and}$$
$$(ON_2, m_2^1), (ON_2, m_2^2), (ON_2, m_2^3), (ON_2, m_2^4)$$

The symbol m_1^i is a marking of ON_1 with one token in place q_i and no other tokens, and m_2^j is a marking of ON_2 with a token in place r_j and no other tokens.

A condensed notation is used for arc labels of the system net. Considering Figure 6, an object net denotation (i.e. ON_1, ON_2 or ON_1+ON_2) on an arc label means an arc variable whose type comprises the object net paired with every possible marking. So ON_1 is shorthand for a variable of type $\{(ON_1, m_1^1), (ON_1, m_1^2)\}$ while ON_2 is shorthand for a variable of type $\{(ON_2, m_2^1), \ldots, (ON_2, m_2^4)\}$. The arc marking $ON_1 + ON_2$ is a variable whose type comprises every multiset of size two containing marked object nets (ON_1, m_1^i) and (ON_2, m_2^j).

$$\text{Let } M := \{\emptyset, \{\!|(ON_1, m_1^i)|\!\}_{i \in \{1,2\}}, \{\!|(ON_2, m_2^j)|\!\}_{j \in \{1,2,3,4\}}\}. \tag{7}$$

Now suppose the constraint is:

$$\mathfrak{m}(p_3) + \mathfrak{m}(p_4) \in M. \tag{8}$$

$$\text{Then} \qquad \mathfrak{m}(p_3) + \mathfrak{m}(p_4) + \mathfrak{m}(p_c) \tag{9}$$

$$= \biguplus_{i \in \{1,2\}} \{\!|(ON_1, m_1^i)|\!\} + \biguplus_{j \in \{1,2,3,4\}} \{\!|(ON_2, m_2^j)|\!\}. \tag{10}$$

Note that if $m_0(p_3) = \emptyset$ and $m_0(p_4) = \emptyset$ then $m_0(p_c) = M$.

The constraint demands that two object nets of the same kind not be in the marked zone at any moment. This has many possible parallels in real manufacturing processes. For example, there may be sufficient machinery in the marked zone to process one fibreglass job and one aluminium job at any moment, but no more than one of each. In addition, it was mentioned above that the number of tokens can increase without bound if left unchecked. The constraint protects the marked zone from being forced to accommodate an unlimited number of tokens.

When a marked object net appears with a particular marking in a cell of a transition matrix, then that cell represents a synchronised transition. Such a marking can be specified only because the object nets used in this example are simple, so there is only one possible marking that could enable any given transition in ON_1 or ON_2. In a general object Petri net with synchronization, there are many possible object net markings which will enable a synchronised object net transition.

Now $L = \begin{bmatrix} 0\,0\,1\,1\,0\,0 \end{bmatrix}$, since the coefficients of $m(p_3)$ and of $m(p_4)$ are 1 in the constraint equation while the coefficient of each $m(p_i)$ for $i \in \{1, 2, 5, 6\}$ is zero. In order to determine how the control place is connected to the existing transitions, just as in (6), the following can be used:

$$\Delta_c = -L \cdot \Delta_p \tag{11}$$
$$= -\begin{bmatrix} 0\,0\,1\,1\,0\,0 \end{bmatrix} \cdot \Delta_p \tag{12}$$

where $\Delta_p =$

$$
\begin{bmatrix}
-(ON_2, m_2^x) & -(ON_1, m_1^x) & 0 & 0 & 0 & 0 & 0 \\
(ON_2, m_2^x) & 0 & 0 & -(ON_2, m_2^2) & 0 & 0 & (ON_2, m_2^x) \\
0 & 0 & (ON_1, m_1^1) & \begin{matrix}-(ON_1, m_1^x)\\-(ON_1, m_1^y)\end{matrix} & 0 & 0 & 0 \\
0 & (ON_1, m_1^x) & -(ON_1, m_1^2) & (ON_1, m_1^x) & -(ON_1, m_1^x) & \begin{matrix}(ON_1, m_1^x)\\+(ON_2, m_2^2)\end{matrix} & 0 \\
0 & 0 & 0 & (ON_1, m_1^y) & (ON_1, m_1^x) & \begin{matrix}-(ON_1, m_1^x)\\-(ON_2, m_2^y)\end{matrix} & 0 \\
0 & 0 & 0 & (ON_2, m_2^3) & 0 & 0 & -(ON_2, m_2^x)
\end{bmatrix}
$$

Applying (12) gives Δ_c equal to the following row vector:

$$\begin{bmatrix} 0 & (ON_1, m_1^x) & (ON_1, m_1^1) - (ON_1, m_1^2) & -(ON_1, m_1^y) & \cdots \end{bmatrix}$$

$$\begin{bmatrix} \cdots & -(ON_1, m_1^x) & (ON_1, m_1^x) + (ON_2, m_2^y) & 0 \end{bmatrix}$$

which yields Δ using $\Delta = \begin{bmatrix} \Delta_p \\ \Delta_c \end{bmatrix}$. For the initial marking of the control place,

$$\mathfrak{m}_0(p_c) = N - L \cdot \mathfrak{m}_0(p) \ \text{where } N \in M$$
$$= N -$$
$$L \begin{bmatrix} (ON_1, m_1^1) + (ON_1, m_1^1) + (ON_2, m_2^1) + (ON_2, m_2^1) \\ 0 \\ 0 \\ 0 \\ 0 \\ 0 \end{bmatrix}$$
$$= N - \emptyset$$
$$\mathfrak{m}_0(p_c) = N \ \text{where } N \in M.$$

The system net equipped with the control place is shown in Figure 9. Object nets with indeterminate markings (represented in the transition matrix by (ON_1, m_1^x) and (ON_2, m_2^y)) have been omitted from Figure 9 for clarity.

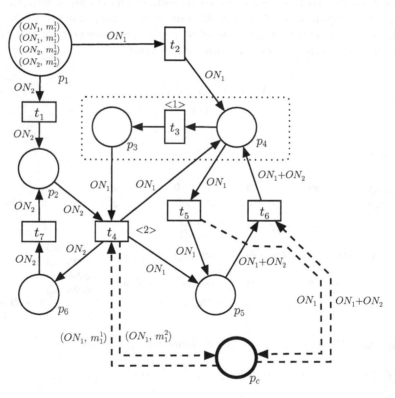

Fig. 9. System net augmented with control place p_c.

Figure 9 displays the system net in Figure 6 with the control place p_c added and with control arcs (shown with dotted lines) inserted between p_c and the t_4, t_5 and t_6 transitions. The multiset sum of the tokens in places p_3, p_4 and p_c is constant at $m(p_3) + m(p_4) + m(p_c)$ from (10) as a result of the consruction of the control arcs. Thus, the constraint (8) is always satisfied.

In a case such as this the power of the method for synthesizing controllers for object Petri nets becomes apparent. For the standard Petri net by Yamalidou *et al* [YMLA96], it was shown in Figure 3 that the occurrence graph is quite simple. By contrast, the occurrence graph of the relatively simple object Petri net in Figures 6 and 7 has over 100 states in its finite, non-repeating subgraph, though the entire occurrence graph is infinite.

The case study presented was constructed by the authors. A second case study was developed and will appear in the third author's PhD thesis to illustrate controller synthesis for object Petri nets in a more pragmatic setting. The second case study is based on an object Petri net extension of the flexible manufacturing system modelled by Holloway and Krogh [HK91].

5   Conclusion and Outlook

Nearly all real-world systems have restrictions on their functioning. Thus, in order to faithfully model such systems, Petri nets (or, in the case of complex systems, object Petri nets) need to be augmented with some mechanism to ensure that undesired or forbidden states are avoided. Without a solution to the forbidden state problem, object Petri nets are limited in their usefuless for modelling practical systems. A relatively straightforward method has been presented for synthesizing a controller for an object Petri net in order to ensure that forbidden states are avoided.

The following three main contributions are made in this work:

1. A method for controller synthesis is given for object Petri net models, so addressing the forbidden state problem for object Petri nets.
2. For the first time, place invariants are defined for object Petri nets.
3. A linear-algebraic calculus is defined for object Petri net evolution.

The method for computing object Petri net controllers was illustrated in a simple system modelled by an object Petri net equipped with synchronization.

The work of Yamalidou *et al* using place invariants for controller synthesis for P/T nets was extended to object Petri nets. This motivated the second contribution. It was necessary to have a definition for place invariants for object Petri nets in order to extend the work of Yamalidou.

In turn, the third contribution was motivated by the second. That is, it was necessary to introduce a new calculus for object Petri net evolution so that a suitable notation was available for defining place invariants. The calculus presented is essentially linear-algebraic and so lends itself to implementation in linear algebra software packages. Thus, calculations on evolution of object Petri nets can be made as tractable as those for P/T nets.

Other restrictions in the method presented are that object net markings must be bounded and that the constraint expressions are limited to the form given in (1) which is recalled here:

$$k_{j_1} m(p_{j_1}) + \cdots + k_{j_{n_j}} m(p_{j_{n_j}}) \in M_j$$

Requiring that object nets are bounded is not an onerous restriction as practical applications are generally finite. Restricting constraints, however, does limit the range of specifications of forbidden states which could be accommodated. In particular, not all constraints take the form in (1). For example, consider:

$$k_1 \mathfrak{m}(p_1) + \cdots + k_n \mathfrak{m}(p_n) \in M_1 \vee \cdots \vee M_j. \tag{13}$$

Therefore, future work should extend the new method to object Petri net constraints obtained by generalizing the expression (1). Generalizing to the kind of constraint in (13) would be straightforward. Howwever, the problem quickly becomes complex when combining several constraints each involving parentheses, conjunction and disjunction (represented by asterisks) in the following way:

$$k_{11}\mathfrak{m}(p_1) + \cdots + k_{1n}\mathfrak{m}(p_n) \in *_{11}m_1^1 \cdots *_{1n_1} M_{1n_1} *_{1n_1+1}$$

$$\vdots$$

$$k_{n_c1}\mathfrak{m}(p_1) + \cdots + k_{n_cn}\mathfrak{m}(p_n) \in *_{n_c1}M_{n_c1} \cdots *_{n_cn_{n_c}} M_{n_cn_{n_c}} *_{n_cn_{n_c}+1}.$$

Nonetheless, such generalization would be invaluable in catering for the complexity that is possible in flexible manufacturing systems as well as other processes that could be modelled by object Petri nets.

Future work should also extend the method given for controller synthesis to more general synchronization expressions, as defined in Section 2.2. It might also be worthwhile extending the method to object Petri nets which have nesting deeper than two levels, as such object Petri nets provide the modularization and comprehensibility benefits of object Petri nets to a greater extent. In particular, using object nets which are themselves object Petri nets is beneficial when a standard object net is so large or complex that greater clarity will be gained by re-expressing it as an object Petri net. A prerequisite to achieving either of these is to extend the calculus in Section 2.4 to accommodate more general synchronizations and deeper nesting.

References

[ADR01]   G. Agha, F. DeCindio, and G. Rozenberg, editors. *Concurrent Object-Oriented Programming and Petri Nets*. Number 2001 in Lecture Notes in Computer Science. Springer, 2001.

[BBNB95] R. Boel, L. Ben-Naoum, and V. Van Breusegem. On the forbidden state problem for a class of controlled Petri nets. *IEEE Transactions on Automatic Control*, 40(10):1717–1731, 1995.

[Far99]   B. Farwer. A linear logic view of object Petri nets. *Fundamenta Informaticae*, 37:225–246, 1999.

[FM02]   B. Farwer and K. Misra. Hierarchical Object Systems. In H.-D. Burkhard, L. Czaja, G. Lindemann, A. Skowron, and P. Starke, editors, *Proceedings of Concurrency, Specification and Programming—CS&P*, number 161, pages 143–163, Berlin, October 2002. Informatik-Berichte Humboldt-Universität zu Berlin.

[FM03]   B. Farwer and K. Misra. Dynamic Modification of System Structures using
            LLPNs. In *Proceedings of the Fifth Andrei Ershow International Conference
            Perspectives of System Informatics*, Lecture Notes in Computer Science.
            Springer-Verlag, 2003. To appear.

[FMGV02]   B. Farwer, D. Moldt, and F. García-Vallés. An Approach to Modelling
            FMS [Flexible Manufacturing Systems] with Dynamic Object Petri Nets.
            In *Proceedings of the 2002 IEEE International Conference on Systems, Man
            and Cybernetics*, pages 1–9. IEEE, October 2002.

[HK91]   L. Holloway and B. Krogh. Synthesis of Feedback Control Logic for Discrete
            Manufacturing Systems. *Automatica*, 27(4):641–651, July 1991.

[HKG97]   L. Holloway, B. Krogh, and A. Giua. A survey of Petri net methods for
            controlled discrete event systems. *Discrete Dynamic Systems: Theory and
            Applications*, 7(2):151–190, 1997.

[IH88]   A. Ichikawa and K. Hiraishi. Analysis and control of discrete event systems
            represented by Petri nets. In *Lecture Notes in Control and Information
            Sciences*, volume 103, pages 115–134. Springer-Verlag, 1988.

[J03]   J. Jorgensen. Coloured petri nets in development of a pervasive health care
            system. In *Proceedings of the 24th International Conference on Applica-
            tion and Theory of Petri Nets*, volume 2679 of *Lecture Notes in Computer
            Science*. Springer, 2003.

[KNX97]   T. Kis, K.-P. Neuendorf, and P. Xirouchakis. Scheduling with Chameleon
            Nets. In B. Farwer, D. Moldt, and M.-O. Stehr, editors, *Proceedings of the
            Workshop on Petri Nets in System Engineering (PNSE'97)*, pages 67–77.
            Universität Hamburg, 1997.

[Kro87]   B. Krogh. Controlled Petri nets and maximally permissive feedback logic.
            In *Proceedings of the 25thAnnual Allerton Conference on Communication,
            Control and Computing*, pages 317–326, 1987. Monticello, Illinois.

[Lak97]   C. A. Lakos. Object Oriented Modelling with Object Petri nets. In *Advances
            in Petri nets*, Lecture Notes in Computer Science. Springer, Berlin, 1997.

[LLKM95]   C. Lakos, J. Lamp, C. Keen, and B. Marriott. Modelling Network Protocols
            with Object Petri Nets. In *Workshop on Petri Nets Applied to Protocols*,
            pages 31–42, 1995.

[LWC01]   Y. Lu, G. Wei, and T.-Y. Cheung. Managing Feature Interactions in
            Telecommunications Systems by Temporal Colored Petri Nets. In *Proceed-
            ings of the Seventh International Conference on Engineering of Complex
            Computer Systems*, number 83, page 260. IEEE Computer Society, 201.

[MBSD99]   M. Makungu, M. Barbeau, and R. St-Denis. Synthesis of controllers of
            processes modelled as colored Petri nets. *Discrete Event Systems: Theory
            and Applications*, 9:147–169, 1999.

[Mur89]   T. Murata. Petri nets: Properties, Analysis and Applications. *Proceedings
            of the IEEE*, 77(4):541–580, April 1989.

[Pet66]   C. Petri. *Kommunikation mit Automaten (Communicating with Automata)*.
            PhD thesis, University of Darmstadt, 1966. English translation in technical
            report RADC-TR-65377, Griss Air Force Base, 1966.

[Red94]   V. Reddy. Modeling Biological Pathways: A discrete event systems ap-
            proach. Master's thesis, Institute for Systems Research, University of Mary-
            land, 1994.

[RW89]   P. Ramadge and W. Wonham. The control of discrete event systems. *Pro-
            ceedings of the IEEE*, 77(1):81–98, 1989.

[Sre97]   R. Sreenivas. On the existence of supervisory policies that enforce liveness in discrete-event dynamic systems modelled by controlled Petri nets. *IEEE Transactions on Automatic Control*, 42(7):928–945, 1997.

[TUK94]   S. Takai, T. Ushio, and S. Kodama. Concurrency and Maximally Permissive Feedback in Petri nets with External Input Place. *International Journal of Control*, 60(4):617–629, 1994.

[Val98]   R. Valk. Petri nets as token objects. an introduction to elementary object nets. In J. Desel and M. Silva, editors, *Applications and Theory of Petri Nets 1998. Proceedings*, volume 1420, pages 1–25. Springer-Verlag, 1998.

[Val99]   R. Valk. Reference and value semantics for object petri nets. In H. Weber, H. Ehrig, and W. Reisig, editors, *Colloquium on Petri Net Technologies for Modelling Communication Based Systems*, pages 169–188. Fraunhofer Institute for Software and Systems Engineering ISST, Berlin, 1999.

[Val00]   R. Valk. Relating Different Semantics for Object Petri nets. Technical Report B-226-00, TGI - Theoretical Foundations of Computer Science Group, Computer Science, University of Hamburg, June 2000.

[Val01]   R. Valk. Concurrency in Communicating Object Petri nets. In G. Agha, F. de Cindio, and G. Rozenberg, editors, *Concurrent Object-Oriented Programming and Petri Nets*, Lecture Notes in Computer Science, pages 164–195. Spring-Verlag, 2001.

[VG03]   R. Valk and C. Girault, editors. *Petri Nets for Systems Engineering—A Guide to Modeling, Verification, and Applications*. Springer-Verlag, 2003.

[Yam91]   K. Yamalidou. *Modeling, Optimization and Control of Discrete-Event Chemical Processes Using Petri Net Theory*. PhD thesis, University of Notre Dame, Notre Dame, Indiana, 1991.

[YMLA96] K. Yamalidou, J. Moody, M. Lemmon, and P. Antsaklis. Feedback control of Petri nets based on place invariants. *Automatica*, 32(1):15–28, 1996.

Towards a Workflow Model
of Real-Time Cooperative Systems

Yuyue Du[1,2,3] and Changjun Jiang[1,3]

[1] Department of Computer Science & Engineering, Tongji University
Shanghai 200092, P.R.China
[2] Department of Computer Science, Liaocheng University, Liaocheng 252059, P.R.China
[3] Lab. of Computer Science, ISCAS, Beijing 100080, P.R.China
`yydu001@163.com, cjjiang@online.sh.cn`

Abstract. The purpose of this paper is to provide the designers of cooperative
workflows with a formalism that has a high expressive power and a strong
theoretical basis. The existing techniques for correctness analysis of real-time
cooperative systems, however, are not suitable to representing passing value
indeterminacy and batch data processing function. Moreover, the correct
behaviors of cooperative systems depend on not only the logical correctness of
the results obtained but also the time of producing them before critical deadlines. To deal with previous problems, logical time Petri nets (LTPN) are first
introduced based on time Petri nets and temporal logic. It can reduce the state
explosion problem to a certain extent. Then logical time workflow nets
(LTWN) and interorganizational LTWNs (ILTWN) are presented for specifying and verifying real-time cooperative systems. Their soundness properties are
formally defined and analyzed. A rigorous approach for correctness analysis of
ILTWNs is given based only on their static net structures. The use of our concepts and techniques is illustrated with a example of modeling and analysis of
an offer-order–deliver-pay system.

1 Introduction

Due to the enhancement of reliability and safety of communication networks, the
number of entities, and the heterogeneity of real-time cooperative systems are un-
precedented and require new approaches to model and verify their correctness and
temporal properties. It is inspiring that today's workflow management systems support business processes of complex real-time systems via electronic networks, and are
widely used by organizations to coordinate the execution of various applications
representing their day-to-day tasks. A workflow is a representation of a given process
that consists of well-defined set of activities, referred to as tasks. Each of the tasks in
the process represented by a workflow serves a given function, and has some information input requirements and may also generate information as a part of its output.
The tasks in a workflow are usually related and dependent on one another. These task
dependencies are called intra-workflow dependencies. Task dependencies may also

J.S. Dong and J. Woodcock (Eds.): ICFEM 2003, LNCS 2885, pp. 452–470, 2003.
© Springer-Verlag Berlin Heidelberg 2003

exist across workflows where multiple organizations are involved in shared business processes, such task dependencies are referred to as inter-workflow dependencies. In general, task dependencies are divided into three types: control dependencies, value dependencies and external dependencies.

It is very important to use an established framework for modeling and analyzing workflow processes [1,9], since processes are a main factor in workflow management systems. Petri nets [10] have been used to model and analyze all kinds of workflow processes, and provide a perfect framework [1]. Therefore, many previous formal approaches and tools of workflows based on Petri nets are given and developed [1,2,4,5,8]. However, existing techniques on Petri nets and workflow are not suitable to representing passing value indeterminacy and batch data processing function, since they focus on using traditional Petri nets or high-level Petri nets and associated tools to analyze the properties of workflows. Moreover, the correct behaviors of cooperative workflow systems depend on not only the logical correctness of the results obtained by running workflows but also the time of producing these results before critical deadlines. Thereby, in this paper, we introduce a new formalism for modeling and analyzing real-time cooperative systems based on Logical Time Petri Nets (LTPN) and Logical Time Workflow Nets (LTWN), which are the abstraction and extension of traditional time Petri nets (TPN) [12] and high-level time Petri nets (HLTPN) [4]. It is of abstract and succinct representation, and can mitigate the problem of state space explosion to a certain extent. This paper focuses on cooperative workflows, i.e., there exist external dependencies between the entities in a cooperative system, and each entity has a local workflow process related to the workflow processes of the other entities. We add hard deadlines to certain individual tasks of the workflow, so that one can guarantee the tasks being completed before the given deadlines. LTWNs can process data in batch and describe the passing value indeterminacy between organizations in real-time cooperative systems. For a class of OR-restricted LTWNs, we discuss how they are combined to ensure that their interorganizational logical time workflow net (ILTWN) is sound. Our results can be more expediently used by the designers of cooperative workflows, when compared with the analyzing approach of interorganizational workflows based on message sequence charts [2,3]. Because the static logical sequence of the cooperative tasks between two related workflows is only analyzed, this method can reduce consumedly the analysis complexity of ILTWNs. The use of our concepts and techniques is illustrated with a useful example of a simple offer-order-deliver-pay system.

The rest of this paper is organized as follows. In Section 2, we present the formal definition of logical time Petri nets, and give their temporal formula semantics and equivalent representations in TPNs and HLTPNs. In Section 3, we define formally LTWNs, and propose their constructing algorithm. Section 4 introduces the formal definition of ILTWNs. The properties of ILTWNs are analyzed in Section 5. Also, we illustrate the application of these techniques to verification of the LTWN and ILTWN models of an offer-order-deliver-pay system. Section 6 concludes this paper.

2 Logical Time Petri Nets

In this section, we first show a brief introduction to TPNs [12] and define their temporal formula semantics. We then introduce formally logical time Petri nets and discuss functionally their equivalent representations in TPNs and HLTPNs.

2.1 Time Petri Nets

For TN=(P,T,B,F,A,SI), a tuple TPN=(TN,M_0) is a time Petri net if and only if [12]

P is a finite nonempty set of places;

T is a finite nonempty set of transitions, and P∩T=∅;

B: P×T→N is the backward incidence function, where N is a set of natural numbers;

F: T×P→N is the forward incidence function;

M_0: P→N∪{0} is the initial marking; (P,T,B,F and M_0 together define a Petri net.)

A⊆P×T is a set of inhibitor arcs;

SI is a mapping called static interval. ∀t∈T, SI(t)=[SEFT(t),SLFT(t)], where SEFT(t) and SLFT(t) are the static earliest and latest firing time, respectively.

In the graphic representation, places are drawn as circles, transitions as bars, and inhibitor arcs as roundlet-terminated arcs. The flow relations between the nodes (i.e. places and transitions) are represented as directed arcs, and the tokens of the making as dots inside places. Incidence functions B and F are annotated close to their corresponding directed arcs and static firing intervals close to their corresponding transitions. But ∀t∈T, p∈P, if B(p,t)=1 or F(t,p)=1, B or F is graphically omitted for the sake of concision. We use the following symbols for the pre-set and post-set of a node x∈P∪T: •x={y| (y,x) ∈ (P×T) ∪(T×P)}, x•={y| (x,y) ∈ (P×T) ∪(T×P)}.

The state of a TPN is made up of a marking M and a dynamic firing interval FI associating each transition with an earliest and a latest dynamic firing time: state =(M,FI), where M∈R(M_0) is a marking reachable from M_0, ∀t∈T, FI(t)=[EFT(t), LFT(t)], and FI(t) is the relative-time firing interval of t. EFT(t) is the enabled delay time from the moment that t is enabled. (M,FI) ∈R((M_0,SI)) means that (M,FI) is a state reachable from (M_0,SI).

A transition t is enabled if each p∈•t contains B(p,t) tokens at least and none of the places connected to it through an inhibitor arc contains any token. t is firable at time τ if t is enabled and τ is neither lower than the earliest firing time EFT(t), or longer than the latest firing time LFT(t′) of any other enabled transition t′, i.e., EFT(t)≤τ≤LFT(t′).

When t fires at time τ, the marking of the net is changed from the current marking M to next reachable marking M′, i.e. (M,FI)[(t,τ)>(M′, FI′), and the values associated with the dynamic firing intervals of enabled transitions are also changed, where when p∈ •t∩t•, M′(p)=M(p)-B(p,t)+F(t,p); when p∈ t•-•t, M′(p)=M(p)+F(t,p); when p∈•t-t•, M′(p)=M(p)-B(p,t); otherwise M′(p)=M(p). Also, firing interval FI′ here is updated by means of the following rules. The enabled transitions are divided into two groups: inherited enabled transitions that were enabled before M′ is reached and newly enabled transitions that were enabled after M′ is reached. For any inherited enabled transition t′≠t, its firing interval is replaced with EFT(t′)=max{0, EFT(t′)-τ}and

$LFT(t')=\max\{0, LFT(t')-\tau\}$; for any newly enabled transition t' (including t), its firing interval is reset to the value of its static firing interval.

2.2 Temporal Formula Semantics of TPNs

To analyze the temporal properties of logical time workflow nets, in the following, the temporal formula semantics of TPNs is defined in terms of temporal logic [6].

Given any reachable state (M,FI) in a TPN, S^* represents a set of its all finite firing sequences at (M,FI), including the empty sequence λ; S^ω represents a set of its all infinite firing sequences at (M,FI). $S^\infty=S^\omega\cup S^*$. $|\alpha|$ is the length of $\alpha\in S^*$. $\alpha\beta$ denotes the concatenation of sequences α and β. If $\alpha\in S^\omega$, the length of α is denoted by symbol ω and $i<\omega$ for any integer i. For $\alpha\in S^\omega$ and each $i:0\le i\le|\alpha|$, suppose that β_i and γ_i are the firing sequences where $|\beta_i|=i$ and $\alpha=\beta_i\gamma_i$, β_i is the prefix of α with length i, and γ_i is the postfix of α excluding β_i. Let f be a TPN formula, $<(M,FI), \alpha> \models f$ means that f is satisfied by the pair of (M,FI) and α.

Definition 1. Let (M,FI) be a reachable state from (M_0,SI) in a TPN, α a firing sequence at (M,FI), f and g TPN formulae, then TPN formulae are defined recursively as follows:

(1) $<(M,FI), \alpha> \models p$ iff there are B(p,t) tokens at least in place p at (M,FI), where $(p,t) \in P\times T$;

(2) $<(M,FI), \alpha> \models (t,\tau)_{fir}$ iff transition t is firable at time τ and (M,FI);

(3) $<(M,FI), \alpha> \models (t,\tau)$ iff transition t fires at time τ and (M,FI);

(4) $<(M,FI), \alpha> \models f \vee g$ iff $<(M,FI), \alpha> \models f$ or $<(M,FI), \alpha> \models g$;

(5) $<(M,FI), \alpha> \models f \wedge g$ iff $<(M,FI), \alpha> \models f$ and $<(M,FI), \alpha> \models g$;

(6) $<(M,FI), \alpha> \models \neg f$ iff not $<(M,FI), \alpha> \models f$;

(7) $<(M,FI), \alpha> \models f \Rightarrow g$ iff $<(M,FI), \alpha> \models f$ implies $<(M,FI), \alpha> \models g$;

(8) $<(M,FI), \alpha> \models \bigcirc f$ iff $\alpha\neq\lambda$ and $<(M_1,FI_1),\gamma_1> \models f$;

(9) $<(M,FI), \alpha> \models \square f$ iff $<(M_i,FI_i),\gamma_i> \models f$ for each $i:0\le i \le |\alpha|$;

(10) $<(M,FI), \alpha> \models \Diamond f$ iff $<(M_i,FI_i),\gamma_i> \models f$ for some $i:0\le i \le |\alpha|$;

(11) $<(M,FI), \alpha> \models f \Delta g$ iff if $<(M,FI), \alpha> \models f$ and $<(M,FI), \alpha> \models g$, then symbol Δ is replaced with $\wedge$, else with $\vee$.

Here, symbols $\neg$, $\wedge, \vee$ and $\Rightarrow$ are the Boolean connectives. Formula $\bigcirc f$ (next) means that f becomes true in the next state reachable from (M,FI). Formula $\square f$ (henceforth) means that f becomes true in each state reachable from (M,FI). Formula $\Diamond f$ (eventually) means that f becomes true at some state reachable from (M,FI). Symbol Δ is a substitutive operator. If f and g become true at (M,FI), then $f \Delta g$ is equivalent to $f \wedge g$, otherwise it is equivalent to $f \vee g$. In this paper, •T• or 1 is used to represent logical true in logical expressions. For instance, $1\Delta1=1\wedge1$.

2.3 Logical Time Petri Nets (LTPN)

Logical time Petri nets (LTPN) are the extension and abstraction of TPNs and high-level time Petri nets (HLTPN) on batch data processing function and passing value indeterminacy. In LTPNs, there are two kinds of logical transitions, logical input and output transitions. The input places of a logical input transition t1 and the output places of a logical output transition t2 are restricted by logical expressions $f_I(t1)$ and

$f_O(t2)$, respectively. The logical expressions describe efficiently the passing value indeterminacy in real-time systems, such as the indeterminacy of arrival purchasing orders or actual trading volume in the runtime of a trading system in electronic commerce. This indeterminacy cannot be expressed by the variable symbol sums in HLTPNs, since they indicate clearly the types of passing or generating values.

In LTPNs, we need usually to convert a logical input/output expression $f_I(t)$ /$f_O(t)$ into a disjunctive normal form, such that each of its disjunctive clauses is a conjunct in which each conjunctive clause contains only a place name. If the input places of a logical input transition t satisfy $f_I(t)$ at time τ, this means that a conjunct at least becomes true at τ in its disjunctive normal form. When two or more conjuncts of $f_I(t)$ become true at τ, it corresponds with the conditional routing construction in workflow nets and here one of the conjuncts is only selected to fire t at τ. However, which conjunct of $f_O(t)$ is satisfied by the output places of a logical output transition t at τ depends on the newly generating values after firing t.

Definition 2. For LTN=(P,T,B,F,SI,I,O), LTPN=(LTN,M_0) is a logical time Petri net iff

(1) P is a finite set of places;
(2) $T=T_G \cup T_I \cup T_O$ is a finite set of transitions, $T \cup P \neq \varnothing$, $\forall t \in T_I \cup T_O$: $\bullet t \cap t \bullet = \varnothing$, and sets P, T_G, T_I and T_O are disjunct each other, where
  (a) T_G denotes a set of general time transitions in T;
  (b) T_I denotes a set of logical input transitions in T, and $\forall t \in T_I$, all input places of t are restrained by a logical input expression $f_I(t)$;
  (c) T_O denotes a set of logical output transitions in T, and $\forall t \in T_O$, all output places of t are restrained by a logical output expression $f_O(t)$;
(3) Definitions of symbols B, F, SI and M_0 are the same as in Section 2.1;
(4) I is a logical restriction input function, and $\forall t \in T_I$, $I(t)=f_I(t)$ is a logical input expression;
(5) O is a logical restriction output function, and $\forall t \in T_O$, $O(t)=f_O(t)$ is a logical output expression;
(6) Transition firing rules:
  (a) $\forall t \in T_G$, the firing rules of t are the same as in TPNs;
  (b) $\forall t \in T_I$, $I(t)= f_I(t)$, t is enabled if $f_I(t)|_M= \bullet T \bullet$, i.e., all input places of t satisfy the logical input expression $f_I(t)$ at the current marking M. t is firable at time τ if t is enabled and τ is neither lower than EFT(t), or longer than LFT(t'), where $t' \neq t$ and t' is enabled. After t fires at τ, the current marking M of the LTPN and the dynamic firing interval of enabled transitions are changed. Let M' be a new marking generated by firing t, then for $\forall p \in \bullet t$, if p is contained in a conjunctive clause of $f_I(t)$, where $f_I(t)$ becomes true, then M'(p)=M(p)-B(p,t), else M'(p)=M(p); $\forall p \in t\bullet$: M'(p)=M(p)+F(t,p); $\forall p \notin \bullet t \cup t\bullet$: M'(p)=M(p). The computation rules of the new dynamic firing interval are the same as in Section 2.1;
  (c) $\forall t \in T_O$, $O(t)=f_O(t)$, the enabled and firable conditions of t, and the algorithm of the new dynamic firing interval are the same as in Section 2.1. But after t fires at τ and (M,FI), the new generated marking M' must satisfy $f_O(t)$, i.e, $f_O(t)|_{M'}= \bullet T \bullet$, and $\forall p \in \bullet t$: M'(p)=M(p)-B(p,t); $\forall p \notin t\bullet \cup \bullet t$: M'(p)=M(p).

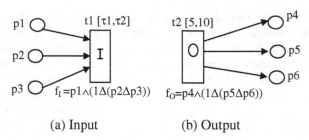

(a) Input   (b) Output

Fig. 1. Representations of logical input/output transitions in LTPNs

In the graphic representation of LTPNs, logical input and output transitions are drawn as the rectangles in which the symbols "I" and "O" are embedded respectively, and logical input or output expression is marked close to the corresponding rectangle (see Fig.1). Logical input transition t1 is enabled at M if $f_I(t)|_M = \bullet T\bullet$, where $M(p1)=1$, and $M(p2)=1 \wedge M(p3)=1$ or $M(p2)=1 \vee M(p3)=1$ in Fig.1(a). If $\tau1 \leq \tau \leq \tau2$, t1 is firable at τ. After firing t1, there is no token in p1, p2 and p3. In Fig.1 (b), p4 generates one token, and one token is included in one or each of p5 and p6 in terms of newly generating values by firing t2 at $\tau \in [5,10]$.

In this definition, we assume that all input and output place sets of each transition in $T_I \cup T_O$ are disjunct, in order to mainly apply logical input and output transitions to the modeling of receiving and sending actions, respectively, in cooperative systems.

2.4 Equivalent Representations of LTPNs in TPNs and HLTPNs

As mentioned in Introduction, LTPNs are the abstraction and extension of TPNs and HLTPNs. In fact, each LTPN exists an equivalent representation in TPNs or HLTPNs. Table 1 reports that two building blocks of LTPNs are represented functionally by their equivalent forms in TPNs and HLTPNs, respectively.

In Table 1, x is a variable of token colors, $<x>+<y>$ a variable symbol sum in HLTPNs. Place pijk denotes that it deposits the tokens of places pi, pj and pk in LTPNs. n, m and l are three positive integer variables. But the value of the variable annotating an input arc of a transition t must be determined when t fires at time τ and (M,FI), and it is equal to the number of the current tokens (same color tokens in HLTPNs) in the related place of the arc. For instance, $B(p,t)=n<p1>+m<p2>$ means that firing t consumes n tokens with color p1 and m tokens with color p2 in p. Table 1 shows that the building block of a logical input (output) transition may be represented functionally by two or more transition building blocks in TPNs and HLTPNs respectively. Therefore, LTPNs can compress the net structure of a modeled system, and some properties of the system can be easily analyzed at a conceptual level. Thereby, the modeling and analysis of cooperative systems based on LTPNs can mitigate the problem of state space explosion to a certain extent.

Table 1. Illustration of LTPN's equivalent expressions in TPNs and HLTPNs

Building blocks in LTPNs	Corresponding representations in TPNs	Corresponding representations in HLTPNs
p1 ◯ n t [τ1,τ2] p2 ◯ n ▸ I p3 ◯ n $f_I = p1 \wedge (1\Delta(p2\Delta p3))$	p1 ◯ n t p2 ◯ p3 ◯ [τ1,τ2] or P1 ◯ n t P2 ◯ n n P3 ◯ n [τ1,τ2]	t p123 ◯ n<p1> ▸| [τ1,τ2] or t p123 ◯ n<p1>+m<x> ▸| [τ1,τ2] or p123 ◯ n<p1>+m<p2>+l<p3> t [τ1,τ2]
t [τ1,τ2] 0 n ▸◯p1 n ▸◯p2 n ▸◯p3 $f_O = p1 \wedge (1\Delta(p2\Delta p3))$	t n |—— ▸◯p1 [τ1,τ2] or t n ◯p1 n n n ▸◯p2 [τ1,τ2] n n ▸◯ p3	t n<p1> |—— ▸◯ [τ1,τ2] p123 or t n<p1>+m<x> |—— ▸◯ [τ1,τ2] p123 or t n<p1>+m<p2>+l<p3> |—— ▸◯ [τ1,τ2] p123

3 Logical Time Workflow Nets

In this section, we first define formally logical time workflow nets (LTWN) within an organization according to LTPNs and workflow techniques. Then the constructing algorithm of LTWNs is given, which is an important guidance for the designers of cooperative workflows. Finally, we introduce and analyze the correctness of LTWNs.

3.1 Formal Definition

In real-time cooperative systems, we focus on analyzing the relations between cooperative organizations. Thus, value dependencies and external dependencies together are called passing value dependencies, since the value dependencies within an organization are usually omitted to model and analyze cooperative systems at a conceptual level. That is, passing value dependencies describe the task dependencies crossing organizational boundaries. Therefore, two types of places are introduced in LTWNs, control places and data places. Control places are used to deposit control tokens, data places to deposit data tokens. Data places are also called interface places according to the previous discussion in this paper.

A Petri net is strongly connected if and only if for every pair of nodes x and y, there is a path leading from x to y.

Definition 3. For LTN=(P,T,B,F,SI,I,O), an LTPN=(LTN,M_0) is called an LTWN iff

(1) The LTPN has two disjunct subsets, P_C and P_I, and $P=P_C \cup P_I$, where P_C is a set of control places, P_I a set of interface places, and $\forall p \in P_I: |(\bullet p \cup p \bullet) \cap T|=1$;

(2) P_C includes two special places: i and o. Place i is a source place: $\bullet i=\varnothing$. Place o is a sink place: $o\bullet=\varnothing$;

(3) $\forall t \in T$, $\bullet t$ and $t\bullet$ include one control place at least, respectively;

(4) If we add a transition t^* to the LTPN which connects place o with i (i.e. $\bullet t^*=\{o\}$ and $t^*\bullet=\{i\}$), then its inner logical net ILN=(IP, IT,IB,IF,SI,I,O) is strongly connected, where IP=P_C, IT=$T\cup\{t^*\}$, IB:IP×IT→N and IF: IT×IP→N are the backward and forward incidence functions, respectively.

In LTWNs, task dependencies are depicted based on control dependencies or both control dependencies and passing value dependencies. Thereby, a whole run of an LTWN means that a control token flows from a source place i to a sink place o. In workflow processes, there are four kinds of basic routing constructions: sequential routing, parallel routing, conditional routing and iterative routing [1]. To model parallel routing and conditional routing constructions, we need two pairs of basic building blocks: AND-split and AND-join, OR-split and OR-join. Fig.2 shows two kinds of equivalent LTWN representations in each building block. One is represented by a transition in T_G, the other by a logical transition. Note that there is a same graphical representation between building blocks AND-split and OR-split or between building blocks AND-join and OR-join. However, they have different logical expressions.

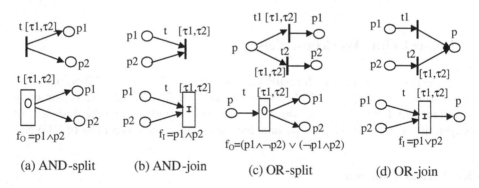

| (a) AND-split | (b) AND-join | (c) OR-split | (d) OR-join |

Fig.2. Basic building blocks in LTWNs

3.2 Constructing Algorithm of LTWNs

Suppose that the task set of an entity and the requirements specifications of all kinds of task dependencies are given, in this subsection, we show how workflow designers construct the LTWN model of the entity.

Algorithm 1. Construct the LTWN model of an entity

(1) Model each task in the given task set based on the corresponding building block of a transition t, and guarantee that •t and t• include one control place at least respectively;

(2) Order all building blocks according to the control dependencies among the tasks;

(3) If the input places of a transition t contain one or more interface places, then it is modeled by a logical input transition and its static firing time interval [SEFT(t), SLFT(t)] satisfies the condition 0<SEFT(t)<SLFT(t);

(4) Add a source place i to the input places of the first transition (task), a sink place o to the output places of the latest transition (task);

(5) Add a transition t* to the net which connects place o with i such that •t*={o} and t*•={i}.

In Algorithm 1, the preference relation of all tasks will be arranged based only on the control dependencies among them within an entity. If a task is responsible for receiving messages from the other entities, it is represented by a logical input transition in step (3), and the time difference SLFT(t)-SEFT(t) is positive, in order to fulfil batch data processing function and to avoid waiting for a long time to accept the messages. That is, a logical input transition t can fire at enabled delay time τ when $\tau \geq$EFT(t). However, during the enabled delay time of t, the new messages from the other entities can arrive in its interface places, and t will continue to be enabled. This means that more data can be processed when t fires. An additional transition t* is used to run the LTWN repeatedly in step (4).

3.3   Properties Analysis of LTWNs

In the following, we focus on the properties analysis of LTWNs within an organization. The correctness, effectiveness and efficiency of the real-time cooperative system supported by a workflow management system are vital to an organization. Thus, one of main aims in our formalism is to verify whether the static structure and dynamic behavior of a given LTWN are consistent with the requirements specification of the modeled entity, and to test whether the LTWN can terminate in an acceptable state. For this purpose, we will first define the correctness property of LTWNs, called soundness property. Then we concentrate on analyzing how to establish a sound LTWN based on its static net structure, Petri net analysis techniques and temporal logic.

Definition 4. Let X be a finite alphabet, $Y \subseteq X$. $\Gamma_{X \to Y}$ is a projection mapping from X to Y if for $\Gamma_{X \to Y:} X^* \to Y^*$, $\forall \sigma \in X^*$, $\Gamma_{X \to Y}(\sigma)$ represents the rest part of σ after deleting the characters in X-Y. Specially, for $Z \subseteq X$, $\Gamma_{X \to Y}(Z)$ denotes the alphabet consisting of the rest characters of Z excluding the characters in Z -Y.

In an LTWN, we should ensure that a control token in place i arrives eventually in place o via a firing transition sequence after a whole and correct run. And when place o has one control token, $\forall p \in P_c-\{o\}$, p is empty. Let M_0 be the initial marking of an LTWN and $M_0(i)=1$, then $\Gamma_{P \to IP}(M_0)=IM_0$ is an initial marking of its ILN and $IM_0(i)=1$.

Definitions 5. An LTWN is sound iff in (ILN, IM_0)

(1) $\forall(IM, FI) \in R((IM_0, SI))$, there exist a firing sequence α, a firing interval FI_0 and firing time τ such that $<(IM, FI), \alpha> \models \Diamond(o \wedge ((t^*, \tau) \Rightarrow \bigcirc(IM_0, FI_0)))$;

(2) $\forall t \in IT$, $\exists(IM, FI) \in R((IM_0, SI))$, there exist a firing sequence α and firing time τ such that $<(IM, FI), \alpha> \models \Diamond(t, \tau)$.

In the above definition, requirement (1) means that there is a firing sequence α such that $(IM_1, FI_1)[\alpha > (IM_2, FI_2)$, $IM_2(o) = 1$ and $\forall p \in IP - \{o\}: IM_2(p) = 0$. Here t^* is enabled and firable, and the next marking reachable from (IM_2, FI_2) is the initial marking IM_0 after firing t^*. However, requirement (2) means that there is no dead transition in the inner logical marking net (ILN, IM_0) of the LTWN, i.e., $\forall t \in IT$, $\exists(IM, FI) \in R((IM_0, SI))$, t is firable at τ and (IM, FI). Since the interface places and their related arcs are omitted in an ILN, we can think of net (ILN, IM_0) as its private workflow process, i.e., the corresponding organization has full control over the local part of the LTWN.

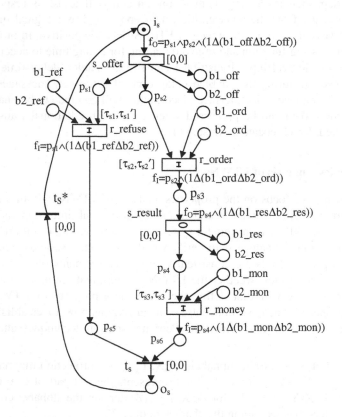

Fig. 3. LTWN$_s$ modeling the behaviors of a seller S

Fig.3 models the behavior of a seller S in a simple offer-order-deliver-pay system [7], which consists of two buyers (B1 and B2) and a seller (S). Some private and cooperative tasks within an entity are omitted for the sake of simplicity in this example, such as preparation for goods, request for offer. Here, S has five tasks related to buyers B1 and B2: send offer (s_off), receive refuse (r_ref), receive order (r_ord), send result (goods) (s_res) and receive money (r_mon). $P_C=\{p_{s1},p_{s2},\dots, p_{s6},i_s,o_s\}$, $P_I=\{bi\_off, bi\_ord, bi\_ref, bi\_res, bi\_mon, i=1,2\}$, $IM_0(i_s)= M_0(i_s)=1$, $\forall p \in P_C \cup P_I -\{i_s\}$: $M_0(p)=0$ and $\forall p \in P_c -\{i_s\}$: $IM_0(p)=0$. t_s is added to perform a parallel routing structure. It is proved easily that the two requirements in Definition 5 are satisfied in $LTWN_s$. Accordingly, it is sound.

We give below a sufficient and necessary condition satisfied by sound LTWNs.

Theorem 1. An LTWN is sound if and only if (ILN,IM_0) is live and bounded.

Proof: The necessity is proved via a reduction to absurdity. If it is not live, there are two cases. Case 1: $\forall(IM,FI) \in R((IM_0,SI))$, $\exists t \in IT$, for any firing sequence α, there exist a state (IM',FI') reachable from (IM,FI) and firing time τ such that $(IM,FI)[\alpha>(IM',FI') \wedge \neg((IM',FI')[(t,\tau)>)$. This is in contradiction with the requirement (2) of Definition 5. Case 2: $\exists(IM,FI) \in R((IM_0,SI))$, $\forall t \in IT$, for any firing sequence α and any time τ, $\exists(IM',FI') \in R((IM_0,SI))$ such that $(IM,FI)[\alpha>(IM',FI') \wedge \neg((IM',FI')[(t,\tau)>)$. Here $IM'(o)=0$ in terms of Algorithm 1, i.e., $\forall(IM',FI') \in R((IM_0,SI))$, $IM'(o)=0$. This contradicts the requirement (1) in Definition 5.

If (ILN,IM_0) is not bounded, then for $\forall k \in N$, $\exists(IM,FI) \in R((IM_0,SI))$, $p \in IP$: $IM(p)>k$. Thus $\exists t \in p\bullet$, t may fire at IM twice successively. By Definition 3, $\forall k \in N$, $\exists p' \in IP \cap t\bullet$, there are $\tau1$ and $\tau2$ such that $(IM,FI)[(t, \tau1)(t, \tau2)>(IM',FI') \wedge IM'(p')>k$. If the previous process is done repeatedly, then for $\forall(IM',FI') \in R((IM,FI))$, $\exists p \in IP \wedge IM'(p)>k$. Hence there exists a firing sequence α at IM such that $(IM,FI)[\alpha>(IM',FI') \wedge IM'(o)>k$. This contradicts that there are τ and FI_0 such that $(t^*,\tau) \Rightarrow O(IM_0,FI_0)$. Therefore, the (ILN,IM_0) is live and bounded .

The sufficiency is proved as follows. Suppose (ILN,IM_0) is live, the requirement (2) in Definition 5 is satisfied apparently. The requirement (1) will be verified below. Actually, only place i has a control token at IM_0, i.e. $IM_0(i)=1$ and $\forall p \subset IP-\{i\}:IM_0(p)=0$. Thus, $\forall(IM,FI) \in R((IM_0,SI))$, there is a firing sequence α such that $<(IM,FI), \alpha> \models \Diamond o$.

Here t^* is firable at time τ based on the structure of the ILN, and $\exists(IM',FI') \in R((IM_0,SI))$, $(IM,FI) [(t^*,\tau)>(IM',FI') \wedge IM'(i)=1$. If $\exists p \in IP-\{i\}$: $IM'(p)>0$, then $\exists t \in \bullet p$ such that $F(t,p)$ tokens are added in p after firing α again. This results in contradiction with the boundedness of (ILN,IM_0). Thereby, $<(IM,FI),\alpha> \models \Diamond((t^*,\tau) \Rightarrow O(IM_0,FI_0))$ and the requirement (1) is satisfied. Therefore, the LTWN is sound. ∎

Since it is easily verified that the (ILN,IM_0) in Fig.3 is live and bounded, $LTWN_s$ is sound in terms of Theorem 1.

Definition 6. Let TPN be a time Petri net. C is a path leading from a node n_1 to a node n_k iff there is a node sequence $<n_1,n_2,\dots,n_k>$ in the TPN such that $(n_i,n_{i+1}) \in (T \times P) \cup (P \times T)$, $i=1,2,\dots,k-1$. Assume that $\&(C)$ denotes the alphabet of a path C, i.e. $\&(C)=\{n_1,n_2,\dots,n_k\}$. C is an elementary path iff $\forall n_i, n_j \in \&(C)$, if $i \neq j$, then $n_i \neq n_j$. Node n_j is an inheritor of node n_i in C (notation $n_i \prec_C n_j$) iff there are nodes $n_i,n_{i+1},\dots,$ $n_j \in \&(C)$ such that (n_i,n_{i+1}), $(n_{i+1},n_{i+2}),\dots,(n_{j-1},n_j) \in (T \times P) \cup (P \times T)$.

The concept of well-structured LTWNs is introduced in the following, in order to analyze the relations between the static structure of an LTWN and soundness. Building blocks AND/OR-splits and AND/OR-joins must be well paired in a well-structured LTWN, respectively.

Definition 7. A TPN is well-structured iff for any pair of nodes x and y (one is a place, the other a transition), if there exist two elementary paths C_1 and C_2 leading from x to y such that $\&(C_1) \cap \&(C_2) = \{x,y\}$, then $C_1 = C_2$. An LTWN is well-structured iff its ILN is well-structured.

According to the above definition, any two of the parallel routing and conditional routing structures cannot intersect in a well-structured LTWN, but one can be embedded in the other. A well-structured LTWN can be verified for soundness in polynomial time [1]. We assume that all LTWNs are well-structured in the rest of this paper.

4 Interorganizational Logical Time Workflow Nets

In the previous section, we model and analyze the workflows within an organization on the basis of LTPNs. In this section, we consider how to construct the cooperative workflow net of the LTWNs modeling all organizations in a real-time cooperative system, called an interorganizational logical time workflow net (ILTWN). In fact, each cooperative entity has itself private workflow process and can full control over the control flows in its LTWN. However, there exist the passing value dependencies between some tasks belonging cooperative entities in a real-time cooperative system. There are two interaction ways: synchronous communication and asynchronous communication. But for a number of real-time cooperative systems, only asynchronous communication is usually performed, such as electronic contracts [7] and heterogeneous purchase processes [11] in electronic commerce. Therefore, asynchronous communication between organizations is only considered in this paper.

Since the interface places in LTWNs are used to fulfil message exchange, their ILTWN can be achieved based on the interface places between the related LTWNs.

Definition 8. Let $LTWN_j = (P_j, T_j, B_j, F_j, SI_j, I_j, O_j, M_{0j})$ be an LTWN of the jth cooperative entity, $j=1,2,\ldots,n$. $ILTWN = (P,T,B,F,SI,I,O, M_0)$ is an interorgnizational logical time workflow net iff

(1) $P = \cup_{j \in \{1,2,\ldots,n\}} P_j$; $T = \cup_{j \in \{1,2,\ldots,n\}} T_j$;

(2) $\forall p \in P_j$, $\forall t \in T_j$, $B(p,t) = B_j(p,t)$, $j=1,2,\ldots,n$;

(3) $\forall p \in P_j$, $\forall t \in T_j$, $F(t,p) = F_j(t,p)$, $j=1,2,\ldots,n$;

(4) $\forall t \in T_j$, $SI(t) = SI_j(t)$, $j=1,2,\ldots,n$;

(5) $\forall t \in T_{Ij}$, $I(t) = I_j(t)$, and $\forall t \in T_{Oj}$, $O(t) = O_j(t)$, where T_{Ij} is a set of logical input transitions in T_j, T_{Oj} a set of logical output transitions in T_j, $j=1,2,\ldots,n$;

(6) M_0 is the initial marking, and $\forall p \in P_j$: $M_0(p) = M_{0j}(p)$, $j=1,2, \ldots,n$;

(7) Transition firing rules. The transition firing rules in ILTWNs are the same as in Definition 2.

Based on the above definition, if the workflow processes of each cooperative organization are modeled by an LTWN in a real-time cooperative system, an ILTWN can be obtained through superposing the interface places between the related LTWNs. However, the correctness of an ILTWN may be destroyed, since the passing values in an asynchronous communication may be subjected to order errors. We can use Theorem 1 to prove the two logical time workflow nets in Fig.4 are correct, i.e., LTWN1 and LTWN2 are sound. Nevertheless, their ILTWN is not live, because t11, t12, t21 and t22 are dead transitions. But if the order of a receiving action and a sending action is exchanged in one of two LTWNs, the ILTWN is live. For instance, if (p2,t21) and (t22,p1) are replaced with (p2,t22) and (t21,p1), respectively, the ILTWN becomes live in Fig.4.

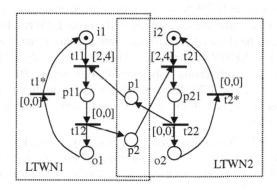

Fig. 4. An ILTWN composed of two LTWNs.

5   Verification of Interorganizational Logical Time Workflow Nets

Given all LTWNs in a real-time cooperative system, we can construct their ILTWN in terms of Definition 8. However, the ILTWN may be not live even though every LTWN is sound (see Fig.4). In the following, therefore, we first introduce formally the soundness of ILTWNs based on the soundness of LTWNs. Then we discuss how to verify the soundness of an ILTWN by means of its static structure.

Definition 9. Let $P_I = \cup_{j \in \{1,2,\ldots,n\}} P_{Ij}$, where P_{Ij} is a set of the interface places in P_j. r: $T \rightarrow T$ is a renaming function if $\forall p \in P_I$, $\forall t \in T$, $j \in \{1,2,\ldots,n\}$:

(1) $t \in p \bullet \cap T_j$, $r(t) = r_j(p)$, i.e., $r_j(p)$ denotes the output transition of p in T_j;
(2) $t \in \bullet p \cap T_j$, $r(t) = s_j(p)$, i.e., $s_j(p)$ denotes the input transition of p in T_j;
(3) $t \notin (\bullet p \cup p \bullet) \cap T_j$, $r(t) = t$.

In the above definition, the transitions connecting with the interface places are only renamed by a renaming function, in order to analyze the soundness of ILTWNs. Since the soundness of an LTWN implies its correctness, if all LTWNs in an ILTWN are sound, the correctness of the ILTWN depends on the liveness of the transitions related to the places in P_I and their precedence order in every local workflow process. Based on Definition 8, however, the order cannot be updated when an ILTWN is constructed, i.e. the structural order of the transitions in every LTWN is the same as in the ILTWN. Consequently, when all LTWNs are sound in an ILTWN, if the ILTWN is not live, this means that the incorrect order of the transitions related to the interface places in some LTWNs leads to some dead ones in the ILTWN.

Definition 10. An ILTWN is sound iff

(1) Each of its LTWNs is sound;

(2) $\forall p \in P_I, \forall r_j(p) \in p\bullet, r_j(p)$ is live.

In Fig.4, $P_I = \{p1, p2\}$, since there are transitions $r_1(p1) = t11 \in p1\bullet, r_2(p2) = t21 \in p2\bullet$ such that $\forall (M,FI) \in R((M_0,SI)), \forall \tau 1, \tau 2 \in [2,4], r_1(p1)$ at time $\tau 1$ and $r_2(p2)$ at time $\tau 2$ are not firable at (M,FI), the ILTWN is not sound in terms of Definition 10. Actually, soundness is related to the dynamic behavior of a real-time cooperative system. To verify the soundness of an ILTWN based on its static structure, we consider the relations between soundness and the elementary paths in its LTWNs. In fact, the soundness of ILTWNs can be decided for arbitrary interorganizational logical time workflow nets, but it is EXPSPACE-hard [2]. Thereby, we analyze the soundness of ILTWNs only for some interesting subclasses in this paper. Therefore, we restrict analysis of soundness to the ILTWNs in which none of sending and receiving actions between collaborative organizations is included in any conditional routing (OR-split/join) construction.

Definition 11. An LTWN is OR-restricted iff for any $p_1, p_2 \in P_C$, if there exist two elementary paths C_1 and C_2 ($C_1 \neq C_2$) leading from p_1 to p_2, and $\&(C_1) \cap \&(C_2) = \{p_1, p_2\}$, then for $\forall t \in T \cap (\bullet P_1 \cup P_1 \bullet)$: $t \notin \&(C_1) \cup \&(C_2)$. An ILTWN is OR-restricted iff each of its LTWNs is OR-restricted.

According to the above definition, $LTWN_s$ in Fig.3 is OR-restricted. In the following, we first discuss the soundness of a simple ILTWN consisting of two LTWNs.

Theorem 2. Let ILTWN be an OR-restricted interorganizational logical time workflow net composed of two sound LTWNs: $LTWN_1$ and $LTWN_2$. ILTWN is sound if for any elementary path C_j leading from i_j to o_j in $LTWN_j$, $j=1,2$, and $l \in \{0,1\}$, there exists no pair of interface places p and q such that $r_{l+1}(p) \prec_{C_{l+1}} s_{l+1}(q)$ and $r_{2-l}(q)$

$\prec_{C_{2-l}} s_{2-l}(p)$ become true simultaneously.

Proof: Since $LTWN_1$ and $LTWN_2$ are sound and OR-restricted, each of their ILNs is live and bounded, and any $t \in T \cap (\bullet P_I \cup P_I \bullet)$ is not in conditional routing structures. By Definition 10, we need only to prove that each $t \in T \cap (\bullet P_I \cup P_I \bullet)$ is live and that each $p \in P_I$ is bounded. We use notation C_{lj} to represent $\Gamma_{T_j \cup P_j \to \bullet P_l \cup P_l \bullet}(C_j)$, $j=1,2$. For $j \in \{1,2\}$, if $C_{lj} = \phi$, then $\Gamma_{T_j \cup P_j \to T_j}(C_j)$ is a firing sequence of the ILTWN, as each transition in it is not concerned in external dependencies. Thus, we assume below that $C_{lj} \neq \phi$, $j=1,2$, and the liveness of each $t \in T \cap (\bullet P_I \cup P_I \bullet)$ will be proved in terms of the following two cases.

Case 1: If $(\bullet(\&C_{11}) \cup (\&C_{11})\bullet) \cap (\bullet(\&C_{12}) \cup (\&C_{12})\bullet) = P_I$, this means that the sending and receiving actions between $LTWN_1$ and $LTWN_2$ are only in sequential routing in $LTWN_1$ and $LTWN_2$, respectively. By means of the conditions of the theorem, $\forall p, q \in P_I, r_{l+1}(p) \prec_{C_{l+1}} s_{l+1}(q)$ and $r_{2-l}(q) \prec_{C_{2-l}} s_{2-l}(p)$ are not satisfied simultaneously, $l \in \{0,1\}$, i.e., there exists no time τ such that $LTWN_{l+1}$ waits to receive the data to be not sent by $LTWN_{2-l}$ at τ in p and $LTWN_{2-l}$ waits to receive the data to be not sent by $LTWN_{l+1}$ at τ in q. Thereby, each transition in C_{l1} and C_{l2} is live in the ILTWN.

Case 2: For $l \in \{1,2\}$, because $LTWN_l$ is OR-restricted, if $\bullet(\&C_{lI}) \cup (\&C_{lI}) \bullet \neq P_l$, then there are k_l elementary paths $C_l^{(1)}, \ldots, C_l^{k_l}$ ($k_l \in N$) leading from i_l to o_l such that $\cup_{j \in \{0,1,\ldots,k/l\}} \bullet (\&C_{lI}^{(j)}) \cup (\&C_{lI}^{(j)}) \bullet = P_l$ (let $C_{lI} = C_{lI}^{(0)}$), $\&(C_{lI}) \neq \&(C_{lI}^{(j)})$, $\&(C_{lI}^{(j)}) - \&(C_{lI}) \cap \&(C_{lI}^{(j)}) \neq \phi$, and $\Gamma_{T_l \cup P_l \to \&(C_{lI}) - \&(C_{lI}) \cap \&(C_{lI}^{(j)})} (C_l)$ and

$\Gamma_{T_l \cup P_l \to \&(C_{lI}^{(j)}) - \&(C_{lI}) \cap \&(C_{lI}^{(j)})} (C_l^{(j)})$ are in the same parallel routing structures, $j=1,\ldots,k_l$.

Therefore, for any whole and correct running and any $t \in \&(C_{l1}) \cup \&(C_{l2})$, t must fire only once. For $l \in \{0,1\}$, if there exists $p \in P_l$ such that $r_{l+1}(p) \in r(\&(C_{l(l+1)}))$, then there is $j \in \{0,1,\ldots,k_{l+1}\}$ such that $s_{2-l}(p) \in r(\&(C_{l(2-l)}^{(j)}))$. Since $C_{l(l+1)}^{(u)}$ and $C_{l(l+1)}^{(v)}$ ($u \neq v$, $0 \leq u,v \leq k_{l+1}$) fire concurrently and there is a synchronization at $t \in \&(C_{l(l+1)}^{(u)}) \cap \&(C_{l(l+1)}^{(v)})$ in $LTWN_{l+1}$, if for any $j \in \{0,1,\ldots,k_{2-l}\}$, $(\bullet(\&C_{l(l+1)}^{(j)}) \cup (\&C_{l(l+1)}^{(j)}) \bullet) \cap (\bullet(\&C_{l(2-l)}^{(j)}) \cup (\&C_{l(2-l)}^{(j)}) \bullet) \neq \phi$, then we can assert that $C_{l(l+1)}$ is live through doing the analysis similar to that in Case 1.

Consequently, $\forall t \in T \cap (\bullet P_l \cup P_l \bullet)$, t is live. Because for any $p \in P_l$, if there is $j \in \{0,1,\ldots,k_{l+1}\}$ such that $r_{l+1}(p) \in r(\&(C_{l(l+1)}^{(j)}))$, then there must exist $j \in \{0,1,\ldots,k_{2-l}\}$ such that $s_{2-l}(p) \in r(\&(C_{l(2-l)}^{(j)}))$, and $r_{l+1}(p)$ and $s_{2-l}(p)$ must fire in each complete running. Thereby, for $\forall p \in P_l$, p is explicitly bounded. ∎

According to Theorem 2, we obtain below a general result on the ILTWN composed of n ($n \geq 2$) LTWNs. In this case, an LTWN may communicate asynchronously with more than one other LTWNs.

Theorem 3. Let ILTWN be an OR-restricted interorganizational logical time workflow net composed of n sound LTWNs: $LTWN_1, \ldots, LTWNn$. ILTWN is sound if for any $u,v \in \{1,\ldots,n\}$, $u \neq v$, $P_{Iu} \cap P_{Iv} \neq \phi$, and any two elementary paths C_u and C_v leading from a source place to a sink place in $LTWN_u$ and $LTWN_v$, respectively, there exists no pair of interface places p and q in $P_{Iu} \cap P_{Iv}$ such that for $k,l \in \{u,v\}$ and $k \neq l$, relations $r_k(p) \prec_{C_k} s_k(q)$ and $r_l(q) \prec_{C_l} s_l(p)$ are true simultaneously.

Proof: If $u,v \in \{1,\ldots,n\}$, $u \neq v$ and $P_{Iu} \cap P_{Iv} \neq \phi$, then there exists asynchronous communication between $LTWN_u$ and $LTWN_v$, and they can be combined in terms of Definition 8. Here we think of the net composed of them as a new logical time workflow net of the ILTWN, represented by notation $LTWN_{uv}$. Thus, the ILTWN is consist of n-1 LTWNs: $LTWN_{uv}$ and $LTWN_j$, $j=1,\ldots,n$, $j \notin \{u,v\}$. The interface place set of $LTWN_{uv}$ is $P_{Iuv} = P_{Iu} \cup P_{Iv} - P_{Iu} \cap P_{Iv}$. Since ILN_u and ILN_v are live and bounded, the inner logical net ILN_{uv} of $LTWN_{uv}$ is also live and bounded at $\Gamma_{P \to P_u \cup P_v - P_{Iuv}} (M_0)$ based on Theorem 2, i.e., $LTWN_{uv}$ is sound, where M_0 is the initial marking of the ILTWN. If the above procedure is done repeatedly for the n-1 LTWNs, then the ILTWN made up of $LTWN_1$, $LTWN_2$, $\ldots$, and $LTWN_n$ is live and bounded. ILTWN is sound by Definition 10. ∎

According to Theorem 3, although that the correctness of a real-time cooperative system is concerned in its dynamic behavior, it may be verified efficiently by its static net structure, when the system can be modeled by an OR-restricted ILTWN. That is, Theorem 3 means that we can verify the soundness of an OR-restricted ILTWN only through checking the preference relation of the transitions related to the interface places on each elementary path of the two related LTWNs in terms of their static net structures.

We continue to analyze the offer-order-deliver-pay system presented in Section 3.3. We depict the LTWN models of a buyer Bj ($1 \le j \le 2$) and the communication system (see Fig.5 and Fig.6). Fig.5 models the behaviors of a buyer Bj ($j \in \{1,2\}$). Since buyer Bj purchases goods only from one seller S, we can use a traditional time Petri net to construct its LTWN model $LTWN_{bj}$. In $LTWN_{bj}$, its interface place set P_{Ibj} consists of places bj_s_off, bj_s_ref, bj_s_ord, bj_s_res and bj_s_mon. Task set T_{bj} contains five tasks: receive offer (r_offer), send offer refuse (s_refuse), send order (s_order), receive result (goods) (r_result) and send money (s_money). $ILN_{bj}= (IP_{bj}, IT_{bj}, IB_{bj}, IF_{bj}, I_{bj}, O_{bj})$ can be easily verified for liveness and boundedness properties. Therefore, $LTWN_{bj}$ is sound on the basis of Theorem 1.

To demonstrate the function of the communication system in this example, it is also modeled as an organization (see Fig.6). It works such that each message sent by an organization is delivered to the other organizations. We assume here that it is safe, i.e., that the message sent is bound to the result in its receipt on the other side and that receiving a message is bound to be a result of sending it by the other side. Its LTWN model $LTWN_c$ is shown in Fig.6. Its interface place set P_{Ic} is the union of the interface place sets in $LTWN_s$, $LTWN_{b1}$ and $LTWN_{b2}$, i.e. $P_{Ic}=P_{Is} \cup P_{Ib1} \cup P_{Ib2}$. It is easily verified that ILN_c is live and bounded. Thus, $LTWN_c$ is sound according to Theorem 1.

In the following, we consider the soundness property of their cooperative workflow net ILTWN (notation $ILTWN_{sb}$). Because three sets P_{Is}, P_{Ib1} and P_{Ib2} are disjunct each other, there exists only asynchronous communication between $LTWN_c$ and each of $LTWN_s$, $LTWN_{b1}$ and $LTWN_{b2}$. Therefore, $ILTWN_{sb}$ can be built through overlapping the interface places in P_{Is} to combine $LTWN_c$ with $LTWN_s$, and the places in P_{Ibi} to combine $LTWN_c$ with $LTWN_{bi}$, i=1,2, based on Definition 8. However, $ILTWN_{sb}$ will be omitted to save space.

Since each LTWN is sound and OR-restricted, according to Theorem 3, we only need to verify whether the preference relations of the transitions, which connect with the common interface places in each pair of related LTWNs, satisfy the condition of Theorem 3 in any pair of elementary paths leading from source places to sink places to prove that $ILTWN_{sb}$ is sound.

We now analyze the combination of $LTWN_c$ and $LTWN_{b1}$. Their common interface places are the places in $P_{Ib1}=\{b1\_s\_off,$

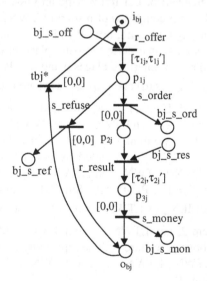

Fig. 5. $LTWN_{bj}$ modeling the behaviors of a buyer Bj (j=1,2)

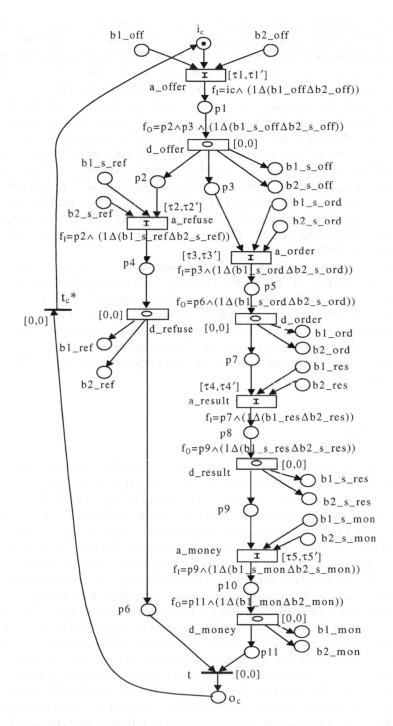

Fig.6. LTWN$_c$ modeling the behaviors of the communication system

$b1\_s\_ref$, $b1\_s\_ord$, $b1\_s\_res$, $b1\_s\_mon\}$, while the transitions related to them are all transitions in $LTWN_{b1}$ and the transitions: d_offer, a_refuse, a_order, d_result and a_money in $LTWN_c$ (see Fig.5 and Fig.6). In $LTWN_{b1}$, there are only two elementary paths from i_{b1} to o_{b1}, i.e., $C_{b1}= i_{b1}{\to}r\_offer{\to}p_{11}{\to}s\_refuse{\to}o_{b1}$ and $C'_{b1}= i_{b1}{\to}r\_offer{\to}p_{11}{\to}$ $s\_order{\to}$ $p_{21}{\to}$ $r\_result{\to}p_{31}{\to}s\_money{\to}o_{b1}$. $\Gamma_{Tb1\cup Pb1\to Tb1}(C_{b1})= r\_offer{\to}s\_refuse$, $\Gamma_{Tb1\cup Pb1\to Tb1}(C'_{b1}) = r\_offer{\to}s\_order{\to}r\_result{\to}s\_money$. By the definition of renaming function r, $r(\Gamma_{Tb1\cup Pb1\to Tb1}(C_{b1}))=r_{b1}(b1\_s\_off){\to}s_{b1}(b1\_s\_ref)$, $r(\Gamma_{Tb1\cup Pb1\to Tb1}(C'_{b1}))=r_{b1}(b1\_s\_off){\to}s_{b1}(b1\_s\_ord){\to}r_{b1}(b1\_s\_res){\to}s_{b1}(b1\_s\_mon)$.

In $LTWN_c$, there are also only two elementary paths C_c and C_c' from i_c to o_c. $r(\Gamma_{Tc\cup Pc\to Tc}(C_c))=a\_offer{\to}s_c(b1\_s\_off){\to}r_c(b1\_s\_ref){\to}d\_refuse{\to}t$, $r(\Gamma_{Tc\cup Pc\to Tc}(C_c')) =a\_offer{\to}s_c(b1\_s\_off){\to}r_c(b1\_s\_ord){\to}d\_order{\to}a\_result{\to}s_c(b1\_s\_res){\to}r_c(b1\_s\_mon){\to}d\_money{\to}t$. Therefore, for $\forall C_1\in\{C_{b1}, C_{b1}'\}$, $C_2\in\{C_c,C_c'\}$, $\forall p,q\in P_{lb1}$, then C_1, C_2, p and q satisfy the condition in Theorem 3. Similarly, we can verify the composite net between $LTWN_c$ and one of $LTWN_s$ and $LTWN_{b2}$ satisfies also the condition. Consequently, $ILTWN_{sb}$ is sound.

In $LTWN_c$, the batch data processing function and passing value indeterminacy are explicitly represented in Fig.6. For instance, $f_t(a\_order)=p3\wedge(1\ (b1\_s\_ord\ b2\_s\_ord))$, if p3 and $b1\_s\_ord$ contain one token respectively, and $b2\_s\_ord$ is empty, then transition a_order is enabled because $f_t(a\_order)= \bullet T\bullet$. But even if $b2\_s\_ord$ is empty, a_order can fire, when its enabled delay time $\tau \geq \tau3$. However, a data token sent by buyer B2 may arrive in $b2\_s\_ord$ among the enabled delay time, and the data can be processed together by communication system $LTWN_c$ when a_order fires.

6 Conclusion

In real-time cooperative systems, it is very important that the messages between the organizations are exchanged successfully. Thus, this paper focuses on cooperative workflows, i.e., a number of cooperative organizations are involved in shared workflow processes. The objective of this paper is to provide the designers of cooperative workflows with a formalism that on one hand has a high expressive power and on the other hand has a strong theoretical basis. In interorganizational workflows, each cooperative organization has own private workflow processes and control-flows. An interorganizational workflow consists of local workflows, whereas the exchange of messages between the cooperative organizations is implemented through passing value dependencies. In order to model the passing value indeterminacy and batch processing function, Logical Time Petri Nets are first introduced in this paper. It can mitigate the problem of state explosion to a certain extent. Then we present the concept of logical time workflow nets based on LTPNs and workflow techniques, and construct formally the LTWN model of a real-time cooperative system, Interorganizational Logical Time Workflow Net. For a class of OR-restricted LTWNs, the inheritable conditions of the soundness are obtained. By means of our concepts and techniques, therefore, the designers of cooperative workflows can verify easily the soundness property of an ILTWN only from its net structure. The use of the methods and techniques has been demonstrated through analyzing the example of an offer-order-deliver-pay system.

Further research work will be to formally verify soundness of the ILTWNs that are not OR-restricted. Also, we intend to develop a tool for the modeling and analysis of ILTWN models.

Acknowledgements

This work is supported partially by projects of National Preeminent Youth Foundation (No. 60125205); National Key Basic Science Foundation of China (863 Plan, 2001AA413020, 2002AA4Z3430); Open project of Laboratory of Computer Science, Institute of Software, Chinese Academy of Sciences (SYSKF0205, SYSKF0309); Excellent Ph.D Paper Author Foundation of China (199934).

References

1. van der Aalst, W. M.P.: The application of Petri nets to workflow management. The Journal of Circuits, Systems and Computers 1 (1998) 21-66
2. van der Aalst, W.M.P.: Loosely coupled interorganizational workflows: modeling and analyzing workflows crossing organizational boundaries. Information &Management 1 (2000) 67-75
3. Alur, R., Yannakakis, M.: Model checking of message sequence charts. Software Concepts and Tools 2 (1999) 70-77
4. Atluri, V., Huang, H.K.: A Petri net based safety analysis of workflow authorization models. Journal of Computer Security 2-3 (2000) 209-240
5. Derks, W., Dehnert, J., Grefen, P., Jonker, W.: Customized atomicity specification for transactional workflows. In Proceedings 3rd International symposium on Cooperative Database Systems for Advanced Applications, Beijing, China (2001) 155-164
6. Du, Y.Y., Jiang, C.J.: Formal analysis of an online stock trading system by temporal Petri nets. In: Proc. Int. Workshop on Computer Networks and Mobile Computing, IEEE Computer Society Press, Beijing, China (2001) 197-202
7. Grimm, R., Ochsenschlager, P.: Binding telecooperation – a formal model for electronic commerce. Computer Networks 2 (2001) 171-193
8. Hauschildt, D., Verbeek, H.M.W., van der Aalst, W.M.P.: WOFLAN: a Petri-net-based workflow analyzer. Computing Science Reports 97/12, Eindhoven University of Technology, Eindhoven (1997)
9. Lawrence, P., editor. Workflow handbook 1997. Workflow Management Coalition. John Wiley and Sons, New York (1997)
10. Murata, T.: Petri nets: properties, analysis and applications. Proceedings of the IEEE, 4 (1989) 541-580
11. Popovici, A., Schuldt, H., Schek, H.J.: Generation and verification of heterogeneous purchase processes. In: Proceedings of the International Workshop on Technologies for E-Services (TES'01), Cairo, Egypt (2000)
12. Vicario, E.: Static analysis and dynamic steering of time-dependent systems. IEEE Transactons on Software Engineering 8 (2001) 728-748

New Developments in Closed-Form Computation for GSPN Aggregation

Jörn Freiheit and Jonathan Billington

Computer Systems Engineering Centre (CSEC)
University of South Australia
Mawson Lakes, SA, 5095
{jorn.freiheit,j.billington}@unisa.edu.au

Abstract. Petri nets are useful for modelling complex concurrent systems. While modelling using Petri nets focusses on local states and actions, the analysis methods are concerned with global states and their transitions. Unfortunately generation of the complete state space suffers from the well-known state space explosion problem. This paper presents a method to overcome the state-space explosion problem for a class of Generalised Stochastic Petri Nets (GSPNs). Large complex GSPN models are transformed into smaller, less complex ones with smaller state spaces than the original models. This transformation is called aggregation. The aim of aggregation is to reduce the state space while preserving the desired behaviour of the original model. In this paper we investigate the aggregation of GSPNs preserving time dependent behaviour by using recent [5,6] and newly developed transformation rules. These rules are used to merge several single timed transitions into one *merged* transition. The firing rate of the merged transition turns out to be dependent on the marking of the net. Beside the introduction of a new method for the aggregation of exponential transitions with fixed firing rates, new formulae to aggregate transitions with marking-dependent firing rates are presented. Successive aggregation becomes possible to transform very complex models into models in which either a closed-form computation of the stationary state distribution is available or which has a very small state space. A prototype implementation is used to demonstrate both the drastically reduced state space for suitable models and the general limits of the method.

1 Introduction

A suitable formal method to model and analyse complex concurrent systems are Petri nets [13]. Generalised Stochastic Petri Nets (GSPN) [9] extend Petri nets to handle the time- and stochastic-dependent behaviour of systems. Most analysis methods are based on generating the complete state space of the investigated model. Due to their large state spaces, many practical systems cannot be analysed. Overcoming this limitation is an important topic in discrete event system analysis. Replacing large, complex model structures by smaller, less complex ones is known as *aggregation*, an important class of reduction techniques [7,10,12]. To

J.S. Dong and J. Woodcock (Eds.): ICFEM 2003, LNCS 2885, pp. 471–490, 2003.
© Springer-Verlag Berlin Heidelberg 2003

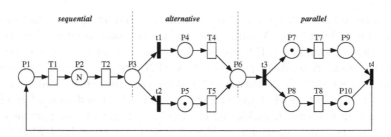

Fig. 1. A GSPN example with three different structures.

be useful these techniques must preserve the desired properties of the original model.

This paper presents an aggregation technique that preserves the stationary token distribution [9,14] for a special class [2,4] of GSPN models. Recently developed formulae [5,6] are presented that compute marking-dependent firing rates of aggregated transitions. Moreover, formulae to aggregate transitions with marking-dependent firing rates are presented in this paper for the first time. Three different fundamental structures of Petri nets are investigated: sequential, alternative and parallel. Figure 1 shows a Petri net example with these three structures.

The method proposed in [5,6] is restricted in that transitions with marking-dependent firing rates cannot be aggregated. Hence, multi-step aggregation is impossible. This paper presents new formulae to overcome this restriction. This allows transitions to be aggregated independently of whether their firing rates are marking-dependent or fixed.

Using our formulae for the special class of *Product-Form* Petri nets [2], models with huge numbers of states are analysable. We discuss the capabilities and limitations of our closed-form aggregation method using examples throughout the paper. It is shown that, as opposed to sequential and alternative structures, there is no aggregation for parallel structures that preserves the stationary token distribution of the environment [5].

Most of the known aggregation techniques yield approximate results [8,10,12]. They are based on an iterative computation involving several aggregated nets derived from the original net. In contrast, we present a closed-form computation of the firing rates of merged transitions used in the aggregated model, thus an iterative computation is avoided. For the presented class of Petri nets the aggregation technique yields exact results.

The paper is organized as follows. Section 2 presents an introduction to GSPNs and their analysis methods. In Sections 3 and 4 the formulae for the aggregation of sequential and alternative structures, respectively are introduced. Section 5 summarises the paper and suggests areas of future work.

2   GSPNs

Assuming that the reader is familiar with the basic concepts of Petri nets [13] we briefly introduce GSPNs. GSPNs consist of places (depicted as circles) and transitions (depicted as rectangles and bars) with directed arcs connecting elements of these two disjoint sets. A number of *tokens* are associated with places (depicted as dots or numbers). If there are one or more tokens in a place, the place is *marked*. Considering all the places of the GSPN, the *marking*, M, of each place gives the current state in a distributed fashion (as opposed to Markov chains). It is exactly this feature that makes Petri nets ideally suited to modelling complex concurrent systems. Considering the model in Figure 1, the current state is described by the marking $M(\text{P2}) = N, M(\text{P5}) = 1, M(\text{P7}) = 1, M(\text{P10}) = 1$ and $M(\text{p}) = 0$ for $\text{p} \in \{\text{P1}, \text{P3}, \text{P4}, \text{P8}, \text{P9}\}$.

A transition is enabled if each of its input places contains one or more tokens. The marking in Figure 1 enables three transitions: T2, T5, T7. An enabled transition may occur. When it occurs, one token is removed from each of its input places and one token is added to each of its output places. This happens in an atomic step. In GSPNs there are two different types of transitions: timed (depicted as unfilled rectangles) and immediate (depicted as black bars). If a timed transition is enabled, it may fire after a delay governed by the exponential distribution. The firing itself does not use any time. The (probability density function of the) exponential distribution function (for an introduction see e.g. [16]) is given by:

$$f_X(x) = \begin{cases} \lambda \cdot e^{-\lambda x} & x > 0 \\ 0 & x \leq 0 \end{cases}$$

The exponential distribution is uniquely specified by the *firing rate* λ (in terms of GSPNs the reciprocal value λ^{-1}, called the *delay*, is also used).

As opposed to exponential transitions, immediate transitions do not consume any time between enabling and firing. If there is a state in which both exponential and immediate transitions are enabled, always the immediate transitions may fire and the exponential ones do not. Thus immediate transitions have priority over the exponential transitions. These two types of transitions lead to two types of states. In *vanishing* states, at least one immediate transition is enabled, while in *tangible* states only exponential transitions can fire. The probability that the modelled system is in a vanishing state is zero, while the probability that the system is in one of the tangible states is nonzero.

2.1   Reduced Reachability Graph

Figure 2 shows the reachability graph of the GSPN of Figure 1, with just one token in P1 as the given initial marking. The ellipses with solid lines represent tangible markings and the dashed ellipses stand for vanishing states. If a place name is included in an ellipse, then this means that the place has one token in it. The absence of a place indicates it has no tokens in it.

A firing probability (*weight*) is associated with each immediate transition. It is used if two or more immediate transitions are enabled at the same time. If there are two immediate transitions $t1$ and $t2$, with firing weights $w1$ and $w2$ respectively, enabled at the same time, then $t1$ fires with probability $w1/(w1 + w2)$ while $t2$ fires with the probability $w2/(w1 + w2)$.

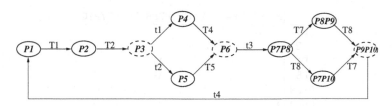

Fig. 2. The reachability graph of the GSPN of Figure 1 with only one circulating token.

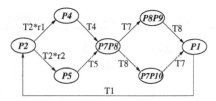

Fig. 3. The reduced reachability graph of the reachability graph of Figure 2.

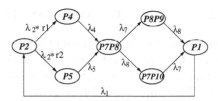

Fig. 4. The directed state graph – isomorphic to a continuous time Markov chain.

To analyse the modelled system it is necessary to generate the *reduced* reachability graph (RRG), which is obtained by removing the vanishing states from the reachability graph while preserving the firing probabilities of all enabled immediate transitions.

Figure 3 shows the reduced reachability graph of the GSPN of Figure 1 with only one circulating token. $r1$ and $r2$ represent the relative firing probabilities of transitions t1 and t2 respectively. The firing probability of $t3$ and $t4$ is each one and hence is omitted.

2.2   Generator Matrix Q

The reduced reachability graph is isomorphic to a continuous time Markov chain (CTMC) [9]. A CTMC can be described either by a directed state transition graph or by its equivalent state transition matrix **G**. Figure 4 shows the directed state graph and Figure 5 its corresponding state transition matrix.

λ_l in Figure 4 stands for the firing rate of transition Tl. The left column in Figure 5 represents the source states and the top row represents the destination states of the transitions. Hence, an entry g_{ab} in the ath row and the bth column

	P1	P2	P4	P5	P7P8	P8P9	P7P10
P1		λ_1					
P2			$\lambda_2 * r_1$	$\lambda_2 * r_2$			
P4					λ_4		
P5					λ_5		
P7P8						λ_7	λ_8
P8P9	λ_8						
P7P10	λ_7						

Fig. 5. The state transition matrix $\mathbf{G}$ – isomorphic to a continuous time Markov chain.

	P1	P2	P4	P5	P7P8	P8P9	P7P10
P1	$-\lambda_1$	λ_1					
P2		$-(\lambda_2 * r_1 + \lambda_2 * r_2)$	$\lambda_2 * r_1$	$\lambda_2 * r_2$			
P4			$-\lambda_4$		λ_4		
P5				$-\lambda_5$	λ_5		
P7P8					$-(\lambda_7 + \lambda_8)$	λ_7	λ_8
P8P9	λ_8					$-\lambda_8$	
P7P10	λ_7						$-\lambda_7$

Fig. 6. The generator matrix $\mathbf{Q}$ – derived from $\mathbf{G}$ in Figure 5.

represents the transition from state a to b. If there is no transition from state a to state b, the entry g_{ab} in $\mathbf{G}$ is zero. In Figure 5 all zeros are omitted.

The state transition matrix is used to obtain the so-called *infinitesimal generator matrix* [14] $\mathbf{Q}$ (see Figure 6), which differs from the state transition matrix only in the diagonal. Let n be the number of (tangible) states of the model, then the state transition matrix $\mathbf{G}$ and the generator matrix $\mathbf{Q}$ are of dimension $n \times n$. Then for all $a \in \{1, \ldots, n\}$, $q_{aa} = -\sum_{1 \leq b \leq n} g_{ab}$ while for all $a, b \in \{1, \ldots, n\}$ and $a \neq b$, $q_{ab} = g_{ab}$.

2.3 Stationary State Probabilities

Using $\mathbf{Q}$, the vector $\boldsymbol{\pi} = (\pi_1, \pi_2, \ldots, \pi_n)$ of state probabilities can be derived [14]. π_i is the probability that the modelled system is in state i for all $i \in \{1, \ldots, n\}$. The values for $\boldsymbol{\pi}$ are computed by $\boldsymbol{\pi}\mathbf{Q} = \mathbf{0}$ and $\sum_i \pi_i = 1$.

Accordingly, the stationary analysis of GSPNs consists of three steps:

1. generation of the reduced reachability graph
2. generation of the generator matrix Q
3. finding normalized solutions for the equation system $\boldsymbol{\pi}\mathbf{Q} = \mathbf{0}$

For our example (Figure 1) we assume that the firing rates $\lambda_1 = \frac{1}{1}$, $\lambda_2 = \frac{1}{2}$, $\lambda_4 = \frac{1}{4}$, $\lambda_5 = \frac{1}{5}$, $\lambda_7 = \frac{1}{7}$, $\lambda_8 = \frac{1}{8}$ are the firing rates associated with the exponential transitions T1, T2, T4, T5, T7, T8 respectively and the firing weights of $t1$ and $t2$ are 1 and 2 respectively. The resulting values of $\boldsymbol{\pi}$ are $\pi_{P1} = 0.052817$, $\pi_{P2} = 0.105634$, $\pi_{P4} = 0.070423$, $\pi_{P5} = 0.176056$, $\pi_{P7P8} = 0.197183$, $\pi_{P7P10} = 0.172535$, $\pi_{P8P9} = 0.225352$. That means e.g. that the probability that the system is in the state P8P9 is four times the probability that the system is in state P1.

2.4 Stationary Token Distribution

Using the state probabilities important performance measures of the model can be determined, e.g. the mean value (expected value) of the number of tokens in a place P: $E\{M(\text{P})\} = \sum_{M \in [M_0\rangle} M(\text{P}) \cdot \pi_M$ or the probability that exactly x tokens are in place P: $P\{M(\text{P}) = x\} = \sum_{M \in [M_0\rangle : M(\text{P}) = x} \pi_M$ where $[M_0\rangle$ stands for the set of markings reachable from the initial marking M_0.

Obviously, one requirement for stationary analysis of GSPNs is that the state space is finite. This requires *bounded (k-bounded)* GSPNs. A Petri net is k-bounded, if there are at most k tokens in any place of the net for every reachable state (marking). For all $x \in \{0, ..., k\}$ $P\{M(\text{P}) = x\}$ is called the *stationary token distribution* of the GSPN. In GSPNs modelling and evaluation, the state probabilities are only computed to derive the stationary token distribution. Examples of the importance of the probability that exactly x tokens are in a place are the probability that a buffer is full, a channel has a certain number of messages or the system is idle or busy.

The mean value $E\{M(\text{P})\}$ then can be computed by $E\{M(\text{P})\} = \sum_x x \cdot P\{M(\text{P}) = x\}$. Mean values are important to answer questions like: What is the mean number of items in a buffer? What is the average number of messages in a channel? On average how many processors are idle or busy?

We show the computation of the token distribution for our example (Figure 1) for place P7 only: $P\{M(\text{P7}) = 1\} = \pi_{\text{P7P8}} + \pi_{\text{P7P10}} = 0.369718$ while $P\{M(\text{P7}) = 0\} = 1 - P\{M(\text{P7}) = 1\} = 1 - (\pi_{\text{P7P8}} + \pi_{\text{P7P10}}) = 0.630282$.

As described, the stationary analysis of GSPNs is a state space based method. The size of the state space depends on the number of places and the initial numbers of tokens in the GSPN and may grow exponentially. The size of the state space and thus the dimension of the generator matrix is the main limitation concerning numerical analysis of GSPNs. Realistic models with more than a million states become intractable.

We can reduce the size of the state space by aggregating parts of the GSPN [6,8,10,12]. Our new aggregation method is the subject of the following sections.

3 Aggregation of Sequential Structures

A Petri net model consists of a number of basic structures. The three most common ones are displayed in Figure 1. Our aggregation method transforms these simple elementary structures into one single transition each preserving the stochastic behaviour of the structure's environment.

3.1 General Considerations

This section describes the aggregation of a structure in which transitions and places are arranged sequentially. The only known approach (for an introduction see e.g. [1,16]) to aggregate a simple sequential structure into a single transition is to associate a special phase-type distribution of order n (if n sequentially ordered exponential transitions are aggregated) with the aggregated transition. If all exponential transitions have identical firing rates, the Erlang-n distribution becomes applicable [16]. However, the derived stochastic Petri net does not belong to the class of GSPNs and thus does not contribute to reducing the size of the state space nor to providing easier to handle analysis algorithms. Hence, we define the following two requirements for our aggregation method:

- The aggregation of parts of a GSPN leads to another GSPN.
- The term 'stochastic equivalent behaviour' is relaxed in the sense that the stationary token distribution in places of the non-aggregated environment is preserved by aggregation.

Note that the stochastic equivalence considered here is restricted to the token distribution of the remaining non-aggregated environment. Higher moments like variance of the dwelling times of single tokens in the environment are different in the original and in the aggregated model. However, the main important performance measures of investigated systems like throughput, mean values, or probabilities of buffer fill levels are computable using the stationary token distribution.

To illustrate the main concept let us consider a very simple GSPN model shown in Figure 7.

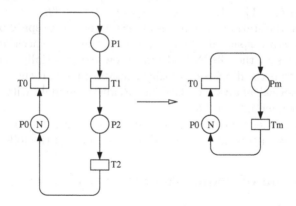

Fig. 7. Aggregation of a sequence: reference model.

In Figure 7, the original model is displayed on the left. Observing the above requirements, the aggregation of T1, P1 and T2 into a single transition Tm must ensure that the firing time is exponentially distributed and that the stationary token distribution is preserved in place P0. Additionally, the firing rate of Tm must be independent of the environment T0. To satisfy all these requirements so-called *marking-dependent* firing rates [3] are associated with Tm. That means that the firing rate of the exponential transition Tm depends on the number of tokens ($M(\text{Pm})$) in the place Pm in the preset of the transition Tm.

3.2   Formulae for the Firing Rate of the Aggregated Transition

To present the general idea of deriving the formula for the computation of λ_m the state transition graphs of the original model (left side) and of the aggregated one (right side) are displayed in Figure 8.

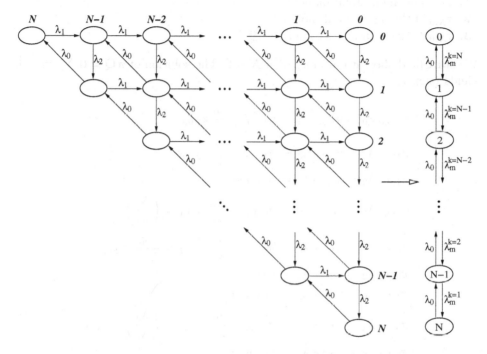

Fig. 8. State transition graphs of the reference model and its aggregation.

The top row above the state transition graph of the original model indicates the number of tokens in place P1 and the right column represents the number of tokens in P0. The states of the aggregated model's state transition graph are labelled with the number of tokens in P0. $\lambda_m^{k=N}$ stands for the marking-dependent firing rate λ_m of transition Tm if there are N tokens in Pm (note the place-invariant $M(\text{P0}) + M(\text{Pm}) = N$ of the aggregated model and the labelling for P0 in the state transition graph). Each original state in the state transition graph is unique identified by its place in the state transition graph. If it is in the rth row in the sth column, then the state is described by the marking in which $M(\text{P0}) = r$ and $M(\text{P1}) = s$. From the place-invariant $M(\text{P0}) + M(\text{P1}) + M(\text{P2}) = N$ follows that then $M(\text{P2}) = N - r - s$ where $r, s \geq 0, r + s \leq N$. Stationary probabilities are denoted by $\pi_{r,N-r}$ for the aggregated model and by $\pi_{r,s,N-r-s}$ for the original model. Hence e.g. $\pi_{1,2,3}$ is the probability that the original model of Figure 7 is in the state in which exactly one token is in place P0, two tokens are in P1 and three tokens are in P2. $\pi_{1,2}$ describe the probability that the aggregated model is in a state in which there is one token in P0 and there are two tokens in Pm.

To derive the formula for λ_m we compute $\pi_{N,0,0}$ and $\pi_{N,0}$ symbolic, using the system of linear equations $\boldsymbol{\pi Q} = \mathbf{0}, \sum_i \pi_i = 1$. After obtaining $\pi_{N,0,0}$ and $\pi_{N,0}$ we equate them in order to derive the marking-dependent rates of the aggregated transition Tm.

1. $\pi_{N,0,0}$ of the original model
2. $\pi_{N,0}$ of the aggregated model
3. $\pi_{N,0,0} = \pi_{N,0}$ in order to derive $\lambda_m^{k=N}$.

We start (and show it only for) with $N = 2$. The solution of $\boldsymbol{\pi Q} = \mathbf{0}, \sum_i \pi_i = 1$ yields (step 1):

$$\pi_{2,0,0}\,\lambda_0 = \pi_{1,0,1}\,\lambda_2 \Rightarrow \pi_{1,0,1} = \frac{\lambda_0}{\lambda_2}\,\pi_{2,0,0}$$

$$\pi_{1,1,0}\,\lambda_1 = \pi_{2,0,0}\,\lambda_0 \Rightarrow \pi_{1,1,0} = \frac{\lambda_0}{\lambda_1}\,\pi_{2,0,0}$$

$$\pi_{1,0,1}\,\lambda_2 = \pi_{1,1,0}\,\lambda_1 \Rightarrow \text{(not used)}$$

$$\pi_{1,0,1}\,\lambda_0 = \pi_{0,0,2}\,\lambda_2 \Rightarrow \pi_{0,0,2} = \frac{\lambda_0}{\lambda_2}\,\pi_{1,0,1} = \left(\frac{\lambda_0}{\lambda_2}\right)^2 \pi_{2,0,0}$$

$$\pi_{0,1,1}\,\lambda_1 = \pi_{1,0,1}\,\lambda_0 \Rightarrow \pi_{0,1,1} = \frac{\lambda_0}{\lambda_1}\,\pi_{1,0,1} = \frac{\lambda_0^2}{\lambda_1\lambda_2}\,\pi_{2,0,0}$$

$$\pi_{0,0,2}\,\lambda_2 = \pi_{0,1,1}\,\lambda_1 \Rightarrow \text{(not used)}$$

$$\pi_{1,1,0}\,\lambda_0 = \pi_{0,1,1}\,\lambda_2 \Rightarrow \text{(not used)}$$

$$\pi_{0,2,0}\,\lambda_1 = \pi_{1,1,0}\,\lambda_0 \Rightarrow \pi_{0,2,0} = \frac{\lambda_0}{\lambda_1}\,\pi_{1,1,0} = \left(\frac{\lambda_0}{\lambda_1}\right)^2 \pi_{2,0,0}$$

$$\pi_{0,1,1}\,\lambda_2 = \pi_{0,2,0}\,\lambda_1 \Rightarrow \text{(not used)}$$

Normalization yields:

$$1 = \sum_{r=0}^{2}\sum_{s=0}^{2-r} \pi_{r,s,2-r-s} = \pi_{2,0,0}\left(1 + \frac{\lambda_0}{\lambda_2} + \frac{\lambda_0}{\lambda_1} + \left(\frac{\lambda_0}{\lambda_2}\right)^2 + \frac{\lambda_0^2}{\lambda_1\lambda_2} + \left(\frac{\lambda_0}{\lambda_1}\right)^2\right)$$

$$\Rightarrow \quad \pi_{2,0,0} = \frac{1}{1 + \lambda_0\left(\frac{1}{\lambda_1} + \frac{1}{\lambda_2}\right) + \lambda_0^2\left(\frac{1}{\lambda_1^2} + \frac{1}{\lambda_1\lambda_2} + \frac{1}{\lambda_2^2}\right)}$$

which is the probability $\pi_{2,0,0}$ that exactly two tokens are in place P0 of the original reference model.

The (local balance) equations of the corresponding aggregated GSPN are given by (step 2):

$$\pi_{2,0}\,\lambda_0 = \pi_{1,1}\,\lambda_m^{k=1} \Rightarrow \pi_{1,1} = \frac{\lambda_0}{\lambda_m^{k=1}}\,\pi_{2,0}$$

$$\pi_{1,1}\,\lambda_0 = \pi_{0,2}\,\lambda_m^{k=2} \Rightarrow \pi_{0,2} = \frac{\lambda_0}{\lambda_m^{k=2}}\,\pi_{1,1} = \frac{\lambda_0^2}{\lambda_m^{k=1}\lambda_m^{k=2}}\,\pi_{2,0}$$

With normalization:

$$1 = \sum_{r=0}^{2} \pi_{r,2-r} = \pi_{2,0}\left(1 + \frac{\lambda_0}{\lambda_m^{k=1}} + \frac{\lambda_0^2}{\lambda_m^{k=1}\lambda_m^{k=2}}\right)$$

$$\Rightarrow \pi_{2,0} = \frac{1}{1 + \lambda_0 \frac{1}{\lambda_m^{k=1}} + \lambda_0^2 \frac{1}{\lambda_m^{k=1}\lambda_m^{k=2}}} .$$

Equating $\pi_{2,0,0}$ to $\pi_{2,0}$ (step 3) we obtain:

$$(\pi_{2,0,0} = \pi_{2,0})$$

$$1 + \lambda_0\left(\frac{1}{\lambda_1} + \frac{1}{\lambda_2}\right) + \lambda_0^2\left(\frac{1}{\lambda_1^2} + \frac{1}{\lambda_1\lambda_2} + \frac{1}{\lambda_2^2}\right) = 1 + \lambda_0\frac{1}{\lambda_m^{k=1}} + \lambda_0^2\frac{1}{\lambda_m^{k=1}\lambda_m^{k=2}} \quad (1)$$

$$\Rightarrow \quad \lambda_m^{k=1} = \frac{1}{\frac{1}{\lambda_1} + \frac{1}{\lambda_2}} = \lambda_1\frac{1}{1 + \frac{\lambda_1}{\lambda_2}}$$

$$\Rightarrow \quad \lambda_m^{k=2} = \frac{1}{\lambda_m^{k=1}\left(\frac{1}{\lambda_1^2} + \frac{1}{\lambda_1\lambda_2} + \frac{1}{\lambda_2^2}\right)} = \frac{\frac{1}{\lambda_1} + \frac{1}{\lambda_2}}{\frac{1}{\lambda_1^2} + \frac{1}{\lambda_1\lambda_2} + \frac{1}{\lambda_2^2}} = \lambda_1\frac{1 + \frac{\lambda_1}{\lambda_2}}{1 + \frac{\lambda_1}{\lambda_2} + \left(\frac{\lambda_1}{\lambda_2}\right)^2}$$

because Equation (1) is true for all $\lambda_0 \geq 0$ if the coefficients of the quadratic polynomials are equal.

Note that $\lambda_m^{k=N}$ is independent of λ_0 (from the aggregation environment) for the reference model. Moreover, the induction for arbitrary N yields [5]:

$$\lambda_m^{k=3} = \lambda_1\frac{1 + \frac{\lambda_1}{\lambda_2} + \left(\frac{\lambda_1}{\lambda_2}\right)^2}{1 + \frac{\lambda_1}{\lambda_2} + \left(\frac{\lambda_1}{\lambda_2}\right)^2 + \left(\frac{\lambda_1}{\lambda_2}\right)^3} = \frac{1}{\lambda_m^{k=1}\lambda_m^{k=2}\left(\frac{1}{\lambda_1^3} + \frac{1}{\lambda_1^2\lambda_2} + \frac{1}{\lambda_1\lambda_2^2} + \frac{1}{\lambda_2^3}\right)}$$

$$\vdots$$

$$\lambda_m^{k=x} = \lambda_1\frac{\sum_{i=0}^{x-1}\left(\frac{\lambda_1}{\lambda_2}\right)^i}{\sum_{i=0}^{x}\left(\frac{\lambda_1}{\lambda_2}\right)^i} = \frac{\displaystyle\sum_{\substack{i,j\geq 0 \\ i+j=x-1}}\left(\frac{1}{\lambda_1}\right)^i\left(\frac{1}{\lambda_2}\right)^j}{\displaystyle\sum_{\substack{i,j\geq 0 \\ i+j=x}}\left(\frac{1}{\lambda_1}\right)^i\left(\frac{1}{\lambda_2}\right)^j} \quad (2)$$

A further generalization [5] of that formula is the aggregation of not only two but n sequential ordered transitions:

$$\lambda_m^{k=x} = \frac{\displaystyle\sum_{\substack{i_1,i_2,...,i_n\geq 0 \\ i_1+i_2+...+i_n=x-1}}\frac{1}{\lambda_1^{i_1}\lambda_2^{i_2}\ldots\lambda_n^{i_n}}}{\displaystyle\sum_{\substack{i_1,i_2,...,i_n\geq 0 \\ i_1+i_2+...+i_n=x}}\frac{1}{\lambda_1^{i_1}\lambda_2^{i_2}\ldots\lambda_n^{i_n}}} \quad (3)$$

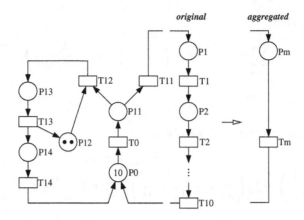

Fig. 9. Sequence aggregation in a complex environment.

3.3 Example of Aggregating Sequential Transitions with Fixed Firing Rates

Figure 9 shows a simple manufacturing system with a sequential assembly line at the right side of the original model. The sequence consists of 10 exponential transitions T1... T10, associated with a firing rate $\lambda_l = 1/l$ for $l \in \{1, \ldots, 10\}$. These 10 transitions are aggregated into one single transition Tm in the aggregated model. The transition T0 models the delivery of finished work pieces. Hence, we are interested in the throughput of transition T0 ($TP = E\{M(\text{P0})\} \cdot \lambda_0$) where $\lambda_0 = 1/5$ is the firing rate of transition T0 and in the probability that there is no token in P0 ($P\{M(\text{P0}) = 0\}$) to determine the workload of the system.

Table 1 shows the marking-dependent firing rates $\lambda_m^{k=x}$ and their reciprocal values (delays) of the aggregated transition Tm computed using Equation (3). x stands for the number of tokens in Pm.

Table 1. Values of rates $\lambda_m^{k=x}$/mean delays $\frac{1}{\lambda_m^{k=x}}$ in the example of Figure 9.

x	$\lambda_m^{k=x}$	$\frac{1}{\lambda_m^{k=x}}$	x	$\lambda_m^{k=x}$	$\frac{1}{\lambda_m^{k=x}}$
1	0.01818182	55	6	0.06535393	15.30129870
2	0.03225807	31	7	0.07024348	14.23619670
3	0.04335664	23.06451613	8	0.07432426	13.45455691
4	0.05224164	19.14181818	9	0.07775486	12.86093251
5	0.05944664	16.82180851	10	0.08065740	12.39811804

The numerical analysis of the model for $N = 10$ takes almost 4 days (323.278 sec) on a Pentium-III PC with 512 MB main memory using the software tool TimeNET [17]. Achieving identical results, the performance evaluation of the aggregated model takes only 0.683 sec! An analysis of the original model for $N > 10$ is impossible, because the number of states for $N = 10$ is already

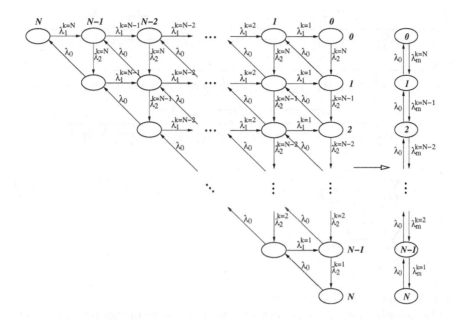

Fig. 10. State transition graphs of the reference model and its aggregation (marking-dependent).

1.066.546. With firing rates set equal to $\frac{1}{5}$ for each of the transitions T11...T14, the throughput of transition T0 is 0.31 and the probability that no token is in place P0 is 0.3399.

3.4   Aggregation of Sequential Marking-Dependent Transitions

If different structures of a GSPN are aggregated in a first step using the formulae to compute marking-dependent firing rates from transitions with a fixed firing rate it is often desirable to aggregate the model further. However, a further aggregation was not possible before, because there were no formulae to handle the aggregation of transitions with marking-dependent firing rates. In this section we present newly developed formulae to close this gap.

Let us consider Figure 7 again and assume, that T1 and T2 have associated marking-dependent firing rates $\lambda_1^{k=x}$ and $\lambda_2^{k=y}$ where $x, y \in \{1, 2, \dots N\}$. Applying the same derivation of the formula as above (see Figure 10) the marking-dependent firing rates for Tm are:

$$\lambda_m^{k=1} = \frac{1}{\frac{1}{\lambda_1^{k=1}} + \frac{1}{\lambda_2^{k=1}}}$$

$$\lambda_m^{k=2} = \frac{1}{\lambda_m^{k=1}\left(\frac{1}{\lambda_1^{k=1}\lambda_1^{k=2}} + \frac{1}{\lambda_1^{k=1}\lambda_2^{k=1}} + \frac{1}{\lambda_2^{k=1}\lambda_2^{k=2}}\right)}$$

$$= \frac{\dfrac{1}{\lambda_m^{k=1}}}{\dfrac{1}{\lambda_1^{k=1}\lambda_1^{k=2}} + \dfrac{1}{\lambda_1^{k=1}\lambda_2^{k=1}} + \dfrac{1}{\lambda_2^{k=1}\lambda_2^{k=2}}} = \frac{\dfrac{1}{\lambda_1^{k=1}} + \dfrac{1}{\lambda_2^{k=1}}}{\dfrac{1}{\lambda_1^{k=1}\lambda_1^{k=2}} + \dfrac{1}{\lambda_1^{k=1}\lambda_2^{k=1}} + \dfrac{1}{\lambda_2^{k=1}\lambda_2^{k=2}}}$$

$$\lambda_m^{k=3} = \frac{1}{\lambda_m^{k=1}\lambda_m^{k=2}\left(\dfrac{1}{\lambda_1^{k=1}\lambda_1^{k=2}\lambda_1^{k=3}} + \dfrac{1}{\lambda_1^{k=1}\lambda_1^{k=2}\lambda_2^{k=1}} + \dfrac{1}{\lambda_1^{k=1}\lambda_2^{k=1}\lambda_2^{k=2}} + \dfrac{1}{\lambda_2^{k=1}\lambda_2^{k=2}\lambda_2^{k=3}} \right)}$$

$$= \frac{\dfrac{1}{\lambda_1^{k=1}\lambda_1^{k=2}} + \dfrac{1}{\lambda_1^{k=1}\lambda_2^{k=1}} + \dfrac{1}{\lambda_2^{k=1}\lambda_2^{k=2}}}{\dfrac{1}{\lambda_1^{k=1}\lambda_1^{k=2}\lambda_1^{k=3}} + \dfrac{1}{\lambda_1^{k=1}\lambda_1^{k=2}\lambda_2^{k=1}} + \dfrac{1}{\lambda_1^{k=1}\lambda_2^{k=1}\lambda_2^{k=2}} + \dfrac{1}{\lambda_2^{k=1}\lambda_2^{k=2}\lambda_2^{k=3}}}$$

$$\vdots$$

$$\lambda_m^{k=x} = \frac{\displaystyle\sum_{\substack{i,j\geq 0 \\ i+j=x-1}} \dfrac{1}{\lambda_1^{\to i}\lambda_2^{\to j}}}{\displaystyle\sum_{\substack{i,j\geq 0 \\ i+j=x}} \dfrac{1}{\lambda_1^{\to i}\lambda_2^{\to j}}}$$

where $\lambda^{\to i}$ means $\lambda^{k=1}\lambda^{k=2}\ldots\lambda^{k=i}$.

The following formula generalises the formula above in that not only two but n sequentially ordered transitions with marking-dependent firing rates can be aggregated.

$$\lambda_m^{k=x}(\lambda_1,\lambda_2) = \frac{\displaystyle\sum_{\substack{i_1,i_2\geq 0 \\ i_1+i_2=x-1}} \dfrac{1}{\lambda_1^{\to i_1}\lambda_2^{\to i_2}}}{\displaystyle\sum_{\substack{i_1,i_2\geq 0 \\ i_1+i_2=x}} \dfrac{1}{\lambda_1^{\to i_1}\lambda_2^{\to i_2}}}$$

$$\lambda_m^{k=x}(\lambda_1,\lambda_2,\lambda_3) = \frac{\displaystyle\sum_{\substack{i_1,i_2,i_3\geq 0 \\ i_1+i_2+i_3=x-1}} \dfrac{1}{\lambda_1^{\to i_1}\lambda_2^{\to i_2}\lambda_3^{\to i_3}}}{\displaystyle\sum_{\substack{i_1,i_2,i_3\geq 0 \\ i_1+i_2+i_3=x}} \dfrac{1}{\lambda_1^{\to i_1}\lambda_2^{\to i_2}\lambda_3^{\to i_3}}}$$

$$\vdots$$

$$\lambda_m^{k=x}(\lambda_1,\lambda_2,\ldots,\lambda_n) = \frac{\displaystyle\sum_{\substack{i_1,i_2,\ldots,i_n\geq 0 \\ i_1+i_2+\ldots+i_n=x-1}} \dfrac{1}{\lambda_1^{\to i_1}\lambda_2^{\to i_2}\ldots\lambda_n^{\to i_n}}}{\displaystyle\sum_{\substack{i_1,i_2,\ldots,i_n\geq 0 \\ i_1+i_2+\ldots+i_3=x}} \dfrac{1}{\lambda_1^{\to i_1}\lambda_2^{\to i_2}\ldots\lambda_n^{\to i_n}}} \qquad (4)$$

where $\lambda^{\to i}$ means $\lambda^{k=1}\lambda^{k=2}\ldots\lambda^{k=i}$.

Please note the strong similarity to Equation (3). Hence, if a sequence is aggregated containing both transitions with fixed and transitions with marking-

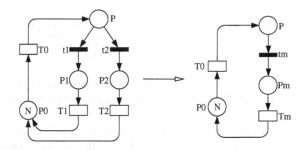

Fig. 11. Aggregation of an alternative structure: reference model.

dependent rates, Equation (4) is used where $\lambda^{\to i}$ means $\lambda^{k=1}\lambda^{k=2}\ldots\lambda^{k=i}$ for the marking-dependent rates and $\lambda^{\to i}$ means λ^i for the fixed firing rates.

We show an example that applies formula (4) at the end of the next section.

4   Aggregation of Alternative Structures

In the first stochastic Petri net approaches [11,15] there were no immediate transitions. However, it turned out that conflict situations could not be handled adequately with timed transitions. Therefore immediate transitions, with associated weights, were introduced to handle a conflict situation in an appropriate way. Figure 11 shows such a model of a stochastic decision. If P is marked, either t1 or t2 fires. Assume both transitions are associated with weights w_1 and w_2 respectively, t1 fires with probability $w_1/(w_1+w_2)$ while t2 has the firing probability $w_2/(w_1+w_2)$ (see also Section 2). Figure 11 shows the simplest alternative structure of a GSPN, which we use as a reference model for the aggregation of alternative structures. Note that the immediate transition on the right-hand side aggregated model is redundant, as the model has the same behaviour without P and tm. However, to make the formula we are presenting applicable in a general environment, we also observe the weight of the aggregated immediate transitions. Although the original model in Figure 11 has only two alternatives ($n = 2$) again we are interested in a general formula for both an arbitrary n and an arbitrary number N of circulating tokens.

4.1   Formulae for the Firing Rate of the Aggregated Transition

Please recall that we are looking for a formula which keeps the token distribution for the remaining environment (in the reference model: P0) unchanged. As discussed, that requirement is weaker than 'stochastic equivalence', because we do not preserve higher moments. However, the only known distribution of Tm for which an aggregation is applicable is the hyperexponential distribution, but only for the case $N = 1$ [1,16].

$$F_{\text{hyp}}(t) = \sum_{i=1}^{n} \frac{w_i}{\sum_{i=1}^{n} w_i} \left(1 - e^{-\lambda_i t}\right) = 1 - \frac{1}{\sum_{i=1}^{n} w_i} \sum_{i=1}^{n} \left(w_i e^{-\lambda_i t}\right)$$

with expectation $1/\sum_{i=1}^{n} w_i \cdot \left(\sum_{i=1}^{n} w_i/\lambda_i\right)$. Parameter w_i is the weight of immediate transition `ti`, while λ_i is the rate of exponential transition `Ti` for all $i \in \{1, \ldots, n\}$.

Due to the space limitations and because the way of obtaining the formulae is as same as the one presented before, we do not derive the formulae in detail. We note that there is a strong similarity to Equation (2) for sequentially ordered transitions (λ_l replaced by $\lambda_l \frac{w_1 + w_2}{w_l}$ for $l = 1, 2$):

$$\lambda_m^{k=x} = \frac{w_1 + w_2}{w_1} \lambda_1 \frac{\displaystyle\sum_{i=0}^{x-1} \left(\frac{\lambda_1}{\lambda_2} \frac{w_2}{w_1}\right)^i}{\displaystyle\sum_{i=0}^{x} \left(\frac{\lambda_1}{\lambda_2} \frac{w_2}{w_1}\right)^i} = \frac{\displaystyle\sum_{\substack{i,j \geq 0 \\ i+j=x-1}} \left(\frac{w_1}{\lambda_1}\right)^i \left(\frac{w_2}{\lambda_2}\right)^j}{\displaystyle\sum_{\substack{i,j \geq 0 \\ i+j=x}} \left(\frac{w_1}{\lambda_1}\right)^i \left(\frac{w_2}{\lambda_2}\right)^j} \cdot (w_1 + w_2)$$

As mentioned above, in the reference model of Figure 11, the immediate transition is redundant, but for the required case in conflict settings in more complex environments a computation of the weight w_m of the transition `tm` is given:

$$w_m = \sum_{i=1}^{n} w_i$$

A further generalization concerning the number of alternatives, n, gives the following formula:

$$\lambda_m^{k=x} = \frac{\displaystyle\sum_{\substack{i_1,i_2,\ldots,i_n \geq 0 \\ i_1+i_2+\ldots+i_n=x-1}} \left(\frac{w_1}{\lambda_1}\right)^{i_1} \left(\frac{w_2}{\lambda_2}\right)^{i_2} \cdots \left(\frac{w_n}{\lambda_n}\right)^{i_n}}{\displaystyle\sum_{\substack{i_1,i_2,\ldots,i_n \geq 0 \\ i_1+i_2+\ldots+i_n=x}} \left(\frac{w_1}{\lambda_1}\right)^{i_1} \left(\frac{w_2}{\lambda_2}\right)^{i_2} \cdots \left(\frac{w_n}{\lambda_n}\right)^{i_n}} \cdot \sum_{i=1}^{n} w_i$$

4.2 Aggregation of Alternative Marking-Dependent Transitions

In the same way that there was no formula for sequentially ordered transitions, there was no formula to aggregate transitions with marking-dependent firing rates for alternatives before. Bridging that gap, now it is possible for instance to aggregate sequential or alternative ordered structures of sequences and alternatives by aggregating the sequences and alternatives first, and then aggregating the marking-dependent transitions. In the example at the end of this section this method is presented using the following formula for the aggregation of n alternative ordered transitions T1, T2, ... Tn with marking-dependent firing rates

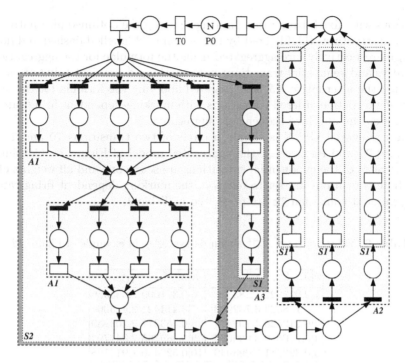

Fig. 12. Successive aggregation – original model.

$\lambda_1^{k=x}, \lambda_2^{k=x}, \ldots, \lambda_n^{k=x}$, respectively with up to N tokens in the preset of the transitions, each.

$$
\lambda_m^{k=x} = \frac{\displaystyle\sum_{\substack{i_1,i_2,\ldots,i_n \geq 0 \\ i_1+i_2+\ldots+i_n=x-1}} \left(\frac{w_1}{\lambda_1}\right)^{\to i_1} \left(\frac{w_2}{\lambda_2}\right)^{\to i_2} \cdots \left(\frac{w_n}{\lambda_n}\right)^{\to i_n}}{\displaystyle\sum_{\substack{i_1,i_2,\ldots,i_n \geq 0 \\ i_1+i_2+\ldots+i_n=x}} \left(\frac{w_1}{\lambda_1}\right)^{\to i_1} \left(\frac{w_2}{\lambda_2}\right)^{\to i_2} \cdots \left(\frac{w_n}{\lambda_n}\right)^{\to i_n}} \cdot \sum_{i=1}^{n} w_i
$$

where $\left(\dfrac{w_i}{\lambda_i}\right)^{\to j}$ means $\dfrac{w_i^j}{\lambda_i^{k=1}\lambda_i^{k=2}\ldots\lambda_i^{k=j}}$.

4.3   Example of Successive Aggregating Transitions

In this section we apply our formulae successively. Figure 12 shows a GSPN model of a manufacturing system containing different assembly lines, test stations, repair stations etc. The model consists of several sequential and alternative structures. The inner basic structures are aggregated first. The dashed rectangles labelled by *A1* highlight the inner alternatives while the dotted rectangles labelled with *S1* cover the inner sequences. These structures are aggregated in the first step using the formulae to aggregate sequential and alternative ordered transitions with fixed firing rates. In a second step the obtained alternative and sequential structures (highlighted by the $A2$ and $S2$ labelled dashed and dotted rectangles respectively) are aggregated using the formulae for the aggregation of alternative and sequential transitions with marking-dependent firing rates. In a third step the alternative $A3$ is aggregated applying the formula for the aggregation of alternative ordered transitions with marking-dependent firing rates. In the last step the obtained sequence is aggregated.

The aggregated GSPN is simply a circle of two transitions T0 and Tm and two places P0 and Pm (see e.g. the aggregated model of Figure 7). Considering all firing rates of the exponential transitions are set to one and all weights of the immediate transitions are set to one too, the marking-dependent firing rates of the aggregated transition Tm are presented in Table 2.

Table 2. Values of rates $\lambda_m^{k=x}$/mean delays $\frac{1}{\lambda_m^{k=x}}$ in example of Figure 12.

x	$\lambda_m^{k=x}$	$\frac{1}{\lambda_m^{k=x}}$	x	$\lambda_m^{k=x}$	$\frac{1}{\lambda_m^{k=x}}$
1	0.077922	12.833327	6	0.371009	2.695356
2	0.148523	6.732953	7	0.414421	2.413006
3	0.212520	4.705434	8	0.453877	2.203239
4	0.270556	3.696086	9	0.489765	2.041794
5	0.323211	3.093949	10	0.522436	1.914108

Table 3 shows a comparison both of the number of states and the duration of computation of the entire numerical analysis of the original and the aggregated model for a variable number N of initial tokens in P0. For $N > 5$ an analysis of the original model is impossible because the state space is too large. For $N > 6$ even the state space is too large to generate the reachability graph of the model. Opposed to the original model, the number of states of the aggregated model is only $N + 1$. Note the dramatic speedup of processing times with no loss in accuracy.

The simple structure of the aggregated model allows a closed-form solution to be obtained without generating the state space of the model. The stationary state probabilities of the aggregated model (see e.g. right-hand side of Figure 7) are computed by

$$\pi_{r,N-r} = \frac{\frac{\Pi_{j=1}^{r} \lambda_m^{k=N-j+1}}{\lambda_0^r}}{\sum_{l=0}^{N} \frac{\Pi_{j=1}^{l} \lambda_m^{k=N-j+1}}{\lambda_0^l}}$$

where $\pi_{r,N-r}$ describes the probability of being in a state in which r tokens are in P0 and $N - r$ are in Pm. Hence, for $N = 3$, the probability that no token is in P0 is computed by

$$\pi_{0,3} = \frac{1}{1 + \frac{\lambda_m^{k=3}}{\lambda_0} + \frac{\lambda_m^{k=3}}{\lambda_0}\frac{\lambda_m^{k=2}}{\lambda_0} + \frac{\lambda_m^{k=3}}{\lambda_0}\frac{\lambda_m^{k=2}}{\lambda_0}\frac{\lambda_m^{k=1}}{\lambda_0}} = 0.802217$$

Table 3. Comparison performance evaluation of original and aggregated model (Figure 12).

N	number of states of original model	duration of computation	number of states of aggregated model	duration of computation
1	32	0.15 sec	2	0.007 sec
2	528	0.36 sec	3	0.007 sec
3	5.984	259.1 sec	4	0.007 sec
4	52.360	≈ 13 hours	5	0.007 sec
5	376.992	≈ 3.5 days	6	0.008 sec
6	2.324.784	-	7	0.008 sec
7	≈ 12.500.000	-	8	0.008 sec
8	≈ 72.000.000	-	9	0.009 sec
9	≈ 350.000.000	-	10	0.009 sec
10	≈ 1.600.000.000	-	11	0.010 sec

which is exactly the same result as achieved by analysis of the original model or of the aggregated model.

The example shows that with the new formulae we are able to handle very large and complex GSPNs in an exact way. The computation of the marking-dependent rates requires only simple additions and multiplications, so that computational overhead is low. As shown, for models containing only sequences and alternatives, the application of the new formulae lead to aggregated models, that are so simple, that even a closed-form computation of the stationary state distribution is possible.

5 Conclusions

Aggregation is one of the main methods to overcome the state space explosion problem. Net-level based aggregation can allow the state space of the original model to be reduced drastically. The most important known aggregation methods either obtain approximate results or are based on iterative algorithms with large computational overhead. This paper presents formulae to aggregate basic structures of Petri nets into single transitions, which preserve the stationary token distribution of the non-aggregated environment. The derived aggregated Petri nets are still GSPNs and therefore numerical analysis techniques are applicable. When a GSPN is reduced, sequential and alternative subnets are replaced by transitions that have marking-dependent firing rates. Additionally, we present newly developed formulae that aggregate structures consisting of transitions with marking-dependent firing rates. Hence, successive or multi-step aggregation becomes possible. The inner basic structures are aggregated first and step-by-step the outer structures are aggregated. Using this technique we are able to aggregate large complex models into models for which either closed-form computation of the stationary state distribution is possible, without generating the state space, or the state space is drastically reduced.

Our aggregation techniques not only reveal exact quantitative properties related to stationary state distributions, but also can be used efficiently in a modular and non-iterative fashion.

The power of the aggregation method presented in this paper is shown by several examples using a prototype implementation of the technique in combination with the stochastic Petri net modelling and analysis tool, TimeNET [17].

There are no formulae applicable for parallel structures that preserve the stationary token distribution exactly [5]. Nevertheless, in many cases, parallel structures can be retained with still a huge decrease in the size of the state space or an approximate aggregation of parallel structures can be used with reasonable results [5].

As discussed, the formulae yield exact results for stationary token distributions for the class of so-called Product-Form Petri nets [4]. An unproven, but experimentally validated condition related to independent subnets [2] characterises the environments in which the aggregation steps can be applied. An important future task is to find net-level based properties to identify the Petri net class for which the aggregation yields exact results.

Acknowledgements

The authors would like to thank Guy Gallasch of the Computer Systems Engineering Centre for finding and implementing a recursive algorithm for the formulae presented in this paper and Armin Heindl of the Technische Universität Berlin for his fruitful comments. Many thanks also to the anonymous reviewers whose constructive criticisms have helped to improve this paper.

References

1. G. Bolch, S. Greiner, H. de Meer, and K. Trivedi. *Queueing Networks and Markov Chains. Modeling and Performance Evaluation with Computer Science Applications.* John Wiley & Sons, 1998.
2. R. Boucherie. A characterization of independence for competing Markov chains with applications to stochastic Petri nets. *IEEE Transactions on Software Engineering*, 20(7):536–544, 1994.
3. M. Curiel and R. Puigjaner. Using load-dependent servers to reduce the complexity of large client-server simulation models. In *Performance Engineering: State of the Art and Current Trends*, LNCS 2047, pages 131–147. Springer Verlag, 2001.
4. S. Donatelli and M. Sereno. On the product-form solution for stochastic Petri nets. In *Proc. 13th Int. Conf. on Application and Theory of Petri Nets*, pages 154–172, 1992.
5. J. Freiheit. *Matrizen- und zustandsraumreduzierende Verfahren zur Leistungsbewertung großer stochastischer Petrinetze.* PhD thesis, TU Berlin, June 2002.
6. J. Freiheit and A. Heindl. Novel formulae for GSPN aggregation. In *The Tenth IEEE/ACM International Symposium on Modeling, Analysis and Simulation of Computer and Telecommunication Systems (MASCOTS 2002)*, pages 209–216, Fort Worth, Texas, 2002.

7. W. Henderson and D. Lucic. Exact results in the aggregation and disaggregation of stochastic Petri nets. In *Proc. 4th Int. Workshop on Petri Nets and Performance Models*, pages 166–175, Melbourne, Australia, 1991.

8. H. Jungnitz, B. Sánchez, and M. Silva. Response time approximation for the performance analysis of manufacturing systems modeled with stochastic marked graphs. In *Proc. Int. Conf. on Robotics and Automation*, pages 1000–1005, Nice, 1992.

9. M. Ajmone Marsan, G. Balbo, G. Conte, S. Donatelli, and G. Franceschinis. *Modelling with Generalized Stochastic Petri Nets*. John Wiley and Sons, 1995.

10. C. Murray Woodside and Yao Li. Performance Petri net analysis of communications protocol software by delay-equivalent aggregation. In *Proc. 4th Int. Workshop on Petri Nets and Performance Models*, pages 64–73, Melbourne, Australia, 1991.

11. S. Natkin. *Les Reseaux de Petri Stochastiques et leur Application a L'evaluation des Systémes Informatiques*. Dissertation, Conservatoire National des Arts et Metiers (CNAM), Paris, 1980.

12. C. J. Pérez-Jiménez and J. Campos. On state space decomposition for the numerical analysis of stochastic Petri nets. In *Proceedings of the 8th International Workshop on Petri Nets and Performance Models*, pages 32–41, Zaragoza, Spain, September 1999.

13. W. Reisig. Petri nets. *EATCS Monographs on Theoretical Computer Science*, 4, 1985.

14. W.J. Stewart. *Introduction to the numerical solution of Markov chains*. Princeton University Press, 1994.

15. F.J.W. Symons. *Modeling and analysis of communication protocols using numerical Petri nets*. Dissertation, University of Essex, 1978.

16. K.S. Trivedi. *Probability and Statistics with Reliability, Queueing, and Computer Science Applications*. Prentice-Hall, Inc., 1982.

17. A. Zimmermann, J. Freiheit, R. German, and G. Hommel. Petri net modelling and performability evaluation with TimeNET 3.0. In *Proc. 11th Int. Conf. on Modelling Techniques and Tools for Computer Performance Evaluation*, pages 188–202, Chicago, USA, 2000.

On Clock Difference Constraints and Termination in Reachability Analysis of Timed Automata

Johan Bengtsson and Wang Yi

Department of Information Technology, Uppsala University, Sweden
{johanb,yi}@it.uu.se

Abstract. The key step to guarantee termination of reachability analysis for timed automata is the normalisation algorithms for clock constraints i.e. zones represented as DBM's (Difference Bound Matrices). It transforms DBM's which may contain arbitrarily large integers (the source of non-termination) into their equivalent according to the maximal constants of clocks appearing in the input timed automaton to be analysed. Surprisingly, though the zones of a timed automaton are essentially difference constraints in the form of $x - y \sim n$ [1], as shown in this paper, it is a non-trivial task to normalise the zones of timed automata that allows difference constraints in the enabling conditions (i.e. guards) on transitions. In fact, the existing normalisation algorithms implemented in tools such as Kronos and UPPAAL [2] can only handle timed automata (as input) allowing simple constraints in the form of $x \sim n$. For a long time, this has been a serious restriction for the existing tools. Difference constraints are indeed needed in many applications e.g. in solving scheduling problems. In this paper, we present a normalisation algorithm to remove the limitation, that based on splitting, transforms DBM's according to not only maximal constants of clocks but also the set of difference constraints appearing in an input automaton. The algorithm has been implemented and integrated in the UPPAAL tool, demonstrating that little run-time overhead is needed though the worst case complexity is the same as in the construction of region automata.

1 Introduction

Following the work of Alur and Dill on timed automata [AD94], a number of model checkers have been developed for modelling and verification of timed systems with timed automata as the core of their input languages [DOTY95,Yov97,LPY97,ABB$^+$01] based on reachability analysis. The foundation for decidability of reachability problems for timed automata is Alur and Dill's region technique, by which the infinite state space of a timed automaton due to the density of time, may be partitioned into finitely many equivalence classes i.e. according to *regions* in such a way that states within each class will always evolve to states within the same classes. However, analysis based on the region technique is practically infeasible due to the large number of equivalence

---

[1] Where x is a clock, $\sim \in \{\leq, <, =, >, \geq\}$, and n is a natural number.

[2] For example, the current released version of UPPAAL can only provide an inconclusive answer in verifying automata containing difference constraints.

J.S. Dong and J. Woodcock (Eds.): ICFEM 2003, LNCS 2885, pp. 491–503, 2003.

classes [LPY95], which is highly exponential in the number of clocks and their maximal constants.

One of the major advances in the area after the pioneering work of Alur and Dill is the symbolic technique [Dil89,YL93,HNSY94,YPD94,LPY95], which transforms the reachability problem to that of solving simple constraints. It adopts the idea from symbolic model checking for untimed systems, which uses logical formulas to represent set of states and operations on formulas to represent state transitions. It is proven that the infinite state-space of timed automata can be finitely partitioned into symbolic states which are represented and manipulated using a class of linear constraints known as zones and represented as *Difference Bound Matrices* (DBM) [Bel57,Dil89]. The reachability relation over symbolic states can be represented and computed by a few efficient operations on zones. From now on, we shall not distinguish the terms: constraint, zone and DBM.

The technique can be simply formulated in an abstract reachability algorithm[3] as shown in Algorithm 1. The algorithm is to check whether a timed automaton may reach a final location l_f. It explores the state space of the automaton in terms of *symbolic states* in the form (l, D) where l is a location and D is a zone (represented as a DBM).

Algorithm 1 Symbolic reachability analysis.

PASSED $= \emptyset$, WAIT $= \{\langle l_0, D_0 \rangle\}$
while WAIT $\neq \emptyset$ **do**
  take $\langle l, D \rangle$ from WAIT
  if $l = l_f$ **then return** "YES"
  if $D \not\subseteq D'$ for all $\langle l, D' \rangle \in$ PASSED **then**
    add $\langle l, D \rangle$ to PASSED
    for all $\langle l', D' \rangle$ such that $\langle l, D \rangle \rightsquigarrow \langle l', D' \rangle$ **do**
      add $\langle l', D' \rangle$ to WAIT
    end for
  end if
end while
return "NO"

Having a closer look at the algorithm, one will realize that termination is not guaranteed unless the number of constraints generated is finite or the constraints form a well quasi-ordering with respects to set-inclusion (over solution sets for clock constraints) [Hig52]. There have been several normalisation algorithms for clock constraints represented as DBMs (e.g. [Rok93,Pet99]) that are the key step to guarantee termination for the existing tools. They transform DBMs which may contain arbitrary constants into their equivalent with respect to maximal constants appearing in clock constraints. The transformation respects region equivalence and therefore the number of DBMs explored is finite. However a restriction of the existing normalisation algorithms is that clock constraints in the syntax of timed automata must be in the form [AD94] of $x \sim n$

---

[3] Several verification tools for timed systems (e.g. UPPAAL [BLL+96]) have been implemented based on this algorithm.

where x is a clock variable, $\sim$ is a relational operator and n is a natural number. It was discovered recently that the existing tools were either providing incorrect answers or not terminating when they are used to verify automata containing difference constraints of the form: $x - y \sim n$ (that are indeed needed in many applications e.g. in solving scheduling problems).

A normalisation algorithm based on region equivalence treats clock values above a certain constant as equivalent. This is correct only when no guard of the form: $x - y \sim n$ is allowed in an automaton. Otherwise the normalisation operation may enlarge a zone so that the guard (a difference constraint) labelled on a transition is made true and thus incorrectly enables the transition. For automata containing difference constraints as guards, we need a finer partitioning, since the difference constraints introduce diagonal lines that split the entire clock space, even above the maximum constants for clocks. The partitioning and related normalisation operation based on region construction is too crude.

We demonstrate this by an example. Consider the automaton shown in Fig. 1. The final location of the automaton is not reachable according to the semantics. This is because in location s_2, the clock zone is $(x - y > 2$ and $x > 2)$ where the guard is $(x - z < 1$ and $z - y < 1)$ which is equivalent to $(x - z < 1$ and $z - y < 1$ and $x - y < 2)$ can never be true and thus disables the last transition. However, because the maximal constants for clock x is 1 (and 2 for y), the zone in location s_2: $(x - y > 2$ and $x > 2)$ will be normalised to $(x - y > 1$ and $x > 1)$ by the maximal constant 1 for x, which enables the guard $(x - z < 1$ and $z - y < 1)$ leading to the final location. Thus the symbolic reachability analysis based on a standard normalisation algorithm would incorrectly conclude that the last location is reachable.

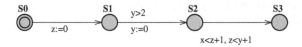

Fig. 1. A counter example.

In [BDGP98], it has been proved that a timed automaton with constraints on clock differences can be transformed to an equivalent automaton without constraints on differences. However, it is impractical to implement this approach in tools that support debugging of models since the transformation change the syntax of the original automaton. In this paper, we present a normalisation algorithm that allows not only clock comparison with naturals but also comparison between clocks i.e. constraints on clock differences. The algorithm transforms DBMs according to not only the maximal constants of clocks but also difference constraints appearing in an automaton. To our knowledge, this is the first published normalisation algorithms for timed automata containing difference constraints. The algorithm has been implemented in UPPAAL. Our experiments demonstrate that almost no extra overhead is added to deal with difference constraints.

The paper is organised as follows: Section 2 reviews timed automata and reachability analysis. Section 3 introduces the problem in normalising symbolic states for timed automata with constraints over clock differences. Section 4 presents the new normalisation algorithm. Section 5 concludes the paper.

2 Preliminaries

In this section we briefly review the notation for timed automata and its semantics. More extensive descriptions can be found in *e.g.* [AD94,Yov98,Pet99].

2.1 Timed Automata Model

Let Σ be a finite set of labels, ranged over by a, b etc. A timed automaton is a finite state automaton over alphabet Σ extended with a set of real valued clocks, to model time dependent behaviour. Let $\mathcal{C}$ denote a set of clocks, ranged over by x, y, z, and define $\mathcal{B}(\mathcal{C})$ as the set of conjunctions of atomic constraints of the form $x \sim n$ and $x - y \sim n$ for $\sim \in \{\leq, <, =, >, \geq\}$ and $n \in \mathbb{N}$. We use $\mathcal{B}_{\mathrm{df}}(\mathcal{C})$ for the subset of $\mathcal{B}(\mathcal{C})$ where all atomic constraints are of the form $x \sim n$ and let g range over this set.

Definition 1 (Timed Automaton). *A timed automaton A is a tuple $\langle N, l_0, \rightarrow, I \rangle$ where N is a set of control nodes, $l_0 \in N$ is the initial node, $\rightarrow \in N \times \mathcal{B}_{\mathrm{df}}(\mathcal{C}) \times \Sigma \times 2^{\mathcal{C}} \times N$ is the set of edges and $I : N \longrightarrow \mathcal{B}(\mathcal{C})$ assign invariants to locations. As a simplification we will use $l \xrightarrow{g,a,r} l'$ to denote $\langle l, g, a, r, l' \rangle \in \rightarrow$.*

The clocks values are formally represented as functions, called clock assignments, mapping $\mathcal{C}$ to the non-negative reals $\mathbb{R}_+$. We let u, v denote such functions, and use $u \in g$ to denote that the clock assignment u satisfy the formula g. For $d \in \mathbb{R}_+$ we use $u + d$ for the clock assignment that maps all clocks x in $\mathcal{C}$ to the value $u(x) + d$, and for $r \subseteq \mathcal{C}$ we let $[r]u$ denote the clock assignment that maps all clocks, x, in r to 0 and agree with u for the other clocks in $\mathcal{C}$.

The semantics of a timed automaton is a timed transition-system where the states are pairs $\langle l, u \rangle$, with two types of transitions, corresponding to delay transitions and discrete action transitions respectively:

– $\langle l, u \rangle \xrightarrow{\epsilon(t)} \langle l, u + t \rangle$ if $u + t' \in I(l)$ for all $t' \in [0, t]$
– $\langle l, u \rangle \xrightarrow{a} \langle l', u' \rangle$ if $l \xrightarrow{g,a,r} l'$, $u \in g$, $u' = [r]u$ and $u' \in I(l')$

It is easy to see that the state space for such a transition system is infinite and thus not adequate for algorithmic verification. However, efficient algorithms may be obtained using a *symbolic semantics* based on *symbolic states* of the form $\langle l, D \rangle$, where $D \in \mathcal{B}(\mathcal{C})$ [HNSY92,YPD94]. The symbolic counterpart of the transitions are given by:

– $\langle l, D \rangle \rightsquigarrow \langle l, D^{\uparrow} \wedge I(l) \rangle$
– $\langle l, D \rangle \rightsquigarrow \langle l', r(D \wedge g) \wedge I(l') \rangle$ if $l \xrightarrow{g,a,r} l'$

where $D^{\uparrow} = \{u + d \mid u \in D \wedge d \in \mathbb{R}_+\}$ and $r(D) = \{[r]u \mid u \in D\}$. It can be shown that the set of constraint systems is closed under these operations, in the sense that the result of the operations can be expressed by elements of $\mathcal{B}(\mathcal{C})$.

Moreover the symbolic semantics corresponds closely to the standard semantics in the sense that if $\langle l, D \rangle \rightsquigarrow \langle l', D' \rangle$ then, for all $u' \in D'$ there is $u \in D$ such that $\langle l, u \rangle \rightarrow \langle l', u' \rangle$.

2.2   Reachability Analysis

Given a timed automaton with symbolic initial-state $\langle l_0, D_0 \rangle$ and a symbolic state $\langle l, D \rangle$, $\langle l, D \rangle$ is said to be *reachable* if $\langle l_0, D_0 \rangle \rightsquigarrow^* \langle l, D_n \rangle$ and $D \cap D_n \neq \emptyset$ for some D_n. This problem may be solved using a standard reachability algorithm for graphs. However the unbounded clock values may render an infinite zone graph and thus might the reachability algorithm not terminate. The solution to this problem is to obtain a finite symbolic semantics by normalising the states with respect to the maximum constant each clock is compared to in the automaton. For details we refer the reader to [Pet99,Rok93] but the main fact and the intuition behind it is described here. In order to do this we first have to introduce the notion of closed constraint systems. We say that a constraint system $D \in \mathcal{B}(C)$ is *closed under entailment* or just closed, for short, if no constraint in D can be strengthened without reducing the solution set.

Proposition 1. *For each constraint system $D \in \mathcal{B}(C)$ there is a unique constraint system $D' \in \mathcal{B}(C)$ such that D and D' have exactly the same solution set and D' is closed under entailment.*

From this proposition we conclude that a closed constraint system can be used as a canonical representation of a zone.

Given a zone D and a set of maximal constants $k = \{k_x, k_y, \ldots\}$ where k_x denotes the maximal constant for clock x, the normalisation of D, denoted $\mathsf{norm}_k(D)$, is computed from the closed representation of D by

1. Removing all constraints of the form $x < m$, $x \leq m$, $x - y < m$ and $x - y \leq m$ where $m > k_x$,
2. Replacing all constraints of the form $x > m$, $x \geq m$, $y - x > m$ and $y - x \geq m$ where $m > k_x$ with $x > k_x$ and $y - x > k_x$ respectively.

This can then be used to define a notion of normalised symbolic transitions ($\rightsquigarrow_k$) by modifying the transitions of the standard symbolic semantics to preserve normalisation. The discrete action transition already preserves this so there is no need to modify it, but the delay transition should be modified to $\langle l, D \rangle \rightsquigarrow_k \langle l, \mathsf{norm}_k(D^{\uparrow} \wedge I(l)) \rangle$.

Proposition 2. *Assume a timed automaton A with initial-state $\langle l_0, D_0 \rangle$ and let k be the set of maximal constants used to compare with respective clocks in A. Then l is reachable from $\langle l_0, D_0 \rangle$ if and only if there is a sequence of normalised transitions $\langle l_0, D_0' \rangle \rightsquigarrow_k^* \langle l, D_n' \rangle$, where $D_0' = \mathsf{norm}_k(D_0)$.*

Using this we get a finite symbolic state-space where we can apply a standard reachability algorithm for graphs, such as the one in Algorithm 1 with the symbolic transition relation $\rightsquigarrow$ being replaced with the normalised version $\rightsquigarrow_k$.

3   Constraints on Clock Differences and Normalisation

It is well known how to extend timed automata to allow guards where the difference between two clocks is compared, *i.e.* allowing the guards to be taken from the full set $\mathcal{B}(\mathcal{C})$, not only from $\mathcal{B}_{df}(\mathcal{C})$. It has also been shown that this extension do not give more expressive power; there exists algorithms (*e.g.* in [BDGP98]) that transforms a timed automaton with difference constraints into an equivalent automaton without difference constraints.

We note that for diagonal-free timed automata the normalisation algorithm described earlier is based on the so called region equivalence.

Definition 2 (Region Equivalence). *For a clock $x \in \mathcal{C}$, let k_x be a constant (the ceiling of clock x). For a real number t, let $\{t\}$ denote the fractional part of t, and $\lfloor t \rfloor$ denote its integer part. Two clock assignments u, v are region-equivalent, denoted $u \stackrel{.}{\sim} v$, iff*

1. for each clock x, either $\lfloor u(x) \rfloor = \lfloor v(x) \rfloor$ or $(u(x) > k_x$ and $v(x) > k_x)$, and
2. for all clocks x, y if $u(x) \le k_x$ and $u(y) \le k_y$ then
   (a) $\{u(x)\} = 0$ iff $\{v(x)\} = 0$ and
   (b) $\{u(x)\} \le \{u(y)\}$ iff $\{v(x)\} \le \{v(y)\}$

For the extended version we need a finer partitioning, since the difference constraints in the guards introduce diagonal lines that split the entire clock space, even above the maximum constants for the clocks. The partitioning used for diagonal-free automata, and the connected normalisation operation norm_k is too crude. We demonstrate this by studying the zones explored when exploring the state-space of the counter example in Fig. 1. The zones are shown, in canonical form, in Fig. 2. The implicit constraints that all clocks are non-negative are not shown.

We note that for S_0 and S_1 the normalised and unnormalised zones are identical. The automaton may idle in location S_0 and then, after performing the first action step, reach location S_1. In location S_1 the automaton will stay until the clock y is at least greater than two before it takes the step to location S_2. This will introduce constraints in the DBM that are above the maximum constant for x. In the normalised semantics these bounds will then be lowered to the maximum constant for x, which will, erroneously, add time assignments satisfying both of the guards on the transition to S_3, and thus make S_3 reachable. The conclusion is that the normalisation procedure has to be adapted to handle timed automata with difference constraints.

4   New Normalisation Algorithm

In this section we will present how to normalise the symbolic states for a timed automaton with difference constraints. The key issue for the extended normalisation algorithm is to honour the equivalence classes that are introduced by difference constraints in the guards. We note that difference constraints in the guards may introduce equivalence classes in the clock space that reach beyond any maximum constant. Thus we need to refine the region equivalence from Definition 2 to take the difference constraints into account.

$$S_0 : \begin{cases} x - y = 0 \\ y - z = 0 \\ z - x = 0 \end{cases} \qquad S_0 : \begin{cases} x - y = 0 \\ y - z = 0 \\ z - x = 0 \end{cases}$$

$$S_1 : \begin{cases} x - y = 0 \\ z - x \le 0 \\ z - y \le 0 \end{cases} \qquad S_1 : \begin{cases} x - y = 0 \\ z - x \le 0 \\ z - y \le 0 \end{cases}$$

$$S_2 : \begin{cases} y - x < -2 \\ y - z \le 0 \\ z - x \le 0 \\ 0 - x < -2 \end{cases} \qquad S_2 : \begin{cases} y - x < -1 \\ y - z \le 0 \\ z - x \le 0 \\ 0 - x < -1 \end{cases}$$

$$S_3 : \begin{cases} y - x < -1 \\ y - z < 0 \\ z - x < 0 \\ 0 - x < -1 \\ 0 - z < 0 \\ x - z < 1 \\ z - y < 1 \\ x - y < 2 \end{cases}$$

(a) Without normalisation   (b) Normalised with norm_k

Fig. 2. Zones for the counter example in Fig. 1.

Definition 3 (Refined Region Equivalence). *Let G be a finite set of constraints of the form $x - y \sim n$ for $x, y \in C$, $\sim \in \{\le, <, =, >, \ge\}$ and $n \in \mathbb{N}$. Two clock assignments u, v are equivalent, $u \approx v$ iff $u \sim v$ and $\forall g \in G : u \in g \Leftrightarrow v \in g$*

We note that since the number of regions defined by $\sim$ is finite and there are only finitely many constraints in G this refined region equivalence will define finitely many regions.

4.1 The Core of Normalisation

We can now use the refined region equivalence from Definition 3 to obtain the core of a normalisation algorithm. From the region equivalence we get the need to ensure that if a difference constraint is not satisfied by any point in the unnormalised zone, D, then it should not be satisfied by any point in the normalised zone, $\mathsf{norm}_d(D)$, and if all points in D satisfy a difference constraint then so should all points in $\mathsf{norm}_d(D)$. This leads to a core normalisation algorithm consisting of three stages:

1. Collect all difference constraints from A that are not satisfied by any point in the zone and the negation of all difference constraints that are satisfied by all points in the zone.
2. Perform normalisation with respect to the maximum constants of A.
3. Apply the negation of all the collected constraints to the normalised zone to make sure that none of the collected constraints are satisfied after normalisation.

In Algorithm 2 this core normalisation is given as pseudo code. The set G_d referred to in the algorithm is the set of difference constraints in A and the operation norm_k refers to normalisation with respect to the maximum constants of A.

Algorithm 2 Core normalisation algorithm ($\text{norm}_d(D)$).

$G_{\text{unsat}} := \emptyset$
for all $g \in G_d$ **do**
  if $D \wedge g = \emptyset$ **then**
    $G_{\text{unsat}} := G_{\text{unsat}} \cup \{g\}$
  end if
  if $D \wedge \neg g = \emptyset$ **then**
    $G_{\text{unsat}} := G_{\text{unsat}} \cup \{\neg g\}$
  end if
end for
$D := \text{norm}_k(D)$
for all $g \in G_{\text{unsat}}$ **do**
  $D := D \wedge \neg g$
end for
return D

However, there are cases where this algorithm is incorrect with respect to the equivalence classes. For some cases when a difference constraint split the zone to be normalised, the ideal normalisation may not be represented using a single zone. This problem only occurs when a difference constraint divides the unnormalised zone, *i.e.* some of the time assignments in the zone satisfy the difference constraint and some do not. Thus, if all such zones are split along dividing difference constraints before normalisation, *e.g.* using Algorithm 3, the problem can be avoided.

Algorithm 3 Zone splitting algorithm ($\text{split}(D)$).

$Q := \{D\}, Q' := \emptyset$
for all $g \in G_d$ **do**
  for all $D' \in Q$ **do**
    if $D' \wedge g$ and $D' \wedge \neg g$ **then**
      $Q' := Q' \cup \{D' \wedge g, D' \wedge \neg g\}$
    else
      $Q' := Q' \cup \{D'\}$
    end if
  end for
  $Q := Q', Q' := \emptyset$
end for
return Q

The complete normalisation procedure is presented in Algorithm 4. The splitting, denoted by split in the description, is used as a preprocessing step and then the basic normalisation algorithm, norm_d, is applied to all the resulting zones. We use Norm_d to denote this normalisation operation and we use this operation to define a normalised symbolic transition relation.

Definition 4. *Let A be a timed automaton with the symbolic semantics $\leadsto$. The s-normalised version of $\leadsto$ ($\leadsto_s$) for A is defined by: whenever $\langle l, D \rangle \leadsto \langle l', D'' \rangle$ then $\langle l, D \rangle \leadsto_s \langle l', D' \rangle$ for all $D' \in \text{Norm}_d(D'')$.*

Algorithm 4 Normalisation algorithm.

$Q := \emptyset$
for all $D' \in \mathsf{split}(D)$ **do**
   $Q := Q \cup \{\mathsf{norm}_d(D')\}$
end for
return Q

To demonstrate the normalisation procedure we apply it to the zone for location S_2 in our counter example. The difference constraints in the example are $g_1 = x - z < 1$ and $g_2 = z - y < 1$. The initial zone contains both time assignments satisfying g_1 and assignments satisfying its negation, and thus we have to split the zone with respect to this constraint prior to normalisation, giving the zones below.

$$
\begin{cases}
y - x < -2 \\
y - z < -1 \\
z - x \le 0 \\
0 - x < -2 \\
0 - z < -1 \\
x - z < 1
\end{cases}
\qquad
\begin{cases}
y - x < -2 \\
y - z \le 0 \\
0 - x < -2 \\
z - x \le -1
\end{cases}
$$

(a) satisfying g_1 (b) satisfying $\neg g_1$

Zone (a) above does not contain any time assignments satisfying g_2 and thus it will not be split further. Zone (b) however needs to be split into assignments satisfying g_2 and assignments satisfying $\neg g_2$. This gives us the following zones to normalise.

$$
\begin{cases}
y - x < -2 \\
y - z < -1 \\
z - x \le 0 \\
0 - x < -2 \\
0 - z < -1 \\
x - z < 1
\end{cases}
\qquad
\begin{cases}
y - x < -2 \\
y - z \le 0 \\
0 - x < -2 \\
z - x \le -1
\end{cases}
\qquad
\begin{cases}
y - x < -2 \\
y - z \le -1 \\
z - x \le -1 \\
0 - x < -2 \\
0 - z \le -1
\end{cases}
$$

(a) g_1 and $\neg g_2$ (b) $\neg g_1$ and g_2 (c) $\neg g_1$ and $\neg g_2$

After splitting we can apply the Norm_d algorithm. The set of unsatisfied difference constraints for the different zones are: $G^{(a)}_{unsat} = \{\neg g_1, g_2\}$, $G^{(b)}_{unsat} = \{g_1, \neg g_2\}$, $G^{(c)}_{unsat} = \{g_1, g_2\}$. After collecting this information we are ready to apply norm_k to the zones, giving:

$$
\begin{cases}
y - x < -1 \\
y - z < -1 \\
z - x \le 0 \\
0 - x < -1 \\
0 - z < -1 \\
x - z < 1
\end{cases}
\qquad
\begin{cases}
y - x < -1 \\
y - z \le 0 \\
0 - x < -1 \\
x - z \ge 1
\end{cases}
\qquad
\begin{cases}
y - x < -1 \\
y - z \le -1 \\
z - x \le -1 \\
0 - x < -1 \\
0 - z \le -1
\end{cases}
$$

(a) g_1 and $\neg g_2$ (b) $\neg g_1$ and g_2 (c) $\neg g_1$ and $\neg g_2$

Since applying norm_k to the parts of the split zone does not enable any constraint in G_{unsat}, we do not have to conjunct the corresponding difference constraints to the zones. We note that, as the unnormalised zone, none of the normalised zones include time assignments satisfying both g_1 and g_2; the transition from S_2 to S_3 is not erroneously enabled by the normalisation procedure.

Before proving the correctness of the s-normalised transition relation, we need to establish some properties of the Norm_d operator.

Lemma 1. *Assume a timed automaton A, with associated* Norm_d *operator. For any zone D the following holds.*

(1) For all constraints g mentioned in A, $\mathsf{Norm}_d(D \wedge g) = \{D' \wedge g \,|\, D' \in \mathsf{Norm}_d(D)\}$
(2) $\mathsf{Norm}_d(D^\uparrow) = \{(D')^\uparrow \,|\, D' \in \mathsf{Norm}_d(D)\}$
(3) $D' \in \mathsf{Norm}_d(D) \Rightarrow \mathsf{Norm}_d(r(D')) \subseteq \mathsf{Norm}_d(r(D))$

Proof. (sketch) These properties are proved by reasoning about how the $\wedge$, $\uparrow$ and r operations modify the zones with respect to the two types of constraints that effect normalisation, *i.e.* non-difference constraints with bounds above the maximum constants and difference constraints.

(1) Adding a guard of the form $x_i - x_j \sim n$ will cut the zone along one of the normalisation split lines. If this is done before normalisation the result will be that normalisation produce a subset of the zones that it would originally have produced. If the guard is added after normalisation a number of entire zones from the normalisation will be removed giving the same final result.
Adding a guard of the form $x_i \sim n$ will cut away a part of the zone that is not affected by the normalisation since, by definition, $n \leq k_i$
(2) Difference constraints are not effected at all by the $\uparrow$ operation. Further $\uparrow$ do not introduce any new non-difference constraints.
(3) $r(D)$ operations are projections of a D on a hyperplane defined by r. This projection has the property that points that were added by normalisation are mapped to other that would be added by renormalisation.

Finally we prove that the s-normalised transition relation is correct.

Theorem 1. *Let A be a timed automaton and for each clock* $x_i \in C$ *let* k_i *be the largest number* x_i *is compared to in A.*

- *(Soundness) whenever* $\langle l_0, \{u_0\} \rangle \leadsto_s^* \langle l_f, D_f \rangle$ *then* $\langle l_0, u_0 \rangle \to^* \langle l_f, u_f \rangle$ *for some* $u_f \in D_f$
- *(Completeness) whenever* $\langle l_0, u_0 \rangle \to^* \langle l_f, u_f \rangle$ *then* $\langle l_0, \{u_0\} \rangle \leadsto_s^* \langle l_f, D_f \rangle$ *for some* D_f *such that* $u_f \in D_f$

Proof. Both soundness and completeness are proven by induction on the length of the transition sequences.

(Soundness) As induction hypothesis, assume $\langle l_0, \{u_0\} \rangle \leadsto_s^n \langle l_n, D_n^s \rangle \Rightarrow \exists D_n$ such that $\langle l_0, \{u_0\} \rangle \leadsto^n \langle l_n, D_n \rangle$ and $D_n^s \in \mathsf{Norm}_d(D_n)$. Further assume $\langle l_n, D_n^s \rangle \leadsto_s$ $\langle l_{n+1}, D_{n+1}^s \rangle$. We now need to prove that $\exists D_n$ such that $D_n^s \in \mathsf{Norm}_d(D_n)$, $\langle l_n, D_n \rangle \leadsto \langle l_{n+1}, D_{n+1} \rangle$ and $D_{n+1}^s \in \mathsf{Norm}_d(D_{n+1})$. We have two cases: delay transitions and action transitions.

– (Delay) By the assumption $\langle l_n, D_n^s \rangle \leadsto_s \langle l_n, D_{n+1}^s \rangle$ by delay, and the definition of $\leadsto_s$ we get $D_{n+1}^s \in \mathsf{Norm}_d(D_n^{s\uparrow} \wedge I(l_n))$. Combining this with Lemma 1 (1+2) gives $D_{n+1}^s \in \mathsf{Norm}_d(\{D \wedge I(l_n) \mid \{(D')^\uparrow \mid D' \in \mathsf{Norm}_d(D_n^s)\}\})$, and since D_n^s is already normalised we get $D_{n+1}^s \in \{D_n^{s\uparrow} \wedge I(l_n)\}$, i.e. $D_{n+1}^s = D_n^{s\uparrow} \wedge I(l_n)$. Now assume that for all D_n^i such that $D_n^s \in \mathsf{Norm}_d(D_n^i)$ and $\langle l_n, D_n \rangle \leadsto \langle l_n, D_{n+1} \rangle$ by delay, $D_{n+1}^s \notin \mathsf{Norm}_d(D_{n+1})$. By the definition of $\leadsto$ we have $D_{n+1} = D_n^{i\uparrow} \wedge I(l_n)$, which gives $\mathsf{Norm}_d(D_{n+1}) = \mathsf{Norm}_d(D_n^{i\uparrow} \wedge I(l_n))$. Expansion using Lemma 1 (1+2) yields $\mathsf{Norm}_d(D_{n+1}) = \{D \wedge I(l_n) \mid D \in \{(D')^\uparrow \mid D' \in \mathsf{Norm}_d(D_n^i)\}\}$. By our assumption, $D_n^s \in \mathsf{Norm}_d(D_n^i)$ and $D_{n+1}^s \notin \mathsf{Norm}_d(D_{n+1})$, for all D_n^i, but this lead to a contradiction.

– (Action) By assumption we know that $\langle l_n, D_n^s \rangle \leadsto_s \langle l_{n+1}, D_{n+1}^s \rangle$ by $l_n \xrightarrow{gar} l_{n+1}$. From the definitions of Norm_d and $\leadsto$ we can derive that for all D_n^i such that $D_n^s \in \mathsf{Norm}_d(D_n^i)$, $\langle l_n, D_n^i \rangle \leadsto \langle l_{n+1}, D_{n+1} \rangle$ by $l_n \xrightarrow{gar} l_{n+1}$ Now we need to prove that $\exists D_{n+1}$ such that $D_{n+1}^s \in \mathsf{Norm}_d(D_{n+1})$. By the definition of $\leadsto$, $\mathsf{Norm}_d(D_{n+1}) = \mathsf{Norm}_d(r(D_n^i \wedge g) \wedge I(l_{n+1}))$. Expansion by Lemma 1(1) gives $\mathsf{Norm}_d(D_{n+1}) = \{D \wedge I(l_{n+1}) \mid D \in \mathsf{Norm}_d(r(D_n^i \wedge g))\}$. According to Lemma 1(1+3) and $D_n^s \in \mathsf{Norm}_d(D_n^i)$ we have $\mathsf{Norm}_d(r(D_n^s \wedge g)) \subseteq \mathsf{Norm}_d(r(D_n^i \wedge g))$. And since we know, by the definition of $\leadsto$, that $D_{n+1}^s \in \mathsf{Norm}_d(r(D_n^i \wedge g))$ we conclude that $D_{n+1}^s \in \mathsf{Norm}_d(D_{n+1})$.

(Completeness) As induction hypothesis, assume $\langle l_0, u_0 \rangle \rightarrow^n \langle l_n, u_n \rangle \Rightarrow \exists D_n$ such that $\langle l_0, \{u_0\} \rangle \leadsto_s^n \langle l_n, D_n \rangle$ and $u_n \in D_n$. Further assume $\langle l_n, u_n \rangle \xrightarrow{\alpha} \langle l_{n+1}, u_{n+1} \rangle$. We need to prove that $\exists D_n^i$ such that $u_n \in D_n^i, \langle l_n, D_n^i \rangle \leadsto_s \langle l_{n+1}, D_{n+1} \rangle$ and $u_{n+1} \in D_{n+1}$. There are two cases, $\alpha = \epsilon(d)$ or $\alpha \in \Sigma$.

– ($\alpha = \epsilon(d)$) By the assumption $\langle l_n, u_n \rangle \xrightarrow{\epsilon(d)} \langle l_n, u_n + d \rangle$ we know $(u_n + d) \in I(l_n)$, i.e. $\exists u_n : u_n \in D_n^i \wedge u_n + d \in I(l_n)$. From the definition of $\leadsto_s$ we have $\langle l_n, D_n \rangle \leadsto_s \langle l_n, D_{n+1} \rangle$ by delay, if $D_{n+1} \in \mathsf{Norm}_d(D_n^\uparrow \wedge I(l_n))$. Expansion by the definition of $\uparrow$ yields $D_{n+1} \in \mathsf{Norm}_d(\{u + d \mid u \in D_n \wedge u + d \in I(l_n)\})$. By the definition of Norm_d we know that for all zones D, $D \Rightarrow \bigwedge_{D' \in \mathsf{Norm}_d(D)} D'$. Thus there is a zone $D_{n+1} \in \mathsf{Norm}_d(D_n^\uparrow \wedge I(l_n))$ such that $u_{n+1} \in D_{n+1}$

– ($\alpha \in \Sigma$) By the assumption $\langle l_n, u_n \rangle \xrightarrow{\alpha} \langle l_{n+1}, [r]u_n \rangle$ we know $l_n \xrightarrow{g,\alpha,r} l_{n+1}$, $u_n \in g$, $[r]u_n \in I(l_{n+1})$. From the definition of $\leadsto_s$ we have $\langle l_n, D_n^i \rangle \leadsto_s \langle l_{n+1}, D_{n+1} \rangle$ by $l_n \xrightarrow{g,\alpha,r} l_{n+1}$ if $D_{n+1} \in \mathsf{Norm}_d(r(D_n \wedge g) \wedge I(l_{n+1}))$. Expanding this by the definition of the r-operation yields $D_{n+1} \in \mathsf{norm}_k(\{[r]u \mid u \in D_n^i \wedge u \in g \wedge [r]u \in I(l_{n+1})\})$. By the definition of Norm_d we know that for all zones D, $D \Rightarrow \bigwedge_{D' \in \mathsf{Norm}_d(D)} D'$. Thus there is a zone $D_{n+1} \in \mathsf{Norm}_d(r(D_n \wedge g) \wedge I(l_{n+1}))$ such that $u_{n+1} \in D_{n+1}$.

5   Conclusion

In modelling and verifying timed systems, using timed automata, constraints over clock differences are useful and needed in many applications e.g. solving scheduling problems. In this paper, we have reported a problem in the existing (published) symbolic reachability algorithms for timed automata. The problem is that the existing normalisation algorithms (implemented by several verification tools for timed automata e.g. UPPAAL) for clock constraints based on region equivalence are incorrect in the sense that they may provide wrong answers in verifying timed automata containing constraints on clock differences. The reason is that the normalisation operations may enlarge a zone such that the guard (a difference constraint) labelled on a transition is made true and therefore incorrectly enables the transition. Thus the normalisation operation should be based on a finer equivalence relation than region equivalence. We propose to use the region equivalence which is further refined by difference constraints. Based on this, we have developed a normalisation algorithm that allow not only clock comparison with naturals but also comparison between clocks i.e. constraints on clock differences. The algorithm transforms DBMs according to not only the maximal constants of clocks but also difference constraints appearing in an automaton. To our knowledge, this is the first published normalisation algorithm for timed automata containing difference constraints. The algorithm have been implemented in UPPAAL showing that almost no extra overhead is added to deal with difference constraints[4].

References

[ABB+01]   Tobias Amnell, Gerd Behrmann, Johan Bengtsson, Pedro R. D'Argenio, Alexandre David, Ansgar Fehnker, Thomas Hune, Bertrand Jeannet, Kim G. Larsen, M. Oliver Möller, Paul Pettersson, Carsten Weise, and Wang Yi. UPPAAL - Now, Next, and Future. In *Modelling and Verification of Parallel Processes*, number 2067 in Lecture Notes in Computer Science, pages 100–125. Springer-Verlag, 2001.

[AD94]   Rajeev Alur and David L. Dill. A theory of timed automata. *Journal of Theoretical Computer Science*, 126(2):183–235, 1994.

[BDGP98]   Beatrice Bérard, Volker Diekert, Paul Gastin, and Antoine Petit. Characterization of the expressive power of silent transitions in timed automata. *Fundamenta Informaticae*, 36:145–182, 1998.

[Bel57]   Richard Bellman. *Dynamic Programming*. Princeton University Press, 1957.

[BLL+96]   Johan Bengtsson, Kim G. Larsen, Fredrik Larsson, Paul Pettersson, and Wang Yi. UPPAAL in 1995. In *Proc. of the* 2nd *Workshop on Tools and Algorithms for the Construction and Analysis of Systems*, number 1055 in Lecture Notes in Computer Science, pages 431–434. Springer–Verlag, March 1996.

[Dil89]   David L. Dill. Timing assumptions and verification of finite-state concurrent systems. In *Proceedings, Automatic Verification Methods for Finite State Systems*, volume 407 of *Lecture Notes in Computer Science*, pages 197–212. Springer-Verlag, 1989.

[DOTY95]   Conrado Daws, Alfredo Olivero, Stavros Tripakis, and Sergio Yovine. The tool kronos. In *Proceedings, Hybrid Systems III: Verification and Control*, volume 1066 of *Lecture Notes in Computer Science*. Springer-Verlag, 1995.

[Hig52]   Graham Higman. Ordering by divisibility in abstract algebras. *Proceedings of the London Mathematical Society, Ser. 3*, 2:326–336, 1952.

[HNSY92]   Thomas A. Henzinger, Xavier Nicollin, Joseph Sifakis, and Sergio Yovine. Symbolic model checking for real-time systems. In *Proceedings, Seventh Annual IEEE Symposium on Logic in Computer Science*, pages 394–406, 1992.

---

[4] For timed automata without difference constraints the improved algorithm performs identical to the classic algorithm.

[HNSY94]   Thomas A. Henzinger, Xavier Nicollin, Joseph Sifakis, and Sergio Yovine. Symbolic model checking for real-time systems. Technical Report TR94-1404, Cornell Computer Science Technical Report Collection, 1994.

[LPY95]   Kim G. Larsen, Paul Pettersson, and Wang Yi. Compositional and Symbolic Model-Checking of Real-Time Systems. In *Proc. of the 16th IEEE Real-Time Systems Symposium*, pages 76–87. IEEE Computer Society Press, December 1995.

[LPY97]   Kim G. Larsen, Paul Petterson, and Wang Yi. Uppaal in a nutshell. *Journal on Software Tools for Technology Transfer*, 1997.

[Pet99]   Paul Pettersson. *Modelling and Verification of Real-Time Systems Using Timed Automata: Theory and Practice*. PhD thesis, Uppsala University, 1999.

[Rok93]   Tomas Gerhard Rokicki. *Representing and Modeling Digital Circuits*. PhD thesis, Stanford University, 1993.

[YL93]   Mihalis Yannakakis and David Lee. An efficient algorithm for minimizing real-time transition systems. In *Proceedings, Fifth International Conference on Computer Aided Verification*, volume 697 of *Lecture Notes in Computer Science*, pages 210–224. Springer-Verlag, 1993.

[Yov97]   Sergio Yovine. Kronos: A verification tool for real-time systems. *Journal on Software Tools for Technology Transfer*, 1, October 1997.

[Yov98]   Sergio Yovine. Model checking timed automata. In *European Educational Forum: School on Embedded Systems*, volume 1494 of *Lecture Notes in Computer Science*, pages 114–152. Springer-Verlag, 1998.

[YPD94]   Wang Yi, Paul Petterson, and Mats Daniels. Automatic verification of real-time communicating systems by constraint-solving. In *Proceedings, Seventh International Conference on Formal Description Techniques*, pages 223–238, 1994.

Analyzing the Redesign
of a Distributed Lift System in UPPAAL*

Jun Pang[1], Bart Karstens[1], and Wan Fokkink[1,2]

[1] CWI, Department of Software Engineering
P.O. Box 94079, 1090 GB Amsterdam, The Netherlands
{pangjun,bart,wan}@cwi.nl
[2] Vrije Universiteit Amsterdam
Department of Computer Science
De Boelelaan 1081a, 1081 HV Amsterdam
The Netherlands
wanf@cs.vu.nl

Abstract. An existing distributed lift system was analyzed using the process algebraic language μCRL [7]. Four problems were found, three of which were also found independently by the developers in the testing phase. They solved these problems in an *ad hoc* manner, because the causes of the problems were unclear. The analysis in [7] revealed the reasons for those problems, and proposed solutions.

In this paper, we checked the developers' solutions using UPPAAL. We show that the solutions of the developers do not solve these problems completely, while a refined version of our solution proposed in [7] does.

1   Introduction

As is well known, distributed algorithms form a major aspect of system design. Verifying the correctness of the protocols that regulate the behavior of distributed systems is usually a formidable task, as even simple behaviors become wildly complicated when they are carried out in parallel. Formal verification is a suitable approach to check whether a system meets its requirements.

In a formal model of a real-life system, details irrelevant to the requirements under scrutiny can be abstracted away. With the formal model at hand, one is able to reason about the system in a systematic and automatic way, using for example a model checker or a theorem prover. This formal reasoning can detect errors and suggest ways in which the system can be improved or optimized. A model is never completely equal to the original system, because it describes the system at a certain level of abstraction. This means that we can never be hundred percent sure that the system is correct with respect to the checked requirements. To achieve more confidence with the verified system, the model can be refined

---

* This research is partly supported by the Dutch Technology Foundation STW under the project CES5008: Improving the quality of embedded systems using formal design and systematic testing.

J.S. Dong and J. Woodcock (Eds.): ICFEM 2003, LNCS 2885, pp. 504–522, 2003.

by adding more details. In this paper, we report some experience related to this topic by analyzing the redesign of a distributed lift system.

This lift system is used in real life for lifting lorries, railway carriages, buses etc. A system consists of a number of lifts: each wheel is supported by one lift and each lift has its own micro controller. This system has been designed and implemented by a small Dutch company (for commercial reasons we are not at liberty to reveal the company name). A special protocol has been developed to let the lifts operate synchronously. When testing their implementation the developers found three problems, but the causes of two of them were unclear. They solved these problems in an *ad hoc* manner. In order to explain the reasons and to make sure there are no more errors, the lift system was specified and verified in μCRL [8] and its toolset [5] in close cooperation with the developers. The three problems that were found by the developers were also found in the μCRL model. This indicated that the specification is actually close to the implementation. Another new problem was found in the model, which is indeed present in the system. The causes for the problems were detected, and solutions were proposed and included in the μCRL specification. The modified μCRL specification was shown to satisfy all the requirements by model checking. However, this happened independently of the developers, who decided not to wait for the results of the formal analysis and to redesign their implementation based on their own solutions. To distinguish between the two lift systems in this paper, we call the first lift system 'original design' and the one with the solutions of the developers 'redesign'.

The developers experienced a new problem in the redesign. Again the reason was unclear. Since the error traces displayed a regular pattern in time, the developers thought modeling exact timing might reveal the reason for this problem. In the μCRL specification, time is abstracted away. We could extend the μCRL model with exact timing information, but there is no automated verification toolset for timed process algebras. Therefore it was decided to use UPPAAL [11], which is a toolset for validation and model checking of real time systems.

The UPPAAL model of the redesign is achieved in several steps. First the μCRL model is translated into UPPAAL. Then the UPPAAL model is refined to move it closer to the real system; each lift is split into two components, where one component communicates with the other lifts and the other component can receive input from the environment. The developers' solutions for the aforementioned problems are adopted. After discussions with the developers, exact timing information is added. The requirements for the lift system are formulated in UPPAAL, using its requirement specification language and test automata, and model checked. Using the graphic simulation tool in UPPAAL, we detect the reason for the new problem, which the developers encountered in the redesign. We propose a new solution, which is based on the solution that was already put forward in [7]. The UPPAAL model with the new solution satisfies all the requirements.

The developers acknowledge the efficiency and usefulness of formal verification for their redesign. Our solution will be implemented in the new release of the lift system; they are now more confident in the correct functioning of the redesigned lift system. The developers stress that formal methods should be applied in the early design phases to save testing effort and cost.

2   The Lift System

2.1   Layout of the Lift System

The lift system consists of an arbitrary number of lifts. Each lift supports one wheel of a vehicle. Different lift systems may have a different number of lifts, but this has no influence on the analysis, since this network should operate in the same way regardless how many lifts are connected.

Every lift has its own buttons. Three buttons are taken into account in the model: UP, DOWN and SETREF. If an UP or DOWN button on a certain lift is pressed, all lifts in the system should move up or down. Pressing a SETREF button on a lift is the only way a run of the system can start.

The movement of a lift system is controlled by means of a micro controller. Each lift has its own micro controller, called station. The stations can adopt four different states: STARTUP, STANDBY, UP and DOWN. The state of a lift can change in two ways: when a button on the lift is pressed, or by receiving a message from the network.

In the lift system, the data field of the messages transferred over the bus can contain two pieces of information: the position of the sender station, and the type of the message. There are two types of messages: SYNC messages and state messages. State messages broadcast the state of the sending station to the other stations. SYNC messages initiate physical movement. In response to a SYNC message, each station will immediately transfer its state to the motor of the lift, which causes movement. If the station is in UP, the lift will move up a fixed distance; if it is in DOWN, the lift will move down.

All the stations are connected to a CAN (Controller Area Network) bus [6]. The CAN bus is a simple, low-cost, multi-master serial bus with error detection capabilities. The bus transmits messages to the stations. Whenever a station wants to send a message, it is said to claim the bus. Stations can receive messages at any moment, but when a station wants to send a message it has to wait until it is its turn to use the bus. In the CAN bus, all stations can claim the bus at each cycle and several stations can claim the bus simultaneously. A non-destructive arbitration mechanism is used to determine which station may send its message. The resulting usage of the bus is ordered, and the stations take fixed turns to send their messages. To achieve this orderly usage of the bus, before the real use of the lift system we call 'normal operation', a start-up phase has been designed. In this phase each station finds out its position in the network and the total number of lifts in the network. When each station has been assigned a unique position, a virtual token can pass among the stations in the same order cycle after cycle. A station knows whether it is its turn to use the bus by checking the position of the sender station in the received message. The orderly usage of the bus during normal operation plays a crucial role in the analysis of the requirements and in the problems the lift system faces.

Control of the Lift: Start-Up. The start-up phase has two functions. First it assigns a unique position to each lift in the network. This position works as an identity. When each lift has got its own position, an orderly usage of the bus is possible. To assure that all lifts move simultaneously in the same direction, the station initiating a certain movement must verify whether all stations are in the appropriate state before it sends the SYNC message. In order to do this, each station must know how many stations there are in the network.

There is a relay between every pair of adjacent stations and each relay is controlled by the station at its left side. When the system is switched on all the relays are open.

The start-up phase is initialized by the station where the SETREF button is pressed. This station will behave differently from the other stations in the network. It will act as follows (chronological order):

1. it stores that it has position 1,
2. it adopts the STARTUP state,
3. it closes its relay,
4. it broadcasts a STARTUP message,
5. it opens its relay,
6. it waits for a STARTUP message,
7. it stores the position of the sender of that message as the number of stations in the network,
8. it adopts the STANDBY state,
9. it broadcasts this state.

The other stations receive a STARTUP message from another station. The first time a station receives a STARTUP message, it will act as follows:

1. it adds 1 to the position of the sender of that message and stores this as its own position,
2. it stores its own position as the number of stations in the network,
3. it adopts the STARTUP state,
4. it closes its relay,
5. it sends a STARTUP message,
6. – if it receives another STARTUP message, it stores the position of the sender of that message as the number of stations in the network,
   – if it receives a STANDBY message, it adopts the STANDBY state (if the station has position 2 it will in addition initiate normal operation by broadcasting its state).

Assume that in the left part of Fig. 1, the SETREF button of station B is pressed. The end result is that all stations are connected in the manner pictured in the right part of Fig. 1. All stations know their position and all stations know that there are four lifts in the network. More explanation about the start-up phase can be found in [7].

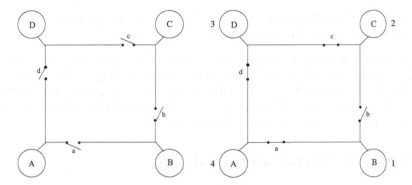

Fig. 1. State of the relays before (left) and after (right) initialization.

Control of the Lift: Normal Operation. When the start-up phase is finished, all the stations are in STANDBY. During the normal operation phase, the first station broadcasts its state, then the next station broadcasts its state and so on, until the last station has broadcast its state, after which the first station starts again. The state of a lift is changed if its UP or DOWN button is pressed. The station where this happens is called an active station. The active station will send an UP or DOWN message, according to the button that was pressed at the station. Passive stations change their state according to the messages they receive, and when it is their turn to use the bus they broadcast a message according to their state. These messages are received by all the other stations, and the active station is the only one that will count them. When it counts enough state messages, the active station will send a SYNC message, after which all the lifts move. The ordered sending of messages makes sure that the active station counts no more than one message from each station. In contrast to the passive stations, the state of the active station can only change if the pressed button is released again. In that case its state changes to STANDBY and the station becomes passive again. More details about this phase, including what happens when two UP or DOWN buttons at different lifts are pressed at the same time, will be discussed in Section 3.

2.2 Requirements

The desired behavior of the system is formulated in five requirements it has to fulfill. These requirements are listed below:

1. Deadlock freeness: The system never ends up in a state where it cannot perform any action.
2. Liveness I: It is always possible for the system to get to a state in which pressing UP or DOWN will yield the appropriate response.
3. Liveness II: If exactly one UP or exactly one DOWN button is pressed and not released, then all the lifts will eventually move up or down.
4. Safety I: If one of the lifts moves, all the other lifts should simultaneously move in the same direction.

5. Safety II: If the lifts move, an appropriate button was pressed. The lifts will not move if no one has pressed an UP or DOWN button.

The two liveness requirements make sure that buttons can always be pressed and in response the lifts will always move. The two safety requirements make sure that the system will move properly. In Section 3, we present four problems in the original lift system. If the lift system satisfies the five requirements above, those four problems are guaranteed to be resolved.

3   UPPAAL Model of the Redesign

UPPAAL [11] is a toolset for validation and model checking of real time systems, which are modeled as networks of timed automata [2] extended with global shared variables. It consists of a number of tools including a graphic editor for system description, a simulator and a model checker. The idea of the UPPAAL toolset is to model a system using timed automata, simulate it and then verify properties of the system. During the design phase, the graphic simulator is used intensively to validate the dynamic behavior of each design sketch, in particular for fault detection, and later on for debugging the generated diagnostic traces. The verifier mainly checks for invariants and reachability properties. It does so by exploring the state space of a system using 'on the fly' searching techniques. It uses symbolic techniques to reduce the verification of modal logic formulas to solving simple reachability constraints. Some notable recent case studies with UPPAAL are [9,12,3].

The UPPAAL model presented in this section is the result of a few steps. First the μCRL model of the original design is translated into UPPAAL. This model is then changed into a representation of the redesign by adding the developers' solutions to the problems, that were found in the original design. The UPPAAL model of the redesign is also more specific, since interactions between the environment and the lift system are added that were abstracted away in the μCRL model of the original design. Furthermore, the model is extended with exact timing information. With respect to the explanation of the original design in Section 2, the redesign can be viewed as a refinement of the μCRL model. However, the desired behavior of the lift is basically the same as explained in Section 2. The redesign should therefore meet the same requirements as the original design.

The UPPAAL model contains four components. They are automata: *Station*, *Bus*, *Interface* and *Timer*. In UPPAAL, an automaton can be instantiated an arbitrary number of times. As explained in Section 2, the lift system consists of one bus and an arbitrary number of lifts. The automaton *Bus* models the CAN bus. For each lift in the system, we create two automata: *Station* and *Interface*. The automaton *Station* models the micro controller. In automaton *Interface*, the pressing and releasing of buttons on the lift is modeled. The automaton *Timer* is used to model time delay. In this section we will walk through the model. Due to space limitation, pictures of these automata are presented with only superficial explanation. Detailed information can be found in [10].

3.1   Transforming the μCRL Model

The original lift system has been analyzed in μCRL [8], which combines the process algebra ACP [4] with equational abstract data types. To analyze the redesign of this system, first we transform the μCRL model into UPPAAL. In this section, we discuss some model choices that have been made.

Value Passing. The μCRL specification of a process is constructed from action names, recursion variables and process algebraic operators. Actions and recursion variables carry zero or more data parameters. Parallel composition $p \parallel q$ interleaves the actions of processes p and q; moreover, actions from p and q may also synchronize to a communication action, when this is explicitly allowed by a predefined communication function. Two actions can only synchronize if they occur at the same time, and if their data parameters are semantically the same, which means that communication can be used to represent data transfer from one process to another. The communication function was used heavily in the μCRL specification in [7] to model the communications between the bus and stations. However in UPPAAL, data transfer (or value passing) between processes (or automata) cannot be modeled in this way.

We define two channels between the bus and stations: *bustolift* and *lifttobus*, and declare several global variables for data transfer when communication happens. When a station wants to send a message to the bus, it has to instantiate the values for some global variables in the message, for instance the state and the sender's position. When communication takes place, the values of those global variables are saved to the variables used by the bus. After communication, those global variables are provided with default values. In a similar fashion, messages are sent from the bus to stations. Detailed information can be found in the automata *Station* and *Bus* (see Fig. 2, Fig. 4 and Fig. 5).

Messages Broadcasting. In μCRL, summation $\sum_{d:D} p(d)$ provides the possibly infinite choice over a data type D. In the μCRL specification of the bus, when the bus gets a message from a station, it can compute the set of stations who can get this message via closed relays. Then the bus can choose one station from the set nondeterministically, and send it the message. By this way, we can model the broadcasting of a message. In UPPAAL, the summation operator is absent. We set a kind of fix order for the bus to broadcast a message. The relay controlled by a station is modeled as a flag. When the relay is closed, the flag is set to 1; otherwise it is 0. When a bus broadcasts a message, it starts to check the flag at the position of the message sender. If the flag is 1, it sends a message to the station connected by this relay, and continues to check the flag of this station. As soon as it reaches a flag with value 0, it continues at the station preceding the message sender. If the flag at this station is 1, the message is sent to the station, and the bus continues to check the flag at the preceding station. This procedure moves on until the bus reaches another flag with value 0. Recall that in both phases of the lift system, there is at least one open relay, which guarantees that the broadcasting procedure terminates. In the automaton *Bus*

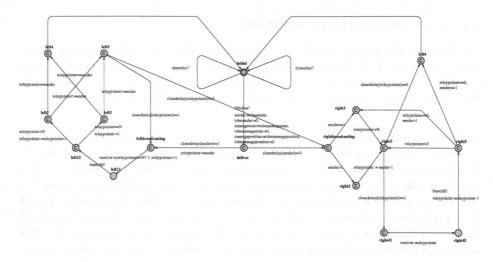

Fig. 2. The automaton *Bus.*

(see Fig. 2), when a bus gets a message at the 'initial' node, it starts broadcasting the message from the left part of the picture, then continues at the right part, and finally goes back to the 'initial' node.

One SETREF Button Pressed. In [7], the second problem of the original design was found during the start-up phase. It occurs if the SETREF buttons at two lifts are pressed. The result of the problem is that after the start-up phase there will be two lift systems instead of one. The situation may lead to the violation of all the requirements. Given the chosen bus it seems impossible to solve this problem satisfactorily. The developers chose to emphasize in the manual that it is important to make sure that in the start-up phase the SETREF button of only one lift is pressed. We also take this assumption into our analysis of the redesign.

In the UPPAAL model it is impossible to press another SETREF button after one is pressed. We use guards on transitions to block pressing of SETREF buttons after one SETREF button has been pressed. In the automaton *Interface* (see Fig. 3), a variable *onesetref* is used as a guard on both transitions from the initial state. Initially the variable is zero, so one *Interface* can take the transition with the guard 'onesetref==0', if the SETREF button on the lift is pressed. The variable *onesetref* is now set to 1. In order to leave their initial state, the other *Interface* automata have to take the other transition with the guard 'onesetref>0'. Therefore it is simply made impossible to press more than one SETREF button in our UPPAAL model.

3.2   Adding the Solutions

In the automaton *Station*, the two phases of the lift system as explained in Section 2 are clearly distinguishable.

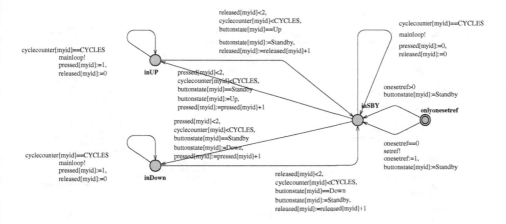

Fig. 3. The automaton *Interface*.

Start-Up. Until all the stations have reached the node 'normaloperation', it is in the start-up phase. The main role of the start-up phase is to find out which position a lift has in the network and how many lifts there are in the network. The variables *position* and *number* are assigned to each lift to store this information.

The station where the SETREF button is pressed will move clockwise in Fig. 4 from the 'initial' node. It gets position 1, closes its relay, and sends a STARTUP message to the bus. After that it opens its relay and waits for a STARTUP message. When it gets the STARTUP message, it adopts the value of the variable *number* in this message; this way it gets to know how many lifts there are in the system. Then, it sends a STANDBY message and reaches the 'normaloperation' node. The other stations will move anti-clockwise in Fig. 4 from the 'initial' node. They first get a STARTUP message, increase the sender of the message by one, and save it as their own *position*. They close their own relay and send a STARTUP message. There is a small loop in Fig. 4, to indicate that the stations keep getting STARTUP messages and changing the knowledge of the number of lifts in the system. In the end, they will get a STANDBY message, and end up in the 'normaloperation' node. When all the stations have reached the 'normaloperation' node, all the stations are STANDBY. They all have a unique value for *position*, and the value of *number* of all the lifts is equal to the total number of lifts in the network.

Some time delays are added into the start-up phase to solve one problem found during testing. The timing information will be discussed in Section 3.3.

Normal Operation. At node 'normaloperation', a station enters the normal operation phase, which is depicted in Fig. 5. In the normal operation phase, a distinction is made between two loops which a station can perform. One is the 'main loop', which takes place at the node 'normaloperation' in Fig. 5; and the other one we will call 'internal loop', which is the other part of Fig. 5. The difference between the main loop and the internal loop can be stated as follows: in a main loop the station receives state messages from its *Interface* and can

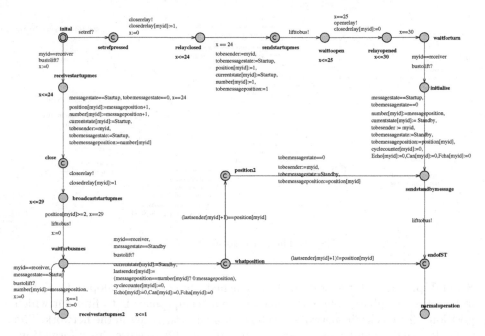

Fig. 4. The automaton *Station*: Start-up phase.

change its state accordingly, and in an internal loop the station exchanges state messages with *Bus* and changes its state accordingly.

The main loop is a short loop in which the automaton *Station* synchronizes with its *Interface*. Executing the main loop is the only way the station can get information about which button on the lift (if any) is pressed or released. This main loop takes place after a fixed number of internal loops, which is modeled as a constant *CYCLES* in the UPPAAL model. And a counter *cyclecounter* is used to record the number of internal loops that have happened after the last main loop. When 'cyclecounter==CYCLES', the main loop takes place and *cyclecounter* is reset to 0. If the station detects a difference between its current state (modeled by variable *currentstate*) and the state of the *Interface* (modeled by variable *buttonstate*), the station may change its state and adopt the one from the *Interface*. The main loop is also part of the original design, but it was abstracted away in the µCRL model in [7]. In the UPPAAL model of the redesign it could not be left out, because as we will see the solutions from the developers interact in a critical way with the main loop.

In an internal loop, a station can do several things. First a station can get messages from the bus. Second, a station can send a message to the other stations, if it gets the turn to use the bus. Third, the active station can count state messages and initiate a movement of the whole system. In that case the active station will enter the node 'activemovement', while the other stations get a SYNC message and enter the node 'passivemovement'. A variable *move* is associated to each station to indicate the direction of the current movement.

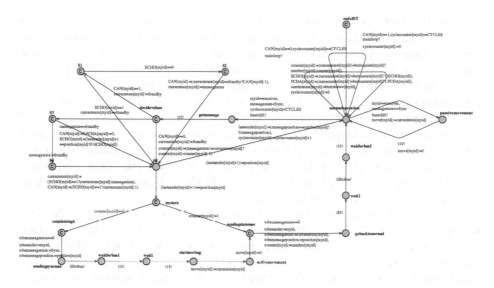

Fig. 5. The automaton *Station*: Normal operation.

Flags. Problem three and four found in [7] occur in the normal operation phase. The third problem happens when an UP or DOWN button is pressed and released at an inappropriate moment. The lift system will end up in the situation that all stations are in UP or DOWN state, but there is no active station. This means that all the lifts will remain in that state until the system is shut down. This problem violates property Liveness II in Section 2.2. The reason for this problem is that in the original system a station becomes passive as soon as the pressed button on this lift is released. This problem was discovered by the developers when testing the system, and they solved it by means of flags.

The fourth problem occurs when two UP or DOWN buttons on different lifts are pressed at the same time and one of them is released at an inappropriate moment. As a result, some lifts will move, and one lift (where the button is released) remains at the same height. This violates property Safety I in Section 2.2. The reason for this problem is that a station becomes active as soon as a button on this lift is pressed. This problem was unknown to the developers and found its way into the final implementation of the original system. The detailed description of each problem can be found in [7]. We proposed to solve this problem by allowing a station to decide to be active or passive only when it is its turn to use the bus. In this paper, we focus on the solutions from the developers, and explain how they fail to solve the problems in Section 4. Furthermore, in Section 5 we refine our solution from [7], and show that it does solve the problems.

The developers attempted to solve the third problem with flags. When they are set their value is 1, and when they are reset their value is 0. The flags serve as blocks: they can prevent state changes when they are set. Two type of flags are used in the redesign, i.e. CAN, ECHO. Every station has its own flags. Initially all flags are 0. The CAN flag is set when a station receives a state message from the bus. An exception is the STANDBY message. If a station receives this message, the opposite happens: CAN is reset, but only when the current state of the station is also STANDBY; otherwise CAN is left unchanged. The idea of the developers was to use the CAN flag to block state changes by the main loop. If CAN is set, the main loop cannot change the state of the station. In Fig. 5, we have two main loops with different guards. One is 'CAN==1', and the other 'CAN==0'. If 'CAN==0' the main loop is taken. The current state of the station is compared with the *Interface*. In Fig. 3, *Interface* can communicate with *Station* when it is in the nodes 'inUp' (the UP button is pressed), 'inDown' (the DOWN button is pressed) or 'inSby' (no button is pressed). If 'CAN==1', some counters such as *cyclecounter* are reset, but nothing else happens.

The ECHO flag can only be set via the main loop with guard 'CAN==0'. When the station detects a difference between its current state and the state of the button, ECHO is set. When ECHO is set, the state of the station cannot change by messages it receives from the bus. Like CAN, ECHO can only be reset when the state of the station is STANDBY and a STANDBY message is received from the bus. But for ECHO, there is an extra requirement that has to be fulfilled before it can be reset: it has to be the station's turn to use the bus.

3.3 Adding Timing Information

The time model in UPPAAL is continuous or dense. Clocks are used to capture time in UPPAAL. They can be associated with a transition or a node. In a transition, clock variables can be reset or used as a guard. In a node, clock variables can be used as a hold up to let the process stay in that node for a certain amount of time. Such nodes are said to be labeled with an invariant.

The way we modeled the time information of the lift system is influenced by the developers' solution to solve one problem found in the start-up phase. It is also influenced by the fact that during normal operation the stations take fixed turns to use the bus. During the start-up phase there is no such order. This difference has led to a different treatment of the timing information in the two phases. We first discuss the start-up phase and then normal operation.

Start-Up. The first problem found in [7] occurs in the start-up phase. It has to do with the re-opening of the relay between the first and second lift at the wrong moment. Consider Fig. 1 in Section 2 again. The SETREF button is pressed on station B, which closes its relay and sends a STARTUP message to station C. If station C sends a STARTUP message before the relay between station B and station C is opened, this message is received by station B, which draws the incorrect conclusion that there are only two lifts in the network.

The solution to this problem is to let station C (or in general the station with position 2) wait until the relay between the first station and the second station is opened, before sending the STARTUP message. The developers added delays to the original design to make sure this happens.

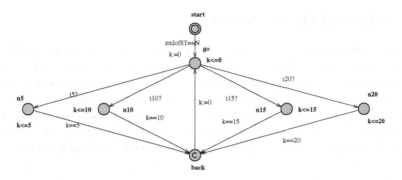

Fig. 6. The automaton *Timer*.

In the redesign, during the start-up phase, a local clock 'x' is assigned to each station. The local clock is reset when a station gets a STARTUP message, or a SETREF button is pressed. This is used to capture the moment when the stations join the network. Receiving a message from the bus or sending a message to the bus costs 1 millisecond. The opening and closing of a relay cost 5 milliseconds. There is a delay of 24 milliseconds before sending a STARTUP message. This is all the timing information in the start-up phase.

Normal Operation. During normal operation, the local clocks used during the start-up phase are not used anymore. Instead we use one global. We create an extra automaton *Timer* depicted in Fig. 6.

Transitions normally don't take time in UPPAAL, but this does happen in the lift system. Each main loop consumes 1 millisecond. After each main loop, the station waits 0.5 millisecond to get messages from the bus. During the internal loop, the receiving and sending messages take 1 millisecond. Before sending a SYNC message, stations delay 1.5 milliseconds. Before sending a state message, stations delay 2 milliseconds. This is all the timing information in the normal operation phase. We use *Timer* to express time consumption by transitions; this idea is borrowed from [9]. The guard 'endofST==N' makes sure that the *Timer* is only used in normal operation, where N is the number of lifts in the system. In node 'go', time is constrained to not progress at all. This means that in order for time to progress, one of the edges 'tn?' must be taken; where $n \in \{5, 10, 15, 20\}$ expresses the amount time of delay. These edges then lead to nodes where time can progress with the corresponding number of time units, where after control returns immediately to the 'go' node.

Concluding, the four problems in the original system are:

1. The relay between the first and second lift is re-opened at the wrong moment;
2. The SETREF buttons at two lifts are pressed in the start-up phase;
3. An UP or DOWN button is pressed and released at an inappropriate moment;
4. Two UP or DOWN buttons at different lifts are pressed at the same time, and one is released at an inappropriate moment.

4   Analysis of the Redesign

Since the redesign does not change the desired external behavior of lifts, the UPPAAL model of the redesign should satisfy all the requirements in Section 2.2. We formulate those requirements in the UPPAAL requirement specification language, and verify them, sometimes with the help of test automata, to check whether the redesign solves problems 3 and 4. We do not give the definition and explanation of the UPPAAL requirement specification language [11]; we expect that the formulas in this section can be understood without difficulties.

4.1   Expressing the Requirements

We first check deadlock freeness. This can be translated into the UPPAAL requirement specification language directly:

– A[] not deadlock

The redesign satisfies this property, which indicates that the solution from the developers solves the first problem found in [7]. In the implementation of the lift system, the delay for each STARTUP message is 24 milliseconds. In the UPPAAL model, a delay of 6 milliseconds for each STARTUP message is already enough to solve this problem.

Liveness I says that buttons on a lift can be pressed and released whenever the user wants, and that the system will respond to this. After implementing the main loop in the UPPAAL model, it is always possible to press or release buttons. So for the redesign, Liveness I becomes trivial.

Liveness II says that if an UP or DOWN button is pressed and not released and no other button is pressed, all lifts will move. In the UPPAAL requirement specification language, it is impossible to express this property. Fortunately, according to [1], we can transform this property into a test automaton, in which an approach is developed to model-checking of timed automata via reachability testing. The idea is to create a 'bad' state in the test automaton and let the verifier check whether the system can reach this state. If it does, the system violates a certain property.

The test automaton may need some extra 'decorations' for the verification purpose. In principle, with the test automaton we can express all scenarios we want to check. As this would lead to a possibly infinite state space, some scenarios which are not interesting can be abstracted away. For example, in the lift system, the buttons can be pressed and released many times. We consider only those scenarios where a button on one lift is pressed and released at most once. The automaton for the Liveness II requirement is depicted in Fig. 7.

We add new synchronizations between the *Interface* automata and the test automaton via *press* and *release* channels, to model the number of pressing and releasing actions. In the test automaton only one pressing and releasing per lift can take place. *nomore* is a variable that is used to block more pressing and releasing actions. This test automaton is used to express that if a button is pressed and not released any more, after some period of time (modeled by

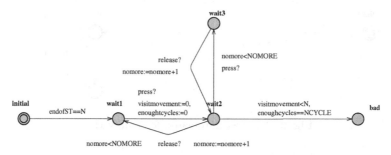

Fig. 7. The test automaton for Liveness II.

Fig. 8. The test automaton for Safety I.

variable *enoughcycles*) all the lifts will move. We now check whether the test automaton can reach the node 'bad'. If the test automaton reaches the node 'bad', it means that not all the lifts have moved and the system violates property Liveness II.

– A[] not testautomaton.bad

Test automata are also used to model and check the other two safety properties.

With Liveness II, we could check that if one button is pressed, all the lifts reach their 'activemovement' or 'passivemovement' node within a certain amount of time. What we do not check is whether they move in the same direction. Safety I demands that whenever a lift moves, all the other lifts move simultaneously in the same direction. The corresponding test automaton is depicted in Fig. 8. This test automaton waits for one lift to reach the 'activemovement' node, which is detected by a synchronization on channel 'go?' between *Station* and this test automaton. The test automaton then checks whether the other lifts move in the same direction (modeled by guard 'visitmovement!=N') within a certain amount of time (modeled by 'enoughcycles==NCYCLES').

Safety II states that there will be no movement when no button has been pressed. The corresponding test automaton is depicted in Fig. 9. The variable *noupdown* (meaning no UP or DOWN button pressed) is used to block all pressings of buttons in the *Interfaces*. Now we can check whether it is still possible for the lifts to reach movement nodes (modeled by 'visitmovement≥0').

The redesign satisfies requirement Safety II, and violates requirements Liveness II and Safety I. We will discuss the diagnostic traces and the reasons in the next section.

Fig. 9. The test automaton for Safety II.

4.2   Problems

The developers invented flags to solve the third problem found in [7]. These flags seem to solve the error scenario described in [7]. But during the testing phase, the developers encountered a new error; again the cause for this error was not clear to them. We have built a UPPAAL model (see Section 3) for the redesign and checked it. Liveness II turns out to be violated. We first investigate the diagnostic trace generated by the model checker in UPPAAL, and then give the reason why the solution from the developers fails. The generated diagnostic trace contains 256 transitions; we used the graphic simulation tool in UPPAAL to analyze it.

Initially all the flags are 0. When an UP button is pressed on one station (A), ECHO will be set and the state of station A will change to UP. Station A sends an UP message. The other stations will set the CAN flag and change their state to UP. Suppose the button is released again. The flag of station A does not change, but its state will change to STANDBY (see the main loop in Fig. 5). Station A will send a STANDBY message which the others will adopt. When they have adopted this state, and if they receive another STANDBY message, the CAN flags of the other stations will be reset. After a short while all CAN flags in the network are 0, ECHO of station A is 1, and all the states of the stations are STANDBY. Suppose now that an UP button of another station (B) is pressed. Station B will send an UP message. Station A will receive this but cannot change its state because ECHO is set. When it is station A's turn to use the bus it will therefore send a STANDBY message. Station B will receive this STANDBY message, and it will not count enough UP messages. The whole counting procedure has to start over again. Station B will send an UP message. The other stations will adopt this state and send a UP message. But when it is station A's turn, again since ECHO is set, it will send a STANDBY message and station B will again not count enough UP messages. It is clear that the ECHO of station A should be reset to get out of this situation, but that can only happen when the state of the station is STANDBY, a STANDBY message is received, and it is this station's turn to use the bus. For station A this never happens. As a result, the whole system will never move, even when an UP button is pressed.

The test automaton detects this problem. Even though the solution of the developers has some virtue, they seem not to have taken into account that the main reason for the third problem lies in the fact that the active station immediately changes its state to STANDBY after a button is released. Their solution was directed to block state changes to the active station after its state has changed to STANDBY. This is not the heart of the problem and therefore the problem remains in the redesign.

The fourth problem found in [7] is also still in the redesign. The redesign violates Safety I property. The reason resembles what is already explained in [7]. This is not very surprising, since the fourth problem was unknown to the developers at the time of the redesign.

5   A New Solution

In this section, we refine the solution proposed in [7] in such a way that it corresponds with UPPAAL and resemble to the solution from the developers. The key point why our solution differs from the flags added into the redesign is that our solution creates a link between the state change of a station and the turn of the station to use the bus. This idea was already mentioned in the μCRL model [7], but it was not further specified. With the more exact model of the redesign, including the main loop, and using the idea of the flags the developers came up with, now we work out the idea in detail.

The new flags are called CHANGE and ACTIVE. They are assigned to each station. CAN and ECHO are no longer a part of the new solution. When ACTIVE is 1, the corresponding station is active; otherwise, the station is passive. CHANGE of a station is set when there is a button pressed or released at this station (through the main loop). This is used to remember that the ACTIVE flag at this station must change from active to passive, or vice versa. Only when the station gets its turn to use the bus, this change will actually happen. If one station wants to become active, it has to make sure that there are no other active stations in the system, by checking whether the state of the message from the bus is STANDBY. If the CHANGE of a station is set, this station does not change its state until it is its turn to use the bus to make a decision. CHANGE is reset together with a setting or resetting of ACTIVE.

Changing the new flags has no effect on the automata *Interface*, *Bus* and *Timer*. They are exactly the same as in the redesign. Only the automaton *Station* has undergone crucial changes. We will not explain the new *Station* automaton in detail, more information can be found in [10]. All requirements have been checked successfully on the model with this new solution. In particular, problem three and four are resolved.

6   Concluding Remarks

In this paper, we have reported an industrial case study on applying formal techniques for the design and analysis of a distributed system for lifting trucks. Our work can be considered as one piece of evidence that formal verification techniques are mature enough to be applied in industrial projects.

The lift system has been analyzed in the process algebraic language μCRL [7]. Four problems were found. Three of them were also found by the developers during the testing phase. They proposed solutions and made a redesign. But they faced a new problem. The redesign was then modeled in UPPAAL. The analysis in Section 4 has produced some interesting results. The first is that the redesign does not satisfy all the requirements. Second, the redesign does not solve all the problems with the original design. Only one problem is solved by adding time delays. The third problem, for which those flags were developed, and the fourth problem are not solved. Third, our solution in [7] was refined, and will be implemented in the new release of the lift system.

Since more details of the lift system are taken into account in the UPPAAL model, the state space of the redesign increases dramatically. In [7], we could analyze the μCRL model with up to five lifts. With the current version of the μCRL toolset, we can get up to seven lifts on a cluster at CWI, owing to a distributed state space generation algorithm. For the UPPAAL model of the redesign, we could only manage the analysis for systems with three lifts. The requirements were checked on a 1.4 GHz AMD Althlon^{TM} Processor with 512 Mb memory.

Acknowledgments

We thank the developers of the lift systems for their collaboration and fruitful discussions. We thank the anonymous referees for their useful comments.

References

1. L. Aceto, A. Burgueno and K.G. Larsen. Model checking via reachability testing for timed automata. In *Proceedings of 4th International Conference on Tools and Algorithms for Construction and Analysis of Systems*, LNCS 1384, pp. 263-280. Springer-Verlag, 1998.
2. R. Alur and D.L. Dill. A theory of timed automata. *Theoretical Computer Science*, 126(2):183–235, 1994.
3. J. Bengtsson, W.O.D. Griffioen, K.J. Kristoffersen, K.G. Larsen, F. Larsson, P. Pettersson, and Y. Wang. Automated analysis of an audio control protocol using UPPAAL. *Journal of Logic and Algebraic Programming*, 52-53:163–181, 2002.
4. J.A. Bergstra and J.W. Klop. Process algebra for synchronous communication. *Information and Computation*, 60:109–137, 1984.
5. S.C.C. Blom, W.J. Fokkink, J.F. Groote, I.A. van Langevelde, B. Lisser, and J.C. van de Pol. μCRL: A toolset for analysing algebraic specifications. In *Proceedings of 13th Conference on Computer Aided Verification*, LNCS 2102, pp. 250–254. Springer, 2001.
6. Robert Bosch Gmbh, Postfach 30 02 40, D-70442 Stuttgart, Germany. *CAN Specification. Version 2.0*, 1991.
7. J.F. Groote, J. Pang, and A.G. Wouters. Analysis of a distributed system for lifting trucks. *Journal of Logic and Algebraic Programming*, 55(1/2):21–56, 2003.
8. J.F. Groote and A. Ponse. The syntax and semantics of μCRL. *Algebra of Communicating Processes '94*, Workshops in Computing Series, pages 26–62. Springer-Verlag, 1995.

9. K. Havelund, K.G. Larsen and A. Skou. Formal verification of a power controller using the real-time model checker UPPAAL. In *Proceedings of 5th International AMAST Workshop on Formal Methods for Real-Time and Probabilistic Systems*, LNCS 1601, pp. 277-298. Springer-Verlag, 1999.
10. B. Karstens. *Formal verification of the redesign of a distributed lift system using UPPAAL*. Master thesis, Utrecht University, 2003. Available at `http://www.cwi.nl/~pangjun/research/liftredesign.ps`
11. K.G. Larsen, P. Pettersson, and Y. Wang. UPPAAL in a nutshell. *International Journal on Software Tools for Technology Transfer*, 1(1–2):134–152, 1997.
12. M. Lindahl, P. Pettersson, and Y. Wang. Formal design and analysis of a gear controller. *International Journal on Software Tools for Technology Transfer*, 3(3):353–368, 2001.

Verification of Timeliness QoS Properties in Multimedia Systems

Behzad Bordbar[1] and Kozo Okano[2]

[1] University of Birmingham
B.Bordbar@cs.bham.ac.uk
[2] Osaka University
okano@ist.osaka-u.ac.jp

Abstract. One of the main challenges of the design of object-based Distributed Multimedia Systems is to address the performance related issues such as the Quality of Service (QoS). The specification of QoS is a crucial part of architectural object-based methods such as Open Distributed Processing (ODP). In the ODP, a QoS property assigned to an object is modelled via two clauses of *required* and *provided* QoS statements, which specify the level of QoS required/provided by an object from/to its environment, respectively. An over-demanding QoS statement can be beyond the physical limitation of the system and might result in inconsistencies. In particular, to produce a correct design, it is crucial to study the effect of QoS statements of components on the overall behaviour of the system in earlier stages of the design.

This paper develops a theory for the verification of *Timeliness QoS* properties such as Jitter, Throughput and Latency. The approach adopted is based on the idea of *Test Automata*. We shall present a formal definition of *Timeliness QoS* properties, which is used for the creation of Test Automata. Such Test Automata, which we shall refer to as *QoS Timed Automata*, can be used to verify the corresponding QoS Timeliness property. The method is illustrated by the verification of Throughput in a Video Player systems via the model checker UPPAAL.

Keywords: QoS, Network of Timed Automata, Real-time System, Verification, Model checker UPPAAL

1 Introduction

Since modern Distributed Multimedia systems are object-based, functional behaviour of such systems is encapsulated within multiple components. Quality of Service (QoS) properties, which can be seen as a set of contracts on the system, are end-to-end issues, i.e. a QoS requirement is related to the systems as a whole. As a result, a major challenge of the integration of QoS in the design process of object-based distributed systems is to specify suitable QoS characteristics for each component of the system such that; if the QoS characteristics of components are satisfied, then the QoS requirement of the whole system is satisfied. In particular, it is important to ensure that under the specification of the functional behaviour of the system the QoS is achievable.

J.S. Dong and J. Woodcock (Eds.): ICFEM 2003, LNCS 2885, pp. 523–540, 2003.

The current paper builds on earlier works [1, 11, 12], which present a method of specification of QoS in ODP [21] design of Distributed Multimedia Systems. Our aim is to present a method of verification of *Timeliness* QoS statements such a Jitter, Throughput and Latency, which are boolean functions on the set of sequences of time of occurrence of events. The adopted approach is based on the idea of *Test Automata* [2–4, 16]. Assume that the functional behaviour of the system is modelled via (a network of) Timed Automata [5, 9] $\mathscr{A}$. Starting from a Timeliness property ϕ related to the time of occurrence of external event $e_1, \ldots, e_K$ of $\mathscr{A}$, we shall present a network of Timed Automata $QTA(\phi, e_1, \ldots, e_K)$, called *QoS Timed Automata,* which will be used to verify the property ϕ on $\mathscr{A}$. The QoS Timed Automata is such that $\mathscr{A}$ satisfies the property ϕ if and only if $QTA(\phi, e_1, \ldots, e_K) \parallel \mathscr{A}$ does not reach to a global state with a coordinate **failure**, where the location **failure** of $QTA(\phi, e_1, \ldots, e_K)$ represents the violation of ϕ. In practice, using QTA transfers the problem of verifying a QoS statement of a distributed system into a reachability analysis in a network of Timed Automata, which can be carried out via model checkers. In this paper, we shall use UPPAAL [6, 9], which has been successfully applied to the verification of real-time systems [8, 14, 18].

The paper is organised as follows. Section 2 presents a brief introduction to Timed Automata and UPPAAL. Section 3, presents a formal definition for QoS Timeliness properties and QoS Timed Automata (QTA). Theorem 1, the main result of the paper, proves that a QTA is a Test Automata [2–4, 16]. Section 4 applies our approach to the verification of throughput in an example of a Video Player system. Section 5 presents a proof for **Theorem** 1. The final two sections discuss some related works and draw a conclusion.

2   Timed Automata with Data Variables and UPPAAL

In this section, we shall review a variation of Timed Automata model proposed by Alur and Dill [5], which is used in UPPAAL [6, 9, 16, 17], a tool for the verification of behavioural properties of real-time systems.

Consider a set of *Completed Actions*, denoted by CA, which specify internal actions of a component of the system modelled via Timed Automata. In the UPPAAL model, Timed Automata (components) communicate via simple CCS [20] style point-to-point communication. As a result, consider a set of *Half Actions*, $HA = \{x?, x! \mid x \in CA\}$. Let $\mathbb{A}$ denotes the set of *all* actions of the system consist of all half actions and complete actions, i.e. $\mathbb{A} = HA \cup CA$. $x \in CA$. Underlying actions are defined via the function $\downarrow : \mathbb{A} \to \mathbb{A}$ defined by $\downarrow (x!) = \downarrow (x?) = \downarrow (x) = x$ for all $x \in CA$. If there is no fear of confusion, we shall sometimes drop parentheses and write $\downarrow x!, \downarrow x?$ or $\downarrow x$. Moreover, for $A \subset \mathscr{A}$, $\downarrow A = \{\downarrow y \mid y \in A\}$.

Suppose that $\mathscr{C}$ is a set of clock variables, with values in $\mathbb{R}^{\geq 0}$ and $\mathscr{D}$ is a set of data variables, with integer values. Let $c(\mathscr{C} \cup \mathscr{D})$ denotes the conjunction of boolean expressions over atomic formulae of the form $x \sim q$ or $x - y \sim q$ or $i \sim n$, where $x, y \in \mathscr{C}$, $i \in \mathscr{D}$, q is a rational number, $n \in \mathbb{N} = \{0, 1, \ldots\}$ a natural number and $\sim\, \in \{\leq, \geq, =, <, >\}$. In what follows the term *variable* refers to both data and clock variables.

A *valuation (variable assignment)* is a map $v : c(\mathscr{C} \cup \mathscr{D}) \to \mathbb{R}^{\geq 0} \cup \mathbb{N}$, which assigns to each clock a non-negative real-number and to a data variable a natural number. For a valuation v, a delay $d \in \mathbb{R}^{\geq 0}$, which is denoted by $v + d$, is defined as $(v+d)(x) = v(x)+d$, if x is a clock and $(v+d)(i) = v(i)$, if i is a data variable. In other words, all clocks operate with the same speed and data variables are time-insensitive. If $A \neq \emptyset$ is a set of variables, i.e. $A \subset \mathscr{C} \cup \mathscr{D}$, the set of valuations on A is denoted by $\mathscr{V}(A)$. For nonempty sets of variables A, B and valuations $v_1 \in \mathscr{V}(A)$ and $v_2 \in \mathscr{V}(B)$ if $v_1(x) = v_2(x)$ for all $x \in A \cap B$, we define $v_1 \cup v_2 \in \mathscr{V}(A \cup B)$ by $v_1 \cup v_2(x) = v_1(x)$ if $x \in A$ and $v_1 \cup v_2(y) = v_2(y)$ if $y \in B$.

The value of clock or data variable can be *reset*. A reset statement is of the form $x := e$, where x is a clock or a data variable and e is an expression. In the current version of UPPAAL, for a clock, e must be a natural number, and for a data variable, e must be in the form of $cy + c'$, where c and c' are constant integer and y is a data variable. A set of reset statements is called a *reset-set* or *reset* if each variable is assigned at most once. The result of applying a reset r to a valuation v is denoted by the valuation $r(v)$. If a variable x is such that no assignment of r changes its value then $v(x) = r(v)(x)$. Let $\mathscr{R}$ denotes the set of all resets. If $r_1, r_2 \in \mathscr{R}$, then $r_1 \cup r_2 \in \mathscr{R}$, if $r_1 \cup r_2$ assigns at most one value to each variable. A *Timed Automaton* $\mathscr{A}$ is a 6-tuple (L, l_0, T, I, C, D, A) such that

- L is a finite set of *locations* and $l_0 \in L$ is a designated location called the *initial location*.
- $C \subset \mathscr{C}$, $D \subset \mathscr{D}$ and $A \subset \mathbb{A}$ are finite sets of clock variables, data variables and actions, respectively.
- $T \subset L \times A \times c(C \cup D) \times \mathscr{R} \times L$ is a transition relation. An element of T is of the form of (l_1, a, g, r, l_2), where $l_1, l_2 \in L$ are locations of Timed Automaton, $a \in \mathbb{A}$ is an action, $g \in c(C \cup D)$ is called a *guard*, and $r \in \mathscr{R}$ is a set of reset statement. We sometimes write $l_1 \xrightarrow{e,g,r} l_2$ to depict that $\mathscr{A}$ evolves from a location l_1 to a new location l_2, if the guard g is evaluated *true*, the action a is performed and clocks and data variables are reset according to r.
- $I : L \to c(C \cup D)$ is a function that assigns to each location an *invariant*. Intuitively, a timed automata can stay in a location while its invariants are satisfied. The default invariant for a location is *true* ($x \geq 0$).

For each Timed Automaton $\mathscr{A}$, we shall write $Location(\mathscr{A})$, $Clock(\mathscr{A})$, $Data(\mathscr{A})$ and $Act(\mathscr{A})$ to denote the set of *locations*, *clocks*, *data variables* and *actions* of $\mathscr{A}$, respectively.

The semantics of Timed Automata can be interpreted over transition systems, i.e. triple $(S, s_0, \Rightarrow)$, where

- $S \subset L \times \mathscr{V}$ is the set of *states*, i.e. each state is a pair (l, v), where l is a location and v is a valuation
- $s_0 \in S$ is an *initial state*, and
- $\Rightarrow \subset S \times (Act(\mathscr{A}) \cup \mathbb{R}^{\geq 0}) \times S$ is a *transition relation*.

A transitions can be either a *discrete transitions*, e.g. (s_1, e, s_2), where $e \in Act(\mathscr{A})$ or a *time transitions*, e.g. (s_1, d, s_2), where $d \in \mathbb{R}^{>0}$ and denotes the passage of d time units. Transitions are written: $s_1 \xrightarrow{e} s_2$ and $s_1 \xrightarrow{d} s_2$, respectively, and are defined according of the following inference rules:

$$\frac{l_1 \xrightarrow{e,g,r} l'_1, g(v)}{(l_1, v) \xrightarrow{e} (l_2, r(v))} \qquad \frac{\forall d' \leq d \quad I(l)(v + d')}{(l, v) \xrightarrow{d} (l, v + d)}$$

A direct results of the above definition is the Time Additivity Axiom [23].

Time Additivity Axiom: For every $s_1, s_2 \in S$ and $d_1, d_2 \in \mathbb{R}^{\geq 0}$, $s_1 \xrightarrow{d_1 + d_2} s_2$ if and only if there is a state s_3 such that $s_1 \xrightarrow{d_1} s_3$ and $s_3 \xrightarrow{d_2} s_2$.

To model concurrency and synchronisation between Timed Automaton, CCS [20] style parallel composition operators are introduced, which synchronise over half actions. Suppose that $\mathscr{A}_1, \ldots, \mathscr{A}_n$ are Timed Automata, the parallel composition $\mathscr{A} := \mathscr{A}_1 \parallel \mathscr{A}_2 \parallel \cdots \parallel \mathscr{A}_n$ is referred to as a *network of Timed Automata* [6, 9, 16, 17]. The semantics of a network of Timed Automata can be expressed via a transition system $(S, s_0, \Rightarrow)$. A state $s \in S$ is of the form $s = (l, v)$ where $l = (l_1, \ldots, l_n)$, in which each l_i is location of $\mathscr{A}_i$ and v is a valuation on $\cup_i(Clock(\mathscr{A}_i) \cup Data(\mathscr{A}_i))$. $s_0 = (l_0, v_0)$ is the *initial location*, where l_0 is the vector of initial location of the components and v_0 is the a valuation compatible with the initial valuation of the components, i.e. $v_0 \mid_{Clock(\mathscr{A}_i) \cup Data(\mathscr{A}_i)}$ is the initial valuation of the i-th component.

Let for a vector of location $l = (l_1, \ldots, l_n)$, $l[l'_i/l_i]$ denotes the vector of location created by replacing l_i with l'_i, then $\Rightarrow$ is defined via the following inference rules:

- For a completed action a which belongs to a component $\mathscr{A}_i$, i.e. $a \in Act(\mathscr{A}_i) \cap CA$, $(l, v) \xrightarrow{a} (l[l'_i/l_i], r_i(v))$, if $l_i \xrightarrow{a, g_i, r_i} l'_i$ and $g_i(v)$ [1]
- Suppose that $x!$ and $x?$ are half actions of $\mathscr{A}_i$ and $\mathscr{A}_j$ where $i \neq j$. $(l, v) \xrightarrow{x}$ $(l[l'_i/l_i, l'_j/l_j], r_i \cup r_j(v))$, if $l_i \xrightarrow{x!, g_i, r_i} l'_i$, $l_j \xrightarrow{x?, g_j, r_j} l'_j$, $g_i(v), g_j(v)$ and $r_i \cup r_j \in \mathscr{R}$.
- For $d \in \mathbb{R}^{\geq 0}$, $(l, v) \xrightarrow{d} (l, v + d)$, if $I(l_i)(v + d')$ for all i, and all $d' \leq d$.

Presence of urgent channels and committed locations may overrule the above transitions as follows. In a state where two components may synchronise of an urgent channel, no further delay is allowed. If in a state, one of the components is in a location labelled as being committed, no delay is allowed to occur and any discrete transition *must* invoke. In this paper, we shall not use any urgent action or committed state.

Assume that $\mathscr{A}$ is a network of Timed Automata. A *run* σ of $\mathscr{A}$ is a finite/infinite sequence of transitions of the form $s_0 \xrightarrow{\lambda_1} s_1 \xrightarrow{\lambda_2} s_2 \cdots$ where s_0 is the initial state and $\lambda_i \in Act(\mathscr{A}) \cup \mathbb{R}^{\geq 0}$. For each state s_j of the run σ, define

---

[1] Note that g_i is a function defined on valuations of the a component timed automata $\mathscr{A}_i$. As a result, $g_i(v)$ is an abbreviation for $g_i(v \mid_{Clock(\mathscr{A}_i) \cup Data(\mathscr{A}_i)})$.

$TimeStamp(\sigma, s_j) = \sum_{i=1}^{j-1}\{\lambda_i \mid \lambda_i \in \mathbb{R}^{\geq 0}\}$. Similarly, for an action λ_j define $TimeStamp(\sigma, \lambda_j) := TimeStamp(\sigma, s_j)$, which denotes the time of occurrence of λ_j. We shall denote the set of all runs of $\mathscr{A}$ with $Run(\mathscr{A})$. Assume that σ_1 and $\sigma_2 \in Run(\mathscr{A})$ are such that $\sigma_1 := s_0^1 \overset{\lambda_1}{\Rightarrow} s_1^1 \overset{\lambda_2}{\Rightarrow} s_2^1 \cdots$ and $\sigma_2 := s_0^2 \overset{\mu_1}{\Rightarrow} s_1^2 \overset{\mu_2}{\Rightarrow} s_2^2 \cdots$. We say σ_1 and σ_2 are *identical* if they have the same length, i.e. either both are infinite length or both have the same length, and for each i, $s_i^1 = s_i^2$ and $\lambda_i = \mu_i$. However, by Time Additivity Axiom, two runs $\sigma_1 := s_0 \overset{\frac{1}{2}}{\Rightarrow} s_1 \overset{\frac{1}{2}}{\Rightarrow} s_2$ and $\sigma_2 := s_0 \overset{1}{\Rightarrow} s_2$, although not identical, are equal. In this paper, two runs are called **equal,** if they are equal up to Time Additivity Axiom, i.e. applying Time Additivity Axiom to one of them results in an identical run with the other. If l is a location of $\mathscr{A}$, we say a run $\sigma \in Run(\mathscr{A})$ *meets* the location l, if there is a state $s_i = (l, v)$ in σ.

3   Verification of QoS Timeliness Properties

Assume that e is an action of the system, a Timeliness property for e is defined to be a property related to the time of occurrence of e [10]. For example, if the action e marks the dispatch of frames from a communication channel, the throughput of 25 frames per sec. can be seen as a property of the time sequence $\{t_1, t_2, \ldots\}$ of the time of the occurrence of e such that

$$\forall n \quad \mid t_{n+25} - t_n \mid < 1000, \tag{1}$$

where time is measured in msec.

In general, the sequence of time of occurrence of events are finite or infinite sequences of non-decreasing, non-negative real numbers.

Definition 1. *For $n \in \mathbb{N}$, let $\Gamma^n = \{\{t_i\}_{i=1}^n \mid 0 \leq t_1 \leq t_2 \leq \cdots \leq t_n\}$.*
Let $\Gamma = \bigcup_{n=1}^{\infty} \Gamma^n \cup \{\emptyset\}$, where $\emptyset$ is the empty set.

Suppose that $\mathscr{A}$ is a a network of Timed Automata and $\sigma = s_0 \overset{\lambda_1}{\Rightarrow} \cdots \overset{\lambda_n}{\Rightarrow} s_n \cdots$ is a finite/infinite run of $\mathscr{A}$, where for each i, s_i is a state and $\lambda_i \in act(\mathscr{A}) \cup \mathbb{R}^{\geq 0}$.

Definition 2. *For each action $e \in Act(\mathscr{A})$, if e is an event occurring as $\{\lambda_i\}$, let $Time(\sigma, e, n)$ denotes the time of n-th occurrence of e in the run σ, i.e. $Time(\sigma, e, n) = TimeStamp(\sigma, s_j) = \sum_{i=1}^{j-1}\{\lambda_i \mid \lambda_i \in \mathbb{R}^{\geq 0}\}$. Let the sequence $Time(\sigma, e) := \{Time(\sigma, e, n) \mid n \in \mathbb{N}\}$.*

Clearly, for each run σ and each action $e \in \mathscr{A}$, $Time(\sigma, e) \in \Gamma$. In particular, if e does not appear in σ, then $Time(\sigma, e) = \emptyset (\in \Gamma)$ is the empty sequence. Now, we shall present a formal definition of Timeliness properties as boolean functions on the set of time sequences.

Definition 3. *A Timeliness property of degree $K \geq 1$, is a function $\phi : \Gamma^K \longrightarrow \{\mathbf{T}, \mathbf{F}\}$, where $\Gamma^K = \overbrace{\Gamma \times \Gamma \times \cdots \times \Gamma}^{K}$.*

Example 1. The throughput of 25 frames per sec. for e can be expressed via the Timeliness property ϕ of degree 1, defined by

$$\phi(t) = \begin{cases} \mathbf{T} & \forall n \quad |\ t_{n+25} - t_n\ | < 1000 \\ \mathbf{F} & \text{otherwise} \end{cases} .$$

As a result, throughput is a Timeliness property of degree 1. It can be seen QoS statements such as various types of Jitter [13] are Timeliness properties of degree 1, whereas latency is a Timeliness property of degree 2. In general, it seems that, any property related to the relative time of occurrence of K events can be evaluated via a Timeliness property function of degree K. Assume that the functional behaviour of system is modelled via a network of Timed Automata. For a property to satisfy, it must satisfy for all runs of the network of Timed Automata.

Definition 4. *Assume that $\mathscr{B}$ is a Timed Automaton such that $e_1, \ldots, e_K \in Act(\mathscr{B})$. Suppose that ϕ is a Timeliness property of the degree K. $\mathscr{B}$ satisfies ϕ for $e_1, \ldots, e_K$ iff for each run σ of $\mathscr{B}$, $\phi(\text{Time}(\sigma, e_1), \ldots, \text{Time}(\sigma, e_K)) = \mathbf{T}$. In this case, we say σ satisfies ϕ.*

The main focus of this paper is on Timeliness properties which express QoS statements. The outline of our approach is as follows. We start from a Timeliness statement ϕ and create a network of Timed Automata such that all its runs that do not meet a state called **failure**, satisfy ϕ. Moreover, all runs of the network of Timed Automata that *meet* **failure** violate ϕ. This ensures that the network of Timed Automata fully represents the property ϕ.

Definition 5. *Assume that ϕ is a Timeliness properties of degree K expressing a QoS statement on the set of actions $e_1, e_2, \ldots, e_K$. A QoS Timed Automaton corresponding to ϕ and $e_1, \ldots, e_K$ is a network of Timed Automaton $\mathscr{A} = QTA(\phi, e_1, e_2, \ldots, e_K)$ such that*

1. *$\mathscr{A}$ contains a distinct location **failure**;*
2. *for each run σ of $\mathscr{A}$, if σ does not meet a **failure** state, i.e. a vector of locations with at least one co-ordinate **failure**, σ satisfies ϕ.*
3. *for sequences, $t^1, t^2, \ldots t^K \in \Gamma$ that satisfy ϕ, there is a run σ of $\mathscr{A}$ such that*
   *(a) σ does not meet **failure**; and*
   (b) for each i $\text{Time}(\sigma, e_i) = t_i$;
4. *for finite sequences $t^1, t^2, \ldots, t^K \in \Gamma$, if ϕ does not satisfy $t^1, t^2, \ldots, t^K$, then there is a finite run σ of $\mathscr{A}$ such that σ ends in **failure** and $t^i = \text{Time}(\sigma, e_i)$.*

It poses as a question that which Timeliness properties correspond to QoS Timed Automata (QTA). Since Timeliness properties are boolean functions on Γ^K, the cardinality of the set of Timeliness properties is $\geq 2^{2^{\aleph_0}}$. Notice, the cardinality of Γ^K is the same as the cardinality of Γ, which is $\geq 2^{\aleph_0}$. The cardinality of the set of timed automata is $2^{\aleph_0}$ the majority of Timeliness properties are not in correspondence with any QTA. The question of characterisation of all timeliness properties which can be translated to QTA is highly nontrivial. [2–4] adapts a Temporal logic approach to characterise all properties which are testable via timed automata. However, considering that the Timed Automata model of [2–4] does not include data variables, further research is required to characterise all Timeliness properties corresponding to QTA.

A Timeliness property ϕ deals with the time of occurrence of external events $e_1, \ldots e_K$. Since actions are atomic, two consecutive external actions in a run σ have identical Timestamps. As a result, the order of occurrence of such events has no effect on "σ satisfies ϕ," when ϕ is of degree ≥ 2, i.e. the property ϕ can not differentiate between two runs which are identical except the order of consecutive actions with the same Timestamp. Consequently, it is important for a QTA to include all permutations of such actions.

Definition 6. *Suppose that $\mathscr{A}$ is a QTA corresponding to a Timeliness property ϕ and events $e_1, \ldots e_K$. $\mathscr{A}$ is called a* Complete QTA *if for each run $\sigma := s_0 \overset{\lambda_1}{\Rightarrow} s_1 \overset{\lambda_2}{\Rightarrow} s_2 \cdots \overset{\lambda_n}{\Rightarrow} s_n$ of $\mathscr{A}$ with consecutive actions $\lambda_i, \lambda_{i+1} \in Act(\mathscr{A}) \cap \{e_1, \ldots e_K\}$, the run $\sigma' := s_0 \overset{\lambda_1}{\Rightarrow} s_1 \overset{\lambda_2}{\Rightarrow} s_2 \cdots s_i \overset{\lambda_{i+1}}{\Rightarrow} s' \overset{\lambda_i}{\Rightarrow} s_{i+1} \cdots \overset{\lambda_n}{\Rightarrow} s_n$, which is created from changing the order of occurrence of λ_i and λ_{i+1}, is also a run of $\mathscr{A}$.*

The next theorem which is the main result of the paper, uses parallel composition of a QTA and the network of Timed Automata representing the functional behaviour of the system to verify Timeliness properties. In effect, the next theorem states that each QTA is a Test Automata [2–4].

Theorem 1. *Assume that $\mathscr{B}$ is a network of Timed Automaton such that $e_1, \ldots, e_K \in Act(\mathscr{B})$. Suppose that ϕ is a Timeliness property of the degree K, for which a complete QTA $\mathscr{A}$ exists. $\mathscr{B}$ satisfies ϕ for $e_1, \ldots, e_K$ if and only if no run of $\mathscr{A}' \parallel \mathscr{B}'$ meet the state* **failure***, where $\mathscr{A}' = QTA(\phi, e_1, e_2, \ldots, e_K)$ $[e_1?/e_1, \ldots, e_K?/e_K]$ and $\mathscr{B}' = \mathscr{B}[e_1!/e_1, \ldots e_K!/e_K]$, created from $\mathscr{A}$ and $\mathscr{B}$, respectively, by replacing $e_1, \ldots, e_K$ with half actions.*

Proof: See section 5.

4   Verification of QoS for a Video Player System

In this section, we shall apply our results to verification of Timeliness QoS statements on a model of a Video Player system. Fig. 1 depicts a process oriented view of a Video Player system. The system consists of four components *Video Source, Buffer, Decoder* and *QoS Controller* that can be explained as follows.

Video Source: models the application that produces streams of video packets. The dispatch of each video packet is abstracted as the emission of a signal *packet!*. Fig. 2 depicts the behaviour of the *Video Source* as a Timed Automaton, which dispatches *packet!* signals with the periods T_0. The variable R_P, which models the rate of the creation of the packets, is used by the *QoS controller*.

Buffer: (in Fig. 3) receives *packet?* signals and emits *o_packet!* signals in periods of T_0. The number of *packet?* in the buffer is denoted by c. If c is equal to L,

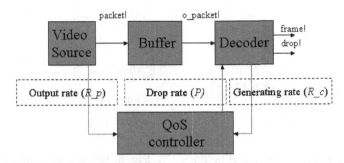

Fig. 1. A Process Oriented View of the Video Player System.

the length of the buffer, the buffer is full and the next signal causes an overflow of the buffer, which results an *Exception* being thrown. One of the objectives of the design of functional behaviour is to avoid an overflow of the buffer.

Decoder: (in Fig. 5) is used to convert arriving packets into video frames. For the purpose of simplicity, we assume that each frame consists of a single packet. On creation of a frame a half action *frame!* is emitted, which can be used to synchronise with the display driver. It takes at most T_1 unit of time and at least T_0 unit time to generate a frame from an arriving packet. The Decoder also generates *drop!* signals, which mark failure of generation of a frame. The emission of a *drop!* signal is controlled by two local variables r and p, and a global variable P. The value of variable P represents the drop rate ratio. For example for the drop rate of $\frac{1}{5}$, the value of P is equal to five, which denotes that one out of five frames are dropped. In this case the Timed Automaton creates one *drop!* in every five output signals.

The value of a global variable R_c, which shows the current rate of performance of Decoder, is incremented to mark the creation of a frame. The value is also periodically reset by QoS controller.

QoS Controller: (in Fig. 4) controls the drop rate P of the *Decoder*. To synthesise the controller, within each *unit* time, the current rate of the system performance R_p and R_c are compared. If $R_p - R_c > \theta_0$, the value of P is incremented. If $R_c - R_p > \theta_1$, the value of P is decremented. θ_0 and θ_1 are constant threshold values.

One of the outputs of the above Video Player example is a signal *frame!* representing the creation of a single frame. This signal is used to synchronise the Video Player with a display drive. For a display drive to present a high quality pictures, it is required that signals *frame!* are dispatched with a suitable throughput. In general, the QoS characteristic throughput of an event e is referred to as a lower bound or an upper bound time on the number of occurrences of the event e [10]. For the rest of the current section, we shall demonstrate our approach by an example of verification of the QoS Throughput. Formally, a Throughput of $k \in \mathbb{N}\setminus\{0\}$ within T_0 and T_1 unit of time ($T_0 < T$) is defined by

$$\forall n \ T_0 \leq \tau(e?, n + K) - \tau(e?, n) \leq T, \tag{2}$$

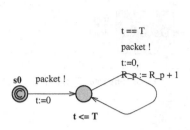

Fig. 2. Video Source represented in TA.

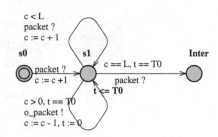

Fig. 3. RBuff represented in TA.

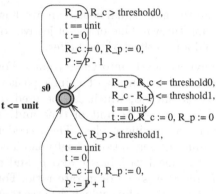

Fig. 4. QoS controller represented in TA.

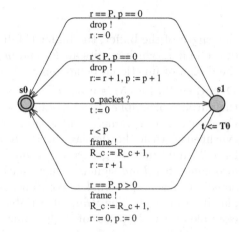

Fig. 5. Decoder represented in TA.

where $\tau(e?, n)$ denotes the time of the n-th occurrence of the event $e?$ in the system.

Example 1 expresses the throughput of 25 frames per sec. as a Timeliness property. Similarly, the general form of throughput, equation (2), can be written as a Timeliness property of degree 1. Our next aim is to present a QTA $\mathscr{A}$ corresponding to throughput that satisfies the definition 5. The first requirement is that all runs of $\mathscr{A}$ should be such that the time for the occurrence of e satisfies the equation 2. A solution is to create k clocks $t_0, t_1, \ldots, t_{k-1}$ and use each clock t_i to measure the time difference between the j-th and $i + k$-th occurrence of e, in a periodic form.

Fig. 6 represents a Timed Automata that checks if two consecutive occurrences of a signal $e?$ are within T_0 and T_1 units of each other. In order to check the Throughput, we require k parallel composition copies of the Timed Automata of Fig. 6. Each such copy of the Timed Automata of Fig. 6 has an index, denoted by i, which acts as an *identifier*. There is a global variable c, which determines which copy can fire an action $e?$. For example, in location **active**, if $c == i$ and $e?$ occurs within the period of $[T_0, T]$, a transition fires which sets the value

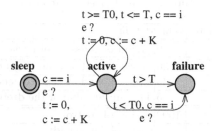

Fig. 6. QTA to measure time difference between corresponding events e.

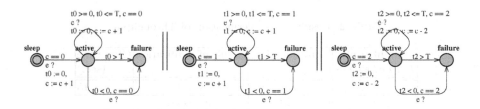

Fig. 7. QTA for the Throughput with $K = 3$.

of c to $c + K$. This means that, if the condition $T_0 \le t \le T$ is satisfied, *only* the copy of the Timed Automata of Fig. 6 with the index $i + K$ can fire. For example, the QTA for the Throughput of at least $K = 3$ within L unit of time, *i.e.*, $\forall n \quad 0 \le \tau(e, n + 2) - \tau(e?, n) \le T$ can be modelled via the network of Timed Automata depicted in Fig. 7.

The QTA of Fig. 7 works as follows. At first the value of the counter c is 0, therefore, if an action $e?$ occurs, then the Left Hand Side (LHS) Timed Automata changes its location to **active**, because condition $c == 0$ holds. Thus, LHS Timed Automata increments counter c by 1 resetting its own clock t_0. At this moment, if another action $e?$ occurs, then the Timed Automata in the middle changes its location due to *active*. It also increments the counter c by 1. Finally, the Right Hand Side Timed Automata changes its location on arriving the third action $e?$, because condition $c == 2$ holds. At this point, since $c := c - 2$, the value of c is set to 0. Now, if the fourth action e occurs within the period $[0, T]$, LHS Timed Automata again fires and c is again incremented from 0 to 1.

It can easily be seen that the network of Timed Automata of Fig. 7 satisfies the definition 5 and hence is the QTA for the throughput.

The rest of the current section demonstrates our method for the verification of Throughput of *frame?* signals in the Video Player system. In what follows, we have used UPPAAL (ver. 3.2.13) on SUN WS (Ultra SPARC Memory:4G) with the parameters specified in Table 1.

One of the requirements of the design is to ensure that the Buffer never overflows, i.e. the location **Inter** of the Buffer of Fig. 3 is not reachable. This has been verified checking the deadlock-freeness of the model.

Table 1. Video Player Parameters.

sub-system	parameter	value	details
Video Source	T_0	40	period of emission of packets
Decoder	T_0	30	Lower bound of time to generate a frame
Decoder	T_1	40	Upper bound of time to generate a frame
Decoder	P	5	The initial value of the drop-rate of the frames
Qos Controller	unit	1000	period of control
Qos Controller	θ_0, θ_1	5	Control Thresholds
Buffer	T_0	40	fixed period for the dispatch of packets
Buffer	L	5	length of the Buffer

Table 2. Result of the Verification of Throughput.

Number of frame? signals	Duration time	Result of verification	CPU time (sec.)
1	130	valid	15
1	129	not valid	
2	170	valid	30
2	169	not valid	
3	210	valid	120
3	209	not valid	
5	250	valid	60
5	249	not valid	
6	290	valid	100
6	289	not valid	
7	330	valid	600
7	329	not valid	

Checking the Throughput of K *frame?* signals per T msec. is straight forward. We only need to include K parallel composition copies of the Timed Automata of Fig. 6 and check for deadlock-freeness. Since, we have already verified that the buffer will not overflow, the only likely deadlock can occur from reaching a global state with a coordinate **failure**. But, how can we calculate K and T?

In general, estimating the Throughput of a given system is non-trivial. Here, we can see that the system produces at most K *frame?* signals every $T = 130 + (K-1) \times 40$ msec. To see, this noticing that the system has a drop rate of one in five, we need to look for the worst possible delay between *frame?* signals. The worst scenario happens when two consecutive *o_packets* are dropped. For example, consider the case that the 3-rd *frame?* signal is created in the possible time, i.e. 30 msec. after the arrival of the corresponding buffered packet. The 5-th and 6-th *frame?* signals are dropped and the 7-th is created at the latest possible time, i.e. 40 msec. after the arrival of the corresponding buffered packet. In this case, the time difference between the 4-th and 7-th *frame?* is equal to $130 = 3 \times 40 + 10$.

Table 2 depicts the result of the verification. It can be seen that Throughput of 1 frames in 130 msec., 2 frames in 170 msec., ... are verified, while the Throughput of 1 frames in 129 msec., 2 frames in 169 msec., ... are not valid. We have also included the CPU time for each experiment, which indicates an exponential increase in time. As a result, there is a clear scope in the research for finding faster method of verification of QoS Timeliness properties.

Of course UPPAAL itself is not a system development tool. However, in the early stages of the system design, it can be a strong tool for detecting time related design errors in the specification. For example, often choosing a wrong value for a constant or using $<$ instead of $\leq$ may creates a dead-lock. Such system errors can be easily detected using UPPAAL. When the designer developes an implementation as an executable code or a hardware logic design, it is hard to detect such errors.

5   Proof of Theorem 1

The aim of this section is to present a proof of the Theorem 1. Our first result establishes the relationship between runs of the parallel composition of two networks of Timed Automata with runs of each component. The idea is to *project* each run of the parallel composition to a run of the components. We shall start with the definition of a projection map.

Definition 7. *Suppose that $\mathscr{A}$ and $\mathscr{B}$ are two network of Timed Automata that share actions $e_1, e_2, \ldots, e_K$. Let $\pi_{\mathscr{A}} : Act(\mathscr{A} \parallel \mathscr{B}) \cup \mathbb{R}^{\geq 0} \longrightarrow Act(\mathscr{A}) \cup \mathbb{R}^{\geq 0}$*

$$
\pi_{\mathscr{A}}(\lambda) = \begin{cases} \lambda & \lambda \in \mathbb{R}^{\geq 0} \\ 0 & \lambda \in Act(\mathscr{B}) \backslash Act(\mathscr{A}) \\ \lambda & \lambda \in Act(\mathscr{A}) \backslash Act(\mathscr{B}) \\ \downarrow \lambda & \lambda \in Act(\mathscr{A}) \cap Act(\mathscr{B}) \end{cases} .
$$

It can be seen that the projection function $\pi_{\mathscr{A}}$ maps all actions $\lambda \notin Act(\mathscr{A})$ to 0. This can be interpreted by considering that the occurrence of such λ has no effect on the dynamics of $\mathscr{A}$ and takes zero-time. The projection map $\pi_{\mathscr{B}}$ can be defined similarly.

If $s = (l, v)$ is a state of $\mathscr{A} \parallel \mathscr{B}$, then the vector of location l consists of coordinates representing locations in both $\mathscr{A}$ and $\mathscr{B}$. Also, the valuation is a map on the set of clock variables and data variables belonging to both $\mathscr{A}$ and $\mathscr{B}$.

Definition 8. *Suppose that $s = (l, v)$ is a state of $\mathscr{A} \parallel \mathscr{B}$, define $pr_{\mathscr{A}}(s)$, called the* projection of the state s to $\mathscr{A}$, *as a pair $(l_{\mathscr{A}}, v_{\mathscr{A}})$ such that $l_{\mathscr{A}}$ is the restriction of l to the set of coordinates of locations in $\mathscr{A}$ and $v_{\mathscr{A}}$ is the restriction of v to the clocks and data variables in $\mathscr{A}$.*

The next lemma states that the projection of each run of $\mathscr{A} \parallel \mathscr{B}$ to $\mathscr{A}$ is a run of $\mathscr{A}$. Assume that $\mathscr{A}$ and $\mathscr{B}$ are networks of Timed Automata with shared actions $\{e_1, e_2, \ldots, e_K\}$.

Lemma 1. *If* $\sigma := s_0 \overset{\lambda_1}{\Rightarrow} s_1 \overset{\lambda_2}{\Rightarrow} \cdots \overset{\lambda_n}{\Rightarrow} s_n \cdots$ *is a finite/infinite of* $\mathscr{A} \parallel \mathscr{B}$, *then* $pr_{\mathscr{A}}(s_0) \overset{\pi_{\mathscr{A}}(\lambda_1)}{\Rightarrow} pr_{\mathscr{A}}(s_1) \overset{\pi_{\mathscr{A}}(\lambda_2)}{\Rightarrow} \cdots \overset{\pi_{\mathscr{A}}(\lambda_n)}{\Rightarrow} pr_{\mathscr{A}}(s_n) \cdots$, *which we shall denote with* $proj(\sigma, \mathscr{A})$, *is a run of* $\mathscr{A}' = \mathscr{A}[\downarrow e_1/e_1, \ldots, \downarrow e_K/e_K]$ *created from* $\mathscr{A}$ *by replacing each half action with its complete form.*

Proof. The proof is by induction on n. We must show that if $s_n \overset{\lambda_{n+1}}{\Rightarrow} s_{n+1}$ then $pr_{\mathscr{A}}(s_n) \overset{\pi_{\mathscr{A}}(\lambda_{n+1})}{\Rightarrow} pr_{\mathscr{A}}(s_{n+1})$. Let $s_n = (\boldsymbol{l_n}, v_n)$ and $s_{n+1} = (\boldsymbol{l_{n+1}}, v_{n+1})$.

Case 1: $\lambda_{n+1} \in \mathbb{R}^{\geq 0}$, is trivial. As $s_n \overset{\lambda_{n+1}}{\Rightarrow} s_{n+1}$ implies that for each coordinate l_i of the vector of locations $\boldsymbol{l_n}$, $I(l_i)(v+d')$ for all $d' \leq \lambda_{n+1}$. This is true specially for the coordinates l_i of $\mathscr{A}$.

Case 2: $\lambda_{n+1} \in Act(\mathscr{B}) \backslash Act(\mathscr{A})$ i.e. λ_{n+1} is an internal action of $\mathscr{B}$ and occurrence of λ_{n+1} has no effect on $\mathscr{A}$. Consequently, none of the locations, valuation of clocks or data variable of $\mathscr{A}$ is changed i. e. $pr_{\mathscr{A}}(s_n) = pr_{\mathscr{A}}(s_{n+1})$ and we can write $pr_{\mathscr{A}}(s_n) \overset{0}{\Rightarrow} pr_{\mathscr{A}}(s_{n+1})$.

Case 3: $\lambda_{n+1} \in Act(\mathscr{A}) \backslash Act(\mathscr{B})$, then there is a location $l_i \in Location(\mathscr{A})$ such that $l_i \overset{\lambda_{n+1}, g_i, r_i}{\longrightarrow} l_i'$. As a result, $\boldsymbol{l_{n+1}} = \boldsymbol{l}[l_i'/l_i]$, $v_{n+1} = r(v_n)$, and $g_i(v) = g_i(v \mid_{Clock(\mathscr{A}_i) \cup Data(\mathscr{A}_i)})$, $pr_{\mathscr{A}}(s_n) \overset{\lambda_i}{\Rightarrow} pr_{\mathscr{A}}(s_{n+1})$.

Case 4: $\downarrow \lambda_{n+1} \in \downarrow Act(\mathscr{A}) \cap \downarrow Act(\mathscr{B})$. In this case, λ_{n+1} is a shared action and there is an $e_n (1 \leq n \leq K)$, such that $\lambda_{n+1} = \downarrow e_n$. For example, $l_i \overset{e_n?, g_i, r_i}{\longrightarrow} l_i'$ and $l_i \overset{e_n!, g_j, r_j}{\longrightarrow} l_i'$ in $\mathscr{A}$ and $\mathscr{B}$, respectively. Moreover, $g_i(v_n), g_j(v_n)$ and $r_i \cup r_j \in \mathscr{R}$. As a result, replacing $e_n?$ with $\downarrow e_n (=\downarrow \lambda_n)$, we have $l_i \overset{e_n?, g_i, r_i}{\longrightarrow} l_i'$, $g_i(v_n), r_i \in \mathscr{R}$. Hence, $pr_{\mathscr{A}}(s_n) \overset{\lambda_i}{\Rightarrow} pr_{\mathscr{A}}(s_{n+1})$. $\qquad\square$

The converse of the above lemma is not valid. In other word, it is not possible to start with *any* two runs $\sigma_1 \in \mathscr{A}$ and $\sigma_2 \in \mathscr{B}$ and *merge* them to create a run of the parallel composition. For σ_1 and σ_2 to synchronise, one of the requirements is that the order of the occurrence of the shared actions to be identical.

Definition 9. *Assume that $\mathscr{A}$ and $\mathscr{B}$ are two networks of Timed Automata with shared actions $e_1, \ldots, e_K$. Assume that σ_1 and σ_2 are finite runs of $\mathscr{A}$ and $\mathscr{B}$, respectively. σ_1 and σ_2 are called Shared Action Compatible if the order of the occurrence of shared actions in them are identical. i.e. if $\{\mu_1^1, \mu_2^1, \ldots, \mu_n^1\}$ and if $\{\mu_1^2, \mu_2^2, \ldots, \mu_m^2\}$ are ordered sequences of shared actions in σ_1 and σ_2, respectively, then $n = m$ and for each i, μ_i^1 and μ_i^2 are half actions of the same complete action, i.e. . $\downarrow \mu_i^1 = \downarrow \mu_i^2$.*

The following Lemma studies a special case under which it is possible to merge a run σ_1 of $\mathscr{A}$ and a run σ_2 of $\mathscr{B}$. For σ_1 and σ_2 to merge into a run of the the parallel composition $\mathscr{A} \parallel \mathscr{B}$, they must have the same *time sequences*, for the corresponding shared actions *and* the order of the occurrence of shared actions with equal Timestamps must be identical.

Lemma 2. *Assume that $\mathcal{A}$ and $\mathcal{B}$ are network of Timed Automata with shared actions $e_1, e_2, \ldots e_K$. Assume that $\mathcal{A}$ and $\mathcal{B}$ have no shared clocks or data variables. Suppose that σ^1 and σ^2 are finite runs of $\mathcal{A}$ and $\mathcal{B}$ that*

1. *σ^1 and σ^2 are Shared Action Compatible and;*
2. *for each i, $Time(\sigma^1, e_i) = Time(\sigma^2, e_i)$,*

then there is $\sigma \in Run(\mathcal{A} \| \mathcal{B})$ such that $proj(\sigma, \mathcal{A}) = \sigma^1$ and $proj(\sigma, \mathcal{B}) = \sigma^2$.

Sketch of the Proof: suppose that $\sigma^1 = s_0^1 \overset{\alpha_1}{\Rightarrow} s_1^1 \overset{\alpha_2}{\Rightarrow} \cdots \overset{\alpha_N}{\Rightarrow} s_N^1$ and $\sigma^2 = s_0^2 \overset{\beta_1}{\Rightarrow} s_1^2 \overset{\beta_2}{\Rightarrow} \cdots \overset{\beta_M}{\Rightarrow} s_M^2$, where for each i, $\alpha_i \in Act(\mathcal{A}) \cup \mathbb{R}^{\geq 0}$ and $\beta_i \in Act(\mathcal{B}) \cup \mathbb{R}^{\geq 0}$.

Let us assume that $Timestamp(\sigma^1, S_N^1) \leq Timestamp(\sigma^2, S_M^2)$; the symmetric case of $Timestamp(\sigma^1, S_N^1) \geq Timestamp(\sigma^2, S_M^2)$ can be treated similarly. Also, without any loss of generality, we can assume that the set of all Timestamps of all states σ^1 and the Timestamps of the states of σ^2 that occurs before the Timestamp of the last state of σ^1 are identical, i.e.

$$\{Timestamp(\sigma^1, s_j^1) \mid 0 \leq j \leq N\} = \{Timestamp(\sigma^2, s_j^2) \mid \\ Timestamp(\sigma^2, s_j^2) \leq Timestamp(\sigma^1, s_N^1)\}. \tag{3}$$

The above can be achieved by using Time Additive Axiom to modify a run and adding extra states. The proof of the lemma is by induction, we shall use the following notations in the rest of the proof:

- for $0 \leq p \leq N$, let $\sigma^{1,p} := s_0^1 \overset{\alpha_1}{\Rightarrow} s_1^1 \overset{\alpha_2}{\Rightarrow} \cdots \overset{\alpha_p}{\Rightarrow} s_p^1$,
- for $0 \leq q \leq M$, let $\sigma^{2,q} := s_0^2 \overset{\beta_1}{\Rightarrow} s_1^2 \overset{\beta_2}{\Rightarrow} \cdots \overset{\beta_q}{\Rightarrow} s_q^2$,
- also assume that for $0 \leq n$, $\sigma^n := s_0 \overset{\lambda_1}{\Rightarrow} s_1 \overset{\lambda_2}{\Rightarrow} \cdots \overset{\lambda_n}{\Rightarrow} s_n$ donates a run of $\mathcal{A} \| \mathcal{B}$.

Since the induction base is trivial, we only need to prove the following claim, which implies the induction step.

CLAIM: for $p+q < M+N$, if $proj(\sigma^n, \mathcal{A}) = \sigma^{1,p}$ and $proj(\sigma^n, \mathcal{B}) = \sigma^{2,q}$, there is $\sigma^{n+1} \in Run(\mathcal{A} \| \mathcal{B})$ such that $proj(\sigma^{n+1}, \mathcal{A}) = \sigma^{1,p'}$ and $proj(\sigma^{n+1}, \mathcal{B}) = \sigma^{2,q'}$, where $p \leq p' \leq N$, $q \leq q' \leq M$ and $p + q < p' + q'$.

Proof of the CLAIM: The proof of above claim involves a number of cases. Let $s_p^1 = (l^1, v^1)$, $s_q^2 = (l^2, v^2)$ and $s_n = (l, v)$, where l consists of coordinates of l^1 and l^2 and $v = v^1 \cup v^2$.

Case I: $\alpha_{p+1} = 0$ or $\beta_{q+1} = 0$ is trivial. For example if $\alpha_{p+1} = 0$ then $s_p^1 = s_{q+1}^1$. In this case, the sequence $\sigma^{n+1} = s_0 \overset{\lambda_1}{\Rightarrow} s_1 \overset{\lambda_2}{\Rightarrow} \cdots \overset{\lambda_n}{\Rightarrow} s_n \overset{\alpha_{p+1}}{\Rightarrow} s_{n+1}$ is such that $proj(\sigma^{n+1}, \mathcal{A}) = \sigma^{1,p+1}$ and $proj(\sigma^{n+1}, \mathcal{B}) = \sigma^{2,q}$. We see that $p' = p + 1$ and $q' = q + 1$.

Case II: α_{p+1} and β_{q+1} are both nonnegative real numbers. Using equation 3 we can show that $\alpha_{p+1} = \beta_{q+1} = d$. Now, if $\sigma^{n+1} := s_0 \overset{\lambda_1}{\Rightarrow} s_1 \overset{\lambda_2}{\Rightarrow} \cdots \overset{\lambda_n}{\Rightarrow} s_n \overset{d}{\Rightarrow} s_{n+1}$, we can see that $proj(\sigma^{n+1}, \mathcal{A}) = \sigma^{1,p+1}$ and $proj(\sigma^{n+1}, \mathcal{B}) = \sigma^{2,q+1}$. Consequently, $p' = p + 1$ and $q' = q + 1$.

Case III: One of α_{p+1} or β_{q+1} is a completed action. For example, if α_{p+1} is a completed action and enabled under s_n, α_{p+1} is enabled under s_p^1. Hence, if $\sigma^{n+1} := s_0 \overset{\lambda_1}{\Rightarrow} s_1 \overset{\lambda_2}{\Rightarrow} \cdots \overset{\lambda_n}{\Rightarrow} s_n \overset{\alpha_{p+1}}{\Rightarrow} s_{n+1}$ then $proj(\sigma^{n+1}, \mathscr{A}) = \sigma^{1,p+1}$ and $proj(\sigma^{n+1}, \mathscr{B}) = \sigma^{2,q}$. In this case, $p' = p+1$ and $q' = q$.

Case IV: Both α_{p+1} and β_{q+1} are half actions. By the Shared Action Compatibility, α_{p+1} and β_{q+1} are half actions of the same actions, *i.e.*, there is i such that $\downarrow \alpha_{p+1} = \downarrow \beta_{q+1} = e_i$ for $1 \leq i \leq K$. Then let $\sigma^{n+1} := s_0 \overset{\lambda_1}{\Rightarrow} s_1 \overset{\lambda_2}{\Rightarrow} \cdots \overset{\lambda_n}{\Rightarrow} s_n \overset{e_i}{\Rightarrow} s_{n+1}$. We can see that $proj(\sigma^{n+1}, \mathscr{A}) = \sigma^{1,p+1}$ and $proj(\sigma^{n+1}, \mathscr{B}) = \sigma^{2,q+1}$. Notice that $p' = p+1$ and $q' = q+1$.

Case V: One of α_{p+1} or β_{q+1} is a half action and other is in $\mathbb{R}^{\geq 0}$. Let $\alpha_{p+1} \in HA$ and $\beta_{q+1} \in \mathbb{R}^{\geq 0}$. By the Shared Action Compatibility, there is $r > q+1$, such that β_r and α_{p+1} are half actions of the same actions, *i.e.*, $\downarrow \alpha_{p+1} = \downarrow \beta_r = e_i$. This implies that $\beta_{q+1} = 0$, since $\beta_{q+1} \leq \text{Timestamp}(\sigma^2, s_{r-1}^2) - \text{Timestamp}(\sigma^1, s_p^1) = 0$. Using case I, there is nothing to prove. □

We shall end this section with the proof of **Theorem** 1.

Proof of Theorem 1 $\Rightarrow$: We shall prove by contradiction. Suppose that $\mathscr{B}$ satisfies the property ϕ but there is a run σ of $\mathscr{A}' \parallel \mathscr{B}'$ ending in **failure**. Then by **Lemma** 1 $\sigma_{\mathscr{A}} = proj(\sigma, \mathscr{A})$ is a run of $\mathscr{A}$ ending in a **failure** state of $\mathscr{A}$, i.e. a state of $\mathscr{A}$ with a failure coordinate. As a result, $\phi(\text{Time}(\sigma_{\mathscr{A}}, e_1), \ldots, \text{Time}(\sigma_{\mathscr{A}}, e_K)) = \mathbf{F}$. Now, consider $\sigma_{\mathscr{B}} = proj(\sigma, \mathscr{B})$ which is a run of $\mathscr{B}$. Since, $\text{Time}(\sigma_{\mathscr{A}}, e_i) = \text{Time}(\sigma_{\mathscr{B}}, e_i)$, for each i, $\phi(Time(\sigma_{\mathscr{B}'}, e_1), \ldots, Time(\sigma_{\mathscr{B}'}, e_K)) = \mathbf{F}$. Consequently, by definition 5, $\sigma_{\mathscr{B}}$ does not satisfy ϕ, which is a contradiction.

Conversely: The proof of this case is also by contradiction. Assume that no run of the parallel composition meets any **failure** state, but $\mathscr{B}$ does not satisfy ϕ. Then there is a run σ_2 of $\mathscr{B}$ such that $\phi(\text{Time}(\sigma_2, e_1), \ldots, \text{Time}(\sigma_2, e_K)) = \mathbf{F}$. Suppose that $t^1 = \text{Time}(\sigma_2, e_1), \ldots, t^K = \text{Time}(\sigma_2, e_K)$. Since $\phi(t^1, \ldots, t^K) = \mathbf{F}$ by Definition 5. There is a finite run σ_1 of $\mathscr{A}$ such that σ_1 ends in **failure** and $t_1 = \text{Time}(\sigma_1, e_1), \ldots, t_K = \text{Time}(\sigma_1, e_K)$. Moreover, since $\mathscr{A}$ is a Complete QTA, σ_1 can be chosen such that σ_1 and σ_2 are Shared Action Compatible. Now, using σ_1, σ_2 and Lemma 2, we can conclude that there is a run of $\mathscr{A}' \parallel \mathscr{B}'$ ending in **failure**. This is a contradiction. □

6 Related Works

Formal specification of QoS in a distributed system via modelling languages such as Unified Modelling Language (UML) is an active area of research [22, 7, 15, 1, 11, 12]. In particular, the idea of specifying the QoS requirements as contracts [19] on the behaviour of the system is proposed [15] as a part of Model Driven Architecture, the new initiative by the Object Management Group (www.omg.org). However, the current research mainly deals with the issue of verifying of QoS property via Test Automata. The question that, which properties can be analysed by Test Automata is discussed in details in [2–4]. In particular, [3] presents a property language, called SBLL which is suitable for expressing safety and liveness properties of the real-time systems. SBLL is a testable language, in the

538   Behzad Bordbar and Kozo Okano

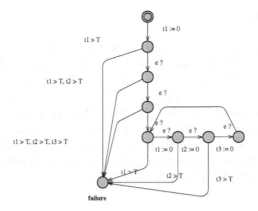

Fig. 8. QTA for checking Throughput of K occurrence of e? in T unit of time.

sense that [4] presents an algorithm for the translation of SBLL formulae to Test Automata. SBLL has the following grammar:

$\phi ::= \mathbf{ff} \mid \phi_1 \wedge \phi_2 \mid g \vee \phi \mid \mathbb{W}\phi \mid [a]\phi \mid \langle a \rangle \mathbf{tt}(a \in \mathscr{U}) \mid x \underline{\text{in}} \phi \mid X \mid \max(X, \phi),$

where $\mathbf{ff}$ and $\mathbf{tt}$ stand for *false* and *true*, respectively. g is a guard expression on the clocks, $x \underline{\text{in}} \phi$ stands for resetting a clock x before evaluating ϕ, $\max(X, \phi)$ is the maximal fixed point solution on X in ϕ, $\mathscr{U}$ is a set of urgent actions and $\mathbb{W}\phi$ stands for ϕ holds *forever*.

The following formula represents the Throughput as an SBLL formula

$$\phi = t_1 \underline{\text{in}} \ [e?](t_1 \geq T \vee (t_2 \underline{\text{in}} \ [e?]t_1 \geq T \vee t_2 \geq T \vee (\cdots (t_1 \geq T \vee \cdots t_{K-1} \geq T$$

$$\vee t_K \ _1 \underline{\text{in}} \ [e?](\phi'')) \cdots)))$$

$$\phi'(X) =$$

$$t_1 \geq T \vee t_1(\underline{\text{in}} \ [e?](t_2 \geq T \vee t_2 \underline{\text{in}} \ [e?](\cdots t_{K-1} \geq T \vee t_{K-1} \underline{\text{in}} \ [e?](X) \cdots)))$$

$$\phi'' = \max(X, \phi').$$

Fig. 8 depicts the Test Automaton for the Throughput for $K = 3$, created via the algorithm [4], in which all redundant transitions are omitted. Fig. 7 depicts the equivalent QTA created earlier. It can be seen that the QTA of Fig. 7 has the advantage of being *scalable*, i.e. the Test Automaton for the throughput of K signals e? in T units of time can be created from the parallel composition of K copies of the QTA of Fig. 6. The reason behind scalability of our model is that, unlike SBLL, our model of Timed Automata includes data variables. There is a clear scope for research to extended the SBLL to include data variables. In particular, since $L_{\forall s}$, an extension of SBLL, completely characterises testable properties [2-4], an extension of SBLL to include data variables will enable to characterize the Timeliness properties which are testable.

7 Conclusion

This paper presents a formal approach to the verification of Timeliness QoS properties, such as Throughput, Jitter and Latency, in object-based models of Distributed Multimedia Systems. For each Timeliness property ϕ, we define a QoS Timed Automata (QTA) such that all its runs that do not meet a failure location, satisfy ϕ. Moreover, all runs of the QTA that meet a failure location violate ϕ. The main result of the paper proves that a QTA is a Test Automata, i.e. it can be used to verify the property ϕ over a network of Timed Automata via parallel composition. We have demonstrated our approach by the verification of Throughput in a Video Player system.

References

1. D. H. Akehurst, B. Bordbar, J. Derrick, and a. g. waters: *design support for distributed systems: dse4ds* in J. Finney, M. Haahr, and A. Montressor, editors, proceedings of the 7th Cabernet Radicals Workshop, October 2002.
2. L. Ageto, P. Bouyer, A. Burgueño and K. G. Larsen: *The Power of Reachability Testing for Timed Automata*, In Proceedings of 18th Conference of Fundamental of Software Technology and Theoretical Computer Science (FST and TCS '98), LNCS **1530** pp.245–256, 1998.
3. L. Ageto, P. Bouyer, A. Burgueño and K. G. Larsen: *Model-Checking via Reachability Testing for Timed Automata*, In Proceedings 4th Conference of Tools and Algorithms for Construction and Analysis of Systems (TACAS '98), LNCS **1384** pp.263–280, 1998.
4. L. Ageto, P. Bouyer, A. Burgueño and K. G. Larsen: *The Power of Reachability Testing for Timed Automata*, available from
   http://www.lsv.ens-cachan.fr/Publis/publis-y3-2003.php,
   to appear in Theoretical Computer Science.
5. R. Alur and D.L. Dill: *A Theory for Timed Automata*, In Theoretical Computer Science **125** pp.183–235, 1994.
6. T. Amnell, G. Behmann, J. Bengtsson, P. R. D'Argenio, A. David, A. Fehnker, T. Hune, B. Jeannet, K. G. Larsen, O. Möller, P. Pettersson, C. Weise and W. Yi: *UPPAAL—Now, Next and Future* In proceedings of Modelling and Verification of Parallel Processes (MOVEP2k), LNCS **2067** pp.100–125, 2001.
7. J. Øyvind Aagedal and E. F. Ecklund Jr. *Modelling QoS: Towards a UML Profile* UML 2002, pp. 275–289, 2003.
8. J. Bengtsson, W. O. D. Griffioen, K.J. Kristoffersen, K. G. Larsen, F. Larsson, P. Pettersson and W. Yi: *Verification of an Audio Protocol with Bus Collision Using UPPAAL*, In Proceedings of the 8th International Conference on Computer-Aided Verification, LNCS **1102** pp.244–256, 1996.
9. J. Bengtsson, K. G. Larsen, F. Larsson, P. Pettersson and W. Yi: *UPPAAL, a Tool suite for automatic verification of real-time systems* In Proceedings of Workshop on Hybrid Systems III: Verification and Control, LNCS **1066** pp.232–243, 1995.
10. G. Blair, J.-B. Stefani: *Open Distributed Processing and Multimedia* Addison-Wesley, Boston, MA, 1997.
11. B. Bordbar, J. Derrick, and A. G. Waters: *A UML approach to the design of open distributed systems* In Chris George and Huaikou Miao, editors, Formal Methods and Software Engineering, LNCS **2495** pp.561–572, 2002.

12. B. Bordbar, J. Derrick, and A. G. Waters: *Using UML to specify QoS constraints in ODP* Computer network and ISDN systems **40** pp.279–304 2002.
13. H. Bowman, G. Faconti, and M. Massink: *Specification and verification of media constraints using UPPAAL*, In Proceedings of Design, Specification and Verification of Interactive Systems '98, Markopoulos and P. Johnos, editors, pp. 261–277 Springer, 1998.
14. K. Havelund, A. Skou, K. G. Larsen and K. Lund: *Formal Modelling and Analysis of an Audio/Video Protocol: An Industrial Case Study Using UPPAAL* In Proceedings of the 18th IEEE Real-Time Systems Symposium, pp.2–13, 1997.
15. J.-M. Jézéquel *Model-driven engineering with contracts, patterns, and aspects* In Tutorial Program of AOSD 2003: 2nd International Conference on Aspect-Oriented Software Development, ACM-IEEE, March 2003.
16. K. G. Larsen, Paul Pettersson and W. Yi: *UPPAAL in a Nutshell*, In Springer International Journal of Software Tools for Technology Transfer **1(1+2)** 1997.
17. M. Lindahl, Paul Pettersson and W. Yi: *Formal Design and Analysis of a Gear Controller*, In Springer International Journal of Software Tools for Technology Transfer, volume 3, issue 3, pp. 353-368, 2001.
18. H. Lönn and P. Pettersson: *Formal Verification of a TDMA Protocol Start-Up Mechanism*, In Proceedings of 1997 IEEE Pacific Rim International Symposium on Fault-Tolerant Systems, pp.235–242, 1997.
19. Stephane Lorcy, Noel Plouzeau, and Jean-Marc Jézéquel *Reifying quality of service contracts for distributed software*, In 26th Conference on Technology of Object-Oriented Systems (TOOLS USA'98), August 1998
20. R. Milner, *Communication and concurrency*, Prentice Hall, Upper Saddle River, NJ, 1989.
21. *ITU Recommendation X.901-904 ISO/IEC 10746 1-4.* Open Distributed Processing Reference Model - Parts **1-4**, July, 1995.
22. R. Staehli, F. Eliassen, J. Øyvind Aagedal and G. S. Blair *Quality of Service Semantics for Component-Based Systems* The 1st International Workshop on Middleware for Grid Computing, pp. 153-157, 2003.
23. W. Yi, *Real-Time Behaviour of Asynchronous Agents*, In Proceeding of 1st Int. Conf. Theory of Concurrency (CONCUR90), LNCS **458**, pp. 502-520, 1990.

A Calculus for Set-Based Program Development

Georg Struth

Institut für Informatik, Universität Augsburg
D-86135 Augsburg, Germany
struth@informatik.uni-augsburg.de

Abstract We propose an algebraic calculus for set-based program development. First, we reconstruct a fragment of set theory via atomic distributive lattices (ADL). Semantically, ADL extends boolean reasoning about sets by element-wise reasoning; it avoids presupposing a universal set. Operationally, ADL yields abstract, concise, elegant proofs from few elementary principles. Second, we develop a focused automated proof-search procedure for ADL with simple deduction and powerful reduction and simplification rules. Proof-search is guided by rewriting techniques. The procedure decides several subclasses. Main application is the proof-support for formal methods like B or Z.

1   Introduction

Intuitive or naive set theory is both an official mathematical ontology and a universal mathematical tool. In computer science, it is the basis of popular and successful formal methods like Z [17] and B [1]. Therefore, the integration of intuitive set-theoretic reasoning into efficient focused automated deduction systems is an important question. There are a few systems that implement axiomatic set theory (e.g. [7,16,14,15]), but these are either interactive or designed for foundations rather than applications as automated formal methods. Hines [10] proposes a resolution calculus for restricted reasoning with some set-theoretic operations, but the problems of characterizing the underlying fragment of set theory and proving completeness of his calculus are now open for more than a decade. So the apparent lack of answer to the above question indicates an interesting gap both in the field of formal methods and in automated deduction.

We propose a calculus to close this gap. Besides, it solves the longstanding open problem related to [10]. Our first main contribution is a core calculus for set theory as used in formal methods. The second one is the integration of this calculus into a focused resolution-based automated deduction procedure.

In opposition to the usual logical approaches, our core calculus is algebraic. It is the calculus of atomic distributive lattices (ADL). Appropriateness of ADL for reasoning with sets follows from the representation theorem for this class. Accordingly, every atomic distributive lattice can be isomorphically embedded into a field of sets; the zero of the lattice represented by the empty set, join and meet by union and intersection, the lattice order by set inclusion. But reasoning with ADL differs from boolean reasoning about sets: The ontological commitment

J.S. Dong and J. Woodcock (Eds.): ICFEM 2003, LNCS 2885, pp. 541–559, 2003.
© Springer-Verlag Berlin Heidelberg 2003

to a universal set is avoided, since there need not be a maximal element. Set-difference can nevertheless be expressed, since ADL has unique sectional complements. More important, ADL supports element-wise reasoning: elements of sets are in one-to-one correspondence with singleton sets, which represent atoms. Using techniques from the representation theorem we also show that atomicity of the lattice expresses precisely extensionality of the set theory. Our approach shares the usual benefits of other algebraic calculi for reasoning about programs (c.f. [6,11,13]): Economy of axioms, support of abstract, concise, elegant calculations from few elementary principle and relation to standard algebraic decision procedures. It is therefore particularly suited for automation.

We also propose a focused ordered resolution calculus (ADC) for ADL. Focusing means integrating mathematical and procedural knowledge, here via specific inference rules, rewriting techniques, ordering constraints and simplification techniques. The inference rules are specific ordered chaining rules (c.f. [3]) for ADL that extend a Knuth-Bendix completion procedure for distributive lattices [18]. They are restricted to manipulations with maximal terms in maximal atoms. Focusing seems indispensable for structures like ADL. Axiomatic reasoning would lead to an explosion of the search space. Our term-oriented ordering constraints, for instance, control the proliferation by theory unifications that would otherwise arise for joins and meets. We develop ADC with the derivation method from [19]. Its main idea is to internalize axioms into inference rules by establishing a separation property on axioms in refutations by ordered resolution and then internalizing the axioms into derived inference rules by inspecting their proof-patterns with non-theory clauses. Completeness of the resulting focused calculus then follows from faithfulness of the construction. Fortunately, since the derivation method is modular with respect to extensions, the development of ADC need not be done from scratch: we can base it on a focused calculus for distributive lattices [20]. By carefully choosing an appropriate representation of ADL, all inference rules of ADC are restrictions of those for distributive lattices. Using a variant of extensionality for eliminating all negative literals, the most prolific rules of the previous calculus even disappear. Moreover, the ADL-axioms dealing with atoms are entirely casted into simplification and reduction rules. Part of the efficiency of ADC is also due to the fact that atoms are only lazily introduced instead of boiling down the whole structure. Intuitively, new atoms are only used to witness that two sets are different. This feature also causes the specialization of ADC to decision procedures for certain subclasses, in particular finite structures.

Forgetting the ordering constraints, the inference rules of ADC are essentially those of [10]. We can also transfer the two main simplification techniques of [10] to the ordered resolution framework and to ADL. However, the ordering constraints give restrictions on certain inferences on variables for free that would otherwise be difficult to verify; the simplification rules of ADL can be justified using the standard generic notion of redundancy [2].

In this extended abstract, we can only outline the main ideas of our approach. Formal details can be found in technical reports [21,22].

2 Lattices

A *lattice* [4,9] is a partially ordered set $(L, \le)$ closed under least upper bounds or joins (denoted by $\sqcup$) and under greatest lower bound or meets (denoted by $\sqcap$) for all pairs of elements. Formally, for all $a, b, c \in L$,

$$a \le c \wedge b \le c \Leftrightarrow a \sqcup b \le c, \tag{1}$$
$$c \le a \wedge c \le b \Leftrightarrow c \le a \sqcap b. \tag{2}$$

The *dual* of a statement about lattices is obtained by interchanging joins and meets and converting the ordering. Thus (1) and (2) are dual statements. L is *distributive*, if

$$a \sqcap (b \sqcup c) \le (a \sqcap b) \sqcup (a \sqcap c)$$

holds for all $a, b, c \in L$ or its dual and therewith both.

We denote the minimal and the maximal elements with respect to $\le$ of L, if they exist, by 0 and 1. A lattice with 0 and 1 is called *bounded*. Formally, for all $a \in L$,

$$0 \le a. \tag{3}$$

The class of lattices is denoted by L, the class of distributive lattices by DL. If K is a class of lattices, then K_0 denotes the subclass that has a zero, K_1 the subclass that has a one and K_{01} the subclass that is bounded.

We consider lattices as orderings. Alternatively, the class can also be axiomatized equationally. The translation between the two classes is given by

$$a \le b \Leftrightarrow a \sqcup b = b \Leftrightarrow a \sqcap b = a. \tag{4}$$

In the equational definition, joins and meets are associative, commutative, idempotent ($a \sqcap a = a = a \sqcup a$) and absorptive ($a \sqcup (a \sqcap b) = a = a \sqcap (a \sqcup b)$) operations. Experience shows that order-based reasoning with lattices is more natural than equational reasoning.

Let $L_1, L_2 \in L$. A mapping $h : L_1 \to L_2$ *preserves joins*, if $h(a \sqcup b) = h(a) \sqcup h(b)$ for all $a, b \in L_1$. It *preserves meets*, if $h(a \sqcap b) = h(a) \sqcap h(b)$ for all $a, b \in L_1$. A *lattice-homomorphism* (or *homomorphism*) preserves joins and meets. We also require $h(0) = 0$ and $h(1) = 1$, if present. An injective lattice homomorphism is called a *(lattice-)embedding*, a surjective lattice embedding a *(lattice-)isomorphism*. Every join or meet preserving mapping is *monotone*, that is $a \le b$ implies $h(a) \le h(b)$ for all $a, b \in L_1$.

Example 1.

(i) A family of subsets of some set is called *ring of sets*, if it is closed under (set-theoretic) union and intersection. Every ring of sets is a distributive lattice. A finite lattice is distributive iff it is isomorphic to a ring of sets.
(ii) Every chain (for example the chain of natural numbers) is a distributive lattice.

3 Complements

Let $L \in \mathsf{L}_{01}$. A *complement* of an element $a \in L$ is an element $b \in L$ such that $a \sqcup b = 1$ and $a \sqcap b = 0$. L is *complemented*, if every element has a complement. A *boolean lattice* is a complemented distributive lattice. The class of boolean lattices is denoted by BL.

Our main interest are lattices with a weaker notion of complementation. Let $L \in \mathsf{L}_0$ and consider the sublattice $L|a = \{b \in L : b \leq a\}$. L is *sectionally complemented*, if $L|a$ is complemented for every $a \in L$.

In DL, sectional complements and complements are uniquely determined (if they exist). In DL_0, we write $b - a$ for the sectional complement of a in $L|(a \sqcup b)$. In DL_{01}, we write a' for the complement of a. Every complemented distributive lattice is sectionally complemented with $b - a = a' \sqcap (a \sqcup b)$ and $a' = 1 - a$. Every sectionally complemented distributive lattice with 1 is boolean. In Section 5 we will see that sectional complementation is very natural for atomic distributive lattices. Also in the context of intuitive set theory, sectional complements are natural concepts. There, the empty set corresponds to the zero, but we would like to avoid assuming the existence of a one, that is a universal set.

Example 2.

(i) In a ring of sets, $s_1 - s_2$ denotes set-difference, that is $s_1 - s_2$ is the set of all elements of s_1 that are not elements of s_2.

(ii) A ring of set is called *field of sets*, if it closed under set-difference. Every field of sets is a sectionally complemented distributive lattice.

We now present laws for computing with sectional complements. First, we introduce some identities for simplifying expressions with sectional complements. Then we generalize some standard laws for complements to sectional complements: de Morgan laws, monotonicity laws and shunting laws. Some of them can be found in the literature [9,5]. Most of the laws are based on the following property of sectional complements, which is immediate from the definition.

$$a = b - c \Leftrightarrow a \sqcup c = b \sqcup c \wedge a \sqcap c = 0.$$

– Simplification of sectional complement expressions.

$$(a - b) \sqcup b = a \sqcup b, \tag{5}$$
$$(a - b) \sqcap b = 0, \tag{6}$$
$$a \sqcap (a - b) = a - b, \tag{7}$$
$$a \sqcup (a - b) = a, \tag{8}$$
$$a - a = 0, \tag{9}$$
$$a - (b - c) = (a - b) \sqcup (a \sqcap c), \tag{10}$$
$$a - (a - b) = a \sqcap b. \tag{11}$$

– Generalized de Morgan laws.

$$a - (b \sqcap c) = (a - b) \sqcup (a - c), \tag{12}$$
$$a - (b \sqcup c) = (a - b) \sqcap (a - c), \tag{13}$$
$$(a \sqcap b) - c = (a - c) \sqcap (b - c), \tag{14}$$
$$(a \sqcup b) - c = (a - c) \sqcup (b - c). \tag{15}$$

– Generalized monotonicity laws.

$$a \leq b \Rightarrow a - c \leq b - c, \tag{16}$$
$$a \leq b \Rightarrow c - b \leq c - a. \tag{17}$$

– Generalized shunting laws.

$$(a - b) \leq c \Leftrightarrow a \leq b \sqcup c, \tag{18}$$
$$a \sqcap (c - b) \leq d \Leftrightarrow a \sqcap c \leq b \sqcup d, \tag{19}$$
$$a \leq (c - b) \sqcup d \Leftrightarrow a \leq c \sqcup d \wedge a \sqcap b \leq d, \tag{20}$$
$$a \leq c - b \Leftrightarrow a \leq c \wedge a \sqcap b \leq 0. \tag{21}$$

(7) is very useful in the form $a - b \leq a$. Each of these laws can be proven in a few lines of lattice calculus. The usual laws for complements are recovered by setting $a' = 1 - a$.

The laws (5)–(21) are interesting for two reasons. First, they are used in the normal form computations of our focused calculus in Section 9. There they allow us to completely eliminate sectional complements. Second, they support abstract algebraic reasoning with sets, for instance in set-based program development methods like Z and B.

4 Atoms

Intuitively, an atom of a lattice with zero is an element that lies immediately above (hence *covers*) the zero. Formally, let $L \in L_0$. Then $\alpha \in L$ is an *atom* of L, if for all $b \in L$,

$$\alpha \nleq 0, \tag{22}$$
$$b \leq \alpha \Rightarrow \alpha \leq b \vee b \leq 0. \tag{23}$$

Simple lattice calculus shows that (23) is equivalent to

$$\alpha \leq a \sqcup b \Leftrightarrow \alpha \leq a \vee \alpha \leq b, \tag{24}$$

if L is also distributive and sectionally complemented. $A(L)$ denotes the set of atoms of L.

(24) relates atoms with join-irreducible elements. An element a in a lattice L is *join-irreducible*, if for all $b, c \in L$, $a = b \sqcup c$ implies $a = b$ or $a = c$. All atoms

of a lattice are join-irreducible and all join-irreducible elements of a distributive sectionally complemented lattice with zero are atoms. Example 3 (ii) presents a finite distributive lattice with join-irreducible elements that are not atoms.

The following properties are helpful as rewrite rules for eliminating certain negative inequalities.

Lemma 1. *Let $L \in L_0$. For all $\alpha, \beta \in A(L)$ and $a, b \in L$,*

$$\alpha \nleq b \Leftrightarrow \alpha \sqcap b \leq 0, \tag{25}$$
$$\alpha \sqcap \beta \nleq 0 \Leftrightarrow \alpha = \beta, \tag{26}$$
$$\alpha \sqcap a \leq b \Leftrightarrow \alpha \sqcap a \leq 0 \vee \alpha \leq b, \tag{27}$$
$$\alpha \sqcap a \nleq b \Leftrightarrow \alpha \sqcap b \leq 0. \tag{28}$$

Example 3.

(i) In a field of sets, the atoms are precisely the singleton sets.
(ii) In the interval $[0, n]$ of natural numbers, all elements except 0 are join-irreducible. 1 is the only atom.
(iii) Consider the finite boolean lattice L_n generated by $a_1, \ldots, a_n$. The atoms of L_n are the elements $c_1 \sqcap \ldots \sqcap c_n$, where c_i is one of a_i and a_i'. By distributivity, every element $s \in L_n$ is equivalent to some $t \in L_n$ which is a join of meets of a_i and a_i'. If the join contains at least two elements, then t has at least two lower covers and is not join-irreducible. If the join has only one element, then $t = c_1 \sqcap \ldots \sqcap c_k$, where c_i is one of a_i and a_i' and $k \leq n$. If $k = n$, then t is an atom, hence join-irreducible. If $k < n$, then $t \sqcap a_{k+1}$ and $t \sqcap a_{k+1}'$ are lower covers of t. Thus t is not join-irreducible. Consequently, the join-irreducible elements of L_n are precisely the atoms.

5   Atomicity

A lattice $L \in L_0$ is *atomic*, if for each non-zero $a \in L$ there is a nonempty $T \subseteq A(L)$ such that $a = \bigsqcup T$. For a class K of lattices, the subclass of atomic lattices is denoted by AK. We also define a mapping $\eta : L \to 2^{A(l)}$ that associates with each element $a \in L$ the set of atoms below it.

$$\eta(a) = \{\alpha \in A(L) : \alpha \leq a\}. \tag{29}$$

L is *η-stable*, iff $a = \bigsqcup \eta(a)$ holds for all $a \in L$.

It is easy to show that a lattice with zero is atomic iff it is η-stable. Using (24) is also easy to show that η is a homomorphism, if $L \in DL$. If L is is non-distributive, η preserves zero and joins, but not necessarily meets.

Lemma 2. *Let L be a lattice with at least two elements. If η is injective, then $\eta(a) \neq \emptyset$ for all $a \in L$, $a \neq 0$.*

Proof. If L has at least two elements, then $A(L) \neq \emptyset$, since these elements have different images under η by injectivity. Moreover, $0 \in L$, since the definition of atoms presupposes a zero. Since $\eta(0) = \emptyset$, $\eta(a)$ must, for all $a \neq 0$ contain at least one atom. $\square$

We now present an alternative characterization of atomicity. $L \in L_0$ is *extensional*, if for all $a, b \in L$,

$$a \leq b \Leftrightarrow \forall \alpha \in A(L).(\alpha \leq a \Rightarrow \alpha \leq b). \tag{30}$$

By (25) and first-order logic, (30) is equivalent to

$$a \not\leq b \Leftrightarrow \exists \alpha \in A(L).(\alpha \leq a \wedge \alpha \sqcap b \leq 0). \tag{atomic}$$

Theorem 1. *A lattice with zero (and at least two elements) is atomic iff it is extensional.*

Proof. (Sketch) The key is to show the following claim: Lattice L is atomic iff

$$a \leq b \Leftrightarrow \eta(a) \subseteq \eta(b) \tag{31}$$

for all $a, b \in L$, which is equivalent to

$$a = b \Leftrightarrow \eta(a) = \eta(b), \tag{32}$$

since η preserves meets. To establish the claim, we first remember that atomicity is equivalent to η-stability. So let L be η-stable. Then

$$\eta(a) \subseteq \eta(b) \Rightarrow \bigsqcup \eta(a) \leq \bigsqcup \eta(b) \Leftrightarrow a \leq b.$$

The other direction of (31) is just monotonicity of η.

We now show the converse direction of the claim, that (32) implies η-stability. First, by Lemma 2, we know that $\eta(a)$ and $\eta(b)$ are non-empty.

We verify that a is a least upper bound of $\eta(a)$. Since η is an embedding of L into some subsemilattice of $2^{A(L)}$ (η preserves meets), we can carry out the proof entirely on the set-side. Obviously, a is an upper bound of $\eta(a)$. To show that it is a least upper bound, assume, by reductio ad absurdum, another upper bound b of $\eta(a)$ such that $a \not\leq b$. Thus $\eta(a) \not\subseteq \eta(b)$ by (31) and by boolean reasoning $\eta(a) \cap (A(L) - \eta(b)) \neq \emptyset$. So there is some atom $\alpha \in \eta(a) \cap (A(L) - \eta(b))$. Consequently, $\alpha \in \eta(a)$ and $\alpha \in A(L) - \eta(b)$, hence on the one hand $\alpha \notin \eta(b)$. On the other hand, $\alpha \in \eta(a)$ implies $\alpha \in \eta(b)$, a contradiction. This proves our claim.

It now remains to show that (32) is equivalent to extensionality. But

$$a \leq b \Leftrightarrow \eta(a) \subseteq \eta(b) \Leftrightarrow \forall \alpha \in A(L).(\alpha \leq a \Rightarrow \alpha \leq b)$$

$$\square$$

Note that there is a finite $L \in \mathsf{DL}$ with $\eta(a) \neq \emptyset$ for all $a \neq 0$ that is not extensional and therefore not atomic (c.f [21]).

We can restate Theorem 1 as follows. Define the relation $\sim$ for all $a, b \in L$ by

$$a \sim b \Leftrightarrow \forall \alpha \in A(L).(\alpha \leq a \Leftrightarrow \alpha \leq b). \tag{33}$$

$\sim$ is a congruence on sectionally complemented distributive lattices and $L \in \mathsf{L}$ is atomic iff $a = b \Leftrightarrow a \sim b$ holds for all $a, b \in L$. This congruence is interesting in its own right. For non-atomic lattices, it yields a notion of observational equivalence induced by measurements of lattice properties via atoms.

Algebraically, (30) expresses an *extensionality principle*: two elements of an atomic lattice are equal, iff they are built from the same atoms. Similarly, (atomic) expresses a *separability principle*: two elements of an atomic lattice are different, iff they can be distinguished by an atom.

Operationally, (30) allows the transition between atom-free and atom-wise reasoning. Moreover, in Section 9, (30) and (atomic) are important for normal form computations with our focused calculi. (atomic) allows us to replace all negative inequalities by positive ones.

The following statement shows that atoms of distributive lattices induce sectional complements.

Lemma 3. *Every atomic distributive lattice is sectionally complemented. For $L \in \mathsf{ADL}$ and $a, b \in L$, $a \leq b$, $\bigsqcup(\eta(b) - \eta(a))$ is the sectional complement of a in $L|b$.*

Proof. First, we show that $b \sqcap c = 0$. Since $\eta(b)$ and $\eta(a) - \eta(b)$ are disjoint, $(\bigsqcup \eta(b)) \sqcap (\bigsqcup(\eta(a) - \eta(b))) = 0$, using Lemma 1 (ii). Therefore, $b \sqcap c = 0$.

Now we show that $b \sqcup c = a$.

$$
\begin{aligned}
b \sqcup c &= (\bigsqcup \eta(b)) \sqcup (\bigsqcup(\eta(a) - \eta(b))) \\
&= \bigsqcup(\eta(b) \sqcup (\eta(a) - \eta(b))) \\
&= \bigsqcup \eta(a) \\
&= a.
\end{aligned}
$$

Thus c is a sectional complement of b with respect to a. By distributivity of the lattice, this complement is unique. $\square$

Consequently, we can use (24) instead of (23) in ADL and we need no special axioms for sectional complements.

Example 4.

(i) The set of all subsets of some set is an atomic boolean lattice.
(ii) In every field of sets, the singleton sets are precisely the atoms. Hence instead of the set-theoretic expression $a \in s$ we can write $\{a\} \subseteq s$ according to set theory and more abstractly $\alpha_a \leq s$ in AL. Existence of this atom is guaranteed by atomicity. Conversely, in a field of sets, we can write $a \in s \Rightarrow a \in t$ instead of $\alpha_a \leq s \Rightarrow \alpha_a \leq t$. Then (30) is equivalent to the standard axiom of extensionality of set theory,

$$
a = b \Leftrightarrow \forall x.(x \in a \Leftrightarrow x \in b).
$$

Conversely again, we can introduce the $\in$-relation as syntactic sugar for $L \in \mathsf{AL}$, defining $\alpha \in s \Leftrightarrow \alpha \leq s$ for all $\alpha \in A(L)$ and $a \in L$.

(iii) In Example 2 (i) we have stated that in a field of sets, $s_1 - s_2$ denotes the set of all elements of s_1 that are not in s_2. This can be easily verified in ADL. First, we replace every statement of the form $a \in s$ by $\alpha_a \leq s$, using atomicity. Then, it remains to show that $\alpha \leq s_1 - s_2$ iff $\alpha \leq s_1 \wedge \alpha \not\leq s_2$. This follows immediately from (21) and (25).

6   Representation

The techniques of Theorem 1 usually serve for proving the well-known representation theorems for atomic lattices, which are variants of Stone's theorem (c.f [4]). The following facts are proven in [21] for $L \in \mathsf{L}$.

- If L is finite, then $\eta(a) \neq \emptyset$ for every non-zero $a \in L$.
- If $\eta(a) \neq \emptyset$ for every non-zero $a \in L$ and L is sectionally complemented, then L is atomic.
- L is distributive iff all sectional complements are unique.

It follows that every finite sectionally complemented lattice is atomic and distributive and therefore boolean. Moreover, every finite boolean lattice is atomic.

Theorem 2.

(i) Every atomic distributive lattice and every atomic boolean lattice L can be embedded into the field of sets $2^{A(L)}$.

(ii) Every finite atomic distributive lattice and every finite boolean lattice is isomorphic with the field of sets $2^{A(L)}$.

Our previous examples show that ADL has at least sets as models. The representation theorem shows that it has at most these models. Thus first-order reasoning about fields of sets is precisely first-order reasoning about ADL. But this is more than boolean reasoning. It is stronger, since via atoms, we are able to reason element-wise and it is weaker, since we avoid the ontological commitment to a universal set.

Given the representation theorems and the standard translation between objects of of set theory and those of ADL, we can prove all statements of Section 3 to Section 5 entirely at the set-side.

Finally, well-known size bounds for finite lattices follow immediately from the representation theorems. The free boolean lattice with n generators, for instance, has 2^n atoms (c.f Example 3 (iii)) and therefore 2^{2^n} elements.

7   Ordered Resolution and Redundancy

We now come to the second part of our abstract, the discussion of the focused calculus for ADL. Ordered resolution is not only one of its main ingredients, it is also used as a metaprocedure for its development. We first recall some basic facts about ordered resolution and redundancy elimination (c.f. [2]). Ordered resolution calculi are among the most powerful and successful automated deduction procedures. Particular benefits are their potential to decide many problem classes and to integrate theory-specific reasoning facilities.

Let $T_\Sigma(X)$ be a set of terms with signature Σ and variables in X. A term is *ground*, if it contains no variables. An *atomic formula* is an expression $p(t_1, \ldots, t_n)$, where p is an n-ary predicate symbol and $t_1, \ldots, t_m \in T_\Sigma(X)$. A *literal* is an atomic formula ϕ (*positive literal*) or its negation $\neg\phi$ (*negative literal*). A *clause* is a finite multiset of literals. A *Horn clause* contains at most one positive literal. A *clause set* is a set of clauses. If Γ is a clause and ϕ a literal, we write Γ, ϕ instead of $\Gamma \cup \{\phi\}$.

We consider calculi constrained by syntactic orderings. This may considerably narrow the search space. A *term* and a *literal ordering* $\prec$ is a well-founded total ordering on the respective ground expressions. $\prec$ is lifted to non-ground expressions by stipulating $e_1 \prec e_2$ iff $e_1\sigma \prec e_2\sigma$ for all ground substitutions σ. A literal l is *maximal* with respect to a multiset Γ of literals, if $l \not\prec l'$ for all $l' \in \Gamma$. It is *strictly maximal* with respect to Γ, if $l \not\preceq l'$ for all $l' \in \Gamma$. The non-ground orderings are still well-founded, but need no longer be total.

Literal orderings are extended to clauses, measuring clauses as multisets of literals and comparing them via the multiset extension of the literal ordering. A literal is assigned greater weight when it is negative than when it is positive. See Section 10 for more details. A clause ordering inherits totality and well-foundedness from the literal ordering. Again, the non-ground extension need not be total. We usually denote all syntactic orderings by $\prec$.

Definition 1. *Let $\prec$ be a literal ordering. The ordered resolution calculus OR consists of the deduction inference rules*

$$\frac{\Gamma, \phi \qquad \Delta, \neg\psi}{\Gamma\sigma, \Delta\sigma}, \quad \text{(Res)} \qquad \frac{\Gamma, \phi, \psi}{\Gamma\sigma, \phi\sigma}. \quad \text{(Fact)}$$

- *In the ordered resolution rule (Res), σ is a most general unifier of ϕ and ψ, $\phi\sigma$ is strictly maximal with respect to $\Gamma\sigma$ and maximal with respect to $\Delta\sigma$.*
- *In the ordered factoring rule (Fact), σ is a most general unifier of ϕ and ψ and $\phi\sigma$ is strictly maximal with respect to the set of positive literals and maximal with respect to the set of negative literals in $\Gamma\sigma$.*

In all inference rules, *side formulas* are the parts of clauses denoted by capital Greek letters. Literals occurring explicitly in the premises are called *minor formulas*, those in the conclusion *principal formulas*.

Let S be a clause set and $\prec$ a clause ordering. A clause Γ is $\prec$-*redundant* or simply redundant in S, if it is a semantic consequence of instances from S which are all smaller than Γ with respect to $\prec$. A ground inference is *redundant* in S, if either the maximal premise is redundant or else its conclusion is a semantic consequence of instances from S which are all smaller than the maximal premise with respect to $\prec$. An inference is *redundant*, if all its ground instances are. Closing S under OR up to redundant inferences and eliminating redundant clauses on the fly transforms S in the limit into an *ordered resolution basis* (an *orb*).

As usually, an OR-proof is defined inductively as a finite tree whose nodes are labeled by clauses and whose edges are determined by OR-inferences. An OR-*refutation* from a clause set S is an OR-proof with all leaves in S and with the empty clause as root.

Proposition 1.

 (i) *Orbs of inconsistent clause sets contain the empty clause.*
 (ii) *Fair* OR-*implementations refute inconsistent clause sets in finite time.*
 (iii) *For every inconsistent clauses set containing an orb there is a refutation in which no* OR-*inference has both premises from the orb.*

8   The Derivation Method

We now briefly sketch the main ideas of the derivation method for focused calculi. At the clause level, our intention is the internalization of axioms into focused, that is theory-specific, inference rules. At the term level, we would like to integrate theory-specific simplification rules, rewriting techniques and decision procedures. The method has a syntactic and a semantic side.

At the syntactic side, consider a set T of *theory clauses* and a set S of *non-theory* clauses that is disjoint from T such that $S \cup T$ is inconsistent. We intend to internalize T into a set of derived inference rules in refutations. The (ground) chaining rule

$$\frac{\Gamma, a \leq b \qquad \Delta, b \leq c}{\Gamma, \Delta, a \leq c}, \tag{34}$$

for instance, internalizes the instance $a \not\leq b, b \not\leq c, a \leq c$ of the transitivity law in the resolution proof

$$\frac{\dfrac{\Gamma, a \leq b \quad a \not\leq b, b \not\leq c, a \leq c}{\Gamma, b \not\leq c, a \leq c} \qquad \Delta, b \leq c}{\Gamma, \Delta, a \leq c}$$

With appropriate ordering constraints, (34) is an extension of a critical pair computation of a Knuth-Bendix completion procedure for transitive relations to the clausal level (c.f. [19]). Chaining calculi are resolution-based calculi that use (34) and similar focused inference rules for reasoning about transitivity. It is a well-known fact that such focused inference rules are operationally superior to plain axiom-based reasoning. Ordered resolution inferences with two instances of the transitivity law, for instance, would eagerly introduce fresh variables into the theorem-proving process, which may lead to search-space explosion. See [19] for a discussion of the advantage of focusing and its relation to traditional theorem-proving strategies.

In general, the above internalization is possible, if there exists an OR- refutation of $S \cup T$ with the following properties.

- The refutation is *T-separable*: For every premise $\Gamma \in T$ with k literals, the following $k - 1$ inferences do not have another premise from T.
- The refutation is *T-serial*: For every premise $\Gamma \in T$ with k literals, the following $k - 1$ inferences have one minor formula that is an instance of a literal of Γ.

Intuitively, T-separability guarantees that there is enough distance between premises from T to partition a refutation into subproofs that consume all but one literal from each premise from T separately. T-seriality guarantees that this consumption is not interrupted by inferences with minor formulas from non-theory clauses.

In our application, theory clauses have at most three literals. Thus only subproofs of size at most 2 must be inspected with respect to separability and seriality and, by Proposition 1 (iii), only subproofs of size at least 2, if T is an orb. This suggests the following three-step scenario. Let T be an input theory.

1. Construct an orb of T.
2. Establish separability and seriality for the ground case; extract inference rules.
3. Lift the inference rules to the non-ground case.

The derivation method is modular. When a set T of axioms is added to an orb B and the changes of the syntactic ordering do not affect B, then only inferences between B and T must be inspected for extending B. Also separability and seriality need only be checked with respect to T. In particular, if B is a subset of the orb of B and T and the second step succeeds, then the inference rules for B will at most be restricted in the extension.

At the semantic side, we use three ways to integrate declarative and procedural background knowledge. The first way is the selection of an appropriate theory specification. Our axioms for sectional complements and atoms in Section 3 to Section 5 are equivalences that act as clausal simplification rules. The second way is the extension of related procedures. In Section 11 we will extend a chaining calculus DC for DL [20]. The third way is the adaptation of the syntactic orderings $\prec$. We will reuse that of DC.

9   Reduction of Lattice Inequalities

Let $L = \{\sqcup, \sqcap, -, \alpha, 0\}$ be a signature for ADL. In particular, the unary function α denotes that some element is an atom. For the sake of simplicity, we flatten terms, that is we consider join and meet as operation symbols of polyadic arity. We also consider terms modulo associativity and commutativity (AC). Let Σ be a signature of free functions disjoint from L. As usually, we identify terms with trees. A term $t \in T_{\Sigma \cup L}(X)$ is *pure*, if for all subterms t' of t, if the root of t' has a label from Σ, then $t' \in T_\Sigma(x)$. A literal, clause or clause set is *pure*, if all terms that occur in it are pure. A *lattice term* is a pure term whose root is labeled by a lattice operation symbol. A term is *elementary*, if it is pure and the label of its root is neither $\sqcup$, $\sqcap$ or $-$.

An inequality $s \leq t$ is *reduced* if s is a (polyadic) join and t a (polyadic) meet of elementary terms. We write

$$s_1 \ldots s_m \leq t_1 \ldots t_m$$

instead of $s_1 \sqcap \ldots \sqcap s_m \leq t_1 \sqcup \ldots \sqcup t_m$. A clause or clause set is *reduced* if all the inequalities it contains are reduced. A formula is in *reduced clause normal form* (in $RCNF$), if it is in clause normal form (CNF) and every clause is reduced. A clause set is in *positive reduced clause normal form* (in $RCNF^+$), if it is in $RCNF$ and all literals are positive.

We now present an equivalence transformation ν from CNF to $RCNF^+$ for ADL. Since the transformation has more than 20 rules, we only discuss its main features. Details can be found in [22]. The rules of ν purify terms, eliminate negative lattice inequalities, split certain terms containing atoms, eliminate sectional complements, split with respect to joins and meets, discard literals and clauses and simplify lattice terms.

1. Purification. If in clause Γ, l the literal l contains an impure term t, then its subterm t' whose root is labeled by L is replaced by a fresh variable x in t and the clause Γ, l is replaced by $\Gamma, x \not\leq t', t' \not\leq x, l[x]$. This renaming is justified, since in first-order logic

$$\phi(s) \Leftrightarrow \forall x.(x = s \Rightarrow \phi(x)),$$
$$\phi(s) \Leftrightarrow \exists x.(x = s \wedge \phi(x)).$$

2. Elimination of negative inequalities. If in $\Gamma, s \not\leq t$ the term s does not contain an atom symbol, then the clause is replaced by the clauses $\Gamma, \alpha(f(\overline{x})) \leq s$ and $\Gamma, \alpha(f(\overline{x})) \sqcap t \leq 0$, where f is a fresh Skolem function and $\overline{x}$ denotes the free variables in s and t. This is justified by (atomic). If s contains an atom term α, the replacement is based on (28) and (25); α is reused[1].

3. Atom-based splitting. A clause $\Gamma, \alpha \leq t_1 \sqcup t_2$ is replaced by $\Gamma, \alpha \leq t_1, \alpha \leq t_2$. This is justified by (24).

4. Elimination of sectional complements. These rules, for positive and negative literals, are justified by the generalized shunting rules (18)–(20). $\Gamma, s \not\leq r \sqcup (t_1 - t_2)$, for instance, is replaced by $\Gamma, s \not\leq r \sqcup t_1, s \sqcap t_2 \not\leq r$.

5. Join- and meet-based splitting. These rules, for positive and negative literals, are justified by (1), (2) and distributivity. $\Gamma, r \sqcap (s_1 \sqcup s_2) \not\leq t$, for instance, is replaced by $\Gamma, r \sqcap s_1 \not\leq t, r \sqcap s_2 \not\leq t$.

6. Clause simplification. These rules, for positive and negative literals, are justified by reflexivity of $\leq$, (3) and (22). A clause $\Gamma, 0 \leq s$, for instance, is discarded; a clause $\Gamma, \alpha \leq 0$ is replaced by Γ.

7. Term simplification. Subterms $s \sqcap s$, $s \sqcup s$, $s - 0$ and $s \sqcup 0$ are replaced by s; $0 - s$ and $s \sqcap 0$ by 0.

---

[1] Remember that according to the conventions of this section, α is now a unary function symbol.

Note that also positive inequalities can be further reduced by (30). This is discussed in [22]. One can also use the generalized de Morgan laws and the simplification rules for sectional complements for further reduction.

All concrete rules of ν are so designed that they produce clauses. All axioms of ADL that deal with atoms are used in ν. In the elimination of negative inequalities, the introduction of new atoms is restricted as far as possible. The respective rule can be applied only finitely many times. It can be shown that ν terminates. By induction on the structure of lattice terms it is easy to see that some rule of ν is applicable, whenever a clause set is not in $RCNF^+$.

Finally, ν is not optimized. In several rules, lattice terms and clauses are copied. This could be avoided by renaming subterms, using an extension of the purification rule together with a Tseitin transformation at the clause level [24].

10   A Focused Calculus for DL

In this section we sketch the ordered chaining calculus DC for distributive lattices from [20] and further motivate the semantic side of the derivation method.

We first consider the orb D for DL. First, using the rules in ν for purification, join- and meet-based splitting and the appropriate clause and term simplifiction rules, we may assume that all clauses are reduced. Therefore, D can be restricted to axiomatize the reduced clausal theory of DL. Here, we may use D as a black-box. There are only two important points. First, D supposes normalization with respect to idempotence. This has been integrated into ν. Second, D uses the rule

$$x_1 \not\leq y_1 z, x_2 z \not\leq y_2, x_1 x_2 \leq y_1 y_2 \qquad \text{(cut)}$$

for characterizing distributivity. This may be understood as a lattice-theoretic variant of (Res). With appropriate ordering constraints, (cut) is a critical pair computation of a Knuth-Bendix completion procedure for DL (c.f. [18]). Extension to the clause level yields the focused ground inference rules

$$\frac{\Gamma, s_1 \leq a \qquad \Gamma', [s_2]a \leq t_2}{(\Gamma, \Gamma', s_1[s_2] \leq t_2)\nu} \qquad \text{(Cut)}$$

$$\frac{\Gamma, s \leq t_1 a, s \leq t_1 t_2}{(\Gamma, [s]a \not\leq t_2, s \leq t_1 t_2)\nu} \qquad \text{(DF)}$$

- In (Cut), the terms containing a are strictly maximal in the minor formulas. The minor formulas are strictly maximal wrt. the side formulas in the premises.
- In (DF), a is an elementary term, either t_1 is strictly maximal in the minor formulas or s is strictly maximal in the minor formulas and s is removed in the antecedent of the conclusion. The leftmost minor formula is strictly maximal with respect to the side formulas and the rightmost minor formula.

The brackets in the rules denote that an expression $[r]s \leq t$ can be read either as $s \leq t$ or as $rs \leq t$. Brackets in premises and conclusions are synchronized.

The inference rule (Cut) is derived by a two-step OR-proof with inference rule (Res) and axiom (cut) that characterizes distributivity, just like the chaining rule (34) has been derived by a two-step proof with the transitivity law in Section 8. In particular, (34) arises as a special case of (Cut) when setting s_2 to 0. In this sense, (Cut) is a chaining rule that has been refined to distributive lattices.

Similarly, the inference rule (DF) is derived by a two-step OR-proof with axiom (cut), in which the first step uses (Res) and the second step uses (Fact).

In addition, there is a dual rule to (DF). There are also several rules that resolve with negative literals. We do not mention these rules here, since for ADL, we may assume $RCNF^+$, such that these rules are not applicable.

The construction of the syntactic ordering $\prec$ on terms and literals again follows our intention to model (cut) as a lattice-theoretic variant of (Res) and (Cut) as an extension of (34). To this end we compare joins and meets of elementary terms as multisets in the term ordering. Elementary terms are compared with respect to some standard term ordering. The literal ordering compares inequalities lexicographically with respect to the tuple (t_ν, p, s, t_μ). Here, t_ν denotes the maximal term in the inequality: t_μ the minimal term. p assigns to negative inequalities greater weight than to positive ones. s assigns greater weight to inequalities in which the maximal term occurs at the left-hand side. See [20] for a formal definition and a discussion. All these orderings are well-founded by construction; terms which are equal modulo associativity and commutativity are assigned the same measure. All these orderings are extended to the non-ground level and the clause level according to Section 7.

11   A Focused Calculus for **ADL**

We now extend DC to an ordered chaining calculus for finite atomic distributive lattices. In the finite case, all non-theory clauses are ground, since existential and universal quantification can be replaced by joins and meets. The extension to the non-ground case is discussed in Section 12. We use the bracket notation introduced in Section 10.

We reuse the syntactic ordering for DC with one moderate local modification that has no impact on completeness of DC. In the term ordering, we also force atom terms to be smaller than all other terms, for example using a pair (a, g), such that $a = 1$ if the respective term denotes an atom and otherwise $a = 0$. g is the usual measure for a term.

Definition 2. *Let $\succ$ be the atom and clause ordering defined above. Let all clauses be in $RCNF^+$. Let ν be the transformation defined in Section 9. The ordered chaining calculus for finite atomic distributive lattices* ADC *consists of the deductive inference rules and the redundancy elimination rules of* OR [2] *and the focused inference rules (Cut), (DF) and the rule dual to (DF). The calculus is meant modulo associativity and commutativity at the lattice level.*

---

[2] Section 7 only defines a semantic *notion* of redundancy. Every set of inference rules implementing this notion is admitted. Many such rules have already been encoded into ν'.

Comparing ADC with DC, it turns out that addition of mathematical structure has simplified the calculus. The elimination of negative inequalities by (atomic) is very beneficial, since the negative chaining rules are the most prolific rules of DC (c.f. [20] for a discussion). Moreover, the entire impact of sectional complements, atoms and atomicity could be integrated into the simplification rules of ν. This justifies the mathematical efforts from Section 3 and 5.

We now sketch the soundness and completeness proofs of ADC. Soundness is obvious relative to soundness of DC (c.f. [20]) and correctness of ν (c.f Section 9). Completeness is shown using the derivation method relative to previous results for DC according to our remarks at the end of Section 8. Complete proofs can be found in [22].

Lemma 4. *Every ordered resolution inference with a clausal variant of (3), (22), (24) and (atomic) is redundant.*

Proof. (Sketch) Inspection with respect to $\prec$ show that every such inference yields a clause set that is smaller than and equivalent to the premise clause.   □

Lemma 4 and the fact that our black box D is already an orb for distributive lattices immediately imply the following result, which yields the first step of our derivation method from Section 8, the construction of an orb.

Proposition 2. *Let AD be the set D extended with clausal variants of (3), (22), (24) and (atomic). AD is an orb for the reduced clausal theory of ADL.*

Remember that by definition all inferences among members of an orb are redundant.

We now proceed to the second step of the derivation method, the derivation of the focused inference rules.

Lemma 5. *For every set S in $RCNF^+$ such that $S \cup AD$ is inconsistent, there exists an AD-separable and AD-serial OR-refutation.*

Proof. Completeness of DC provides the focused inference rules for DL. Lemma 4 prohibits all interferences of (3), (22), (24) and (atomic) inside of the macros corresponding to DC-inference rules and among these axioms. This establishes AD-separability. In [18], existence of T-serial OR-refutations has been shown for arbitrary T (In fact, T-seriality is shown only relative to local violations of the ordering constraints, which are, however, all inside of macros and therefore disappear in the derived rules.).   □

The main idea of the generic proof of T-seriality is that the needed good ordered resolution inference on a literal from the theory clause can be permuted up in the refutation tree, whereas the bad ordered resolution inference on a non-theory literal prescribed by the ordering constraints can be permuted down. This yields a new refutation with the desired macro inference at the appropriate place. Due to factoring it may be the case that some subtrees of the proof tree must be copied. This construction is iterated on the proof tree. The proof immediately applies to the present case.

We are now prepared for our main theorem.

Theorem 3. *Let all clauses be in $RCNF^+$. The ground ordered chaining calculus* ADC *is refutationally complete for finite atomic distributive lattices: For every ground reduced clause set that is inconsistent in the first-order theory of finite atomic distributive lattices, there exists a refutation in* ADC.

Proof. DC is refutationally complete for DL, but only the rules (Cut) and (DF) apply to clauses in $RCNF^+$. By Lemma 4 and Lemma 5, the axioms (3), (22), (24) and (atomic) do not interfere with these derived rules; they can be completely internalized into ν.

Conclusions of (Cut) must possibly be normalized by ν with respect to idempotence and negative inequalities must be eliminated by ν from conclusions of (DF). This explains the integration of ν into the inference rules.   □

12   Discussion

In this section we briefly discuss further results that are formally proven in [22].

- We have developed an alternative proof-search procedure to ADC in which, using (30), reduced terms can be further *atomized* to the form either $\alpha \leq s$ for s elementary or $\alpha s \leq 0$.
- The ordering constraints on (Cut) can be strengthened such that a is strictly maximal in the respective inequalities. This is shown by a proof transformation by induction on the structure of refutations. This restriction is very important for pruning the search space. We do not know a similar restriction for DC.
- ADC can be easily extended to a calculus for finite boolean lattices, thus improving a result from [20]. It can be immediately used as a calculus for finite sectionally complemented lattices (c.f Section 6).
- ADC (and its extension) decide the reduced clausal theories of finite ADL, finite BL, the universal theories of ADL and ABL and solve the uniform word problems for ADL and ABL. This follows from inspection of the rules in ν that eliminate negative inequalities. In fact, ν has been designed especially for this purpose. Since for the above problems, the input specification is ground, Skolemization does not introduce non-ground terms. Since Skolemization is needed only for negative inequalities with atom-free left-hand sides, the number of Skolemizations is bounded by the number of subterms that appear in the specification. Moreover, the ADC-inferences neither add any new symbols, nor do they shuffle atoms from left-hand to right-hand sides. Therefore only finitely many inferences lead to irredundant conclusions. The resulting orb contains the empty clause if and only if the initial clause set was inconsistent. It seems very interesting to extend these decision procedures to further classes, for instance by integrating more simplification rules into ADC. The elementary theory of distributive lattices, for instance, is undecidable [8], while the elementary theory of boolean lattices and atomic boolean lattices is decidable [23,12].

- We have extended ADC to the non-ground case, using standard lifting techniques. Now, some rules from ν are no longer simplifications. Idempotence of join and meet, for instance, must be taken out of ν, new deduction rules must be added to ADC. These are ordered factoring rules at the level of lattice terms. Moreover, also (Cut) inferences that cut out variables must be considered. Although such inferences can to a certain extent be restricted by the ordering constraints and circumvented by further simplification and redundancy elimination techniques, it is open whether they can be completely avoided.
- Hines [10], in his related calculus, has presented two simplification techniques. One is based on *chainless sets*. In ADL, these are atoms that appear only at left-hand sides of inequalities. Since ν and the inference rules of ADL are designed such that atoms are never shuffled from left-hand sides of inequalities to right-hand sides, the atoms introduced by elimination of negative inequalities are chainless. It is easy to show that the chainless set technique integrates in the redundancy elimination framework. The other technique depends on an axiom that excludes a universal set. It allows the elimination of certain inequalities with variables that could otherwise lead to prolific (cut) inferences. We show that this technique also works in ADC.

13 Conclusion

We have proposed atomic distributive lattices as an algebraic core calculus for reasoning about sets in program development methods like B or Z. We have developed an axiomatization that supports the effective reduction and simplification of terms, inequalities and clauses and yields a modular extension of a focused ordered resolution calculus for distributive lattices. In particular, this extension simplifies its predecessor. This nicely mirrors the fact that atomic lattices are mathematically simpler than non-atomic ones. We do not know of any other theory of comparable complexity that has been integrated into an automated proof-search procedure so far.

We envision the following further work. First the calculus and the associated proof-search method should be implemented and integrated into an applicable formal method. Second, more structure should be added, for instance, types for sets, pairs, comprehension, infinite sets, a choice function (c.f. [1]). Third, the transformation ν should be optimized, further simplification techniques should be developed. The theoretical results in this paper then open the way for practical automated reasoning about sets in the context of industrial-strength formal methods.

References

1. J.-R. Abrial. *The B-Book*. Cambridge University Press, 1996.
2. L. Bachmair and H. Ganzinger. Rewrite-based equational theorem proving with selection and simplification. *J. Logic and Computation*, 4(3):217–247, 1994.

3. L. Bachmair and H. Ganzinger. Rewrite techniques for transitive relations. In *Ninth Annual IEEE Symposium on Logic in Computer Science*, pages 384–393. IEEE Computer Society Press, 1994.
4. G. Birkhoff. *Lattice Theory*, volume 25 of *Colloquium Publications*. American Mathematical Society, 1984. Reprint.
5. R. P. Dilworth. Lattices with unique complements. *Trans. Amer. Math. Soc.*, 57:123–154, 1945.
6. H. Doornbos, R. C. Backhouse, and J. van der Woude. A calculation approach to mathematical induction. *Theoretical Computer Science*, 179:103–135, 1997.
7. M. Gordon. Set theory, higher-order logic or both? In J. Grundy and J. Harrison, editors, *Theorem Proving in Higher-Order Logic: 9th International Conference*, volume 1125 of *LNCS*, pages 191–202. Springer-Verlag, 1996.
8. A. Grzegorczyk. Undecidability of some topological theories. *Fund. Math.*, 38:137–152, 1951.
9. H. Hermes. *Einführung in die Verbandstheorie*. Springer-Verlag, 1967.
10. L. Hines. Str+ve⊆: The Str+ve-based Subset Prover. In M. E. Stickel, editor, *10th International Conference on Automated Deduction*, volume 449 of *LNAI*, pages 193–206. Springer-Verlag, 1990.
11. C. A. R. Hoare and B. von Karger. Sequential calculus. *Information Processing Letters*, 53(3):123–130, 1995.
12. D. Kozen. Complexity of Boolean algebras. *Theoretical Computer Science*, 10:221–247, 1980.
13. D. Kozen. Kleene algebra with tests. *Transation on Programming Languages and Systems*, 19(3):427–443, 1997.
14. L. C. Paulson. Set theory for verification: I. From foundations to functions. *J. Automated Reasoning*, 11:353–389, 1993.
15. A. Quaife. Automated deduction in von-Neumann-Bernays-Gödel set theory. *J. Automated Deduction*, 8:91–147, 1993.
16. P. Rudnicki. An overwiev of the MIZAR project. Technical report, Department of Computing Science, University of Alberta, 1992.
17. J. M. Spivey. *Understanding Z*. Cambrigde University Press, 1988.
18. G. Struth. An algebra of resolution. In L. Bachmair, editor, *Rewriting Techniques and Applications, 11th International Conference*, volume 1833 of *LNCS*, pages 214–228. Springer-Verlag, 2000.
19. G. Struth. Deriving focused calculi for transitive relations. In A. Middeldorp, editor, *Rewriting Techniques and Applications, 12th International Conference*, volume 2051 of *LNCS*, pages 291–305. Springer-Verlag, 2001.
20. G. Struth. Deriving focused lattice calculi. In S. Tison, editor, *Rewriting Techniques and Applicaions, 13th International Conference*, volume 2378 of *LNCS*, pages 83–97. Springer-Verlag, 2002.
21. G. Struth. A calculus for set-based program development I: Mathematical foundations. Technical Report 2003-15, Institut für Informatik; Universität Augsburg, 2003.
22. G. Struth. A calculus for set-based program development II: Proof search. Technical Report 2003-16, Institut für Informatik; Universität Augsburg, 2003.
23. A. Tarski. Arithmetical classes and types of Boolean algebras. *Bull. Am. Math. Soc.*, 55(64):1192, 1949.
24. G. S. Tseitin. On the complexity of derivations in propositional calculus. In J. Siekmann and G. Wrightson, editors, *Automation of Reasoning: Classical Papers on Computational Logic*, pages 466–483. Springer-Verlag, 1983. reprint.

Compositional Verification of a Switch Fabric from Nortel Networks

Hong Peng, Sofiène Tahar, and Yassine Mokhtari

Dept. of Electrical & Computer Engineering,
Concordia University
1455 de Maisonneuve W., Montreal, Quebec, H3G 1M8 Canada
{pengh,tahar,mokhtari}@ece.concordia.ca

Abstract. With the development of ASIC designs, simulation cannot cover all the corner cases in a complicated design. Model checking is a fully automatic approach to verify a finite state machine against its temporal specifications. However, its application is limited by the size of the system to be verified. Compositional verification and model reduction are two possible methods to tackle this problem. In this paper, we propose a verification framework based on assume-guarantee compositional model checking, where we can apply model checking to do exhaustive verification at the module level and conduct global properties via compositional reasoning. In this framework, temporal specifications are synthesized into Verilog modules. In case a module under verification is beyond the capability of model checking, the proposed model reduction algorithm is used. We implemented the framework on top of the VIS tool and applied it on an ATM switch fabric from Nortel Networks.

1 Introduction

With the development of ASIC designs, simulation cannot cover all the corner cases in a complicated design. Model checking [6] is a fully automatic approach to verify a finite state machine against its temporal specifications. However, its application is limited by the size of the system to be verified. Current model checking tools [2,13,3] are limited to several hundred Boolean state variables due to state space explosion. There are two main methods to tackle this problem: *compositional verification* and *model reduction*. Compositional verification is to verify each partition in the system separately and then derive the system specification from the partial proofs. Model reduction is to reduce the size of the system such that it can be handled by a verification tool. One active research area is on how to introduce model checking into the verification flow of a complicated design.

In this paper, we propose a framework to perform model checking by integrating compositional reasoning and model reduction. To illustrate our approach, we used a Nortel ATM (Asynchronous Transfer Mode) switch fabric as a real case study. Using this framework, we succeed to verify the switch fabric whose size is beyond the capability of current model checking tools. Our main contributions in this paper are to integrate two novel techniques: environment (stimulus) synthesis [14] and syntactic model reduction [17] into the framework, and make the verification by conducting global properties from module level local properties [18].

J.S. Dong and J. Woodcock (Eds.): ICFEM 2003, LNCS 2885, pp. 560–578, 2003.

In the compositional verification [18], properties are only true under certain environments. One of the problems in the compositional reasoning approach is to generate the *environment assumption*, i.e., stimulus for the module (partition) under verification. In our approach, we provide the environment assumptions as temporal logic formulas in **ACTL** [7] and then synthesize the formulas into Verilog modules [14]. We then compose this environment module with the RTL block under verification and feed it into a model-checking tool (here VIS [2]). However, in case the size of the composed module is still beyond the capability of model checking, we use a new syntactic model reduction algorithm based on cone of influence reduction and which analyzes the (Verilog) source code and removes the redundant variables and values [17].

The rest of paper is structured as follows. Section 2 introduces the verification flow we adopt. Section 3 describes the compositional verification and the environment synthesis. Section 4 presents the model reduction method. Section 5 introduces the ATM Switch Fabric case study and discusses its modeling and verification. In Section 5, we compare the experimental results obtained using our framework with those using the FormalCheck [3] tool. Finally Section 6 concludes the paper.

2 Verification Flow

Traditionally, outgoing from the requirement specification of a product, a design group starts to implement the RTL design, while verification groups develop a behavioral model and a test suite by using either HDLs such as Verilog and VHDL or HVLs such C, e, and OpenVera. The test suite endeavors to cover all test cases. The behavioral model is written at a higher level and cannot be synthesized, but only simulated, which can be developed much quicker than the RTL model. Test benches generate test vectors for both behavior and RTL models, and thus after simulation, their outputs can be compared. The test benches are tested using the behavioral model. Because of the increasing complexity of modern ASIC chips, this verification methodology cannot discover all the bugs and takes too long. Moreover, the behavioral model itself can be bug-proned.

As a complementary approach to simulation, formal methods, in particular model checking, have proven to be very useful in design verification coverage. However, the size of the blocks that can be actually verified is very limited. In this paper, we propose a model-checking framework based on an assume-guarantee [19] compositional reasoning and model reduction. In this framework, temporal specifications are synthesized into Verilog modules acting as "test benches" in module level model checking [14], and then module level local properties are composed into global properties by using compositional reasoning [18]. In case the module under model-checking is beyond the capability of model checking, syntactic model reduction is used [17]. The proposed verification flow is illustrated in Figure 1.

1. Given an RTL design and global properties derived from the specification. If the size of the RTL design, even after the reduction, is beyond the capability of model checking, then we will do the following compositional verification steps.
2. Partition the RTL design into modules.
3. Obtain local properties with respect to each RTL module (this is derived from the RTL design and the global property).

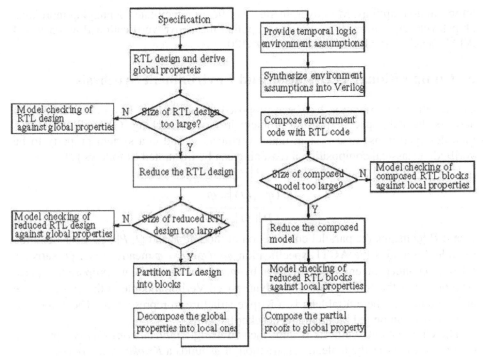

Fig. 1. Compositional Verificatioin Frameworks

4. Derive the environment assumptions (stimulus in temporal logic **ACTL** formulas) with respect to each RTL module, and then synthesize the formulas into Verilog environment modules as illustrated in [14]. Later, compose the RTL block and the Verilog environment module.
5. In case the size of the composed code is beyond the capability of the model-checking tool, apply the syntactic model reduction in [17] with respect to the local properties, and get the reduced composed model.
6. Verify the reduced composed model against the corresponding local properties using model checking, respectively.
7. Deduce the satisfaction of the global properties on the RTL design from these local properties using compositional reasoning rules illustrated in [18].

For our framework, we have chosen the model checker VIS [2] as our evaluation tool because it provides neither compositional reasoning nor model reduction options. Furthermore, VIS has a Verilog front-end such that we can feed our design into the tool directly. Throughout the compositional verification, the global properties are correct if and only if all the local properties are correct. For now, in terms of verification, partitioning the RTL design, deriving environment assumption formulas and local properties have to be done manually. Once we have the local properties and the corresponding environment assumptions, the following verification steps, i.e., the environment synthesis, the syntactic model reduction, and model checking, then are executed *automatically*. Another advantage of this framework is that the compositional reasoning allows us to do design verification at the system level even before the RTL modules are implemented since we can replace the missing modules by their temporal assumptions. Moreover, module verification facilitates debugging more than chip level verification does. We have applied the above verification flow on a 4*4 ATM switch fabric from Nortel Networks [20].

3 Compositional Verification and Environment Synthesis

Compositional verification has been proposed for some time as an efficient way to address the state space explosion problem in model checking. Given P and Q two modules (partitions) of a system under verification, and φ a system property to be verified, a classical compositional reasoning can be illustrated as follows [7]

$$\frac{P \models \varphi_p \qquad (\varphi_p, Q) \models \varphi}{P \| Q \models \varphi}$$

where $P\|Q$ means the parallel composition of module P and Q; $P \models \varphi_p$ means that the module P satisfies the **ACTL** specification φ_p; $(\varphi_p, Q) \models \varphi$ means model Q satisfies formula φ under the environment given by φ_p. In our approach, we propose to replace $(\varphi_p, Q) \models \varphi)$ by the composition of the synthesized Verilog module of the *tableau* of φ_p and module Q, where a tableau is a Kripke structure to represent φ_p. The composed system then can be fed into a model checker like VIS.

The environment synthesis is implemented using a *tableau construction* approach. Given a formula φ, the tableau construction of φ builds a *Kripke structure* (state transition graph) $\mathcal{K}$ consisting of states labeled by atomic propositions derived from φ and transitions between states, such that every model of φ is represented as an infinite path in $\mathcal{K}$.

As is often the case with tableaus for temporal logics, e.g., [7,12], a state of the tableau consists of a set of formulas that are supposed to hold along all paths leaving the state. We propose therefore to define a reduced tableau of **ACTL** formulas consisting of less states and transitions but accepting precisely the models of the formulas. Here, the formulas in the states are interpreted over a formula or its negation, or none of them. If the latter occurs, it reflects a don't care situation, and we call this state a *dummy state*.

In [6], E. M. Clarke et al. proposed the method of constructing concurrent programs from **CTL** formulas. The result program covers one, but not all, behavior of the formulas. A. Arora et al. [1] used the same approach for real-time applications. In [11,7], D. Long et al. proposed a tableau construction approach to connect the simulation relation and the satisfaction of an **ACTL** formula. However their tableau size is exponential to the size of the formula. In [16], C. S. Pasareanu et al. proposed an environment synthesis approach for LTL formulas in the context of software model checking using the same tableau construction approach as that in SPIN [8].

Our work distinguishes itself from the above through the following facts: (1) We are constructing the tableau for the full range of **ACTL** formulas; (2) We obtain a smaller tableau by interpreting states over a three-valued domain; (3) We apply rewriting rules to reduce the tableau size further more; (4) We describe the fairness constraint by generalized Buchi conditions; (5) We synthesize the tableau into Verilog code. In [14], we have proved the following theorem:

*Given a simulation relation ≤ and an **ACTL** formula φ, for every structure $\mathcal{K}'_\varphi$, $\mathcal{K}'_\varphi$*
|= φ iff $\mathcal{K}'_\varphi \le \mathcal{K}_\varphi$, where $\mathcal{K}_\varphi$ is the reduced tableau of φ.

Based on the above ideas, we implemented in Java a tableau construction and Verilog synthesis for the model checker VIS [2]. We hence support here the Verilog subset of VIS.

An overview of the proposed approach is depicted in Figure 2, where "Rewriting formulas" is a pre-processor to remove the redundancy in the input **ACTL** formulas [14].

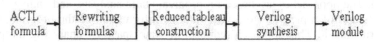

Fig. 2. Reduced tableau construction and Verilog synthesis

4 Syntactic Model Reduction

Beyond compositional approaches, model reduction is the most important technique for solving the state explosion problem. Model reduction is a general approach [5,4], which allows to reduce a concrete system (M) under verification to a more abstract and smaller one (M'). Both systems M and M' are connected by an abstraction relation which is *safe* with respect to a given property φ, namely it preserves the property. This means if the property holds for the abstract system, it holds for the concrete one as well. More formally, the property φ is either *weakly* preserved if $M'|=\varphi \Rightarrow M|=\varphi$, or *strongly* preserved if $M|=\varphi \equiv M|=\varphi$. It should be intuitively clear that the more weakly the property is preserved, the more reduction can be achieved.

One popular abstraction technique is the *cone of influence reduction* (COI) [10]. This method decreases the size of the concrete system by focusing on the variables of the concrete system that are referred to in the property and eliminating variables that do not influence the variables of interest in the property. In this way, the property satisfaction is preserved, while the size of the model that needs to be verified is smaller. However, sometimes, there are still lots of redundant information in the COI reduced model. We can easily find a case in practice where a variable A depends on variable B, but the value of variable B does not affect the value of variable A. For example, a two-input AND gate, if one of the inputs is set to zero, then no matter what value the other input takes, the output of the gate is always at zero.

Based on the above observation, we give a refined dependency definition by examining the values of the variables that influence the truth of the property. In this approach, a system under verification is considered as a program, which syntactic and semantic structure will be analyzed. Throughout the analysis, the value domains of the state variables are extracted based on the *control flow diagram* (CFD), and the values of state variables in the program are partitioned into *active values*, and *deactive values* according to their dependency in the property. The deactive values then can be replaced by a typical *abstract* value, and thus the value domains of the variables are much smaller than the original ones. Accordingly, we can have a reduced program with respect to the abstracted variables. After the above procedures, the state space of the reduced program is smaller than that of the original one, while the correctness of the properties are preserved. In [17], we have proved the following theorem.

There is a simulation relation between the models $\mathcal{K}_P$ and $\mathcal{K}_{P^\wedge}$ where P and P^ are the concrete model and the reduced model, respectively. Namely $\mathcal{K}_P \leq \mathcal{K}_{P^\wedge}$

In [5], abstract interpretation is a classical static program analysis approach. It has been used intensively in formal verification and model reduction [4,9]. Our proposed approach distinguishes itself from the above through the fact that the abstract domain of a variable is generated throughout the analysis of the program, which makes the reduction automatic. In [21], K. Yorav proposed ways to use the high level description (program text) of a system in order to improve the model checking process by reduction. The approaches are based on program static analysis, and analyze the control flow graph of a program to reveal runtime information of the program, without actually running it. This approach reduces the state space by analyzing the path between breakpoints where a breakpoint is a state that influence the specification. Hence, the states between these breakpoints are removed. In a similar way, we identify the breakpoints but our approach is focused on the dependency between values that influence the specification. In [15], K. S. Namjoshi et. al. proposed a reduction approach which translates a variable with large value domain, for example an integer, into a set of predicates. These predicates are determined by the automated syntactic analysis of the program under verification. Our reduction is different from this approach since we work on the finite domain, and will not generate predicates but abstract domains. Moreover, we keep only one value in the abstract domain. Our approach is also related to other works on cone-of-influence reduction [10]. However, our method is more efficient because we analyze the dependency between the *values* of variables in addition to the dependency between variables, thus the dependency relation is more accurate.

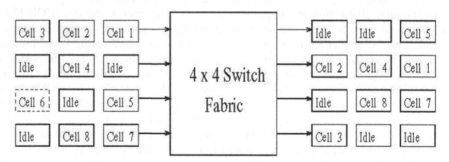

Fig. 3. ATM switch fabric

5 Case Study: Nortel ATM Switch Fabric

The basic purpose of an ATM (Asynchronous Transfer Mode) switch fabric is to transport valid (i.e., uncorrupted) ATM cells arriving at its ingress ports to the designated egress ports as shown in Figure 3 where cell 6 is a corrupted cell. Invalid ATM cells are to be discarded. Besides valid and invalid ATM cells, ATM cell streams may also contain idle cells, which serve to adapt the cell streams to the transmission bit rates employed. Cell type identification and cell switching is based on the contents of

ATM cells. More precisely, an ATM cell is a fixed-length cell consisting of a 5 octet header field and a 48 octet payload field. The payload field is available for actual user information. The header field carries the information for identification and transportation of the cell. The header of an ATM cell is further decomposed into subfields as illustrated in Figure 4.

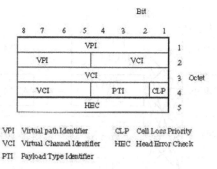

Fig. 4. ATM cell header

The virtual path identifier (VPI) and the virtual channel identifier (VCI) together constitute the routing fields of the cell head. The payload type identifier (PTI) and cell loss priority (CLP) fields are not used explicitly for cell switching purposes. The last octet of the cell header contains the header error check (HEC) sequence used to check the integrity of the other header subfields. ATM cell switching can now be described in brief as follows. After receiving a cell at one of its ingress ports, an ATM switch fabric determines whether the cell is a corrupted or idle cell. A corrupted cell is a cell with an incorrect HEC sequence. An idle cell is a cell with its VPI, VCI and PTI bits all set to 0 and its CLP bit set to 1, and with a correct HEC sequence. If the ingress ATM cell is not corrupt or idle, an attempt is made to translate the value of the VPI/VCI field into a new VPI/VCI value and an egress port number by means of a VPI/VCI routing table. If the routing table contains an enabled entry for the VPI/VCI value of the ingress cell, this value is replaced by the new VPI/VCI value and a new correct HEC sequence is generated. The resulting cell (i.e., with the new VPI/VCI value and HEC sequence) is then placed in the cell queue and switched onto the designated egress port.

5.1 Modeling the Switch Fabric

There are mainly four modules in the Nortel ATM switch fabric at hand, *ATM_SWITCH*, *ATM_MON*, *FIFO_QUEUE*, and *ATM_GEN* as shown in Figure 5. *ATM_SWITCH* is the root module, which includes the ATM cell routing functions. *ATM_MON* is the ingress part of the fabric, which includes the ATM cell monitor and detection functions. *FIFO_QUEUE* is the queuing module. *ATM_GEN* is the egress part of the fabric, which includes the ATM cell restructure functions.

The major property of such an ATM switch fabric is that "Valid cells (with good HEC and matching VPI/VCI) are switched correctly". Trying to prove this property directly using model checking will fail because of state space explosion, even after model reduction. In order to prove this property, compositional verification is necessary. Here, since all the cells are queued in the *FIFO_QUEUE* module, we specify the ingress part and the egress part separately and extract the local properties respectively. Namely, in the ingress part, valid cells (with good HEC and matching VPI/VCI) are switched into the queue, and in the egress part, cells in the queue are restructured and sent.

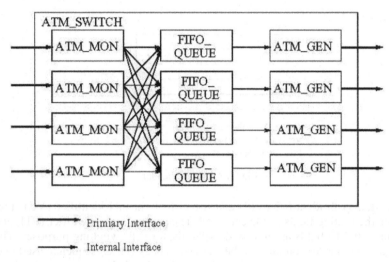

Fig. 5. Nortel ATM switch fabric structure

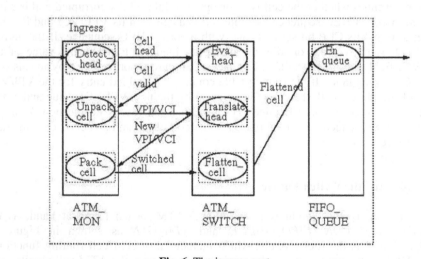

Fig. 6. The ingress part

In order to verify the ingress part, we decompose the ingress part as shown in Figure 6 where we can see that the system is partitioned into some blocks, namely *Detect_head*, *Unpack_cell*, *Pack_cell*, and so on. Hence, we can check the local properties of these blocks to derive the global property. For example, in order to check block *Translate_head*, we put the local property as

$Ingress_\varphi$: $AF\ (((VPI\_VCI\_IN[27:4] = 0)\ AND\ (MATCH\_FOUND = 1)))$

where VPI_VCI_IN is the VPI/VCI of incoming cells. The incoming cell can find a match VPI/VCI ($MATCH\_FOUND = 1$) when $VPI\_VCI\_IN[27:4] = 0$. In order to verify the egress part, we partition it as shown in Figure 7. For example, in order to check block *Restruct_cell*, we put the local property as

$Ingress_\psi$: $AG\ ((RESTRUCTED\_CELL[0] = FLATTENED\_CELL[7:0])\ AND$
$(RESTRUCTED\_CELL[53] = FLATTENED\_CELL\ [423:416]))$

where $FLATTENED\_CELL$ is the cell from the queue and $RESTRUCTED\_CELL$ is the restructed cell. The detailed properties of the blocks in the ingress and egress parts are in **Appendix B**.

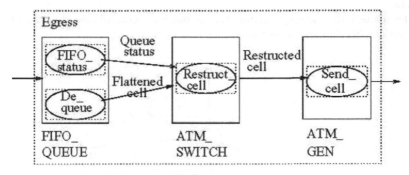

Fig. 7. The egress part

5.2   Verification of the Switch Fabric

We need to verify that the blocks in the ingress part, i.e., *Detect_head*, *Eva_head*, *Translate_head*, etc., and the blocks in the egress part, i.e., *FIFO_status*, *De_queue*, etc., satisfy their local properties given a cell coming in. Here in this section, we only show how to prove a sample local property $Ingress_\varphi$. The other properties can be proved in a similar way.

In the verification of $Ingress_\varphi$, what we want to check is that the correct VPI_VCI of the incoming cell can find a match in the routing table, while the corrupted VPI_VCI of the incoming cell cannot find a match. Hence, the environment assumption is the value of the VPI_VCI of incoming cell, i.e., VPI_VCI_IN. Since in the switch fabric, only those VPI_VCI_IN with bit 27 to 4 being 0 can find a match, the corresponding environment **ACTL** formula is:

$$AF\ (VPI\_VCI\_IN\ [27:4] = 0)$$

This assumption is discharged if the blocks before "Translate_head" can be proved. We construct the reduced tableau of this assumption shown in Figure 8, where "p" menas "$(VPI\_VCI\_IN\ [27:4] = 0)$" and "0" mean Buchi states. The states with double circles are initial states and the state without prepositional label (p or ~p) means that "p" can be either true or false in this state. As we proved in [14], this tableau contains less states than a normal tableau, but covers every possible model of the formula.

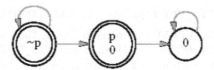

Fig. 8. Reduced tableau of the assumption

This above reduced tableau then can be synthesized into Verilog behavior code (see **Appendix A**). This code then can be composed with the block under verification, i.e., *Translate_head*. However, since the routing table is involved in the verification, and the size of the routing table is 1024*58-bit, no model checking tool can accept such a large model. We have to apply syntactic model reduction [17] with respect to the properties.

In order to make the model reduction, we construct the control flow diagram of module *Translate_head* as shown as follows.

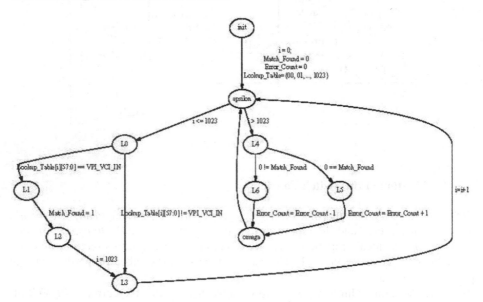

Fig. 9. Control flow diagram of Translate_head

By observing property *Ingress$_\varphi$*, we find that we are just verifying the behavior of variable *MATCH_FOUND*. The value of *MATCH_FOUND* is changed in node "L2" in the above diagram, which we call "key node". According to the model reduction approach proposed in [17], we traverse the diagram and find those values that do not affect *MATCH_FOUND*, namely those values from which node "L2" is not reachable. Then those values can be abstracted using one typical value. In the diagram, only the first item in the routing table with bit 27 to 4 equaling to 0 can change the value of *MATCH_FOUND*, so this value is kept as *active values*, while all other values in the routing table, which do not affect the behavior of *MATCH_FOUND* can be removed. So, we can keep only two items in the routing table and remove the other 1022 items.

In this way, the model under verification is reduced. Then we can compose the reduced model and its environment, and check it against the local property using VIS.

The verification results of sample properties are shown in the Table 1, where the CPU time reported is the real time; the BDD size in the table represents those states of the system that satisfy the formula.

Table 1. Verification Results of Sample Properties in VIS

Properties	Status	Model Checking		
		CPU(S)	Memory(MB)	BDD nodes
Ingress_P_1	Verified	19.5	0.908	42722
Ingress_P_2	Verified	272.4	1.908	18446
Ingress_P_3	Verified	1.4	1.308	15073
Ingress_P_4	Verified	3.8	9.9	7130
Ingress_P_5	Verified	11.3	8.54	164033
Ingress_P_6	Verified	11.6	8.54	383969
Ingress_P_7	Verified	3.7	9.918	7104
Ingress_P_8	Failed	-	-	-
Ingress_P_9	Verified	15.1	100.6	490923
Egress_P_1	Verified	2.5	1.44	15764
Egress_P_2	Verified	16.5	112.3	632434
Egress_P_3	Failed	-	-	-
Egress_P_4	Verified	6.7	12.2	137724

Table 2. Verification Results of Sample Properties in FormalCheck

Properties	Status	CPU(S)	Memory(MB)	States
Ingress_P_1	Failed	-	-	-
Ingress_P_2	Verified	1036	29.64	2.02e+03
Ingress_P_3	Verified	4	3.121	4
Ingress_P_4	Verified	22	6.71	1.02e+03
Ingress_P_5	Non-terminated	-	-	-
Ingress_P_6	Non-terminated	-	-	-
Ingress_P_7	Verified	32	13.75	3.36e+07
Ingress_P_8	Verified	8	3.69	1.31e+05
Ingress_P_9	Non-terminated	-	-	-
Egress_P_1	Verified	365	0.55	2.62e+05
Egress_P_2	Non-terminated	-	-	-
Egress_P_3	Verified	605	115.07	6.67e+02
Egress_P_4	Failed	-	-	-

The verification is performed using the VIS model checker on a SUN Enterprise server with 6GB memory. Through out the model checking, we set VIS with the options: implicit clocking and advanced ordering. In the Table, "-"means that VIS does not accept the model because of VIS internal bugs. In this case, we conducted the particular property verification in another tool (here FormalCheck) to make sure that it is really sound. Also, for the purpose of comparison, we verified the same models in FormalCheck on the same machine. However, this time, we do not do the reduction using our model reduction approach. The verification results are shown in Table 2. The reduction algorithm selected in FormalCheck is iterated with empty reduction seed because there are no constraints on the primary inputs, and the run option is symbolic BDD because it allows a more efficient model checking. The CPU time in the table is the real time and "States" are the states reachable.

In the Table, *"Non-terminated"* means that the verification failed due to state space explosion. The reason for this is either that the property under verification involves so many variables in the program that the reduction algorithms in FormalCheck are of no help (in this case, FormalCheck gives an internal bug report), or the model under verification is too large to be even complied by the tool (in this case, the tool will stay in a dead lock state until all the memory is consumed).

The *"Failed"* in the table means that the property cannot be verified by this tool because the environment assumptions could not be specified. We can translate the environment assumption into FormalCheck format by dropping 'A' operator.

Overall, since the verification in VIS is based on the reduced model while the verification in FormalCheck is based on the concrete model, the former is efficient with respect to CPU time and memory because the latter has to do the reduction work by itself.

Through out the verification, we also found some bugs in the design.

For example, a statement in the *Translate_head* block

```
while (!MATCH_FOUND && i <= MAX_CONNECTIONS)
    if (LOOKUP_TABLE[i].VPI_VCI_IN == VPI_VCI_IN ) begin
        MATCH_FOUND = 1;
......
```

is mistaken as

```
while (!MATCH_FOUND && i <= MAX_CONNECTIONS)
    if   (LOOKUP_TABLE[i].VPI_VCI_IN   ==   VPI_VCI_IN   &
28'hFF7FFFF) begin
        MATCH_FOUND = 1;
......
```

where *MAX_CONNECTIONS* is the number of items in the *LOOKUP_TABLE* and 28 is the length of *VPI_VCI_IN*. In this case, cells with *VPI_VCI* equaling to *008000* are matched, but should not, since according to the specification, only the cells with *VPI_VCI* equaling to *000000* can be matched. This bug actually is difficult to be found using simulation because one has to simulate that all the cells with *VPI_VCI* not equaling to *000000* cannot be matched. With formal verification, one can easily detect this bug using property *Ingress_P$_6$*. According to this property, every state in the state space should be *(VPI_VCI_IN != 000000) AND (MATCH_FOUND = 0)*, provided that the incoming *VPI_VCI_IN* does not equal to *000000*. This bug is also corrected by simply removing *28'hFF7FFFF* in the while loop.

After the above verification, we actually proved that every block satisfies its local properties, given certain environment assumptions. Moreover, because these environment assumptions are the outputs of the blocks in the system, they are discharged in the verification of the local properties. We apply the compositional rule as follows.

Where $\mathcal{T}\varphi$ means the synthesized Verilog module of formula φ, Actually, the global property: "Valid cells (with good HEC and matching VPI/VCI) are switched correctly" is given by assuming P_{valid_cells} and deducing $Egress\_P_4$ (correct switch). This way, we are checking the satisfaction of the global property against the whole design.

$$T_{Pvalid\_cell} \parallel Detect\_head \models Ingress\_p1$$
$$Eva\_head \parallel T_{Ingress\_p1} \models Ingress\_p2$$
$$Eva\_head \parallel T_{Ingress\_p1} \models Ingress\_p3$$
$$Unpack\_cell \parallel T_{Ingress\_p3} \models Ingress\_p4$$
$$Translate\_head \parallel T_{Ingress\_p4} \models Ingress\_p5$$
$$Translate\_head \parallel T_{Ingress\_P4} \models Ingress\_p6$$
$$Pack\_cell \parallel T_{Ingress\_P5} \parallel T_{Ingress\_p6} \models Ingress\_p7$$
$$Flattened\_cell \parallel T_{Ingress\_P7} \models Ingress\_p8$$
$$En\_queue \parallel T_{Ingress\_P8} \models Ingress\_P9$$
$$FIFO\_status \models Egress\_p1$$
$$De\_queue \models Egress\_p2$$
$$Re\,struct\_cell \parallel T_{Egress\_p1} \parallel T_{Egress\_p2} \models Egress\_p3$$
$$Send\_cell \mid T_{Egress\_p3} \models Egress\_p4$$

$$\overline{T_{Pvalid\_cell} \parallel Detect\_head \parallel Eva\_head \parallel Unpack\_cell \parallel Translate\_cell \parallel}$$
$$Pack\_cell \parallel Flatten\_cell \parallel En\_queue \parallel FIFO\_status \parallel De\_queue \parallel$$
$$Re\_struct\_cell \parallel Send\_cell \models Egress\_p4$$

6 Conclusion

In this paper, we proposed a compositional verification framework including environment synthesis and model reduction techniques. Using this framework, we verified an ATM switch fabric from Nortel Networks, which cannot be verified by plain model checking due to state space explosion. Here, we use VIS as target model checker, however, we can still use some other alternatives, such as SMV [13]. Through out the verification, we found bugs in the design, which were not caught through simulation. Because of the advantages in the environment synthesis and the model reduction, this framework is efficient in the verification with respect to the CPU time and memory resources. The framework is implemented in Java running on SUN Solaris OS.

Reference

1. A.Arora, P.C. Attie, and E.A. Emerson. Synthesis of fault-tolerant concurrent programs. In *Proceedings of the 17th Annual ACM Symposium on Principles of Distributed Computing*, pages 173--182, Puerto Vallarta, Mexico, June 1998.
2. R.K. Brayton et al.VIS: A system for verification and synthesis. In T.Henzinger and R.Alur, editors, *Computer-aided Verification'96*, volume 1102 of *Lecture Notes in Computer Science*, pages 428--432. Springer Verlag, Rutgers University, NY, USA, July 1996.
3. Cadence Design Systems. *Technical manual of FormalCheck*, v2.3 edition, 1987-1999.

4. E.M. Clarke, O.Grumberg, and D.Long. Model checking and abstraction. *ACM Transactions on Programming Languages and Systems*, Vol.16(No. 5):1512--1542, Sept 1994.
5. P.Cousot and R.Cousot. Abstract interpretation: a unified lattice model for static analysis of programs by construction or approximation of fixpoints. *Conference Record of the Fourth Annual ACM SIGPLAN-SIGACT Symposium on Principles of Programming Languages*, pages 238--252, Los Angeles, California, USA, 1977.
6. E.A. Emerson and E.M. Clarke. Using branching time temporal logic to synthesize synchronization skeletons. *Science of Computer Programming*, 2(3):241--266, 1982.
7. O.Grumberg and D.E. Long. Model checking and modular verification. *ACM Transactions on Programming Languages and Systems*, 16(3):843--871, May 1994.
8. G.J. Holzmann. *Design and validation of computer protocols*. Prentice hall, 1991.
9. Y.Kesten and A.Pnueli. Modularization and abstraction: the key to practical formal verification. *23rd Int. Symp. Mathematical Foundations of Computer Science*, Brno, Czech Republic, 1998.
10. R.P. Kurshan. *Computer-aided verification of coordinating processes*. Princeton University Press, 1994.
11. D.E. Long. *Model Checking, Abstraction, and Compositional Verification*. PhD thesis, CMU, 1993.
12. Z.Manna and A.Pnueli. *The Temporal Logic of Reactive and Concurrent Systems: Safety*. Springer-Verlag, New York, 1991.
13. K.L. McMillan. *Symbolic M}odel Checking*. Kluwer, 1993.
14. H.Peng, Y.Mokhtari, and S.Tahar. *Environment synthesis for compositional model checking*. In *Proceeding of IEEE International Conference on Computer Design*, Freiburg, Germany, September 2002. IEEE computer society Press.
15. K.S. Namjoshi and R.P. Kurshan. Syntactic program transformations for automatic abstraction. In E.Allen Emerson and A.Prasad Sistla, editors, *Computer-aided Verification'00*, volume 1855 of *Lecture Notes in Computer Science*, pages 433--449, Chicago, IL, USA, July 2000. Springer Verlag.
16. C.S. Pasareanu, M.B. Dwyer, and M.Huth. Assume-guarantee model checking of software: A comparative case study. *SPIN Workshop 1999*, pages 168--183, Trento, Italy, June 1999.
17. H.Peng, Y.Mokhtari, and S.Tahar. Model reduction based on value dependency. In *Proceeding of IEEE International ASIC/SOC Conference*, Washigton, DC, USA, September 2001.
18. H.Peng and S.Tahar. Compositional verification of IP based designs. In *Proceedings of IFIP International Workshop on IP Based Synthesis and System Design*, Grenoble, France, December 1999.
19. A.Pnueli. In transition for global to modular temporal reasoning about programs. In K.R. Kurshan, editor, *Logics and Models of Concurrent Systems*, volume 13 of *NATO ASI series. Series F*. Springer Verlag, 1984.
20. Northern Telecom. *Specification of a 4*4 ATM switch*, November 1998.
21. K.Yorav. *Exploiting syntactic structure for automatic verification*. PhD thesis, Israel institute of technology, June 2000.

A Synthesized Environment of *Ingress_φ*

The **ACTL** environment assumption of properties *Ingress_φ* is "**AF**(VPI_VCI_IN [27:4] = 0)". The synthesized Verilog code (Verilog subset acceptable in VIS model checker) of this assumption is shown as follows. Lines 0 to 5 are comments. *VPI_VCI_IN[27:4]* is set as an output of the module *tableau*. Lines 9 to 12 are to declare the variables. Lines 14 to 18 are to set the initial states, where *S_INIT_W* indicates the initial states and *S_INIT_W_TMP* is a temporary variable. In Lines 19 to 25, wire variables *Sx_NEXT_W* describe the transitions of the states, i.e., what is the next state of current state *Sx*. *Sx_NEXT_W_TMP* are the temporary variables. Lines 26 to 49 are the non-deterministic assignment of *VPI_VCI_IN[27:4]*. Lines 50 to 70 are the behaviors of this environment.

```
L0:  //'define TRUE 1
L1:  //'define FALSE 0
L2:  //'define S0 0
L3:  //'define S1 1
L4:  //'define S2 2
L5:  //'define S3 3
L6:  module tableau(VPI_VCI_IN);
L7:  output[27:4] VPI_VCI_IN;
L8:  //Variable declaration
L9:  reg [27:4] VPI_VCI_IN;
L10: wire [27:4] VPI_VCI_INND_W;
L11: reg [1:0] STATE;
L12: wire [1:0] S_INIT_W_TMP, S_INIT_W,
                S0_NEXT_W, S1_NEXT_W,
                S2_NEXT_W, S3_NEXT_W;
L13: //Initializaation
L14: assign S_INIT_W_TMP = $ND(0, 1, 2, 3);//$
L15: assign S_INIT_W = ((S_INIT_W_TMP == 3)) ?
            2 : S_INIT_W_TMP;
L16: initial begin
L17:     STATE = S_INIT_W;
L18: end // Initial

L19: //Combinational part
L20: assign S2_NEXT_W = 3;
L21: assign S3_NEXT_W = 3;
L22: assign S1_NEXT_W = 1;
L23: wire [1:0] S0_NEXT_W_TMP;
L24: assign S0_NEXT_W_TMP = $ND (0,1,2,3);//$
L25: assign S0_NEXT_W = ((S0_NEXT_W_TMP == 1)
        || (S0_NEXT_W_TMP == 3)) ?
            2 : S0_NEXT_W_TMP;
L26: assign VPI_VCI_INND_W[4] = $ND( 0, 1);
```

```
L27: assign VPI_VCI_INND_W[5] = $ND( 0, 1);
L28: assign VPI_VCI_INND_W[6] = $ND( 0, 1);
L29: assign VPI_VCI_INND_W[7] = $ND( 0, 1);
L30: assign VPI_VCI_INND_W[8] = $ND( 0, 1);
L31: assign VPI_VCI_INND_W[9] = $ND( 0, 1);
L32: assign VPI_VCI_INND_W[10] = $ND( 0, 1);
L33: assign VPI_VCI_INND_W[11] = $ND( 0, 1);
L34: assign VPI_VCI_INND_W[12] = $ND( 0, 1);
L35: assign VPI_VCI_INND_W[13] = $ND( 0, 1);
L36: assign VPI_VCI_INND_W[14] = $ND( 0, 1);
L37: assign VPI_VCI_INND_W[15] = $ND( 0, 1);
L38: assign VPI_VCI_INND_W[16] = $ND( 0, 1);
L39: assign VPI_VCI_INND_W[17] = $ND( 0, 1);
L40: assign VPI_VCI_INND_W[18] = $ND( 0, 1);
L41: assign VPI_VCI_INND_W[19] = $ND( 0, 1);
L42: assign VPI_VCI_INND_W[20] = $ND( 0, 1);
L43: assign VPI_VCI_INND_W[21] = $ND( 0, 1);
L44: assign VPI_VCI_INND_W[22] = $ND( 0, 1);
L45: assign VPI_VCI_INND_W[23] = $ND( 0, 1);
L46: assign VPI_VCI_INND_W[24] = $ND( 0, 1);
L47: assign VPI_VCI_INND_W[25] = $ND( 0, 1);
L48: assign VPI_VCI_INND_W[26] = $ND( 0, 1);
L49: assign VPI_VCI_INND_W[27] = $ND( 0, 1);
L50: //Sequential part
L51: always begin
L52:    case (STATE)
L53:    0: begin

L54:        VPI_VCI_IN[27:4] = 1;
L55:        STATE = S0_NEXT_W;
L56:       end
L57:    1: begin
L58:        VPI_VCI_IN[27:4] = 1;
L59:        STATE = S1_NEXT_W;
L60:       end
L61:    2: begin
L62:        VPI_VCI_IN[27:4] = 0;
```

```
L63:           STATE = S2_NEXT_W;
L64:           end
L65:      3: begin
L66:           VPI_VCI_IN = VPI_VCI_INND_W;
L67:           STATE = S3_NEXT_W;
L68:           end
L69:      endcase // case (STATE)
L70: end // always begin
L71: endmodule // tableau
```

The fairness constraint file is shown as follows, namely one of the following states has to be asserted infinitely often.

```
(tableau.STATE = 1
|| tableau.STATE = 2
|| tableau.STATE = 3
);
```

B Ingress and Egress Properties

Ingress_P_1
In this property, we require that the ingress port will receive a cell if a cell is coming into the port.Formally,

$$AF \; (New\_cell\_recieved = 1)$$

Where *New_cell_recieved* is set when a cell with integral structure is received.

Ingress_P_2
In this property, we check the HEC detection mechanism in the ingress part, given there is a cell ready. Namely,

$$AG \; (HEC\_OK = 1)$$

where *HEC_OK* is set if the cell under test has a good HEC value.

Ingress_P_3
In this property, we check the IDLE detection mechanism in the ingress part, given there is a cell ready. Formally,

$$AG((\; WORD[0]=0) \; AND \; (WORD[1] = 0) \; AND \; (WORD[2] = 0) \; AND$$
$$(WORD[3][7:1] = 0) \; AND \; (WORD[3][0] = 1) \rightarrow (IS\_IDLE = 1))$$

meaning that when the byte stream (*WORD*) in a cell satisfying the above format (all 0 except the last bit), then this cell is judged to be an idle cell.

Ingress_P_4
In this property, we check that a cell is unpacked correctly. Formally,

$$AG \; ((VPI[11:4] = WORD[0]) \; AND \; (VCI[11:4] = WORD[2]) \; AND \; (VPI[3:0] =$$
$$WORD[1][7:4]) \; AND \; (VCI[15:12] = WORD[1][3:0]) \; AND \; (VCI[3:0] =$$
$$WORD[3][7:4]) \; AND \; (PTI[2:0]=WORD[3][3:1]) \; AND \; (CLP = WORD[3][1]))$$

where *WORD* is the input byte stream and *VPI, VCI, CLP, PTI* are the formatted cell headers.

Ingress_P_5
In this property, we check that if the incoming *VPI_VCI* satisfies our specification (bit 27 to 4 are 0), then it will find a match in the routing table. Formally,
$$AF\,(((VPI\_VCI\_IN[27:4] = 0)\,AND\,(MATCH\_FOUND = 1))))$$
where *VPI_VCI_IN* is the *VPI_VCI* value of the input cell. *MATCH_FOUND* is set when *VPI_VCI_IN* can find a match in the routing table.

Ingress_P_6
In this property, we check that all incoming *VPI_VCI* that do not satisfy our specification cannot find a match in the routing table. Formally,
$$AG\,((NOT(VPI\_VCI\_IN[27:4] = 0)) \rightarrow (MATCH\_FOUND = 0)))$$
This is a safety property of the routing table, which has the similar form as *Ingress_P_5*.

Ingress_P_7
In this property, we check that the cell is packed correctly. Formally,
$$AG\,((VPI[11:4] = WORD[0])\,AND\,(VCI[11:4] = WORD[2])\,AND\,(VPI[3:0] =$$
$$WORD[1][7:4])\,AND\,(VCI[15:12] = WORD[1][3:0])\,AND\,(VCI[3:0] =$$
$$WORD[3][7:4])\,AND\,(PTI[2:0]=WORD[3][3:1])\,AND\,(CLP = WORD[3][1]))$$
This property is similar with *Ingress_P_4*.

Ingress_P_8
In this property, we check that the cell is flattened correctly, namely the word structure of a cell can be correctly flattened into a bit stream. Formally,
$$AG((FLATTENED\_CELL[7:0] = WORD[0])\,AND\,(FLATTENED\_CELL[15:8] =$$
$$WORD[1])\,)$$
where *FLATTENED_CELL* is the corresponding bit stream of the cell.

Ingress_P_9
In this property, we check that the flattened cell can be enqueued correctly, namely the flattened cell is put into the queue and the pointer of the queue is changed accordingly. Formally,
$$AG(\,NOT\,IS\_FULL \rightarrow AF\,((Queue.HEAD = FLATTENED\_CELL)\,AND\,(HEAD =$$
$$HEAD + 1)))$$
Where *IS_FULL* is set when the queue is full; the property means that if the queue is not full, then the cell will find a place in the queue.

Egress_P_1
In this property, we check that the status of the queue is empty if the head pointer equals to the tail pointer. Formally,
$$AG\,((HEAD = TAIL) \rightarrow (EMPTY = 1))$$
where *EMPTY* is set when the queue is empty.

Egress_P_2
In this property, we check that the flattened bit stream cell can be restructured into a word format cell. Formally,
$$AG\,((RESTRUCTED\_CELL[0] = FLATTENED\_CELL[7:0])\,AND$$
$$(RESTRUCTED\_CELL[53] = FLATTENED\_CELL\,[423:416]))$$
meaning that the dequeued cell (*FLATTENED_CELL*) can be restructured into a formatted cell (*RESTRUCTED_CELL*);

Egress_P$_3$

In this property, we check that the flattened bit stream cell can be restructured into a word format cell. Formally,

$$AG\ ((RESTRUCTED\_CELL[0] = FLATTENED\_CELL[7:0])\ AND$$
$$(RESTRUCTED\_CELL[53] = FLATTENED\_CELL\ [423:416]))$$

meaning that the dequeued cell (*FLATTENED_CELL*) can be restructured into a formatted cell (*RESTRUCTED_CELL*);

Egress_P$_4$

In this property, we check that the de-queued cell can be sent out to the egress port. Formally,

$$AF\ (NEWCELL\_READY = 1)$$

where *NEWCELL_READY* is set when a cell has been sent out successfully.

Constraint-Based Model Checking of Data-Independent Systems*

Beata Sarna-Starosta and C. R. Ramakrishnan

Department of Computer Science
State University of New York at Stony Brook
Stony Brook, New York, 11794-4400, USA
{bss,cram}@cs.sunysb.edu

Abstract. Data-independent systems are an important class of infinite-state systems which can be subject to model checking by first building finite-state property-preserving abstractions. Exploiting data independence in practice involves user guidance, either in terms of the abstraction itself or in terms of symmetry properties of the system. In this paper we present a constraint-based verification technique that automatically handles data-independent systems. Our technique introduces a unified, automata-based model for infinite-state systems and LTL formulas. The technique can be seen as a generalization of explicit state model checker for reachability and LTL properties. We have implemented our technique using logic programming with tabulation and constraints. We also describe an extension to the automata model that permits verification of a richer class of systems. We show its power by analyzing configuration (security) vulnerabilities in a computer system.

1 Introduction

Many real-world systems and designs are naturally modeled as systems with infinite state space. Systems that have a finite number of control locations (analogous to program counter values) but manipulate data ranging over arbitrary unbounded domains are used to model software artifacts and control systems such as communication protocols or hardware controllers. Such systems can be modeled as extended finite automata (EFA) where each control location has a set of local variables and the transitions have (i) a guard that tests the valuation of variables in the source location and (ii) a relation that maps values of variables in the source location to the variables in the destination location. For instance, Figure 1 shows an EFA model for a two-place FIFO buffer. Many infinite-state systems use only operations such as input, output and copy that do not inspect the individual values themselves. Notice for instance, that input values to the buffer in Figure 1 do not affect the system's observable behavior except for the corresponding changes to the output values. Such infinite-state systems are called *data-independent* [27].

---

* This research was supported in part by NSF grants EIA-9705998, CCR-9876242, IIS-0072927, CCR-0205376, CCR-0311512, and ONR grant N000140110967.

J.S. Dong and J. Woodcock (Eds.): ICFEM 2003, LNCS 2885, pp. 579–598, 2003.

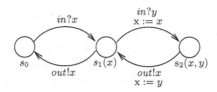

Fig. 1. Example EFA for 2-place FIFO buffer.

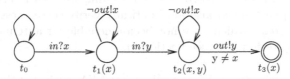

Fig. 2. Automaton representing a run with "out of order" message delivery.

The State of the Art: Since the control behavior of data-independent systems does not depend on the actual values of the data, such systems can be verified using traditional model checking techniques as follows. First, temporal properties of such systems can be specified using only data values drawn from a finite domain. Then a data-independent system can be abstracted to a finite-state system by restricting the data variables to take values only over this finite data domain. The crucial problem in verifying data-independent systems is, then, to identify the appropriate (finite) data domain that makes the abstraction property-preserving. In the seminal work of [27], this abstraction is performed manually. Since then, several techniques [12,10,13,18] for identifying the appropriate abstraction have been developed. However, existing techniques either require user guidance or expect the temporal properties to be solely about the control behavior of the system. (These issues are explored in more detail in Section 7.)

Summary of Our Approach: We model data-independent systems, as well as their temporal properties, as extended finite automata. For instance, Figure 2 shows an EFA representing runs that deliver messages "out-of-order", i.e. where there are two data objects, x and y, such that x is read before y, but y is written out before x. The structure of EFAs is such that a product of two such automata is also an EFA. Following the automata-based approach we can verify properties of systems by looking for particular runs in their product EFAs: safety and liveness can be verified using reachability analysis, while LTL properties can be checked by good cycles detection.

We represent EFAs as constraint logic programs; analyzing the runs can be then posed as query evaluation over these programs. Note that, resolution, the widely-used query evaluation mechanism, ensures that the variables in the EFA are bound only to the extent necessary to answer the query. This follows our earlier approaches to constructing model checkers of finite and infinite-state systems based on query evaluation over (constraint) logic programs. Moreover, the EFA product construction itself can be encoded as a constraint logic program, meaning that the product automaton itself is constructed on demand: only portions of the product automaton needed to answer the particular query are materialized. Finally, interpreting the query over a domain of equalities and negated equalities (commonly referred to as *disequalities*, see e.g. [24]) ensures that we can verify temporal properties of data-independent systems without attempting to enumerate specific valuations of the data variables. This approach can be used to automatically verify the data-independent systems that have been reported in the literature [27,10,13] without needing any user intervention or annotations. Our approach can also automatically verify correctness properties of cache-memory systems which have not been amenable for automatic treatment using the existing techniques (see Section 4).

Extensions and Applications: We initially define EFAs such that they manipulate only equality and disequality constraints (Section 3). Even these relatively simple models are expressive enough to represent data-independent systems as defined in [27], as well as their extensions [13]. We describe the verification of cache-memory systems using such EFAs in Section 4. We further extend EFAs to use membership constraints (e.g. $x \in y$) in order to represent a richer class of systems (Section 5). With these constraints, the model checking problem is no longer decidable. We hence devise abstractions that ensure termination of the analysis but with very little loss of information in practice. We use this technique to verify properties of a generalized cache-memory system, as well as to detect vulnerabilities in computer system configurations (Section 6).

The technique presented in this paper provides a way for direct and automatic verification of data-independent systems. The system models may in fact be specified in a familiar process algebraic notation that can be automatically translated to the underlying EFAs. This enables direct application of our technique on system models constructed for use in finite-state model checkers such as XMC [23]. The systems handled by the model checker include those that compare data variables using equality (e.g. $x = y$ where x and y are data variables) and disequality (e.g., $x \neq y$) tests. The temporal properties can naturally express both data and control behaviors of these systems. Furthermore, our implementation of this technique can be seen as an extension to an explicit-state model checker for LTL properties [2,21].

2   Preliminaries

We assume the standard notion of variables, function symbols, predicates, terms, substitutions, and unification [16]. Variables range over an enumerable set $\mathcal{V}$; we use $x, y, \ldots$ to denote variables. Function symbols range over $\mathcal{F}$; 0-ary function symbols are called constants (denoted by the set $\mathcal{C}$). We use $\mathcal{T}$ to denote the set of all terms constructed from $\mathcal{V}$ and $\mathcal{F}$; σ, θ to denote substitutions; and mgu to denote the most general unifier of a set of terms. A term t under a substitution σ is denoted by $t\sigma$. By $\sigma[t/x]$ we denote a substitution σ' that maps x to t and is identical to σ everywhere else.

Constraints, Constraint Languages and Assertions: A formal definition of extended finite automata (see Section 3) is based on a language of constraints. Constraint languages are parameterized with respect to a set of *primitive constraints PC*. For instance, *equality* and *disequality* constraints are defined using the following set of primitive constraints:

$$PC_{\{=\}} = \{v_1 = v_2, v_1 \neq v_2\}$$

where $v_1, v_2 \in \mathcal{V} \cup \mathcal{C}$. A constraint language L defined with respect to PC is built using the constraints in PC, Boolean connectives $\wedge$ and $\vee$, and existential quantification $\exists$ over variables. Elements of L are also called *assertions* and are denoted by φ (possibly primed and/or subscripted). Formally, L_s, the language of constraints defined over PC_s is the smallest set such that (i) $PC_s \subseteq L_s$; (ii) $\varphi_1 \wedge \varphi_2, \varphi_1 \vee \varphi_2 \in L_s$ if $\varphi_1, \varphi_2 \in L_s$; and (iii) $\exists v.\ \varphi \in L_s$ if $\varphi \in L_s$ and $v \in \mathcal{V}$. As $PC_{\{o_i\}}$ includes negations of constraints formed by each o_i, we do not have an explicit connective for negation.

The set of variables in an assertion φ is denoted by $vars(\varphi)$. We use the standard notion of bound and free variables (due to quantifiers) in assertions. The set of bound variables in an assertion φ is denoted by $bv(\varphi)$ and the set of free variables by $fv(\varphi)$. We also use the standard notion of *meaning* of assertions in $L_{\{=\}}$, by interpreting them over the data domain $\mathcal{C}$. With each assertion φ we associate a set $[\![\varphi]\!]$ of substitutions mapping $fv(\varphi)$ to $\mathcal{C}$. Note that we define the meaning by substituting only the free variables of an assertion. Each substitution σ in $[\![\varphi]\!]$ is said to "satisfy" φ (written as $\sigma \models \varphi$).

In the first part of the paper, we use only equality and disequality constraints, since they suffice to describe and analyze data-independent systems. We subsequently expand our techniques to analyze systems whose control behaviors are dependent on certain infinite-domain values. We model such systems using an expanded constraint language $L_{\{=,\in\}}$ which considers two distinguished set constants, $\{\}$ (empty set) and $\mathcal{U}$ (the universal set) in $\mathcal{C}$, and has the following set of primitive constraints:

$$PC_{\{=,\in\}} = \{v_1 = v_2, v_1 \neq v_2, v_1 \in v_2, v_1 \notin v_2\}$$

where $v_1, v_2 \in \mathcal{V} \cup \mathcal{C}$. Assertions in $L_{\{=,\in\}}$ are interpreted by first classifying variables into many sorts: base variables that take values over $\mathcal{C}$, first-order set variables that take values over $2^{\mathcal{C}}$, etc.

Expressions and Assignments: Given a substitution that associates values with variables, expressions compute new values. For data-independent systems, we consider the constraint language $L_{\{=\}}$ and the set of expressions $\mathcal{E}_{\{=\}} = \mathcal{V} \cup \mathcal{C}$. When considering the constraint language $L_{\{=,\in\}}$, we will use a richer expression language $\mathcal{E}_{\{=,\in\}}$ which is the smallest set such that (i) $\mathcal{V} \cup \mathcal{C} \subseteq \mathcal{E}_{\{=,\in\}}$; (ii) $2^{\mathcal{V}} \cup 2^{\mathcal{C}} \subseteq \mathcal{E}_{\{=,\in\}}$; and (iii) if $e_1, e_2 \in \mathcal{E}_{\{=,\in\}}$ then $e_1 \cup e_2, e_1 \cap e_2, e_1 - e_2$

are all in $\mathcal{E}_{\{=,\,\in\}}$. The value of an expression e with respect to a substitution σ is denoted by $e\sigma$.

Assignments are written as $x := e$ where $x \in V$ and $e \in \mathcal{E}$. The *meaning* of an assignment $x := e$ can be captured as a binary relation between substitutions such that $(\sigma, \sigma') \in [\![x := e]\!]$ iff $\sigma' = \sigma[e\sigma/x]$. Simultaneous assignments are denoted by $\bar{V} := \bar{E}$ where $\bar{V}$ and $\bar{E}$ are (equal-length) sequences of variables and expressions respectively. An assignment can also be seen as transforming assertions: from one that is satisfied before the assignment to another that is satisfied after the assignment. This assertion mapping corresponding to an assignment ρ is denoted by Ξ_ρ.

Standard Forms and Equivalence: We say that two assertions are identical if they differ only in the names of bound variables. Two assertions are *equivalent* if and only if they are satisfied by the same set of substitutions. Note that while identical assertions will be equivalent, the converse does not always hold: e.g. $\varphi_1 = (x = y \wedge y = z)$ and $\varphi_2 = (x = y \wedge x = z)$ are equivalent but not identical.

When processing assertions, it is often useful to reduce them to equivalent *standard form*, defined as follows:

Definition 1 [Standard Form of Assertions] An assertion $\varphi \in L_{\{=\}}$ is said to be in standard form if the following hold:

- *Structure:* φ is in disjunctive normal form, i.e., is of the form $\varphi_1 \vee \varphi_2 \cdots \varphi_n$ such that each φ_i itself is of the form $\exists V.\varphi_{i,1} \wedge \varphi_{i,2} \wedge \cdots \wedge \varphi_{i,k_i}$ where $\varphi_{i,j} \in PC_{\{=\}}$; the assertions φ_i are called the disjuncts of φ.
- *Non-redundancy:* A primitive constraint occurs at most once in any disjunct in φ.
- *Naming:* $bv(\varphi) \cap fv(\varphi) = \{\}$;
- *Order:* For each disjunct φ_i in φ, if $x = y$ occurs in φ_i then there are no primitive constraints of the form $y = z$, $z = y$, $y \neq z$ or $z \neq y$ in φ_i for any variable z. □

Given a conjunction φ of primitive constraints over $PC_{\{=\}}$, it is easy to see that we can group its variables in several equivalence classes ($x = y$ in φ means that x and y belong to the same class). Moreover, φ is satisfiable (when interpreted over an infinite data domain) if and only if whenever $x \neq y$ occurs in φ, x and y belong to different classes. These observations immediately yield a procedure to convert every assertion into an equivalent standard form.

Proposition 1 *For every satisfiable assertion* $\varphi \in L_{\{=\}}$ *there is an equivalent assertion* φ' *such that* φ' *is in standard form.*

An assertion φ in standard form is said to be quantifier-free if it has no bound variables. For any disjunct $\exists V.\ \varphi$ let $\exists V.\ \varphi'$ be an equivalent standard form such that for every $x = y$ in φ', $x \in V$ implies $y \in V$. Let φ'' be the assertion obtained by dropping from φ' every primitive constraint that contains a variable in V. It can then be shown that φ'' is equivalent to $\exists V\varphi$ whenever the assertions are interpreted over an infinite domain of constants.

Example 1 Consider $\varphi : \exists y . x = y \wedge y \neq z \wedge z \neq w \wedge y \neq w$.

- The assertion $\varphi_1 : \exists y . x = y \wedge x \neq z \wedge z \neq w \wedge x \neq w$ is in standard form, and is equivalent to φ.
- Shrinking the scope of the quantifier yields the assertion $\varphi_2 : (\exists y . x = y) \wedge x \neq z \wedge z \neq w \wedge x \neq w$ which is equivalent to φ_1 and hence φ.
- Since $(\exists y . x = y)$ is satisfiable (under interpretation over any domain), the assertion $\varphi_3 : x \neq z \wedge z \neq w \wedge x \neq w$, and φ_2 are equivalent. ∎

In the above example, the assertion $(\exists y . \ x = y)$ is always satisfiable and hence the final quantifier-free form φ_3 is always equivalent to the initial assertion φ. In general, however, the dropped assertion may be satisfiable only over domains that are sufficiently large. For instance, $\exists y, z . \ x \neq y \wedge x \neq z \wedge y \neq z$ is satisfiable only when the data domain has at least two elements. However, the dropped assertions are always satisfiable when interpreted over an infinite data domain. Hence we have:

Proposition 2 *For every satisfiable assertion $\varphi \in L_{\{=\}}$ there is assertion φ' such that φ and φ' are equivalent over infinite data domains and φ' is in quantifier-free standard form.*

Quantifier-free standard forms are important since they allow us to finitely represent all possible assertions over a finite set of free variables.

Proposition 3 *Let V be a set of variables and $\Phi \subseteq L_{\{=\}}$ be the set of all assertions in quantifier-free standard form such that $fv(\varphi) = V$ for all $\varphi \in \Phi$. Then the set Φ is finite.*

3   Extended Finite Automata

We now describe an automata-based model to specify infinite-state systems with finite number of control locations. The automaton's behavior can be observed based on the labels, called *actions*, on the transitions taken by the automaton. We distinguish between *input actions* (denoted by $c?x$), *output actions* (denoted by $c!e$) and *internal actions* (denoted by special symbol τ) where $c \in \mathcal{C}$, $x \in \mathcal{V}$, and $e \in \mathcal{V} \cup \mathcal{C}$. The set of actions is denoted as *Act*; we use α to range over actions. We refer to the sets of free and bound variables involved in an action α as $fv(\alpha)$ and $bv(\alpha)$, respectively. These sets are defined as follows: $fv(c?x) = \emptyset$, $bv(c?x) = \{x\}$, $fv(c!e) = vars(e)$, $bv(c!e) = \emptyset$.

Definition 2 [Extended Finite Automaton (EFA)] An *extended finite automaton* over the constraint language $L_{\{=\}}$ is defined by the sextuple $\mathcal{A} = \langle \mathcal{L}, \delta, \iota, \ell_0, \varrho, \mathcal{F} \rangle$ where:

- $\mathcal{L}$ is a finite set of (control) *locations*;
- $\delta = \mathcal{L} \times 2^{\mathcal{V}}$, the variable map, is a function that maps each location ℓ_i to a finite set of variables local to ℓ_i;

- ι is a function that maps each location to an assertion (invariant) such that $\iota(\ell_i) \in L_{\{=\}}$ and $\iota(\ell_i)$ must be satisfied by $\delta(\ell_i)$ whenever ℓ_i is reached;
- $\ell_0 \in \mathcal{L}$ is the *initial location*;
- ϱ is the *transition relation* such that for all $(\ell_i, \ell_j, \langle \gamma, \alpha, \rho \rangle) \in \varrho$,
  - $\ell_i, \ell_j \in \mathcal{L}$ are the source and destination locations of the transition, respectively
  - $\langle \gamma, \alpha, \rho \rangle$ is the label on the transition consisting of:
    * $\gamma \in L_{\{=\}}$, the *enabling condition*: an assertion over $\delta(\ell_i)$ which specifies the condition under which the transition may be taken
    * $\alpha \in Act$, the *action* associated with the transition, such that $bv(\alpha) \cap \delta(\ell_i) = \emptyset$
    * ρ, the *update relation*: a set of simultaneous assignments defining the values assumed by the variables $\delta(\ell_j)$ of the destination location in terms of values of variables $\delta(\ell_i)$ in the source location;
- $\mathcal{F} \subseteq \mathcal{L}$ is the set of *final locations*. $\qquad\qquad\square$

Example 2 The 2-place FIFO buffer shown in Figure 1 is formally represented as the EFA $\mathcal{S} = \langle \mathcal{L}, \delta, \iota, \ell_0, \varrho, \mathcal{F} \rangle$ where $\mathcal{L} = \{s_0, s_1, s_2\}$, the variable map $\delta(s_0) = \emptyset$, $\delta(s_1) = \{x\}$ and $\delta(s_2) = \{x, y\}$; the invariants $\iota(s_0) = \iota(s_1) = \iota(s_2) = true$, the initial location $\ell_0 = s_0$, the transition relation is defined as $\varrho = \{(s_0, s_1, \langle true, in?x, \{\} \rangle), (s_1, s_0, \langle true, out!x, \{\} \rangle), (s_1, s_2, \langle true, in?y, \{x := x\} \rangle), (s_2, s_1, \langle true, out!x, \{x := y\} \rangle)\}$, and the set of final locations $\mathcal{F} = \emptyset$. $\qquad\blacksquare$

Behaviors of an EFA: Note that an EFA is analogous to a program: control locations correspond to program counter values (program points) and the local variables correspond to the data variables live at each program point. We call $q = \langle \ell, \theta \rangle$ a *concrete state* of an automaton if ℓ is a location and θ is a ground substitution of variables in $\delta(\ell)$ defined over a data domain D. We can define behaviors of an EFA with respect to specific valuations of its variables, as follows.

Definition 3 [Concrete run of an EFA] A *concrete run* ω_D of $\mathcal{A}$ is a (possibly infinite) sequence of alternating concrete states and actions $\langle \ell_0, \theta_0 \rangle \, \alpha_0 \, \langle \ell_1, \theta_1 \rangle \, \alpha_1 \ldots$ such that:

- ℓ_0 is the initial location of $\mathcal{A}$ and θ_0 is a ground substitution of variables in $\delta(\ell_0)$ to D such that $\theta_0 \models \iota(\ell_0)$
- for all i $(\ell_i, \ell_{i+1}, \langle \gamma, \alpha, \rho \rangle) \in \varrho$ such that:
  - *Transition is enabled:* $\theta_i \models \gamma$
  - *Input Value is bound:* θ'_i is a ground extension of θ_i to $vars(\alpha)$ such that $\alpha_i = \alpha[\theta'_i]$
  - *Data is transferred from source to destination:* $(\theta_i, \theta''_i) \in [\![\rho]\!]$
  - *Input value is transferred:* $\theta'_{i+1} = \theta''_i \circ \sigma$ where σ is such that $\theta'_i = \theta_i \circ \sigma$, and
  - *Destination invariant holds:* $\theta_{i+1} \models \iota(\ell_{i+1})$. $\qquad\qquad\square$

```
reach(A, Ls,Ss, Ld,Sd) :-          gtrans(A, Ls,Ss, Act, Ld,Sd) :-
  gtrans(A, Ls,Ss, Act, Ld,Sd).      inv(A, Ls,Ss),
reach(A, Ls,Ss, Ld,Sd) :-            trans(A, Ls,Ss, Act, Ld,Sd),
  gtrans(A, Ls,Ss, Act, Lm,Sm),      ground(Act),
  reach(A, Lm,Sm, Ld,Sd).            inv(A, Ld,Sd).
```

Fig. 3. Relation describing the reachability of concrete states in an EFA.

EFA as a Logic Program: An EFA can be readily represented as a set of Prolog rules. The following relations specify an EFA A:

- init(A, L): a relation with a single tuple, specifying the initial location L.
- inv(A, L,V): a relation specifying the invariants at each location.
- trans(A, Ls,Vs, Act, Ld,Vd): a relation defining transitions from source location Ls, with the list Vs representing Ls's variables, to destination location Ld, with variables Vd. Act denotes the action taken by the automaton. The body of each rule corresponds to transition's enabling condition γ (i.e. facts imply $\gamma = true$). Finally, the update relation is specified either by unifying corresponding variables in Vs and Vd or using additional predicates in the body of the rule.
- final(A, L): a relation specifying the final locations.

Example 3 The EFA $\mathcal{S} = \langle \mathcal{L}, \delta, \iota, \ell_0, \varrho, \mathcal{F} \rangle$ from Example 2 can be represented as the following logic program:

```
init(S, s₀).                    trans(S, s₀,[], in(X), s₁,[X]).
                                trans(S, s₁,[X], out(X), s₀,[]).
inv(S, s₀,[]).                  trans(S, s₁,[X], in(Y), s₂,[X,Y]).
inv(S, s₁,[X]).                 trans(S, s₂,[X,Y], out(X), s₁,[Y]).
inv(S, s₂,[X,Y]).                                                    ∎
```

The reachability of a concrete state of an EFA can be computed using the transitive closure relation **reach** over the transitions of A shown in Figure 3. In the figure, the relation **gtrans** nondeterministically selects an applicable transition and binds any variables in its action (i.e. if Act is an input action, binds the input variable to some value in the data domain), and ensures that the invariants at the source and destination states hold. The relation **reach** admits a state (Ld,Sd) reachable from (Ls,Ss) whenever there exists a transition from (Ls,Ss) to (Ld,Sd) (the first clause), or if (Ls,Ss) has a transition to some state (Lm,Sm), from which (Ld,Sd) can be reached (the second clause). The set of all concrete states of an automaton A that are reachable from a given concrete state $\langle \ell, \theta \rangle$ can be computed as answers to the query **reach**(A, $\ell, \delta(\ell)\theta$, Ld,Sd) over the concrete reachability program. It can be easily shown that evaluating the above query using resolution is step-wise equivalent to computing concrete runs using Definition 3.

A run that reaches a concrete state can be easily computed based on the resolution steps needed to establish the reachability of the state using the above program (e.g. using the notion of *justification* of a logic programming proof [25]).

Abstracting the Behaviors of an EFA: To ensure that behaviors of an EFA can be analyzed even when it has an infinite number of concrete states, we use an alternative representation of the behaviors. For this, we introduce the notion of an abstract state: a pair $\langle \ell, \varphi \rangle$ where ℓ is a control location and $\varphi \in L_{\{=\}}$ is an assertion (representing constraints on the valuations of the local variables at ℓ) such that $fv(\varphi) \subseteq \delta(\ell)$.

Definition 4 [Abstract run of an EFA] An *abstract run* ω of $\mathcal{A}$ is a (possibly infinite) sequence of alternating abstract states and actions $\langle \ell_0, \varphi_0 \rangle \, \alpha_0 \, \langle \ell_1, \varphi_1 \rangle \, \alpha_1 \dots$ such that:

- ℓ_0 is the initial location of $\mathcal{A}$ and $\varphi_0 = \iota(\ell_0)$.
- for all i $(\ell_i, \ell_{i+1}, \langle \gamma, \alpha, \rho \rangle) \in \varrho$ such that:
  - *Transition is enabled:* $\varphi_i \wedge \gamma$ is satisfiable
  - *Constraint is transferred to destination:* $\varphi_i' = \varXi_\rho(\varphi_i)$ and $\varphi_{i+1} = (\exists V \varphi_i') \wedge \iota(\ell_{i+1})$ where $V = vars(\varphi_i') - \delta(\ell_{i+1})$ □

An abstract state $q = \langle \ell, \varphi \rangle$ of an EFA corresponds to a (possibly infinite) set S of concrete states over value domain D such that $\forall \langle \ell, \theta \rangle \in S.\theta \models \varphi$; in other words, φ cannot distinguish between the valuations of the concrete states in S. We say that each element $\langle \ell, \theta \rangle$ of S is a *concretization* of q, and q is an *abstraction* of S.

Given the relationship between abstract and concrete states, we can construct an abstract run from a concrete run and vice versa. The close correspondence between abstract and concrete states is formalized by the following theorem:

Theorem 4 *A concrete state $\langle \ell_n, \theta_n \rangle$ is reachable in a concrete run ω_D of an extended finite automaton, iff there exists an abstract state $\langle \ell_n, \varphi_n \rangle$ which is reachable in an abstract run ω such that $\theta_n \models_D \varphi_n$.*

Finiteness: Two abstract states $\langle \ell, \varphi \rangle$, $\langle \ell', \varphi' \rangle$ are equivalent iff $\ell = \ell'$ and φ and φ' are equivalent. Since all assertions at location ℓ can be written in quantifier-free standard form with free variables from $\delta(\ell)$, from Proposition 3 we know that there are only finite number of abstract states involving ℓ. This immediately leads to the following result:

Proposition 5 *Reachability of any abstract state of an EFA is decidable.*

From Theorem 4 and Proposition 5 we have:

Corollary 6 *Reachability of a concrete state of an EFA is decidable.*

Data Domain Size: Note that the finiteness results above used quantifier-free standard forms for assertions, and hence are valid when we interpret EFAs over infinite data domains. These results also carry over to finite domains that are "large enough". A domain size above which the results always hold can be estimated as follows. Consider all the quantifier elimination steps applied while

```
reach(A, Ls,Ss, Ld,Sd) :-           atrans(A, Ls,Ss, Act, Ld,Sd) :-
    atrans(A, Ls,Ss, Act, Ld,Sd).       inv(A, Ls,Ss),
reach(A, Ls,Ss, Ld,Sd) :-               trans(A, Ls,Ss, Act, Ld,Sd),
    atrans(A, Ls,Ss, Act, Lm,Sm),       inv(A, Ld,Sd).
    reach(A, Lm,Sm, Ld,Sd).
```

Fig. 4. Abstract reachability relation for EFAs.

computing an abstract run. At each step, say to eliminate the quantifier in $\exists V \varphi$, let φ be in standard form, and let N_D be the number of variables of V in disequality constraints. Then the quantifier-free form is equivalent to the original assertion for all domains of size N_D or greater. Thus the above correctness results hold for domains of size N or greater, where N is the largest N_D among all quantifier elimination steps used in computing the run.

Query Evaluation for Abstract State Reachability: Reachability of abstract states can be computed using the reachability relation shown in Figure 4. The relation **atrans** in the figure selects an applicable transition and ensures that the invariants at source and destination states hold. However, in order to ensure that query evaluation using resolution w.r.t. the abstract reachability program is equivalent to computing abstract runs using Definition 4, we need to first augment the evaluation mechanism with constraint solving. Traditional logic programming systems resolve queries by keeping track of substitutions. When a subgoal such as $x \neq y$ is encountered, these mechanisms will fail if x and y are not already bound to specific values in the data domain. Constraint Logic Programming (CLP)[11] provides a very expressive framework to resolve such queries by generalizing substitutions to assertions in a constraint language. We can check for reachability of abstract states by resolving queries w.r.t. the reachability program in a CLP system that handles constraints over $L_{\{=\}}$. Tabled resolution [26] can be used to ensure the termination of query evaluation. We built such a query evaluation system as a tabled constraint meta-interpreter that handles constraints over $L_{\{=\}}$.

Verification Using EFAs

For EFAs that model systems to be verified, we are typically interested in all-possible runs. Hence all locations in an EFA representing system models will be final locations. Such automata can be seen as equivalent to Symbolic Transition Systems (STS [3]) and generalizations of Symbolic Transition Graphs (STGs [9]) and STGs with Assignments (STGAs [14]).

Property Specification Using EFAs: Liveness properties and negations of safety properties can be simply encoded as EFAs.

Example 4 Consider the "ordered message delivery" property which states that for any two messages x, y such that x is read before y, x will be written out before

```
init((A₁,A₂), (L₁,L₂)) :-            trans((A₁,A₂), (Ls₁,Ls₂),Vs, Act, (Ld₁,Ld₂),Vd) :-
   init(A₁, L₁), init(A₂, L₂).          trans(A₁, Ls₁,Vs₁, Act, Ld₁,Vd₁),
                                         trans(A₂, Ls₂,Vs₂, Act, Ld₂,Vd₂),
                                         append(Vs₁,Vs₂,Vs), append(Vd₁,Vd₂,Vd).
inv((A₁,A₂), (L₁,L₂), V) :-
   inv(A₁, L₁,V₁), inv(A₂, L₂,V₂),    final((A₁,A₂), (L₁,L₂)) :-
   append(V₁,V₂,V).                      final(A₁, L₁), final(A₂, L₂).
```

Fig. 5. Relations describing the product of two EFAs.

y. Note that this is a safety property and hence has to hold throughout a run. The negation of this property, called "out-of-order delivery" is expressed by the nondeterministic EFA in Figure 2. Note that "out-of-order delivery" is a liveness property that is satisfied on a run if it is satisfied at some point in the run (a live-guarantee property according to [17]). Properties of this kind can be simply verified by checking for reachability of final states.   ∎

When an EFA is interpreted as an automaton over finite words, a (concrete/abstract) run of an EFA is said to be accepting if it is finite and ends in a final state. Using this interpretation, we can verify safety and liveness properties of EFA models. We can easily expand this framework to verify linear-time properties with data values, by using the Büchi acceptance condition: a run is accepting only if it is infinite and visits a final state infinitely often. We call EFAs with Büchi acceptance condition as constraint Büchi automata (CBA). Language detection in case of a CBA proceeds as for non-value-passing Büchi automata, i.e. by first constructing a corresponding state graph, and then checking it for strongly connected components containing final (accepting) states that are reachable from the initial state.

The definition of CBA is apparently similar to Pnueli's Büchi Automaton with Data (BAD) [20], differing mainly by treating data variables as local to a control location. Moreover, a CBA allows finite number of data variables to be introduced (new or temporary locals) into states during system execution. Data variables in a CBA have the following properties:

- they may be generated in the states or introduced by the transitions: for any $\ell_i, \ell_j \in \mathcal{L}$ such that $(\ell_i, \ell_j, \langle \gamma, \alpha, \rho \rangle) \in \varrho$, $\delta(\ell_j) \subseteq \delta(\ell_i) \cup vars(\alpha)$;
- whenever a variable x is introduced to ℓ, it overwrites the value of x previously assigned to ℓ; another way to say this is that the interpretation of x is different upon every visit to a location containing x (this in particular applies to self loops);
- initial location ℓ^0 may contain a non-empty, finite set of variables.

Product Construction: Automata-based model checkers pose the verification problem in terms of checking whether the intersection of two automata's languages is empty. Critical to this formulation is the construction of a product automaton $\mathcal{A} = (\mathcal{A}_1 \times \mathcal{A}_2)$ whose language corresponds to the intersection of the languages of $\mathcal{A}_1$ and $\mathcal{A}_2$. We can construct the product of two EFAs such that the result is also an EFA. In fact, given two EFAs A_1 and A_2 represented as logic programs, the product EFA (A_1, A_2) can be computed using a logic program given in Figure 5. Each location in the product automaton is defined as a pair (L_1, L_2) consisting of the locations of the component automata. The non-trivial part of the encoding is the handling of action labels: the label on a transition in the product automaton is obtained by unifying the action labels the two component automata. This ensures that every transition in the product represents matching transitions in the two components, and the source and destination locations of the product transitions result from combining respective locations of the components. Moreover, the variable sets of component automata are merged (with action variables being unified) into corresponding sets of variables of the product. It is easy to show that two automata A_1 and A_2 have a common run if and only if their product has a run.

Example 5 Consider instance of the FIFO buffer from Figure 1 with all locations considered final, and the "out-of-order delivery" property from Figure 2. From the rules in Figure 5, it is easy to see that the following sequence is a run of a product of these two EFAs.

$$\langle (s_0, t_0), tt \rangle \ in(X) \ \langle (s_1, t_1), tt \rangle \ in(Y) \ \langle (s_2, t_2), tt \rangle$$

Note that the above run does not reach any final location of the product EFA $((s_0, t_3), (s_1, t_3)$ or $(s_2, t_3))$, nor it can be extended to do so. In fact, the automaton has no successful runs, which means that the FIFO buffer never satisfies the error condition. ∎

4   Example: Verifying a Write-Back Cache

Below we describe an EFA model of a memory system with a write-back cache. We use this model to verify that a memory read at an arbitrary but specific address retrieves the value previously written to that address. The model captures the behavior of a memory system with potentially infinite memory addresses and an infinite domain of data values. We first build a model for a system with a single-line cache: exactly one address-value pair is stored in the cache. We generalize this model to cache with an arbitrary size in Section 5.

The data state of a single-line cache is denoted as a triple (CA, CV, CD) representing the address CA in the cache, a current data value CV at that address, and a "dirty bit" CD that is 1 if the value in the cache has been modified (and hence possibly different from the value in the main memory) and 0 otherwise. The cache services read and write requests received from the processor.

Upon a request $write?(A, V)$ to write value V to address A, if A is in the cache (i.e. $A = CA$), then the value in the cache is replaced with V (i.e. $CV :=V$) and CD is set to 1. Otherwise, the current cache entry is flushed to memory if CD is 1, and the data state of the cache is set to $(A, V, 1)$. Read requests are processed similarly (flushing the current cache contents to memory on a cache miss); details are omitted.

```
% receive request to write value V to address A
trans(cm, c₀,[CA,CV,CD, MA,MV], write?(A,V), c₁,[CA,CV,CD, MA,MV, A,V]).

% A is in cache: update cache value to V and set dirty bit to 1
trans(cm, c₁,[CA,CV,CD, MA,MV, A,V], tau, c₀,[CA,V,1, MA,MV]) :-
   A = CA.

% A is not in cache, but either cache value has not been modified,
% or cache address is different from that in the memory:
% replace cache contents with the tuple (A,V,1)
trans(cm, c₁,[CA,CV,CD, MA,MV, A,V], tau, c₀,[A,V,1, MA,MV]) :-
   A ≠ CA, (CD ≠ 1; CA ≠ MA).

% A is not in cache, cache value has been modified,
% and cache address is the same as the address in the memory:
% update value in the memory to current cache value
trans(cm, c₁,[CA,CV,CD, MA,MV, A,V], tau, c₂,[CA,CV,CD, MA,CV, A,V]) :-
   A ≠ CA, CD = 1, CA = MA.

% write new tuple, with dirty bit set to 1, to the cache
trans(cm, c₂,[CA,CV,CD, MA,MV, A,V], tau, c₀,[A,V,1, MA,MV]).
```

Fig. 6. Transition rules for handling writes in the cache-memory system.

Note that we are interested in verifying whether a read to a specific memory address returns the previously written value. This enables us to model a memory of arbitrary capacity by a single memory cell with a distinguished address. The data state of the memory is represented by a tuple (MA,MV). The memory responds to read and write requests from the cache. A write to (A,V) changes the data state to (MA,V) if $A = MA$, and leaves the data state unchanged otherwise. A read request to address A returns MV if $A = MA$; otherwise the read returns an arbitrary value.

The cache-memory system can be readily modeled as an EFA; Figure 6 shows the a fragment of a logic program that represents the transition relation of the EFA model (more specifically, the portion of the relation that pertains to write requests). Note that all locations in the EFA for the system model are final locations.

The correctness condition for the cache-memory system is that after a read from an arbitrary address A will return V where V is most recent value written to address A. We represent the negation of this safety property by the EFA in Figure 7.

To verify whether the cache-memory system observes the correctness condition, we check whether a final location in the product of the system EFA and the property EFA is reachable. This check is done using the query

```
reach( (cm,p), (c₀,t₀),[CA,CV,CD, MA,MV, PA], (_,t₃),_), MA=PA.
```

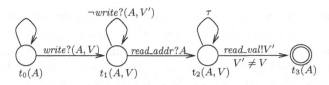

Fig. 7. EFA for the correctness condition of cache-memory system.

over a program consisting of the abstract reachability relation (Figure 4), the product construction relations (Figure 5) and the relations representing the system and property EFAs. In the query, PA is the address of interest to the property. Note that the unification MA=PA in the query ensures that the address of interest to the property is same as the address maintained by the memory. From the results of Section 3, we know that the above query evaluation will terminate and hence we can verify the given correctness property of the cache-memory model.

Comparison with Other Work: It should be noted that the verification of the cache-memory system as described above is not possible with any of the methods of [27,12,10,13,15]. Specifically, the definition of data independence in [27,12] does not admit any comparisons between data objects, so neither of them can handle a problem that requires equality tests.

The cache can be modeled in the scalarset-based approach of [10] as an array storing data values and indexed by the memory addresses. However, since they are used as array indices, the domain of memory addresses themselves cannot be reduced to a small, finite set of elements required for automatic verification.

The method of [13] is applicable to the problem only after a series of manual transformations of its specification that reduce memory addresses and data values to range over finite domains.

Finally, the system as specified above cannot be directly encoded as a symbolic transition graph with assignments [15], as STGAs require all variables in output transitions from a state to be present in the source state; note that the behavior of a memory cell upon receiving a read request needs the ability to output arbitrary values.

5   EFAs: Beyond Equalities

EFAs have been defined only using the constraint language $L_{\{=\}}$. This choice turns out to be crucial in being able to accurately verify systems and properties specified as EFAs. However, this choice also restricts the class of systems that can be modeled using DFAs. Below we describe the consequences of augmenting EFAs with richer constraint languages such as $L_{\{=,\in\}}$.

Computational Aspects of Using Assertions over $L_{\{=,\in\}}$: The ability to finitely represent the potentially infinite set of assertions using quantifier-free standard forms in $L_{\{=\}}$ is a key factor that makes the verification problem of

EFAs decidable. Assertions over $L_{\{=,\in\}}$, in contrast, do not have equivalent quantifier-free representations in general. For example, consider the assertion $\varphi = \exists x.\ x \neq y \wedge x \in z \wedge y \in z$ which states that $y \in z$ and there is another element distinct from y that is also in z. This assertion cannot be expressed using only variables y and z without bound variables. The assertion $y \in z$ is an approximation of φ but fails to capture the fact that z has at least two elements.

This example illustrates that one can maintain counts (as number of elements in a set) in $L_{\{=,\in\}}$ and hence there is no finite representation of assertions in $L_{\{=,\in\}}$. For instance, consider the assignment $z := z \cup \{x\}$ evaluated under the constraint $x \notin z$. This assignment increases the cardinality of the set represented by z and hence simulates counting.

A classic approach to deal with problems due to counts is to approximate the counts: for instance, a widely-used approach is to maintain counts using the finite domain $\{0, 1, many\}$. This abstraction corresponds to representing assertions in $L_{\{=,\in\}}$ using at most one bound variable. We call assertions with a fixed ceiling on the number of bound variables as assertions in limited quantifier form. We can represent every $\varphi \in L_{\{=,\in\}}$ by an assertion $\varphi^\flat$ in limited quantifier form such that $\varphi \implies \varphi^\flat$ (i.e. by "relaxing" the meaning of the assertion). The direction of the approximation ensures that for every concrete run in an EFA there is an abstract run, but the converse may not hold. Consequently, identifying an accepting abstract run during verification simply means that the property "may" hold; conversely, failure to find an an accepting abstract run means that the property "definitely" does not hold.

Extended Data Types: As the primitive constraints of $L_{\{=\}}$ involve only variables and constants, all data elements we have been considering so far are taken from $\mathcal{V} \cup \mathcal{C}$. When modeling systems with membership constraints and sets, it is useful to consider non-recursive compound terms (e.g. tuples) to represent data records. This improves the expressiveness without unduly complicating its formal framework. Therefore, in the following, we assume that constraints in $L_{\{=,\in\}}$ are built over variables, constants, and shallow, non-recursive compound terms. Such structures are used in both examples presented below.

Application: Mutli-line Cache: We augment the EFA model of cache-memory system (Section 4) to handle cache with an arbitrary number of cache lines. The contents of the cache are now represented as a set Cs of tuples (CA, CV, CD) each corresponding to one cache line, where CA, CV and CD are address, value and dirty bit of that cache line. There are several modifications necessary for the transition rules to accommodate the extended specification. Checking for a presence of a tuple in the cache will now use membership constraints rather than equality. Upon cache miss, the line to be flushed to memory is chosen from the set nondeterministically (again using membership constraints). Finally, updating value in the cache upon a write hit requires first locating the appropriate cache line (using a membership constraint), and then updating its data value and dirty bit (using set difference and union operations, and equality constraints).

6   Example: Detecting Vulnerabilities in Computer Systems

A computer system consists of concurrent, interacting processes and services and users. Unexpected interactions between these entities often lead to subtle vulnerabilities that can be exploited to compromise system security. For example, comsat is a mail notification program, which prints the initial lines of incoming mails on a user's terminal. It obtains the user's terminal information from a system file /etc/utmp (containing terminal information stored as records). Misconfiguration of this file may permit any system user to obtain root privileges as follows. If records in /etc/utmp can be changed by a user, then an attacker can replace their terminal in the file with '/etc/passwd'. The attacker can then send mail to self, thereby overwriting the password file. By choosing the mail message appropriately, the user can obtain root privileges.

In [22] we presented a model of this system in a value-passing process algebra with four processes: a user, the mailer service, comsat, and the file system fs. The first three processes interact via the file system. The model of the file system, thus, is central and most interesting. There are several distinct infinite-domain data types involved in this model: names of files and users, contents of files, etc. Some of the components of the system, such as the mailer and comsat are data-independent (in the type of message contents) in the sense of [27]. Similarly, the file system's control behavior is independent of the contents of the files. Below we describe an EFA model of the file system using assertions from $L_{\{=,\in\}}$.

Figure 8 shows a logic program encoding the transition relation of an EFA model of the file system. In the model, the variable FS holds the current state of the file system — the files and their contents. Its value is represented as a set of triples $(FN, FPerm, FCont)$, each triple expressing the state of a particular file with name FN, permissions $FPerm$, and contents $FCont$. File's permissions, in turn, are given by a set of pairs (U, P), denoting that user U has permission P ($P \in \{w, r\}$). The contents of a file are defined as a set of data records.

The program in Figure 8 uses several predicates representing the following assertions:

– exists(FS, N) checks for existence of file named N in the file system FS:

$$\exists P, C . (N, P, C) \in FS$$

– access(FS, U, N, T) verifies that user U has access of type T to file named N in the file system:

$$\exists P, C . (N, P, C) \in FS \land (U, T) \in P$$

– r_rec(FS, U, N, R) extracts record R from file named N in the file system:

$$\exists P, C . (N, P, C) \in FS \land (U, r) \in P \land R \in C$$

```
trans(fs, s0,[FS], read?(U,N), s1,[FS,U,N]).
trans(fs, s1,[FS,U,N], tau, s0,[FS]) :-
   not(exists(FS,N), access(FS,U,N,r)).
trans(fs, s1,[FS,U,N], tau, s2,[FS,U,R]) :-
   exists(FS,N), access(FS,U,N,r), r_rec(FS,U,N,R).
trans(fs, s2,[FS,U,R], read_return!(U,R), s0,[FS]).

trans(fs, s0,[FS], write?(U,N,D), s3,[FS,U,N,D]).
trans(fs, s3,[FS,U,N,D], tau, s0,[FS]) :-
   not(access(FS,U,N,w)).
trans(fs, s3,[FS,U,N,D], tau, s0,[FS']) :-
   access(FS,U,N,w), add_rec(FS,U,N,D,FS').
```

Fig. 8. Transition relation for an EFA model of a file system.

- add_rec(FS, U, N, D, FS') adds record D to file named N in the file system FS, giving the modified file system in FS':

$$\exists P, C, C'. (N,P,C) \in FS \wedge (U,w) \in P \wedge C' = C \cup \{D\}$$
$$\wedge \; FS' = FS - \{(N,P,C)\} \cup \{(N,P,C')\}$$

One of the simplest safety properties expected to hold in a model of a computer system is that there are no unauthorized writes to /etc/passwd. We begin by checking a straightforward reachability property: whether there are any writes to /etc/passwd in the above EFA model. The analysis shows that writes to /etc/passwd are indeed possible, but many of the runs that are witnesses to this property show "normal" behavior that does not reveal the vulnerability. For instance, one of the runs corresponds to root issuing an explicit write to /etc/passwd. Hence we refine the property to rule out expected runs (called the "intentions model" [22]). We then observe writes to /etc/passwd using a sequence of operations — overwriting /etc/utmp and then sending mail — that exploit the vulnerability described earlier.

Note that the EFA model uses assertions over $L_{\{=, \in\}}$ and hence abstract runs may not have corresponding concrete runs. Thus a detected vulnerability may not, in general, actually exist in the model. However, given an abstract run, we can estimate whether or not the abstract states represent approximations; for instance, loss of accuracy in manipulating assertions in $L_{\{=, \in\}}$ occurs when we eliminate bound variables to derive assertions in limited quantifier form. We can therefore modify the order in which transitions are taken during reachability analysis, preferring transitions that involve no loss of information. Abstract runs composed solely of transitions whose effects are computed losslessly always have corresponding concrete runs. Using this heuristic, we can isolate vulnerabilities that exist in the model despite using an expressive constraint language. With the presence of an approximation our verification is conservative, i.e. if no vulnerability is reported for the abstraction, there cannot be one in the original system, but if a vulnerability in the abstracted system is found, the result for the original system is unknown. This heuristic is not limited to reachability analysis alone and can be readily extended to good cycle detection in CBA.

7   Related Work and Discussion

In this paper we presented an automata-based approach to the analysis of behavior of infinite-state systems. We used EFAs as a unified model for infinite-state systems and their properties. Our technique can be used to automatically verify properties of data-independent systems, and can be extended to analyze more general infinite-state systems as well.

Considerable research has been done on generating a finite-state, property-preserving abstraction of data-independent systems. The method of [27] relies on the user to identify a data-independent program and manually transform its specification. A similar method was suggested in [1] to verify the alternating bit protocol. An automatic abstraction is proposed in [12] where a special countable set of values, called *schematic names* are used to bind data variables. However, this method is applicable only to programs that do not have tests on the values of data variables. A similar set of "symbolic values" is used in [15] which gives an algorithm for model checking data-independent value-passing processes. Because of working on process variables rather than inventing an extra set of values, we can claim our approach more directly implementable than the one presented in this work. Data independence is considered as a form of symmetry in [10] where a method is given to reduce the size of the data domain. The reduction is automatic once the user identifies a data-independent program and specifically annotates data-independent types ("data scalarsets"). Moreover, the approach works only for safety properties.

In [13], algorithms for refinement checking among data-independent systems are developed. They are based on the notion of *threshold collections*: finite collections of data types such that if the refinement holds for each of these types substituted for the data domain of the processes, it holds for an arbitrary data domain. The threshold collections must be identified manually before applying the appropriate refinement algorithms. Finally, an automatic method to abstract a large class of systems including data-independent systems is developed in [18]. That method is analogous to predicate abstraction [8] and constructs a finite-state system by introducing Boolean variables for every predicate in the original system. It is shown that for data-independent systems the method will terminate, producing a finite Boolean program which simulates the original system (with respect to control behaviors).

Our technique is most closely related to the abstraction method of [18]: the constraints in our case correspond to the Boolean variables introduced by [18]. However, note that [18] abstracts only the system and preserves only control flow properties. Thus, given an arbitrary property φ of a data-independent system S, one must first construct a product system S' and pose the verification of φ in S in terms of an appropriate control flow property of S'. In contrast, our technique constructs the product space, performs the necessary abstraction, and verifies the appropriate property on the product system, all in one phase. Such "on demand" abstraction is especially advantageous when the properties can be proved without constructing the entire abstract state space of the system.

There have been several works on constraint-based model checking and the use of constraint (logic) programming for verification of infinite-state systems (e.g. [5,4,6]). We have developed verification techniques for infinite-state systems based on tabled resolution and constraint processing: for timed systems [7,19], systems with mobility [28], and for symbolic bisimulation of systems [3]; each of those techniques can be seen as a conservative extension to our finite state model checker, XMC [23]. This paper presents a model checker for data-independent systems using a similar approach, but uses an LTL-based logic to specify properties. We are currently investigating easy-to-implement tableau-based techniques to verify a general class of value passing systems (to model mobility as well as data independence). Our current work also includes modeling other security-related problems to further the application and development of infinite-state verification techniques.

References

1. S. Aggarwal, R.P. Kurshan, and K. Sabnani. A calculus for protocol specification and validation. *Protocol Specification, Testing and Verification, III*, 1983.
2. S. Basu, K. Narayan Kumar, L.R. Pokorny, and C.R. Ramakrishnan. Resource-constrained model checking of recursive programs. In *TACAS*, 2002.
3. S. Basu, M. Mukund, C.R. Ramakrishnan, I.V. Ramakrishnan, and R.M. Verma. Local and symbolic bisimulation using tabled constraint logic programming. In *ICLP*, 2001.
4. T. Bultan, R. Gerber, and W. Pugh. Symbolic model checking of infinite state systems using presburger arithmetic. In *CAV*, 1997.
5. W. Chan, R.J. Anderson, P. Beame, and D. Notkin. Combining constraint solving and symbolic model checking for a class of systems with non-linear constraints. In *CAV*, 1997.
6. G. Delzanno and A. Podelski. Model checking in CLP. In *TACAS*, 1999.
7. X. Du, C. R. Ramakrishnan, and S. A. Smolka. Tabled resolution + constraints: A recipe for model checking real-time systems. In *RTTS*, 2000.
8. S. Graf and H. Saidi. Construction of abstract state graphs with PVS. In *CAV*, 1997.
9. M. Hennessy and H. Lin. Symbolic bisimulations. *Theoretical Computer Science*, 138:353–389, 1995.
10. C. Norris Ip and D. L. Dill. Better verification through symmetry. *FMSD*, 1996.
11. J. Jaffar and J.-L. Lassez. Constraint logic programming. In *POPL*, 1987.
12. B. Jonsson and J. Parrow. Deciding bisimulation equivalences for a class of non-finite-state programs. *Information and Computation*, 107(2), December 1993.
13. R. S. Lazić. *A Semantic Study of Data Independence with Applications to Model Checking*. PhD thesis, Oxford University, 1999.
14. H. Lin. Symbolic transition graphs with assignments. In *CONCUR*, 1996.
15. H. Lin. Model checking value-passing processes. In *APSEC*, 2001.
16. J. W. Lloyd. *Foundations of Logic Programming*. Springer, 1984.
17. Z. Manna and A. Pnueli. *The Temporal Logic of Reactive and Concurrent Systems*. Springer, 1992.

18. K.S. Namjoshi and R.P. Kurshan. Syntactic program transformations for automatic abstractions. In *CAV*, 2000.
19. G. Pemmasani, C. R. Ramakrishnan, and I. V. Ramakrishnan. Efficient model checking of real time systems using tabled logic programming and constraints. In *ICLP*, 2002.
20. A. Pnueli, Y. Kesten, and M. Vardi. Yes, Matilda! Abstraction can Replace Deduction, even for Computational Models which are BAD (Buchi Automata with Data). In *VHS Meeting*, Grenoble, 1999.
21. L. Robert Pokorny and C. R. Ramakrishnan. Model checking linear temporal logic using tabled logic programming. In *TAPD*, 2000.
22. C. R. Ramakrishnan and R. Sekar. Model-based analysis of configuration vulnerabilities. *Journal of Computer Security (JCS)*, 10(1 / 2):189–209, 2002.
23. C.R. Ramakrishnan, I.V. Ramakrishnan, S.A. Smolka, et al. XMC: A logic-programming-based verification toolset. In *CAV*, 2000.
24. Y. Rodeh and O. Shtrichman. Finite instantiations in equivalence logic with uninterpreted functions. In *CAV*, Paris, 2001.
25. A. Roychoudhury, C. R. Ramakrishnan, and I. V. Ramakrishnan. Justifying proofs using memo tables. In *PPDP*, 2000.
26. H. Tamaki and T. Sato. OLDT resolution with tabulation. In *ICLP*, 1986.
27. P. Wolper. Expressing interesting properties of programs in propositional temporal logic. In *POPL*, 1986.
28. P. Yang, C. R. Ramakrishnan, and S. A. Smolka. A logical encoding of the pi-calculus: Model checking mobile processes using tabled resolution. In *VMCAI*, 2003.

A Formal Model for the Block Device Subsystem of the Linux Kernel

Peter T. Breuer

Universidad Carlos III de Madrid

Abstract. A formal model of the block-device subsystem of the Linux operating system kernel is set out here, as an introduction to the kernel for formal methods people and a preliminary to further formal methods work. The model is abstract, but executable, and it is faithful to the detail of the real Linux kernel code. The model is used here to analyse kernel behavior. It is proved of the model that the kernel block device system cannot deadlock.

1 Introduction

The several releases of the Linux 2.4 kernel source code in 2002-3 each contained about 3.5 million lines of C code. This article provides a formal model of a small but important part of that code – the block subsystem that driver writers deal with when they write for a device that does its read/write transfers in blocks, that is to say in groups of 1024 bytes or more at a time, instead of byte per byte. The aim of this article is to succinctly describe to a formal methods audience how that part of the kernel works, because while many theoreticians could write this article if they already knew how the kernel worked, they presently do not know. Moreover, the C code of the kernel is (intentionally) the only authoratative design document for it, and the intrinsic difficulty of interpreting the code cannot be overemphasized. The kernel code is complex beyond the capacity all but the very best C coders, who also have to be experts in many aspects of operating system design and implementation. Even those qualifications are not enough, because much hands-on experience in the Linux kernel itself is additionally required in order to understand the appropriate context for each (individually opaque) piece of kernel code.

The real experience of kernel code development is in practice possessed by a small elite, perhaps a few hundred strong. But only a core few, perhaps forty or fifty in number, possess a full picture of the current design for important parts of the kernel. The rest of us scrabble for an imperfect and belated understanding of the parts of the kernel that concern us at any moment. This article describes the content of the block device kernel subsystem code, at a level of abstraction that reveals the architectural design behind it, and at the same time is faithful to the real kernel code itself, down to the details of function names and the low-level separation of tasks into different functions.

Most new kernel code authors do firstly attempt to obtain some understanding of the *generic* kernel mechanisms that pertain to their task. Rubini's book [5],

J.S. Dong and J. Woodcock (Eds.): ICFEM 2003, LNCS 2885, pp. 599–619, 2003.
© Springer-Verlag Berlin Heidelberg 2003

in particular, has been helpful in providing insight as well as detail to many programmers. There are other well-known sources of information: for example, the block commenting at the head of functions in the kernel code has lately become much more extensive and regular in form, with argument and usage information being included for the first time. There are also several "hacker's guides" available on the web, but their contents have dated quickly, even though they have usually been written by the kernel code author directly responsible for a subsystem. The kernel is a moving target! But between the very few books published over the last decade, the ageing and sketchy guides, and the block commentary in the code itself, the sources of documentation about exhaust themselves.

As a primary source of information, new authors tend first to read other authors work, abstracting out general patterns of use. The simpler and more unsophisticated driver codes are the most helpful in this regard, because they are the most transparant. But even the simpler drivers leave open questions that cannot be settled by "peephole" examination of the code. Many kernel mechanisms arise through calls through function pointers held in one structure, and intialized to a default value in one place and reset in another. Such a design, while flexible in programming practice, inadvertently makes understanding difficult to obtain via examination of the code. The more sophisticated drivers, which use such techniques by design, thus appear very obscure to those who lack the basic information on what the intent of each piece of code is and when and how it will be used.

The value of the model described in this article lies principally in the understanding that it imparts. It reduces a complex design to a simple, regular abstraction. But the abstraction can then itself be used to attack some important questions about the kernel design. Is the kernel design fundamentally flawed, for example? Is it capable of "deadlock by design"? Is the kernel "real-time" in some sense? The model will be used to demonstrate in particular that the portion of the kernel considered is not capable of deadlock by design. Whether the conclusion is accurate for some version of the kernel code is not so important – the code at any moment expresses an underlying design but changes at a great rate in response to bug reports, pressures from efficiency concerns, and in response to desires for more maintainability or legibility or flexibility. Design is the only relative constant in the kernel.

The structure of this article is as follows: Section 2 describes how drivers and core kernel work together at a high level, without entering into implementational detail. It derives simple results on the behavior of the composite of driver and kernel given reasonable hypotheses on the behavior of the two components, including the key result that the composite system described is deadlock-free, and a guarrantee that user requests and system responses correspond, overall, albeit not in a 1-1 way. Section 3 describes the core kernel block-device system and also supplies the support required in Section 2. Section 4 provides examples produced by simulation of the model described. Section 5 generalises the simple model analysed to the case of multiple device drivers, and derives equivalent results to those achieved in Section 2. Section 6 shows that a simplified model of the virtual memory system may be added without incurring excessive complication illustrating the compositional nature of the model and the analysis that it is intended to support. With the virtual memory system in place, the kernel can now deadlock under certain conditions.

Notation

Type declarations are written $x :: \tau$, where τ is the type being declared for object x. We write $[\tau]$ for the type of (finite) lists of elements of type τ, and $\langle \tau \rangle$ for the type of infinite lists, or streams. Both kinds of lists may be written $(x : xs)$, where x is the head element, and xs is the remainder of the list. Written out element by element, a finite list is $[x_1, \ldots, x_n]$, and a stream is $\langle x_1, x_2, \ldots \rangle$. Lists (or streams) may be generated by expressions of the form $[b | x \leftarrow a]$, which means $[b[x_1/x], b[x_2/x], \ldots]$ where $a = [x_1, x_2, \ldots]$ is an enumeration of the list a.

Function types will be written $\tau_1 \to \tau_2$. Functional application is indicated by juxtaposition, thus: $f\ x$. Tuple types are written (τ_1, τ_2), (τ_1, τ_2, τ_3), etc., and their elements are written (x_1, x_2), (x_1, x_2, x_3), etc., respectively. Abstract types will be named with a leading capital and declared $Name ::= \ldots$. Their abstract structures will be written $Name(v_1, \ldots, v_n)$, where the name usually coincides with that of the type and the $v_1, \ldots, v_n$ are the field values.

The refinement relation on a domain is written $x \sqsubseteq y$, and the bottom element of the domain is $\perp$ such that $\perp \sqsubseteq x$, for any x.

2   Outline

A goal of the model in this article is to separate driver and core kernel concerns. On the one hand, a driver writer is usually not an expert in other parts of the kernel code and therefore wishes to treat the rest of the kernel as only a black box that does a well-defined job. The core kernel authors, on the other hand, also wish to treat driver codes as black boxes, because they really do know nothing particular about them! The driver may not yet have been written when the core kernel authors wrote their code. Thus the aim of separating driver concerns from core kernel concerns reflects a real-world schism in approaches, code, authors, attitudes, areas of competence, and knowledge about internal state.

The interaction between the core kernel and a driver will be pictured as involving two distinct and disjoint states: (i) the state of the kernel, incorporating counts of available kernel buffers, pending kernel requests, values for key behavior-determining parameters, and so on, and (ii) the state of the device that the driver is driving, which only the driver knows about. Type names Kernel and Device will be assigned to the two state spaces, without here going into detail about their internal structure:

$$Kernel ::= \ldots$$
$$Device ::= \ldots$$

602   Peter T. Breuer

The kernel behavior affects only a Kernel structure, while the driver behavior affects only a Device structure.

How does a device driver author see the kernel? The author of a block-device driver, at least, knows only that the kernel will from time to time call a driver method known as the *request function* for the device, and the driver code has to be written to expect that the request function will be called whenever the kernel has work for the device to do. At each call of this function, the kernel will have readied a linked list of *kernel requests* at a designated location. The request function must unlink the requests immediately, process them in an appropriate way, and return control to the kernel. Some time later the driver will signal to the kernel that it is finished with each request in turn by running a special *end request* function on it. Drivers with fast devices can run end request during the call from the kernel to the request function, thereby avoiding having to call back later.

The driver's request function is modelled here as taking as input a list of pending kernel requests, and returning as output a list of *driver responses* reflecting the results of processing those requests. Statuses reported in the responses will later be used in the end request processing, so, if end processing of a request is delayed, then the list of responses from the request function may well be shorter than the list of requests presented to it at that time. The remainder will be stored internally in the driver until they can be treated. The driver may deal with kernel requests in any order, but it is normal to deal with them in order of arrival. As it processes a request the driver may change the internal state of the device. Thus the request function semantics is that of a *side-effecting function* on the devices internal state, taking a list of pending kernel requests as its single input, and producing a list of driver responses as its single output. That type will be written as follows, where Req is the type of kernel requests, Res is the type of the driver responses, and Device is the type of the statespace of the device:

$$\text{request\_fn} :: [\text{Req}] \rightarrow S \text{ Device } [\text{Res}]$$

The S type notation here means a "side-effecting function with argument a list of requests, acting on the state Device and returning as result a list of status reports":

$$S \text{ Device } [\text{Res}] = \text{Device} \rightarrow (\text{Device}, [\text{Res}])$$

So the request function takes the device state as an extra "hidden" parameter, and returns the altered state as an extra hidden result.

The driver itself looks to the kernel like a continuous sequence of calls to the request function. Thus it has the action of a series of repeats of the request function side-effect. Each call transforms a list of kernel requests to a list of status reports, and the driver therefore transforms a *stream* (i.e., an infinite list) of lists of kernel requests to a stream of lists of status reports, changing the device state as it goes:

$$\text{driver} :: \langle[\text{Req}]\rangle \rightarrow S \text{ Device } \langle[\text{Res}]\rangle$$

The stream of inputs represents successive states of the kernel pending request queue at each successive call to the driver request function by the kernel. The following is the driver semantics: it receives as input a stream of lists of requests; designate the first list rqs and the future lists $rqss$, so the input stream is (rqs : $rqss$). It produces as output a stream of lists of responses; designate the first list res and the future lists $ress$, so the output stream is (res : $ress$). The driver passes the first list rqs of requests to its request function, which causes a change of state in the device from dev to dev', and receives back the first list res of responses. The driver emits this first list of responses res on its output stream, and then repeats forever, emitting the rest $ress$ of the output stream in the fullness of time, and "finishing up" with the device in state dev''. That is:

$$\text{driver } (rqs : rqss) \ dev = (dev'', res : ress) \tag{1}$$
$$(dev', res) = \text{request\_fn } rqs \ dev$$
$$(dev'', ress) = \text{driver } rqss \ dev'$$

Note that one element in the input stream gives rise to one element in the output stream, where "an element" is respectively a list of kernel requests and a list of driver responses. This is a causal property:

Proposition 1. *The generic block-device driver described in (1) is causal in its stream of inputs and outputs. That is, it needs no knowledge of the future inputs to produce the present output.*

The proof depends on Axiom 1 below on driver request function behavior:

Axiom 1 *The driver request function does not block – it always constructs a fully formed list of responses from a fully formed list of requests.*

A point on notation: the driver semantics (1) can be written much more neatly in terms of the request function using the "monadic" notation from Gofer [3] for composing the abstract side-effecting functions in a fully formally defined way, but giving the appearance of an ordinary imperative programming language construct:

$$\text{driver } :: \ \langle [\text{Req}] \rangle \rightarrow S \text{ Device } \langle [\text{Res}] \rangle$$
$$\text{driver } (rqs : rqss) = \textbf{do } \{$$
$$res \ \leftarrow \text{request\_fn } rqs;$$
$$ress \leftarrow \text{driver } rqss;$$
$$\textbf{result } (res : ress)$$
$$\}$$

or, in terms of process algebra:

$$\text{driver} = \text{rqs? request\_fn(rqs)! driver}$$

The formal semantics given for the notation in Figure 1 makes the driver code above equal in semantics to that expressed directly in equation (1).

What does a kernel look like to a driver? The kernel feeds it a request, and receives a report back from the driver. To the driver, the kernel's input-output

$$a :: S \; \tau \; \tau_x \; \& \; x :: \tau_x \Rightarrow b[x] :: S \; \tau \; \tau_y \Rightarrow \mathbf{do} \; \{ \; x \leftarrow a; \; b[x] \; \} :: S \; \tau \; \tau_y$$
$$x :: \tau_x \Rightarrow \mathbf{result} \; x :: S \; \tau \; \tau_x$$

$$[\mathbf{do} \; \{ \; x \leftarrow a; \; b[x] \; \}] = \lambda s.[b[x]] \; s' \; \mathbf{where} \; (s', x) = [a] \; s$$
$$[\mathbf{result} \; x] = \lambda s.(s, x)$$

Fig. 1. Notation – type laws, side-effecting semantics of the **do** and **result** syntax.

directionality looks exactly the reverse of its own. This might be impossible to represent as a function, but it is not. Enough information is included in the response that the driver sends to the kernel to be able to (re)construct from it what request the kernel must have sent the driver. So the relation response to request across the kernel is functional. Formalising it in the anti-causal direction simplifies the description of the composition of kernel and driver given below.

The kernel is also sensitive to a stream of external events: user read and write requests, timer clocks, and so on. These drive the kernel to produce the requests that the driver sees. The Linux kernel has to be given the following type:

$$\text{kernel} :: \langle \text{Event} \rangle \rightarrow \langle [\text{Res}] \rangle \rightarrow S \; \text{Kernel} \; \langle [\text{Req}] \rangle$$

and then driver and kernel functions can be placed in parallel, with the kernel feeding the driver with a stream of requests, and consuming the driver's stream of responses, and vice versa, the combined unit being driven by a stream of external events.

The *communicating parallelism* – each component's outputs connected to the other component's inputs – described above is set out formally in Figure 2. Note that we choose to expose the internal communication in the output from the combinator. Then we can define the complete operating system, linux, as the communicating parallel composition of kernel and driver, as follows:

$$\text{linux} :: \langle \text{Event} \rangle \rightarrow S \; (\text{Kernel}, \text{Device}) \; (\langle [\text{Req}] \rangle, \langle [\text{Res}] \rangle) \qquad (2)$$
$$\text{linux} \; evs = \text{kernel} \; evs \, \| \, \text{driver}$$

Note that the equation (2) always results in streams of well defined outputs provided that at least one of the two components is capable of generating "something from nothing" – an output without having to first look at its input. In the case of equation (2), the contributor is the kernel component, because it receives external events which cause it to generate requests for the driver without yet having read the driver's response to those requests. The kernel does need to read the driver's response eventually, but not until just before it prepares the next request to send out.

Proposition 2. *The linux kernel and driver combination defined in (2) never blocks – that is, it generates an infinite sequence of outputs – if*

1. *the incoming stream of external events contains an infinite number of DiskTQ commands,*

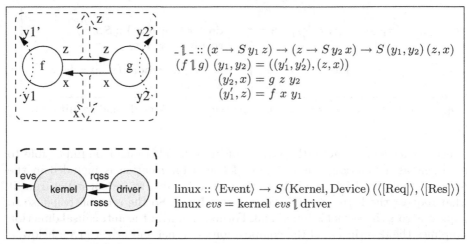

Fig. 2. The side-effecting communicating parallelism construct, in which internal communications are exported, and the linux operating system expressed as a side-effecting communicating parallel composite of kernel core and driver.

   2. the kernel component, when it receives a DiskTQ command, always generates a list (possibly empty) of kernel requests to be treated by the driver,

   3. the driver's request function does not block.

The proof is by the lemma below and Proposition 1.

Lemma 3. *The communicating parallel composition of two side-effecting stream filters as in (2) generates a well defined infinite output stream provided, for each n, at least one of the components satisfies (i) below, and the other satisfies (ii):*

   i. $(y_1', z_1 : \ldots : z_{n+1} : \bot) \sqsubseteq f\ (x_1 : x_2 : \ldots : x_n : \bot)\ y_1$
  ii. $(y_2', x_1 : \ldots : x_n : \bot) \sqsubseteq g\ (z_1 : z_2 : \ldots : z_n : \bot)\ y_2$

The lemma is proved by considering the length of approximants to solutions for (2).

   This proposition answers the question posed at the outset: is the kernel capable of "deadlock by design"? No, it is not.

   Note that the proposition does not say that the kernel does not block user space, but only that the kernel continues to work. It is quite possible that the kernel may not be able to flush existing requests to the driver, and then further user space requests to the device will be blocked, possibly forever. This happens often in running computers, particularly in connection with failed network file system mounts.

   In order to give concrete examples, the types Event, Req and Res will now be detailed. Events are either (3) user requests to read (or write) from the device, at given offsets and with given dimension, to (or from) a byte buffer; these are prefixed with the command UserReq, or are (4) the single command DiskTQ

606   Peter T. Breuer

```
struct request {              struct buffer_head {
   struct list_head queue;        struct buffer_head *b_next;
   int elevator_sequence;         unsigned long b_blocknr;
   volatile int rq_status;        unsigned short b_size;
   kdev_t rq_dev;                 unsigned short b_list;
   int cmd; /* READ or WRITE */   kdev_t b_dev;
   ...                            ...
   request_queue_t *q;            unsigned long b_rsector;
};                                wait_queue_head_t b_wait;
                                  struct inode * b_inode;
                                  struct list_head b_inode_buffers;
                               };
```

Fig. 3. The real Linux kernel's request and buffer head structs (C code).

("Disk Task Queue"), which instructs the kernel to pass to the i/o execution context and execute the driver request function.

$$
\begin{aligned}
\text{Event} ::= {}& \text{UserReq}(o, s, t, b), \quad o \leftarrow \text{Offset}, \ s \leftarrow \text{Size}, \ t \leftarrow \text{Type}, \ b \leftarrow \text{Buffer} \quad (3) \\
& \mid \ \text{DiskTQ} \quad\quad\quad\quad\quad\quad\quad\quad\quad\quad\quad\quad\quad\quad\quad\quad\quad\quad\quad\quad\quad (4) \\
\text{Offset} = {}& \text{Int}, \ \text{Size} = \text{Int}, \ \text{Type} ::= \text{R} \mid \text{W} \\
\text{Buffer} = {}& [c_0, \dots, c_n], \ c_i \leftarrow \text{Byte}
\end{aligned}
$$

Kernel requests delivered to the device driver have a two-tier structure. Each request specifies the offset and dimension of the read/write request, and its type. But instead of a byte buffer, the request contains a linked list of *buffer heads*. These are byte buffers plus extra information. The extra information consists of the buffers intended offset and dimension, and whether it is a read or write buffer.

$$
\begin{aligned}
\text{Req} ::= {}& \text{Request}(o, s, t, [h_0, \dots, h_n]) \\
\text{BH} ::= {}& \text{BH}(o, s, t, b), \quad o \leftarrow \text{Offset}, \ s \leftarrow \text{Size}, \ t \leftarrow \text{Type}, \ h_i \leftarrow \text{BH}, \ b \leftarrow \text{Buffer}
\end{aligned}
$$

In the kernel code, both requests and buffer heads are C structs with considerably more fields (see Figure 3) than modelled above. The Offset field corresponds to the **sector** field in the kernel request struct, except that the count here is in bytes, and the kernel count is in sectors. The Size field corresponds to the kernel's **nr_sectors** field, with the count again being in bytes against sectors. The other fields in the C code struct are mostly concerned with aspects of kernel accounting and state, and request and buffer accounting in particular. Each request details in full its target device, the number of contiguous segments it contains, which kernel queue it came from, whether it is locked, dirty, etc. Each buffer head likewise also contains a number of flags and counters that serve to allow the kernel to manage it correctly. But a device driver will normally not concern itself with these.

Responses returned by the driver to the kernel are simply kernel requests, with an error code appended. The error code zero indicates success.

$$\text{Res} ::= \text{EndReq}(rq, e), \ rq \leftarrow \text{Req}, \ e \leftarrow \text{Error} \tag{5}$$
$$\text{Error} = \text{Int}$$

Now an example can be given. Consider the sequence of events consisting of a write request of 8 bytes "abcdefgh" at the beginning of the device, then a read request for the same range (in this case, the buffer is empty, or null, and will be filled by the driver), then a command to run the driver request function, then the halt command to finish the emulation:

$$\text{UserReq}(0, 8, \text{W}, \text{"abcdefgh"}), \ \text{UserReq}(0, 8, \text{R}, [\,]), \ \text{DiskTQ}$$

Both user requests will be converted to kernel requests and placed on the driver's request queue by the kernel, then, when the request function is called, they will be resolved and acknowledged, in the order that they were queued. Supposing the driver to react inmediately, a single run of the request function will return two responses indicating tha the two have been treated. Both responses here carry error code zero. The return for the read request contains the data written in the preceding write.

	Req	Res
0	Request$(0, 8, \text{W}, [\text{BH}(0, 8, \text{W}, \text{"abcdefgh"})])$	EndReq$(\text{Request}(0, 8, \text{W}, [\text{BH}(0, 8, \text{W}, \text{"abcdefgh"})]), 0)$
1	Request$(0, 8, \text{R}, [\text{BH}(0, 8, \text{R}, [\,])])$	EndReq$(\text{Request}(0, 8, \text{R}, [\text{BH}(0, 8, \text{R}, \text{"abcdefgh"})]), 0)$

Adding an extra DiskTQ between the two user requests only changes the timing of the results. Instead of a single input list and a single output list, there will be two input and two output lists, one for each request function call, each a singleton.

The example above illustrates that the kernel plus driver satisfies a delicate progress requirement: each user request that enters is responded to with an EndReq call, eventually. In principle, the driver responds once for each request and maintains the original request order, but that it does so may be masked by "request merging". To phrase the idea formally, let f, g, h be functions (h partial) that discard the actual buffers from the kernel requests, driver responses and user requests, respectively, leaving only an indication of where they went or came from:

$$f, \ g :: \text{Req} \rightarrow (\text{Offset}, \text{Size}, \text{Type}) \qquad h :: \text{Event} \rightarrow (\text{Offset}, \text{Size}, \text{Type})$$
$$f \ (\text{Request}(o, s, t, bhs)) = (o, s, t) \qquad h \ (\text{UserReq}(o, s, t, b)) = (o, s, t)$$
$$g \ (\text{EndReq}(rq, e)) \qquad = f \ rq$$

The kernel, should not be expected to precisely emit one kernel request for each user request that arrives, or to maintain the order, because it reorders and/or aggregates requests in order to optimise the head-travel on hard disk devices, for example. However, the disorder introduced is always only local. Overall there is still a relation between user requests entering and kernel requests leaving the kernel.

Definition 4. *Say that the sequence* (o_i, s_i, t_i) *of user requests is* covered *by the sequence* (o'_i, s'_i, t'_i) *of kernel requests if there is a (computable) surjection* $p : Int \rightarrow Int$ *with the following properties. Call the user requests* i *such that* $p(i) = p$ *the* p'*th* group *of user requests, then the properties are:*

1. *the group is finite and the types of the user requests in the group are all the same and the same as the type of the* p'*th kernel request,*
2. *the address spaces of the user requests in the group exactly cover the address spaces of the* p'*th kernel request,*
3. *the address spaces of the user requests in the group are all disjoint.*

Then, letting kernel$_0$ be the initial state of the kernel, the kernel's behavior is described by the following condition – user requests entering the kernel *are covered by* the kernel requests emitted to the driver:

$$[h \ es_0, \ldots] \ is \ covered \ by \ [f \ rq \mid rq \leftarrow rqs_0 + \!\!+ \ldots] \tag{6}$$
$$\textbf{where} \ (\_, [rqs_0, \ldots]) = \text{kernel} \ [ev_0, \ldots] \ [rss_0, \ldots] \ \text{kernel}_0$$

and identifying rss_m, rqs_m across (6), as they are combined in the linux operating system equation (2), under the mappings induced by f, g, the two infinite sequences are identical, and indeed cover the sequence of user requests as mapped by h. So:

Proposition 5. *The linux kernel and driver combination defined in (2) produces responses EndReq corresponding to every user request UserReq, not necessarily 1-1 or in the same order, but in such a manner that the user requests are* covered *by the responses (if the conditions of Proposition 2 are satisfied).*

This result follows from the preceding remarks and the following axiom of driver behavior, and a lemma, which will be proved later.

Axiom 2 *The driver eventually produces one EndReq response for every kernel request that it receives, and maintains their order.*

Lemma 6. *The kernel component eventually produces kernel requests corresponding to every user request that it receives, not necessarily 1-1 or in the same order, but in such a manner that the user requests are* covered *by the kernel requests.*

3   The Kernel

The abstraction here of the kernel and its internal structures is approximate. Its important trait is that the kernel has a limited number of request structures available for use by a given driver. This imposes a bound on the number of outstanding user requests that can be converted into kernel requests at one go. Further user requests must wait upon the processing of some of the pending kernel requests by the driver.

The number of unallocated request structures available will be represented by a counter of type NFreeRQ in the kernel data structyre. Typically this number is initially 128 per device in a real kernel. The request structures allocated out and queued for the device driver will be represented by a linked list.

$$\text{Kernel} ::= \text{Kernel}(\mathit{nfrq}, \ [rq_0, \dots, rq_n]), \ \mathit{nfrq} \leftarrow \text{NFreeRQ}, rq_i, \leftarrow \text{Req}$$
$$\text{NFreeRQ} \ = \ \text{Int}$$

A kernel feature that will be ignored until Section 6 is that the kernel is also limited in the number of buffers that it can supply for buffer head structures. The limit is enforced by the amount of available physical memory, at least. It is unusual that the limit will be reached in practice under standard operating conditions, however.

When the kernel receives a new user request, it tries to merge the contents of the request at the beginning or end of an existing pending kernel request. Only if it fails will it call for a new kernel request. Then it will fail if there are no kernel requests available, and in that case the kernel must wait for a kernel request to become free, blocking user space in the meantime. Adding or merging a user request into the queue of pending kernel requests is handled by the *make request* function, which calls for an *elevator merge*. This leaves the queue requests ordered according to their offset on the device itself. This allows disk heads to sweep in only one direction across the disk at a time, like an elevator delivering passengers to their floors.

The model has make_request returning a failure notification in case there is no merge possible and no request free. There is then nothing to do but wait for something else to free a request. In the model, there is nothing else but the kernel and the driver, so a DiskTQ command is pushed on to the front of the event sequence, simulating the postponement of the treatment of the user request. In case the user request is successfully incorporated into the pending queue by make_request, the kernel is allowed to continue processing.

$$\text{kernel} :: \langle \text{Event} \rangle \rightarrow \langle [\text{Res}] \rangle \rightarrow S \text{ Kernel } \langle [\text{Req}] \rangle$$
$$\qquad \text{kernel } (\text{UserReq}(o, s, t, b) : evs) \ rsss = \mathbf{do}\{ \qquad\qquad (7)$$
$$\qquad\qquad\qquad v \leftarrow \text{make\_request } (\text{BH}(o, s, t, b));$$
$$\qquad\qquad\qquad \mathbf{if} \ v \ \mathbf{then} \quad \text{kernel } evs \ rsss$$
$$\qquad\qquad\qquad \mathbf{else} \quad \text{kernel } (\text{DiskTQ} : \text{UserReq}(o, s, t, b) : evs) \ rsss$$
$$\qquad\qquad \}$$

Or, in terms of process algebra:

$$\text{kernel} = \text{UserReq}(o, s, t, b)? \ \mathbf{if} \ (\text{make\_request } (\text{BH}(o, s, t, b)) \ \mathbf{then} \ \text{kernel}$$
$$\qquad\qquad | \ \text{DiskTQ}? \ \dots \ \text{kernel}$$

where the precise action on a DiskTQ event will be detailed below.

The make request function itself is only a wrapper for the function that does the elevator merge. In the kernel code, it passes a pointer to the front of the pending requests queue, so that the elevator merge function may move the pointer through the queue, looking for places to merge a new entry. In the model here, we pass an extra empty queue as parameter, and go through the kernel queue taking requests off that queue and onto the extra queue. When a place to merge is found, we reassemble the kernel queue from the two parts.

$$\text{make\_request} :: \text{BH} \rightarrow S \text{ Kernel Bool} \qquad (8)$$
$$\text{make\_request } bh = \text{elevator\_merge } bh \,[\,]$$

The aim of the elevator merge function is to slip the new buffer head contiguously onto one end of an existing queued request, or if that is impossible, to place a new request containing the buffer between two existing requests, in order. Thus, if the requests in the kernel queue are already ordered the elevator merge maintains that order. Details are omitted here.

Requests are resolved early in the kernel virtual memory system so that never, for example, do two writes to the same address range fall through to the block device queue. The writes will be performed in a kernel buffer and the last write alone will eventually fall through to the queue. Thus write (or read) requests reaching the devices kernel queue are necessarily all disjoint from each other.

Unloading the pending requests to the device driver is called *unplugging* the kernel device queue. The queue is normally *plugged*, and when it is plugged the kernel's make request function uses the elevator merge function to merge new requests into existing ones on the queue.

In the real kernel code, a scheduled task periodically unplugs the queue and runs the driver's request function (see Figure 4). Correspondingly, the model here calls the unplug function whenever it receives DiskTQ. The driver treats those requests and, in the kernel C code, the driver then helps finish off by calling the generic end request function. But in the model we call do_end_request from the kernel code and it then calls the end request function for each request. So the end request function has changed places between the real C code and the model. Migrating it across the boundary between driver and kernel here allows it to be located with the data that it affects – the kernel buffer counts and free lists. This is the only structural difference between the model and the real kernel code.

$$\text{kernel} :: \langle \text{Event} \rangle \rightarrow \langle [\text{Res}] \rangle \rightarrow S \text{ Kernel } \langle [\text{Req}] \rangle$$
$$\text{kernel (DiskTQ} : evs) \; rsss = \textbf{do} \; \{$$
$$\qquad rqs \leftarrow \text{unplug};$$
$$\qquad (\_, rsss') \leftarrow \text{do\_end\_request } rsss;$$
$$\qquad rqss \leftarrow \text{kernel } evs \; rsss';$$
$$\qquad \textbf{result } (rqs : rqss)$$
$$\}$$

$$\text{unplug} :: S \text{ Kernel [Req]} \qquad (9)$$
$$\text{unplug (Kernel}(nfrq, krqs)) = (\text{Kernel}(nfrq, [\,]), krqs)$$

```
      static inline void __generic_unplug_device(request_queue_t *q) {
        if (q->plugged) {
          q->plugged = 0;
          if (!list_empty(&q->queue_head))
            q->request_fn(q);
        }
      }
```

Fig. 4. The real kernel code for the unplug function. Note the request function call.

Or, in terms of process algebra, referring to the list of requests aimed at the device and pending in the kernel by kernel.rqs:

$$\text{kernel} = \dots \mid \text{DiskTQ? unplug; do\_end\_request; kernel}$$

$$\text{unplug} = \text{kernel.rqs! kernel.rqs} := [\,]$$

The do_end_request operation is responsible for absorbing further driver responses to requests from the kernel, converting them into individual EndIO actions on individual buffers. For the moment, we can discard the EndIO outputs, since they will only be used for accounting elsewhere in the kernel. The following process expression references the number of free requests remaining in the kernel as *kernel.nfrq*:

$$\text{do\_end\_request} = [\text{EndReq}(rq_1, e_1), \dots, \text{EndReq}(rq_n, e_n)]? \text{ kernel.nfrq} \mathrel{+}= n$$

The kernel can now be seen to satisfy the third of the conditions of Proposition 2, namely that a DiskTQ event always causes the kernel to emit a list of requests *rqs*. The unplug function cannot block, which is sufficient to produce the single output corresponding to the DiskTQ event. Can the kernel block between DiskTQ events? On receiving a user request it runs the make request function, which will either return success, moving the kernel on to treat more events without emitting anything, or failure, which will cause a DiskTQ event. So the only way that the kernel can block between DiskTQ events is to receive an infinite number of user requests, all of which it treats successfully. And it cannot receive an infinite number of user requests between two DiskTQ events. So Proposition 2 now gives rise to:

Corollary 7. *The linux kernel and driver combination defined in (2) and the kernel and driver described here and in the previous section never blocks – that is, it generates an infinite sequence of outputs – if*

1. *the incoming stream of external events contains an infinite number of DiskTQ commands,*
2. *the driver's request function does not block.*

The requests that are produced are the result of merging incoming user requests using the elevator algorithm. Each kernel request is the agglomeration of several disjoint, contiguous, user requests, and the user requests cannot have been delayed more that nr_requests * max_sectors elements with respect to the sequentialization, as plugging will not endure beyond nr_requests requests, and each request will not grow beyond max_sectors in size. Thus Lemma 6 is now satisfied.

4   Simple Examples

Suppose that the driver initial state consists of a zeroed memory area of defined size, and its size denominator, the size in KB (blk_size) times 1024:

$$\text{device}_0 :: \text{Device}$$
$$\text{device}_0 = \text{Device}(n, [\overbrace{000, \ldots, 000}^{n}])$$
$$\textbf{where } n = \text{blk\_size} * 1024$$

The kernel initial state is determined by the number of free requests structures to be made available to the driver. To make problems visible, we set the number at 4, although 128 is the number in the real kernel.

$$\text{nr\_requests} :: \text{NFreeRQ}$$
$$\text{nr\_requests} = 4$$
$$\text{kernel}_0 :: \text{Kernel}$$
$$\text{kernel}_0 = \text{Kernel}(\text{nr\_requests}, [\,])$$

Consider an event sequence of several interleaved read and write events, none of them contiguous, so they will not be merged by the elevator algorithm:

$$\text{UserReq}(0, 8, W, \text{``abcdefgh''}), \quad \text{UserReq}(0, 8, R, [\,]),$$
$$\text{UserReq}(16, 8, W, \text{``ijklmnop''}), \quad \text{UserReq}(16, 8, R, [\,]),$$
$$\text{UserReq}(32, 8, W, \text{``qrstuvwx''}), \quad \text{UserReq}(32, 8, R, [\,]),$$
$$\text{DiskTQ}$$

This sequence overflows the kernel's number of free requests after four kernel requests have been issued, and before the single DiskTQ. Therefore the kernel issues an extra DiskTQ in order to free up some requests, and emulation shows not one firing of the driver's request function, but two, grouped as four plus two requests and responses, as shown in the table below.

	Req	Res
0	Request(0,8,W,[BH(0,8,W,"abcdefgh")])	EndReq(Request(0, 8,W,[BH(0,8,W,"abcdefgh")]),0)
1	Request(0,8,R,[BH(0,8,R,[ ])])	EndReq(Request(0,8,R,[BH(0,8,R,"abcdefgh")]),0)
2	Request(16,8,W,[BH(16,8,W,"ijklmnop")])	EndReq(Request(16,8,W,[BH(16,8,W,"ijklmnop")]),0)
3	Request(16,8,R,[BH(16,8,R,[ ])])	EndReq(Request(16,8,R,[BH(16,8,R,"ijklmnop")]),0)
4	Request(32,8,W,[BH(32,8,W,"qrstuvwx")])	EndReq(Request(32,8,W,[BH(32,8,W,"qrstuvwx")]),0)
5	Request(32,8,R,[BH(32,8,R,[ ])])	EndReq(Request(32,8,R,[BH(32,8,R,"qrstuvwx")]),0)

To see that the kernel is vulnerable to driver faults, we may observe what happens if the driver code is changed so that it goes into an infinite loop on being requested a read at offset 16. The result is shown in the table below:

	Req	Res
0	Request(0,8,W,[BH(0,8,W, "abcdefgh")])	EndReq(Request(0, 8,W,[BH(0,8,W, "abcdefgh"]),0)
1	Request(0,8,R,[BH(0,8,R,[ ])])	EndReq(Request(0,8,R,[BH(0,8,R, "abcdefgh"]),0)
2	Request(16,8,W,[BH(16,8,W, "ijklmnop"])	EndReq(Request(16,8,W,[BH(16,8,W, "ijklmnop"]),0)
3	Request(16,8,R,[BH(16,8,R,[ ])])	{blocked!}

The entire kernel locks after treating three requests in this case. The real kernel code makes no attempt to time out driver responses, and is vulnerable to such bugs.

More subtle lock-ups are also possible. A driver may not block, but may fail to run end request, perhaps due to an untrapped error condition. In that case, eventually there will be no free requests left for the kernel to allocate in the make request function, and the make request function will postpone actions past the next DiskTQ event continuously. The result is livelock. The kernel is alive and the driver is dead.

5   Multiple Drivers

Incorporating multiple drivers in the kernel model implies a small modification of the request and buffer head structures to include a major number, indicating which driver the request or buffer is aimed at. It corresponds to (part of) the rq_dev and b_dev fields in the corresponding C structs (see Figure 3). User requests also have to be elaborated to match.

$$\text{Req} ::= \text{Request}(m, o, s, t, [h_0, \ldots, h_n])$$
$$\text{BH} ::= \text{BH}(m, o, s, t, b)$$
$$\text{Event} ::= \text{UserReq}(m, o, s, t, b) \mid \text{DiskTQ}$$
$$m \leftarrow \text{Major}, \ o \leftarrow \text{Offset}, \ s \leftarrow \text{Size}, \ t \leftarrow \text{Type}, \ h_i \leftarrow \text{BH}, \ b \leftarrow \text{Buffer}$$
$$\text{Major} = \text{Int}$$

The real kernel counts request structures for different majors separately, and maintains different free lists for them, and different device queues. This means that the model here can be made to support two drivers by placing two copies of the model for one driver in parallel, and directing incoming user requests to one or the other as appropriate. Support for n drivers is not more complicated. The parameter defining the number of supported block-device majors is max_blkdev, and it is 255 in the real kernel (this number will rise in the future, but there are currently only 8 bits available for the major number), but it will be set to 2 here, for purposes of illustration.

$$\text{max\_blkdev} = 2$$

So the n-kernel model runs n = max_blkdev unit copies of the simple kernel core block-device unit in parallel (see Figure 7). The copies share no state, as the only state is the count and list of free request structures available for the

$$\langle \_, \ldots, \_\rangle :: S\ x_1\ y_1 \to \ldots \to S\ x_n\ y_n \to S\ (x_1, \ldots, x_n)\ (y_1, \ldots, y_n)$$
$$\langle k_1, \ldots, k_n \rangle\ (x_1, \ldots, x_n) = ((x_1', \ldots, x_n'), (y_1, \ldots, y_n))$$
$$\textbf{where}\ (x_m', y_m) = k_m\ x_m$$

Fig. 5. Disjoint parallelism.

```
void generic_make_request (int rw, struct buffer_head * bh) {
    ...
    do {
        q = blk_get_queue(bh->b_rdev);
        if (!q) {
            printk(KERN_ERR ...);
            buffer_IO_error(bh);
            break;
        }
    } while (q->make_request_fn(q, rw, bh));
}
```

Fig. 6. The real kernel's front-end to the make request function, showing the deferral to a device-registered replacement at the end.

device major, and the kernel does not (in kernel version 2.4) share these free lists between majors. Each unit in the n-kernel receives those input events relevant to its major, plus all incoming EndIO commands. The events are filtered from the incoming event stream and directed to the individual unit majors by the demux function described below:

$$\text{demux} :: \langle \text{Event} \rangle \to \langle \text{Event} \rangle^n \tag{10}$$
$$\text{demux}\ evs = (evs_1, \ldots, evs_n)$$
$$\textbf{where}\ evs_m \qquad\qquad = \langle ev \mid ev \leftarrow evs,\ p_m(ev) \rangle$$
$$p_m\ (\text{UserReq}(m', o, s, t, b)) = (m = m')$$
$$p_m\ \_ \qquad\qquad\qquad = \text{True}$$

The n-kernel's construction can be expressed in terms of an n-ary disjoint parallelism operator, shown in Figure 5. The operator leaves all inputs and outputs of its n component units visible and internally unconnected, available for external connections:

$$\text{nkernel} :: \langle \text{Event} \rangle \to \langle [\text{Res}] \rangle^n \to S\ \text{Kernel}^n\ \langle [\text{Req}] \rangle^n \tag{11}$$
$$\text{nkernel}\ evs\ (rss_1, \ldots, rss_n) = \langle\ \text{kernel}\ evs_1\ rss_1, \ldots, \text{kernel}\ evs_n\ rss_n\ \rangle$$
$$\textbf{where}\ (evs_1, \ldots, evs_n) = \text{demux}\ evs$$

The real kernel does the job of selecting which requests go where at the point where it runs the generic make request function, which finishes by placing a kernel request on the appropriate driver queue. So in the real kernel, target

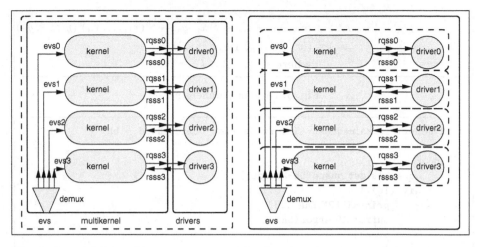

Fig. 7. A multi-driver Linux system can either be viewed as the communicating composition (thick dotted lines) of two disjointly parallel agglomerates (thick full lines), left, or as the agglomeration of several communicating compositions, right.

selection occurs inside a single generic make request function, and in the model here it occurs just prior to that point, and is then passed to a make request function particular to the device. The kernel's generic make request function sleeps when it cannot get a request structure, which allows other threads to clear any logjam, and *never* returns with error. In contrast, in the model, make request may return a failure code, and in that case the model itself emits an extra DiskTQ event, which emulates exactly what happens when make request sleeps in the real kernel.

Now the multi-driver linux kernel can be expressed as the combination of the n-kernel and the various block-drivers (see Figure 7):

$$\text{nlinux} :: \langle\text{Event}\rangle \to S\ (\text{Kernel}^n, \text{Device}^n)\ (\langle[\text{Req}]\rangle^n, \langle[\text{Res}]\rangle^n) \qquad (12)$$

$$\text{nlinux}\ evs = \text{nkernel}\ evs\ \text{⑂}\ \lambda(rqs_1, \ldots, rqs_n).\langle\!\!\langle\ \text{driver}_1\ rqs_1, \ldots, \text{driver}_n\ rqs_n\ \rangle\!\!\rangle$$

This is the same, up to a reformatting isomorphism, as combining the simple kernel core block-device unit with the individual driver, then compounding the pairs:

$$\text{nlinux}' :: \langle\text{Event}\rangle \to S\ (\text{Kernel}, \text{Device})^n\ (\langle[\text{Req}]\rangle, \langle[\text{Res}]\rangle)^n \qquad (13)$$

$$\text{nlinux}'\ evs = \langle\!\!\langle\ \text{kernel}\ evs_1\ \text{⑂}\ \text{driver}_1, \ldots, \text{kernel}\ evs_n\ \text{⑂}\ \text{driver}_n\ \rangle\!\!\rangle$$

$$\textbf{where}\ (evs_1, \ldots, evs_n) = \text{demux}\ evs$$

Proposition 8. *The two constructions of the multi-driver linux kernel shown in (12) and (13) above are isomorphic.*

The natural 1-1 and onto functions $f :: (u^n, v^n) \to (u, v)^n$ reformat appropriately:

$$(\lambda(s, x).(f\ s, f\ x)) \circ \text{nlinux}\ evs = \text{nlinux}'\ evs \circ f$$

Corollary 9. *The n-kernel plus drivers combination defined in (12) never blocks – that is, it generates an infinite sequence of outputs – if*

1. *the incoming stream of external events contains an infinite number of DiskTQ commands,*
2. *none of the drivers' request functions block.*

The corollary clearly holds of the function nlinux′, because it is composed via the independent composition in parallel of simple kernel core plus driver units which have the property asserted, according to Corollary 7. And the proposition asserts that the function is isomorphic to the nlinux function, so that proves the corollary.

Proposition 5 on the relation between user requests and kernel requests extends:

Corollary 10. *The n-kernel plus drivers combination defined in (12) responds to user requests with EndReq responses in such a way that the subsequence of user requests for each device is covered by the corresponding stream of EndReq responses.*

This means that the stream of responses may be locally disordered with respect to the incoming order, and that a single response may correspond to several merged user requests. In the absence of elevator-merging, the streams will correspond 1-1.

Now consider the example sequence of user requests examined before, three pairs of write then read requests. Let the first two pairs be directed at major 0 and the third pair be directed at major 1, followed by a DiskTQ event. Suppose that the drivers for both the majors 0 and 1 are instances of the same simple storage driver:

$$
\begin{aligned}
&\text{UserReq}(0,0,8,\text{W},\text{``abcdefgh''}), \quad \text{UserReq}(0,0,8,\text{R},[\ ]), \\
&\text{UserReq}(0,16,8,\text{W},\text{``ijklmnop''}), \quad \text{UserReq}(0,16,8,\text{R},[\ ]), \\
&\text{UserReq}(1,32,8,\text{W},\text{``qrstuvwx''}), \quad \text{UserReq}(1,32,8,\text{R},[\ ]), \\
&\text{DiskTQ}
\end{aligned}
$$

This time the sequence does not overflow the number of free requests available at any point, as there are four available in the kernel per device. So all the requests are serviced at the single DiskTQ event, albeit by two different drivers. The time-wise order in which they are treated between the drivers is not defined. The specification here assigns requests for different major's drivers to different streams, and the order of evaluation between streams is purely a function of the printout order chosen, since there is no communication between devices.

	Req	Res
0	Request(0,0,8,W,[BH(0,0,8,W, "abcdefgh")])	EndReq(Request(0,0, 8,W,[BH(0,0,8,W, "abcdefgh"]),0)
1	Request(0,0,8,R,[BH(0,0,8,R,[ ])])	EndReq(Request(0,0,8,R,[BH(0,0,8,R, "abcdefgh"]),0)
2	Request(0,16,8,W,[BH(0,16,8,W, "ijklmnop"])	EndReq(Request(0,16,8,W,[BH(0,16,8,W, "ijklmnop"]),0)
3	Request(0,16,8,R,[BH(0,16,8,R,[ ])])	EndReq(Request(0,16,8,R,[BH(0,16,8,R, "ijklmnop"]),0)
4	Request(1,32,8,W,[BH(1,32,8,W, "qrstuvwx"])	EndReq(Request(1,32,8,W,[BH(1,32,8,W, "qrstuvwx"]),0)
5	Request(1,32,8,R,[BH(1,32,8,R,[ ])])	EndReq(Request(1,32,8,R,[BH(1,32,8,R, "qrstuvwx"]),0)

The situation would be different if one device talked to another, or if other parts of the kernel intervened in the operation of the devices – an example would be when a block device used the kernel's TCP/IP networking layer as its transmission medium. Then causal dependencies may lead to subtle deadlocks.

6   The Virtual Memory System

Briefly, the virtual memory system (VMS) is responsible for managing the random access memory and any "swap space" on disk. Importantly, the VMS allocates out the buffers that are referenced within buffer heads within kernel requests. Buffers represent an important physical resource limitation. A fast process writing to a slow device may fill the VMS with *dirty* buffers that have to be flushed to the target device before they can be reclaimed for other uses. This is potentially a deadlock situation, and the VMS must manage it appropriately.

The VMS was changed at version 2.4.10 of the kernel, and the new VMS is still being tuned and debugged (at time of writing, we are at version 2.4.19 and 2.5.17 of the kernel). Some interesting memory deadlock conditions have only recently been discovered, and may require further changes. The VMS exerts a limiting influence only under conditions of extreme memory pressure.

By the time user requests arrive at the block-device subsystem, they already have their buffers attached to them, having passed through the VMS. The VMS acts as a cache: user processes trying to read from a block device may be satisfied directly from the VMS if the data to be read is cached there, either because it has just been written, or because it has already been read. Only if the data is not cached will the requests fall through to the kernel block-device layer below. Writes also lodge in the VMS initially, and only fall through to the kernel's block-device layer when the buffer *ages* sufficiently, which it normally does after about thirty seconds.

We cannot model the VMS in detail here, it is too complex. We can give a type for it, however: the VMS acts as a stateful two-way filter, letting user events through if it cannot satisfy them itself, and receiving the kernel's acknowledgements and passing them on to the user as necessary (see Figure 8). The kernel's acknowledgements come in separate streams, one emanating from each device. So the type is as follows:

$$\text{vms} :: \langle \text{Event} \rangle \rightarrow \langle \text{EndIO} \rangle^n \rightarrow S \text{ VMS } (\langle \text{Event} \rangle, \langle \text{EndIO} \rangle)$$

How does a VMS affect the analysis given? It is now possible to block the kernel if a driver requests memory from within its request function. If there are no buffers free then the VMS system will block the allocation, and the request function will block. With the request function blocked, other drivers will continue running and may release memory, which will unblock the system. But what if the driver is the *only* driver receiving i/o? I.e. VMS has been filled with dirty buffers aimed at the driver, and then the driver blocks asking for more memory?

In that situation, there is no way out – the kernel is deadlocked. Can the model described here exhibit that condition? No, it cannot. Drivers have been

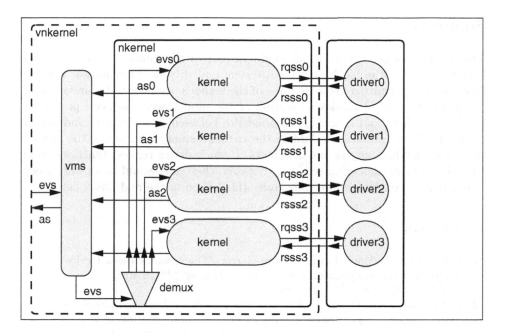

Fig. 8. The virtual memory system fits on the front of the block-device layers.

modelled as only reacting to kernel requests, not also interacting with other subsystems. This is true of the vast majority of real kernel drivers. In order to allow deadlock, it is firt necessary to extend the driver model. That would also require a more detailed model of the VMS and its distinct layers. However, the real kernel can deadlock this way in some drivers. For example, the NBD (Network Block Device) driver does call for memory while running its request function! It does so indirectly, by calling for a TCP network transfer, but TCP requires buffers, so the driver is able to block the kernel by the mechanism above. Some other drivers which need memory manage their own pools, obtained at driver startup.

To avoid the NBD/TCP deadlock, the kernel briefly raises the priority with which the kernel process involved with NBD calls for memory just before doing TCP. Then it cannot be deadlocked by priority inversion, where the high priority i/o process writing to NBD is blocked by the lower priority of the NBD kernel process. But it can be blocked by pure memory deadlock, when the only process doing i/o is the one writing to NBD. If memory fills up with its dirty buffers, then the NBD kernel process cannot get yet more buffers to do the TCP that would flush them. The NBD driver cannot avoid this deadlock unless memory is reserved for the use of its TCP socket, at all times, and there is currently no facility in the kernel VMS. So it seems likely that Linux will have to evolve some mechanisms for reserving memory in association with processes or other objects. However, the deadlock being discussed here has only very recently been discovered, and it is not clear how significant it is.

Summary

This article has set out a formal model of part of the Linux operating system kernel, featuring the block-device subsystem and drivers. The analysis is sufficient to have permitted gross features of the kernel's behavior to be understood. In particular, the block device section of the model here has been proven to be deadlock-free, and a firm correspondence between user requests and kernel replies has been established. Adding the virtual memory system into the picture does not introduce any kernel deadlocks. If block driver request functions were to make memory allocation requests, however, then that would be another story – and it is currently possible to exercise this option in the real Linux kernel.

References

1. P.T. Breuer, A. Marín Lopez, Arturo García. 'The Network Block Device'. http://www2.linuxjournal.com/lj-issues/issue73/3778.html
   The Linux Journal, #73, May 2000.
2. P. Cousot and R. Cousot. 'Abstract interpretation: A unified lattice model for static analysis of programs by construction or approximation of fixpoints'. In *Proc. 4th ACM Symposium on the Principles of Programming Languages*, pages 238–252, 1977.
3. Mark P. Jones. *Introduction to Gofer*. Technical report, Department of Computer Science, Yale University, USA, September 1991. (part of the Gofer distribution, anonymous ftp from ftp.cs.nott.ac.uk in the directory nott-fp/languages/gofer, rev. Oct. 1994).
4. E.S. Raymond. *The Cathedral and the Bazaar*. http://www.tuxedo.org/~esr/writings/cathedral-bazaar/cathedral-bazaar/ Linux Kongress, May 1997.
5. A. Rubini. *Linux Device Drivers*. O'Reilly, Sebastopol CA, Feb. 1998.

A Mathematical Framework for Safecharts

Hamdan Dammag and Nimal Nissanke

South Bank University
103 Borough Road, London SE1 0AA, UK
{dammagh,nissanke}@sbu.ac.uk
http://www.sbu.ac.uk/scism

Abstract. Safecharts is a variant of Statecharts intended exclusively for safety critical systems design. Its specific features include an explicit representation of risks posed by different hazardous states, a separation of functional and safety concerns, a representation of component failures and characterisation of transitions based on the nature of their risk. This paper presents a rigorous mathematical framework for enabling greater clarity and accuracy in Safecharts. It contains a study of the representation chosen for risks and associated concepts such as risk graphs and safety oriented classification of transitions. The step semantics is also defined in relation to Safecharts. As lower level abstractions of states are brought into focus, a way of constructing risk graphs for AND states is suggested. As a case study, the use of Safecharts in the domain of security is illustrated, in particular in modelling the Role-Based Access Control.

Keywords: Safety, Security, Statecharts, Step Semantics, RBAC

1 Introduction

Statecharts, introduced by Harel [6] and extensively studied by others, is widely used for modelling reactive systems. Safecharts [2] is a variant of Statecharts developed originally for exclusive use in the safety critical domain, namely, in relation to systems design. The objectives of this paper are two–fold. On the one hand, the paper aims at providing a mathematical exposition of Safecharts that matches the level of rigour and clarity sought in critical domains such as safety. On the other hand, it attempts to place Safecharts on a new, more general, footing so that it can serve system design with respect to safety, as well as other critical system attributes such as security broadly in a similar manner. This generality is an important goal in itself. It allows the transfer of methodological experience, as well as the associated human expertise, from one domain to another easily, thus mutually enriching the practices of domains concerned in the long run. Despite this generalisation being sought, this paper continues to use, generally, a single 'safety attribute' to mean whatever the critical system attribute under study, whether it is safety, security, or any other system attribute, unless where a reference to a specific system attribute is required.

The basic ideas of Safecharts have been discussed in [2,12], with illustrations of concepts and usage using case studies. Safecharts aspires to the same goals

J.S. Dong and J. Woodcock (Eds.): ICFEM 2003, LNCS 2885, pp. 620–640, 2003.

as Statecharts: visual appeal, ease of abstraction, modular and hierarchical representation of systems, mathematical rigour, etc. In addition, Safecharts aspires to fulfil the needs specific to safety critical systems design; these include representation of risks posed by system states and equipment failures, provision of additional safeguards against them, a systematic, rigorous and disciplined approach to design, and so on. These attributes are central to the design philosophy adopted in Safecharts.

For achieving a systematic, rigorous and disciplined approach, Safecharts adopts a twin–track strategy. On the one hand, Safecharts uses as its foundation Statecharts – a formalism with an appealing mathematical basis. On the other hand, it separates the aspects of the safety from those of the function, in order to allow the designers to focus on critical and functional features independently and in a systematic manner, and the reviewers to concentrate on safety without being distracted by functional issues. The separation of function and safety is achieved by having two 'layers' in Safecharts representations. The purpose is, on the one hand, to disambiguate between requirements and features devoted to safety and function and, on the other, to highlight the interdependencies between the two. The *functional layer* is devoted to functional issues and utilises Statecharts as used conventionally. The *safety layer* is devoted exclusively to safety issues and deals with issues such as equipment failures, risks posed by hazardous states, representation of safety features and mechanisms and reduction of unpredictable patterns of behaviour due to any non-determinism in a safe manner. In the case of security, safety layer deals with security risks posed by system states and with security mechanisms.

A key feature in realising the above is an ordering of system states according to risks posed by them relative to one another. Mathematically, this corresponds to a *risk ordering relation* on states. As a matter or prudence, Safecharts does not permit transitions between states of unknown risk levels. Recognising the possibility of such a situation arising from omissions, inaccuracies and inconsistencies in the risk ordering relation, for example, due to human error or the lack of knowledge, Safecharts imposes an additional clustering of states into *risk bands* and constructs a *risk graph* of these states. In doing so, any state with a possible inadequate consideration of risk is placed conservatively in a higher risk band by default, alerting the designer to reconsider its risk nature if such an interpretation is undesirable. A classification of transitions into *safe, unsafe* and *neutral* transitions based on the risk graph provides a sound basis for calling for additional safeguards against unsafe transitions and prompt enforcement of safe transitions. It also provides a safety-oriented resolution of non-determinism between any conflicting transitions favouring transitions that are more likely to bring the system down to a safer level. Representation of equipment failures and subsequent repair fits in neatly with the proposed framework and allows the incorporation of fail–soft features in functioning equipment in response to failures elsewhere and fail–safe mechanisms in extreme cases.

Correct interpretation of Safecharts requires a sound understanding of several important aspects of its semantics. This paper extends previous work [2,12] on

Safecharts, firstly, by formulating a mathematical framework for dealing with the above issues and, secondly, enriching it with a unique step semantics appropriate to the needs of Safecharts and a set of more refined rules for resolving non-determinism between conflicting transitions. As a new contribution, the papers makes an advance to the security domain by demonstrating the applicability of Safecharts to modelling of Role Based Access Control [14].

The paper has the following structure. Section 2 introduces basic concepts of Statecharts and the notation used here in relation to Statecharts. Section 3 prepares the ground for the subsequent discussion, introducing the key concepts of Safecharts related only to risks posed by hazardous states. Section 4 presents an integral mathematical view of Safecharts, including its step semantics. Section 5 presents a case study drawn from the domain of security both to illustrate the general use of Safecharts and to point out how it can be used in the security context, while Section 6 concludes the paper.

2   Statecharts

Primary purpose of this section is to place Statecharts in the setting of the mathematical framework used later for defining Safecharts. It is not intended as a formalisation of Statecharts, for which there are widely known other sources. Our formalisation, however, introduces certain restrictions to Statecharts, without greatly inhibiting its generality and yet serving the clarity or simplifications sought in Safecharts. Below is a brief informal introduction to Statecharts.

2.1   Statecharts in Brief

Statecharts is a visual specification formalism introduced by David Harel [6] for modelling the behaviour of complex reactive systems. Statecharts is an extension of finite-state machines with enhanced capabilities such as hierarchical decomposition of system's states, explicit representation of concurrency and broadcast communication. Statecharts is a kind of directed graph, with nodes denoting states and arrows denoting labelled transitions. Labels of transitions take the form $e[c]/a$, e being the triggering event of the transition, c a guarding condition and a an action generated precisely if and when the transition takes place. For a transition to take place, its source state must be an active state. Once generated, the action a is broadcasted to the whole Statechart, triggering, if applicable, other transitions in the diagram. In Statecharts, there are three types of states: AND, OR and BASIC states. Similar to states in state–transition diagrams, BASIC states are non–decomposable. Both AND and OR states consist of a number of substates. Being in an OR state means being in exactly one of its substates while being in an AND state means being in all of its substates simultaneously. The substates of an AND state are indicated by a dashed line and are known as *orthogonal* states.

For example, in Figure 1(a), state S is an AND state with two (orthogonal) substates A and B, each being of type OR. Being in S means being in A and

B simultaneously. States D, E, F, G, J and K are BASIC states that cannot be decomposed into further substates. The *default* state, pointed by a dangling arrow, is a substate of an OR state to be entered if a transition arriving at the OR state does not have an explicit entry state. In Figure 1(a), states C and G are the default states of A and B respectively. At initialisation, state S is in its default configuration, namely $\{J, G\}$. If the event e occurs, the transition J↝K takes place. As a consequence, the state J is exited, the state K is entered and the event a is generated and broadcasted throughout the Statecharts. Consequently, the action a triggers transition G↝F, and hence moving to state F inside state B. As a result, a new configuration of state S is realised, namely $\{K, F\}$.

2.2 The Basic Structure of States in Statecharts

As with any *state–based* formalism, fundamental to any definition of semantics of Statecharts are the notions of *state* and *transition*. This approach allows a compositional view of the structure of states at any given level of abstraction, ignoring the internal details of their substates at lower levels of abstraction.

Given an application, let $\mathbb{S}$ denote the set of all relevant states as understood in Statecharts, $\mathbb{T}$ the set of all possible transitions, $\mathbb{E}$ the set of all events, Θ the set of possible types of states in Statecharts, that is, $\Theta = \{OR, AND, BASIC\}$, SN a set of names used for labelling states, and Φ the set of (logical) formulae consisting of variables, logical operators and relational operators. When it stands in for an element of a set, let λ be a *null value*, standing in for an unspecified component, or a component irrelevant to a given specification, belonging to that set. Let S be an arbitrary state in $\mathbb{S}$. It has the general form:

$$S = (id, \theta, C, d, A, \alpha, T, \ell, E) \tag{1}$$

where

id – $id \in SN$ is a name uniquely identifying S.
θ – the type of the state S; $\theta \in \Theta$.
C – a finite set of direct substates of S, referred to as *child states* of S.
d – $d \in C$ and is referred to as the *default state* of S.
    It applies only to OR states.
A – a finite set of currently active child states.
α – a status flag indicating whether or not S is active; $\alpha \in \{active, inactive\}$.
T – a finite subset of $\mathbb{S} \times \mathbb{S}$, referred to as explicitly *specified transitions* of S.
ℓ – a function $T \to \mathbb{E} \times \Phi \times \mathbb{F}E$, labelling each and every specified transition
    in T with a triple, $\mathbb{F}E$ denoting the set of all finite subsets of E.
E – the finite set of events relevant to the specified transitions of S; $E \subseteq \mathbb{E}$

When dealing with several states simultaneously, various components of a given state S_i are referred to using the form $S_i.C, S_i.T$, etc. When it makes no confusion, we will denote these components simply as θ, C, etc. Intuitively, an active basic state S has the structure

$$S = (id, BASIC, \emptyset, \lambda, \emptyset, active, T, \ell, E) \tag{2}$$

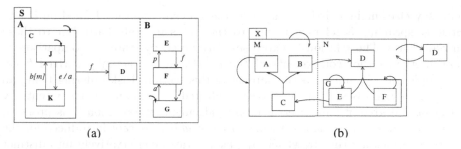

(a)   (b)

Fig. 1. An Example of Statecharts and invalid transitions.

Components in (1) have various interdependencies; their formal definitions and interrelationships are beyond the scope of this paper but are given in [3]. Due to the existence of many different variants of Statecharts (see [15] for a review) transitions have been introduced and interpreted differently. Hence, it is important here to clarify what are valid transitions of Statecharts as understood in Safecharts. Given a transition $t \in \mathbb{T}$, its label is denoted by $\ell(t) = (e, c, a)$, written conventionally as $e[a]/a$. e, c and a in the latter, denoted also as $trg(t) = e$, $con(t) = c$, and $gen(t) = a$, represent respectively the triggering event, the guarding condition and the set of generated actions. Note that since the elements of the label are optional, these functions may return λ to signify the absence of a particular element of the label. The source state of a transition t is denoted by $sc(t)$ while its target state is denoted by $tg(t)$. When it is more appropriate, a transition will be represented by a pair containing its source and target states, and is indicated as an arrow in the form $sc(t) \rightsquigarrow tg(t)$. For a transition $t \in \mathbb{T}$ to be a *valid* transition, the following conditions must be satisfied: (i) t has only one unique source state and one unique target state. In other words, unlike many statecharts variants, e.g. [7,9], t cannot have multiple source states or multiple target states, (ii) t does not span between substates of an AND states which is a common ancestor state of its source and target states, and (iii) the source state and the target state of t must not be ancestrally related. For example, according to the above conditions, all transitions in Figure 1(b) are invalid transitions in Safecharts.

3   Risk Frame

Turning to the subject matter of this paper, that is, the safety critical systems design, Safecharts treats the hazardous states and the risks posed by them as a fundamentally important issue. In this respect, this section lays the foundation for our subsequent discussion by examining separately several key concepts related to risks posed by states. In the context of a state S, *risk frame* is a 5-tuple and can be defined as:

$$F = (\sqsubseteq, n, \mathcal{B}, \beta, \sqsubseteq_\beta) \tag{3}$$

The key element in F is $\sqsubseteq$, which is a *risk ordering relation* defined on $\mathbb{S} \times \mathbb{S}$. Strictly speaking, $\mathbb{S}$ refers here not to the states in Statecharts but to those in Safecharts. The relation $\sqsubseteq$ expresses risks posed by states in comparison to one another. Other components of the risk frame are actually derived from, or supplement, $\sqsubseteq$ and form the subject of this section. Risk ordering being an outcome of risk assessment, a process conducted by domain experts potentially carrying a degree of human error or misjudgement, the relation $\sqsubseteq$ is prone to gaps, inaccuracies and inconsistencies. *Risk band* is a concept introduced for the purpose of tackling this drawback by placing states conservatively into distinct bands, or clusters, with some numerical indexing for comparative purposes. n in (3) represents the total number of risk bands of a given state. $\mathcal{B}$ and β are two related functions, the former from $\mathbb{N}$ to $\mathbb{PS}$ and the latter from $\mathbb{S}$ to $\mathbb{N}$. Given a risk band i and a state s, $\mathcal{B}(i)$ gives the set of states in the ith risk band, while $\beta(s)$ gives the risk band index of the state s. $\sqsubseteq_\beta$ in (3) is a binary relation on $\mathbb{N}_1^k$, with $\mathbb{N}_1 = \mathbb{N} - \{0\}$ and $k = \#S.C$. It is a subsidiary relation for risk ordering in AND states only and is defined using risk band indices of their child states.

3.1   Risk Ordering Relation

Given a state S, its risk ordering relation is denoted by $\sqsubseteq_S$, or simply by $\sqsubseteq$ where it causes no confusion. Given that S is an OR state and the states $s_1, s_2 \in S.C$, the risk ordering relation of S is defined such that $s_1 \sqsubseteq s_2$ is true if and only if the risk level of s_1 is known to be less than, or equal to, the risk level of s_2. The relation $\sqsubseteq$ may consist of pairs of states which are known to be either of two distinct risk levels or of an identical risk level. This can be represented mathematically by decomposing $\sqsubseteq$ into two relations: a partial order relation and an equivalence relation, denoted by $\prec$ and $\approx$ respectively. The interpretation of this notation is such that, given two distinct states s_1 and s_2,
$s_1 \prec s_2$ – the risk level of s_1 is known to be strictly lower than that of s_2.
$s_1 \approx s_2$ – the risk levels of s_1 and s_2 are known to be identical.
The relation $\sqsubseteq$ is reflexive and transitive. However, $\sqsubseteq$ may not necessarily be symmetric or antisymmetric. This is because there can be symmetrical pairs in $\sqsubseteq$, denoting states which are at the same risk level.

However, in the case of S being an AND state, it is impossible to define the risk ordering relation $\sqsubseteq$ on its parallel child states in C. Alternatively, the risk ordering relation $\sqsubseteq$ is defined on the set C' containing the child states of the equivalent flattened OR state of S, namely S', as mentioned in Section (3.2). The risk ordering relation can be represented as a graph; see Figure 2(a). In order to reduce the clutter in its visual presentations, arcs in graphs $\sqsubseteq$ and $\prec$ are assumed to run implicitly upwards and loops at nodes corresponding to reflexive terms are not shown.

3.2   The Risk Graph of OR and AND States

The risk graph of an OR-state S, denoted by $\mathcal{G}(S)$ is constructed on the basis of the risk ordering relation $\sqsubseteq_S$. However, in $\mathcal{G}(S)$, each state is placed in a unique risk band. As an example, Figure 2(b) shows the risk graph of a set of states defined by the relation ⊑ depicted in Figure 2(a). The concept of risk band and its formal definition is given in [3,12]. Two states s and s' are said to be *risk–comparable* if and only if they are comparable by $\approx$ (i.e. $s \approx s'$) or they lie in different risk bands. Otherwise, they are said to be *risk–noncomparable*. Note that risk–comparable states in the risk graph may be noncomparable by the relation ⊑.

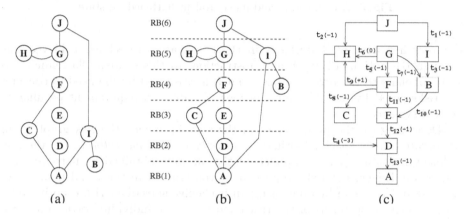

Fig. 2. (a) Risk ordering relation (b) Risk graph (c) Risk distances of transitions.

In general, risk ordering of an AND state can be quite complicated and may not be a viable option in practice when dealing potentially with a large number of orthogonal child states. This is because risk ordering in an individual orthogonal child OR state would no longer make sense unless due attention is paid to risk ordering in the adjoining child OR states. However, this difficulty can be overcome by *flattening* the AND state, that is, by converting the AND state into its equivalent OR state. In doing so, the risk ordering relation can be applied to the resulting OR state and, hence, the risk graph can be constructed in the usual manner.

An AND state S, with a set of direct substates C, can be flattened into an equivalent OR state S' whose C' consists of tuples drawn from the unordered Cartesian product of all orthogonal states in C. Each such tuple consists of a number of *parallel* states, equal to the number of orthogonal states in C and corresponds to a conventional state. The transitions associated with the equivalent OR state can be derived using the canonical mapping approach of [5]. For example, Figure 3(a) shows an AND state with two orthogonal substates M and N, while Figure 3(b) shows the equivalent OR state as well as its interpreted transitions.

When flattening an AND state, the number of interpreted transitions rises rapidly, especially if the AND state consists of many orthogonal states. This is a well–known problem of state–transitions diagrams – a problem that led to

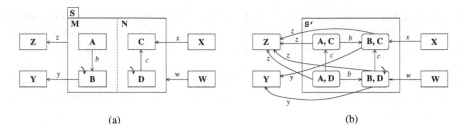

Fig. 3. An AND state and its equivalent flattened OR state.

the very invention of Statecharts in the first place. Statecharts achieved this through the notions of depth and abstraction. In this context, flattening AND state amounts to the reverse process but is necessitated by the need to consider the risks posed by possible combinations of states – a requirement peculiar to critical systems.

Depending on the performance of the domain expert, the risk graph of an AND state can be specified either: (i) *directly*, or (ii) *indirectly*. In (i), the risk ordering relation $\sqsubseteq$ can be applied to the OR state obtained by flattening the AND state. Hence, the risk graph can be constructed in the usual manner. In (ii), risk ordering can be done using an irreflexive subsidiary risk ordering relation $\sqsubseteq_\beta$ defined in terms of the risk band indices of individual orthogonal risk graphs. Thus, (ii) does not require flattening the AND state for the purpose of specification of $\sqsubseteq$. A formal definition of the direct and indirect approaches is given in [3].

3.3 Node Replacement in the Risk Graph

The hierarchical structure of states in Statecharts, achieved by the AND and OR composition, is also reflected in risk graphs. Analogous to a state in Statecharts being composed of a number of other child states, a node in a risk graph may in turn consist of a risk graph corresponding to the structure of the state represented by that node. When dealing with the system under consideration at a lower level of abstraction, there may be a need to expand the risk graph to the same level of abstraction. In this case, it is necessary to replace the node concerned with the risk graph it represents. This section outlines how to perform such node replacement. Given that x is a non BASIC state and $x \in S.C$, the node corresponding to x in $\mathcal{G}(S)$ can be replaced by its risk graph $\mathcal{G}(x)$ in the following manner. Let $\mathcal{G}'(S)$ denote the revised risk graph of S after the node replacement. Nodes in the highest risk band of a risk graph are referred to as its 'highest nodes' while its 'lowest nodes' are those nodes in the lowest risk band:

(a) The node x, as well as arcs incident on it, are removed from $\mathcal{G}(S)$.
(b) The highest node(s) in $\mathcal{G}(x)$ are connected to immediate successor nodes of x in $\mathcal{G}(S)$, if any.
(c) The lowest node(s) in $\mathcal{G}(x)$ are connected to immediate predecessor nodes of x in $\mathcal{G}(S)$, if any.

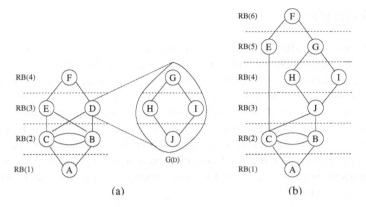

Fig. 4. Replacing node D with its risk graph $\mathcal{G}(\mathrm{D})$.

(d) If there exists a node representing a state x' in $\mathcal{G}(S)$ such that $x' \approx x$
   (i) if x' is a BASIC state then the lowest node(s) of $\mathcal{G}(x)$ are connected to x' by the $\approx$ relation,
   (ii) if x' is a non-BASIC state then the lowest node(s) of $\mathcal{G}(x)$ are connected to the lowest node(s) of x', by the $\approx$ relation.
(e) In the event of x having no direct successor in $\mathcal{G}(S)$ but there being a node x' in $\mathcal{G}(S)$ such that $\beta_S(x') = \beta_S(x) + 1$ in $\mathcal{G}(S)$, highest node(s) of $\mathcal{G}(x)$ are to be placed in $\mathcal{G}'(S)$ at least one risk band lower than that of x' in $\mathcal{G}'(S)$.
(f) In the event of x having no direct predecessor in $\mathcal{G}(S)$ but there being a node x' in $\mathcal{G}(S)$ such that $\beta_S(x') = \beta_S(x) - 1$ in $\mathcal{G}(S)$, lowest node(s) of $\mathcal{G}(x)$ are to be placed in $\mathcal{G}'(S)$ at least one risk band higher than that of x' in $\mathcal{G}'(S)$.

The risk graph $\mathcal{G}(x)$ intended to replace the node x is obtained depending on the nature of the node x such that: (i) if x denotes an AND or an OR state then $\mathcal{G}(x)$ is obtained as described in Section (3.2), or (ii) if x denotes a tuple then $\mathcal{G}(x)$ is obtained analogous to the risk graph of an AND state. This is achieved by considering x as being an AND state and the elements of the tuple as being its orthogonal states. However, in contrast to our definition of AND states, in this case, the set $x.C$ (the elements in the tuple) might contain one, or more BASIC state(s). In this case, the risk graph $\mathcal{G}(x)$, is constructed as follows: (a) all BASIC states in the tuple x are to be excluded and a risk graph $\mathcal{G}(x')$ of the remaining non-BASIC states is to be conventionally constructed, and (b) every excluded BASIC states is to be attached to every node in $\mathcal{G}(x')$. In the case where all the elements in x are BASIC states then no node replacement takes place.

In the interest of maintaining an identical level of abstraction, it makes sense to perform any node replacement on all non-BASIC nodes at a given level of the state hierarchy simultaneously. This is in line with maintaining the degree of the depth and abstraction obtained by the Safecharts diagram. As an example, Figure 4(a) shows the risk graph of S with node D to be replaced by its risk graph, that is by $\mathcal{G}(\mathrm{D})$. The revised risk graph of S, that is $\mathcal{G}'(S)$, obtained after the node replacement is shown in Figure 4(b).

4   Safecharts

Safecharts was introduced in [2] as a safety-oriented variant of Statecharts developed especially for the specification and design of safety-critical systems. One of its unique features is the maintenance of two separate layers of representation: a *functional layer* and a *safety layer*. The aim of the former is to capture system's transformational behaviour purely from a functional point of view, by using Statecharts in the conventional sense, while that of the latter is to capture the risk involved in such behaviour. The safety layer contains a *risk graph* of the states of the system under description and a *safety annotation* associated with transitions between these states. The concept of *risk graph* is based on our discussion in Section 3.

4.1   States in Safecharts

In dealing with failures in safety–critical systems, each component is represented in the form of an OR state with two distinguished substates, denoted generically by IN and OUT, meaning respectively that the component is functioning correctly or has failed. The nature of these two states are such that IN is strictly safer than OUT (IN $\preccurlyeq$ OUT). Associated with these states are also two generic events: a non-deterministic event ε signifying a failure, and an event μ signifying a maintenance or repair action which returns the component back to service. A component may have more than one failure mode, in which case OUT may itself be an OR state with a distinct substate for each of the failure modes, possibly with further transitions to model failure propagation.

Let us refer to the notation introduced in Section 2.2 in relation to **State**charts using the subscript *stc*, and to the notation introduced here in relation to **Safe**charts using the subscript *sfc*. First let us define a predicate *sys* on $\mathbb{S}_{stc}$ such that $sys(S)$ is true of S exactly if it models the state of a system, or the state of an item of equipment. For each such state in $\mathbb{S}_{stc}$, let there be a corresponding state $\mathbb{S}_{sfc}$ with three further states SYS_S, IN_S and OUT_S. Informally, SYS_S denotes the state of an extended *failure-prone* version of S. The $\mathbb{S}_{sfc}$, and likewise the $\mathbb{E}_{sfc}$, can be extended as follows:

$$\mathbb{S}_{sfc} = \mathbb{S}_{stc} \cup \{\text{SYS}_S, \text{IN}_S, \text{OUT}_S \mid S \in \mathbb{S}_{stc} \wedge sys(S)\} \tag{4}$$

$$\mathbb{E}_{sfc} = \mathbb{E}_{stc} \cup \{\epsilon_S, \mu_S \mid S \in \mathbb{S}_{stc} \wedge sys(S)\} \tag{5}$$

where $\text{IN}_S, \text{OUT}_s, \epsilon_S$ and μ_S are as introduced above. Where it causes no confusion, the subscripts in these new elements will be dropped. The states in Safecharts have an extended structure and include, in addition to what was discussed in section 2.2, the components of the risk frame as well as the associated relations $\sqsubseteq$ and $\approx$. The extended structure has the form

$$S = (id, \text{OR}, C, d, A, \alpha, T, \ell_s, E_s, \sqsubseteq, n, \mathcal{B}, \beta, \lambda) \tag{6}$$

$$S = (id, \text{AND}, C, \lambda, A, \alpha, T, \ell_s, E_s, \sqsubseteq, n, \mathcal{B}, \beta, \sqsubseteq_\beta) \tag{7}$$

$$S = (id, \text{BASIC}, \emptyset, \lambda, \emptyset, \alpha, T, \ell_s, E_S, \lambda, \lambda, \lambda, \lambda, \lambda) \tag{8}$$

where $E_s \in \mathbb{E}_{sfc}$ and every component is defined using the sets (4) and (5) with extended versions defined above. When dealing with the two special states IN and OUT, let us separate the functional and safety requirements concerning the state S as follows:

$$\text{IN} = S_f +\!\!+ S_s \tag{9}$$

$$S_f = (id, \theta, C, \lambda, A, \alpha, T_f, \ell_f, \mathbb{E}_{stc}, \lambda, \lambda, \lambda, \lambda) \tag{10}$$

$$S_s = (id, \theta, \lambda, d, \lambda, \alpha, T_s, \ell_s, \mathbb{E}_{sfc}, \lambda, \sqsubseteq, n, \beta, \sqsubseteq_\beta) \tag{11}$$

S_f and S_s being two partially completed templates of state specifications in Safecharts. The operator $+\!\!+$ which 'glues' the two templates together, is intended to have the following effect: $\theta_{\text{IN}} = \theta_{S_f} = \theta_{S_s}$, $C_{\text{IN}} = C_{S_f}$, $d_{\text{IN}} = d_{S_s}$, $A_{\text{IN}} = A_{S_f}$, $T_{\text{IN}} = T_{S_f} \cup T_{S_s}$, $E_{\text{IN}} = E_f \cup E_s$ and $\ell_{\text{IN}} = \{(t, \ell_f(t) \frown \ell_s(t)) \mid t \in T_{\text{IN}}\}$. The risk frame components in state IN are identical to those in S_s. If necessary, state OUT may also be defined as an OR state for modelling failure propagation from one mode to another. The extended failure–prone version SYS for a given state $S \in \mathbb{S}_{stc}$ is an OR state that can be defined as follows:

$$\begin{aligned} \text{SYS} = (id, \text{OR}, \{\text{IN}, \text{OUT}\}, \text{IN}, A, \alpha, \{(\text{IN}, \text{OUT}), (\text{OUT}, \text{IN})\}, \\ \ell_s, \{\epsilon, \mu\}, \{(\text{IN} \prec \text{OUT})\}, 2, \{(\text{IN}, 1), (\text{OUT}, 2)\}, \lambda) \end{aligned} \tag{12}$$

Features SYS (12), IN (9) and S_s (11) represent the contents of the safety layer, whereas S_f (10) represents the content of the functional layer. It is clear that S_f in (10) is based purely on Statecharts as understood conventionally. Thus, its non-null values are identical to the corresponding ones given in (1) for dealing with functional requirements. The default state d in S_s (11) is defined such that $\beta(d) = 1$ and is referred to as the *safe default* state of IN, which is itself being the default state of SYS (12). This forms a safe initialisation feature in Safecharts.

4.2 Transitions in Safecharts

A transition $t \in T$ in Safecharts is a *legal* transition if and only if $sc(t)$ and $tg(t)$ are risk-comparable states in a common risk graph. Based on the risk graph, Safecharts classifies transitions according to the nature of risks they carry and, accordingly, extends the specification (labelling) of transitions with additional guards and enforcement conditions. Transitions belong to three categories: *safe* (hi-to-lo risk), *unsafe* (lo-to-hi risk) and *neutral* (between states of the same risk level). In terms of the function β, introduced informally in Section 3, this classification can be made as: a transition t is considered *safe* if $\beta(tg(t)) < \beta(sc(t))$, *unsafe* if $\beta(tg(t)) > \beta(sc(t))$, and *neutral* if $\beta(tg(t)) = \beta(sc(t))$. Thus, ε introduced in Section 4.1 triggers an unsafe transition, while μ triggers a safe transition.

Transition labelling in Safecharts has the general form $e\,[c]/a\,[l, u)\,\Psi[G]$, with e, c and a remaining the same as in Section 2 and certain components being mandatory depending on the risk classification of the transition concerned. $[l, u)$ is a right-open time interval from time l to time u. Ψ is a safety enforcement pattern specified using two alternative symbols: ⌐ and ↾, and $[G]$ is a safety clause. $t \;↾ [G]$ is mandatory for unsafe transitions and means that the transition t is forbidden to execute as long as G holds. $t[l, u) ↾ [G]$ is mandatory for safe transitions and means that the transition t is forced to execute within $[l, u)$ from whenever G begins to hold irrespective of the occurrence of its triggering event.

The *risk distance* of a transition $t \in T_S$ is the number of band boundaries between the source and target states of t in $\mathcal{G}(S)$. Denoting it by $\mathcal{D}(t)$, it can be defined as: $\mathcal{D}(t) = \beta(sc(t)) - \beta(tg(t))$, the positive and negative signs of $\mathcal{D}(t)$ thus signifying respectively an increasing, or decreasing, risk; see Figure 2(c). The risk nature of transitions plays an important role in determining their *safety enabling conditions*. For a neutral transition to be enabled, it must be *functionally enabled*, that is, its source state is active, its triggering event e has occurred and its guarding condition c, if any, is true. However, for an unsafe transition to be enabled, it must be both functionally enabled and its safety clause G must be false. Likewise, for a safe transition to be enabled, it must be either functionally enabled or its safety clause G is true.

The enabling time of a transition t, denoted by $EnTime(t)$, is defined as the earliest time when t becomes safety enabled, as defined above. The time interval $[l, u)$ associated with safe transitions, introduced above, is a real-time constraint on t and imposes the condition that t does not execute until at least l time units have elapsed since it most recently became safety enabled, that is, since $EnTime(t)$, and must execute before u time units since $EnTime(t)$. If l and u have not been specified explicitly then t is assumed to be *spontaneous* with an open-ended $[0, 1)$ time interval. This implies that t executes as soon as it is enabled by G, in other words, as soon as $EnTime(t)$ is realised. In Safecharts, a transition t is *executed* if and only if it is safety enabled within its associated time interval and, either t is not in conflict with any other enabled transition or t has the highest priority among its conflicting transitions.

In Safecharts, two transitions t_1 and t_2 are said to be in conflict if $sc(t_1) = sc(t_2)$ and they become functionally enabled simultaneously. In Safecharts, non-deterministic choice between two, or more, conflicting transitions can be resolved by giving higher priority to the transition with the shortest risk distance. This approach is different from other approaches, for example in [13], where priorities are given according to the scope[1] of the conflicting transitions while in [4] priorities are given according to the hierarchy of their source states.

Let $conflict(t)$ be the set of all possible transitions which are in conflict with transition t. In the case of transitions with equal risk distances, prioritisation is based on the *cumulative* risk distances of future transitions of conflicting transitions. A transition t' is said to be a *future* transition of the transition t if the source state of t' is the target state of t. The set of future transitions of t can be defined as $future(t) = \{t' \mid sc(t') = tg(t)\}$. There is a greater likelihood of a future transition t' being executed if its source state becomes active as a result of the execution of a transition t among those in

---

[1] The scope of a transition t is the lowest common OR ancestor state containing both $sc(t)$ and $tg(t)$.

conflict, and its triggering event was generated by the execution of t. We refer to such transitions as *expected* future transitions and introduce the set: $expected(t) = \{t' \mid t' \in future(t) \wedge trg(t') \in gen(t)\}$.

Any nondeterminism between two, or more, conflicting transitions can now be resolved by giving highest priority to the competing transition with the smallest cumulative risk distance. The way cumulative risk distances of competing transitions are calculated is as follows: $\forall x \in (conflict(t) \cup \{t\})$

(1) if $expected(x) \neq \emptyset$ then select any transition y from the set $\{y \mid y \in expected(x) \wedge \forall y' \in expected(x) \Rightarrow \mathcal{D}(y) \leq \mathcal{D}(y')\}$

(2) if $expected(x) = \emptyset \wedge future(x) \neq \emptyset$ then select any transition y from the set $\{y \mid y \in future(x) \wedge \forall y' \in future(x) \Rightarrow \mathcal{D}(y) \geq \mathcal{D}(y')\}$

(3) In both above cases, resolve the non-determinism on the basis of $\mathcal{D}(x) + \mathcal{D}(y)$, otherwise on $\mathcal{D}(x)$ alone.

Nevertheless, non-determinism may still continue to persist even after considering the future transitions as shown above, for example, if all, or some, transitions in $conflict(t)$ have equal accumulative risk distances. However, this kind of non-determinism is considered a *safe non-determinism* since all outcomes are identical in terms of the risks involved.

4.3   The Step Semantics of Safecharts

There exists many different semantics for Statecharts, centering mostly around the concept of *step*. The step semantics has been a much debated issue, primarily because of the anomalous and counter–intuitive behavioural patterns of Statecharts resulting from some of the interpretations. These debates concern the central issue as to whether the changes, such as the generated actions or updating values of data items that occur in a given step, should take effect in the current step or in the next step. The reader is referred to [15,10,11,13] for more details about the different step semantics and the problems associated with their definitions.

In defining the step semantics of Safecharts, our aim here is to adopt the most appropriate standpoint in relation to the sole concern of Safecharts, namely the design of critical systems from whatever the perspective, whether it is from safety, security or any other system attribute. The step semantics of Safecharts retains certain characteristics of the conventional step semantics such as the synchronous hypothesis, while at the same time maintaining an intuitive relationship between external and internal events so that it corresponds to the operational reality of reactive systems. It is based on the treatment of external and internal events in an identical manner, but it also requires the introduction of the concept of *postponed transitions* and two separate notions of time, namely a *synchronous time* metric and a *real time* metric. The step semantics in Safecharts is based on the synchronous time model of STATEMATE [7]. The system evolves from one step to the next after considering a set of *input events* at consecutive intervals separated by a granularity of Δ time units, referred to as Δ-interval. The synchronous time model has the advantage of avoiding infinite loop of triggering transitions enabled by infinitely generated internal events, and preventing the occurrence of *racing conditions*.

The set of input events at the end of the current Δ-interval consists of the external events sent by the environment during the current interval as well as the internal events generated by the execution of the previous step. Input events last only for the duration of a single Δ-interval. Once the step has been taken, all input events are consumed and the set of input events becomes empty. In its initial state (initial configuration), the system waits for the environment to produce external events. At the end of the first Δ-interval, the input events consist of only the external events sent by the environment and are sensed and reacted to by executing the initial step. As a result of the initial step, the system moves to a new configuration, provided that the step is a 'status step' (in the sense discussed later), the generated internal events, if any, are added to the set of input events of the next step, and the clock is incremented by Δ-interval. The set of input events of the next step consists of the internal events, if any, generated by the initial step together with the external events, if any, received by the environment during the following Δ-interval. In the example shown in Figure 5, the set of input events of *step1* consists of the internal event e_1 as well as the external events e_2 and e_3. At the end of the Δ-interval, *step1* is executed and all the input events are consumed. This process continues in each step.

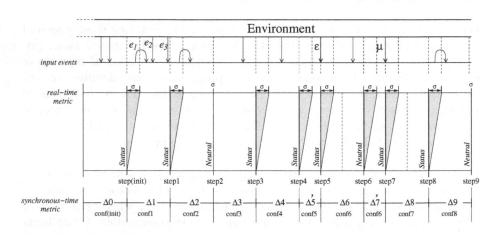

Fig. 5. The step semantics of Safecharts.

In the cases where there are no external events generated by the environment during the Δ-interval prior to the step, the set of input events comprises only the internal events generated in the previous step. In this case, the step is taken by consuming all input events and triggering relevant transitions. Consequently, internal events are possibly generated again for the next step, leading to a new configuration. In the case where there are neither external nor internal events from the previous step, that is, where the set of input events is empty, after Δ-interval the step is taken anyway without executing any transition and, consequently, with no change in the configuration of the system. For the system to move to a new configuration, the environment has to produce a new set of external events during the subsequent Δ-intervals. In this connection, our step semantics distinguishes two types of steps, namely *status* steps and *neutral* steps, the former causing a material change in the configuration of the system while the latter causing no change.

Analogous to several other definitions of step semantics, the step semantics of Safecharts eliminates many undesirable features, for example, negated events and instantaneous states. Safecharts also maintains a clear causality ordering and global consistency. Similar to the semantics of Statecharts introduced by [7] and adopted by many variants, the execution of a step in Safecharts takes zero time unit, and thus transitions triggered by input events are taken instantaneously once the step is taken. However, as stated in [8], the synchronous hypothesis does not reflect the intuitive operational reality of reactive systems, where transformations between the states of the system usually take some *real time*, during which the environment can send some external events. In order to reconcile the mismatch between the synchronous hypothesis and the reality of transformational behaviour of real-time reactive systems, we propose two notions of time metrics: a *synchronous-time* metric and a *real-time* metric. In the synchronous-time metric, the duration of the step, denoted by σ, is always taken to be zero (in other words, σ is too fine to be detected), while in the real-time metric σ is either zero in the case of the step being neutral step, or a non-zero constant in the case of the step being a status step.

With reference to the real-time metric, the assumption underlying the adoption of the synchronous hypothesis is that, once a step is taken at the end of a Δ-interval, any external events sent by the environment during the σ time unit are postponed until the elapse of σ interval. Due to their importance in modelling the safety aspects of the system's behaviour, it is a feature in Safecharts that generic events, namely ε and μ, must be taken as soon as they occur. Thus, in this context, generic events are treated differently from other input events, and are considered as interrupt events. Once they occur and are added to the set of input events, the step does not wait until the end-time of the current Δ-interval, but rather executes immediately consuming all input events gathered so far. The Δ-interval during which generic events occur is called an *irregular* interval, and denoted by Δ'. The step that follows Δ' is called an *interrupt* step. For example, in Figure 5, $step_5$ and $step_7$ are two episodic steps executed as a result of the occurrence of events ε and μ respectively.

5   Case Study: Safecharts in the Security Domain

Alongside availability and reliability, safety and security are two closely related properties of dependable systems. The design of dependable systems is often required to satisfy several of these critical properties simultaneously. There is a growing interest in the degree to which techniques from one domain could complement, or conflict with, those from another. In this section, we investigate the applicability of Safecharts and its various safety-oriented techniques and mechanisms for dealing with security issues. More specifically, we examine the use of the concept of risk graph, and the various safety enforcement applied to transitions, in the field of security.

5.1   RBAC and Its Modelling in Safecharts

In computer security, access control is the concept of managing authorisations, by which resources (objects) are accessed by individuals (subjects) with a specific set of operations. Role Base Access Control (RBAC) is a well-established approach in computer security for controlling access by users to various resources; see [14]. It is increasingly relevant to modern commercial, business and other domains. Our approach to modelling RBAC, however, is applicable to systems where security requirements are predominantly dependent on the state of the system. An exemplar of such systems is reactive systems which Statecharts and, hence, Safecharts are intended for. RBAC is based on the concept of *role* – a representation of job functions performed by individuals in an organisation [1]. Unlike in traditional access control mechanisms, such as those used in operating systems, RBAC assigns access rights to the roles rather than to the individuals directly. In other words, the subjects are able to access objects only by virtue of their roles. A subject can be associated with more than one role and a role can be assigned to many subjects.

Permitted access rights of different roles to objects are maintained in an Access Control List (ACL) against which requests by subjects to perform various operations or tasks (e.g a *write* operation) on an object are checked. If a role authorising the access of the object concerned by the required operation is found, then the access right associated with this role is granted, otherwise, denied. The model of RBAC permits the temporary *delegation* of access rights by one party to another in order to perform one or more specific functions. Figure 6(a) depicts such a scenario in the context of an engineering organisation, where a manager A delegates some, or all, of his tasks (access rights) to a subordinate engineer Q, enabling Q to perform A's tasks on his behalf. This mechanism is vulnerable to potential security risks as ACL makes no distinction as to whether a subject requesting a certain mode of access is doing so in the capacity of his own role, for example, as originally assigned by the security officer, or in the capacity of a role acquired through a delegation.

As presented in [14], RBAC may be treated as a hierarchy of four models: $RBAC_0$ (flat model), $RBAC_1$ (hierarchical model), $RBAC_2$ (constrained model) and $RBAC_3$ (symmetric model). $RBAC_0$ is a model depicting simply various permissions allocated to various roles and, thereby, to different users. $RBAC_1$, on the other hand, depicts a seniority relation on roles, whereby senior roles automatically inherits the rights permitted to more junior roles to perform various tasks, reflecting the lines of authority or responsibility in a given organisation. Going further, $RBAC_2$ enforces separation of duties and $RBAC_3$ introduces the capability to review assignment of permission with changing circumstances.

In this work, we consider only the models, RBAC_0 and RBAC_1. RBAC involves generally three types of entities: users U, roles R and permissions P. Assignment of permissions (allocation of tasks) to roles is given by a function $\alpha \in R \to \mathbb{P}\,P$ so that, for any $r \in R$, $\alpha(r)$ gives the set of permissions assigned to the role r. Likewise, assignment of users to roles may be given by a function from U to $\mathbb{P}\,R$, though its detailed elaborartion is not required in this particular work. Since no restrictions are imposed on these functions, their representations are all that is required in RBAC_0. Turning to RBAC_1, in addition to its conventional features, our model considers here the relative risks associated with situations when users belonging to different roles performs different tasks. This is represented by risk ordering relations $\sqsubseteq$ and $\preccurlyeq$ on $R \times P$ with the same meaning as that given in Section 3.1. For example, the interpretation of $\preccurlyeq$ is such that for any $r_1, r_2 \in R$ and $p_1, p_2 \in P$, $(r_1, p_1) \preccurlyeq (r_2, p_2)$ is true if and only if the security risk level associated with a user in role r_1 performing the task p_1 is known to be strictly lower than that of with a user in role r_2 performing a task p_2, unless r_1 and r_2, and p_1 and p_2, each denote the same entity. Let $\leqslant$ denote the hierarchical ordering on R such that, for any $r_1, r_2 \in R$, $r_1 \leqslant r_2$ is true if and only if the role r_1 is of a lower, or an identical, hierarchy compared to the role r_2. In our model, $r_1 \leqslant r_2$ if and only if

$$\alpha(r_1) \subseteq \alpha(r_2) \wedge (\forall\, p \in P \bullet p \notin \alpha(r_1) \wedge p \in \alpha(r_2) \Rightarrow (r_2, p) \preccurlyeq (r_1, p)) \qquad (13)$$

In other words, each role of any given higher hierarchy consists of some specific tasks not permitted by the roles of the lower hierarchies on security grounds, for example, based on criteria such as trustworthiness, required competence level and so forth. The above thus expresses in our model a principle of *permission assignment* to roles. This is a capability not found in the formal representation of conventional RBAC_1 [14]. In fact, classification of role hierarchies has to be based on some sort of risk assessment and, in this respect, the concept of risk graph in Safecharts provides a formal basis for achieving this. In the remainder of this section, we illustrate the use of Safecharts in modelling temporary delegation of a higher rank role to a user of a lower rank role in RBAC and the use of the principle (13) in establishing assignment of permissions to roles and, hence, the determination of enforcement conditions appearing in certain transition labels. Figure 6(a) shows the example being considered – a scenario involving just two users, a manager A in role M and an engineer Q in role E, accessing a particular object O, for example, a file or a database. The following operations are permitted: *read* (read only), *write* (both read and write), *priv_writing* (privilege writing from a read–only mode). The two roles are such that $E \leqslant M$, though the actual role–permission relation shown in the figure is to be established later. Figure 6(b) shows a Safecharts model for part of it, depicting how the two users access *Object*1, modelled as an AND state. Substates of *Object*1 are two OR states: *Status* showing possible states the object can be in, and *User* signifying that the object can be accessed by the two users in an exclusive mode. The order in which the states are placed vertically in the diagram of any OR state corresponds to an implicit risk ordering. For example, the object

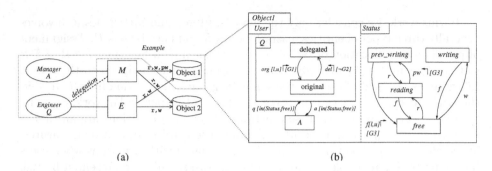

(a)   (b)

Fig. 6. An example of delegation in RBAC and the safety layer.

being in the state *free* is considered safer (more secure) than being in the state
reading, while being in the state *reading* safer than being in the states *writing* or
priv_writing. In contrast, states *writing* and *priv_writing* are assumed to be risk
non-comparable. In other words, a risk ordering of the form (*free* $\preccurlyeq$ *reading*),
(*reading* $\preccurlyeq$ *writing*) and (*reading* $\preccurlyeq$ *pre_writing*) is assumed in *Status*. Similarly,
for the state Q, a risk ordering of the form (*original* $\preccurlyeq$ *delegated*) is assumed,
indicating that the user Q accessing the object in his original role is safer than
accessing the same object in a delegated capacity. Accordingly, the transition
original$\leadsto$*delegated*, signifying the delegation of a role, is an unsafe (unsecure)
transition, whereas the transition *delegated*$\leadsto$*original*, signifying revocation of
the role delegation, is a safe (secure) transition.

Though the risk ordering described above has some significance in an isolated
context, it is not adequate for describing the risks involved in access control. This
is because the interdependencies of risks, depending on the roles of the users involved and the operations being performed by them, need to be considered. In
other words, we need to consider risks posed by different combinations of states.
Technically speaking, this amounts to flattening of the AND state *Object*1 into an
equivalent OR state and developing a risk graph for the flattened state. As was
mentioned in Section 3.2, the required risk graph can be constructed either directly or indirectly; in this example, we follow the former. The set of sub-states of
the resulting equivalent OR state and, hence, the nodes of the resulting risk graph,
consists of eight (pairs of) states: (Q, *writing*), (Q, *prev_writing*), (Q, *reading*),
(Q, *free*), (A, *writing*), (A, *prev_writing*), (A, *reading*), (A, *free*). Furthermore,
since Q is itself an OR state, each node involving Q in the risk graph needs
to be refined and replaced by its risk graph, that is $\mathcal{G}(Q)$. As a result, the
node (Q, *writing*), for example, must be replaced by a risk graph consisting of
two nodes, possibly, with a risk ordering of the form ($Q.delegated$, *writing*) $\preccurlyeq$
($Q.original$, *writing*). Hence, the resulting risk graph will consist of a total twelve
nodes.

The direct approach adopted here to construct the risk graph for the flattened state provides an opportunity to review the risks involved, ideally, based
on a proper security analysis of the problem concerned. For illustrative purposes, we have assumed that (A, *priv_writing*) $\prec$ ($Q.original$, *priv_writing*);

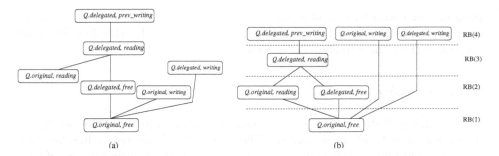

Fig. 7. The risk ordering relation and the risk graph of the user Q.

no other distinctions are being made otherwise between A and Q when Q is acting in his original role. For reasons of space, we have also chosen to concentrate here only on the behaviour of Q and, thus limiting ourselves to the risk graph shown in Figure 7(a) giving risk ordering related to Q only. Note that the states $(Q.original, writing)$ and $(Q.delegated, writing)$ are treated as non-comparable by $\sqsubseteq$ with many other states (nodes). As a precaution against this being possibly due to an inadequacy of the risk assessment process, the banded risk graph in Figure 7(b) has placed these states conservatively in the highest risk band. This is to be taken as a flag, alerting the designer to reconsider the risk levels of these states if the circumstances do not warrant such an interpretation. Due to the positions of their source and target states in the risk graph, transitions such as $(Q.original, free) \rightsquigarrow (Q.original, writing)$, $(Q.original, free) \rightsquigarrow (Q.delegated, writing)$ and $(Q.original, free) \rightsquigarrow (Q.delegated, prev\_writing)$ have equal risk distances. An implication of this is that in the event of a conflict, selecting either of these transitions is considered as a safe non-determinism. If this is unacceptable on security grounds, then the designer needs to verify the security policy and/or the relative risk levels of their target states, namely $(Q.original, writing)$, $(Q.delegated, writing)$ and $(Q.delegated, prev\_writing)$.

Turning to the permission assignment, the two roles can now be distinguished in accordance with the principle (13). It can be seen, for example, that $\alpha(E) = \{read, write\}$ and $\alpha(M) = \{read, write, priv\_writing\}$ satisfies (13). As a result, a user belonging to the role E will no longer have access to the operation $priv\_writing$ in his $original$ capacity. However, this can be allowed in a delegated capacity provided that he satisfies a suitably specified condition G_2 expressing, perhaps, that additional measures have been taken to ensure his temporary security credentials, for example, that he has been given additional training. Hence, the prohibition condition $(\neg G_2)$ appearing in the label of the transition $original \rightsquigarrow delegated$ and the enforcement condition G_1 appearing in that of $delegated \rightsquigarrow original$, G_1 being identical to G_2 or being a timeout. Likewise, a pair of prohibition and enforcement conditions involving a predicate G_3, G_3 being defined as $in(Q.original)$, have been added to the labels of the transitions $reading \rightsquigarrow prev\_writing$ and $priv\_writing \rightsquigarrow free$ respectively. Thus, role classification arrived above allows us to deal with temporary delegation of tasks of senior roles to individuals of more junior roles. The above is a systematic approach for avoiding problems such as the one mentioned earlier in relation to the conventional implementation of ACL.

6   Conclusion

Correct interpretation of Safecharts requires a sound understanding of several important aspects of its semantics. The objective of this paper has been to present a mathematical framework for Safecharts, with the primary aim of giving greater clarity and accuracy to key concepts used in Safecharts. These include separation of function and safety, risk ordering, the risk graph, failures, risk nature of transitions and resolution of non-determinism. In extending the notion of risk ordering to include composite OR and AND states, the paper also extends previous work by showing how to deal with interdependencies of risk at lower levels of abstraction; this involves flattening AND states and node replacement in risk graphs. In this paper, the step semantics of Safecharts has been defined and the mismatch between the synchronous hypothesis and the reality of transformational behaviour of real-time reactive systems has been reconciled. Rules on resolution of non-determinism between any conflicting transitions have also been refined to include triggering events of transitions. Although Safecharts was originally developed explicitly for safety-critical systems design, its various features and mechanisms used to ensure safety are found to be equally valid in the security domain. This has been demonstrated in this paper using, for illustrative purposes, a simple but realistic example of delegation of roles as understood in Role Based Access Control (RBAC) in security. On–going work investigates *situational events* – a special kind of events which calls for alteration to the risk ordering relation dynamically to account for unfolding scenarios brought about by a chain of failure events.

References

1. Barka E. and Sandhu R. *Framework for Role-Based Delegation Models*. Proceedings of the 16th IEEE Annual Computer Security Applications Conference, pp: 168–175, New Orleans, Louisiana, USA, December, 2000.
2. Dammag H. and Nissanke N. *Safecharts for specifying and designing safety critical systems*. Proceedings of the 18th IEEE Symposium on Reliable Distributed Systems, pp: 78–87, Lausanne, Switzerland, 1999.
3. Dammag H. and Nissanke N. *A Mathematical Definition for Safecharts*. Technical Report, South Bank University, SBU-CISM-03-02 March, 2003.
4. Day N. *A Model Checker for Statecharts (Linking CASE tools with formal Methods)*. Technical Report 93-35, University of British Columbia , Vancouver, Canada, 1993.
5. Glinz, M. *An Integrated Formal Model of Scenarios Based on Statecharts*. LNCS, Vol. 989, pp: 254–271, Springer, 1995.
6. Harel D. *Statecharts: A Visual Formalism For Complex Systems*. Science of Computer Programming, Vol. 8, No. 3, pp: 231–274, North-Holland 1987.

7. Harel D. and Naamad A. *The STATEMATE Semantics of Statecharts.* In ACM Transactions on Software Engineering and Methodology, Vol. 5, Issue 4, pp: 293–333, October 1996.
8. Huizing C. and de Roever W. *Introduction to Design Choices in the Semantics of Statecharts.* Information Processing Letters, Vol. 37, Issue 4, pp: 205–213, 1991.
9. Hong H. S., Kim J. H, Cha S. D and Kwon Y. R. *Static Semantics and Priority Schemes for Statecharts.* Proceedings of the 19th International Computer Software and Applications Conference COMPSAC'95, pp: 114–120, Texas, USA, 1995.
10. Lüttgen G. and Mendler M. *The Intuitionism Behind Statecharts Steps.* In ACM Transactions on Computational Logic, Vol. 3, Issue 1, pp: 1–41, 2002.
11. Maggiolo-Scheltini A., Peron A. and Tini S. *A Comparison of Statecharts Step Semantics.* Theoretical Computer Science Journal, Vol. 290, Issue 1, pp: 465–498, January, 2003.
12. Nissanke N. and Dammag .H *Design for safety in Safecharts with risk ordering of states.* Safety Science, Vol. 40, Issue 9, pp: 753–763, December 2002.
13. Pnueli A. and Shalev A. *What is in a Step: On the Semantics of Statecharts.* In Ito T. and Meyer A.R., editors, Theoretical Aspects of Computer Software, LNCS 526, pp: 244–265. Springer, 1991.
14. Sandhu R., Ferraiolo D. and Kuhn R. *The NIST Model for Role-Based Access Control: Towards A Uinfied Standard.* In Proceedings of 5th ACM Workshop on Role-Based Access Control, pp: 47–64, Berlin, Germany, July, 2000.
15. Von der Beck M. *A Comparison of Statecharts variants.* LNCS 863, pp: 128–148, Springer, Berlin, 1996.

A Relational Model for Formal Object-Oriented Requirement Analysis in UML

Zhiming Liu[1,3], He Jifeng[1], Xiaoshan Li[2], and Yifeng Chen[3]

[1] International Institute for Software Technology
The United Nations University, Macau
{hjf,lzm}@iist.unu.edu
[2] Faculty of Science and Technology
The University of Macau, Macau
xsl@umac.mo
[3] Department of Mathematics and Computer Science
The University of Leicester, UK
{zl2,yc10}@mcs.le.ac.uk

Abstract. This paper is towards the development of a methodology for object-oriented software development. The intention is to support effective use of a formal model for specifying and reasoning during the requirements analysis and design of a software development process. The overall purpose is to enhance the application of the Unified Modelling Language (UML) with a formal semantics in the Rational Unified Software Development Process (RUP). The semantic framework defines the meaning of some UML submodels. It identifies both the *static* and *dynamic* relationships among these submodels. Thus, the focus of this paper is the development of a semantic model to consistently combine a *use-case model* and a *conceptual class diagram* to form a system specification.

Keywords: Object-orientation, UML, use-cases, conceptual models, requirement specification

1 Introduction

Object orientation is now a popular approach in the software industries. UML [11] is the de-facto standard modelling language for the development of software with a broad range of applications, covering the early development stages of requirements analysis and specification and with strong support for design and implementation [16, 5]. Driven by this trend, computer scientists are now intensifying the research to help better understanding and use of OO methods and UML, e.g. [18, 10, 2, 12, 26, 17].

A main feature of UML is that different modelling diagrams are used to represent a system from various views at different levels of abstraction. This however gives rise to the questions of whether different models used in a system development are consistent and how they are related. In [7], problems concerning consistency among the models for different views are classified as *horizontal consistency*, and those about models at different levels of abstraction as *vertical consistency*. Furthermore, consistency of each kind is divided into *syntactical consistency* and *semantic consistency*.

J.S. Dong and J. Woodcock (Eds.): ICFEM 2003, LNCS 2885, pp. 641–664, 2003.

Conditions of syntactical consistency are expressed in UML in terms of the well-formedness rules of OCL (Object Constraint Language) [28]. Obviously semantic consistency requires syntactical consistency. Article [7] studies a particular kind of *behavioral consistency* among different statecharts of a system by translating them into Hoare's CSP. The work in [6] deals with automated checking of horizontal syntactical consistency between a design class diagram and a sequence diagrams of a system at the design level.

In this paper, we provide a unified framework for formal specification for the models used in different activities in RUP [16, 19]. The framework enables us to identify the distinguishable features of different models and to relate and manipulate them as well. These models are UML requirement models including *use-case models* and *class diagrams*, and the design models that are *interaction diagrams* and *design class diagrams*. Our long term aim is to support formal use of UML in requirement specification and analysis, and transformation of requirement models to design models. When it is used within the incremental and iterative RUP, the method allows stepwise refinement and supports object-oriented and component-based software development. We believe this will help to change today's situation that OO software development in practice is usually done in a non-scientific manner based on pragmatics and heuristics. On the other hand, with the incorporation of our model into the incremental and iterative RUP, we hope to improve the use of formal methods in the development of large scale systems.

Our formalization follows the Unifying Theories of Programming of Hoare and He [15] and is based on the relational model for object-oriented programming in [13]. It uses a simple set theory and predicate logic, rather than a particular formal specification language, such as Z or VDM.

In this paper, we focus on only conceptual aspects of object orientation. Most syntactical and semantic consistency conditions defined in this paper have straightforward algorithms for checking and hence support from necessary automated tools. We have started our effort to build such as tool [22].

In the rest of this paper, Section 2 briefly discusses the activities and models in RUP that we intend to formalize. Section 3 introduces a computational model that is similar to the notation of action systems in [25]. Section 4 defines a syntax and a semantics for a conceptual model. Section 5 defines a syntax for use-case model using the relational model developed in [13]. Section 6 gives a semantics for a use case and a *canonical form* of system specification. It shows how a use case behaves in the context of a conceptual model, and captures the consistency between the two models. Finally conclusions and discussion are given in Section 7. Simple examples are used to illustrate the ideas and formalization.

2   Models in Rational Development Process

Requirements capture, analysis, design and modelling are the main technical activities in the early stage of a RUP cycle. Requirements analysis mainly involves the creation and analysis of *use-case models* and *conceptual models* [16, 20, 5].

A *use-case model* consists of a set of *use-case diagrams*, and a family of *use-case descriptions* in text, each describing one use case. Each use-case description specifies a required functional service that the system is expected to provide for certain kinds of users called *actors*. It describes a *use case* in terms of a pattern of interactions between the actors and the system. The use-case diagrams do not provide much semantic information. They only illustrate which actors use which use cases and which use cases are *included* as parts of a use case. Therefore, a use-case model specifies the systems's required functional services, the users of these services, and the dependency relationships among these services. A library system, for example, has use cases to, *Borrow a copy*, *Make a Reservation* and *Validate User Identification* for the actor called **User**. Both *Borrow a Copy* and *Make a Reservation* includes *Validate User Identification*.

A conceptual model for an application is a class diagram consisting of *classes* (also called *concepts*), and *associations* between classes. A class represents a set of *conceptual objects* and an association determines how the objects in the associated classes are related (or *linked*).

For example, the library system has **User**, **Loan**, **Publication** and **Copy**. They are associated so that a *user takes* (currently) a number of loans and a loan *borrows* a copy *of* a publication. Different library systems have different conceptual models and provide different services. A "small" library does not allow a user to make a reservation, while a "big" library may provide this service. A conceptual class diagram is given in Figure 1. In addition to associations between concepts, a concept may have some

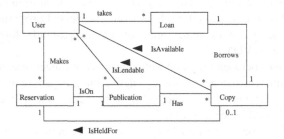

Fig. 1. A conceptual class diagram.

properties represented by *attributes*. For example, **User** has a *name* as an attribute, and **Loan** has a *date* as an attribute.

We say a class diagram is conceptual at this level because it is not concerned with what an object does, how it behaves, or how an attribute is represented. The decision on these issues will be made during design when the *responsibilities* of a use case are decomposed and assigned to appropriate objects. Use case decomposition is carried out according to the *knowledge* that the objects maintain. *What an object can do depends on what it knows, though an object does not have to do all that it can do*. What an object knows is determined by its attributes and associations with other objects. Only when the responsibilities of the objects are decided in the design, can the directions of the associations (i.e. *navigation* and *visibility* from one object to another) be determined. This indicates that an association at the conceptual level are simply sets of pairs of objects and has no direction or equivalently two directions. Therefore, a conceptual model is a *static model* of the *structure* of the application domain.

The relationship between a use-case model and a conceptual model is that the conceptual model specifies the environment, i.e. *the state space*, under which the use cases are to be carried out. A *state* is an *object diagram* that consists of a set of objects and a set of *links* between these objects. Each object and each link in a state must be respectively an instance of a class and an association declared in the conceptual model. An execution step in a use case transforms a state into another. A conceptual model is consistent with a use-case model if it is *adequate* to realize the functional services required by the use-case model.

In *system design*, a requirement specification is realized by a design specification consisting of a *design class diagram* and a family of *interaction diagrams*. The design class diagram models the *software structure* that realizes the conceptual model of the requirement specification. The interaction diagrams (i.e. collaboration diagrams or a sequence diagrams) model the interactions between objects and realize the use cases of the requirement specification. The creation and manipulation of these design models mainly involve use case decomposition and assignment of responsibilities to objects. The interaction diagrams must meet the requirements. This can be proved by showing that the use cases are indeed correctly realized by the interactions between objects. Experience [20] shows that once a design class diagram is obtained, code can be easily produced from it. It is possible to develop a tool to help in transforming a design into a code of implementation.

3   Computational Model

We use a notation similar to a transition or action system [25] to combine the two models together to model a system. A *system* is defined by a tuple $(\alpha, \Phi, \Theta, P)$ where

- α denotes the set of program variables known to the program.
- P is a set of *operations*, each of which is a predicate that relates the initial values of program variables. The predicate is of the form $p(x) \vdash R(x, x')$ (called a design in [15]):

$$p(x) \vdash R(x, x') \stackrel{def}{=} ok \wedge p(x) \Rightarrow ok' \wedge R(x, x')$$

  where x and x' represent the initial and final values of x respectively; ok asserting that the operation is started well and ok' means that the operation terminated; $p(x)$ is called the precondition, and $R(x, x')$ the post-condition or the transition relation.
- Θ is a predicate over α, called the *initial condition* and defines the initial state(s) of the system.
- Φ is a predicate over α, called the *invariant*. It must be true in any initial state and preserved by each operation in P.

An action only changes a subset of variables declared in α. The *normal form* of a design is thus a *framed design* of the form $V : (p \vdash R)$, that denotes $p \vdash R \wedge (\underline{w}' = \underline{w})$, where V and $\underline{w}$ are subsets of α, and $\underline{w} = \alpha - V$. When there is no confusion, we will omit the frame in a design by assuming that a variable x can be changed by a design only if its primed version x' occurs in the design.

The above model has to take into account the following OO aspects.

1. A use case is composed from a number of operations, while a conceptual model determines the following variables on which a use case operates:
   - for every concept, a *class variable* that takes values of sets of objects of the concept;
   - for every object of a concept, a variable for each attribute of the concept;
   - for every association, an *association variable* that take values of sets of links (i.e. pairs) between objects of the associated concepts.
2. Due to the inheritance mechanism, the effect of a use case on a variable depends on its current type during execution, rather than its originally declared type.
3. As in imperative languages, a state of a variable is its current value. An object is represented as a finite tuple that records its *identity*, current type, and the values of its attributes. As an object has no attributes of object types in a conceptual model, there is no recursive nesting needed here. Association variables are used to represent links between objects, which may be realized as object attributes in the later design and implementation.

In summary, a model of an OO requirement is a system $\mathbf{S} = (\alpha, \Phi, \Theta, P)$ where

- P consists of a set of use cases.
- α identifies the variables on which the use cases in P operate and it is determined by the conceptual class diagram and the input and output variables of the program.
- The invariant Φ formally models the invariant constraint. The pair (α, Φ) thus gives the formalization of the conceptual model.
- Θ is a condition to be established when starting up the system.

In the following sections, we formulate these four components of a system specification.

4   Conceptual Model

A conceptual model is a pair $CM = (\mathcal{D}, \Phi)$, where $\mathcal{D}$ is a *class diagram* and Φ is the state constraint on the classes and associations enforced by $\mathcal{D}$.

4.1   Conceptual Class Diagram

A conceptual class diagram $\mathcal{D}$ of an application identifies the environment in which the use cases operate. This environment consists of four parts:

1. The first part provides the *static* information on classes and their inheritance relationships:
   - **CN**: the finite set of classes identified in the diagram. We use bold capital letters to represent arbitrary classes and types.
   - **super**: the partial function which maps a class to its *direct* superclass, i.e. $\mathbf{super}(\mathbf{C}) = \mathbf{D}$ if $\mathbf{D}$ is the direct superclass of $\mathbf{C}$.

2. The second part describes the structure of each class and for $\mathbf{C} \in \mathbf{CN}$, it includes **attr(C)**: the set of $\{< a_1 : \mathbf{T}_1 >, \ldots, < a_m : \mathbf{T}_m >\}$ attributes of **C**, where $\mathbf{T}_i$ stands for the type of attribute a_i of class **C**, and will be referred by $type(\mathbf{C}.a_i)$. As in [1], the type of an attribute is assumed to be a built-in *simple data type*, such as the natural numbers **Nat**. We use **DT** to denote the set of these assumed data types. Each class **C** defines a type, also denoted by **C**. We allow the construction of a type from the direct product of two types, and the power set $\mathbb{P}(\mathbf{T})$ of a type **T**.

3. The third part identifies the relationships among the classes: **AVar**: the finite set of associations captured in the diagram and declared as *association variables*

$$\{A_1 : \mathbb{P}(\mathbf{C}_{11} \times \mathbf{C}_{12}), \ldots, A_m : \mathbb{P}(\mathbf{C}_{m1} \times \mathbf{C}_{m2})\}$$

The type of each A_i, referred by $type(A_i)$, is the powerset $\mathbb{P}(\mathbf{C}_{i1} \times \mathbf{C}_{i2})$. We use **AN** to denote the list $A_1, \ldots, A_m$ of the association names in **AVar**. The separation of the treatments of attributes and associations supports a more flexible design of the interactions or connection between objects [8, 12, 1]. For simplicity, we only deal with binary associations. General relations among classes can be modelled in the same way.

4. For each class name $\mathbf{C} \in \mathbf{CN}$, there is one state variable, denoted by C, whose value records the objects of class **C** currently existing in the system:

$$\mathbf{CVar} \stackrel{def}{=} \{C : \mathbb{P}(\mathbf{C}) | \mathbf{C} \in \mathbf{CN}\}$$

The type of C, denoted by $type(C)$, is $\mathbb{P}(\mathbf{C})$.

The multiplicities of the roles of an association will be specified in the invariant of the conceptual model.

Example The formalization of class diagram in Figure 1 is given as follows, where every class is a subclass of class **Object** and we omit **attr(C)** when **C** has no attributes:

$$
\begin{aligned}
\mathbf{CN} &= \{\mathbf{User}, \mathbf{Loan}, \mathbf{Copy}, \mathbf{Publ}, \mathbf{Resv}\} \\
\mathbf{super(C)} &= \mathbf{Object}, \text{ for all } \mathbf{C} \in \mathbf{CN} \\
\mathbf{attr(User)} &= \{< Id : \mathbf{String}, name : \mathbf{String} >\} \\
\mathbf{attr(Loan)} &= \{< date : \mathbf{Date} >\} \\
\mathbf{AVar} &= \{Takes : \mathbb{P}(\mathbf{User} \times \mathbf{Loan}), Borrows : \mathbb{P}(\mathbf{Loan} \times \mathbf{Copy}), \\
&\quad IsAvailable : \mathbb{P}(\mathbf{Copy} \times \mathbf{User}), \\
&\quad IsLendable : \mathbb{P}(\mathbf{Publ} \times \mathbf{User}), Has : \mathbb{P}(\mathbf{Publ} \times \mathbf{Copy}), \\
&\quad IsHeldFor : \mathbb{P}(\mathbf{Copy} \times \mathbf{Resv}), Makes : \mathbb{P}(\mathbf{User} \times \mathbf{Resv})\} \\
\mathbf{CVar} &= \{User : \mathbb{P}(\mathbf{User}), Copy : \mathbb{P}(\mathbf{Copy}), Loan : \mathbb{P}(\mathbf{Loan}), \\
&\quad Publ : \mathbb{P}(\mathbf{Publ}), Resv : \mathbb{P}(\mathbf{Resv})\}
\end{aligned}
$$

A refinement of the model allows us to add more details, such as attributes and associations [14].

4.2 Inheritance and Well-Formedness Conditions

Every attribute of a class in a conceptual model is inherited by its subclasses. Formally speaking, we require

$$\mathbf{super(C)} = \mathbf{D} \Rightarrow \mathbf{attr(C)} \supseteq \mathbf{attr(D)}$$

Thus, when drawing or describing a class diagram, we do not repeat the attributes of a class in its subclasses.

A class diagram is *well-formed* when following conditions are met:

1. The function **super** does **not** cause circularity:

$$NoCirc \stackrel{def}{=} \mathbf{super}^+ \cap Id = \emptyset$$

where we abuse the notation by treating **super** as a binary relation, with Id denoting the identity relation and the definition using relation composition ";".

$$\mathbf{super}^+ \stackrel{def}{=} \bigcup_{n \geq 1} \mathbf{super}^n, \quad \mathbf{super}^1 \stackrel{def}{=} \mathbf{super}$$
$$\mathbf{super}^{n+1} \stackrel{def}{=} \mathbf{super}^n; \mathbf{super}$$

We use $\mathbf{N} < \mathbf{M}$ to denote that $\mathbf{N}$ is a subclass of $\mathbf{M}$.

2. An association only relate classes in the diagram, i.e.:

$$WFAsso \stackrel{def}{=} \forall(A : \mathbb{P}(\mathbf{C}_1 \times \mathbf{C}_2)) \in \mathbf{AVar} \bullet (\mathbf{C}_1 \in \mathbf{CN} \wedge \mathbf{C}_2 \in \mathbf{CN})$$

3. The association names are all distinct:

$$DistAssoName \stackrel{def}{=} dist(\mathbf{AN})$$

4. Classes should not be related by attributes, i.e. the type of an attribute should not be a class:

$$AssoDistAttr \stackrel{def}{=} \forall \mathbf{C} \in \mathbf{CN}, a \in \mathbf{attr}(\mathbf{C}) \bullet type(\mathbf{C}.a) \in \mathbf{DT}$$

5. The attribute names of a class are distinct:

$$DistAttrName \stackrel{def}{=} \forall \mathbf{C} \in \mathbf{CN} \bullet dist(\pi_1(\mathbf{attr}(\mathbf{C})))$$

where π_1 returns the *list* of the attribute names in $\mathbf{attr}(\mathbf{C})$, and $dist$ is true if the elements in the list are distinct.

Let $W(\mathcal{D}) \stackrel{def}{=} NoCirc \wedge WFAsso \wedge DistAssoName \wedge AssoDistAttr \wedge DistAttrName$ and it defines the well-formedness condition for a class diagrams $\mathcal{D}$.

4.3   Object Diagrams as System States

An object diagram of a class diagram is a state over the $\mathbf{CVar} \cup \mathbf{AVar}$, i.e. a *well typed* mapping from $\mathbf{CVar} \cup \mathbf{AVar}$ to $\mathbb{P}(\mathbf{Object}) \cup \mathbb{P}(\mathbf{Object} \times \mathbf{Object})$.

For an association $A : \mathbb{P}(\mathbf{C}_1 \times \mathbf{C}_2)$ and an object $o_i \in C_i$, $i = 1, 2$, let $A(o_i)$ be the set of objects in the class that is associated with $\mathbf{C}_i$. Formally,

$$A(o_i) \stackrel{def}{=} \{o_{i \oplus 1} \mid o_{i \oplus 1} \in C_{i \oplus 1} \wedge (o_1, o_2) \in A\}$$
$$A(\mathbf{C}_i) \stackrel{def}{=} \bigcup_{o \in C_i} A(o)$$

where $1 \oplus 1 = 2$ and $2 \oplus 1 = 1$. The multiplicities of the roles of an association can now be defined as a state property. Let M_1 and M_2 be subsets of **Int**. We assign M_1 and M_2 as respectively the *multiplicities* of $\mathbf{C}_1$ and $\mathbf{C}_2$ to the association A to enforce the following state property:

$$Multiplicity(A) \stackrel{def}{=} \bigwedge_{i=1,2} \forall o_i \in C_i \bullet (|A(o_i)| \in M_{i\oplus})$$

asserting that the number of objects in C_1 (or C_2 resp.) linked to an object in C_2 (or C_1) is bounded by the range of M_1 (or M_2). We use $A : (M_1, \mathbf{C}_1, \mathbf{C}_2, M_2)$ to represent an association between $\mathbf{C}_1$ and $\mathbf{C}_2$ with multiplicities M_1 and M_2.

It is also required that an association A only links objects that currently exist in the state: for every association $A : \mathbb{P}(\mathbf{C}_1 \times \mathbf{C}_2)$ in $\mathcal{D}$,

$$LinkObjects(A) \stackrel{def}{=} A(\mathbf{C}_1) \subseteq C_1 \wedge A(\mathbf{C}_2) \subseteq C_2$$

A state of a class diagram is *valid* if each association A of the class diagram satisfies both condition $Multiplicity(A)$ and condition $LinkObjects(A)$. In subsequent discussion, we use the term state to refer to a valid state when there is no confusion.

Conditions $Multiplicity(A)$ and $LinkObjects(A)$ define the precise meaning of an association A and the multiplicities of its roles depicted in a UML class diagram. However, only classes, associations, and their multiplicities are not enough to express all the constraints required by an application. In particular, multiplicity restrictions do not allow relationships between associations to be expressed. For example, the library application requires that a copy c that "is held" for a reservation r be a copy of the publication p reserved by the reservation r. UML uses a OCL statement to describes such as constraints. Because OCL is not expressive enough to specify the semantics of use cases, this paper uses a relational logic to specify state assertions. The above constraint in the library application can be described as the state assertion:

$$\forall c \in Copy, r \in Resv, p \in Publ \bullet IsHeldFor(c, r) \wedge IsOn(r, p) \Rightarrow Has(p, c)$$

where $R(a, b)$ iff $< a, b > \in R$. Furthermore, this constraint can be equivalently written in terms of the algebra of relations

$$IsHeldFor \circ IsOn \subseteq Has^{-1}$$

where "$\circ$" is the *composition* operation of relations, and Has^{-1} is the inverse of Has.

4.4   Conceptual Model

A *conceptual model* can now be formally defined as a pair $CM = (\mathcal{D}, \Phi)$ where $\mathcal{D}$ is a class diagram formalized above, and Φ is a state constraint on the states of $\mathcal{D}$. We can use the following Java-like format to specify a conceptual model as follows.

Conceptual Model CM
Class $\mathbf{C}_{11}$ **Extends** $\mathbf{C}_{12}$ $\{\mathbf{T}_{11}\ x_1; \ldots; \mathbf{T}_{1m}\ x_m\}$

$\ldots\ldots$

Class $\mathbf{C}_{n1}$ **Extends** $\mathbf{C}_{n2}$ $\{\mathbf{T}_{n1}\ y_1; \ldots; \mathbf{T}_{nk}\ y_k\}$
Association $(M_1^1, \mathbf{C}_1^1, \mathbf{C}_1^2, M_1^2)\ A_1;\ \ldots;\ (M_j^1, \mathbf{C}_j^1, \mathbf{C}_j^2, M_j^2)\ A_j$
Invariant Φ
End CM

where $\mathbf{C}_1$ **Extends** $\mathbf{C}_2$ denotes that $\mathbf{super}(\mathbf{C}_1) = \mathbf{C}_2$. M_i^1 and M_i^2 are sets of natural numbers and represent the *multiplicities* of the roles $\mathbf{C}_i^1$ and $\mathbf{C}_i^2$ of association A_i, $i = 1, \ldots, j$.

The following syntax can be followed when we write the specification of a conceptual class diagram *ccdec*:

$$ccdec ::= empty | cdec | adec | ccdec;\, ccdec$$

where *empty* denotes the empty diagram, *cdec* a class declaration, and *adec* an association declaration. From such a specification of a diagram $\mathcal{D}$, we can easily calculate the categories of the formal model. An alternative format would be to declare associations as classes with two attributes of the types as the associated classes.

Although we cannot present the formal UML syntax of a class diagram in this paper because of the space limit, the translation *between* a class diagram to its formalization is straightforward and can be automated. Relating the graphic presentation and the formal specification of a model in this way allows the user to obtain the later without necessarily knowing the detailed formality of the specification language.

For a state constraint Ψ, we write $CM \vdash \Psi$ iff $\Phi \Rightarrow \Psi$, meaning that Ψ can be proven from Φ in the relational calculus. This allows us to reason about properties of a conceptual model and relationships between two conceptual models. For example, we can define transformations between conceptual diagrams that have to preserve a state constraint.

4.5 Special Classes and Associations

We also use *state constraints* or *invariants* to specify some special classes and associations.

Abstract Classes. In a conceptual class diagram D, a class $\mathbf{C}$ is called an *abstract class*, if $C = C_1 \cup C_2 \cup \ldots \cup C_k$ is an invariant of the system, where $\mathbf{C}_1, \ldots, \mathbf{C}_k$ are all the direct subclasses of $\mathbf{C}$ and $k \geq 2$. This means an object in the abstract class can only be created as an instance of one of its direct subclasses.

Association Classes. UML allows *association classes* to represent associations that have data properties too. An example is shown in Diagram (a) of Figure 2. **JobContract** is about the association *Employs*. This fact can be modelled by decomposing the association into two associations as shown in Diagram (b) of Figure 2. Notice the multiplicities of **Company** in the association *Has* and **People** in the association *IsFor* are both 1 to ensure that an instance of **JobContract** only relates

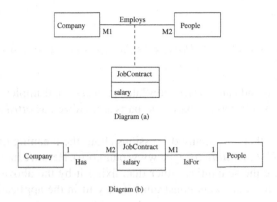

Fig. 2. Example of an association class.

one company and one person. However, we relate the association $Employs$ with the two newly introduced associations by the constraint

$$Has \circ IsFor = Employs$$

In general, we model an association class **AClass** for an association $A : (M_1, \mathbf{C}_1, \mathbf{C}_2, M_2)$ by introducing two fresh associations

$$A_1 : (\{1\}, \mathbf{C}_1, \mathbf{AClass}, M_2) \text{ and } A_2 : (M_1, \mathbf{AClass}, \mathbf{C}_2, \{1\})$$

such that $A_1 \circ A_2 = A$. The decomposition also changes the many-to-many association into one-to-many associations that are much easier to realize in the later design. This treatment of association classes can be also used in applications where an association class relates a number of classes.

Aggregations. An *aggregation* can be safely treated as a general association. Its special properties, such as the visibility of the *whole* class to its *part classes*, are more relevant in the design and implementation and thus should be deferred till the time when we deal with the design. However, the property that a *part* of a *composite whole* exists if and only when the whole itself exists, i.e. parts are created or destroyed when the whole is created or destroyed, can be specified as a state invariant. Assume **Composite** and **Part**$_1, \ldots,$ **Part**$_n$ are classes, and $IsPart_i : (\{m_i\}, \mathbf{Part}_i, \mathbf{Composite}, \{1\})$ are associations in a conceptual class diagram. We say that **Composite** is *composite aggregation* of **Part**$_i$, $i = 1, \ldots, n$, if the following state invariants are true

$$HasParts \stackrel{def}{=}$$
$$\forall c \in Composite \Rightarrow \quad \exists o_{11} \ldots o_{1m_1} \in Part_1, \ldots o_{n1}, \ldots o_{nm_n} \in Part_n \bullet$$
$$IsPart_1(o_{11}, c) \wedge \ldots \wedge IsPart_1(o_{1m_1}, c)$$
$$\wedge \ldots$$
$$\wedge IsPart_n(o_{n1}, c) \wedge \ldots \wedge IsPart_n(o_{nm_n}, c)$$

$$HasWhole \stackrel{def}{=} \bigvee_{i=1}^{n} \exists o \in Part_i \Rightarrow \exists c \in Composite \bullet IsPart_i(o, c)$$

$$NoShare \stackrel{def}{=}$$
$$\bigwedge_{i=1}^{n} (\forall c_1, c_2 \in Composite, o \in Part_i \bullet IsPart_i(o, c_1) \wedge Part_i(o, c_2) \Rightarrow c_1 = c_2)$$

And these invariants indicates a decision later in design and implementation that the whole should the visibility to the parts and parts are realized as *attributes* of the whole class.

Please note that there are many discussions about the meaning of an aggregation, particular on the *pUML mailing list* (see www.puml.org). Here we have provided a way of formally defining the semantics rather than fixing it by the above three invariants. One can of course have different constraints if they fit in the application better. If one wants to avoid any confusion, we suggest the use of a general association and specify the constraints as required.

5   Use-Case Model

A use case model consists of a use-case diagram and a textual description of each use case in the use case diagram. As said earlier, a use-case diagram provides only static information about the use cases. The dynamic semantic aspects are described in the textual descriptions of the use cases as sequences of interactions between actors and the system. Therefore, for a formal design it is more important to formalize the textual description.

An actor of a use case can be any entity external to the system. It interacts with the system by calling a *system operation* to request a service of the system. The system may also require services from actors to carry out a requested service. A UML *system sequence diagram* is used to describe the order of the interaction between the actors of in a use case and the system treated as a black box, but it does not describe the change of the system state caused by such an interaction. It is important to note that a system sequence diagram does not and should not provide information about interaction among objects inside the system [5, 20]. The main task in the system design is in fact to *realize* the use cases by interactions among objects inside the system. This is done by decomposing the responsibilities of the use cases and assigning them to objects as methods.

5.1   System Operations

When an actor calls a system operation to carry out a step of a use case, the execution of the called operation changes the system state, by creating new objects, deleting existing objects; forming or breaking links between objects; modifying attributes of objects. We therefore treat the system under consideration as a *component* and a system operation a *provided method* of the component [3]. We model this component as a *use-case handler class* [20] that encapsulates the classes in the conceptual model:

Class Use-Case-Name-Handler {
     Attr : $\underline{x}$: $\underline{\mathbf{T}}$;
     Method : $op_1(\mathbf{val}\ x_1 : \mathbf{T}_{11}, \mathbf{res}\ y_1 : \mathbf{T}_{21})\{c_1\}$;
             $\ldots$;
     Method : $op_n(\mathbf{val}\ x_n : \mathbf{T}_{1n}, \mathbf{res}\ y_n : \mathbf{T}_{2n})\{c_n\}$
}

where the attributes $\underline{x}$ may include state control variables so that the use case can be defined by a state machine; and for each method $op_i(\mathbf{val}\ x_i : \mathbf{T}_{1i}, \mathbf{res}\ y_i : \mathbf{T}_{2i})\ \{c_i\}$, **val** x_i is a list of value parameters and **res** y_i a list of result parameters. The command c_i in an operation allows us to specify the effect of the operation at different levels of abstractions and is in one of the following forms:

$$c ::= d|\ x := e\ |\ c; c$$
$$\ \ \ \ \ \ |\ \mathbf{var}\ x : \mathbf{T}\ |\ \mathbf{end}\ x \quad \text{variable declaration and undeclaration}$$
$$\ \ \ \ \ \ |\ c \lhd b \rhd c \quad\quad\quad \text{conditional}$$
$$\ \ \ \ \ \ |\ b * c \quad\quad\quad\quad \text{iteration}$$
$$\ \ \ \ \ \ |\ c \sqcap c \quad\quad\quad\quad \text{non-deterministic choice}$$
$$\ \ \ \ \ \ |\ Actor.m \quad\quad\quad \textit{a call to a required method of an actor Actor}$$
$$\ \ \ \ \ \ |\ o.\bar{a}(y)\ |\ o.a(e) \quad \text{reading and resetting attribute}$$

where d is a framed design, b is a Boolean expression and e is an expression. In general, an expression can be in one of the following forms:

$$e ::= x|\mathbf{null}|\mathbf{new}\ \mathbf{C}|\mathbf{self}|e.a|f(e)$$

We use a command **var** x : $\mathbf{T}$ to introduce local variables in a block, and a command **end** x to end the variable block. A set of program variables, denoted by **locvar**, is needed to record the set of local variables in scope in a state. The value of **locvar** is of the form $\{v_1 : \mathbf{T}_1, \ldots, v_m : \mathbf{T}_m\}$.

5.2 Actors

An actor of a use case calls system operations in the use case controller. However, some actors provide services to the system too. We thus can treat an actor as a component which may provide services as well as to request services. As we are only required to design the system under consideration, we only specify an actor's services required by the system in terms of methods in the actor class.

Class Actor {
     Attr : $\underline{x}$: $\underline{\mathbf{T}}$;
     Method $m_1(\mathbf{val}\ x_1 : \mathbf{T}_{11}, \mathbf{res}\ y.\mathbf{T}_{12})\{c_1\}$;
             $\ldots$;
     Method $m_k(\mathbf{val}\ x_k : \mathbf{T}_{k1}, \mathbf{res}\ y_k : \mathbf{T}_{k2})\{c_k\}$;
}

where attributes $\underline{x}$: $\underline{\mathbf{T}}$ may include control state variables; m_i is a method that can be called by the system, but the command c_i in such a method is only a framed design to avoid infinite recursive method calls.

5.3 System Specification

To specify a use case H, we specify its handler **H-Handler** and actors $\mathbf{Actor}_1, \ldots,$ $\mathbf{Actor}_m$. Putting these together we have a specification $Spec(H)$. Suppose that for the design of a system S we have identified the use cases $H_1, \ldots, H_\ell$ and constructed a conceptual model CM. We combine the specification of the conceptual model CM, the use-case handlers and the actors $CM; Spec(H_1); \ldots; Spec(H_\ell)$ to form the *structural specification* of the system, i.e. the conceptual model, the use-handlers, and its environment that consists of the actors classes. This specification can be illustrated graphically in the diagram in Figure 3.

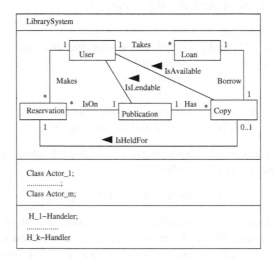

Fig. 3. A system specification.

Each *scenario* or *instance* of a use case is an execution sequence of calls (by actors) to methods in the use-case handler with given input values to the **val** parameters. To describe all possible scenarios of all use cases, we introduce a set **IN** of variables for the input values and a set **OUT** of variables for the output values. Let **L** be a set of *control variables* that are used to control the order of the execution of the use *case actions* (that will be formally defined soon). In general, scenarios of a use case can be executed concurrently and this needs multiple instances of the use-case handler class.

Let the system state variables be those declared in the conceptual model **CVar**, that now includes the use-case handler and the actor classes, **AVar** that now includes an association between a use-case handler and an actor if the use-case handler requires services from the actor.

Now define $\alpha \overset{def}{=} \mathbf{AVar} \cup \mathbf{CVar} \cup \mathbf{IN} \cup \mathbf{OUT} \cup \mathbf{L}$. Let Φ be the state constraint of the conceptual model conjoining with the condition that each actor class has a single instance. We use a predicate Θ to specify the initial states for starting up the system. Θ has to imply some instances of each use-case handler class **H-Handler**, and the instance of each actor class **Actor**, denoted by $Actor$, have already been created.

A *use case action* is a guarded command $g \longrightarrow c$, where g is a boolean expression over **IN** $\cup$ **OUT** $\cup$ **L** and c is a command on **IN** $\cup$ **OUT** $\cup$ **L** to process the input and output values, or a call $h.op$ to a method op of an instance of a use-case handler **H-Handler**. A *use case* is a set U_h of use case actions that contains calls to the same use-case handler instance h. Let P be a set of use cases, a *system requirement specification* S is then of the *canonical form*

$$Spec(S) \stackrel{def}{=} CM; Spec(H_1); \ldots; Spec(H_\ell) \bullet P$$

We thus have obtained the transition system model $(\alpha, \Phi, \Theta, P)$ for the system S.

In the case for sequential programs, only one instance h of a use-case handler **H-Handler** is needed and $h.op$ is simply written as op. Then each use case U_H is a piece of sequential program, and whole program P is an iterative deterministic choice among the use cases:

$$\neg stop * (read(service); \mathbf{if} \, \{service = H \longrightarrow U_H\} \, \mathbf{fi}; read(stop))$$

where $read(x) \stackrel{def}{=} true \vdash x' \in type(x)$.

A call to a system operation $m(\mathbf{val} \, x, \mathbf{res} \, y)$ can also be written as a CSP-like process

$$m?x \longrightarrow m(x, y); m!y$$

Then use case H as a whole can be written as a CSP process U_H and the program P in the canonical system specification can be specified as an iterative process $(U_{H_1} [] \cdots [] U_{H_\ell})^*$.

Therefore our methodology is:

- For a sequential software development, after the system operations are identified and specified in the use-case handler classes, writing the formal specification of the use cases becomes writing a specification of the *main method* P of the object-oriented software.
- For a concurrent system, writing the formal specification of the use cases is to write the specification of the *run methods* of the concurrent actors that requires services from the system.
- However, as suggested in RUP and UML, the development takes a sequential view first and treats concurrency in the implementation stage by using *activity diagrams*. Then the design and implementation of the system is mainly to design and implement the system operations by decomposing them into interactions between objects of the system.

This is a typical top-down development, but the use cases and system operations can be taken in turns in an iterative process.

Example. For the library application, use case *BorrowCopy* is about how an actor *Borrower* can borrow a copy of a publication. Obviously, its pre-conditions are: an user and the copy are currently known to the system, the publication of the copy is lendable to the user, and the copy is currently available. The effect of the use case is to create a loan to record the fact that the user has taken this loan on the copy, and the copy not available anymore. The system has to record the date of the loan. For this, the system needs to interact with the system clock to get the date. Therefore this use case has another actor, and we call it *Clock* that is *partially* specified here as follows

$$\textbf{Class Clock} \{$$
$$\textbf{Attr} : \textbf{Date} \ date, \ \textbf{Time} \ time;$$
$$\textbf{Method} : \ getDate(\textbf{res} \ out : \textbf{Date})\{true \vdash out' = date\}$$
$$\}$$

The use-case handler can be given below

$$\textbf{Class BorrowCopy-Handler} \{$$
$$\textbf{Method} \ BorrowCopy(\textbf{val String} \ Cid, \ \textbf{String} \ Uid)\{$$
$$\textbf{Pre} \ \exists c \in Copy, u \in User \bullet c.Id = Cid \wedge u.Id = Uid \wedge$$
$$IsLendableTo(Has(c), u) \wedge IsAvailable(c, u);$$
$$\textbf{var Loan} \ \ell; \ell := \textbf{New Loan}();$$
$$\textbf{var Date} \ date; Clock.getDate(date); \ell.(date); \textbf{end} \ date;$$
$$Loan := Loan \cup \{\ell\};$$
$$Borrow := Borrow \cup \{< \ell, c >\}; Takes := takes \cup \{< u, \ell >\};$$
$$IsAvailable := IsAvailable / \bigcup_{u \in User} \{< c, u >\}$$
$$\textbf{end} \ \ell$$
$$\}$$
$$\}$$

Strictly speaking, use case *BorrowCopy* is not well-formed regarding to the given conceptual model in Section 4.1, as class **Copy** has no attribute Id declared. However, if we refine (following a refinement rule in [14]) the conceptual model by adding this attribute to class **Copy**. The specification becomes well-formed.

Introducing input variables Uid and Cid and assuming BorrowCopy-Handler is the instance of the given use-case handler class already created, use case *BorrowCopy* is programmed by the following statement:

$$read(Uid, Cid); BorrowCopy(Cid, Uid)$$

This corresponds to a system sequence diagram in which actor *Borrower* calls method *BorrowCopy* of the system and the system calls $getDate()$ method of the clock.

Suppose we declare in the use-case handler class three operations $FindU()$ that finds the user for a given user identifier, $FindC()$ that finds the copy for an input copy identifier, and $RecordL()$ that checks whether a loan can be made and records it if so. The *BorrowCopy* use case can be refined to or *zoomed in* [5] the following use cases

$$read(Uid, Cid); Find(Uid, u); FindC(Cid, cp);$$
$$RecordL(u, cp) \triangleleft (u \neq null \wedge cp \neq null) \triangleright \bot$$

The system calls the $getDate()$ method of the clock in $RecordL()$. Thus the above program corresponds to the system sequence diagram in which actor *Borrower* calls method $FindUser()$, then $FindC()$ and then $RecordL()$ of the system, after receiving the call of $RecordL()$, the system calls $getDate()$ of actor $Clock$. This sequence diagram is a refinement of the earlier one. This refinement is carried out without changing the underlying conceptual model.

Another dimension of refinement is to refine the conceptual model together with the use cases. For example, the association $Isavailable$ can be realized by a boolean attribute IsA of class **Copy** such that for every copy c and every user u, $Isavailable(c, u)$ iff $IsA = true$. Then checking the availability off a copy becomes simply checking this variable. This kind of refinement corresponds the traditional data refinement. Both refinements we have just discussed are not involved with allocation of parts of the computation of a system operation to internal objects of the system [14]. We have a *delegation rule* in [14] to deal with delegating part of a method of an object to an object in another class. Formal transformation of a use-case model into a UML object sequence diagrams is out of the scope of this paper.

6 Semantics

This section defines a semantics of a system specification. We start with showing how to validate an expression and determine its value.

6.1 Expressions

To validate an expression e, we introduce a predicate $W(e)$ which is true just in those circumstances in which e can be successfully evaluated.

A state binds variables in α to their values. A variables of type **DT** simply takes a value of that type. However, a variable of a class **C** takes an object of **C** as it value. An object is defined in terms of its *identity*, values of its attributes, and its current type:

$$\{identity \mapsto id\} \cup \{class \mapsto \mathbf{C}\} \cup \{a \mapsto value | a \in \mathbf{attr}(\mathbf{C})\}$$

For the identities of objects, we require that $o_1(identity) = o_2(identity)$ iff $o_1 = o_2$. $W(e)$, $type(e)$, and the value of e are defined as follows:

- x is well-formed if it is known in the environment of the use case: $W(x) \stackrel{def}{=} x \in \alpha$.
- $W(\mathbf{null}) \stackrel{def}{=} true$, and $type(\mathbf{null}) \stackrel{def}{=} \mathbf{NULL}$. **NULL** is a reserved class name and a subclass of all classes. The identity of **null** is undefined and **null** is the only object without an identity.
- The variable **self** is only used as local variable when defining $o.\bar{a}(y)$ and $o.a(e)$:

$$W(\mathbf{self}) \stackrel{def}{=} \mathbf{self} \in \mathbf{locvar}$$

- **new C** is well-formed if **N** is declared:

$$W(\mathbf{new\ C}) \stackrel{def}{=} \mathbf{C} \in \mathbf{CN} \qquad type(\mathbf{new\ C}) \stackrel{def}{=} \mathbf{C}$$
$$\mathbf{new\ C}(class) \stackrel{def}{=} \mathbf{C}$$
$$\mathbf{new\ C}(identity) \notin \{id | \exists o \in C\bullet\ o(identity) = id\}$$

new$C(identity)$ is *fresh* and this will be also specified by **newC** $\notin C$.

- $e.a$ is well formed if e is an object, and a is a declared attribute of the class of e:

$$W(e.a) \overset{def}{=} W(e) \wedge type(e) \in \mathbf{CN} \wedge a \in \mathbf{attr}(type(e))$$
$$type(e.a) \overset{def}{=} type(type(e).a)$$
$$e.a \overset{def}{=} e(a)$$

- Well-formedness of built-in expressions $f(e)$ is defined by the building rules. For example, for two association variables $A_i : (M_{i1}, \mathbf{C}_{i1}, \mathbf{C}_{i2}, M_{i2})$, $i = 1, 2$,

$$W(A_1 \circ A_2) \overset{def}{=} W(A_1) \wedge W(A_2) \wedge \mathbf{C}_{21} \leq \mathbf{C}_{12}$$

This means if we want to derive a composition association from two given associations A_1 and A_2 the target class C_{12} of A_1 should be the source class A_{21} or a superclass of it.

6.2   Commands

Each command c is defined as a predicate of the form $W(c) \Rightarrow D(c)$. $W(c)$ is true when the command is well-formed in the initial state and captures the consistency of the conceptual model with the command. $D(c)$ is of the form a framed design $V :$ $p(x) \vdash R(x, x')$ and captures the dynamic behavior of the command c. This integrates syntactic consistency and semantic consistency check mechanism with the traditional specification-oriented semantics. Let $skip \overset{def}{=} \varnothing : (true \vdash true)$ be the command that does nothing and terminates successfully, and the command $chaos \overset{def}{=} \varnothing : (false \vdash true)$ that has unpredictable behaviour:

Let P and Q be designs. The notation $P \lhd b \rhd Q$ describes a design which behaves like P if b is true in the initial state, and like Q otherwise.

$$P \lhd b \rhd Q \overset{def}{=} W(b) \wedge (type(b) = \mathbf{B}) \Rightarrow (P \wedge b \vee Q \wedge \neg b)$$

We use the condition $\mathbf{Pre}\ b \overset{def}{=} (skip \lhd b \rhd chaos)$ to represent a Floyd assertion, which behaves like $chaos$ if the initial value of b is false, otherwise it has no effect. This is useful when we specify the precondition of a use case.

Let $\{P_i | 1 \leq i \leq n\}$ be a family of designs. The multiple conditional choice

$$\mathbf{if}\ \{(b_i \rightarrow P_i) | 1 \leq i \leq n\}\ \mathbf{fi}$$

selects P_i to execute if its guard b_i is true. When all the guards are false it behaves like $chaos$:

$$\mathbf{if}\ \{(b_i \rightarrow P_i) | 1 \leq i \leq n\}\ \mathbf{fi} \overset{def}{=}$$
$$\bigwedge_{i:1...n}(W(b_i) \wedge type(b_i) = \mathbf{B}) \Rightarrow (\bigvee_{i:1...n}(b_i \wedge P_i) \vee \neg(\bigvee_{i:1...n} b_i) \wedge chaos)$$

For the non-determinism, let P and Q be designs. $P \sqcap Q \overset{def}{=} P \vee Q$ stating that it behaves either like P or Q.

The command $P; Q$ is executed by first executing P followed by executing Q when P terminates. The final state of P is passed on as the initial state of Q.

$$P(x, x'); Q(x, x') \stackrel{def}{=} \exists m \bullet P(x, m) \wedge Q(m, x')$$

If b is a condition, the iteration $b * P$ repeats P as long as b is true before each iteration:

$$b * P \stackrel{def}{=} \mu X \bullet (P; X) \lhd b \rhd skip$$

where $\mu X \bullet F(X)$ denotes the weakest fixed point of the recursive equation $X = F(X)$. The semantics of an assignment is defined by the following design:

$$x := e \stackrel{def}{=} W(x) \wedge W(e) \wedge (type(e) \leq type(x)) \Rightarrow \{x\} : (true \vdash (x' = e))$$

Declaration **var** $x : \mathbf{T}$ introduces a new program variable x to allow x of type $\mathbf{T}$ to be used in the portion of the program that follows it. The complementary command takes the form **end** x. It terminates the region of allowable use of x:

$$\mathbf{var}\ x : \mathbf{T} \stackrel{def}{=} x \notin \alpha \Rightarrow \mathbf{locvar} : (true \vdash \mathbf{locvar}' = \mathbf{locvar} \cup \{x : \mathbf{T}\})$$

$$\mathbf{end}\ x \stackrel{def}{=} x \in \mathbf{locvar} \Rightarrow \mathbf{locvar} : (true \vdash \mathbf{locvar}' = \{x\} \lhd \mathbf{locvar})$$

where $\{x\} \lhd \mathbf{locvar}$ denotes the set **locvar** after removing variable x. For convenience, we allow variables to be declared together in a list **var** $x_1 : \mathbf{T}_1, \ldots, x_k : \mathbf{T}_k$ as the short hand of **var** $x_1 : \mathbf{T}_1; \ldots;$ **var** $x_k : \mathbf{T}_k$.

To avoid direct access to object attributes in order for further implementation, we use an attribute reading command to get the value of an object's attribute, and an attribute resetting command to update an object's attribute. This is important for further refinement. The behavior of these two commands are defined as follows.

$$o.\overline{a}(y) \stackrel{def}{=} (W(o) \wedge W(y) \wedge type(o) \in \mathbf{CN} \wedge a \in \mathbf{attr}(o(class))) \Rightarrow$$

$$\mathbf{if}\ \{(o(class) = \mathbf{C}) \rightarrow \begin{pmatrix} \mathbf{var}\ z : \mathbf{T}, \mathbf{self} : \mathbf{C}; \mathbf{self} := o; \\ \{z\} : (\mathbf{T} = type(\mathbf{C}.a) \vdash z' = \mathbf{self}.a); \\ y := z; \mathbf{end}\ z, \mathbf{self} \end{pmatrix}$$

$$| \mathbf{C} \in \mathbf{CN}\} \mathbf{fi}$$

$$o.a(e) \stackrel{def}{=} (W(o) \wedge W(e) \wedge type(o) \in \mathbf{CN} \wedge a \in \mathbf{attr}(o(class))) \Rightarrow$$

$$\mathbf{if}\ \{(o(class) = \mathbf{C}) \rightarrow \begin{pmatrix} \mathbf{var}\ z : \mathbf{T}, \mathbf{self} : \mathbf{C}; z := e; \mathbf{self} := o; \\ \{\mathbf{self}.a\} : (\mathbf{T} = type(\mathbf{C}.a) \vdash \mathbf{self}'.a = z); \\ o := \mathbf{self}; \mathbf{end}\ z, \mathbf{self} \end{pmatrix}$$

$$| \mathbf{C} \in \mathbf{CN}\} \mathbf{fi}$$

6.3 Declarations

In Section 4.4, a syntax of the specification of a conceptual model was given, which is composed from class declarations and association declarations. We treat the semantics of a declaration in the same way as treating a command, i.e. we define its semantics as a design.

A class declaration **Calass C_1 Extends C_2 $\{T_1\ a_1; \ldots; T_m\ a_m\}$** modifies the logic variables **Cvar**, **super** and **Attr** according to the following design

$$\left(\begin{array}{l} C_1, C_2 \in CN \\ \land\ C_2 \in CVar \\ \land\ \bigwedge_{i+1}^{m} a_i \notin Attr(C_2) \end{array} \right) \vdash \left(\begin{array}{l} CVar' = CVar \cup \{C_1 : \mathbb{P}C_1\} \\ \land\ super' = super \cup \{C_1 \mapsto C_2\} \\ \land\ Attr' = Attr\cup \\ \quad \{C_1 \mapsto \{a_i : T_i | 1 \le i \le m\} \cup Atrr(C_2)\} \end{array} \right)$$

This design says that the declaration declares a new class C_1 as a subclass of C_2 and the newly added attributes of C_1.

Similarly, an association declaration **Association** $(M_1, C_1, C_2, M_2)\ A$ adds a new association to **AVar** and the state constraints on this association into the set **Invariant**:

$$C_1, C_2 \in CVar \land A \notin AVar \vdash \left(\begin{array}{l} AVar' = AVar \cup \{A : \mathbb{P}(C_1 \times C_2)\} \\ \land\ Invariant' = Invariant \\ \quad \land Multiplicity(A) \land LinkObjects(A) \end{array} \right)$$

A declaration of an actor or a use-case handler introduces methods as well as class variables and attributes. For this, we introduce a logic variable **Meth** that is a function from **CN** to the set of method definitions of the form

$$op(\mathbf{var}\ x : T_1, \mathbf{res}\ y : T_2)\{c\}$$

Now, given a declaration of an actor or a use-case handler class

> **Class A {**
>   **Attr** : $\underline{x}$: $\underline{T}$;
>   **Method** $m_1(\mathbf{val}\ x_1 : T_{11}, \mathbf{res}\ y_1 : T_{12})\{c_1\}$;
>   ...;
>   **Method** $m_k(\mathbf{val}\ x_k : T_{k1}, \mathbf{res}\ y_k : T_{k2})\{c_k\}$;
> **}**

Its semantics is defined by the design

$$A \in CN \vdash \left(\begin{array}{l} CVar' = CVar \cup \{A\} \\ \land\ Attr' = Attr \cup \{A \mapsto \underline{x} : \underline{T}\} \\ \land\ Meth' = Meth \cup \{A \mapsto \{m_i def \mid 1 \le i \le k\}\} \end{array} \right)$$

where $m_i def$ is $m_i(\mathbf{var}\ x_i : T_{1i}, \mathbf{res}\ y_i : T_{2i})\{c_i\}$.

According to the semantics of sequential definition given in the previous subsection, the semantics of the structural specification of a system $CM; Spec(H_1); \ldots; Spec(H_\ell)$ given in Section 5.3 is now well defined and calculates the alphabet α and the state invariant Φ of the transition system $S = (\alpha, \Phi, \Theta, P)$.

6.4   Call to a Required Method

Let *vale* and *rese* be lists of expressions. A call *Actor.m(vale, rese)* to a method of an actor assigns the values of the actual parameters *vale* to the formal value parameters

val x of the declared method m. After it terminates, the values of the result parameters **res** y of op are passed back to the actual value parameters $rese$.

$$Actor.m(vale, rese) \stackrel{def}{=} m \in \mathbf{Meth}(type(Actor)) \Rightarrow \begin{pmatrix} \mathbf{var}\ x : \mathbf{T}_1, y : \mathbf{T}_2; \\ x := vale; y := rese; \\ type(Actor).m; \\ rese := y; \mathbf{end}\ x, y \end{pmatrix}$$

where

- $\mathbf{Meth}(type(Actor))$ is the set of methods declared in the class of $Actor$.
- x, y are the value and result parameters of the method m.
- $type(Actor).m$ stands for the design associated with the command of m defined in the actor class $type(Actor)$.

Notice that $type(Actor) = \mathbf{Actor}$.

6.5 System Specification

An action of a use case that is a call to a method of a use-case handler $h.op(val, res)$ is defined similar to a call to a method of an actor by a use-case handler:

$$op \in \mathbf{Meth}(type(h)) \Rightarrow \begin{pmatrix} \mathbf{var}\ x : \mathbf{T}_1, y : \mathbf{T}_2; \\ x := vale; y := rese; type(type(h)).op; \\ rese := y; \mathbf{end}\ x, y \end{pmatrix}$$

The semantics of a guarded action $g \longrightarrow c$ is $W(g) \Rightarrow g \wedge c$, where $W(g)$ is true g is a Boolean expression over $\mathbf{IN} \cup \mathbf{OUT} \cup \mathbf{L}$.

We define the semantics of a system $S = (\alpha, \Psi, \Theta, P)$ be the set of infinite state sequences

$$[\![\mathbf{S}]\!] \stackrel{def}{=} \{\sigma_0, \sigma_1 \ldots, \mid \sigma_i \in \Sigma_\alpha\}$$

such that

- Σ_α is the set of states over α.
- σ_0 satisfies the initial condition Θ and each state transition (σ_{i-1}, σ_i) is carried out by an enabled call to a method in the use-case handler, i.e. there an action $U \in P$ such that $(\sigma_{i-1}, \sigma_i) \models U$.
- Ψ is a proof obligation that each action $U \in P$ preserves this invariant in the sense that $(g \wedge Pre(U) \wedge \Psi) \Rightarrow (Post(U) \Rightarrow \Psi')$, where g is the guard of action U, $Pre(U)$ is the precondition and $Post(U)$ the post-condition of design U, and Ψ' is the predicate obtained from Ψ by replacing each free variable x with it primed version x'.

A *refinement* of a system can be carried out by refining a method in a use-case handler.

7   Conclusion and Related Work

7.1   Conclusion

We have given a relational model for UML conceptual diagrams and use cases. The conceptual model of a system declares the system variables, and its object diagrams form the system state space. We formally define a use-case model of a system to describe the interactions between the system and its external environment that consists of the actors of the use cases. Both the actors and the system are treated as components that have *required services* as well as *provided services*. The execution of a call to a system service by an actor will cause a change of the system state with some new objects created, some existing objects deleted, some new links between object established, some existing links between objects removed, and values of some object attributes modified. It enhances RUP for OO software development with a formal method roughly as follows: we first write a use case informally; then construct a conceptual model based on the use case; then draw a system sequence diagram and identify the methods of the use-case handler class; transform the conceptual model into a formal specification and formally specify these methods are in the notation provided in this paper; then check the consistency of these methods with the conceptual model with the method provided in this paper; refine the conceptual model and the use-case specification if they are not consistency; for an executable specification[1], test it by running it for some input values; finally we can take this specification into the design, implementation, and testing. This completes a cycle. Then new use cases can then be specified, analyzed, and the existing conceptual model is refined to support the newly added use cases. During the design of a new use case, one can reuse the methods of classes that have already been designed. For more details about the integration of the formal method in this paper with RUP can be found in [23].

The formalism is based on the design calculus in Hoare and He's Unifying Theories of Programming [15]. Some of the mathematics may seem rather theoretical at first, but the approach is quite practical. For example, the choice of a java-like syntax for the specification language is a pragmatic solution to the problems of representing name spaces and (the consequences of) inheritance in a notation such as CSP.

7.2   Related Work

Instead of taking a process view, such as that in [9, 4], we keep an object-oriented and state-based approach and the specification in a java-like style. We specify consistency between the models in the preconditions in terms of well-formedness conditions of use cases.

Our work [24] establishes the soundness and (implicity) the completeness of the action systems for both conceptual and use-case modelling. This paper, extend that work with a formal notation for the specification. Our related work [21] demonstrates that our method supports stepwise refinement and reflects the informal way of using UML

---

[1] If the program specification is not executable but realizable, refine it into an executable specification.

for requirement analysis. Use-case refinement can be carried out using the traditional refinement calculus of imperative programs, and can be done by refining the methods provided in the use case-case handlers one by one [14].

We take a similar schema of the semantics of UML proposed in [26], where different kinds of diagrams of a UML model are given individual semantics and then such semantics are composed to get the semantics of the overall model. However, unlike [26] that uses an universal algebraic approach, we use a simple predicate theory to define a specification language with a syntax similar to Java programming language. We believe that this feature makes the method more accessible to people who are familiar to the general theory of programming languages. The main difference between our work and that in [7, 6] is that we study formal semantic relationships between different models of UML, rather than only formalization of individual diagrams. The paper [12] also treats a class as a set of objects and an association as a relation between objects, but it does not consider use cases. This model of associations can also be used in the specification of *connectors* in architecture models [8, 27, 1]. Our work also shares some common ideas with [2] in the treatment of use cases. However, our treatment of use cases is at the system interface level without referring to the design details about how internal objects of the system behave, or what methods that a class of the system provides. We believe our model is simpler and addresses the tight relationships among different models more clearly. Also in our model, actors are not only users of the system but also service providers. We will carry out the design of the system by decomposing the methods in the use-case handlers, in turns one by one, and assign the decomposed responsibilities to classes of the conceptual model. This is the main task in the creation of UML interaction diagrams, i.e. *object sequence diagrams* or *collaboration diagrams*. The formalization of such a design within our framework in [14] is given in [23]. The main difference between our work and most of the work of the precise UML consortium (see www.puml.org) is that, rather than trying to formalize individual views of UML, we aim to tightly combine different views in a unified formal language, and our formal language provided built-in facilities to naturally capture the object-oriented features of UML, rather than using a traditional formalism which were not designed for object-oriented systems to derive the definitions of classes, objects, inheritance, etc.

In this paper, we have focused on only conceptual aspects of object orientation. The transformation of a UML conceptual model into a formal specification can be easily automated. We can refine a use case specified in our notation to executable specification without the need the the details of inter-object interaction or the internal behavior of objects. We can thus execute the use case to generate the post state (i.e. the post object diagrams) from the pre-state (i.e. pre-object diagram) of the use case to validate the use case and to check the consistency between the use case and the conceptual model. Then based on the generated object-diagrams and our work on the refinement calculus for object systems [14], we can decompose the use cases by "zooming them in" [5]. In [22], we have developed a method for automatic generation of a prototype from a formal specification of a UML requirement model. A prototype generated that way can be used for the validation of a use-case model and a conceptual model, as well as to check the state invariants and the consistency between a use-case model and a conceptual model.

Acknowledgement

We would like to thank Chris George for his useful comments on the work, and the referees for their comments that has helped us to improve the presentation.

References

1. N. Aguirre and T. Maibaum. A temporal logic approach to component-based system specification and verification. In *Proc. ICSE'02*, 2002.
2. R.J.R. Back, L. Petre, and I.P. Paltor. Formalizing UML use cases in the refinement calculus. Technical Report 279, Turku Centre for Computer Science, Turku, Finland, May 1999.
3. J. Cheesman and J. Daniels. *UML Components. Component Software series*. Addison-Wesley, 2001.
4. J. Davies and C. Crichton. Concurrency and refinement in the unified modelling language. In *Preliminary Proceedings of REFINE'02: An FME Sponsored Refinement Workshop in Collaboration with BCS FACS*, Copenhagen, Denmark, 2002.
5. D. D'Souza and A.C. Wills. *Objects, Components and Framework with UML: The Catalysis Approach*. Addison-Wesley, 1998.
6. A. Egyed. Scalable consistency checking between diagrams: The Viewintegra approach. In *Proc. of the 16th IEEE International Conference on Automated Software Engineering*, San Diego, USA, 2001.
7. G. Engels, J.M. Kuster, R. Heckel, and L. Groenewewegen. A methodology for specifying and analyzing consistency of object-oriented behavioral models. In *The Proc. of International Conference on Foundation of Software Engineering, FSE-10*, Austria, 2001.
8. J. Fiadeiro and T. Maibaum. Design structures for object-based systems. In S. Goldsack and S. Kent, editors, *Fomal Methods and Object Technology*. Springer-Verlag, 1996.
9. C. Fischer, E-R. Olderog, and H. Wehrheim. A CSP view on UML-RT structure diagrams. In Heinrich Hussmann, editor, *4th FASE, Genova, Italy, 2001, Proceedings*, volume 2029 of *LNCS*, pages 91–108. Springer, 2001.
10. R. France, A. Evans, K. Lano, and B. Rumpe. The UML as a formal modeling notation. *Computer Standards & Interfaces*, 19:325–334, 1998.
11. Object Modelling Group. Unified Modelling Language Specification, version 1.3. URL: uml.shl.com:80/docs/UML.1.3/99-06-08.pdf, 1999.
12. D. Harel and B. Rumpe. Modeling languages: Syntax, semantics and all that stuff - part I: The basic stuff. Technical Report MCS00-16, The Weizmann Institute of Science, Israel, September 2000.
13. J. He, Z. Liu, and X. Li. A relational model for object-oriented programming. Technical Report UNU/IIST Report No 231, UNU/IIST, P.O. Box 3058, Macau, March 2001.
14. J. He, Z. Liu, and X. Li. Towards a refinement calculus for object-oriented systems. In *Proc. ICCI02, Alberta, Canada*. IEEE Computer Scociety, 2002.
15. C.A.R. Hoare and J. He. *Unifying theories of programming*. Prentice-Hall International, 1998.
16. I. Jacobson, G. Booch, and J. Rumbaugh. *The Unified Software Development Process*. Addison-Wesley, 1999.
17. J. Jürjens. Formal semantics for interacting UML subsystems. In *FMOODS 2002*, pages 29–44, 2002.
18. S. Kent. Constraint diagrams: Visualising invariants in object-oriented models. In *OOPSLA97*. ACM Press, 1997.
19. P. Kruchten. *The Rational Unified Process – An Introduction. 2nd edition*.

20. C. Larman. *Applying UML and Patterns*. Prentice-Hall International, 2001.
21. X. Li, Z. Liu, and J. He. Formal and use-case driven requirement analysis in UML. In *COMPSAC01*, pages 215–224, Illinois, USA, October 2001. IEEE Computer Society.
22. X. Li, Z. Liu, and J. He. Generating a prototype from a UML model of system requirements. Submitted for publication, 2003.
23. J. Liu, Z. Liu, X. Li, and J. He. Towards an integrating a formal method with the Rational Unified Process. Submitted for publication, 2003.
24. Z. Liu, X. Li, and J. He. Using transition systems to unify uml models. In Chris George, editor, *The Proceedings of 4th International Conference on Formal Engineering Methods, ICFEM2002, in LNCS 2495*, pages 535–547, Shanghai, China, October 2002. Springer-Verlag.
25. Z. Mana and A. Pnueli. The temporal framework for concurrent programs. In R.S. Boyer and J.S. Moore, editors, *The Correctness Problem in Computer Science*, pages 215–274. Academic Press, 1981.
26. G. Reggio, M. Cerioli, and E. Astesiano. Towards a rigorous semantics of UML supporting its multiview approach. In H. Hussmann, editor, *Proc. FASE 2001, number 2029, Lecture Notes in Computer Science*. Springer Verlag, 2001.
27. B. Selic. Using UML for modelling complex real-time systems. In F. Muller and A. Bestavros, editors, *Languages, compilers, and Tools for Embedded Systems, Volume 1474 of Lecture Notes in Computer Science*, pages 250–262. Springer Verlag.
28. J. Warmer and A. Kleppe. *the Object Constraint Language: precise modeling with UML*. Addison-Wesley, 1999.

From Specification to Hardware Device: A Synthesis Algorithm

Vincenza Carchiolo, Michele Malgeri, and Giuseppe Mangioni

Dipartimento di Ingegneria Informatica e delle Telecomunicazioni
V.le A. Doria, 6 – I95125 Catania, Italy
{VCarchiolo,MMalgeri,GMangioni}@diit.unict.it

Abstract. Raising complexity of hardware devices being developed and increasing time-to-market constraints has scaled up the risk of designing bug-affected devices augmenting the interest into formal design techniques. This approach considerably improves early error detection, giving good guaranties on the effectiveness of the devices produced. To deploy the design some techniques must be provided to synthesise the device preserving its features. The proposed technique defines an hardware translation of LOTOS specifications into a Register Transfer Level language. To preserve LOTOS synchronisation semantics an handshake protocol is defined.

Keywords: Hardware Design, Synthesis, Rapid System Prototyping

1 Introduction

Until a few years ago hardware systems were designed using CAD tools, mainly based on graphic editors, which enabled designers to define the electrical scheme of the connections between the various components, and programs whereby it was possible to extract a certain amount of information from them. This information was used to test and simulate the behaviour of the device. Interpretation of the results depended on the ability of designers who used their experience to guarantee the correctness of the design.

Recent technologies allow the development of very complex hardware devices. This complexity, together with increasing time-to-market constraints, has scaled up the risk of designing bug-affected devices. In fact, they can cause serious damage and also do harm in the case of critical safety devices.

For this reason the need has been felt, in the last few decades to update design techniques in order to use formal techniques. This approach considerably improves early error detection, giving good guarantees on the effectiveness of the devices produced. A widely used design path starts with a requirement specification and validation step devoted to formalising and verifying the device requirements. Formal techniques allows us to perform device validation with mathematical techniques rather then simulation-based techniques. This validation step is followed by device synthesis that allows to map the formal specification onto the device implementation.

J.S. Dong and J. Woodcock (Eds.): ICFEM 2003, LNCS 2885, pp. 665–681, 2003.

In [1] we proposed a direct-synthesis approach of a formal specification. The proposed approach used a Formal Description Technique (FDT) named Language Of Temporal Ordering Specification (LOTOS [2]). LOTOS is successfully used for hardware specification as illustrated by [3][4]. Our approach starts with the LOTOS specification of the device, then it is validated (by means of model checking or theorem proving) and finally, the specification of the device is synthesised into a Register Transfer Level (RTL) Language. The synthesis algorithm proposed is a syntax-direct one, that is for each LOTOS operator a corresponding hardware implementation is defined. In this paper we describe the translation into RTL of the basic LOTOS operators. In LOTOS, it is possible to describe several synchronisation mechanisms featuring the presence of one or more processes that can transmit or receive information. Translation of the synchronisation mechanisms from LOTOS to RTL is accomplished only in the presence of a single transmitter and one or more receivers. The other LOTOS synchronisation mechanisms are not taken into account, because they are of little interest in hardware applications. Translation of the complex LOTOS synchronisation into RTL requires the use of several signals to guarantee the semantic correctness of the translation. The need for two signals for synchronisation is due to the fact that communication in LOTOS is a rendez-vous between events.

In literature there exist other examples of synthesis of LOTOS specifications into hardware devices. In [5] a technique to transform a LOTOS specifications into a VHDL specification is presented, but it is restricted to two-way synchronisation. In [6] a LOTOS synthesis algorithm that uses an EFSM model of a LOTOS specification is presented. This approach implements the multi-way synchronisation among processes using a rendezvous table that models the synchronisation mechanism.

Section 2 introduces LOTOS peculiarities. Section 3 discusses the implementation model of the synchronisation. Section 6 describes the synthesis algorithm and in section 7 a case study is shown.

2   LOTOS

LOTOS basic idea is that the behaviour of a system can be described by observing from the outside the temporal order in which events occur. In practise, the system is seen as a black-box which interacts with the environment by means of events, the occurrence of which is described by LOTOS behaviour expressions.

The language has two components: the first is the description of the behaviour of processes and their interaction, and is mainly based on the CCS[7] and CSP[8]; the second is the description of the data structure and expressions, and is based on ACT ONE[9].

In LOTOS distributed systems are described in terms of processes; the system as a whole is represented as a process, but it may consist of a hierarchy of processes (often called subprocesses) which interact with each other and the environment. LOTOS models a process by its interaction with the environment.

The atomic forms of interaction take the name of events. The definition of a process in LOTOS is:

```
process <proc-id> <par-list> := <behaviour-expression>
endproc
where:  <proc-id>    is the name to be assigned to the process;
        <par-list>   is the list of gates with which the
                     process can interact with the environment;
```

`<behaviour-expression>`s are the LOTOS expressions which define the behaviour of the process The recursive occurrence of a process-identifier in a behaviour expression makes it possible to define infinite behaviour (both auto- and mutual recursion are possible). A completely inactive process, i.e. one which cannot execute any event, is represented by `stop`. In the following we describe the basic operators by which it is possible to describe any system.

The action prefix represents the basic synchronisation. This operator produces a new behaviour expression from an existing one, prefixing it with the name of an event. If B is a behaviour expression and a is the name of an event, the expression a;B indicates that the process containing it first takes part in the event a and then behaves as indicated by the expression B.

The choice operator models the nondeterministic behaviours which takes place when two (or more) event are available. If B1 and B2 are two behaviour expressions, then B1 [] B2 denotes a process which can behave either B1 or B2. Choice between the two forms of behaviour is made by the environment.

To simplify the description of the system being specified a lot of derived operator are present in LOTOS. They can be easily rewritten in term of the basic one but the resulting specification is longer and difficult to understand. Some of the derived operators are described in the following.

The arbitrary interleaving represents the independent composition of two processes, B1 and B2 and is indicated as B1 ||| B2. If the two processes have some event in common, B1 ||| B2 indicates their capacity to synchronise with the environment but not with each other.

The parallel operator is indicated as B1 || B2 and it means that the two processes have to synchronise with each other in all events. B1 || B2 can take part in an event if and only if both B1 and B2 can participate. The general parallel composition is a general, way of expressing the the parallel composition of several events and is denoted with the expression B1 |[a_1,...,a_n]| B2.

The sequential composition of two processes, B1 and B2, is indicated as B1>>B2 and model the fact that when the execution of B1 terminates successfully B2 is executed ("`>>`" is also known as an enabling operator). To mark successful termination, there is a special LOTOS process called `exit`.

Every LOTOS behaviour expression can be preceded by a Boolean condition, called guard, which determines whether the expression is to be executed or not.

The introduction of types makes it possible to describe structured events. They consist of a label or gate name which identifies the point of interaction, or gate (i.e. an event), and a finite list of attributes. Two types of attributes

Table 1. Type of interactions among processes.

process B_1	process B_2	sync condition	int. sort	effect
$g!E_1$	$g!E_2$	value(E_1) = value(E_2)	matching	synchronisation
$g!E$	$g?x : t$	value(E) $\in$ domain(t)	passing	after synch. x = value(E)
$g?x : t$	$g?y : u$	$t = u$	generation	after synchronisation
				$x = y = v,\ \forall v \in$domain($t$)

are possible: value declaration and variable declaration. Table 1 presents the permitted interactions.

3   Implementation Model of Synchronisation

In this section the model of the complex LOTOS synchronisation mechanism is illustrated. As discussed in section 2, the synchronisation among LOTOS processes takes place through interaction points named *gate*. Three kind of synchronisation can be modelled in LOTOS:

1. synchronisation with no data exchange;
2. *value declaration* $g!x$, in which a gate is ready to synchronise itself offering a data x. In this case we refer to the gate as *transmitter*;
3. *variable declaration* $g?y$, in which a gate is ready to synchronise itself accepting a data that will be stored in y. In this case we refer to the gate as *receiver*;

In this paper we discuss about synchronisation model under the hypothesis that in each randez-vous mechanism are involved no more than a transmitter (with the same name), whereas, can be involved several receiver. Synchronisation in which are involved only receivers or with more than one transmitter are out of scope of this paper, in fact in describing hardware device these cases are not remarkable.

LOTOS *choice* operator describes the nondeterminism among the occurrence a set of events. The synthesis algorithm solve the nondeterministic choice with a policy discussed in 6.1.

Each gate involved in an event is modelled with four signals (READY, ACK, ENABLE, DATA ENABLE) used to implement the multi-way rendezvous. These signals take up different sense according to whether gate is a *transmitter* or a *receiver*.

Receiver

Let a_i, a gate, refer to:

- $[a_i]_r$ an output signal through gate a_i (READY signal). When it is raised denotes to the *transmitter*, the receiver availability to take part in the synchronisation.
- $[a_i]_a$ an input signal through gate a_i (ACK signal). When it is raised denotes the *transmitter* availability to take part in the synchronisation.

- $[a_i]_e$ an output signal (ENABLE signal). It is meaningful only in the case of nondeterminism in a *choice* This signal is used to select one among several events offered.
- $[a_i]_v$ an output signal through a_i (DATA ENABLE signal). It enables data storing in x_i.

Transmitter

Let a_i, a gate, refer to:

- $[a_i]_r$ an input signal through gate a_i (READY signal), it notifies to a_i the availability of all *receiver* to take part in the synchronisation. It is the result of the logic AND among all READY signals emitted by the *receivers*.
- $[a_i]_a$ an output signal through gate a_i (ACK signal). It became high to notify *receivers transmitter* availability to take part in the synchronisation. This signal is emitted after the READY signal reception from all *receivers* involved.
- $[a_i]_e$ an input signal through gate a_i (ENABLE signal). It is meaningful only in the case of nondeterministic *choice*. It is the result of the logic AND among all ENABLE signals emitted by the *receivers*.
- $[a_i]_v$ an output signal through a_i (DATA ENABLE signal). It enables the data reading of x_i.

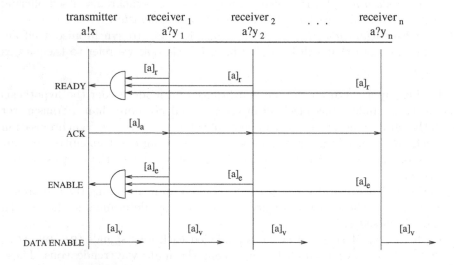

Fig. 1. Interactions among transmitter and receivers.

Now, we discuss our approach in the more general case, that is the one-to-many synchronisation, in which are involved one transmitter and n receivers. The synchronisation it is solved in four phases (see figure 1):

1. all the *receivers* set high the READY signal to notify their availability to take part in synchronisation. The *transmitter* READY signal is equal to the logic AND of all *receivers* READY signals. The READY signal is raised, the transmitter will be certain that all receiver are ready to synchronise.

2. In this phase the *transmitter* raises the ACK signal to notify the receiver of the rendezvous starting.
3. In this phase each *receiver* raises his ENABLE signal. Whereas the ENABLE signal of the *transmitter* is the logic AND of all *receiver* ENABLE signals. As said above, this signal is used to manage the selection among all the possible synchronisation event.
4. Each gate (both *transmitter* or *receiver*) that take part in synchronisation raises its DATA ENABLE signal to allow the data transfer.

4   Notation

Each LOTOS behaviour-expression can be expresses in term of a set of *choice-expressions*. For this reason, the synthesis algorithm is based on direct synthesis of a generic choice expression. In this section, we introduce several useful notation.

Given a *choice* expression:

- let be N the total number of branches;
- let be M the branches guarded by an event;
- let be K the branches being *transmitter* (!) and $M - K$ being *receivers* (?);
- let be $\mathcal{A}$ the finite set of atomic actions;
- let be $\mathcal{P}$ the finite set of LOTOS processes names (included stop and exit).

Definition

1. we denote $\mathcal{TRANS}$ as the ordered set (with signature K) of 4-uple $(a_i, B_i, x_i, cond_i)$ for $i = 1..K \mid [cond_i] \rightarrow a_i!x_i; B_i$ is a transmitter branch of *choice*, where:
   - $a_i \in \mathcal{A}$ denotes the event if the $i - th$ branch;
   - B_i denotes the *behaviour expression* following action a_i;
   - $!x_i$ denotes the *value offering* by variable x_i thought gate a_i;
   - $cond_i$ denoted the boolean guard of $i - th$ branches;
   In the following we denote with $\mathcal{T}_i$ each 4-uple $\in \mathcal{TRANS}$.
2. we denote $\mathcal{RECVS}$ as the ordered set (with signature $M - K$) of 5-uple $(a_i, B_i, x_i, type_i, cond_i)$ for $i = K + 1..M \mid [cond_i] \rightarrow a_i?x_i : type_i; B_i$ is a receiver branch of the *choice* where:
   - $a_i \in \mathcal{A}$ denotes the event if the $i - th$ branch;
   - B_i denotes the *behaviour expression* following action a_i;
   - $?x_i : type_i$ denotes a *variable offering* of the variable x_i of type $type_i$
   - $cond_i$ denotes the boolean guard of $i - th$ branches;
   In the following we denote with $\mathcal{R}_i$ each 5-uple $\in \mathcal{RECVS}$.
3. we denote $\mathcal{PROCS}$ as the ordered set (with signature $N - M$) of 2-uple $(P_i, cond_i)$ for $i = M + 1..N \mid [cond_i] \rightarrow P_i$ is the branch of the *choice* with process P_i instantiation, where:
   - $cond_i$ denotes the boolean guard of $i - th$ branch;
   - $P_i \in \mathcal{P}$ denotes the instantiation of a process.

In the following we denote with $\mathcal{PR}_i$ the 2-uple $\in \mathcal{PROCS}$.

Using the above notation, a generic *choice* can be written as follows (where we use $\sum$ instead of $[\,]$):

$$choice(\mathcal{TRANS}, \mathcal{RECV}, \mathcal{PROCS}) = \sum_{\mathcal{T}_i \in \mathcal{TRANS}} [cond_i] \rightarrow a_i!x_i; B_i +$$

$$\sum_{\mathcal{R}_i \in \mathcal{RECVS}} [cond_i] \rightarrow a_i?x_i : type_i; B_i +$$

$$\sum_{\mathcal{PR}_i \in \mathcal{PROCS}} [cond_i] \rightarrow P_i \qquad (1)$$

Definition

- Given a 4-uple $\mathcal{T}_i \in \mathcal{TRANS}$, we define a function $S_{\mathcal{T}}^k$ which returns the l'*kth* element of $\mathcal{T}_i$ with $k = 1..4$.
- Given a 5-uple $\mathcal{R}_i \in \mathcal{RECVS}$, we define a function $S_{\mathcal{R}}^k$ which return the l'*kth* element of $\mathcal{R}_i$ with $k = 1..5$.
- Given a 2-uple $\mathcal{PR}_i \in \mathcal{PROCS}$, we define a function $S_{\mathcal{PR}}^k$ which return the *kth* element of $\mathcal{PR}_i$ with $k = 1..2$.

Using the previous notation, each choice can be modelled using (1).

Value Offering
A behaviour expression in which a gate a offers a value x and then behaves like process B (that is $a!x; B$) is a sub-cases of generic *choice* and can be obtained by (1) with the following parameters :

$$choice(\{(a, B, x, true)\}, \{\}, \{\})$$

Variable Offering
A behaviour expression in which a gate a able to accept a value x of type *type* and then behaves like process B (that is $a?x : type; B$) is a sub-cases of generic *choice* and can be obtained by (1) with the following parameters:

$$choice(\{\}, \{(a, B, x, type, true)\}, \{\})$$

Example
The following *choice* expression:

```
[guard1] -> a1!x1;B1
[]
[guard2] -> a2?x2:type2;B2
[]
[guard3] -> P1
```

can be expressed by (1) with the following parameters:

$$choice(\{(a1, B1, x1, guard1)\}, \{(a2, B2, x2, type2, guard2)\}, \{(P1, guard3)\})$$

5   The Target RTL Language

The RTL language used throughout this paper is a language which can define the structure of a generic digital system. Any digital system is modelled by using a functional block which receives information from the external environment by using signals and processes them producing output signals (the response to the environment). Each functional block is implemented by the *control unit* and the *processing unit*. The first unit provides the signal to synchronise the operations performed by the second. The full system is based on a single *clock* which provides the synchronisation. The basic hypothesis is that the circuit must be stable before the clock cycle finishes. The RTL module is defined by the following sections:

- components: it contains the declaration of the components which make up the processing unit.
- control sequence: it defines the internal command sequence which must be emitted by the control unit.
- permanent assignment: it defines an operation which must be repeated every clock cycle.

The control sequence is made up of steps; each one is numbered and must be executed in a single clock unit. Each step is made up of one or more commands which are executed in parallel. All the commands belonging to a step are separated by ;. Therefore the control sequence has the following form:

```
i:   op1; op2; op3
j:   op4; op5
```

where i and j are the generic step i and step j and op_i are the commands.

The main constructs of the language are the assignment and the conditional. The first represents the transfer of a value between two registers. The right hand side of the operation can contain any Boolean operation. The two operators are represented as follows:

```
i:   targetRegister := sourceRegister
j:   targetRegister := sourceRegister_1 and sourceRegister_2 or...
k:   if( c1; c2 ) then (op1; op2)
h:   if( c3; c4 ) goto (n; m)
```

To describe a direct connection between elements, the language allows us to describe the assignment of a value to a line; in this case the assignment is only valid for one clock cycle. It is described by the operator "=" and it is also used to describe the assignment to output lines.

The *exit*(< *parameter* >) construct denotes the termination of the module; this is signalled on the wire called < *parameter* > setting it high.

6   Synthesis Algorithm

6.1   Restrictions

In this paragraph we present some of the hypothesis on which the synthesis process is based, and in particular which restrictions we impose in the use of LOTOS.

The basic element of LOTOS is the event, which consists of the interaction between processes based on a rendez-vous mechanism. As said in section 2 three different types of interaction are present in LOTOS: *value matching, value generation* and *value passing*. The only one which is meaningful for our application is value passing because it has a correspondence with the physical reality of devices, thus it is the only one we have taken into account.

The instantiation of processes in LOTOS plays a fundamental role in the specification of systems; some situations which are syntactically correct cannot be used due to the static nature of hardware. The main limit imposed on the use of processes lies in the use of recursion and in the form of the gate list. Recursion requires the use of the same gate list for any instantiation of the process.

Mutual recursion must be avoided because it can generate a dynamic structure and therefore it has no correspondence in hardware. Moreover, self- instantiation is only allowed if the gate list is not modified.

In the implementation of the choice operator we have to solve the nondeterminism typical of this operator because it cannot be easily implemented in either hardware or software.

Moreover in a choice all the guards related to a process instantiation must be mutually exclusive with respect to all other guards (we consider all branches without guards as they are guarded by TRUE). More formally:

$$\forall\, i, j, l \; where \; i = 1..K, \; j = K + 1..M, \; l = M + 1..N$$

$$valueOf(S^2_{\mathcal{PR}}(\mathcal{PR}_l)) \neq valueOf(S^4_{\mathcal{T}}(\mathcal{T}_i))$$

$$AND$$

$$valueOf(S^2_{\mathcal{PR}}(\mathcal{PR}_l)) \neq valueOf(S^5_{\mathcal{R}}(\mathcal{R}_j))$$

Where function $valueOf(arg)$ returns the value of the expression arg. We are working on discarding some of the above limitations.

6.2   Translation of Choice into RTL

In this section the synthesis of a generic LOTOS choice and some simple examples are presented. The proposed technique is valid under the restrictions discussed in section 6.1.

The following RTL module is the synthesis of a generic choice, parametrised with respect to the number and types of branches.

RTL instruction labelled by 1 implements the first phase of synchronisation (see section 3). In this phase the selection among synchronisation that can take place is performed. Depending on the selected branch (*transmitter* or *receiver* or *process instantiation*) one of next blocks will be executed. In particular, first block (beginning from line $(3i - 1)$ for $i = 1 \ldots K$) implements the *i-th transmitter*, second block (beginning from line $(K + 2i)$ for $i = (K + 1) \ldots M$) implements the *i-th receiver* and third block (beginning from line $(M + K + i + 1)$ for $i = (M + 1) \ldots N$) implements the *i-th process instantiation* branch.

$$choice(\mathcal{TRANS}, \mathcal{RECVS}, \mathcal{PROCS})_{RTL} =$$

$$1: \bigcup_{i=K+1}^{M} [S_{\mathcal{R}}^{1}\mathcal{R}_i)]_r = 1;$$

$$if \Bigg(not \ \Big(\bigvee_{i=1}^{K} ([S_{\mathcal{T}}^{1}(\mathcal{T}_i)]_r \ and \ S_{\mathcal{T}}^{4}(\mathcal{R}_i)) \ or \ \bigvee_{i=K+1}^{M} ([S_{\mathcal{R}}^{1}(\mathcal{R}_i)]_a \ and \ S_{\mathcal{R}}^{5}(\mathcal{R}_i)) \ or \ \bigvee_{i=M+1}^{N} (S_{\mathcal{PR}}^{2}(\mathcal{PR}_i)));$$

$$\bigcup_{i=1}^{K} \Big(([S_{\mathcal{T}}^{1}(\mathcal{T}_i)]_r \ and \ S_{\mathcal{T}}^{4}(\mathcal{T}_i)) \quad and \quad \bigwedge_{j=1}^{i-1} not \ ([S_{\mathcal{T}}^{1}(\mathcal{T}_j)]_r \ and \ S_{\mathcal{T}}^{4}(\mathcal{T}_j)));$$

$$\bigcup_{i=K+1}^{M} \Big(([S_{\mathcal{R}}^{1}(\mathcal{R}_i)]_a \ and \ S_{\mathcal{R}}^{5}(\mathcal{R}_i)) \quad and \quad \bigwedge_{j=1}^{K} not([S_{\mathcal{T}}^{1}(\mathcal{T}_j)]_r \ and \ S_{\mathcal{T}}^{4}(\mathcal{T}_j))$$

$$and \quad \bigwedge_{j=K+1}^{i-1} not([S_{\mathcal{R}}^{1}(\mathcal{R}_j)]_a \ and \ S_{\mathcal{R}}^{5}(\mathcal{R}_j)));$$

$$\bigcup_{i=M+1}^{N} \Big(((S_{\mathcal{PR}}^{2}(\mathcal{PR}_i)) \ and \ \bigwedge_{j=1}^{K} not([S_{\mathcal{T}}^{1}(\mathcal{T}_j)]_r \ and \ S_{\mathcal{T}}^{4}(\mathcal{T}_j))$$

$$and \quad \bigwedge_{j=K+1}^{M} not([S_{\mathcal{R}}^{1}(\mathcal{R}_j)]_a \ and \ S_{\mathcal{R}}^{5}(\mathcal{R}_j)) \ and \ \bigwedge_{j=M+1}^{i-1} not(S_{\mathcal{PR}}^{2}(\mathcal{PR}_j))); \Big)$$

$$goto\Big(1; \bigcup_{i=1}^{K} (2 + 3(i - 1)); \bigcup_{i=K+1}^{M} ((2 + 3K) + 2(i - (K + 1))); \bigcup_{i=M+1}^{N} ((2M + K + 2) + (i - (M + 1))); \Big)$$

$$for \quad i = 1 \ldots K$$

$$(3i - 1) : [S_{\mathcal{T}}^{1}(\mathcal{T}_i)]_a = 1$$

$$(3i - 1) + 1 : if \ (not[S_{\mathcal{T}}^{1}(\mathcal{T}_i)]_e; [S_{\mathcal{T}}^{1}(\mathcal{T}_i)]_e) \ goto(1; (3i - 1) + 2)$$

$$(3i - 1) + 2 : [S_{\mathcal{T}}^{1}(\mathcal{T}_i)]_v = S_{\mathcal{T}}^{3}(\mathcal{T}_i); exit(i)$$

$$\ldots$$

$$for \quad i = (K + 1) \ldots M$$

$$(K + 2i) : [S_{\mathcal{R}}^{1}(\mathcal{R}_i)]_e = 1$$

$$(K + 2i) + 1 : S_{\mathcal{R}}^{3}(\mathcal{R}_i) := [S_{\mathcal{R}}^{1}(\mathcal{R}_i)]_v; exit(i)$$

$$\ldots$$

$$for \quad i = (M + 1) \ldots N$$

$$(M + K + i + 1) : exit(i)$$

In the following the above formula is used to produce the RTL description of the simple examples presented in section 4.

Value Offering

$$choice(\{(a, B, x, true)\}, \{\}, \{\})_{RTL} =$$

$$1 : if \ (not \, (a_r \ and \ true); \ a_r \ and \ true) \quad goto \ (1; 2)$$

$$2 : a_a = 1$$

$$3 : if \ (not \ a_e; \ a_e) \quad goto \ (1; 4)$$

$$4 : a_v = x; \ exit(1)$$

Variable Offering

$$choice(\{\}, \{(a, B, x, type, true)\}, \{\})_{RTL} =$$

$1 : a_r = 1; \ if \ (not\,(a_a \ and \ true)\,; \ a_a \ and \ true) \quad goto \ (1; 2)$

$2 : a_e = 1$

$3 : x := a_v; \ exit(1)$

Example

$$choice(\{a1, B1, x1, guard1\}, \{(a2, B2, x2, type2, guard2)\}, \{P1, guard3\})_{RTL} =$$

$1 : a1_r = 1;$

   $if \ ($

      $not\,((a1_r \ and \ guard1) \quad or \quad (a2_a \ and \ guard2) \quad or \quad ((guard3))\,;$

      $(a1_r \ and \ guard1)\,;$

      $((a2_a \ and \ guard2) \ and \ not \ (a1_r \ and \ guard1))\,;$

      $((guard3) \ and \ not\,(a2_a \ and \ guard2) \ and \ not \ (a1_r \ and \ guard1))\,;$

   $) \ goto \ (1; 2; 5; 7)$

$2 : a1_a = 1$

$3 : if \ (not \ a1_e; \ a1_e) \ goto \ (1; 4)$

$4 : a1_v = x1; \ exit(1)$

$5 : a2_e = 1$

$6 : x2 := a2_v; \ exit(2)$

$7 : exit(3)$

6.3   Graphic Layout

RTL being a representation of actual devices, it is possible to draw a netlist using proper blocks. Each block represents a choice operator, the unique difference lies in number of input/output terminals which actually depends on the number of branches.

Figure 2 shows the generic choice block, the signals are grouped as follows:

- *transmitter.* For each gate (a_i) needs five signals to implement the synchronisation model of transmitters: $[a_i]_r$, $[a_i]_a$, $[a_i]_e$, $[a_i]_v$, $cond_i$;
- *receiver.* For each gate (a_i) needs five signals: $[a_i]_r$, $[a_i]_a$, $[a_i]_e$, $[a_i]_v$, $cond_i$;
- *processes/guards.* These groups collects all the signals needed to implement the synchronisation of branch where a process instantiation is present. Only one signal is needed and it is $cond_i$;
- *control.* This group collects signals needed to drive the block:

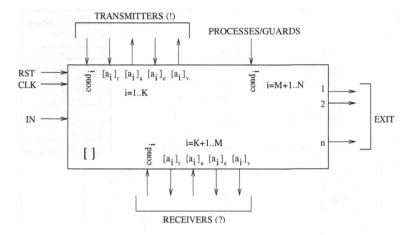

Fig. 2. Generic *choice* Block.

- IN. When it is raised the choice starts, usually it is connected to the exit signal of another block;
- EXIT. When it is raised active choice has finished and is going to activate the next. They are equal to the number of branches;
- RST. It resets the block;
- CLK. The clock.

7   Case Study

In order to show the applicability of the methodology, we will use the example of the traffic light controller [10] (see figure 3).

The problem consists of the creation of a device for controlling the traffic lights of a crossroad between a small farm road and a big highway road, in order to maximise the time during which the green signal remains on the highway. This device must operate in order to keep the traffic light of the highway with the green signal for at least a time equal to "long". At any moment after "long", if there are cars waiting on the farm road, the traffic light on the farm road must switch to the green signal. This condition must persist until there are still some cars on the farm road, or until a time equal to "long" has passed.

In both traffic lights the yellow signal must persist for a time equal to "short". The system consists of 5 modules:

1. block that generates the times "short" and "long" (Clock);
2. farm road traffic light;
3. highway road traffic light;
4. sensor that communicates, through signals "CP" and "CnP", whether cars are present or not on the farm road;
5. traffic light controller.

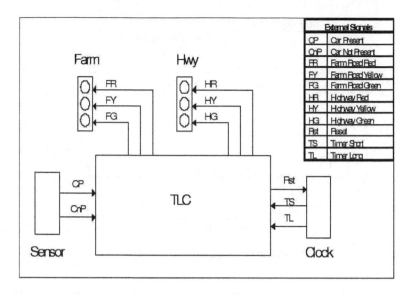

Fig. 3. Traffic light controller schema.

The block Clock, after receiving the reset (Rst) signal, emits a "TS" signal after a time equal to "short", and then emits a "TL" signal after a time equal to "long". Let us assume that the traffic light in the farm road is at the beginning in the red state, while the one in the highway road is in the green state. The Traffic Light Controller manages the synchronization between the two traffic lights and the sensor. The traffic light on the highway is kept in the green state for at least a time equal to "long". **Da modificare** It then remains green while no cars are in the farm road; otherwise, it switches to yellow, and remains in that state for a time equal to "short", and it then becomes red. The traffic light in the farm road becomes green when the one in the highway becomes red. It remains green until there are still some cars, or until a time equal to "long" passes. Then it switches to yellow for a time equal to "short" and becomes red again, enabling the traffic light in the highway road at the same time. Let us assume that modules Clock, Sensor and the two traffic lights already exist. The module TLC must be synthetized according to what has been informally specified before.

In figure 4 the LOTOS TLC specification is shown. It is divided in two main blocks: Timer and Controller, each one subdivided into other subprocesses. The Timer works as an interface between the external Clock and the module Controller. The module Controller implements the control functions of traffic lights, by interfacing with the module Timer and with the external Sensor module. The Controller consists of four other modules, each representing a state of the system. For the sake of semplicity we discuss the synthesis of the process FarmGreen only. As can be seen in figure 4 the process FarmGreen is a four-way choice:

```
(" Traffic Light Controller Specification ")
specification TLC [Rst, TS, TL, CP, CnP, FR, FY, FG, HR, HY, HG]:noexit
behaviour
Hide Str, LG, SH in
  Timer[TS, TL, Rst, SH, LG, Str]
    |[Str, LG, SH]|
  Controller [Str, CP, CnP, FY, FG, FR, HY, HG, HR, LG, SH]
where
process Timer [TS, TL, Rst, SH, LG, Str] : noexit :=
        Str; Rst; (TS; SH; Timer01 [TS, TL, Rst, SH, LG, S]
                  []
                      Timer[TS, TL, Rst, SH, LG, Str]
                  )
      where
      process Timer01 [TS, TL, Rst, SH, LG, Str] : noexit :=
              TL; (LG; Timer [TS, TL, Rst, SH, LG, Str]
                  []
                      Timer[TS, TL, Rst, SH, LG, Str]
                  )
              []
              Timer[TS, TL, Rst, SH, LG, Str]
          endproc
endproc

process Controller [Str, CP, CnP, FY, FG, FR, HY, HG, HR, LG, SH] : noexit :=
        FR; HG; FarmRed [Str, CP, CnP, FY, FG, FR, HY, HG, HR, LG, SH]
      where
      process FarmRed [Str, CP, CnP, FY, FG, FR, HY, HG, HR, LG, SH] : noexit :=
          Str; SH; LG; WaitCar [Str, CP, CnP, FY, FG, FR, HY, HG, HR, LG, SH]
        where
        process WaitCar [Str, CP, CnP, FY, FG, FR, HY, HG, HR, LG, SH] : noexit :=
            CP; HY; Str; SH; HR; FG; Str; FarmGreen [Str, CP, CnP, FY, FG, FR, HY, HG, HR, LG, SH]
          []
          CnP; WaitCar [Str, CP, CnP, FY, FG, FR, HY, HG, HR, LG, SH]
          where
          process FarmGreen [Str, CP, CnP, FY, FG, FR, HY, HG, HR, LG, SH] : noexit :=
              CP; FarmGreen [Str, CP, CnP, FY, FG, FR, HY, HG, HR, LG, SH]
            []
            LG; FarmYellow [Str, CP, CnP, FY, FG, FR, HY, HG, HR, LG, SH]
            []
            SH; FarmGreen [Str, CP, CnP, FY, FG, FR, HY, HG, HR, LG, SH]
            []
            CnP; FarmYellow [Str, CP, CnP, FY, FG, FR, HY, HG, HR, LG, SH]
            where
            process FarmYellow [Str, CP, CnP, FY, FG, FR, HY, HG, HR, LG, SH] : noexit :=
                FY; Str; SH; FR; HG; FarmRed [Str, CP, CnP, FY, FG, FR, HY, HG, HR, LG, SH]
              endproc (" Farm Yellow ")
            endproc (" Farm Green ")
          endproc (" WaitCar ")
        endproc (" Farm Red ")
    endproc (" Controller ")

endspec (" TLC ")
```

Fig. 4. Traffic light controller specification.

1. synchronizes on CP and behaves as FarmGreen;

2. synchronizes on LG and behaves as FarmYellow;

3. synchronizes on SH and behaves as FarmGreen;

4. synchronizes on CnP and behaves as FarmYellow.

Therefore the process FarmGreen is synthetised by two blocks: the former is RTL translation of the four-way choice, the latter is the FarmYellow process implementation. RTL translation of the four-way choice is as follow:

$choice(\ \{\},$

$\qquad \{\ \ (CP, FarmGreen, null, void, true),$

$\qquad\qquad (LG, FarmYellow, null, void, true),$

$\qquad\qquad (SH, FarmGreen, null, void, true),$

$\qquad\qquad (CnP, FarmYellow, null, void, true)\},$

$\qquad \{\}\ )_{RTL} =$

$1\ :\ [CP]_r = 1;\ [LG]_r = 1;\ [SH]_r = 1;\ [CnP]_r = 1;$

$\qquad if\ ($

$\qquad\qquad not([CP]_a\ or\ [LG]_a\ or\ [SH]_a\ or\ [CnP]_a);$

$\qquad\qquad ([CP]_a);$

$\qquad\qquad ([LG]_a\ and\ not\ [CP]_a);$

$\qquad\qquad ([SH]_a\ and\ not\ [LG]_a\ and\ not\ [CP]_a);$

$\qquad\qquad ([CnP]_a\ and\ not\ [SH]_a\ and\ not\ [LG]_a\ and\ not\ [CP]_a);$

$\qquad)\ goto(1;\ 2;\ 4;\ 6;\ 8)$

$2\ :\ [CP]_e = 1$

$3\ :\ null; exit(1)$

$4\ :\ [LG]_e = 1$

$5\ :\ null; exit(2)$

$6\ :\ [SH]_e = 1$

$7\ :\ null; exit(3)$

$8\ :\ [CnP]_e = 1$

$9\ :\ null; exit(4)$

The label *null* in the above RTL code means that no value is exchanged during synchronizations, according to LOTOS specification of the process FarmGreen. Actually this label is a dummy operation then it can be removed. Figure 5 shows the schematic of the synthetised FarmGreen. As can be seen, signals $exit(1)$ and $exit(3)$ are directly connected to the input of the choice because firing either CP or SH leads to the re-instantiation of the same process. This fact is equivalent to substitute $exit(1)$ and $exit(3)$ with $goto(1)$. Instead $exit(2)$ and $exit(4)$ jumps to the first instruction of the module FarmYellow. Figure 5 show the HW synthesis of all other modules that form the TLC.

8 Conclusions

Designing hardware devices is an hard task due to the complexity of the system, strictly time-to-market constraints and risk linked to safety application. Using formal techniques to help designer to develop error-free devices represents a good solution but several tools are needed to make comfortable this approach.

In this paper we focus on the synthesis of the specification starting from LO-TOS. First, we describe the structure of the hardware device implementing the

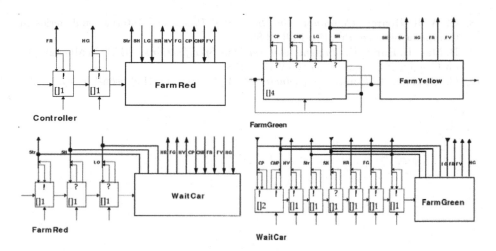

Fig. 5. Hw implementation of TLC.

LOTOS *choice* operator, than, thanks to the LOTOS features, the specification of the device being implemented is transformed in order to use only *choices* operators. *Choice* translation is described by a parametric RTL expression which covers all possible type of synchronisation. Finally, an example of application of the proposed synthesis technique is presented.

Currently a prototype implementation of the synthesis algorithm is under testing in order to develope a full design tool.

Further study needs to optimise resulting devices in order to reduce either wire or flip-flop number.

References

1. V. Carchiolo, M. Malgeri, and G. Mangioni. Hardware/Software synthesis of formal specifications in Codesign of embedded systems. *ACM Transactions on Design Automation of Electronic Systems (TODAES)*, 6, January 2001.
2. ISO-IS-8807. *Information Processing Systems, Open System Interconnection, LOTOS, A Formal Description Technique Based on the Temporal Ordering of Observational Behaviour*. ISO, June 1988.
3. M. Faci and L. Logrippo. Specifying Hardware in LOTOS. In *Proceedings of CHDL'93, IFIP Conference on Hardware Description Languages and their Applications*, Ottawa, April 1993.
4. K.J. Turner. DILL – Digital logic in LOTOS. In *Formal Description Techniques, FORTE VII, Boston*. North-Holland, October 1993.
5. IEEE std 1076-1987. *Standard VHDL Language Reference Manual*. IEEE, 1988.
6. H. Katagiri, K. Yasumoto, T. Higashino, and K. Taniguchi. Hardware implementation of communication protocols modeled by concurrent EFSM with multi-way synchronization. In *Proceedings of 37th Design Automation Conference*, Los Angelese, CA, June 2000.
7. R. Milner. *A Calculus of communicating systems*. LCNS 92. Springer Verlag, New York, 1980.

8. C. A. R. Hoare. *Communicating Sequential Processes*. International Series in Computer Science. Prentice-Hall, 1985.
9. B. Mahr H. Ehrig. *Fundamentals of Algebraic Specifications*. 1 EATCS Monographs on Computer Science. Springer-Verlag, 1985.
10. C. Mead and L. Conway. *introduction to VLSI systems*. Haddison-Wesley, 1980.

Author Index